WASHOE COUNTY LIBRARY

3 1235 02982 9012

sl

S0-ATD-149

GM CELEBRITY/CENTURY/CUTLASS CIERA/6000
1982-95 REPAIR MANUAL

CHILTON'S

President, Chilton Enterprises	David S. Loewith
Senior Vice President	Ronald A. Hoxter
Publisher and Editor-In-Chief	Kerry A. Freeman, S.A.E.
Executive Editors	Dean F. Morgantini, S.A.E., W. Calvin Settle, Jr., S.A.E.
Managing Editor	Nick D'Andrea
Special Products Manager	Ken Grabowski, A.S.E., S.A.E.
Senior Editors	Jacques Gordon, Michael L. Grady, Debra McCall, Kevin M. G. Maher, Richard J. Rivele, S.A.E., Richard T. Smith, Jim Taylor, Ron Webb
Project Managers	Martin J. Gunther, Will Kessler, A.S.E., Richard Schwartz
Production Manager	Andrea Steiger
Product Systems Manager	Robert Maxey
Director of Manufacturing	Mike D'Imperio
Editor	Dawn Hoch

CHILTON BOOK COMPANY

ONE OF THE **DIVERSIFIED PUBLISHING COMPANIES,**
A PART OF **CAPITAL CITIES/ABC, INC.**

Manufactured in USA
© 1995 Chilton Book Company
Chilton Way, Radnor, PA 19089
ISBN 0-8019-8681-8
Library of Congress Catalog Card No. 94-069434
2345678901   5432109876

SPARKS LIBRARY   AUG 1 9 2004

Contents

SPARKS LIBRARY AUG. 1 9 2004

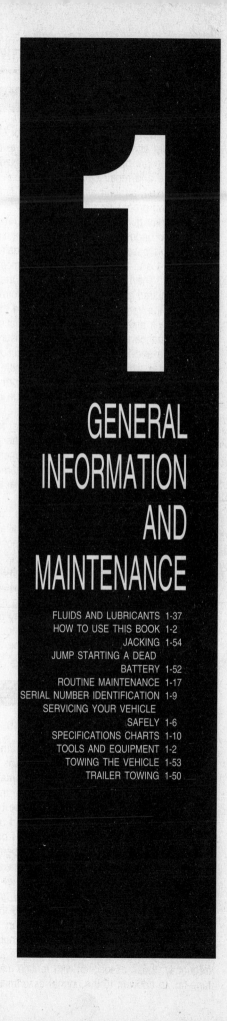

1

GENERAL INFORMATION AND MAINTENANCE

HOW TO USE THIS BOOK

This Chilton's Total Car Care manual for Celebrity, Century, Cutlass Ciera and 6000 cars is designed to teach you some of the operating principles of your car, and guide you through maintenance and repair operations. You can perform many repairs yourself, as long as you have the time, initiative, patience, and proper assortment of tools.

A secondary purpose of this book is a reference for owners who want to understand their car and/or their mechanics better. In this case, no tools at all are required.

Sections 1 and 2 will probably be the most frequently used in the book. The first section contains all the information that may be required at a moment's notice-information such as the location of the various serial numbers and the proper towing instructions. It also contains all the information on basic day-to-day maintenance that you will need to ensure good performance and long component life. Section 2 covers tune-up procedures which will assist you not only in keeping the engine running properly and at peak performance levels, but also in restoring some of the more delicate components to operating condition in the event of a failure. Sections 3 through 10 cover repairs (rather than maintenance) for various portions of the car, with each section covering either one system or two related systems. When repair of a component is not considered practical, we tell you how to remove the part and then how to install the new or rebuilt replacement. In this way, you at least save the labor costs.

In using the Table of Contents, refer to the bold listings for the beginning of the section. See the smaller listings or the index for information on a particular component or specifications.

Before removing any bolts, read through the entire procedure. This will give you the overall view of what tools and supplies will be required. There is nothing more frustrating than having to walk to the bus stop on Monday morning because you were short one bolt on Sunday afternoon. So read ahead and plan ahead. Each operation should be approached logically and all procedures thoroughly understood before attempting any work.

Cautions and notes will be provided where appropriate to help prevent you from injuring yourself or damaging your car. Therefore, you should read through the entire procedure before beginning the work, and make sure that you are aware of the warnings. Since no number of warnings could cover every possible situation, you should work slowly and try to envision what is going to happen in each operation ahead of time.

When it comes to tightening things, there is generally a slim area between too loose to properly seal or resist vibration and so tight as to risk damage or warping. When dealing with major engine parts, or with any aluminum component, it pays to procure a torque wrench and go by the recommended figures.

When reference is made in this book to the right side or left side of the car, it should be understood that the positions are always to be viewed from the front seat. Thus, the left side of the car is always the driver's side and the right side is always the passenger's side, even when facing the car, as when working on the engine.

We have attempted to eliminate the use of special tools whenever possible, substituting more readily available hand tools. However, in some cases the tools are necessary. These can be purchased from your General Motors dealer, or from an automotive parts store.

Always be conscious of the need for safety in your work. Never get under the car unless it is firmly supported by jackstands or ramps. Never smoke near or allow flame to get near the battery or the fuel system. Keep your clothing, hands and hair clear of the fan and pulleys when working near the engine, if it is running. Most importantly, try to be patient; even in the midst of an argument with a stubborn bolt, reaching for the largest hammer in the garage is usually a cause for later regret and more extensive repair. As you gain confidence and experience, working on your car can become a source of pride and satisfaction.

TOOLS AND EQUIPMENT

▶ **See Figures 1, 2, 3, 4, 5, 6, 7, 8, 9, 10, 11, 12 and 13**

It would be impossible to catalog each and every tool that you may need to perform all the operations included in this book. It would also not be wise for the amateur to rush out and buy an expensive set of tools on the theory that he/she may need one of them at some time. The best approach is to proceed slowly, gathering together a good quality set of those tools that are used most frequently. Don't be misled by the low cost of bargain tools. It is far better to spend a little more for quality, name brand tools. Forged wrenches, 6 or 12-point sockets and fine-tooth ratchets are a better investment than their less expensive counterparts. As any good mechanic can tell you, there are few worse experiences than trying to work on a vehicle with bad tools. Your monetary savings will be far outweighed by frustration and mangled knuckles.

Begin accumulating those tools that are used most frequently, those associated with routine maintenance and tune-up. In addition to the normal assortment of screwdriver's and pliers, you should have the following tools for routine maintenance jobs:

- SAE (or Metric) or SAE/Metric wrenches-sockets and combination open end/box end wrenches in sizes from ⅛ in. (3mm) to ¾ in. (19mm) and a spark plug socket ⅝ in. (16mm). If possible, buy various length socket drive extensions. One break in this department is that the metric sockets available in the U.S. will all fit the ratchet handles and extensions you may already have (¼ in., ⅜ in., and ½ in. drive);
- Jackstands for support.
- Oil filter wrench.
- Oil filler spout for pouring oil.
- Grease gun for chassis lubrication.
- A container for draining oil.
- Many rags for wiping up the inevitable mess.

In addition to the above items there are several others that are not absolutely necessary, but handy to have around. These include oil dry some form of oil-absorbent are one, a transmission funnel and the usual supply of lubricants, antifreeze and fluids, although these can be purchased as needed. This is a basic list for routine maintenance, but only your personal needs and desires can accurately determine your list of tools.

A more advanced set of tools, suitable for tune-up work, can be drawn up easily. While the tools are slightly more sophisticated, they need not be outrageously expensive. The key to these purchases is to make them with an eye towards adaptability and wide range. A basic list of tune-up tools could include:

- Tachometer
- Spark plug socket
- Spark plug gauge and gapping tool
- Timing light

The choice of a timing light should be made carefully. A light which works on the DC current supplied by the car battery is the best choice; it should have a xenon tube for brightness. Since all these cars have an electronic ignition system, the timing light should have an inductive pickup which clamps around the No. 1 spark plug cable (the timing light illustrated has one of these pickups).

In addition to these basic tools, there are several other tools and gauges which, though not particularly necessary for basic tune-up work, you may find to be quite useful. These include:

- A compression gauge. The screw-in type seals easily and eliminates the need for a remote starting switch during compression testing.
- Manifold vacuum gauge.
- A 12 VDC test light.
- Combination volt/ohmmeter.
- An induction meter, used to determine whether or not there is current flowing through a wire.

Finally, you will find a torque wrench necessary for all but the most basic of work. The beam-type models are perfectly adequate. The newer click-type (breakaway) and digital torque wrenches are more accurate, but are also much more expensive. All torque wrenches must be periodically recalibrated.

TCCS1201

Fig. 2 In addition to ratchets, a good set of wrenches and hex keys will be necessary

TCCS1202

Fig. 3 A hydraulic floor jack and a set of jackstands are essential for lifting and supporting the vehicle

TCCS1200

Fig. 1 All but the most basic procedure will require an assortment of ratchets and sockets

TCCS1203

Fig. 4 An assortment of pliers will be handy, especially for old rusted parts and stripped bolt heads

TCCS1204

Fig. 5 Various screwdriver's, a hammer, chisels and prybars are necessary to have in your toolbox

TCCS1003

Fig. 8 Compression gauge and a combination vacuum/fuel pressure test gauge

TCCS1001

Fig. 6 Dwell/tachometer unit (typical)

DEFLECTING BEAM

RUGID CASE, DIAL INDICATOR

CLICK TYPE

86811015

Fig. 9 Many repairs will require the use of a torque wrench, here are three types that are commonly used

TCCS1002

Fig. 7 Inductive type timing light

TCCS1209

Fig. 10 Although not always necessary, using specialized brake tools will save time

TCCS1210

Fig. 11 A few inexpensive lubrication tools will make regular service easier

TCCS1211

Fig. 12 Various pullers, clamps and separator tools are needed for the repair of many components

TCCS1212

Fig. 13 A variety of tools and gauges are needed for spark plug service

Special Tools

▶ See Figure 14

Most of the jobs covered in this guide can be accomplished with commonly available hand tools. However, in some cases special tools are required. Your General Motors dealer can probably supply the necessary tools, or they can be ordered from:

Kent-Moore Corporation
1501 South Jackson St.
Jackson, MI. 49203
1-800-345-2233

T - INTERNAL DRIVE
E - EXTERNAL

86811016

Fig. 14 A view of special lobed sockets and fasteners used by General Motors on later models

SERVICING YOUR VEHICLE SAFELY

It is virtually impossible to anticipate all of the hazards involved with automotive maintenance and service, but car and common sense will prevent most accidents.

The rules of safety for mechanics range from "don't smoke around gasoline," to "use the proper tool for the job." The trick to avoiding injuries is to develop safe work habits and take every possible precaution.

Do's

▶ See Figures 15, 16, 17 and 18

• Do keep a fire extinguisher and first aid kit handy.

• Do wear safety goggles when cutting, drilling, grinding or prying, even if you have 20/20 vision. If you wear glasses for the sake of vision, then wear safety goggles over your glasses.

• Do shield your eyes whenever you work around the battery. Batteries contain sulfuric acid; in case of contact with the eyes or skin, flush the area with water or a mixture of water and baking soda and get medical attention immediately.

• Do use jackstands for any undercar service. Jacks are for raising vehicles; jackstands are for making sure the vehicle stays raised. Whenever the vehicle is raised, block the wheels remaining on the ground and set the parking brake.

• Do use adequate ventilation when working with chemicals. Like carbon monoxide, asbestos dust resulting from some brake lining wear can be poisonous in sufficient quantities.

• Do disconnect the negative battery cable when working on the electrical system. The secondary ignition system can contain up to 50,000 volts.

• Do follow manufacturer's directions whenever working with potentially hazardous materials. Most fluids are poisonous if taken internally.

• Do maintain your tools. Loose hammerheads, mushroomed punches and chisels, frayed or poorly grounded electrical cords, excessively worn screwdriver's, spread wrenches (open end), cracked sockets, slipping ratchets, or faulty droplight sockets can cause accidents.

• Do use the proper size and type of tool for the job at hand.

• Do when possible, pull on a wrench handle rather than push on it, and adjust your stance to prevent a fall.

• Do be sure that adjustable wrenches are fit tightly on the nut or bolt and are pulled so the force is on the fixed jaw.

• Do select a tool that fits the nut or bolt. The wrench or socket should sit straight, not cocked.

• Do strike squarely with a hammer — avoid glancing blows.

• Do set the parking brake and block the drive wheels if the work requires that the engine be running.

Don'ts

▶ See Figures 19 and 20

• Don't run an engine in a garage without proper ventilation — EVER! Carbon monoxide is poisonous; it takes a long time to leave the body and you can build up a deadly supply of it in your system by simply breathing in a little every day. You may not realize you are slowly poisoning yourself. Always use vents, windows, fans and/or open the garage doors.

• Don't work around moving parts while wearing a necktie or loose clothing. Short sleeves are much safer than long, loose sleeves and hard-toed shoes with neoprene soles protect your toes and give a better grip on slippery surfaces. Jewelry such as watches, belt buckles, or body adornment of any kind is not safe for working on a car. Long hair should be hidden under a hat or cap.

• Don't use pockets for toolboxes. A fall or bump can push a screwdriver deep into your body. Even a rag hanging from your back pocket can wrap around a spinning shaft or fan.

• Don't smoke at any time when working with gasoline, cleaning solvent or other flammable materials.

• Don't smoke when working around the battery. When the battery is being charged, it gives off explosive hydrogen gas.

• Don't use gasoline to wash your hands; there are excellent soaps available. Gasoline contains many additives which are harmful. Gasoline also removes all the natural oils from the skin so that bone dry hands will suck up oil and grease.

• Don't service the air conditioning system unless you are equipped with the necessary tools and training. The refrigerant is extremely cold and when exposed to the air, will instantly freeze any surface it comes in contact with, including your eyes. Although the refrigerant is normally non-toxic, R-12 becomes a deadly poisonous gas in the presence of an open flame. One good whiff of the vapors from burning refrigerant can be fatal. Remember, it is advisable for a reputable service station to work on your air conditioning system.

86811017

Fig. 15 Jackstands should be always used when working under your vehicle

TWO-WIRE CONDUCTOR
THIRD WIRE GROUNDING
THE CASE

THREE-WIRE CONDUCTOR
GROUNDING THRU
A CIRCUIT

THREE-WIRE CONDUCTOR
ONE WIRE TO A GROUND

THREE-WIRE CONDUCTOR
GROUNDING THRU
AN ADAPTER PLUG

86811018

Fig. 16 Make certain that all electrical tools are grounded properly

A

B

86811019

Fig. 17 When using a screwdriver, make certain that it is the correct size and the tip is in good condition. (A) is a good screwdriver, (B) should be thrown away

86811020

Fig. 18 When using a wrench, make sure you use the correct size. If not, you could strip the nut

86811036

Fig. 19 Identification chart of various bolts and nuts

A - Length
B - Diameter (major diameter)
C - Threads per inch
D - Thread length
E - Size of the wrench required
F - Root diameter (minor diameter)

86811035

Fig. 20 Figure out the dimensions of bolts in this way

SERIAL NUMBER IDENTIFICATION

Vehicle

▶ See Figures 21, 22 and 23

The Vehicle Identification Number (VIN) is a seventeen digit alpha/numeric sequence stamped on a plate which is located at the top, left hand side of the instrument panel.

As far as the car owner is concerned, many of the digits in the VIN are of little or no value. At certain times, it may be necessary to refer to the VIN to interpret certain information, such as when ordering replacement parts or determining if your vehicle is involved in a factory service campaign (recall). In either of these instances, the following information may be helpful:

• 1ST DIGIT — Indicate the country of manufacture. A **1** designates the USA; **2** designates Canada.
• 8TH DIGIT — Indicates the type and the manufacturer of the original engine which was installed in the vehicle.
• 10TH DIGIT — Indicates the model year of the vehicle. **C** designates a 1982 model, **D** is for 1983, and so on. Certain letters such as I, O and Q are not used due to possible confusion with numbers.
• 11TH DIGIT — Indicates the specific plant at which the vehicle was assembled.
• 12TH-17TH DIGITS — This is the plant sequential number, which identifies the specific number of each vehicle within a production run. In the event of engineering change or a recall involving only a certain quantity of vehicles within a production run, the affected vehicles can be identified with this number.

The Vehicle Emission Control Information (VECI) tag is located on the front of the strut tower on most vehicles. This tag identifies the information needed to tune-up your vehicle.

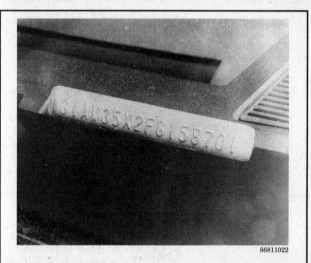

86811022

Fig. 21 The VIN tag is located on the dash, behind the windshield, in the upper left hand corner

Body

▶ See Figure 24

An identification plate for body-related items is attached to the front tie bar, just behind the passenger side headlamp. Information on the body identification plate would rarely be useful to the owner. An illustration of the plate is provided.

Engine

▶ See Figures 25 and 26

The engine identification code will sometimes be required to order replacement engine parts. The code is stamped in different locations, depending upon the size of the engine. Refer to the accompanying illustrations to determine the code location for your engine.

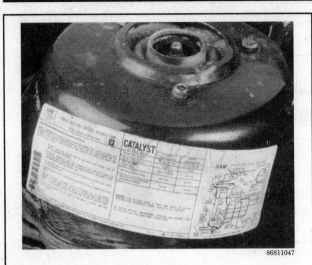

Fig. 22 An engine emissions tag is sometimes located on the front strut tower of your car

Transaxle

▶ See Figures 27 and 28

The transaxle code serves the same purpose as the engine identification code. Transaxle code locations may be determined by referring to the accompanying illustrations.

Drive Axle

The drive axle code is stamped onto the axle shaft near the CV-boot.

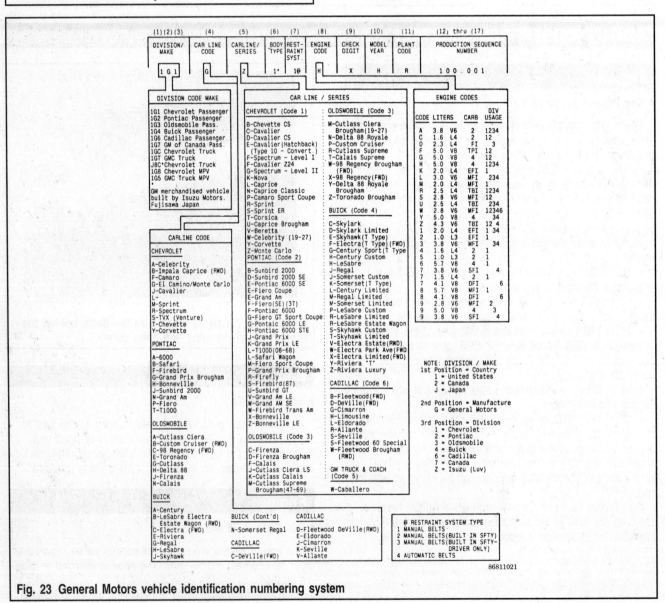

Fig. 23 General Motors vehicle identification numbering system

1 — BODY STYLE
2 — ASSEMBLY PLANT
3 — UNIT NUMBER
4 — PAINT TYPE
5 — ROOF OPTION
6 — SEAT OPTION
7 — TRIM COMBINATION
8 — UPPER BODY
9 — UPPER COLOR
10 — LOWER BODY
11 — REMAINING LINES
   — AVAILABLE FOR
   —PLANT USE
12 — LOWER COLOR
13 — MODEL YEAR
14 — TIME BUILD CODE
15 — DIVISION
16 — BODY TYPE

86811023

Fig. 24 General Motors body plate identification numbering system

2.5L L-4 (CODE R)

VIEW A

2.8L V-6 (CODES W & X & 9)

2.5L L-4 (CODE 2)

4.3L V-6 (CODE T)

4.3L V-6 (CODE Z)

1—V.I.N. NUMBER LOCATION

2—OPTIONAL V.I.N. NUMBER LOCATION

86811024

Fig. 25 Engine identification tag locations

1 Optional VIN location
2 Primary VIN location

3100 ENGINE

2.2L ENGINE

86811025

Fig. 26 Engine identification tag locations

Fig. 27 Manual transaxle identification tag locations

Fig. 28 Automatic transaxle identification tag locations

ENGINE IDENTIFICATION

Year	Model	Engine Displacement Liters (cc)	Engine Series (ID/VIN)	Fuel System	No. of Cylinders	Engine Type
1982	Celebrity	2.5 (2475)	R	TBI	4	OHV
	Celebrity	2.5 (2475)	5	2BC	4	OHV
	Celebrity	2.8 (2835)	X	2BC	6	OHV
	Celebrity	4.3 (4293)	T	DSL	6	OHV
	Century	2.5 (2475)	R	TBI	4	OHV
	Century	2.8 (2835)	X	2BC	6	OHV
	Century	3.0 (2999)	E	2BC	6	OHV
	Century	4.3 (4293)	T	DSL	6	OHV
	Cutlass Ciera	2.5 (2475)	R	TBI	4	OHV
	Cutlass Ciera	2.8 (2835)	X	2BC	6	OHV
	Cutlass Ciera	3.0 (2999)	E	2BC	6	OHV
	Cutlass Ciera	4.3 (4293)	T	DSL	6	OHV
	6000	2.5 (2475)	R	TBI	4	OHV
	6000	2.8 (2835)	X	2BC	6	OHV
	6000	4.3 (4293)	T	DSL	6	OHV
1983	Celebrity	2.5 (2475)	R	TBI	4	OHV
	Celebrity	2.5 (2475)	5	2BC	4	OHV
	Celebrity	2.8 (2835)	X	2BC	6	OHV
	Century	4.3 (4293)	T	DSL	5	OHV
	Century	2.5 (2475)	R	TBI	4	OHV
	Century	2.8 (2835)	X	2BC	6	OHV
	Century	3.0 (2999)	E	2BC	6	OHV
	Century	4.3 (4293)	T	DSL	6	OHV
	Cutlass Ciera	2.5 (2475)	R	TBI	4	OHV
	Cutlass Ciera	2.8 (2835)	X	2BC	6	OHV
	Cutlass Ciera	3.0 (2999)	E	2BC	6	OHV
	Cutlass Ciera	4.3 (4293)	T	DSL	6	OHV
	6000	2.5 (2475)	R	TBI	4	OHV
	6000	2.8 (2835)	X	2BC	6	OHV
	6000	4.3 (4293)	T	DSL	6	OHV
1984	Celebrity	2.5 (2475)	R	TBI	4	OHV
	Celebrity	2.5 (2475)	5	2BC	4	OHV
	Celebrty	2.8 (2835)	X	2BC	6	OHV
	Celebrity	4.3 (4293)	T	DSL	6	OHV
	Century	2.5 (2475)	R	TBI	4	OHV
	Century	2.8 (2835)	X	2BC	6	OHV
	Century	3.0 (2999)	E	2BC	6	OHV
	Century	3.8 (3785)	3	MFI	6	OHV
	Century	4.3 (4293)	T	DSL	6	OHV
	Cutlass Ciera	2.5 (2475)	R	TBI	4	OHV
	Cutlass Ciera	3.8 (3875)	3	MFI	6	OHV
	Cutlass Ciera	3.0 (2999)	E	2BC	6	OHV
	Cutlass Ciera	4.3 (4293)	T	DSL	6	OHV
	6000	2.5 (2475)	R	TBI	4	OHV
	6000	2.8 (2835)	X	2BC	6	OHV
	6000	2.8 (2835) HO	Z	2BC	6	OHV
	6000	4.3 (4293)	T	DSL	6	OHV

86811027

ENGINE IDENTIFICATION

Year	Model	Engine Displacement Liters (cc)	Engine Series (ID/VIN)	Fuel System	No. of Cylinders	Engine Type
1985	Celebrity	2.5 (2475)	R	TBI	4	OHV
	Celebrity	2.8 (2835)	X	2BC	6	OHV
	Celebrity	2.8 (2835)	W	MFI	6	OHV
	Celebrity	4.3 (4310)	T	DSL	6	OHV
	Century	2.5 (2474)	R	TBI	4	OHV
	Century	2.8 (2835)	X	2BC	6	OHV
	Century	3.0 (2999)	E	2BC	6	OHV
	Century	3.8 (3785)	3	MFI	6	OHV
	Century	4.3 (4293)	T	DSL	6	OHV
	Cutlass Ciera	2.5 (2474)	R	TBI	4	OHV
	Cutlass Ciera	3.0 (2999)	E	2BC	6	OHV
	Cutlass Ciera	3.8 (3785)	3	MFI	6	OHV
	Cutlass Ciera	4.3 (4293)	T	DSL	6	OHV
	6000	2.5 (2475)	R	TBI	4	OHV
	6000	2.8 (2835)	X	2BC	6	OHV
	6000	2.8 (2835) HO	W	MFI	6	OHV
	6000	4.3 (4294)	T	DSL	6	OHV
1986	Celebrity	2.5 (2475)	R	TBI	4	OHV
	Celebrity	2.8 (2835) HO	W	MFI	6	OHV
	Celebrity	2.8 (2835)	X	2BC	6	OHV
	Century	2.5 (2474)	R	TBI	4	OHV
	Century	2.8 (2835)	X	2BC	6	OHV
	Century	3.8 (3785)	3	MFI	6	OHV
	Century	3.8 (3785)	B	MFI	6	OHV
	Cutlass Ciera	2.5 (2474)	R	TBI	4	OHV
	Cutlass Ciera	2.8 (2835)	X	2BC	6	OHV
	Cutlass Ciera	2.8 (2835)	W	MFI	6	OHV
	Cutlass Ciera	3.8 (3785)	3	MFI	6	OHV
	Cutlass Ciera	3.8 (3785)	B	MFI	6	OHV
	6000	2.5 (2475)	R	TBI	4	OHV
	6000	2.8 (2835)	X	2BC	6	OHV
	6000	2.8 (2835) HO	W	MFI	6	OHV
1987	Celebrity	2.5 (2474)	R	TBI	4	OHV
	Celebrity	2.8 (2835)	W	MFI	6	OHV
	Century	2.5 (2474)	R	TBI	4	OHV
	Century	2.8 (2835)	W	MFI	6	OHV
	Century	3.8 (3785) HO	3	MFI	6	OHV
	Cutlass Ciera	2.5 (2474)	R	TBI	4	OHV
	Cutlass Ciera	2.8 (2835)	W	MFI	6	OHV
	Cutlass Ciera	3.8 (3785)	3	MFI	6	OHV
	6000	2.5 (2475)	R	TBI	4	OHV
	6000	2.8 (2835)	W	MFI	6	OHV
1988	Celebrity	2.5 (2474)	R	TBI	4	OHV
	Celebrity	2.8 (2835)	W	MFI	6	OHV
	Century	2.5 (2474)	R	TBI	4	OHV
	Century	2.8 (2835)	W	MFI	6	OHV
	Century	3.8 (3785) HO	3	MFI	6	OHV

86811028

ENGINE IDENTIFICATION

Year	Model	Engine Displacement Liters (cc)	Engine Series (ID/VIN)	Fuel System	No. of Cylinders	Engine Type
1988	Cutlass Ciera	2.5 (2474)	R	TBI	4	OHV
	Cutlass Ciera	2.8 (2835)	W	MFI	6	OHV
	Cutlass Ciera	3.8 (3785)	3	MFI	6	OHV
	6000	2.5 (2475)	R	TBI	4	OHV
	6000	2.8 (2835)	W	MFI	6	OHV
1989	Celebrity	2.5 (2474)	R	TBI	4	OHV
	Celebrity	2.8 (2835)	W	MFI	6	OHV
	Century	2.5 (2474)	R	TBI	4	OHV
	Century	2.8 (2835)	W	MFI	6	OHV
	Century	3.3 (3342)	N	MFI	6	OHV
	Cutlass Ciera	2.5 (2474)	R	TBI	4	OHV
	Cutlass Ciera	2.8 (2835)	W	MFI	6	OHV
	Cutlass Ciera	3.3 (3342)	N	MFI	6	OHV
	Cutlass Cruiser	2.5 (2474)	R	TBI	4	OHV
	Cutlass Cruiser	2.8 (2835)	W	MFI	6	OHV
	Cutlass Cruiser	3.3 (3342)	N	MFI	6	OHV
	6000	2.5 (2475)	R	TBI	4	OHV
	6000	2.8 (2835)	W	MFI	6	OHV
	6000	3.1 (3136)	T	MFI	6	OHV
1990	Celebrity	2.5 (2475)	R	TBI	4	OHV
	Celebrity	3.1 (3130)	T	MFI	6	OHV
	Century	2.5 (2474)	R	TBI	4	OHV
	Century	3.3 (3342)	N	MFI	6	OHV
	Cutlass Ciera	2.5 (2474)	R	TBI	4	OHV
	Cutlass Ciera	3.3 (3342)	N	MFI	6	OHV
	Cutlass Cruiser	2.5 (2474)	R	TBI	4	OHV
	Cutlass Cruiser	3.3 (3342)	N	MFI	6	OHV
	6000	2.5 (2475)	R	TBI	4	OHV
	6000	3.1 (3136)	T	MFI	6	OHV
1991	Century	2.5 (2474)	R	TBI	4	OHV
	Century	3.3 (3342)	N	MFI	6	OHV
	Cutlass Ciera	2.5 (2474)	R	TBI	4	OHV
	Cutlass Ciera	3.3 (3342)	N	MFI	6	OHV
	Cutlass Cruiser	2.5 (2474)	R	TBI	4	OHV
	Cutlass Cruiser	3.3 (3342)	N	MFI	6	OHV
	6000	2.5 (2475)	R	TBI	4	OHV
	6000	3.1 (3136)	T	MFI	6	OHV
1992	Century	2.2 (2195)	4	MFI	4	OHV
	Century	3.3 (3342)	N	MFI	6	OHV
	Cutlass Ciera	2.5 (2474)	R	TBI	4	OHV
	Cutlass Ciera	3.3 (3342)	N	MFI	6	OHV
	Cutlass Cruiser	2.5 (2474)	R	TBI	4	OHV
	Cutlass Cruiser	3.3 (3342)	N	MFI	6	OHV
1993	Century	2.2 (2195)	4	MFI	4	OHV
	Century	3.1 (3130)	M	SFI	6	OHV
	Cutlass Ciera	2.2 (2195)	4	MFI	4	OHV
	Cutlass Ciera	3.3 (3342)	N	MFI	6	OHV

86811029

ENGINE IDENTIFICATION

Year	Model	Engine Displacement Liters (cc)	Engine Series (ID/VIN)	Fuel System	No. of Cylinders	Engine Type
1993	Cutlass Cruiser	2.2 (2195)	4	MFI	4	OHV
	Cutlass Cruiser	3.3 (3342)	N	MFI	6	OHV
1994	Century	2.2 (2195)	4	MFI	4	OHV
	Century	3.1 (3130)	M	SFI	6	OHV
	Cutlass Ciera	2.2 (2195)	4	MFI	4	OHV
	Cutlass Ciera	3.1 (3130)	M	SFI	6	OHV
	Cutlass Cruiser	2.2 (2195)	4	MFI	4	OHV
	Cutlass Cruiser	3.1 (3130)	M	SFI	6	OHV
1995	Cutlass Ciera	2.2 (2195)	4	MFI	4	OHV
	Cutlass Ciera	3.1 (3130)	M	SFI	6	OHV
	Cutlass Cruiser	2.2 (2195)	4	MFI	4	OHV
	Cutlass Cruiser	3.1 (3130)	M	SFI	6	OHV

BC - Barrel carburetor
DSL - Diesel
HO - High output
MFI - Multi-Port Fuel Injection

OHV - Overhead valve
SFI - Sequential Fuel Injection
TBI - Throttle Bodyl fuel injection

86811030

ROUTINE MAINTENANCE

Proper maintenance of any vehicle is the key to long and trouble-free vehicle life. As a conscientious car owner, set aside a Saturday morning, say once a month, to check or replace items which could cause major problems later. Keep your own personal log to jot down which services you performed, how much parts cost you, the date, and the exact odometer reading at the time. Keep all receipts for such items as engine oil and filters, so that they may be referred to in case of related problems or to determine operating expenses. As a do-it-yourselfer, these receipts are the only proof you have that the required maintenance was performed. In the event of a warranty problem, these receipts will be invaluable.

The literature provided with your car when it was originally delivered includes the factory recommended maintenance schedule. If you do not have the factory schedule, we have provided a mirror image of the GM schedule which should be used. No matter which schedule is used, follow it to the letter.

Air Cleaner

REMOVAL & INSTALLATION

▶ See Figures 29, 30 and 31

The air cleaner element should be checked periodically. Regular air cleaner element replacement is a must, since a partially clogged element will cause a performance loss, decreased fuel mileage, and engine damage (if enough dirt gets into the cylinders and contaminates the engine oil.

1. Replacement of the element is simply a matter of removing the wing nut(s) or clamps from the air cleaner lid. Some assemblies have screws to hold down the lid along with the clamps.

Fig. 29 Loosen an remove the air cleaner wing nut from the cleaner lid on a 2.8L engine

Fig. 30 Lifting out the filter element on the 2.8L engine

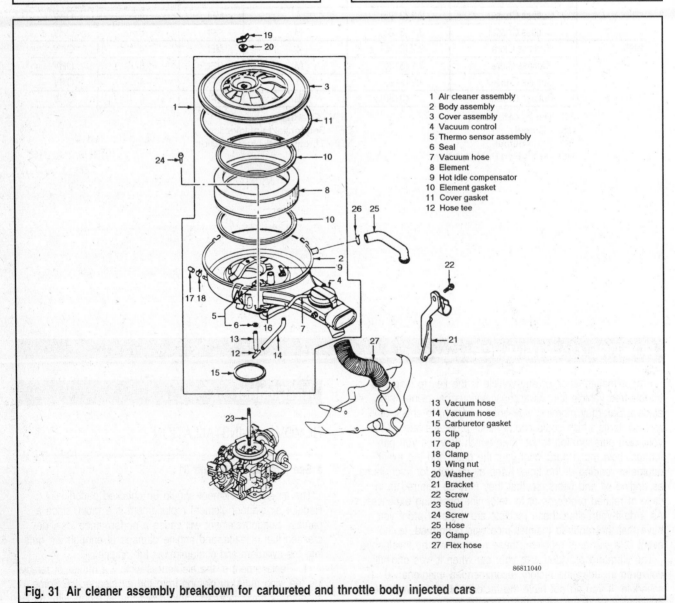

1 Air cleaner assembly
2 Body assembly
3 Cover assembly
4 Vacuum control
5 Thermo sensor assembly
6 Seal
7 Vacuum hose
8 Element
9 Hot idle compensator
10 Element gasket
11 Cover gasket
12 Hose tee

13 Vacuum hose
14 Vacuum hose
15 Carburetor gasket
16 Clip
17 Cap
18 Clamp
19 Wing nut
20 Washer
21 Bracket
22 Screw
23 Stud
24 Screw
25 Hose
26 Clamp
27 Flex hose

Fig. 31 Air cleaner assembly breakdown for carbureted and throttle body injected cars

2. Once this is done lift off the lid, and remove the old filter element.

To install:

3. Wipe the inside of the housing with a damp cloth before placing the new element into the housing.

4. Place the new element in the housing.

5. Install the lid and tighten. On vehicles with wing nut(s), just snug it down with moderate finger pressure. Excessive tightening of the wing nut(s) will damage components.

6. On vehicles with screws and clamps, simply tighten the screws and hook the clamps.

➡**Never attempt to clean or soak the element in gasoline, oil, or cleaning solvent. The element is designed to be a throw-away item.**

Fuel Filter

REMOVAL & INSTALLATION

Gasoline Engines

CARBURETORS

▶ **See Figure 32**

An internal filter is located in the inlet fitting of all carburetors. The elements are spring loaded and are held against the inlet fitting gasket surface.

1. Disconnect the negative battery cable.

2. Disconnect the fuel line at the fuel inlet filter nut. Remove the inlet filter nut, the filter and the spring.

To install:

3. Install a new filter (with the check valve end facing the fuel line), the spring, the gasket and the fuel line nut.

4. Torque the fuel filter nut to 18 ft. lbs. (24 Nm), then install the fuel line.

5. Connect the negative battery cable. Check for leaks.

FUEL INJECTED

▶ **See Figure 33**

On throttle body vehicles, there are two kinds of in-line filters available. From 1982-85 the filter is located in the engine compartment. From 1986 the filter is located to the left of the fuel tank. On the MFI engines, the filter is located on the left side of the fuel tank also.

1. Disconnect the negative battery cable.

2. Relieve the fuel system pressure.

3. For engines other than early TBI with an engine compartment mounted filter, raise and safely support the vehicle.

4. Remove the filter bracket attaching screw(s) and filter bracket.

5. Grasp the filter and 1 fuel line fitting. Twist the quick-connect fitting ¼ turn in each direction to loosen any dirt within the fitting. Repeat for the other fuel line fitting.

6. Use compressed air, blow out dirt from the quick-connect fittings at both ends of the fuel filter.

✳✳CAUTION

Always wear safety goggles when using compressed air.

7. To disconnect the fuel line fittings, squeeze the plastic tabs on the male end of the connector and pull the fitting apart. Repeat for the other fitting.

8. Remove the fuel filter.

To install:

9. Remove the protective caps from the new filter.

10. Connect the filter retainers on the filter inlet and outlet pipes.

11. Install the filter and quick-connect fittings.

12. On rear mounted filters, align the filter bracket on the frame, then attach with mounting screw(s).

13. Lower the vehicle, if raised. Tighten the fuel filler cap.

14. Connect the negative battery cable.

15. Turn the ignition **ON** and inspect for leaks.

16. Reset the clock, radio and any other accessaries if required.

Fig. 32 Removing an internal fuel filter on a carbureted engine

Fig. 33 TBI fuel filter assembly in the engine compartment

Diesel Engines
▶ **See Figure 34**

The fuel filter is located on the left fender front wheel house.

1. Disconnect the negative battery cable.
2. Disconnect the fuel lines from the inlet and the outlet ports. Disconnect the drain hose and, if equipped, the electrical harness at the filter.
3. Remove the filter assembly clamp-to-bracket bolts and the clamp. Rotate the filter assembly to disengage it from the bracket, then remove the filter assembly.
4. Cover the assembly with a cloth and clamp it in a vise (using the line openings and the flat on the opposite side.)
5. Remove the filter and clean the gasket mounting surface.
6. Coat the new filter gasket with engine oil or diesel fuel. Install the filter on the cover and tighten it to ⅔ turn beyond the gasket contact.

```
 1  Water in fuel module
 2  Cover assembly
 3  Drain valve - 7 Nm (5 lbs. ft.) min.
 4  Water in fuel probe (part of No.2)
 5  Filter
 6  Fully driven, seated and not stripped
 7  Fuel heater (optional)
 8  "O" ring
 9  Bracket lock tab (part of No. 2)
10  Outlet pipe fitting - 23 Nm (17 lbs.ft.)
11  Inlet pipe fitting - 27 Nm (20 lbs.ft.)
12  Outlet pipe "O" ring
13  Inlet pipe "O" ring
14  Air bleed seal
15  Air bleed
```

86811046

Fig. 34 Exploded view of the diesel engine fuel filter assembly

7. Place the assembly into the bracket and engage the lock tab into the bracket. Install new O-rings and loosely attach the fuel lines to the unit.
8. To complete the installation, reverse the removal procedures.
9. Open the air bleed screw, turn the ignition switch to the **RUN** position (the pump will run) and close the air bleed screw when fuel flows from the opening.
10. Connect the negative battery cable.
11. Start the engine and check for leaks.
12. Reset the clock, radio and any other accessaries if required.

➡ **The inline filter should be changed when changing the fuel filter.**

WATER IN FUEL

✳✳CAUTION

The water/diesel fuel mixture is flammable, and could be HOT. When opening the drain valve, do not touch the fuel coming out. Most of all do not expose the fuel to open flames or sparks.

The system has a red WATER IN FUEL warning light which is designed to come on to warn of excessive water in the system. It will also come ON as you start your vehicle to let you know the bulb is working. If the light comes on at any other time, there is water in the fuel, (and possibly other contaminants). You must drain the system within one hour of operation after the light comes ON.

✳✳WARNING

Continuing to drive the vehicle with the warning light on can result in serious damage to the fuel injection system or other parts of the engine.

If the light comes on after a few minuets after refueling, this means water has entered the tank. Turn the engine **OFF** and remove the water immediately.

1. Stop and park the vehicle in a safe place. Turn the engine **OFF** and apply the parking brake.
2. Turn the key to the **RUN** position, but do not start the engine. This will engage the electric fuel pump.
3. Open the hood.
4. The drain valve is on the driver's side of the engine compartment. Place a fuel-resistant container under the vehicle's drain valve.
5. Open the valve a full two turns, then push the button on the fuel filter (located on the driver's side of the engine, at the front). Fuel and water should begin flowing out from the drain valve.
6. Hold in the button until the liquid coming from the valve looks like clean fuel. This can take about 15-20 seconds.
7. Release the button and close the valve tightly. Dispose of the mixture in a suitable manner.

If the warning light does not go out after draining, or it comes back on within seconds after repeated drainings, turn the engine **OFF** and see an authorize service station immediately.

PCV System

The Positive Crankcase Ventilation (PCV) valve regulated crankcase pressure during various engine running conditions. At high vacuum (idle speed and partial load range) it will open slightly and at low vacuum (full throttle) it will open fully. This allows vapors to be drawn from the crankcase by engine vacuum and then sucked into the combustion chamber where they are burned.

REMOVAL & INSTALLATION

PCV Valve

♦ See Figures 35 and 36

The PCV valve must be replaced every 30,000 miles (48,300 km). Details on the PCV system, including system tests, are given in Section 4.

The valve is located in a rubber grommet on the valve cover, connected to the air cleaner housing by a large diameter rubber hose.

1. Pull the valve (with the hose attached) from the rubber grommet in the valve cover.
2. Remove the valve from the hose.
3. Inspect the rubber grommet that houses the valve for deterioration, replace if needed.

To install:
4. Install a new valve into the hose.
5. Press the valve back into the rubber grommet in the valve cover.

PCV Filter

Some vehicles are equipped with a PCV filter which is located in the air cleaner housing and must be replaced every 50,000 miles (80,000 km).

1. Remove the air cleaner housing lid.

Fig. 36 Remove the PCV valve, inspect and replace if needed

2. Slide back the filter retaining clip and remove the old filter.
3. Install the new filter, attach the retaining clip, then install the housing lid.

Evaporative Canister

SERVICING

♦ See Figure 37

The evaporator canister should be checked every 12 months or 15,000 miles (24,000 km). Check the fuel vapor lines and the vacuum hoses for proper connections and correct routing, as well as condition. Replace clogged, damaged or deteriorated parts as necessary.

For more details on the evaporative emissions system, please refer to Section 4.

CRANKCASE VENTILATION VALVE

PCV CONTROL VALVE

⇨ CLEAN AIR
→ VOLATILE OIL FUMES
--→ MIXTURE OF AIR AND FUMES

Fig. 35 PCV valve system operation

Fig. 37 Check the vapor lines and vacuum hoses for proper connection and correct routing, as well as condition. Replace clogged, damaged or deteriorated parts, as necessary

Battery

The single battery used in models equipped with gasoline engines is located at the driver's side front corner of the engine compartment. Because of the added cranking loads, diesel models use two batteries; one in each front corner of the engine compartment. All models were originally equipped with a Delco Freedom II battery. Though this battery is considered to be maintenance-free due to the fact that it will never need water added, the battery should be given some periodic attention.

Since batteries have a limited life-span, you may have already purchased a battery for your car at one point in time. Many aftermarket batteries are not maintenance-free (meaning they may require the periodic addition of distilled water), and some maintenance-free batteries are not sealed. Any non-sealed battery has caps which can be removed for access to the battery cells. You can remove the caps to check fluid level and specific gravity or to add water.

GENERAL MAINTENANCE

♦ See Figures 38, 39 and 40

The major cause of slow engine cranking or a no-start condition is battery terminals which are loose, dirty, or corroded. Every 3 months or so, disconnect the battery and clean the terminals of both the battery and the cables. Cleaning tools for this purpose are available at most any auto parts store. When you buy a cleaning tool, be sure to specify whether you have a top terminal or side terminal battery, as the type of tool differs depending upon the style of battery.

❋❋CAUTION

When loosening or tightening the positive battery cable screw(s) at the battery, DO NOT touch the wrench to any metal surface. Personal injury and/or component damage will result.

➡To use a terminal cleaning tool on the battery, it will probably be necessary to remove the windshield washer bottle (all models) or the coolant recovery tank (diesel only) to gain the necessary clearance.

CABLES

♦ See Figure 41

Check the battery cables for signs of wear or chafing. If corrosion is present on the cable or if the wire is visible through the jacket, the cable assembly should be replaced. If cable replacement is necessary, it is best to purchase a high quality part that has the cable jacket sealed to the terminal ends.

Batteries themselves can be cleaned using a solution of baking soda and water. Surface coatings on battery cases can actually conduct electricity which will cause a slight voltage drain, so make sure the battery case is clean.

Fig. 38 The underside of this special battery tool has a wire brush to clean post terminals

Fig. 39 Place the tool over the terminals and twist to clean the post

Fig. 40 Cleaning a side mounted battery is done in a similar matter as a top mount

Fig. 41 Battery maintenance may be accomplished with household items (such as baking soda to neutralize spilled acid) or with special tools such as this post and terminal cleaner

TESTING

The quickest test of a battery, without expensive tools, is a by using voltmeter set on the 15 volt dc scale. Attach the leads across the battery terminals it should read about 13 volts with the engine and lights off. If turning the headlights and defogger on lowers the reading below 10.5 volts the battery is too low. Before replacing the battery, charge the battery on a low ampere charger over for several hours, and repeat the test. The voltmeter should not drop below 10.5 volts when cranking the engine with the starter either, but caution must be used to prevent injury and the test could be misleading if the starter is defective causing a greater voltage drop.

➡If the car engine cranks over normally when cold, but cranks slowly when hot the problem is often NOT the battery. The starter and battery cables should be the first items suspected.

※※CAUTION

Keep flame or sparks away from the battery; it gives off explosive hydrogen gas. Battery electrolyte contains sulfuric acid. If you should splash any on your skin or in your eyes, flush the affected area with plenty of clear water. NO MATTER WHAT! If it gets in your eyes, get medical help IMMEDIATELY.

Specific Gravity
▶ See Figures 42 and 43

Most maintenance-free batteries are sealed, therefore it is not possible to check the specific gravity using a typical automotive hydrometer. Instead, the indicator built into the top of the case must be relied on to display any signs of battery deterioration. If the indicator is dark, the battery can be assumed to be OK. If the indicator is light, the specific gravity is low, and the battery should be charged or replaced. The indicator on some aftermarket batteries may vary, so be sure to check the instructions included with your battery if in doubt.

If your battery is of the non-sealed type, various inexpensive hydrometers are available at most auto supply stores to check the condition of your battery. Follow the instructions which come with the hydrometer and carefully check the gravity in each of the battery's cells.

Load Test

A true test of a battery's condition is the load test. It requires the use of a special carbon pile to simulate an electrical load on the battery. Normally, a battery is tested at half it's cold cranking amps rating or at three times the amp-hour rating for 15 seconds.

Fig. 42 Test indicator location on the Maintenance Free battery

Fig. 43 Carefully pry off the battery filler caps on non-sealed batteries ONLY

NOTE: ALWAYS TAP HYDROMETER LIGHTLY ON TOP TO DISLODGE ANY AIR BUBBLES THAT MIGHT GIVE A FALSE INDICATION

86811052

Fig. 44 Maintenance free batteries may have a built-in hydrometer

Generally, if after 15 seconds the battery voltage is not at 9.6 volts or more, the battery either needs to be recharged or replaced.

✳✳CAUTION

Never load test a battery unless the electrolyte level is sufficiently full, otherwise it may explode causing personal injury.

CHARGING

▸ See Figures 44 and 45

Any time the engine won't crank, check the color of the battery condition indicator (which is actually a built-in hydrometer). If the indicator is green, the battery is sufficiently charged and in good condition. A complete check of the starter and related wiring should be performed. If the indicator is darkened, the battery is discharged. In this case, the reason for the discharge should be determined (e.g. low alternator output, voltage draw, etc.) then the battery itself should be tested and recharged. If the indicator is light without a green dot visible or if it is yellow in color, the battery must be replaced — DO NOT attempt to test or recharge a battery with this indicator condition. Test the electrical system after the battery has been replaced. A battery should be charged at a slow rate to keep the plates inside from getting too hot.

REPLACEMENT

▸ See Figures 46 and 47

1. Raise the hood and remove the front end diagonal brace(s) from above the battery.
2. Disconnect the cables from the battery. It may be necessary to use a small box end wrench or a ¼ in. drive ratchet to

Charging Rate Amps	Time
75	40 min
50	1 hr
25	2 hr
10	5 hr

Battery	Test Load (Amps)
83 - 50	150
83 - 60	180
85A - 60	170
87A - 60	230
89A - 60	270
1981103	200
1981104	250
1981105	270
1981577	260

Temperature (°F)	Minimum Voltage
70 or above	9.6
60	9.5
50	9.4
40	9.3
30	9.1
20	8.9
10	8.7
0	8.5

86811060

Fig. 45 Charging rates for batteries

sneak in between the battery and the windshield washer (or coolant recovery) tank.

✳✳CAUTION

When loosening or tightening the positive battery cable screw(s) at the battery, DO NOT touch the wrench to any metal surface. Personal injury and/or component damage will result.

3. Loosen and remove the battery hold-down bolt and block. The use of a long extension which places the ratchet above the battery makes it very easy to get to the hold-down bolt.

4. Carefully lift the battery from the engine compartment. It may be necessary to remove the air cleaner intake duct (except 4-cyl.) or the intake resonator (4-cyl. only) for clearance.

5. Clean the battery and the battery tray thoroughly with the baking soda/water solution. Don't allow the solution to get into the small vent holes of the battery.

6. Rinse the battery with clear water and wipe it dry with a couple of clean paper towels. Don't use the towels for anything else, they probably have traces of sulfuric acid on them. Dispose of the paper towels.

7. Thoroughly flush the battery tray and the surrounding area with a baking soda/water solution. Using a wire brush, remove any rust which may be on the tray. Clear away the rust and dry the tray.

8. Coat the battery tray liberally with anti-rust paint.

9. Thoroughly clean the battery and cable terminals BEFORE installing the battery.

10. Install the battery in the reverse of steps 1-4. Tighten the hold-down bolt snugly-don't overtighten it.

After you clean the terminals and reconnect the battery, apply a corrosion inhibitor to the terminals. Stay away from using any substance which is not meant specifically for this purpose. Do not apply the corrosion inhibitor to the mating surfaces of the terminals unless specified by the chemical manufacturer.

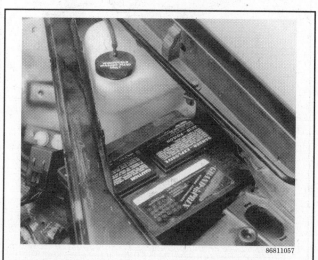

Fig. 46 Remove the front end diagonal brace(s) from above the battery

Fig. 47 Installation of a side mount battery

Belts

INSPECTION

Every 12 months or 15,000 miles (24,100 km) on gasoline engines or every 5000 miles (8000 km) on diesel engines, not dependent upon a period in months, check the drive belts for proper tension. Also look for signs of wear, fraying, separation, glazing and so on, and replace the belts as required.

ADJUSTMENT

◆ **See Figure 48**

Belt tension should be checked with a gauge made for that purpose. If a gauge is not available, tension can be checked with moderate thumb pressure applied to the belt at its longest span midway between pulleys. If the belt has a free span less than 12 in. (305mm), it should deflect approximately 1/8-1/4 in. (3-6mm). If the span is longer than 12 in. (305mm), deflection can range between 1/8 in. (3mm) and 3/8 in. (10mm).

➡**Models with a serpentine belt are automatically adjusted by a spring loaded belt tensioner. Adjustments are not normally required.**

1. Loosen the driven accessory's pivot and mounting bolts.

2. Move the accessory toward or away from the engine until the tension is correct. You can use a wooden hammer handle as a lever, but do not use anything metallic.

3. Tighten the bolts and recheck the tension. If new bolts have been installed, run the engine for a few minutes, then recheck and readjust, as necessary.

It is better to have belts too loose than too tight, because overtight belts will lead to bearing failure, particularly in the water pump and alternator. However, loose belts place an extremely high impact load on the driven component due to the whipping action of the belt.

Fig. 48 Checking a belt tension can be done with the use of your own thumb if a gauge is not available

REMOVAL & INSTALLATION

Except Serpentine Belt

➡It may be necessary to loosen more than one pulley or remove another belt to access the drive belt, such as the power steering and air conditioning.

1. Loosen the driven accessory's pivot and mounting bolts.
2. Move the accessory toward or away from the engine until there is enough slack in the belt to slip it over the pulley of the driven accessory.
3. Remove the belt from the engine.
4. Install the new belt and move the accessory toward or away from the engine until the tension is correct. You can use a wooden hammer handle as a lever, but do not use anything metallic.
5. Adjust the belt tension, then tighten the bolts.

Serpentine Belt

1. Place a tool over the tensioner pulley axis bolt.
2. Rotate the tool counterclockwise to relieve belt tension.
3. Remove the drive belt.
4. Carefully release the tensioner pulley and remove the tool.

To install:
5. Route the belt over the pulleys, except tensioner.
6. Place tool over tensioner, rotate counterclockwise and install belt.
7. Remove the tool, then check alignment of tension and belt.

Hoses

▸ **See Figures 49, 50, 51, 52, 53, 54, 55, 56, 57 and 58**

The upper and lower radiator hoses, along with the heater hoses should be checked periodically for deterioration, leaks, and loose clamps. GM recommends that this be done every 12 months or 15,000 miles (24,100 km). For your own peace of mind, it may be wise to check these items at least every

spring and fall, since the summer and winter months wreak the most havoc with your cooling system. Expect to replace the hoses about every 24 months or 30,000 miles (48,300 km).

REMOVAL & INSTALLATION

1. Drain the cooling system.

❄❄CAUTION

When draining the coolant, keep in mind that cats and dogs are attracted by ethylene glycol antifreeze, and are quite likely to drink any that is left in an uncovered container or in puddles on the ground. This will prove fatal in sufficient quantity. Always drain the coolant into a sealable container. Coolant should be reused unless it is contaminated or several years old.

2. Loosen the hose clamps at each end of the hose to be removed. If the clamps are of the type which have a screw

1 Charcoal canister hose
2 Pipe asm. outlet
3 Hose outlet (module)
4 Clamp
5 Hose outlet (engine)
6 Hose inlet (module)
7 Intake manifold fitting
8 Pipe asm. inlet (engine)
9 Bracket (with cruise cont. only)

Fig. 49 Heater hose routing — 1982-85 2.5L (VIN R)

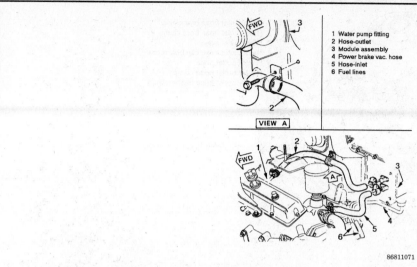

1 Water pump fitting
2 Hose-outlet
3 Module assembly
4 Power brake vac. hose
5 Hose-inlet
6 Fuel lines

86811071

Fig. 50 Heater hose routing — 1982-86 2.8L (VIN X and Z)

1 Outlet hose
2 Power brake
  booster
3 Pipe
4 Pipe assembly
5 Inlet hose assembly
6 Clip

86811072

Fig. 51 Heater hose routing — 1983-85 4.3L Diesel (VIN T)

1 Heater inlet hose rear clamp
2 Heater inlet hose front clamp
3 Heater inlet hose
4 Heater inlet hose clip bolt/screw
5 Heater outlet hose
6 Heater outlet hose clamp
7 Heater outlet hose heater clamp

86811073

Fig. 52 Heater hose routing — 1993-95 3.1L (VIN M)

1 Heater inlet hose rear clamp
2 Heater inlet hose
3 Heater inlet hose front clamp
4 Heater outlet hose bolt/screw
5 Heater outlet hose engine clamp
6 Heater pipe retainer
7 Heater outlet pipe assembly
8 Heater inlet hose clip bolt/screw
9 Heater outlet hose heater clamp

86811A74

Fig. 53 Heater hose routing — 1992-95 2.2L (VIN 4)

1 Heater pipes
2 Clamps
3 Heater hoses
4 Bolt/screw
5 Water pump (engine)
6 Nut

86811A75

Fig. 54 Heater hose routing — 1982-92 2.5L (VIN R)

1 Coolant outlet
2 Outlet hose
3 Clamp
4 Inlet hose
5 Inlet

86811077

Fig. 55 Coolant hose routing — 1982-92 2.5L (VIN R)

1' Radiator inlet hose clamp assembly
2 Radiator inlet hose
3 Radiator assembly
4 Radiator outlet hose engine clamp
   assembly
5 Radiator outlet hose

86811079

Fig. 57 Coolant hose routing — 1992-95 2.2L (VIN 4)

positioned vertically in relation to the hose, loosen the screw and gently tap the head of the screw towards the hose. Repeat this until the clamp is loose enough. If corrosion on the clamp prevents loosening in this manner, carefully cut the clamp off with cutters and replace the clamp with a new one.

3. Once the clamps are out of the way, grasp the hose and twist it off of the tube connection using only moderate force. If the hose won't break loose, DON'T use excessive force — doing so can easily damage the heater core and/or radiator tubes. Using a razor blade, carefully slit the portion of the hose which covers the connection point, peel the hose off of the connection and disconnect the hose.

4. Remove the hose and clean the connection points.

5. Slip the (loosened) clamps onto the hose ends and install the new hose, being careful to position it so that no interference.

6. Position the clamps at the ends of the hoses, beyond the sealing bead, and centered on the clamping surface. Tighten the hose clamps with a screwdriver — don't use a wrench on the screw heads to tighten them, as overtightening can damage the hose and/or connections points.

7. Refill the cooling system (detailed later) and check for leakage.

8. If so equipped, disconnect the routing clamps from the hose.

1 Clamp 3 Nm (27 lb.in.)
2 Inlet hose
3 Radiator asm.
4 Outlet hose

86811078

Fig. 56 Coolant hose routing — 1989-93 3.3L (VIN N)

1 Radiator inlet hose
2 Radiator assembly
3 Radiator outlet hose

86811080

Fig. 58 Coolant hose routing — 1993-95 3.1L (VIN M)

TCCS1010

Fig. 60 A torn boot should be replaced immediately

CV-Boots

▶ See Figures 59 and 60

INSPECTION

The CV (Constant Velocity) boots should should be checked for damage each time the oil is changed, between 3000 and 5000 miles, and anytime the vehicle is raised for service. These boots keep water, grime, dirt and other damaging matter from entering the CV-joints. Any of these can cause early CV-joint failure which can be expensive to repair. Heavy grease thrown around the inside of the front wheel(s) and on the brake caliper/drum can be an indication of a torn boot. Thoroughly check the boots for missing clamps and tears. If the boot is damaged, it should be replaced immediately. Please refer to Section 7 for procedures.

TCCS1011

Fig. 59 CV-Boots must be inspected periodically for damage

Air Conditioning

SAFETY PRECAUTIONS

Because of the inherent dangers involved with working on air conditioning systems and refrigerant, the following safety precautions must be strictly adhered to in order to service the system safely.

• Avoid contact with a charged refrigeration system, even when working on another part of the air conditioning system or vehicle. If a heavy tool comes into contact with a section of tubing or a heat exchanger, it can easily cause the relatively soft material to rupture.

• When it is necessary to apply force to a fitting which contains refrigerant, as when checking that all system couplings are securely tightened, use a wrench on both parts of the fitting involved, if possible. This will avoid putting torque on refrigerant tubing. (It is advisable, when possible, to use tube or line wrenches when tightening these flare nut fittings.)

➡ **R-12 refrigerant is a chlorofluorocarbon which, when released into the atmosphere, can contribute to the depletion of the ozone layer in the upper atmosphere. Ozone filters out harmful radiation from the sun.**

• Do not attempt to discharge the system by merely loosening a fitting, or removing the service valve caps and cracking these valves. Precise control is possible only when using the service gauges and a proper A/C refrigerant recovery station. Wear protective gloves when connecting or disconnecting service gauge hoses.

➡ **Be sure to consult the laws in your area before servicing the air conditioning system. In some states, it is illegal to perform repairs involving refrigerant unless the work is done by a certified technician.**

• Discharge the system only in a well ventilated area, as high concentrations of the gas which might accidentally escape can exclude oxygen and act as an anesthetic. When leak testing or soldering, this is particularly important, as toxic gas is formed when R-12 contacts any flame.

• Never start a system without first verifying that both service valves are properly installed, and that all fittings throughout the system are snugly connected.

• Avoid applying heat to any refrigerant line or storage vessel. Charging may be aided by using water heated to less than 125°F (50°C) to warm the refrigerant container. Never allow a refrigerant storage container to sit out in the sun, or near any other source of heat, such as a radiator.

• Always wear goggles to protect your eyes when working on a system. If refrigerant contacts the eyes, it is advisable in all cases to see a physician as soon as possible.

• Frostbite from liquid refrigerant should be treated by first gradually warming the area with cool water, and then gently applying petroleum jelly. A physician should be consulted.

• Always keep refrigerant drum fittings capped when not in use. If the container is equipped with a safety cap to protect the valve, make sure the cap is in place when the can is not being used. Avoid sudden shock to the drum, which might occur from dropping it, or from banging a heavy tool against it. Never carry a drum in the passenger compartment of a car.

• Always completely discharge the system into a suitable recovery unit before painting the vehicle (if the paint is to be baked on), or before welding anywhere near refrigerant lines.

• When servicing the system, minimize the time that any refrigerant line or fitting is open to the air in order to prevent moisture or dirt from entering the system. Contaminants such as moisture or dirt can damage internal system components. Always replace O-rings on lines or fittings which are disconnected. Prior to installation coat, but do not soak, replacement O-rings with suitable compressor oil.

GENERAL SERVICING PROCEDURES

▶ See Figure 61

The most important aspect of air conditioning service is the maintenance of a pure and adequate charge of refrigerant in the system. A refrigeration system cannot function properly if a significant percentage of the charge is lost. Leaks are common because the severe vibration encountered underhood in an automobile can easily cause a sufficient cracking or loosening of the air conditioning fittings; allowing, the extreme operating pressures of the system to force refrigerant out.

The problem can be understood by considering what happens to the system as it is operated with a continuous leak. Because the expansion valve regulates the flow of refrigerant to the evaporator, the level of refrigerant there is fairly constant. The receiver/drier stores any excess of refrigerant, and so a loss will first appear there as a reduction in the level of liquid. As this level nears the bottom of the vessel, some refrigerant vapor bubbles will begin to appear in the stream of liquid supplied to the expansion valve. This vapor decreases the capacity of the expansion valve very little as the valve opens to compensate for its presence. As the quantity of liquid

in the condenser decreases, the operating pressure will drop there and throughout the high side of the system. As the R-12 continues to be expelled, the pressure available to force the liquid through the expansion valve will continue to decrease, and, eventually, the valve's orifice will prove to be too much of a restriction for adequate flow even with the needle fully withdrawn.

At this point, low side pressure will start to drop, and severe reduction in cooling capacity, marked by freeze-up of the evaporator coil, will result. Eventually, the operating pressure of the evaporator will be lower than the pressure of the atmosphere surrounding it, and air will be drawn into the system wherever there are leaks in the low side.

Because all atmospheric air contains at least some moisture, water will enter the system and mix with the R-12 and the oil. Trace amounts of moisture will cause sludging of the oil, and corrosion of the system. Saturation and clogging of the filter/drier, and freezing of the expansion valve orifice will eventually result. As air fills the system to a greater and greater extent, it will interfere more and more with the normal flows of refrigerant and heat.

From this description, it should be obvious that much of the technicians time will be spent detecting leaks, repairing them, and then restoring the purity and quantity of the refrigerant charge. A list of general rules should be followed in addition to all safety precautions:

• Keep all tools as clean and dry as possible.

• Thoroughly purge the service gauges and hoses of air and moisture before connecting them to the system. Keep them capped when not in use.

• Thoroughly clean any refrigerant fitting before disconnecting it, in order to minimize the entrance of dirt into the system.

• Plan any operation that requires opening the system beforehand, in order to minimize the length of time it will be exposed to open air. Cap or seal the open ends to minimize the entrance of foreign material.

• When adding oil, pour it through an extremely clean and dry tube or funnel. Keep the oil capped whenever possible. Do not use oil that has not been kept tightly sealed.

• Use only R-12 refrigerant. Purchase refrigerant intended for use only in automatic air conditioning systems. Avoid the use of R-12 that may be packaged for other purposes, such as cleaning, or powering a horn, as it is impure.

• Completely evacuate any system that has been opened to replace a component, or that has leaked sufficiently to draw in moisture and air. This requires evacuating air and moisture with a good vacuum pump for at least one hour. If a system has been open for a considerable length of time it may be advisable to evacuate the system for up to 12 hours (overnight).

• Use a wrench on both halves of a fitting that is to be disconnected, so as to avoid placing torque on any of the refrigerant lines.

• When overhauling a compressor, pour some of the oil into a clean glass and inspect it. If there is evidence of dirt or metal particles, or both, flush all refrigerant components with clean refrigerant before evacuating and recharging the system. In addition, if metal particles are present, the compressor should be replaced.

"HPV" — HIGH PRESSURE VAPOR LEAVING COMPRESSOR.

"HPL" — VAPOR IS COOLED DOWN BY CONDENSER AIR FLOW AND LEAVES AS HIGH PRESSURE LIQUID.

"LPL" — ORIFICE METERS THE LIQUID R-12, INTO EVAPORATOR, REDUCING ITS PRESSURE, AND
WARM BLOWER AIR ACROSS EVAPORATOR CORE CAUSES BOILING OFF OF LIQUID INTO VAPOR.

"LPV" — LEAVES EVAPORATOR AS LOW PRESSURE VAPOR AND RETURNS WITH THE
SMALL AMOUNT OF . . .

"lpl" — . . . LOW PRESSURE LIQUID THAT DIDN'T BOIL OFF COMPLETELY BACK TO
THE COMPRESSOR TO BE COMPRESSED AGAIN.

86811085

Fig. 61 The air conditioning system functional layout

• Schrader valves may leak only when under full operating pressure. Therefore, if leakage is suspected but cannot be located, operate the system with a full charge of refrigerant and look for leaks from all Schrader valves. Replace any faulty valves.

Additional Preventive Maintenance Checks

ANTIFREEZE

In order to prevent heater core freeze-up during A/C operation, it is necessary to maintain permanent type antifreeze protection of +15°F (9°C), or lower. A reading of -15°F (-9°C) is ideal since this protection also supplies sufficient corrosion inhibitors for the protection of the engine cooling system.

➡**The same antifreeze should not be used longer than the antifreeze or car specifies.**

RADIATOR CAP

For efficient operation of an air conditioned car's cooling system, the radiator cap should have a holding pressure which meets car manufacturer's specifications. A cap which fails to hold these pressures should be replaced.

CONDENSER

Any obstruction of or damage to the condenser configuration will restrict the air flow which is essential to its efficient operation. It is therefore a good rule to keep this unit clean and in proper physical shape.

➡**Bug screens are regarded as obstructions.**

CONDENSATION DRAIN TUBE

This single molded drain tube expels the condensation, which accumulates on the bottom of the evaporator housing, into the engine compartment. If this tube is obstructed, the air conditioning performance can be restricted and condensation buildup can spill over onto the vehicle's floor.

SYSTEM INSPECTION

➡**R-12 refrigerant is a chlorofluorocarbon which, when released into the atmosphere, can contribute to the depletion of the ozone layer in the upper atmosphere. Ozone filters out harmful radiation from the sun.**

The easiest and often most important check for the air conditioning system consists of a visual inspection of the system components. Visually inspect the air conditioning system for refrigerant leaks, damaged compressor clutch, compressor drive belt tension and condition, plugged evaporator drain tube, blocked condenser fins, disconnected or broken wires, blown fuses, corroded connections and poor insulation.

A refrigerant leak will usually appear as an oily residue at the leakage point in the system. The oily residue soon picks up dust or dirt particles from the surrounding air and appears greasy. Through time, this will build up and appear to be a heavy dirt impregnated grease. Most leaks are caused by damaged or missing O-ring seals at the component connections, damaged charging valve cores or missing service gauge port caps.

For a thorough visual and operational inspection, check the following:

1. Check the surface of the radiator and condenser for dirt, leaves or other material which might block air flow.

2. Check for kinks in hoses and lines. Check the system for leaks.

3. Make sure the drive belt is under the proper tension. When the air conditioning is operating, make sure the drive belt is free of noise or slippage.

4. Make sure the blower motor operates at all appropriate positions, then check for distribution of the air from all outlets with the blower on **HIGH**.

➡**Keep in mind that under conditions of high humidity, air discharged from the A/C vents may not feel as cold as expected, even if the system is working properly. This is because the vaporized moisture in humid air retains heat more effectively than does dry air, making the humid air more difficult to cool.**

5. Make sure the air passage selection lever is operating correctly. Start the engine and warm it to normal operating temperature, then make sure the hot/cold selection lever is operating correctly.

REFRIGERANT LEVEL CHECKS

The factory installed air conditioning unit has no sight glass for system checks. It is recommended that all air conditioning service work be entrusted to a qualified mechanic.

DISCHARGING, EVACUATING AND CHARGING

Discharging, evacuating and charging the air conditioning system must be performed by a properly trained and certified mechanic in a facility equipped with refrigerant recovery/recycling equipment that meets SAE standards.

Windshield Wipers

▶ See Figure 62

For maximum effectiveness and longest life, the windshield and wiper elements should be kept clean. Dirt, tree sap, road tar, etc., will cause streaking, smearing, and wiper element deterioration. Hardening of the elements will cause the wipers to chatter as they wipe the windshield. Wash the windshield thoroughly with a glass cleaner at least once a month. Wipe off the rubber element with a wet rag afterwards.

Obviously, the item most frequently requiring replacement is the element. It is very rarely necessary to replace the blade or arm unless they become accidentally bent or damaged in some other manner.

Your car is equipped from the manufacture with one of three types of elements: the first type is commonly referred to as the Anco® style; the second type is the Trico® style; and the third is the plastic style which uses a plastic blade assembly. Replacement of any element type is very simple and requires only a few minutes to do.

86811087

Fig. 62 TRICO ® insert replacement

REPLACEMENT

Wiper arm replacement is covered in Section 6.

ANCO® Style Blade

1. Locate the red release button at the top of one of the yokes (free yoke), push the button, and separate the free yoke from the blade.
2. Pull the element out of the other yoke (attached yoke).
3. Transfer the free yoke to the new element, being sure to engage the element into all of the yoke jaws.
4. Feed the other end of the element into the attached yoke, again being sure that the element is fully engaged.
5. Push the button and snap the free yoke into place on the blade. Release the button and double-check that the element is fully engaged into all of the yoke jaws.

Trico® Style Blade

▶ See Figure 63

1. Squeeze the sides of the element retainer (located on only one side of the element) and pull the element out of the blade/yoke assembly.
2. To install the new element, guide the new element into all of the blade/yoke jaws. The element must be positioned in the same manner as the one which was removed. When the retainer comes in contact with the end of the blade, make sure that each side of the retainer is positioned on the inside of the jaws, then snap the element into place.
3. Check that the element is fully engaged to all of the jaws before operating the wipers.

Plastic

▶ See Figure 64

1. Remove the wiper blade and element assembly from the wiper arm.
2. Pull the wiper blade and the element apart, then pull the element downward. This will disengage the element from the retaining tabs.
3. Pull the element out, guide the new element into place, and release the hand pressure on the blade to engage the retaining tabs. Be sure that the element is completely engaged. Snap the wiper blade and element assembly into place on the arm.

Tires and Wheels

TIRE ROTATION

▶ See Figure 65

Tire rotation is the moving of the tires from wheel-to-wheel position in order to even wear. Tire rotation is recommended every 6000 miles (10,000 km), and then every 15,000 miles (25,000 km) there after to obtain maximum tire wear. The pattern you use depends on whether or not your car has a usable spare. Radial tires can be cross-switched (from one side of the car to the other). Be careful though if you have

1. Wiper arm
2. Transmission shaft
3. Wiper arm retaining latch
4. Wiper blade removal
5. Wiper insert removal
6. Wiper blade assembly
7. Wiper insert
8. Screwdriver
9. Blade retainer
10. Insert retainer

86811089

Fig. 63 Wiper blade assembly removal and installation

86811088

Fig. 64 Slide the plastic insert into the claws to replace

directional tires on your car, they can not be cross-switched. Snow tires sometimes have directional arrows molded into the side of the carcass. The arrow shows the direction of rotation. They will wear very rapidly if the rotation is reversed. Studded tires will lose their studs if their rotational direction is reversed.

➡Mark the wheel position or direction of rotation on radial tires or studded snow tires before removing them.

TIRE DESIGN

▸ See Figures 66 and 67

For maximum satisfaction, tires should be used in sets of five. Mixing different types (radial, bias-belted, fiberglass belted) should be avoided. Conventional bias tires are constructed so that the cords run bead to bead at an angle. Alternate plies run at an opposite angle. This type of construction gives rigidity to both tread and side wall. Bias belted tires are similar in construction to conventional bias ply tires. Belts

RECOMMENDED ROTATION PATTERN FOR FRONT WHEEL DRIVE CARS

LF   RF

LR   RR

DO NOT INCLUDE "TEMPORARY USE ONLY" SPARE TIRE IN ROTATION

86811091

Fig. 65 Tire rotation

run at an angle and also at a 90° angle to the bead, as in radial tires. Tread life is improved considerably over the conventional bias tire. The radial tire differs in construction, but instead of the carcass running at an angle of 90° at each other they run at an angle of 90° to the bead. This gives the tread a great deal of rigidity and the side wall a great deal of flexibility (which accounts for the characteristic bulge associated with radial tires).

TIRE STORAGE

Store the tires at the proper inflation pressure if they are mounted on wheels. Keep them in a cool dry place, on their sides. If the tires are stored in the garage or basement, do not let them stand on a concrete floor, and make sure there is no danger of water collecting inside them. Set them on strips of wood. Keep tires away from from sources of heat and ozone such as hot pipes and electric generators. Be sure tires surfaces on which the tires are stored are clean and free from

grease, gasoline or other substances which could deteriorate the rubber.

TIRE INFLATION

▶ **See Figures 68 and 69**

Tire inflation is the most ignored item of auto maintenance. Gasoline mileage can drop as much as 0.8% for every 1 pound per square inch (6.9 kPa) of under inflation.

Two items should be a permanent fixture in every glove compartment: a tire pressure gauge and a tread depth gauge. Check the tire air pressure (including the spare) regularly with a pocket type gauge. Kicking the tires won't tell you a thing, and the gauge on the service station air hose is notoriously inaccurate. General Motors recommends checking your tire inflation once a month.

The tire pressures recommended for your car are usually found on the left door or in the owner's manual. Ideally, inflation pressure should be checked when the tires are cool. When the air becomes heated it expands and the pressure

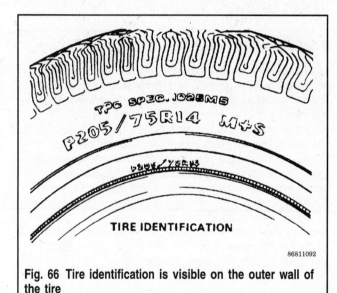

Fig. 66 Tire identification is visible on the outer wall of the tire

Fig. 67 Tire size explanation

A Date
B Gross vehicle weight rating
C Gross axle weight rating - FRT & RR
D Certification statement
E Vehicle identification number
F Vehicle class type: "Pass." car"
g Maximum occupants
H Maximum vehicle capacity weight
I Maximum loading at GVWR
J Tire size
K Spare tire size
L Tire label code
M Tire press. with max. occupants FRT & RR
N Spare tire pressure

Fig. 68 This is the tire placard which is located on the rear face of the driver's door of the car. This card specifies what size tires and the maximum tire pressures etc.

Fig. 69 Proper inflation is very important for tire tread life.

increases. Every 10°F (rise (or drop) in temperature means a difference of 1 psi (6.9 kPa), which also explains why the tire appears to lose air on a very cold night. When it is impossible to check the tires cold, allow for pressure build-up due to heat. If the hot pressure exceeds the cold pressure by more than 15 psi (103.4 kPa), reduce your speed, load or both. Otherwise internal heat is created in the tire. When the heat approaches the temperature at which the tire was cured, during manufacture, the tread can separate from the body.

✳✳CAUTION

Never counteract excessive pressure build-up by bleeding off air pressure (letting some air out). This will only further raise the tire operating temperature.

Before starting a long trip with lots of luggage, you can add about 2-4 psi (13.8-27.6 kPa) to the tires to make them run cooler, but never exceed the maximum inflation pressure on the side of the tire.

CARE OF SPECIAL WHEELS

▶ **See Figure 70**

If you have invested money in magnesium, aluminum alloy or sport wheels, special precautions should be taken to make sure your investment is not wasted, and that your special wheels look good for the lifetime of the car.

Special wheels are easily scratched and/or damaged. Occasionally check the rim for cracks, damage or air leaks. If any of these conditions are found, replace the wheel. In order to prevent this type of damage, and the costly replacement of a special wheel, observe the following precautions:

• Take special care not to damage the wheels during removal, installation, balancing, etc. After removal of the wheels from the car, place them on a rubber mat or other protective surface.

• While the vehicle is being driven, be careful not to drive over sharp obstacles or allow the wheels to contact the shoulder of the road. Hitting a pothole can damage your wheels by

causing a stress crack. These cracks are not necessarily on the outside of the wheel in visible sight. You could have a crack on the inner portion of the rim and this can be dangerous.

• When washing, use a mild detergent and water. Avoid using cleansers with abrasives, or hard brushes. And a little metal polish or wax after washing will help your wheels keep that new look.

• If possible, remove your special wheels from the car during the winter months, and replace them with regular steel rims. Salt and sand that is applied to the roadways for snow removal during these months can do severe damage to special wheels.

• Make sure that the recommended lug nut torque is never exceeded, or you may crack your wheels. And never use snow chains with special wheels.

• If you intend to store the wheels, lay them flat on a protective surface and cover them. Do not stack them on top of each other and do not place anything else, except a protective cover, on them.

TREAD DEPTH

▶ **See Figures 71, 72 and 73**

All tires made since 1968, have 7 built-in tread wear indicator bars that show up as ½ in. (13mm) wide smooth bands across the tire when ½ in. (0.8mm) of tread remains. The appearance of tread wear indicators means that the tires should be replaced. In fact, many states have laws prohibiting the use of tires with less than 13/32 in. (0.8mm) tread.

You can check your own tread depth with an inexpensive gauge or by using a Lincoln head penny. Slip the Lincoln penny into several tread grooves. If you can see the top of Lincoln's head in 2 adjacent grooves, the tires have less than 13/32 in. (0.8mm) tread left and should be replaced. You can measure snow tires in the same manner by using the tails side of the Lincoln penny. If you can see the top of the Lincoln memorial, it's time to replace the snow tires.

Fig. 70 Always keep your eyes open for any signs of tire damage; a cut sidewall, such as this, could lead to a serious accident

Fig. 71 Tread wear indicators are a very important indicator that you need new tires

Fig. 72 Use a tread wear depth gauge to speculate the need of new tires

Fig. 73 The use of Lincoln head on a penny is an inexpensive gauge

BUYING NEW TIRES

When buying new tires, give some thought to the following points, especially if you are considering a switch to larger tires or a different profile series:

1. All four tires must be of the same construction type. This rule cannot be violated. Radial, bias, and bias-belted tires must not be mixed.

2. The wheels should be the correct width for the tire. Tire dealers have charts of tire and rim compatibility. A mismatch will cause sloppy handling and rapid tire wear. The tread width should match the rim width (inside bead to inside bead) within an inch. For radial tires, the rim width should be 80% or less of the tire (not tread) width.

3. The height (mounted diameter) of the new tires can change speedometer accuracy, engine speed at a given road speed, fuel mileage, acceleration, and ground clearance. Tire manufacturers furnish full measurement specifications.

4. The spare tire should be usable, at least for short distance and low speed operation, with the new tires.

5. There shouldn't be any body interference when loaded, on bumps, or in turns.

FLUIDS AND LUBRICANTS

Fluid Disposal

Used fluids such as engine oil, transmission fluid, antifreeze and brake fluid are hazardous wastes and must be disposed of properly. Before draining any fluids, consult with local authorities; in many cases, waste oil, etc., is accepted in recycling programs. A number of service stations and auto parts stores are also accepting waste fluids for recycling.

Be sure of the recycling center's policies before draining the fluids, as many will not accept mixed fluids such as oil and antifreeze.

Fuel and Engine Oil Recommendations

FUEL RECOMMENDATIONS

Gasoline

All cars covered by this manual must use unleaded fuel. The use of leaded fuel will plug the catalyst rendering it imperative, and will increase the exhaust back pressure to the point where engine output will be severely reduced. The minimum octane for all engines is 87 RON. All unleaded fuels sold in the U.S. and Canada are required to meet this minimum octane rating.

Use of a fuel too low in octane (a measurement of anti-knock quality) will result in spark knock. Since many factors affect operating efficiency, such as altitude, terrain, air temperature and humidity, knocking may result even though the recommended fuel is being used. If persistent knocking occurs, it may be necessary to switch to a slightly higher grade of unleaded gasoline. Continuous or heavy knocking may result in serious engine damage, for which the manufacturer is not responsible.

➡**Your car's engine fuel requirement can change with time, due to carbon buildup, which changes the compression ratio. If your car's engine knocks, pings, or runs on, switch to a higher grade of fuel, if possible, and check the ignition timing. Sometimes changing brands of gasoline will cure the problem. If it is necessary to retard timing from specifications, don't change it more than a few degrees. Retarded timing will reduce power output and fuel mileage, and will increase engine temperature.**

Diesel

✳✳WARNING

Failure to use specified fuels will result in engine damage for which the manufacturer is not responsible. Use of fuel additives is NOT recommended.

At any outside temperature above 20°F (-7°C), Number 2-D diesel fuel should be used, since it will give better fuel economy then Number 1-D. When the outside temperature is below 20°F (-7°C), use either Number 1-D fuel (preferred if available) or a blended Number 2-D. The blended Number 2-D has 1-D fuel in it, but will usually be called just Number 2-D. Check with the service station operator to be sure you get the proper fuel.

➡**Diesel fuel may foam during filling, which is normal. The foam may cause the automatic pump nozzle to turn off before the tank is actually filled. The foaming effect can be reduced by slowing the fill rate.**

OPERATING IN COLD WEATHER

All types of diesel fuel have a certain paraffin content. The paraffin components are high in energy content and help to improve fuel economy. Below about 20°F (-7°C), the trouble with paraffin begins. At this temperature, the paraffin components begin turning to wax flakes. Depending upon the temperature, the wax flakes can block either or both of the two fuel filters (tank or engine) and stop fuel from reaching the engine.

Since Number 2-D fuel has more paraffin than Number 1-D (or blended Number 2-D), Number 2-D would be more apt to cause waxing problems (See Fuel Recommendations).

If the fuel tank filter plugs due to waxing, a check valve inside of the fuel tank will open and allow fuel to flow to the engine. Because of the check valve location, not all of the fuel in the tank can be used if the filter remains clogged (check valve remains open). About 4 gallons of fuel will remain in the tank when you run out of fuel. When driving in temperatures below 20°F (-7°C), be sure to keep the tank more than ¼ full to help prevent running out of fuel if the filter plugs.

If equipped, the fuel line heater should be used when temperatures are expected to be below 10°F (-12°C) and you have Number 2-D fuel in the tank.

WATER IN THE FUEL

Diesel fuel should be purchased from a reputable dealer, since the majority of the water found in a diesel fuel system gets into the system during refueling. Water can cause extensive (and expensive) damage to the diesel fuel system.

This car has a water separator system in the fuel tank and a Water-In-Fuel indicator on the instrument panel. The indicator is designed to illuminate when starting the engine (as a bulb check), or when water is detected in the tank. If the light comes on at any other time, there is probably a fault in the detector circuit. If the engine loses power and begins to run rough without the detector light on, there is probably water in the system. Both the fuel system and the detector circuit should be checked.

If the indicator light comes on immediately after refueling, a large amount of water was pumped into the tank, DON'T run the engine; the fuel system must be purged right away.

If the indicator lights after braking, cornering, etc., a moderate amount of water is in the system. In this case, the water should be removed within one or two days.

OIL RECOMMENDATIONS

Gasoline Engine

◗ **See Figures 74, 75 and 76**

Under normal conditions, the engine oil and the filter should be changed at the first 7500 miles (12,000 km) or once a year whichever comes first. GM recommends that the oil filter be changed at every other oil change thereafter. For the small price of an oil filter, it's cheap insurance to replace the filter at every oil change. One of the larger filter manufacturers points out in its advertisements that not changing the filter leaves one quart of dirty oil in the engine. This claim is true and should be kept in mind when changing your oil.

Under severe conditions, such as:
- Driving in dusty areas
- Trailer towing
- Frequent idling or idling for extended periods
- Frequently driving short distances — 4 miles (6 km) or so in freezing weather

The engine oil and filter should be changed every 3 months or 3000 miles (4800 km), whichever comes first. If dust storms are ever encountered in your area, change the oil and filter as soon as possible after the storm.

The American Petroleum Institute (API) designation (printed on the oil container) indicates the classification of engine oil for use under certain operating conditions. Oils having an API service designation of SG should be used in your car. The SG rating designates the highest quality oil meant for passenger car usage. It is okay to use an SG oil having a combination rating such as SG/CC or SG/CD for gasoline powered engines. In addition, GM recommends the use of SG/Energy Conserving oil. Oils labeled, Energy Conserving (or Saving); Fuel (Gas or Gasoline) Saving, etc., are recommended due to their superior

	Anticipated Temperature Range	SAE Viscosity
Multi-grade	Above 32°F	10W—40 10W—50 20W—40 20W—50 10W—30
	May be used as low as −10°F	10W—30 10W—40
	Consistently below 10°F	5W—20 5W—30
Single-grade	Above 32°F	30
	Temperature between +32°F and −10°F	10W

86811098

Fig. 74 Oil viscosity selection chart — vehicles since 1987 are designed to use 5W-30 all year

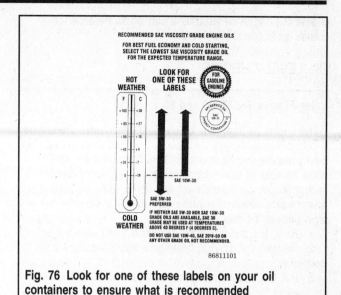

86811101

Fig. 76 Look for one of these labels on your oil containers to ensure what is recommended

86811099

Fig. 75 Gasoline oil selection chart

86811100

Fig. 77 Diesel engine oil selection chart

lubricating qualities (less friction = easier and more efficient engine operation) and fuel saving characteristics. Use of engine oil additives is not recommended, because if the correct oil is purchased to begin with, the additives will be of no value.

➡️Use of engine oils without an SG rating, or failing to change the oil and filter at the recommended intervals will cause excessive engine wear and could affect your warranty.

Diesel Engines

♦ See Figure 77

The engine oil requirements for diesel engines are more stringent than those for gasoline engines, since contaminant build-up in the engine oil occurs much faster in the diesel engine. Also, the diesel contaminants are more damaging to the engine oil.

Under normal operating conditions, the engine oil and filter MUST be changed every 5000 miles (8000 km), regardless of the time period involved.

Under severe operating conditions, such as those mentioned previously under Gasoline Engines, the oil and filter must be changed every 2500 miles (4000 km) or 3 months, whichever comes first.

In the diesel equipped car, ONLY an engine oil having one of the two following API designations should be used: SG/CC or SG/CD. Period! Don't use any other type of oil.

✳✳CAUTION

Failure to use an SG/CC or SG/CD oil will result in excessive engine wear and will probably void the engine warranty. Failure to change the oil and filter at the recommended intervals will have the same results.

In diesel engines, the use of oil in regard to its viscosity is limited. With a diesel, you only have three choices: 10W-30, 15W-40, or straight 30W. Refer to the accompanying chart to choose the engine oil viscosity according to the expected outside air temperature.

OIL LEVEL CHECK

▶ **See Figures 78, 79, 80 and 81**

The engine oil level may be checked either when the engine is cold or warm, though the latter is preferred. If you check the level while the engine is cold, DO NOT start the engine first, since the cold oil won't drain back to the engine oil pan fast enough to give an accurate reading. Even when the engine is warm, wait a couple of minutes after turning it off to let the oil drain back to the pan.

1. Raise the hood, pull the dipstick out and wipe it clean.
2. Reinsert the dipstick, being sure that you push it back in completely.
3. Pull the dipstick back out, hold it horizontally, and check the level at the end of the dipstick. Some dipsticks are marked with ADD and FULL lines, others with ADD 1 QT and OPERATING RANGE. In either case, the level must be above the ADD line. Reinsert the dipstick completely.
4. If oil must be added, it can be poured in through the rocker (valve) cover after removing the filler cap on the cover. Recheck the level a few minutes after adding oil.
5. Be sure that the dipstick and oil filler cap are installed before closing the hood.

OIL AND FILTER CHANGE

Screw On Oil Filter

▶ **See Figures 82, 83, 84, 85 and 86**

1. Drive the car until the engine is at normal operating temperature. A run to the parts store for oil and a filter should accomplish this. If the engine is not hot when the oil is changed, most of the acids and contaminants will remain inside the engine.

Fig. 79 When checking the oil level it should appear to be clean, not dark in color or thick. The level should be between the add and full marks

Fig. 80 Turn and remove the oil filler cap

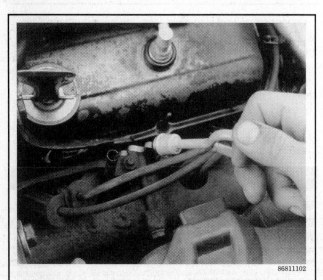

Fig. 78 Remove the oil dipstick and wipe clean

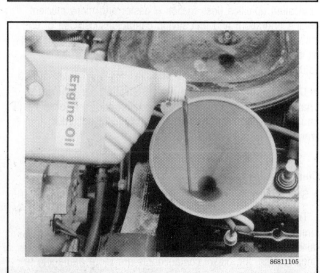

Fig. 81 Insert a funnel into the valve cover and add the appropriate amount of engine oil needed

2. Raise and support the front of the vehicle safely on jackstands to access the oil filter.

3. Slide a pan of at least six quarts capacity under the oil pan.

4. Remove the drain plug from the engine oil pan, after wiping the plug area clean. The drain plug is the bolt inserted at an angle into the lowest point of the oil pan.

5. Use a rag to protect your hands from the hot plug.

6. The oil from the engine will be HOT. It will probably not be possible to hold onto the drain plug. You may have to let it fall into the pan and fish it out later. Allow all the oil to drain completely. This will take a few minutes.

7. Wipe off the drain plug, removing any traces of metal particles. Check the condition of the plastic drain plug gasket. If it is cracked or distorted in any way, replace it. Reinstall the drain plug and gasket. Tighten the drain plug snugly.

8. The oil filter for the V6 gasoline engine is right up front, just behind the radiator. The four cylinder oil filter is at the back of the engine, it is impossible to reach it from above. It is almost as inaccessible from below. It may be easiest to remove the right front wheel and reach through the fender opening to get at the four cylinder oil filter. The oil filter of the diesel V6 engine is located on the passenger side face of the engine block. Use an oil strap wrench to loosen the oil filter; these are available at auto parts stores. It is recommended that you purchase one with as thin a strap as possible, to get into tight areas. Place the drain pan on the ground, under the filter. Unscrew and discard the old filter. It will be VERY HOT, so be careful.

9. If the oil filter is on so tightly that it collapses under pressure from the wrench, drive a long punch or a nail through it, across the diameter and as close to the base as possible, and use this as a lever to unscrew it. Make sure you are turning it counterclockwise.

10. Clean off the oil filter mounting surface with a rag. Apply a thin film of clean engine oil to the new filter gasket.

11. Screw the filter on by hand until the gasket makes contact. Then tighten it by hand an additional ½-¾ of a turn. Do not overtighten.

12. Remove the filler cap on the rocker (valve) cover, after wiping the area clean.

Fig. 83 Install the plug and gasket snugly

Fig. 84 Using a wrench loosen and remove the oil filter. Don't forget there is still a small amount of oil inside the filter

Fig. 82 Make sure you have a pan ready, loosen the drain plug with a wrench, then place the plug into the drain pan

Fig. 85 Before installing a new oil filter, coat the rubber gasket with clean oil

Fig. 86 Using your hands install and tighten the filter onto the car

13. Add the correct number of quarts of oil specified in the Capacities chart. If you don't have an oil can spout, you will need a funnel. Be certain you do not overfill the engine, which can cause serious damage. Replace the cap.

14. Check the oil level on the dipstick. It is normal for the level to be a bit above the full mark. Start the engine and allow it to idle for a few minutes.

✳✳CAUTION

Do not run the engine above idle speed until it has built up oil pressure, indicated when the oil light goes out.

15. Shut off the engine, allow the oil to drain for a minute, and check the oil level.

16. Check around the filter and and drain plug for any leaks.

Cartridge Oil Filter

▶ See Figure 87

This cartridge type filter is found on some of the mid — model year 2.5L engines.

1. Drive the car until the engine is at normal operating temperature. A run to the parts store for oil and a filter should accomplish this. If the engine is not hot when the oil is changed, most of the acids and contaminants will remain inside the engine.

2. Raise the car and support on jackstands.

3. Remove the oil pan drain plug.

4. Drain the oil into a drain pan.

5. Slowly turn the plug to begin removal and pull downwards.

➡**Be sure to stand clear of the flowing oil from this next step.**

6. With a pair of pliers, applied to the tab/boss, remove the filter.

7. Make sure the O-ring/gasket was removed with the filter; if not remove it.

Fig. 87 Cartridge type oil filter

To install:

8. Coat the O-ring/gasket on the end of the filter with clean engine oil.

9. Press the filter into position in the housing by hand.

10. Make sure the filter is fully seated.

11. Check the oil filter O-ring/gasket for any damage and replace it, if necessary. Lube with oil the gasket and install the drain plug.

12. Tighten the plug 1/4 turn after gasket contacts, then tighten another 1/4 turn.

13. Lower the car, fill engine with proper amount of oil and check for leaks.

After completing this job, you will have several quarts of oil to dispose of. The best thing to do with it is to funnel it into old plastic milk containers or bleach bottles. Then, you can locate a service station with a recycling barrel.

Manual Transaxle

FLUID RECOMMENDATIONS

Under normal conditions, the lubricant used in the manual transaxle does not require periodic changing. The fluid level in the transaxle should be checked every 12 months or 7500 miles (12,000 km), whichever comes first. The manual transaxle is designed for use with Dexron®III automatic transmission. Don't use standard manual transmission lubricant in the transaxle.

LEVEL CHECK

▶ See Figures 88 and 89

1. Park the car on a level surface. Before proceeding, the transaxle case must be cool to the touch. Due to the expansion characteristics of the Dexron®III fluid, it will be above the level of the filler plug when the transmission is hot. On your HM-282 manual 5 speeds, there is a dipstick.
2. The dipstick type can be removed in the same manner as an oil dipstick. On the drain plug type, slowly remove the filler plug from the driver's side of the transaxle (see the illustration). The lubricant level should be right at the bottom of the filler plug hole. If the fluid trickles out as the plug is removed, or if you can just touch the fluid through the filler plug hole, the level is correct.
3. If you cannot feel the fluid level with your finger through the filler plug hole, add Dexron®III automatic transmission through the hole until the fluid begins to trickle out of the hole.
4. When the level is correct, install the filler plug and tighten it snugly.

Fig. 89 Most models use a filler plug to fill and check the fluid level on a manual transaxle

DRAIN AND REFILL

1. Park the car on a level surface, turn **OFF** engine and apply the parking brake.
2. Place a container of adequate capacity beneath the drain plug which is located underneath the car, on the bottom of the transaxle housing.
3. Use the proper size wrench to loosen the drain plug slowly, while maintaining a slight upward pressure, to keep the oil from leaking out around the plug.
4. Allow all of the lubricant to drain from the transaxle, then clean the plug area thoroughly. Install the drain plug and gasket (if so equipped).
5. Remove the transaxle dipstick and add slowly checking the level often. Do not overfill.
6. Check the oil level as outlined above.

Automatic Transaxle

FLUID RECOMMENDATIONS

Under normal operating conditions, the automatic transmission fluid only needs to be changed every 100,000 miles (161,000 km), according to GM If one or more of the following driving conditions is encountered the fluid and filter should be changed every 15,000 miles (24,100 km):

• Driving in heavy city traffic when the outside temperature regularly reached 90°F (32°C)
• Driving regularly in hilly or mountainous areas
• Towing a trailer
• Using the vehicle as a taxi or police car, or for delivery purposes.

Remember, these are the factory recommendations, and in this case are considered to be the minimum. You must determine a change interval which fits your driving habits. If your vehicle is never subjected to these conditions, a 100,000 mile (161,000 km) change interval is adequate. If you are a normal driver, a two-year/30,000 mile (48,300 km) interval will be more

Fig. 88 Some manual transaxles have a dipstick to check the fluid level

than sufficient to maintain the long life for which your automatic transaxle was designed.

When replacing or adding fluid, use only fluid labeled Dexron®III or Dexron®IIE. Use of other fluids could cause erratic shifting and transmission damage.

LEVEL CHECK

▶ **See Figures 90, 91 and 92**

The fluid level may be checked with the transaxle cold, warm, or hot, as this is accounted for on the dipstick graduations.

➡**If the vehicle has just been driven in extreme conditions, allow the fluid to cool for about 30 minutes.**

1. Park the car on a level surface and set the parking brake.
2. Start the engine, apply the brake, and move the shift lever through all of the gear ranges, ending up in Park.
3. Let the engine idle for at least 5 minutes with the transaxle in Park.
4. The dipstick is located on the driver's side of the engine compartment, ahead of the engine.
5. Raise the hood, pull the dipstick out and wipe it off with a clean cloth.
6. Reinsert the dipstick, being sure that it is fully seated.
7. Again, remove the dipstick. Hold it horizontally and read the fluid level. Touch the fluid-if it feels cold or warm, the level should be between the dimples above the **FULL HOT** mark. If the fluid feels hot, the level should be in the hatched area, between the **ADD 1 PT** and **FULL HOT** marks.
8. If required, add just enough Dexron®II automatic transmission fluid to bring the level to where it should be. One pint of fluid will raise the level from **ADD** to **FULL** when the transaxle is hot. Recheck the level.

Fig. 91 Notice the fluid level, smell it to make sure it is not burnt. Add only to the full mark, NEVER overfill

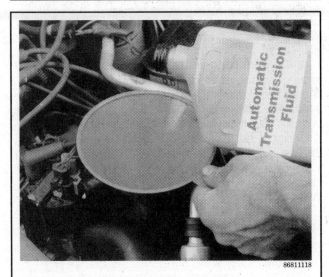
Fig. 92 A funnel is handy for adding fluid

9. Reinsert the dipstick, again making sure that it is fully seated. Lower the hood.

※※WARNING

NEVER overfill the transaxle, as fluid foaming and subsequent transaxle damage can occur!

DRAIN, FILTER SERVICE AND REFILL

▶ **See Figures 93, 94, 95, 96, 97 and 98**

➡**Some transaxle use RTV sealer in place of a gasket. Do not attempt to replace the sealer with a gasket.**

1. Jack up the front of your vehicle and support it with jackstands.
2. Remove the front and side pan bolts.
3. Loosen the rear bolts about 4 turns.

Fig. 90 Locate the dipstick, remove and wipe clean before reinserting

Fig. 93 The transaxle fluid pan is usually located behind the engine oil pan (as shown here)

Fig. 95 Remove the pan after the fluid has drained, be careful, there is still some fluid in the pan

Fig. 94 Loosen and remove the pan bolts

Fig. 96 Discard the gasket (if equipped)

4. Carefully pry the oil pan loose, allowing the fluid to drain.

5. Remove the remaining bolts, the pan, and the gasket or RTV. Discard the gasket.

6. Clean the pan with solvent and dry thoroughly, with compressed air.

7. Remove the strainer and O-ring seal.

To install:

8. Install new strainer and new O-ring seal locating the strainer against the dipstick stop.

9. Install a new gasket or RTV. Tighten the pan bolts to: 15 ft. lbs. (20 Nm) for the 440-T4, 8 ft. lbs. (11 Nm) for the 3T40, 13 ft. lbs. (17 Nm) for the 4T60.

10. Lower the car. Add about 4 quarts of Dexron®IIE or Dexron®III transmission fluid, check your owners manual.

11. Start the engine; let it idle. Block the wheels and apply the parking brake.

12. Move the shift lever through the ranges.

Fig. 97 Remove the strainer

Fig. 98 Insert a new O-ring seal on the new strainer

13. With the lever in PARK check the fluid level. If necessary, add fluid.

➡Always replace the filter with a new one, don't attempt to clean the old filter. The transmission fluid currently being used may appear to be darker and have a strong odor. This is normal and not a sign of required maintenance or transmission failure.

Cooling System

General Motors recommends that you check your cooling system every 12 months or 15,000 miles (24,100 km). The following services should be performed:

1. Wash and inspect the radiator cap and the filler neck.
2. Check the coolant level and the degree of freezing protection.
3. If a pressure tester is available, pressure test the system and the radiator cap.
4. Inspect the hoses of the cooling system. Expect to replace the hoses at 24 months/30,000 miles (48,200 km).
5. Check the fins of the radiator for blockage.

FLUID RECOMMENDATIONS

▸ See Figure 99

The coolant used in any General Motors engine must:
• Be a high quality ethylene glycol-based solution. Do not use alcohol or methanol-based solutions at any time.
• Have built-in rust inhibitors.
• Be designed for year-round use.
• Offer complete protection for a minimum of 12 months/30,000 miles (48,300 km), without replacement, as long as the proper concentration is maintained.
• Meet GM Specification 1825-M (as specified on the container). This point is critical for diesel engines; coolant meeting other specifications could result in cooling system damage and engine damage due to overheating.
• Be mixed in the proper proportions: 50% coolant/50% water for gasoline engines; 64% coolant/36% water for diesel engines.

❋❋CAUTION

Adding only plain water to your cooling system can be dangerous. Plain water, or any other liquid like alcohol, can boil before the proper coolant fluid will. Your car's cooling system is designed to operate properly only with the proper coolant mixture. With plain water or the wrong mixture, your engine could get too hot but you wouldn't get the overheat warning.

➡On diesels, this proportion can be accurately attained only when refilling the system entirely. See Draining and Refilling.

The use of self-sealing coolants is not recommended. Also, the use of a coolant meeting the above requirements negates the need for supplemental additives. Use of such supplemental products is an unnecessary expense and may cause less than optimum cooling system performance.

LEVEL CHECK

▸ See Figure 100

Any time the hood is raised, check the level of the coolant in the see-through plastic coolant recovery tank. With the engine cold, the coolant level should be near the ADD mark on the tank. At normal engine operating temperature, the level should be at the FULL mark on the bottle. If coolant must be added to the tank, use a 50/50 mix of coolant/water to adjust the fluid level on models with gasoline engines. On models with diesel engines, use straight, undiluted coolant to adjust the level in the tank.

An inexpensive tester may be purchased to test the freezing protection of the coolant. Follow the instructions provided with the tester. The coolant used in models with gasoline engines

Fig. 99 Notice the markings on your coolant reservoir

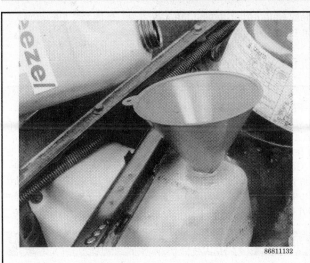

Fig. 100 Fill the coolant bottle using a funnel and proper a mixture of anti freeze and water

should protect to -34°F (-37°C); diesels must have protection to -75°F (-59°C).

DRAIN AND REFILL

At least every 24 months or 30,000 miles (50,000 km)-whichever comes first. The cooling system should be completely drained and refilled with the proper mixture of coolant and water. Many mechanics recommend that this be done once a year for extra protection against corrosion and subsequent overheating.

Though most coolants are labeled permanent, this only means that the coolant will retain its anti-freezing characteristics. The required rust inhibitors and other chemicals which were added to the coolant during its manufacture will become less effective over a period of time.

➡️**If you are only replacing the hoses, perform steps 1-3, and 11-16 as required.**

✳✳CAUTION

To avoid being burned, DO NOT remove the radiator cap while the engine is at operating temperature. The cooling system will release HOT scalding fluid and steam under pressure if the cap is removed while the radiator is still hot. This could result in personal injury.

1. Park the car a level surface.
2. Remove the radiator cap. Slowly rotate the pressure cap counterclockwise to detent. Wait until the pressure (indicated by a hissing sound) is completely gone.
3. After the pressure is relieved, press down on the cap and continue to rotate counterclockwise.
4. Raise the front of the vehicle and support it safely with jackstands.
5. Place a drain pan under the car to collect the drained coolant.
6. Open the radiator fitting (located at the bottom of the radiator) by turning it counterclockwise. It may be wise to coat

the fitting with penetrating lubricant before you attempt to turn it. Allow the coolant to drain from the radiator.
7. On the 3.1L engine open the air bleed vent on the throttle body return pipe (above the coolant pump). The air bleed vent should be opened two to three turns.

✳✳CAUTION

When draining coolant, keep in mind that cats and dogs are attracted to ethylene glycol antifreeze, and are quite likely to drink any that is left in an uncovered container or in puddles on the ground. This will prove fatal in sufficient quantity. Always drain the coolant into a sealable container. Coolant should be reused unless it is contaminated or several years old.

8. Remove the drain plug(s) from the engine block (located on the engine block, above the engine oil pan) and allow the coolant to drain.
9. Close the radiator drain fitting and reinstall the engine block plugs.
10. On the 3.1L close the bleed valve on the throttle body.
11. Add clear water to the system until it is filled.
12. Start the engine and repeat steps 7-12 until the drained water is almost colorless. Turn the engine OFF.
13. Allow the system to drain completely and repeat step 10. Remove the cap from the coolant recovery tank, leaving the hoses connected to the cap.
14. Unbolt and remove the coolant recovery tank, drain it, and flush it with clear water. Reinstall the tank.
15. Fill the radiator to the base of the radiator filler neck with a 50/50 mixture of coolant/water. On diesel equipped models, add a gallon of undiluted coolant first, then add the 50/50 solution.

➡️**If only the radiator was drained, use a 50/50 solution to refill it, then check the freezing protection after the level stabilizes.**

16. Fill the coolant recovery tank to the FULL mark with the 50/50 solution.
17. With the radiator cap still removed, start the engine and allow it to idle until the upper radiator hose becomes hot, indicating that the thermostat has opened.
18. With the engine still idling, fill the radiator to the base of the filler neck with the 50/50 solution.
19. Install the radiator cap, being sure to align the arrows on the cap with the overflow tube.
20. Turn the engine OFF, check for leakage, and double check that the radiator drain is closed and the drain plug(s) is (are) tightened.

FLUSHING AND CLEANING THE SYSTEM

Several aftermarket radiator flushing and cleaning kits can be purchased at your local auto parts store. It is recommended that the radiator be cleaned and flushed of sludge and any rust build-up once a year. Manufacturers directions for proper use, and safety precautions, come in each kit.

RADIATOR CAP

▶ See Figure 101

Before removing the cap, squeeze the upper radiator hose. If it compresses easily (indicating little or no pressure in the system), the cap may be removed by turning it counterclockwise until it reaches the stop. If any hissing is noted at this point (indicating the release of pressure), wait until the hissing stops before you remove the cap. To completely remove the cap, press downward and turn it counterclockwise.

✳✳CAUTION

To avoid being burned, DO NOT remove the radiator cap while the engine is at operating temperature. The cooling system will release HOT scalding fluid and steam under pressure if the cap is removed while the radiator is still hot. This could result in personal injury and loss of coolant.

If the upper radiator hose is hard, pressure is indicated within the system. In this case, a greater degree of caution should be used in removing the cap. Cover the radiator cap with a thick cloth, and while wearing a heavy glove, carefully turn the cap to the stop. This will allow the pressure to be relieved from the system. After the hissing stops, completely remove the cap (press and turn counterclockwise).

Check the condition of the radiator cap gasket and the seal inside of the cap. The radiator cap is designed to seal the cooling system under normal operating conditions which allows the system to build-up a certain amount of pressure (this pressure rating is stamped or printed on the cap). The pressure in the system raises the boiling point of the coolant to help prevent overheating. If the radiator cap does not seal properly, the boiling point of the coolant will be lowered and overheating will occur. If the cap must be replaced, purchase the new cap according to the pressure rating which is specified for your vehicle.

Prior to installing the cap, inspect and clean the radiator filler neck. If you are reusing the old cap, clean it thoroughly with

Fig. 101 Make sure you take extra care before opening a radiator. The cautions are right on the cap

clear water. After turning the cap, make sure that the arrows on the cap align with the overflow hose.

CLEANING RADIATOR OF DEBRIS

Periodically clean any debris - leaves, paper, insects, etc. from the radiator fins. Pick the large pieces off by hand. The smaller pieces can be washed away with water pressure from a hose.

Carefully straighten any bent radiator fins with a pair of needle nose pliers. Be careful, the fins are very soft. Don't wiggle the fins back and forth too much. Straighten them once and try not to move them again.

Master Cylinder

FLUID RECOMMENDATIONS

Only extra-heavy duty fluid meeting DOT-3 specifications must be used. Using an inferior fluid will result in component damage and reduced braking capabilities.

✳✳CAUTION

DOT-5 silicone brake fluid can damage your car, DO NOT use it.

LEVEL CHECK

▶ See Figure 102

About once a month, the fluid level in the master cylinder should be checked.

1. Park the car on a level surface, turn it **OFF** and raise the hood.
2. Wipe off the master cylinder cover before you remove it, to prevent contaminating the fluid with dirt.

➡**On most models, a see-through reservoir is used, eliminating the need to remove the cover.**

3. Two types of lids are used on these master cylinders. One cover is snapped into place on the master cylinder. To remove this type, just press up on the two tabs at the side of the cover, then tilt and remove it. Be careful not to damage the rubber seal under the cover. Another type of cylinder cover has a screw on cap, simply turn the cap to remove.

✳✳CAUTION

If you value the paint on your car, don't spill brake fluid on the finish. Brake fluid destroys paint. Should a spill accidently occur, thoroughly flush the area with clean water.

➡**Don't leave the cover off of the master cylinder or the cap off of the brake fluid container any longer than necessary.**

4. The fluid level in each master cylinder reservoir should be ¼ in. (6mm) below the lowest edge of the filler opening. If necessary, use fresh brake fluid to adjust the level.

It is normal for the master cylinder fluid level to drop as the brake linings wear about ⅛ in. (3mm) every 10,000 miles (16,100 km). If the fluid level is constantly low, the system should be checked for leaks.

5. Carefully seat the seal into the cover, then snap the cover into place on the master cylinder. Be sure that all four snaps latch completely.

Power Steering Pump

FLUID RECOMMENDATIONS

▶ See Figure 103

When adding power steering fluid use GM part #1050017, 1052884 or their equal. In cold climates, use GM part #12345867 and 12345866 (the system should be flushed and bled prior to using this fluid).

LEVEL CHECK

▶ See Figures 104 and 105

The power steering fluid level should be checked at every oil change. On models with gasoline engines, the power steering pump and reservoir are integrated into one unit that is bolted to the front of the engine. On models with diesel engines, the pump is mounted on the engine, and a separate, translucent reservoir is attached to the firewall in the engine compartment.

To check the fluid level, run the engine until it reaches normal operating temperature, then turn the engine **OFF**. Remove the reservoir filler cap and check the oil level on the dipstick. The fluid level must be between the HOT and COLD marks on the filler cap indicator. Add power steering fluid as required then reinstall the cap.

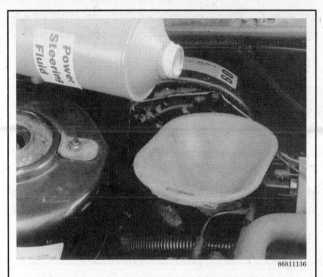

Fig. 103 Fill the power steering pump using a funnel

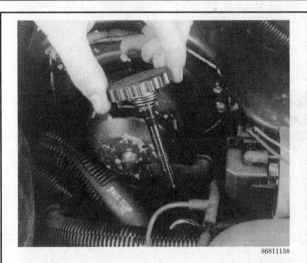

Fig. 104 The power steering cap has a built-in dipstick to check the fluid level

Fig. 102 Fill with only DOT-3 fluid

Fig. 105 Make sure the level is in between the HOT and COLD lines on the dipstick

Steering Gear

FLUID RECOMMENDATIONS AND LEVEL CHECK

All models use integral rack and pinion power steering. The power steering pump delivers hydraulic pressure through two hoses to the steering gear itself. Refer to the power steering pump fluid recommendation and level check procedures to check the steering gear fluid level.

Chassis Greasing

FRONT SUSPENSION AND STEERING LINKAGE

These parts should be greased every 12 months or 7500 miles (12,000 km) with an EP grease meeting GM specification NLGI Grade 2, Category LB or GC-LB, or an equivalent.

If you choose to do this job yourself, you will need a hand operated grease gun, and a long flexible extension hose to reach the various grease fittings. You will also need a cartridge of the appropriate grease.

Press the fitting of the grease gun hose onto the grease fitting (zerk fitting) of the suspension or steering linkage component. Pump a few shots of grease into the fitting (zerk fitting), until the rubber boot on the joint begins to expand, indicating that the joint is full. Remove the gun from the fitting. Be careful not to overfill the joints, which will rupture the rubber boots, allowing the entry of dirt.

TRANSAXLE SHIFT LINKAGE

Lubricate the manual transaxle shift linkage contact points with the EP grease used for chassis greasing (that meets GM specification 6031M). The automatic transaxle linkage should be lubricated with clean engine oil.

Trailer Towing

General Recommendations

✳✳CAUTION

If you don't use the correct equipment and drive properly, you can lose control when you pull a trailer. If a trailer is too heavy, the brakes could not work properly or even not at all. You and your passengers/loved ones could be seriously injured. Pull a trailer only if you have followed all the steps in your owners manual.

There are many different laws having to do with towing a trailer. Make sure your rig will be legal for not only your area,

Body Lubrication

Clean the latch surfaces and apply clean engine oil to the latch pilot bolts and the spring anchor. Use the engine oil to lubricate the hood, door, liftgate hinges, and rear folding seats. Use a chassis grease to lubricate all the pivot points in the latch release mechanism.

DOOR HINGES

The gas tank filler door, car door, and rear hatch or trunk lid hinges should be wiped clean and lubricated with clean engine oil. Silicone spray also works well on these parts, but must be applied more often. Use engine oil to lubricate the trunk or hatch lock mechanism and the lock bolt and striker. The door lock cylinders can be lubricated easily with a shot of silicone spray or one of the many dry penetrating lubricants commercially available.

PARKING BRAKE LINKAGE

Use chassis grease on the parking brake cable where it contacts the guides, links, levers, and pulleys. The grease should be water resistant for durability under the car.

ACCELERATOR LINKAGE

Lubricate the carburetor stud, carburetor lever, and the accelerator pedal lever at the support inside the car with clean engine oil.

Rear Wheel Bearings

The bearing assembly used on these vehicles doesn't need periodic grease service, the following procedures can be used if a problem with the rear bearing assembly is suspected. See Section 8 for more detail.

but wherever it is your planning on going. Contact your state or providence police department for regulations.

• Ask your hitch dealer about sway controls.

• Don't tow a trailer during the first 500 miles (800 km) of the cars life. This could cause serious damage to the vehicles powertrain.

• In the first 500 miles (800 km) that you do tow a trailer DO NOT drive over 50 mph (80 km/h) and don't make starts at full throttle.

• Check periodically to see that all hitch nuts and bolts are tight.

Your car is designed and intended to be used mainly to carry people. Towing a trailer will affect handling, durability and economy.Your safety and satisfaction depend upon proper use and correct equipment. You should also avoid overloads and other abusive use.

Information on trailer towing ability, special equipment required and optional equipment available should be obtained from your dealer.

Necessary Equipment

Hitches are an important piece of equipment to have. With crosswinds, large trucks, and rough roads are a few reasons you will need the right hitch. Make sure you follow the rules of the road for using a hitch:

• Will you have to install any holes in the body of your car to install a trailer hitch? If you do, make sure you remember to seal the holes when you remove hitch. If not, you may have deadly carbon monoxide entering your car. This can kill you. Besides that, you can get dirt and water in the car which will rust the car out prematurely.

• Most bumpers are not capable of attaching a hitch to these days. And DO NOT attach a rental hitch or other bumper hitches to them. Use only a frame mounted hitch that does not attach to the bumper.

• Safety chains should always be attached to the car and the trailer. Cross the safety chain under the tongue of the trailer so that the tongue will not drop to the road if it becomes separated from the hitch. (we have all seen at least one car/trailer on the side of the road do to this). Instructions about safety chains are provided by the manufacturer, follow them carefully.

• Trailer brakes, does your trailer have it's own brakes? Contact your dealer to install and maintain them properly.

Maintenance

Your car will need service more frequently when you're towing a trailer. See the maintenance schedule for more on this.

Trailer Weight

The weight of the trailer is the most important factor. A good weight-to-horsepower ratio is about 35:1, 35 lbs. of GCW (Gross Combined Weight) for every horsepower your engine develops. Multiply the engine's rated horsepower by 35 and subtract the weight of the car, passengers, and luggage. The result is the approximate ideal maximum weight you should tow, although a numerically higher axle ratio can help compensate for heavier weight.

Hitch (Tongue) Weight

▶ See Figure 106

Select the proper hitch based on the anticipated hitch tongue weight. Hitch weight is usually 9-11% of the trailer gross weight and should be measured with the trailer loaded. Hitches fall into various categories: those that mount on the frame and rear bumper, the bolt-on type or the weld-on distribution type used for larger trailers. Axle mounted or clamp-on bumper hitches should never be used.

Check the gross weight rating of your trailer. Tongue weight is usually figured as 10% of gross trailer weight. Therefore, a trailer with a maximum gross weight of 2000 lbs. will have a

Fig. 106 Calculating proper tongue weight for you trailer

maximum tongue weight of 200 lbs. Class I trailers fall into this category. Class II trailers are those with a gross weight rating of 2000-3000 lbs., while Class III trailers fall into the 3500-6000 lbs. category. Class IV trailers are those over 6000 lbs. and are for use with fifth wheel trucks, only.

When you've determined the hitch that you'll need, follow the manufacturer's installation instructions exactly, especially when it comes to fastener torques. The hitch will subjected to a lot of stress and good hitches come with hardened bolts. Never substitute an inferior bolt for a hardened bolt.

Cooling

ENGINE

One of the most common, if not THE most common, problems associated with trailer towing is engine overheating. If you have a standard cooling system, without' an expansion tank, you'll definitely need to get an aftermarket expansion tank kit, preferably one with at least a 2 quart capacity. These kits are easily installed on the radiator's overflow hose, and come with a pressure cap designed for expansion tanks.

Another helpful accessory for vehicles using a belt-driven radiator fan is a flex fan. These fans are large diameter units designed to provide more airflow at low speeds, from blades that have deeply cupped surfaces. The blades then flex, or flatten out, at high speed, when less cooling air is needed. These fans are far lighter in weight than stock fans, requiring less horsepower to drive them. Also, they are far quieter than stock fans. If you do decide to replace your stock fan with a flex fan, note that if your car has a fan clutch, a spacer will be needed between the flex fan and water pump hub.

Aftermarket engine oil coolers are helpful for prolonging engine oil life and reducing overall engine temperatures. Both of these factors increase engine life. While not absolutely necessary in towing Class I and some Class II trailers, they are recommended for heavier Class II and all Class III towing. Engine oil cooler systems usually consist of an adapter, screwed on in place of the oil filter, a remote filter mounting and a multi-tube, finned heat exchanger, which is mounted in front of the radiator or air conditioning condenser.

TRANSMISSION

An automatic transmission is usually recommended for trailer towing. Modern automatics have proven reliable and, of course, easy to operate, in trailer towing. The increased load of a trailer, however, causes an increase in the temperature of the automatic transmission fluid. Heat is the worst enemy of an automatic transmission. As the temperature of the fluid increases, the life of the fluid decreases.

It is essential, therefore, that you install an automatic transmission cooler. The cooler, which consists of a multi-tube, finned heat exchanger, is usually installed in front of the radiator or air conditioning compressor, and hooked in-line with the transmission cooler tank inlet line. Follow the cooler manufacturer's installation instructions.

Select a cooler of at least adequate capacity, based upon the combined gross weights of the car and trailer.

JUMP STARTING A DEAD BATTERY

Whenever a vehicle must be jump started, precautions must be followed in order to prevent the possibility of personal injury. Remember that batteries contain a small amount of explosive hydrogen gas which is a by product of battery charging. Sparks should always be avoided when working around batteries, especially when attaching jumper cables. To minimize the possibility of accidental sparks, follow the procedure carefully.

❋❋CAUTION

NEVER hook the batteries up in a series circuit or the entire electrical system will go up in smoke, especially the starter!

Cars equipped with a diesel engine utilize two 12 volt batteries, one on either side of the engine compartment. The batteries are connected in a parallel circuit (positive terminal to positive terminal, negative terminal to negative terminal). Hooking the batteries up in parallel circuit increases battery cranking power without increasing total battery voltage output. Output remains at 12 volts. On the other hand, hooking two 12 volt batteries up in a series circuit (positive terminal to negative terminal, positive terminal to negative terminal) increases total battery output to 24 volts (12 volts plus 12 volts).

Jump Starting Precautions

▶ **See Figure 107**

• Be sure that both batteries are of the same voltage. All vehicles covered by this manual and most vehicles on the road today utilize a 12 volt charging system.
• Be sure that both batteries are of the same polarity (have the same grounded terminal; in most cases NEGATIVE).
• Be sure that the vehicles are not touching or a short circuit could occur.
• On serviceable batteries, be sure the vent cap holes are not obstructed.

Cooler manufacturers recommend that you use an aftermarket cooler in addition to, and not instead of, the present cooling tank in your radiator. If you do want to use it in place of the radiator cooling tank, get a cooler at least two sizes larger than normally necessary.

➡**A transmission cooler can, sometimes, cause slow or harsh shifting in the transmission during cold weather, until the fluid has a chance to come up to normal operating temperature. Some coolers can be purchased with or retrofitted with a temperature bypass valve which will allow fluid flow through the cooler only when the fluid has reached above a certain operating temperature.**

Handling A Trailer

Towing a trailer with ease and safety requires a certain amount of experience. It's a good idea to learn the feel of a trailer by practicing turning, stopping and backing in an open area such as an empty parking lot.

• Do not smoke or allow sparks anywhere near the batteries.
• In cold weather, make sure the battery electrolyte is not frozen. This can occur more readily in a battery that has been in a state of discharge.
• Do not allow electrolyte to contact your skin or clothing.

Jump Starting Procedure

1. Make sure that the voltages of the 2 batteries are the same. Most batteries and charging systems are of the 12 volt variety.
2. Pull the jumping vehicle (with the good battery) into a position so the jumper cables can reach the dead battery and that vehicle's engine. Make sure that the vehicles do NOT touch.

TCCS1080

Fig. 107 Connect the jumper cables to the batteries and engine in the order shown

3. Place the transmissions of both vehicles in NEUTRAL or PARK, as applicable, then firmly set their parking brakes.

➡️If necessary for safety reasons, both vehicle's hazard lights may be operated throughout the entire procedure without significantly increasing the difficulty of jump starting the dead battery.

4. Turn lights and accessories off on both vehicles. Make sure the ignition switches on both vehicles are turned to the **OFF** position.

5. Cover the battery cell caps with a rag, but do not cover the terminals.

6. Make sure the terminals on both batteries are clean and free of corrosion or proper electrical connection will be impeded. If necessary, clean the battery terminals before proceeding.

7. Identify the positive (+) and negative (-) terminals on both batteries.

8. Connect the first jumper cable to the positive (+) terminal of the dead battery, then connect the other end of that cable to the positive (+) terminal of the booster (good) battery.

9. Connect one end of the other jumper cable to the negative (-) terminal of the booster battery and the other cable clamp to an engine bolt head, alternator bracket or other solid, metallic point on the dead battery's engine. Try to pick a ground on the engine that is positioned away from the battery, in order to minimize the possibility of the 2 clamps touching

should one loosen during the procedure. DO NOT connect this clamp to the negative (-) terminal of the bad battery.

❄❄CAUTION

Be very careful to keep the jumper cables away from moving parts (cooling fan, belts, etc.) on both engines.

10. Check to make sure that the cables are routed away from any moving parts, then start the donor vehicle's engine. Run the engine at moderate speed for several minutes to allow the dead battery a chance to receive some initial charge.

11. With the donor vehicle's engine still running slightly above idle, try to start the vehicle with the dead battery. Crank the engine for no more than 10 seconds at a time and let the starter cool for at least 20 seconds between tries. If the vehicle does not start within 3 tries, it is likely that something else is also wrong.

12. Once the vehicle is started, allow it to run at idle for a few seconds to make sure that it is operating properly.

13. Turn on the headlights, heater blower and, if equipped, the rear defroster of both vehicles in order to reduce the severity of voltage spikes and subsequent risk of damage to the vehicles' electrical systems when the cables are disconnected.

14. Carefully disconnect the cables in the reverse order of connection. Start with the negative cable that is attached to the engine ground, then the negative cable on the donor battery. Disconnect the positive cable from the donor battery, then disconnect the positive cable from the formerly dead battery. Be careful when disconnecting the cables from the positive terminals not to allow the alligator clips to touch any metal on either vehicle or a short circuit and sparks will occur.

TOWING THE VEHICLE

◆ **See Figure 108**

DO NOT attempt to start your car by pushing or towing as damage to the catalytic convertor or other components may result. If the battery is weak, the vehicle may be jump started, using the procedure found earlier in this section.

As long as the driveline and steering are normally operable, your car may be towed on all four wheels. If this is done, don't exceed 35 mph or travel further than 50 miles (80 km). The steering wheel must be unlocked, the transaxle in Neutral, and the parking brake released. Never attach towing equipment to the bumpers or bumper brackets, the equipment must be attached to the main structural members of the car.

➡️Remember that there will be no power assist for brakes and steering with the engine OFF. Also, be sure to check into state and local towing laws before flat-towing your vehicle.

If the car is to be towed by a wrecker, instructions supplied by the wrecker manufacturer should be followed. Because of the front wheel drive, towing on a flat-bed or on the rear wheels is preferred. If absolutely necessary, the car may be towed on the front wheels as long as the speed does not exceed 25 mph and the towing distance does not exceed 10 miles (16 km).

❄❄CAUTION

Don't exceed the speed or distance limits which are outlined here. Severe transaxle damage could result.

86811147

Fig. 108 Various ways of towing your car

JACKING

Precautions

▶ **See Figures 109 and 110**

• NEVER use the jack supplied with the vehicle for anything but changing tires.
• NEVER crawl underneath the vehicle while it is supported by a jack.
• NEVER start or run the engine while the car is supported by a jack.
• ALWAYS secure the spare tire, jack, etc., to prevent loose parts from causing personal injury during hard braking.

Instructions

▶ **See Figure 111**

Please refer to the accompanying illustrations for detailed jacking instructions and spare tire/jack stowage instructions.

✳✳CAUTION

Be especially careful not to damage the catalytic convertor when jacking from the floor side rails.

The accompanying illustrations depict the preferred jacking and jack stand support points underneath the vehicle. When using a floor jack, either the center of the engine cradle cross-member or the center of the rear axle bar can be used as jacking points in addition to the previous hoisting points.

SUSPENSION CONTACT HOIST
(UNDER FRONT LOWER CONTROL ARM)

86811148

Fig. 109 Procedure for storage of the wagons tire and jack

Fig. 110 Wagons have basically the same jacking points as sedans

■ FRAME CONTACT HOIST
▫ FLOOR JACK
▨ SUSPENSION CONTACT HOIST

WHEN USING FLOOR JACK, LIFT
ON CENTER OF FRONT CROSSMEMBER

WHEN USING FLOOR JACK, LIFT
ON REAR SUSPENSION AXLE

FRAME CONTACT HOIST
(REARWARD OF FRONT TIRE)

FRAME CONTACT HOIST
(FORWARD OF REAR TIRE)

SUSPENSION CONTACT HOIST
(LIFTING ON REAR TIRES)

SUSPENSION CONTACT HOIST
(UNDER FRONT LOWER CONTROL ARM.

86811152

Fig. 111 Proper lifting locations for your vehicle

Follow Schedule I if the vehicle is mainly operated under one or more of the following conditions:
When most trips are less than 4 miles (6 kilometers)
When most trips are less than 10 miles (16 kilometers) and outside temperatures - remain below freezing
When most trips include extended idling and/or frequent low-speed operation as in stop-and-go traffic
Towing a trailer**
Operating in dusty areas

Schedule I should also be followed if the vehicle is used for delivery service, police, taxi or other commercial applications

TO BE SERVICED	WHEN TO PERFORM Miles (Kilometers) or Months whichever Occurs First	The services shown in this schedule up to 60,000 miles (100,000 km) are to be performed after 60,000 miles (100,000 km) at the same intervals																			
	MILES (000)	3	6	9	12	15	18	21	24	27	30	33	36	39	42	45	48	51	54	57	60
	KILOMETERS (000)	5	10	15	20	25	30	35	40	45	50	55	60	65	70	75	80	85	90	95	100
Engine Oil & Oil Filter Change *	Every 3,000 (5000 km) or 3 mos	•	•	•	•	•	•	•	•	•	•	•	•	•	•	•	•	•	•	•	•
Chassis Lubrication	Every other oil change		•		•		•		•		•		•		•		•		•		•
Services To Be Performed At Least Twice A Year (See Explanation)																					
Services To Be Performed At Least Once A Year (See Explanation)																					
Throttle Body Mount Bolt Torque (Some Models)*	At 6,000 mi (10,000 km) only		•																		
Tire & Wheel Insp and Rotation	At 6,000 mi (10,000 km) and then every 15,000 mi (25,000 km)		•					•					•					•			
Engine Accessary Drive Belt(s) Insp *	Every 30,000 mi (50,000 km) or 24 mos										•										•
Cooling System Service*	Every 30,000 mi (50,000 km) or 24 mos										•										•
Transaxle Service	See explanation for service interval																				
Spark Plug Replacement*	LN2 every 100,000 mi (166,000 km) LB2 every 30,000 mi (50,000 km)										•										•
Spark Plug Wire Insp (Some Models)*	Every 30,000 mi. (50,000 km)										•										•
EGR System Insp *††	Every 30,000 mi (50,000 km) or 36 mos										•										•
Air Cleaner Replacement	Every 30,000 mi (50,000 km) or 36 mos										•										•
Eng. Timing Check (Some Models)*	Every 30,000 mi (50,000 km)										•										•
Fuel Tank, Cap & Lines Insp *††	Every 30,000 mi (50,000 km)										•										•

FOOTNOTES: * An Emission Control Service
†† The U.S. Environmental Agency or the California Air Resources Board has determined that the failure to perform this maintenance item will not nullify the emission warranty or limit recall liability prior to the completion of vehicle useful life. General Motors, however, urges that all recommended maintenance services be performed at the indicated intervals and the maintenance be recorded in Section C of the owner's Maintenance Schedule.

** Trailering is not recommended for some models, see the Owner's Manual for details.

86811154

• Follow Schedule II only is none of the driving conditions specified in Schedule I apply

TO BE SERVICED	WHEN TO PERFORM Miles (Kilometers) or Months whichever Occurs First	The services shown in this schedule up to 60,000 miles (100,000 km) are to be performed after 60,000 miles (100,000 km) at the same intervals							
	MILES (000)	7.5	15	22.5	30	37.5	45	52.5	60
	KILOMETERS (000)	12.54	25	37.5	50	62.5	75	87.5	100
Engine Oil Change•, Plus Other Required Services (See Explanation)	Every 7,500 mi. (12,500 km) or 12 mos.	•	•	•	•	•	•	•	•
Oil Filter Change•	At first and every other oil change or 12 mos	•		•		•		•	
Chassis Lubrication	Every 7,500 mi. (12,500 km) or 12 mos.	•	•	•	•	•	•	•	•
Services To Be Performed At Least Twice A Year (See Explanation)									
Services To Be Performed At Least Once A Year (See Explanation)									
Throttle Body Mount Bolt Torque (Some Models)•	At 7,500 mi (12,500 km) only	•							
Tire & Wheel Insp. and Rotation	At 7,500 mi (12,500 km) and then every 15,000 mi. (25,000 km)	•		•		•		•	
Engine Accessory Drive Belt(s) Insp.•	Every 30,000 mi. (50,000 km) or 24 mos.				•				•
Cooling System Service•	Every 30,000 mi. (50,000 km) or 24 mos.				•				•
Transaxle Service	See explanation for service interval								
Spark Plug Replacement•	LN2 every 100,000 mi (166,000 km) LB2 every 30,000 mi (50,000 km)				•				
Spark Plug Wire Insp. (Some Models)•	Every 30,000 mi. (50,000 km)				•				•
EGR System Insp. •††	Every 30,000 mi. (50,000 km) or 36 mos.				•				•
Air Cleaner Replacement	Every 30,000 mi. (50,000 km) or 36 mos.				•				•
Fuel Tank, Cap & Lines Insp •††	Every 30,000 mi. (50,000 km)				•				•

FOOTNOTES: • An Emission Control Service

†† The U. S. Environmental Agency or the California Air Resources Board has determined that the failure to perform this maintenance item will not nullify the emission warranty or limit recall liability prior to the completion of vehicle useful life, life General Motors. however urges that all recommended maintenance services be performed a the indicated intervals and the maintenance be recorded in Section C of the owner's Maintenance Schedule

86811155

CAPACITIES

Year	Model	Engine ID/VIN	Engine Displacement Liters (cc)	Engine Oil with Filter (qts.)	Transmission (pts.) 4-Spd	5-Spd	Auto.	Transfer Case (pts.)	Drive Axle Front (pts.)	Rear (pts.)	Fuel Tank (gal.)	Cooling System (qts.)
1982	Celebrity	R	2.5 (2474)	3.0 [1]	-	-	2	-	-	-	16.0	10.0
	Celebrity	X	2.8 (2835)	4.0	-	-	2	-	-	-	16.0	12.5
	Celebrity	T	4.3 (4293)	6.0	-	-	2	-	-	-	16.0	13.1
	Century	R	2.5 (2474)	3.0	6.0	-	2	-	-	-	15.7	[9]
	Century	X	2.8 (2835)	4.0	-	-	2	-	-	-	16.0	12.5
	Cutlass Ciera	R	2.5 (2474)	3.0	6.0	-	2	-	-	-	15.7	10.0
	Cutlass Ciera	X	2.8 (2835)	4.0	6.0	-	2	-	-	-	16.5	12.0
	6000	R	2.5 (2474)	3.0	6.0	-	2	-	-	-	15.7	10.0
	6000	X	2.8 (2835)	4.0	6.0	-	2	-	-	-	16.4	11.5
1983	Celebrity	R	2.5 (2474)	3.0	-	-	2	-	-	-	16.0	10.0
	Celebrity	5	2.5 (2474)	3.0	-	-	2	-	-	-	16.0	10.0
	Celebrity	X	2.8 (2835)	4.0	-	-	2	-	-	-	16.0	12.5
	Celebrity	T	4.3 (4293)	6.0	-	-	2	-	-	-	16.0	13.0
	Century	R	2.5 (2474)	3.0	6.0	-	2	-	-	-	15.7	[2]
	Century	X	2.8 (2835)	4.0	-	-	2	-	-	-	16.0	12.5
	Century	E	3.0 (2998)	4.0	6.0	-	2	-	-	-	15.7	13.0
	Century	T	4.3 (4293)	6.0	-	-	2	-	-	-	16.4	13.0
	Cutlass Ciera	R	2.5 (2474)	3.0	6.0	-	2	-	-	-	15.7	10.0
	Cutlass Ciera	X	2.8 (2835)	4.0	6.0	-	2	-	-	-	16.5	12.0
	Cutlass Ciera	E	3.0 (2998)	4.0	6.0	-	2	-	-	-	15.7	12.5
	Cutlass Ciera	T	4.3 (4293)	6.0	-	-	2	-	-	-	16.5	13.0
	6000	R	2.5 (2474)	3.0	6.0	-	2	-	-	-	15.7	10.0
	6000	X	2.8 (2835)	4.0	6.0	-	2	-	-	-	16.4	11.5
	6000	T	4.3 (4293)	6.0	-	-	2	-	-	-	16.5	13.0
1984	Celebrity	R	2.5 (2474)	3.0	-	-	10.0	-	-	-	16.0	10.0
	Celebrity	5	2.5 (2474)	3.0	-	-	10.0	-	-	-	16.0	10.0
	Celebrity	X	2.8 (2835)	4.0	-	-	10.0	-	-	-	16.0	12.5
	Celebrity	T	4.3 (4293)	6.0	-	-	10.0	-	-	-	16.0	13.0
	Century	R	2.5 (2474)	3.0	6.0	-	2	-	-	-	15.7	[3]
	Century	X	2.8 (2835)	4.0	-	-	10.0	-	-	-	16.5	12.5
	Century	E	3.0 (2998)	4.0	6.0	-	2	-	-	-	15.7	13.0
	Century	3	3.8 (3785)	4.0	6.0	-	2	-	-	-	[10]	13.0
	Century	T	4.3 (4293)	6.0	-	-	2	-	-	-	16.5	13.0
	Cutlass Ciera	R	2.5 (2474)	3.0	6.0	-	2	-	-	-	15.7	10.0
	Cutlass Ciera	3	3.8 (3785)	4.0	6.0	-	2	-	-	-	15.7	13.0
	Cutlass Ciera	E	3.0 (2998)	4.0	6.0	-	2	-	-	-	15.7	13.0
	Cutlass Ciera	T	4.3 (4293)	6.0	-	-	2	-	-	-	16.6	13.0
	6000	R	2.5 (2474)	3.0	6.0	-	2	-	-	-	15.7	9.5
	6000	X	2.8 (2835)	4.0	6.0	-	2	-	-	-	16.5	11.5
	6000	Z	2.8 (2835)	4.0	6.0	-	2	-	-	-	16.5	11.5
	6000	T	4.3 (4293)	6.0	-	-	2	-	-	-	16.5	13.0
1985	Celebrity	R	2.5 (2474)	3.0 [1]	-	6.0	5	-	-	-	16.0	[3]
	Celebrity	W	2.8 (2835)	4.0 [1]	-	-	5	-	-	-	16.0	13.0
	Celebrity	T	4.3 (4310)	6.5 [1]	-	-	5	-	-	-	16.0	13.0
	Century	R	2.5 (2474)	3.0 [1]	-	-	5	-	-	-	15.7	[3]
	Century	X	2.8 (2835)	4.0 [1]	-	-	5	-	-	-	16.4	12.0
	Century	E	3.0 (2999)	4.0 [1]	-	-	5	-	-	-	15.7	13.1
	Century	3	3.8 (3785)	4.0 [1]	-	-	5	-	-	-	16.6	13.0
	Century	T	4.3 (4293)	6.5 [1]	-	-	5	-	-	-	16.4	13.0
	Cutlass Ciera	R	2.5 (2474)	3.0 [1]	-	-	5	-	-	-	16.0	[3]
	Cutlass Ciera	E	3.0 (2999)	4.0 [1]	-	-	5	-	-	-	16.5	13.1
	Cutlass Ciera	3	3.8 (3785)	4.0 [1]	-	-	5	-	-	-	16.5	13.0
	Cutlass Ciera	T	4.3 (4293)	6.0 [1]	-	-	5	-	-	-	16.6	13.0

86811180

CAPACITIES

Year	Model	Engine ID/VIN	Engine Displacement Liters (cc)	Engine Oil with Filter (qts.)	Transmission (pts.) 4-Spd	5-Spd	Auto.	Transfer Case (pts.)	Drive Axle Front (pts.)	Drive Axle Rear (pts.)	Fuel Tank (gal.)	Cooling System (qts.)
1985	6000	R	2.5 (2474)	3.0 [1]	6.0	-	5	-	-	-	15.7	3
	6000	X	2.8 (2835)	4.0 [1]	6.0	-	5	-	-	-	16.5	12.0
	6000	Z	2.8 (2835)	4.0 [1]	6.0	-	5	-	-	-	16.5	12.0
	6000	T	4.3 (4294)	6.0 [1]	-	-	5	-	-	-	16.5	13.0
1986	Celebrity	R	2.5 (2474)	4.0 [1]	-	6.0	5	-	-	-	16.0	10.0
	Celebrity	W	2.8 (2835)	4.0 [1]	-	-	2	-	-	-	16.0	12.0
	Celebrity	X	2.8 (2835)	4.0 [1]	5.9	-	2	-	-	-	16.5	12.0
	Century	R	2.5 (2474)	4.0 [1]	-	-	8.0	-	-	-	15.5	10.0
	Century	X	2.8 (2835)	4.0 [1]	-	-	2	-	-	-	16.5	6
	Century	3	3.8 (3785)	4.0 [1]	-	-	8.0	-	-	-	15.5	6
	Century	B	3.8 (3785)	4.0 [1]	-	-	8.0	-	-	-	15.5	6
	Cutlass Ciera	R	2.5 (2474)	4.0 [1]	-	-	2	-	-	-	15.8	10.0
	Cutlass Ciera	X	2.8 (2835)	4.0 [1]	-	-	2	-	-	-	16.5	12.0
	Cutlass Ciera	W	2.8 (2835)	4.0 [1]	-	-	2	-	-	-	15.8	12.0
	Cutlass Ciera	3	3.8 (3785)	4.0 [1]	-	-	2	-	-	-	15.8	6
	Cutlass Ciera	B	3.8 (3785)	4.0 [1]	-	-	2	-	-	-	15.8	6
	6000	R	2.5 (2474)	4.0 [1]	6.0	-	8.0	-	-	-	15.8	10.0
	6000	W	2.8 (2835)	4.0 [1]	6.0	-	2	-	-	-	16.5	13.0
	6000	X	2.8 (2835)	4.0 [1]	6.0	-	2	-	-	-	16.5	13.0
1987	Celebrity	R	2.5 (2474)	3.0 [1]	-	4.5	8.0	-	-	-	15.8	3
	Celebrity	W	2.8 (2835)	4.0 [1]	-	-	13.0	-	-	-	16.0	13.0
	Century	R	2.5 (2474)	3.0 [1]	-	-	12.0	-	-	-	15.8	3
	Century	W	2.8 (2835)	4.0 [1]	-	-	13.0	-	-	-	16.0	13.0
	Century	3	3.8 (3785)	4.0 [1]	-	-	12.0	-	-	-	16.0	13.0
	Cutlass Ciera	R	2.5 (2474)	3.0 [1]	-	-	2	-	-	-	15.8	3
	Cutlass Ciera	W	2.8 (2835)	4.0 [1]	-	-	2	-	-	-	16.0	13.0
	Cutlass Ciera	3	3.8 (3785)	4.0 [1]	-	-	2	-	-	-	16.0	13.0
	6000	R	2.5 (2474)	4.0 [1]	6.0	-	2	-	-	-	15.8	3
	6000	W	2.8 (2835)	4.0 [1]	6.0	-	2	-	-	-	16.5	13.0
1988	Celebrity	R	2.5 (2474)	3.0 [1]	-	4.5	8.0	-	-	-	16.0	3
	Celebrity	W	2.8 (2835)	4.0 [1]	-	5.3	10.0	-	-	-	16.0	13.0
	Century	R	2.5 (2474)	3.0 [1]	-	-	12.0	-	-	-	15.5	3
	Century	W	2.8 (2835)	4.0 [1]	-	-	4	-	-	-	15.5	13.0
	Century	3	3.8 (3785)	4.0 [1]	-	-	12.0	-	-	-	15.8	12.0
	Cutlass Ciera	R	2.5 (2474)	3.0 [1]	-	-	2	-	-	-	15.8	3
	Cutlass Ciera	W	2.8 (2835)	4.0 [1]	-	-	2	-	-	-	15.8	13.0
	Cutlass Ciera	3	3.8 (3785)	4.0 [1]	-	-	2	-	-	-	15.8	12.0
	6000	R	2.5 (2474)	4.0 [1]	-	6.0	2	-	-	-	15.8	3
	6000	W	2.8 (2835)	4.0 [1]	-	6.0	2	-	-	-	15.8	13.5
1989	Celebrity	R	2.5 (2474)	4.0 [1]	-	4.5	12.0	-	-	-	16.0	10.0
	Celebrity	W	2.8 (2835)	4.0 [1]	-	-	5	-	-	-	16.0	13.0
	Century	R	2.5 (2474)	4.0 [1]	-	-	12.0	-	-	-	15.8	10.0
	Century	W	2.8 (2835)	4.0 [1]	-	-	5	-	-	-	15.8	13.0
	Century	N	3.3 (3342)	4.0 [1]	-	-	13.0	-	-	-	15.8	13.0
	Cutlass Ciera	R	2.5 (2474)	4.0 [1]	-	-	2	-	-	-	15.8	3
	Cutlass Ciera	W	2.8 (2835)	4.0 [1]	-	-	2	-	-	-	15.8	13.0
	Cutlass Ciera	N	3.3 (3342)	4.0 [1]	-	-	2	-	-	-	15.8	13.0
	Cutlass Cruiser	R	2.5 (2474)	4.0 [1]	-	-	2	-	-	-	15.8	3
	Cutlass Cruiser	W	2.8 (2835)	4.0 [1]	-	-	2	-	-	-	15.8	13.0

86811181

CAPACITIES

Year	Model	Engine ID/VIN	Engine Displacement Liters (cc)	Engine Oil with Filter (qts.)	Transmission (pts.) 4-Spd	5-Spd	Auto.	Transfer Case (pts.)	Drive Axle Front (pts.)	Rear (pts.)	Fuel Tank (gal.)	Cooling System (qts.)
1989	Cutlass Cruiser	N	3.3 (3342)	4.0 [1]	-	-	[2]	-	-	-	15.8	13.0
	6000	R	2.5 (2474)	4.0 [1]	-	-	[2]	-	-	-	15.8	[3]
	6000	W	2.8 (2835)	4.0 [1]	-	-	[2]	-	-	-	15.8	13.0
	6000	T	3.1 (3136)	4.0 [1]	-	-	[2]	-	-	-	15.8	13.0
1990	Celebrity	R	2.5 (2474)	4.0 [1]	-	-	13.0	-	-	-	15.8	10.0
	Celebrity	T	3.1 (3130)	4.0 [1]	-	-	13.0	-	-	-	15.8	13.0
	Century	R	2.5 (2474)	3.0 [1]	-	-	12.0	-	-	-	15.5	10.0
	Century	N	3.3 (3342)	4.0 [1]	-	-	13.0	-	-	-	15.5	13.0
	Cutlass Ciera	R	2.5 (2474)	3.0 [1]	-	-	[2]	-	-	-	15.8	10.0
	Cutlass Ciera	N	3.3 (3342)	4.0 [1]	-	-	[2]	-	-	-	15.8	10.0
	Cutlass Cruiser	R	2.5 (2474)	3.0 [1]	-	-	[2]	-	-	-	15.8	10.0
	Cutlass Cruiser	N	3.3 (3342)	4.0 [1]	-	-	[2]	-	-	-	15.8	13.0
	6000	R	2.5 (2474)	4.0 [1]	-	-	[2]	-	-	-	15.8	10.0
	6000	T	3.1 (3136)	4.0 [1]	-	-	[2]	-	-	-	15.8	13.0
1991	Century	R	2.5 (2474)	4.0 [1]	-	-	[7]	-	-	-	15.7	10.0
	Century	N	3.3 (3342)	4.0 [1]	-	-	[7]	-	-	-	15.7	13.0
	Cutlass Ciera	R	2.5 (2474)	4.0 [1]	-	-	[7]	-	-	-	15.7	10.0
	Cutlass Ciera	N	3.3 (3342)	4.0 [1]	-	-	[7]	-	-	-	15.7	13.0
	Cutlass Cruiser	R	2.5 (2474)	4.0 [1]	-	-	[7]	-	-	-	15.7	10.0
	Cutlass Cruiser	N	3.3 (3342)	4.0 [1]	-	-	[7]	-	-	-	15.7	13.0
	6000	R	2.5 (2474)	4.0 [1]	-	-	[7]	-	-	-	15.7	10.0
	6000	T	3.1 (3136)	4.0 [1]	-	-	[7]	-	-	-	15.7	13.1
1992	Century	R	2.5 (2474)	4.0 [1]	-	-	[8]	-	-	-	15.7	10.0
	Century	N	3.3 (3342)	4.0 [1]	-	-	[8]	-	-	-	15.7	13.0
	Cutlass Ciera	R	2.5 (2474)	4.0 [1]	-	-	[8]	-	-	-	15.7	10.0
	Cutlass Ciera	N	3.3 (3342)	4.0 [1]	-	-	[8]	-	-	-	15.7	13.0
	Cutlass Cruiser	R	2.5 (2474)	4.0 [1]	-	-	[8]	-	-	-	15.7	10.0
	Cutlass Cruiser	N	3.3 (3342)	4.0 [1]	-	-	[8]	-	-	-	15.7	13.0
1993	Century	4	2.2 (2195)	4.0 [1]	-	-	[8]	-	-	-	16.5	8.0
	Century	N	3.3 (3342)	4.0 [1]	-	-	[8]	-	-	-	16.5	13.0
	Cutlass Ciera	4	2.2 (2195)	4.0 [1]	-	-	[8]	-	-	-	16.5	8.0
	Cutlass Ciera	N	3.3 (3342)	4.0 [1]	-	-	[8]	-	-	-	16.5	13.0
	Cutlass Cruiser	4	2.2 (2195)	4.0 [1]	-	-	[8]	-	-	-	16.5	8.0
	Cutlass Cruiser	N	3.3 (3342)	4.0 [1]	-	-	[8]	-	-	-	16.5	13.0
1994	Century	4	2.2 (2195)	4.0 [1]	-	-	[8]	-	-	-	16.5	9.0
	Century	M	3.1 (3130)	4.0 [1]	-	-	[8]	-	-	-	16.5	12.0
	Cutlass Ciera	4	2.2 (2195)	4.0 [1]	-	-	[8]	-	-	-	16.5	9.0
	Cutlass Ciera	M	3.1 (3130)	4.0 [1]	-	-	[8]	-	-	-	16.5	12.0
	Cutlass Cruiser	4	2.2 (2195)	4.0 [1]	-	-	[8]	-	-	-	16.5	9.0
	Cutlass Cruiser	M	3.1 (3130)	4.0 [1]	-	-	[8]	-	-	-	16.5	12.0

86811182

CAPACITIES

Year	Model	Engine ID/VIN	Engine Displacement Liters (cc)	Engine Oil with Filter (qts.)	Transmission (pts.)			Transfer Case (pts.)	Drive Axle		Fuel Tank (gal.)	Cooling System (qts.)
					4-Spd	5-Spd	Auto.		Front (pts.)	Rear (pts.)		
1995	Century	4	2.2 (2195)	4.0 [1]	-	-	8	-	-	-	16.5	9.0
	Century	M	3.1 (3130)	4.0 [1]	-	-	8	-	-	-	16.5	12.0
	Cutlass Ciera	4	2.2 (2195)	4.0 [1]	-	-	8	-	-	-	16.5	9.0
	Cutlass Ciera	M	3.1 (3130)	4.0 [1]	-	-	8	-	-	-	16.5	12.0
	Cutlass Cruiser	4	2.2 (2195)	4.0 [1]	-	-	8	-	-	-	16.5	9.0
	Cutlass Cruiser	M	3.1 (3130)	4.0 [1]	-	-	8	-	-	-	16.5	12.0

1 Capacity is without filter replacement make sure to check fluid level to add
2 With AT 125C: 8.0
  With AT 440-T4: 13.0
3 With std. and A/C cooling: 10.0
  With heavy duty cooling (all): 12.0
4 With AT 125C: 12.0
  With AT 440-T4:13.0
5 With AT 125C: 8.0
  With AT 440-T4: 12.0
6 With std. cooling: 12.0
  With A/C: 13.0
7 With 3T-40 trans: 14.0
  With 4T-60 trans: 12.0
8 With 3T-40 trans:8.0
  With 4T-60 trans.: 12.0
9 Std. cooling: 10.0
  Heavy duty cooling: 13.0
10 Sedan: 16.6 gal.
   Wagon: 15.7 gal.

86811183

TORQUE SPECIFICATIONS

Component		US	Metric
Automatic Transaxle			
Oil pan retaining nuts:			
1982-88		15 ft. lbs.	20 Nm
1989-95		8 ft. lbs.	11 Nm
Drive Belt Tensioner Bolt:			
2.2L		37 ft. lbs.	50 Nm
2.5L		37 ft. lbs.	50 Nm
2.8L		40 ft. lbs.	54 Nm
3.1L		40 ft. lbs.	54 Nm
3.3L		33 ft. lbs.	45 Nm
4.3L		77 ft. lbs.	105 Nm
Fuel Pipe Nut Fittings:			
2.5L	1990-92	22 ft. lbs.	30 Nm
3.1L	1990-91	17 ft. lbs.	23 Nm
3.1L	1993-95	13 ft. lbs.	17 Nm
3.3L	1990-93	20 ft. lbs.	27 Nm
Glow Plugs:			
4.3L		15 ft. lbs.	21 Nm
Oil Pan Drain Plug:			
2.2L		35 ft. lbs.	45 Nm
2.5L		25 ft. lbs.	34 Nm
2.8L		18 ft. lbs.	25 Nm
3.0L		30 ft. lbs.	41 Nm
3.1L	Vin-M	18 ft. lbs	25 Nm
3.3L		30 ft. lbs.	41 Nm
3.8L		30 ft. lbs.	41 Nm
4.3L		26 ft. lbs.	36 Nm
Oil Filter Access Plug:			
2.5L		Hand tighten + 1/4 turn	Hand tighten + 1/4 turn
Spark Plugs:			
2.2L		11 ft. lbs.	15 Nm
2.5L	to 1991	20 ft. lbs.	27 Nm
2.5L	1992 on	11 ft. lbs.	15 Nm
2.8L		15 ft. lbs.	20 Nm
3.1L	Vin-M	11 ft. lbs.	15 Nm
3.1L	Vin-T	18 ft. lbs.	24 Nm
3.3L	to 1991	20 ft. lbs.	27 Nm
3.3L	1992 on	11 ft. lbs.	15 Nm
Wheel Lug Nuts:		100 ft. lbs.	138 Nm

86811575

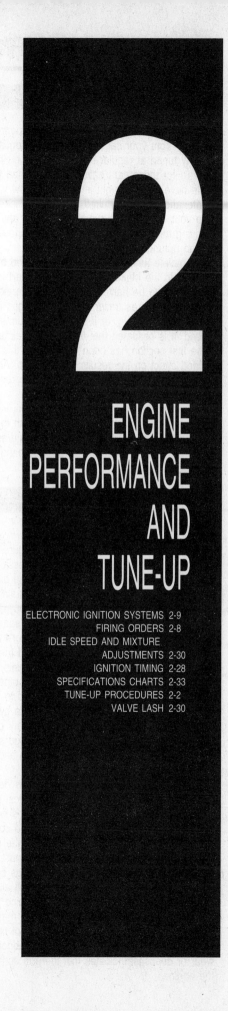

2

ENGINE PERFORMANCE AND TUNE-UP

TUNE-UP PROCEDURES

In order to extract the full measure of performance and economy from your car's engine it is essential that it be properly tuned at regular intervals. Although the tune-up intervals for these cars have been stretched to limits which would have been thought impossible a few years ago, periodic maintenance is still required. A regularly scheduled tune-up will keep your car's engine running smoothly and will prevent the annoying minor breakdowns and poor performance associated with an untuned engine.

A complete tune-up should be performed at the interval specified in the Maintenance Intervals chart in Section 1. This interval should be halved if the car is operated under severe conditions, such as trailer towing, prolonged idling, continual stop-and-start driving, or if starting and running problems are noticed. It is assumed that the routine maintenance described in the first section has been kept up, as this will have a decided effect on the results of a tune-up. All of the applicable steps should be followed in order, as the result is a cumulative one.

If the specifications on the tune-up label in the engine compartment of your vehicle disagree with the Tune-Up Specifications chart in this section, the figures on the sticker must be used. The label often reflects changes made during the production run.

Spark Plugs

▶ **See Figures 1, 2 and 3**

Spark plugs ignite the air and fuel mixture in the cylinder as the piston reaches the top of the compression stroke. The controlled explosion that results forces the piston down, turning the crankshaft and the rest of the drive train.

The average life of a spark plug 30,000 miles (48,300 km). On the 2.2L (LN2),engine the life of the spark plug is 100,000 miles (166,000 km). Part of the reason for this extraordinarily long life is the exclusive use of unleaded fuel, which reduces the amount of deposits within the combustion chamber and on the spark plug electrodes themselves, compared with the deposits left by the leaded gasoline used in the past. An additional contribution to long life is made by the High Energy Ignition (HEI) system, which fires the spark plugs with over 35,000 volts of electricity. The high voltage serves to keep the electrodes clear, which suffer less pitting and wear compared to breaker point ignitions.

Nevertheless, the life of a spark plug is dependent on a number of factors, including the mechanical condition of the engine, driving conditions, and the driver's habits.

When you remove the plugs, check the condition of the electrodes, they are a good indicator of the internal state of the engine. Since the spark plug wires must be checked every 15,000 miles (24,000 km), the spark plugs can be removed and examined at the same time. This will allow you to keep an eye on the mechanical status of the engine.

A small deposit of light tan or rust/red material on a spark plug that has been used for any period of time is to be considered normal. Any other color, or abnormal amounts of wear or deposits, indicates that there is something amiss in the engine.

Fig. 1 Breakdown of a common spark plug

The gap between the center electrode and the side or ground electrode can be expected to increase not more than 0.001 in. (0.025mm) every 1000 miles (1609 km) under normal conditions.

When a spark plug is functioning normally or, more accurately, when the plug is installed in an engine that is functioning properly, the plugs can be taken out, cleaned, regapped, and reinstalled in the engine without doing the engine any harm.

When, and if, a plug fouls and begins to misfire, you will have to investigate, correct the cause of the fouling, and either clean or replace the plug.

There are several reasons why a spark plug will foul and you can learn which is at fault by just looking at the plug. A few of the most common reasons for plug fouling, and a description of the fouled plug's appearance, are listed in a picture in this section.

Fig. 2 Heat range on spark plugs explained

Spark plugs suitable for use in your car's engine are offered in a number of different heat ranges. The amount of heat which the plug absorbs is determined by the length of the lower insulator. The longer the insulator, the hotter the plug will operate; the shorter the insulator, the cooler it will operate. A spark plug that absorbs (or retains) little heat and remains too cool will accumulate deposits of oil and carbon, because it is not hot enough to burn them off. This leads to fouling and consequent misfiring. A spark plug that absorbs too much heat will have no deposits, but the electrodes will burn away quickly and, in some cases, pre-ignition may result. Pre-ignition occurs when the spark plug tips get so hot that they ignite the fuel/mixture before the actual spark fires. This premature ignition will usually cause a pinging sound under conditions of low speed and heavy load. In severe cases, the heat may become high enough to start the fuel/air mixture burning throughout the combustion chamber rather than just to the front of the plug. In this case, the resultant explosion (detonation) will be strong enough to damage pistons, rings, and valves.

In most cases, the factory recommended heat range is correct; it is chosen to perform well under a wide range of operating conditions. However, if most of your driving is long distance, high speed travel, you may want to install a spark plug one range colder than standard. If most of your driving is of the short trip variety, when the engine may not always reach operating temperature, a hotter plug may help burn off the deposits normally accumulated under those conditions.

REMOVAL & INSTALLATION

▶ **See Figures 4, 5, 6, 7, 8, 9, 10, 11 and 12**

Before you replace your spark plugs make sure your engine is cool. If you do attempt to remove the plugs on a hot engine, several things could occur. The spark plugs could seize, causing damage to the cylinder head threads which can be expensive. You can also burn yourself severely. Also, make sure you clean the recess area thoroughly *before* removing the plugs. Any dirt entering the plug area will prevent the plug not to seat properly.

1. Number the wires with pieces of adhesive tape so that you won't cross them when you replace them.

2. The spark plug boots have large grips to aid in removal. Grasp the wire by the rubber boot and twist the boot ½ turn in either direction to break the tight seal between the boot and the plug. Then twist and pull on the boot to remove the wire from the spark plug. Do not pull on the wire itself or you will damage the carbon cord conductor.

3. Some of the engines may have a plug that is difficult to access. This requires the use of a special tool to aid in the removal and installation. There are two tools which are made for these kinds of problems: J-38491, to prevent damage to the wire by breaking the plug/boot bond, J-39294, to remove the plug wire from the rear bank of the engine.

4. If compressed air is available, apply it to the area around the spark plug holes. Otherwise, use a rag or a brush to clean the area. Doing this now will help from dirt entering into the plug chamber after removal.

5. Use a correct size spark plug socket to loosen all of the plugs about two turns. A universal joint installed at the socket end of the extension will ease the process. If removal of the

Fig. 3 Explanation of the spark plugs numbering system

Fig. 4 Tool J-38491

Fig. 6 The correct size socket is VERY important. You do not want to strip plug and not be able to remove it. This could be an expensive plug replacement

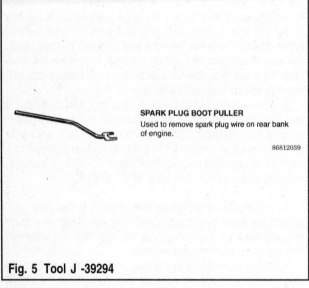

Fig. 5 Tool J -39294

Fig. 7 Spark plugs can be removed with your hands after you have loosened them enough

plugs is difficult, apply a few drops of penetrating oil or silicone spray to the area around the base of the plug, and allow it a few minutes to work.

6. Remove the plugs by unscrewing them the rest of the way.

To install:

7. Check and adjust the gap. This includes old and new plugs. Never rely on "pre-gapped" plugs. Also, use a wire gauge as opposed to a flat feeler gauge.

8. Lubricate the threads of the spark plugs with a drop of oil or a shot of silicone spray. Install the plugs and tighten them hand-tight. Take care not to cross-thread them.

9. Tighten the spark plugs with the socket. Do not apply the same amount of force you would use for a bolt; just snug them in. These spark plugs do not use gaskets, and over-tightening will make future removal difficult. If a torque wrench is available, tighten to 10-20 ft. lbs. (13-27 Nm).

Fig. 8 A variety of tools and gauges are needed for spark plug service

Fig. 9 Checking the spark plug gap with a feeler gauge

Fig. 10 Replacing the plug wires is easy when you have taken the time to mark everything

Tracking Arc
High voltage arcs between a fouling deposit on the insulator tip and spark plug shell. This ignites the fuel/air mixture at some point along the insulator tip, retarding the ignition timing which causes a power and fuel loss.

Wide Gap
Spark plug electrodes are worn so that the high voltage charge cannot arc across the electrodes. Improper gapping of electrodes on new or "cleaned" spark plugs could cause a similar condition. Fuel remains unburned and a power loss results.

Flashover
A damaged spark plug boot, along with dirt and moisture, could permit the high voltage charge to short over the insulator to the spark plug shell or the engine. AC's buttress insulator design helps prevent high voltage flashover.

Fouled Spark Plug
Deposits that have formed on the insulator tip may become conductive and provide a "shunt" path to the shell. This prevents the high voltage from arcing between the electrodes. A power and fuel loss is the result.

Bridged Electrodes
Fouling deposits between the electrodes "ground out" the high voltage needed to fire the spark plug. The arc between the electrodes does not occur and the fuel air mixture is not ignited. This causes a power loss and exhausting of raw fuel.

Cracked Insulator
A crack in the spark plug insulator could cause the high voltage charge to "ground out." Here, the spark does not jump the electrode gap and the fuel air mixture is not ignited. This causes a power loss and raw fuel is exhausted.

Fig. 11 Used spark plugs which show damage may indicate engine problems

GAP BRIDGED

IDENTIFIED BY DEPOSIT BUILD—UP CLOSING GAP BETWEEN ELECTRODES.

CAUSED BY OIL OR CARBON FOULING. REPLACE PLUG, OR, IF DEPOSITS ARE NOT EXCESSIVE THE PLUG CAN BE CLEANED.

OIL FOULED

IDENTIFIED BY WET BLACK DEPOSITS ON THE INSULATOR SHELL BORE ELECTRODES.

CAUSED BY EXCESSIVE OIL ENTERING COMBUSTION CHAMBER THROUGH WORN RINGS AND PISTONS, EXCESSIVE CLEARANCE BETWEEN VALVE GUIDES AND STEMS, OR WORN OR LOOSE BEARINGS. CORRECT OIL PROBLEM. REPLACE THE PLUG.

CARBON FOULED

IDENTIFIED BY BLACK, DRY FLUFFY CARBON DEPOSITS ON INSULATOR TIPS, EXPOSED SHELL SURFACES AND ELECTRODES.

CAUSED BY TOO COLD A PLUG, WEAK IGNITION, DIRTY AIR CLEANER, DEFECTIVE FUEL PUMP, TOO RICH A FUEL MIXTURE, IMPROPERLY OPERATING HEAT RISER OR EXCESSIVE IDLING. CAN BE CLEANED.

NORMAL

IDENTIFIED BY LIGHT TAN OR GRAY DEPOSITS ON THE FIRING TIP

PRE-IGNITION

IDENTIFIED BY MELTED ELECTRODES AND POSSIBLY BLISTERED INSULATOR. METALIC DEPOSITS ON INSULATOR INDICATE ENGINE DAMAGE.

CAUSED BY WRONG TYPE OF FUEL, INCORRECT IGNITION TIMING OR ADVANCE, TOO HOT A PLUG, BURNT VALVES OR ENGINE OVERHEATING. REPLACE THE PLUG.

OVERHEATING

IDENTIFIED BY A WHITE OR LIGHT GRAY INSULATOR WITH SMALL BLACK OR GRAY BROWN SPOTS AND WITH BLUISH-BURNT APPEARANCE OF ELECTRODES.

CAUSED BY ENGINE OVER-HEATING, WRONG TYPE OF FUEL, LOOSE SPARK PLUGS, TOO HOT A PLUG, LOW FUEL PUMP PRESSURE OR INCORRECT IGNITION TIMING. REPLACE THE PLUG.

FUSED SPOT DEPOSIT

IDENTIFIED BY MELTED OR SPOTTY DEPOSITS RESEMBLING BUBBLES OR BLISTERS.

CAUSED BY SUDDEN ACCELERATION. CAN BE CLEANED IF NOT EXCESSIVE, OTHERWISE REPLACE PLUG.

TCCS2002

Fig. 12 Inspect the spark plug to determine engine running conditions

➡️**While over-tightening the spark plug is to be avoided, under-tightening is just as bad. If combustion gases leak past the threads, the spark plug will overheat and rapid electrode wear will result.**

10. Install the wires on their respective plugs. Make sure the wires are firmly connected. You will be able to feel them click into place. Spark plug wiring diagrams are in this section if you get into trouble.

Spark Plug Wires

INSPECTION & TESTING

Every 15,000 miles (24,000 km), inspect the spark plug wires for burns, cuts, or breaks in the insulation. Check the boots and the nipples on the distributor cap. Replace any damaged wiring. General Motors requests that you replace your spark plug wires every 30,000 miles (50,000 km).

The resistance of the wires should be checked with an ohmmeter. Wires with excessive resistance will cause misfiring, and may make the engine difficult to start in damp weather.

To check resistance, remove the distributor cap, leaving the wires in place. Connect one lead of an ohmmeter to an electrode within the cap; connect the other lead to the corresponding spark plug terminal (remove it from the spark plug for this test). The following chart gives resistance values as a function of length. Replace any wire which shows a resistance over 30,000 ohms.

- 0-15 in. (0-38cm): 3,000-10,000 ohms
- 15-25 in. (38-64cm): 4,000-15,000 ohms
- 25-35 in. (64-89cm): 6,000-20,000 ohms
- Over 35 in. (89cm): 25,000 ohms

It should be remembered that resistance is a function of length; the longer the wire, the greater the resistance. Thus, if the wires on your car are longer than the factory originals, resistance will be higher, quite possibly outside these limits.

REMOVAL & INSTALLATION

▶ See Figures 13, 14 and 15

When installing new wires, replace them one at a time to avoid mixups. Start by replacing the longest one first. Install the boot firmly over the spark plug. Route the wire over the the same path as the original. Insert the nipple firmly onto the tower on the distributor cap or coil, then install the cap cover and latches to secure the wires, if applicable.

1 Insert screwdriver to unlock
2 Retainer - Do not pull on wire with retainer locked

86812016

Fig. 13 In order to replace the plug wires, you must first unlock the plastic retainers

86812017

Fig. 14 Grasp only the boot when removing the wires, never tug on the wire itself!

1 Bump stop
2 Spark plug wire
3 Spark plug
4 Lower tabs
5 Heat sheild

86812015

Fig. 15 Make sure the heat shield is seated against the bump stop and lower the tabs extended over the hex on the spark plug — 3.3L engine

FIRING ORDERS

▶ See Figures 16, 17, 18, 19, 20, 21, 22 and 23

➡ To avoid confusion, remove and tag the wires one at a time, for replacement.

Fig. 16 3.0L and 3.8L engines with distributor
Firing order: 1-6-5-4-3-2
Distributor rotation clockwise

Fig. 17 2.5L engine with distributor
Firing order: 1-3-4-2
Distributor rotation clockwise

Fig. 18 2.8L engine with distributor
Firing order: 1-2-3-4-5-5
Distributor rotation clockwise

Fig. 19 2.5L engine without distributor
Firing order: 1-3-4-2
Distributorless ignition

Fig. 20 3.3L engine without distributor
Firing order: 1-6-5-4-3-2
Distributorless ignition

Fig. 22 3.1L (VIN T and M) engine without distributor
Firing order: 1-6-5-4-3-2
Distributorless ignition

Fig. 21 3.8L engine without distributor
Firing order: 1-6-5-4-3-2
Distributorless ignition

Fig. 23 2.2L engine without distributor
Firing order: 1-3-4-2
Distributorless ignition

ELECTRONIC IGNITION SYSTEMS

Description and Operation

General Motors uses two basic ignition systems on these vehicles. A high energy distributor type system or a high energy distributorless type system. The High Energy Ignition (HEI) system is virtually maintenance free, since it is electronic and, therefore, uses no breaker points. The only required service for the HEI distributor is to check the distributor cap and rotor for cracks, carbon tracking, and corrosion every 30,000 miles (48,300 km).

On distributorless systems, even less maintenance is required. Since there is no distributor, there is no cap or rotor to wear out. The only normal maintenance required on these systems will be the spark plug and wires. Diagnosis of no start

conditions may require testing the ignition module or coil assemblies. These items are not much different than the ignition module or coil used on HEI systems.

The distributorless ignition systems used by General Motors goes by two names, either DIS or C^{3}I. DIS simple stands for Distributorless Ignition System while C^{3}I stands for Computer Controlled Coil Ignition. Both of these systems function the same way; by connecting a coil pack to a pair of spark plugs and firing the proper coil each time the a specific plug should spark, instead of using a distributor cap and rotor.

The distributorless ignition system is far better than previous system. It allows for more accurate spark control and a higher spark output. This is important at high engine speeds which newer engines are capable of.

HIGH ENERGY IGNITION (HEI) SYSTEM

▶ **See Figure 24**

The General Motors HEI system is a pulse-triggered, transistor-controlled, inductive discharge ignition system. The entire HEI system is contained within the distributor cap.

The distributor, contains the ignition coil, the electronic control module, and the magnetic pick-up assembly contains a permanent magnet, a pole piece with internal teeth, and a pick-up coil (not to be confused with the ignition coil).

For 1982 and later an HEI distributor with Electronic Spark Timing (EST) is used (for more information on EST, refer to Section 4).

All spark timing changes in the 1982 and later distributors are done electronically by the Ignition Control Module (ICM) which monitors information from various engine sensors, computes the desired spark timing and then signals the distributor to change the timing accordingly. No vacuum or mechanical advance systems are used whatsoever.

In the HEI system, as in other electronic ignition systems, the breaker points have been replaced with an electronic switch, (a transistor), which is located within the control module. This switching transistor performs the same function the points did in a conventional ignition system; it simply turns coil primary current on and off at the correct time. Essentially then, electronic and conventional ignition systems operate on the same principle.

The module which houses the switching transistor is controlled (turned on and off) by a magnetically generated impulse induced in the pick-up coil. When the teeth of the rotating timer align with the teeth of the pole piece, the induced voltage in the pick-up coil signals the electronic module to open the coil primary circuit. The primary current then decreases, and a high voltage is induced in the ignition coil secondary windings which is then directed through the rotor and spark plug wires to fire the spark plugs.

In essence then, the pick-up coil module system simply replaces the conventional breaker points and condenser. The condenser found within the distributor is for radio suppression purposes only and has nothing to do with the ignition process. The module automatically controls the dwell period, increasing it with increasing engine speed. Since dwell is automatically controlled, it cannot be adjusted. The module itself is non-adjustable and non-repairable and must be replaced if found defective.

DISTRIBUTORLESS IGNITION SYSTEMS

▶ **See Figures 25, 26, 27 and 28**

Starting in 1987, some models came with engines equipped with a Computer Controlled Coil Ignition (C3I) or Distributorless Ignition System (DIS).

Both DIS and C3I system consists of the coil pack, ignition module, crankshaft sensor, interrupter rings and ignition control module (ICM). All components are serviced as complete assemblies, although individual coils are available for Type 2 coil packs. Since the ICM controls the ignition timing, no timing adjustments are necessary or possible.

Fig. 25 Triggering system used on the C3I fast start system

Fig. 24 Coil packs for Distributorless ignitions on 4 and 6 cylinder engines

Fig. 26 Electrical schematic on C³I ignition system

Fig. 27 Wiring schematic used on the C³I ignition system

Fig. 28 Notch effect on the output signal used on the crankshaft sensor

Diagnosis and Testing

▶ See Figure 29

The ignition, fuel, electrical and emission systems are all interrelated on vehicles that have computer control engines. Testing these systems has become very involved because of this. When using this manual it's important to realize that these systems overlap. Some testing or component replacement that may effect the ignition system may be in the emissions section 4. If a component test or symptom is not found in the section of the book that you expect, check the other related sections and you should find the necessary procedures.

HEI PRECAUTIONS

▶ See Figure 30

This is an extremely high voltage system and contact with the spark plug wires with the ignition switch **ON** can give a very dangerous shock. Never service the or test the spark plug wires, distributor cap or coil with the key **ON** or engine running unless instructed to perform a specific test. Before going on to troubleshooting, it might be a good idea to take note of the following precautions:

➡**To avoid damage to the ICM or other ignition system components, do not use electrical test equipment such as battery or AC powered voltmeter, ohmmeter, etc. or any type of tester other than specified.**

• When performing electrical tests on the system, use a high impedance multimeter, digital voltmeter (DVM) J-34029-A or equivalent.
• To prevent electrostatic discharge damage, when working with the Computer Control Module (ECM/PCM), do not touch the connector pins or soldered components on the circuit board.
• When handling a PROM, CAL-PAK or MEM-CAL, do not touch the component leads. Also, do not remove the integrated circuit from the carrier.

• Never pierce a high tension lead or boot for any testing purpose; otherwise, future problems are guaranteed.
• Leave new components and modules in the shipping package until ready to install them.
• Never disconnect any electrical connection with the ignition switch **ON** unless instructed to do so in a test.

Timing Light Use
▶ See Figure 31

Inductive pick-up timing lights are the best kind of use with HEI. Timing light which connect between the spark plug and the spark plug wire occasionally (not always) give false readings.

DISTRIBUTOR COMPONENT TESTING

▶ See Figure 32

Not all tachometers will operate or indicate correctly when used on a HEI system. While some tachometers may give a reading, this does not necessarily mean the reading is correct. In addition, some tachometers hook up differently from others. If you can't figure out whether or not your tachometer will work on your car, check with the tachometer manufacturer. The following procedure is for internal coils, see the illustrations for external coils.

✴✴CAUTION

Never ground the TACH terminal; serious module and ignition coil damage will result. If there is any doubt as to the correct tachometer hookup, check with the tachometer manufacturer.

1. Connect an ohmmeter between the TACH and BAT terminals in the distributor cap. The primary coil resistance should be less than 1 ohm.
2. To check the coil secondary resistance, connect an ohmmeter between the rotor button and BAT terminal. Note the reading. Connect the ohmmeter between the rotor button and the TACH terminal. Note the reading. The resistance in both

Fig. 29 Direct ignition system on 2.8L engine

VOLTMETER - Voltage Position Measures amount of voltage. When connected in parallel to an existing circuit. A digital voltmeter with 10 meg ohm input impedence is used because this type of meter will not load down the circuit and result in faulty readings.some circuits require accurate low voltage readings, and some circuits in the ECM have a very high resistance .

AMMETER - When used as ammeter, this meter also accurately measures extremely low current flow. Refer to meter instructions for more information.
- Selector must be set properly for both function and range. DC is used for most automotive measurements.

OHMMETER - Measures resistance of circuit directly in ohms. Refer to meter for more information.
- OL Display in all ranges indicates open circuit.
- Zero display in all ranges indicates a short circuit.
- Intermittent connection in circuit may be indicated by digital reading that will not stabilize on circuit.
- Range Switch.
  - ☐ 200Ω – Reads ohms directly
  - 2K,20K,200KΩ – Reads ohms in thousands
  - 2M and 20MΩ - Reads ohms in millions

86812040

HIGH IMPEDANCE MULTIMETER (DIGITAL VOLTMETER-DVM) J34029-A

Fig. 30 Tool J-34029-A

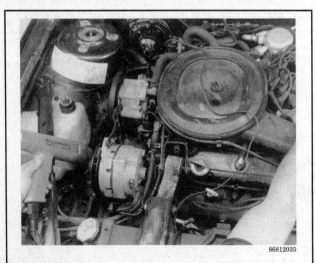

86812035

Fig. 31 Aim the Inductive timing light at the timing marks on the engine and pulley

cases should be 6000-30,000 ohms. Be sure to test between the rotor button and both the BAT and TACH terminals.

3. Replace the coil only if the readings in Step 1 and 2 are infinite.

➡These resistance checks will not disclose shorted coil windings. This condition can only be detected with scope analysis or a suitably designed coil tester. If these instruments are unavailable, replace the coil with a known good coil as a final test.

4. To test the pick-up coil, first disconnect the white and green module leads. Set the ohmmeter on the high scale and connect it between a ground and either the white or green lead. Any resistance measurement less than infinity requires replacement of the pick-up coil.

5. Pick-up coil continuity is tested by connecting the ohmmeter (on low range) between the white and green leads. Normal resistance is between 800-1500 ohms. Move the vacuum advance arm while performing this test, if equipped. This will detect any break in coil continuity. Such a condition can

cause intermittent misfiring. Replace the pick-up if the reading is outside the specified limits.

6. If no defects have been found at this time, and you still have a problem, then the module will have to be checked. If you do not have access to a module tester, the only possible alternative is a substitution test or have the module tested by a professional.

HEI System Testers

Instruments designed specifically for testing HEI systems are available from several tool manufacturers. Some of these will even test the module itself.

If the engine cranks but doesn't start additional tests are in Section 4. Use the A-Charts especially Charts A-2 to A-7. These charts provide step by step instruction for testing for spark and fuel.

HEI Parts Replacement

REMOVAL & INSTALLATION

Integral Coil
▶ **See Figures 33, 34 and 35**

1. Disconnect the negative battery cable.

2. Disconnect the feed and module wire terminal connectors from the distributor cap.
3. Remove the ignition set retainer.
4. Remove the 4 coil cover-to-distributor cap screws.
5. Using a blunt drift, press the coil wire spade terminals out of the distributor cap.
6. Lift the coil out of the distributor cap.
7. Remove and clean the coil spring, rubber seal washer and coil cavity of the distributor cap.

To install:
8. Coat the rubber seal with a dielectric lubricant furnished. This is usually in the replacement ignition coil package.
9. Install the coil spring, rubber seal washer and coil cavity into the distributor cap.
10. Place the coil into the cap, connect the spade terminals.
11. Install the 4 cover-to distributor cap screws, install the ignition set retainer.
12. Connect the feed and module wire terminal connectors to the distributor cap.
13. Connect the negative battery cable.
14. Reset the clock, radio and any other accessaries if required.

Fig. 32 Electronic distributor modules used by General Motors

DISTRIBUTOR DISASSEMBLY
TEST AND REASSEMBLY
(COIL IN CAP)

"COIL IN CAP" DISTRIBUTOR

COIL AND CAP ASSEMBLY

TERMINALS
C. B+

LATCH (4)

4 TERMINAL CONNECTOR

CONNECTOR (DISCONNECTED FROM CAP)

1. A 6-cyl. EST distributor with coil-in-cap is illustrated.
2. Detach wiring connector from cap, as shown.
3. Turn four latches and remove cap and coil assembly from lower housing.

TESTING IGNITION COIL

1 OHMMETER   2 OHMMETER

4. Connect ohmmeter. Test 1.
5. Reading should be zero. or nearly zero. If not. replace coil. Step 8.
6. Connect ohmmeter both ways. Test 2. Use high scale. Replace coil only if both readings are infinite. Step 8.
7. If coil is good. go to Step 13.

IGNITION COIL ATTACHING SCREWS

COIL ATTACHING SCREW (4)

IGNITION COIL

GROUND LEAD COIL SECONDARY

C. GRD. B+
TERMINALS

8. Remove coil-cover attaching screws and lift off cover.

86812046

Fig. 33 The distributor coil in the cap testing, disassembly and assembly

IGNITION COIL REMOVED FROM CAP

SEAL
GROUND
CONNECTOR

IGNITION
COIL

9. Remove ignition coil attaching screws and lift coil with leads from cap.
10. Remove ignition coil arc seal.
11. Clean with soft cloth and inspect cap for defects. Replace, if needed.
12. Assemble new coil and cover to cap.

TESTING PICKUP COIL

OHMMETER   OHMMETER
1   2

PICKUP COIL LEADS
DISCONNECTED
FROM MODULE

4-TERMINAL
CONNECTOR
LATCH

MODULE

PICKUP COIL
ASSEMBLY

"P"
TERMINAL

13. On all distributors, including distributors with Hall Effect Switch identified in Step 27, remove rotor and pickup coil leads from module.
14. Connect ohmmeter Test 1 and then Test 2.
15. If vacuum unit is used, connect vacuum source to vacuum unit. Replace unit if inoperative. Observe ohmmeter throughout vacuum range; flex leads by hand without vacuum to check for intermittent opens.
16. Test 1 — should read infinite at all times.
    Test 2 — should read steady at one value within 500-1500 ohm range.
    NOTE: Ohmmeter may deflect if operating vacuum unit causes teeth to align. This is not a defect.
17. If pickup coil is defective, go to Step 18. If okay, go to Step 23.

DRIVING PIN FROM SHAFT

ROLL
PIN

18. Mark distributor shaft and gear so they can be reassembled in same position.
19. Drive out roll pin.

SHAFT ASSEMBLY REMOVED

THREE
ATTACHING
SCREWS

MAGNETIC
SHIELD

MODULE

PICKUP COIL
LEADS DIS-
CONNECTED
FROM MODULE

20. Remove gear and pull shaft assembly from distributor.

86812047

Fig. 34 The distributor coil in the cap testing, disassembly and assembly continued

Fig. 35 The distributor coil in the cap testing, disassembly and assembly continued

External Coil

▶ See Figures 36, 37, 38, 39 and 40

1. Disconnect the negative battery cable.
2. Loosen the bolts securing the coil assembly.
3. Remove the wires attached to the mounting screw.
4. Disconnect the wire harnesses connected to the coil assembly
5. Disconnect the coil wire from the coil.

To install:

6. Place the new coil in position, attach the mounting wires to the mounting bolts and tighten.
7. Install the wiring harnesses to the coil, and connect the coil wire.
8. Connect the negative battery cable.
9. Reset the clock, radio and any other accessaries if required.

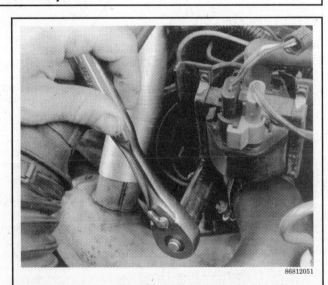

Fig. 36 Loosening the external coil hold-down bolts . . .

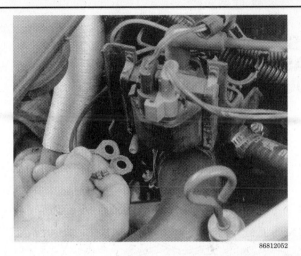

Fig. 37 . . . remove the wires attached to the mounting bolts

Fig. 38 Remove the wire harnesses

Distributor Cap

INTEGRAL COIL

1. Disconnect the negative battery cable.
2. Remember to number the cap and wires before removal.
3. Remove the feed and module wire terminal connectors from the distributor cap.
4. Remove the retainer and spark plug wires from the cap.
5. Depress and release the 4 distributor cap-to-housing retainers and lift off the cap assembly.
6. Remove the 4 coil cover screws and cover.
7. Using a finger or a blunt drift, push the spade terminals out of the distributor cap.
8. Remove all 4 coil screws and lift the coil, coil spring and rubber seal washer out of the cap coil cavity.

To install:

9. Position the new cap on the distributor. Clean and lubricate the rubber seal washer with dielectric lubricant.
10. Install the coil spring, rubber seal washer and coil cavity into the distributor cap.

11. Position the coil into the cap, connect the spade terminals.
12. Install the 4 cover-to distributor cap screws, install the ignition set retainer.
13. Connect the feed and module wire terminal connectors to the distributor cap.
14. Connect the negative battery cable.
15. Reset the clock, radio and any other accessaries if required.

EXTERNAL COIL

▶ **See Figures 41 and 42**

1. Disconnect the negative battery cable.
2. Remember to number the cap and wires before removal. It might be a good idea to match the caps up and insert the wires into the new cap prior to installation. This could aid you in replacing the wires on the correct terminals.
3. Remove the spark plug wires from the cap.
4. Remove the 2 cap screws and lift the cap off.

To install:

5. Install the new distributor cap using the cap screws and tighten until snug.
6. Replace the wires to the proper terminals.
7. Connect the negative battery cable.
8. Reset the clock, radio and any other accessaries if required.

Rotor

▶ **See Figures 43 and 44**

1. Disconnect the negative battery cable.
2. Remove the distributor cap.
3. Remove the two rotor attaching screws and rotor.

To install:

4. Insert the new rotor in place and tighten the mounting screws until snug.
5. Install the distributor cap.
6. Connect the negative battery cable.
7. Reset the clock, radio and any other accessaries if required.

Ignition Module

▶ **See Figures 45, 46 and 47**

1. Disconnect the negative battery cable.
2. Remove the distributor cap and rotor as previously described.
3. Unplug the harness connector and pick-up coil spade connectors from the module. Be careful not to damage the wires when removing the connector.
4. Remove the two screws and module from the distributor housing.

To install:

5. Coat the bottom of the new module with dielectric lubricant. This is usually supplied with the new module.
6. Install the module and tighten the screws until snug.
7. Engage the harness connector and pick-up coil spade connectors to the module.
8. Install the cap and rotor.
9. Connect the negative battery cable.
10. Reset the clock, radio and any other accessaries if required.

DISTRIBUTOR DISASSEMBLY
TEST AND REASSEMBLY
(SEPARATELY MOUNTED COIL)

HEI/EST DISTRIBUTOR

B+ C−
CONNECTOR

4 TERMINAL
CONNECTOR

1. A TYPICAL DISTRIBUTOR USED WITH A SEPARATELY MOUNTED COIL IS SHOWN.

TESTING IGNITION COIL

OHMMETER   OHMMETER   OHMMETER

2. CHECK IGNITION COIL WITH OHMMETER FOR OPENS AND GROUNDS:
   STEP 1. — USE HIGH SCALE. SHOULD READ VERY HIGH (INFINITE). IF NOT, REPLACE COIL.
   STEP 2. — USE LOW SCALE. SHOULD READ VERY LOW OR ZERO. IF NOT, REPLACE COIL.
   STEP 3. — USE HIGH SCALE. SHOULD NOT READ INFINITE. IF IT DOES, REPLACE COIL.

TESTING PICKUP COIL

PICKUP COIL LEADS

OHMMETER

3. REMOVE ROTOR AND PICKUP COIL LEADS FROM MODULE.
   4. CONNECT OHMMETER PART 1 AND PART 2.
   5. OBSERVE OHMMETER. FLEX LEADS BY HAND TO CHECK FOR INTERMITTENT OPENS.
      STEP 1 — SHOULD READ INFINITE AT ALL TIMES. IF NOT, PICKUP COIL IS DEFECTIVE.
      STEP 2 — SHOULD READ ONE STEADY VALUE BETWEEN 500-1500 OHMS AS LEADS ARE FLEXED BY HAND. IF NOT, PICKUP COIL IS DEFECTIVE.

DRIVING PIN FROM SHAFT

ROLL PIN

6. DRIVE ROLL PIN FROM GEAR AND REMOVE SHAFT ASSEMBLY. MARK GEAR AND SHAFT FOR CORRECT REASSEMBLY.

86812049

Fig. 39 Distributor testing and disassembly on the external coil

DISTRIBUTOR DISASSEMBLY TEST AND REASSEMBLY (SEPARATELY MOUNTED COIL)

REMOVE PICKUP COIL

PRY OFF RETAINER

POLE PIECE

PICKUP COIL

7. TO REMOVE PICKUP COIL, REMOVE RETAINER.
8. LIFT PICKUP COIL ASSEMBLY STRAIGHT UP TO REMOVE FROM DISTRIBUTOR.

REMOVING MODULE

MODULE

APPLY SILICONE LUBRICANT

9. DISCONNECT WIRING CONNECTORS FROM MODULE. REMOVE TWO SCREWS TO REMOVE MODULE TEST MODULE WITH AN APPROVED MODULE TESTER.

REASSEMBLY

10. WIPE DISTRIBUTOR BASE AND MODULE CLEAN, APPLY SILICONE LUBRICANT BETWEEN MODULE AND BASE FOR HEAT DISSIPATION.
11. ATTACH MODULE TO BASE. ATTACH PICKUP CONNECTOR TO MODULE.
12. ASSEMBLE PICKUP POLE PIECE AND RETAINER.
13. ASSEMBLE SHAFT, GEAR PARTS AND ROLL PIN.
14. SPIN SHAFT TO INSURE THAT TEETH DO NOT TOUCH.
15. INSTALL ROTOR AND CAP.

86812050

Fig. 40 Distributor testing and disassembly on the external coil continued

IGNITION COIL CONNECTOR TERMINALS

C-

B+

LATCH

LATCH (2)

4-TERMINAL CONNECTOR

86812056

Fig. 41 HEI external mounted coil distributor assembly

86812054

Fig. 42 Remove the bolts that secure the cap for removal

Fig. 43 Lift the cap off

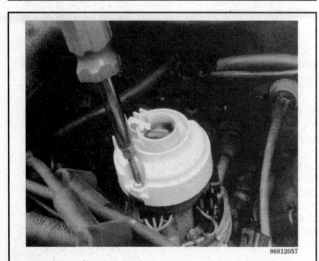

Fig. 44 Remove the two mounting screws from the rotor

Fig. 45 Electronic distributor modules used by General Motors

2A MODULE USED WITH INTEGRAL COIL DISTRIBUTOR
2B MODULE USED WITH REMOTE COIL DISTRIBUTOR
2C MODULE USED WITH NEW 72 AND 80 MM REMOTE COIL DISTRIBUTORS.

Fig. 46 Module replacement is always in need of silicone lubricant

Fig. 47 Pick up coil with distributor shaft removed

DIS Parts Replacement

IDLE LEARN PROCEDURE

This procedure allows the ICM memory to be updated with the correct IAC valve pintle position. The Idle Learn procedure must be performed on the 3.1L engine as follows:
1. Place the transaxle in **P** or **N**.
2. Install the Tech 1 scan tool or equivalent.
3. Turn the ignition switch **ON**, engine OFF.
4. Select IAC system, then Idle Learn in the MISC Test mode.
5. Proceed with the Idle Learn as directed by the scan tool.

REMOVAL & INSTALLATION

DIS Assembly

2.2L, 2.5L, 2.8L, 3.1L AND 3.8L ENGINES

▶ See Figures 48 and 49

1. Disconnect the negative battery cable.
2. Unplug the DIS electrical connectors.
3. Tag and disconnect the spark plug wires.
4. Remove the DIS assembly attaching bolts.
5. Remove the DIS assembly from the engine.

To install:

6. Install the DIS assembly and attaching bolts.
7. Connect the spark plug wires.
8. Engage the DIS electrical connectors.
9. Connect the negative battery cable.
10. On 3.1L (VIN-T) engine, perform the idle learn procedure.

1 Bracket	4 1-4 ignition coil
2 Ignition control	5 Screw (4)
3 2-3 ignition coil	4.5 Nm (40 lb.in.)

86812062

Fig. 48 DIS system assembly on 2.2L engine

1 Upper intake manifold assembly
2 Ignition coil assembly
3 Bolt/Screw
4 Nut
5 Evap purge solenoid valve bracket
6 Stud

86812063

Fig. 49 DIS system assembly on 3.1L (VIN-M) engine

11. Reset the clock, radio and any other accessaries if required.

Ignition Coils

2.2L ENGINE

1. Disconnect the negative battery cable.
2. Raise the car and support with jackstands.
3. Disconnect the ICM electrical connectors.
4. Mark and disconnect the spark plug wires.
5. Remove the 3 coil assembly-to-block bolts.
6. Remove the coil assembly from the engine.

To install:

7. Install the coil assembly to the engine with the mounting bolts.
8. Connect the 3 ignition coil assembly-to-the block bolts.
9. Tighten the coil assembly mounting bolts to 15-22 ft. lbs. (20-30 Nm).
10. Install the plug wires to the proper coils.
11. Install the ICM connectors.
12. Lower the car, connect the negative battery cable.
13. Reset the clock, radio and any other accessaries if required.

2.5L, 2.8L, 3.1L AND 3.8L ENGINES

1. Disconnect the negative battery cable.
2. Disconnect and tag spark plug wires.
3. Remove ignition coil attaching bolts, then the ignition coil from the module.

To install:

4. Install the coil(s) and attaching bolts, tighten to 40 inch lbs. (4-5 Nm).
5. Connect the spark plug wires.
6. Connect the negative battery cable.
7. On 3.1L engine perform the idle learn procedure.
8. Reset the clock, radio and any other accessaries if required.

3.3L ENGINE

1. Disconnect the negative battery cable.
2. Tag and disconnect spark plug wires.
3. Remove ignition coil(s) attaching bolts, then the ignition coil from the module.

To install:

4. Install the coil(s) and attaching bolts, torque to 27 inch lbs. (3 Nm).
5. Connect the spark plug wires.
6. Connect the negative battery cable.
7. Reset the clock, radio and any other accessaries if required.

Ignition Module

2.2L ENGINE

1. Disconnect the negative battery cable.
2. Raise and support the car.
3. Remove the ignition coil assembly from the engine. Disconnect the coils from the assembly.
4. Remove the module from the assembly plate.

To install:

5. Install the new module to the plate.

6. Install the coils to the assembly, and install the coil assembly on the engine.

7. Lower the car. Connect the negative battery cable, then reset the clock, radio and any other accessaries.

2.5L, 2.8L, 3.1L (VIN-T) AND 3.8L ENGINES

1. Disconnect the negative battery cable.
2. Remove the DIS assembly from the engine.
3. Remove the coils from the assembly.
4. Remove DIS module from the assembly plate.

To install:

5. Install the DIS module to the assembly plate.
6. Install the coils to the assembly.
7. Install the DIS assembly to the engine.
8. Connect the negative battery cable, then reset the clock, radio and any other accessaries.
9. On 3.1L engine perform the idle learn procedure.

3.1L (VIN-M) ENGINE

1. Disconnect the negative battery cable.
2. Remove the 6-way, 3-way and 2-way connectors at the ignition control module.
3. Remove the plug wires from the coil assembly.
4. Disconnect the 6 screws that secure the coil assemblies to the ICM.
5. Remove the nuts and washers securing the ICM assembly to the bracket and remove the ICM.

To install:

6. Install the coils to the ICM installing the 6 screws.
7. Tighten the screws to 40 inch lbs. (4-5 Nm).
8. Install the nuts and washers securing the assembly to the bracket and torque them to 70 inch lbs. (8 Nm).
9. Engage the 2, 3, and 6 way connectors to the ICM.
10. Connect the negative battery cable, then reset the clock, radio and any other accessaries.

Crankshaft Position Sensor (CKP)

2.2L ENGINE

1. Disconnect the negative battery cable.
2. Raise the car and support.
3. Disconnect the harness at the sensor.
4. Remove the bolt to the sensor.
5. Remove the sensor from the engine.

To install:

6. Inspect the O-ring and replace if needed. Lubricate the O-ring with engine oil.
7. Install the sensor to the block.
8. Insert the bolt and tighten to 71 inch lbs. (8 Nm).
9. Engage the harness on the sensor.
10. Lower the car, Connect the negative battery cable, then reset the clock, radio and any other accessaries.

2.5L, 2.8L, 3.1L (VIN-T) AND 3.8L ENGINES

1. Disconnect the negative battery cable.
2. Disconnect crankshaft sensor electrical connector.
3. Remove the crankshaft sensor attaching bolt, then remove the crankshaft sensor from the vehicle.

To install:

4. Inspect the sensor O-ring for wear, cracks or leakage. Replace as necessary. Lubricate the new O-ring with engine oil prior to installation.

5. Install the sensor into the hole in the engine block and install retaining bolt.
6. Engage the electrical connector.
7. Connect the negative battery cable, then reset the clock, radio and any other accessaries.
8. On 3.1L engine perform the idle learn procedure.

3.1L (VIN-M) ENGINE WITH 3X CKP

▶ See Figure 50

➡**On cars equipped with manual transaxles, the CKP is easily accessed from beneath the engine. For automatic transaxles, the rack and pinion heat shield and the converter intermediate exhaust assembly must be removed.**

1. Disconnect the negative battery cable.
2. Unplug the sensor connector.
3. Remove the sensor bolts and the sensor from the engine.
4. Inspect the O-ring and replace if needed. This is always advisable anyway.

To install:

5. Install the sensor to the engine, tighten the mounting bolt to 88 inch lbs. (10 Nm).
6. Insert the connector to the sensor, then connect the negative battery cable.
7. Reset the clock, radio and any other accessaries.

3.1L (VIN-M) ENGINE WITH 24X CKP

▶ See Figures 51 and 52

1. Disconnect the negative battery cable.
2. Remove the serpentine belt from the crankshaft pulley.
3. Raise the car on a hoist.
4. Remove the crankshaft harmonic balancer retaining bolt. Use tool J-38197 or equivalent.
5. Unplug the crankshaft sensor connector.
6. Remove the 2 sensor mounting bolts, remove the sensor.

To install:

7. Connect the sensor with the 2 mounting bolts. Torque the bolts to 8 ft. lbs. (10 Nm).
8. Reattach the sensor connector.

1 Engine block assembly
2 Crankshaft position (CKP) sensor

86812067

Fig. 50 3X CKP mounting on 3.1L Vin-M

1 Front engine cover
2 24x crankshaft position sensor assembly
3 Bolt (2) torque 10 Nm (8 lb.ft.)

86812066

Fig. 51 24X CKP mounting 3.1L Vin-M

BALANCER REMOVER
Used to remove crankshaft pulley.

86812065

Fig. 52 Special tool to remove the balancer

9. Install the balancer on the crankshaft.
10. Apply thread sealer GM# 1052080 or it's equivalent to the threads of the balancer bolt. Torque the bolt to 110 ft. lbs. (150 Nm).
11. Lower the car.
12. Install the serpentine belt.
13. Connect the negative battery cable, then reset the clock, radio and any other accessaries.

Camshaft Position Sensor

3.1L ENGINE (VIN-M)

▶ **See Figures 53, 54 and 55**

1. Disconnect the negative battery cable.
2. Remove the serpentine belt.
3. Remove the power steering pump.
4. Unplug the connector to the sensor.
5. Remove the mounting bolt for the sensor, and remove the sensor.

1 Camshaft position sensor
2 Bolt/Screw - torque to 10 Nm (8 lb.ft.)
3 Engine block assembly

86812070

Fig. 53 Camshaft sensor mounting location on 3.1L engine — Vin-M

To install:

6. Install the camshaft sensor.

7. Insert the bolt, tighten down to 8 ft. lbs. (10 Nm).

8. Insert the electrical connector to the sensor.

9. Install the power steering pump, and the serpentine belt.

10. Connect the negative battery cable, then reset the clock, radio and any other accessaries.

C³I System Parts Replacement

The 3.3L engine is the only one with the C³I system.

REMOVAL & INSTALLATION

C³I Module

▶ **See Figure 56**

1. Disconnect the negative battery cable.

Fig. 54 Conventional ignition system function

86812072

86812073

Fig. 55 Distributorless ignition system function

2. Unplug the 14-way connector at the ignition module.

3. Tag and disconnect the spark plug wires at the coil assembly.

4. Remove the nuts and washers securing the C³I module assembly to the bracket.

5. Remove the 6 bolts attaching the coil assemblies to the ignition module.

To install:

6. Install the coil assemblies to the ignition module and install the 6 attaching bolts.

7. Install the nuts and washers attaching the assembly to the bracket.

8. Connect the spark plug wires.

9. Engage the 14-way connector to the module.

10. Connect the negative battery cable, then reset the clock, radio and any other accessaries.

Ignition Coil(s)

1. Disconnect the negative battery cable.

2. Tag and disconnect the spark plug wires.

3. Remove ignition coil attaching bolts, then the ignition coil from the module.

To install:

4. Install the coil(s) and attaching bolts.

5. Connect the spark plug wires.

6. Connect the negative battery cable, then reset the clock, radio and any other accessaries.

Dual Crankshaft Sensor

▶ **See Figures 57, 58 and 59**

1. Disconnect battery negative cable.

2. Remove serpentine belt from crankshaft pulley.

3. Raise and safely support the vehicle.

4. Remove right front tire and wheel assembly, then the inner access cover.

5. Remove crankshaft harmonic balancer retaining bolt and crankshaft harmonic balancer.

6. Unplug the electrical connector from the sensor and remove the crankshaft sensor from the vehicle.

86812071

Fig. 56 Distributorless C³I coils and module system — 3.3L Engine

86812074

Fig. 57 Harmonic balancer with interrupter rings on C³I system

86812075

Fig. 58 Dual crankshaft sensor — C³I system

To install:

7. Loosely install the crankshaft sensor on the pedestal.

8. Position the sensor with the pedestal attached on special tool J-37089.

9. Position the tool on the crankshaft.

10. Install the bolts to hold the pedestal to the block face. Tighten to 14-28 ft. lbs. (20-40 Nm).

11. Tighten the pedestal pinch bolt to 30-35 inch lbs. (3-4 Nm).

12. Remove special tool J-37089.

13. Place special tool J-37089 on the harmonic balancer and turn. If any vane of the harmonic balancer touches the tool, replace the balancer assembly.

➡A clearance of 0.025 inch is required on either side of the interrupter ring. Be certain to obtain the correct clearance. Failure to do so will damage the sensor. A mis-

adjusted sensor of bent interrupter ring could cause rubbing of the sensor, resulting in potential driveability problems, such as rough idle, poor performance, or a no start condition.

14. Install the balancer on the crankshaft and install the crankshaft balancer bolt. Tighten to 200-239 ft. lbs. (270-325 Nm).

15. Install the inner fender shield.

16. Install the tire and wheel assembly. Tighten to 100 ft. lbs. (140 Nm).

17. Lower the vehicle.

18. Install the serpentine belt.

19. Connect the negative battery cable, then reset the clock, radio and any other accessaries.

J 37089

86812076

Fig. 59 Distributorless C³I positioning tool J-37089 for installing dual crankshaft sensor. system — 3.3L Engine

IGNITION TIMING

General Information

GASOLINE ENGINES

♦ **See Figures 60, 61, 62 and 63**

Ignition timing is the point at which each spark plug fires in relation to its respective piston, during the compression stroke of the engine.

As far as ignition timing is concerned, the position of the piston can be related (in degrees) to the following reference terms: Top Dead Center (TDC), After Top Dead Center (ATDC), and Before Top Dead Center (BTDC). The movement of the piston is expressed in degrees due to the rotation of the crankshaft. Even though the crankshaft turns 720° to complete one entire 4-stroke cycle, all we're concerned about here is the compression stroke, since this is when the ignition of the air/fuel mixture takes place (or more accurately, should take place).

Because it takes a fraction of a second for the spark (at the spark plug) to ignite the air/fuel mixture and for the mixture to burn completely, the spark should ideally occur just before the piston reaches TDC. If the spark didn't occur until exactly TDC or ATDC, the piston would already be on its way down before the mixture explosion and would not exert as much downward force on the piston as it would if the ignition timing was properly set. The result of this would be reduced power and fuel economy.

Should ignition of the air/fuel mixture occur too far BTDC (advanced), the mixture explosion will try to force the piston downward before it can mechanically do so. This contest between the explosion forcing the piston downward and the crankshaft forcing the piston upward will result in a pinging sound if you're lucky; severe engine damage if you're not so

Fig. 61 Magnetic probe timing hole and marks

lucky. If you experience pinging, check with a reputable mechanic to determine if the pinging is mild or severe. Only a trained car mechanic can safely determine this.

➡**Pinging can also be caused by inferior gasoline, since lower octane gas burns at a faster, more uncontrolled rate than a higher octane fuel.**

In order to compensate for low quality gas, the ignition timing may be retarded a couple of degrees, though this is not recommended since performance and fuel economy will suffer.

On federal emissions engines, after the initial (base) timing is set, the computer and related components electronically determine and adjust the degree of spark advance under all conditions. On Canadian models, total ignition timing advance is determined by three things: initial timing setting, distributor vacuum control and distributor mechanical control.

Fig. 60 Ignition timing using the average method — 4 cylinder with distributor

Fig. 62 Timing mark location on a 2.8L engine

DIESEL ENGINES

▶ See Figure 64

The timing meter picks up the engine speed and crankshaft position from the crankshaft balancer. It uses a luminosity signal through a glow plug probe to determine the combustion timing. Certain engine malfunctions may cause a incorrect timing reading. An engine malfunction should be corrected before a timing adjustment is made. The marks on the pump and adapter flange will normally be aligned within 1.27mm (.050 in.). A timing meter Tool J-33075 is recommended for this job.

Inspection and Adjustment

DIS AND C³I SYSTEMS

On vehicles equipped with either the Direct or Distributorless Ignition System (DIS) or the Computer Controlled Coil Ignition

Fig. 64 Special tool J-33075 for timing on diesel engines

(C³I) system, timing advance and retard are accomplished through the ICM with the Electronic Spark Timing (EST) and Electronic Spark Control (ESC) circuitry. No ignition timing adjustment is required or possible.

HEI SYSTEM

Because your car has electronic ignition, you should use a timing light which has an inductive pick-up. This type of pick-up merely clamps around the No. 1 spark plug wire, eliminating any kind of adapter. Other types of timing lights may cause false timing readings when used with ignition systems.

❋❋CAUTION

NEVER use a timing light which requires piercing of the spark plug wire.

Fig. 63 The crankshaft sensor has no timing adjustment if you have no distributor

1. Refer to the instructions listed on the emission control label inside the engine compartment. Follow all instructions on the label.

2. Locate the timing marks on the front of the engine and on the crankshaft balances.

3. Clean off the marks so that they are readable. Chalk or white paint on the balancer mark (line) and at the correct point on the timing scale will make the marks much easier to accurately align.

4. If specified on the emissions label, attach a tachometer to the engine according to the tachometer manufacturer's instructions.

➡**On 4-cylinder engines, the TACH terminal is at the brown wire connection at the ignition coil; on V6's, it is next to the BAT connector on the distributor cap.**

5. Attach a timing light according to the timing light manufacturer's instructions. Remember that the inductive pick-up is clamped around the No. 1 spark plug wire.

6. Check that all wiring is clear of the fan, then start the engine. Allow the engine to reach normal operating temperature.

7. Aim the timing light at the timing marks. The line on the crankshaft balancer should align the correct timing mark. If the line is within 1° of where it should be, no adjustment is necessary.

8. If adjustment is necessary, loosen the distributor hold-down bolt slightly. Slowly rotate the distributor until the proper setting is attained.

9. Tighten the hold-down bolt, recheck the timing and readjust if required.

10. Turn the engine off and disconnect the timing light (and tachometer, if in use).

➡**Disregard the short tube which may be integral with the timing scale on some engines. This tube is used to connect magnetic timing equipment which is marketed to professional shops.**

DIESEL

1. Shut the engine **OFF**.

2. Note the relative position of the marks on the pump flange and either the pump intermediate adapter.

3. Loosen the nuts or bolts holding the pump to a point where the pump can just be rotated. You may need a wrench with a slight offset to clear the fuel return line.

4. Rotate the pump to the left to advance the timing and to the right to retard the timing. The width of the mark on the intermediate adaptor is about $2/3°$. Move the pump the amount that is needed and tighten the pump retaining nuts to 35 ft. lbs. (47 Nm).

5. Start the engine and recheck the timing as described earlier. Reset the timing if necessary.

6. Reset the fast and curb idle speeds.

➡**Wild needle fluctuations on the timing meter indicate a cylinder not firing properly. Correction of this condition must be made prior to adjusting the timing.**

7. If after resetting the timing, the timing marks are far apart and the engine still runs poorly, the dynamic timing could still be off. It is possible that a malfunctioning cylinder will cause incorrect timing. If this occurs, it is essential that timing be checked in cylinder 1 or 4. If different timing exists between cylinders, try both positions to determine which timing works best.

VALVE LASH

Adjustment

All models utilize an hydraulic valve lifter system to obtain zero lash. No adjustment is necessary. An initial adjustment is required anytime that the lifters are removed or the valve train is disturbed, this procedure is covered in Section 3.

IDLE SPEED AND MIXTURE ADJUSTMENTS

Gasoline Engines

IDLE SPEED

Carbureted Models

On non-A/C models not equipped with Idle Speed Control (ISC), the idle speed is adjusted at the idle speed screw on the carburetor. Before adjusting, check the underhood sticker for any preparations required. On A/C equipped models which do not have an ISC motor, an idle speed solenoid is used. This solenoid is adjusted at the solenoid screw. Consult the underhood specifications sticker for special instructions. If the sticker is missing, consult your dealer for specifications.

1. All idle settings are made with the engine operating in the closed loop. The air cleaner must be removed, along with the A/C and cooling fan **OFF**.

2. Apply the parking brake and block the drive wheels.

3. Disconnect and plug the vacuum hoses at the EGR valve and purge hose at the canister.

4. For the fast idle speed adjustment:

a. With the automatic in PARK, manual in NEUTRAL, place the adjusting screw on the highest step of the fast idle cam.

b. Adjust if needed, to recommended rpm in PARK or NEUTRAL.

5. For the curb idle speed adjustment:

a. Adjust the curb idle speed screw to recommended rpm in DRIVE (AT) or NEUTRAL (MT).

6. For the idle speed actuator plunger adjustment:

a. Disconnect and plug the vacuum hose at the actuator.

b. Connect a vacuum source (a hand vacuum pump) and apply, 6 in. Hg. vacuum minimum to the actuator. The actuator plunger must be fully extended.

c. Adjust if needed, recommended rpm in DRIVE (AT) or NEUTRAL (MT).

7. Unplug and reconnect the all the vacuum hoses: EGR valve, canister purge, and the idle speed actuator.

Fuel Injected Models

THROTTLE BODY

No idle speed or mixture adjustments are possible on fuel injected engines unless the following: This procedure should be performed only when the throttle body parts have been replaced. Newer models may not provide for this adjustment as the computer is responsible for idle control.

➡**The following procedure requires the use of a special tool.**

1. Remove the air cleaner and gasket.

2. Plug the vacuum port on the TBI marked THERMAC.

3. If the car is equipped with a tamper resistant plug cover the throttle stop screw, the TBI unit must be removed as instructed above, to remove the plug.

4. Remove the throttle valve cable from the throttle control bracket to allow access to the throttle stop screw.

5. Connect a tachometer to the engine.

6. Start the engine and run it to normal operating temperature.

7. Install tool J-33047 into the idle air passage of the throttle body. Be sure that the tool is fully seated and that no air leaks exist.

8. Using a #20 Torx bit (0.16 in.-4mm), turn the minimum air screw until the engine rpm is 675-725 with automatic in PARK, and 725-825 with manual in NEUTRAL.

9. Stop the engine and remove the special tool.

10. Install the cable on the throttle body.

11. Use RTV sealant to cover the throttle stop screw.

MULTI-PORT/SEQUENTIAL INJECTION

The engine should be at normal operating temperature before making this adjustment. Newer engines do not provide for this adjustment as the idle is completely computer controlled. If the computer cannot control the idle, the most likely cause a defective idle air control valve. Test the IAC valve, check the engine for mechanical problems (for basic tune-up, vacuum leaks, proper compression) and check the rest of the fuel control system. The least likely cause is the computer itself, unless someone has recently worked on the computer or the electrical system. For models that are adjustable following the following procedures:

1. Using an awl, pierce the idle stop screw plug (located on the side of the throttle body) and remove it by prying it from the housing.

2. Using a jumper wire, ground the diagnostic lead of the IAC motor.

3. Turn on the ignition, DO NOT start the engine and wait for 30 seconds, then disconnect the IAC electrical connector. Remove the diagnostic lead ground lead and start the engine. Allow the system to go to closed loop.

4. Adjust the idle set screw to 550 rpm for the automatic transaxle in Drive, and 650 rpm for the manual transaxle in Neutral.

5. Turn the ignition **OFF** and reconnect the IAC motor lead.

6. Using a voltmeter, adjust the TPS to 0.45-0.65 volt and secure the TPS.

7. Recheck the setting, then start the engine and check for proper idle operation.

8. Seal the idle stop screw with silicone sealer.

MIXTURE ADJUSTMENT

Carbureted Models

▶ **See Figure 65**

Mixture adjustments are a function of the Computer Command Control (CCC) system. The idle speed on models equipped with an Idle Speed Control (ISC) motor is also automatically adjusted by the Computer Command Control System, making manual adjustment unnecessary. The underhood specifications sticker will indicate ISC motor use. We strongly recommend that mixture adjustments be referred to a qualified, professional technician.

The idle mixture screws are concealed under hardened plugs and mixture adjustments are not normally required. Since carburetor removal is necessary in order to gain access to the screws, the plug removal and adjustment procedures are covered in Section 5.

1. Preform the carburetor pre-set procedure. See Section 5.

2. Run the engine on high step of the fast idle cam. until the engine cooling fan starts to cycle.

3. Run the engine at 3000 rpm and adjust the lean mixture screw slowly in small increments allowing time for dwell to stabilize after turning the screw to obtain an average dwell of 35°. If the dwell is too low, back the screw out, if too high, turn it in. If you are unable to adjust it to specifications, inspect the main metering circuit for leaks or restrictions.

4. Return to idle.

5. Adjust the mixture screw to obtain the average dwell of 25° with the cooling fan in the off cycle. If the reading is too low, back the screw out. If the reading is too high, turn it in. Allow time for reading to stabilize after each adjustment. Adjustment is very sensitive. Make a final check with the adjusting tool removed.

6. If you are unable to adjust to specifications, inspect the idle system for leaks, or restrictions.

7. Disconnect the mixture control solenoid when the cooling fan is in the off cycle, then check for an rpm change of at least 50 rpm. If the rpm does not change enough, inspect the idle air bleed circuit for restrictions or leaks.

8. Run the engine at 3000 rpm for a few moments, then note the dwell reading. Dwell should be varying with the average reading of 35°.

9. If the 35° is not the average dwell, reset the lean mixture screw pre step 3. Then reset the idle mixture screw to obtain a 25° dwell per steps 5 and 6.

Fig. 65 Common label for a carbureted engine

10. If you have an average dwell, reconnect the systems disconnected (purge and vent hoses, EGR valve etc..), then reinstall the vent screen and set the idle speed.

Fuel Injected Models

▶ See Figure 66

No mixture adjustments are possible on fuel injected engines.

Diesel Engines

IDLE ADJUSTMENT

▶ See Figures 67 and 68

Adjustments to diesel fuel injection units are to be performed only in the case of parts replacement on the injection unit.

➡The following procedure requires the use of a special tool.

1. Apply the parking brake, place the transmission selector lever in Park and block the drive wheels.

2. Start engine and allow it to run until warm, usually 10-15 minutes.

➡Failure to have the engine fully warmed up will result in sooting of the probe which will cause an incorrect reading and adjustment for the timing.

3. Shut off the engine, and remove the air cleaner assembly. Install the cover tool J-26996-1. Make sure the EGR hose is disconnected.

4. Clean the front cover RPM counter (probe holder) and the crankshaft balancer rim.

5. Clean the both ends of the glow plug probe and the lens to the photo-electric pick-up. Scrape the carbon from the combustion chamber side of the glow plug probe. Look thorough the probe to make sure it is clean. Retarded readings will be obtained if the probe is not clean.

6. Install the magnetic pick-up probe of tool J-26925 fully into the rpm counter. Connect the battery leads; red to positive (+) and black to negative (-).

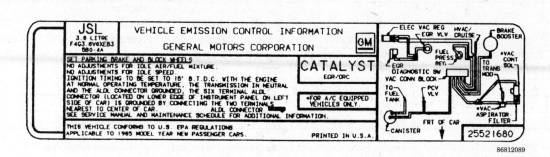

Fig. 66 Common label for a fuel injected engine

7. Disconnect the two-lead connector at the generator.

8. Turn off all electrical accessories.

9. Allow no one to touch either the steering wheel or service brake pedal.

10. Start the engine and place the transmission selector lever in **D** (Drive).

11. Check the slow idle speed reading against the one given on the underhood emission control sticker. Reset if required.

12. Unplug the connector from the fast idle cold advance (engine temp.) switch and install a jumper between the connector terminals. Do not allow the jumper to touch ground.

Fig. 67 Cover — Tool # J-26996-1

Fig. 68 Tachometer tool # J-26925 for a diesel engine

13. Check the fast idle solenoid speed against the one given on the underhood sticker and reset if required.

14. Remove the jumper and reconnect the connector to the temperature switch.

15. Recheck and reset the slow idle speed if necessary.

16. Shut off the engine.

17. Reconnect the lead at the generator.

18. Disconnect and remove the tachometer.

19. If equipped with cruise control, adjust the servo throttle cable to minimum slack then install the clip on the servo stud.

DIESEL ENGINE TUNE-UP SPECIFICATIONS

Year	Engine ID/VIN	Engine Displacement cu. in. (cc)	Valve Clearance Intake (in.)	Valve Clearance Exhaust (in.)	Intake Valve Opens (deg.)	Injection Pump Setting (deg.)	Injection Nozzle Pressure (psi) New	Injection Nozzle Pressure (psi) Used	Idle Speed (rpm)	Cranking Compression Pressure (psi)
1983	T	262 (4293)	HYD	HYD	16B	[1]	1000	850	650	300
1984	T	262 (4293)	HYD	HYD	16B	[1]	1000	850	650	300
1985	T	262 (4293)	HYD	HYD	16B	[1]	1000	850	650	300

NOTE: The Vehicle Emission Control Information label often reflects specification changes made during production. The label figures must be used if they differ from those in this chart

B - Before top dead center

HYD - Hydraulic

1 Refer to underhood sticker

86812102

GASOLINE ENGINE TUNE-UP SPECIFICATIONS

Year	Engine ID/VIN	Engine Displacement Liters (cc)	Spark Plugs Gap (in.)	Ignition Timing (deg.) MT	AT	Fuel Pump (psi)	Idle Speed (rpm) MT	AT	Valve Clearance In.	Ex.
1982	R	2.5 (2474)	0.060	8B	8B	6-8	950	750	HYD	HYD
	X	2.8 (2835)	0.045	10B	10B	6-7.5	800	600	HYD	HYD
	Z [7]	2.8 (2835)	0.045	6B	10B	6-7.5	850 [7]	750	HYD	HYD
	E	3.0 (2999)	0.080	-	15B	6-8	-	-	HYD	HYD
1983	R	2.5 (2474)	0.060	8B	8B	6-8	950	750	HYD	HYD
	X	2.8 (2835)	0.045	10B	10B	6-7.5	800	600	HYD	HYD
	Z [7]	2.8 (2835)	0.045	6B	10B	6-7.5	850 [7]	750	HYD	HYD
	E	3.0 (2999)	0.080	-	15B	6-8	-	-	HYD	HYD
1984	R	2.5 (2474)	0.060	8B	8B	6-8	950	750	HYD	HYD
	X	2.8 (2835)	0.045	10B	10B	6-7.5	800	600	HYD	HYD
	Z [7]	2.8 (2835)	0.045	6B	10B	6-7.5	850 [7]	750	HYD	HYD
	E	3.0 (2999)	0.080	-	15B	6-8	-	-	HYD	HYD
1985	R	2.5 (2474)	0.060	8B	8B	9-13	900-1000	675-775	HYD	HYD
	X	2.8 (2835)	0.045	10B	10B	6-7	800	600D	HYD	HYD
	W	2.8 (2835)	0.045	10B	10B	30-37	600-700	500-600D	HYD	HYD
	E	3.0 (2999)	0.060	15B	15B	4-6.5	-	- [2]	HYD	HYD
	3	3.8 (3785)	0.080	-	15B	34-40	-	- [2]	HYD	HYD
1986	R	2.5 (2474)	0.060	8B	8B	9-13	850-950	750-850D	HYD	HYD
	X	2.8 (2835)	0.045	10B	10B	5.5-6.5	775	600D	HYD	HYD
	W	2.8 (2835)	0.045	10B	10B	30-37	600-700	500-600D	HYD	HYD
	B	3.8 (3735)	0.045	-	[1]	34-40	-	[2]	HYD	HYD
	3	3.8 (3735)	0.080	-	[1]	34-40	-	[2]	HYD	HYD
1987	R	2.5 (2474)	0.060	[1]	[1]	9-13	600 [3]	600 [3]	HYD	HYD
	W	2.8 (2835)	0.045	[1]	[1]	40-46	-	550D [3]	HYD	HYD
	3	3.8 (3785)	0.045	[1]	[1]	34-44	-	500D [3]	HYD	HYD
1988	R	2.5 (2474)	0.060	[1]	[1]	9-13	550-650 [3]	550-650 [3]	HYD	HYD
	W	2.8 (2835)	0.045	[1]	[1]	40-46	550-650 [3]	500-600D [3]	HYD	HYD
	3	3.8 (3785)	0.045	[1]	[1]	34-40	-	500D [3]	HYD	HYD
1989	R	2.5 (2474)	0.060	[1]	[1]	9-13	550-650 [3]	550-650 [3]	HYD	HYD
	W	2.8 (2835)	0.045	[1]	[1]	41-47	600-700 [3]	500-600D [3]	HYD	HYD
	T	3.1 (3146)	0.045	[1]	[1]	41-47	[4]	[4]	HYD	HYD
	N	3.3 (3342)	0.045	[1]	[1]	41-47	[4]	[4]	HYD	HYD
1990	R	2.5 (2474)	0.060	[1]	[1]	9-13	550-650 [3]	550-650 [3]	HYD	HYD
	T	3.1 (3146)	0.045	[1]	[1]	41-47	[4]	[4]	HYD	HYD
	N	3.3 (3342)	0.060	[1]	[1]	41-47	[4]	[4]	HYD	HYD
1991	R	2.5 (2474)	0.060	[1]	[1]	9-13	550-650 [6]	550-650 [6]	HYD	HYD

86812100

GASOLINE ENGINE TUNE-UP SPECIFICATIONS

Year	Engine ID/VIN	Engine Displacement Liters (cc)	Spark Plugs Gap (in.)	Ignition Timing (deg.) MT	AT	Fuel Pump (psi)	Idle Speed (rpm) MT	AT	Valve Clearance In.	Ex.
1991	T	3.1 (3146)	0.045	1	1	41-47	9	9	HYD	HYD
	N	3.3 (3342)	0.060	1	1	41-47	5	5	HYD	HYD
1992	4	2.2 (2195)	0.045	1	1	41-47	5	5	HYD	HYD
	R	2.5 (2474)	0.060	1	1	9-13	550-650 4	550-650 4	HYD	HYD
	N	3.3 (3342)	0.060	1	1	41-47	5	5	HYD	HYD
1993	4	2.2 (2195)	0.045	1	1	41-47	5	5	HYD	HYD
	N	3.3 (3342)	0.060	1	1	41-47	4	4	HYD	HYD
	M	3.1 (3130)	0.060	1	1	41-47	4	4	HYD	HYD
1994	4	2.2 (2195)	0.060	1	1	41-47	5	5	HYD	HYD
	M	3.1 (3130)	0.060	1	1	41-47	5	5	HYD	HYD
1995	4	2.2 (2195)	0.060	1	1	41-47	5	5	HYD	HYD
	M	3.1 (3130)	0.060	1	1	41-47	5	5	HYD	HYD

NOTE: The Vehicle Emission Control Information label often reflects specification changes made during production. The label figures must be used if they differ from those in this chart.

B - Before top dead center

D - Drive

HYD - Hydraulic

1   Direct ignition system timing is not adjustable

2   Minimum idle speed: 450-550 in drive; Refer to manual for adjustment procedure

3   Minimum idle speed setting; Refer to manual for procedure

4   Idle speed is controlled by ECM; Minimum air rate is adjusted by IAC centering; Refer to manual for procedure

5   Idle speed is maintained by the ECM. There is no recommended adjustment procedure

6   Idle specification is minimum air rate: Refer to manual for procedure

7   High output

8   California: 750

9   Refer to emmisions label

86812101

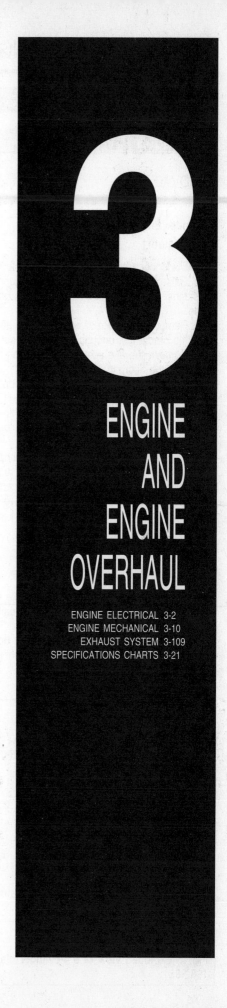

3

ENGINE
AND
ENGINE
OVERHAUL

ENGINE ELECTRICAL

Distributor

REMOVAL

4-Cylinder Engines

▶ **See Figure 1**

1. Disconnect the negative battery cable.
2. Raise the front of the vehicle and support is safely with jackstands. DO NOT place the jackstands under the engine cradle.
3. Remove the two rear engine cradle attaching bolts and lower the cradle just enough to gain access to the distributor.
4. Remove the five screws which attach the brake line support to the floorpan.
5. Remove the coil wire from the distributor.
6. Remove the distributor cap.
7. Mark the position of the rotor firing tip on the distributor body, then mark the relationship between the distributor body and the engine.
8. Loosen the distributor hold-down clamp bolt and slide the hold-down clamp aside to clear the distributor body.
9. Lift the distributor out of the engine and mark the point at which the rotor stops turning while you're pulling upward. The rotor will have to be positioned at this same spot in order to install the distributor correctly.

V6 Engines

▶ **See Figure 2**

1. Disconnect the negative battery cable at the battery.
2. Release the distributor and ignition coil electrical connections at the distributor cap.
3. Remove the distributor clamp screw and hold-down clamp. Note position of the rotor. Pull distributor up until the

1 Distributor cap		10 Screw	
2 Screw		11 Pickup coil	
3 Rotor		12 Pickup coil shield	
4 Main shaft		13 Pole piece	
5 Retainer		14 Pin	
6 O-ring		15 Distributor gear	
7 Distributor housing		16 Under gear washer	
8 Pin		17 Tang under gear washer	
9 Module			

86813021

Fig. 2 Distributor assembly used on 1985-86 2.8L (VIN W) engines

rotor just stops turning clockwise. Note the position of rotor again.

➡ **The rotor will have to be positioned at this same spot in order to install the distributor correctly.**

INSTALLATION

Engine Disturbed

1. Remove the spark plug from the No. 1 cylinder.
2. Place your thumb over the spark plug hole and turn the crankshaft by hand with a wrench until pressure is felt at the plug hole.
3. Look at the timing marks on the front of the engine and check to see if the balancer slash is aligned with the **0** on the timing scale. If necessary, turn the crankshaft until it does align.

1 Distributor cap	9 Pole piece and plate assy. (pick-up coil)
2 Screw	10 Seal
3 Rotor	11 Module
4 Bushing	12 Housing assembly
5 Distributor shaft	13 O-ring
6 Retainer	14 Washer
7 Distributor shaft	15 Distributor gear
8 Wiring harness	16 Pin

86813020

Fig. 1 Exploded view of a 4-cylinder distributor — 1982-86

4. Position the firing tip of the rotor between the No.1 and 6 towers of the cap on 6-cylinder engines or the No. 1 tower, on 4-cylinder engine.

5. Install the distributor into the engine.

6. Reposition the hold-down clamp on the distributor body and tighten the bolt until the distributor is snug, but can be moved with a little effort.

7. On 4-cylinder models, jack the engine cradle back into place. Install the engine cradle bolts and the brake line support bolts.

8. Connect all wiring to the distributor.

9. Connect the battery cable, tighten the cable bolt to 11 ft. lbs. (15 Nm).

10. Adjust the ignition timing.

Engine Not Disturbed

1. Align the ignition rotor with the mark made during the removal procedure.

2. Install the distributor into the engine, noting that the marks made previously must align. If they don't line up the first time, remove the distributor and try again.

3. Reposition the hold-down clamp on the distributor body and tighten the bolt until the distributor is snug, but can be moved with a little effort.

4. On 4-cylinder models, jack the engine cradle back into place. Install the engine cradle bolts and the brake line support bolts.

5. Connect all wiring to the distributor.

6. Connect the battery cable, tighten the cable bolt to 11 ft. lbs. (15 Nm).

7. Adjust the ignition timing.

The Charging System

The automobile charging system provides electrical power for operation of the vehicle's ignition and starting systems and all the electrical accessories. The battery serves as an electrical surge or storage tank, storing (in chemical form) the energy originally produced by the engine driven A.C. (alternator). The system also provides a means of regulating alternator output to protect the battery from being overcharged and to avoid excessive voltage to the accessories.

The storage battery is a chemical device incorporating parallel lead plates in a tank containing a sulfuric acid/water solution. Adjacent plates are slightly dissimilar, and the chemical reaction of the two dissimilar plates produces electrical energy when the battery is connected to a load such as the starter motor. The chemical reaction is reversible, so that when the alternator is producing a voltage (electrical pressure) greater than that produced by the battery, electricity is forced into the battery, and the battery is returned to its fully charged state.

The vehicle's alternator is driven mechanically, through belts, by the engine crankshaft. It consists of two coils of fine wire, stationary (the stator), and one movable (the rotor). The rotor may also be known as the armature, and consists of fine wire wrapped around an iron core which is mounted on a shaft. In an alternator, the field rotates while all the current produced passes only through the stator windings. The brushes bear against continuous slip rings. This causes the current produced to periodically reverse the direction of its flow. Diodes (electrical one-way switches) block the flow of current from traveling in the wrong direction. A series of diodes is wired together to permit the alternating flow of the stator to be converted to a pulsating, but unidirectional flow at the alternator output. The alternator's field is wired in series with the voltage regulator. Alternators are self-limiting as far as maximum current is concerned.

SYSTEM PRECAUTIONS

Observing these precautions will ensure safe handling of the electrical system components, and will avoid damage to the vehicle's electrical system:

1. Be absolutely sure of the polarity of a battery before making connections. Connect the cables positive to positive, and negative to negative. Connect positive cables first and disconnect negative cables first.

2. Disconnect both vehicle battery cables before attempting to charge a battery.

3. Never ground the alternator output or battery terminal. Be cautious when using metal tools around a battery to avoid creating a short circuit between the terminals.

4. Never run an alternator without load unless the field circuit is disconnected.

5. Never attempt to polarize an alternator.

Alternator

PRECAUTIONS

1. When installing a battery, make sure that the positive and negative cables are not reversed.

2. When jump-starting the car, be sure that like terminals are connected. This also applies to using a battery charger. Reverse polarity will burn out the alternator and regulator in a matter of seconds.

3. Never operate the alternator with the battery disconnected or on an otherwise uncontrolled open circuit.

4. Do not short across or ground any alternator or regulator terminals.

5. Do not try to polarize the alternator.

6. Do not apply full battery voltage to the field (brown) connector.

7. Always disconnect the battery ground cable before disconnecting the alternator lead.

8. Always disconnect the battery (negative cable first) when charging it.

9. Never subject the alternator to excessive heat or dampness. If you are steam cleaning the engine, cover the alternator.

10. Never use arc-welding equipment on the car with the alternator connected.

REMOVAL & INSTALLATION

▶ See Figures 3, 4, 5 and 6

SI Series

4-CYLINDER ENGINES

1. Disconnect the negative battery cable.
2. Remove the two-terminal plug and the battery leads from the rear of the alternator.
3. Remove the adjusting bolt from the alternator.
4. Remove the drive belt.
5. Remove the upper alternator bracket.
6. Loosen and remove the alternator pivot bolt, remove the alternator.

To install:

7. Position the alternator and install the pivot bolt.
8. Install upper mounting bracket, insert the adjusting bolt.
9. Place belt into position.
10. Be sure to adjust the tension of the drive belt properly, then tighten the adjusting bolt(s).
11. Install alternator terminal plug and battery leads to the alternator.
12. Connect the negative battery cable, tighten the cable bolt to 11 ft. lbs. (15 Nm).

6-CYLINDER GASOLINE ENGINES

1. Disconnect the negative battery cable.
2. Remove the two-terminal plug and the battery leads from the rear of the alternator.
3. Remove the adjusting bolt from the alternator.
4. Move the alternator to loosen the drive belt, then remove the belt.
5. On some modes you may need to remove the upper alternator bracket.
6. Remove the alternator pivot bolt and remove the alternator.

To install:

7. Position the alternator and install the pivot bolt.
8. Insert upper mounting bracket with the adjusting bolt.
9. Place the belt into position.
10. Be sure to adjust the tension of the drive belt properly, then tighten the adjusting bolt.
11. Install the terminal plug and battery leads to the alternator.
12. Connect the negative battery cable, tighten the cable bolt to 11 ft. lbs. (15 Nm).

DIESEL ENGINES

1. Disconnect the negative battery cable.
2. Remove the two-terminal plug and the battery leads from the rear of the alternator.
3. Fit the end of a ratchet extension into the square hole of the belt tensioner bracket. Attach a ratchet to the extension. Lever the tensioner towards the firewall side of the engine compartment and remove the serpentine drive belt from the alternator.
4. Remove the alternator brace bolt from the rear of the alternator.
5. Remove both alternator attaching bolts and remove the alternator.

Fig. 3 Unplug the field terminal connector from the alternator

Fig. 4 Loosen the nut to disconnect the "BAT" lead

Fig. 5 Remove the adjusting bolt to release the belt

Fig. 6 After disconnecting all terminals and removing the mounting bolts, pull the alternator from its bracket

To install:

6. Install the alternator with both attaching bolts.

7. Install the brace and insert bolt from the rear of alternator.

8. Install belt.

9. Tighten the adjusting bolt(s).

10. Install the terminal plug and battery leads to the alternator.

11. Connect the negative battery cable, tighten the cable bolt to 11 ft. lbs. (15 Nm).

CS Series

> ✳✳**CAUTION**

Failure to disconnect the negative battery cable when working on the CS alternator can result in personal injury. If a tool is shorted at the alternator output or battery terminal, the tool will heat up enough to cause skin damage.

2.2L ENGINE

▶ See Figure 7

1. Disconnect the negative battery cable.

2. Disconnect the electrical connector at the alternator.

3. Lift or rotate the tensioner using a 15mm socket to remove the belt.

4. Loosen and remove all the bolts to alternator.

5. Remove bolts from brace(s) to alternator.

6. Remove the nut from alternator battery terminal BAT.

7. Remove the alternator.

To install:

8. Install the alternator with mounting bolts. Tighten the front bolts to, 37 ft. lbs. (50 Nm) and rear bolts 18 ft. lbs. (25 Nm).

9. Connect battery positive lead and nut to alternator output BAT terminal. Tighten nut 71 inch lbs. (8 Nm).

10. Insert electrical connector to alternator.

11. Install drive belt by lifting or rotating tensioner using a 15mm socket.

12. Connect the negative battery cable, tighten the cable bolt to 11 ft. lbs. (15 Nm).

1 Drive belt tensioner bracket
2 Generator bolt/screw
3 Generator rear bracket bolt/screw
4 Generator rear bracket
5 Generator assembly
6 Generator bolt/screw
7 Generator bolt/screw

Fig. 7 Alternator mounting on the 2.2L engine

2.5L ENGINE

▶ See Figure 8

1. Disconnect the negative battery cable.

2. Remove the belt by lifting or rotating the tensioner using a 15mm socket.

3. Disconnect the electrical connector at the alternator.

4. Remove the nut from alternator battery terminal BAT.

5. Remove the rear attaching bolt, front attaching bolt and rear brace.

6. Remove the alternator.

To install:

7. Install the alternator with mounting bolts but do not tighten.

8. Install the rear brace and attaching bolt.

9. Tighten the long bolts 37 ft. lbs. (50 Nm), short bolts 18 ft. lbs. (25 Nm), rear bolts 18 ft. lbs. (25 Nm).

10. Connect battery positive lead and nut to alternator output BAT terminal. Tighten nut 71 inch lbs. (8 Nm).

11. Insert electrical connector to alternator.

1 Generator
2 Bolt 25 Nm (18 lbs.ft.)
3 Bolt 50 Nm (37 lbs.ft.)
4 Brace

Fig. 8 Alternator mounting on the 2.5L engine

12. Install drive belt by lifting or rotating tensioner using a 15mm socket.

13. Connect the negative battery cable, tighten the cable bolt to 11 ft. lbs. (15 Nm).

3.1L ENGINE

▶ See Figure 9

1. Disconnect the negative battery cable.
2. Detach the electrical connector at the alternator.
3. Disconnect the belt shield bolt, remove shield (if equipped).
4. Lift or rotate tensioner using a breaker bar.
5. Untighten and remove the nuts, bolt along with the stud for alternator braces.
6. The alternator bolts may be removed now.
7. Remove the nut from alternator battery terminal BAT.
8. Remove the alternator, bracket bolts and the bracket.

To install:

9. Install bracket to alternator, tighten to 37 ft. lbs. (50 Nm).
10. Position the alternator. Install the BAT lead and nut on alternator. Tighten to 71 inch lbs. (8 Nm).

1 Generator assembly
2 Generator bolt/screw
3 Generator bracket
4 Generator (pivot) bolt/screw
5 Generator rear brace stud
6 Generator rear brace nut
7 Generator rear brace
8 Generator front brace
9 Engine wiring harness

86813032

Fig. 9 Alternator mounting used on the 3.1L engine

11. Install the alternator bolt, do not tighten.
12. Install the brace stud, nuts and bolts to alternator.

➡**Make sure when tightening the brace stud, it does not bind the alternator.**

13. Tighten the alternator pivot to 37 ft. lbs. (50 Nm), the other bolts to 18 ft. lbs. (25 Nm), Install brace nuts and studs to 18 ft. lbs. (25 Nm).
14. Lift or rotate tensioner with breaker bar and install the belt. Install the bolt shield, tighten to 89 inch lbs. (10 Nm).
15. Connect the electrical connector at alternator.
16. Connect the negative battery cable, tighten the cable bolt to 11 ft. lbs. (15 Nm).

3.3L ENGINE

1. Disconnect the negative battery cable.
2. Disconnect the electrical connector at the alternator.
3. Lift or rotate the tensioner to remove the belt.
4. Loosen and remove all the bolts to alternator.
5. Next remove bolts from brace(s) to alternator.
6. Remove the nut from alternator battery terminal BAT, remove alternator.

To install:

7. Connect battery positive lead and nut to alternator output BAT terminal. Tighten nut to 71 inch lbs. (8 Nm).
8. Install the alternator with mounting bolts but do not tighten.
9. After inserting all bolts, tighten the long bolts to 37 ft. lbs. (50 Nm), short bolts to 18 ft. lbs. (25 Nm), and the brace bolt to 37 ft. lbs. (50 Nm). Make sure when tightening brace bolt, it does not bind the alternator.
10. Install drive belt by lifting or rotating tensioner using a 15mm socket.
11. Insert electrical connector to alternator.
12. Connect the negative battery cable, tighten the cable bolt to 11 ft. lbs. (15 Nm).

Regulator

A solid-state regulator is mounted within the alternator. It is non-adjustable.

REMOVAL & INSTALLATION

1982-1987 SI Series

1. Remove the alternator from the vehicle. Position the assembly in a suitable holding fixture.
2. Make scribe marks on the case end frames to aid in reassembly.
3. Remove the through bolts. Separate the drive end frame assembly from the rectifier end frame assembly.
4. Remove the rectifier attaching nuts and the regulator attaching screws from the end frame assembly. Note the position of the screws with the insulated washers for reassembly.
5. Remove the voltage regulator from the end frame assembly.

To install:

6. Position the brushes in the brush holder and retain them in place using a brush retainer wire or equivalent.

7. Assemble the brush holder, regulator, resistor, diode trio and rectifier bridge to the end frame. Be sure to assemble the screws with the insulated washers in the correct locations.

8. Assemble the end frames together with the through bolts. Remove the brush retainer wire.

1988-1995 CS Series

TYPE 130

1. Remove the alternator from the vehicle. Scribe marks on the end frames to facilitate assembly. Remove the through bolts and separate the end frames.

2. Remove the cover rivets or pins and remove the cover.

3. Unsolder the stator leads at the three terminals on the rectifier bridge. Avoid excessive heat, as damage to the assembly will occur. Remove the stator.

4. Remove the brush holder screw. Disconnect the terminal and remove the brush holder assembly.

5. Unsolder and pry open the terminal between the regulator and the rectifier bridge. Remove the terminal and the retaining screws. Remove the regulator and the rectifier bridge from the end frame.

To install:

6. Position the brushes in the brush holder and retain them in place using a brush retainer wire or equivalent.

7. Assembly is the reverse of disassembly. Be sure to remove the brush retainer wire when the alternator has been reassembled.

TYPE 144

1. Remove the alternator from the vehicle. Scribe marks on the end frames to facilitate assembly. Remove the through bolts and separate the end frames.

2. Remove the stator attaching nuts and the stator from the end frame.

3. Unsolder the connections, remove the retaining screws and connector from the end frame. Separate the regulator and brush holder from the end frame.

To install:

4. Position the brushes in the brush holder and retain them in place using a brush retainer wire or equivalent.

5. Assembly is the reverse of disassembly. Be sure to remove the brush retainer wire when the alternator has been reassembled.

Battery

REMOVAL & INSTALLATION

1. Raise the hood and remove the front end diagonal brace(s) from above the battery(ies).

2. On some vehicles, it will be necessary to remove the air cleaner and duct assembly.

3. Disconnect the battery cables from the battery(ies). Use a small box end wrench or a 1/4 in. (6mm) drive ratchet. Avoid using an open-end wrench for the cable bolts.

4. Loosen and remove the battery hold-down bolt and block. The use of a long extension which places the ratchet above the battery makes it easier to reach to the hold-down bolt.

5. Carefully lift the battery from the engine compartment.

To install:

6. Install the new battery in the vehicle. Attach the retainer and hold-down bolt. Tighten to 13 ft. lbs. (17 Nm).

7. Connect the positive battery cable, tighten to 11 ft. lbs. (15 Nm).

8. Connect the negative battery cable, tighten to 11 ft. lbs. (15 Nm).

9. Attach the air cleaner and duct assembly if removed.

10. Install the cross brace and bolts, then tighten to 52 ft. lbs. (70 Nm).

11. Reset the radio, clock and any other components in need.

Starter

REMOVAL & INSTALLATION

Diesel Engines

1982 MODELS

1. Disconnect the negative battery cable(s).

2. Raise the front of the vehicle and support it safely with jackstands.

3. Remove the lower starter shield nut and flex the starter shield for access during removal.

4. Tag, then disconnect the wires from the starter.

5. Remove the front starter attaching bolt.

6. Loosen the rear starter attaching bolt and remove the starter assembly, leaving the rear bolt in the starter housing.

To install:

7. Position and install then new starter assembly into the vehicle.

8. Insert the starter bolts, tighten to specification.

9. Attach the starter wires in the proper locations.

10. Reinstall the lower starter shield, tighten the nut.

11. Lower the vehicle, connect the negative battery cable, then reset the radio and clock.

1983-85 MODELS

1. Disconnect the negative battery cable(s) from the battery(s).

2. Install tool J-28467 to the engine, then raise the vehicle on a hoist.

3. Remove the left and the center engine mounting stud nuts.

4. Move the intermediate shaft seal upwards, then remove the intermediate shaft-to-stud shaft pinch bolt and disconnect the shaft from the gear.

✳✳CAUTION

It is necessary to disconnect the intermediate shaft from the rack and pinion stud shaft; otherwise, damage to the steering gear and/or the intermediate shaft can occur, which may result in the loss of steering control.

5. Remove the 2 front cradle mounting bolts, then lower the cradle at the front to gain access to the flywheel cover bolts.

6. Remove the flywheel cover bolts and the cover.

7. Remove the starter shield nut from the starter and the flex shield.

8. Tag and disconnect the wires from the starter. Remove the starter mounting bolts and the starter.

9. To install, reverse the removal procedures. Tighten the stub shaft pinch bolt to 45 ft. lbs. (62 Nm) and the starter-to-engine bolts to 32 ft. lbs. (43 Nm).

1982-85 Gasoline Engines

1. Disconnect the negative battery cable.

2. Raise the front of the vehicle and support it safely with jackstands.

3. From underneath the vehicle, remove the two starter motor-to-engine bolts and carefully lower the starter. Note the location of shims (if so equipped). On the four cylinder engine, remove the nut that holds the starter bracket to the rear of the starter.

4. Mark and disconnect all wiring at the starter.

To install:

5. Position and install then new starter assembly into the vehicle.

6. Insert the starter bolts, tighten to specification.

7. Attach the starter wires in the proper locations.

8. Lower the vehicle, connect the negative battery cable, then reset the radio and clock.

1986-95 Models

2.2L ENGINE

1. Disconnect the negative battery cable.

2. Remove the engine torque strut brace.

3. Raise and support the vehicle.

4. Loosen and remove the bolts for the inspection cover, then the cover itself.

5. Remove the bolt from the bracket, then the bolts from the starter motor.

6. If used remove the shims from the starter as you lower the starter from the vehicle, then disconnect the starter wiring.

7. Remove the starter bracket.

To install:

➡Before you install the starter to the vehicle, be sure the solenoid battery terminal is secure. Tighten the nut next to the cap on the solenoid battery terminal. If it is not tight in the solenoid cap, the cap may be damaged during installation of the electrical connection and cause the starter to fail later.

8. Connect the wiring and nuts to the solenoid battery terminal and the solenoid S terminal. Tighten the nuts on the solenoid battery terminal to 84 inch lbs. (10 Nm). Then tighten the nut on the S terminal to 22 inch lbs. (3 Nm).

9. Attach the bracket to the starter, tighten the nuts to 76 inch lbs. (9 Nm).

10. Install the shims (if used).

11. Position the starter on the engine, then tighten the two starter mounting bolts to 32 ft. lbs. (43 Nm).

12. Install the starter bracket to engine bolt, tighten to 26 ft. lbs. (32 Nm).

13. Install the flywheel cover and tighten the bolts to 89 inch lbs. (10 Nm).

14. Lower the vehicle, then install the engine torque strut brace.

15. Connect the negative battery cable, tighten the cable bolt to 11 ft. lbs. (15 Nm).

2.5L AND 2.8L ENGINES

▶ **See Figures 10, 11 and 12**

1. Disconnect the negative battery cable.

2. Raise and safely support the vehicle.

3. Disconnect the solenoid wires and battery cable from the starter.

4. Remove the bolt from the engine cross brace.

5. Place a prybar tool between the upper engine mount and engine to pry rearward. Support the engine.

6. Remove the 4 bolts holding the dust covers. Remove the dust covers.

7. Remove the 2 bolts attaching the starter.

8. On the 2.5L engine, remove the bolt attaching the starter bracket to the engine.

9. Remove the starter and any shims.

Fig. 10 Disconnect the wires from the solenoid. Limited access can make this difficult

Fig. 11 Remove the bolts securing the starter to the engine

86813052

Fig. 12 When removing the starter, be careful not to lose any shims which may be used

To install:

➡If replacing the starter, transfer the starter bracket to the new starter.

10. Install the starter and any applicable shims.
11. Install the 2 starter attaching bolts.
12. On the 2.5L engine, install the bolt attaching the starter bracket to the engine.
13. Install the dust cover and 4 attaching bolts.
14. Connect the battery cable and solenoid wires.
15. Lower the vehicle.
16. Roll the engine forward and install the engine brace bolts.
17. Connect the negative battery cable.

3.1L ENGINE (VIN T)

1. Disconnect the negative battery cable.
2. Raise and safely support the vehicle.
3. If equipped, remove the nut from the brace at the air conditioning compressor.
4. If equipped, remove the nuts from the starter-to-engine brace.
5. Remove the drain pan under the engine oil pan.
6. Disconnect the oil pressure sending unit electrical connector. Remove the oil pressure sending unit.
7. Remove the oil filter.
8. Remove the bolts from the flywheel inspection cover. Remove the inspection cover.
9. Remove the bolts from the starter motor.
10. Remove the starter motor and any shims.
11. Disconnect the starter motor electrical connectors.
To install:
12. Connect the starter motor electrical connectors.
13. Install the starter motor and any shims.
14. Install the starter motor attaching bolts. Tighten to 32 ft. lbs. (43 Nm).

15. Install the flywheel inspection cover and attaching bolts.
16. Install the oil filter.
17. Attach the oil pressure sending unit. Connect the electrical wire.
18. Bolt on the drain pan.
19. Install the nuts to the starter-to-engine brace.
20. Install the nut to brace at the air conditioner compressor.
21. Lower the vehicle.
22. Connect the negative battery cable.
23. Check the engine oil level, add as required.

3.1L ENGINE (VIN M)

1. Disconnect the negative battery cable.
2. Raise and safely support the vehicle.
3. Remove the starter mounting bolts and lower the starter until the solenoid wiring is accessible.
4. Disconnect the electrical leads.
5. Remove the starter.
To install:
6. Install the starter.
7. Connect the electrical leads to the starter.
8. Install the starter mounting bolts and tighten to 32 ft. lbs. (43 Nm).
9. Lower the vehicle.
10. Connect the negative battery cable.

3.3L ENGINE

1. Disconnect the negative battery cable.
2. Properly discharge the air conditioning system into a recycling recovery machine. Refer to Section 1.
3. Remove the cooling fan assembly.
4. Remove the front exhaust manifold.
5. Raise and support the vehicle safely.
6. Remove the bolts from the flywheel inspection cover and remove the cover.
7. Disconnect the air conditioner condenser hose from the compressor and position aside. Cap the opening.
8. Disconnect the starter motor electrical wiring.
9. Remove the 2 bolts attaching the starter.
10. Remove the starter and any shims.
To install:
11. Install the starter motor and any shims.
12. Install the 2 bolts attaching the starter. Tighten to 30 ft. lbs. (40 Nm).
13. Connect the starter motor electrical wiring.
14. Replace the condenser O-ring. Lubricate with refrigerant oil. Connect the air conditioner condenser hose to the compressor.
15. Install the flywheel inspection cover and attaching bolts.
16. Lower the vehicle.
17. Install the front exhaust manifold.
18. Install the cooling fan assembly.
19. Evacuate, recharge and leak test the air conditioning system.
20. Connect the negative battery cable.

ENGINE MECHANICAL

Engine Overhaul Tips

Most engine overhaul procedures are fairly standard. In addition to specific parts replacement procedures and specifications for your individual engine, this section also is a guide to acceptable rebuilding procedures. Examples of standard rebuilding practice are shown and should be used along with specific details concerning your particular engine.

Competent and accurate machine shop services will ensure maximum performance, reliability and engine life. In most instances it is more profitable for the do-it-yourself mechanic to remove, clean and inspect the component, buy the necessary parts and deliver these to a shop for actual machine work.

On the other hand, much of the rebuilding work (crankshaft, block, bearings, piston rods, and other components) is well within the scope of the do-it-yourself mechanic's tools and abilities. You will have to decide for yourself the depth of involvement you desire in an engine repair or rebuild.

TOOLS

The tools required for an engine overhaul or parts replacement will depend on the depth of your involvement. With a few exceptions, they will be the tools found in a mechanic's tool kit (see Section 1 of this manual). More in-depth work will require some or all of the following:
- a dial indicator (reading in thousandths) mounted on a universal base
- micrometers and telescope gauges
- jaw and screw-type pullers
- scraper
- valve spring compressor
- ring groove cleaner
- piston ring expander and compressor
- ridge reamer
- cylinder hone or glaze breaker
- Plastigage®
- engine stand

The use of most of these tools is illustrated in this chapter. Many can be rented for a one-time use from a local parts jobber or tool supply house specializing in automotive work.

Occasionally, the use of special tools is called for. See the information on Special Tools and the Safety Notice in the front of this book before substituting another tool.

INSPECTION TECHNIQUES

Procedures and specifications are given in this chapter for inspecting, cleaning and assessing the wear limits of most major components. Other procedures such as Magnaflux® and Zyglo® can be used to locate material flaws and stress cracks. Magnaflux® is a magnetic process applicable only to ferrous materials. The Zyglo® process coats the material with a fluorescent dye penetrant and can be used on any material. Checking for suspected surface cracks can be more readily made using spot check dye. The dye is sprayed onto the suspected area, wiped off and the area sprayed with a developer. Cracks will show up brightly.

OVERHAUL TIPS

Aluminum has become extremely popular for use in engines, due to its low weight. Observe the following precautions when handling aluminum parts:
- Never hot tank aluminum parts (the caustic hot tank solution will eat the aluminum.
- Remove all aluminum parts (identification tag, etc.) from engine parts prior to the tanking.
- Always coat threads lightly with engine oil or anti-seize compounds before installation, to prevent seizure.
- Never overtighten bolts or spark plugs especially in aluminum threads.

Stripped threads in any component can be repaired using any of several commercial repair kits (Heli-Coil®, Microdot®, Keenserts®, etc.).

When assembling the engine, any parts that will be exposed to frictional contact, the parts must be prelubed to provide lubrication at initial start-up. Any product specifically formulated for this purpose can be used, but engine oil is not recommended as a prelube in most cases.

When semi-permanent (locked, but removable) installation of bolts or nuts is desired, threads should be cleaned and coated with Loctite® or other similar, commercial non-hardening sealant.

REPAIRING DAMAGED THREADS

▶ See Figures 13, 14, 15, 16 and 17

Several methods of repairing damaged threads are available. Heli-Coil® (shown here), Keenserts® and Microdot® are among the most widely used. All involve basically the same principle — drilling out stripped threads, tapping the hole and installing a prewound insert — making welding, plugging and oversize fasteners unnecessary.

Two types of thread repair inserts are usually supplied: a standard type for most inch coarse, inch fine, metric course and metric fine thread sizes and a spark lug type to fit most spark plug port sizes. Consult the individual manufacturer's catalog to determine exact applications. Typical thread repair kits will contain a selection of prewound threaded inserts, a tap (corresponding to the outside diameter threads of the insert) and an installation tool. Spark plug inserts usually differ because they require a tap equipped with pilot threads and a combined reamer/tap section. Most manufacturers also supply blister-packed thread repair inserts separately in addition to a master kit containing a variety of taps and inserts plus installation tools.

Before attempting to repair a threaded hole, remove any snapped, broken or damaged bolts or studs. Penetrating oil can be used to free frozen threads. The offending item can be removed with locking pliers or using a screw/stud extractor. After the hole is clear, the thread can be repaired, as shown

Fig. 13 Damaged bolt hole threads can be replaced with thread repair inserts

Fig. 14 Standard thread repair insert (left), and spark plug thread insert

Fig. 15 Drill out the damaged threads with the specified drill. Be sure to drill completely through the hole or to the bottom of a blind hole

Fig. 16 Using the kit, tap the hole in order to receive the thread insert. Keep the tap well oiled and back it out frequently to avoid clogging the threads.

Fig. 17 Screw the threaded insert onto the installer tool until the tang engages the slot. Thread the insert into the hole until it is 1/4 or 1/2 turn below the top surface, then remove the tool and break off the tang using a punch.

in the series of accompanying illustrations and in the kit manufacturer's instructions.

Checking Engine Compression

▶ See Figure 18

A noticeable lack of engine power, excessive oil consumption and/or poor fuel mileage measured over an extended period are all indicators of internal engine war. Worn piston rings, scored or worn cylinder bores, blown head gaskets, sticking or burnt valves and worn valve seats are all possible culprits here. A check of each cylinder's compression will help you locate the problems.

As mentioned in the Tools and Equipment section of Section 1, a screw-in type compression gauge is more accurate that the type you simply hold against the spark plug hole, although it takes slightly longer to use. It's worth it to obtain a more accurate reading.

TCCS3801

Fig. 18 A screw-in type compression gauge is more accurate and easier to use without an assistant

GASOLINE ENGINES

1. Warm up the engine to normal operating temperature.
2. Remove all spark plugs.
3. Disconnect the high tension lead from the ignition coil.
4. Fully open the throttle either by operating the carburetor throttle linkage by hand or by having an assistant floor the accelerator pedal.
5. Screw the compression gauge into the No.1 spark plug hole until the fitting is snug.

➡**Be careful not to crossthread the plug hole. On aluminum cylinder heads use extra care, as the threads in these heads are easily ruined.**

6. While you read the compression gauge, ask the assistant to crank the engine two or three times in short bursts using the ignition switch.
7. Read the compression gauge at the end of each series of cranks, and record the highest of these readings. Repeat this procedure for each of the engine's cylinders. Compare the highest reading of each cylinder to the compression pressure specification in the Tune-Up Specifications chart in Section 2. The specs in this chart are maximum values. A cylinder's compression pressure is usually acceptable if it is not less than 80% of maximum. The difference between each cylinder should be no more than 12-14 psi (83-97 kPa).
8. If a cylinder is unusually low, pour a tablespoon of clean engine oil into the cylinder through the spark plug hole and repeat the compression test. If the compression comes up after adding the oil, it appears that the cylinder's piston rings or bore are damaged or worn. If the pressure remains low, the valves may not be seating properly (a valve job is needed), or the head gasket may be blown near that cylinder. If compression in any two adjacent cylinders is low, and if the addition of oil doesn't help the compression, there is leakage past the head gasket. Oil and coolant water in the combustion chamber can result from this problem. There may be evidence of water droplets on the engine dipstick when a head gasket has blown.

DIESEL ENGINES

Checking cylinder compression on diesel engines is basically the same procedure as on gasoline engines except for the following:

1. A special compression gauge adaptor suitable for diesel engines (because these engines have much greater compression pressures) must be used.
2. Remove the injector tubes and remove the injectors from each cylinder.

➡**Don't forget to remove the washer underneath each injector; otherwise, it may get lost when the engine is cranked.**

3. When fitting the compression gauge adaptor to the cylinder head, make sure the bleeder of the gauge (if equipped) is closed.
4. When reinstalling the injector assemblies, install new washers underneath each injector.

Engine

REMOVAL & INSTALLATION

❈❈CAUTION

When draining the coolant, keep in mind that cats and dogs are attracted by ethylene glycol antifreeze, and are quite likely to drink any that is left in an uncovered container or in puddles on the ground. This will prove fatal in sufficient quantity. Always drain the coolant into a sealable container. Coolant should be reused unless it is contaminated or several years old.

2.2L Engine

❈❈CAUTION

The fuel system is under pressure and must have the pressure relieved prior to disconnecting the fuel lines. Failure to properly bleed the system can lead to personal injury.

1. Relieve the fuel pressure.
2. Disconnect the negative battery cable.
3. Drain the cooling system into a suitable container.
4. While supporting the hood, disconnect the hydraulic shock from the cowl pan and secure the hood in a fully open position.
5. Remove the air cleaner and air duct assembly.
6. Disconnect the control cables from the throttle body and remove the control cable bracket from the intake manifold and rocker arm cover. Set the assembly out of the way.
7. Disconnect and cap the fuel lines from the throttle body and manifold mounting bracket.
8. Tag and disconnect any vacuum hoses that will interfere with the engine removal.
9. Remove the upper and lower radiator hoses.

10. Disconnect the heater hoses from the intake manifold and the water pump, then secure them out of the way.

11. Remove the torque strut.

12. Disconnect the engine harness wiring, then rotate the engine forwards.

13. Remove the power steering pump from the engine an support it out of the way with the power steering lines attached.

14. Disconnect the electrical wiring from the rear of the engine.

15. Remove the transaxle oil fill tube.

16. Remove the transaxle-to-engine bolts leaving in only the two upper bolts.

17. Rotate the engine to it's normal position.

18. Loosen the right front wheel lug nuts, then raise and support the vehicle.

19. Remove the right front tire and wheel assembly.

20. Remove the right inner fender well splash shield.

21. Disconnect the exhaust pipe from the exhaust manifold.

22. Remove the flywheel cover.

23. Disconnect and remove the starter.

24. Remove the engine mount-to-frame nuts.

25. Remove the torque converter-to-flywheel bolts.

26. Remove the A/C compressor from the mounting bracket and secure out of the way to the side without disconnecting the refrigerant lines.

27. Remove the front pipe support bracket from the transaxle.

28. Remove the transaxle support bracket from the transaxle and frame.

29. Lower the vehicle.

30. Remove the two remaining engine-to-transaxle mounting bolts.

31. Attach a suitable lifting device and slowly remove the engine. While lifting out the engine, make sure that no hoses or electrical connectors are still attached.

To install:

32. Lower the engine into the vehicle and connect the engine to the transaxle.

33. Install the two upper engine-to-transaxle bolts. Tighten the bolts only until snug.

34. Raise and safely support the vehicle.

35. Install the transaxle support bracket and tighten the mounting bolts to 38 ft. lbs. (52 Nm).

36. Install the front exhaust pipe-to-transaxle mounting bolt.

37. Install the A/C compressor in the mounting bracket.

38. Secure the torque converter-to-flywheel bolts, then tighten to 46 ft. lbs. (62 Nm).

39. Secure the engine mount-to-frame nuts, then tighten them to 33 ft. lbs. (45 Nm).

40. Connect and install the starter, then tighten the mounting bolts to 33 ft. lbs. (45 Nm).

41. Connect the exhaust pipe to the exhaust manifold, then tighten the mounting bolts to 22 ft. lbs. (30 Nm).

42. Attach the right inner fender well splash shield.

43. Install the tire and wheel assembly, then lower the vehicle.

44. Tighten the lug nuts to 100 ft. lbs. (136 Nm).

45. Install the remainder of the engine-to-transaxle bolts, then tighten all the bolts to 37 ft. lbs. (50 Nm).

46. Insert the transaxle fill tube.

47. Connect the electrical harness to the rear of the engine.

48. Install the power steering pump onto it's mounting bracket.

49. Connect the engine harness.

50. Attach the power steering pump onto the bracket.

51. Install the torque strut, then tighten the mounting bolts to 41 ft. lbs. (51 Nm).

52. Attach the heater hoses to the intake manifold and the water pump.

53. Attach the upper and lower radiator hoses.

54. Connect any vacuum hoses disconnected at removal.

55. Connect the fuel lines to the throttle body and the fuel line brackets.

56. Install the throttle cable bracket on the intake manifold and rocker arm cover, then connect the control cables to the throttle body.

57. Install the air cleaner and air inlet duct work.

58. Connect the hood hydraulic shock to the cowl panel.

59. Refill the cooling system and engine oil if needed.

60. Connect the negative battery cable.

61. Start the vehicle, top the cooling system as it warms up.

62. Check for leaks.

2.5L Engine with Manual Transaxle

✳✳CAUTION

The fuel system is under pressure and must have the pressure relieved prior to disconnecting the fuel lines. Failure to properly bleed the system can lead to personal injury.

1. Relive the fuel pressure.

2. Disconnect the battery cables at the battery.

3. Raise and support the vehicle.

4. Remove the front mount-to-cradle nuts.

5. Remove the forward exhaust pipe.

6. Remove the starter assembly, make sure the wires are attached, then swing to the side.

7. Remove the flywheel inspection cover.

8. Lower the car.

9. Remove the air cleaner assembly.

10. Remove all the bell housing bolts.

11. Remove the forward torque rod from the engine and the core support.

12. If equipped with air conditioning, remove the air conditioning belt and compressor, then put to the side.

13. Unfasten the emission hoses at the canister.

14. Remove the power steering hoses (if so equipped).

15. Detach the vacuum hoses and the electrical harness at solenoid.

16. Remove the heater blower motor.

17. Disconnect the throttle cable.

18. Drain the heater hose.

19. Disconnect the heater hose.

20. Disconnect the radiator hoses.

21. Disconnect engine harness at the bulkhead.

22. With an engine lifting tool, hoist the engine (remove heater hose at intake manifold, then disconnect the fuel line).

To install:

23. Lower the engine into the engine compartment.

24. Connect engine the harness at the bulkhead.

25. Install the radiator hoses.

26. Connect the heater hoses.
27. Attach the throttle cable.
28. Install the heater blower motor.
29. Install the vacuum hoses and electrical connectors at the solenoid.
30. Connect the power steering hose.
31. Install the emission hoses at the canister.
32. Install the air conditioning compressor and belt.
33. Install the forward torque reaction rod to the engine and core support.
34. Secure all of the bell housing bolts.
35. Install the air cleaner.
36. Raise and support the vehicle.
37. Install the flywheel inspection cover.
38. Install the starter assembly.
39. Connect the forward exhaust pipe.
40. Install the front mount-to-cradle nuts.
41. Lower the vehicle and install the battery.
42. Fill the engine oil and cooling system, start the engine, then top off the fluids.

2.5L Engine with Automatic Transaxle

✳✳CAUTION

The fuel system is under pressure and must have the pressure relieved prior to disconnecting the fuel lines. Failure to properly bleed the system can lead to personal injury.

1. Relive the fuel pressure.
2. Disconnect the battery cables at battery.
3. Drain the cooling system.
4. Remove the air cleaner and pre-heat tube.
5. Disconnect the engine harness.
6. Disconnect and tag all of the external vacuum hoses.
7. Remove the throttle and transaxle linkage at E.F.I. assembly and the intake manifold.
8. Remove the upper radiator hose.
9. If equipped with air conditioning, remove the air conditioning compressor from it's mounting brackets, then set aside. Do not disconnect the hoses.
10. Unsecure and remove the front engine strut assembly.
11. Disconnect the heater hose at intake manifold.
12. Remove the transaxle-to-engine bolts, make sure to leave the upper two bolts in place.
13. Remove the front mount-to-cradle nuts.
14. Disconnect and drop the forward exhaust pipe.
15. Remove the flywheel inspection cover, then remove the starter motor.
16. Remove the torque converter-to-flywheel bolts.
17. Remove the power steering pump and bracket, then move aside.
18. Detach the heater hose and lower radiator hose.
19. Remove the two rear transaxle support bracket bolts.
20. Remove the fuel supply line at the fuel filter.
21. Using a floor jack, and a block of wood placed under the transaxle, raise engine and transaxle until the engine front mount studs clear the cradle.
22. Connect the engine lift equipment and put tension on engine.
23. Remove the two remaining transaxle bolts.

24. Slide the engine forwards and lift it from the vehicle.
To Install:
25. Lower the engine into the vehicle. Do not completely lower the engine while the jack is supporting the transaxle.
26. Install the two transaxle bolts.
27. Remove the floor jack and lower the engine completely into the vehicle.
28. Connect the fuel supply line and install the filter.
29. Install the two transaxle rear support bracket bolts.
30. Install the heater and lower radiator hoses.
31. Connect the power steering bracket and pump.
32. Install the torque converter-to-flywheel bolts.
33. Install the starter motor and the flywheel inspection cover.
34. Connect the forward exhaust pipe.
35. Install the front mount-to-cradle nuts.
36. Install the transaxle to engine bolts.
37. Connect the heater hose at intake manifold.
38. Install the front engine strut assembly.
39. Install the air conditioning compressor mounting brackets and the compressor.
40. Install the upper radiator hose.
41. Connect the throttle and transaxle linkage at the E.F.I. assembly and intake manifold.
42. Connect all the external vacuum hose connections.
43. Connect the engine harness.
44. Install the air cleaner and pre-heat tube.
45. Fill the cooling system.
46. Connect battery cables at battery.
47. Start the engine, top the cooling system, check for leaks.

2.8L Engine with Manual Transaxle

✳✳CAUTION

The fuel system is under pressure and must have the pressure relieved prior to disconnecting the fuel lines. Failure to properly bleed the system can lead to personal injury.

1. Relieve the fuel pressure.
2. Disconnect the cables from the battery.
3. Remove the air cleaner assembly.
4. Drain the cooling system.
5. Disconnect and tag the vacuum hoses to all of the non-engine mounted components.
6. Disconnect the accelerator linkage from the carburetor.
7. Disconnect the engine harness from the ECM/PCM, then pull the connector through the front of the dash.
8. Disconnect the radiator hoses from radiator.
9. Disconnect the heater hoses from the engine.
10. If equipped, remove the power steering pump and bracket assembly from the engine.
11. Disconnect the clutch cable from the transaxle.
12. Disconnect the shift linkage from the transaxle shift levers. Remove the cables from the transaxle bosses.
13. Disconnect the speedometer cable from the transaxle.
14. Raise and support the vehicle on jackstands.
15. Remove the exhaust crossover pipe.
16. Remove all but one of the transaxle-to-engine retaining bolts.
17. Remove the side and crossmember assembly.

18. Disconnect the exhaust pipe.
19. Remove all the powertrain mount-to-cradle attachments.
20. Disconnect the engine harness from the junction block at the left side of the dash.
21. Lower the vehicle. If equipped with MFI, disconnect the throttle, T.V. and cruise control cables at the throttle body.
22. Install the engine support fixture. Raise the engine until the weight is relieved from the mount assembled.
23. Lower the left side of the engine/transaxle assembly.
24. Place a jack under the transaxle.
25. Remove the final transaxle-to-engine attaching bolt, then separate the transaxle from the engine and lower.
26. Lower the vehicle.
27. Install the engine lifting device.
28. If equipped with air conditioning, remove the compressor from the mounting bracket and swing aside.
29. Disconnect the forward strut bracket from the radiator support. Swing aside.
30. Lift the engine out of the vehicle.

To Install:

31. Lower the engine into the vehicle.
32. Connect the forward strut bracket to radiator support.
33. Install the air conditioning compressor and mounting bracket.
34. Raise the vehicle and place the transaxle jack under the transaxle.
35. Raise the transaxle flush with the engine, then install the engine-to-transaxle attaching bolts.
36. Remove the transaxle jack and lower the vehicle just enough to install the engine support fixture.
37. Raise the engine until the weight is relieved from the mount assemblies.
38. Connect all of the powertrain mount-to-cradle attachments.
39. Connect the exhaust pipe.
40. Install the side and crossmember assembly. Connect the engine harness to the junction block at the left side of the dash.
41. Install all remaining transaxle-to-engine retaining bolts.
42. Install the exhaust crossover.
43. Remove the engine support fixture.
44. Lower the vehicle.
45. Connect the speedometer cable to the transaxle.
46. Install the cables to the transaxle bosses.
47. Connect the transaxle shift linkage.
48. Connect the clutch cable.
49. Install the power steering bracket and pump assembly.
50. Connect the heater hoses to the engine.
51. Install the radiator hoses to the radiator.
52. Feed the engine harness through the front of the dash, then attach it to the ECM/PCM.
53. Connect the throttle, T.V. and the cruise control cables at the throttle body.
54. Connect the accelerator linkage to the carburetor.
55. Connect vacuum hosing to all non-engine mounted components.
56. Fill the cooling system.
57. Install the air cleaner.
58. Connect the battery cables.
59. Start the engine, top off the cooling system, check for leaks.

2.8L Engine with Automatic Transaxle

✳✳CAUTION

The fuel system is under pressure and must have the pressure relieved prior to disconnecting the fuel lines. Failure to properly bleed the system can lead to personal injury.

1. Relieve the fuel pressure.
2. Disconnect the battery cables from the battery.
3. Remove the air cleaner.
4. Drain the cooling system.
5. Disconnect and tag the vacuum hoses to all non-engine mounted components.
6. Disconnect the detent cable from the carburetor lever.
7. Disconnect the accelerator linkage. If equipped with MFI, disconnect the throttle at the T.V. and the cruise control cables at the throttle body.
8. Disconnect the engine harness from the ECM/PCM, then pull the connector through the front of the dash, then disconnect it from the junction block at the left side of the dash.
9. Disconnect the ground strap from the engine at the engine forward strut.
10. Remove the radiator hoses from radiator.
11. Disconnect the heater hoses from engine.
12. Remove the power steering pump and bracket assembly from the engine, if equipped.
13. Raise and support the vehicle.
14. Disconnect the exhaust pipe.
15. Disconnect the fuel lines at their rubber hose connections at the right side of the engine.
16. Remove the engine front mount-to-cradle retaining nuts (right side of vehicle).
17. Disconnect the battery cables from the engine (starter and transaxle housing bolt).
18. Remove the flex plate cover, then disconnect the torque convertor from the flex plate.
19. Remove the transaxle case-to-cylinder case support bracket bolts.
20. Lower the vehicle. Place a support under the transaxle rear extension.
21. Remove the engine strut bracket from the radiator support and swing rearward.
22. Remove the exhaust crossover pipe.
23. Remove the transaxle-to-cylinder case retaining bolts. Make note of ground stud location.
24. If air conditioning equipped, remove the compressor from the mounting bracket and lay aside.
25. Install a lift fixture to the engine, then remove engine from the vehicle.

To Install:

26. Lower the engine into the vehicle.
27. Install the compressor mounting bracket and the compressor.
28. Install the transaxle to cylinder case retaining bolts and the ground stud.
29. Install the exhaust crossover pipe.
30. Install the engine stud bracket to the radiator support.
31. Raise the vehicle and remove the support from the transaxle rear extension.

32. Install the transaxle case to cylinder case support bracket bolts.

33. Connect the torque converter to the flex plate and install the flex plate cover.

34. Connect the battery cables to the engine (starter and transaxle housing bolt).

35. Install the engine front mount to cradle retaining nuts (right side of vehicle).

36. Connect the fuel lines at the rubber hose connections at the right side of the engine.

37. Connect the exhaust pipe.

38. Lower the vehicle.

39. Install the power steering pump and bracket assembly to the engine.

40. Connect the heater hoses to the engine.

41. Connect the radiator hoses to the radiator.

42. Attach the ground strap to the engine at the engine forward strut.

43. Connect the engine harness connector to the junction block at the left side of the dash then push the connector through the front of the dash and connect it to the ECM/PCM.

44. Attach the accelerator linkage. If equipped with MFI, connect the throttle at the T.V. and the cruise control cables at the throttle body.

45. Connect the detent cable from the carburetor lever.

46. Connect the vacuum hosing to all non-engine mounted components.

47. Fill the cooling system.

48. Install the air cleaner.

49. Connect battery cables.

50. Start the engine, top off the cooling system, then check for leaks.

3.0L Engine

※※CAUTION

The fuel system is under pressure and must have the pressure relieved prior to disconnecting the fuel lines. Failure to properly bleed the system can lead to personal injury.

1. Relieve the fuel pressure.
2. Disconnect the battery cables from the battery.
3. Remove the air cleaner.
4. Drain the cooling system.
5. Disconnect and tag the vacuum hoses to all non-engine mounted components.
6. Remove the detent cable from the carburetor lever.
7. Unsecure the accelerator linkage.
8. Disconnect the engine harness.
9. Loosen and remove the ground strap from the engine at the engine forward strut.
10. Disconnect the radiator hoses from radiator.
11. Disconnect all heater hoses from engine.
12. Remove the power steering pump and bracket assembly from the engine.
13. Raise and support the vehicle.

14. Disassemble the exhaust pipe at the manifold.

15. Disconnect all fuel lines at the rubber hose connections.

16. Remove the engine front mount-to-cradle retaining nuts (right side of vehicle).

17. Disconnect the battery cables from engine (starter and transaxle housing bolt).

18. Remove the flex plate cover, then disconnect the torque converter from the flex plate.

19. Remove the transaxle case-to-cylinder case support bracket bolts.

20. Lower the vehicle. Place a support under the transaxle rear extension.

21. Remove the engine strut bracket from the radiator support and swing rearwards.

22. Remove transaxle to cylinder case retaining bolts. Make note of ground stud location.

23. If air conditioning equipped, remove the compressor from the mounting bracket and lay aside.

24. Install a lift fixture to the engine.

25. Remove the engine from the vehicle.

To Install:

26. Lower the engine into the vehicle.

27. Attach the compressor mounting bracket and the compressor to the vehicle.

28. Install the transaxle-to-cylinder case retaining bolts and the ground stud.

29. Install the exhaust crossover pipe.

30. Install the engine stud bracket to the radiator support.

31. Raise the vehicle and remove the support from the transaxle rear extension.

32. Install the transaxle case to cylinder case support bracket bolts.

33. Connect the torque converter to the flex plate and install the flex plate cover.

34. Connect the battery cables to the engine (starter and transaxle housing bolt).

35. Install the engine front mount to cradle retaining nuts (right side of vehicle).

36. Connect fuel lines at rubber hose connections at right side of engine.

37. Connect exhaust pipe.

38. Lower the vehicle.

39. Install the power steering pump and bracket assembly to the engine.

40. Connect the heater hoses to the engine.

41. Connect the radiator hoses to the radiator.

42. Assemble the ground strap to the engine at the engine forward strut.

43. Connect the engine harness connector to the junction block at the left side of the dash then push the connector through the front of the dash and connect it to the ECM/PCM.

44. Connect the accelerator linkage.

45. Connect detent cable from carburetor lever.

46. Connect vacuum hosing to all non-engine mounted components.

47. Fill the cooling system.

48. Install the air cleaner.

49. Connect battery cables.

3.1L Engine (VIN T)

❋❋CAUTION

The fuel system is under pressure and must have the pressure relieved prior to disconnecting the fuel lines. Failure to properly bleed the system can lead to personal injury.

1. Relieve the fuel system pressure.
2. Disconnect the negative battery cable. Scribe reference marks at the hood supports and remove the hood. Install covers on both fenders.
3. Remove the airflow tube at the air cleaner and throttle valve.
4. Drain the cooling system.
5. Disconnect and tag all vacuum hoses from all non-engine mounted components.
6. Disassemble the accelerator linkage and TV cable, then disconnect the cruise control cable, if equipped.
7. Disconnect the engine harness connector from the ECM/PCM and pull the connector through the front of dash. Disconnect the engine harness from the junction block at the dash panel.
8. Remove the engine strut bracket from the radiator support and position aside, as required.
9. Disconnect the radiator hoses from radiator and heater hoses from engine. Disconnect and plug the transaxle cooler lines.
10. Remove the serpentine belt cover and belt.
11. On vehicles with the air conditioning compressor mounted on the upper portion of the engine, remove the AIR pump and bracket. Then, remove the air conditioning compressor from the mounting bracket and position aside.
12. If equipped, remove power steering pump from engine and set it aside. Disconnect and cap any power steering lines.
13. Disconnect and plug the fuel lines.
14. Disconnect the EGR at the exhaust, as required.
15. Raise and safely support the vehicle.
16. On vehicles with the air conditioning compressor mounted on the lower portion of the engine, remove the air conditioning compressor from the engine. Do not discharge the air conditioning system.
17. Remove the engine front mount-to-cradle and mount-to-engine bracket retaining nuts, as required.
18. Disconnect and tag all electrical wiring at the starter. Remove the starter retaining bolts and remove the starter.
19. If equipped with automatic transaxle, remove the transaxle inspection cover and disconnect the torque converter from the flexplate.
20. Disconnect the exhaust pipe.
21. Remove the 1 transaxle-to-engine bolt from the back side of the engine.
22. Disconnect the power steering cut-off switch, if equipped.
23. Lower the vehicle.
24. Remove the exhaust crossover pipe.
25. Remove the remaining transaxle-to-engine bolts.
26. Support the transaxle by positioning a floor jack and a block of wood under the transaxle. Install an engine lift tool and remove the engine from the vehicle.

To install:

27. Position the engine in the vehicle while aligning the transaxle. Install the transaxle-to-engine bolts.
28. Position the front engine mount studs in the cradle and engine bracket.
29. Remove the engine lift tool. Raise and support the vehicle safely.
30. Install the engine mount retaining nuts.
31. If equipped, connect the power steering cut-off switch.
32. Install the 1 transaxle-to-engine bolt from the back side of the engine.
33. Connect the exhaust pipe.
34. If equipped with automatic transaxle, connect the torque converter to the flexplate and install the transaxle inspection cover.
35. Install the starter and retaining bolts. Connect the starter electrical connectors.
36. Install the engine front mount-to-cradle and mount-to-engine bracket retaining nuts.
37. On vehicles with the air conditioning compressor mounted on the lower portion of the engine, install the air conditioning compressor.
38. Lower the vehicle.
39. Connect the EGR at the exhaust, if removed.
40. Connect the fuel lines.
41. If equipped, install power steering pump.
42. On vehicles with the air conditioning compressor mounted on the upper portion of the engine, install the air conditioner compressor. Install the AIR pump and bracket.
43. Install the serpentine belt cover and belt.
44. Connect the radiator and heater hoses. Connect the transaxle cooler lines.
45. Install the engine strut bracket to the radiator support.
46. Connect the engine harness connector to the ECM/PCM.
47. Connect the accelerator linkage and TV cable. Connect the cruise control cable, if equipped.
48. Connect vacuum hoses to all non-engine mounted components.
49. Install the airflow tube at the air cleaner and throttle valve.
50. Install the hood using the reference marks made upon removal.
51. Connect the negative battery cable.
52. Fill cooling system and check for leaks. Start the engine and allow to come to normal operating temperature. Check for leaks and refill the cooling system.

3.1L Engine (VIN M)

❋❋CAUTION

Fuel Injection systems remain under pressure, even after the engine has been turned OFF. The fuel system pressure must be relieved before disconnecting any fuel lines. Failure to do so may result in fire and/or personal injury.

1. Relieve the fuel system pressure.
2. Disconnect the negative battery cable.
3. Remove the top half of the air cleaner assembly and the throttle body inlet duct.
4. Drain the cooling system.
5. Remove the upper and lower radiator hoses.

6. Disconnect the coolant inlet line from the coolant surge tank.

7. Disconnect and tag the vacuum hoses from the EVAP canister purge valve, vacuum modulator and power brake booster.

8. Disconnect the heater outlet hose from the water pump.

9. Remove the serpentine drive belt.

10. Disconnect the control cables from the throttle body lever and intake manifold bracket and position the cables out of the way.

11. Disconnect the following electrical connectors from their related components:
   - Ignition assembly
   - Oxygen sensor
   - Fuel injectors
   - Idle Air Control valve (IAC)
   - Throttle position sensor (TPS)
   - Coolant sensor
   - Park neutral switch
   - TCC solenoid
   - Shift solenoid
   - EGR valve
   - Transaxle ground

12. Remove the alternator.

13. Disconnect and cap the power steering lines from the power steering pump.

14. Disconnect and cap the fuel lines from the fuel rail.

15. Remove the cooling fan assembly.

16. Disconnect the shift control cable from the transaxle shift lever and cable bracket.

17. Detach the transaxle vent tube from the transaxle.

18. Disconnect the vacuum hose from the vacuum reservoir.

19. Install an engine support fixture, J-28467-A, or the equivalent.

20. Loosen, but do not remove the top 2 A/C compressor mounting bolts.

21. Raise and safely support the vehicle.

22. Remove the front tire and wheel assemblies.

23. Remove the right and left inner fender splash shields.

24. Remove the engine mount strut.

25. Disconnect the ABS sensor wires from the wheel sensors and suspension member supports, if equipped.

26. Remove the cotter pins and castle nuts from the lower ball joints. Using a suitable tool, separate the lower ball joints from the steering knuckles.

27. Remove the lower suspension support assemblies with the lower control arms attached.

28. Disconnect the halfshafts from the transaxle and support out of the way.

29. Remove the oil filter and oil filter adapter.

30. Remove the flywheel cover.

31. Remove the starter.

32. Disconnect the following electrical connectors from their related components:
   - Knock sensor
   - Front crankshaft position sensor
   - Side crankshaft position sensor
   - Oil level sensor
   - Vehicle speed sensor
   - Transaxle ground

33. Disconnect the heater hoses from the heater core.

34. Remove the A/C compressor lower mounting bolts and remove the compressor from the mounting bracket and position aside. DO NOT disconnect the refrigerant lines from the compressor or allow the lines top support the weight of the compressor.

35. Remove the vacuum reservoir tank.

36. Disconnect the exhaust pipe from the exhaust manifold and position the pipe aside.

37. Remove the engine mount strut bracket from the engine.

38. Disconnect the transaxle cooler lines from the radiator.

39. Remove the transaxle oil fill tube.

40. Lower the vehicle until the powertrain assembly is resting on a suitable engine table.

41. Unbolt the transaxle mount-to-body bolts.

42. Remove the intermediate bracket from the right engine mount.

43. Remove the engine support fixture.

44. Raise the vehicle leaving the powertrain assembly on the engine table.

45. Separate the engine and transaxle assemblies.

To install:

46. Connect the transaxle to the engine and tighten the mounting bolts to 55 ft. lbs. (75 Nm).

47. Position the powertrain assembly under the vehicle and lower the vehicle into position.

48. Loosely install the serpentine belt.

49. Install the intermediate bracket to the right side engine mount.

50. Install the transaxle-to-body bolts.

51. Raise and safely support the vehicle.

52. Install the transaxle fill tube.

53. Connect the transaxle cooler lines to the radiator.

54. Install the engine strut bracket to the engine and tighten the mounting bolts to 44 ft. lbs. (60 Nm).

55. Connect the exhaust pipe to the exhaust manifold and tighten the mounting bolts to 18 ft. lbs. (25 Nm).

56. Install the vacuum reserve tank.

57. Install the A/C compressor in the mounting bracket. Install the upper bolts loosely and tighten the lower bolts.

58. Connect the heater hoses to the heater core.

59. Connect the following electrical connectors to their related components:
   - Knock sensor
   - Front crankshaft position sensor
   - Side crankshaft position sensor
   - Oil level sensor
   - Vehicle speed sensor
   - Transaxle ground

60. Attach the starter to the engine.

61. Install the flywheel cover.

62. Install the oil filter adapter and after coating the oil filter seal with clean engine oil, install the oil filter.

63. Connect the drive axles to the transaxle.

64. Install the suspension support assemblies and lower control arms.

65. Connect the lower ball joints to the steering knuckles and tighten the castle nuts to 41 ft. lbs. (55 Nm).

66. Connect the ABS sensor wires to the wheel sensors and suspension support wire clips.

67. Install the engine mount strut.

68. Reinstall the left and right inner fender splash shields.

69. Install the right front tire and wheel assemblies.

70. Lower the vehicle.
71. Tighten the upper A/C compressor mounting bolts.
72. Remove the engine support fixture.
73. Connect the vacuum hose to the reservoir.
74. Connect the transaxle vent hose to the transaxle.
75. Connect the shift cable linkage to the cable bracket and shift lever on the transaxle.
76. Install the cooling fan assembly.
77. Connect the fuel lines to the fuel rail.
78. Connect the power steering lines to the power steering pump.
79. Install the alternator.
80. Connect the following electrical connectors to their related components:
   - Ignition assembly
   - Oxygen sensor
   - Fuel injectors
   - Idle Air Control valve (IAC)
   - Throttle position sensor (TPS)
   - Coolant sensor
   - Park neutral switch
   - TCC solenoid
   - Shift solenoid
   - EGR valve
   - Transaxle ground
81. Connect the control cables to the throttle body lever and cable bracket.
82. Install the serpentine belt.
83. Connect the heater outlet hose to the water pump.
84. Connect the vacuum hoses to the power brake booster, vacuum modulator and EVAP purge solenoid.
85. Connect the coolant inlet line to the surge tank.
86. Install the upper and lower radiator hoses.
87. Install the top half of the air cleaner assembly and the throttle body air inlet duct.
88. Connect the negative battery cable.
89. Check and fill all the engine fluids as necessary.
90. Start the vehicle and bleed the power steering system.

3.3L Engine

❈❈CAUTION

The fuel system is under pressure and must have the pressure relieved prior to disconnecting the fuel lines. Failure to properly bleed the system can lead to personal injury.

1. Disconnect the negative battery cable. Scribe reference marks at the hood supports and remove the hood. Install covers on both fenders.
2. Relieve the fuel system pressure.
3. Disconnect the negative battery cable.
4. Drain the cooling system. Disconnect the radiator and heater hoses. Disconnect and plug the transaxle cooler lines.
5. Remove the upper engine strut and engine cooling fan.
6. Remove the intake duct from the throttle body. Disconnect and tag the vacuum hoses from all non-engine mounted components. Disconnect all electrical connections.
7. Remove the cable bracket and cables from the throttle body.

8. Remove the serpentine belt. If equipped, remove the power steering pump and locate to the side.
9. Unfasten the upper transaxle-to-engine retaining bolts.
10. Raise and support the vehicle safely.
11. Remove the air conditioning compressor and locate to the side.
12. Remove the engine mount-to-frame nuts, flywheel dust cover and flywheel-to-converter bolts.
13. Remove the lower engine-to-transaxle bolts; 1 bolt is located behind the transaxle case and engine block.
14. Lower the vehicle. Install an engine lift tool and remove the engine from the vehicle.
To install:
15. Install the engine in the engine compartment. Install the upper engine-to-transaxle bolts. Remove the engine lift tool.
16. Raise and safely support the vehicle.
17. Install the lower engine-to-transaxle bolts; 1 bolt is located behind the transaxle case and engine block.
18. Install the flywheel-to-converter bolts, flywheel dust cover and engine mount-to-frame nuts.
19. Install the air conditioning compressor.
20. Lower the vehicle.
21. If equipped, install the power steering pump. Install the serpentine belt.
22. Install the cable bracket and cables to the throttle body.
23. Install the intake duct to the throttle body. Connect vacuum hoses to all non-engine mounted components. Connect all electrical connections.
24. Install the upper engine strut and engine cooling fan.
25. Connect the radiator and heater hoses. Connect the transaxle cooler lines.
26. Install the hood.
27. Connect the negative battery cable.
28. Fill cooling system and check for leaks. Start the engine and allow to come to normal operating temperature. Recheck for leaks and fill the cooling system.

3.8L Engine

❈❈CAUTION

The fuel system is under pressure and must have the pressure relieved prior to disconnecting the fuel lines. Failure to properly bleed the system can lead to personal injury.

1. Relive the fuel pressure.
2. Disconnect the negative battery cable. Scribe reference marks at the hood supports and remove the hood. Install covers on both fenders.
3. Remove the air cleaner assembly and drain the cooling system.
4. Disconnect and tag the vacuum hoses to all non-engine mounted components.
5. Disconnect the detent cable and accelerator linkage.
6. Disconnect the engine electrical harness and ground strap.
7. Disconnect the heater hoses from the engine and radiator hoses from the radiator. Disconnect the transaxle cooler lines, if equipped.
8. If equipped, remove the power steering pump and bracket assembly.

9. Raise and safely support the vehicle.

10. Disconnect the exhaust pipe from the manifold.

11. Disconnect the fuel lines.

12. Remove the engine front mount-to-cradle retaining nuts.

13. Disconnect and tag all electrical wiring at the starter. Remove the starter retaining bolts and remove the starter.

14. Remove the flexplate cover and disconnect the flexplate from the torque converter.

15. Remove the retaining bolts from the transaxle rear support bracket.

16. Lower the vehicle and place a support under the transaxle rear extension.

17. Remove the engine strut bracket from the radiator support and position aside.

18. Remove the transaxle-to-engine retaining bolts.

19. If equipped with air conditioning, remove the air conditioning compressor from the mounting bracket and lay aside.

20. Install an engine lift tool and remove the engine from the vehicle.

To install:

21. Position the engine in the vehicle and align the engine front mount studs. Align the transaxle and install the transaxle-to-engine retaining bolts.

22. Remove the engine lift tool.

23. If equipped, install the air conditioning compressor to the mounting bracket.

24. Raise and safely support the vehicle. Install the retaining bolts to the transaxle rear support bracket.

25. Connect the flexplate to the torque converter and install the flexplate cover.

26. Install the starter and retaining bolts. Connect the starter electrical connectors.

27. Install the engine front mount-to-cradle retaining nuts.

28. Connect the fuel lines.

29. Connect the exhaust pipe to the manifold.

30. Lower the vehicle.

31. If equipped, install the power steering bracket assembly and pump.

32. Connect the heater and radiator hoses. Connect the transaxle cooler lines, if equipped.

33. Connect the engine electrical harness and ground strap.

34. Connect the detent cable and accelerator linkage.

35. Connect vacuum hoses to all non-engine mounted components.

36. Install the air cleaner assembly.

37. Install the hood.

38. Connect the negative battery cable.

39. Fill cooling system and check for leaks. Start the engine and allow to come to normal operating temperature. Check for leaks and refill the cooling system.

4.3L Diesel Engine

1. Drain the cooling system. Remove the serpentine drive belt (and vacuum pump drive belt, if air conditioning equipped).

2. Remove the air cleaner and install cover J-26996.

3. Disconnect the negative battery cable(s) at the batteries, and the ground wires at the inner fender panel. Disconnect the engine ground strap, at the rear (right) head to cowl.

4. Raise and support the vehicle.

5. Remove the flywheel cover.

6. Remove the flywheel-to-torque converter bolts.

7. Disconnect the exhaust pipe from the rear exhaust manifold.

8. Remove the engine-to-transaxle brace.

9. Remove the engine mount-to-cradle retaining nuts and washers.

10. Disconnect the leads to the starter motor, the No. 2 cylinder glow plug, and the battery ground cable at the transaxle-to-engine bolt.

11. Disconnect the lower oil cooler hose and cap the openings.

12. Remove the accessible power steering pump bracket fasteners.

13. Lower the car.

14. Remove the remaining power steering pump bracket/brace fasteners and lower the power steering pump with hoses out of the way.

15. Remove the heater water return pipe.

16. Disconnect all of the remaining glow plug leads, at the glow plugs.

17. Disconnect all other leads at the engine, disconnect the engine harness at the cowl connector and body mounted relays, then position the engine harness aside.

18. If air conditioning equipped, disconnect the compressor with brackets and lines attached, then position them aside.

19. Disconnect the fuel and vacuum hoses, cap all fuel line openings.

20. Disconnect the throttle and T.V. cables at the injection pump, and the cable bracket. Position all cables aside.

21. Disconnect the upper oil cooler hose and cap the openings.

22. Remove the exhaust crossover pipe heat shield.

23. Disconnect and move aside the transaxle filler tube.

24. Remove the exhaust crossover pipe.

25. Remove the engine mounting strut and strut brackets.

26. Install a suitable engine lifting device. Make certain that when installing chains to the cylinder heads that washers are used under the chains and bolt heads. Tighten the bolts to 20 ft. lbs. (27 Nm).

✳✳CAUTION

Failure to properly secure the engine lift to the aluminum cylinder heads can result in personal injury.

27. Position a support under the transaxle rear extension. It may be necessary to raise the support as the engine is being removed.

28. Remove the engine to transaxle bolt, then remove the engine.

29. To install, reverse the removal process noting the following:

   a. Before installing the flex plate-to-converter bolts, make sure that the weld nuts on the converter are flush with the flex plate, and the converter rotates freely by hand.

   b. Use only new O-rings at all connections.

   c. Adjust the throttle valve cable as outlined in the Section 7.

GENERAL ENGINE SPECIFICATIONS

Year	Engine ID/VIN	Engine Displacement Liters (cc)	Fuel System Type	Net Horsepower @ rpm	Net Torque @ rpm (ft. lbs.)	Bore x Stroke (in.)	Compression Ratio	Oil Pressure @ rpm
1982	R	2.5 (2474)	TBI	92@4000	134@2800	4.00x3.00	8.2:1	38.5@2000
	X	2.8 (2835)	2BC	112@4800	145@2100	3.50x3.00	8.5:1	50-65@1200
	Z	2.8 (2835) HO	2BC	135@5400	145@2400	3.50x3.00	8.9:1	50-65@1200
	E	3.0 (2999)	2BC	110@4800	145@2600	3.80x2.66	8.45:1	35-42@2000
1983	R	2.5 (2474)	TBI	92@4000	134@2800	4.00x3.00	8.2:1	37.5@2000
	X	2.8 (2835)	2BC	112@4800	145@2100	3.50x3.00	8.5:1	50-65@1200
	Z	2.8 (2835) HO	2BC	135@5400	145@2400	3.50x3.00	8.9:1	50-65@1200
	E	3.0 (2999)	2BC	110@4800	145@2600	3.80x2.66	8.45:1	35-42@2000
	T	4.3 (4293)	DSL	85@3600	165@1600	4.05x3.38	21.6:1	40-45@2000
1984	R	2.5 (2835)	TBI	92@4000	164@2800	4.00x3.00	9.0:1	38.5@2000
	X	2.8 (2835)	2BC	112@4800	145@2100	3.50x3.00	8.5:1	50-65@1200
	Z	2.8 (2835) HO	2BC	135@5400	145@2400	3.50x3.00	8.9:1	50-65@2000
	E	3.0 (2999)	2BC	110@4800	145@2600	3.80x2.66	8.45:1	35-42@2000
	T	4.3 (4293)	DSL	85@3600	165@1600	4.05x3.38	21.6:1	40-45@2000
1985	R	2.5 (2835)	TBI	92@4000	134@2800	4.00x3.00	9.0:1	38.5@2000
	X	2.8 (2835)	2BC	112@4800	145@2100	3.50x3.00	8.5:1	50-65@1200
	E	3.0 (2999)	2BC	110@4800	145@2600	3.80x2.66	8.45:1	35-42@2000
	3	3.8 (3785)	MFI	150@4400	200@2000	3.80x3.40	8.5:1	37@2400
	T	4.3 (4293)	DSL	85@3600	165@1600	4.06x3.39	21.6:1	40-45@2000
1986	R	2.5 (2474)	TBI	92@4000	134@2800	4.00x3.00	9.0:1	38.5@2000
	X	2.8 (2835)	2BC	112@4800	144.5@2100	3.50x3.00	8.5:1	50-65@1200
	3	3.8 (3785)	MFI	150@4400	200@2000	3.80x3.40	8.5:1	37@2400
	B	3.8 (3785)	MFI	150@4400	200@2000	3.80x3.40	8.5:1	37@2400
1987	R	2.5 (2474)	TBI	98@4800	135@3200	4.00x3.00	8.3:1	38.5@2000
	W	2.8 (2835)	MFI	125@4800	160@3600	3.50x2.99	8.9:1	50-65@2400
	3	3.8 (3785)	MFI	150@4400	200@2000	3.80x3.40	8.5:1	37@2400
1988	R	2.5 (2474)	TBI	92@4000	134@2800	4.00x3.00	8.3:1	50.@2000
	W	2.8 (2835)	MFI	130@4800	155@3600	3.50x2.99	8.9:1	50-65@2400
	3	3.8 (3785)	MFI	150@4400	200@2000	3.80x3.40	8.5:1	37@2400
1989	R	2.5 (2474)	TBI	98@4500	134@2800	4.00x3.00	8.3:1	50@2000
	W	2.8 (2835)	MFI	125@4500	160@3600	3.50x2.99	8.9:1	15@1100
	N	3.3 (3342)	MFI	160@5200	185@3200	3.70x3.16	9.0:1	45@2000
	T	3.1 (3130)	MFI	120@4200	175@2200	3.50x3.31	8.8:1	15@1100
1990	R	2.5 (2474)	MFI	110@5200	135@3200	4.00x3.00	8.3:1	26@800
	T	3.1 (3130)	MFI	120@4200	175@2200	3.50x3.31	8.8:1	15@1100
	N	3.3 (3342)	MFI	160@5200	185@2200	3.70x3.16	9.0:1	40@1850
1991	R	2.5 (2474)	TBI	110@5200	135@3200	4.00x3.00	8.3:1	26@800
	N	3.3 (3342)	MFI	160@5200	185@2000	3.70x3.16	9.0:1	60@1850
	T	3.1 (3130)	MFI	120@4200	175@2200	3.50x3.31	8.8:1	15@1100
1992	4	2.2 (2195)	MFI	110@5200	130@3200	3.50x3.346	9.0:1	56@3000
	R	2.5 (2474)	TBI	110@5200	135@3200	4.00x3.00	8.3:1	26@800
	N	3.3 (3342)	MFI	160@5200	185@2000	3.70x3.16	9.0:1	60@1850
1993	4	2.2 (2195)	MFI	110@5200	130@3200	3.50x3.346	9.0:1	56@3000
	M	3.1 (3130)	MFI	160@5200	185@4000	3.50x3.31	9.5:1	15@1100
	N	3.3 (3342)	MFI	160@5200	185@4000	3.50x3.31	9.5:1	15@1100
1994	4	2.2 (2195)	MFI	120@5200	130@4000	3.50x3.46	9.0:1	56@3000
	M	3.1 (3130)	MFI	160@5200	185@4000	3.50x3.31	9.5:1	15@1100
1995	4	2.2 (2195)	MFI	120@5200	130@4000	3.50x3.46	9.0:1	56@3000
	M	3.1 (3130)	MFI	160@5200	185@4000	3.50x3.31	9.5:1	15@1100

TBI - Throttle body fuel injection
MFI - Multiport fuel injection
BC - barrel carburetor
DSL - Diesel

86813080

VALVE SPECIFICATIONS

Year	Engine ID/VIN	Engine Displacement Liters (cc)	Seat Angle (deg.)	Face Angle (deg.)	Spring Test Pressure (lbs. @ in.)	Spring Installed Height (in.)	Stem-to-Guide Clearance (in.) Intake	Stem-to-Guide Clearance (in.) Exhaust	Stem Diameter (in.) Intake	Stem Diameter (in.) Exhaust
1982	R	2.5 (2474)	46	45	176@1.254	1.660	0.0010-0.0027	0.0010-0.0027	0.3418-0.3425	0.3418-0.3425
	X, Z	2.8 (2835)	46	45	155@1.160	1.610	0.0010-0.0027	0.0010-0.0027	0.3410-0.3416	0.3410-0.3416
	E	3.0 (2999)	45	45	220@1.340	1.727	0.0015-0.0035	0.0015-0.0032	0.3412-0.3401	0.3412-0.3405
1983	R	2.5 (2474)	46	45	176@1.254	1.660	0.0010-0.0027	0.0010-0.0027	0.3418-0.3425	0.3418-0.3425
	X, Z	2.8 (2835)	46	45	195@1.181	1.575	0.0010-0.0027	0.0010-0.0027	0.3410-0.3416	0.3410-0.3416
	E	3.0 (2999)	45	45	220@1.340	1.727	0.0015-0.0035	0.0015-0.0032	0.3412-0.3401	0.3412-0.3405
	T	4.3 (4293)	[1]	[2]	203-217@1.220	1.670	0.0010-0.0027	0.0015-0.0032	0.3425-0.3432	0.3420-0.3428
1984	R	2.5 (2474)	46	45	176@1.254	1.660	0.0010-0.0027	0.0010-0.0027	0.3418-0.3425	0.3418-0.3425
	X, Z	2.8 (2835)	46	45	195@1.181	1.575	0.0010-0.0027	0.0010-0.0027	0.3410-0.3416	0.3410-0.3416
	E	3.0 (2999)	45	45	220@1.340	1.727	0.0015-0.0035	0.0015-0.0032	0.3412-0.3401	0.3412-0.3405
	T	4.3 (4293)	[1]	[2]	203-217@1.220	1.670	0.0010-0.0027	0.0015-0.0032	0.3425-0.3432	0.3420-0.3428
1985	R	2.5 (2474)	46	45	176-180@1.260	1.69	0.0010-0.0027	0.0010-0.0027	0.3420-0.3430	0.3420-0.3430
	X	2.8 (2835)	46	45	195@1.181	1.575	0.0010-0.0027	0.0010-0.0027	0.3410-0.3416	0.3410-0.3416
	W	2.8 (2835)	46	45	195@1.181	1.575	0.0010-0.0027	0.0010-0.0027	0.3410-0.3416	0.3410-0.3416
	E	3.0 (2999)	45	45	220@1.340	1.727	0.0015-0.0035	0.0015-0.0032	0.3412-0.3401	0.3412-0.3405
	T	4.3 (4293)	[1]	[2]	203-217@1.220	1.670	0.0010-0.0027	0.0015-0.0032	0.3425-0.3432	0.3420-0.3428
1986	R	2.5 (2474)	46	45	176-180@1.260	1.690	0.0010-0.0027	0.0010-0.0027	0.3420-0.3430	0.3420-0.3430
	X	2.8 (2835)	46	45	195@1.181	1.575	0.0010-0.0027	0.0010-0.0027	0.3410-0.3416	0.3410-0.3416
	B	3.8 (3785)	45	45	185@1.340	1.727	0.0015-0.0035	0.0015-0.0032	0.3412-0.3401	0.3412-0.3405
	3	3.8 (3785)	45	45	185@1.340	1.727	0.0015-0.0035	0.0015-0.0032	0.3412-0.3401	0.3412-0.3405
1987	R	2.5 (2474)	46	45	158-170@1.040	1.440	0.0010-0.0027	0.0010-0.0027	0.3130-0.3140	0.3120-0.3130
	W	2.8 (2835)	46	45	215@1.291	1.575	0.0010-0.0027	0.0010-0.0027	0.3412-0.3416	0.3412-0.3416

VALVE SPECIFICATIONS

Year	Engine ID/VIN	Engine Displacement Liters (cc)	Seat Angle (deg.)	Face Angle (deg.)	Spring Test Pressure (lbs. @ in.)	Spring Installed Height (in.)	Stem-to-Guide Clearance (in.)		Stem Diameter (in.)	
							Intake	Exhaust	Intake	Exhaust
	3	3.8 (3785)	46	45	175-195@ 1.340	1.697- 1.757	0.0015- 0.0035	0.0015- 0.0032	0.3412- 0.3401	0.3412- 0.3405
1988	R	2.5 (2474)	46	45	158-170@ 1.040	1.440	0.0010- 0.0027	0.0010- 0.0027	0.3130- 0.3140	0.3120- 0.3130
	W	2.8 (2835)	46	45	215@1.291	1.575	0.0010- 0.0027	0.0010- 0.0027	NA	NA
	3	3.8 (3785)	46	45	185@1.340	1.720	0.0015- 0.0035	0.0015- 0.0032	0.3412- 0.3401	0.3412- 0.3405
1989	R	2.5 (2474)	46	45	173@1.240	1.680	0.0010- 0.0026	0.0013- 0.0041	NA	NA
	W	2.8 (2835)	46	45	215@1.291	1.575 [1]	0.0010- 0.0027	0.0010- 0.0027	NA	NA
	T	3.1 (3146)	46	45	215@1.291	1.701 [1]	0.0010- 0.0027	0.0010- 0.0027	NA	NA
	N	3.3 (3342)	45	45	200-220@ 1.315	1.690- 1.750	0.0015- 0.0035	0.0015- 0.0032	NA	NA
1990	R	2.5 (2474)	46	45	173@1.240	1.680	0.0010- 0.0026	0.0013- 0.0041	NA	NA
	T	3.1 (3146)	46	45	215@1.291	1.575	0.0010- 0.0027	0.0010- 0.0027	NA	NA
	N	3.3 (3342)	45	45	200-220@ 1.315	1.690- 1.750	0.0015- 0.0032	0.0015- 0.0032	NA	NA
1991	R	2.5 (2474)	46	45	173@1.240	1.680	0.0010- 0.0026	0.0013- 0.0041	NA	NA
	T	3.1 (3146)	46	45	215@1.291	1.575	0.0010- 0.0027	0.0010- 0.0027	NA	NA
	N	3.3 (3342)	45	45	210@1.315	1.690- 1.720	0.0015- 0.0035	0.0015- 0.0032	NA	NA
1992	4	2.2 (2195)	46	45	215-233@ 1.247	1.637	0.0011- 0.0026	0.0014- 0.0031	NA	NA
	R	2.5 (2474)	46	45	173@1.240	1.680	0.0010- 0.0028	0.0013 0.0041	NA	NA
	T	3.1 (3146)	46	45	215@1.291	1.575	0.0010- 0.0027	0.0010- 0.0027	NA	NA
	N	3.3 (3342)	45	45	210@1.315	1.690- 1.720	0.0015- 0.0035	0.0015- 0.0032	NA	NA
1993	4	2.2 (2195)	46	45	215-233@ 1.247	1.637	0.0011- 0.0026	0.0014- 0.0031	NA	NA
	M	3.1 (3130)	45	45	250@1.239	1.710	0.0001- 0.0027	0.0010- 0.0027	NA	NA
	N	3.3 (3342)	45	45	210@1.315	1.690- 1.720	0.0015- 0.0035	0.0015- 0.0035	NA	NA
1994	4	2.2 (2195)	46	45	220-236@ 1.278	1.710	0.0001- 0.0027	0.0014- 0.0031	NA	NA
	M	3.1 (3130)	45	45	250@1.239	1.710	0.0001- 0.0027	0.0010- 0.0027	NA	NA
1995	4	2.2 (2195)	46	45	220-236@ 1.278	1.710	0.0001- 0.0027	0.0014- 0.0031	NA	NA
	M	3.1 (3130)	45	45	250@1.239	1.710	0.0001- 0.0027	0.0010- 0.0027	NA	NA

NA - Not Available

1 Intake seat angle: 45

   Exhaust seat angle: 31

2 Intake face angle: 44

   Exhaust face angle: 30

86813082

CAMSHAFT SPECIFICATIONS
All measurements given in inches.

Year	Engine ID/VIN	Engine Displacement Liters (cc)	Journal Diameter					Elevation		Bearing Clearance	Camshaft End Play
			1	2	3	4	5	In.	Ex.		
1982	R	2.5 (2474)	1.8690	1.8690	1.8690	1.8690	1.8690	0.398	0.398	0.0001-0.0027	0.0015-0.0050
	X	2.8 (2835)	1.8678-1.8815	1.8678-1.8815	1.8678-1.8815	1.8678-1.8815	1.8678-1.8815	0.231	0.263	0.0010-0.0040	NA
	Z	2.8 (2835)	1.8690	1.8690	1.8690	1.8690	NA	0.231	0.263	0.0010-0.0040	NA
	E	3.0 (2999)	1.7860	1.7860	1.7860	1.7860	1.7860	0.406	0.406	1	NA
1983	R	2.5 (2474)	1.8690	1.8690	1.8690	1.8690	1.8690	0.398	0.398	0.0001-0.0027	0.0015-0.0050
	X	2.8 (2835)	1.8678-1.8815	1.8678-1.8815	1.8678-1.8815	1.8678-1.8815	1.8678-1.8815	0.231	0.263	0.0010-0.0040	NA
	Z	2.8 (2835)	1.8690	1.8690	1.8690	1.8690	NA	0.231	0.263	0.0010-0.0040	NA
	E	3.0 (2999)	1.7860	1.7860	1.7860	1.7860	1.7860	0.406	0.406	1	NA
	T	4.3 (4293)	3 2.0150-2.0160	1.9960-1.9950	1.9760-1.9750	NA		0.252	0.279	0.0020-0.0043	0.0080-0.0220
1984	R	2.5 (2474)	1.8690	1.8690	1.8690	1.8690	1.8690	0.398	0.398	0.0001-0.0027	0.0015-0.0050
	X	2.8 (2835)	1.8678-1.8815	1.8678-1.8815	1.8678-1.8815	1.8678-1.8815	1.8678-1.8815	0.231	0.263	0.0010-0.0040	NA
	Z	2.8 (2835)	1.8690	1.8690	1.8690	1.8690	NA	0.231	0.263	0.0010-0.0040	NA
	E	3.0 (2999)	1.7860	1.7860	1.7860	1.7860	1.7860	0.406	0.406	1	NA
	T	4.3 (4293)	3 2.0150-2.0160	1.9960-1.9950	1.9760-1.9750	NA		0.252	0.279	0.0020-0.0043	0.0080-0.0220
1985	R	2.5 (2474)	1.8690	1.8690	1.8690	1.8690	1.8690	0.398	0.398	0.0001-0.0027	0.0015-0.0050
	X	2.8 (2835)	1.8678-1.8815	1.8678-1.8815	1.8678-1.8815	1.8678-1.8815	1.8678-1.8815	0.231	0.263	0.0010-0.0040	NA
	Z	2.8 (2835)	1.8690	1.8690	1.8690	1.8690	NA	0.231	0.263	0.0010-0.0040	NA
	E	3.0 (2999)	1.7860	1.7860	1.7860	1.7860	1.7860	0.406	0.406	1	NA
	3	3.8 (3785)	1.7850-1.7860	1.7850-1.7860	1.7850-1.7860	1.7850-1.7860	1.7850-1.7860	0.368	0.384	1	NA
	T	4.3 (4293)	3 2.0150-2.0160	1.9960-1.9950	1.9760-1.9750	-		0.252	0.279	0.0020-0.0043	0.0080-0.0220
1986	R	2.5 (2474)	1.8690	1.8690	1.8690	1.8690	1.8690	0.398	0.398	0.0001-0.0027	0.0015-0.0050
	X	2.8 (2835)	1.8678-1.8815	1.8678-1.8815	1.8678-1.8815	1.8678-1.8815	1.8678-1.8815	0.231	0.263	0.0010-0.0040	NA
	B	3.8 (3785)	1.7850-1.7860	1.7850-1.7860	1.7850-1.7860	1.7850-1.7860	1.7850-1.7860	0.392	0.392	1	NA
	3	3.8 (3785)	1.7850-1.7860	1.7850-1.7860	1.7850-1.7860	1.7850-1.7860	1.7850-1.7860	0.368	0.384	1	NA
1987	R	2.5 (2474)	1.8690	1.8690	1.8690	1.8690	1.8690	0.398	0.398	0.0001-0.0027	0.0015-0.0050
	W	2.8 (2835)	1.8678-1.8815	1.8678-1.8815	1.8678-1.8815	1.8678-1.8815	1.8678-1.8815	0.263	0.273	0.0010-0.0040	NA
	3	3.8 (3785)	1.7850-1.7860	1.7850-1.7860	1.7850-1.7860	1.7850-1.7860	1.7850-1.7860	0.397	0.397	1	NA
1988	R	2.5 (2474)	1.8690	1.8690	1.8690	1.8690	1.8690	0.232	0.232	0.0007-0.0027	0.0015-0.0050

86813083

CAMSHAFT SPECIFICATIONS

All measurements given in inches.

Year	Engine ID/VIN	Engine Displacement Liters (cc)	Journal Diameter					Elevation		Bearing Clearance	Camshaft End Play
			1	2	3	4	5	In.	Ex.		
	W	2.8 (2835)	1.8670-1.8690	1.8670-1.8690	1.8670-1.8690	1.8670-1.8690	1.8670-1.8690	0.263	0.273	0.0010-0.0030	NA
	3	3.8 (3785)	1.7850-1.7860	1.7850-1.7860	1.7850-1.7860	1.7850-1.7860	1.7850-1.7860	0.210	0.240	0.0005-0.0035	NA
1989	R	2.5 (2474)	1.8690	1.8690	1.8690	1.8690	1.8690	0.248	0.248	0.0007-0.0027	0.0015-0.0050
	W	2.8 (2835)	1.8678-1.8815	1.8678-1.8815	1.8678-1.8815	1.8678-1.8815	1.8678-1.8815	0.263	0.273	0.0010-0.0040	NA
	T	3.1 (3146)	1.8678-1.8815	1.8678-1.8815	1.8678-1.8815	1.8678-1.8815	1.8678-1.8815	0.263	0.273	0.0010-0.0040	NA
	N	3.3 (3342)	1.7850-1.7860	1.7850-1.7860	1.7850-1.7860	1.7850-1.7860	1.7850-1.7860	0.250	0.255	0.0005-0.0035	NA
1990	R	2.5 (2474)	1.8690	1.8690	1.8690	1.8690	1.8690	0.248	0.248	0.0007-0.0027	0.0020-0.0090
	T	3.1 (3146)	1.8678-1.8815	1.8678-1.8815	1.8678-1.8815	1.8678-1.8815	1.8678-1.8815	0.2626	0.2732	0.0010-0.0040	NA
	N	3.3 (3342)	1.7850-1.7860	1.7850-1.7860	1.7850-1.7860	1.7850-1.7860	1.7850-1.7860	0.250	0.255	0.0005-0.0035	NA
1991	R	2.5 (2474)	1.8690	1.8690	1.8690	1.8690	1.8690	0.248	0.248	0.0007-0.0027	0.0020-0.0090
	T	3.1 (3146)	1.8678-1.8815	1.8678-1.8815	1.8678-1.8815	1.8678-1.8815	1.8678-1.8815	0.2626	0.2732	0.0010-0.0040	NA
	N	3.3 (3342)	1.7850-1.7860	1.7850-1.7860	1.7850-1.7860	1.7850-1.7860	1.7850-1.7860	0.250	0.255	0.0005-0.0035	NA
1992	R	2.5 (2474)	1.8690	1.8690	1.8690	1.8690	1.8690	0.248	0.248	0.0007-0.0027	0.0015-0.0050
	T	3.1 (3146)	1.8678-1.8815	1.8678-1.8815	1.8678-1.8815	1.8678-1.8815	1.8678-1.8815	0.262	0.273	0.0010-0.0040	NA
	N	3.3 (3342)	1.7850-1.7860	1.7850-1.7860	1.7850-1.7860	1.7850-1.7860	1.7850-1.7860	0.250	0.255	0.0005-0.0035	NA
1993	4	2.2 (2195)	1.8670-1.8690	1.8670-1.8690	1.8670-1.8690	1.8670-1.8690	1.8670-1.8690	0.259	0.250	0.0010-0.0039	NA
	M	3.1 (3130)	1.8680-1.8690	1.8680-1.8690	1.8680-1.8690	1.8680-1.8690	1.8680-1.8690	0.273	0.273	0.0010-0.0040	NA
	N	3.3 (3342)	1.7850-1.7860	1.7850-1.7860	1.7850-1.7860	1.7850-1.7860	1.7850-1.7860	0.250	0.255	0.0005-0.0035	NA
1994	4	2.2 (2195)	1.8680-1.8690	1.8680-1.8690	1.8680-1.8690	1.8680-1.8690	1.8680-1.8690	0.288	0.288	0.0010-0.0039	NA
	M	3.1 (3130)	1.8680-1.8690	1.8680-1.8690	1.8680-1.8690	1.8680-1.8690	1.8680-1.8690	0.273	0.273	0.0010-0.0040	NA
1995	4	2.2 (2195)	1.8680-1.8690	1.8680-1.8690	1.8680-1.8690	1.8680-1.8690	1.8680-1.8690	0.288	0.288	0.0010-0.0039	NA
	M	3.1 (3130)	1.8680-1.8690	1.8680-1.8690	1.8680-1.8690	1.8680-1.8690	1.8680-1.8690	0.273	0.273	0.0010-0.0040	NA

NA - Not Available

1 No. 1 bearing: 0.0005-0.0025
  Bearing Nos. 2-5: 0.0005-0.0035
2 0 Spring loaded thrust bearing
3 No. 1 bearing is not boreable and must be replaced separately

86813084

CRANKSHAFT AND CONNECTING ROD SPECIFICATIONS

All measurements are given in inches.

Year	Engine ID/VIN	Engine Displacement Liters (cc)	Crankshaft				Connecting Rod		
			Main Brg. Journal Dia.	Main Brg. Oil Clearance	Shaft End-play	Thrust on No.	Journal Diameter	Oil Clearance	Side Clearance
1982	R	2.5 (2474)	2.9995-2.3005	0.0005-0.0022	0.0035-0.0085	5	1.9995-2.0005	0.0005-0.0026	0.0060-0.0220
	X, Z	2.8 (2835)	2.4397-2.4946	0.0017-0.0030	0.0020-0.0067	3	1.9984-1.9994	0.0014-0.0036	0.0060-0.0170
	E	3.0 (2999)	2.4990-2.5000	0.0003-0.0018	0.0030-0.0090	2	2.2487-2.2495	0.0005-0.0026	0.0023-0.0220
1983	R	2.5 (2474)	2.9995-2.3005	0.0005-0.0022	0.0035-0.0085	5	1.9995-2.0005	0.0005-0.0026	0.0060-0.0220
	X, Z	2.8 (2835)	2.4397-2.4946	0.0017-0.0030	0.0020-0.0067	3	1.9984-1.9994	0.0014-0.0036	0.0060-0.0170
	E	3.0 (2999)	2.4990-2.5000	0.0003-0.0018	0.0030-0.0090	2	2.2487-2.2495	0.0005-0.0026	0.0023-0.0220
	T	4.3 (4293)	2.9993-3.0003	[2]	0.0035-0.0135	4	2.2498-2.2490	0.0004-0.0026	0.0080-0.0214
1984	R	2.5 (2474)	2.9995-2.3005	0.0005-0.0022	0.0035-0.0085	5	1.9995-2.0005	0.0005-0.0026	0.0060-0.0220
	X, Z	2.8 (2835)	2.4397-2.4946	0.0017-0.0030	0.0020-0.0067	3	1.9984-1.9994	0.0014-0.0036	0.0060-0.0170
	E	3.0 (2999)	2.4990-2.5000	0.0003-0.0018	0.0030-0.0090	2	2.2487-2.2495	0.0005-0.0026	0.0023-0.0220
	T	4.3 (4293)	2.9993-3.0003	[2]	0.0035-0.0135	4	2.2498-2.2490	0.0004-0.0026	0.0080-0.0214
1985	R	2.5 (2474)	2.9995-2.3005	0.0005-0.0022	0.0035-0.0085	5	1.9995-2.0005	0.0005-0.0026	0.0060-0.0220
	X	2.8 (2835)	[1]	0.0016-0.0033	0.0020-0.0033	3	1.9993-1.9983	0.0014-0.0037	0.0060-0.0170
	E	3.0 (2999)	2.4990-2.5000	0.0003-0.0090	0.0030-0.0090	2	2.2487-2.2495	0.0005-0.0026	0.0060-0.0220
	3	3.8 (3785)	2.4995	0.0003-0.0018	0.0030-0.0110 [3]	2	2.2487-2.2495	0.0005-0.0026	0.0060-0.0230
	T	4.3 (4293)	2.9993-3.0003	[2]	0.0035-0.0135	4	2.2498-2.2490	0.0004-0.0026	0.0080-0.0214
1986	R	2.5 (2474)	2.9995-2.3005	0.0005-0.0022	0.0035-0.0085	5	1.9995-2.0005	0.0005-0.0026	0.0060-0.0220
	X	2.8 (2835)	[1]	0.0016-0.0033	0.0020-0.0033	3	1.9993-1.9983	0.0014-0.0037	0.0060-0.0170
	B	3.8 (3785)	2.4995	0.0003-0.0018	0.0030-0.0110 [3]	2	2.2487-2.2495	0.0005-0.0026	0.0060-0.0230
	3	3.8 (3785)	2.4995	0.0003-0.0018	0.0030-0.0110	2	2.2487-2.2495	0.0005-0.0026	0.0060-0.0230
1987	R	2.5 (2474)	2.9995-2.3005	0.0005-0.0022	0.0035-0.0085	5	1.9995-2.0005	0.0005-0.0026	0.0060-0.0220
	W	2.8 (2835)	2.6473-2.6483	0.0016-0.0032	0.0024-0.0083	3	1.9994-1.9983	0.0013-0.0026	0.0060-0.0170
	3	3.8 (3785)	2.4995	0.0003-0.0018	0.0030-0.0090	2	2.2487-2.2495	0.0005-0.0026	0.0040-0.0150

86813085

CRANKSHAFT AND CONNECTING ROD SPECIFICATIONS

All measurements are given in inches.

Year	Engine ID/VIN	Engine Displacement Liters (cc)	Crankshaft Main Brg. Journal Dia.	Crankshaft Main Brg. Oil Clearance	Crankshaft Shaft End-play	Crankshaft Thrust on No.	Connecting Rod Journal Diameter	Connecting Rod Oil Clearance	Connecting Rod Side Clearance
1988	R	2.5 (2474)	2.9995-2.3005	0.0005-0.0022	0.0035-0.0085	5	1.9995-2.0005	0.0005-0.0026	0.0060-0.0220
	W	2.8 (2835)	2.6473-2.6438	0.0016-0.0033	0.0020-0.0080	3	1.9983-1.9993	0.0013-0.0026	0.0066-0.0170
	3	3.8 (3785)	2.4988-2.4998	0.0003-0.0018	0.0030-0.0110 [4]	2	2.2487-2.2499	0.0003-0.0028	0.0030-0.0150
1989	R	2.5 (2474)	2.3000	0.0005-0.0022	0.0006-0.0110	5	2.0000	0.0005-0.0030	0.0060-0.0220
	W	2.8 (2835)	2.6473-2.6483	0.0012-0.0027	0.0024-0.0083	3	1.9994-1.9983	0.0014-0.0036	0.0140-0.0270
	T	3.1 (3146)	2.6473-2.6483	0.0012-0.0027	0.0024-0.0083	3	1.9994-1.9983	0.0014-0.0036	0.0140-0.0270
	N	3.3 (3342)	2.4988-2.4998	0.0003-0.0018	0.0030-0.0110	2	2.2487-2.2495	0.0003-0.0026	0.0030-0.0150
1990	R	2.5 (2474)	2.3000	0.0005-0.0022	0.0006-0.0110	5	2.0000	0.0005-0.0030	0.0060-0.0240
	T	3.1 (3146)	2.6473-2.6483	0.0012-0.0030	0.0024-0.0083	3	1.9983-1.9994	0.0110-0.0340	0.0140-0.0270
	N	3.3 (3342)	2.4988-2.4998	0.0003-0.0018	0.0030-0.0110	2	2.2487-2.2499	0.0003-0.0026	0.0030-0.0150
1991	R	2.5 (2474)	2.3000	0.0005-0.0022	0.0006-0.0110	5	2.0000	0.0005-0.0030	0.0060-0.0240
	T	3.1 (3146)	2.6473-2.6483	0.0012-0.0030	0.0024-0.0083	3	1.9983-1.9994	0.0011-0.0034	0.0140-0.0270
	N	3.3 (3342)	2.4988-2.4998	0.0003-0.0018	0.0030-0.0110	2	2.2487-2.2499	0.0003-0.0026	0.0030-0.0150
1992	4	2.2 (2195)	2.4945-2.4954	0.0006-0.0019	0.0020-0.0070	4	1.9983-1.9994	0.0010-0.0031	0.0039-0.0149
	R	2.5 (2474)	2.3000	0.0005-0.0022	0.0005-0.0100	5	2.0000	0.0005-0.0030	0.0060-0.0240
	N	3.3 (3342)	2.4988-2.4998	0.0008-0.0022	0.0030-0.0110	2	2.2487-2.2499	0.0008-0.0022	0.0030-0.0150
1993	4	2.2 (2195)	2.4945-2.4954	0.0006-0.0019	0.0020-0.0070	4	1.9983-1.9994	0.0010-0.0031	0.0039-0.0149
	M	3.1 (3130)	2.6473-2.6483	0.0012-0.0030	0.0024-0.0083	3	1.9982-1.9984	0.0011-0.0037	0.0071-0.0173
	N	3.3 (3342)	2.4988-2.4998	0.0008-0.0022	0.0030-0.0110	2	2.2487-2.2499	0.0008-0.0022	0.0030-0.0150
1994	4	2.2 (2195)	2.4945-2.4954	0.0006-0.0019	0.0020-0.0070	4	1.9983-1.9994	0.00098-0.0031	0.0039-0.0149
	3	2.3 (2261)	2.0470-2.0480	0.0005-0.0023	0.0034-0.0095	3	1.8887-1.8897	0.0005-0.0020	0.0059-0.0177
	M	3.1 (3130)	2.6473-2.6483	0.0012-0.0030	0.0024-0.0083	3	1.9982-1.9984	0.0011-0.0037	0.0071-0.0173
1995	4	2.2 (2195)	2.4945-2.4954	0.0006-0.0019	0.0020-0.0070	4	1.9983-1.9994	0.00098-0.0031	0.0039-0.0149
	M	3.1 (3130)	2.6473-2.6483	0.0012-0.0030	0.0024-0.0083	3	1.9982-1.9984	0.0011-0.0037	0.0071-0.0173

1 Engine ID code on front of block
  Codes A, T: 2.6473-2.6483
  Code K: 2.4937-2.4947

2 Nos. 1-3: 0.0005-0.0021
  No. 4: 0.0020-0.0034

3 Measured at thrust bearing
4 No. 1: 2.4988-2.4998

86813086

PISTON AND RING SPECIFICATIONS

All measurements are given in inches.

Year	Engine ID/VIN	Engine Displacement Liters (cc)	Piston Clearance	Ring Gap			Ring Side Clearance		
				Top Compression	Bottom Compression	Oil Control	Top Compression	Bottom Compression	Oil Control
1982	R	2.5 (2474)	0.0025-0.0033	0.010-0.022	0.010-0.027	0.015-0.055	0.0015-0.0030	0.0015-0.0030	SNUG
	X, Z	2.8 (2835)	0.0017-0.0027	0.010-0.020	0.010-0.020	0.020-0.055	0.0012-0.0028	0.0016-0.0037	0.008
	E	3.0 (2999)	0.0008-0.0020	0.013-0.023	0.013-0.023	0.015-0.035	0.0030-0.0050	0.0030-0.0050	0.0035
1983	R	2.5 (2474)	0.0025-0.0033	0.010-0.022	0.010-0.027	0.015-0.055	0.0015-0.0030	0.0015-0.0030	SNUG
	X, Z	2.8 (2835)	0.0017-0.0027	0.010-0.020	0.010-0.020	0.020-0.055	0.0012-0.0028	0.0016-0.0037	0.008
	E	3.0 (2999)	0.0008-0.0020	0.013-0.023	0.013-0.023	0.015-0.035	0.0030-0.0050	0.0030-0.0050	0.0035
	T	4.3 (4293)	0.0030-0.0040	0.015-0.025	0.015-0.025	0.015-0.055	0.0050-0.0070	0.0030-0.0070	0.001-0.005
1984	R	2.5 (2474)	0.0025-0.0033	0.010-0.022	0.010-0.027	0.015-0.055	0.0015-0.0030	0.0015-0.0030	SNUG
	X, Z	2.8 (2835)	0.0017-0.0027	0.010-0.020	0.010-0.020	0.020-0.055	0.0012-0.0028	0.0016-0.0037	0.008
	E	3.0 (2999)	0.0008-0.0020	0.013-0.023	0.013-0.023	0.015-0.035	0.0030-0.0050	0.0030-0.0050	0.0035
	T	4.3 (4293)	0.0030-0.0040	0.015-0.025	0.015-0.025	0.015-0.055	0.0050-0.0070	0.0030-0.0070	0.001-0.005
1985	R	2.5 (2474)	0.0014-0.0022 [1]	0.010-0.020	0.010-0.020	0.020-0.060	0.0020-0.0030	0.0010-0.0030	0.0150-0.0550
	X	2.8 (2835)	0.0007-0.0017	0.010-0.020	0.010-0.020	0.020-0.055	0.0012-0.0027	0.0016-0.0037	0.0078 MAX
	E	3.0 (2999)	[2]	0.010-0.020	0.010-0.020	0.015-0.055	0.0030-0.0050	0.0030-0.0050	0.0035
	3	3.8 (3785)	[2]	0.010-0.020	0.010-0.020	0.015-0.055	0.0030-0.0050	0.0030-0.0050	0.0035
	T	4.3 (4293)	0.0035-0.0045	0.019-0.027	0.013-0.021	0.015-0.055	0.0050-0.0070	0.0030-0.0050	0.0010-0.005
1986	R	2.5 (2474)	0.0014-0.0022 [1]	0.010-0.020	0.010-0.020	0.020-0.060	0.0020-0.0030	0.0010-0.0030	0.0150-0.0550
	X	2.8 (2835)	0.0007-0.0017	0.010-0.020	0.010-0.020	0.020-0.055	0.0012-0.0027	0.0016-0.0037	0.0078 MAX
	3	3.8 (3785)	[2]	0.010-0.020	0.010-0.020	0.015-0.055	0.0030-0.0050	0.0030-0.0050	0.0035
	B	3.8 (3785)	[2]	0.010-0.020	0.010-0.020	0.015-0.055	0.0030-0.0050	0.0030-0.0050	0.0035
1987	R	2.5 (2474)	0.0014-0.0022 [1]	0.010-0.020	0.010-0.020	0.020-0.060	0.0020-0.0030	0.0010-0.0030	0.0150-0.0550
	W	2.8 (2835)	0.0012-0.0022	0.010-0.020	0.010-0.020	0.020-0.055	0.0010-0.0030	0.0010-0.0030	0.0080 MAX

86813087

PISTON AND RING SPECIFICATIONS

All measurements are given in inches.

Year	Engine ID/VIN	Engine Displacement Liters (cc)	Piston Clearance	Ring Gap			Ring Side Clearance		
				Top Compression	Bottom Compression	Oil Control	Top Compression	Bottom Compression	Oil Control
	3	3.8 (3785)	[2]	0.010-0.020	0.010-0.020	0.015-0.055	0.0030-0.0050	0.0030-0.0050	0.0035
1988	R	2.5 (2474)	0.0014-0.0022 [1]	0.010-0.020	0.010-0.020	0.020-0.060	0.0020-0.0030	0.0010-0.0030	0.0150-0.0550
	W	2.8 (2835)	0.0020-0.0028	0.010-0.020	0.010-0.020	0.020-0.055	0.0010-0.0030	0.0010-0.0030	0.0080 MAX
	3	3.8 (3785)	0.0004-0.0022 [2]	0.010-0.020	0.010-0.022	0.015-0.055	0.0010-0.0030	0.0010-0.0030	0.0005-0.0065
1989	R	2.5 (2474)	0.0014-0.0022 [1]	0.010-0.020	0.010-0.020	0.020-0.060	0.0020-0.0030	0.0010-0.0030	0.0150-0.0550
	W	2.8 (2835)	0.0009-0.0022	0.010-0.020	0.010-0.020	0.001-0.020	0.0020-0.0030	0.0020-0.0035	0.0008-0.0035
	T	3.1 (3146)	0.0009-0.0022	0.010-0.020	0.010-0.020	0.001-0.020	0.0020-0.0030	0.0020-0.0035	0.0008-0.0035
	N	3.3 (3342)	0.0004-0.0022	0.010-0.025	0.010-0.025	0.010-0.040	0.0013-0.0031	0.0013-0.0031	0.0011-0.0081
1990	R	2.5 (2474)	0.0028-0.0048	0.010-0.020	0.010-0.020	0.020-0.060	0.0020-0.0030	0.0010-0.0030	0.0150-0.0550
	T	3.1 (3146)	0.0009-0.0022	0.010-0.020	0.020-0.028	0.010-0.030	0.0020-0.0035	0.0020-0.0035	0.0080 MAX
	N	3.3 (3342)	0.0004-0.0220	0.010-0.025	0.010-0.025	0.010-0.040	0.0013-0.0031	0.0013-0.0031	0.0011-0.0081
1991	R	2.5 (2474)	0.0014-0.0022	0.010-0.020	0.010-0.020	0.020-0.060	0.0020-0.0030	0.0010-0.0030	0.0150-0.0550
	T	3.1 (3146)	0.0009-0.0022	0.010-0.020	0.020-0.028	0.010-0.030	0.0020-0.0035	0.0020-0.0035	0.0080 MAX
	N	3.3 (3342)	0.0004-0.0022	0.010-0.025	0.010-0.025	0.010-0.040	0.0013-0.0031	0.0013-0.0031	0.0011-0.0081
1992	4	2.2 (2195)	0.0007-0.0017	0.010-0.020	0.010-0.020	0.010-0.050	0.0019-0.0027	0.0019-0.0027	0.0019-0.0082
	R	2.5 (2474)	0.0014-0.0022	0.010-0.020	0.010-0.020	0.020-0.060	0.0020-0.0030	0.0010-0.0030	0.0150-0.0550
	N	3.3 (3342)	0.0004-0.0022 [1]	0.010-0.025	0.010-0.025	0.015-0.055	0.0013-0.0031	0.0013-0.0031	0.0011-0.0081
1993	4	2.2 (2195)	0.0007-0.0017	0.010-0.020	0.010-0.020	0.010-0.050	0.0019-0.0027	0.0019-0.0027	0.0019-0.0082
	M	3.1 (3130)	0.0013-0.0027	0.007-0.016	0.020-0.028	0.010-0.030	0.0020-0.0035	0.0020-0.0035	0.0080 MAX
	N	3.3 (3342)	0.0004-0.0022 [1]	0.010-0.025	0.010-0.025	0.015-0.055	0.0013-0.0031	0.0013-0.0031	0.0011-0.0081
1994	4	2.2 (2195)	0.0007-0.0017	0.010-0.020	0.010-0.020	0.010-0.050	0.0019-0.0027	0.0019-0.0027	0.0019-0.0082
	M	3.1 (3130)	0.0013-0.0027	0.007-0.016	0.020-0.028	0.010-0.030	0.0020-0.0035	0.0020-0.0035	0.0080 MAX
1995	4	2.2 (2195)	0.0007-0.0017	0.010-0.020	0.010-0.020	0.010-0.050	0.0019-0.0027	0.0019-0.0027	0.0019-0.0082
	M	3.1 (3130)	0.0013-0.0027	0.007-0.016	0.020-0.028	0.010-0.030	0.0020-0.0035	0.0020-0.0035	0.0080 MAX

NA - Not Available

1 Measured 1/8 down from top of piston

2 Measured at top of piston skirt

86813088

TORQUE SPECIFICATIONS
All readings in ft. lbs.

Year	Engine ID/VIN	Engine Displacement Liters (cc)	Cylinder Head Bolts	Main Bearing Bolts	Rod Bearing Bolts	Crankshaft Damper Bolts	Flywheel Bolts	Manifold		Spark Plugs	Lug Nut
								Intake	Exhaust		
1982	R	2.5 (2474)	92	70	32	200	44	29	44	NA	100
	X	2.8 (2835)	70	68	37	75	50	23	25	7-15	100
	Z	2.8 (2835)	70	68	37	75	50	23	25	7-15	100
	E	3.0 (2999)	80	100	40-45	225	60	32	25-37	13	100
1983	R	2.5 (2474)	92	70	32	200	44	29	44	NA	100
	X	2.8 (2835)	70	68	37	75	50	23	25	7-15	100
	Z	2.8 (2835)	70	68	37	75	50	23	25	7-15	100
	E	3.0 (2999)	80	100	40-45	225	60	32	25-37	13	100
	T	4.3 (4293)	[23]	107	42	200	76	41†	29	NA	100
1984	R	2.5 (2474)	92	70	32	200	44	29	44	NA	100
	X	2.8 (2835)	70	68	37	75	50	23	25	7-15	100
	Z	2.8 (2835)	70	68	37	75	50	23	25	7-15	100
	E	3.0 (2999)	80	100	40-45	225	60	32	25-37	13	100
	T	4.3 (4293)	[23]	107	42	200	76	41	29	NA	100
1985	R	2.5 (2474)	[1]	70	32	200 [2]	[22]	[4]	[4]	15	100
	W	2.8 (2835)	65-90	63-74	34-40	67-85	45	23	22-28	11	100
	X	2.8 (2835)	65-90	63-74	34-40	67-85	[6]	23	22-28	11	100
	E	3.0 (2999)	72	97	40	200	60	35	37	20	100
	3	3.8 (3785)	[6]	100	45	200	60	32	37	20	100
	T	4.3 (4293)	[4]	[23]	42	203	76	41	[8]	-	100
1986	R	2.5 (2474)	[2]	70	32	200 [1]	[22]	[4]	[4]	15	100
	X	2.8 (2835)	65-90	63-74	34-40	67-85	[22]	23	22-28	11	100
	B	3.8 (3785)	[6]	100	45	200	60	32	37	20	100
	3	3.8 (3785)	[6]	100	45	200	60	32	37	20	100
1987	R	2.5 (2474)	[2]	70	32	200 [1]	[22]	[4]	[4]	15	100
	W	2.8 (2835)	[5]	63-83	34-40	67-85	25	15-23	15-23	10-25	100
	3	3.8 (3785)	[6]	100	45	219	32	37	37	20	100
1988	R	2.5 (2474)	[7]	70	32	162 [1]	[22]	[4]	[4]	15	100
	W	2.8 (2835)	[5]	70	37	77	45	18	19	10-25	100
	3	3.8 (3785)	[6]	100	45	219	60	32	37	20	100
1989	R	2.5 (2474)	[7]	65	29	162 [1]	[22]	25	[8]	15	100
	W	2.8 (2835)	[5]	70	37	77	45	18	[8]	10-25	100
	T	3.1 (3146)	[5]	70	37	77	45	18	[8]	20	100
	N	3.3 (3342)	[8]	90	[9]	219	61	7	30	20	100
1990	R	2.5 (2474)	[7]	70	32	162 [1]	[22]	25	[8]	15	100
	T	3.1 (3146)	[5]	73	39	76	45	[11]	18	20	100
	N	3.3 (3342)	[10]	90	[9]	219	61	7	30	20	100

86813666

TORQUE SPECIFICATIONS
All readings in ft. lbs.

Year	Engine ID/VIN	Engine Displacement Liters (cc)	Cylinder Head Bolts	Main Bearing Bolts	Rod Bearing Bolts	Crankshaft Damper Bolts	Flywheel Bolts	Manifold Intake	Manifold Exhaust	Spark Plugs	Lug Nut
1991	R	2.5 (2474)	[7]	65	29	162 [1]	[22]	25	[8]	15	100
	T	3.1 (3146)	[5]	73	39	76	52	[11]	18	20	100
	N	3.3 (3342)	[10]	[12]	[9]	[13]	[21]	7	41	20	100
1992	R	2.5 (2474)	[7]	65	29	162 [1]	55	25	[3]	20	100
	N	3.3 (3342)	[10]	[12]	[9]	[14]	[15]	7	38	12	100
1993	4	2.2 (2195)	[17]	66	38	77	54	24	10	11	100
	N	3.3 (3342)	[10]	[12]	[9]	[16]	[15]	7	38	20	100
1994	4	2.2 (2195)	[17]	70	38	77	55	24	10	[18]	100
	M	3.1 (3130)	[5]	[19]	[20]	76	61	[11]	10	[18]	100
1995	4	2.2 (2195)	[17]	70	38	77	55	24	10	[18]	100
	M	3.1 (3130)	[5]	[19]	[20]	76	61	[11]	10	[18]	100

1 Sprocket retaining bolt
2 Step 1: Tighten all head bolts to 18 ft. lbs.
   Step 2: Tighten all bolts to 22 ft. lbs. except No. 9
   Tighten No. 9 to 29 ft. lbs.
   Step 3: Tighten all 120 dgrees (two flats) except No. 9
   Tighten No. 9 1/4 turn (90 degrees)
3 Inner bolts: 37 ft. lbs.
   Outer bolts: 28 ft. lbs.
4 Refer to text
5 Coat threads with sealer. Torque to 33 ft. lbs. then turn 90 degrees
6 Torque all bolts to 25 ft. lbs.
   Tighten 180 degrees in two steps, not exceeding a total of 60 ft. lbs.
7 Step 1: 18 ft. lbs.
   Step 2: 26 ft. lbs. except I bolt. Retorque I bolt to 18 ft. lbs.
   Step 3: Plus 90 degrees
8 Inner bolts: 37 ft. lbs
   Outer bolts: 26 ft. lbs.
9 20 ft. lbs. plus 50 degrees
10 Step 1: 35 ft. lbs.
   Step 2: Plus 130 degrees
   Step 3: Rotate four center bolts an additional 30 degrees
11 Step 1: 15 ft. lbs.
   Step 2: 24 ft. lbs.
12 26 ft. lbs. plus 50 degrees
13 105 ft. lbs. plus 56 degrees
14 100 ft. lbs. plus 76 degrees
15 11 ft. lbs. plus 50 degrees
16 111 ft. lbs. plus 76 degrees
17 Short bolts: 43 ft. lbs. plus 90 degrees
   Long bolts: 46 ft. lbs. plus 90 degrees
18 New cylinder head:
   1st-time installation: 20 ft. lbs.
   All other installations: 11 ft. lbs.
19 37 ft. lbs. plus 77 degrees
20 15 ft. lbs. plus 75 degrees
21 7 ft. lbs. plus 90 degrees
22 Automatic transaxle: 55 ft. lbs.
   Manual transaxle: 69 ft. lbs.
23 All exc. No. 5,6,11,12,13,14:142 ft. lbs.
   No. 5,6,1,12,13,14:59 ft. lbs.

86813667

Valve/Rocker Cover(s)

REMOVAL & INSTALLATION

▶ See Figure 19

❉❉CAUTION

When draining the coolant, keep in mind that cats and dogs are attracted by ethylene glycol antifreeze, and are quite likely to drink any that is left in an uncovered container or in puddles on the ground. This will prove fatal in sufficient quantity. Always drain the coolant into a sealable container. Coolant should be reused unless it is contaminated or several years old.

2.2L Engine
▶ See Figure 20

  1. Clean all the dirt from around the mating area of the valve cover.
  2. Disconnect the PCV valve from the valve cover.
  3. Remove the valve cover bolts.
  4. Remove the valve cover by tapping it with a rubber mallet. This must be done to break the seal. DON'T attempt to pry the cover off, as it is easily damaged.
  5. Clean the sealing surface on the head and the valve cover with a de-greaser.

To install:
  6. Attach a new gasket in the mating area of the head.
  7. Install the valve cover to the head, tighten the cover bolts to 89 inch lbs. (10 Nm).
  8. Install the PCV valve.
  9. Add engine oil if needed. Start the engine and check for leaks.

1 Bolt
2 Rocker cover
3 Gasket
4 Rocker stud
5 Must be free of oil upon rocker cover gasket installation.
6 Pushrod
7 Rocker arm
8 Ball
9 Nut
10 Spark plug wire support

86813101

Fig. 20 Valve cover and rocker assembly on 2.2L engines

2.5L Engine
▶ See Figure 21

  1. Clean all the dirt from around the mating area of the valve cover.
  2. Remove the air cleaner assembly, being sure to tag all disconnected hoses for reassembly purposes.
  3. Remove the PCV valve and hose from the valve cover grommet.
  4. Remove the spark plug wires from the spark plugs and the locating clips. Be sure to tag the wires so that they may be attached properly.
  5. Remove the crankcase vent tube from the cover.
  6. Remove the EGR valve.
  7. Remove the cover retaining bolts, then the valve cover by tapping it with a rubber mallet. This must be done to break the seal. DON'T attempt to pry the cover off, as it is easily damaged.
  8. Clean the mating surface on the head and valve cover assembly.

86813117

Fig. 19 Always make sure you completely remove all traces of gasket and sealant before installing a valve cover

To install:

9. Install a new valve cover gasket on the cylinder head mating surface, then the cover.

10. Install the valve cover bolts, tighten to 80 inch lbs. (9 Nm).

11. Install the EGR valve with a new gasket.

12. Install the crankcase vent tube to the valve cover.

13. Attach the spark plug wires to the spark plugs, then attach the clip on the cover.

14. Install the air cleaner assembly.

15. Start the engine, check for leaks.

2.8L Engine

▶ **See Figures 22 and 23**

1. Disconnect the negative battery cable at the battery.

2. Clean all the dirt from around the mating area of the valve cover.

3. Remove the air cleaner assembly, being sure to tag all disconnected hoses for reassembly purposes.

➡ **If equipped with an MFI system, remove any component which will interfere with the valve cover removal.**

4. Remove the spark plug wires from the spark plugs and the locating clips. Be sure to tag the wires so that they may be attached properly.

5. Disconnect the accelerator linkage and springs from the carburetor.

6. If your vehicle has an automatic transaxle, disconnect the T.V. (throttle valve) linkage at the carburetor.

7. If your vehicle has cruise control, remove the diaphragm actuator mounting bracket.

8. Remove the air management valve and the necessary hoses (see Section 4).

9. Remove the valve cover retaining bolts, then remove the valve cover. If the cover sticks, tap it loose with a rubber mallet. DON'T attempt to pry it off of the head, as the cover may be easily damaged.

To install:

10. Clean the mating surfaces of the cylinder head and intake manifold with degreaser.

11. Place RTV sealer all around the valve cover sealing surface. When going around the holes always follow the inboard side of the holes.

12. Install the cover and tighten the bolts to 8 ft. lbs. (10 Nm).

13. Install the front engine strut bracket-to-cylinder head. Tighten the bolts to 35 ft., lbs. (48 Nm).

14. Connect all the vacuum hoses and the spark plug wires.

15. Install the front engine strut at the radiator support and engine bracket.

16. Install the air cleaner.

17. Connect the negative battery cable, start the engine, check for leaks.

3.0L and 3.8L Engines

FRONT COVER

1. Disconnect the negative battery cable.

1 Rocker arm cover
2 Rocker arm cover gasket
3 Bolt rocker arm cover bolt tightening sequence:
A, B, C, D, E, F, G

86813105

Fig. 21 Valve cover assembly used on 2.5L engines

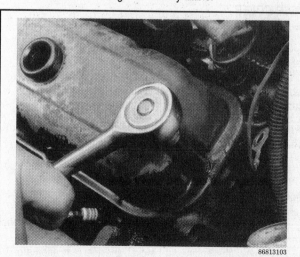

86813103

Fig. 22 Use a deep socket or extension to remove the valve cover retaining bolts

Fig. 23 Lift the valve cover off the head. If necessary, use a rubber mallet to loosen it

2. Clean all the dirt from around the mating area of the valve cover.

3. Remove the crankcase breather tube.

4. Remove the spark plug wire harness cover and disconnect the spark plug wires at the spark plugs.

5. Remove the valve cover nuts, washers, seals and valve cover.

6. Using a putty knife, clean the gasket mounting surfaces.

To install:

7. Install a new gasket to the clean mating area of the cylinder head, then put the valve cover on.

8. Install the valve cover seals, washers and nuts. Tighten the nuts to 7 ft. lbs. (10 Nm).

9. Install the spark plug wire harness on the valve cover, then insert the wires in there proper places. Connect the plug wires to the spark plugs.

10. Connect the crankcase breather tube.

11. Fill the engine oil to the proper fill mark, connect the negative battery cable.

12. Start the engine, check for leaks.

REAR COVER

1. Disconnect the negative battery cable.

2. Clean all the dirt from around the mating area of the valve cover.

3. Remove the C₃I ignition coil module, the spark plug cables, the wiring connectors, the EGR solenoid wiring and vacuum hoses.

➡**If equipped with an MFI system, remove any component which will interfere with the valve cover removal.**

4. Remove the serpentine drive belt.

5. Remove the alternator's wiring connectors, then the mounting bolt and swing the alternator toward the front of the vehicle.

6. Remove the power steering pump from the belt tensioner (move it aside) and the belt tensioner assembly.

7. Remove the engine lift bracket and the rear alternator brace.

8. Drain the cooling system below the level of the heater hose, then disconnect the throttle body heater hoses.

9. Remove the valve cover nuts, the washers, the seals, the valve cover and the gasket.

10. Using a putty knife, clean the gasket mounting surfaces.

11. To install, use a new gasket and reverse the removal procedures. Tighten the valve cover nuts to 7 ft. lbs. (10 Nm.).

3.1L Engine (VIN T)

FRONT COVER

1. Release fuel system pressure and disconnect the negative battery cable.

2. Clean all the dirt from around the mating area of the valve cover.

3. Remove the air cleaner assembly.

4. Drain the cooling system.

5. Disconnect the ignition wire clamps from the coolant tube.

6. Remove the coolant tube mount at head and coolant tube from each end.

7. Remove the coolant tube at the coolant pump and remove the tube.

8. Remove the ignition wire guide.

9. Remove the spark plug wire harness cover and disconnect the spark plug wires at the spark plugs, as needed.

10. Remove the valve cover nuts, washers, seals and valve cover.

11. Using a putty knife, clean the gasket mounting surfaces.

To install:

12. Install a new gasket to the clean mating area of the cylinder head, then put the valve cover on.

13. Install the valve cover seals, washers and nuts. Tighten the nuts to 7 ft. lbs. (10 Nm).

14. Install the spark plug wire harness on the valve cover, then insert the wire in there proper places. Attach the spark plug wires to the plugs if removed.

15. Install the ignition wires and guides.

16. Attach the air cleaner assembly on the engine.

17. Fill the coolant system.

18. Fill the engine oil to the proper fill mark, connect the negative battery cable.

19. Start the engine, top off the cooling system, then check for leaks.

REAR COVER

1. Release fuel system pressure and disconnect the negative battery cable.

2. Drain the cooling system below the level of the heater hose.

3. Clean all the dirt from around the mating area of the valve cover.

4. Remove the hoses at the intake plenum.

5. Remove the airflow tube.

6. Remove the EGR valve crossover pipe.

7. Remove the ignition wire guide.

8. Tag and remove the ignition wires.

9. Disconnect the coolant hoses at the throttle body.

10. Tag and disconnect all electrical connectors to throttle body and that will ease the operation by moving aside.

11. Disconnect the throttle body cables.

12. Remove the bracket at the right side of the intake plenum.

13. Disconnect the power brake booster supply hose.

14. Remove the serpentine belt.
15. Remove the coolant recovery bottle.
16. Remove the exhaust crossover pipe.
17. Remove the alternator and support it out of the way.
18. Remove the PCV valve from the valve cover.
19. Remove the valve cover nuts, the washers, the seals, the valve cover and the gasket.
20. Using a putty knife, clean the gasket mounting surfaces.

To install:

21. Use a new gasket and reverse the removal procedures. Tighten the valve cover nuts to 7 ft. lbs. (10 Nm.).
22. Insert the PCV valve.
23. Install the alternator, exhaust crossover and coolant recovery tank.
24. Install the serpentine drive belt.
25. Attach the brake booster hose.
26. Install the bracket to the right side of the intake plenum.
27. Connect the throttle body cables, electrical connectors and hoses.
28. Install the ignition wires and guides.
29. Install the EGR valve crossover pipe and the airflow tube.
30. Install the vacuum hoses.
31. Fill the radiator and check for leaks.
32. Connect the negative battery cable, install air cleaner. Tighten the air cleaner bolt to 11 ft. lbs. (15 Nm).

3.1L Engine (VIN M)

FRONT COVER

▶ See Figure 24

1. Disconnect the negative battery cable.
2. Drain the cooling system to a level below the coolant pipe on the front of the engine.
3. Remove the coolant bypass hose clamp at the coolant tube.
4. Remove the two bolts and nut securing the coolant tube to the cylinder head and position the tube out of the way.
5. Clean all the dirt from around the mating area of the valve cover.
6. Disconnect the PCV valve from the valve cover.
7. Remove the four valve cover bolts and remove the valve cover.
8. Remove the rocker arm nuts, balls, rocker arms and pushrods.

To install:

9. Clean all the gasket surfaces completely.
10. Coat all the valve train components with engine oil prior to installation.
11. Install the pushrods and install the rocker arms on the studs. Install the rocker arm balls and mounting nuts. Make sure the pushrods are properly seated in the lifter and rocker arm. Tighten the mounting nuts to 18 ft. lbs. (24 Nm).
12. Install the valve cover using a new gasket and tighten the rocker cover bolts to 89 inch lbs. (10 Nm).
13. Connect the PCV valve to the valve cover.
14. Position the coolant tube and connect the thermostat bypass hose.
15. Install the coolant tube mounting nut and bolts. Tighten the screw at the water pump to 106 inch lbs. (12 Nm), the bolt at the corner of the cylinder head to 18 ft. lbs. (25 Nm) and the nut to 18 ft. lbs. (25 Nm).

1 Valve cover and gasket
2 10 Nm (89 lb.in.)
3 Cylinder head
4 Sealer

86813110

Fig. 24 Valve cover assembly used on the 3.1L (VIN M) engine

16. Refill the cooling system.
17. Connect the negative battery cable.
18. Start the vehicle and verify no leaks.

REAR COVER

1. Disconnect the negative battery cable.
2. Disconnect the spark plug wires from the spark plugs and upper intake plenum wire retainer and position out of the way.
3. Disconnect the power brake booster vacuum pipe from the intake plenum.
4. Remove the serpentine belt.
5. Remove the alternator.
6. Disconnect and remove the ignition assembly and EVAP canister purge solenoid as an assembly.
7. Clean all the dirt from around the mating area of the valve cover.
8. Remove the four valve cover bolts and remove the valve cover.
9. Remove the rocker arm nuts, balls, rocker arms and pushrods.

To install:

10. Clean all the gasket surfaces completely.
11. Coat all the valve train components with engine oil prior to installation.
12. Install the pushrods and install the rocker arms on the studs. Install the rocker arm balls and mounting nuts. Make sure the pushrods are properly seated in the lifter and rocker arm. Tighten the mounting nuts to 18 ft. lbs. (25 Nm).
13. Install the valve cover using a new gasket and tighten the rocker cover bolts to 90 inch lbs. (10 Nm).
14. Install the alternator.
15. Install the serpentine belt.
16. Connect the power brake booster vacuum pipe to the plenum.
17. Install the EVAP solenoid and ignition assembly.
18. Connect the spark plug wires to the wire retainers on the plenum and the spark plugs.
19. Refill the cooling system.
20. Connect the negative battery cable.

21. Start the vehicle, top off the cooling system, then verify there are no leaks.

3.3L Engine

FRONT COVER

1. Disconnect the negative battery cable.
2. Remove the serpentine drive belt.
3. Remove the alternator brace bolt and brace.
4. Remove the engine torque strut at the radiator support, then the strut bracket bolts and nuts from the intake and exhaust manifolds.
5. Remove the engine lift bracket, then loosen the engine lift bracket brace bolt.
6. Remove the spark plug wire harness cover and disconnect the spark plug wires at the spark plugs.
7. Clean all the dirt from around the mating area of the valve cover.
8. Remove the valve cover nuts, washers, seals and valve cover.
9. Using a putty knife, clean the gasket mounting surfaces.

To install:

10. Install a new gasket to the cylinder head mating surface, then install the valve cover.
11. Apply thread locking compound to the bolt threads.
12. Insert the valve cover retainer bolts. Tighten the bolts to 89 inch lbs. (10 Nm).
13. Connect the spark plug wires to the plugs and cover.
14. Install the engine lift bracket brace bolt, then the bracket.
15. Secure the engine strut mount bracket bolts and nuts to the intake and exhaust manifolds.
16. Attach the engine torque strut at the radiator support, tighten the bolt to 18 ft. lbs. (24 Nm).
17. Position the alternator, then install the mounting bolts and support brace.
18. Install the serpentine drive belt.
19. Install the negative battery cable, start engine and check for leaks.

REAR COVER

1. Disconnect the negative battery cable.
2. Remove the serpentine drive belt.
3. Loosen the power steering pump bolts and slide the pump forward. Remove the pump braces.
4. Remove the power steering pump from the belt tensioner (move it aside) and the belt tensioner assembly.
5. Clean all the dirt from around the mating area of the valve cover.
6. Remove the valve cover nuts, the washers, the seals, the valve cover and the gasket.
7. Using a putty knife, clean the gasket mounting surfaces.

To install:

8. To install, use a new gasket and reverse the removal procedures. Tighten the valve cover nuts to 7 ft. lbs. (10 Nm.).
9. Reinstall the power steering pump and install the serpentine drive belt.
10. Install the negative battery cable, start engine and check for leaks.

4.3L Diesel Engine

▶ See Figure 25

1. Disconnect the negative battery cable.
2. Remove the fuel injection lines.
3. When removing the right rear cover, disconnect the crankcase ventilation components.
4. Remove the forward engine support strut, which is bolted to the radiator support strut and an engine bracket.
5. Unbolt and remove the strut bracket from the engine.
6. If necessary, remove any additional piece(s) which may interfere with removal of the cover.
7. Clean all the dirt from around the mating area of the valve cover.
8. Unbolt and remove the cover. If the cover sticks, tap it loose with a rubber mallet. DON'T attempt to pry it off of the head, as the cover may be easily damaged.
9. Raise the jack until it just starts to lift the vehicle.
10. Remove the two front body mount bolts from the cradle, along with the cushions and the retainers. Remove the cushions from the bolts.
11. Thread the body mount bolts (with the retainers) back into place, making sure to turn them at least three full turns each.
12. Carefully and slowly lower the jack until the cradle contacts the retainers. While you are lowering the jack, be sure to watch for any component interference and correct as required.

❋❋CAUTION

DO NOT attempt to lower the cradle without the bolts and retainers in place, as this could cause damage of various underhood components.

13. Unbolt and remove the cover. If the cover sticks, tap it loose with a rubber mallet. DON'T attempt to pry it off of the head, as the cover may be easily damaged.

To install:

14. Thoroughly clean the head and valve cover gasket surfaces. Apply RTV sealer or an equivalent to the valve cover.
15. Lubricate the entire valve cover attaching bolt with GM part no. 1052080 or an equivalent.

APPLY LUBE TO ENTIRE BOLT
BOLTS TO BE FULLY DRIVEN,
SEATED AND NOT STRIPPED

APPLY A 3/32" BEAD OF R.T.V. SEALER
ON THE VALVE COVER AS SHOWN

86813111

Fig. 25 Apply RTV sealant to the cover as shown

16. If the right cover was removed, install the crankcase ventilation components.

17. Install the injection lines.

18. Connect the negative battery cable.

Rocker Arm and Pushrod

REMOVAL & INSTALLATION

→When removing the valve train components, they should be kept in the order they were removed.

2.2L Engine

▶ **See Figure 26**

1. Disconnect the negative battery cable.

2. Remove the air cleaner and air duct assembly.

3. Tag and disconnect the spark plug wires from the spark plugs, then disconnect the plug wire clips from the valve cover and position aside.

1 Bolt
2 Rocker cover
3 Gasket
4 Rocker stud
5 Flange, must be free of oil upon rocker cover gasket installation.
6 Pushrod
7 Rocker arm
8 Ball
9 Nut

86813112

Fig. 26 Exploded view of the valve cover and rocker arm assembly on 2.2L engines

4. Disconnect the throttle cables from the throttle body, then remove the cable bracket from the intake plenum and move aside.

5. Remove the valve cover bolts, then remove the cover.

6. Remove the rocker arm nuts, balls and rocker arms.

To install:

7. Clean the gasket surfaces thoroughly.

8. Coat the bearing surfaces of the rocker arms and the arm balls with Molykote® or it's equivalent.

9. Seat the pushrods in the lifters.

10. Install the rocker arms, balls and nuts in the same positions they were removed from. Tighten the nuts to 22 ft. lbs. (30 Nm).

11. Install a new gasket in the valve cover.

12. Install the valve cover on the cylinder head, then tighten the cover bolts to 89 inch lbs. (10 Nm).

13. Install the throttle cable bracket on the intake plenum, then connect the throttle control cables to the throttle body.

14. Attach the spark plug wire clips to the valve cover, then connect the plug wires to the spark plugs.

15. Install the air cleaner an air duct assembly.

16. Connect the negative battery cable.

17. Install fresh oil to the fill line on the dipstick, then start the engine to verify no leaks.

2.5L Engine

▶ **See Figure 27**

1. Remove the air cleaner assembly.

2. Tag and remove the spark plug wires from the plugs and the cover clips.

3. Disconnect and remove the EGR valve.

4. Remove the valve cover.

5. On fuel injected engines relieve pressure in the fuel system before disconnecting any fuel lines.

6. Loosen and remove the rocker arm bolt and balls.

7. Lift the rocker arm off the stud, keeping rocker arms in order for installation.

To install:

8. Position the rocker arms on the studs, then install the arm balls and bolts. Tighten the bolts to 20 ft. lbs. (27 Nm).

9. Attach the valve cover.

10. Install the EGR valve.

11. Attach the plug wire clip to the cover, then attach all the plug wires in there proper locations.

12. Install the air cleaner assembly.

2.8L Engine

▶ **See Figures 28 and 29**

1. Relieve the fuel system pressure.

2. Disconnect the negative battery cable at the battery.

3. Clean all the dirt from around the mating area of the valve cover.

4. Remove the valve cover.

5. Remove the rocker arm nuts, balls and rocker arms, then pull the pushrods from their seats.

To install:

6. Clean the mating surfaces of the cylinder head and intake manifold with degreaser.

7. Coat the bearing surfaces of the rocker arms and the arm balls with Molykote® or it's equivalent.

8. Seat the pushrods in the lifters.

1 Bolt
2 Rocker arm ball
3 Rocker arm
4 Push rod
5 Push rod guide

FRT

86813116

Fig. 27 Rocker arm assembly on 2.5L engines

86813114

Fig. 28 After the nut and ball is removed, lift the rocker arm off the stud

86813115

Fig. 29 If necessary, the pushrod can now be removed as well

9. Install the rocker arms, balls and nuts in the same positions they were removed from. Tighten the nuts to 22 ft. lbs. (30 Nm). Be sure to adjust valve lash after replacing rocker arms.

10. Install the valve covers.

11. Connect the negative battery cable, start the engine, check for leaks.

3.0L and 3.8L Engine

1. Remove the valve cover(s).
2. Remove the rocker arm shaft(s).
3. Place the shaft on a clean surface.
4. Remove the nylon rocker arm retainers.
5. Slide the rocker arms off the shaft and inspect them for wear or damage. Keep them in order!

To install:

6. To install, reverse the removal steps. If new rocker arms are being installed, note that they are stamped R (right) or L (left), meaning that they be used on the right or left of each cylinder, NOT right and left cylinder banks. Each rocker arm must be centered over its oil hole. New nylon retainers must be used.

3.1L Engine (VIN T)

1. Release fuel pressure and disconnect the negative battery cable.
2. Remove the valve covers.
3. Remove the rocker arm nuts.
4. Remove rocker are pivot ball and arms. Keep the parts in order.
5. Remove the pushrods.

➡Keep all components separated. The pushrods are not the same length. Intake pushrods are 6 in. (152mm) long and marked orange, while the exhaust pushrods are 6 ³/₈ in. (162mm) long and marked blue.

To install:

6. Install the pushrods taking care they are in the proper locations.
7. Make sure the pushrods are seated in the lifters.

8. Install the rocker arms, pivots and nuts. They should be coated with prelube (GM 1052365 or equivalent).

9. Tighten the rocker arm nuts to 18 ft. lbs. (25 Nm).

10. Install the valve covers. Install the battery cable.

3.1L Engine (VIN M)

▸ See Figure 30

LEFT SIDE ROCKER ARMS (FRONT)

1. Disconnect the negative battery cable.
2. Remove the valve cover.
3. Remove the rocker arm nuts, balls, rocker arms and pushrods. Keep them in order.

To install:

4. Clean all the gasket surfaces completely.
5. Coat all the valve train components with engine oil prior to installation.
6. Install the pushrods and install the rocker arms on the studs. Install the rocker arm balls and mounting nuts. Make sure the pushrods are properly seated in the lifter and rocker arm. Tighten the mounting nuts to 18 ft. lbs. (24 Nm).
7. Install the valve cover.
8. Connect the negative battery cable.
9. Start the vehicle and verify no leaks.

RIGHT SIDE ROCKER ARMS (REAR)

1. Disconnect the negative battery cable.
2. Remove the valve cover.
3. Remove the rocker arm nuts, balls, rocker arms and pushrods.

To install:

4. Clean all the gasket surfaces completely.
5. Coat all the valve train components with engine oil prior to installation.
6. Install the pushrods and install the rocker arms on the studs. Install the rocker arm balls and mounting nuts. Make sure the pushrods are properly seated in the lifter and rocker arm. Tighten the mounting nuts to 18 ft. lbs. (25 Nm).
7. Install the rocker arm cover using a new gasket and tighten the rocker cover bolts to 90 inch lbs. (10 Nm).
8. Connect the negative battery cable.

1 Pushrod
2 Valve rocker arm stud
3 Valve rocker arm
4 Valve rocker arm pivot ball
5 Valve rocker arm nut

86813118

Fig. 30 Exploded view of the rocker arm assembly used on 3.1L (VIN M) engines

9. Start the vehicle and verify no leaks.

3.3L Engine

1. Release fuel pressure and disconnect the negative battery cable.
2. Remove the valve covers.
3. Remove the rocker arm pedestal bolts.
4. Remove rocker arm and pedestal assembly.

➡**Keep all components in order, if old parts are to be reinstalled they must be installed in the same locations.**

5. Remove the pushrods.

To install:

6. Install the pushrods taking care they are in the proper locations.
7. Make sure the pushrods are seated in the lifters.
8. Install the rocker arm assembly. Coat threads with lock compound (GM 12345493 or equivalent).
9. Tighten the rocker arm bolts to 28 ft. lbs. (38 Nm).
10. Install the valve covers. Install the battery cable.

4.3L Diesel Engine

1. Remove the valve cover(s).
2. Remove the rocker arm nuts, pivot and rocker arms.
3. If rocker arms are being replaced, they must be replaced in cylinder sets. Never replace just one rocker arm per cylinder! If a stud was replaced, coat the threads with locking compound and tighten it to 11 ft. lbs. (15 Nm).

To install:

4. Position the set of rocker arms (for one cylinder) in the proper location.
5. Perform the valve lifter bleed-down procedure. This is absolutely necessary!

✳✳WARNING

If lifters are not bled, engine damage will be unavoidable!

6. Lubricate the wear points with GM part no. 1050169 lubricant or an equivalent, then install the pivots.
7. Install the nuts and tighten alternately. Tighten the bolts to 28 ft. lbs. (37 Nm).

Diesel Engine Valve Lifter Bleed Down

If the rocker arms have been loosened or removed, but the intake manifold was not removed, only the bleed-down procedure need be performed.

REMOVAL

✳✳WARNING

Keep lifters and pushrods in order! This is absolutely necessary for installation, since these parts have differences which could result in engine damage if not installed in their original positions!

1. Remove intake manifold.

2. Remove valve covers, rocker arm assemblies and pushrods.

3. Remove the valve lifter guide retainer bolts.

4. Remove the retainer guides and valve lifters.

DISASSEMBLY

1. Remove the lifters.

2. Remove the retainer ring with a small screwdriver.

3. Remove pushrod seat and oil metering valve.

4. Remove plunger and plunger spring.

5. Remove check valve retainer from plunger, then remove valve and spring.

CLEANING AND INSPECTION

After lifters are disassembled, all parts should be cleaned in clean solvent. A small particle of foreign material under the check valve will cause malfunctioning of the lifter. Close inspection should be made for nicks, burrs or scoring of parts. If either the roller body or plunger is defective, replace with a new lifter assembly. Whenever lifters are removed, check as follows:

1. Roller should rotate freely, but without excessive play.

2. Check for missing or broken needle bearings.

3. Roller should be free of pits or roughness. If present, check camshaft for similar condition. If pits or roughness are evident replace lifter and camshaft.

ASSEMBLY

1. Coat all lifter parts with a coating of clean kerosene or diesel fuel.

2. Assemble the ball check, spring and retainer into the plunger.

3. Install plunger spring over check retainer.

4. Hold plunger with spring up and insert into lifter body. Hold plunger vertically to prevent cocking spring.

5. Submerge the lifter in clean kerosene or diesel fuel.

6. Install oil metering valve and pushrod seat into lifter and install retaining ring.

7. Prime new lifters by working the lifter plunger while submerged in kerosene or diesel fuel.

8. Install the lifters.

9. Preform the bleed-down procedure.

BLEED-DOWN

1. Before installing any removed rocker arms, rotate the engine crankshaft so the No. 1 cylinder is 32° before top dead center. This is a 2 in. (50mm) counterclockwise from the **0** pointer. If only the right valve cover was removed, remove No. 1 cylinder's glow plug to determine if the position of the piston is the correct one. The compression pressure will tell you that you are in the right position. If the left valve cover was re-

moved, rotate the crankshaft until the No. 5 cylinder intake valve pushrod ball is 0.28 in. (7.0mm) above the No. 5 cylinder exhaust valve pushrod ball.

➡**Use only hand wrenches to tighten the rocker arm pivot nuts to avoid engine damage.**

2. If removed, install the No. 5 cylinder pivot and rocker arms. Tighten the nuts alternately between the intake and exhaust valves until the intake valve begins to open, then stop.

3. Install remaining rocker arms except No. 3 exhaust valve. (If this rocker arm was removed).

4. If removed, install, but do not tighten the No. 3 valve pivots beyond the point that the valve would be fully open. This is indicated by strong resistance while still turning the pivot retaining bolts. Going beyond this would bend the pushrod. Tighten the nuts SLOWLY allowing the lifter to bleed down.

5. Finish tightening the No. 5 cylinder rocker arm pivot nut SLOWLY. Do not go beyond the point that the valve would be fully open. This is indicated by strong resistance while still turning the pivot retaining bolts. Going beyond this would bend the pushrod.

6. DO NOT turn the engine crankshaft for at least 45 minutes.

7. Finish reassembling the engine as the lifters are being bled.

➡**Do not rotate the engine until the valve lifters have been bled down, or damage to the engine will occur.**

Thermostat

REMOVAL & INSTALLATION

◆ **See Figures 31, 32, 33 and 34**

1. Disconnect the negative battery cable.

2. Drain the cooling system.

❋❋CAUTION

When draining the coolant, keep in mind that cats and dogs are attracted by ethylene glycol antifreeze, and are quite likely to drink any that is left in an uncovered container or in puddles on the ground. This will prove fatal in sufficient quantity. Always drain the coolant into a sealable container. Coolant should be reused unless it is contaminated or several years old.

3. Some models require you to remove the air cleaner assembly from the throttle body.

4. Some models with cruise control have a vacuum modulator attached to the thermostat housing with a bracket. It your vehicle is equipped as such, remove the bracket from the housing.

5. On the 4-cylinder engines, unbolt the water outlet from the thermostat housing, remove the outlet from the housing and lift the thermostat out of the housing. On all other models, unbolt the water outlet from the intake manifold, remove the outlet and lift the thermostat out of the manifold.

Fig. 31 Loosen the clamp securing the hose to the thermostat housing

Fig. 32 Remove the bolts securing the housing, then pull it away

Fig. 33 Make a note as to which end of the thermostat fits in the housing

To install:

6. Clean both of the mating surfaces and run a ⅛ in. (3mm) bead of R.T.V. (Room Temperature Vulcanizing) sealer in the groove of the water outlet.

7. Install the thermostat (spring towards engine) and bolt the water outlet into place while the R.T.V. sealer is still wet. Tighten the bolts 17-21 ft. lbs. (23-28 Nm) on all but the 2.2L engine. Other engines tighten to 89 inch lbs. (10 Nm).

8. The remainder of the installation is the reverse of removal. Fill the cooling system, start the engine and top off. Check for leaks after the car is started and correct as required.

Intake Manifold

REMOVAL & INSTALLATION

✳✳CAUTION

When draining the coolant, keep in mind that cats and dogs are attracted by ethylene glycol antifreeze, and are quite likely to drink any that is left in an uncovered container or in puddles on the ground. This will prove fatal in sufficient quantity. Always drain the coolant into a sealable container. Coolant should be reused unless it is contaminated or several years old.

2.2L Engine
▶ See Figure 35

UPPER INTAKE

1. Disconnect the throttle body from the air cleaner air inlet duct.

2. Remove the accelerator control cable bracket at the manifold and valve cover.

3. Remove the brake vacuum booster hose from the manifold.

4. Disconnect the MAP sensor connection and, then remove the sensor.

Fig. 34 Make sure both of the mating surfaces are free of any old gasket material

5. Disconnect the vacuum harness at the throttle body.

6. Remove the electrical connections at the throttle body and intake manifold.

7. Remove the intake manifold bolts and studs.

8. Remove the manifold and gasket.

To install:

9. Install the manifold and gasket.

10. Install the bolts and studs, tighten to 22 ft. lbs. (30 Nm).

11. Attach the electrical connections to the throttle body and intake manifold.

12. Reinstall the vacuum harness to the throttle body.

13. Install the MAP sensor and connection.

14. Install the brake booster hose to the manifold.

15. Attach the accelerator cable bracket to the manifold and valve cover. Tighten the bolts to 18 ft. lbs. (25 Nm).

16. Install the throttle body to the air cleaner.

LOWER INTAKE

1. Disconnect the negative battery cable.

2. Drain the cooling system.

3. Remove the air cleaner and duct assembly.

1 Bolt
2 Stud
3 Upper intake manifold assembly
4 Gasket
5 Lower intake manifold
6 EGR valve injector
A Upper intake manifold assembly
  tightening sequence

86813123

Fig. 35 Exploded view of the intake manifold assembly used on 2.2L engines

4. Rotate the engine forwards.

5. Disconnect the throttle control cable bracket.

6. Remove the electrical connections from the:
   - Throttle body
   - Fuel injector
   - Wiring harness clip from under the manifold

7. Remove the vacuum hoses from:
   - Intake manifold
   - Plenum
   - EGR valve

8. Remove the power steering pump bracket from the intake manifold brace.

9. Tag and remove the spark plug wires.

10. Relieve the fuel system pressure. This is extremely important.

11. Disconnect the fuel lines, set aside.

12. Remove the transaxle fluid level indicator tube retaining nut, position aside.

13. Remove the nuts and manifold with the plenum attached, then clean all the gasket surfaces on the cylinder head and intake manifold.

To install:

14. Install a new gasket and intake manifold with the plenum attached, then install and tighten the retaining nuts to 24 ft. lbs. (33 Nm).

15. Install the transaxle fluid level indicator tube retaining nut.

16. Attach the fuel lines.

17. Connect the spark plug wires in ther proper locations.

18. Attach the power steering pump bracket to the intake manifold brace.

19. Install the vacuum hoses from:
   - Intake manifold
   - Plenum
   - EGR valve

20. Attach the electrical connections to the:
   - Throttle body
   - Fuel injector
   - Wiring harness clip from under the manifold

21. Attach the throttle body cable bracket, then connect the cables to the throttle body.

22. Rotate the engine to it's proper position.

23. Assemble the air cleaner and air duct to the engine.

24. Refill the engine coolant.

25. Connect the negative battery cable, then start the engine, top off the coolant.

2.5L Engine

▶ See Figure 36

1. Relieve the fuel system pressure.

2. Remove the air cleaner and the PCV valve.

3. Drain the cooling system into a clean container.

4. Disconnect the fuel and vacuum lines and the electrical connections at the carburetor/throttle body and manifold.

5. Disconnect the throttle linkage at the EFI unit and disconnect the transaxle downshift linkage and cruise control linkage.

6. Remove the carburetor and the spacer.

7. Remove the bell crank and the throttle linkage. Position to the side for clearance.

8. Remove the heater hose at the intake manifold.

1 Intake manifod gasket
2 Intake manifold
3 Bolt to 34 Nm (25 ft.lb.)
4 Engine lift bracket
5 Ignition cable harness bracket

TIGHTENING SEQUENCE

86813124

Fig. 36 Intake manifold assembly used on 2.5L engines

9. Remove the pulse air check valve bracket from the manifold.

10. Remove the manifold attaching bolt and remove the manifold.

11. To install, reverse the removal procedure.

2.8L Engine

CARBURETED ENGINE

▶ **See Figures 37, 38, 39 and 40**

1. Remove the rocker covers.

2. Drain the cooling system.

3. If equipped, remove the AIR pump and bracket.

4. Remove the distributor cap. Mark the position of the ignition rotor in relation to the distributor body, and remove the distributor. Do not crank the engine with the distributor removed.

5. Remove the heater and radiator hoses from the intake manifold.

6. Remove the power brake vacuum hose.

7. Disconnect and label the vacuum hoses. Remove the EFE pipe from the rear of the manifold.

8. Remove the carburetor linkage. Disconnect and plug the fuel line.

9. Remove the manifold retaining bolts/nuts.

10. Remove the intake manifold. Remove and discard the gaskets, and scrape off the old silicone seal from the front and rear ridges.

To install:

11. The gaskets are marked for right and left side installation; do not interchange them. Clean the sealing surface of the engine block, and apply a $\frac{3}{16}$ in. (5mm) bead of silicone sealer to each ridge.

12. Install the new gaskets onto the heads. The gaskets will have to be cut slightly to fit past the center pushrods. Do not cut any more material than necessary. Hold the gaskets in place by extending the ridge bead of sealer $\frac{1}{4}$ in. (6mm) onto the gasket ends.

13. Install the intake manifold. The area between the ridges and the manifold should be completely sealed.

86813139

Fig. 37 Use a deep socket to loosen the manifold retainers

86813141

Fig. 38 Make sure all wiring and hoses are disconnected before removing the manifold

Fig. 39 Always discard the old gasket

14. Install the retaining bolts and nuts, and tighten in sequence to 23 ft. lbs. (31 Nm). Do not overtighten; the manifold is made from aluminum, and can be warped or cracked with excessive force.

15. The rest of installation is the reverse of removal. Adjust the ignition timing after installation, and check the coolant level after the engine has warmed up.

FUEL INJECTED

▶ See Figure 40

1. Relieve the pressure in the fuel system before disconnecting any fuel line connections.
2. Disconnect the negative battery cable.
3. Remove the accelerator and TV cable bracket at the intake plenum.
4. Unsecure the throttle body at the intake plenum.
5. Disconnect the EGR valve at the intake plenum.
6. Remove the intake plenum.
7. Unfasten the fuel inlet and return pipes at the fuel rail.
8. Remove the serpentine belt.
9. Remove the power steering pump and lay it aside.

Fig. 40 Intake manifold tightening sequence for 2.8L engines

10. Disconnect the alternator and lay it aside.
11. Loosen the alternator bracket.
12. Separate the idle air vacuum hose at the throttle body.
13. Unfasten the wires at the injectors.
14. Remove the fuel rail.
15. Remove the breather tube.
16. Remove both rocker covers.
17. Drain the cooling system.
18. Separate the radiator hose at the thermostat housing.
19. Disconnect the wires at the coolant sensor and the oil sending switch.
20. Remove the coolant sensor.
21. Disconnect the bypass hose at the fill neck and head.
22. Loosen the rocker arms and remove the pushrods.
23. Remove the intake manifold bolts and remove the intake manifold.

To install:

24. Place a ⁹⁄₁₆ in. (5mm) diameter bead of GM sealer 1052917 or equivalent, on each ridge.
25. Position a new intake manifold gasket.
26. Install the pushrods and tighten the rocker arm nuts to 14-20 ft. lbs. (19-27 Nm).
27. Install the intake manifold and tighten the bolts in sequence.
28. Connect the bypass hose to the filler neck and head.
29. Install the coolant sensor.
30. Attach the wires to the coolant sensor and the oil sending switch.
31. Connect the radiator hose to the thermostat housing.
32. Install both rocker covers.
33. Install the breather tube.
34. Connect the fuel rail.
35. Connect the wires to the injectors.
36. Connect the idle air vacuum hose to the throttle body.
37. Tighten the alternator bracket.
38. Attach the alternator electrical connectors.
39. Install the power steering pump.
40. Install the serpentine belt.
41. Connect the fuel inlet and return pipes to the fuel rail.
42. Install the intake plenum.
43. Attach the EGR valve to the intake plenum.
44. Connect the throttle body to the intake plenum.
45. Connect the accelerator and TV cable bracket to the intake plenum.
46. Connect the negative battery cable.
47. Fill cooling system and check for leaks. Start the engine and allow to come to normal operating temperature. Check for leaks and top off the coolant.
48. Adjust the valve, as required.

3.0L Engine

▶ See Figure 41

1. Relieve the fuel system pressure.
2. Disconnect the battery ground.
3. Drain the cooling system.
4. Remove the air cleaner.
5. Disconnect all hoses and wiring from the manifold.
6. Disconnect the accelerator linkage and cruise control chain.

➡ **If equipped with an MFI system, remove any component which will interfere with the intake manifold removal.**

7. Disconnect the fuel line.

8. Remove the distributor cap and rotor to remove the Torx® head bolt from the left side of the manifold.

9. Unbolt and remove the manifold.

To install:

10. Place a new intake manifold gasket and rubber manifold seals in position at the front and rear rails of the cylinder block. Make sure the pointed end of the seal fits snugly against the block and head.

11. Before installing the intake seals, apply silicone sealer to each ends of the seals.

12. Install the one piece manifold gasket, then carefully set the intake on the engine block.

13. Insert the head to manifold bolts. A new gasket and seals must be used when a manifold is removed.

14. When installing the manifold, start with number 1 and 2 bolts, then gradually tighten both bolts until snug. Continue with the rest of the bolts in sequence, tighten to 41 ft. lbs. (55 Nm).

15. Reverse the removal for installation.

16. Connect the negative battery cable.

17. Close the drainplug and fill the radiator. Start the engine, top off the coolant.

3.1L Engine (VIN T)

▶ See Figure 42

1. Relieve the pressure in the fuel system before disconnecting any fuel line connections.

2. Disconnect the negative battery cable.

3. Separate the accelerator and TV cable bracket at the intake plenum.

4. Disconnect the throttle body at the intake plenum.

5. Remove the EGR valve at the intake plenum.

6. Remove the intake plenum.

7. Detach the fuel inlet and return pipes at the fuel rail.

8. Remove the serpentine belt.

9. Remove the power steering pump and lay it aside.

10. Disconnect the alternator and lay it aside.

11. Loosen the alternator bracket.

12. Unsecure the idle air vacuum hose at the throttle body.

13. Disconnect the wires at the injectors.

86813126

Fig. 41 Intake manifold tightening sequence for 3.0L engines

14. Separate the fuel rail from the vehicle.

15. Remove the breather tube.

16. Remove both rocker covers.

17. Drain the cooling system.

18. Separate the radiator hose from the thermostat housing.

19. Disconnect the wires at the coolant sensor and the oil sending switch.

20. Remove the coolant sensor.

21. Disconnect the bypass hose at the fill neck and head.

22. Loosen the rocker arms and remove the pushrods.

23. Remove the intake manifold bolts and remove the intake manifold.

To install:

24. Place a ³⁄₁₆ in. (5mm) diameter bead of GM sealer 1052917 or equivalent, on each ridge.

25. Position a new intake manifold gasket.

26. Install the pushrods and tighten the rocker arm nuts to 14-20 ft. lbs. (19-27 Nm).

27. Install the intake manifold and tighten the bolts to specifications.

28. Attach the bypass hose to the filler neck and head.

29. Install the coolant sensor.

30. Connect the wires to the coolant sensor and the oil sending switch.

31. Secure the radiator hose to the thermostat housing.

32. Install both rocker covers.

33. Install the breather tube.

34. Connect the fuel rail.

35. Connect the wires to the injectors.

36. Connect the idle air vacuum hose to the throttle body.

37. Tighten the alternator bracket.

38. Connect the alternator electrical connectors.

39. Install the power steering pump.

40. Install the serpentine belt.

41. Connect the fuel inlet and return pipes to the fuel rail.

42. Install the intake plenum.

43. Connect the EGR valve to the intake plenum.

44. Connect the throttle body to the intake plenum.

45. Connect the accelerator and TV cable bracket to the intake plenum.

46. Connect the negative battery cable.

47. Fill cooling system and check for leaks. Start the engine and allow to come to normal operating temperature. Recheck for leaks. Top-up coolant.

48. Adjust the valve, as required.

3.1L Engine (VIN M)

▶ See Figure 42

❋❋CAUTION

The fuel system is under pressure and must be properly relieved before disconnecting the fuel lines. Failure to properly relieve the fuel system pressure can lead to personal injury and component damage.

1. Relieve the fuel system pressure.

2. Disconnect the negative battery cable.

3. Remove top half of the air cleaner assembly and throttle body duct.

4. Drain the cooling system.

5. Remove the EGR pipe from exhaust manifold.

1 22 N·m (16 LB. FT.)
   THEN 32 N·m (23 LB. FT.)
   RETORQUE 32 N·m
   (23 LB. FT.) IN SEQUENCE

   ⑦ ④ ③ ⑥
   ⑧ ① ② ⑤

86813128

Fig. 42 Tightening sequence for 3.1L engines

6. Remove the serpentine belt.

7. Remove the brake vacuum pipe at the intake plenum.

8. Disconnect the control cables from the throttle body and intake plenum mounting bracket.

9. Remove the power steering lines at the alternator bracket.

10. Remove the alternator.

11. Disconnect the spark plug wires from the spark plugs and wire retainers on the intake plenum.

12. Remove the ignition assembly and the EVAP canister purge solenoid together.

13. Disconnect the upper engine wiring harness connectors at the following components:
   - Throttle Position Sensor (TPS)
   - Idle Air Control (IAC)
   - Fuel Injectors
   - Coolant temperature sensor
   - MAP sensor
   - Camshaft Position (CMP) sensor

14. Disconnect the vacuum lines from the following components:
   - Vacuum modulator
   - Fuel pressure regulator
   - PCV valve

15. Remove the MAP sensor from upper intake manifold.

16. Remove the upper intake plenum mounting bolts and remove the plenum.

17. Disconnect the fuel lines from the fuel rail and fuel line bracket.

18. Install engine support fixture special tool J 28467-A or an equivalent.

19. Remove the right side engine mount.

20. Remove the power steering mounting bolts and support the pump out of the way without disconnecting the power steering lines.

21. Disconnect the coolant inlet pipe from coolant outlet housing.

22. Remove the coolant bypass hose from the water pump and the cylinder head.

23. Disconnect the upper radiator hose at thermostat housing.

24. Remove the thermostat housing.

25. Remove both rocker arm covers.

26. Remove the lower intake manifold bolts. Make sure the washers on the four center bolts are installed in their original locations.

➡**When removing the valve train components they should be kept in order for installation the original locations.**

27. Remove the rocker arm retaining nuts and remove the rocker arms and pushrods.

28. Remove the intake manifold from the engine.

   To Install:

29. Clean gasket material from all mating surfaces. Remove all excess RTV sealant from front and rear ridges of cylinder block.

30. Place a 0.1 in. (3mm) bead of RTV, on each ridge, where the front and rear of the intake manifold contact the block.

31. Using a new gasket, install the intake manifold to the engine.

32. Install the pushrods, rocker arms and mounting nuts. Make sure the pushrods are properly seated in the valve lifters and rocker arms.

33. Install rocker arm nuts and tighten the rocker arm nuts to 18 ft. lbs. (24 Nm).

34. Install lower the intake manifold attaching bolts. Apply sealant GM part no. 12345739 or equivalent to the threads of bolts, and tighten bolts to 115 inch lbs. (13 Nm).

35. Install the front rocker arm cover.

36. Install the thermostat housing.

37. Connect the upper radiator hose to the thermostat housing.

38. Install the coolant inlet pipe to thermostat housing.

39. Install coolant bypass pipe at the water pump and cylinder head.

40. Install the power steering pump in the mounting bracket.

41. Connect the right side engine mount.

42. Remove the special engine support tool.

43. Connect the fuel lines to fuel rail and bracket.

44. Install the upper intake manifold and tighten the mounting bolts to 18 ft. lbs. (25 Nm).

45. Install the MAP sensor.

46. Connect the upper engine wiring harness connectors to the following components:
   - Throttle Position Sensor (TPS)
   - Idle Air Control (IAC)
   - Fuel Injectors
   - Coolant temperature sensor
   - MAP sensor
   - Camshaft Position (CMP) sensor

47. Connect the vacuum lines to the following components:
   - Vacuum modulator
   - Fuel pressure regulator
   - PCV valve

48. Install the EVAP canister purge solenoid and ignition assembly.

49. Install the alternator assembly.

50. Connect the power steering line to the alternator bracket.

51. Install the serpentine belt.

52. Connect the spark plug wires to the spark plugs and intake plenum wire retainer.

53. Install the EGR pipe to the exhaust manifold.

54. Connect the control cables to the throttle body lever and upper intake plenum mounting bracket.

55. Install air intake assembly and top half of the air cleaner assembly.

56. Install the brake vacuum pipe.

57. Fill the cooling system.

58. Connect the negative battery cable.

59. Start the vehicle and verify no leaks exist.

3.3L Engine

♦ See Figure 43

1. Relieve the pressure in the fuel system before disconnecting any fuel line connections.

2. Disconnect the negative battery cable.

3. Drain the cooling system.

4. Remove the serpentine belt, alternator and braces and power steering pump braces.

5. Remove the coolant bypass hose, heater pipe and upper radiator hose.

6. Remove the air inlet duct, throttle cable bracket and cables.

7. Disconnect and tag all vacuum hoses and electrical connectors, as necessary.

8. Remove the fuel rail, vapor canister purge line and heater hose from the throttle body.

9. Remove the intake manifold retaining bolts and intake manifold.

To install:

10. Clean the cylinder head and intake manifold surfaces from any foreign matter, nicks or heavy scratches.

11. Apply sealer GM part no. 12345336 or equivalent, to the ends of the manifold seals. Clean the intake manifold bolts and bolt holes. Apply thread lock compound GM part no. 1052624 or equivalent, to the intake manifold bolt threads before assembly.

12. Install the new gasket and intake manifold. Tighten the intake manifold bolts twice to 88 inch lbs. (10 Nm) in the proper sequence.

13. Install the fuel rail, vapor canister purge line and heater hose from the throttle body.

14. Connect all vacuum hoses and electrical connectors.

15. Install the air inlet duct, throttle cable bracket and cables.

16. Install the coolant bypass hose, heater pipe and upper radiator hose.

17. Install the serpentine belt, alternator and braces and power steering pump braces.

18. Connect the negative battery cable.

19. Fill cooling system and check for leaks. Start the engine and allow to come to normal operating temperature. Recheck for leaks.

3.8L Engine

♦ See Figure 44

1. Relieve the pressure in the fuel system before disconnecting any fuel line connections.

2. Disconnect the negative battery cable.

3. Remove the mass air flow sensor and air intake duct.

4. Remove the serpentine accessory drive belt, alternator and bracket.

5. Remove the ignition coil module, TV cable, throttle cable and cruise control cable.

6. Disconnect and tag all vacuum hoses and electrical wiring, as necessary.

7. Drain the cooling system. Remove the heater hoses from the throttle body and upper radiator hose.

8. Disconnect the fuel lines from the fuel rail and injectors.

9. Remove the intake manifold retaining bolts and remove the intake manifold and gasket.

To install:

10. Clean the cylinder head and intake manifold surfaces from any foreign matter, nicks or heavy scratches.

11. Install the intake manifold gasket and rubber seals. Apply sealer GM part no. 1050026 or equivalent, on the gasket. Apply sealer/lubricant GM part no. 1052080 or equivalent, to all pipe thread fitting.

12. Carefully install the intake manifold to cylinder block. Install the intake manifold bolts and tighten in sequence to the specified value.

13. Connect the fuel lines to the fuel rail and injectors.

14. Install the heater hoses to the throttle body and upper radiator hose.

86813130

Fig. 43 Intake manifold tightening sequence for 3.3L engines

86813129

Fig. 44 Intake manifold tightening sequence for 3.8L engines

15. Connect all vacuum hoses and electrical wiring.
16. Install the ignition coil module, TV cable, throttle cable and cruise control cable.
17. Install the bracket, alternator and serpentine belt.
18. Install the mass air flow sensor and air intake duct.
19. Connect the negative battery cable.
20. Fill cooling system and check for leaks. Start the engine and allow to come to normal operating temperature. Recheck for leaks.

4.3L Diesel Engine

▶ **See Figure 45**

1. Remove the air cleaner assembly.
2. Drain the radiator, then disconnect the upper radiator hose from the water outlet.
3. Disconnect the heater inlet hose from the outlet on intake manifold and disconnect the heater outlet pipe from the intake manifold attachments and move it aside.
4. Remove air crossover and the fuel injection pump.
5. Disconnect wiring as necessary at the alternator and air conditioning compressor (if so equipped).
6. Remove the cruise control servo if so equipped.
7. Remove the air conditioning compressor bracket and brace bolts and position the compressor (if so equipped) with lines attached out of the way.
8. Remove the alternator assembly.
9. Disconnect the engine mounting strut.
10. Remove the fuel lines, filter and brackets. Cap all openings.
11. Disconnect the electrical leads to the glow plug controller and sending units.
12. Disconnect the exhaust crossover pipe heat shield.
13. Remove the left (forward) injection lines and cap all openings. Use backup wrench on the nozzles.
14. Disconnect the throttle and TV cables from the bracket.
15. Remove the drain tube.
16. Remove the intermediate pump adapter.
17. Remove pump adapter and seal.
18. Remove the intake manifold.

To install:

19. Disassemble and bleed-down the lifters. Refer to the procedure earlier in this section.
20. Clean the machined surfaces of cylinder head and intake manifold with a putty knife. Use care not to gouge or scratch the machined surfaces. Clean all bolts and bolt holes.
21. Coat both sides of gasket sealing surface that seal the intake manifold to the head with GM part no. 1050026 sealer or equivalent and position intake manifold gasket. Install end seals, making sure that ends are positioned under the cylinder heads. The seals and mating surfaces must be dry. Any liquid, including sealer will act as a lubricant and cause the seal to move during assembly. Use RTV sealer only on each end of the seal.
22. Position intake manifold on engine. Lubricate the entire intake manifold bolt with lubricant GM part no. 1052080 or equivalent.
23. Tighten the bolts in sequence shown to 20 ft. lbs. (27 Nm). Then retighten to 41 ft. lbs. (56 Nm).
24. Install the drain tube.
25. Install the pump adapter.
26. Apply chassis lube to seal area of intake manifold and pump adapter.
27. Apply chassis lube to inside and outside diameter of seal and seal area of tool J-28425.
28. Install seal on tool and install the seal.
29. Install intermediate pump adapter.
30. Reverse the order of removal and install all other removed parts except the air crossover.
31. Fill the cooling system.
32. Install manifold covers, J-29657.
33. Start engine and check for leaks.
34. Check and if necessary, reset the injection pump timing.
35. Remove screen covers from manifold.
36. Install air crossover.
37. Install the air cleaner.
38. Road test car and inspect for leaks.

Exhaust Manifold

REMOVAL & INSTALLATION

2.2L Engine

▶ **See Figure 46**

1. Disconnect the negative battery cable.
2. Remove the air cleaner and air inlet duct.
3. Remover the lower air inlet duct.
4. Remove the engine drive belt, then remove the alternator.
5. Unsecure the engine torque strut bracket from the cylinder head.
6. Loosen and remove the alternator bracket.
7. Raise and support the vehicle safely.
8. Remove the two bolts securing the exhaust pipe to the exhaust manifold.
9. Lower the vehicle.
10. Remove the dipstick tube mounting bolt, then the dipstick tube and stick.

86813131

Fig. 45 Tightening sequence for the 4.3L engine

11. Disconnect the electrical harness to the Oxygen sensor (O_2) sensor.

12. Unsecure the manifold mounting bolts/nuts, then remove the manifold.

To install:

13. Clean all the gasket surfaces completely.

14. Install the exhaust manifold, then tighten the mounting bolts to 116 inch lbs. (13 Nm).

15. Connect the O_2 sensor harness to the sensor.

16. Attach the dipstick tube with it's mounting bolt.

17. Raise and support the vehicle.

18. Connect the front exhaust pipe to the exhaust manifold, then tighten the mounting bolts to 18 ft. lbs. (25 Nm).

19. Lower the vehicle.

20. Install the alternator rear support bracket, then tighten the three mounting bolts to 74 ft. lbs. (100 Nm).

21. Install the engine torque strut bracket to the engine, then tighten the nuts to 41 ft. lbs. (56 Nm) and the bolt to 40 ft. lbs. (55 Nm).

22. Attach the torque strut, then tighten the bolts to 40 ft. lbs. (55 Nm).

23. Attach the alternator to the engine.

24. Install the drive belt.

25. Attach the lower air intake duct, then the air intake resonator to the upper tie bar.

26. Install the air cleaner and duct work.

27. Connect the negative battery cable.

28. Start the vehicle, then check for leaks.

2.5L Engine

1. Disconnect the negative battery cable. Remove the air cleaner and the preheat tube.

2. Remove the manifold strut bolts from the radiator support panel and the cylinder head.

3. Remove the air conditioning compressor bracket to one side. Do not disconnect any of the refrigerant lines.

4. If necessary, remove the dipstick tube attaching bolt and the engine mount bracket from the cylinder head.

5. Raise the vehicle and support safely. Disconnect the exhaust pipe from the manifold.

6. Remove the manifold attaching bolts, then remove the manifold and gasket.

To install:

7. Clean all the gasket surfaces completely.

8. Install the exhaust manifold and gasket to the cylinder head. Tighten all bolts in sequence to the specified value. The outside bolts to 28 ft. lbs. (38 Nm), and the inside bolts to 37 ft. lbs. (50 Nm).

9. Connect the exhaust pipe to the manifold. Lower the vehicle.

10. Install the dipstick tube attaching bolt and the engine mount bracket to the cylinder head.

11. Install the air conditioning compressor bracket.

12. Install the manifold strut bolts to the radiator support panel and the cylinder head.

13. Install the air cleaner and the preheat tube.

14. Connect the negative battery cable.

2.8L Engine

▶ **See Figures 47 and 48**

LEFT SIDE

1. Remove the air cleaner. Remove the exhaust crossover pipe.

2. Remove the air supply plumbing from the exhaust manifold, if equipped.

3. Raise and support the car. Unbolt and remove the exhaust pipe at the manifold.

4. Unbolt and remove the manifold and gasket.

To install:

5. Clean the mating surfaces of the cylinder head and manifold. Install the manifold and gasket to the head, then install the retaining bolts finger-tight.

6. Tighten the manifold bolts in a circular pattern, working from the center to the ends, to 25 ft. lbs. (34 Nm) in two stages.

7. Connect the exhaust pipe to the manifold.

8. The remainder of installation is the reverse of removal.

RIGHT SIDE

1. Disconnect the negative battery cable.

Fig. 46 Exhaust manifold assembly used on 2.2L engines

1 Stud
2 Gasket
3 Exhaust manifold
4 Nut

86813160

Fig. 47 If necessary, disconnect the crossover pipe from the exhaust manifold

86813151

Fig. 48 Once the retaining bolts are removed, the exhaust manifold can be removed from the engine

2. Raise and safely support the vehicle.
3. Disconnect the exhaust pipe and lower the vehicle.
4. Remove the air cleaner assembly, breather, mass air flow sensor and heat shield.
5. Remove the crossover at the manifold.
6. Remove the accelerator and TV cables and brackets, as required.
7. Remove the exhaust manifold retaining bolts, then remove the manifold and gasket.

To install:
8. Clean all the gasket surfaces completely.
9. Install the exhaust manifold and gasket with the retaining bolts. Tighten to 15-22 ft. lbs. (20-30 Nm).
10. If removed, install the accelerator, TV cables and brackets.
11. Install the crossover at the manifold.
12. Install the air cleaner assembly, breather, mass air flow sensor and heat shield.
13. Raise and safely support the vehicle.
14. Connect the exhaust pipe and lower the vehicle.
15. Connect the negative battery cable.

3.0L Engine

LEFT SIDE

1. Disconnect the battery ground.
2. Unbolt and remove the crossover pipe.
3. Remove the upper engine support strut.
4. Unbolt and remove the manifold and gasket.

To install:
5. Clean all the gasket surfaces completely.
6. Install the exhaust manifold, making sure the new gasket is in place.
7. Tighten the mounting bolts for the manifold to 25 ft. lbs. (34 Nm).
8. Attach the upper engine support to the vehicle.
9. Install the engine crossover pipe.
10. Connect the negative battery cable.

RIGHT SIDE

1. Disconnect the negative battery cable.

2. Remove the intermediate shaft pinch bolt and separate the intermediate shaft from the stub shaft.

> **✳✳CAUTION**
>
> Failure to disconnect the intermediate shaft from the rack and pinion stub shaft can result in damage to the steering gear and/or the intermediate shaft. This damage can cause loss of steering control.

3. Raise the support the vehicle on jackstands.
4. Remove the exhaust pipe-to-manifold bolts, then lower the vehicle.
5. Place a jack under the front crossmember of the cradle, then raise the jack until it starts to raise the vehicle and remove the two front body mount bolts.
6. With the cushions removed, thread the body mount bolts and retainers at least three turns into the cage nuts, then slowly release the jack.
7. Remove the power steering pump and bracket, then move it aside.
8. Disconnect the oxygen sensor connector.
9. Remove the crossover pipe-to-manifold nuts and the exhaust manifold bolts.
10. Remove the manifold and gasket.
11. To install, reverse the removal procedures.
12. Clean all the gasket surfaces completely.

3.1L Engine (VIN T)

▶ **See Figure 49**

LEFT SIDE

1. Disconnect the negative battery cable.
2. Loosen and remove the air supply plumbing from the exhaust manifold, as required.
3. Remove the coolant recovery bottle, if necessary.
4. Remove the serpentine belt cover and belt, as required.
5. Remove the air conditioning compressor and lay aside, if necessary.
6. Remove the right side torque strut, air conditioning and torque strut mounting bracket, as required.
7. Disconnect the heat shield, if equipped.
8. Separate the exhaust crossover pipe at the manifold.
9. Remove the exhaust manifold retaining bolts, then the manifold and gasket.

To install:
10. Clean all the gasket surfaces completely.
11. Attach the exhaust manifold and gasket to the vehicle with the retaining bolts. Tighten to 15-20 ft. lbs. (20-30).
12. Attach the exhaust crossover pipe at the manifold, then tighten the mounting nuts to 18 ft. lbs. (25 Nm).
13. Install the heat shield, if equipped.
14. If removed, install the right side torque strut, air conditioning and torque strut mounting bracket.
15. If removed, install the air conditioning compressor.
16. If removed, install the serpentine belt and cover.
17. If removed, attach the coolant recovery bottle.
18. Install the air supply plumbing to the exhaust manifold.
19. Connect the negative battery cable.

RIGHT SIDE

1. Disconnect the negative battery cable.

```
1 Cylinder head          5 10 Nm (89 lb.in.)
2 Gasket                 6 Heat shield
3 Manifold (right)       7 Manifold (left)
4 25 Nm (18 lb.ft.)
```

86813161

Fig. 49 Left and right side exhaust manifolds used on 3.1L engines

2. Raise and safely support the vehicle.

3. Disconnect the exhaust pipe and lower the vehicle.

4. Remove the air cleaner assembly, breather, mass air flow sensor and heat shield.

5. Remove the crossover at the manifold.

6. Remove the accelerator and TV cables and brackets, as required.

7. Remove the exhaust manifold retaining bolts, then remove the manifold and gasket.

To install:

8. Clean all the gasket surfaces completely.

9. Install the exhaust manifold, gasket and retaining bolts. Tighten to 15-20 ft. lbs. (20-30 Nm).

10. If removed, install the accelerator, TV cables and brackets.

11. Install the crossover at the manifold.

12. Install the air cleaner assembly, breather, mass air flow sensor and heat shield.

13. Raise and safely support the vehicle.

14. Connect the exhaust pipe and lower the vehicle.

15. Connect the negative battery cable.

3.1L Engine (VIN M)

▶ See Figure 49

FRONT

1. Disconnect the negative battery cable.

2. Remove the top half of the air cleaner assembly and throttle cable duct.

3. Partially drain the cooling system.

4. Separate the radiator hose from the thermostat housing.

5. Remove the coolant bypass hose at the coolant pump and from the exhaust manifold.

6. Loosen and remove the exhaust crossover heat shield.

7. Remove the exhaust crossover pipe from the manifold.

8. Tag and disconnect the secondary ignition wires from the spark plugs.

9. Remove the exhaust manifold heat shield.

10. Unsecure the exhaust manifold retaining nuts.

11. Remove the exhaust manifold and gasket.

To Install:

12. Clean mating surfaces at the cylinder head and manifold.

13. Install the exhaust manifold gasket and the exhaust manifold. Tighten the manifold mounting nuts to 12 ft. lbs. (16 Nm).

14. Attach the exhaust manifold heat shield.

15. Install the exhaust crossover pipe to the manifold.

16. Attach the exhaust crossover pipe heat shield.

17. Connect the secondary ignition wires to the appropriate spark plug.

18. Connect the coolant bypass pipe to the coolant pump and exhaust manifold.

19. Secure the radiator hose to the coolant outlet housing.

20. Install the top half of the air cleaner and the throttle body duct.

21. Connect the negative battery cable.

REAR

1. Disconnect the negative battery cable.

2. Remove the top half of the air cleaner assembly and throttle cable duct.

3. Remove the exhaust crossover heat shield.

4. Separate the exhaust crossover pipe from the manifold.

5. Remove the oxygen sensor.

6. Separate the EGR pipe from the exhaust manifold.

7. Raise and safely support the vehicle.

8. Remove the transaxle oil fill tube and lever indicator assembly.

9. Disassemble the front exhaust pipe from the exhaust manifold.

10. Disconnect the exhaust pipe from the converter flange and support the converter.

11. Remove the converter heat shield from the body.

12. Loosen and remove the exhaust manifold heat shield.

13. Unsecure the exhaust manifold nuts.

14. Remove the exhaust manifold from the bottom of vehicle and the gasket.

To Install:

15. Clean mating surfaces at the cylinder head and manifold.

16. Install the exhaust manifold gasket.

17. Install the exhaust manifold loosely and install heat shield at this time.
18. Install the manifold nuts, then tighten to 12 ft. lbs. (16 Nm).
19. Install the exhaust manifold heat shield nuts.
20. Install the converter heat shield to the body.
21. Connect the exhaust pipe to the converter flange.
22. Connect the exhaust pipe to the exhaust manifold.
23. Install the transaxle oil level indicator and fill tube assembly.
24. Safely lower the vehicle.
25. Connect the oxygen sensor.
26. Connect the EGR pipe to exhaust manifold.
27. Install top half of the air cleaner assembly and throttle body duct.
28. Connect the negative battery cable.

3.3L Engine

LEFT SIDE

1. Disconnect the negative battery cable.
2. Remove the air cleaner inlet ducting. Install the spark plug wires.
3. Loosen and remove the 2 bolts attaching the exhaust crossover pipe to the manifold.
4. Remove the engine lift hook, manifold heat shield and oil level indicator.
5. Remove the exhaust manifold retaining bolts and remove the manifold.

To install:
6. Clean all the gasket surfaces completely.
7. Install the exhaust manifold and retaining bolts, then tighten to 30 ft. lbs. (41 Nm).
8. Install the engine lift hook, manifold heat shield and oil level indicator.
9. Secure the 2 bolts attaching the exhaust crossover pipe to the manifold.
10. Install the air cleaner inlet ducting. Install the spark plug wires.
11. Connect the negative battery cable.

RIGHT SIDE

1. Disconnect the negative battery cable.
2. Remove the spark plug wires, oxygen sensor connector, throttle cable bracket and cables.
3. Remove the brake booster hose from the manifold.
4. Unsecure the 2 bolts attaching the exhaust crossover pipe to the manifold.
5. Remove the exhaust pipe-to-manifold bolts, engine lift hook and transaxle oil level indicator tube.
6. Remove the manifold heat shield. Remove the exhaust manifold retaining bolts and remove the manifold.

To install:
7. Clean all the gasket surfaces completely.
8. Install the exhaust manifold and retaining bolts, then tighten to 30 ft. lbs. (41 Nm). Install the manifold heat shield.
9. Install the exhaust pipe-to-manifold bolts, engine lift hook and transaxle oil level indicator tube.
10. Secure the 2 bolts attaching the exhaust crossover pipe to the manifold.
11. Attach the brake booster hose to the manifold.

12. Install the spark plug wires, oxygen sensor connector, throttle cable bracket and cables.
13. Connect the negative battery cable.

3.8L Engine

1. Disconnect the negative battery cable.

✳✳WARNING

Failure to disconnect the intermediate shaft from the rack and pinion stub shaft may result in damage to the steering gear and/or intermediate shaft.

2. Remove the pinch bolt from the intermediate shaft and separate the intermediate shaft from the stub shaft.
3. Raise and safely support the vehicle.
4. Remove the 2 bolts attaching the exhaust pipe to the manifold.
5. Lower the vehicle.
6. Remove the upper engine support strut.
7. Place a jack under the front crossmember of the cradle and raise the jack until it starts to raise the vehicle.
8. Remove the 2 front body mount bolts.
9. With the cushions removed, thread the body mount bolts and retainers a minimum of 3 turns into the cage nuts.
10. Release the jack slowly.

➡To avoid damage, do not lower the cradle without it being restrained.

11. Remove the power steering pump and bracket from the cylinder head and exhaust manifold.
12. Disconnect the oxygen sensor.
13. If removing the left side exhaust manifold, remove the upper engine support strut.
14. Remove the 2 nuts retaining the crossover pipe to the exhaust manifold.
15. Remove the 6 bolts attaching the manifold to the cylinder head.
16. Remove the exhaust manifold.
To install:
17. Carefully, clean the gasket sealing surfaces of old gasket material.
18. Install the exhaust manifold and the manifold-to-cylinder head bolts, then tighten to 37 ft. lbs. (50 Nm).
19. If the left side exhaust manifold was removed, install the crossover pipe to the manifold.
20. If the right side exhaust manifold was removed, install the upper engine support strut.
21. Connect the oxygen sensor wire.
22. Install the power steering pump and bracket.
23. Support the cradle with the jack. Remove the 2 body mount bolts and install the cushions.
24. Raise the cradle into position and install the 2 body mount bolts.
25. Remove the jack.
26. Connect the intermediate shaft to the stub shaft and install the pinch bolt.
27. Raise and safely support the vehicle.
28. Install the exhaust pipe-to-manifold bolts.
29. Lower the vehicle.
30. Connect the negative battery cable.

4.3L Diesel Engine

LEFT SIDE

▶ **See Figure 50**

1. Remove the upper exhaust crossover pipe-to manifold bolts. Loosen the lower crossover pipe bolt at the right rear exhaust manifold.
2. Raise and support the car on jackstands.
3. Remove the remaining left front crossover pipe-to-manifold bolt. Unbolt and remove the manifold and gasket.

To install:

4. Clean all the gasket surfaces completely.
5. Lubricate the entire exhaust manifold-to-cylinder head bolts with lubricant GM part no. 1052080 or equivalent.
6. Attach the new manifold and gasket to the vehicle, tighten the bolts to 29 ft. lbs. (39 Nm).
7. Bend the locktabs over the bolt heads.
8. Install the left front crossover pipe bolt, lower the vehicle.
9. Attach the lower crossover pipe bolt at the right rear exhaust manifold.
10. Install the upper exhaust crossover pipe-to manifold bolts.

RIGHT SIDE

▶ **See Figure 51**

1. Remove the engine support strut.
2. Place a floor jack under the front crossmember and take up the weight of the car.
3. Remove the two front body mount bolts. Remove the cushions from the bolts.
4. Thread the body mount bolts with their retainers into the cage nuts so that the bolts restrict movement of the engine cradle.
5. Lower the jack until the crossmember contacts the body mount bolt retainers. Check for any hose or wire interference.
6. Remove the crossover pipe.
7. Raise and support the car on jackstands.
8. Disconnect the exhaust pipe from the manifold.
9. Lower the car.
10. Unbolt and remove the manifold and gasket.

Fig. 50 Locktabs are used to secure the exhaust manifold bolts

Fig. 51 Right (rear) exhaust manifold used on 4.3L engines

11. Installation is the reverse of removal. Lubricate the entire length of each manifold bolt with lubricant GM part no. 1052080 or its equivalent.

Radiator

REMOVAL & INSTALLATION

▶ **See Figures 52, 53, 54, 55 and 56**

1. Disconnect the negative battery cable. On some vehicles you will need to remove the air cleaner assembly.
2. Drain the cooling system.

✳✳CAUTION

When draining the coolant, keep in mind that cats and dogs are attracted by ethylene glycol antifreeze, and are quite likely to drink any that is left in an uncovered container or in puddles on the ground. This will prove fatal in sufficient quantity. Always drain the coolant into a sealable container. Coolant should be reused unless it is contaminated or several years old.

3. Unplug the fan electrical connector.
4. Remove the attaching bolts for the fan, then remove the fan assembly.
5. Remove the forward strut brace for the engine at the radiator. Loosen the bolt to prevent shearing the rubber bushing, then swing the strut rearward.
6. On 2.5L engine, remove the resonator mounting and resonator. Disconnect the headlamp wiring harness from the fan frame.
7. Some vehicles will require you to scribe the hood latch location on the radiator support, then remove the latch.
8. Disconnect the coolant hoses from the radiator. Keep rags handy for this step. Remove the coolant recovery tank hose from the radiator neck. Disconnect and plug the automatic transmission fluid cooler lines from the radiator, if so equipped. On the diesel engine, disconnect the engine oil cooler hoses.

9. Remove the upper mounting panel mounting bolts and the panel.

10. Remove the radiator attaching bolts and remove the radiator. If the car has air conditioning, if first may be necessary to raise the left side of the radiator so that the radiator neck will clear the compressor.

To install:

➡ **If a new radiator is going to be installed, check that all the fittings and brackets from the old radiator are removed, you'll need them on the new one.**

11. Install the radiator in the car, tightening the mounting bolts to 7 inch lbs. (0.8 Nm). Connect the transmission cooler lines and hoses. Install the coolant recovery hose.

12. Secure the upper and lower radiator hoses.

13. Install the hood latch. Tighten to 6 ft. lbs. (8 Nm).

14. Install the fan, making sure the bottom leg of the frame fits into the rubber grommet at the lower support. Tighten the fan bolts to 80 inch lbs. (10 Nm).

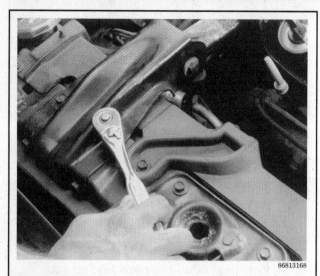
Fig. 52 Remove the bolts securing the engine strut . . .

Fig. 53 . . . then lift and position it aside

Fig. 54 On automatic transaxles, disconnect the cooler lines from the radiator

Fig. 55 Remove the bolts securing the upper mouting panel

Fig. 56 After the attaching bolts are removed, the radiator can be pulled from the engine compartment

15. Install the fan wires and the headlamp wiring harness. Swing the strut and brace forward, tightening the bolt to 11-18 ft. lbs. (15-24 Nm) and the nut to 39 ft. lbs. (53 Nm).
16. Connect the negative battery cable.
17. Fill the cooling system with clean coolant.
18. Start the vehicle, top off the coolant.
19. Pressure test the system to verify no leaks.

Electric Cooling Fan

REMOVAL & INSTALLATION

▶ **See Figures 57 and 58**

1. Disconnect the negative battery cable.
2. Drain the cooling system.
3. Remove the cooling fan mounting bolt.
4. Disconnect the electrical connector from the fan.
5. Remove the radiator inlet hose from the radiator.

Fig. 57 Remove the attaching bolts for the fan . . .

Fig. 58 . . . then remove the fan assembly

6. Remove the radiator mounting bolt.
7. On some models you may need to pull the windshield washer fluid bottle fill tube from the bottle.
8. Remove the vacuum tank, then the bracket if needed.
9. Remove the cooling fan by sliding fan leg into area left from the vacuum tank.
To Install:
10. Install the cooling fan assembly.
11. Install the vacuum tank bracket.
12. Secure the vacuum tank.
13. Attach the windshield washer fluid bottle fill tube, if removed.
14. Install the radiator mounting bolt.
15. Connect the radiator inlet hose to the radiator.
16. Connect the electrical connector to cooling fan.
17. Install the cooling fan mounting bolt.
18. Install the air intake duct assembly.
19. Connect the negative battery cable.

Auxiliary Engine Cooling Fan

REMOVAL & INSTALLATION

➡**Only the 3.1L (VIN M) engine uses the auxiliary fan.**

1. Remove the grille assembly from the vehicle.
2. Disconnect the electrical harness from the cooling fan.
3. Unbolt the front end upper support.
4. Remove the bolts from the top of the fan.
5. Raise and support the vehicle safely.
6. Unbolt the front end lower bolts.
7. Remove the bolts from the bottom of the fan.
8. Remove the fan.
To Install:
9. Attach the fan to the vehicle, then tighten the bolt at the bottom of the fan to 80 inch lbs.
10. Attach the front end lower support bolts, then lower the vehicle.
11. Attach the remaining bolts to the fan, tighten them to 80 inch lbs. (9 Nm).
12. Attach the bolts for the front end upper support.
13. Install the electrical harness for the fan.
14. Install the grille to the front of the vehicle.

Water Pump

REMOVAL & INSTALLATION

✳✳CAUTION

When draining the coolant, keep in mind that cats and dogs are attracted by ethylene glycol antifreeze, and are quite likely to drink any that is left in an uncovered container or in puddles on the ground. This will prove fatal in sufficient quantity. Always drain the coolant into a sealable container. Coolant should be reused unless it is contaminated or several years old.

2.2L Engine

▸ **See Figure 59**

1. Partially drain the engine coolant from the vehicle.
2. Remove the serpentine drive belt from the vehicle.
3. Loosen and position the alternator to one side.
4. Unbolt the water pump pulley, then remove the pulley.
5. Unbolt the water pump, then remove the pump and gasket.
6. Clean the gasket areas thoroughly.

To install:

7. Install a new gasket to the water pump mating surface.
8. Attach the water pump to the engine with the retaining bolts, tighten them to 18 ft. lbs. (25 Nm).
9. Attach the water pump pulley, then tighten the bolts to 22 ft. lbs. (30 Nm).
10. Properly position the alternator.
11. Install the serpentine drive belt.
12. Fill the coolant system, start the engine, then top off the fluid.

2.5L Engine

1. Disconnect the negative battery cable.
2. Drain the cooling system.
3. Remove the serpentine belt. Removal of the alternator and/or bracket may help give more room for easier access.
4. Remove water pump attaching bolts and nut, then remove pump.

To install:

5. Clean the sealing surfaces, then place a ³/₃₂ in. (2mm) bead of RTV sealant or equivalent on the water pump sealing surface.
6. Coat the bolt threads with a pipe sealant GM part no. 1052080 or equivalent.
7. Install the water pump, then tighten the bolts to 10-24 ft. lbs. (14-33 Nm).
8. Connect the negative battery cable.
9. Fill the cooling system, then check for leaks. Start the engine and allow to come to normal operating temperature. Recheck for leaks. Top off the coolant.

2.8L Engine

▸ **See Figure 60**

1. Disconnect battery negative cable.
2. Drain cooling system and remove heater hose.
3. Remove the pump pulley.
4. When replacing the water pump, the timing cover must be clamped to the cylinder block prior to removing the water pump bolts. Use special tool J29176 or its equivalent.
5. Remove water pump attaching bolts and nut and remove pump.

To install:

6. With the sealant surfaces cleaned, place a ³/₃₂ in. (2mm) bead of sealant GM part no. 1052357 or equivalent on the water pump sealing surface.
7. Coat bolt threads with pipe sealant GM part no. 1052080 or equivalent.
8. Install the new water pump, then tighten the bolts to 10-18 ft. lbs. (14-24 Nm).
9. Attach the pulley to the water pump, tighten the bolts to 15 ft. lbs. (21 Nm).
10. Connect the negative battery cable.

3.0L Engine

1. Disconnect the negative battery cable, then drain the coolant.
2. Remove accessory drive belts. Remove the radiator and heater hoses from the water pump.
3. Remove the water pump attaching bolts.
4. Remove the engine support strut.
5. Place a floor jack under the front crossmember of the cradle and raise the jack until the jack just starts to raise the car.
6. Disconnect the front two body mount bolts with the lower cushions and retainers.
7. Remove the cushions from the bolts.
8. Thread the body mount bolts with retainers a minimum of three (3) turns into the cage nuts so that the bolts restrain cradle movement.
9. Release the floor jack slowly until the crossmember contacts the body mount bolts retainers. As the jack is being

1 Water pump gasket
2 Water pump assembly
3 Water pump bolt/screw

86813177

Fig. 59 Water pump used on 2.2L engines

86813175

Fig. 60 After the water pump attaching bolts are removed, the pump can be pulled from its housing

lowered watch and correct any interference with hoses, lines, pipes and cables.

➡**Do not lower the cradle without its being restrained as possible damage can occur to the body and underhood items.**

10. Remove water pump from engine.

To install:

11. To install, reverse the removal procedure. Tighten the water pump bolts to 25 ft. lbs. (34 Nm).

12. Connect negative battery cable.

13. Fill with coolant, start the engine. Top off the coolant system and check for leaks.

3.1L Engine (VIN T)

1. Disconnect the negative battery cable.
2. Drain cooling system in to a drain pan.
3. Remove the serpentine belt.
4. Remove the heater hose and radiator hose.
5. Remove the water pump cover attaching bolts and remove the cover.
6. Remove the water pump attaching bolts and remove the water pump.

To install:

7. Position the water pump on the engine and install the attaching bolts. Tighten bolts to 89 inch lbs. (10 Nm).
8. Install the water pump cover and attaching bolts.
9. Install the heater hose and radiator hose.
10. Install the serpentine belt.
11. Connect the negative battery cable.
12. Fill cooling system and check for leaks. Start the engine and allow to come to normal operating temperature. Recheck for leaks.

3.1L Engine (VIN M)

1. Partially drain the coolant from the vehicle.
2. Remove the serpentine drive belt from the vehicle.
3. Unbolt the pulley from the pump.
4. Remove the water pump mounting bolts.
5. Remove the pump from the engine, then clean the gasket area.

To install:

6. Attach the water pump with gasket to the engine with the mounting bolts.
7. Tighten the mounting bolts to 89 inch lbs. (10 Nm).
8. Attach the pulley with it's mounting bolts. Tighten them to 18 ft. lbs. (25 Nm).
9. Install the serpentine drive belt.
10. Fill the coolant system, start the engine and top off the fluid. Check for leaks.

3.3L Engine

1. Disconnect the negative battery cable.
2. Drain the cooling system.
3. Remove the serpentine drive belt.
4. Disconnect the coolant hose at the water pump.
5. Unsecure the water pump pulley bolts. The long bolt should be removed through the access hole provided in the body side rail. Remove the pulley.
6. Remove the water pump attaching bolts, then remove the water pump.

To install:

7. Install the water pump with the attaching bolts. Tighten the bolts to 22 ft. lbs. (30 Nm).
8. Install the pulley. Install the water pump pulley bolts. The long bolt should be installed through the access hole provided in the body side rail.
9. Install the coolant hose at the water pump.
10. Install the serpentine drive belt.
11. Connect the negative battery cable.
12. Fill cooling system and check for leaks. Start the engine and allow to come to normal operating temperature. Recheck for leaks.

3.8L Engine

1. Disconnect the negative battery cable.
2. Drain the cooling system.
3. Remove the serpentine drive belt.
4. Disconnect the radiator and heater hoses at the water pump.
5. Remove the water pump pulley bolts, the long bolt is removed through the access hole provided in the body side rail. Remove the pulley.
6. Remove the water pump attaching bolts, then remove the water pump.

To install:

7. Clean all gasket mating surfaces.
8. Using a new gasket, install the water pump to the engine.
9. Install the water pump pulley.
10. Connect the radiator and heater hoses to the water pump.
11. Install the serpentine drive belt.
12. Connect the negative battery cable.
13. Fill cooling system and check for leaks. Start the engine and allow to come to normal operating temperature. Check for leaks and top-off the coolant.

4.3L Diesel Engine

1. Drain radiator. Remove the negative battery cable.
2. Disconnect lower radiator hose at water pump.
3. Disconnect the heater return hose at the water pump. Remove the bolt retaining the heater water return pipe to the intake manifold and position the pipe out-of-the-way.
4. If equipped with A/C, remove the vacuum pump drive belt.
5. Remove the serpentine drive belt.
6. Remove the alternator, air conditioning compressor or vacuum pump brackets.
7. Remove the water pump attaching bolts and remove the water pump assembly.
8. Using tools J-29785 and J-29786, remove the water pump pulley.

To install:

9. Clean the gasket material from engine block.
10. Apply a thin coat of GM part. no. 1050026 sealer or equivalent to the water pump housing to retain the gasket.
11. Position a new gasket on the housing.
12. Position the new water pump, then apply sealer to the water pump mounting bolts. Tighten the bolts to 12-15 ft. lbs. (16-20 Nm).

13. Attach the alternator, air conditioning compressor or vacuum pump brackets.

14. Install the serpentine drive belt.

15. Attach the vacuum pump drive belt, if equipped with A/C.

16. Connect the heater return hose at the water pump, attach the bolt retaining the heater water return pipe to the intake manifold.

Cylinder Head

REMOVAL & INSTALLATION

❊❊CAUTION

When draining the coolant, keep in mind that cats and dogs are attracted by ethylene glycol antifreeze, and are quite likely to drink any that is left in an uncovered container or in puddles on the ground. This will prove fatal in sufficient quantity. Always drain the coolant into a sealable container. Coolant should be reused unless it is contaminated or several years old.

2.2L Engine

▶ See Figure 61

1. Relieve the fuel system pressure.
2. Disconnect the negative battery cable.
3. Drain the cooling system into a suitable container.
4. Separate the air cleaner and air duct assembly from the vehicle.
5. Remove the lower air inlet.
6. Remove the serpentine drive belt.
7. Unsecure the alternator, and remove from the vehicle.
8. Remove the power steering pump, then position it aside without disconnecting the power steering lines.
9. Disconnect the spark plug wires, lay them aside.
10. Detach the control cables from the throttle body, then remove the cable bracket at the throttle body and valve cover.

➡**When removing the valve train components, they must be kept in order for installation, in the same locations as they were removed from.**

11. Remove the valve cover, rocker arm nuts, rocker arms and pushrods.
12. Disconnect the electrical harness from the intake manifold, throttle body and cylinder head.
13. Remove the O_2 sensor connection.
14. Unsecure the power steering pump bracket from the intake brace, located under the manifold.
15. Remove the torque strut and the engine side torque strut mounting bracket.
16. Unfasten the alternator rear bracket.
17. Tag and disconnect the vacuum lines at the intake manifold and cylinder head.
18. Disconnect the upper radiator hose from the engine.
19. Raise and safely support the vehicle.
20. Disconnect the exhaust pipe from the exhaust manifold.
21. Lower the vehicle.

22. Disconnect and cap the fuel lines at the quick disconnects.
23. Remove the transaxle fill tube.
24. Remove the cylinder head bolts.
25. Remove the cylinder head with both manifolds, then remove the intake and exhaust manifolds from the cylinder head.

To install:

26. Clean all the gasket surfaces completely. Clean the threads on the cylinder head bolts and the block threads.
27. Install the intake and exhaust manifolds on the cylinder head.
28. Place a new cylinder head gasket in position over the dowel pins on the block. Carefully guide the cylinder head into position.
29. Install the head bolts finger-tight. The long bolts go in bolts positions 1, 4, 5, 8, and 9. The short bolts are in the positions 2, 3, 6 and 7. The stud is in position 10.
30. Tighten the bolts in sequence. The long bolts to 23 ft. lbs. (32 Nm) and the short bolts and stud to 22 ft. lbs. (29 Nm). Make a second pass tightening the long bolts to 46 ft. lbs. (58 Nm). Maker a final pass over all the bolts tightening each an additional 100°.
31. Install the transaxle fill tube.
32. Connect the fuel lines to the throttle body.
33. Raise and support the vehicle.
34. Connect the exhaust pipe to the exhaust manifold. Tighten the mounting bolts to 22 ft. lbs. (30 Nm).
35. Lower the vehicle.
36. Attach the upper radiator hose.
37. Install the vacuum lines to the intake manifold.
38. Attach the engine side torque strut bracket and torque strut to the engine.
39. Install the alternator rear bracket.
40. Install the power steering pump bracket to the intake manifold brace, located under the intake manifold.
41. Connect the electrical harness at the intake manifold, throttle body and cylinder head.
42. Attach the O_2 sensor wiring harness.
43. Install the pushrods, rocker arms and rocker arm nuts, then tighten to 22 ft. lbs. (30 Nm).
44. Install the valve cover.
45. Connect the control cables to the throttle body, then install the cables brackets at the throttle body and valve cover.
46. Attach the spark plug wires to there proper locations.
47. Install the power steering pump in the mounting bracket.
48. Attach the alternator to the engine.
49. Install the serpentine drive belt.
50. Connect the lower air inlet duct.
51. Attach the air inlet resonator tie bar.
52. Install the air cleaner and duct assembly.
53. Refill the cooling system.
54. Connect the negative battery cable.
55. Start the vehicle, top off the coolant. Verify there are no leaks.

2.5L Engine

▶ See Figure 62

❊❊CAUTION

On fuel injected engines, relieve the pressure in the fuel system before disconnecting any fuel line connections.

1 Long bolts
2 Short bolts
3 Stud
4 Numbers on gasket
  indicate torque sequence

86813180

Fig. 61 Tightening sequence for cylinder head bolts on 2.2L engines

➡ **The engine should be not be warm, it is best to leave engine sit overnight to cool before removing the cylinder head.**

1. Drain the cooling system into a clean container.
2. Remove the air cleaner, the negative battery cable, the oil dipstick tube, the ignition coil, the engine-to-upper strut rod bolt and the power steering pump bracket.
3. Remove the intake and exhaust manifolds as previously outlined.
4. Remove the alternator bracket bolts.
5. Remove the air conditioning compressor bracket bolts and position the compressor to one side. Do not disconnect any of the refrigerant lines.
6. Disconnect and tag all vacuum and electrical connections from the cylinder head.
7. Disconnect the upper radiator hose.
8. Disconnect the spark plug wires and remove the plugs.
9. Remove the valve cover, rocker arms, and pushrods.
10. Unbolt and remove the cylinder head.
11. Clean the gasket surfaces thoroughly.
12. Install a new gasket over the dowels with the right side facing up.
13. Coat the head bolt threads with sealer and install finger-tight.
14. Tighten the bolts in sequence, in equal steps to the specified torque.
15. On vehicles from:
   a. 1982-84 final torque is 85 ft. lbs. (115 Nm).
   b. 1985-86 final torque is 92 ft. lbs. (125 Nm).
   c. 1987-92 first torque to 18 ft. lbs. (25 Nm), then repeat 26 ft. lbs. (35 Nm) excluding No. 9, which is 18 ft. lbs. (25 Nm).
16. Reverse the removal procedure to install.

2.8L Engine

▶ **See Figures 63 and 64**

LEFT SIDE

1. Disconnect the negative battery cable.
2. Raise and support the car.
3. Drain the coolant and lower the car.

4. Remove the valve covers.
5. Remove the intake manifold and plenum.
6. Remove the crossover pipe.
7. Remove the left exhaust manifold.
8. Remove the oil dipstick.
9. Remove the alternator and AIR pump brackets.
10. Remove the dipstick tube.
11. Loosen the rocker arm bolts and remove the pushrods. Keep the pushrods in the same order as removed.
12. Remove the cylinder head bolts in stages using the reverse order of the tightening sequence.
13. Remove the cylinder head. Do not pry on the head to loosen it.

   To install:
14. Clean all mating surfaces on the cylinder head block and intake manifold.
15. Place the gasket into position over the dowel pins, with the correct side facing up, if marked.
16. Install the cylinder head.
17. Coat the head bolt threads with GM part no. 1052080 sealer or an equivalent.
18. Tighten the head bolts in proper sequence to 70 ft. lbs. (90 Nm) on 1982-86 models and 1987-89 models to 33 ft. lbs. (45 Nm).
19. Attach the intake manifold gasket.
20. Install the pushrods loosely retained with the rocker arms. Make sure the pushrods seat in the lifter.
21. Install the rocker arm nuts.
22. Attach the intake manifold and plenum.
23. Install the valve covers, then connect the oil level indicator tube bracket.
24. Install the crossover pipe and the left exhaust manifold.
25. Connect the engine strut bracket top the engine.
26. Fill the cooling system, connect the negative battery cable.
27. Double check no connections have been missed.
28. Start the vehicle, top off the coolant, then check for leaks.

RIGHT SIDE

1. Raise the car and drain the coolant from the block.

1—APPLY SEALING COMPOUND PART NUMBER 1052080 OR EQUIVALENT TO THREADS ON BOLTS SHOWN.

2—MOUNTING SURFACES OF BLOCK ASM., HEAD ASM. AND BOTH SIDES OF GASKET MUST BE FREE OF OIL AND FOREIGN MATERIAL.

3—LOCATING PINS

NUMBERS SHOWN DESIGNATE BOLT POSITIONS AND BOLT TIGHTENING SEQUENCE.

Fig. 62 Tightening sequence for cylinder head bolts on 2.5L engines

Fig. 63 Remove the cylinder head. Do not pry on the head to loosen it

Fig. 64 Tightening sequence for cylinder head bolts on 2.8L engines

2. Disconnect the exhaust pipe and lower the car.

3. If equipped, remove the cruise control servo bracket.

4. Remove the air management valve and hose.

5. Remove the intake manifold.

6. Remove the exhaust crossover.

7. Loosen the rocker arm nuts and remove the pushrods. Keep the pushrods in the order in which they were removed.

8. Remove the cylinder head bolts in stages using the reverse order of the tightening sequence.

9. Remove the cylinder head. Do not pry on the cylinder head to loosen it.

To install:

10. Clean all mating surfaces on the cylinder head block and intake manifold.

11. Place the gasket into position over the dowel pins, with the correct side facing up, if marked.

12. Install the cylinder head.

13. Coat the head bolt threads with GM part no. 1052080 sealer or an equivalent.

14. Tighten the head bolts in proper sequence to 70 ft. lbs. (90 Nm) on 1982-86 models and 1987-89 models to 33 ft. lbs. (45 Nm).

15. Attach the intake manifold gasket.

16. Install the pushrods loosely retained with the rocker arms. Make sure the pushrods seat in the lifter.

17. Install the rocker arm nuts.

18. Attach the intake manifold and plenum.

19. Install the valve covers, then connect the spark plug wires.

20. Install the crossover pipe and the right exhaust manifold. The crossover heat shield needs to be installed.

21. Raise and support the vehicle.

22. Install the exhaust at the crossover. Lower the vehicle.

23. Attach the cruise control servo bracket, if removed.

24. Fill the cooling system, connect the negative battery cable.

25. Double check no connections have not been missed.

26. Start the vehicle, top off the coolant, then check for leaks.

3.0L Engine

▶ See Figure 65

1. Disconnect negative battery cable.

2. Remove intake manifold.

3. Loosen and remove the belt(s).

4. When removing LEFT cylinder head;

   a. Remove oil dipstick.

   b. Remove air and vacuum pumps with mounting bracket if present, and move out of the way with hoses attached.

5. When removing RIGHT cylinder head:

   a. Remove alternator.

   b. Disconnect power steering gear pump and brackets attached to cylinder head.

6. Disconnect wires from spark plugs, and remove the spark plug wire clips from the valve cover studs.

7. Remove exhaust manifold bolts from head being removed.

8. Clean dirt off cylinder head and adjacent area to avoid getting dirt into engine. It is extremely important to avoid getting dirt into the hydraulic valve lifters.

Fig. 65 Tightening sequence for cylinder head bolts on 3.0L engines

9. Remove valve cover and rocker arm and shaft assembly from cylinder head. Lift out pushrods.

10. Loosen all cylinder head bolts, then remove bolts and lift off the cylinder head.

11. With cylinder head on bench, remove all spark plugs for cleaning and to avoid damaging them during work on the head.

12. Installation is the reverse of removal. Clean all gasket surfaces thoroughly. Always use a new head gasket. The head gasket is installed with the bead downward. Coat the head bolt threads with heavy-bodied thread sealer. Tighten the head bolts in equal stages. Recheck head bolt torque after the engine has been warmed to operating temperature.

3.1L Engine (VIN T)

▶ See Figure 66

LEFT SIDE

✳✳CAUTION

Care should be taken when working around the fuel system. DO NOT smoke or expose the fuel system to any flames or sparks. The fuel system is under pressure and must be relieved prior to performing any service work on the system components. Failure to properly bleed the system can lead to personal injury or component damage. Always keep a suitable fire extinguisher handy when servicing the fuel system.

1. Relieve the pressure in the fuel system before disconnecting any fuel line connections. Disconnect the fuel lines.

2. Disconnect the negative battery cable.

3. Remove the air cleaner assembly. Raise and safely support the vehicle.

4. Drain the cylinder block and lower the vehicle.

5. Remove the oil level indicator tube, valve cover, intake manifold and plenum, as required.

6. Remove the exhaust crossover, alternator bracket, AIR pump and brackets.

7. Disconnect and tag all electrical wiring and vacuum hoses that may interfere with the removal of the left cylinder head.

8. Loosen the rocker arm until the pushrods can be removed. Remove the pushrods. Keep the pushrods in the same order as removed.

9. Remove the cylinder head bolts. Remove the cylinder head. Do not pry on the head to loosen it.

To install:

10. Clean the cylinder head and block from any foreign matter, nicks or heavy scratches. Clean the cylinder head bolt threads and threads in the cylinder block.

11. Place the gasket into position over the dowel pins, with the correct side facing up, if marked.

12. Install the cylinder head bolts and tighten in sequence to 33 ft. lbs. (45 Nm). Turn an additional 90° in sequence.

13. Install the pushrods. Make sure the lower ends of the pushrods are in the lifter seats. Install the rocker arm nuts and tighten the nuts to 14-20 ft. lbs. (20-27 Nm).

14. Install the intake manifold.

15. Connect all electrical wiring and vacuum hoses.

16. Install the exhaust crossover, alternator and AIR pump brackets, alternator and AIR pump.

17. If removed, install the oil level indicator tube, valve cover, intake manifold and plenum.

18. Connect the fuel lines.

19. Connect the negative battery cable.

20. Adjust the valve lash, as required.

21. Install the air cleaner assembly.

RIGHT SIDE

1. Relieve the pressure in the fuel system before disconnecting any fuel line connections.

2. Disconnect the negative battery cable. Remove the air cleaner assembly. Raise the vehicle and support it safely.

3. Drain the cylinder block and lower the vehicle.

4. If equipped, remove the cruise control servo bracket, the air management valve and hose and the intake manifold.

5. Remove the exhaust pipe at crossover, crossover and heat shield, as required.

6. Disconnect and tag all electrical wiring and vacuum hoses that may interfere with the removal of the right cylinder head.

7. Remove the rocker cover. Loosen the rocker arm nuts and remove the pushrods. Keep the pushrods in the order in which they were removed.

8. Remove the cylinder head bolts. Remove the cylinder head. Do not pry on the head to loosen it.

To install:

9. Clean the cylinder head and block from any foreign matter, nicks or heavy scratches. Clean the cylinder head bolt threads and threads in the cylinder block.

10. Place the gasket into position over the dowel pins, with the correct side facing up, if marked.

11. Install the cylinder head bolts and tighten in sequence to 33 ft. lbs. (45 Nm). Turn an additional 90° in sequence.

12. Install the pushrods. Make sure the lower ends of the pushrods are in the lifter seats. Install the rocker arm nuts and tighten the nuts to 14-20 ft. lbs. (20-27 Nm).

13. Install the intake manifold.

14. Install the rocker cover.

15. Connect all electrical wiring and vacuum hoses.

16. If removed, install the crossover exhaust pipe and heat shield.

17. If equipped, install the cruise control servo bracket, the air management valve and hose.

18. Connect the negative battery cable.

19. Fill cooling system and check for leaks. Start the engine and allow to come to normal operating temperature. Recheck for leaks.

20. Adjust the valve lash, as required.

21. Install the air cleaner assembly.

3.1L Engine (VIN M)

LEFT SIDE (FRONT)

▶ See Figure 66

❋❋CAUTION

Fuel Injection systems remain under pressure, even after the engine has been turned OFF. The fuel system pressure must be relieved before disconnecting any fuel lines. Failure to do so may result in fire and/or personal injury.

1. Relieve the fuel system pressure.

2. Disconnect the negative battery cable.

3. Drain the cooling system.

4. Remove the top half of the air cleaner assembly and remove the throttle body air inlet duct.

5. Remove the exhaust crossover pipe heat shield and crossover pipe.

6. Disconnect the spark plug wires from spark plugs and wire looms and route the wires out of the way.

7. Remove the rocker arm covers.

8. Remove upper intake plenum and lower intake manifold.

9. Remove the left side exhaust manifold.

10. Remove oil level indicator tube.

➡**When removing the valve train components they must be kept in order for installation in the same locations they were removed from.**

11. Remove rocker arms nut, rocker arms, balls and pushrods.

Fig. 66 Tightening sequence for cylinder head bolts on 3.1L engines

1 Engine block assembly
2 Cylinder head gasket
3 Cylinder head assembly
4 Cylinder head bolt/screw
5 Cylinder head bolt/screw
6 Cylinder head locating pin

86813184

12. Remove the cylinder head bolts evenly.

13. Remove the cylinder head.

To Install:

14. Clean all the gasket surfaces completely. Clean the threads on the cylinder head bolts and block threads.

15. Place the gasket into position over the dowel pins, with the correct side facing up, if marked.

16. Coat the bolt threads with sealer and install finger-tight.

17. Tighten the cylinder head bolts in sequence to 33 ft. lbs. (45 Nm). With all the bolts tightened make a second pass tightening all the bolts an additional 90°.

18. Install the pushrods, rocker arms, balls and rocker arm nuts. Tighten the rocker arm nuts to 18 ft. lbs. (25 Nm).

19. Install the lower intake manifold and upper intake plenum.

20. Install the rocker arm covers.

21. Install the oil level indicator tube.

22. Connect the spark plug wires to spark plugs and wire looms.

23. Install the left side exhaust manifold.

24. Install the exhaust crossover pipe and crossover pipe heat shield.

25. Refill the cooling system.

26. Install the top half of the air cleaner assembly and the throttle body air inlet duct.

27. Connect negative battery cable.

28. Start vehicle and verify no leaks.

RIGHT SIDE (REAR)

✳✳CAUTION

Fuel Injection systems remain under pressure, even after the engine has been turned OFF. The fuel system pressure must be relieved before disconnecting any fuel lines. Failure to do so may result in fire and/or personal injury.

1. Relieve the fuel system pressure.

2. Disconnect the negative battery cable.

3. Drain the cooling system.

4. Remove the top half of the air cleaner assembly and remove the throttle body air inlet duct.

5. Remove the exhaust crossover pipe heat shield and crossover pipe.

6. Raise and safely support the vehicle.

7. Disconnect the oxygen (O_2) sensor connector.

8. Disconnect the exhaust pipe from the exhaust manifold.

9. Remove the right side exhaust manifold.

10. Lower the vehicle.

11. Disconnect the spark plug wires from spark plugs and wire looms and route the wires out of the way.

12. Remove the rocker arm covers.

13. Remove upper intake plenum and lower intake manifold.

➡**When removing the valve train components they must be kept in order for installation in the same locations they were removed from.**

14. Remove rocker arms nut, rocker arms, balls and pushrods.

15. Remove the cylinder head bolts evenly.

16. Remove the cylinder head.

To Install:

17. Clean all the gasket surfaces completely. Clean the threads on the cylinder head bolts and block threads.

18. Place the gasket into position over the dowel pins, with the correct side facing up, if marked.

19. Coat the bolt threads with sealer and install finger-tight.

20. Tighten the cylinder head bolts in sequence to 33 ft. lbs. (45 Nm). With all the bolts tightened make a second pass tightening all the bolts an additional 90°.

21. Install the pushrods, rocker arms, balls and rocker arm nuts. Tighten the rocker arm nuts to 18 ft. lbs. (25 Nm).

22. Install the lower intake manifold and upper intake plenum.

23. Install the rocker arm covers.

24. Connect the spark plug wires to spark plugs and wire looms.

25. Raise vehicle and safely support.

26. Install the exhaust manifold.

27. Connect the exhaust pipe to the exhaust manifold.

28. Lower the vehicle.

29. Connect the oxygen (O_2) sensor connector.

30. Install the exhaust crossover pipe and heat shield.

31. Refill the cooling system.

32. Install the top half of the air cleaner assembly and the throttle body air inlet duct.

33. Connect negative battery cable.

34. Start vehicle and verify no leaks.

3.3L Engine

◆ See Figure 67

RIGHT SIDE

1. Relieve the pressure in the fuel system before disconnecting any fuel line connections.

2. Disconnect the negative battery cable. Raise the vehicle and support it safely.

3. Drain the cylinder block and lower the vehicle.

4. Remove the intake manifold.

5. Remove the exhaust crossover pipe.

6. Disconnect the heater pipe retaining nut, then slide the pipe from the front of the cover housing.

7. Unsecure the power steering pump bolts at the mounting bracket, then remove the ground wires.

8. Unsecure the engine lift bracket and coolant pipe.

9. Remove the exhaust manifold heat shield.

10. Unbolt the transaxle fill tube.

11. Remove the spark plug loom, wires and spark plugs.

12. Raise and support the vehicle.

13. Disconnect the exhaust pipe to the manifold.

14. Lower the vehicle.

15. Unbolt the exhaust manifold and the heat shield, then remove.

16. Remove the valve cover, then remove the rocker arm assemblies.

17. Disconnect and tag all electrical wiring and vacuum hoses, as necessary.

18. If equipped with air conditioning, remove the air conditioning compressor and position to the side.

19. Remove the cylinder head bolts, then remove the cylinder head.

To install:

20. Clean the cylinder head and block of any foreign matter, nicks or heavy scratches. Clean the cylinder head bolt threads and threads in the cylinder block.

21. Position the new cylinder head gasket on the block. Apply sealant GM part no. 1052080, to the under side of the bolt heads, and thread locker GM part no. 12345382, to the bolt threads.

22. Carefully guide the cylinder head into place.

23. Coat the cylinder head bolts with sealing compound and install into the head. Tighten the cylinder head bolts according to the following procedure:

 a. Tighten in sequence to 35 ft. lbs. (47 Nm).

 b. Using an appropriate torque angle gauge, rotate each bolt in sequence an additional 130°.

 c. Rotate the center 4 bolts an additional 30° in sequence.

24. Install the pushrods, guide plate and rocker arm assembly. Tighten the rocker arm pivot bolts to 28 ft. lbs. (38 Nm).

25. Install the exhaust manifold and heat shield, tighten the mounting bolts to 38 ft. lbs. (52 Nm).

26. Raise and support the vehicle.

27. Attach the exhaust pipe to the manifold.

28. Lower the vehicle.

29. Install the spark plug, wires and looms to the engine.

30. Bolt the transaxle fill tube to the engine.

31. Attach the exhaust manifold heat shield.

32. Install the coolant pipe and the engine lift bracket.

33. Connect the ground wires, then install the power steering pump bolts to the mounting bracket.

34. Slide the heater pipe to the front of the cover housing, then install the pipe retaining nut.

35. Attach the exhaust crossover pipe.

36. Install the intake manifold.

37. Connect all electrical wiring and vacuum hoses.

38. If equipped with air conditioning, install the air conditioning compressor.

39. Connect the negative battery cable.

40. Fill cooling system and check for leaks. Start the engine and allow to come to normal operating temperature. Recheck for leaks.

LEFT SIDE

1. Relieve the pressure in the fuel system before disconnecting any fuel lines.

2. Disconnect the negative battery cable. Raise the vehicle and support it safely.

3. Drain the cylinder block and lower the vehicle.

4. Unbolt the intake manifold.

5. Remove the spark plug loom and wires.

6. Unsecure the engine lift bracket and coolant pipe.

7. Unbolt the valve cover.

8. Remove the spark plugs.

9. Unfasten the exhaust crossover pipe.

10. Remove the oil level indicator.

11. Remove the cooling fan assembly.

12. Disconnect the exhaust manifold heat shield.

13. Remove the exhaust manifold support bracket.

14. Unbolt the exhaust manifold.

15. Remove the rocker arm assemblies.

16. Disconnect the A/C bracket bolt from the cylinder head.

Fig. 67 Tightening sequence for cylinder head bolts on 3.3L engines

17. Disconnect the bolts holding the alternator and ignition coil mounting bracket, push aside.

18. Remove the vacuum line bolt at the cylinder head (rear).

19. Remove the cylinder head bolts, then remove the cylinder head.

To install:

20. Clean the cylinder head and block of any foreign matter, nicks or heavy scratches. Clean the cylinder head bolt threads and threads in the cylinder block.

21. Position the new cylinder head gasket on the block. Apply sealant GM part no. 1052080, to the under side of the bolt heads, and thread locker GM part no. 12345382, to the bolt threads.

22. Carefully guide the cylinder head into place.

23. Coat the cylinder head bolts with sealing compound and install into the head. Tighten the cylinder head bolts according to the following procedure:

 a. Tighten in sequence to 35 ft. lbs. (47 Nm).

 b. Using an appropriate torque angle gauge, rotate each bolt in sequence an additional 130°.

 c. Rotate the center 4 bolts an additional 30° in sequence.

24. Attach the vacuum line bolt at the cylinder head.

25. Connect the A/C bracket bolt from the head.

26. Install the pushrods, guide plate and rocker arm assembly. Tighten the rocker arm pivot bolts to 28 ft. lbs. (38 Nm).

27. Install the exhaust manifold, gasket and heat shield, tighten the mounting bolts to 38 ft. lbs. (52 Nm).

28. Attach the manifold support bracket and the heat shield, tighten the nuts fro the heat shield to 20 ft. lbs. (27 Nm).

29. Install the cooling fan assembly.

30. Attach the oil level indicator, tighten to 20 ft. lbs. (27 Nm).

31. Install the exhaust crossover.

32. Install the spark plugs.

33. Attach the intake manifold and gasket.

3.8L Engine

▶ **See Figure 68**

1. Relieve the pressure in the fuel system before disconnecting any fuel lines.

2. Disconnect the negative battery cable. Raise the vehicle and support it safely.

3. Drain the cylinder block and lower the vehicle.

4. Remove the serpentine belt.

5. Remove the alternator, AIR pump, oil indicator and power steering pump, as required. Position to the side.

6. Remove the throttle cable. Remove the cruise control cable, if equipped.

7. Disconnect the fuel lines and fuel rail, as required.

8. Loosen and remove the heater hoses and radiator hoses.

9. Disconnect and tag all vacuum and electrical wiring.

10. Remove the radiator and cooling fan, if necessary.

11. Remove the intake manifold and valve cover.

12. Disconnect the exhaust manifold(s).

13. Remove the rocker arm assembly and pushrods.

14. Unbolt the cylinder head, then remove the cylinder head and gasket.

To install:

15. Clean the cylinder head and block from any foreign matter, nicks or heavy scratches. Clean the cylinder head bolt threads and threads in the cylinder block.

16. Position the new cylinder head gasket on the block.

17. Carefully guide the cylinder head into place. Coat the cylinder head bolts with sealing compound and install.

18. Tighten the cylinder head bolts according to the following procedure:

a. Tighten the cylinder head bolts in sequence to 25 ft. lbs. (34 Nm).

b. Do not exceed 60 ft. lbs. (81 Nm) at any point during the next 2 steps.

c. Using a torque angle gauge, tighten each bolt an additional 90° in sequence.

19. Install the exhaust manifold.

20. Install the intake manifold, pushrods and rocker arm assembly.

21. Install the valve cover.

22. Install the radiator and cooling fan, as required.

23. Connect all vacuum and electrical wiring.

24. Install the heater hoses and radiator hoses.

25. Connect the fuel lines and fuel rail.

26. Attach the throttle cable. Install the cruise control cable, if equipped.

27. Install the alternator, AIR pump, oil indicator and power steering pump.

28. Install the serpentine belt.

29. Connect the negative battery cable.

30. Fill cooling system and check for leaks. Start the engine and allow to come to normal operating temperature. Check for leaks and top off the coolant.

4.3L Diesel Engine

▶ **See Figure 69**

1. Remove intake manifold.

2. Remove valve cover. Loosen or remove any accessory brackets or pipe clamps which interfere.

➡ **If removing the left cylinder head, remove the oil level indicator guide.**

3. Disconnect glow plug wiring (and block heater lead if so equipped on rear bank).

4. Remove the ground strap from the rear cylinder head. Remove the fuel lines at the injector nozzles.

5. Remove rocker arm nuts, pivots, rocker arms and pushrods. Scribe pivots and keep rocker arms separated so they can be installed in their original locations.

6. Disconnect the exhaust crossover pipe from the exhaust manifold on the side being worked on and loosen it on the other.

7. Remove engine block drain plug, from side of the block where head is being removed.

8. Remove the plugs covering the upper cylinder head bolts.

9. Remove all the cylinder head bolts and remove the cylinder head.

10. If necessary to remove the prechamber, remove the glow plug and injection nozzle, then tap out with a small blunt ⅛ in. (3mm) drift. Do not use a tapered drift.

To install:

11. Install the cylinder head gaskets using a special composition gasket that must be used without a sealer.

12. Attach the cylinder head, head bolts, pipe thread plugs. Coat the plug threads, bolt threads and the area under the bolt heads with GM part no. 1052080 sealer or equivalent.

✳✳WARNING

Failure to coat the bolts with the correct sealer will result in coolant leaks and loss of clamping force on the cylinder head gasket due to thread and bolt-to-head friction. This will cause cylinder head damage.

13. Tighten the cylinder head bolts to:

• Except No. 5, 6, 11, 12, 13 and 14 — 100 ft. lbs. (135 Nm)

• No. 5, 6, 11, 12, 13 and 14 — 41 ft. lbs. (55 Nm)

Then retighten the cylinder head bolts to:

• Except No. 5, 6, 11, 12, 13 and 14 — 142 ft. lbs. (193 Nm)

• No. 5, 6, 11, 12, 13 and 14 — 59 ft. lbs. (80 Nm)

TIGHTENING SEQUENCE

1 Engine block assembly
2 Cylinder head gasket
3 Cylinder head assembly
4 Cylinder head bolt/screw
5 Cylinder head bolt/screw
6 Cylinder head locating pin

86813184

Fig. 68 Tightening sequence for cylinder head bolts on 3.8L engines

TORQUE ALL BOLTS (EXCEPT 5, 6, 11, 12, 13 & 14) TO 193 Nm (142 FT.LBS.). NUMBERS 5, 6, 11, 12, 13 & 14 TORQUE TO 80 Nm (59 FT.LBS.).

86813187

Fig. 69 Cylinder head bolt tightening sequence on 4.3L engines

TCCS3132

Fig. 70 Use a gasket scraper to remove the bulk of the old head gasket from the mating surface

14. Install the pipe thread plugs, install the plug so that the bottom of the plug is flush with the bottom of the hole to 0.250 in. (6.35mm) above.

15. Install the engine coolant drain plug.

16. Attach the engine crossover pipe to the vehicle.

17. Install the pushrods and rocker arms.

18. Bleed the valve lifters. Refer to the procedure outlined in this section.

19. Attach the ground strap.

20. Connect the glow plug wiring.

21. Install the fuel lines to injection nozzles.

22. Bolt on the oil level indicator tube.

23. Install the valve covers.

24. Install the intake manifold.

25. Fill the cooling system, start the vehicle, top off the coolant.

26. Check for leaks.

CLEANING AND INSPECTION

▶ See Figures 70 and 71

Chip carbon away from the valve heads, combustion chambers, and ports, using a chisel made of hardwood. Remove the remaining deposits with a stiff wire brush.

✳✳WARNING

DO NOT use a steel wire brush to clean an aluminum cylinder head. Special brushes are sold just for use on aluminum. Always wear eye protection when grinding chipping or wire brushing.

Be sure that the deposits are actually removed, rather than burnished. Have the cylinder head cleaned to remove grease, corrosion, and scale from the water passages. Clean the remaining cylinder head parts in an engine cleaning solvent. Do not remove the protective coating from the springs.

TCCS3133

Fig. 71 An electric drill equipped with a wire wheel will expedite complete gasket removal

RESURFACING

▶ See Figures 72 and 73

➡**All machine work should be performed by a competent, professional machine shop.**

Place a straightedge across the gasket surface of the cylinder head. Using feeler gauges, determine the clearance at the center of the straightedge. If warpage is between 0.002 in. (0.05mm) to 0.010 in. (0.25mm) in a 6 in. (152mm) span, or 0.004 in. (0.1mm) to 0.010 in. (0.25mm) over all, resurface the cylinder head. If warpage exceeds 0.010 in. (0.25mm) in a 6 in. (152mm) span, the cylinder head must be replaced.

➡**If warpage exceeds the manufacturer's maximum tolerance for material removal, the cylinder head must be replaced. When milling the cylinder heads of V-type engines, the intake manifold mounting position is altered, and must be corrected by milling the manifold flange a proportionate amount.**

Fig. 72 Check the cylinder head for warpage along the center using a straightedge and a feeler gauge

Fig. 73 Be sure to check for warpage across the cylinder head at both diagonals

Valves and Springs

ADJUSTMENT

➡This procedure must be performed on V6 engines anytime the rocker arms have been loosened or removed.

1. Remove the valve cover and the No. 1 spark plug.
2. Rotate the engine until the **0** mark on the crankshaft pulley aligns with the timing tab and the No. 1 cylinder is on the TDC of the compression stroke.
3. With the engine in this position, adjust the exhaust valves of No. 1, 2 and 3 and the intake valves of No. 1, 5 and 6. Back out the adjusting nut until lash is felt at the pushrod, then turn the nut to remove the lash. With the lash removed, turn the nut an additional 1½ turns.
4. Rotate the engine 1 complete revolution until the **0** mark on the crankshaft pulley aligns with the timing tab and the No. 4 piston is on the TDC of the compression stroke.

5. With the engine in this position, adjust the exhaust valves of No. 2, 3 and 4; adjust the valves the same way as in Step No. 3.
6. Install the valve covers and the spark plugs.

REMOVAL & INSTALLATION

▶ **See Figures 74 and 75**

1. Remove the cylinder head(s) from the vehicle as previously outlined.
2. Using a suitable valve spring compressor, compress the valve spring and remove the valve keys using a magnetic retrieval tool.
3. Slowly release the compressor and remove the valve spring caps (or rotators) and the valve springs.
4. Fabricate a valve arrangement board to use when you remove the valves, which will indicate the port in which each valve was originally installed (and which cylinder head on V6 models). Also note that the valve keys, rotators, caps, etc.

Fig. 74 A small magnet will help in removal of the valve keys

Fig. 75 Once the spring has been removed, the O-ring may be removed from the valve stem

should be arranged in a manner which will allow you to rein-stall them on the valve on which they were originally used.

5. Remove and discard the valve seals. On models using the umbrella type seals, note the location of the large and small seals for assembly purposes.

6. Thoroughly clean the valves on the wire wheel of a bench grinder, then clean the cylinder head mating surface. Avoid using a metallic scraper, since this can cause damage to the cylinder head mating surface, especially on models with aluminum heads.

7. Using a valve guide cleaner chucked into a drill, clean all of the valve guides.

To install:

8. Lubricate all of the valve stems with a light coating of engine oil, then install the valves into the proper ports/guides.

9. Install the valve seals. Be sure to use a seal protector to prevent damage to the seals as they are pushed over the valve keeper grooves. Install O-ring seals in the second groove closest to the head.

10. Install the valve springs and the spring retainers (or rotators), and using the valve compressing tool, compress the springs.

11. After all of the valves are installed and retained, tap each valve spring retainer with a rubber mallet to seat the keepers in the retainer.

INSPECTION

▶ **See Figures 76, 77 and 78**

1. Reinstall each valve into its respective port (guide) of the cylinder head.

2. Mount a dial indicator so that the stem is at 90° to the valve stem, as close to the valve guide as possible.

3. Move the valve off its seat, and measure the valve guide-to-stem clearance by rocking the stem back and forth to actuate the dial indicator.

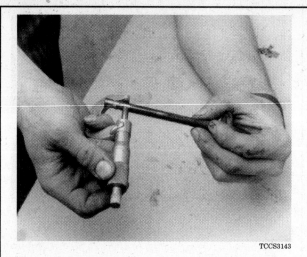

Fig. 77 Use a micrometer to measure the valve stem diameter

4. Measure the valve stems using a micrometer, and compare to specifications, to determine whether stem or guide wear is responsible for excessive clearance.

REFACING

Using a valve grinder, resurface the valves according to specifications in this section. All machine work should be performed by a competent, professional machine shop.

➡**Valve face angle is not always identical to valve seat angle.**

A minimum margin of $\frac{3}{32}$ in. (0.8mm) should remain after grinding the valve. The valve stem top should also be squared and resurfaced, by placing the stem in the V-block of the grinder, and turning it while pressing lightly against the grinding wheel. Be sure to chamfer the edge of the tip so that the squared edges don't dig into the rocker arm.

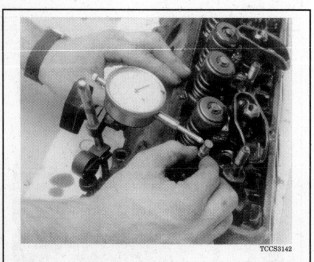

Fig. 76 A dial gauge may be used to check valve stem-to-guide clearance

Fig. 78 Valve stems may be rolled on a flat surface to check for bends

LAPPING

This procedure should be performed after the valves and seats have been machined, to insure that each valve mates to each seat precisely.

1. Invert the cylinder head, lightly lubricate the valve stems, and install the valves in the head as numbered.
2. Coat valve seats with fine grinding compound, and attach the lapping tool suction cup to a valve head.

➡**Moisten the suction cup.**

3. Rotate the tool between the palms, changing position and lifting the tool often to prevent grooving.
4. Lap the valve until a smooth, polished seat is evident.
5. Remove the valve and tool, and rinse away all traces of grinding compound.

Valve Seals

REPLACEMENT

▶ **See Figure 79**

The valve seals can be replaced with the cylinder head on or off the engine. But great care and skill must be used to perform this procedure with the cylinder head on the engine. With the cylinder head off the engine,compress the valve spring using tool J26513 or equivalent. Remove the keeper, spring and seal. All parts must be return to their original locations.

If the cylinder head is on the vehicle, 60 psi or more of compressed air must be used. The procedure will require bringing the piston of the cylinder to be serviced up to top dead center on compression stoke. Then apply compressed air

through the spark plug hole using a compressor gauge fitting. The valve spring and seal can now be removed.

➡**If the air pressure is too low or drops during this procedure the valve will fall into the engine, requiring complete removal of the cylinder head. Also if the valve is pressed downward at all, pressure will be lost and the valve will fall in.**

Valve Spring Testing

Place the spring on a flat surface next to a square. Measure the height of the spring and rotate it against the edge of the square to measure distortion. If spring height varies (by comparison) by more than $\frac{1}{16}$ in. (1.6mm) or if distortion exceeds $\frac{1}{16}$ in. (1.6mm), replace the spring. In addition to evaluating the spring as above, test the spring pressure at the installed and compressed (installed height minus valve lift) height using a valve spring tester. Spring pressure should be within 1 lb. (0.45kg) of all other springs in either position.

Valve Seat Service

The valve seats are integral with the cylinder head on all engines except the V6 diesel with aluminum cylinder heads. On all engines except that particular diesel, the seats are machined into the cylinder head casting itself. On the aluminum head diesel, the valve seats are separate inserts, which may be replaced by a competent machine shop if required. The reason for using inserts on this engine is basically because the aluminum could not withstand the constant pounding of the valves opening and closing as well as the hardened steel insert which is used.

Machining of the valve seats, or replacement of the seats in the case of the diesel, should be referred to a professional machine shop.

Valve Guide Service

The valve guides used in these engines are integral with the cylinder head, that is, they cannot be replaced.

Valve guides are most accurately repaired using the bronze wall rebuilding method. In this operation, threads are cut into the bores of the valve guide and bronze wire is turned into the threads. The bronze wall is then reamed to the proper diameter. This method is well received for a number of reasons:

• It is relatively inexpensive
• It offers better valve lubrication (the wire forms channels which retain oil)
• It offers less valve friction
• It preserves the original valve guide-to-seat relationship.

Another popular method of repairing valve guides is to have the guides knurled. The knurling entails cutting action raises metal off of the guide bore which actually narrows the inner diameter of the bore, thereby reducing the clearance between the valve guide bore and the valve stem. This method offers the same advantages as the bronze wall method, but will generally wear faster.

Another method of repairing the guides is to ream the bores and install oversize valves.

TCCS3252

Fig. 79 An umbrella type seal is used on some engines

All of the above services must be performed by a professional machine shop which has the specialized knowledge and tools necessary to perform the service.

Valve Lifters

REMOVAL & INSTALLATION

2.2L Engine

1. Disconnect the negative battery cable.
2. Drain the engine coolant in a suitable container.
3. Remove the valve cover and gasket.
4. Loosen and remove the rocker arm nuts. Remove the rocker arms and balls.
5. Remove the pushrods.
6. Remove the engine lift bracket from the rear of the engine.
7. Disconnect the spark plug wires, route them under the intake manifold.
8. Remove the cylinder head with the intake and exhaust manifolds attached.
9. Unbolt the anti-rotation brackets then remove them.
10. Remove the lifters. Keep all components separated so they may be reinstalled in the same location.

To install:

When ever new valve lifters are being installed, coat the foot of the valve lifters with camshaft assembly lube GM part no. 1052365 or equivalent.

The lifter foot is slightly convex. This can be detected by holding a straight edge to the surface while looking into a light source. If the lifter foot is worn flat or grooved, it must be replaced.

11. Lubricate the bearing surfaces with GM part no. 1052365 or equivalent.
12. Install the lifters in the same bores they were taken from.
13. Install the anti-rotation brackets, tighten the mounting bolts to 97 inch lbs. (11 Nm).
14. Install the spark plug wires to the correct plugs.
15. Install the pushrods making sure they seat in the lifters correctly.
16. Install the rocker arms, balls and mounting nuts, tighten the nuts to 22 ft. lbs. (30 Nm).
17. Secure the valve cover and gasket, tighten the bolts to 89 inch lbs. (10 Nm).
18. Connect the negative battery cable.

2.5L Engine

1. Disconnect the negative battery cable.
2. Remove the intake manifold, valve and side covers.
3. Loosen the rocker arms and rotate to clear the pushrods.
4. Remove the pushrods, retainer and guide.
5. Remove the lifters. Keep all components separated so they may be reinstalled in the same location.

To install:

6. Lubricate the lifters with engine oil and install the lifters in their bore.
7. Install the guides, retainers and pushrods.
8. With the lifter on the base circle of the camshaft, tighten the rocker arm bolts to 24 ft. lbs. (32 Nm).
9. Install the intake manifold, valve and side covers.
10. Connect battery negative cable.

3.1L Engine (VIN M)

1. Disconnect the negative battery cable.
2. Drain the cooling system.
3. Remove the rocker arm covers and the intake manifold.

➡ **Be sure to keep all valve train parts in order so they may be reinstalled in their original locations and with the same mating surfaces as when removed.**

4. Remove the rocker arm retaining nuts, rocker arm balls, rocker arms and pushrods.
5. Remove the 2 bolts from the right or left side lifter guide and remove the guide.
6. Remove the valve lifter(s) from the lifter bores.

To install:

7. Lubricate the bearing surfaces with Molykote® or equivalent.
8. Install the lifters in their original locations.
9. Install the lifter guide and lifter guide bolts and tighten the guide bolts to 89 inch lbs. (10 Nm).
10. Install the pushrods, rocker arms, rocker balls and rocker arm nuts. Tighten the rocker arm nuts to 18 ft. lbs. (25 Nm).
11. Install the intake manifold and rocker arm covers.
12. Refill the cooling system.
13. Connect the negative battery cable.
14. Start the vehicle and verify no leaks.

All Other Engines

1. Disconnect the negative battery cable.
2. Drain the cooling system.
3. Remove the valve cover and the intake manifold.
4. If the engine is equipped with individual rocker arms, loosen the rocker arm adjusting nut and rotate the arm so as to clear the pushrod.
5. If the engine is equipped with a rocker shaft assembly, remove the rocker shaft retaining bolts/nuts and remove the shaft assembly.

➡ **Be sure to keep all valve train parts in order so they may be reinstalled in their original locations and with the same mating surfaces as when removed.**

6. Remove the pushrods and valve lifters using tool J-3049 or equivalent.

To install:

7. Lubricate the bearing surfaces with Molykote® or equivalent.
8. Install the lifters in their original locations.
9. With the lifter on the base circle of the camshaft, tighten the rocker arm bolts to 14-20 ft. lbs. (20-27 Nm).
10. Connect the negative battery cable.
11. Adjust the valves, as required.

Oil Pan

REMOVAL & INSTALLATION

✱✱CAUTION

The EPA warns that prolonged contact with used engine oil may cause a number of skin disorders, including cancer! You should make every effort to minimize your exposure to used engine oil. Protective gloves should be worn when changing the oil. Wash your hands and any other exposed skin areas as soon as possible after exposure to used engine oil. Soap and water, or waterless hand cleaner should be used.

2.2L Engine

▶ **See Figure 80**

1. Disconnect the negative battery cable.
2. Remove the air cleaner and air duct form the vehicle.
3. Remove the serpentine belt.
4. Detach the engine torque strut.
5. Install the engine support fixture J-28467-A.
6. Loosen the right front lug nuts.
7. Raise and support the vehicle safely.
8. Remove the right front tire.
9. Detach the right front inner fender well splash shield.
10. Remove the flywheel cover bolts.
11. Disconnect and remove the starter and starter bracket.
12. Unbolt the A/C compressor mounting bolts, then set the compressor aside without detaching the lines.
13. Remove the front engine mount nuts from the frame.
14. Remove the front engine mount bolts from the engine.
15. Lower the vehicle.
16. Raise the engine about three inches using the support fixture.
17. Raise and safety support the vehicle.
18. Drain the engine oil.
19. Remove the front engine mount bracket.

1 Seal
2 Bolt
3 Nut
4 Oil pan
5 Oil lever sensor

END   SEALER
EAR
VIEW A

86813212

Fig. 80 Unbolt the oil pan, then lower the pan. Once the pan is removed, don't forget to discard the gasket

20. Unbolt the oil pan, then lower the pan.
To install:
21. Clean all the gasket surfaces completely.
22. Apply a thin bead of sealer around the outside edge of the oil pan and install the oil pan gasket onto the sealer.
23. Install the oil pan onto the engine and loosely install all the fasteners.
24. Tighten the nuts and bolts to 89 inch lbs. (10 Nm).
25. Install the front engine mount bracket and loosely install the mount-to-engine bolts.
26. Lower the vehicle.
27. Lower the engine into place.
28. Raise and safely support the vehicle.
29. Tighten the front engine mount bolts.
30. Install and tighten the engine mount nuts to 33 ft. lbs. (45 Nm).
31. Install the A/C compressor in the mounting bracket and tighten to 37 ft. lbs. (50 Nm).
32. Install the exhaust pipe and converter.
33. Connect the starter and install the starter and support bracket.
34. Install the flywheel cover and cover mounting bolts.
35. Install the right fender well splash shield.
36. Install the right front tire and wheel assembly and tighten to specification.
37. Lower the vehicle.
38. Remove the engine support fixture.
39. Install the engine torque strut.
40. Refill the crankcase with oil.
41. Install the serpentine belt.
42. Install the air cleaner and air duct assembly.
43. Connect the negative battery cable.
44. Start the vehicle and verify no leaks.

2.5L Engine

1982-85 MODELS

▶ **See Figure 81**

1. Raise and support the car. Drain the oil.
2. Remove the engine cradle-to-front engine mounts.
3. Disconnect the exhaust pipe at both the exhaust manifold and at the front of the converter.
4. Disconnect and remove the starter. Remove the flywheel housing or torque converter cover.
5. Remove the alternator upper bracket. Remove the splash shield.
6. Install an engine lifting chain and raise the engine. If equipped, remove the power steering pump and bracket and move it aside.
7. Remove the lower alternator bracket. Remove the engine support bracket.
8. Remove the oil pan retaining bolts and remove the pan.
To install:
9. Clean all gasket surfaces thoroughly.
10. Install the rear oil pan gasket into the rear main bearing cap, then apply a thin bead of silicone sealer to the pan gasket depressions.
11. Install the front pan gasket into the timing cover.
12. Install the side gaskets onto the pan, not the block. They can be retained in place with grease. Apply a thin bead of silicone seal to the mating joints of the gaskets.

13. Install the oil pan, then attach the timing gear bolts last, after the other bolts have been snugged down.

14. Attach the alternator bracket and the engine support bracket.

15. Reverse to install the remaining components.

1986-92 MODELS

▶ See Figure 81

1. Disconnect the negative battery cables.
2. Remove the coolant recovery reservoir.
3. Unbolt and remove the engine torque strut.
4. If needed detach the air cleaner and air inlet assemblies.
5. Remove the serpentine drive belt.
6. If equipped, remove the air conditioning compressor from it's brackets and set aside.
7. Remove the oil level indicator.
8. Raise and support the vehicle.
9. Drain the engine oil from the vehicle.
10. On some models you may need to remove the nuts from the engine mount-to-cradle.

11. Detach the exhaust pipe at the manifold and front of the converter.

12. Detach the starter and flywheel cover, then set aside.

13. Turn the front wheels to the extreme right, then disconnect the engine wiring harness screws under the oil pan right and left sides.

14. Detach the right side engine splash shield.

15. On some models you will need to remove the power steering pump and bracket.

16. Lower the vehicle, then support the engine and raise approximately 2 inches.

17. Disconnect the engine front mount and bracket.

18. Unbolt the oil pan, then lower the pan from the vehicle.

19. Clean the oil pan mounting area and oil pan of any old gasket material (RTV).

20. Reverse to install. Using RTV, apply as shown in the illustration to the oil pan. Tighten the mounting bolts on the oil pan to 89 inch lbs. (10 Nm).

21. Fill the crank case with fresh engine oil.

22. Connect the negative battery cable, then start the engine and check for leaks.

APPLY RTV SEALANT AS SPECIFIED

1	5/16" WIDE × 1/8" THICK
2	9/64" WIDE × 3/32" THICK
3	5/64" BEAD IN AREAS SHOWN

BLOCK

PAN

FWD

86813217

Fig. 81 Apply the correct amount of RTV on the oil pan mating surfaces as shown

2.8L Engine

▶ See Figures 82 and 83

1. Disconnect the battery ground.
2. Raise and support the car on jackstands.
3. Drain the oil.
4. Remove the bellhousing cover.
5. Remove the starter.
6. Support the engine.
7. Unbolt the engine from its mounts.
8. Remove the oil pan bolts.
9. Raise the engine with a jack, just enough to remove the oil pan.
10. Installation is the reverse of removal. The pan is installed using RTV gasket material in place of a gasket. Make sure that the sealing surfaces are free of old RTV material. Use a ⅛ in. (3mm) bead of RTV material on the pan sealing

Fig. 82 An extension is necessary to reach many of the bolts

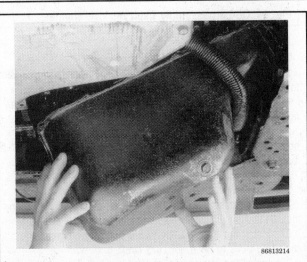

Fig. 83 The oil pan will require some maneuvering before it will come off

flange. Tighten the pan bolts to 6mm bolts to 6-9 ft. lbs. (8-12 Nm) and 8mm bolts to 14-22 ft. lbs. (19-30 Nm).
11. Fill the crank case with fresh engine oil.
12. Connect the negative battery cable, then start the engine and check for leaks.

3.0L Engine

1. Disconnect the battery ground cable.
2. Raise and support the car on jackstands.
3. Drain the oil.
4. Remove the bellhousing cover.
5. Unbolt and remove the oil pan.

To install:

6. Clean the mating area well, then install RTV gasket material in place of a gasket.
7. Make sure that the sealing surfaces are free of all old RTV material. Use a ⅛ in. (3mm) bead of RTV material on the oil pan sealing flange.
8. Install the oil pan to the block, then tighten the pan bolts to 10 ft. lbs. (14 Nm).
9. Attach the bellhousing cover.
10. Lower the vehicle.
11. Add engine oil to the engine.
12. Connect the negative battery cable.
13. Start the engine, check for leaks.

3.1L Engine (VIN T)

▶ See Figure 84

1. Disconnect the battery ground.
2. Remove the serpentine belt cover, belt and tensioner.
3. Support the engine with tool J-28467-A or equivalent, using an extra support leg.
4. Raise and safely support the vehicle.
5. Drain the oil.
6. Remove the right tire and wheel assembly. Remove the splash shield.
7. Remove the steering gear pinch bolt, as required.

✳✳CAUTION

Failure to disconnect the intermediate shaft from the rack and pinion stub shaft can result in damage to the steering gear and/or the intermediate shaft. This damage can result in loss of steering control, this could cause personal injury.

8. Remove the transaxle mount retaining nuts and engine-to-frame mount retaining nuts, as required.
9. Remove the front engine horse collar bracket from the block, as required.
10. Remove the bellhousing cover and remove the starter.
11. Position a jackstand under the frame front center crossmember.
12. Loosen but do not remove the rear frame bolts.
13. Remove the front frame bolts and lower the front frame.
14. Remove the DIS sensor wire.
15. Remove the oil pan retaining bolts and nuts, then remove the oil pan.

To install:

16. Clean and inspect the oil pan flanges, oil pan rail, front cover, rear main bearing cap and the threaded holes.

➡**The oil pan on some vehicles may not require a gasket. If a gasket is not required, the oil pan is installed using RTV gasket material. Make sure the sealing surfaces are free of old RTV material. Use a 1/8 inch (3mm) bead of RTV material on the pan sealing flange.**

17. Install the oil pan using a new gasket or RTV gasket material. Tighten the pan nuts to 89 inch lbs. (10 Nm), rear bolts; 18 ft. lbs. (25 Nm) and remaining bolts to 89 inch lbs. (10 Nm).
18. Attach the DIS sensor wire.
19. Raise the front frame and install the the front frame bolts.
20. Tighten the rear frame bolts.
21. Remove the jackstand from the front center crossmember.
22. Install the starter and bellhousing cover.
23. If removed, install the front engine horse collar bracket from the block.
24. Install the transaxle mount retaining nuts and engine to frame mount retaining nuts.
25. If removed, install the steering gear pinch bolt.
26. Install the splash shield. Install the right tire and wheel assembly.
27. Lower the vehicle.
28. Install the tensioner, serpentine belt and cover.
29. Fill the crankcase with oil.
30. Connect the negative battery cable.
31. Start the vehicle and check for leaks.

3.1L Engine (VIN M)

▶ **See Figure 84**

1. Disconnect the negative battery cable.
2. Remove the serpentine belt.
3. Unbolt the upper A/C compressor bolts, if equipped.
4. Raise and safely support the vehicle.
5. Drain the engine oil.
6. Remove the right front tire and wheel assembly.
7. Detach the right inner fender splash shield.
8. Remove the engine mount strut from the suspension support.
9. Remove the cotter pin and castle nut from the lower ball joint and separate the joint from the steering knuckle.
10. Unbolt and remove the right side sway bar link.
11. Disconnect the ABS sensor from the right subframe.
12. Remove the right side subframe mounting bolts and remove the right side subframe and control arm as an assembly.
13. Remove the lower A/C compressor mounting bolts and position the compressor aside. DO NOT disconnect the refrigerant lines or allow the compressor to hang unsupported.
14. Remove the engine mount strut bracket from the engine.
15. Remove the engine to transaxle brace.
16. Remove the oil filter.
17. Remove the starter.
18. Remove the flywheel cover.
19. Remove the oil pan flange retaining bolts and the oil pan side retaining bolts. Remove the oil pan.

1 Nut 8 Nm (71 lb.in.)
2 Bolt 8 Nm (71 lb.in.)
3 Oil pan
4 Bolt 25 Nm (18 lb.ft.)
5 Apply sealer
6 Stud 8 Nm (71 lb.in.)

86813218

Fig. 84 Oil pan assembly used on 3.1L engines

To install:

20. Clean the gasket mating surfaces.
21. Install a new gasket on the oil pan. Apply silicon sealer to the portion of the pan that contacts the rear of the block.
22. Install the oil pan and install the mounting bolts finger-tight.
23. With all the bolts in place, tighten the oil pan flange bolts to 18 ft. lbs. (25 Nm) and the oil pan side bolts to 37 ft. lbs. (50 Nm).
24. Install the flywheel cover.
25. Install the starter.
26. Coat the seal on the oil filter with clean engine oil and install the filter on the engine.
27. Install the engine-to-transaxle brace and tighten the mounting bolts to 68 ft. lbs. (93 Nm).
28. Install the engine mount strut bracket. Tighten the mounting bolt at the engine bracket to 85 ft. lbs. (115 Nm).
29. Install the A/C compressor in the mounting bracket and tighten the lower mounting bolts.

30. Attach the right side subframe and control arm assembly. Tighten the subframe mounting bolts to 89 ft. lbs. (120 Nm).

31. Install the right side sway bar link and tighten to 22 ft. lbs. (30 Nm).

32. Connect the ball joint to the steering knuckle and tighten the castle nut to 48 ft. lbs. (60 Nm). Install a new cotter pin.

33. Connect the ABS sensor from the right subframe assembly.

34. Connect the engine mount strut bracket and tighten the mounting bolt at the frame to 89 ft. lbs. (120 Nm).

35. Install the right inner fender well splash shield.

36. Install the right front tire and wheel assembly and tighten to specification.

37. Lower the vehicle.

38. Install the serpentine belt.

39. Fill the crankcase to the correct level.

40. Connect the negative battery cable.

41. Start the vehicle and verify no leaks.

3.3L Engine

1. Disconnect the negative battery cable.
2. Raise and support the vehicle safely.
3. Drain the engine oil.
4. Remove the transaxle converter cover and starter motor.
5. Remove the oil filter, oil pan retaining bolts and oil pan assembly.

To install:

6. Clean the oil pan and cylinder block mating surfaces.
7. Install a new oil pan gasket to the oil pan flange.
8. Install the oil pan and tighten the retaining bolts 8-10 ft. lbs. (11-14 Nm).
9. Lower the vehicle.
10. Fill the crankcase with oil.
11. Connect the negative battery cable.

3.8L Engine

1. Disconnect the battery ground cable.
2. Raise and safely support the vehicle.
3. Drain the oil.
4. Remove the bellhousing cover.
5. Unbolt and remove the oil pan.

To install:

6. RTV gasket material is used in place of a gasket. Make sure the sealing surfaces are free of all old RTV material. Use a 1/8 inch (3mm) bead of RTV material on the oil pan sealing flange. Tighten the pan bolts to 10-14 ft. lbs. (14-19 Nm).
7. Install the bellhousing cover.
8. Lower the vehicle.
9. Fill the crankcase with oil.
10. Connect the negative battery cable.

4.3L Diesel Engine

✳✳CAUTION

The following procedure will be personally hazardous unless the procedures are followed exactly.

1. Install the engine support fixture tool J-28467. Be certain to arrange washers on the fixture so that the bolt securing the chain to the cylinder head can be tightened to 20 ft. lbs. (27 Nm). THIS IS ABSOLUTELY NECESSARY!

2. Raise the front and rear of the car and support it on jackstands with the rear slightly lower than the front. The front jackstands should be located at the front lift points shown in your owner's manual.

3. Turn the intermediate steering shaft so that the steering gear stub shaft clamp bolt is in the UP position. Remove the clamp bolt and disconnect the two shafts. Drain the oil.

4. Remove the left side steering gear cradle bolt, then loosen the right side cradle bolt.

5. Remove the front stabilizer bar.

6. Using a 1/2 in. (13mm) drill bit, drill through the spot weld located between the rear holes at the left front stabilizer bar mounting.

7. Remove the nuts securing the engine and transaxle to its cradle.

8. Disconnect the left lower ball joint from the knuckle.

9. Place a wood block on a floor jack and raise the transaxle under the pan until the mount studs clear the cradle.

10. Remove the bolts securing the front crossmember to the right side of the cradle.

11. Remove the bolts from the left side front body mounts.

12. Remove the left side and front crossmember assemblies. It will be necessary to lower the rear crossmember below the left side of the body through the careful use of a large pry bar.

13. Remove the bellhousing cover.

14. Remove the starter.

15. Remove the engine from mount bracket.

16. Unbolt and remove the oil pan.

17. Installation is the reverse of removal. Apply sealer to both sides of the oil pan gasket and make sure that the tabs on the gaskets are installed in the seal notches. Apply RTV sealer to the front cover oil pan seal retainer, and to each seal where it contacts the block. Wipe the seal area of the pan with clean engine oil before installing the pan. Tighten the pan bolts to 10 ft. lbs. (14 Nm)., then the steering clamp bolt to 40 ft. lbs. (54 Nm).

Oil Pump

REMOVAL & INSTALLATION

✳✳CAUTION

The EPA warns that prolonged contact with used engine oil may cause a number of skin disorders, including cancer! You should make every effort to minimize your exposure to used engine oil. Protective gloves should be worn when changing the oil. Wash your hands and any other exposed skin areas as soon as possible after exposure to used engine oil. Soap and water, or waterless hand cleaner should be used.

2.2L Engine
▶ See Figure 85

1. Disconnect the negative battery cable.
2. Raise and support the vehicle safely.
3. Drain the engine oil into a suitable container.

4. Remove the oil pan.

5. Remove the oil pump-to-main bearing cap bolt, then the oil pump and extension shaft.

To install:

> ## ❋❋WARNING
>
> Heat the extension shaft retainer in hot water prior to assembly. Be sure the retainer does not crack upon installation. Wear heavy gloves when handling the hot retainer.

> ## ❋❋WARNING
>
> To avoid engine damage, all oil pump cavities must be filled with petroleum jelly before installing the gears into the pump body. Also use only original equipment gaskets. Gasket thickness is critical to proper oil pump operation.

1 Bracket
2 Bolt
3 Oil pump drive assembly
4 O-ring
5 Shaft
6 Reatiner; Heat and water soak prior to installation
7 Bolt
8 Oil pump
9 Cylinder block

86813219

Fig. 85 Oil pump assembly used on 2.2L engines

6. Install the extension shaft, oil pump and pump-to-rear main cap bolt. Tighten the oil pump-to-bearing cap bolt to 25-38 ft. lbs. (34-54 Nm) and the upper oil pump drive bolt to 14-22 ft. lbs. (19-30 Nm).

7. Install the oil pan and attaching bolts.

8. Lower the vehicle.

9. Fill the crankcase with clean engine oil.

10. Connect the negative battery cable.

11. Start the engine, check the oil pressure, then check for leaks.

12. Check the oil level, add as needed.

2.5L Engine

1. Disconnect the negative battery cable.

2. Raise and support the vehicle safely.

3. Drain the engine oil and remove the oil pan.

4. Remove the 2 flange mounting bolts and nut from the main bearing cap bolt.

5. Remove the pump and screen as an assembly.

To install:

6. Remove the 4 cover attaching screws and cover from the oil pump assembly.

7. Pack the space around the oil pump gears completely full of petroleum jelly. There must be no air space left inside the pump. If the pump is not packed, it may not begin to pump oil as soon as the engine is started and engine damage may result.

> ## ❋❋WARNING
>
> To avoid engine damage, all oil pump cavities must be filled with petroleum jelly before installing the gears into the pump body. Also use only original equipment gaskets. Gasket thickness is critical to proper oil pump operation.

8. Align the oil pump shaft to match with the oil pump drive shaft tang, then install the oil pump to the block positioning the flange over the oil pump driveshaft lower bushing. Do not use any gasket. Tighten the bolts to 20 ft. lbs. (30 Nm).

9. Install the oil pan using a new gasket and seals.

10. Install the 2 flange mounting bolts and nut to the main bearing cap bolt.

11. Lower the vehicle.

12. Fill the crankcase with oil.

13. Connect the negative battery cable.

2.8L Engine

▶ See Figures 86, 87 and 88

1. Disconnect the negative battery cable.

2. Raise and support the vehicle safely.

3. Drain the engine oil and remove the oil pan.

4. Remove the pump-to-rear main bearing cap bolt and remove the pump and extension shaft.

To install:

5. Remove the 4 cover attaching screws and cover from the oil pump assembly.

6. Pack the space around the oil pump gears completely full of petroleum jelly. There must be no air space left inside the pump. If the pump is not packed, it may not begin to

Fig. 86 Once the oil pan is removed you have access to the oil pump

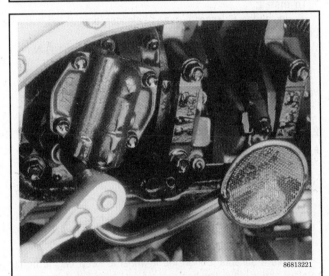

Fig. 87 Remove the bolts securing the oil pump

Fig. 88 The pump assembly may now be pulled out

pump oil as soon as the engine is started and engine damage may result.

✳✳WARNING

To avoid engine damage, all oil pump cavities must be filled with petroleum jelly before installing the gears into the pump body. Also use only original equipment gaskets. Gasket thickness is critical to proper oil pump operation.

7. Assemble the pump and extension shaft with retainer to rear main bearing cap, aligning the top end of the extension shaft with the lower end of the drive gear.
8. Install the pump-to-the rear bearing cap bolt. Tighten to 30 ft. lbs. (40 Nm).
9. Install the oil pan.
10. Lower the vehicle.
11. Fill the crankcase with oil.
12. Connect the negative battery cable.

3.0L Engines

1. Remove the oil filter.
2. Unbolt the oil pump cover from the timing chain cover.
3. Slide out the oil pump gears. Clean all parts thoroughly in solvent and check for wear. Remove the oil pressure relief valve cap, spring and valve.
4. Installation is the reverse of removal. Tighten the pressure relief valve cap to 35 ft. lbs. (47 Nm). Place a straight-edge across the face of the pump cover and check that it is flat to within 0.001 in. (0.025mm). Pack the oil pump cavity with petroleum jelly so that there is no air space. Install the cover and tighten the bolts to 10 ft. lbs. (14 Nm).

✳✳WARNING

To avoid engine damage, all oil pump cavities must be filled with petroleum jelly before installing the gears into the pump body. Also use only original equipment gaskets. Gasket thickness is critical to proper oil pump operation.

3.1 Engine (VIN T)

1. Disconnect the negative battery cable.
2. Raise and support the vehicle safely.
3. Drain the engine oil and remove the oil pan.
4. Remove the pump-to-rear main bearing cap bolt and remove the pump and extension shaft.

To install:

5. Remove the 4 cover attaching screws and cover from the oil pump assembly.
6. Pack the space around the oil pump gears completely full of petroleum jelly. There must be no air space left inside the pump. If the pump is not packed, it may not begin to pump oil as soon as the engine is started and engine damage may result.

✳✳WARNING

To avoid engine damage, all oil pump cavities must be filled with petroleum jelly before installing the gears into the pump body. Also use only original equipment gaskets. Gasket thickness is critical to proper oil pump operation.

7. Assemble the pump and extension shaft with retainer to rear main bearing cap, aligning the top end of the extension shaft with the lower end of the drive gear.

8. Install the pump-to-the rear bearing cap bolt. Tighten to 30 ft. lbs. (41 Nm).

9. Install the oil pan.

10. Lower the vehicle.

11. Fill the crankcase with oil.

12. Connect the negative battery cable.

3.1 Engine (VIN M)

1. Disconnect the negative battery cable.

2. Raise and safely support the vehicle.

3. Drain the engine oil into a suitable container.

4. Unbolt the oil pan, then remove it from the vehicle.

5. Remove the crankshaft oil deflector bolts.

6. Remove the crankshaft oil deflector.

7. Remove the oil pump retaining bolts and remove the oil pump and pump driveshaft.

To Install:

8. Install the oil pump and pump driveshaft. Tighten the oil pump mounting bolts to 30 ft. lbs. (41 Nm).

9. Install the crankshaft oil deflector and mounting nuts. Tighten the mounting nuts to 18 ft. lbs. (25 Nm).

10. Attach the oil pan.

11. Lower the vehicle.

12. Fill the crankcase to the correct level with oil.

13. Start the engine, check the oil pressure and check for leaks.

3.3L and 3.8L Engines

1. Disconnect the negative battery cable.

2. Drain the engine oil.

3. Remove the oil filter adapter, pressure regulator valve and spring.

4. Remove the oil pump cover attaching screws and cover.

5. Remove the gears.

To install:

6. Lubricate the gears with petroleum jelly.

7. Assemble the gears in the housing.

8. Pack the gear cavity with petroleum jelly.

9. Install the oil pump cover and screws. Tighten to 97 inch lbs. (11 Nm).

10. Install the pressure regulator and spring valve.

11. Install the oil filter adapter with a new gasket. Tighten the oil filter adapter bolts to 24 ft. lbs. (33 Nm).

12. Install the front cover on the engine.

13. Fill the crankcase with oil.

14. Connect the negative battery cable.

4.3L Diesel Engine

1. Remove the oil pan.

2. Unbolt and remove the oil pump and drive extension.

To install:

3. Pack the gear cavity with petroleum jelly.

4. Insert the drive shaft extension through the opening in the main bearing cap and block until the shaft mates into the oil pump drive gear.

5. Position the pump onto the rear main bearing cap and install the attaching bolts. Tighten the bolts to 18 ft. lbs. (24 Nm).

6. Install the oil pan assembly.

Crankshaft Damper

REMOVAL & INSTALLATION

2.2L Engine

1. Remove the drive belt from the vehicle.

2. Loosen the lug nuts on the right front tire.

3. Raise and support the vehicle safely.

4. Remove the right front tire and wheel from the vehicle.

5. Detach the right engine splash shield.

6. Loosen and remove the crankshaft bolt.

7. Pull the crankshaft balancer hub and balancer off the vehicle. Make sure to use a suitable tool to hold the flywheel from rotating.

8. Remove the balancer using a suitable puller.

To install:

9. Install the balancer hub and balancer, tighten the hub bolts to 37 ft. lbs. (40 Nm).

10. Install the balancer bolt, tighten to 77 ft. lbs. (105 Nm).

11. Attach the right engine splash shield.

12. Install the right front tire and wheel assembly, lower the vehicle, then tighten the lug nuts to 100 ft. lbs. (136 Nm).

13. Install the drive belt.

2.5L, 3.3L and 3.8L Engines

▶ See Figure 89

1. Disconnect the negative battery cable, and remove the serpentine belt.

2. Raise and safely support the vehicle.

3. Remove the flywheel or torque converter cover.

4. Remove the right front tire and wheel assembly.

5. Detach the right front engine splash shield.

6. Use a suitable tool on the flywheel to keep engine from rotating and remove the bolt and washer from the damper.

7. Remove the balancer and the key using a suitable puller.

To install:

8. Install the key and balancer.

9. Install the bolt and washer, tighten the bolt to 162 ft. lbs. (220 Nm).

10. Attach the engine splash shield.

11. Install the tire and wheel assembly.

12. Install the flywheel or torque converter cover.

13. Lower the vehicle.

14. Install the serpentine belt.

15. Connect the negative battery cable.

2.8L Engine

1. Disconnect the negative battery cable, and remove the serpentine belt.

2. Raise and safely support the vehicle.

3. Remove the flywheel or torque converter cover.

4. Right front tire and wheel assembly.

5. Remove the right front engine splash shield.

6. Remove the AIR pump, if equipped.

1 220 Nm (162 lb.ft.)
2 Washer
3 Crankshaft balancer
4 Key
5 Front cover

86813238

Fig. 89 The damper assembly is secured by a large bolt

7. Use a suitable tool on the flywheel to keep engine from rotating and remove the bolt and washer from the damper.

8. With tool J-29113, or equivalent, installed on the damper, turn the puller screw.

➡**The inertia weight section of the damper is assembled to the hub with a rubber sleeve. A proper puller must be used to avoid damaging the damper assembly.**

9. Remove the damper.

To install:

10. Coat the cover seal with clean engine oil before installing the damper using tool J-29113 or equivalent.

11. Apply sealant to the key and keyway.

12. Place the damper into position and pull into place with tool.

13. Install the retaining bolt and tighten to 110 ft. lbs. (149 Nm).

14. Install the right front tire and wheel.

15. Install the AIR pump, inner splash shield and lower the vehicle.

16. Tighten the lug nuts on the right front to 100 ft. lbs. (136 Nm).

17. Install the serpentine drive belt.

18. Install the negative battery cable.

3.1L Engine (VIN T)

1. Disconnect the negative battery cable, and remove the serpentine belt.

2. Raise and safely support the vehicle.

3. Remove the flywheel or torque converter cover.

4. Right front tire and wheel assembly.

5. Remove the right front engine splash shield.

6. Use a suitable tool on the flywheel to keep engine from rotating and remove the bolt and washer from the damper.

7. Remove the balancer and the key. With tool J-24420-B or equivalent, turn the puller screw to remove the balancer.

To install:

8. Install the key and balancer.

9. Install the bolt and washer, tighten the bolt to 76 ft. lbs. (103 Nm).

10. Attach the engine splash shield.

11. Install the tire and wheel assembly.

12. Install the flywheel or torque converter cover.

13. Lower the vehicle.

14. Tighten the right wheel lug nuts to 100 ft. lbs. (136 Nm).

15. Install the serpentine belt.

16. Connect the negative battery cable.

4.3L Diesel Engine

1. Remove the serpentine belt.

2. Raise and support the vehicle.

3. Remove the right splash shield.

4. Unbolt the four pulley-to-crankshaft balancer bolts, then remove the pulley assembly.

5. Unbolt the balancer-to-crankshaft bolt and washer.

6. Remove the balancer assembly by pulling it off. If the balancer is tight on the crankshaft, remove using a puller.

To install:

7. Apply sealer to the inside diameter of the pulley hub and to the crankshaft key to prevent possible oil leakage. Coat the outside area of the pulley hub which enters the seal with lubricant.

8. Attach the balancer on the crankshaft. If it will not slip on with hand pressure, remove the burrs present on the balancer, key or crankshaft, then lightly tap the balancer in place with a rawhide or soft faced hammer.

9. Install the washer and bolt, tighten to 203-350 ft. lbs. (275-474 Nm).

10. Install the pulley assembly, tighten the four bolts to 29 ft. lbs. (40 Nm).

11. Attach the right splash shield.

12. Install the serpentine drive belt.

13. Add engine oil if needed, road test the vehicle and check for leaks.

Timing Gear/Chain Cover

REMOVAL & INSTALLATION

2.2L Engine

1. Disconnect the negative battery cable.

2. Remove the serpentine drive belt.

3. Remove the drive belt tensioner as follows:

   a. Remove the coolant reservoir.

   b. Unbolt the front alternator mounting bolts.

   c. Remove the three power steering pump mounting bolts. These bolts can be accessed by working through the holes in the drive pulley on the pump. Lay the pump aside, without disconnecting the power steering lines.

   d. Unsecure the four tensioner mounting bolts, then remove the tensioner.

4. Raise and safely support the vehicle.

5. Remove the oil pan.

6. Remove the crankshaft pulley and hub as follows:

   a. Remove the right front tire and wheel assembly.

   b. Detach the right inner fender well splash shield.

   c. Remove the bolts from the crankshaft pulley and hub, then remove the pulley from the pulley hub.

   d. Install tool J-24420-B, or an equivalent puller and remove the hub from the crankshaft.

7. Unbolt the front cover.

8. Lift the front cover off. If it is difficult to remove, use a soft faced mallet to lightly strike the cover loose.

9. After removing the timing cover, pry oil seal from front of cover. Lubricate the seal lip and install new lip seal with lip, open side of seal, facing toward the cylinder block. Carefully drive or press seal into place.

To install:

10. Clean all gasket surfaces completely.

11. Apply a thin bead of sealer around the gasket area of the front cover, then install a new front cover gasket on the cover.

12. Attach the front cover making sure the dowel pins line up with the holes in the cover. Tighten the mounting bolts to 97 inch lbs. (11 Nm).

13. Attach the crankshaft pulley and hub as follows;

   a. Coat the seal contact area of the hub with clean engine oil.

   b. Line up the notch in the hub with the crankshaft key, then slide the hub on until the key is in the notch.

   c. Using a suitable puller, J-29113 or an equivalent, seat the hub on the crankshaft.

   d. Install the pulley on the hub. Tighten the three pulley mounting bolts to 37 ft. lbs. (50 Nm) and the center hub bolt to 77 ft. lbs. (105 Nm).

   e. Install the right fender splash shield.

   f. Install the right tire and wheel assembly.

14. Attach the oil pan, then lower the vehicle.

15. Tighten the lug nuts to 100 ft. lbs. (136 Nm).

16. Install the serpentine drive belt tensioner as follows:

   a. Attach the tensioner on the front of the engine, then tighten the mounting bolts to 37 ft. lbs. (50 Nm).

   b. Position the power steering pump against the tension so the bolt hoes are lined up. Mount the three bolts tightening them to 25 ft. lbs. (34 Nm).

   c. Install the two alternator bolts removed. Tighten the upper bolt to 22 ft. lbs. (30 Nm) and the lower bolt to 37 ft. lbs. (50 Nm).

   d. Install the coolant reservoir.

17. Install the serpentine drive belt.

18. Connect the negative battery cable.

19. Top off the coolant reservoir as needed.

20. Start the vehicle and verify there are no oil or coolant leaks.

2.5L Engine

▶ **See Figures 90 and 91**

1. Relieve the pressure in the fuel system before disconnecting any fuel line connections.

2. Disconnect the negative battery cable.

3. On some models you will need to remove the drive belt tensioner.

4. Raise and support the vehicle.

5. Remove the right tire assembly.

6. Remove the inner fender splash shield. Remove the crankshaft balancer.

7. On some models you will need to:

   a. Remove the alternator lower bracket and the front engine mounts.

   b. Using a floor jack, raise the engine.

   c. Remove the engine mount mounting bracket-to-cylinder block bolts. Remove the bracket and mount as an assembly.

8. Remove the oil pan-to-front cover screws and front cover-to-block screws.

9. Pull the cover slightly forward, just enough to allow cutting of the oil pan front seal flush with the block on both sides.

10. Remove the front cover and attached portion of the pan seal.

11. Clean all of the gasket surfaces thoroughly.

To install:

12. Pry oil seal from front of cover, then lubricate the seal lip. Install the new lip seal facing toward the cylinder block. Carefully drive or press seal into place with tool J-34995 or equivalent will help.

13. Coat the new gasket with sealer and position it on the front cover.

14. Apply a 1/8 in. (3mm) bead of silicone sealer to the joint formed at the oil pan and stock.

86813236

Fig. 90 Coat the new gasket with sealer and position it on the front cover

TIGHTEN IN PROPER SEQUENCE
"A" THROUGH "G".

1 Bolt 10 Nm (89 in.lb.)
2 Front cover

86813237

Fig. 91 Make sure to tighten the mounting screws in proper sequence

15. Attach the front cover, partially tighten the two opposing cover screws. Install the remaining block to cover screws, then tighten those screws in proper sequence. See the illustration.

16. Remove the tool J-34995.

17. If removed:

a. Install the alternator lower bracket and the front engine mounts.

b. Using a floor jack, raise the engine.

c. Attach the bracket and mount as an assembly, by installing the engine mount mounting bracket-to-cylinder block bolts.

18. Install the harmonic balancer.

19. Attach the right splash shield.

20. Install the right tire assembly.

21. Lower the vehicle, then tighten the lug nuts.

22. Install the drive belt tensioner.

23. Connect the negative battery cable.

2.8L Engine

▶ See Figure 92

1. Relieve the pressure in the fuel system before disconnecting any fuel line connections. Disconnect the negative battery cable.

2. Drain the cooling system.

3. Remove the serpentine belt and tensioner.

4. Remove the alternator and power steering pump. Locate and support these accessories to the side, remove the AIR pump and hoses, as needed.

5. Remove the A/C compressor without disconnecting any air conditioning lines and lay it aside. If equipped, remove the A.I.R. pump. Raise and support the vehicle safely.

6. Remove the inner splash shield. Remove the torsion damper using tool J-24420-B or equivalent.

7. Remove the flywheel cover at the transaxle and starter.

8. Remove the serpentine belt idler pulley.

9. Drain the engine oil. Remove the oil pan and lower front cover bolts.

10. Lower the vehicle.

11. Remove the radiator hose at the water pump. Remove the heater hose at fill pipe.

12. Remove the bypass hose and overflow hoses. Remove the canister purge hose.

13. Remove the crankshaft damper.

14. Remove the upper front cover retaining bolts and remove the front cover.

15. Pry the oil seal from the front of the cover. Lubricate the seal lip and install new lip seal facing toward the cylinder block. Carefully drive or press seal into place.

To install:

16. Clean the mating surfaces of the front cover and cylinder block.

17. Install a new gasket. Make sure not to damage the sealing surfaces. Apply sealer GM part no. 1052080 or equivalent, to the sealing surface of the front cover.

18. Position the front cover on the engine block and install the upper cover bolt.

19. Raise and safely support the vehicle. Install the oil pan and lower cover bolts.

20. Install the serpentine belt idler pulley.

21. Bolt the flywheel cover to the transaxle. Install the starter.

Fig. 92 Remove the upper front cover retaining bolts and remove the front cover

22. Install the torsion damper. Install the inner splash shield.

23. Lower the vehicle.

24. Attach the bypass hose and overflow hoses. Install the canister purge hose.

25. Connect the radiator hose to the water pump. Connect the heater hose to fill pipe.

26. Mount the alternator and power steering pump.

27. Install the tensioner serpentine belt.

28. Connect the negative battery cable.

3.0L Engine

▶ See Figure 93

1. Drain the cooling system.

2. Disconnect the radiator hoses and the heater hose at the water pump.

3. Remove the water pump pulley and all drive belts. Remove the front engine mount-to-cradle bolts and raise the engine.

4. Unbolt the alternator and brackets.

5. Remove the distributor.

6. Remove the balancer bolt and washer, and using a puller, remove the balancer.

7. Unsecure the cover-to-block bolts. Remove the two oil pan-to-cover bolts.

8. Remove the cover and gasket.

9. Installation is the reverse of removal. Always use a new gasket coated with sealer. Tighten the timing cover bolts to 30 ft. lbs. (41 Nm).

3.1L Engine (VIN M)

▶ See Figure 94

1. Disconnect the negative battery cable.

2. Drain the cooling system into a suitable container.

3. Remove the right engine mount bracket.

4. Remove the serpentine belt.

5. Remove the crankshaft balancer.

6. Remove the serpentine belt tensioner mounting bolt and tensioner.

7. Remove the oil pan.

Fig. 93 Bolt locations for the 3.0L engine on the timing cover

8. Remove coolant bypass pipe from the water pump and the intake manifold.

9. Disconnect the lower radiator hose to from the front cover outlet.

10. Remove the front cover mounting bolts and remove the front cover.

To Install:

11. Clean all gasket surfaces completely.

12. Apply a thin bead of sealer around the gasket sealing area of the front cover. Install a new front cover seal on the front cover.

13. Install the front cover on the engine and tighten the mounting bolts to 15 ft. lbs. (21 Nm).

14. Connect the radiator hose to the coolant outlet.

15. Install coolant bypass pipe to the water pump and the intake manifold.

16. Install the oil pan following the recommended procedure.

17. Install crankshaft balancer.

18. Install the serpentine belt tensioner and tighten the mounting bolt to 40 ft. lbs. (54 Nm).

19. Install the serpentine belt.

20. Install the right engine mount bracket and tighten the bracket-to-mount bolts to 96 ft. lbs. (130 Nm).

21. Refill the cooling system.

22. Check the engine oil level and top off as necessary.

23. Connect the negative battery cable.

24. Start the vehicle and verify no oil leaks.

3.1L Engine (VIN T)

1. Relieve the pressure in the fuel system before disconnecting any fuel line connections. Disconnect the negative battery cable.

2. Drain the cooling system.

3. Remove the serpentine belt and tensioner.

4. Remove the alternator and power steering pump. Locate and support these accessories to the side, remove the AIR pump and hoses, as needed.

5. Remove the A/C compressor without disconnecting any air conditioning lines and lay it aside. If equipped, remove the A.I.R. pump. Raise and support the vehicle safely.

6. Remove the inner splash shield. Remove the torsion damper using tool J-24420-B or equivalent.

7. Remove the flywheel cover at the transaxle and starter.

8. Remove the serpentine belt idler pulley.

9. Remove the crankshaft damper.

10. Drain the engine oil. Remove the oil pan and lower front cover bolts.

11. Lower the vehicle.

12. Remove the radiator hose at the water pump. Remove the heater hose at fill pipe.

13. Remove the bypass hose and overflow hoses. Remove the canister purge hose.

14. Remove the upper front cover retaining bolts and remove the front cover.

To install:

15. Pry the oil seal from the front of the cover. Lubricate the seal lip and install new lip seal with lip, open side of seal, facing toward the cylinder block. Carefully drive or press seal into place.

16. Clean the mating surfaces of the front cover and cylinder block.

17. Install a new gasket. Make sure not to damage the sealing surfaces. Apply sealer GM part no. 1052080 or equivalent, to the sealing surface of the front cover.

18. Position the front cover on the engine block and install the upper cover bolt.

19. Raise and safely support the vehicle. Install the oil pan and lower cover bolts.

20. Install the crankshaft damper.

21. Install the serpentine belt idler pulley.

22. Bolt the flywheel cover to the transaxle. Install the starter.

23. Install the torsion damper. Install the inner splash shield.

24. Lower the vehicle.

25. Attach the bypass hose and overflow hoses. Install the canister purge hose.

26. Connect the radiator hose to the water pump. Connect the heater hose to fill pipe.

27. Mount the alternator and power steering pump.

28. Install the tensioner serpentine belt.

29. Connect the negative battery cable.

3.3L Engine

1. Relieve the pressure in the fuel system before disconnecting any fuel line connections. Disconnect the negative battery cable.

2. Drain the cooling system.

3. Remove the serpentine belt.

4. Remove the heater pipes. Remove the coolant bypass hose and lower radiator hose from cover.

5. Raise and support the vehicle safely.

6. Remove the inner splash shield.

7. Remove the crankshaft balancer.

8. Disconnect all electrical connectors at the camshaft sensor, crankshaft sensor and oil pressure sender.

9. Remove the oil pan-to-front cover retaining bolts, front cover retaining bolts and remove the front cover.

To install:

10. Pry the oil seal from the front of the cover. Lubricate the seal lip and install new lip seal with lip, open side of seal,

1 Apply sealant
2 Crankshaft
3 Front cover oil seal
4 Front cover small bolt
5 Front coverage bolt
6 Front cover
7 Front cover gasket
8 Front cover dowel pin

86813257

Fig. 94 When installing the cover, make sure you put the small bolts into the correct positions on the cover

facing toward the cylinder block. Carefully drive or press seal into place.

11. Clean the mating surfaces of the front cover and cylinder block.

12. Install a new gasket on the cylinder block. Install the front cover. Apply sealer to the threads of the cover retaining bolts and secure the cover. Tighten the bolts to 22 ft. lbs. (30 Nm).

13. Install the oil pan-to-front cover bolts. Tighten the bolts to 88 inch lbs. (10 Nm).

14. Reconnect the camshaft sensor, crankshaft sensor and oil pressure sender electrical connectors. Adjust the crankshaft sensor using tool J-37087 or equivalent.

15. Install the crankshaft balancer.

16. Install the inner splash shield.

17. Lower the vehicle.

18. Install the heater pipes. Install the coolant bypass hose and lower radiator hose from cover.

19. Install the serpentine belt.

20. Connect the negative battery cable.

21. Fill cooling system and check for leaks. Start the engine and allow to come to normal operating temperature. Recheck for leaks.

3.8L Engine

1. Relieve the pressure in the fuel system before disconnecting any fuel line connections. Disconnect the negative battery cable.

2. Drain the cooling system.

3. Disconnect the lower radiator hose and the heater hose from the water pump.

4. Remove the 2 nuts from the front engine mount from the cradle and raise the engine using a suitable lifting device.

5. Remove the water pump pulley and the serpentine belt.

6. Unbolt the alternator and brackets.

7. Remove the balancer bolt and washer. Using a puller, remove the balancer.

8. Unbolt the cover-to-block bolts. Remove the 2 oil pan-to-cover bolts.

9. Remove the cover and gasket.

To install:

10. Pry the oil seal from the front of the cover. Lubricate the seal lip and install new lip seal with lip, open side of seal, facing toward the cylinder block. Carefully drive or press seal into place.

11. Clean the mating surfaces of the front cover and cylinder block.

➡**Remove the oil pump cover and pack the space around the oil pump gears completely with petroleum jelly. There must be no air space left inside the pump. If the pump is not packed, it may not begin to pump oil as soon as the engine is started and engine damage may result.**

12. Install a new gasket to the oil pan and cylinder block. Install the front cover. Apply sealer to the threads of the cover retaining bolts and secure the cover.

13. Install the cover-to-block bolts, then the 2 oil pan-to-cover bolts.

14. Install the balancer, washer and balancer bolt.

15. Attach the alternator brackets and the alternator.

16. Install the water pump pulley and the serpentine belt.

17. Lower the engine into position and install the 2 nuts to the front engine mount at the cradle.

18. Connect the lower radiator hose and the heater hose to the water pump.

19. Connect the negative battery cable.

20. Fill cooling system and check for leaks. Start the engine and allow to come to normal operating temperature. Check for leaks.

4.3L Diesel Engine
▶ **See Figure 95**

1. Drain the cooling system.

2. Disconnect the radiator hoses and the heater hoses at the water pump. Disconnect the heater outlet pipe at the manifold.

3. Disconnect the power steering pump, vacuum pump, belt tensioner, air conditioning compressor and alternator brackets.

✳✳CAUTION

Do not disconnect any refrigerant lines.

4. Remove the crankshaft balancer using a puller.

5. Remove the front cover to block bolts and the probe holder (RPM counter).

6. Remove the front cover and both of the dowel pins. It may be necessary to grind a flat on the pins to get a rough surface for gripping.

7. Installation is the reverse of removal. Grind a chamfer on the end of each dowel pin to aid in cover installation. Trim 1/8 in. (3mm) from the ends of the new front pan seal. Apply RTV sealer to the oil pan seal retainer. After the cover gasket is in place, apply sealer to the junction of the pan, gasket and block. When installing the cover, rotate it right and left while guiding the pan seal into place with a small flat bladed tool.

Oil Seal

REMOVAL & INSTALLATION

Cover Removed

EXCEPT 3.0L AND 3.8L ENGINES

1. After removing the timing cover, pry oil seal out of front of cover.

2. Install new lip seal with lip (open side of seal) inside and drive or press seal carefully into place. The use of tools J-34995, J-35468 or an equivalent can be helpful.

3.0L AND 3.8L ENGINES

1. Using a drift punch, drive the oil seal and the shedder from the front toward the rear of the timing cover.

2. To install the new oil seal, coil it around the opening with the ends toward the top. Using a punch, drive in the oil seal and stake it at three places. Rotate a hammer handle inside the seal until the crankshaft balancer can be inserted through the opening.

3. To complete the installation, reverse the removal procedures. Tighten the balancer bolt to proper torque.

Cover Installed

EXCEPT DIESEL ENGINE

The oil seal may be removed from the timing cover without removing the cover. To do this, remove the damper pulley and pry the oil seal from the timing cover, using a small pry bar.

Place a seal installation tool J-34995, J-35468 or equivalent on the crankshaft (to prevent damaging the seal) when installing the new oil seal or the front cover. To install the new oil seal, place the seal's open end toward the inside of the cover and drive it into the cover. Tighten the damper pulley bolt to proper torque.

4.3L DIESEL ENGINE
▶ **See Figures 96 and 97**

1. Remove the crankshaft balancer from the crankshaft.

2. Using tools J-1859-03 and J-23129 or equivalent, press the oil seal from the timing cover.

3. Remove the burrs from the front cover with a tapered reamer or bearing scraper so that when the seal is installed the seals outside diameter is not scratched. This also form's a chamfer at the opening so that the seal will enter the front of the cover squarely.

4. Lubricate the seal lip with engine oil and the outer edge with sealant GM no. 1050026. Using tool J-29659 or equivalent, press the new oil seal into the timing cover until it seats.

5. To complete the installation, reverse the removal procedures. Tighten the crankshaft balancer bolt to 203-350 ft. lbs. (275-474 Nm).

1 Camshaft
2 Crankshaft
3 Camshaft sprocket key
4 Injection pump drive gear
5 Crankshaft sprocket key
6 Front camshaft bearing retainer
7 65 Nm (48 ft.lbs.)
8 Crankshaft sprocket
9 Timing chain
10 Camshaft sprocket
11 Washer
12 87 Nm (64 ft.lbs.)
13 Slinger
14 Gasket
15 Front cover

16 55 Nm (41 ft.lbs.)
17 28 Nm (21 ft.lbs.)
18 Probe holder (RPM counter)
19 Crankshaft balancer
20 Washer
21 217-475 Nm (160-350 ft.lbs.)
22 Pulley assembly
23 40 Nm (30 ft.lbs.)
24 Cover

86813239

Fig. 95 Exploded view of the 4.3L diesel engine timing cover and chain assembly

Fig. 96 Special tools are available to remove the oil seal on the 4.3L diesel

Fig. 97 This tool should be used to press the oil seal evenly

Timing Gear

REMOVAL & INSTALLATION

➡ **On the 2.5L engine, which does not use a timing chain, the camshaft gear is press fitted on the camshaft. If replacement of the camshaft gear is necessary, the engine must be removed from the vehicle and the camshaft and gear removed from the engine.**

1. Relieve the pressure in the fuel system before disconnecting any fuel line connections.
2. Disconnect the negative battery cable.
3. Remove the engine from the vehicle.
4. Remove the camshaft and gear assembly from the engine block.
5. Using an arbor press and adapter, remove the gear from the camshaft. Position the thrust plate to avoid damage by interference with the Woodruff® key as the gear is removed.

To install:
6. Support the camshaft at the back of the front journal in the arbor press using press plate adapters.
7. Position the spacer ring thrust plate over the end of the shaft and key.
8. Press the gear on the shaft with the bottom against the spacer ring. Measure the end clearance at the thrust plate. Clearance should be within 0.0015-0.0050 in. (0.0381-1.270mm).
   a. If the clearance is less than 0.0015 in. (0.0381mm), replace the spacer ring.
   b. If more than 0.0050 in. (1.270mm), make certain the gear is seated properly against the spacer. If the clearance is still excessive, replace the thrust plate.
9. Lubricate the camshaft journals with a high quality engine oil supplement. Install the camshaft and gear into the engine block.
10. Rotate the camshaft and crankshaft so the timing marks on the gear teeth align. The engine is now in No. 4-cylinder firing position.

11. Install the camshaft thrust plate-to-block screws and tighten to 90 inch lbs. (10 Nm).
12. Install the engine in the vehicle.
13. Connect the negative battery cable.

Timing Chain and Sprocket

REMOVAL & INSTALLATION

2.2L Engine

▶ See Figure 98

1. Disconnect the negative battery cable.
2. Remove the timing chain front cover.
3. Rotate the crankshaft until the piston in No. 1 cylinder is at TDC on the compression stroke. The marks on the camshaft and crankshaft sprockets should be in alignment.
4. Loosen but do not remove, the timing chain tensioner nut.
5. Unbolt the camshaft sprocket bolt, then remove the sprocket and chain together. If the sprocket does not slide from the camshaft easily, a light blow with a soft mallet at the lower edge of the sprocket will dislodge it.
6. Use a puller such as J-22888 or equivalent and remove the crankshaft sprocket.

To install:

7. Install the crankshaft sprocket, using the installation tool J-5590 or equivalent.
8. Install the timing chain over the camshaft sprocket and then around the crankshaft sprocket. Make sure the marks on the two sprockets are in alignment.
9. Lubricate the thrust surface with Molykote® or it's equivalent.
10. Align the dowel in the camshaft with the dowel hole in the sprocket and then install the sprocket onto the camshaft. Use the mounting bolt to draw the sprocket onto the camshaft and then tighten to 77 ft. lbs. (105 Nm).
11. Lubricate the timing chain with clean engine oil. Tighten the bolts on the chain tensioner to 18 ft. lbs. (24 Nm).
12. Install the timing chain front cover.
13. Connect the negative battery cable.

2.5L Engine

▶ See Figure 99

1. Disconnect the negative battery cable.
2. Remove the crankcase front cover.
3. Loosen the camshaft bolt.
4. Place the No. 1 piston at TDC with the marks on the camshaft and crankshaft sprockets aligned.
5. Remove the camshaft sprocket and chain.

➡If the sprocket does not come off easily, a light blow with a plastic mallet on the lower edge of the sprocket should dislodge the sprocket.

To install:

6. Aligning the timing marks with the engine at TDC, install the timing chain and sprocket.
7. Insert and tighten the camshaft bolt to 43 ft. lbs. (58 Nm).

1	BOLT
2	CAMSHAFT SPROCKET
3	BOLT
4	TENSIONER
5	BOLTS
6	CRANKSHAFT SPROCKET

A ALIGN TABS ON TENSIONER WITH MARKS ON CAMSHAFT & CRANKSHAFT SPROCKETS.

86813245

Fig. 98 Timing chain assembly and timing mark alignment

8. Lubricate the timing chain with engine oil. Install the crankcase front cover. Connect battery negative cable.

2.8L Engine

1. Relieve the pressure in the fuel system before disconnecting any fuel line connections. Disconnect the negative battery cable.
2. Remove the crankcase front cover.
3. Place the No. 1 piston at TDC with the marks on the camshaft and crankshaft sprockets aligned.
4. Remove the camshaft sprocket and chain.

➡If the sprocket does not come off easily, a light blow with a plastic mallet on the lower edge of the sprocket should dislodge the sprocket.

5. Remove the crankshaft sprocket.

To install:

6. Install the crankshaft sprocket. Apply Molykote® or equivalent, to the sprocket thrust surface.
7. Hold the sprocket with the chain hanging down and align the marks on the camshaft and crankshaft sprockets.

Fig. 99 Exploded view of the 2.5L timing chain and marks

1 Camshaft
2 Key
3 Tensioner
4 Bolt 25 Nm (43 ft.lb.)
5 Bolt 58 Nm (43 ft.lb.)
6 Washer
7 Sprocket and chain assembly
8 Bolt 10 Nm (89 in.lb.)
9 Bearing
10 Timing marks to be
   aligned as shown
   when engine is rotated
   to T.D.C

86813246

8. Align the dowel in the camshaft with the dowel hole in the camshaft sprocket.

9. Draw the camshaft sprocket onto the camshaft using the mounting bolts. Tighten the camshaft sprocket mounting bolts to 18 ft. lbs. (25 Nm).

10. Lubricate the timing chain with engine oil. Install the crankcase front cover. Connect battery negative cable.

3.0L Engine

▶ See Figures 100 and 101

1. Remove the timing chain cover.
2. Turn the crankshaft so that the timing marks are aligned.
3. Remove the crankshaft oil slinger.
4. Remove the camshaft sprocket bolts.
5. Use two prybars to alternately pry the camshaft and crankshaft sprocket free along with the chain.
6. Installation is the reverse of removal. If the engine was turned, make sure that the No. 1 cylinder is at TDC.

Fig. 100 Exploded view of the 3.0L and 3.8L timing chain

86813251

Fig. 101 Timing marks for the 3.0L and 3.8L timing chain

3.1L Engine (VIN M)

♦ **See Figure 102**

1. Disconnect the negative battery cable.
2. Drain the cooling system into a suitable container.
3. Remove the timing chain front cover.
4. Rotate the crankshaft until the timing marks on the camshaft and crankshaft sprockets are in alignment at their closest approach.
5. Remove the camshaft sprocket mounting bolt and remove the camshaft sprocket and timing chain.
6. Remove the crankshaft sprocket with a gear puller, J-5825-A, or the equivalent.
7. Remove the two bolts and remove the timing chain damper.

To Install:

8. Install the timing chain damper and tighten the mounting bolts to 15 ft. lbs. (21 Nm).
9. Install the crankshaft sprocket onto the crankshaft making sure the notch in the sprocket fits over the crankshaft key. Fully seat the sprocket on the crankshaft using J-38612, or an equivalent gear installer.
10. Make sure the timing mark on the crankshaft sprocket is still pointing straight up.
11. Install the camshaft sprocket inside the timing chain.
12. Pick up the chain and sprocket and hold the sprocket in such a way that the timing mark is pointing down and the timing chain is hanging down off of the sprocket.
13. Loop the timing chain under the crankshaft sprocket and install the camshaft sprocket on the camshaft. The sprocket will only fit on the camshaft if the dowel on the camshaft lines up with the hole in the sprocket.
14. Verify the timing marks are aligned. If the marks are not in alignment proceed as follows:
    a. Remove the chain and sprocket.
    b. Install the sprocket and mounting bolt loosely.
    c. Rotate the crankshaft and camshaft until the marks are in alignment.
    d. Remove the camshaft sprocket and mounting bolt.
15. Repeat steps 13 and 14.
16. Tighten the camshaft sprocket mounting bolt to 74 ft. lbs. (100 Nm).

17. Lubricate the timing chain components with engine oil.
18. Install the timing chain front cover.
19. Refill the cooling system.
20. Connect the negative battery cable.
21. Start the vehicle and verify no leaks.

3.1L Engine (VIN T)

♦ **See Figure 103**

1. Disconnect the negative battery cable.
2. Remove the crankcase front cover.
3. Place the No. 1 piston at TDC with the marks on the camshaft and crankshaft sprockets aligned.
4. Remove the camshaft sprocket and chain.

➡**If the sprocket does not come off easily, a light blow with a plastic mallet on the lower edge of the sprocket should dislodge the sprocket.**

5. Remove the crankshaft sprocket.

To install:

6. Install the crankshaft sprocket. Apply Molykote® or equivalent, to the sprocket thrust surface.
7. Hold the sprocket with the chain hanging down and align the marks on the camshaft and crankshaft sprockets.
8. Align the dowel in the camshaft with the dowel hole in the camshaft sprocket.
9. Draw the camshaft sprocket onto the camshaft using the mounting bolts. Tighten the camshaft sprocket mounting bolts to 18 ft. lbs. (25 Nm).
10. Lubricate the timing chain with engine oil. Install the crankcase front cover. Connect battery negative cable.

3.3L Engine

♦ **See Figure 104**

1. Relieve the pressure in the fuel system before disconnecting any fuel line connections.
2. Disconnect the negative battery cable.
3. Remove the crankcase front cover and camshaft thrust bearing.
4. Turn the crankshaft so the timing marks are aligned.
5. Remove the timing chain damper and camshaft sprocket bolts.
6. Remove the camshaft sprocket and chain. Remove the crankshaft sprocket.

To install:

7. Make sure the crankshaft is positioned so No. 1 piston is at TDC on compression stroke.
8. Rotate the camshaft with the sprocket temporarily installed, so the timing mark is straight down.
9. Assembly the timing chain on the sprockets with the timing marks aligned. Install the timing chain and sprocket.
10. Install the camshaft sprocket bolts. Tighten the bolts to 27 ft. lbs. (37 Nm).
11. Install the timing chain damper and engine front cover. Connect battery negative cable.

3.8L Engine

♦ **See Figures 100 and 101**

1. Relieve the pressure in the fuel system before disconnecting any fuel line connections.
2. Disconnect the negative battery cable.

Fig. 102 The 3.1L (VIN M) engine exploded view of the timing chain

1 Crankshaft sprocket
2 Timing chain
3 Crankshaft key
4 Crankshaft
5 Timing chain damper bolt/screw
6 Timing chain damper
7 Camshaft sprocket bolt/screw
8 Camshaft sprocket
9 Camshaft thrust plate bolt/screw
10 Camshaft thrust plate
11 Camshaft
12 Alignment marks

86813248

Fig. 103 View of the 3.1L (VIN T) timing chain marks

86813249

#1 CYLINDER
AT T.D.C.

#4 CYLINDER
AT T.D.C.

Fig. 104 Exploded view of the 3.3L timing chain and timing marks

1 Bolt
2 Timing chain
3 Camshaft sprocket
4 Key
5 Damper assembly
6 Crankshaft sprocket

ALIGN MARKS

86813252

3. Remove the crankcase front cover.

4. Turn the crankshaft so the timing marks are aligned.

5. Remove the crankshaft oil slinger, as required.

6. Remove the camshaft sprocket bolts.

7. Remove the cam sensor magnet assembly.

8. Use 2 prybars to alternately pry the camshaft and crankshaft sprocket free along with the chain.

To install:

9. Make sure the crankshaft is positioned so No. 1 piston is at TDC.

10. Rotate the camshaft with the sprocket temporarily installed, so the timing mark is straight down.

11. Assemble the timing chain on the sprockets with the timing marks aligned. Install the timing chain and sprocket.

12. Install the cam sensor magnet assembly.

13. Install the oil slinger with the large part of the cone toward the front of the engine, as required.

14. Secure the camshaft sprocket bolt, thrust button and spring.

15. Attach the timing chain damper and engine front cover.

4.3L Diesel Engine

➡**The following procedure requires the bleed-down of the valve lifters. Read that procedure before proceeding.**

1. Remove the front cover.

2. Loosen all the rocker arms.

3. Remove the crankshaft oil slinger.

4. Remove the camshaft sprocket-to-camshaft bolt and washer.

5. Using two prybars, work the camshaft and crankshaft sprockets alternately off their shafts along with the chain. It may be necessary to remove the crankshaft sprocket with a puller.

To install:

6. If the camshaft sprocket to cam key should come out with the camshaft sprocket, remove the front camshaft bearing retainer and install the key into the injection pump drive gear. Install the bearing retainer and tighten the bolts to 48 ft. lbs. (65 Nm).

7. Install the key in the crankshaft, if removed.

8. Install the camshaft sprocket, crankshaft sprocket and timing chain together, then align the marks.

9. Tighten the camshaft sprocket bolt to 64 ft. lbs. (87 Nm).

10. Install the oil slinger.

11. After installing the front cover, you will need to bleed down the valve lifters. See the procedure in this section.

12. Install the valve covers, then check and reset the injection pump timing.

13. Road test and check for leaks.

Camshaft

REMOVAL & INSTALLATION

2.2L Engine

▶ See Figure 105

The engine must be removed from the vehicle for this procedure.

1. Disconnect the negative battery cable.

2. Remove the engine assembly from the vehicle. Mount the engine on a suitable engine stand.

3. Remove the serpentine drive belt.

4. Remove the serpentine drive belt tensioner assembly with the alternator attached.

5. Detach the strut bracket and the rear alternator bracket.

6. Unbolt the front engine mount bracket.

7. Remove the oil level indicator tube.

8. Unbolt and remove the oil pan.

9. Remove the crankshaft balancer and front cover.

10. Remove the timing chain and camshaft sprocket.

11. Disconnect the spark plug wires.

12. Remove the rocker arm cover.

➡**When removing the valve train components they must be kept in order for installation in the same locations from which they were removed.**

13. Remove the rocker arm nuts, rocker arms, balls and pushrods.

14. Remove the power steering pump brace.

15. Disconnect the cylinder head with the intake and exhaust manifolds attached.

16. Remove the valve lifters.

17. Remove the camshaft thrust plate mounting bolts and the thrust plate.

18. Remove the oil pump assembly.

19. Remove the camshaft carefully from the engine.

86813256

Fig. 105 Camshaft and timing chain assembly on the 2.2L engine

To install:

20. Coat the camshaft lobes and bearings with GM Engine Oil Supplement (E.O.S.) 1051396 or equivalent, then insert the camshaft carefully into the engine.

21. Install the oil pump drive assembly.

22. Install the thrust plate, then tighten the mounting bolts to 106 inch lbs. (12 Nm).

23. Install the valve lifters.

24. Attach the cylinder head and manifold assemblies to the engine.

25. Connect the power steering pump brace.

26. Install the pushrods, rocker arms, balls and rocker arms nuts. Tighten the nuts to 22 ft. lbs. (30 Nm).

27. Install the valve cover.

28. Connect the spark plug wires.

29. Install the timing chain and camshaft sprocket. Verify that the camshaft and crankshaft sprocket timing marks are correctly aligned.

30. Install the timing chain front cover and crankshaft balancer.

31. Install the oil pan.

32. Bolt down the oil level indicator.

33. Attach the front engine bracket, rear alternator bracket and strut bracket.

34. Install the drive belt tensioner and alternator assembly, then install the serpentine drive belt.

35. Install the engine assembly into the vehicle.

36. Attach a new oil filter on the engine, then fill the engine crankcase with clean oil.

37. Connect the negative battery cable.

38. Fill the cooling system with new coolant.

39. Start the vehicle, top off the coolant, check for leaks.

2.5L Engine

▶ **See Figures 106, 107 and 108**

1. Relieve the pressure in the fuel system before disconnecting any fuel line connections.

2. Disconnect the negative battery cable.

3. Remove the engine as previously outlined, and support it on a suitable engine stand.

4. Unbolt the rocker cover, rocker arms and pushrods.

5. Remove the spark plugs and fuel pump on carbureted models.

6. Unsecure the pushrod cover and gasket. Remove the lifters.

7. Remove the alternator, the alternator lower bracket and the front engine mount bracket assembly.

8. Remove the oil pump driveshaft and gear assembly.

9. Remove the crankshaft hub and timing gear cover.

10. Unfasten and remove the 2 camshaft thrust plate screws by working through the holes in the gear.

11. Remove the camshaft and gear assembly by pulling it through the front of the block. Take care not to damage the bearings.

12. If replacement of the camshaft gear is necessary, use the following procedure:

    a. Remove the camshaft gear using an arbor press and adapter.

    b. Position the thrust plate to avoid damage by interference with the key as the gear is removed.

Fig. 106 Remove the camshaft thrust plate screws by working through the holes in the gear

Fig. 107 A press is needed to remove the camshaft timing gear

1 Arbor press
2 J-21474-13 or J-21795-1

Fig. 108 Measure the end clearance of the thrust plate

c. When assembling the gear onto the camshaft, support the camshaft at the back of the front journal in the arbor press using press plate adapters.

d. Press the gear on the shaft until it bottoms against the spacer ring.

e. Measure the end clearance of the thrust plate. End clearance should be 0.0015-0.0050 in. (0.0381-0.1270mm).

f. If clearance is less than 0.0015 in. (0.0381mm), replace the spacer ring.

g. If clearance is more than 0.0050 in. (0.127mm), replace the thrust plate.

To install:

13. Lubricate the camshaft journals with a high quality engine oil supplement and carefully install the camshaft and gear into the cylinder block.

14. Rotate the camshaft and crankshaft so the timing marks on the gear teeth align. The engine is now in No. 4-cylinder firing position.

15. Install the camshaft thrust plate-to-block screw. Tighten the screw to 90 inch lbs. (10 Nm).

16. Attach the crankshaft hub and timing gear cover.

17. Install the oil pump driveshaft and gear assembly.

18. Attach the lower alternator bracket, alternator and the front engine mount bracket assembly.

19. Install the spark plugs and fuel pump.

20. Install the lifters. Install the pushrod cover and gasket.

21. Install the pushrods, rocker arms and rocker cover.

22. Place and attach the engine in the vehicle.

23. Connect the negative battery cable.

2.8L Engine

1. Relieve the pressure in the fuel system before disconnecting any fuel line connections.

2. Disconnect the negative battery cable.

3. Remove the engine as previously outlined, and support it on a suitable engine stand.

4. Remove the intake manifold, valve cover, rocker arms, pushrods and valve lifters.

5. Remove the crankshaft balancer and front cover.

6. Remove the timing chain and sprockets.

7. Carefully remove the camshaft. Avoid marring the camshaft bearing surfaces.

To install:

8. Coat the camshaft with lubricant 1052365 or equivalent, and install the camshaft.

9. Install the timing chain and sprocket.

10. Install the camshaft thrust button and front cover.

11. Install the crankshaft balancer.

12. Install the intake manifold, valve cover, rocker arms, pushrods and valve lifters.

13. Install the engine in the vehicle.

14. Connect the negative battery cable.

15. Adjust the valves, as required.

3.0L Engine

1. Disconnect the battery cables.

2. Remove the engine as described earlier.

3. Remove the intake manifold.

4. Remove the valve covers.

5. Remove the rocker arm assemblies, pushrods and lifters.

6. Remove the timing cover, chain and camshaft sprocket. This will avoid burring of the camshaft journals by the crankshaft during removal. Slide the camshaft forward out of the bearing bores carefully to avoid marring the bearing surfaces.

To install:

7. When replacing the camshaft, take extra care to avoid marring the bearing surfaces.

8. Install the valve mechanism.

9. Attach the intake manifold to the engine.

10. Install the engine.

11. Connect the battery cables, start the engine, and check for leaks.

3.1L Engine (VIN T)

1. Remove the engine as previously outlined earlier in this section.

2. Remove the valve lifters, then remove the front cover.

3. Remove the timing chain and sprocket.

4. Slide the camshaft from the engine, take care not to damage the camshaft bearings. The journals are the same diameter.

To install:

5. Coat the camshaft lobes and bearings with GM Engine Oil Supplement (E.O.S.) 1051396 or equivalent, then insert the camshaft carefully into the engine.

6. Lubricate the camshaft journals with engine oil.

7. Install the camshaft.

8. Attach the timing chain and sprocket.

9. Install the crankcase front cover.

10. Install the lifters.

11. Install the engine.

12. Fill the engine crankcase with clean engine oil. Fill the cooling system.

13. Double check everything has been connected, start the engine, top off the cooling system, then check for leaks.

3.1L Engine (VIN M)

✳✳CAUTION

Fuel Injection systems remain under pressure, even after the engine has been turned OFF. The fuel system pressure must be relieved before disconnecting any fuel lines. Failure to do so may result in fire and/or personal injury.

1. Relieve the fuel system pressure.

2. Disconnect the negative battery cable.

3. Remove the engine assembly.

➡**When removing valve train components they must be marked for installation in the same location they are removed from. When the camshaft is being replaced the valve lifters should also be replaced.**

4. Remove the intake manifold, valve cover, rocker arms, pushrods and valve lifters.

5. Remove the crankshaft balancer and front cover.

6. Remove the timing chain and sprockets.

7. Remove the oil pump driven gear mounting bolt and remove the oil pump driven gear.

8. Remove the two bolts and remove the camshaft thrust plate.

9. Carefully remove the camshaft. Avoid marring the camshaft bearing surfaces.

To install:

10. Coat the camshaft with lubricant 1052365 or equivalent, and install the camshaft.

11. Attach the camshaft thrust plate and tighten the mounting bolts to 89 inch lbs. (10 Nm).

12. Install the oil pump driven gear and tighten the mounting bolt to 27 ft. lbs. (36 Nm).

13. Install the timing chain and sprocket.

14. Attach the camshaft thrust button and front cover.

15. Install the crankshaft balancer.

16. Install the intake manifold, valve cover, rocker arms, pushrods and valve lifters.

17. Install the engine assembly.

18. Connect the negative battery cable.

19. Adjust the valves, as required.

20. Add engine and coolant as required.

21. Start the engine and verify no oil leaks.

3.8L Engine

1. Relieve the pressure in the fuel system before disconnecting any fuel line connections.

2. Disconnect the negative battery cable.

3. Remove the engine as previously outlined, and support it on a suitable engine stand.

4. Remove the intake manifold.

5. Unbolt and remove the valve covers.

6. Remove the rocker arm assemblies, pushrods and lifters.

7. Unbolt and remove the timing chain cover.

➡**Align the timing marks of the camshaft and crankshaft sprockets to avoid burring the camshaft journals by the crankshaft.**

8. Remove the timing chain, camshaft sensor magnet assembly and sprockets.

To install:

9. Coat the camshaft with lubricant 1052365 or equivalent, and install the camshaft.

10. Install the timing chain, camshaft sensor magnet assembly and sprockets.

11. Install the camshaft thrust button and front cover.

12. Complete installation by reversing the removal procedure.

13. Add engine oil and coolant as required.

14. Connect battery negative cable.

4.3L Diesel Engine

➡**This procedure requires the removal, disassembly, cleaning, reassembly and bleed-down of all the valve lifters. Read that procedure, described earlier, before proceeding.**

1. Remove the engine as described earlier.

2. Remove the intake manifold.

3. Remove the oil pump drive assembly.

4. Unbolt the timing chain cover.

5. Align the timing marks.

6. Remove the rocker arms, pushrods and lifters, keeping them in order for reassembly.

7. Remove the timing chain and camshaft lifters, keeping them in order for reassembly.

8. Remove the camshaft bearing retainer.

9. Remove the cam sprocket key.

10. Remove the injection pump drive gear.

11. Remove the injection pump driven gear, intermediate pump adapter and pump adapter. Remove the snapring and selective washer. Remove the driven gear and spring.

12. Carefully slide the camshaft out of the block.

13. If the camshaft bearings are being replaced, you'll have to remove the oil pan.

14. Installation is the reverse of removal. Perform the complete valve lifter bleed-down procedure mentioned earlier.

INSPECTION

Degrease the camshaft, using solvent, and clean out all oil holes. Visually inspect cam lobes and bearing journals for excessive wear. If a lobe is questionable, check all lobes as indicated below. If a journal or lobe is worn, the camshaft must be reground or replaced.

Inspect the sprocket, key way and threads, bearing surfaces and lobes for: wear, galling, gouges, and overheating. Do not attempt to repair a camshaft, replace it if damaged. If a new camshaft is installed, all the valve lifters must be replaced.

Measure the bearing journals, with a micrometer, measure the diameter and runout. If out of specification, replace the camshaft. Measure the camshaft lift, lubricate the journal bearings with GM 1052365 or equivalent. Carefully set the camshaft on "V" blocks or between the camshaft centers. With dial indicators, measure the cam lift. If out of specification, replace the cam.

Camshaft Bearings

REMOVAL & INSTALLATION

2.2L Engine

▶ **See Figure 109**

1. Remove the engine from the vehicle.

2. Remove the camshaft from the engine as previously outlined.

3. Assemble the camshaft remover and installer tool, J-33049 or an equivalent.

4. Select the proper pilot, nut and thrust washer.

5. Make sure the puller nut engages a sufficient number of threads.

6. Pull out the bearings.

➡**It is very important that you do not use the old camshaft bearings once they are removed from the engine.**

To install:

7. Separate the front, rear and intermediate camshaft bearings.

8. Assemble the camshaft remover and installer tool, J-33049 or an equivalent.

9. Place the bearing onto the J-33049 and index the oil hole(s) of the bearing with the oil passage(s) in the cylinder block. Pull the bearing into place.

CHECKING OIL HOLE ALIGNMENT WITH BRASS
ROD. MAKE AS SHOWN USING 3/32" ROD
ABOUT 762MM (30") LONG.

1 90° bend

86813263

Fig. 109 Inspect the oil hole alignment with a brass rod

10. Select the proper pilot, nut and thrust washer.

➡**Proper alignment of the oil holes is critical. Restriction of the oil flow will cause severe engine damage.**

11. Install the camshaft plug, then apply GM sealer 1052914 or equivalent to the plug before installing.

12. Inspect with a piece of ³/₃₂ inch brass rod with a 90° bend at the end. Probe the bearing oil holes and verify that they are properly aligned.

2.5L Engine

1982-90 MODELS

1. Remove the engine from the vehicle as previously outlined.

2. Remove the camshaft from the engine as previously outlined.

3. Unbolt and remove the engine flywheel.

4. Drive the rear camshaft expansion plug out of the engine block from the inside.

5. Using a camshaft bearing service tool, J-21473-1 (1982-84) or J-33049 (1985-90), drive the front camshaft bearing towards the rear and the rear bearing towards the front.

6. Install the appropriate extension tool J-21054-1 on the service tool and drive the center bearing out towards the rear.

To install:

7. Drive all of the new bearings into place in the opposite direction of which they were removed, making sure to align the oil holes of each bearing with each of the feed holes in the engine block bores.

➡**The front camshaft bearing must be driven approximately ⅛ in. (3mm) behind the front of the cylinder block to uncover the oil hole to the timing gear oiling nozzle.**

8. Install the camshaft into the engine then reinstall the engine as previously outlined.

1991-93 MODELS

1. Remove the engine from the vehicle.

2. Remove the camshaft from the engine as previously outlined.

3. Assemble the camshaft remover and installer tool, J-33049 or an equivalent.

4. Select the proper pilot, nut and thrust washer.

5. Make sure the puller nut engages a sufficient number of threads.

6. Pull out the bearings.

➡**It is very important that you do not use the old camshaft bearings once they are removed from the engine.**

To install:

7. Separate the front, rear and intermediate camshaft bearings.

8. Assemble the camshaft remover and installer tool, J-33049 or an equivalent.

9. Place the bearing onto the J-33049 and index the oil hole(s) of the bearing with the oil passage(s) in the cylinder block. Pull the bearing into place.

10. Select the proper pilot, nut and thrust washer.

➡**Proper alignment of the oil holes is critical. Restriction of the oil flow will cause sever engine damage.**

11. Install the camshaft plug, then apply GM sealer 1052914 or equivalent to the plug before installing.

12. Inspect with a piece of ³/₃₂ inch brass rod with a 90° bend at the end, probe the bearing oil holes and verify that they are properly aligned.

2.8L Engine

1. Remove the camshaft rear cover.

2. Using Tool J-6098 (1982-84) or J-33049 (1985-88 and later) or its equivalent, index the pilot in the camshaft front bearing, then install the puller screw through the pilot.

3. Install the remover and installer tool with the shoulder towards the bearing, make sure a sufficient amount of threads are engaged.

4. Using two wrenches, hold puller the screw while turning the nut. When the bearing has been pulled from the bore, remove the remover and installer tool, then the bearing from the puller screws.

5. Remove the remaining bearings (except front and rear) in the same manner. It will be necessary to index the pilot in the camshaft rear bearing to remove the rear intermediate bearing.

6. Assemble the remover and installer tool on the driver handle and remove the camshaft front and rear bearings by driving towards the center of the cylinder block.

The camshaft front and rear bearings should be installed first. These bearings will act as guides for the pilot and center the remaining bearings being pulled into place.

To install:

7. Assemble the remover and installer tool on the driver handle, then install the camshaft front and rear bearings by driving towards center of the cylinder block.

8. Use tool set J-6098 (1982-84) or J-33049 (1985 and later), or its equivalent, index the pilot in the camshaft front bearing, then install the puller screw through the pilot.

9. Index the camshaft bearing in the bore (with oil hole aligned as outlined below), then install the remover and in-

staller tool on the puller screw with the shoulder towards the bearing.

• The rear and intermediate bearing oil holes must be aligned at the 2:30 o'clock position.

• The front bearing oil holes must be aligned at the 1:00 and 2:30 o'clock (two holes) positions.

10. Using two wrenches, hold the puller screw while turning the nut. After the bearing has been pulled into the bore, remove the remover and installer tool from the puller screw, then check alignment of the oil hole in the camshaft bearing.

11. Install the remaining bearings in the same manner. It will be necessary to index pilot in the camshaft rear bearing to install the rear intermediate bearing. Clean the rear cover mating surfaces and bolt holes then apply a ⅛ in. (3mm) bead of R.T.V. to the cover. Install the cover.

3.0L Engine

1. Remove the camshaft as previously outlined.
2. Assemble the puller screw to the required length.
3. Select the proper size expanding collet and back-up nut.
4. Install the expanding collet on the expanding mandrel. Install the back-up nut.
5. Insert this assembly into the camshaft bearing to be removed. Tighten the back-up nut to expand the collet to fit the I.D. of the bearing.
6. Thread the end of the puller screw assembly into the end of the expanding mandrel and collet assembly.
7. Install the pulling plate, thrust bearing, and pulling nut on the threaded end of the puller screw.
8. The bearing can then be removed by turning the pulling nut.

➡ **Make certain to grip the ⅝ in. hex end of the puller screw with a wrench to keep it from rotating when the pulling nut is turned. Failure to do this will result in the locking up of all threads in the pulling assembly and possible over expansion of the collet.**

9. Repeat the above procedure to remove any other bearings, except the front bearing, which may be pulled from the rear of the engine.

➡ **When removing rear cam bearing, it is necessary to remove welch plug at the back of cam bore. However, if only the front bearing is being replaced, it is not necessary to remove the engine or welch plug. The front bearing can be removed by using a spacer between the pulling plate and the cylinder block.**

To install:
10. Assemble the puller screw to the required length.
11. Select the proper size expanding collet and back-up nut.
12. Install the expanding collet on the expanding mandrel.
13. Install the back-up nut.
14. Place the new camshaft bearing on the collet and GENTLY hand-tighten the back-up nut to expand the collet to fit the bearing. Do not over-tighten the back-up nut. A loose sliding fit between the collet and the bearing surface is adequate. This will provide just enough clearance to allow for the collapse which will occur when the new bearing is pulled into the engine block.
15. Slide the mandrel assembly and bearing into the bearing bore as far as it will go without force.

16. Thread the end of puller screw onto the end of the mandrel. Make certain to align the oil holes in bearing and block properly. One of the collet separation lines may be used as a reference point.
17. Install the pulling plate, thrust bearing and pulling nut on threaded end of puller screw.
18. Install the bearing in the same manner as described in the previous under bearing removal.

➡ **When installing rear cam bearing, install new welch plug at back of cam bore. Coat outside diameter of plug with non-hardening sealer before installation.**

3.1L Engine (VIN T)

1. Remove the engine from the vehicle as previously outlined.
2. Remove the camshaft from the engine as previously outlined.
3. Remove the camshaft rear plug.
4. Assemble the removal tool. Using care and follow proper tool instructions remove camshaft bearings.
5. Select the proper pilot, nut and thrust washer.
6. Assemble to J-33049. Make certain the puller engages a sufficient number of threads and pull the bearing.
7. Install the appropriate extension tool J-21054-1 on the service tool and drive the center bearing out towards the rear.

3.1L Engine (VIN M)

1. Remove the engine from the vehicle.
2. Remove the camshaft from the engine as previously outlined.
3. Assemble the camshaft remover and installer tool, J-33049 or an equivalent.
4. Select the proper pilot, nut and thrust washer.
5. Make sure the puller nut engages a sufficient number of threads.
6. Pull out the bearings.

➡ **It is very important that you do not use the old camshaft bearings once they are removed from the engine.**

To install:
7. Separate the front, rear and intermediate camshaft bearings.
8. Assemble the camshaft remover and installer tool, J-33049 or an equivalent.
9. Place the bearing onto the J-33049 and index the oil hole(s) of the bearing with the oil passage(s) in the cylinder block. Pull the bearing into place.
10. Select the proper pilot, nut and thrust washer.

➡ **Proper alignment of the oil holes is critical. Restriction of the oil flow will cause sever engine damage.**

11. Install the camshaft plug, then apply GM sealer 1052914 or equivalent to the plug before installing.
12. Inspect with a piece of ³⁄₃₂ inch brass rod with a 90° bend at the end, probe the bearing oil holes and verify that they are properly aligned.

3.3L Engine

1. Remove the engine from the vehicle as previously outlined.

2. Remove the camshaft from the engine as previously outlined.

3. Remove the camshaft rear plug.

4. Assembly the removal tool. Using care and follow proper tool instructions remove camshaft bearings.

5. Select the proper pilot, nut and thrust washer.

6. Assemble to J-33049. Make certain the puller engages a sufficient number of threads and pull the bearing.

7. Install the appropriate extension tool J-21054-1 on the service tool and drive the center bearing out towards the rear.

3.8L Engine

1. Remove the camshaft as previously outlined.

2. Assemble the puller screw to the required length.

3. Select the proper size expanding collet and back-up nut.

4. Install the expanding collet on the expanding mandrel. Install the back-up nut.

5. Insert this assembly into the camshaft bearing to be removed. Tighten the back-up nut to expand the collet to fit the I.D. of the bearing.

6. Thread the end of the puller screw assembly into the end of the expanding mandrel and collet assembly.

7. Install the pulling plate, thrust bearing, and pulling nut on the threaded end of the puller screw.

8. The bearing can then be removed by turning the pulling nut.

➡**Make certain to grip the ⅝ in. hex end of the puller screw with a wrench to keep it from rotating when the pulling nut is turned. Failure to do this will result in the locking up of all threads in the pulling assembly and possible over expansion of the collet.**

9. Repeat the above procedure to remove any other bearings, except the front bearing, which may be pulled from the rear of the engine.

➡**When removing rear cam bearing, it is necessary to remove welch plug at the back of cam bore. However, if only the front bearing is being replaced, it is not necessary to remove the engine or welch plug. The front bearing can be removed by using a spacer between the pulling plate and the cylinder block.**

To install:

10. Assemble the puller screw to the required length.

11. Select the proper size expanding collet and back-up nut.

12. Install the expanding collet on the expanding mandrel.

13. Install the back-up nut.

14. Place the new camshaft bearing on the collet and GENTLY hand-tighten the back-up nut to expand the collet to fit the bearing. Do not over-tighten the back-up nut. A loose sliding fit between the collet and the bearing surface is adequate. This will provide just enough clearance to allow for the collapse which will occur when the new bearing is pulled into the engine block.

15. Slide the mandrel assembly and bearing into the bearing bore as far as it will go without force.

16. Thread the end of puller screw onto the end of the mandrel. Make certain to align the oil holes in bearing and block properly. One of the collet separation lines may be used as a reference point.

17. Install the pulling plate, thrust bearing and pulling nut on threaded end of puller screw.

18. Install the bearing in the same manner as described in under bearing removal.

➡**When installing rear cam bearing, install new welch plug at back of cam bore. Coat outside diameter of plug with non-hardening sealer before installation.**

4.3L Diesel Engine

Camshaft Bearing Remover and Installer Set BT-6409 and camshaft bearing pilot spacer BT-7817 are available tools. This set can be used to remove can bearings. To replace bearings with engine in car, proceed as follows:

➡**The equivalents of special tools mentioned here may be used.**

1. Remove the camshaft as previously outlined.

2. Remove the rear camshaft plug:

   a. Drill a 12mm or ½ in. hole in the center of the plug.

   b. Drive the plug inward carefully just enough to loosen it in the block.

   c. Place a punch or screwdriver in the drilled hole and remove the plug.

   d. Remove all the metal particles that entered the block and all traces of the old sealer.

➡**Failure to remove the metal particles will result in engine damage.**

3. Front bearing removal and installation:

   a. To remove the front (No. 1) camshaft bearing, support the retainer in a vise and drive the bearing out using BT-6409-2 with driver BT-6409-7.

   b. To install the bearing, use the same tools but make certain that the oil hole in the bearing is in alignment with the oil hole in the retainer.

4. For numbers 2, 3, & 4 bearing removal and installation:

   a. Install tool BT-6409-2 on handle BT-6409-7 and drive out the No. 2 cam bearing.

   b. Remove the No. 3 bearing in the same manner using BT-6409-3 on handle BT-6409-7.

   c. Remove the No. 4 bearing using puller BT-6409-8.

   d. To aid aligning the bearings with the oil passages, place each bearing in the front of the bore with tapered edge toward the block and align the oil hole in the bearing with the center of the oil slot in the bore. Mark the bottom of the bearing. When installing the bearings, the mark will act as a guide.

   e. Using pilot BT-6409-1 will aid in installing the No. 4 and 3 bearings by preventing cocking of the bearings. Install the No. 4 bearing using tool BT-6409-4.

➡**Drive the bearing in carefully, stopping to make certain that the oil holes are in alignment, otherwise it is possible to drive the bearing in beyond the oil passage opening. Use a piece of ³⁄₃₂ in. (2.4mm) brass rod with a 90° bend at the end to check the oil hole opening.**

   f. Install the No. 3 bearing using tool BT-6409-3 until the oil holes are in alignment.

   g. Install the No. 2 bearing using tool BT-6409-2 carefully until the oil holes are in alignment.

h. Use a piece of $\frac{3}{32}$ in. (2.4mm) brass rod with a 90° bend at the end to check all oil hole openings. Wire must enter hole or the bearing will not receive sufficient lubrication.

5. Install the rear plug:

a. Coat the block with R.T.V. sealer.

b. Drive the plug into the block until it is flush or no more than 0.5mm (0.020 in.) concave.

c. Install the camshaft and engine assembly. Road test the car and inspect for leaks.

Pistons and Connecting Rods

✳✳CAUTION

The EPA warns that prolonged contact with used engine oil may cause a number of skin disorders, including cancer! You should make every effort to minimize your exposure to used engine oil. Protective gloves should be worn when changing the oil. Wash your hands and any other exposed skin areas as soon as possible after exposure to used engine oil. Soap and water, or waterless hand cleaner should be used.

REMOVAL

♦ **See Figures 110, 111, 112 and 113**

1. Disconnect the negative battery cable.

2. Remove the engine assembly from the vehicle and secure on a suitable workstand.

3. Remove the intake manifold and cylinder heads.

4. Remove the oil pan and oil pump.

5. The position of each piston, connecting rod and connecting rod cap should be noted before any are removed, so they can be reinstalled in the same location.

6. Check the tops of the pistons and the sides of the connecting rods for identifying marks. In some engines, the top of the piston will be numbered to correspond with the cylinder number. The connecting rod and connecting rod cap should have numbers stamped on the machined surfaces next to the rod bolts that correspond with their cylinder number.

7. If no numbers are visible, use a number punch set and stamp the cylinder number on the connecting rod and connecting rod cap. The 2.2L and 2.5L engines are numbered 1-4 front to rear. On the 3.0L, 3.3L, 3.8L and 4.3L diesel V6s, the right (rear) bank is numbered 2,4,6, left (front) bank 1,3,5. The 2.8L and 3.1L engine are numbered 1,3,5 on the right bank, 2,4,6 on the left bank.

8. Rotate the crankshaft until the piston to be removed is at the bottom of the cylinder. Examine the cylinder bore above the ring travel. If the bore is worn so that a shoulder or ridge exists at the top of the cylinder, remove the ridge with a ridge reamer to avoid damaging the rings or cracking the ring lands in the piston during removal. Before operating the ridge

reamer, place a shop towel on top of the piston to catch the metal shavings.

✳✳WARNING

Be very careful when using a ridge reamer. Only remove the cylinder bore material that is necessary to remove the ridge. If too much cylinder bore material is removed, cylinder overboring and piston replacement may be necessary.

9. Loosen the connecting rod bolt nuts until the nuts are flush with the ends of the bolts. Using a hammer and a brass drift or piece of wood, lightly tap on the nuts/bolts until the connecting rod cap is loosened from the connecting rod. Remove the nuts, rod cap and lower bearing shell.

➡**All caps and rods are matched pairs and must be assembled together. They must also return to their original locations. Match mark all caps to rods, for both location and direction. Installing the caps on the wrong rod or facing the wrong way will cause permanent engine damage.**

10. Slip a piece of snug fitting rubber hose over each rod bolt, to prevent the bolt threads from damaging the crankshaft during removal. Using a hammer handle or piece of wood or plastic, push the rod and piston upward in the bore until the connecting rod is clear of the crankshaft journal.

11. Inspect the rod bearings for scoring, chipping or other wear.

12. Inspect the crankshaft rod bearing journal for wear. Measure the journal diameter in several locations around the journal and compare to specification. If the crankshaft journal is scored or has deep ridges, or its diameter is below specification, the crankshaft must be removed from the engine and reground.

13. If the crankshaft journal appears usable, clean it and the rod bearing shells until they are completely free of oil. Blow any oil from the oil hole in the crankshaft.

➡**The journal surfaces and bearing shells must be completely free of oil to get an accurate reading with Plastigage®.**

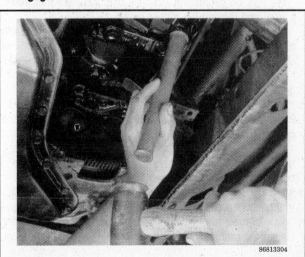

86813304

Fig. 110 Use a brass drift and hammer to loosen the cap

Fig. 111 Remove the nuts, rod cap and lower bearing shell

Fig. 112 Place lengths of rubber hose over the connecting rod studs in order to protect the crankshaft and cylinders from damage

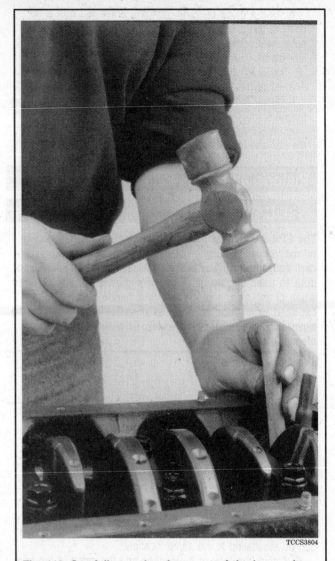

Fig. 113 Carefully tap the piston out of the bore using a wooden dowel

14. Pull the connecting rod back onto the crankshaft rod journal and remove the rubber hoses.

15. Place a strip of Plastigage® lengthwise along the bottom center of the lower bearing shell, then install the cap with the shell and torque the connecting rod nuts to specification. Do not turn the crankshaft with the Plastigage® installed in the bearing.

16. Remove the bearing cap with the shell. The flattened Plastigage® will either be sticking to the bearing shell or the crankshaft journal.

17. Using the printed scale on the Plastigage® package, measure the flattened Plastigage® at its widest point. The number on the scale that most closely corresponds to the width of the Plastigage® indicates the bearing clearance in thousandths of an inch or hundredths of a millimeter.

18. Compare the actual bearing clearance with the bearing clearance specification. If the bearing clearance is excessive,

the bearing must be replaced or the crankshaft must be ground and the bearing replaced.

➡If the crankshaft is still at standard size (has not been ground undersize), bearing shell sets of 0.001, (0.0254mm) 0.002 (0.050mm) and 0.003 in. (0.0762mm) over standard size may be available to correct excessive bearing clearance.

19. After clearance measuring is completed, be sure to remove the Plastigage® from the crankshaft and/or bearing shell.

20. Again remove the connecting rod cap and install the rubber hose on the rod bolts. Push the rod and piston upward in the bore until the piston rings clear the cylinder block. Remove the piston and connecting rod assembly from the top of the cylinder bore.

CLEANING AND INSPECTION

▶ **See Figures 114, 115, 116, 117 and 118**

1. Remove the piston rings from the piston. The compression rings must be removed using a piston ring expander, to prevent breakage.

2. Clean the ring grooves with a ring groove cleaner, being careful not to cut into the piston metal. Heavy carbon deposits can be cleaned from the top of the piston with a scraper or wire brush, however, do not use a wire wheel on the ring grooves or lands. Clean the oil drain holes in the ring grooves. Clean all remaining dirt, carbon and varnish from the piston with a suitable solvent and a brush; do not use a caustic solution.

3. After cleaning, inspect the piston for scuffing, scoring, cracks, pitting or excessive ring groove wear. Replace any piston that is obviously worn.

4. If the piston appears okay, measure the piston diameter using a micrometer. Measure the piston diameter in the thrust

Fig. 116 You can use a piece of an old ring to clean the ring grooves, BUT be careful the ring is sharp

direction, 90° to the piston pin axis, 3/4 in. below the center line of the piston pin bore.

5. Measure the cylinder bore diameter using a bore gauge, or with a telescope gauge and micrometer. The measurement should be made in the piston thrust direction at the top, middle and bottom of the bore.

➡ **Piston diameter and cylinder bore measurements should be made with the parts at room temperature, 70°F (21°C).**

6. Subtract the piston diameter measurement made in Step 4 from the cylinder bore measurement made in Step 5. This is the piston-to-bore clearance. If the clearance is within specification, light finish honing is all that is necessary. If the clearance is excessive, the cylinder must be bored and the piston replaced. If the pistons are replaced, the piston rings must also be replaced.

7. If the piston-to-bore clearance is okay, check the ring groove clearance. Roll the piston ring around the ring groove in which it is to be installed and check the clearance with a feeler gauge. Compare the measurement with specification. High points in the ring groove that may cause the ring to bind

Fig. 114 Use a ring expander tool to remove the piston rings

Fig. 115 Clean the piston grooves using a ring groove cleaner

Fig. 117 A telescoping gauge may be used to measure the cylinder bore diameter

Fig. 118 Measure the piston's outer diameter using a micrometer

may be cleaned up carefully with a points file. Replace the piston if the ring groove clearance is not within specification.

8. Check the connecting rod for damage or obvious wear. Check for signs of fractures and check the bearing bore for out-of-round and taper.

9. A shiny surface on the pin boss side of the piston usually indicates that the connecting rod is bent or the wrist pin hole is not in proper relation to the piston skirt and ring grooves.

10. Abnormal connecting rod bearing wear can be caused by either a bent connecting rod, an improperly machined journal, or a tapered connecting rod bore.

11. Twisted connecting rods will not create an easily identifiable wear pattern, but badly twisted rods will disturb the action of the entire piston, rings, and connecting rod assembly and may be the cause of excessive oil consumption.

12. If the piston must be removed from the connecting rod, mark the side of the connecting rod that corresponds with the side of the piston that faces the front of the engine, so the new piston will be installed facing the same direction. Most pistons have an arrow or notch on the top of the piston, indicating that this side should face the front of the engine. If the original piston is to be reinstalled, use paint or a marker to indicate the cylinder number on the piston, so it can be reinstalled on the same connecting rod.

13. The piston pin is a press fit in the connecting rod. If the piston and/or connecting rod must be replaced, the pin must be pressed into the connecting rod using a fixture that will not damage or distort the piston and/or connecting rod. The piston must move freely on the pin after installation.

HONING

▶ **See Figures 119 and 120**

1. After the piston and connecting rod assembly have been removed, check the clearances as explained in the cleaning and inspection procedure, to determine whether boring and honing or just light honing are required.

2. Honing is best done with the crankshaft removed. This prevents damage to the crankshaft and makes post-honing

cleaning easier, as the honing process will scatter metal particles. However, if the crankshaft is in the cylinder block, position the connecting rod journal for the cylinder being honed as far away from the bottom of the cylinder bore as possible, and wrap a shop cloth around the journal.

3. Honing can be done either with a flexible glaze breaker type hone or with a rigid hone that has honing stones and guide shoes. The flexible hone removes the least amount of metal, and is especially recommended if the piston-to-cylinder bore clearance is on the loose side. The flexible hone is useful to provide a finish on which the new piston rings will seat. A rigid hone will remove more material than the flexible hone and requires more operator skill.

4. Regardless of the type of hone used, carefully follow the manufacturers instructions for operation.

5. The hone should be moved up and down the bore at sufficient speed to obtain a uniform finish. A rigid hone will provide a more definite cross-hatch finish; operate the rigid hone at a speed to obtain a 45° included angle in the cross-

Fig. 119 Removing cylinder glazing using a flexible hone

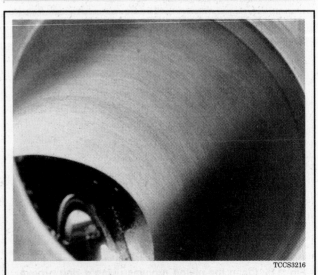

Fig. 120 A properly cross-hatched cylinder bore

hatch. The finish marks should be clean but not sharp, free from embedded particles and torn or folded metal.

6. Periodically during the honing procedure, thoroughly clean the cylinder bore and check the piston-to-bore clearance with the piston for that cylinder.

7. After honing is completed, thoroughly wash the cylinder bores and the rest of the engine with hot water and detergent. Scrub the bores well with a stiff bristle brush and rinse thoroughly with hot water. Thorough cleaning is essential, for if any abrasive material is left in the cylinder bore, it will rapidly wear the new rings and the cylinder bore. If any abrasive material is left in the rest of the engine, it will be picked up by the oil and carried throughout the engine, damaging bearings and other parts.

8. After the bores are cleaned, wipe them down with a clean cloth coated with light engine oil, to keep them from rusting.

PISTON PIN REPLACEMENT

Gasoline Engines
▶ See Figure 121

Use care at all times when handling and servicing connecting rods and pistons To prevent possible damage to these units, do not clamp rod or piston is vise since they may become distorted. Do not allow pistons to strike against one another, against hard objects or bench surfaces, since distortion of piston contour or nicks in the soft aluminum material may result.

1. Remove the piston rings using a suitable piston ring remover.

2. Install the guide bushing of the piston pin removing and installing tool.

3. Install the piston and connecting rod assembly on the support, then place the assembly in an arbor press. Press the pin out of the connecting rod, using tool J-24086-B or equivalent.

4. Clean all disassembled parts completely.

86813290

Fig. 121 Pressing the pin out of the connecting rod

5. Use a mircometer to measure the diameter of the piston pin. Use an inside mircometer to measure to piston pin bore.

➡**If the piston pin-to-piston clearance is in excess of 0.001 in. (0.0254mm), the piston and pin assembly must be replaced.**

6. Lubricate the piston and pin assembly and press fit together.

➡**Never exceed 5000 lbs. of pressure when press fitting piston and pins.**

7. After installing the piston pins, check that the piston has freedom of motion.

Diesel Engines

The piston pin is free floating. The pin bore in the piston is 0.0003-0.0005 in. (0.0076-0.0127mm) and 0.003-0.0013 in. (0.0076-0.033mm) in the rod. If the pin-to-piston clearance is to the high limit (0.005 in./0.0127 piston or 0.0013 in./0.033mm rod), the pin can be inserted in the piston or rod with very little hand pressure and will fall through the piston or rod by its own weight. If the clearance is okay, the pin will not fall through. It is important that the piston and rod pin hole be clean and free of oil when checking pin fit.

The rod may be installed in the piston with either side facing up. Whenever the replacement of a piston pin is necessary, remove the snapring retaining the pin. Then remove pin.

It is very important that after installing the piston pin retaining snaprings that the rings be rotated to make sure they are fully seated in their grooves. The snapring must be installed with the flat side out.

PISTON RING REPLACEMENT

1. After the cylinder bores have been finish honed and cleaned, check the piston ring end-gap. Compress the piston rings to be used in the cylinder, one at a time, into that cylinder. Using an inverted piston, push the ring down into the cylinder bore area where normal ring wear is not encountered.

2. Measure the ring end-gap with a feeler gauge and compare to specification. A gap that is too tight is more harmful than one that is too loose (If ring end-gap is excessively loose, the cylinder bore is probably worn beyond specification).

3. If the ring end-gap is too tight, carefully remove the ring and file the ends squarely with a fine file to obtain the proper clearance.

4. Install the rings on the piston, lowest ring first. The lowest (oil) ring is installed by hand; the top 2 (compression) rings must be installed using a piston ring expander tool. There is a high risk of breaking or distorting the compression rings if they are installed by hand.

5. Install the oil ring expander in the bottom ring groove. Make sure the ends butt together and do not overlap. The expander end-gap should be parallel to the piston pin, facing the right cylinder bank.

6. Start the end of an oil ring rail ring into the oil ring groove above the expander. The rail end-gap should be positioned 135° from the expander end-gap. Finish installing the rail ring by spiraling it the remainder of the way on. Repeat the rail installation with the other rail ring. Its gap position must

be 135° from the other side of the expander end-gap, 90° from the other rail ring end-gap.

➡**If the instructions on the ring packaging differ from this information regarding ring gap positioning, follow the ring manufacturers instructions.**

7. Install the lower compression ring in the piston ring expander tool with the proper side up (usually the manufacturer's mark faces UP). The piston ring packaging should contain instructions as to the directions the ring sides should face. Spread the ring with the expander tool and install it on the piston. Position the end-gap 180° from the oil ring expander end-gap.

8. Repeat Step 7 to install the top compression ring. Position the end-gap in line with the oil ring expander end-gap. The compression ring end-gaps must not be aligned.

ROD BEARING REPLACEMENT

If you have already removed the connecting rod and piston assemblies from the engine, follow only steps 3-7 of the following procedure.

The connecting rod bearings are designed to have a slight projection above the rod and cap faces to insure a positive contact. The bearings can be replaced without removing the rod and piston assembly from the engine.

1. Remove the oil pan. It may be necessary to remove the oil pump to provide access to rear connecting rod bearings.

2. With the connecting rod journal at the bottom, stamp the cylinder number on the machined surfaces of connecting rod and cap for identification when reinstalling, then remove caps.

3. Inspect journals for roughness and wear. Slight roughness may be removed with a fine grit polishing cloth saturated with engine oil. Burrs may be removed with a fine oil stone by moving the stone on the journal circumference. Do not move the stone back and forth across the journal. If the journals are scored or ridged, the crankshaft must be replaced.

4. The connecting rod journals should be checked for out-of-round and correct size with a micrometer.

➡**Crankshaft rod journals will normally be standard size. If any undersized crankshafts are used, all will be 0.254mm undersize and 0.254mm will be stamped the number 4 counterweight.**

If a plastic gaging material (Plastigage® or equivalent) is to be used:

5. Clean oil from the journal bearing cap, connecting rod and outer and inner surface of the bearing inserts. Position insert so that tang is properly aligned with notch in rod and cap.

6. Place a piece of plastic gaging material in the center of lower bearing shell.

7. Remove bearing cap and determine bearing clearances by comparing the width of the flattened plastic gaging material at its widest point with the graduation on the container. The number within the graduation on the envelopes indicates the clearance in thousandths of an inch or millimeters. If this clearance is excessive, replace the bearing and recheck clearance with plastic gaging material. Lubricate bearing with engine oil before installation. Repeat Steps 2 through 7 on remaining

connecting rod bearings. All rods must be connected to their journals when rotating the crankshaft to prevent engine damage.

INSTALLATION

1. Make sure the connecting rod and rod cap bearing saddles are clean and free of nicks or burrs. Install the bearing shells in the connecting rod, making sure the bearing shell tangs are seated in the notches.

➡**Be careful when handling any bearings. Hands and working area should be clean. Dirt is easily embedded in the bearing surface and the bearings are easily scratched or damaged.**

2. Make sure the cylinder bore and crankshaft journal are clean.

3. Position the crankshaft journal at its furthest position away from the bottom of the cylinder bore.

4. Coat the cylinder bore with light engine oil.

5. Install the rubber hoses over the connecting rod bolts to protect the crankshaft during installation.

6. Make sure the piston rings are properly installed and the ring end-gaps are correctly positioned. Install a piston ring compressor over the piston and rings and compress the piston rings into their grooves. Follow the ring compressor manufacturers instructions.

7. Place the piston and connecting rod assembly into the cylinder bore. Make sure the assembly is the correct one for that bore and that the piston and connecting rod are facing in the proper direction. Most pistons have an arrow or notch on the top of the piston, indicating that this side should face the front of the engine.

8. Make sure the ring compressor is seated squarely on the block deck surface. If the compressor is not seated squarely, a ring could pop out from beneath the compressor and hang up on the deck surface. As the piston is tapped into the bore, possibly breaking the ring.

9. Make sure that the connecting rod is not hung up on the crankshaft counterweights and is in position to come straight on to the crankshaft.

10. Tap the piston slowly into the bore, making sure the compressor remains squarely against the block deck. When the piston is completely in the bore, remove the ring compressor.

➡**If the connecting rod bearings were replaced, recheck the bearing clearance as described during the removal procedure, before proceeding further.**

11. Coat the crankshaft journal and the bearing shells with engine assembly lube or clean engine oil. Pull the connecting rod onto the crankshaft journal. After the rod is seated, remove the rubber hoses.

12. Install the rod bearing cap, making sure it is the correct one for the connecting rod. Lightly oil the connecting rod bolt threads and install the rod nuts, then tighten the nuts.

13. After each piston and connecting rod assembly is installed, turn the crankshaft over several times and check for binding. If there is a problem and the crankshaft will not turn, or turns with great difficulty, it will be easier to find the prob-

lem (rod cap on backwards, broken ring, etc.) than if all the assemblies are installed.

14. Check the clearance between the sides of the connecting rods and the crankshaft using a feeler gauge. Spread the rods slightly with a screwdriver to insert the gauge. If the clearance is below the minimum specification, the connecting rod will have to be removed and machined to provide adequate clearance. If the clearance is excessive, substitute an unworn rod and recheck. If the clearance is still excessive, the crankshaft must be welded and reground, or replaced.

15. Install the oil pump and oil pan.

16. Install the cylinder heads and intake manifold.

17. Install the engine in the vehicle.

18. Run the engine and check for leaks and proper engine operation.

Freeze Plugs

REMOVAL & INSTALLATION

▶ See Figures 122 and 123

1. Remove the negative battery cable.
2. Drain the cooling system.

✳✳CAUTION

When draining the coolant, keep in mind that cats and dogs are attracted by ethylene glycol antifreeze, and are quite likely to drink any that is left in an uncovered container or in puddles on the ground. This will prove fatal in sufficient quantity. Always drain the coolant into a sealable container. Coolant should be reused unless it is contaminated or several years old.

3. If equipped with drain plugs on the engine remove them. They would be located at the bottom of the block near the oil pan.

4. Remove any components that restrict access to the freeze plugs, like the starter or motor mounts.

5. Wearing proper eye protection, tap the bottom edge of the freeze plug with a punch and hammer. This should tilt the freeze plug, not cut it. Then use pliers to pull or pry the freeze plug from its bore. Another method is to drill the freeze plug and use a slide hammer, but often there's not enough room to do that.

6. After the plug is removed, clean the area completely. Coat the freeze plug and/or bore with gasket sealant.

To install:

7. Install the freeze plug into the hole, it must be done in evenly or it will keep popping back out as you tap on it. Using a plug installer or socket that fits the edge of the plug can help keep it straight as you tap it in place.

8. Fill the engine with coolant, connect the battery cable. Start engine and check for leaks.

Block Heater

REMOVAL & INSTALLATION

Factory block heaters are not installed on these models. If an aftermarket heater has been installed the following procedure will most likely work. There are two basic types, one for the oil and one for the coolant. The oil heater usually just slips into the dipstick tube or replaces the oil drain plug. The following procedure is for the coolant type.

1. Remove the negative battery cable.
2. Drain the cooling system.

✳✳CAUTION

When draining the coolant, keep in mind that cats and dogs are attracted by ethylene glycol antifreeze, and are quite likely to drink any that is left in an uncovered container or in puddles on the ground. This will prove fatal in sufficient quantity. Always drain the coolant into a sealable container. Coolant should be reused unless it is contaminated or several years old.

Fig. 122 Using a punch and hammer, the freeze plug can be loosened in the block

Fig. 123 Once the freeze plug has been loosened, it can be removed from the block

3. Remove the block heater in the same way as the freeze plugs. Some heater units have a bolt that must be loosened or a V-Clamp that must be removed to remove the heating element.

4. Disconnect the heater connector and remove the heater element.

To install:

5. Coat the new heater with sealant, then install the reverse order of removal.

6. Fill the engine with coolant, connect the battery cable. Start engine and check for leaks.

Rear Main Seal

REMOVAL & INSTALLATION

2.2L and 2.5L Engines

▶ See Figures 124 and 125

The rear main bearing seal is a one piece seal and can be removed without removal of the oil pan or the crankshaft.

1. Disconnect the negative battery cable.
2. Drain the engine oil from the vehicle.
3. Support the engine and remove the transaxle and flywheel.
4. Loosen the seal by inserting a flat bladed tool into the dust lip. Pry the seal out by moving the tool around the seal as required until the seal is removed.

➡Care must be taken not to damage the crankshaft seal surface with the prytool.

5. Clean all of the block and cranshaft-to-seal mating areas.
6. Inspect the inside diameter bore for nicks or burrs.
7. Inspect the crankshaft for nicks or burrs on the seal contact surface. Repair or replace the crankshaft as needed.

To install:

8. Lubricate the seal bore to the seal surface with engine oil.

Fig. 124 Loosen the seal by inserting a flat-bladed tool into the dust lip. Pry the seal out by moving the tool around the seal as required until the seal is removed

Fig. 125 Install the new seal using tool J-34686 or equivalent

9. Install the new seal using tool J-34686 or equivalent.
10. Slide the new seal over the mandrell until the dust lip bottoms squarely against the tool collar.
11. Next align the dowel pin of the tool with the dowel pin hole in the crankshaft, then attach the tool to the crankshaft. Tighten the screws to 45 inch lbs. (5 Nm).
12. Tighten the T-handle of the tool. Push the seal into the bore. Continue until the collar is flush against the cylinder block.
13. Loosen the T-handle completely, then remove the attaching screws and the tool.
14. Check to be sure the seal is seated properly into the bore.
15. Install the flywheel, then reverse to install the remaining components.
16. Add engine oil to the crankcase, as necessary.
17. Connect the negative battery cable.
18. Start the engine and check for leaks.

2.8L Engine

2 PIECE SEAL

▶ See Figures 126 and 127

1. Drain the engine oil.
2. Remove the oil pan and pump.
3. Remove the rear main bearing cap.
4. Gently pack the upper seal into the groove approximately 1/4-3/4 in. (6-19mm) on each side.
5. Measure the amount the seal was driven in on one side, then add 1/16 in. (1.6mm). Cut this length from the old lower cap seal. Be sure to get a clean cut. Repeat for the other side.
6. Place the piece of cut seal into the groove and pack the seal into the block. Do this for each side.

➡GM makes a guide tool (J-29114-1) which bolts to the block via an oil pan bolt hole, and a packing tool (J-29114-2) which is machined to provide a built-in stop for the installation of the short cut pieces. Using the packing tool, work the short pieces of seal onto the guide tool, then pack them into the block with the packing tool.

Fig. 126 Gently pack the upper seal into the groove

AFTER CORRECTLY POSITIONING
SEAL, ROTATE TOOL SLIGHTLY AND
CUT OFF EACH END OF SEAL FLUSH
WITH BLOCK

86813313

Fig. 127 Installing the new lower seal

7. Install a new lower seal in the rear main cap.

8. Install a piece of Plastigage® or the equivalent on the bearing journal. Install the rear cap and tighten to 70 ft. lbs. (95 Nm). Remove the cap and check the gauge for bearing clearance. If out of specification, the ends of the seal may be frayed or not flush, preventing the cap from proper sealing. Correct as required.

9. Clean the journal, and apply a thin film of sealer to the mating surfaces of the cap and block. Do not allow any sealer to get onto the journal or bearing. Install the bearing cap and tighten to 70 ft. lbs. (95 Nm), Install the pan and pump.

10. Add engine oil to the crankcase.

11. Start the engine and check for leaks.

1 PIECE SEAL

1. Drain the engine oil.
2. Remove the transaxle and the flexplate.

3. Using a small pry bar, pry the seal from the block.

✳✳CAUTION

Be careful not to damage the crankshaft surface when removing the oil seal.

4. Clean and inspect the seal mounting surface for nicks and burrs.

5. Coat the new seal with engine oil. Using tool J-34686, press the seal into the block, until it seats.

6. To complete the installation, reverse the removal procedures.

7. Add engine oil to the crankcase.

8. Start the engine and check for leaks.

3.0L Engine

LOWER OIL SEAL

1. Remove the crankshaft.

2. Remove the old seal and place a new seal in the groove with both ends projecting the surface of the cap.

3. Force the seal into the groove rubbing down with a hammer handle or smooth stick until the seal projects above the groove not more than $1/16$ in. (1.6mm). Cut ends off flush with surface of cap, using sharp knife or razor blade.

4. The engine must be operated at slow speed when first started after a new braided seal is installed. Neoprene composition seals are placed in grooves in the sides of bearing cap to seal against leakage in the joints between cap and crankcase. The neoprene composition swells in the presence of oil and heat. The seals are undersize when newly installed and may even leak for a short time until the seals have had time to swell and seal the opening.

5. The neoprene seals are slightly longer than the grooves in the bearing cap. The seals must not be cut to length. Before installation of seals, soak for 1 to 2 minutes in light oil or kerosene. After installation of bearing cap in crankcase, install seal in bearing cap.

6. To help eliminate oil leakage at the joint where the cap meets the crankcase, apply sealer, to the rear main bearing cap split line. When applying sealer, use only a thin coat as an over abundance will not allow the cap to seat properly.

UPPER OIL SEAL

1. Drain the engine oil.
2. Remove oil pan.

3. Insert packing tool (J-21526-2 or equivalent) against one end of the seal in the cylinder block. Drive the old seal gently into the groove until it is packed tight. This varies from $1/4$ in. (6mm) to $3/4$ in. (19mm) depending on the amount of pack required.

4. Repeat on the other end of the seal in the cylinder block.

5. Measure the amount the seal was driven up on one side and add $1/16$ in. (1.6mm). Using a single edge razor blade, cut that length from the old seal removed from the rear main bearing cap. Repeat the procedure for the other side. Use the rear main bearing cap as a holding fixture when cutting the seal.

6. Install guide tool (J-21526-1 or equivalent) onto cylinder block.

7. Using packing tool, work the short pieces cut previously into the guide tool and then pack into cylinder block. The guide tool and packing tool have been machined to provide a built-in stop. Use this procedure for both sides. It may help to use oil on the short pieces of the rope seal when packing into the cylinder block.

8. Remove the guide tool.

9. Install a new fabric seal in the rear main bearing cap. Install cap and tighten to specifications.

10. Install oil pan.

11. Add engine oil to the crankcase, as necessary.

12. Start the engine and check for leaks.

3.1L and 3.3L Engines

1. Disconnect the negative battery cable.

2. Drain the engine oil.

3. Remove the transaxle.

4. Remove the flywheel mounting bolts and remove the flywheel and spacer.

5. Using a small pry bar, pry the seal from the block.

❋❋CAUTION

Be careful not to damage the crankshaft surface when removing the oil seal.

6. Clean the seal mounting surface.

To install:

7. Coat the inside and outside of the new rear main oil seal with engine oil.

8. Install the new seal on tool J-34686 (or equivalent) until the seal bottom is squarely against the collar of the tool.

9. Align the dowel pin of the tool with the dowel pin hole in the crankshaft. Tighten the attaching screws to 45 inch lbs. (5 Nm).

10. Turn the handle of the tool until the collar is tight against the case. This will ensure the seal is fully seated.

11. Back the tool off and remove the attaching screws.

12. Install the flywheel and spacer and tighten the flywheel mounting bolts.

13. Install the transaxle assembly.

14. Connect the negative battery cable.

15. Add engine oil to the crankcase.

16. Start the engine and check for leaks.

3.8L Engine

1. Disconnect the negative battery cable.

2. Raise and support the vehicle safely.

3. Drain the engine oil and remove the oil pan.

4. Remove the rear main bearing cap. Remove the oil seal from the bearing cap.

To install:

5. Insert a packing tool (J-21526-2 or equivalent) against one end of the seal in the cylinder block. Pack the old seal in until it is tight. Pack the other end of seal in the same manner.

6. Measure the amount the seal was driven up into the block on one side and add approximately $3/32$ in. (2mm). With a single edge razor blade, cut this amount off of the old lower seal. The bearing cap can be used as a holding fixture.

7. Install the packing guide tool J-21526-1 or equivalent, onto the cylinder block.

8. Using the packing tool, work the short pieces of the seal into the guide tool and pack into the cylinder block until the tool hits the built in stop. Repeat this step on the other side. A small amount of oil on the pieces of seal may be helpful when packing into the cylinder block.

9. Remove the guide tool.

10. Install a new rope seal in the bearing cap and install the cap. Tighten the retaining bolts to specification.

11. Install the oil pan.

12. Fill the crankcase with oil.

13. Connect the negative battery cable.

14. Start the vehicle and check for leaks.

4.3L Diesel Engine

LOWER OIL SEAL

1. Remove the rear main bearing cap.

2. Remove the old seal and place a new seal in the groove with both ends projecting the surface of the cap.

3. Force the seal into the groove rubbing down with a hammer handle or smooth stick until the seal projects above the groove not more than $1/16$ in. (1.6mm). Cut ends off flush with surface of cap, using sharp knife or razor blade.

4. The engine must be operated at slow speed when first started after a new braided seal is installed. Neoprene composition seals are placed in grooves in the sides of bearing cap to seal against leakage in the joints between cap and crankcase. The neoprene composition swells in the presence of oil and heat. The seals are undersize when newly installed and may even leak for a short time until the seals have had time to swell and seal the opening.

5. The neoprene seals are slightly longer than the grooves in the bearing cap. The seals must not be cut to length. Before installation of seals, soak for 1 to 2 minutes in light oil or kerosene. After installation of bearing cap in crankcase, install seal in bearing cap.

6. To help eliminate oil leakage at the joint where the cap meets the crankcase, apply sealer to the rear main bearing cap split line. When applying sealer, use only a thin coat as an over abundance will not allow the cap to seat properly.

UPPER OIL SEAL

1. Drain the engine oil.

2. Remove oil pan.

3. Insert packing tool (J-21526-2 or equivalent) against one end of the seal in the cylinder block. Drive the old seal gently into the groove until it is packed tight. This varies from $1/4$ in. (6mm) to $3/4$ in. (19mm) depending on the amount of pack required.

4. Repeat on the other end of the seal in the cylinder block.

5. Measure the amount the seal was driven up on one side and add $1/16$ in. (1.6mm). Using a single edge razor blade, cut that length from the old seal removed from the rear main bearing cap. Repeat the procedure for the other side. Use the rear main bearing cap as a holding fixture when cutting the seal.

6. Install Guide Tool (J-21526-1) onto cylinder block.

7. Using packing tool, work the short pieces cut previously into the guide tool and then pack into cylinder block. The guide tool and packing tool have been machined to provide a built-in stop. Use this procedure for both sides. It may help to

use oil on the short pieces of the rope seal when packing into the cylinder block.

8. Remove the guide tool.

9. Install a new fabric seal in the rear main bearing cap. Install cap and tighten to specification.

10. Install oil pan.

11. Add engine oil to the crankcase.

12. Start the engine and check for leaks.

Crankshaft and Main Bearings

REMOVAL & INSTALLATION

▶ **See Figure 128**

1. Remove the engine assembly as previously outlined.
2. Remove the engine front cover.
3. Remove the timing chain and sprockets or gears.
4. Remove the oil pan.
5. Remove the oil pump.
6. Stamp the cylinder number on the machined surfaces of the bolt bosses of the connecting rods and caps for identification when reinstalling. If the pistons are to be removed from the connecting rod, mark cylinder number on piston with a silver pencil or quick drying paint for proper cylinder identification and cap to rod location.
7. Remove the connecting rod caps and install thread protectors.
8. Mark the main bearing caps so that they can be reinstalled in their original positions.
9. Remove all the main bearing caps. They all must go back to their original locations and they must all face the same direction. Any cap install incorrectly will cause engine damage when reassembled.
10. Note position of keyway in crankshaft so it can be installed in the same position.
11. Lift crankshaft out of block. Rods will pivot to the center of the engine when the crankshaft is removed.
12. Remove both halves of the rear main oil seal if two piece design. If a one piece design, remove the seal.

To install:

13. Clean all of the oil sludge and carbon deposits. Probe the oil passages for any obstructions.
14. Inspect the bearing journals for; cracks, chips, gouges, roughness, grooves, and overheating (discoloration).
15. Inspect the corresponding bearing inserts for any imbedded foreign materials, then determine it's source.
16. If cracks, burned spots or gouges are found, you must replace the crankshaft.
17. Measure the crankshaft journals with a micrometer to determine the correct size rod and main bearings to be used. Whenever a new or reconditioned crankshaft is installed, new connect rod bearings and main bearings should be installed.
18. Clean all oil passages in the block (and crankshaft if it is being reused).

➡**A new rear main seal should be installed anytime the crankshaft is removed or replaced. If any engine repair is made, any related seals or gaskets should be replaced. It's not worth the time lost to repeat a repair job due to an old seal or gasket leaking.**

1 Cylinder block
2 Crankshaft
3 Seal
4 Seal
5 Rear cap
6 Bolt
7 Front cap
8 Bearing

86813315

Fig. 128 The crankshaft is secured in the block by the main bearing caps

19. Install sufficient oil pan bolts in the block to align with the connecting rod bolts. Use rubber bands between the bolts to position the connecting rods as required. Connecting rod position can be adjusted by increasing the tension on the rubber bands with additional turns around the pan bolts or thread protectors.

20. Position the upper half of main bearings in the block and lubricate with engine oil.

21. Position crankshaft keyway in the same position as removed and lower into block. The connecting rods will follow the crank pins into the correct position as the crankshaft is lowered.

22. Lubricate the thrust flanges with GM part no. 1050169 lubricant or equivalent. Install caps with lower half of bearings lubricated with engine oil. Lubricate cap bolts with engine oil and install, but do not tighten.

23. With a block of wood, bump the shaft in each direction to align thrust flanges of main bearing. After bumping shaft in

each direction, wedge the shaft to the front and hold it while tightening the thrust bearing cap bolts.

➡**In order to prevent the possibility of cylinder block and/or main bearing cap damage, the main bearing caps are to be tapped into their cylinder block cavity using a brass or leather mallet before attaching bolts are installed. Do not use attaching bolts to pull main bearing caps into their seat.**

24. Tighten all main bearing caps to specification.
25. Remove the connecting rod bolt thread protectors and lubricate the connecting rod bearings with engine oil.
26. Install the connecting rod bearing caps in their original position. Tighten the nuts to specification.
27. Complete the installation by reversing the removal steps.

CHECKING BEARING CLEARANCE

1. Remove bearing cap and wipe oil from crankshaft journal and outer and inner surfaces of bearing shell.
2. Place a piece of plastic gaging material (Plastigage® or equivalent) in the center of bearing. Position the crankshaft in the saddles.
3. Reinstall bearing cap and bearing. Place engine oil on cap bolts and install. Tighten bolts to specification.
4. Remove bearing cap and determine bearing clearance by comparing the width of the flattened plastic gaging material at its widest point with graduations on the gaging material container. The number within the graduation on the envelope indicates the clearance in millimeters or thousandths of an inch. If the clearance is greater than allowed, REPLACE BOTH BEARING SHELLS AS A SET. Recheck clearance after replacing shells.

BEARING REPLACEMENT

Engine Installed

Main bearing clearances must be corrected by the use of selective upper and lower shells. To install main bearing shells, proceed as follows:
1. Remove the oil pan. On some models, the oil pump may also have to be removed.
2. Loosen all main bearing caps.
3. Remove bearing cap and remove lower shell.
4. Insert a flattened cotter pin or roll out pin in the oil passage hole in the crankshaft in the direction opposite to cranking rotation. The pin will contact the upper shell and roll it out.
5. The main bearing journals should be checked for roughness and wear. Slight roughness may be removed with a fine grit polishing cloth saturated with engine oil. Burrs may be

removed with a fine oil stone. If the journals are scored or ridged, the crankshaft must be replaced.
6. Clean crankshaft journals and bearing caps thoroughly before installing new main bearings.
7. Apply lubricant GM part no.1050169 or equivalent to the thrust flanges of bearing shells.
8. Place new upper shell on crankshaft journal with locating tang correctly positioned and rotate shaft to turn it into place. Use the cotter pin or roll out pin as during removal.
9. Place new bearing shell in bearing cap.
10. Install a new oil seal in the rear main bearing cap and block.
11. Lubricate the removed or replaced main bearings with engine oil. Lubricate the thrust surface with lubricant GM part no.1050169 or equivalent.
12. Lubricate the main bearing cap bolts with engine oil.

➡**In order to prevent the possibility of cylinder block and/or main bearing cap damage, the main bearing caps are to be tapped into their cylinder block cavity using a brass or leather mallet before attaching bolts are installed. Do not use attaching bolts to pull main bearing caps into their seats.**

13. Tighten the main bearing cap bolts.

Engine Removed

The bearings can easily be replaced after the crankshaft is removed. Simply remove the bearing inserts from the saddles and main bearing caps, and install the new ones. Be sure to check for proper bearing clearances.

Flywheel and Ring Gear

REMOVAL & INSTALLATION

The ring gear is an integral part of the flywheel and is not replaceable.
1. Remove the transaxle.
2. Remove the bolts attaching the flywheel to the crankshaft flange. Remove the flywheel.
3. Inspect the flywheel for cracks, and inspect the ring gear for burrs or worn teeth. Replace the flywheel if any damage is apparent. Remove burrs with a mill file.
4. Clean the flywheel bolt threads and bolt holes.
To install:
5. Apply thread locker GM part no.12345382 or an equivalent to all of the flywheel bolts.
6. Attach the flywheel and start bolts. The flywheel will only attach to the crankshaft in one position, as the bolt holes are unevenly spaced. Use a suitable tool to prevent the rotation of the crankshaft.
7. Tighten the bolts to specifications.
8. Install the transaxle.

EXHAUST SYSTEM

General Information

➡Safety glasses should be worn at all times when working on or near the exhaust system. Older exhaust systems will almost always be covered with loose rust particles which will shower you when disturbed. These particles are more than a nuisance and could injure your eye.

Whenever working on the exhaust system always keep the following in mind:

1. Check the complete exhaust system for open seams, holes loose connections, or other deterioration which could permit exhaust fumes to seep into the passenger compartment.

2. The exhaust system is usually supported by free-hanging rubber mountings which permit some movement of the exhaust system, but does not permit transfer of noise and vibration into the passenger compartment. Do not replace the rubber mounts with solid ones.

3. Before removing any component of the exhaust system, ALWAYS squirt a liquid rust dissolving agent onto the fasteners for ease of removal. A lot of knuckle skin will be saved by following this rule. It may even be wise to spray the fasteners and allow them to sit overnight.

4. Annoying rattles and noise vibrations in the exhaust system are usually caused by misalignment of the parts. When aligning the system, leave all bolts and nuts loose until all parts are properly aligned, then tighten, working from front to rear.

5. When installing exhaust system parts, make sure there is enough clearance between the hot exhaust parts and pipes and hoses that would be adversely affected by excessive heat. Also make sure there is adequate clearance from the floor pan to avoid possible overheating of the floor.

Front Pipe

REMOVAL & INSTALLATION

Pipe Without Catalytic Converter

♦ See Figure 129

1. Before removing any component of the exhaust system, always squirt a liquid rust dissolving agent onto the fasteners for ease of removal..

2. Raise and support the front of the vehicle on jackstands.

3. Remove the exhaust pipe-to-manifold nuts.

4. Support the catalytic converter, then disconnect the pipe from the converter. Remove the pipe.

5. Remove the exhaust gaskets.

To install:

6. Be sure to use all new gaskets when required. Assemble the system, check the clearance and tighten the bolts to about 15-30 ft. lbs. (20-41 Nm).

7. All clamps should be tightened to about 18-25 ft. lbs. (24-34 Nm). Do over-tighten the clamps. If pipes become dented they can leak.

Fig. 129 Front exhaust pipe connection common on vehicles with the catalytic converter not included

Pipe With Catalytic Converter

1. Before removing any component of the exhaust system, always squirt a liquid rust dissolving agent onto the fasteners for ease of removal.

2. Raise and support the vehicle.

3. On some vehicles you will need to remove the brace from the transaxle.

4. Remove the exhaust pipe nuts from the manifold.

5. Support the catalytic converter pipe bolts from the rear of the converter.

6. Lower the catalytic converter/front pipe assembly from the vehicle.

To install:

7. Be sure to use all new gaskets when required.

8. Attach the new catalytic converter/front pipe assembly to the vehicle. Tighten the pipe to manifold nuts to 20-40 ft. lbs. (27-55 Nm).

9. Attach the bolts at the rear of the catalytic converter/front pipe. Tighten them to 30-35 ft. lbs. (41-47 Nm).

10. Connect the brace at the transaxle if removed.

11. Lower the vehicle.

Crossover Pipe

REMOVAL & INSTALLATION

V6 Engines

✳✳CAUTION

Fuel Injection systems remain under pressure, even after the engine has been turned OFF. The fuel system pressure must be relieved before disconnecting any fuel lines. Failure to do so may result in fire and/or personal injury.

1. Drain the cooling system.

2. Remove the air cleaner assembly. Relieve the fuel system pressure.

3. Disconnect the fuel lines.

4. Remove the upper radiator hose.

5. Disconnect the shift control cables, then remove the bracket.

6. Detach the electrical connectors.

7. Unfasten the heat shield.

8. Remove the crossover pipe nuts, then remove the crossover pipe.

To install:

9. Attach the new crossover pipe to the vehicle, then tighten the mounting nuts to 18 ft. lbs. (25 Nm).

10. Attach the heat shield.

11. Connect the electrical harness to the vehicle.

12. Install the shift control cables and bracket in their proper locations.

13. Attach the upper radiator hose.

14. Connect the fuel lines that were detached.

15. Install the air cleaner assembly.

16. Refill the cooling system.

17. Start the engine. Fill the cooling system, then check for exhaust and cooling leaks.

Intermediate Pipe

REMOVAL & INSTALLATION

▶ **See Figure 130**

1. Before removing any component of the exhaust system, always squirt a liquid rust dissolving agent onto the fasteners for ease of removal.

2. Raise and support the front of the vehicle.

3. Support the exhaust system.

4. Disconnect the intermediate pipe from the catalytic converter. If the pipe is original you may have to cut the pipe from the catalytic converter.

1 Replacement pipe
2 Guillotine clamp
3 Existing converter
4 26 lbs.ft. (35 Nm)

86813325

Fig. 130 Attaching the intermediate pipe to the converter

5. At the muffler, remove the clamp and the intermediate pipe.

To install:

6. Use a new clamp, nuts and bolts, then assemble the system. Be sure to use all new gaskets when required. Check the clearances, then tighten the connectors.

7. All clamps should be tightened to about 18-25 ft. lbs. (24-34 Nm). Do over-tighten the clamps. If pipes become dented they can leak.

Catalytic Converter

REMOVAL & INSTALLATION

▶ **See Figure 131**

For vehicles with the catalytic converter included with the front pipe, see front pipe removal and installation.

1. Before removing any component of the exhaust system, always squirt a liquid rust dissolving agent onto the fasteners for ease of removal.

2. Raise and support the front of the vehicle on jackstands and place a support under the catalytic converter.

3. Remove the clamp at the front of the converter. then cut the pipe at the front of the converter.

4. Remove the converter-to-intermediate pipe nuts/bolts.

5. Disconnect the converter-to-crossover pipe or front pipe.

To install:

6. Reverse to install.

7. Use new clamps and nuts/bolts. Make sure to use all new gaskets if required. Assemble the system, then check the clearances and tighten all of the attachments.

8. All clamps should be tightened to about 18-25 ft. lbs. (24-34 Nm). Do over-tighten the clamps. If pipes become dented they can leak.

Muffler

REMOVAL & INSTALLATION

1. Before removing any component of the exhaust system, always squirt a liquid rust dissolving agent onto the fasteners for ease of removal.

2. Raise and support the vehicle on jackstands.

3. On the single pipe system, cut the exhaust pipe near the front of the muffler. On the dual pipe system, remove the U-bolt clamp at the front of the muffler and disengage the muffler from the exhaust pipe.

➡ **Before cutting the exhaust pipe, measure the service muffler exhaust pipe extension and make certain to allow 1½ in. (38mm) for the exhaust pipe-to-muffler extension engagement.**

4. At the rear of the muffler, remove the U-bolt clamp and disengage the muffler from the tailpipe.

5. Remove the tailpipe clamps and the tailpipe.

6. Inspect the muffler and the tailpipe hangers, replace if necessary.

1 Converter
2 Hanger
3 Front exhaust pipe
4 Intermediate pipe
5 35 lbs.ft. (48 Nm)

86813326

Fig. 131 Catalytic converter installation

To install:

7. Always use all new gaskets if required when installing an exhaust system.

8. Assemble the system. Check the clearances, then tighten all of the attachments.

9. All clamps should be tightened to about 18-25 ft. lbs. (24-34 Nm). Do over-tighten the clamps. If pipes become dented they can leak.

Tailpipe

REMOVAL & INSTALLATION

1. Before removing any component of the exhaust system, always squirt a liquid rust dissolving agent onto the fasteners for ease of removal.

2. Raise and support the vehicle on jackstands.

3. Remove the hanger clamps from the tail pipe.

4. Remove the tailpipe-to-muffler clamp.

5. Disengage the tailpipe from the muffler and remove the tailpipe.

6. Inspect the tailpipe hangers and replace, if necessary.

To install:

7. Assemble the system. Check the clearances, then tighten all of the attachments.

8. All clamps should be tightened to about 18-25 ft. lbs. (24-34 Nm). Do over-tighten the clamps. If pipes become dented they can leak.

L82

LN2

86813341

Fig. 132 Exhaust system for the 1993-95 2.2L and 3.1L excluding the wagon

Fig. 133 Exhaust system for the 1993-95 3.1L wagon

Fig. 134 Exhaust system for the 1982-85 2.5L excluding the wagon

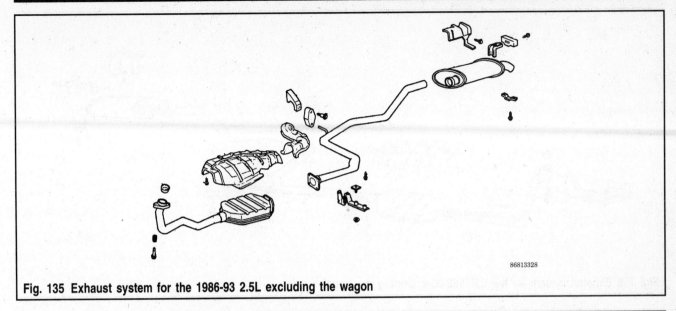
86813328

Fig. 135 Exhaust system for the 1986-93 2.5L excluding the wagon

86813329

Fig. 136 Exhaust system for the 1982-85 2.5L wagon

86813330

Fig. 137 Exhaust system for the 1986-93 2.5L wagon

86813331

Fig. 138 Exhaust system for the V6 1982-86 excluding the wagon

86813332

Fig. 139 Exhaust system for the V6 1982-86 wagon

86813333

Fig. 140 Exhaust system for the V6 1986-92 excluding the wagon

86813331

Fig. 141 Exhaust system for the V6 1986-92 wagon

86813335

Fig. 142 Exhaust system for the diesel excluding the wagon

86813331

Fig. 143 Exhaust system for the diesel wagon

TORQUE SPECIFICATIONS

Component		US	Metric
Alternator bolts:			
	Front:	37 ft. lbs.	50 Nm
	Rear:	18 ft. lbs.	25 Nm
Battery cable:		11 ft. lbs.	15 Nm
Camshaft sprocket:			
	2.2L	77 ft. lbs.	105 Nm
	2.8L	15-20 ft. lbs.	20-27 Nm
	3.1L- T	15-20 ft. lbs.	20-27 Nm
	3.1L- M	74 ft. lbs.	100 ft. lbs.
	3.3L, 3.8L, 4.3L	52 ft. lbs. + 110°	70 Nm + 110°
Camshaft thrust bolt:			
	2.2L	106 inch lbs.	12 Nm
	2.5L, 2.8L, 3.0L, 3.1L	89 inch lbs.	10 Nm
	3.3L, 3.8L, 4.3L	110 inch lbs.	15 Nm
Camshaft sensor:		8 ft. lbs.	10 Nm
Camshaft rear cover:		6-9 ft. lbs.	8-12 Nm
Connecting rod cap nuts:			
	2.2L	38 ft. lbs.	52 Nm
	2.5L	29 ft. lbs.	40 Nm
	2.8L-W	34-40 ft. lbs.	46-54 Nm
	2.8L-X	34-40 ft. lbs.	46-54 Nm
	2.8L-Z	34-40 ft. lbs.	46-54 Nm
	3.0L	40-45 ft. lbs.	54-61 Nm
	3.1L-T	34-40 ft. lbs.	46-54 Nm
	3.1L-M	15 ft. lbs. + 75°	20 Nm + 75°
	3.3L	20 ft. lbs. + 50°	27 Nm + 50°
	3.8L	45 ft. lbs.	61 Nm
	4.3L	40-45 ft. lbs.	54-61 Nm
Crankshaft dampner/balancer:			
	2.5L 1982-87	200 ft. lbs.	260 Nm
	2.5L 1988-93	162 ft. lbs.	220 Nm
	2.8L	75 ft. lbs.	102 Nm
	3.0L	200 ft. lbs.	260 Nm
	3.1L-T	75 ft. lbs.	102 Nm
	3.1L-M	76 ft. lbs.	103 Nm
	3.3L	105 ft. lbs. + 56°	140 Nm + 56°
	3.8L	220 ft. lbs.	290 Nm
	4.3L	40-45 ft. lbs.	54-61 Nm
Crankshaft sensor:			
	2.2L	71 inch lbs.	8 Nm
	3.1L-M	8 ft. lbs.	10 Nm
Engine mount-to-engine:			
	2.2L	39 ft. lbs.	53 Nm
	2.5L, 2.8L, 3.0L, 3.1L	40 ft. lbs.	54 Nm
	3.3L, 3.8L, 4.3L	70 ft. lbs.	95 Nm
Engine mount-to-frame:			
	2.2L, 3.3L, 3.8L, 4.3L	32 ft. lbs.	43 Nm
	2.5L, 2.8L, 3.0L, 3.1L	35 ft. lbs.	47 Nm

TORQUE SPECIFICATIONS

Component			US	Metric
Exhaust manifold:				
	2.2L		39 ft. lbs.	53 Nm
	2.5L	Inner:	37 ft. lbs.	50 Nm
		Outer:	28 ft. lbs.	38 Nm
	2.8L-W		15-23 ft. lbs.	20-30 Nm
	2.8L-X		25 ft. lbs.	34 Nm
	2.8L-Z		25 ft. lbs.	34 Nm
	3.0L		25-37 ft. lbs.	34-50 Nm
	3.1L-N		15-23 ft. lbs.	20-30 Nm
	3.1L-T		35 ft. lbs.	47 Nm
	3.3L		39 ft. lbs.	55 Nm
	3.8L		37 ft. lbs.	50 Nm
	4.3L		29 ft. lbs.	37 Nm
Exhaust clamps:			20-25 ft. lbs.	27-34 Nm
Flywheel bolts:				
	2.2L		55 ft. lbs.	75 Nm
	2.5L	1982-86	47 ft. lbs.	61 Nm
		1987-93	55 ft. lbs.	75 Nm
	2.8L		52 ft. lbs.	70 Nm
	3.0L		60 ft. lbs.	80 Nm
	3.1L-T		76 ft. lbs.	108 Nm
	3.1L-M		61 ft. lbs.	83 Nm
	3.3L		89 inch lbs + 90 °	10 Nm + 90°
	3.8L		60 ft. lbs.	80 Nm
	4.3L		76 ft. lbs.	108 Nm
Front cover:				
	2.2L		97 inch lbs.	11 Nm
	2.5L, 2.8L, 3.0L, 3.1L-T		89 inch lbs.	10 Nm
	3.1L-M	Large	35 ft. lbs.	47 Nm
		Small	15 ft. lbs.	21 Nm
Ignition coil:				
	2.2L		15-22 ft. lbs.	20-30 Nm
	2.5L, 2.8L, 3.1L-T		40 inch lbs.	4-5 Nm
	3.1L-M		40 inch lbs.	4-5 Nm
	3.3L		27 inch lbs.	3 Nm
Intake manifold:				
	2.2L	Lower	24 ft. lbs.	33 Nm
		Upper	22 ft. lbs.	30 Nm
	2.5L, 2.8-W, 3.1-T		25 ft. lbs.	32 Nm
	3.0L, 3.8L		47 ft. lbs.	65 Nm
	3.1L-M		115 inch lbs.	13 Nm
	3.3L		89 inch lbs.	10 Nm
	4.3L		41 ft. lbs.	55 Nm
Lifter guide retaining stud:			89 inch lbs.	10 Nm
Main bearing caps:				
	2.2L		70 ft. lbs.	95 Nm
	2.5L	1982-89	70 ft. lbs.	95 Nm
		1990-93	65 ft. lbs.	88 Nm
	2.8L-W		63-83 Nm	85-112 Nm
	2.8L-X		68 ft. lbs.	90 Nm
	2.8L-Z		68 ft .lbs.	90 Nm
	3.0L		100 ft. lbs.	85-112 Nm
	3.1L-T		63-83 ft. lbs.	85-112 Nm

86813730

TORQUE SPECIFICATIONS

Component	US	Metric
3.1L-M	37 ft. lbs + 77°	50 Nm + 77°
3.3L	26 ft. lbs.+ 45°	35 Nm +45°
3.8L	100 ft. lbs.	135 Nm
4.3L	107 ft. lbs.	145 Nm
Oil pan:		
2.2L	89 inch lbs.	10 Nm
3.1L-M	18 ft. lbs.	25 Nm
3.3L	124 inch lbs.	14 Nm
All others		
M6	6-9 ft. lbs.	8-12 Nm
M8	15-23 ft. lbs.	20-30 Nm
Oil pump hold down:	67-85 ft. lbs.	27-41 Nm
Oil cover-to-timing cover:	89 inch lbs.	11 Nm
Oxygen sensor:	30 ft. lbs.	41 Nm
Spark plugs:		
2.2L		
new	20 ft. lbs.	27 Nm
used	11 ft. lbs.	15 Nm
2.5L	10-25 ft. lbs.	
2.8L-W	10-25 ft. lbs.	
2.8L-X, Z	7-15 ft. lbs.	
3.0L	7-15 ft. lbs.	
3.1L-T	10-25 ft. lbs.	
3.1L-M		
new	20 ft. lbs.	27 Nm
used	11 ft. lbs.	15 Nm
3.3L, 3.8L, 4.3L	20 ft. lbs.	27 Nm
Starter mounting bolts:	32 ft. lbs.	43 Nm
Thermostat housing:	8-23 ft. lbs.	10-30 Nm
Timing chain dampner:	14-19 ft. lbs.	18-24 Nm
Water pump:		
2.2L	18 ft. lbs.	25 Nm
2.5L		
1982-86	25 ft. lbs.	30 Nm
1987-93	10 ft. lbs.	11 Nm
3.0L	8 ft. lbs.	10 Nm
M6 bolts	6-9 ft. lbs.	8-12 Nm
M8 bolts	25 ft. lbs.	34 Nm
Valve cover:		
2.2L	89 inch lbs.	10 Nm
2.5L	80 inch lbs.	9 Nm
2.8L-W	6-9 ft. lbs.	8-12 Nm
2.8L-X	10 ft. lbs.	11 Nm
2.8L-Z	10 ft. lbs.	11 Nm
3.0L	14 ft. lbs.	19 Nm
3.1L-T	6-9 ft. lbs.	8-12 Nm
3.1L-M	18 ft. lbs.	24 Nm
3.3L	14 ft. lbs.	19 Nm
3.8L	14-20 ft. lbs.	19-27 Nm
4.3L	14-20 ft. lbs.	19-27 Nm

86813731

ENGINE REBUILDING SPECIFICATIONS CHART

Component	US	Metric
CAMSHAFT		
2.2L (VIN 4)		
End play:	NA	NA
Bearing diameter:	1.868-1.869 in.	47.45-47.48 mm
Bearing clearance:	0.001-0.0039 in.	0.026-0.101 mm
Lobe lift		
Intake:	0.288 in.	7.309 mm
Exhaust:	0.288 in.	7.307 mm
2.5L (VIN R)		
End play:	0.0015-0.005 in.	NA
Bearing diameter:	1.869 in.	47.45-47.48 mm
Bearing clearance:	0.0007-0.0027 in.	0.026-0.101 mm
Lobe lift (1982-88)		
Intake:	0.398 in.	7.309 mm
Exhaust:	0.398 in.	7.307 mm
Lobe lift (1989)		
Intake:	0.232 in.	5.8882 mm
Exhaust:	0.232 in.	5.8882 mm
Lobe lift (1990-93)		
Intake:	0.248 in.	6.302 mm
Exhaust:	0.248 in.	6.302 mm
2.8L (VIN W)		
End play:	NA	NA
Bearing diameter:	1.8678-1.8815 in.	47.44-47.79 mm
Bearing clearance:	0.001-0.004 in.	0.026-0.101 mm
Lobe lift		
Intake:	0.2626 in.	6.67 mm
Exhaust:	0.2732 in.	6.94 mm
2.8L (VIN X)		
End play:	NA	NA
Bearing diameter:	1.8876-1.8996 in.	47.44-47.49 mm
Bearing clearance:	0.001-0.004 in.	0.026-0.101 mm
Lobe lift		
Intake:	0.2348 in.	5.87 mm
Exhaust:	0.2668 in.	6.67 mm
2.8L (VIN Z)		
End play:	NA	NA
Bearing diameter:	1.8876-1.8996 in.	47.44-47.49 mm
Bearing clearance:	0.001-0.004 in.	0.026-0.101 mm
Lobe lift		
Intake:	0.2348 in.	5.87 mm
Exhaust:	0.2668 in.	6.67 mm
3.0L (VIN E)		
End play:	NA	NA
Bearing diameter:	1.785-1.786 in.	45.339-45.364 mm
Bearing clearance:		
Number 1:	0.0005-0.0025 in.	0.0127-0.0635 mm
Numbers 2, 3, 4:	0.0005-00035 in.	0.0127-0.0889 mm
3.1L (VIN T)		
End play:	NA	NA
Bearing diameter:	1.8678-1.8815 in.	47.44-47.79 mm

86813900

ENGINE REBUILDING SPECIFICATIONS CHART

Component		US	Metric
3.1L (VIN T)	Bearing clearance:	0.001-0.004 in.	0.026-0.101 mm
	Lobe lift		
	Intake:	0.2626 in.	6.67 mm
	Exhaust:	0.2732 in.	6.94 mm
3.1L (VIN M)			
	End play:	NA	NA
	Bearing diameter:	1.871-1.872 in.	47.523-47.549 mm
	Bearing clearance:	0.001-0.004 in.	0.026-0.101 mm
	Lobe lift		
	Intake:	0.2727 in.	6.9263 mm
	Exhaust:	0.2727 in.	6.9256 mm
3.3L (VIN N)			
	End play:	NA	NA
	Bearing diameter:	1.785-1.786 in.	45.339-45.364 mm
	Bearing clearance:	0.0005-0.0035 in.	0.013-0.089 mm
	Lobe lift		
	Intake:	0.250 in.	6.43 mm
	Exhaust:	0.255 in.	6.48 mm
3.8L (VIN 3)			
	End play:	NA	NA
	Bearing diameter:	1.785-1.786 in.	45.339-45.364 mm
	Bearing clearance		
	Number 1:	0.0005-0.0025 in.	0.0127-0.0635 mm
	Numbers 2, 3, 4:	0.0005-0.0035 in.	0.0127-0.0889 mm
4.3L (VIN T)			
	End clearance:	0.0008-0.0228 in.	0.02-0.58 mm
	Bearing diameter:		
	Cam sprocket	2.035-2.036 in.	51.707-51.727 mm
	Number 2:	2.015-2.016 in.	51.219-51.199 mm
	Number 3:	1.995-1.995 in.	50.71-50.60 mm
	Number 4:	1.976-1.975 in.	50.20-50.18 mm
	Bearing clearance:	0.0020-0.0043 in.	0.05-0.11 mm
	Lobe lift		
	Intake:	0.252 in.	6.40 mm
	Exhaust:	0.279 in.	7.09 mm
VALVES			
2.2L (VIN 4)			
	Face angle:	45 °	45 °
	Face runout:	0.0012 in.	0.03 mm
	Seat angle:	46 °	46 °
	Seat runout:	0.002 in.	0.05 mm
	Seat width		
	Intake:	0.049-0.059 in.	1.25-1.50 mm
	Exhaust:	0.063-0.075 in.	1.60-1.90 mm
	Stem clearance		
	Intake:	0.0010-0.0027 in.	0.025-0.069 mm
	Exhaust:	0.0014-0.0031 in.	0.035-0.081 mm
2.5L (VIN R)			
	Face angle:	45 °	45 °
	Seat angle:	46 °	46 °
	Seat runout:	0.002 in.	0.05 mm

86813901

ENGINE REBUILDING SPECIFICATIONS CHART

Component	US	Metric
2.5L (VIN R) Seat width		
Intake:	0.035-0.075 in.	0.889-1.905 mm
Exhaust: (1982-89)	0.058-0.097 in.	1.473-2.642 mm
Exhaust: (1990-93)	0.058-0.105 in.	1.473-2.667 mm
Stem clearance		
Intake:	0.001-0.0028 in.	0.028-0.071 mm
Exhaust: (1982-89)	0.0013-0.0041 in.	0.033-0.104 mm
Exhaust: (1990-93)	0.0013-0.0041 in.	0.033-0.104 mm
2.8L (VIN W)		
Face angle:	45°	45°
Seat angle:	46°	46°
Seat runout:	0.001 in.	0.25 mm
Seat width		
Intake:	0.061-0.073 in.	1.550-1.850 mm
Exhaust:	0.067-0.079 in.	1.70-2.0 mm
Stem clearance		
Intake:	0.001-0.0027 in.	0.026-0.068 mm
Exhaust:	0.001-0.0027 in.	0.026-0.068 mm
2.8L (VIN X)		
Face angle:	45°	45°
Seat angle:	46°	46°
Seat runout:	0.002 in.	0.05 mm
Seat width		
Intake:	0.049-0.059 in.	1.250-1.50 mm
Exhaust:	0.049-0.059 in.	1.250-1.50 mm
Stem clearance		
Intake:	0.001-0.0027 in.	0.026-0.068 mm
Exhaust:	0.001-0.0027 in.	0.026-0.068 mm
2.8L (VIN Z)		
Face angle:	45°	45°
Seat angle:	46°	46°
Seat runout:	0.002 in.	0.05 mm
Seat width		
Intake:	0.049-0.059 in.	1.250-1.50 mm
Exhaust:	0.049-0.059 in.	1.250-1.50 mm
Stem clearance		
Intake:	0.001-0.0027 in.	0.026-0.068 mm
Exhaust:	0.001-0.0027 in.	0.026-0.068 mm
3.0 (VIN E)		
Face angle:	45°	45°
Seat angle:	46°	46°
Seat runout:	0.002 in.	0.05 mm
Seat width		
Intake:	0.3412-0.3401 in.	8.666-8.638 mm
Exhaust:	0.3412-0.3405 in.	8.666-8.649 mm
Stem clearance		
Intake:	0.0015-0..0035 in.	0.038-0.089 mm

86813902

ENGINE REBUILDING SPECIFICATIONS CHART

Component		US	Metric
3.0L (VIN E)	Exhaust:	0.0015-0.0032 in.	0.038-0.081 mm
3.1L (VIN T)			
	Face angle:	45°	45°
	Seat angle:	46°	46°
	Seat runout:	0.001 in.	0.25 mm
	Seat width		
	Intake:	0.061-0.073 in.	1.150-1.850 mm
	Exhaust:	0.067-0.079 in.	1.70-2.0 mm
	Stem clearance		
	Intake:	0.001-0.0027 in.	0.026-0.068 mm
	Exhaust:	0.001-0.0027 in.	0.026-0.068 mm
3.1L (VIN M)			
	Face angle:	45°	45°
	Seat angle:	45°	45°
	Seat runout:	0.001 in.	0.025 mm
	Seat width		
	Intake:	0.061-0.071 in.	1.55-1.80 mm
	Exhaust:	0.067-0.079 in.	1.70-2.0 mm
	Stem clearance		
	Intake:	0.001-0.0027 in.	0.026-0.068 mm
	Exhaust:	0.001-0.0027 in.	0.026-0.068 mm
3.3L (VIN N)			
	Face angle:	45°	45°
	Seat angle:	45°	45°
	Seat runout:	0.002 in.	0.05 mm
	Seat width		
	Intake:	0.060-0.080 in.	1.53-2.030 mm
	Exhaust:	0.090-0.110 in.	2.29-2.79 mm
	Stem clearance		
	Intake:	0.0015-0.0035 in.	0.038-0.089 mm
	Exhaust:	0.0015-0.0032 in.	0.038-0.081 mm
3.8L (VIN 3)			
	Face angle:	45°	45°
	Seat angle:	46°	46°
	Seat runout:	0.002 in.	0.05 mm
	Seat width		
	Intake:	0.3412-0.3401 in.	8.666-8.638 mm
	Exhaust:	0.3412-0.3405 in.	8.666-8.649 mm
	Stem clearance		
	Intake:	0.0015-0.0035 in.	0.038-0.089 mm
	Exhaust:	0.0015-0.0035 in.	0.038-0.081 mm
4.3L (VIN T)			
	Face angle		
	Intake:	44°	44°
	Exhaust:	30°	30°

86813903

ENGINE REBUILDING SPECIFICATIONS CHART

Component		US	Metric
4.3L (VIN T)	Seat angle		
	Intake:	45 °	45 °
	Exhaust:	31 °	31 °
	Overall length		
	Intake:	5.120 in.	130.048 mm
	Exhaust:	5.029 in.	127-7366 mm
	Seat runout		
	Intake:	0.004 in.	0.10 mm
	Exhaust:	0.002 in.	0.05 mm
	Head diameter		
	Internal EGR		
	Intake:	1.875 in.	47.01 mm
	Exhaust:	1.622 in.	41.20 mm
	External EGR		
	Intake:	1.750 in.	44.45 mm
	Exhaust:	1.500 in.	38.20 mm
	Stem diameter		
	Intake:	0.3425-0.3432 in.	8.6995-8.7376 mm
	Exhaust:	0.3420-0.3428 in.	8.6870-8.7070 mm
	Clearance in guide		
	Intake:	0.0010-0.0027 in.	0.026-0.068 mm
	Exhaust:	0.0015-0.0032 in.	0.038-0.081 mm
	Seat width		
	Intake cast:	0.0037-0.075 in.	0.94-1.9 mm
	Intake aluminum:	0.0032-0.077 in.	0.81-1.97 mm
	Exhaust:	0.0046-0.840 in.	1.17-2.14 mm
VALVE SPRING			
2.2L (VIN 4)			
	Free length	1.95 in.	49.5 mm
2.5L (VIN R)			
	Free length:	2.01 in.	51 mm
	Installed height:	1.68 in.	42.64 mm
2.8L (VIN W)			
	Free length:	1.191 in.	48.5 mm
	Installed height:	1.5748 in.	40.0 mm
2.8L (VIN X)			
	Free length:	1.191 in.	48.5 mm
2.8L (VIN Z)			
	Free length:	1.191 in.	48.5 mm
3.1L (VIN T)			
	Free length:	1.191 in.	48.5 mm
	Installed height:	1.5748 in.	40.0 mm
3.1L (VIN M)			
	Free length:	1.89 in.	48.5 mm
	Installed height:	1.710 in.	43 mm

86813904

ENGINE REBUILDING SPECIFICATIONS CHART

Component		US	Metric
3.3 (VIN N)			
	Free length:	1.98 in.	50.32 mm
	Installed height:	1.69-1.72 in.	42.93-44.45 mm
4.3L (VIN T)			
	Free length:	2.09 in.	53.09 mm
SPRING LOAD			
2.2L (VIN 4)			
	Closed	78-81 lbs @ 1.710 in.	332-362 N @ 43.43 mm
	Open	220-236 lbs. @ 1.278 in.	979-1049 N @ 32.47 mm
2.5L (VIN R)			
	Closed	75 lbs. @ 1.68 in.	332 N @ 42.64 mm
	Open	173 lbs. @ 1.24 in.	770 N @ 31.46 mm
2.8L (VIN W)			
	Closed	90 lbs. @ 1.70 in.	400 N @ 43.0 mm
	Open	215 lbs. @ 1.29 in.	956 N @ 33.0 mm
2.8L (VIN X)			
	Closed	88 lbs. @ 1.70 in.	40 Kg @ 40.0 mm
	Open	195 lbs. @ 1.57 in.	88 Kg @ 30.0 mm
2.8L (VIN Z)			
	Closed	88 lbs. @ 1.70 in.	40 Kg @ 40.0 mm
	Open	195 lbs. @ 1.57 in.	88 Kg @ 30.0 mm
3.0L (VIN E)			
	Closed	93 lbs. @ 1.727 in.	413 N @ 43.9 mm
	Open	220 lbs. @ 1.340 in.	978 N @ 34.0 mm
3.1L (VIN T)			
	Closed	90 lbs. @ 1.701 in.	400 N @ 43.0 mm
	Open	215 lbs. @ 1.291 in.	956 N @ 33.0 mm
3.1L (VIN M)			
	Closed	80 lbs @ 1.710 in.	356 N @ 43 mm
	Open	250 lbs. @ 1.239 in.	1111 N @ 31.5 mm
3.3L (VIN N)			
	Closed	80 lbs @ 1.750 in.	356 N @ 43.7 mm
	Open	210 lbs. @ 1.315 in.	935 N @ 33.4 mm
3.8L (VIN 3)			
	Closed	64 lbs @ 1.727 in.	285 N @ 43.9 mm
	Open	182 lbs. @ 1.340 in.	810 N @ 34 mm
4.3L (VIN T)			
	Closed	90 lbs @ 1.670 in.	400 N @ 42.4 mm
	Open	208 lbs. @ 1.220 in.	935 N @ 31.0 mm
LIFTER			
2.2L (VIN 4)		NA	NA
2.5L (VIN R)			
	Body diameter:	0.841-0.843 in.	211.3668-21.4046 mm
	Bore diameter:	0.844-0.845 in.	21.425-21.450 mm
	Bore clearance:	0.002-0.0006 in.	0.06-0.016 mm

86813905

ENGINE REBUILDING SPECIFICATIONS CHART

Component	US	Metric
2.8L (VIN W)	NA	NA
2.8L (VIN X)	NA	NA
2.8L (VIN Z)	NA	NA
3.0L (VIN E)		
Body diameter:	0.820-0.8427 in.	21.3668-21.4046 mm
Bore clearance:	0.008-0.0025 in.	0.0203-0.0635 mm
3.1L (VIN T)	NA	NA
3.1L (VIN M)	NA	NA
3.3 (VIN N)	NA	NA
4.3L (VIN T)		
Body diameter:	0.920-0.922 in.	23.39-23.41 mm
Bore clearance:	0.0003-0.002 in.	0.009-0.054 mm
Length:	2.706 in.	68.73 mm
OIL PUMP		
2.2L (VIN 4)		
Gear pocket depth:	1.195-1.198 in.	30.36-30.44 mm
Gear pocket diameter:	1.503-1.506 in.	38.18-38.25 mm
Gear lash:	0.004-0.008 in.	0.094-0.195 mm
Gear length:	1.199-1.20 in.	30.45-30.48 mm
Gear diameter:	1.498-1.5 in.	38.05-38.10 mm
Side clearance:	0.0015-0.004 in.	0.038-0.102 mm
End clearance:	0.002-0.007 in.	0.05-0.18 mm
Valve to bore:	0.0015-0.0035 in.	0.038-0.089 mm
2.5L (VIN R)		
Gear pocket depth:	0.512-0.516 in.	13.05-13.10 mm
Gear pocket diameter:	0.511-0.512 in.	12.973-12.998 mm
2.8L (VIN W)	NA	NA
2.8L (VIN X)		
Gear pocket depth:	1.195-1.198 in.	30.36-30.44 mm
Gear pocket diameter:	1.503-1.506 in.	38.18-38.25 mm
Gear length:	1.200-1.199 in.	30.48-30.45 mm
Gear diameter:	1.498-1.500 in.	38.05-38.10 mm
Side clearance:	0.003-0.004 in.	0.08-0.10 mm
End clearance:	0.002-0.005 in.	0.05-0.13 mm
Valve to bore:	0.0015-0.0035 in.	0.089-0.038 mm
2.8L (VIN Z)		
Gear pocket depth:	1.195-1.198 in.	30.36-30.44 mm
Gear pocket diameter:	1.503-1.506 in.	38.18-38.25 mm
Gear length:	1.200-1.199 in.	30.48-30.45 mm
Gear diameter:	1.498-1.500 in.	38.05-38.10 mm
Side clearance:	0.003-0.004 in.	0.08-0.10 mm
End clearance:	0.002-0.005 in.	0.05-0.13 mm
Valve to bore:	0.0015-0.0035 in.	0.089-0.038 mm
3.0L (VIN E)	NA	NA
3.1L (VIN T)	NA	NA

86813906

ENGINE REBUILDING SPECIFICATIONS CHART

Component	US	Metric
3.1L (VIN M)		
Gear pocket depth:	1.202-1.204 in.	30.52-30.58 mm
Gear pocket diameter:	1.503-1.505 in.	38.176-38.226 mm
Gear length:	1.199-1.200 in.	30.45-30.48 mm
Gear diameter:	1.498-1.500 in.	38.05-38.10 mm
Side clearance:	0.001-0.003 in.	0.038-0.088 mm
End clearance:	0.002-0.005 in.	0.040-0.125 mm
Valve to bore:	0.0015-0.0035 in.	0.038-0.089 mm
3.3L (VIN N)		
Gear pocket depth:	0.461-0.4625 in.	11.71-11.75 mm
Gear pocket diameter:	3.508-3.512 in.	89.10-89.20 mm
Inner gear clearance:	0.006 in.	0.152 mm
Outer gear end clearance:	0.001-0.0035 in.	0.025-0.089 mm
Diameter clearance:	0.08-0.015 in.	0.203-0.381 mm
Valve to bore:	0.0015-0.0035 in.	0.089-0.038 mm
3.8L (VIN 3)	NA	NA
4.3L (VIN T)		
Gear pocket depth:	1.505-1.509 in.	38.1-38.125 mm
Gear pocket diameter:	1.534-1539 in.	38.960-39.096 mm
Gear length:	1.505-1.5095 in.	38.29-38.341 mm
Gear diameter:	1.529-1.531 in.	38.887-38.836 mm
Side clearance:	0.0015-0.0045 in.	0.04-0.12 mm
Valve to bore:	0.0025-0.0050 in.	0.063-0.127 mm
CYLINDER BORE		
2.2L (VIN 4)		
Diameter:	3.5036-3.5043 in.	88.991-89.009 mm
Out of round:	0.0005 in.	0.013 mm
Taper:	0.0005 in.	0.013 mm
2.5 L (VIN R)		
Diameter:	4.0 in.	101.6 mm
Out of round:	0.001 in	0.02 mm
Taper:	0.005 in.	0.13 mm
2.8L (VIN W)		
Diameter:	3.504-3.5033 in.	89.016-89.034 mm
Out of round:	0.0005 in.	0.13 mm
Taper:	0.0005 in.	0.13 mm
2.8L (VIN X)		
Diameter:	3.504-3.5033 in.	88.90-89.07 mm
Out of round:	0.001 in.	0.02 mm
Taper:	0.001 in.	0.02 mm
2.8L (VIN Z)		
Diameter:	3.504-3.5033 in.	88.90-89.07 mm
Out of round:	0.001 in.	0.02 mm
Taper:	0.001 in.	0.02 mm

ENGINE REBUILDING SPECIFICATIONS CHART

Component		US	Metric
3.0L (VIN E)	Diameter:	3.8 in.	96.52 mm
	Out of round:	0.001 in.	0.02 mm
	Taper:	0.001 in.	0.02 mm
3.1L (VIN T)			
	Diameter:	3.504-3.5033 in.	88.90-89.07 mm
	Out of round:	0.0005 in.	0.13 mm
	Taper:	0.0005 in.	0.13 mm
3.1L (VIN M)			
	Diameter:	3.504-3.5033 in.	89.016-89.034 mm
	Out of round:	0.0005 in.	0.014 mm
	Taper:	0.0008 in.	0.020 mm
3.3L (VIN N)			
	Diameter:	3.7 in.	93.9 mm
	Out of round:	0.0004 in.	0.10 mm
	Taper:	0.0005 in.	0.13 mm
3.8L (VIN 3)			
	Diameter:	3.8 in.	96.52 mm
	Out of round:	0.001 in.	0.02 mm
	Taper:	0.001 in.	0.02 mm
4.3L (VIN T)			
	Diameter:	4.057 in.	103.05 mm
	Out of round:	0.001 in.	0.025 mm
	Taper:	0.001 in.	0.025 mm
PISTON			
2.2L (VIN 4)			
	Clearance to bore:	0.0007-0.0017 in.	0.015-0.045 mm
2.5 L (VIN R)			
	Clearance to bore:	0.0014-0.0022 in.	0.036-0.056 mm
2.8L (VIN W)			
	Clearance to bore:	0.00093-0.00222 in.	0.0235-0.0565 mm
2.8L (VIN X)			
	Clearance to bore:	0.0017-0.003 in.	0.043-0.069 mm
2.8L (VIN Z)			
	Clearance to bore:	0.0017-0.003 in.	0.043-0.069 mm
3.0L (VIN E)			
	Clearance to bore:	0.0008-0.0020 in.	0.020-0.051 mm
3.1L (VIN T)			
	Clearance to bore:	0.0022-0.0028 in.	0.057-0.072 mm
3.1L (VIN M)			
	Clearance to bore:	0.0013-0.0027 in.	0.032-0.068 mm
3.3L (VIN N)			
	Clearance to bore:	0.0004-0.0022 in.	0.010-0.056 mm
3.8L (VIN 3)			
	Clearance to bore:	0.0008-0.0020 in.	0.020-0.051 mm
4.3L (VIN T)			
	Clearance to bore:	0.0035-0.0045 in.	0.088-0114 mm
PISTON RINGS			

86813908

ENGINE REBUILDING SPECIFICATIONS CHART

Component	US	Metric
2.2L (VIN 4) End gap		
Compression:	0.010-0.020 in.	0.25-0.50 mm
Oil:	0.010-0.050 in.	0.25-1.27 mm
Groove Clearance		
Compression:	0.0019-0.0027 in.	0.05-0.07 mm
Oil:	0.0019-0.0082 in.	0.05-0.21 mm
2.5L (VIN R)		
Gap		
Top:	0.01-0.02 in.	0.30-0.50 mm
Second:	0.01-0.02 in.	0.030-0.050 mm
Oil:	0.02-0.06 in.	0.50-1.50 mm
Side clearance		
Top:	0.002-0.003 in.	0.05-0.08 mm
Second:	0.001-0.003 in.	0.03-0.08 mm
Oil:	0.015-0.055 in.	0.38-1.40 mm
2.8L (VIN W)		
Gap		
Top:	0.01-0.02 in.	0.30-0.50 mm
Second:	0.01-0.02 in.	0.30-0.50 mm
Oil:	0.02-0.55 in.	0.50-1.40 mm
Side clearance		
Top:	0.001-0.003 in.	0.03-0.08 mm
Second:	0.001-0.003 in.	0.03-0.08 mm
Oil:	0.008 in.	0.20 mm
2.8L (VIN X)		
Gap	0.01-0.02 in.	0.30-0.50 mm
Top:	0.02-0.55 in.	0.50-1.40 mm
Second:	NA	NA
Oil:		
Side clearance		
Top:	0.001-0.003 in.	0.03-0.08 mm
Second:	0.001-0.003 in.	0.03-0.08 mm
Oil:	0.008 in.	0.20 mm
2.8L (VIN Z)		
Gap		
Top:	0.01-0.02 in.	0.30-0.50 mm
Second:	0.02-0.55 in.	0.50-1.40 mm
Oil:	NA	NA
Side clearance		
Top:	0.001-0.003 in.	0.03-0.08 mm
Second:	0.001-0.003 in.	0.03-0.08 mm
Oil:	0.008 in.	0.20 mm
3.0L (VIN E)		
Gap		
Top:	0.01-0.20 in.	0.254-0.508-mm
Second:	0.10-0.020 in.	0.254-0.508 mm
Oil:	0.015-0.55 in.	0.381-0.397 mm
Grove width		
Top:	0.0770-0.0780 in.	1.955-1.987 mm
Second:	0.0770-0.0780 in.	1.955-1.981 mm
Oil:	0.183-0.189 in.	4.684-4.80 mm

86813909

ENGINE REBUILDING SPECIFICATIONS CHART

Component		US	Metric
	Ring depth		
	Top:	0.184-0.194 in.	4.674-4.928 mm
	Second:	0.186-0.194 in.	4.724-4.928 mm
	Oil:	0.188-0.196 in.	4.7752-4.987 mm
3.1L (VIN T)			
	Gap		
	Top:	0.01-0.02 in.	0.30-0.50 mm
	Second:	0.01-0.02 in.	0.30-0.50 mm
	Oil:	0.01-0.50 in.	0.25-1.27 mm
	Side clearance		
	Top:	0.002-0.0035 in.	0.05-0.09 mm
	Second:	0.002-0.0035 in.	0.05-0.09 mm
	Oil:	0.008 in.	0.20 mm
3.1L (VIN M)			
	Groove clearance		
	1 st.	0.002-0.0035 in.	0.05-0.08 mm
	2nd.	0.002-0.0035 in.	0.05-0.09 mm
	Gap		
	1 st.	0.007-0.016 in.	0.18-0.41 mm
	2nd.	0.0197-0.0280 in.	0.50-0.71 mm
	Oil groove clearance:	0.008 in.	0.20 mm
	Gap:	0.0098-0.0295 in.	0.25-0.75 mm
3.3L (VIN N)			
	Gap		
	Top:	0.01-0.25 in.	0.30-0.63 mm
	Second:	0.01-0.25 in.	0.30-0.63 mm
	Oil:	0.01-0.40 in.	0.25-0.40 mm
	Side clearance		
	Top:	0.00163-0.0031 in.	0.033-0.079 mm
	Second:	0.0013-0.0031 in.	0.033-0.079 mm
	Oil:	0.0011-0.0081 in.	0.28-0.206 mm
	Ring width		
	Top:	0.0581-0.0589 in.	1.476-1.497 mm
	Second:	0.0581-0.0589 in.	1.476-1.497 mm
	Oil:	0.1122-0.01182 in.	2.850-3.002 mm
3.8L (VIN 3)			
	Gap		
	Top:	0.01-0.20 in.	0.254-0.508-mm
	Second:	0.10-0.020 in.	0.254-0.508 mm
	Oil:	0.015-0.55 in.	0.381-0.397 mm
	Grove width		
	Top:	0.0770-0.0780 in.	1.955-1.987 mm
	Second:	0.0770-0.0780 in.	1.955-1.981 mm
	Oil:	0.183-0.189 in.	4.684-4.80 mm
	Ring depth		
	Top:	0.184-0.194 in.	4.674-4.928 mm
	Second:	0.186-0.194 in.	4.724-4.928 mm
	Oil:	0.188-0.196 in.	4.7752-4.987 mm
4.3L (VIN T)			
	Gap		
	Top:	0.19-0.027 in.	0.4826-0.6858 mm

86813910

ENGINE REBUILDING SPECIFICATIONS CHART

Component		US	Metric
4.3L (VIN T)	Second:	0.013-0.021 in.	0.3302-0.5334 mm
	Oil:	0.015-0.55 in.	0.381-0.397 mm
	Side clearance		
	Top:	0.005-0.007 in.	0.127-0.178 mm
	Second:	0.003-0.005 in.	0.077-0.134 mm
	Oil:	0.001-0.005 in.	0.025-0.127 mm
	Ring width	0.078-0.077 in.	1.958-1.981 mm
PISTON PINS			
2.2L (VIN 4)			
	Diameter:	0.8000-0.8002 in.	20.320-20.325 mm
	Fit in piston:	0.0004-0.0009 in.	0.010-0.022 mm
	Press fit in rod:	0.00098-0.0017 in.	0.025-0.045 mm
2.5 L (VIN R)			
	Diameter:	0.927-0.928 in.	23-546-213.561 mm
	Fit in piston:	0.0003-0.0005 in.	0.008-0.013 mm
	Press fit in rod:	press fit	press fit
2.8L (VIN W)			
	Diameter:	0.9052-0.9056 in.	22.937-23.001 mm
	Fit in piston:	0.00025-0.0037 in.	0.0065-0.091 mm
	Press fit in rod:	0.00078-0.0021 in.	0.020-0.0515 mm
2.8L (VIN X)			
	Diameter:	0.9052-0.9056 in.	22.937-23.001 mm
	Fit in piston:	0.00026-0.00037 in.	0.0065-0.091 mm
	Press fit in rod:	0.00078-0.0021 in.	0.20-0.515 mm
2.8L (VIN Z)			
	Diameter:	0.9052-0.9056 in.	22.937-23.001 mm
	Fit in piston:	0.0002-0.0037 in.	0.0065-0.0091 mm
	Press fit in rod:	0.00078-0.0021 in.	0.020-0.0515 mm
3.0L (VIN E)			
	Diameter:	0.931-0.9394 in.	23.853-23.860 mm
	Fit in piston:	0.0004-0.0007 in.	0.0100-0.0177 mm
	Press fit in rod:	0.00078-0.0017 in.	0.017-0.0432 mm
	Pin off-set:	0.040 in. thrust side	1.016 mm thrust side
3.1L (VIN T)			
	Diameter:	0.9052-0.9054 in.	22.937-22.964 mm
	Fit in piston:	0.0004-0.0008 in.	0.0096-0.0215 mm
	Press fit in rod:	0.00078-0.0021 in.	0.020-0.0515 mm
3.1L (VIN M)			
	Diameter:	0.9052-0.9054 in.	22.9915-22.9964 mm
	Fit in piston:	0.0005-0.0010 in.	0.0126-0.0245 mm
	Press fit in rod:	0.0006-0.0018 in.	0.0165-0.0464 mm
3.3L (VIN N)			
	Diameter:	0.9053-0.9055 in.	22.995-23.000 mm
	Fit in piston:	0.0004-0.0008 in.	0.0096-0.0215 mm
	Press fit in rod:	0.0007-0.0017 in.	0.018-0.043 mm
3.8L (VIN 3)			
	Diameter:	0.9391-0.9394 in.	23.853-23.860 mm
	Fit in piston:	0.0004-0.0007 in.	0.0100-0.0177 mm
	Press fit in rod:	0.00078-0.0017 in.	0.017-0.0432 mm
	Pin off-set:	0.040 in. thrust side	1.016 mm thrust side

86813911

ENGINE REBUILDING SPECIFICATIONS CHART

Component	US	Metric
4.3L (VIN T) Diameter:	1.0949-1.0952 in.	27.81-27.82 mm
Fit in piston:	0.0003-0.0005 in.	0.0076-0.0127 mm
Press fit in rod:	0.0003-0.0013 in.	0.076-0.033 mm
CRANKSHAFT		
2.2L (VIN 4)		
Main journal		
Diameter:	2.4945-2.4954 in.	63.360-63.384 mm
Taper:	0.00019 in.	0.005 mm
Out of round:	0.00019 in.	0.005 mm
Main bearing		
Clearance:	0.0006-0.0019 in.	0.015-0.047 mm
End play:	0.002-0.007 in.	0.0511-0.1780 mm
Connecting rod		
Journal diameter:	1.9983-1.9994 in.	50-758-50.784 mm
Taper:	0.00019 in.	0.005 mm
Out of round:	0.00019 in.	0.0005 mm
Clearance:	0.00098-0.0031 in.	0.025-0.079 mm
Side clearance:	0.0039-0.0149 in.	0.10-0.38 mm
2.5L (VIN R)		
Main journal		
Diameter:	2.3 in.	58.399-58.400 mm
Taper:	0.0005 in.	0.013 mm
Out of round:	0.0005 in.	0.013 mm
Clearance:	0.0005-0.0022 in.	0.013-0.056 mm
End-play:	0.0051-0.010 in.	0.13-0.26 mm
Crankpin		
Diameter:	2.0 in.	50.708-50.805 mm
Taper:	0.0005 in.	0.013 mm
Out of round:	0.0005 in.	0.013 mm
Clearance		
Bearing:	0.0005-0.003 in.	0.013-0.07 mm
Side:	0.006-0.024 in.	0.015-0.06 mm
2.8L (VIN W)		
Main journal		
Diameter:	2.6473-2.4683 in.	67.241-67.265 mm
Taper:	0.0002 in.	0.005 mm
Out of round:	0.0002 in.	0.005 mm
Clearance:	0.0012-0.0027 in.	0.032-0.069 mm
Thrust:	0.0016-0.0031 in.	0.042-0.079 mm
End-play:	0.0024-0.0083 in.	0.06-0.21 mm
Crankpin		
Diameter:	1.9994-1.9983 in.	50-784-50.758 mm
Taper:	0.00002 in.	0.005 mm
Out of round:	0.0002 in.	0.005 mm
Clearance		
Bearing:	0.0015-0.0036 in.	0.038-0.083 mm
Side:	0.014-0.027 in.	0.360-0.680 mm
2.8L (VIN X)		
Main journal		
Diameter:	2.5850-2.5860 in.	63.340-63.364 mm
Taper:	0.0002 in.	0.005 mm

86813912

ENGINE REBUILDING SPECIFICATIONS CHART

Component		US	Metric
2.8L (VIN X)	Out of round:	0.00002 in.	0.005 mm
	Clearance:	0.002-0.003 in.	0.05-0.08 mm
	End-play:	0.002-0.007 in.	0.05-0.18 mm
	Crankpin		
	Diameter:	2.0713-2.0715 in.	50.784-50.758 mm
	Taper:	0.0002 in.	0.005 mm
	Out of round:	0.0002 in.	0.005 mm
	Clearance		
	Bearing:	0.0014-0.0037 in.	0.040-0.083 mm
	Side:	0.0065-0.018 in.	0.160-0.440 mm
2.8L (VIN Z)			
	Main journal		
	Diameter:	2.5850-2.5860 in.	63.340-63.364 mm
	Taper:	0.0002 in.	0.005 mm
	Out of round:	0.00002 in.	0.005 mm
	Clearance:	0.002-0.003 in.	0.05-0.08 mm
	End-play:	0.002-0.007 in.	0.05-0.18 mm
	Crankpin		
	Diameter:	2.0713-2.0715 in.	50.784-50.758 mm
	Taper:	0.0002 in.	0.005 mm
	Out of round:	0.0002 in.	0.005 mm
	Clearnce		
	Bearing:	0.0014-0.0037 in.	0.040-0.083 mm
	Side:	0.0065-0.018 in.	0.160-0.440 mm
3.0L (VIN E)			
	Main journal		
	Diameter:	2.4995 in.	63.4873 mm
	Taper:	0.0002 in.	0.005 mm
	Out of round:	0.0002 in.	0.005 mm
	Clearance:	0.003-0.0018 in.	0.08-0.0457 mm
	End-play:	0.003-0.0011 in.	0.08-0.2794 mm
	Length		
	Numbers 1, 3, 4:	0.864 in.	21.9456 mm
	Number 2:	1.057 in.	28.8478 mm
	Crankpin		
	Diameter:	2.2487-2.2495 in.	57.1169-57.1373 mm
	Taper:	0.0002 in.	0.005 mm
	Out of round:	0.0002 in.	0.005 mm
	Clearnce:	0.0005-0.0026 in.	0.0127-0.066 mm
	Bearing:	0.003-0.015 in.	0.0762-0.381 mm
	Side:	0.654 in.	16.611 mm
3.1L (VIN T)			
	Main journal		
	Diameter:	2.6473-2.6483 in.	67.241-67.265 mm
	Taper:	0.0003 in.	0.008 mm
	Out of round:	0.0002 in.	0.005 mm
	Clearance:	0.0012-0.0027 in.	0.032-0.069 mm
	Thrust:	0.0012-0.0027 in.	0.032-0.069 mm
	End-play:	0.0024-0.0083 in.	0.06-0.21 mm
	Crankpin		
	Diameter:	1.9994-1.9983 in.	50.784-50.758 mm

86813913

ENGINE REBUILDING SPECIFICATIONS CHART

Component		US	Metric
3.1L (VIN T)	Taper:	0.0003 in.	0.008 mm
	Out of round:	0.0002 in.	0.005 mm
	Clearnce		
	Bearing:	0.0013-0.0031 in.	0.032-0.079 mm
	Side:	0.014-0.027 in.	0.360-0.680 mm
3.1L (VIN M)			
	Main journal		
	Diameter:	2.6473-2.6483 in.	67.239-67.257 mm
	Taper:	0.0002 in.	0.005 mm
	Out of round:	0.0002 in.	0.005 mm
	Flange runout:	0.0016 in.	0.04 mm
	Main bearing		
	Bore diameter:	2.8407-2.8412 in.	72.155-72.168 mm
	Inside diameter:	2.6492-2.6502 in.	67.289-67.316 mm
	Bearing clearance:	0.0012-0.0030 in.	0.032-0.077 mm
	Thrust bearing		
	Clearance:	0.0012-0.0030 in.	0.032-0.077 mm
	Crankshaft End-play:	0.0024-0.0083 in.	0.060-0.210 mm
3.3L (VIN N)			
	Main journal		
	Diameter:	2.4988-2.4998 in.	63.47-63.495 mm
	Taper:	0.0003 in.	0.008 mm
	Out of round:	0.0003 in.	0.008 mm
	Clearance:	0.0003-0.0018 in.	0.008-0.045 mm
	End-play:	0.003-0.0011 in.	0.076-0.279 mm
	Crankpin		
	Diameter:	2.2487-2.2499 in.	57.117-57.147 mm
	Taper:	0.0003 in.	0.008 mm
	Out of round:	0.0003 in.	0.008 mm
	Clearnce		
	Bearing:	0.0003-0.0026 in.	0.0076-0.071 mm
	Side:	0.003-0.015 in.	0.076-0.381 mm
3.8L (VIN 3)			
	Main journal		
	Diameter:	2.4995 in.	63.4873 mm
	Taper:	0.0002 in.	0.005 mm
	Out of round:	0.0002 in.	0.005 mm
	Clearance:	0.003-0.0018 in.	0.08-0.0457 mm
	End-play:	0.003-0.0011 in.	0.08-0.2794 mm
	Length		
	Numbers 1, 3, 4:	0.864 in.	21.9456 mm
	Number 2:	1.057 in.	28.8478 mm
	Crankpin		
	Diameter:	2.2487-2.2495 in.	57.1169-57.1373 mm
	Taper:	0.0002 in.	0.005 mm
	Out of round:	0.0002 in.	0.005 mm
	Clearnce:	0.0005-0.0026 in.	0.0127-0.066 mm
	Bearing:	0.003-0.015 in.	0.0762-0.381 mm
	Side:	0.654 in.	16.611 mm
4.3L (VIN T)			
	Main journal		

86813914

ENGINE REBUILDING SPECIFICATIONS CHART

Component		US	Metric
4.3L (VIN T)	Diameter:	2.9993-3.0003 in.	76.181-76.207 mm
	Taper:	0.0005 in.	0.013 mm
	Out of round:	0.0005 in.	0.013 mm
	Clearance:		
	Numbers 1, 2, 3	0.0005-0.002 in.	0.127-0.0533 mm
	Number 4	0.0020-0.0034 in.	0.051-0.086 mm
	End-play:	0.003-0.0135 in.	0.087-0.343 mm
	Shell width		
	Numbers 1, 2	0.970-0.980 in.	21.9456 mm
	Number 3	1.193-1.195 in.	30.302-30.353 mm
	Number 4	1.27 in.	32.26 mm
	Crankpin		
	Diameter:	2.24987-2.2490 in.	57.120-51.146 mm
	Diameter:	2.9993-3.0003 in.	76.181-76.207 mm
	Taper:	0.0005 in.	0.013 mm
	Clearance:	0.0004-0.0026 in.	0.010-0.066 mm
	Side-play:	0.008-0.0214 in.	0.21-0.545 mm

86813915

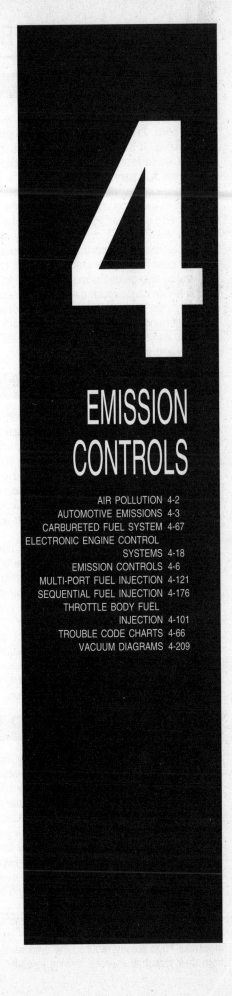

4

EMISSION
CONTROLS

AIR POLLUTION

The earth's atmosphere, at or near sea level, consists of 78% nitrogen, 21% oxygen and 1% other gases, approximately. If it were possible to remain in this state, 100% clean air would result. However, many varied causes allow other gases and particulates to mix with the clean air, causing the air to become unclean or polluted.

Certain of these pollutants are visible while others are invisible, with each having the capability of causing distress to the eyes, ears, throat, skin and respiratory system. Should these pollutants be concentrated in a specific area and under the right conditions, death could result due to the displacement or chemical change of the oxygen content in the air. These pollutants can cause much damage to the environment and to the many man made objects that are exposed to the elements.

To better understand the causes of air pollution, the pollutants can be categorized into 3 separate types: natural, industrial and automotive.

Natural Pollutants

Natural pollution has been present on earth before man appeared and is still a factor to be considered when discussing air pollution, although it causes only a small percentage of the present overall pollution problem existing in our country. It is the direct result of decaying organic matter, wind born smoke and particulates from such natural events as plains and forest fires (ignited by heat or lightning), volcanic ash, sand and dust which can spread over a large area of the countryside.

Such a phenomenon of natural pollution has been recent volcanic eruptions, with the resulting plume of smoke, steam and volcanic ash blotting out the sun's rays as it spreads and rises higher into the atmosphere, where the upper air currents catch and carry the smoke and ash, while condensing the steam back into water vapor. As the water vapor, smoke and ash traveled on their journey, the smoke dissipates into the atmosphere while the ash and moisture settle back to earth in a trail hundred of miles long. In many cases, lives are lost and millions of dollars of property damage result, and ironically, man can only stand by and watch it happen.

Industrial Pollutants

Industrial pollution is caused primarily by industrial processes, the burning of coal, oil and natural gas, which in turn produces smoke and fumes. Because the burning fuels contain much sulfur, the principal ingredients of smoke and fumes are sulfur dioxide (SO_2) and particulate matter. This type of pollutant occurs most severely during still, damp and cool weather, such as at night. Even in its less severe form, this pollutant is not confined to just cities. Because of air movements, the pollutants move for miles over the surrounding countryside, leaving in its path a barren and unhealthy environment for all living things.

Working with Federal, State and Local mandated rules, regulations and by carefully monitoring the emissions, industries have greatly reduced the amount of pollutant emitted from their industrial sources, striving to obtain an acceptable level. Because of the mandated industrial emission clean up, many land areas and streams in and around the cities that were formerly barren of vegetation and life, have now begun to move back in the direction of nature's intended balance.

Automotive Pollutants

The third major source of air pollution is the automotive emissions. The emissions from the internal combustion engine were not an appreciable problem years ago because of the small number of registered vehicles and the nation's small highway system. However, during the early 1950's, the trend of the American people was to move from the cities to the surrounding suburbs. This caused an immediate problem in the transportation areas because the majority of the suburbs were not afforded mass transit conveniences. This lack of transportation created an attractive market for the automobile manufacturers, which resulted in a dramatic increase in the number of vehicles produced and sold, along with a marked increase in highway construction between cities and the suburbs. Multi-vehicle families emerged with much emphasis placed on the individual vehicle per family member. As the increase in vehicle ownership and usage occurred, so did the pollutant levels in and around the cities, as the suburbanites drove daily to their businesses and employment in the city and its fringe area, returning at the end of the day to their homes in the suburbs.

It was noted that a fog and smoke type haze was being formed and at times, remained in suspension over the cities and did not quickly dissipate. At first this "smog," derived from the words "smoke" and "fog," was thought to result from industrial pollution but it was determined that the automobile emissions were largely to blame. It was discovered that as normal automobile emissions were exposed to sunlight for a period of time, complex chemical reactions would take place.

It was found the smog was a photo chemical layer and was developed when certain oxides of nitrogen (NOx) and unburned hydrocarbons (HC) from the automobile emissions were exposed to sunlight and was more severe when the smog would remain stagnant over an area in which a warm layer of air would settle over the top of a cooler air mass at ground level, trapping and holding the automobile emissions, instead of the emissions being dispersed and diluted through normal air flows. This type of air stagnation was given the name "Temperature Inversion."

Temperature Inversion

In normal weather situations, the surface air is warmed by the heat radiating from the earth's surface and the sun's rays and will rise upward, into the atmosphere, to be cooled through a convection type heat expands with the cooler upper air. As the warm air rises, the surface pollutants are carried upward and dissipated into the atmosphere.

When a temperature inversion occurs, we find the higher air is no longer cooler but warmer than the surface air, causing the cooler surface air to become trapped and unable to move. This warm air blanket can extend from above ground level to a few hundred or even a few thousand feet into the air. As the surface air is trapped, so are the pollutants, causing a severe smog condition. Should this stagnant air mass extend to a few thousand feet high, enough air movement with the inversion takes place to allow the smog layer to rise above ground level but the pollutants still cannot dissipate. This inversion can remain for days over an area, with only the smog level rising or lowering from ground level to a few hundred feet high. Meanwhile, the pollutant levels increases, causing eye irritation, respirator problems, reduced visibility, plant damage and in some cases, cancer type diseases.

This inversion phenomenon was first noted in the Los Angeles, California area. The city lies in a basin type of terrain and during certain weather conditions, a cold air mass is held in the basin while a warmer air mass covers it like a lid.

Because this type of condition was first documented as prevalent in the Los Angeles area, this type of smog was named Los Angeles Smog, although it occurs in other areas where a large concentration of automobiles are used and the air remains stagnant for any length of time.

Internal Combustion Engine Pollutants

Consider the internal combustion engine as a machine in which raw materials must be placed so a finished product comes out. As in any machine operation, a certain amount of wasted material is formed. When we relate this to the internal combustion engine, we find that by putting in air and fuel, we obtain power from this mixture during the combustion process to drive the vehicle. The by-product or waste of this power is, in part, heat and exhaust gases with which we must concern ourselves.

AUTOMOTIVE EMISSIONS

Before emission controls were mandated on the internal combustion engines, other sources of engine pollutants were discovered, along with the exhaust emission. It was determined the engine combustion exhaust produced 60% of the total emission pollutants, fuel evaporation from the fuel tank and carburetor vents produced 20%, with the another 20% being produced through the crankcase as a by-product of the combustion process.

Exhaust Gases

The exhaust gases emitted into the atmosphere are a combination of burned and unburned fuel. To understand the exhaust emission and its composition review some basic chemistry.

When the air/fuel mixture is introduced into the engine, we are mixing air, composed of nitrogen (78%), oxygen (21%) and other gases (1%) with the fuel, which is 100% hydrocarbons (HC), in a semi-controlled ratio. As the combustion process is accomplished, power is produced to move the vehicle while the heat of combustion is transferred to the cooling system. The exhaust gases are then composed of nitrogen, a diatomic gas (N_2), the same as was introduced in the engine, carbon dioxide (CO_2), the same gas that is used in beverage carbonation and water vapor (H_2O). The nitrogen (N_2), for the

HEAT TRANSFER

The heat from the combustion process can rise to over 4000°F (2204°C). The dissipation of this heat is controlled by a ram air effect, the use of cooling fans to cause air flow and having a liquid coolant solution surrounding the combustion area and transferring the heat of combustion through the cylinder walls and into the coolant. The coolant is then directed to a thin-finned, multi-tubed radiator, from which the excess heat is transferred to the outside air by one or all of the 3 heat transfer methods: conduction, convection or radiation.

The cooling of the combustion area is an important part in the control of exhaust emissions. To understand the behavior of the combustion and transfer of its heat, consider the air/fuel charge. It is ignited and the flame front burns progressively across the combustion chamber until the burning charge reaches the cylinder walls. Some of the fuel in contact with the walls is not hot enough to burn, thereby snuffing out or quenching the combustion process. This leaves unburned fuel in the combustion chamber. This unburned fuel is then forced out of the cylinder along with the exhaust gases and into the exhaust system.

Many attempts have been made to minimize the amount of unburned fuel in the combustion chambers due to the snuffing out or quenching, by increasing the coolant temperature and lessening the contact area of the coolant around the combustion area. Design limitations within the combustion chambers prevent the complete burning of the air/fuel charge, so a certain amount of the unburned fuel is still expelled into the exhaust system, regardless of modifications to the engine.

most part passes through the engine unchanged, while the oxygen (O_2) reacts (burns) with the hydrocarbons (HC) and produces the carbon dioxide (CO_2) and the water vapors (H_2O). If this chemical process would be the only process to take place, the exhaust emissions would be harmless. However, during the combustion process, other pollutants are formed and are considered dangerous. These pollutants are carbon monoxide (CO), hydrocarbons (HC), oxides of nitrogen (NOx) oxides of sulfur (SOx) and engine particulates.

Lead (Pb), is considered 1 of the particulates and is present in the exhaust gases whenever leaded fuels are used. Lead (Pb) does not dissipate easily. Levels can be high along roadways when it is emitted from vehicles and can pose a health threat. Since the increased usage of unleaded gasoline and the phasing out of leaded gasoline for fuel, this pollutant is gradually diminishing. While not considered a major threat lead is still considered a dangerous pollutant.

HYDROCARBONS

Hydrocarbons (HC) are essentially unburned fuel that have not been successfully burned during the combustion process or have escaped into the atmosphere through fuel evaporation. The main sources of incomplete combustion are rich air/fuel mixtures, low engine temperatures and improper spark timing.

The main sources of hydrocarbon emission through fuel evaporation come from the vehicle's fuel tank and carburetor bowl.

To reduce combustion hydrocarbon emission, engine modifications were made to minimize dead space and surface area in the combustion chamber. In addition the air/fuel mixture was made more lean through improved carburetion, fuel injection and by the addition of external controls to aid in further combustion of the hydrocarbons outside the engine. Two such methods were the addition of an air injection system, to inject fresh air into the exhaust manifolds and the installation of a catalytic converter, a unit that is able to burn traces of hydrocarbons without affecting the internal combustion process or fuel economy.

To control hydrocarbon emissions through fuel evaporation, modifications were made to the fuel tank and carburetor bowl to allow storage of the fuel vapors during periods of engine shut-down, and at specific times during engine operation, to purge and burn these same vapors by blending them with the air/fuel mixture.

CARBON MONOXIDE

Carbon monoxide is formed when not enough oxygen is present during the combustion process to convert carbon (C) to carbon dioxide (CO_2). An increase in the carbon monoxide (CO) emission is normally accompanied by an increase in the hydrocarbon (HC) emission because of the lack of oxygen to completely burn all of the fuel mixture.

Carbon monoxide (CO) also increases the rate at which the photochemical smog is formed by speeding up the conversion of nitric oxide (NO) to nitrogen dioxide (NO_2). To accomplish this, carbon monoxide (CO) combines with oxygen (O_2) and nitric oxide (NO) to produce carbon dioxide (CO_2) and nitrogen dioxide (NO_2). ($CO + O_2S + NO = CO_2 + NO_2$).

The dangers of carbon monoxide, which is an odorless, colorless toxic gas are many. When carbon monoxide is inhaled into the lungs and passed into the blood stream, oxygen is replaced by the carbon monoxide in the red blood cells, causing a reduction in the amount of oxygen being supplied to the many parts of the body. This lack of oxygen causes headaches, lack of coordination, reduced mental alertness and should the carbon monoxide concentration be high enough, death could result.

NITROGEN

Normally, nitrogen is an inert gas. When heated to approximately 2500°F (1371°C) through the combustion process, this gas becomes active and causes an increase in the nitric oxide (NOx) emission.

Oxides of nitrogen (NOx) are composed of approximately 97-98% nitric oxide (NO_2). Nitric oxide is a colorless gas but when it is passed into the atmosphere, it combines with oxygen and forms nitrogen dioxide (NO_2). The nitrogen dioxide then combines with chemically active hydrocarbons (HC) and when in the presence of sunlight, causes the formation of photo chemical smog.

OZONE

To further complicate matters, some of the nitrogen dioxide (NO_2) is broken apart by the sunlight to form nitric oxide and oxygen. (NO_2 + sunlight = NO + O). This single atom of oxygen then combines with diatomic (meaning 2 atoms) oxygen (O_2S) to form ozone (O_3). Ozone is 1 of the smells associated with smog. It has a pungent and offensive odor, irritates the eyes and lung tissues, affects the growth of plant life and causes rapid deterioration of rubber products. Ozone can be formed by sunlight as well as electrical discharge into the air.

The most common discharge area on the automobile engine is the secondary ignition electrical system, especially when inferior quality spark plug cables are used. As the surge of high voltage is routed through the secondary cable, the circuit builds up an electrical field around the wire, acting upon the oxygen in the surrounding air to form the ozone. The faint glow along the cable with the engine running that may be visible on a dark night, is called the "corona discharge." It is the result of the electrical field passing from a high along the cable, to a low in the surrounding air, which forms the ozone gas. The combination of corona and ozone has been a major cause of cable deterioration. Recently, different types and better quality insulating materials have lengthened the life of the electrical cables.

Although ozone at ground level can be harmful, ozone is beneficial to the earth's inhabitants. By having a concentrated ozone layer called the "ozonosphere," between 10 and 20 miles (16-32 km) up in the atmosphere much of the ultra violet radiation from the sun's rays are absorbed and screened. If this ozone layer were not present, much of the earth's surface would be burned, dried and unfit for human life.

There is much discussion concerning the ozone layer and its density. A feeling exists that this protective layer of ozone is slowly diminishing and corrective action must be directed to this problem. Much experimenting is presently being conducted to determine if a problem exists and if so, the short and long term effects of the problem and how it can be remedied.

OXIDES OF SULFUR

Oxides of sulfur (SOx) were initially ignored in the exhaust system emissions, since the sulfur content of gasoline as a fuel is less than $\frac{1}{10}$ of 1%. Because of this small amount, it was felt that it contributed very little to the overall pollution problem. However, because of the difficulty in solving the sulfur emissions in industrial pollutions and the introduction of catalytic converter to the automobile exhaust systems, a change was mandated. The automobile exhaust system, when equipped with a catalytic converter, changes the sulfur dioxide (SO_2) into the sulfur trioxide (SO_3).

When this combines with water vapors (H_2O), a sulfuric acid mist (H_2SO_4) is formed and is a very difficult pollutant to handle and is extremely corrosive. This sulfuric acid mist that is formed, is the same mist that rises from the vents of an automobile storage battery when an active chemical reaction takes place within the battery cells.

When a large concentration of vehicles equipped with catalytic converters are operating in an area, this acid mist will rise and be distributed over a large ground area causing land, plant, crop, paints and building damage.

PARTICULATE MATTER

A certain amount of particulate matter is present in the burning of any fuel, with carbon constituting the largest percentage of the particulates. In gasoline, the remaining percentage of particulates is the burned remains of the various other compounds used in its manufacture. When a gasoline engine is in good internal condition, the particulate emissions are low but as the engine wears internally, the particulate emissions increase. By visually inspecting the tail pipe emissions, a determination can be made as to where an engine defect may exist. An engine with light gray smoke emitting from the tail pipe normally indicates an increase in the oil consumption through burning due to internal engine wear. Black smoke would indicate a defective fuel delivery system, causing the engine to operate in a rich mode. Regardless of the color of the smoke, the internal part of the engine or the fuel delivery system should be repaired to a "like new" condition to prevent excess particulate emissions.

Diesel and turbine engines emit a darkened plume of smoke from the exhaust system because of the type of fuel used. Emission control regulations are mandated for this type of emission and more stringent measures are being used to prevent excess emission of the particulate matter. Electronic components are being introduced to control the injection of the fuel at precisely the proper time of piston travel, to achieve the optimum in fuel ignition and fuel usage. Other particulate after-burning components are being tested to achieve a cleaner particular emission.

Good grades of engine lubricating oils should be used, meeting the manufacturers specification. "Cut-rate" oils can contribute to the particulate emission problem because of their low "flash" or ignition temperature point. Such oils burn prematurely during the combustion process causing emissions of particulate matter.

The cooling system is an important factor in the reduction of particulate matter. With the cooling system operating at a temperature specified by the manufacturer, the optimum of combustion will occur. The cooling system must be maintained in the same manner as the engine oiling system, as each system is required to perform properly in order for the engine to operate efficiently for a long time.

Crankcase Emissions

Crankcase emissions are made up of water, acids, unburned fuel, oil fumes and particulates. The emissions are classified as hydrocarbons (HC) and are formed by the small amount of unburned, compressed air/fuel mixture entering the crankcase from the combustion area during the compression and power strokes, between the cylinder walls and piston rings. The head of the compression and combustion help to form the remaining crankcase emissions.

Since the first engines, crankcase emissions were allowed to go into the air through a road draft tube, mounted on the lower side of the engine block. Fresh air came in through an open oil filler cap or breather. The air passed through the crankcase mixing with blow-by gases. The motion of the vehicle and the air blowing past the open end of the road draft tube caused a low pressure area at the end of the tube. Crankcase emissions were simply drawn out of the road draft tube into the air.

To control the crankcase emission, the road draft tube was deleted. A hose and/or tubing was routed from the crankcase to the intake manifold so the blow-by emission could be burned with the air/fuel mixture. However, it was found that intake manifold vacuum, used to draw the crankcase emissions into the manifold, would vary in strength at the wrong time and not allow the proper emission flow. A regulating type valve was needed to control the flow of air through the crankcase.

Testing, showed the removal of the blow-by gases from the crankcase as quickly as possible, was most important to the longevity of the engine. Should large accumulations of blow-by gases remain and condense, dilution of the engine oil would occur to form water, soots, resins, acids and lead salts, resulting in the formation of sludge and varnishes. This condensation of the blow-by gases occur more frequently on vehicles used in numerous starting and stopping conditions, excessive idling and when the engine is not allowed to attain normal operating temperature through short runs. The crankcase purge control or PCV system will be described in detail later in this section.

Evaporative Emissions

Gasoline fuel is a major source of pollution, before and after it is burned in the automobile engine. From the time the fuel is refined, stored, pumped and transported, again stored until it is pumped into the fuel tank of the vehicle, the gasoline gives off unburned hydrocarbons (HC) into the atmosphere. Through redesigning of the storage areas and venting systems, the pollution factor has been diminished but not eliminated, from the refinery standpoint. However, the automobile still remained the primary source of vaporized, unburned hydrocarbon (HC) emissions.

Fuel pumped form an underground storage tank is cool but when exposed to a warmer ambient temperature, will expand. Before controls were mandated, an owner would fill the fuel tank with fuel from an underground storage tank and park the vehicle for some time in warm area, such as a parking lot. As the fuel would warm, it would expand and should no provisions or area be provided for the expansion, the fuel would spill out the filler neck and onto the ground, causing hydrocarbon (HC) pollution and creating a severe fire hazard. To correct this condition, the vehicle manufacturers added overflow plumbing and/or gasoline tanks with built in expansion areas or domes.

However, this did not control the fuel vapor emission from the fuel tank and the carburetor bowl. It was determined that most of the fuel evaporation occurred when the vehicle was stationary and the engine not operating. Most vehicles carry 5-25 gallons (19-95 liters) of gasoline. Should a large concentration of vehicles be parked in one area, such as a large parking lot, excessive fuel vapor emissions would take place, increasing as the temperature increases.

To prevent the vapor emission from escaping into the atmosphere, the fuel system is designed to trap the fuel vapors while the vehicle is stationary, by sealing the fuel system from the atmosphere. A storage system is used to collect and hold the fuel vapors from the carburetor and the fuel tank when the engine is not operating. When the engine is started, the storage system is then purged of the fuel vapors, which are drawn into the engine and burned with the air/fuel mixture.

The components of the fuel evaporative system will be described in detail later in this section.

EMISSION CONTROLS

You'll find emission controls, ignition controls and fuel system controls are interrelated systems on the newer cars. In this section of the manual you'll find emission components related to exhaust gas recirculation, crankcase fume venting, evaporative. The Electronic Engine Control portion of the section should be be used in conjunction with the Fuel System section of the manual.

Crankcase Ventilation System — Gasoline Engines

OPERATION

All these gasoline vehicles are equipped with a positive crankcase ventilation (PCV) system to control crankcase blow-by vapors. The system functions as follows:

When the engine is running, a small portion of the gases which are formed in the combustion chamber leak by the piston rings and enter the crankcase. Since these gases are under pressure, they tend to escape from the crankcase and enter the atmosphere. If these gases are allowed to remain in the crankcase for any period of time, they contaminate the engine oil and cause sludge to build up in the crankcase. If the gases are allowed to escape into the atmosphere, they pollute the air with unburned hydrocarbons.

The job of the crankcase emission control equipment is to recycle these gases back into the engine combustion chamber where they are reburned.

The crankcase (blow-by) gases are recycled in the following way: as the engine is running, clean, filtered air is drawn through the air filter and into the crankcase. As the air passes through the crankcase, it picks up the combustion gases and carries them out of the crankcase, through the oil separator, through the PCV valve, and into the induction system. As they enter the intake manifold, they are drawn into the combustion chamber where they are reburned.

The most critical component in the system is the PCV valve. This valve controls the amount of gases which are recycled into the combustion chamber. At low engine speeds, the valve is partially closed, limiting the flow of gases into the intake manifold. As engine speed increases, the valve opens to admit greater quantities of gases into the intake manifold. If the valve should become blocked or plugged, the gases will be prevented from escaping from the crankcase by the normal route. Since these gases are under pressure, they will find their own way out of the crankcase. This alternate route is usually a weak oil seal or gasket in the engine. As the gas escapes by the gasket, it also creates an oil leak. Besides causing oil leaks, a clogged PCV valve also allows these gases to remain in the crankcase for an extended period of time, promoting the formation of sludge in the engine.

SERVICE (COMPONENT TESTING)

Inspect the PCV system hose and connections at each tune-up and replace any deteriorated hoses. Check the PCV valve at every tune-up and replace it at 30,000 mile (48,900km) intervals.

1. Remove the PCV valve from the rocker arm cover.
2. Start engine, allow to reach normal temperature and idle speed.
3. Place your thumb over the end of the valve to check for vacuum. If no vacuum, check the valve and hose. Most likely the hose is plugged up.
4. Newer computer controlled vehicles may no show much of a change in engine rpm when the valve is blocked or removed due to the computer compensating almost instantly to the vacuum change.
5. Remove the valve from the engine and hose. Shake the valve; it should rattle. If not, it's plugged up with dirt and must be replaced.
6. When replacing a PCV valve, you MUST use the correct valve. Many valves look alike on the outside, but have different mechanical values. Putting an incorrect PCV valve on a vehicle can cause a great deal of driveability problems. The engine computer assumes the valve is the correct one and may overadjust ignition timing or fuel mixture.

REMOVAL & INSTALLATION

PCV Valve

◗ See Figures 1 and 2

The valve is located in a rubber grommet in the valve cover, connected to the air cleaner housing by a large diameter rubber hose. In replacing the PCV valve, make sure it is fully inserted in the hose, that the clamp is moved over the ridge on the valve so that the valve will not slip out of the hose, and that the valve is fully inserted into the grommet in the valve cover.

1. Pull the valve (with the hose attached) from the rubber grommet in the valve cover.
2. Remove the valve from the hose.
3. Inspect the rubber grommet that houses the valve for deterioration, and replace if necessary.

To install:
4. Install the new (or reusable) PCV valve into the hose.
5. Press the valve back into the rubber grommet in the valve cover.

Fig. 1 PCV system operation

This valve is designed to limit vacuum in the crankcase. The gases are drawn from the valve cover through the CDRV and into the intake manifold.

Fresh air enters the engine through the combination filter, check valve, and oil fill cap. This air mixes with blow-by gases and enters the opposite valve cover. These gases pass through a filter on the valve cover and are drawn into the connected tubing.

Intake manifold vacuum acts against a spring loaded diaphragm to control the flow of crankcase gases. Higher vacuum levels pull the diaphragm closer to the top of the outlet tube. This reduces the amount of gases being drawn from the crankcase and decreases vacuum in the crankcase. As intake vacuum decreases, the spring pushes the diaphragm away from the top of the outlet tube allowing more gases into the manifold.

The diesel Crankcase Ventilation System should be cleaned and inspected every 15,000 miles (24,000 km) or at 12 month intervals.

➡**Do not allow solvent to come in contact with the diaphragm of the CDRV, as it will cause diaphragm damage.**

Fig. 2 Remove the PCV valve, inspect and replace it if necessary

PCV Filter

The PCV filter is located in the air cleaner housing and must be replaced every 50,000 miles (80,000 km).

1. Remove the air cleaner housing lid.
2. Slide back the filter retaining clip and remove the old filter.
3. Install the new filter, replace the retaining clip and replace the housing lid.

Crankcase Ventilation System — Diesel Engines

OPERATION

▶ **See Figures 3 and 4**

A Crankcase Depression Regulator Valve (CDRV) is used to regulate the flow of crankcase gases back into the engine.

Fig. 3 Diesel crankcase ventilation system

1. Inlet port (2) (Gases from crankcase
2. Mounting bracket
3. Cover diaphragm
4. Body
5. Spring
6. Outlet tube (Gases to intake manifold)

CRANKCASE DEPRESSION REGULATOR VALVE
V-TYPE DIESEL ENGINE

86814004

Fig. 4 The Crankcase Depression Regulator Valve (CDRV)

Evaporative Emission Control System

OPERATION

▶ See Figures 5, 6 and 7

The basic Evaporative Emission Control (EEC) system used on all models is the carbon canister storage method. The system is used to reduce emissions of fuel vapors from the car's fuel system. Evaporated fuel vapors are stored for burning during combustion rather than being vented into the atmosphere when the engine is not running. To accomplish this, the fuel tank and the carburetor float bowl are vented through a vapor canister containing activated charcoal. The system utilizes a sealed fuel tank with a dome that collects fuel vapors and allows them to pass on into a line connected with the vapor canister. In addition, the vapors that form above the float chamber in the carburetor also pass into a line connected with the canister. The canister absorbs these vapors in a bed of activated charcoal and retains them until the canister is purged or cleared by air drawn through the filter at its bottom. The absorbing occurs when the car is not running, while the purging or cleaning occurs when the car is running. The amount of vapor being drawn into the engine at any given time is too small to have an effect on either fuel economy or engine performance.

The Computer Control Module (ECM/PCM) controls the vacuum to the canister purge valve by using an electrically operated solenoid valve. When the system is in the "Open Loop" mode, the solenoid valve is energized and blocks all vacuum to the canister purge valve. When the system is in the "Closed Loop" mode, the solenoid valve is de-energized and vacuum is then supplied to operate the purge valve. This releases the fuel vapors, collected in the canister, into the induction system.

It is extremely important that only vapors be transferred to the engine. To avoid the possibility of liquid fuel being drawn into the system, the following features are included as part of the total system:

• A fuel tank overfill protector is provided to assure adequate room for expansion of liquid fuel volume with temperature changes.

• A one point fuel tank venting system is provided on all models to assure that the tank will be vented under any normal car attitude. This is accomplished by the use of a domed tank.

• A pressure-vacuum relief valve is located in the fuel cap.

➡**Some canisters are of the closed design. They draw air from the air cleaner rather than the bottom of the canister.**

REMOVAL & INSTALLATION

Vapor Canister

▶ See Figure 8

1. Loosen the screw holding the canister retaining bracket.
2. If equipped with A/C, loosen the attachments holding the accumulator and pipe assembly.
3. Rotate the canister retaining bracket and remove the canister.
4. Tag and disconnect the hoses leading from the canister.
To install:
5. Connect the canister, attach with the mounting bolts.
6. Attach the tagged hoses leading to the canister. Make sure the connections are correct.

Filter

1. Remove the vapor canister.
2. Pull the filter out from the bottom of the canister.
To install:
3. Install a new filter and then replace the canister.

Evaporative Canister Purge Solenoid Valve

1. Disconnect the negative battery cable.
2. Some vehicles you will need to raise and support the vehicle.
3. Remove the electrical connection and vacuum line from the purge solenoid valve.
4. Some models will have the valve bolted in, remove the bolts to release the valve.
5. On other models, release the locking tab on the solenoid bracket, then remove the purge solenoid valve from the bracket.
To install:
6. Reinstall the valve by inserting the mounting bolts and tightening down, or install the valve to the bracket, then snap the valve down over the locking tabs of the bracket.
7. Connect the vacuum lines and electrical connection to the valve.
8. Lower the vehicle, if raised and supported.
9. Connect the negative battery cable.

1 TBI

2 VAPOR CANISTER

3 FUEL TANK

4 VAPOR RESTRICTION

5 PRESSURE / VACUUM RELIEF VENTED FUEL FILLER CAP

86814006

Fig. 5 Operation of the 2.5L VIN R EEC system

Exhaust Gas Recirculation System (EGR) — Gasoline Engines

OPERATION

➡**Not all vehicles are equipped with an EGR system.**

The EGR system is used to reduce oxides of nitrogen (NOx) emission levels caused by high combustion chamber temperatures. This is accomplished by the use of an EGR valve which opens, under specific engine operating conditions, to admit a small amount of exhaust gas into the intake manifold, below the throttle plate. The exhaust gas mixes with the incoming air charge and displaces a portion of the oxygen in the air/fuel mixture entering the combustion chamber. The exhaust gas does not support combustion of the air/fuel mixture but it takes up volume, the net effect of which is to lower the temperature

of the combustion process. This lower temperature also helps control detonation.

The EGR valve is a mounted on the intake manifold and has an opening into the exhaust manifold. On some vehicles, the EGR valve is opened by manifold vacuum to permit exhaust gas to flow into the intake manifold. On others, the EGR valve is purely electrical and uses solenoid valves to open the flow passage. If too much exhaust gas enters, combustion will not occur. Because of this, very little exhaust gas is allowed to pass through the valve. The EGR system will be activated once the engine reaches normal operating temperature and the EGR valve will open when engine operating conditions are above idle speed and below Wide Open Throttle (WOT). On California vehicles equipped with a Vehicle Speed Sensor (VSS), the EGR valve opens when the VSS signal is greater than 2 mph. The EGR system is deactivated on vehicles equipped with a Torque Converter Clutch (TCC) when the TCC is engaged. There are three basic types of systems as described below, differing in the way EGR flow is modulated.

1 EVAP CANISTER PURGE SOLENOID VALVE VACUUM LINE
2 MANIFOLD VACUUM SOURCE
3 EVAPORATIVE EMISSION CANISTER
4 AIR INLET

5 FUEL TANK VAPOR VACUUM LINE
6 VAPOR RESTRICTION
7 ROLL-OVER VALVE
8 FUEL TANK

86814005

Fig. 6 Operation of the 3.1L VIN M EEC system

Positive Backpressure EGR Valve
▶ See Figure 9

An air bleed valve, located inside the EGR valve assembly acts as a vacuum regulator. The bleed valve controls the amount of vacuum in the vacuum chamber by bleeding vacuum to outside air during the open phase of the cycle. When the EGR valve receives enough backpressure through the hollow shaft, it closes the valve. At this point, maximum available vacuum is applied to the diaphragm and the EGR valve opens. If there is a small amount of vacuum or no vacuum in the vacuum chamber such as wide open throttle or at idle, the EGR valve will not open. The positive backpressure EGR valve also will not open if vacuum is applied to the valve with the engine stopped or idling.

Negative Backpressure EGR Valve
▶ See Figure 10

The negative backpressure EGR valve is similar to the positive backpressure EGR valve except that the bleed valve spring is moved from above the diaphragm to below and the bleed valve is normally closed. The negative backpressure EGR valve varies the amount of exhaust gas flow into the intake manifold depending on manifold vacuum and variations in exhaust backpressure. The diaphragm on the valve has an internal air bleed hole which is held closed by a small spring when there is no exhaust backpressure. Engine vacuum opens the EGR valve against the pressure of a spring. When manifold vacuum combines with negative exhaust backpressure, the vacuum bleed hole opens and the EGR valve closes. This valve will open if vacuum is applied with the engine not running.

Digital EGR Valve
▶ See Figure 11

The digital EGR valve, used on most of the newer engines such as the 3.1L (VIN T) and 3.1L (VIN M), it is designed to control the flow of EGR, independent of intake manifold vacuum. The valve controls EGR flow through 3 solenoid-opened orifices, which increase in size, to produce 7 possible combina-

1 Throttle Body

2 Vapor Canister

3 Fuel Tank

4 Vapor Restriction (.055" orifice)

5 Purge Solenoid Control Assembly

6 Outside Air

86814007

Fig. 7 Operation of the 3.3L VIN N EEC system

1 AIR TUBE (FRESH AIR INLET)
2 PURGE TUBE
3 TANK TUBE
4 CAP - SPLASH

86814008

Fig. 8 Common vapor canister

tions. When a solenoid is energized, the armature with attached shaft and swivel pintle, is lifted, opening the orifice.

The digital EGR valve is opened by the ECM/PCM, grounding each solenoid circuit individually. The flow of EGR is regulated by the ECM/PCM which uses information from the Engine Coolant Temperature Sensor (ECT), Throttle Position Sensor (TPS), Manifold Absolute Pressure (MAP) sensor and Mass Air Flow Sensor (MAF) to determine the appropriate rate of flow for a particular engine operating condition.

Incorrect EGR Operation

Too much EGR flow at idle, cruise, or during cold operation may result in the engine stalling after cold start, the engine stalling at idle after deceleration, vehicle surge during cruise and rough idle. If the EGR valve is always open, the vehicle may not idle. Too little or no EGR flow allows combustion temperatures to get too high which could result in spark knock (detonation), engine overheating and/or emission test failure.

Fig. 9 Positive backpressure EGR valve

Fig. 10 Negative backpressure EGR valve

EGR Valve Identification

• Positive backpressure EGR valves will have a "P" stamped on the top side of the valve below the date built.

• Negative backpressure EGR valves will have a "N" stamped on the top side of the valve below the date built.

• Port EGR valves have no identification stamped below the date built.

REMOVAL & INSTALLATION

▶ **See Figures 12 and 13**

Backpressure EGR valves

1. Disconnect the negative battery cable.
2. Remove the air cleaner assembly.
3. Tag and disconnect the necessary hoses and wiring to gain access to the EGR valve.
4. Remove the EGR valve retaining bolts.
5. Remove the EGR valve. Discard the gasket.

1	SOLENOID & MOUNTING PLATE ASSEMBLY
2	EGR BASE PLATE
3	EGR BASE GASKET
4	INSULATOR GASKET
5	EGR BASE
6	ARMATURE ASSEMBLY
7	SCREW ASSEMBLY

Fig. 11 Digital EGR valve

Fig. 12 Remove the EGR valve retaining bolts with a suitable wrench

Fig. 13 When removing the EGR valve, be sure to also remove all old gasket material and clean off the engine's valve mounting surface

6. Buff the exhaust deposits from the mounting surface and around the valve using a wire wheel.

7. Remove deposits from the valve outlet.

8. Clean the mounting surfaces of the intake manifold and valve assembly.

To install:

9. Install a new EGR gasket.

10. Install the EGR valve to the manifold.

11. Install the retaining bolts and torque to 11-22 ft. lbs. (15-30 Nm).

12. Connect the wiring and hoses.

13. Install the air cleaner assembly.

14. Connect the negative battery cable.

Digital EGR Valves

▶ See Figure 14

1. Disconnect the negative battery cable.

2. Disengage the electrical connector at the solenoid.

3. Remove the 2 base-to-flange bolts.

4. Remove the digital EGR valve.

To install:

5. Install the digital EGR valve.

6. Install the 2 base-to-flange bolts. Tighten to 18-22 ft. lbs. (25-30 Nm).

7. Connect the negative battery cable.

EGR Solenoid

1. Disconnect the negative battery cable.

2. Remove the air cleaner, as required.

3. Some models require the MAP sensor to be removed.

4. Disengage the electrical connector at the solenoid.

5. Disconnect the vacuum hoses.

6. Remove the retaining bolts and the solenoid.

7. Remove the filter, as required.

To install:

8. If removed, install the filter.

9. Install the solenoid and retaining bolts, then tighten to 15-22 ft. lbs. (20-30 Nm).

10. Position and install the MAP sensor if removed.

11. Connect the vacuum hoses.

12. Connect the electrical connector.

13. If removed, install the air cleaner.

14. Connect the negative battery cable.

Exhaust Gas Recirculation (EGR) System — Diesel Engines

▶ See Figures 15 and 16

The diesel EGR systems work in the same basic manner as gasoline engine EGR systems: exhaust gases are introduced into the combustion chambers to reduce combustion temperatures, and thus lower the formation of nitrogen oxides (NOx).

Vacuum from the vacuum pump is modulated by the Vacuum Regulator Valve (VRV) mounted on the injection pump.

The amount of EGR valve opening is further modulated by a Vacuum Modulator Valve (VMV). The VMV allows for an increase in vacuum to the EGR valve as the throttle is closed, up to the switching point of the VMV. The system also employs an RVR valve.

In 1985, the EGR valve was moved to the rear of the engine and has become electronically controlled.

SERVICE (COMPONENT TESTING)

Vacuum Regulator Valve (VRV)

The VRV is attached to the side of the injection pump and regulates vacuum in proportion to throttle angle. Vacuum from the vacuum pump is supplied to port A and vacuum at port **B** (see illustration) is reduced as the throttle is opened. At closed throttle the vacuum should be 15 in. Hg (51 kPa), and at half throttle 6 in. Hg (20 kPa); at wide open throttle there should be zero vacuum.

Exhaust Gas Recirculation Valve

Apply vacuum to the vacuum port. The valve should be fully open at 12 in. Hg (41 kPa) and closed below 6 in. Hg (20 kPa).

1	**BOLT/SCREW**
2	**DIGITAL EGR VALVE**
3	**GASKET**
4	**EGR PAD (PART OF THE UPPER INTAKE MANIFOLD)**
5	**GASKET**
6	**FOLDED TABS**
7	**BRACKET (PART OF THE EGR PIPE ASSEMBLY)**
8	**EXHAUST MANIFOLD**

FRT

86814012

Fig. 14 Unfasten the two base-to-flange bolts to remove the valve

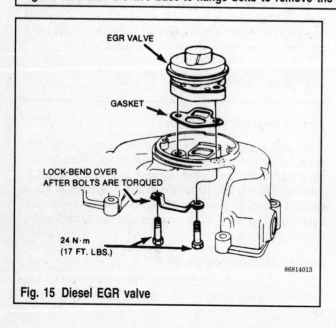

EGR VALVE

GASKET

LOCK-BEND OVER AFTER BOLTS ARE TORQUED

24 N·m
(17 FT. LBS.)

86814013

Fig. 15 Diesel EGR valve

EGR VALVE

EGR VALVE

VACUUM REGULATOR VALVE (VRV)
(ON INJECTION PUMP)

TO GROUND

DIODE

TO TRANSMISSION
T.C.C. DELAY MODULE

TO TERM "D" ON
TRANSMISSION
CASE CONNECTOR

VACUUM SOURCE

VACUUM
MODULATOR
VALVE (VMV)

TO TRANS.
GOV. PRESS.
SWITCH

T.C.C. OPERATED
SOLENOID

VENT

VENT

RESPONSE VACUUM
REDUCER (RVR)

VENT

86814019

Fig. 16 Diesel EGR system

EGR SYSTEM DIAGNOSIS - V-6 DIESEL ENGINE

CONDITION	POSSIBLE CAUSE	CORRECTION
EGR valve will not open	Binding or stuck EGR Valve.	Replace EGR valve.
	No vacuum to EGR valve.	Check VRV, RVR, solenoid, T.C.C. Operation (See Section 7A), Vacuum pump, VMV, and connecting hoses.
EGR valve will not close, or EPR valve will not open. (Heavy smoke on acceleration).	Binding or stuck EGR or EPR valve.	Replace EGR or EPR valve.
	Constant high vacuum to EGR and EPR valve.	Check VRV, RVR, solenoid, VMV and connecting hoses.
EGR valve opens partially.	Binding EGR valve.	Replace EGR valve.
	Low vacuum at EGR valve.	Check VRV, RVR, solenoid, vacuum pump, VMV and connecting hoses.
Loss of power and heavy smoke on acceleration, EGR valve functions normally.	Binding or stuck EPR valve, constant high vacuum to EPR valve.	Replace EPR valve. Check vacuum hose routing.

86814020

Response Vacuum Reducer (RVR)

Connect a vacuum gauge to the port marked To EGR valve or TCC solenoid. Connect a hand operated vacuum pump to the VRV port. Draw 15 in. Hg (51 kPa) of vacuum on the pump and the reading on the vacuum gauge should be lower than the vacuum pump reading by 0.75 in. Hg (2.5 kPa).

Exhaust Pressure Regulator Valve

Apply vacuum to the vacuum port of the valve. The valve should be fully closed at 12 in. Hg (41 kPa) and open below 6 in. Hg (20 kPa).

Vacuum Modulator Valve (VMV)

To test the VMV, block the drive wheels, and apply the parking brake. With the shift lever in Park, start the engine and run at a slow idle. Connect a vacuum gauge to the hose that connects to the port marked **MAN**. There should be at least 14 in. Hg (47 kPa) of vacuum. If not, check the vacuum pump, VRV, RVR, solenoid, and all connecting hoses. Reconnect the hose to the **MAN** port. Connect a vacuum gauge to the **DIST** port on the VMV. The vacuum reading should be 12 in. Hg (40 kPa) except on High Altitude cars, which should be 9 in. Hg (30 kPa).

Emission Control Systems

Emission control system constitute the largest body of emission control devices installed on A-Body cars. Many of these systems are controlled by or engine control computer. Included in this category are: Thermostatic Air Cleaner (THERMAC); Air Management System; Early Fuel Evaporation System (EFE); Exhaust Gas Recirculation (EGR); Computer Command Control System (CCC); Throttle Body Injection (TBI); Multi-Port Fuel Injection (MFI); Deceleration Valve; Mixture Control Solenoid (M/C); Throttle Position Sensor (TPS); Idle Speed Control (ISC); Electronic Spark Timing (EST); Torque Converter Clutch (TCC); Catalytic Converter and the Oxygen Sensor System. A brief description of each system and any applicable service procedures follows.

Many of the component testing is covered in chart format. The Computer Control Module ECM/PCM is capable of storing diagnostic codes. Many of the components test will be cover in the charts related to certain codes. Example is if the ECM/PCM see an improper signal from the coolant temperature sensor it will store a code 14. You would perform the test for Code 14 for the engine in your vehicle. If you wanted to test this component even thought the computer did not store a code you would still use the same chart and procedure.

There are 4 major electronic engine control systems covered in this section: Feedback Carburetor (also called Computer Command Control (CCC) System), Throttle Body Injection, Multi-Port Fuel Injection and Sequential Fuel Injection. You only need use the text and charts for the car's applicable system. Whereas Section 5 (Fuel Systems) covers removal, installation and adjustment procedures, this section contains general descriptions of systems and components, as well as the testing charts needed to diagnose them.

Thermostatic Air Cleaner (THERMAC)

▶ See Figure 17

All Feedback Carbureted, and Throttle Body Injected engines use the THERMAC system. This system is designed to warm the air entering the carburetor when underhood temperatures are low, and to maintain a controlled air temperature into the carburetor at all times. By allowing preheated air to enter the carburetor, the amount of time the choke is on is reduced, resulting in better fuel economy and lower emissions. Engine warm-up time is a also reduced.

The THERMAC system is composed of the air cleaner body, a filter, sensor unit, vacuum diaphragm, damper door, and associated hoses and connections. Heat radiating from the exhaust manifold is trapped by a heat stove and is ducted to the air cleaner to supply heated air to the carburetor. A movable door in the air cleaner case snorkel allows air to be drawn in from the heat stove (cold operation). The door position is controlled by the vacuum motor, which receives intake manifold vacuum as modulated by the temperature sensor.

THERMAL AIR CLEANER ASSEMBLY
SENSOR
VACUUM MOTOR
LINKAGE
AIR BLEED VALVE
VACUUM HOSE TO INTAKE MANIFOLD TEE
SNORKEL
DAMPER ASSEMBLY

86814018

Fig. 17 The thermactor air cleaner is used on carbureted and TBI engines

SYSTEM CHECKS

1. Check the vacuum hoses for leaks, kinks, breaks, or improper connections and correct any defects.

2. With the engine off, check the position of the damper door within the snorkel. A mirror can be used to make this job easier. The damper door should be open to admit outside air.

3. Apply at least 7 in. Hg (24 kPa) of vacuum to the damper diaphragm unit. The door should close. If it doesn't, check the diaphragm linkage for binding and correct hookup.

4. With the vacuum still applied and the door closed, clamp the tube to trap the vacuum. If the door doesn't remain closed, there is a leak in the diaphragm assembly.

Air Management System

The AIR management system, is used to provide additional oxygen to continue the combustion process after the exhaust gases leave the combustion chamber. Air is injected into either the exhaust port(s), the exhaust manifold(s) or the catalytic converter by an engine driven air pump. The system is in operation at all times and will bypass air only momentarily during deceleration and at high speeds. The bypass function is performed by the AIR Management Valve, while the check valve protects the air pump by preventing any backflow of exhaust gases.

The AIR management system helps reduce HC and CO content in the exhaust gases by injecting air into the exhaust ports during cold engine operation. This air injection also helps the catalytic converter to reach the proper temperature quicker during warmup. When the engine is warm (Closed Loop), the AIR system injects air into the beds of a three-way converter to lower the HC and the CO content in the exhaust.

The Air Management system utilizes the following components:

- An engine driven AIR pump
- AIR management valves (Air Control, Air Switching)
- Air flow and control hoses
- Check valves
- A dual-bed, three-way catalytic converter

The belt driven, vane-type air pump is located at the front of the engine and supplies clean air to the AIR system for purposes already stated. When the engine is cold, the Electronic Control Module (ECM) energizes an AIR control solenoid. This allows air to flow to the AIR switching valve. The AIR switching valve is then energized to direct air to the exhaust ports.

When the engine is warm, the ECM/PCM de-energizes the AIR switching valve, thus directing the air between the beds of the catalytic converter. This provides additional oxygen for the oxidizing catalyst in the second bed to decrease HC and CO, while at the same time keeping oxygen levels low in the first bed, enabling the reducing catalyst to effectively decrease the levels of NOx.

If the AIR control valve detects a rapid increase in manifold vacuum (deceleration), certain operating modes (wide open throttle, etc.) or if the ECM/PCM self-diagnostic system detects any problem in the system, air is diverted to the air cleaner or directly into the atmosphere.

The primary purpose of the ECM/PCM's divert mode is to prevent backfiring. Throttle closure at the beginning of deceleration will temporarily create air/fuel mixtures which are too rich to burn completely. These mixtures become burnable when they reach the exhaust if combined with the injection air. The next firing of the engine will ignite this mixture causing an exhaust backfire. Momentary diverting of the injection air from the exhaust prevents this.

The AIR management system check valves and hoses should be checked periodically for any leaks, cracks or deterioration.

REMOVAL & INSTALLATION

Air Pump

▶ **See Figures 18 and 19**

1. Remove the AIR management valves and/or adapter at the pump.
2. Loosen the air pump adjustment bolt and remove the drive belt.
3. Remove the pump pulley.
4. Unscrew the pump mounting bolts and then remove the pump.

To install:

5. Install the pump with the mounting bolts loose.
6. Attach the pump pulley to the pump.
7. Install the pump belt, then adjust.
8. Install the AIR management valves and/or adapter at the pump.
9. Tighten the mounting bolts to 20-35 ft. lbs. (27-56 Nm).

Check Valve

1. Release the clamp and disconnect the air hoses from the valve.
2. Unscrew the check valve from the air injection pipe.

To install:

3. Install the check valve into the air injection pipe.
4. Connect the hoses and tighten with the clamps.

Air Management Valve

1. Disconnect the negative battery cable.

Fig. 18 Loosen the air pump adjustment bolt . . .

Fig. 19 . . . then remove the drive belt

2. Remove the air cleaner.
3. Tag and disconnect the vacuum hose from the valve.
4. Tag and disconnect the air outlet hoses from the valve.
5. Bend back the lock tabs and then remove the bolts holding the elbow to the valve.
6. Tag and disconnect any electrical connections at the valve and then remove the valve from the elbow.

To install:
7. Install the valve to the bracket or adapter and lock tabs if used, with a new gasket.
8. Tighten the attaching screws to 140 inch lbs. (16 Nm).
9. Bend the tab to hex flat against the bolt and screw heads.
10. Install the outlet and vacuum signal hoses and electrical connections, then check for leaks and correct operation.

Emission Service Light

An emissions indicator flag may appear in the odometer window of the speedometer on some vehicles. The flag could say "Sensor," "Emissions" or "Catalyst" depending on the part or assembly that is scheduled for regular emissions maintenance replacement. The word "Sensor" indicates a need for oxygen sensor replacement and the words "Emissions" or "Catalyst" indicate the need for catalytic converter catalyst replacement.

RESETTING

1. Remove the instrument panel trim plate.
2. Remove the instrument cluster lens.
3. Locate the flag indicator reset notches at the driver's side of the odometer.
4. Use a pointed tool to apply light downward pressure on the notches, until the indicator is reset.
5. When the indicator is reset an alignment mark will appear in the left center of the odometer window.

Service Interval Reminder Light

RESETTING

If equipped, the SERVICE REMINDER section of the driver information center (DIC) display shows how many miles remain until service is needed. When the RESET button is pressed twice, a type of service and number of miles remaining until the service is needed will be displayed. Each time the RESET button is pressed, another type of service and mile remaining for it will be displayed.

With the ignition switch in the RUN, BULB, TEST or START position, voltage is applied from the ECM/PCM fuse through a pink/black wire to the ECM/PCM. As the vehicle moves the speed sensor sends pulses to the ECM/PCM. The ECM/PCM then sends signals to the speed input of the DIC module. The DIC module converts these pulses to miles. The module then subtracts the miles travelled from the distance on the DIC display. All four types of service can be displayed at the same time.

To reset the service light it will be necessary to subtract the mileage from the service interval light that is illuminated. The miles remaining for a certain type of service can be decreased by holding the RESET button, and the miles remaining will be decreased in steps of 500 miles (805 km) every 5 seconds. If the RESET button is held in and the miles remaining reach zero, the DIC display will show the service interval for the service selected. The service intervals are: oil filter and change 7500 miles (12,077 km), next oil filter 15,000 miles (24,155 km), tire rotation 7500 miles (12,077 km), next rotation 15,000 miles (24,155 km), tune-up 30,000 miles (48,309 km).

If the RESET button is still held down, the miles will decrease in steps of 500 miles (805 km) from the service interval. When the RESET button is released, the mileage display will be the new distance until the service should be performed.

When the service distance reaches zero, the service reminder item will be displayed. If the service interval is reset within 10 miles (16 km), the display will go out immediately. If more than 10 miles pass before the service interval is reset, the item will remain displayed for another 10 miles before going out.

→On some models it may be necessary to depress the **SYSTEM RECALL** button in order to display the service interval light on the driver information center.

Service Engine Soon (SES) Light

RESETTING

The Service Engine Soon (SES) light or Check Engine light will light if an engine or emission problem is detected. If an emission problem is detected the computer will store a code for that fault. If the fault goes away or is repair the light will go out, but the code will remain in memory. If the problem returns or is not repair the light will not go out and can not be reset. When the problem goes away the light goes out.

Oxygen Sensor (O₂S)

The exhaust oxygen sensor or O_2S is mounted in the exhaust stream where it monitors oxygen content in the exhaust gas. The newer models have a heated oxygen sensor, which is slightly different from the conventional sensor. The oxygen content in the exhaust is a measure of the air/fuel mixture going into the engine. The oxygen in the exhaust reacts with the oxygen sensor to produce a voltage which is read by the ECM/PCM. The voltage output is very low, ranging from 0.1 volt in a high oxygen-lean mixture condition to 0.9 volt in a low oxygen-rich mixture condition.

Testing the oxygen sensor without the use of special scan tools to observe its operation is difficult. The oxygen sensor should not be condemned because of Codes 44, 45, or 131-134. These codes tell you the oxygen sensor is seeing a constant rich or leak mixture. This code is usually not due to a bad oxygen sensor. A rich mixture could be a dirty air filter, stuck choke, leaking injector, burn valve or other problems. A lean mixture could be a vacuum leak, low fuel pressure or even a bad spark plug wire. Follow the proper charts to test the components.

PRECAUTIONS

- Careful handling of the oxygen sensor is essential.
- The electrical pigtail and connector are permanently attached and should not be removed from the oxygen sensor.
- The in-line electrical connector and louvered end of the oxygen sensor must be kept free of grease, dirt and other contaminants.
- Avoid using cleaning solvents of any type on the oxygen sensor.

- Do not drop or roughly handle the oxygen sensor.
- The oxygen sensor may be difficult to remove if the engine temperature is below 120°F (48°C). Excessive force may damage the threads in the exhaust manifold or exhaust pipe.

REMOVAL & INSTALLATION

▸ See Figure 20

→The oxygen sensor must be replaced every 30,000 miles (48,309 km). The sensor may be difficult to remove when the engine temperature is below 120°F (48°C). Excessive removal force may damage the threads in the exhaust manifold or pipe and result in injury; follow the removal procedure carefully.

1. Locate the oxygen sensor; it protrudes from the center of the exhaust manifold at the front of the engine compartment. (The sensor looks somewhat like a spark plug.)
2. Disengage the electrical connector from the oxygen sensor.
3. Spray a commercial heat riser solvent onto the sensor threads and allow it to soak in for at least five minutes.
4. *Carefully* unscrew and remove the sensor.
   To install:
5. Coat the new sensor's threads with GM anti-seize compound No. 5613695 or the equivalent. This is not a conventional anti-seize paste. The use of a regular compound may electrically insulate the sensor, rendering it inoperative. You must coat the threads with an electrically conductive anti-seize compound.
6. Tighten the sensor to 30 ft. lbs. (42 Nm). Do not overtighten.
7. Attach the electrical connector. Be careful not to damage the electrical pigtail. Check the sensor boot for proper fit and installation.

86814021

Fig. 20 The oxygen sensor protrudes from the center of the exhaust manifold at the front of the engine compartment and looks somewhat like a spark plug

ELECTRONIC ENGINE CONTROL SYSTEMS

There are 3 basic fuel control systems used on the General Motors A-Body cars. The feedback carburetor vehicles use a

system called Computer Command Control (CCC) System. The other two systems are fuel injection systems. One system is called Throttle Body Injection (TBI); this system uses an injector built into the throttle body. Throttle body injected vehicles appear very much like carbureted vehicles, but you'll notice there is no choke. The third system is Multi-Port Fuel Injection (MFI), or a variation known as Sequential-Fuel Injection (SFI). This MFI/SFI system has an injector mounted in the intake manifold at each intake valve. There is one injector for each cylinder.

Feedback Carburetor and Computer Command Control (CCC) System

The CCC system monitors engine and vehicle operating conditions which it uses to control engine and emission control systems. This system controls engine operation and lowers the exhaust emissions while maintaining good fuel economy and driveability. The Computer Control Module (ECM/PCM) is the brain of the CCC system. The ECM/PCM controls engine related systems constantly adjusting the engine operation. In addition to maintaining the ideal air/fuel ratio for the catalytic converter and adjusting ignition timing, the CCC system also controls the Air Management System so that the catalytic converter can operate at the highest efficiency possible. The system also controls lock-up on the transaxle's torque converter clutch, adjusts idle speed over a wide range of conditions, purges the evaporative emissions charcoal canister, controls the EGR valve operation and operates the Early Fuel Evaporative (EFE) system. Not all engines use all of the above subsystems.

The CCC system is primarily an emission control system, designed to maintain a 14.7:1 air/fuel ratio under all operating conditions. When this ideal air/fuel ratio is maintained the catalytic converter can control oxides of nitrogen (NOx), hydrocarbon (HC) and carbon monoxide (CO) emissions.

There are 2 operation modes for CCC system: closed loop and open loop fuel control. Closed loop fuel control means the oxygen sensor is controlling the carburetor's air/fuel mixture ratio. Under open loop fuel control operating conditions (wide open throttle, engine and/or oxygen sensor cold), the oxygen sensor has no effect on the air/fuel mixture.

➡️**On some engines, the oxygen sensor will cool off while the engine is idling, putting the system into open loop operation. To restore closed loop operation, run the engine at part throttle and accelerate from idle to part throttle a few times.**

The basic system block diagram shows the catalytic converter located in the exhaust system close to the engine. It is ahead of the muffler and tailpipe. If the converter is to do its job effectively, the engine must receive an air/fuel mixture of approximately 14.7:1.

The carburetor mixes air and gasoline into a combustible mixture before delivering it to the engine. However, carburetors have reached a point where they can no longer control the air/fuel mixture sufficiently close to the ideal 14.7:1 ratio for most operating conditions. Therefore, a different type of control must be used on the carburetor, something that has never been used before.

An electric solenoid in the carburetor controls the air/fuel ratio. The solenoid is connected to an electronic module (ECM/PCM) which is an on board computer. The ECM/PCM

provides a controlling signal to the solenoid. The solenoid controls the metering rod(s) and an idle air bleed valve to closely control the air/fuel ration throughout the operating range of the engine. However, since the engine operates under a wide variety of conditions, the computer must be told what those conditions are. This is so that it will know what to tell the carburetor solenoid to do.

A sensor is located in the exhaust stream close to the engine. It's known as an oxygen sensor or usually refer to as the O_2S sensor. This sensor functions when the engine's exhaust temperature rises above 600°F (315°C). There is a direct relationship between the mixture delivered by the carburetor and the amount of oxygen left in the exhaust gases. The O_2S sensor can determine whether the exhaust is too rich or too lean. It sends a varying voltage signal to the ECM/PCM.

The ECM/PCM will then signal the mixture control solenoid to deliver richer or leaner mixture for the current engine operating conditions. As the carburetor makes a change, the O_2S sensor will sense that change and signal the ECM/PCM whether or not it's too rich or too lean. The ECM/PCM will then make a correction, if necessary. This goes on continually and is what we refer to as Closed Loop operation. Closed loop conditions deliver a 14.7:1 air/fuel mixture to the engine. This makes it possible for the converter to act upon all 3 of the major pollutants in an efficient and effective manner. consider, however, what happens in the morning when it's cold and the vehicle is started. If the system where to keep the air/fuel mixture to the 14.7:1 air/fuel ratio when it's cold the chances are that the engine wouldn't run very well. When the engine is cold, it has to have a richer mixture. An automatic choke is used to give the engine a richer mixture until it is up to normal operating temperature. during this time, the O_2S sensor signals are ignored by the ECM/PCM.

A temperature sensor is located in the water jacket of the engine and connected to the electronic control module. When the engine is cold, the temperature sensor will tell the ECM/PCM to ignore the oxygen sensor signal, since the sensor is too cold to operate. The electronic control module then tells the carburetor to deliver a richer mixture based upon what has already been programmed into the ECM/PCM. The ECM/PCM will also use information from other sensors during cold start operation.

After the engine has been running for some time and has reached normal operating temperature, the temperature sensor will signal the ECM/PCM that the engine is warm and it can accept the oxygen sensor signal. If other system requirements are met, closed loop operations begins. The oxygen sensor will then influence the ECM/PCM as to what mixture it should deliver to the engine. In addition to these 2 conditions, there are 3 other conditions which affect the air/fuel mixture delivered to the engine. First is the load that is placed upon the engine. When an engine is working hard, such as pulling a heavy load up a long grade, it requires a richer air/fuel mixture. This is different from a vehicle that is operating in a cruise condition on a level highway at a constant rate of speed.

Manifold vacuum is used to determine engine load. A manifold pressure sensor is connected to the intake manifold. It detects changes in the manifold pressure which are signalled to the ECM/PCM. As changes occur, the load placed upon the engine varies. The ECM/PCM takes this varying signal into account when determining what mixture the carburetor should be delivering to the engine. The next condition in determining what air/fuel mixture should be is the amount of throttle opening. The more throttle opening at any given time, the richer the mixture required by the engine. On most applications a Throttle Position Sensor (TPS) in the carburetor sends a signal to the ECM/PCM. It tells the ECM/PCM the position of the throttle, whether it it at idle, part throttle, wide open or whatever condition that exists in between.

The last condition, which has a bearing on the mixture that the engine would require, is the speed the engine is running. Certainly when an engine is operating at 600 rpm, it doesn't need as much gasoline as it does when it is operating at 4000 rpm. Therefore, a tachometer signal from the distributor is delivered to the ECM/PCM. This tells the ECM/PCM how fast the engine is running. This signal will also be taken into consideration when the ECM/PCM decides what mixture the carburetor should be delivering to the engine. In the typical CCC system, the ECM/PCM will use various inputs to make decisions that will best control the operation of the mixture control solenoid for maximum system efficiency.

CCC SYSTEM COMPONENTS

Computer Control Module

The Electronic Control Module (ECM) and the Powertrain Control Module (PCM) are one and the same. While older vehicles have the ECM name badge and newer vehicles the PCM, they are both computer control modules. The ECM/PCM is a reliable solid state computer, protected in a metal box. It is used to monitor and control all the functions of the CCC system and is located in on the passenger side kick panel. The ECM/PCM can perform several on-car functions at the same time and has the ability to diagnose itself as well as other CCC system circuits.

The ECM/PCM performs the functions of an on and off switch. It can send a voltage signal to a circuit or connect a circuit to ground at a precise time. Programmed into the ECM/PCM's memory are voltage and time values. These valves will differ from engine to engine. As an example then, if the ECM/PCM sees a proper voltage value for the correct length of time it will perform a certain function. This could be turning the EGR system on as the engine warms up. If however, the voltage or the time interval is not correct, the ECM/PCM will also recognize this. It will not perform its function and in most cases turn the "CHECK ENGINE" or "SERVICE ENGINE SOON" light on.

The other CCC components include the oxygen sensor, an electronically controlled variable-mixture carburetor, a 3-way catalytic converter, throttle position and coolant sensors, a Barometric Pressure (BARO) sensor, a Manifold Absolute Pressure (MAP) sensor, a "CHECK ENGINE" light on the instrument cluster and an Electronic Spark Timing (EST) distributor, which on some engines is equipped with an Electronic Spark Control (ESC) or Knock Sensor (KS), which retards ignition spark under some conditions (detonation, etc.).

Other components used by the CCC system include the Air Injection Reaction (AIR) Management System, charcoal canister purge solenoid, EGR valve control, vehicle speed sensor (located in the instrument cluster), transaxle torque converter clutch solenoid (automatic transaxle models only), idle speed control and Early Fuel Evaporative (EFE) system.

The CCC system ECM/PCM, in addition to monitoring sensors and sending a control signal to the carburetor, also controls the charcoal canister purge, AIR Management System, fuel control, idle speed control, idle air control, automatic transaxle converter clutch lock-up, distributor ignition timing, EGR valve control, EFE control, air conditioner compressor clutch operation, electric fuel pump and the "CHECK ENGINE" light.

The AIR Management System is an emission control which provides additional oxygen either to the catalyst or the exhaust manifold. An AIR Management System, composed of an air switching valve and/or an air control valve, controls the air pump flow and is itself controlled by the ECM/PCM. The AIR system uses vacuum operated, ECM/PCM controlled (grounds to complete the circuit and energize the solenoids) valves to control the AIR switching.

The charcoal canister purge control is an electrically operated solenoid valve controlled by the ECM/PCM. When energized, the purge control solenoid blocks vacuum from reaching the canister purge valve. When the ECM/PCM de-energizes the purge control solenoid, vacuum is allowed to reach the canister and operate the purge valve. This releases the fuel vapors collected in the canister into the induction system.

The EGR valve control solenoid is activated by the ECM/PCM in similar fashion to the canister purge solenoid. When the engine is cold, the ECM/PCM energizes the solenoid, which blocks the vacuum signal to the EGR valve. When the engine is warm, the ECM/PCM de-energizes the solenoid and the vacuum signal is allowed to reach and activate the EGR valve.

The Torque Converter Clutch (TCC) lock-up is controlled by the ECM/PCM through an electrical solenoid in the automatic transaxle. When the vehicle speed sensor in the instrument panel signals the ECM/PCM that the vehicle has reached the correct speed, the ECM/PCM energizes the solenoid which allows the torque converter to mechanically couple the engine to the transmission. When the brake pedal is pushed or during deceleration, passing, etc., the ECM/PCM returns the transaxle to fluid drive.

The idle speed control adjusts the idle speed to load conditions and will lower the idle speed under no-load or low-load conditions to conserve gasoline.

The Early Fuel Evaporative (EFE) system is used on most engines to provide rapid heat to the engine induction system to promote smooth start-up and operation. There are 2 types of system: vacuum servo and electrically heated. They use different means to achieve the same end, which is to pre-heat the incoming air/fuel mixture. They may or may not be controlled by the ECM/PCM.

A/C Wide Open Throttle (WOT) Control: on this system the ECM/PCM controls the A/C compressor clutch to disengage the clutch during hard acceleration. On some engines, the ECM/PCM disengages the clutch during the engine start-up on a warm engine. The WOT control is not installed on all engines.

Electronic Spark Control (ESC) or Knock Sensor (KS): on this system the ECM/PCM controls spark timing on certain engines to allow the engine to have maximum spark advance without spark knock. This improves the driveability and fuel economy. This system is not used on all engines.

Shift Light Control, as equipped on some vehicles, utilizes an ECM/PCM activated light to indicate the best manual transaxle shift point for maximum fuel economy. This control is not used on all engines.

Rochester Feedback Carburetors

The E2ME and E2MC are 2-barrel single stage design. All carburetors are used with the Computer Command Control (CCC) System of fuel control. All Rochester carburetors consist of 3 major assemblies: the air horn, the float bowl and the throttle body. They have 6 basic operating systems: float, idle, main metering, power, pump and choke.

A single float chamber supplies fuel to the carburetor bores. A closed-cell rubber float, brass needle seat and a rubber tipped float valve with pull clip, are used to control fuel level in the float chamber. An electrically operated mixture control solenoid, mounted in the float bowl, is used to control the air and fuel mixture in the primary bores of the carburetor. The plunger in the solenoid is controlled (or pulsed) by electrical signals received from the Computer Control Module (ECM/PCM).

The air valve and metering rods control the air/fuel metering in the secondary bores. A pair of tapered metering rods are attached to a hanger, which operates by cam action resulting from the air valve angle and provides the additional fuel flow necessary during increased engine air flow at wide open throttle.

General Motors Rochester carburetors are identified by their model code. The carburetor model identification number is stamped vertically on the float bowl, near the secondary throttle lever. The letters in the model name describe the specific features of the carburetor. For example: The first letter "E" indicates the the carburetor is Electronically controlled. The second and third digits, "2S" indicates the carburetor is a member of the Varajet family. The last digit "E" indicates an integral Electric choke. The identification code is stamped on the float bowl.

➡**If a carburetor number has an "E" at the end (such as E2ME), that carburetor has an integral Electric Choke.**

For Carburetor repair, overhaul or adjustment, refer to procedures covered in Section 5 (Fuel Systems).

DIAGNOSIS AND TESTING

➡**The following explains how to activate the trouble code signal light in the instrument cluster and gives an explanation of what each code means. This is not a full CCC system troubleshooting and isolation procedure.**

Before suspecting the CCC system or any of its components as faulty, check the ignition system including distributor, timing, spark plugs and wires. Check the engine compression, air cleaner and emission control components not controlled by the ECM/PCM. Also check the intake manifold, vacuum hoses and hose connectors for leaks and the carburetor bolts for tightness.

The following symptoms could indicate a possible problem with the CCC system.

- Detonation
- Stalls or idles rough when cold
- Stalls or idles rough when hot
- Missing
- Hesitation
- Surges
- Poor gasoline mileage
- Sluggish or spongy performance
- Hard starting — cold
- Objectionable exhaust odors (rotten egg smell)
- Cuts out
- Improper idle speed

As a bulb and system check, the "CHECK ENGINE" light will come on when the ignition switch is turned to the **ON** position but the engine is not started. The "CHECK ENGINE" light will also produce the trouble code or codes by a series of flashes which translate as follows. When the diagnostic test terminal under the dash is grounded, with the ignition in the **ON** position and the engine not running, the "CHECK ENGINE" light will flash once, pause, then flash twice in rapid succession. This is a code 12, which indicates that the diagnostic system is working. After a long pause, the code 12 will repeat itself 2 more times. The cycle will then repeat itself until the engine is **STARTED** or the ignition is turned **OFF**.

When the engine is started, the "CHECK ENGINE" light will remain on for a few seconds, then turn off. If the "CHECK ENGINE" light remains on, the self-diagnostic system has detected a problem. If the test terminal is then grounded, the trouble code will flash 3 times. If more than a single problem is found, each trouble code will flash 3 times. Trouble codes will flash in numerical order (lowest code number to highest). The trouble codes series will repeat as long as the test terminal is grounded.

A trouble code indicates a problem with a given circuit. For example, trouble code 14 indicates a problem in the cooling sensor circuit. This includes the coolant sensor, its electrical harness and the Electronic Control Module (ECM). Since the self-diagnostic system cannot diagnose every possible fault in the system, the absence of a trouble code does not mean the system is trouble-free. To determine problems within the system which do not activate a trouble code, a system performance check must be made.

In the case of an intermittent fault in the system, the "CHECK ENGINE" light will go out when the fault goes away, but the trouble code will remain in the memory of the ECM. Therefore, it a trouble code can be obtained even though the "CHECK ENGINE" light is not on, the trouble code must be evaluated. It must be determined if the fault is intermittent or if the engine must be at certain operating conditions (under load, etc.) before the "CHECK ENGINE" light will come on. Some trouble codes will not be recorded in the ECM/PCM until the engine has been operated at part throttle for about 5-18 minutes. On the CCC system, a trouble code will be stored until terminal **R** of the ECM/PCM has been disconnected from the battery for 10 seconds.

An easy way to erase the computer memory on the CCC system is to disconnect the battery terminals from the battery. If this method is used, don't forget to reset clocks and electronic preprogrammable radios. Another method is to remove the fuse marked ECM/PCM in the fuse panel. Not all models have such a fuse.

CCC System Circuit Diagnosis

To diagnose CCC system circuits, use the same general troubleshooting approach that is used for other automotive electrical systems. Finding the fault in a CCC circuit will require the testing tools described in this section. These tools are used with the diagnostic charts for CCC system troubleshooting. Always use a digital voltmeter for accuracy of readings when using CCC diagnostic charts.

Testing CCC System Performance

A dwellmeter is used to analyze operation of the M/C solenoid circuit. The operation of that circuit is controlled by the ECM/PCM, which used information from the sensors.

A chart called the "System Performance Check" is provided in the section. This chart provides step-by-step instructions to determine if the M/C control solenoid circuit, ECM/PCM and various sensors (M/C control system) are functioning properly. If they are not, the chart indicates the steps to take in order to locate and repair the source of the trouble.

Charts for the other systems, such as AIR, EST, EGR, EFE, TCC and canister purge are also provided in the section. Another chart called the "Diagnostic Circuit Check" follows the system performance check. This chart is the starting point for any diagnosis.

The dwellmeter is used to diagnose the M/C control system. Connect a dwellmeter to the pigtail connector in the M/C solenoid wiring harness. In the old contact point style ignition system, the dwellmeter read the period of time that the points were closed (dwell) and voltage flowed to the ignition coil.

In the CCC system the dwellmeter is used to read the time that the ECM/PCM closed the M/C solenoid circuit to ground, allowing voltage to operate the M/C solenoid. Dwell, as used in CCC system performance diagnosis, is the time that the M/C solenoid circuit is closed (or energized). The dwellmeter will translate this time into degrees. The 6-cylinder (0-60 degree) scale on the dwellmeter is used for this reading. The ability of the dwellmeter to perform this kind of conversion makes it an ideal tool to check the amount of time the ECM/PCM,'s internal switch is closed, thus energizing the M/C solenoid. The only difference is that the degree scale on the meter is more like the percent of solenoid ON time rather than actual degrees of dwell.

Connecting the Dwellmeter

First set the dwellmeter on the 6-cylinder position, then connect it to the Mixture Control (M/C) solenoid dwell lead to measure the output of the ECM/PCM. Do not allow the terminal to touch ground, including any hoses. The dwellmeter must be set to the 6-cylinder position when diagnosing all engines, whether working on a 4, 6, or 8-cylinder engine.

➡**Some older dwellmeters may not work properly on CCC. Don't use any dwellmeter which causes a change in engine operation when it is connected to the solenoid lead.**

The 6-cylinder scale on the dwellmeter provides evenly divided points, for example:
- 15 degrees = $\frac{1}{4}$ scale
- 30 degrees = midscale
- 45 degrees = $\frac{3}{4}$ scale

Connect the positive clip lead of the dwellmeter to the M/C solenoid pigtail connector shown in. Attach the other dwellmeter clip lead to ground. Do not allow the clip leads to contact other conductive cables or hoses which could interfere with accurate readings.

After connecting the dwellmeter to a warm, operating engine, the dwell at idle and part throttle will vary between 5-55 degrees. That is, the needle will move continuously up and down the scale. Needle movement indicates that the engine is in closed loop and that the dwell is being varied by signals from the ECM/PCM. However, if the engine is cold, has just been restarted, or the throttle is wide open, the dwell will be fixed and the needle will be steady. Those are signs that the engine is in open loop.

Diagnostic checks to find a condition without a trouble code are usually made on a warm engine (in closed loop) as indicated by a hot upper radiator hose. There are 3 ways of distinguishing open from closed loop operation.

1. A variation in dwell will occur only in closed loop.
2. Test for closed loop operation. Cause the mixture to become richer, by restricting the air flow through into the carburetor or manually closing the choke. If the dwellmeter moves up scale, that indicates closed loop.
3. If a large vacuum leak is created and the dwell drops down, that also indicates closed loop.

Reading the Dwellmeter

The mixture control (M/C) solenoid moves the metering rods up and down 10 times per second. This frequency was chosen to be slow enough to allow full stop-to-stop M/C solenoid travel, but fast enough to prevent any undesirable influence on vehicle response.

The duration of the on period determines whether the mixture is rich (mostly up) or lean (mostly down). When the metering rods are down for a longer period (54 degrees) than they are up (6 degrees), a lean mixture results.

As the solenoid on-time changes, the up time and down time of the metering rods also changes. When a lean mixture is desired, the M/C solenoid will restrict fuel flow through the metering jet 90% of the time, or, in other words, a lean mixture will be provided to the engine.

This lean command will read as 54 degrees on the dwellmeter (54 degrees is 90% of 60 degrees). This means the M/C solenoid has restricted fuel flow 90% of the time. A rich mixture is provided when the M/C solenoid restricts fuel flow only 10% of the time and allows a rich mixture to flow to the engine. A rich command will have a dwellmeter reading of 6 degrees (10% of 60 degrees); the M/C solenoid has restricted fuel flow 10% of the time.

On some engines dwellmeter readings can vary between 5-55 degrees, rather than between 6-54 degrees. The ideal mixture would be shown on the dwellmeter with the needle varying or swinging back and forth, anywhere between 10-50 degrees. Varying means the needle continually moves up and down the scale. The amount it moves does not matter, only the fact that it does move. The dwell is being varied by the signal sent to the ECM by the oxygen sensor in the exhaust manifold.

Under certain operating conditions such as Wide Open Throttle (WOT), or a cold engine, the dwell will remain fixed and the needle will be steady. Remember, a low dwellmeter reading (5-10°) announces the ECM signal to the M/C control solenoid is a rich command, while 55° would indicate a lean command.

Open and Closed Loop Operation

Two terms are often used when referring to CCC system operation. They are closed loop and open loop.

Basically, closed loop indicates that the ECM/PCM is using information from the exhaust oxygen sensor to influence operation of the mixture control (M/C) solenoid. the ECM/PCM still considers other information, such as engine temperature, rpm, barometric and manifold pressure and throttle position, along with the exhaust oxygen sensor information.

During open loop, all information except the exhaust oxygen sensor input is considered by the ECM/PCM to control the M/C solenoid. The diagnostic charts are based on a warmed up engine (closed loop operation) and will generally state, run engine at part throttle for 3 minutes or until there is a varying dwellmeter indication before beginning diagnosis.

It is important to note that the exhaust oxygen sensor may cool below its operational temperature during prolonged idling. This will cause an open loop condition and make the diagnostic chart information not usable during diagnosis. Engine rpm must be increased to warm the exhaust oxygen sensor and re-establish closed loop. Diagnosis should begin again at the first step on the chart after closed loop is resumed.

DIAGNOSTIC PROCEDURES

Following is a complete diagnostic sequence for the CCC system. In all cases, the sequence is begun with routine engine checks. After performing a system diagnostic circuit check, use the code chart (if applicable) or other diagnostic chart. Conduct a system performance check after testing and service are completed.

Diagnostic Charts

This section contains tree-type charts for locating the source of a fault in the CCC system circuits. When using a tree chart, always start at the first step and follow the sequence from top to bottom. Often there will be several branches of the tree to follow. Follow the branch that is applicable to the result obtained in that step. Several charts will be used during diagnosis and this sequential approach should be used in all cases.

➡**The CCC system should not be considered as a possible source of poor engine performance, fuel economy, or excessive emissions until all the routine engine checks, such as ignition, spark plugs, air cleaner and vacuum hoses, have been made.**

SYSTEM DIAGNOSTIC CIRCUIT CHECK

Begin the Diagnostic Circuit Check by making sure that the diagnostic system itself is working. Turn the ignition to **ON** with the engine stopped. If the "CHECK ENGINE" or "SERVICE ENGINE SOON" light comes on, ground the diagnostic code terminal (test lead) under the dash. If the "CHECK ENGINE" or "SERVICE ENGINE SOON" light flashes Code 12, the self-diagnostic system is working and can detect a faulty circuit. If there is no Code 12, see the appropriate chart in this section. If any additional codes flash, record them for later use.

If a Code 51 flashes, use chart 51 to diagnose that condition before proceeding with the Diagnostic Circuit Check. A Code 51 means that the "CHECK ENGINE" or "SERVICE ENGINE SOON" light flashes 5 times, pauses, then flashes once. After a longer pause, code 51 will flash again twice in this same way. To find out what diagnostic step to follow, look up the chart for Code 51 in this section. If there is not a Code 51, follow the "No Code 51" branch of the chart.

Clear the ECM memory by disconnecting the voltage lead either at the fuse panel or the ECM letter connector for 10 seconds. This clears any codes remaining from previous repairs, or codes for troubles not present at this time. Remember, even though a code is stored, if the trouble is not present the diagnostic charts cannot be used. The charts are designed only to locate present faults.

➡**When erasing the computer memory on the CCC system the ignition switch must be turned OFF before removing any fuses, wire connectors or battery cables. If the battery cable is to disconnect from the battery, don't forget to reset clocks and electronic preprogrammable radios.**

Next, remove the TEST terminal ground, set the parking brake and put the transaxle in **P**. Run the warm engine for several minutes, making sure it is run at the specified curb idle. Then, if the "CHECK ENGINE" or "SERVICE ENGINE SOON" light comes on while the engine is idling, ground the TEST lead again and observe (count) the flashing trouble code.

If the "CHECK ENGINE" or "SERVICE ENGINE SOON" light does not come on, check the codes which were recorded earlier. If there were no additional codes, road test the vehicle for the problem being diagnosed to make sure it still exists.

The purpose of the Diagnostic Circuit check is to make sure the "CHECK ENGINE" or "SERVICE SOON SOON" light works, that the ECM is operating and can recognize a fault and to determine if any trouble codes are stored in the ECM memory.

If trouble codes are stored, it also checks to see if they indicate an intermittent problem. This is the starting point of any diagnosis. If there are no codes stored, move on to the System Performance Check.

The codes obtained from the "CHECK ENGINE" or "SERVICE ENGINE SOON" light display method indicate which diagnostic charts provide in the section are to be used.

For example, code 23 can be diagnosed by following the step-by-step procedures on chart 23.

→**If more than a single code is stored in the ECM/PCM, the lowest code number must be diagnosed first. then proceed to the next highest code. The only exception is when a 50 series flashes. 50 series code take precedence over all other trouble codes and must be dealt with first, since they point to a fault in the PROM unit or the ECM/PCM.**

SERVICE

Before suspecting the CCC system, or any of its components as being faulty, check the ignition system (distributor, timing, spark plugs and wires). Check the engine compression, the air cleaner and any of the emission control components that are not controlled by the ECM/PCM. Also check the intake manifold, the vacuum hoses and hose connectors for any leaks. Check the carburetor mounting bolts for tightness.

The following symptoms could indicate a possible problem area with the CCC system:
- Detonation
- Stalling or rough idling when the engine is cold
- Stalling or rough idling when the engine is hot
- Missing
- Hesitation
- Surging
- Poor gasoline mileage
- Sluggish or spongy performance
- Hard starting when engine is cold
- Hard starting when the engine is hot
- Objectionable exhaust odors
- Engine cuts out
- Improper idle speed

As a bulb and system check, the Check Engine light will come on when the ignition switch is turned to the ON position but the engine is not started.

The Check Engine light will also produce the trouble code/codes by a series of flashes which translate as follows: When the diagnostic test terminal under the instrument panel is grounded, with the ignition in the ON position and the engine not running, the Check Engine light will flash once, pause, and then flash twice in rapid succession. This is a Code 12, which indicates that the diagnostic system is working. After a long pause, the Code 12 will repeat itself two more times. This whole cycle will then repeat itself until the engine is started or the ignition switch is turned OFF.

When the engine is started, the Check Engine light will remain on for a few seconds and turn off. If the Check Engine light remains on, the self-diagnostic system has detected a problem. If the test terminal is then grounded, the trouble code will flash (3) three times. If more than one problem is found to be in existence, each trouble code will flash (3) three times and then change to the next one. Trouble codes will flash in numerical order (lowest code number to highest). The trouble code series will repeat themselves for as long as the test terminal remains grounded.

A trouble code indicates a problem with a given circuit. For example, trouble code 14 indicates a problem in the coolant sensor circuit. This includes the coolant sensor, its electrical harness and the Computer Control Module (ECM/PCM).

Since the self-diagnostic system cannot diagnose every possible fault in the system, the absence of a trouble code does not necessarily mean that the system is trouble-free. To determine whether or not a problem with the system exists that does not activate a trouble code, a system performance check must be made. You can follow the symptom charts for the fuel system your car has. If the chart doesn't help you find the problem or instructs you to more involved testing using special tool you may wish to seek a qualified service technician. Guessing which component to test or testing a component incorrectly can be very expensive.

In the case of an intermittent fault in the system, the Check Engine light will go out when the fault goes away, but the trouble code will remain in the memory of the ECM/PCM. Therefore, if a trouble code can be obtained even though the Check Engine light is not on, it must still be evaluated. It must be determined if the fault is intermittent or if the engine must be operating under certain conditions (acceleration, deceleration, etc.) before the Check Engine light will come on. In some cases, certain trouble codes will not be recorded in the ECM/PCM until the engine has been operated at part throttle for at least 5 to 18 minutes.

On the CCC system, a trouble code will be stored until the terminal **R** at the ECM/PCM has been disconnected from the battery for at least 10 seconds, or the battery cable has be removed.

ACTIVATING THE TROUBLE CODE

On the CCC system, locate the test terminal under the instrument panel. Use a jumper wire and ground only the lead.

→**Ground the test terminal according to the instructions given previously in the Basic Troubleshooting section.**

CARBURETOR COMPONENT TESTING

Electric Choke

Check the choke unloader and idle setting adjustments. The choke linkage and fast idle cam must operate freely. Bent, dirty or otherwise damaged linkage must be cleaned, repaired or replaced as necessary. Do not lubricate linkage since lubricant will collect dust and cause sticking.

1. Allow the choke to cool so that when the throttle is opened slightly, the choke blade fully closes.

2. Start the engine and determine the time for the choke blade to reach the full open position.

3. If the the choke blade fails to open fully within 3½ minutes, proceed with Step 4 and 5 below.

4. Check the voltage at the choke heater connection (engine must be running):

a. If the voltage is approximately 12-15 volts, replace the electric choke unit.

b. If the voltage is low or zero, check all wires and connections. If any connections in the oil pressure switch circuitry are faulty, or if pressure switch is failed open, the oil warning light will be on with the engine running. Repair wires or connectors as required.

5. If Steps 4a and 4b do not correct the problem, replace oil pressure switch. No gasket is used between the choke cover and the choke housing due to grounding requirements.

Hot Air Choke

1. With the parking brake applied and the drive wheels blocked, place the transaxle in **P** or **N**, start the engine and allow it to warm up. Visually check to be sure the choke valve fully opens.

2. If the choke fails to open fully, momentarily touch the choke housing and the hot air inlet pipe or hose, to determine if sufficient heat is reaching the choke stat.

✳✳CAUTION

The choke housing and hot air inlet pipe or hose will be HOT to the touch; use caution to prevent burns.

3. If the choke housing and or heat inlet are cool to the touch, check for a loss of vacuum to the housing, restricted heat inlet pipe in the choke housing or choke heat pipe, or restricted passages in the manifold choke heat stove.

4. Replace or correct as necessary.

Float Level

This is an external check procedure.

1. Remove the air horn vent stack.

2. With engine idling and choke wide open, insert gauge J-9789-135, or equivalent, in vent slot or vent hole. Allow the gauge to float freely.

3. Observe the mark on the gauge that lines up with the top of the casting.

4. Setting should be within $\frac{1}{16}$ in. (2mm) of the specified float level setting.

5. If not within specified range, check fuel pressure.

6. If fuel pressure is correct, remove air horn and adjust float.

Mixture Control Solenoid

This is a mixture control solenoid travel test. Before checking the mixture control solenoid travel, it may be necessary to modify the float gauge J-9789-130 or equivalent (used to externally check the float level).

This should be done by filing or grinding the sufficient material off the gauge to allow for insertion down the vertical D-shaped hole in the air horn casting (located next to the idle air bleed valve cover).

Check that the gauge freely enters the D-shaped vent hole and does not bind. The gauge will also be used to determine the total mixture control solenoid travel.

With the engine off and the air cleaner removed, measure the control solenoid travel as follows:

1. Remove the air horn vent stack.

2. Insert a modified float gauge J-9789-130 or equivalent down the D-shaped vent hole. Press down on the gauge and release it.

3. Observe that the gauge moves freely and does not bind. With the gauge released (solenoid in the up position), be sure

to read it at eye level and record the mark on the gauge that lines up with the top of the air horn casting (upper edge).

4. Lightly press down on the gauge until bottomed (solenoid in the down position). Record the mark on the gauge that lines up with the top of the air horn casting.

5. Subtract the gauge up dimension from gauge dimension. Record the difference. This difference is total solenoid travel.

6. If total solenoid travel is not $\frac{1}{16}$-$\frac{1}{8}$ in. (2-3mm), perform the mixture control solenoid adjustments. If the difference is $\frac{1}{16}$-$\frac{1}{8}$ in. (2-3mm), proceed to the idle air bleed valve adjustment.

➡**If adjustment is required, it will be necessary to remove the air horn and drive out the mixture control solenoid screw plug from the under side of the air horn.**

Idle Load Compensator (ILC)

1. Inspect the condition of the tube cap covering the access to plunger travel adjustment screw. If missing or damaged, the diaphragm chamber will lose vacuum.

2. Hold throttle lever half open, to allow ILC to extend fully.

3. Apply finger pressure to the ILC plunger.

4. Apply 20 in. Hg (68 kPa) of vacuum to the ILC, plunger should begin to retract. If not replace the ILC.

5. Observe vacuum gauge, vacuum should hold for at least 20 seconds, if not replace the ILC.

6. Release vacuum from the ILC. The plunger should extend, if not replace the ILC.

Pulse Air Injection (PULSAIR)

All engines use the Pulsair air injection system, which uses exhaust system air pulses to siphon fresh air into the exhaust manifold. The injected air supports continued combustion of the hot exhaust gases in the exhaust manifold, reducing exhaust emissions. A secondary purpose of the Pulsair system is to introduce more oxygen into the exhaust system upstream of the catalytic converter, to supply the converter with the oxygen required for the oxidation reaction.

Air is drawn into the Pulsair valve through a hose connected to the air cleaner. The air passes through a check valve (there is one check valve for each cylinder, all check valves are installed in the Pulsair valve), then through a manifold pipe to the exhaust manifold. All manifold pipes are the same length, to prevent uneven pulsation. The check valves open during pulses of negative exhaust back pressure, admitting air into the manifold pipe and the exhaust manifold. During pulses of positive exhaust back pressure, the check valves close, preventing backfiring into the Pulsair valve and air cleaner.

The Pulsair check valves, hoses and pipes should be checked occasionally for leaks, cracks, or breaks.

REMOVAL & INSTALLATION

1. Remove the air cleaner case. Disconnect the rubber hose(s) from the Pulsair valve(s).

2. Disconnect the support bracket, if present. Some V6 engines have a Pulsair solenoid and bracket, which must be removed.

3. Unscrew the attaching nuts and remove the Pulsair tubes from the exhaust manifold(s).

To install:

4. First apply a light coat of clean oil to the ends of the Pulsair tubes.

5. Install the tubes to the exhaust manifold(s), tightening the nuts to 10-13 ft. lbs. (14-18 Nm). Connect the support bracket and, if applicable, the solenoid and bracket. Connect the rubber hose(s) and install the air cleaner.

Deceleration Valve

▶ See Figure 21

The purpose of the deceleration valve is to prevent backfiring in the exhaust system during deceleration. The normal position of the valve is closed. When deceleration causes a sudden vacuum increase in the vacuum signal lines, the pressure differential on the diaphragm will overcome the closing force of the spring, opening the valve and bleeding air into the intake manifold.

Air trapped in the chamber above the vacuum diaphragm will bleed at a calibrated rate through the delay valve portion of the integral check and delay valve, reducing the vacuum acting on the diaphragm. When the vacuum load on the diaphragm and the spring load equalize, the valve assembly will close, shutting off the air flow into the intake manifold.

The check valve portion of the check and delay valve provides quick balancing of chamber pressure when a sudden decrease in vacuum is caused by acceleration rather than deceleration.

Mixture Control Solenoid (M/C)

The fuel flow through the carburetor idle main metering circuits is controlled by a mixture control (M/C) solenoid located in the carburetor. The M/C solenoid changes the air/fuel mixture to the engine by controlling the fuel flow through the carburetor. The ECM/PCM controls the solenoid by providing a ground. When the solenoid is energized, the fuel flow through the carburetor is reduced, providing a leaner mixture. When the ECM/PCM removes the ground, the solenoid is de-energized, increasing the fuel flow and providing a richer mixture. The M/C solenoid is energized and de-energized at a rate of 10 times per second.

Throttle Position Sensor (TPS)

▶ See Figure 22

The throttle position sensor is mounted in the carburetor body and is used to supply throttle position information to the ECM/PCM. The ECM/PCM memory stores an average of operating conditions with the ideal air/fuel ratios for each of those conditions. When the ECM/PCM receives a signal that indicates throttle position change, it immediately shifts to the last remembered set of operating conditions that resulted in an ideal air/fuel ratio control. The memory is continually being updated during normal operations.

Idle Speed Control (ISC)

▶ See Figure 23

The idle speed control does just what its name implies-it controls the idle. The ISC is used to maintain low engine speeds while at the same time preventing stalling due to engine load changes. The system consists of a motor assembly mounted on the carburetor which moves the throttle lever so as to open or close the throttle blades.

The whole operation is controlled by the ECM/PCM. The ECM/PCM monitors engine load to determine the proper idle speed. To prevent stalling, it monitors the air conditioning compressor switch, the transaxle, the park/neutral switch and the ISC throttle switch. The ECM/PCM processes all this information and then uses it to control the ISC motor which in turn will vary the idle speed as necessary.

Electronic Spark Timing (EST)

All models use EST. The EST distributor, as described in an earlier section, contains no vacuum or centrifugal advance mechanism and uses a seven terminal HEI module. It has four

Fig. 21 Exploded view of the deceleration valve

Fig. 22 Throttle position sensor

Fig. 23 The idle speed control motor (ISC) is mounted on the side of the carburetor

wires going to a four terminal connector in addition to the connectors normally found on HEI distributors. A reference pulse, indicating engine rpm is sent to the ECM/PCM. The ECM/PCM determines the proper spark advance for the engine operating conditions and then sends an EST pulse back to the distributor.

Under most normal operating conditions, the ECM/PCM will control the spark advance. However, under certain operating conditions such as cranking or when setting base timing, the distributor is capable of operating without ECM/PCM control. This condition is called BYPASS and is determined by the BYPASS lead which runs from the ECM/PCM to the distributor. When the BYPASS lead is at the proper voltage (5), the ECM/PCM will control the spark. If the lead is grounded or open circuited, the HEI module itself will control the spark. Disconnecting the 4-terminal EST connector will also cause the engine to operate in the BYPASS mode.

Torque Converter Clutch (TCC)

All models with an automatic transaxle use a TCC. The ECM/PCM controls the converter by means of a solenoid mounted in the transaxle. When the vehicle speed reaches a certain level, the ECM energizes the solenoid and allows the torque converter to mechanically couple the transaxle to the engine. When the operating conditions indicate that the transaxle should operate as a normal fluid coupled transaxle, the ECM/PCM will de-energize the solenoid. Depressing the brake will also return the transaxle to normal automatic operation.

Catalytic Converter

▶ See Figure 24

The catalytic converter is a muffler-like container built into the exhaust system to aid in the reduction of exhaust emissions. The catalyst element consists of individual pellets or a honeycomb monolithic substrate coated with a noble metal such as platinum, palladium, rhodium or a combination. When the exhaust gases come into contact with the catalyst, a

chemical reaction occurs which will reduce the pollutants into harmless substances including water and carbon dioxide.

There are essentially two types of catalytic converters: an oxidizing type and a three-way type. The oxidizing type requires the addition of oxygen to spur the catalyst into reducing the engine's HC and CO emissions into H_2O and CO_2. The oxidizing catalytic converter, while effectively reducing HC and CO emissions, does little, if anything in the way of reducing NOx emissions. Thus, the three-way catalytic converter.

The three-way converter, unlike the oxidizing type, is capable of reducing HC, CO and NOx emissions, all at the same time. In theory, it seems impossible to reduce all three pollutants in one system since the reduction of HC and CO requires the addition of oxygen, while the reduction of NOx calls for the removal of oxygen. In actuality, the three-way system really can reduce all three pollutants, but only if the amount of oxygen in the exhaust system is precisely controlled. Due to this precise oxygen control requirement, the three-way converter system is used only in conjunction with an oxygen sensor system.

There are no service procedures required for the catalytic converter, although the converter body should be inspected occasionally for damage.

PRECAUTIONS

- Use only unleaded fuel.
- Avoid prolonged idling; the engine should run no longer than 20 minutes at curb idle and no longer than 10 minutes at fast idle.
- Do not disconnect any of the spark plug leads while the engine is running.
- Make engine compression checks as quickly as possible.

TESTING

At the present time there is no known way to reliably test catalytic converter operation in the field. The only reliable test

Fig. 24 The catalatic converter is a muffler-like device built into the exhaust system to aid in the reduction of exhaust emissions — 1985 Celebrity wagon shown

is a 12 hour and 40 minute soak test which must be done in a laboratory.

An infrared HC/CO tester is not sensitive enough to measure the higher tailpipe emissions from a failing converter. Thus, a bad converter may allow enough emissions to escape so that the car is no longer in compliance with Federal or state standards, but will still not cause the needle on a tester to move off zero.

The chemical reactions which occur inside a catalytic converter generate a great deal of heat. Most converter problems can be traced to fuel or ignition system problems which cause unusually high emissions. As a result of the increased intensity of the chemical reactions, the converter literally burns itself up.

A completely failed converter might cause a tester to show a slight reading. As a result, it is occasionally possible to detect one of these.

As long as you avoid severe overheating and the use of leaded fuels it is reasonably safe to assume that the converter is working properly. If you are in doubt, take the car to a diagnostic center that has a tester.

Early Fuel Evaporation (EFE)

All models are equipped with this system to reduce engine warm-up time, improve driveability and reduce emissions. The system is electric and uses a ceramic heater grid located underneath the primary bore of the carburetor as part of the carburetor insulator/gasket. When the ignition switch is turned on and the engine coolant temperature is low, voltage is applied to the EFE relay by the ECM/PCM. The EFE relay in turn energizes the heater grid. When the coolant temperature increases, the ECM/PCM de-energizes the relay which will then shut off the EFE heater.

REMOVAL & INSTALLATION

EFE Grid

▶ See Figure 25

1. Remove the air cleaner and disconnect the negative battery cable.
2. Tag and disconnect all electrical, vacuum connections from the carburetor.
3. Unattach the fuel lines and cap them to keep from fuel spilling out, make sure to have a rag handy for any messes.
4. Disconnect the EFE heater electrical lead.
5. Remove the carburetor.
6. Lift off the EFE heater grid.
To install:
7. Clean the surface of the manifold where the grid is to lie, along with the bottom of the carburetor.
8. Install the new EFE grid to the intake manifold.
9. Mount the carburetor, then install all the tagged vacuum lines and electrical leads to the carburetor.
10. Connect the fuel lines.
11. Double check all the lines and hoses are properly connected, then install the air cleaner assembly.
12. Connect the negative battery cable.
13. Adjust the carburetor if needed.

EFE Heater Relay

▶ See Figure 26

1. Disconnect the negative battery cable.
2. Remove the retaining bracket.
3. Tag and disconnect all electrical connections.
4. Unscrew the retaining bolts and remove the relay.
To install:
5. Install the new relay with the retaining bolts, tighten the bolts.
6. Connect the electrical wiring to the appropriate locations, then attach the retaining bracket.
7. Connect the negative battery cable.

CCC SYSTEM DIAGNOSTIC CHARTS

To properly diagnose driveability problems, refer to the diagnostic trouble code charts which appear later in this section. Make certain the charts cover the appropriate engine. If your

Fig. 25 The EFE grid is located under the carburetor

Fig. 26 The EFE heater relay is located near the fender skirt

check engine light is not lit, check for engine stored engine codes. If any codes are stored write them down for reference later. Clear the codes as described earlier. Road test the vehicle to see if any of the codes return. Never try to fix a code problem until you're sure that it comes back. It may have been an old code from years ago that was never cleared or a code that was set do to a rain storm, battery jump, etc.

After clearing any codes and checking that they do not return. If the car drives fine you're finished. But if there are no codes and the car runs poorly you'll need to check the symptoms charts. The problem is most likely not the computer or the devices it controls but the ignition system or engine mechanical.

If you do have a code(s) that returns start with the lowest code and follow the proper chart. You must follow every step of the chart and not jump from test to test or you'll never be certain to find and fix the real problem.

Start with the lowest to highest code chart, making sure to use the charts for your engine. If you have a 50 series code, like code 54. Always check those out first. They are rare but usually indicate a problem with the computer itself or its ability to test itself properly.

➡For carburetor overhaul or service refer to Section 5 (Fuel Systems).

Throttle Body Fuel Injection (TBI)

◆ See Figure 27

The electronic throttle body fuel injection system is a fuel metering system with the amount of fuel delivered by the throttle body injector(s) (TBI) determined by an electronic signal supplied by the Electronic Control Module (ECM) or Powertrain Control Module (PCM). The ECM/PCM monitors various engine and vehicle conditions to calculate the fuel delivery time (pulse width) of the injector(s). The fuel pulse may be modified by the ECM/PCM to account for special operating conditions, such as cranking, cold starting, altitude, acceleration, and deceleration.

The Throttle Body Injection (TBI) system provides a means of fuel distribution for controlling exhaust emissions within legislated limits. The TBI system, by precisely controlling the air/fuel mixture under all operating conditions, provides as near as possible complete combustion.

This is accomplished by using a Computer Control Module (ECM/PCM), a small on-board microcomputer that receives electrical inputs from various sensors about engine operating conditions. An oxygen sensor in the main exhaust stream functions to provide feedback information to the ECM/PCM as to the oxygen content, lean or rich, in the exhaust. The ECM/PCM uses this information from the oxygen sensor, and other sensors, to modify fuel delivery to achieve, as near as possible, an ideal air/fuel ratio of 14.7:1. This air/fuel ratio allows the 3-way catalytic converter to be more efficient in the conversion process of reducing exhaust emissions while at the same time providing acceptable levels of driveability and fuel economy.

COMPUTER CONTROL MODULE

The ECM/PCM program electronically signals the fuel injector in the TBI assembly to provide the correct quantity of fuel for a wide range of operating conditions. Several sensors are used to determine existing operating conditions and the ECM/PCM then signals the injector to provide the precise amount of fuel required.

The ECM/PCM used on TBI vehicles has a learning capability. If the battery is disconnected to clear diagnostic codes, or for repair, the learning process has to begin all over again. A change may be noted in vehicle performance. To teach the vehicle, make sure the vehicle is at operating temperature and drive at part throttle, under moderate acceleration and idle conditions, until performance returns.

The TBI assembly is centrally located on the intake manifold where air and fuel are distributed through a single bore in the throttle body, similar to a carbureted engine. Air for combustion is controlled by a single throttle valve which is connected to the accelerator pedal linkage by a throttle shaft and lever assembly. A special plate is located directly beneath the throttle valve to aid in mixture distribution.

Fuel for combustion is supplied by 1 or 2 fuel injector(s), mounted on the TBI assembly, whose metering tip is located directly above the throttle valve. The injector is pulsed or timed open or closed by an electronic output signal received from the ECM/PCM. The ECM/PCM receives inputs concerning engine operating conditions from the various sensors (coolant temperature sensor, oxygen sensor, etc.). The ECM/PCM, using this information, performs high speed calculations of engine fuel requirements and pulses or times the injector, open or closed, thereby controlling fuel and air mixtures to achieve, as near as possible, ideal air/fuel mixture ratios.

When the ignition key is turned **ON**, the ECM/PCM will initialize (start program running) and energize the fuel pump relay. The fuel pump pressurizes the system to approximately 10 psi. If the ECM/PCM does not receive a distributor reference pulse (telling the ECM/PCM the engine is turning) within 2 seconds, the ECM/PCM will then de-energize the fuel pump relay, turning off the fuel pump. If a distributor reference pulse is later received, the ECM/PCM will turn the fuel pump back on.

The ECM/PCM controls the exhaust emissions by modifying fuel delivery to achieve, as near as possible, and air/fuel ratio of 14.7:1. The injector on-time is determined by various inputs to the ECM/PCM. By increasing the injector pulse, more fuel is delivered, enriching the air/fuel ratio. Decreasing the injector pulse, leans the air/fuel ratio. Pulses are sent to the injector in 2 different modes: synchronized and non-synchronized.

Synchronized Mode

In synchronized mode operation, the injector is pulsed once for each distributor reference pulse. In dual injector throttle body systems, the injectors are pulse alternately.

Non-synchronized Mode
◆ See Figures 28 and 29

In non-synchronized mode operation, the injector is pulsed once every 12.5 milliseconds or 6.25 milliseconds depending on calibration. This pulse time is totally independent of distribu-

"A" CARLINE   RPO: LR8   (VIN R)   2.5L L4 TBI

COMPUTER HARNESS

C1 Electronic Control Module (ECM)
C2 ALDL Diagnostic Connector
C3 "Service Engine Soon" light
C4 ECM Power Fuse
C5 ECM Harness Grounds
C6 Fuse Panel
C8 Fuel Pump Test Connector
C9 Coolant "Temperature" Light

NOT ECM CONNECTED

N1   Crankcase Vent Valve (PCV)
N17 Fuel Vapor Canister

CONTROLLED DEVICES

1   Fuel Injector
2   Idle Air Control (IAC) Valve
3   Fuel Pump Relay
5   TCC Solenoid Connector
8   Cooling Fan Relay
13 A/C Compressor Relay
14 Direct Ignition System (DIS)
    Assembly

    Exhaust Gas Recirculation Valve

INFORMATION SENSORS

A Manifold Absolute Pressure (MAP)
   Sensor (Mounted on Air Cleaner)
B Oxygen (O_2) Sensor
C Throttle Position Sensor (TPS)
D Coolant Temperature Sensor (CTS)
G Vehicle Speed PM Generator
M Park/Neutral (P/N) Switch
S P/S Pressure Switch
T Manifold Air Temperature (MAT)
   Sensor

86814034

Fig. 27 TBI engine component location on the 2.5L (VIN R) engine

tor reference pulses. Non-synchronized mode results only under the following conditions:

- The fuel pulse width is too small to be delivered accurately by the injector (approximately 1.5 milliseconds)
- During the delivery of prime pulses (prime pulses charge the intake manifold with fuel during or just prior to engine starting)
- During acceleration enrichment
- During deceleration leanout

The basic TBI unit is made up of 2 major casting assemblies: (1) a throttle body with a valve to control airflow and (2) a fuel body assembly with an integral pressure regulator and fuel injector to supply the required fuel. An electronically operated device to control the idle speed and a device to provide information regarding throttle valve position are included as part of the TBI unit.

The fuel injector(s) is a solenoid-operated device controlled by the ECM/PCM. The incoming fuel is directed to the lower end of the injector assembly which has a fine screen filter surrounding the injector inlet. The ECM/PCM actuates the sole-

noid, which lifts a normally closed ball valve off a seat. The fuel under pressure is injected in a conical spray pattern at the walls of the throttle body bore above the throttle valve. The excess fuel passes through a pressure regulator before being returned to the vehicle's fuel tank.

The pressure regulator is a diaphragm-operated relief valve with injector pressure on one side and air cleaner pressure on the other. The function of the regulator is to maintain a constant pressure drop across the injector throughout the operating load and speed range of the engine.

The throttle body portion of the TBI may contain ports located at, above, or below the throttle valve. These ports generate the vacuum signals for the EGR valve, MAP sensor, and the canister purge system.

The Throttle Position Sensor (TPS) is a variable resistor used to convert the degree of throttle plate opening to an electrical signal to the ECM/PCM. The ECM/PCM uses this signal as a reference point of throttle valve position. In addition, an Idle Air Control (IAC) assembly, mounted in the throttle body is used to control idle speeds. A cone-shaped valve in the IAC assembly is located in an air passage in the throttle body that leads from the point beneath the air cleaner to below the throttle valve. The ECM/PCM monitors idle speeds and, depending on engine load, moves the IAC cone in the air passage to increase or decrease air bypassing the throttle valve to the intake manifold for control of idle speeds.

Cranking Mode
▶ **See Figure 30**

During engine crank, for each distributor reference pulse the ECM/PCM will deliver an injector pulse (synchronized). The crank air/fuel ratio will be used if the throttle position is less than 80% open. Crank air fuel is determined by the ECM/PCM and ranges from 1.5:1 at 33°F (36°C) to 14.7:1 at 201°F (94°C).

The lower the coolant temperature, the longer the pulse width (injector on-time) or richer the air/fuel ratio. The higher the coolant temperature, the less pulse width (injector on-time) or the leaner the air/fuel ratio.

Clear Flood Mode
▶ **See Figure 31**

If for some reason the engine should become flooded, provisions have been made to clear this condition. To clear the flood, the driver must depress the accelerator pedal enough to open to wide-open throttle position. The ECM/PCM then issues injector pulses at a rate that would be equal to an air/fuel ratio of 20:1. The ECM/PCM maintains this injector rate as long as the throttle remains wide open and the engine rpm is below 600. If the throttle position becomes less than 80%, the ECM/PCM then would immediately start issuing crank pulses to the injector calculated by the ECM/PCM based on the coolant temperature.

Run Mode
▶ **See Figures 32 and 33**

There are 2 different run modes. When the engine rpm is above 400, the system goes into open loop operation. In open loop operation, the ECM/PCM will ignore the signal from the oxygen (O_2) sensor and calculate the injector on-time based

1. Coolant temperature
2. Oxygen sensor
3. MAP
4. ECM
5. Injector
6. Distributor pulses
7. Throttle position sensor

86814031

Fig. 28 This non-synchronized mode of operation is for a single throttle body injection system

1. Coolant temperature
2. Throttle position sensor
3. Injector A
4. Injector B
5. Distributor pulses
6. ECM
7. MAP
8. Oxygen sensor

86814032

Fig. 29 This non-synchronized mode of operation is for a dual throttle body injection system

1. ON
2. Crank
3. Coolant temperature
4. ECM

5. Injector
6. Distributor pulses
7. Throttle position sensor

86814033

Fig. 30 During engine cranking, the ECM/PCM will deliver a synchronized injector pulse for each distributor reference pulse

1. ON
2. Crank
3. Throttle position sensor
4. Injector
5. Distributor pulses
6. ECM

86814035

Fig. 31 The clear flood mode is run through the ECM/PCM and distributor pulses

upon inputs from the coolant and manifold absolute pressure sensors.

During open loop operation, the ECM/PCM analyzes the following items to determine when the system is ready to go to the closed loop mode:

1. The oxygen sensor varying voltage output. (This is dependent on temperature.)

2. The coolant sensor must be above the specified temperature.

3. A specific amount of time must elapse after starting the engine. These values are stored in the PROM.

When these conditions have been met, the system goes into closed loop operation In closed loop operation, the ECM/PCM will modify the pulse width (injector on-time) based upon the signal from the oxygen sensor. The ECM/PCM will decrease the on-time if the air/fuel ratio is too rich, and will increase the on-time if the air/fuel ratio is too lean.

The pulse width, thus the amount of enrichment, is determined by manifold pressure change, throttle angle change, and coolant temperature. The higher the manifold pressure and the

1. Oxygen sensor
2. MAP
3. Coolant temperature
4. Bypass
5. Reference
6. EST
7. Throttle position sensor

86814036

Fig. 32 Run mode with the engine cold in open loop

wider the throttle opening, the wider the pulse width. The acceleration enrichment pulses are delivered non-synchronized. Any reduction in throttle angle will cancel the enrichment pulses. This way, quick movements of the accelerator will not over-enrich the mixture.

Acceleration Enrichment Mode

▶ See Figure 34

When the engine is required to accelerate, the opening of the throttle valve(s) causes a rapid increase in Manifold Absolute Pressure (MAP). This rapid increase in the manifold pressure causes fuel to condense on the manifold walls. The ECM/PCM senses this increase in throttle angle and MAP, then supplies additional fuel for a short period of time. This prevents the engine from stumbling due to too lean a mixture.

Deceleration Leanout Mode

▶ See Figure 35

Upon deceleration, a leaner fuel mixture is required to reduce emission of hydrocarbons (HC) and carbon monoxide

1. Oxygen sensor
2. Coolant temperature
3. ECM
4. Throttle position sensor
5. Injector
6. Distributor pulses
7. MAP

86814037

Fig. 33 Run mode with the engine cold in closed loop

1. A RAPIDLY INCREASING MAP WILL CAUSE FUEL TO CONDENSE ON THE MANIFOLD WALLS.
2. THE ECM WILL INCREASE THE INJECTOR ON TIME TO COMPENSATE.
3. COOLANT SENSOR
4. MAP
5. ACCELERATION ENRICHMENT PULSES ARE DELIVERED ASYCHRONOUSLY BASED UPON MANIFOLD PRESSURE AND THROTTLE ANGLE.
6. ECM
7. INJECTOR
8. DISTRIBUTOR PULSES
9. THROTTLE POSITION SENSOR

86814038

Fig. 34 Schematic of the acceleration enrichment mode

(CO). To adjust the injection on-time, the ECM/PCM uses the decrease in manifold pressure and the decrease in throttle position to calculate a decrease in pulse width. To maintain an idle fuel ratio of 14.7:1, fuel output is momentarily reduced. This is done because of the fuel remaining in the intake manifold during deceleration.

Deceleration Fuel Cut-Off Mode

The purpose of deceleration fuel cut-off is to remove fuel from the engine during extreme deceleration conditions. Deceleration fuel cut-off is based on values of manifold pressure, throttle position, and engine rpm stored in the calibration PROM. Deceleration fuel cut-off overrides the deceleration enleanment mode.

Battery Voltage Correction Mode

The purpose of battery voltage correction is to compensate for variations in battery voltage to fuel pump and injector response. The ECM/PCM modifies the pulse width by a correc-

tion factor in the PROM. When battery voltage decreases, pulse width increases.

Battery voltage correction takes place in all operating modes. When battery voltage is low, the spark delivered by the distributor may be low. To correct this low battery voltage problem, the ECM/PCM can do any or all of the following:
- Increase injector pulse width (increase fuel)
- Increase idle rpm
- Increase ignition dwell time

Fuel Cut-Off Mode

When the ignition is **OFF**, the ECM/PCM will not energize the injector. Fuel will also be cut off if the ECM/PCM does not receive a reference pulse from the distributor. To prevent dieseling, fuel delivery is completely stopped as soon as the engine is stopped. The ECM/PCM will not allow any fuel supply until it receives distributor reference pulses which prevents flooding.

Backup Mode

When in this mode, the ECM/PCM is operating on the fuel backup logic calibrated by the Cal-Pak. The Cal-Pak is used to control the fuel delivery if the ECM/PCM fails. This mode verifies that the backup feature is working properly. The parameters that can be read on a scan tool in this mode are not much use for service.

Highway Mode

When driven at highway speeds the system may enter highway or semi-closed loop mode. This improves fuel economy by leaning out fuel mixture slightly. The ECM/PCM must see correct engine temperature, ignition timing, canister activity and a constant vehicle speed before if will enter this mode. The system will switch back to closed loop periodically to check all system functions.

A scan tool determines highway mode by looking at the integrator/block learn values and oxygen sensor voltage. Integrator and block learn will show very little change and the oxygen sensor voltage is be less than 100 millivolts.

1. COOLANT SENSOR
2. UPON DECELERATION, THE ECM USES THE DECREASE IN MANIFOLD PRESSURE (MAP) AND THE DECREASE IN THROTTLE POSITION TO CALCULATE A DECREASE IN PULSE WIDTH.
3. ECM
4. THROTTLE POSITION SENSOR
5. INJECTOR
6. DISTRIBUTOR PULSES
7. MAP

86814039

Fig. 35 Schematic of the deceleration leanout mode

DLC/ALCL/ALDL Connector

The Assembly Line Communication Link (ALCL) or Assembly Line Diagnostic Link (ALDL) is now called the Data Link Connector (DLC). The diagnostic connector is usually located in the passenger compartment. It has terminals which are used in the assembly plant to check that the engine is operating properly before it leaves the plant. This connector is a very useful tool in diagnosing fuel injected engines. Important information from the ECM/PCM is available at this terminal and can be read with one of the many popular scanner tools.

FUEL INJECTION SUBSYSTEMS

Electronic Fuel Injection (EFI) is the name given to the entire fuel injection system. Various subsystems are combined to form the overall system. These subsystems are:

- Fuel supply system
- Throttle Body Injector (TBI) assembly
- Idle Air Control (IAC)
- Computer Control Module (ECM/PCM)
- Data sensors
- Electronic Spark Timing (EST)
- Emission controls

Fuel Supply System

▶ See Figures 36 and 37

Fuel, supplied by an electric fuel pump mounted in the fuel tank, passes through an in-line fuel filter to the TBI assembly. To control fuel pump operation, a fuel pump relay is used.

When the ignition switch is turned to the **ON** position, the fuel pump relay activates the electric fuel pump for 1.5-2.0 seconds to prime the injector. If the ECM/PCM does not receive reference pulses from the distributor after this time, the ECM/PCM signals the relay to turn the fuel pump off. The relay will once again activate the fuel pump when the ECM/PCM receives distributor reference pulses.

The oil pressure sender is the backup for the fuel pump relay. The sender has 2 circuits, 1 for the instrument cluster

1 FUEL INJECTOR AND PRESSURE REGULATOR	**3** FUEL PUMP AND SENDING UNIT
2 FUEL RETURN LINE	**4** FUEL LINE
	5 FUEL FILTER

86814040

Fig. 37 Fuel pump supply system on a TBI vehicle

light or gauge, the other to activate the fuel pump if the relay fails. If the fuse relay has failed, the sender activates the fuel pump when oil pressure reaches 4 psi. Thus a failed fuel pump relay would cause a longer crank, especially in cold weather. If the fuel pump fails, a no start condition exists.

Throttle Body Injector (TBI) Assembly

The basic TBI model 700 is used on 4-cylinder engines, is made up of 2 major casting assemblies: (1) a throttle body with a valve to control airflow and (2) a fuel body assembly with an integral pressure regulator and fuel injector to supply the required fuel. A device to control idle speed (IAC) and a device to provide information about throttle valve position (TPS) are included as part of the TBI unit.

The model 220 is used on V6 and V8 engines, consists of 3 major castings. (1) fuel meter cover with pressure regulator, (2) Fuel meter body with injectors and (3) throttle body with IAC valve and TPS sensor.

The throttle body portion of the TBI unit may contain ports located at, above, or below the throttle valve. These ports generate the vacuum signals for the EGR valve, MAP sensor, and the canister purge system.

The fuel injector is a solenoid-operated device controlled by the ECM/PCM. The incoming fuel is directed to the lower end of the injector assembly which has a fine screen filter surrounding the injector inlet. The ECM/PCM turns on the solenoid, which lifts a normally closed ball valve off a seat. The fuel, under pressure, is injected in a conical spray pattern at the walls of the throttle body bore above the throttle valve. The excess fuel passes through a pressure regulator before being returned to the vehicle fuel tank.

The pressure regulator is a diaphragm-operated relief valve with the injector pressure on one side, and the air cleaner pressure on the other. The function of the regulator is to maintain constant pressure (approximately 11 psi or 76 kPa) to the injector throughout the operating loads and speed ranges of the engine. If the regulator pressure is too low, below 9 psi (62 kPa), it can cause poor performance. Too high a pressure could cause detonation and a strong fuel odor.

1 OIL LAMP	
2 OIL PRESSURE SWITCH	**6** INSTRUMENT PANEL
3 FUEL PUMP RELAY	**7** IGNITION SWITCH
4 FUEL PUMP	**8** BULKHEAD
5 ECM	**9** ENGINE

86814041

Fig. 36 Fuel pump wiring circuit

Idle Air Control (IAC)

▶ See Figure 38

The purpose of the Idle Air Control (IAC) system is to control engine idle speed while preventing stalls due to changes in engine load. The IAC assembly, mounted on the throttle body, controls bypass air around the throttle plate. By extending or retracting a conical valve, a controlled amount of air can move around the throttle plate. If rpm is too low, more air is diverted around the throttle plate to increase rpm.

During idle, the proper position of the IAC valve is calculated by the ECM/PCM based on battery voltage, coolant temperature, engine load, and engine rpm. If the rpm drops below a specified rate, the throttle plate is closed. The ECM/PCM will then calculate a new valve position.

Three different designs are used for the IAC conical valve. The first design used is single 35 taper while the second design used is a dual taper. The third design is a blunt valve. Care should be taken to insure use of the correct design when service replacement is required.

The IAC motor has 255 different positions or steps. The zero, or reference position, is the fully extended position at which the pintle is seated in the air bypass seat and no air is allowed to bypass the throttle plate. When the motor is fully retracted, maximum air is allowed to bypass the throttle plate. When the motor is fully retracted, maximum air is allowed to bypass the throttle plate.

The ECM/PCM always monitors how many steps it has extended or retracted the pintle from the zero or reference position; thus, it always calculates the exact position of the motor. Once the engine has started and the vehicle has reached approximately 40 mph, the ECM/PCM will extend the motor 255 steps from whatever position it is in. This will bottom out the pintle against the seat. The ECM/PCM will call this position 0 and thus keep its zero reference updated.

The IAC only affects the engine's idle characteristics. If it is stuck fully open, idle speed is too high (too much air enters the throttle bore) If it is stuck closed, idle speed is too low (not enough air entering). If it is stuck somewhere in the middle, idle may be rough, and the engine won't respond to load changes.

SINGLE TAPER VALVE

DUAL TAPER VALVE

BLUNT PINTLE

86814042

Fig. 38 The three different designs of the IAC valve

Idle Speed Control (ISC)

Incorrect diagnosis and/or misunderstanding of the idle speed control systems used on fuel injected engines may lead to unnecessary replacement of the IAC valve. Engine idle speed is controlled by the ECM/PCM which changes the idle speed by moving the IAC valve. The ECM/PCM adjusts idle speed in response to fluctuations in engine load (A/C, power steering, electrical loads, etc.) to maintain acceptable idle quality and proper exhaust emission performance.

The following is provided to help you better understand the system. Asking yourself questions that a mechanic would ask will help you narrow down the problem area.

Rough Idle/Low Idle Speed

The ECM/PCM will respond to increases in engine load, which would cause a drop in idle speed, by moving the IAC valve to maintain proper idle speed. After the induced load is removed the ECM/PCM will return the idle speed to the proper level.

During A/C compressor operation (MAX, BI-LEVEL, NORM or DEFROST mode) the ECM/PCM will increase idle speed in response to an A/C-ON signal, thereby compensating for any drop in idle speed due to compressor load. On some vehicles, the ECM/PCM will also increase the idle speed in response to high power steering loads.

During periods of especially heavy loads (A/C-ON plus parking maneuvers) significant effects on idle quality may be experienced. These effects are more pronounced on 4-cylinder engines. Abnormally low idle, rough idle and idle shake may occur if the ECM/PCM does not receive the proper signals from the monitored systems.

High Idle Speed/Warm-Up Idle Speed (No Kickdown)

Engine idle speeds as high as 2100 rpm may be experienced during cold starts to quickly raise the catalytic converter to operating temperature for proper exhaust emissions performance. The idle speed attained after a cold start is ECM/PCM controlled and will not drop for 45 seconds regardless of driver attempts to kickdown.

It is important to note that fuel injected engines have no accelerator pump or choke. Idle speed during warm-up is entirely ECM/PCM controlled and cannot be changed by accelerator kickdown or pumping.

Abnormally low idle speeds are usually caused by an ECM/PCM system-controlled or monitored irregularity, while the most common cause for abnormally high idle speed is an induction (intake air) leak. The idle air control valve may occasionally lose its memory function, and it has an ECM/PCM programmed method of relearning the correct idle position. This reset, when required, will occur the next time the car exceeds 35 mph (56 km/h). At that time, the ECM/PCM seats the pintle of the IAC valve in the throttle body to determine a reference point. Then it backs out a fixed distance to maintain proper idle speed.

SENSORS

A variety of sensors provide information to the ECM/PCM regarding engine operating characteristics. These sensors and their functions are described below. Be sure to take note that not every sensor described is used with every engine application.

Coolant Temperature (ECT)

The Engine Coolant Temperature Sensor (ECT) is a thermister (a resistor which changes value based on temperature) mounted on the engine coolant stream. As the temperature of the engine coolant changes, the resistance of the coolant sensor changes. Low coolant temperature produces a high resistance (100,000 ohms at 40°C/40°F), while high temperature causes low resistance (70 ohms at 130°C/266°F).

The ECM/PCM supplies a 5 volt signal to the coolant sensor and measures the voltage that returns. By measuring the voltage change, the ECM/PCM determines the engine coolant temperature. The voltage will be high when the engine is cold and low when the engine is hot. This information is used to control fuel management, IAC, spark timing, EGR, canister purge and other engine operating conditions.

A failure in the coolant sensor circuit should either set a Code 14 or 15. These codes indicate a failure in the coolant temperature sensor circuit.

Oxygen

The exhaust oxygen sensor is mounted in the exhaust system where it can monitor the oxygen content of the exhaust gas stream. The oxygen content in the exhaust reacts with the oxygen sensor to produce a voltage output. This voltage ranges from approximately 100 millivolts (high oxygen — lean mixture) to 900 millivolts (low oxygen — rich mixture).

By monitoring the voltage output of the oxygen sensor, the ECM/PCM will determine what fuel mixture command to give to the injector (lean mixture = low voltage and a rich command; rich mixture = high voltage and a lean command).

Remember that oxygen sensor indicates to the ECM/PCM what is happening in the exhaust. It does not cause things to happen. It is a type of gauge: high oxygen content = lean mixture; low oxygen content = rich mixture. The ECM/PCM adjusts fuel to keep the system working.

The oxygen sensor, if open should set a Code 13. A constant low voltage in the sensor circuit should set a Code 44 while a constant high voltage in the circuit should set a Code 45. Codes 44 and 45 could also be set as a result of fuel system problems.

Manifold Absolute Pressure

The Manifold Absolute Pressure (MAP) sensor measures the changes in the intake manifold pressure which result from engine load and speed changes. The pressure measured by the MAP sensor is the difference between barometric pressure (outside air) and manifold pressure (vacuum). A closed throttle engine coastdown would produce a relatively low MAP value (approximately 20-35 kPa), while wide-open throttle would produce a high value (100 kPa). This high value is produced when the pressure inside the manifold is the same as outside the manifold, and 100% of outside air (or 100 kPa) is being measured. This MAP output is the opposite of what you would measure on a vacuum gauge. The use of this sensor also allows the ECM/PCM to adjust automatically for different altitude.

The ECM/PCM sends a 5 volt reference signal to the MAP sensor. As the MAP changes, the electrical resistance of the sensor also changes. By monitoring the sensor output voltage the ECM/PCM can determine the manifold pressure. A higher pressure, lower vacuum (high voltage) requires more fuel, while a lower pressure, higher vacuum (low voltage) requires less fuel. The ECM/PCM uses the MAP sensor to control fuel delivery and ignition timing. A failure in the MAP sensor circuit should set a Code 33 or Code 34.

Intake Air Temperature

The Intake Air Temperature (IAT) and Manifold Air Temperature (MAT) are the same sensor. This sensor is a thermistor mounted in the intake manifold or air intake. A thermistor is a resistor which changes resistance based on temperature. Low manifold air temperature produces a high resistance (100,000 ohms at 40°F/40°C), while high temperature cause low resistance (70 ohms at 266°F/130°C).

The ECM/PCM supplies a 5 volt signal to the MAT/IAT sensor through a resistor in the ECM/PCM and monitors the voltage. The voltage will be high when the manifold air is cold and low when the air is hot. By monitoring the voltage, the ECM/PCM calculates the air temperature and uses this data to help determine the fuel delivery and spark advance. A failure in the MAT/IAT circuit should set either a Code 23 or Code 25.

Vehicle Speed

▶ See Figure 39

➡ **A vehicle equipped with a speed sensor, should not be driven without a the speed sensor connected, as idle quality may be affected. Also extreme poor gas mileage and a code will be stored in the computers memory.**

The Vehicle Speed Sensor (VSS) is mounted behind the speedometer in the instrument cluster or on the transaxle/speedometer drive gear. It provides electrical pulses to the ECM/PCM from the speedometer head. The pulses indicate the road speed. The ECM/PCM uses this information to operate the IAC, canister purge, and TCC.

Some vehicles equipped with digital instrument clusters use a Permanent Magnet (PM) generator to provide the VSS signal. The PM generator is located in the transaxle and replaces the speedometer cable. The signal from the PM generator drives a stepper motor which drives the odometer. A failure in the VSS circuit should set a Code 24.

Throttle Position

▶ See Figure 40

The Throttle Position Sensor (TPS) is connected to the throttle shaft and is controlled by the throttle mechanism. A 5 volt reference signal is sent to the TPS from the ECM/PCM. As the throttle valve angle is changed (accelerator pedal moved), the resistance of the TPS also changes. At a closed throttle position, the resistance of the TPS is high, so the output voltage to the ECM/PCM will be low (approximately 0.5 volts). As the throttle plate opens, the resistance decreases so that, at wide open throttle, the output voltage should be approximately 5 volts. At closed throttle position, the voltage at the TPS should be less than 1.25 volts.

1. Reflector plate
2. Speedometer frame
3. VVS and photo cell
4. Buffer circuit
5. Battery voltage
6. Ground
7. VVS output

86814043

Fig. 39 The vehicle speed sensor is mounted behind the speedometer in the instrument panel or on the transaxle/speedometer drive gear

1. Throttle body
2. Throttle position sensor
3. Throttle valve

86814044

Fig. 40 A 5 volt reference signal is sent to the TPS from the ECM/PCM

By monitoring the output voltage from the TPS, the ECM/PCM can determine fuel delivery based on throttle valve angle (driver demand). The TPS can either be misadjusted, shorted, open or loose. Misadjustment might result in poor idle or poor wide-open throttle performance. An open TPS signals the ECM/PCM that the throttle is always closed, resulting in poor performance. This usually sets a Code 22. A shorted TPS gives the ECM/PCM a constant wide-open throttle signal and should set a Code 21. A loose TPS indicates to the ECM that the throttle is moving. This causes intermittent bursts of fuel from the injector and an unstable idle. On some vehicles, the TPS is adjustable and therefore can be adjusted to correct any complications caused by to high or to low of a voltage signal.

Crankshaft and Camshaft
▶ See Figures 41 and 42

These sensors are mounted on the engine block, near the engine crankshaft, and also near the camshaft on some en-

gines. The sensors are used to send a signal through the Direct Ignition System (DIS) module to the ECM. The ECM uses this reference signal to calculate engine speed and crankshaft position. There are several names for these sensors, 3X and 24X Crankshaft Position Sensor (CPS).

In a typical 4 cylinder engine application, a sensor is mounted with the ignition module and 2 ignition coils to comprise the direct ignition assembly. When mounted on the engine block, the sensor tip is very close to a metal disk wheel with slots which is mounted on the crankshaft.

The sensor tip contains a small magnet and a small coil of wire. As the metal disk wheel with the slots rotates past the sensor tip, the magnetic field of the permanent magnet is changed and a voltage is induced into the coil. This voltage signal is sent to the ignition module. The ignition module is able to determine engine speed from the frequency of the voltage curve, which changes with engine speed.

A 6-cylinder engine may use a different type of sensor called a hall effect switch. With the direct ignition connected to the vehicle electrical system, the system voltage is applied to the hall effect switch located near the tip of the sensor. A small permanent magnet creates a magnetic field in the hall effect switch circuit. As the disc wheel with the slots rotates past the sensor tip, the magnetic field in the hall effect switch changes and a change in the voltage occurs at the hall effect switch output terminal.

Since this terminal is connect to the ignition module, the module senses this change in voltage and correlates the frequency of the voltage curve to determine the engine speed. The ignition module then uses this voltage input to help determine when to close and open the ignition coil primary circuit and fire the spark plug.

SWITCHES

Park/Neutral Switch

➡Vehicle should not be driven with the park/neutral switch disconnected, as idle quality may be affected in PARK or NEUTRAL and a Code 24 (VSS) may be set.

1 Engine block assembly
2 Crankshaft position (CKP) sensor

86812067

Fig. 41 3X Crankshaft Position Sensor (CKP) mounting on 3.1L (VIN M) engine

1 Camshaft position sensor
2 Bolt/Screw - torque to 10 Nm (8 lb.ft.)
3 Engine block assembly

86812070

Fig. 42 Camshaft sensor mounting location on 3.1L (VIN M) engine

This switch indicates to the ECM/PCM when the transaxle is in **P** or **N**. The information is used by the ECM for control on the torque converter clutch, EGR, and the idle air control valve operation.

Air Conditioner Request Signal

This signal indicates to the ECM/PCM that an air conditioning mode is selected at the switch and that the A/C low pressure switch is closed. The ECM/PCM controls the A/C and adjusts the idle speed in response to this signal.

Torque Converter Clutch (TCC) Solenoid

▶ See Figure 43

The purpose of the Torque Converter Clutch (TCC) system is designed to eliminate power loss by the converter (slippage) to increase fuel economy. By locking the converter clutch, a more effective coupling to the flywheel is achieved. The converter clutch is operated by the ECM/PCM controlled torque converter clutch solenoid.

Power Steering Pressure (PSPS)

The Power Steering Pressure Switch (PSPS) is used so that the power steering oil pressure pump load will not effect the engine idle. Turning the steering wheel increase the power steering oil pressure and pump load on the engine. The power steering pressure switch will close before the load can cause an idle problem.

Oil Pressure

The oil pressure switch is usually mounted on the back of the engine, just below the intake manifold. Some vehicles use the oil pressure switch as a parallel power supply, with the fuel pump relay and will provide voltage to the fuel pump, after approximately 4 psi (28 kPa) of oil pressure is reached. This switch will also help prevent engine seizure by shutting off the power to the fuel pump and causing the engine to stop when the oil pressure is lower than 4 psi (28 kPa).

IGNITION

Various components are used in conjunction with the ignition system. Below are the basics for the TBI.

Electronic Spark Timing (EST)

Electronic Spark Timing (EST) is used on all engines. The EST distributor contains no vacuum or centrifugal advance and uses a 7-terminal distributor module. It also has 4 wires going to a 4-terminal connector in addition to the connectors normally found on HEI distributors. A reference pulse, indicating both engine rpm and crankshaft position, is sent to the ECM/PCM. The ECM/PCM determines the proper spark advance for the engine operating conditions and sends an EST pulse to the distributor.

The EST system is designed to optimize spark timing for better control of exhaust emissions and for fuel economy improvements. The ECM/PCM monitors information from various engine sensors, computes the desired spark timing and changes the timing accordingly. A backup spark advance system is incorporated in the module in case of EST failure.

Electronic Spark Control (ESC)

▶ See Figures 44, 45, 46, 47 and 48

When engines are equipped with Electronic Spark Control (ESC) in conjunction with EST, ESC is used to reduce spark advance under conditions of detonation. A knock sensor signals a separate ESC controller to retard the timing when it senses engine knock. The ESC controller signals the ECM/PCM which reduces spark advance until no more signals are received from the knock sensor.

Direct Ignition System (DIS)

▶ See Figures 49 and 50

Components of the Direct Ignition System (DIS) are a coil pack, ignition module, crankshaft reluctor ring, magnetic sensor and the ECM/PCM. The coil pack consists of 2 separate, interchangeable, ignition coils. These coils operate in the same manner as previous coils. Two coils are needed because each coil fires for 2 cylinders. The ignition module is located under

Fig. 43 The converter clutch is operated by the ECM/PCM controlled torque converter clutch solenoid

Fig. 44 Electronic Spark Control (ECS) schematic

Fig. 45 Electronic spark control timing inputs

Fig. 46 Electronic spark control timing circuit during cranking mode

Fig. 47 Electronic spark control timing circuit during running mode

Fig. 48 Electronic spark control knock sensor circuit

the coil pack and is connected to the ECM/PCM by a 6 pin connector. The ignition module controls the primary circuits to the coils, turning them on and off and controls spark timing below 400 rpm and if the ECM/PCM bypass circuit becomes open or grounded.

The magnetic pickup sensor inserts through the engine block, just above the pan rail in proximity to the crankshaft reluctor ring. Notches in the crankshaft reluctor ring trigger the magnetic pickup sensor to provide timing information to the ECM/PCM. The magnetic pickup sensor provides a cam signal to identify correct firing sequence and crank signals to trigger each coil at the proper time.

This system uses EST and control wires from the ECM/PCM, as with the distributor systems. The ECM/PCM controls the timing using crankshaft position, engine rpm, engine temperature and manifold absolute pressure sensing.

EMISSION CONTROL

Various components are used to control exhaust emissions from a vehicle. These components are controlled by the ECM based on different engine operating conditions. These components are described in the following paragraphs. Not all components are used on all engines.

Exhaust Gas Recirculation (EGR) System

EGR is a oxides of nitrogen (NOx) control which recycles exhaust gases through the combustion cycle by admitting exhaust gases into the intake manifold. The amount of exhaust gas admitted is adjusted by a vacuum controlled valve in response to engine operating conditions. If the valve is open, the recirculated exhaust gas is released into the intake manifold to be drawn into the combustion chamber.

The integral exhaust pressure modulated EGR valve uses a transducer responsive to exhaust pressure to modulate the vacuum signal to the EGR valve. The vacuum signal is provided by an EGR vacuum port in the throttle body valve.

Fig. 49 DIS misfire under load schematic — 2.5L (VIN R) engine

Fig. 50 DIS misfire at idle schematic — 2.5L (VIN R) engine

Under conditions when exhaust pressure is lower than the control pressure, the EGR signal is reduced by an air bleed within the transducer. Under conditions when exhaust pressure is higher than the control pressure, the air bleed is closed and the EGR valve responds to an unmodified vacuum signal. Physical arrangement of the valve components will vary depending on whether the control pressure is positive or negative.

Positive Crankcase Ventilation (PCV) System

A closed Positive Crankcase Ventilation (PCV) system is used to provide more complete scavenging of crankcase vapors. Fresh air from the air cleaner is supplied to the crankcase, mixed with blow-by gases and then passed through a PCV valve into the induction system.

The primary mode of crankcase ventilation control is through the PCV valve which meters the mixture of fresh air and blowby gases into the induction system at a rate dependent upon manifold vacuum.

To maintain the idle quality, the PCV valve restricts the ventilation system flow whenever intake manifold vacuum is

designed to allow excessive amounts of blow-by gases to backflow through the breather assembly into the air cleaner and through the throttle body to be consumed by normal combustion.

Thermostatic Air Cleaner (TAC) System

To assure optimum driveability under varying climatic conditions, a heated intake air system is used on engines. This system is designed to warm the air entering the TBI to insure uniform inlet air temperatures. Under this condition, the fuel injection system can be calibrated to efficiently reduce exhaust emission and to eliminate throttle blade icing. The Thermac system used on fuel injected vehicles operates identically to other Thermac systems.

Evaporative Emission Control (EEC) Systems

The basic evaporative emission control system used on all vehicles uses the carbon canister storage method. This method transfers fuel vapor to an activated carbon storage device for retention when the vehicle is not operating. A ported vacuum signal is used for purging vapors stored in the canister.

CONTROLLED CANISTER PURGE

The ECM/PCM controls a solenoid valve which controls vacuum to the purge valve in the charcoal canister. In open loop, before a specified time has expired and below a specified rpm, the solenoid valve is energized and blocks vacuum to the purge valve. When the system is in closed loop, after a specified time and above a specified rpm, the solenoid valve is de-energized and vacuum can be applied to the purge valve. This releases the collected vapors into the intake manifold. On systems not using an ECM/PCM controlled solenoid, a Thermo Vacuum Valve (TVV) is used to control purge. See the appropriate vehicle sections for checking procedures.

AIR MANAGEMENT CONTROL

The air management system aids in the reduction of exhaust emissions by supplying air to either the catalytic converter, engine exhaust manifold, or to the air cleaner. The ECM/PCM controls the air management system by energizing or de-energizing an air switching valve. Operation of the air switching valve is dependent upon such engine operating characteristics as coolant temperature, engine load, and acceleration (or deceleration), all of which are sensed by the ECM/PCM.

PULSAIR REACTOR SYSTEM

▶ See Figure 51

The Pulsair Injection Reactor (PAIR) system utilizes exhaust pressure pulsations to draw air into the exhaust system. Fresh air from the clean side of the air cleaner supplies filtered air to avoid dirt build-up on the check valve seat. The air cleaner also serves as a muffler for noise reduction.The internal mechanism of the Pulsair valve reacts to 3 distinct conditions.

• If the pressure is positive, the disc is forced to the closed position and no exhaust gas is allowed to flow past the valve and into the air supply line.

• If there is a negative pressure (vacuum) in the exhaust system at the valve, the disc will open, allowing fresh air to mix with the exhaust gases.

• Due to the inertia of the system, the disc ceases to follow the pressure pulsations at high engine rpm. At this point, the disc remains closed, preventing any further fresh air flow.

The firing of the engine creates a pulsating flow of exhaust gases which are of positive (+) or negative (-) pressure. This pressure or vacuum is transmitted through external tubes to the Pulsair valve.

CATALYTIC CONVERTER

Of all emission control devices available, the catalytic converter is the most effective in reducing tailpipe emissions. The major tailpipe pollutants are hydrocarbons (HC), carbon monoxide (CO), and oxides of nitrogen (NOx).

SERVICE PRECAUTIONS

When working around any part of the fuel system, take precautionary steps to prevent fire and/or explosion:

• Disconnect negative terminal from battery (except when testing with battery voltage is required).
• When possible, use a flashlight instead of a drop light.
• Keep all open flame and smoking material out of the area.

• Use a shop cloth or similar to catch fuel when opening a fuel system.
• Relieve fuel system pressure before servicing.
• Use eye protection.
• Always keep a dry chemical (class B) fire extinguisher near the area.

➡**Due to the amount of fuel pressure in the fuel lines, before doing any work to the fuel system, the fuel system should be depressurized.**

Electrostatic Discharge Damage

Electronic components used in the control system are often design to carry very low voltage and are very susceptible to damage caused by electrostatic discharge. It is possible for less than 100 volts of static electricity to cause damage to some electronic components. By comparison it takes as much as 4000 volts for a person to even feel the zap of a static discharge.

There are several ways for a person to become statically charged. The most common methods of charging are by friction and induction. An example of charging by friction is a person sliding across a car seat, in which a charge as much as 25,000 volts can build up. Charging by induction occurs when a person with well insulated shoes stands near a highly charged object and momentarily touches ground. Charges of the same polarity are drained off, leaving the person highly charged with the opposite polarity. Static charges of either type can cause damage, therefore, it is important to use care when handling and testing electronic components.

➡**To prevent possible electrostatic discharge damage to the ECM/PCM, do not touch the connector pins or soldered components on the circuit board. When handling a PROM, Mem-Cal or Cal-Pak, do not touch the component leads and remove the integrated circuit from the carrier.**

DIAGNOSTIC ENGINE COMPUTER CODES

Data Link Connector (DLC)

▶ See Figure 52

The Data Link Connector (DLC) is also known as the Assembly Line Communication Link (ALCL) and also known as the Assembly Line Diagnostic Link (ALDL). It is a diagnostic connector located in the passenger compartment usually under the instrument panel, and is sometimes called the DIAGNOSTIC CONNECTOR. The assembly plant were the vehicles originate use the connector to check the engine for proper operation before it leaves the plant. Terminal B is the diagnostic TEST terminal (lead) and it can be connected to terminal A, or ground, to enter the Diagnostic mode or the Field Service Mode.

Reading Codes and Diagnostic Modes

This information is able to be read by putting the ECM/PCM into 1 of 4 different modes. These modes are entered by inserting a specific amount of resistance between the DLC connector terminals A and B. The modes and resistances needed to enter these modes are as follows:

1 VALVE ASM.
2 PIPE ASM.
3 BRACKET
4 GROMMET
5 VALVE
6 ACTUATOR
7 BRACE
8 GROUND STRAP

TO CYLINDER HEAD

FILTERED AIR

DISC

+ PRESSURE

VIEW A

TO CYLINDER HEAD

FILTERED AIR

DISC

− PRESSURE

VIEW B

86814056

Fig. 51 The system and operation of the pulsair injection system

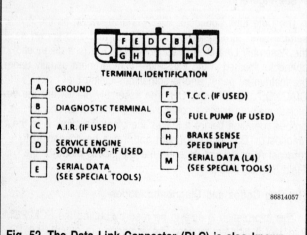

TERMINAL IDENTIFICATION

A	GROUND	F	T.C.C. (IF USED)
B	DIAGNOSTIC TERMINAL	G	FUEL PUMP (IF USED)
C	A.I.R. (IF USED)	H	BRAKE SENSE SPEED INPUT
D	SERVICE ENGINE SOON LAMP - IF USED	M	SERIAL DATA (L4) (SEE SPECIAL TOOLS)
E	SERIAL DATA (SEE SPECIAL TOOLS)		

86814057

Fig. 52 The Data Link Connector (DLC) is also known as the Assembly Line Communication Link (ALCL) and as the Assembly Line Diagnostic Link (ALDL)

DIAGNOSTIC MODES — 0 OHMS

When 0 resistance is between terminals A and B of the DLC connector, the diagnostic mode is entered. There are 2 positions to this mode. One with the engine **OFF**, but the ignition **ON**; the other is when the engine is running called Field Service Mode.

If the diagnostic mode is entered with the engine in the **OFF** position, trouble codes will flash and the idle air control motor will pulsate in and out. Also, the relays and solenoids are energized with the exception of the fuel pump and injector.

As a bulb and system check, the SERVICE ENGINE SOON light will come on with the ignition switch **ON** and the engine not running. When the engine is started, the SERVICE ENGINE SOON light will turn off. If the SERVICE ENGINE SOON light remains on, the self-diagnostic system has detected a problem.

If the B terminal is then grounded with the ignition **ON**, engine not running, each trouble code will flash and repeat 3 times. If more than 1 problem has been detected, each trouble code will flash 3 times. Trouble codes will flash in numeric order (lowest number first). The trouble code series will repeat as long as the B terminal is grounded.

A trouble code indicates a problem in a given circuit (Code 14, for example, indicates a problem in the coolant sensor circuit; this includes the coolant sensor, connector harness, and ECM/PCM). The procedure for pinpointing the problem can be found in diagnosis. Similar charts are provided for each code.

Also in this mode all ECM/PCM controlled relays and solenoids except the fuel pump relay. This allows checking the circuits which may be difficult to energize without driving the vehicle and being under particular operating conditions. The IAC valve will move to its fully extended position on most models, block the idle air passage. This is useful in checking the minimum idle speed.

FIELD SERVICE MODE — 0 OHMS

When the DLC connector terminal B is grounded with the engine running, the ECM/PCM goes into the field service mode. In this mode, the SERVICE ENGINE SOON light flashes closed or open loop and indicates the rich/lean status of the engine. The ECM/PCM runs the engine at a fixed ignition timing advanced above the base setting.

The SERVICE ENGINE SOON light will show whether the system is in Open loop or Closed loop. In Open loop the SERVICE ENGINE SOON light flashes 2 times and one half times per second. In Closed loop the light flashes once per second. Also in closed loop, the light will stay OUT most of the time if the system is too lean. It will stay ON most of the time if the system is too rich. In either case the Field Service mode check, which is part of the Diagnostic circuit check, will lead you into choosing the correct diagnostic chart to refer to.

BACKUP MODE — 3.9 KILO-OHMS

The backup mode is entered by applying 3.9 kilo-ohms resistance between terminals A and B of the DLC connector with the ignition switch in the **ON** position. The DLC scanner tool can now read 5 of the 20 parameters on the data stream. These parameters are as mode status, oxygen sensor voltage, rpm, block learn and idle air control. There are 2 ways to enter the backup mode. Using a scan tool is one way of putting a 3.9 kilo-ohms resistor across terminals A and B of the DLC is another.

SPECIAL MODE — 10 KILO-OHMS

This special mode is entered by applying a 10K ohms resistor across terminals A and B. When this happens the ECM does the following:
- Allows all of the serial data to be read.
- Bypasses all timers.
- Add a calibrated spark advance.
- Enables the canister purge solenoid on some engines.
- Idles at 950-1050 rpm fixed idle air control and fixed base pulse width on the injector.
- Forces the idle air control to reset at part throttle (approximately 2000 rpm).
- Disables the park/neutral restrict functions.

OPEN OR ROAD TEST MODE — 20 KILO-OHMS

On engines that can be monitored in the Open mode, certain parameters can be observed without changing the engine operating characteristics. The parameters capable of being read vary with the engine families. Most Scan tools are programmed so that the system will go directly into the DLC mode if the Open mode is not available.

DLC SCAN TESTER INFORMATION
▶ See Figure 53

A DLC display unit (DLC tester, scanner, monitor, etc), allows you to read the engine control system information from the DLC connector under the instrument panel. It can provide information faster than a digital voltmeter or ohmmeter can. The scan tool does not diagnose the exact location of the problem. The tool supplies information about the ECM/PCM, the information that it is receiving and the commands that it is sending plus special information such as integrator and block learn. To use a DLC display tool you should understand thoroughly how an engine control system operates.

A DLC scanner or monitor puts a fuel injection system into a special test mode. This mode commands an idle speed of 1000 rpm. The idle quality cannot be evaluated with a tester plugged in. Also the test mode commands a fixed spark with no advance. On vehicles with Electronic Spark Control (ECS) and its knock sensor, there will be a fixed spark, but it will be advanced. On vehicles with ESC, there might be a serious spark knock which is bad enough to prevent road testing the vehicle in the DLC test mode. Be sure to check the tool manufacturer for instructions on special test modes which should overcome these limitations.

When a tester is used with a fuel injected engine, it bypasses the timer that keeps the system in Open loop for a certain period of time. When all Closed loop conditions are met, the engine will go into Closed loop as soon as the vehicle is started. This means that the air management system will not function properly and air may go directly to the converter as soon as the engine is started.

These tools cannot diagnose everything. They do not tell where a problem is located in a circuit. The diagnostic charts to pinpoint the problems must still be used. These tester's do not let you know if a solenoid or relay has been turned on. They only tell the ECM/PCM command. To find out if a solenoid has been turned on, check it with a suitable test light or

86814061

Fig. 53 The Data Link Connector (DLC) display unit (DLC tester, scanner, monitor, etc.) allows you to read the engine control system information from the DLC connector under the instrument panel. It can provide information faster than a digital voltmeter or ohmmeter digital voltmeter, or see if vacuum through the solenoid changes.

SCAN TOOLS FOR INTERMITTENT PROBLEMS

In some scan tool applications, the data update rate may make the tool less effective than a voltmeter, such as when trying to detect an intermittent problem which lasts for a very short time. Some scan tools have a snapshot function which stores several seconds or even minutes of operation to located an intermittent problem. Scan tools allow one to manipulate the wiring harness or components under the hood with the engine not running while observing the scan tool's readout.

The scan tool can be plugged in and observed while driving the vehicle under the condition when the SERVICE ENGINE SOON light turns on momentarily or when the engine driveability is momentarily poor. If the problem seems to be related to certain parameters that can be checked on the scan tool, they should be checked while driving the vehicle. If there does not seem to be any correlation between the problem and any specific circuit, the scan tool can be checked on each position. Watching for a period of time to see if there is any change in the reading that indicates intermittent operation.

The scan tool is also an easy way to compare the operating parameters of a poorly operating engine with typical scan data for the vehicle being serviced or those of a known good engine. For example, a sensor may shift in value but not set a trouble code. Comparing the sensor's reading with those of a known good parameters may uncover the problem.

The scan tool has the ability to save time in diagnosis and prevent the replacement of good parts. The key to using the scan tool successfully for diagnosis lies in the ability to understand the system being diagnosed, as well as the scan tool's operation and limitations.

CLEARING TROUBLE CODES

When the ECM/PCM finds a problem with the system, the SERVICE ENGINE SOON light will come on and a trouble code will be recorded in the ECM/PCM memory. If the problem is intermittent, the SERVICE ENGINE SOON light will go out after 10 seconds, when the fault goes away. However the trouble code will stay in the ECM/PCM memory until the battery voltage to the ECM/PCM is removed. Removing the battery voltage for 10 seconds will clear all trouble codes. Do this by disconnecting the ECM/PCM harness from the positive battery terminal pigtail for 10 seconds with the key in the **OFF** position, or by removing the ECM/PCM fuse for 10 seconds with the key **OFF**.

➡**To prevent ECM/PCM damage, the key must be OFF when disconnecting and reconnecting ECM/PCM power.**

INTEGRATOR AND BLOCK LEARN

The integrator and block learn functions of the ECM/PCM are responsible for making minor adjustments to the air/fuel ratio on the fuel injected GM vehicles. These small adjustments are necessary to compensate for pinpoint air leaks and normal wear.

The integrator and block learn are 2 separate ECM/PCM memory functions which control fuel delivery. The integrator makes a temporary change and the block learn makes a more permanent change. Both of these functions apply only while the engine is in CLOSED LOOP. They represent the on-time of the injector. Also, integrator and block learn controls fuel delivery on the fuel injected engines as does the MC solenoid dwell on the CCC carbureted engines.

Integrator

Integrator is the term applied to a means of temporary change in fuel delivery. Integrator is displayed through the DLC data line and monitored with a scanner as a number range between 0 and 255 with an average of 128. The integrator monitors the oxygen sensor output voltage (usually below 450 mV) and adds and subtracts fuel depending on the lean or rich condition of the oxygen sensor. When the integrator is displaying 128, it indicates a neutral condition. This means that the oxygen sensor is seeing results of the 14.7:1 air/fuel mixture burned in the cylinders.

➡**An air leak in the system (a lean condition) would cause the oxygen sensor voltage to decrease while the integrator would increase (add more fuel) to temporarily correct for the lean condition. If this happened the injector pulse width would increase.**

Block Learn

Although the integrator can correct fuel delivery over a wide range, it is only for a temporary correction. Therefore, another control called block learn was added. Although it cannot make as many corrections as the integrator, it does so for a longer period of time. It gets its name from the fact that the operating range of the engine for any given combinations of rpm and load is divided into 16 cell or blocks.

The computer has a given fuel delivery stored in each block. As the operating range gets into a given block the fuel delivery will be based on what value is stored in the memory in that block. Again, just like the integrator, the number represents the on-time of the injector. Also, just like the integrator, the number 128 represents no correction to the value that is stored in the cell or block. When the integrator increases or decreases, block learn which is also watching the integrator will make corrections in the same direction. As the block learn makes corrections, the integrator correction will be reduced until finally the integrator will return to 128 if the block learn has corrected the fuel delivery.

Block Learn Memory

Block learn operates on 1 of 2 types of memories depending on application: non-volatile or volatile. The non-volatile memories retain the value in the block learn cells even when the ignition switch is turned **OFF**. When the engine is restarted, the fuel delivery for a given block will be based on information stored in memory.

The volatile memories lose the numbers stored in the block learn cells when the ignition is turned to the **OFF** position. Upon restarting, the block learn starts at 128 in every block and corrects from that point as necessary.

Integrator/Block Learn Limits

Both the integrator and block learn have limits which will vary from engine to engine. If the mixture is off enough so that the block learn reaches the limit of its control and still cannot correct the condition, the integrator would also go to it's limit of control in the same direction and the engine would then begin to run poorly. If the integrators and block learn are close to or at their limits of control, the engine hardware should be checked to determine the cause of the limits being reached, vacuum leaks, sticking injectors, etc.

If the integrator is lied to, for example, if the oxygen sensor lead was grounded (lean signal) the integrator and block learn would add fuel to the engine to cause it to run rich. However, with the oxygen sensor lead grounded, the ECM/PCM would continue seeing a lean condition eventually setting a Code 44 and the fuel control system would change to open loop operations.

Closed Loop Fuel Control

The purpose of closed loop fuel control is to precisely maintain an air/fuel mixture 14.7:1. When the air/fuel mixture is maintained at 14.7:1, the catalytic converter is able to operate at maximum efficiency which results in lower emission levels.

Since the ECM/PCM controls the air/fuel mixture, it needs to check its output and correct the fuel mixture for deviations from the ideal ratio. The oxygen sensor feeds this output information back to the ECM/PCM.

ENGINE PERFORMANCE DIAGNOSIS

Engine performance diagnostic procedures are guides that will lead to the most probable causes of engine performance complaints. They consider the components of the fuel, ignition, and mechanical systems that could cause a particular complaint, and then outline repairs in a logical sequence.

It is important to determine if the SERVICE ENGINE SOON light is on or has come on for a short interval while driving. If the SERVICE ENGINE SOON light has come on, the Computer Command Control System should be checked for stored **TROUBLE CODES** which may indicate the cause for the performance complaint.

All of the symptoms can be caused by worn out or defective parts such as spark plugs, ignition wiring, etc. If time and/or mileage indicate that parts should be replaced, it is recommended that it be done.

➡**Before checking any system controlled by the Electronic Fuel Injection (EFI) system, the Diagnostic Circuit Check must be performed or misdiagnosis may occur. If the complaint involves the SERVICE ENGINE SOON light, go directly to the Diagnostic Circuit Check.**

Basic Troubleshooting

➡**The following explains how to activate the trouble code signal light in the instrument cluster and gives an explanation of what each code means. This is not a full system troubleshooting and isolation procedure.**

Before suspecting the system or any of its components as faulty, check the ignition system including distributor, timing, spark plugs and wires. Check the engine compression, air cleaner, and emission control components not controlled by the ECM/PCM. Also check the intake manifold, vacuum hoses and hose connectors for leaks.

The following symptoms could indicate a possible problem with the system:
- Detonation
- Stalls or idles rough when cold
- Stalls or idles rough when hot
- Missing
- Hesitation
- Surges
- Poor gasoline mileage
- Sluggish or spongy performance
- Hard starting-cold
- Objectionable exhaust odors (that rotten egg smell)
- Cuts out
- Improper idle speed

As a bulb and system check, the SERVICE ENGINE SOON light will come on when the ignition switch is turned to the **ON** position but the engine is not started. The SERVICE ENGINE SOON light will also produce the trouble code or codes by a series of flashes which translate as follows. When the diagnostic test terminal under the dash is grounded, with the ignition in the **ON** position and the engine not running, the SERVICE ENGINE SOON light will flash once, pause, then flash twice in rapid succession. This is a Code 12, which indicates that the diagnostic system is working. After a long pause, the Code 12 will repeat itself 2 more times. The cycle will then repeat itself until the engine is started or the ignition is turned off.

When the engine is started, the SERVICE ENGINE SOON light will remain on for a few seconds, then turn off. If the SERVICE ENGINE SOON light remains on, the self-diagnostic system has detected a problem. If the test terminal is then grounded, the trouble code will flash 3 times. If more than 1 problem is found, each trouble code will flash 3 times. Trouble codes will flash in numerical order (lowest code number to highest). The trouble codes series will repeat as long as the test terminal is grounded.

A trouble code indicates a problem with a given circuit. For example, trouble Code 14 indicates a problem in the cooling sensor circuit. This includes the coolant sensor, its electrical harness, and the ECM/PCM. Since the self-diagnostic system cannot diagnose every possible fault in the system, the absence of a trouble code does not mean the system is trouble-free. To determine problems within the system which do not activate a trouble code, a system performance check must be made.

In the case of an intermittent fault in the system, the SERVICE ENGINE SOON light will go out when the fault goes away, but the trouble code will remain in the memory of the ECM/PCM. Therefore, it a trouble code can be obtained even though the SERVICE ENGINE SOON light is not on, the trouble code must be evaluated. It must be determined if the fault is intermittent or if the engine must be at certain operating conditions (under load, etc.) before the SERVICE ENGINE SOON light will come on. Some trouble codes will not be recorded in the ECM/PCM until the engine has been operated at part throttle for about 5-18 minutes.

Fuel System Pressure Testing

Due to the varied application of components, a general procedure is outlined. For the exact procedure for the vehicle being service use Chart A7 for the appropriate engine. A fuel system pressure test is part of several of the diagnostic charts and symptom checks.

1. Relieve the fuel pressure from the fuel system. Turn the ignition **OFF** and remove the air cleaner assembly (if necessary).

2. Plug the Thermac vacuum port if required on the TBI unit.

3. Uncouple the fuel supply flexible hose in the engine compartment and install fuel pressure gauge J-29658/BT-8205 or equivalent in the pressure line or install the fuel pressure gauge into the pressure line connector located near the left engine compartment frame rail. Connection of the fuel gauge will vary accordingly to all the different engine application.

4. Be sure to tighten the fuel line to the gauge to ensure that there no leaks during testing.

5. Start the engine and observe the fuel pressure reading. The fuel pressure should be 9-13 psi (62-90 kPa).

6. Relieve the fuel pressure. Remove the fuel pressure gauge and reinstall the fuel line. Be sure to install a new O-ring on the fuel feed line.

7. Start the engine and check for fuel leaks. Stop the engine and remove the plug covering the Thermac vacuum port on the TBI unit and install the air cleaner assembly.

➡**Some vehicles will use more sensors than others. Also, a complete general diagnostic section is outlined. The steps and procedures can be altered as necessary according to the specific model being diagnosed and the sensors it is equipped with. If the battery power is disconnected for any reason, the volatile memory resets and the learning process begins again. A change may be noted in the performance of the vehicle. To teach the vehicle, ensure that the engine is at normal operating temperature. Then, the vehicle should be driven at part throttle, with moderate acceleration and idle conditions until normal performance returns.**

TBI SYSTEM DIAGNOSTIC CHARTS

To properly diagnose driveability problems, refer to the trouble code charts which appear later in this section. Make certain the charts cover the appropriate engine. If your check engine light is not lit, check for engine stored engine codes. If any codes are stored write them down for reference later. Clear the codes as described earlier. Road test the vehicle to see if any of the codes return. Never try to fix a code problem until you're sure that it comes back. It may have been an old code from years ago that was never cleared or a code that was set do to a rain storm, battery jump, etc.

After clearing any codes and checking that they do not return. If the car drives fine you're finished. But if there are no codes and the car runs poorly you'll need to check the symptoms charts. The problem is most likely not the computer or the devices it controls but the ignition system or engine mechanical.

If you do have a code(s) that returns start with the lowest code and follow the proper chart. You must follow every step of the chart and not jump from test to test or you'll never be certain to find and fix the real problem.

Start with the lowest to highest code chart, making sure to use the charts for your engine. If you have a 50 series code, like code 54. Always check those out first. They are rare but usually indicate a problem with the computer itself or its ability to test itself properly.

➡**Whereas component repair and replacement are covered in Section 5 (Fuel System), this section only deals with testing the system for driveability and emission problems.**

Multi-Port Fuel Injection (MFI) and Sequential Fuel Injection (SFI)

Both the MFI and SFI systems are controlled by a Computer Control Module (ECM or PCM) which monitors engine operations and generates output signals to provide the correct air/fuel mixture, ignition timing and engine idle speed control. Input to the control unit is provided by an oxygen sensor, coolant temperature sensor, detonation sensor, hot film mass sensor and throttle position sensor. The ECM/PCM also receives information concerning engine rpm, road speed, transaxle gear position, power steering and air conditioning.

The injectors are located, one at each intake port, rather than the single injector found on the earlier throttle body system. The injectors are mounted on a fuel rail and are activated by a signal from the computer control module. The injector is a solenoid-operated valve which remains open depending on the width of the electronic pulses (length of the signal) from the ECM/PCM. The longer the open time, the more fuel is injected. In this manner, the air/fuel mixture can be precisely controlled for maximum performance with minimum emissions.

Fuel is pumped from the tank by a high pressure fuel pump, located inside the fuel tank. It is a positive displacement roller vane pump. The impeller serves as a vapor separator and precharges the high pressure assembly. A pressure regulator maintains 41-47 psi (282-324 kPa) in the fuel line to the injectors and the excess fuel is fed back to the tank. A fuel accumulator is used to dampen the hydraulic line hammer in the system created when all injectors open simultaneously.

The Mass Air Flow (MAF) Sensor is used to measure the mass of air that is drawn into the engine cylinders. It is located just ahead of the air throttle in the intake system and consists of a heated film which measures the mass of air, rather than just the volume. A resistor is used to measure the temperature of the film at 75°F (24°C) above ambient temperature. As the ambient (outside) air temperature rises, more energy is required to maintain the heated film at the higher temperature and the control unit used this difference in required energy to calculate the mass of the incoming air. The control unit uses this information to determine the duration of fuel injection pulse, timing and EGR.

The throttle body incorporates an Idle Air Control (IAC) that provides for a bypass channel through which air can flow. It consists of an orifice and pintle which is controlled by the ECM/PCM through a step motor. The IAC provides air flow for idle and allows additional air during cold start until the engine reaches operating temperature. As the engine temperature rises, the opening through which air passes is slowly closed.

The Throttle Position Sensor (TPS) provides the control unit with information on throttle position, in order to determine injector pulse width and hence correct mixture. The TPS is connected to the throttle shaft on the throttle body and consists of as potentiometer with on end connected to a 5 volt source from the ECM/PCM and the other to ground. A third wire is connected to the ECM/PCM to measure the voltage output from the TPS which changes as the throttle valve angle is changed (accelerator pedal moves). At the closed throttle position, the output is low (approximately 0.4 volts). As the throttle valve opens, the output increases to a maximum 5 volts at Wide Open Throttle (WOT). The TPS can be misadjusted open, shorted, or loose and if it is out of adjustment, the idle quality or WOT performance may be poor. A loose TPS can cause intermittent bursts of fuel from the injectors and an unstable idle because the ECM/PCM thinks the throttle is moving. This should cause a trouble code to be set. Once a trouble code is set, the ECM/PCM will use a preset value for the TPS and some vehicle performance may return. A small amount of engine coolant is routed through the throttle assembly to prevent freezing inside the throttle bore during cold operation.

COMPUTER CONTROL MODULE

The fuel injection system is controlled by an on-board computer, the Electronic Control Module/Powertrain Control Module (ECM/PCM), usually located in the passenger compartment. The ECM/PCM monitors engine operations and environmental conditions (ambient temperature, barometric pressure, etc.) needed to calculate the fuel delivery time (pulse width/injector on-time) of the fuel injector. The fuel pulse may be modified by the ECM/PCM to account for special operating conditions, such as cranking, cold starting, altitude, acceleration and deceleration.

The ECM/PCM controls the exhaust emissions by modifying fuel delivery to achieve, as nearly as possible an air/fuel ratio of 14.7:1. The injector on-time is determined by the various sensor inputs to the ECM/PCM. By increasing the injector pulse, more fuel is delivered, enriching the air/fuel ratio. Pulses are sent to the injector in 2 different modes, synchronized and non-synchronized.

In synchronized mode operation, the injector is pulsed once for each distributor reference pulse. In non-synchronized mode operation, the injector is pulsed once every 12.5 milliseconds or 6.25 milliseconds depending on calibration. This pulse time is totally independent of distributor reference.

The ECM/PCM constantly monitors the input information, processes this information from various sensors, and generates output commands to the various systems that affect vehicle performance.

The ability of the ECM/PCM to recognize and adjust for vehicle variations (engine, transaxle, vehicle weight, axle ratio, etc.) is provided by a removable calibration unit (PROM) that is programmed to tailor the ECM/PCM for the particular vehicle. There is a specific ECM/PCM — PROM combination for each specific vehicle, and the combinations are not interchangeable with those of other vehicles.

The ECM/PCM also performs the diagnostic function of the system. It can recognize operational problems, alert the driver through the SERVICE ENGINE SOON light, and store a code or codes which identify the problem areas to aid the in making repairs.

➡Instead of an edgeboard connector, newer ECM/PCM's have a header connector which attaches solidly to the ECM/PCM case. Like the edgeboard connectors, the header connectors have a different pinout identification for different engine designs.

The ECM/PCM consists of 3 parts, a Controller (the ECM/PCM without a PROM), a Calibrator called a PROM (Programmable Read Only Memory) and a Cal-Pak.

PROM

To allow 1 model of the ECM/PCM to be used for many different vehicles, a device called a Calibrator (or PROM) is used. The PROM is located inside the ECM/PCM and has information on the vehicle's weight, engine, transaxle, axle ratio and other components.

While one ECM/PCM part number can be used by many different vehicles, a PROM is very specific and must be used for the right vehicle. For this reason, it is very important to check the latest parts book and or service bulletin information for the correct PROM part number when replacing the PROM.

An ECM/PCM used for service (called a controller) comes without a PROM. The PROM from the old ECM/PCM must be carefully removed and installed in the new ECM/PCM.

Cal-Pak
▶ See Figure 54

A device called a Cal-Pak is added to allow fuel delivery if other parts of the ECM/PCM are damaged. It has an access door in the ECM/PCM, and removal and replacement procedures are the same as with the PROM. If the Cal-Pak is missing, a Code 52 will be set. Not all vehicles with MFI/SFI are equipped with a Cal-Pak.

Mem-Cal

This assembly contains the functions of the PROM Cal-Pak and the ESC module used on other GM applications. Like the PROM, it contains the calibrations needed for a specific vehicle as well as the back-up fuel control circuitry required if the rest of the ECM becomes damaged or faulty.

Synchronized Mode

In synchronized mode operation, the injector is pulsed once for each distributor reference pulse.

Non-synchronized Mode

In non-synchronized mode operation, the injector is pulsed once every 12.5 milliseconds or 6.25 milliseconds depending on calibration. This pulse time is totally independent of distributor reference pulses. Non-synchronized mode results only under the following conditions:

1. The fuel pulse width is too small to be delivered accurately by the injector (approximately 1.5 milliseconds)
2. During the delivery of prime pulses (prime pulses charge the intake manifold with fuel during or just prior to engine starting)

GRASP CALPAK
CARRIER AT
NARROW ENDS
ONLY

1. CAL-PAK
2. Removal tool

86814060

Fig. 54 How to remove the Cal-Pak

3. During acceleration enrichment
4. During deceleration leanout

Starting Mode

When the engine is first turned **ON**, the ECM/PCM will turn on the fuel pump relay for 2 seconds and the fuel pump will build up pressure. The ECM/PCM then checks the coolant temperature sensor (ECT), throttle position sensor (TPS) and crank sensor, then the ECM/PCM determines the proper air/fuel ratio for starting. This ranges from 1.5:1 at -33°F (-36°C) to 14.7:1 at 201°F (94°C).

The ECM/PCM controls the amount of fuel that is delivered in the Starting Mode by changing how long the injectors are turned on and off. This is done by pulsing the injectors for very short times.

Clear Flood Mode

If for some reason the engine should become flooded, provisions have been made to clear this condition. To clear the flood, the driver must depress the accelerator pedal enough to position the throttle in its wide-open position. The ECM/PCM then issues a command to completely turn off the fuel flow. The ECM/PCM holds this operational mode as long as the throttle stays in the wide-open position and the engine rpm is below 600. If the throttle position becomes less than 62% (2.9mv) on MFI vehicles or 80% on SFI vehicles, the ECM/PCM returns to the starting mode.

Run Mode

There are 2 different run modes. When the engine is first started and the rpm is above 400, the system goes into Open Loop operation. In open loop operation, the ECM/PCM will ignore the signal from the oxygen sensor (O_2S) and calculate the injector on-time based upon inputs from the coolant sensor (ECT), mass air flow (MAF) and mass air temperature (MAT) sensors.

During Open Loop operation, the ECM/PCM analyzes the following items to determine when the system is ready to go to the Closed Loop mode.

1. The oxygen sensor (O_2S) varying voltage output showing that is is hot enough to operate properly. This is dependent on temperature.

2. The coolant sensor (ECT) must be above specified temperature.

3. A specific amount of time must elapse after starting the engine. These values are stored in the PROM.

4. The engine speed is above 800 rpm since start up.

When these conditions have been met, the system goes into Closed Loop operation In Closed Loop operation, the ECM/PCM will calculate the air/fuel ratio (injector on time) based upon the signal from the oxygen sensor. The ECM/PCM will decrease the on-time if the air/fuel ratio is too rich, and will increase the on-time if the air/fuel ratio is too lean.

Acceleration Mode

When the engine is required to accelerate, the opening of the throttle valve(s) causes a rapid increase in Manifold Absolute Pressure (MAP). This rapid increase in MAP causes fuel to condense on the manifold walls. The ECM/PCM senses this increase in throttle angle and MAP, and supplies additional fuel for a short period of time. This prevents the engine from stumbling due to too lean a mixture.

Deceleration Mode

Upon deceleration, a leaner fuel mixture is required to reduce emission of hydrocarbons (HC) and carbon monoxide (CO). To adjust the injection on-time, the ECM/PCM uses the decrease in MAP and the decrease in throttle position to calculate a decrease in injector on time. To maintain an idle fuel ratio of 14.7:1, fuel output is momentarily reduced. This is done because of the fuel remaining in the intake manifold. The ECM/PCM can cut off the fuel completely for short periods of time.

Battery Voltage Correction Mode

The purpose of battery voltage correction is to compensate for variations in battery voltage to fuel pump and injector response. The ECM/PCM compensates by increasing the engine idle rpm.

Battery voltage correction takes place in all operating modes. When battery voltage is low, the spark delivered by the distributor may be low. To correct this low battery voltage problem, the ECM/PCM can do any or all of the following:

- Increase injector on time (increase fuel)
- Increase idle rpm
- Increase ignition dwell time

Fuel Cut-off Mode

When the ignition is **OFF**, no fuel will be delivered by the injectors. Fuel will also be cut off if the ECM/PCM does not receive a reference pulse from the distributor. To prevent dieseling, fuel delivery is completely stopped as soon as the engine is stopped. The ECM/PCM will not allow any fuel supply until it receives distributor reference pulses which prevents flooding.

Converter Protection Mode

In this mode the ECM/PCM estimates the temperature of the catalytic converter and then modifies fuel delivery to protect the converter from high temperatures. When the ECM/PCM has determined that the converter may overheat, it will cause open loop operation and will enrich the fuel delivery. A slightly richer mixture will then cause the converter temperature to be reduced.

Fuel Backup Mode

The ECM/PCM functions in the fuel backup circuit mode if any one, or any combination, of the following exist:
- The ECM/PCM voltage is lower than 9 volts.
- The cranking voltage is below 9 volts.
- The PROM is missing or not functioning.
- The ECM/PCM circuit fails to insure the computer operating pulse. The computer operating pulse (COP) is an internal ECM/PCM feature designed to inform the fuel backup circuit that the ECM/PCM is able to function.

Some engines run erratically in the fuel backup mode, while others seemed to run very well. Code 52 will be set to indicate a missing Cal-Pak. The fuel backup circuit is ignition fed and senses Throttle Position Sensor (TPS), Engine Coolant Temperature Sensor (ECT) and rpm. The fuel backup circuit controls the fuel pump relay and the pulse width of the injectors. Some vehicles have this mode, not all.

Data Link Connector (DLC/ALDL)

The Data Link Connector (DLC) or Assembly Line Data Link (ALDL), is a diagnostic connector located in the passenger compartment, usually under the instrument panel.

The assembly plant were the vehicles originate use these connectors to check the engine for proper operation before it leaves the plant. Vehicles with the ALDL system, enter the Diagnostic mode or the Field Service Mode by connecting or jumping terminal B, the diagnostic TEST terminal to terminal A, or ground circuit. Vehicles with the check connector, connect or jump terminal TE1, the diagnostic TEST terminal to terminal E1, or ground circuit. This connector is a very useful tool in diagnosing fuel injected engines. Important information from the ECM/PCM is available at this terminal and can be read with one of the many popular scanner tools.

FUEL CONTROL SYSTEM

The fuel control system is made up of the following components:
- Fuel supply system
- Throttle body assembly
- Fuel injectors
- Fuel rail
- Fuel pressure regulator
- Idle Air Control (IAC)
- Fuel pump
- Fuel pump relay
- Inline fuel filter

The fuel control system starts with the fuel in the fuel tank. An electric fuel pump, located in the fuel tank with the fuel gauge sending unit, pumps fuel to the fuel rail through an in-line fuel filter. The pump is designed to provide fuel at a pressure above the pressure needed by the injectors. A pressure regulator in the fuel rail keeps fuel available to the injectors at a constant pressure. Unused fuel is returned to the fuel tank by a separate line.

In order for the fuel injectors to supply a precise amount of fuel at the command of the ECM/PCM, the fuel supply system maintains a constant pressure drop of approximately 41-47 psi (284-325 kPa) across the injectors. As manifold vacuum changes, the fuel system pressure regulator controls the fuel supply pressure to compensate. On the MFI vehicles the fuel is supplied at the same time in a pulse injection timing, on the SFI vehicles the fuel is supplied in the order of the timing. The fuel pressure accumulator used on select models, isolates fuel line noise. The fuel rail is bolted rigidly to the engine and it provides the upper mount for the fuel injectors. It also contains a spring loaded pressure tap for testing the fuel system or relieving the fuel system pressure.

The injectors are controlled by the ECM/PCM. They deliver fuel in one of several modes as previously described. In order to properly control the fuel supply, the fuel pump is operated by the ECM/PCM through the fuel pump relay and oil pressure switch.

Throttle Body Unit
▶ See Figure 55

The throttle body unit has a throttle valve to control the amount of air delivered to the engine. The TPS and IAC valve are also mounted onto the throttle body. The throttle body contains vacuum ports located at, above or below the throttle valve. These vacuum ports generate the vacuum signals needed by various components.

On some vehicles, the engine coolant is directed through the coolant cavity at the bottom of the throttle body to warm the throttle valve and prevent icing.

Fuel Injector
▶ See Figure 56

A fuel injector is installed in the intake manifold at each cylinder. Mounting is approximately 3-4 in. (7.5-10mm) from the

1	VALVE-IDLE AIR CONTROL (IAC)
2	SENSOR-MASS AIR FLOW (MAF)
3	SENSOR-THROTTLE POSITION (TP)

86814066

Fig. 55 Throttle body unit on an SFI vehicle

center line of the intake valve on the V6 and the V8 engine applications. The nozzle spray pattern is on a 25 degree angle. The fuel injector is a solenoid operated device controlled by the ECM/PCM. The ECM/PCM turns on the solenoid, which opens the valve which allows fuel delivery. The fuel, under pressure, is injected in a conical spray pattern at the opening of the intake valve. The fuel, which is not used by the injectors, passes through the pressure regulator before returning to the fuel tank.

An injector that is partly open, will cause loss of fuel pressure after the engine is shut down, so long crank time would be noticed on some engines. Also dieseling could occur because some fuel could be delivered after the ignition is turned to **OFF** position.

There are 2 O-ring seals used. The lower O-ring seals the injector at the intake manifold. The O-rings are lubricated and should be replaced whenever the injector is removed from the intake manifold. The O-rings provide thermal insulation, thus preventing the formation of vapor bubbles and promoting good hot start characteristics. The O-rings also prevent excess injector vibration.

Air leakage at the injector/intake area would create a lean cylinder and a possible driveability problem. A second seal is used to seal the fuel injector at the fuel rail connection. The injectors are identified with an ID number cast on the injector near the top side. Injectors manufactured by Rochester® Products have an **RP** positioned near the top side in addition to the ID number.

Fuel Rail
▶ **See Figure 57**

The fuel rail is bolted rigidly to the engine and it provides the upper mount for the fuel injectors. It distributes fuel to the individual injectors. Fuel is delivered to the input end of the fuel rail by the fuel lines, goes through the rail, then to the fuel pressure regulator. The regulator keeps the fuel pressure to the injectors at a constant pressure. The remaining fuel is then returned to the fuel tank. The fuel rail also contains a spring loaded pressure tap for testing the fuel system or relieving the fuel system pressure.

Pressure Regulator
▶ **See Figure 58**

The fuel pressure regulator contains a pressure chamber separated by a diaphragm relief valve assembly with a calibrated spring in the vacuum chamber side. The fuel pressure is regulated when the pump pressure acting on the bottom spring of the diaphragm overcomes the force of the spring action on the top side.

The diaphragm relief valve moves, opening or closing an orifice in the fuel chamber to control the amount of fuel returned to the fuel tank. Vacuum acting on the top side of the diaphragm along with spring pressure controls the fuel pressure. A decrease in vacuum creates an increase in the fuel pressure. An increase in vacuum creates a decrease in fuel pressure.

An example of this is under heavy load conditions the engine requires more fuel flow. The vacuum decreases under a heavy load condition because of the throttle opening. A decrease in the vacuum allows more fuel pressure to the top

1	INJECTOR ASSEMBLY - FUEL
A	PART NUMBER IDENTIFICATION
B	BUILD DATE CODE
C	MONTH 1-9 (JAN-SEPT) O, N, D (OCT, NOV, DEC)
D	DAY
E	YEAR

86814063

Fig. 56 The injectors are identified with an ID number cast on the injector near the top side. Injectors manufactured by Rochester Products® have an RP positioned near the top side in addition to the ID number

side of the pressure relief valve, thus increasing the fuel pressure.

The pressure regulator is mounted on the fuel rail and serviced separately. If the pressure is too low, poor performance could result. If the pressure is too high, excessive odor and a Code 45 may result.

Idle Air Control (IAC)

The purpose of the Idle Air Control (IAC) system is to control engine idle speeds while preventing stalls due to changes in engine load. The IAC assembly, mounted on the throttle body, controls bypass air around the throttle plate. By extending or retracting a conical valve, a controlled amount of air can move around the throttle plate. If rpm is too low, more air is diverted around the throttle plate to increase rpm.

During idle, the proper position of the IAC valve is calculated by the ECM/PCM based on battery voltage, coolant temperature, engine load, and engine rpm. If the rpm drops below a specified rate, the throttle plate is closed. The ECM/PCM will then calculate a new valve position.

Fig. 57 Fuel rails, like injectors, have an identification number stamped on them

Three different designs are used for the IAC conical valve. The first design used is single taper while the second design used is a dual taper. The third design is a blunt valve. Care should be taken to insure use of the correct design when service replacement is required.

The IAC motor has 255 different positions or steps. The zero, or reference position, is the fully extended position at which the pintle is seated in the air bypass seat and no air is allowed to bypass the throttle plate. When the motor is fully retracted, maximum air is allowed to bypass the throttle plate. When the motor is fully retracted, maximum air is allowed to bypass the throttle plate.

The ECM/PCM always monitors how many steps it has extended or retracted the pintle from the zero or reference position thus, it always calculates the exact position of the motor. Once the engine has started and the vehicle has reached approximately 40 mph, the ECM/PCM will extend the motor 255 steps from whatever position it is in. This will bottom out the pintle against the seat. The ECM/PCM will call this position **0** and thus keep its zero reference updated.

The IAC only affects the engine's idle characteristics. If it is stuck fully open, idle speed is too high (too much air enters the throttle bore) If it is stuck closed, idle speed is too low (not enough air entering). If it is stuck somewhere in the middle, idle may be rough, and the engine won't respond to load changes.

Fuel Pump

The fuel is supplied to the system from an in-tank positive displacement roller vane pump. The pump supplies fuel through the in-line fuel filter to the fuel rail assembly. The pump is removed for service along with the fuel gauge sending unit. Once they are removed from the fuel tank, they pump and sending unit can be serviced separately.

Fuel pressure is achieved by rotation of the armature driving the roller vane components. The impeller at the inlet end serves as a vapor separator and a precharger for the roller vane assembly.

The fuel pump delivers more fuel than the engine can consume even under the most extreme conditions. Excess fuel flows through the pressure regulator and back to the tank via the return line. The constant flow of fuel means that the fuel system is always supplied with cool fuel, thereby preventing the formation of fuel-vapor bubbles (vapor lock).

Fuel Pump Relay Circuit

The fuel pump relay is usually located on the right or left front inner fender (or shock tower) or on the engine side of the firewall (center cowl). The fuel pump electrical system consists of the fuel pump relay, ignition circuit and the ECM/PCM circuits are protected by a fuse. The fuel pump relay contact switch is in the normally open (NO) position.

When the ignition is turned **ON** the ECM/PCM will for 2 seconds, supply voltage to the fuel pump relay coil, closing the open contact switch. The ignition circuit fuse can now supply ignition voltage to the circuit which feeds the relay contact switch. With the relay contacts closed, ignition voltage is supplied to the fuel pump. The ECM/PCM will continue to supply voltage to the relay coil circuit as long as the ECM/PCM receives the rpm reference pulses from the ignition module.

The fuel pump control circuit also includes an engine oil pressure switch with a set of normally open contacts. The switch closes at approximately 4 lbs. of oil pressure and provides a secondary battery feed path to the fuel pump. If the relay fails, the pump will continue to run using the battery feed supplied by the closed oil pressure switch. A failed fuel pump relay will result in extended engine crank times in order to build up enough oil pressure to close the switch and turn on the fuel pump.

In-Line Fuel Filter

The fuel filter is of a 10-20 micron size and is serviced only as a complete unit. O-rings are used at all threaded connections to prevent fuel leakage. The threaded flex hoses connect the filter to the fuel tank feed line.

SENSORS

A variety of sensors provide information to the ECM/PCM regarding engine operating characteristics. These sensors and

1	CAP - FUEL PRESSURE CONNECTION	11	INJECTOR ASSEMBLY - FUEL
2	VALVE ASSEMBLY - FUEL PRESSURE CONNECTION	12	BACKUP - O-RING
3	RAIL ASSEMBLY - RH FUEL	13	O-RING - LOWER INJECTOR (BROWN)
4	BRACKET - RETAINER AND SPACER	14	SCREW - RAIL MOUNTING BRACKET ATTACHING
5	SCREEN - FILTER	15	BRACKET - RAIL MOUNTING (2 EA.)
6	O-RING - PRESSURE REGULATOR INLET	16	RAIL ASSEMBLY - LH FUEL (WITH CROSSOVER TUBE)
7	REGULATOR ASSEMBLY - FUEL PRESSURE	17	CLIP - CROSSOVER TUBE RETAINER
8	SCREW - PRESSURE REGULATOR ATTACHING	18	O-RING - CROSSOVER TUBE
9	O-RING - UPPER INJECTOR (BLACK)		
10	CLIP - INJECTOR RETAINER		

86814065

Fig. 58 The pressure regulator is mounted on the fuel rail and is serviced separately

their functions are described below. Be sure to take note that not every sensor described is used with every GM engine application.

Electronic Spark Timing (EST)

Electronic spark timing (EST) is used on all engines equipped with HEI distributors and direct ignition systems. The EST distributor contains no vacuum or centrifugal advance and uses a 7-terminal distributor module. It also has 4 wires going to a 4-terminal connector in addition to the connectors normally found on HEI distributors. A reference pulse, indicating both engine rpm and crankshaft position, is sent to the ECM/PCM. The ECM/PCM determines the proper spark advance for the engine operating conditions and sends an **EST** pulse to the distributor.

The EST system is designed to optimize spark timing for better control of exhaust emissions and for fuel economy improvements. The ECM/PCM monitors information from various engine sensors, computes the desired spark timing and changes the timing accordingly. A backup spark advance system is incorporated in the module in case of EST failure.

The basic function of the fuel control system is to control the fuel delivery to the engine. The fuel is delivered to the engine by individual fuel injectors mounted on the intake manifold near each cylinder.

The main control sensor is the oxygen sensor which is located in the exhaust manifold. The oxygen sensor tells the ECM/PCM how much oxygen is in the exhaust gas and the ECM/PCM changes the air/fuel ratio to the engine by controlling the fuel injectors. The best mixture (ratio) to minimize exhaust emissions is 14.7:1 which allows the catalytic converter to operate the most efficiently. Because of the constant measuring and adjusting of the air/fuel ratio, the fuel injection system is called a **CLOSED LOOP** system.

➡**Whenever the term Electronic Control Module (ECM) is used in this manual, it refers to the engine control computer, regardless of whether it is a Powertrain Control Module (PCM) or Electronic Control Module (ECM).**

Electronic Spark Control (ESC)

When engines are equipped with ESC in conjunction with EST, ESC is used to reduce spark advance under conditions of detonation. A knock sensor signals a separate ESC controller to retard the timing when it senses knock. The ESC controller signals the ECM/PCM which reduces spark advance until no more signals are received from the knock sensor.

Engine Coolant Temperature (ECT)
▶ See Figure 59

The coolant sensor is a thermister (a resistor which changes value based on temperature) mounted on the engine coolant stream. As the temperature of the engine coolant changes, the resistance of the coolant sensor changes. Low coolant temperature produces a high resistance (100,000 ohms at -40°C/-40°F), while high temperature causes low resistance (70 ohms at 130°C/266°F).

The ECM/PCM supplies a 5 volt signal to the coolant sensor and measures the voltage that returns. By measuring the voltage change, the ECM/PCM determines the engine coolant temperature. The voltage will be high when the engine is cold and low when the engine is hot. This information is used to control fuel management, IAC, spark timing, EGR, canister purge and other engine operating conditions.

A failure in the coolant sensor circuit should either set a Code 14 or 15 on MFI and P0117 or P0118 on SFI. These codes indicate a failure in the coolant temperature sensor circuit. Once the trouble code is set, the ECM/PCM will use a default valve for engine coolant temperature.

Intake Air Temperature (IAT)

The Intake Air Temperature Sensor (IAT) is a thermister which changes the value based on the temperature of air entering the engine. A low temperature produces a high resistance, while a low temperature causes a low resistance. The ECM/PCM supplies a 5 volt signal to the sensor through a resister in the ECM/PCM, then measures the voltage. A failure in the IAT sensor could result in a Code of P0112 or P0113 in the SFI and Codes 23 or 25 in the MFI. The Manifold Air Temperature (MAT) Sensor is another name for the IAT sensor.

Oxygen (O₂S)
▶ See Figures 60 and 61

The exhaust oxygen sensor is mounted in the exhaust system where it can monitor the oxygen content of the exhaust gas stream. The oxygen content in the exhaust reacts with the oxygen sensor to produce a voltage output. This voltage ranges from approximately 100 millivolts (high oxygen — lean mixture) to 900 millivolts (low oxygen — rich mixture).

By monitoring the voltage output of the oxygen sensor, the ECM/PCM will determine what fuel mixture command to give to the injector (lean mixture = low voltage and a rich command, rich mixture = high voltage and a lean command).

Remember that the oxygen sensor only indicates to the ECM/PCM what is happening in the exhaust. It does not cause things to happen. It is a type of gauge: high oxygen content = lean mixture; low oxygen content = rich mixture. The ECM/PCM adjusts fuel to keep the system working.

The oxygen sensor, if open, should set a Code 13. A constant low voltage in the sensor circuit should set a Code 44 in

HARNESS CONNECTOR

COOLANT TEMPERATURE SENSOR

86814068

Fig. 59 The ECT sensor and connector

Fig. 60 A cross-sectional view of the oxygen sensor

Labels:
- WIRE TO ECM
- OPEN TO ATMOSPHERE
- INSIDE SURFACE POSITIVE TERMINAL
- CERAMIC ZIRCONIA ELEMENT
- METAL GASKET - CONNECTS TO POSITIVE TERMINAL
- METAL GASKET - CONNECTS TO (–) NEGATIVE TERMINAL
- OUTSIDE SURFACE GROUND TERMINAL
- PLATINUM COATING
- (+)

86814069

Fig. 61 The heated oxygen sensor looks the same as the non-heated variety

86814070

MFI and P0131 in SFI, while a constant high voltage in the circuit should set a Code 45 in MFI and P0132 or P0131 in SFI. Codes 44, 45, P0132 and P0131 could also be set as a result of fuel system problems. The oxygen sensor on MFI vehicles is not heated, but it is heated on SFI vehicles.

Manifold Absolute Pressure (MAP)

The Manifold Absolute Pressure (MAP) sensor measures the changes in the intake manifold pressure which result from engine load and speed changes. The pressure measured by the MAP sensor is the difference between barometric pressure (outside air) and manifold pressure (vacuum). A closed throttle engine coastdown would produce a relatively low MAP value (approximately 20-35 kPa), while wide-open throttle would produce a high value (100 kPa). This high value is produced when the pressure inside the manifold is the same as outside the manifold, and 100% of outside air (or 100 kPa) is being measured. This MAP output is the opposite of what you would measure on a vacuum gauge. The use of this sensor also

allows the ECM/PCM to adjust automatically for different altitude.

The ECM/PCM sends a 5 volt reference signal to the MAP sensor. As the MAP changes, the electrical resistance of the sensor also changes. By monitoring the sensor output voltage the ECM/PCM can determine the manifold pressure. A higher pressure, lower vacuum (high voltage) requires more fuel, while a lower pressure, higher vacuum (low voltage) requires less fuel. The ECM/PCM uses the MAP sensor to control fuel delivery and ignition timing. A failure in the MAP sensor circuit should set a Code 33 or Code 34.

Manifold Air Temperature (MAT)

The Manifold Air Temperature (MAT) sensor also known as the IAT sensor, is a thermistor mounted in the intake manifold. A thermistor is a resistor which changes resistance based on temperature. Low manifold air temperature produces a high resistance (100,000 ohms at -40°F/-4°C), while high temperature cause low resistance (70 ohms at 266°F/130°C).

The ECM/PCM supplies a 5 volt signal to the MAT sensor through a resistor in the ECM/PCM and monitors the voltage. The voltage will be high when the manifold air is cold and low when the air is hot. By monitoring the voltage, the ECM calculates the air temperature and uses this data to help determine the fuel delivery and spark advance. A failure in the MAT or IAT sensor could result in Codes P0112 or P0113 for SFI vehicles and Codes 23 or 25 for MFI vehicles. Once the trouble code is set, the ECM/PCM will use an artificial default value for the MAT and some vehicle performance will return.

Mass Air Flow (MAF)

The Mass Air Flow (MAF) sensor measures the amount of air which passes through it. The ECM/PCM uses this information to determine the operating condition of the engine, to control fuel delivery. A large quantity of air indicates acceleration, while a small quantity indicates deceleration or idle.

This sensor produces a frequency output between 32 and 150 hertz. A scan tool will display air flow in terms of grams of air per second (gm/sec), with a range from 3gm/sec to 150 gm/sec. A failure in the MAF sensor could produce a Code of P0101 for SFI vehicles.

Vehicle Speed

➡A vehicle equipped with a speed sensor, should not be driven without a the speed sensor connected, as idle quality may be affected.

The Vehicle Speed Sensor (VSS) is mounted behind the speedometer in the instrument cluster or on the transaxle/speedometer drive gear. It provides electrical pulses to the ECM/PCM from the speedometer head. The pulses indicate the road speed. The ECM/PCM uses this information to operate the IAC, canister purge, and TCC.

Some vehicles equipped with digital instrument clusters use a Permanent Magnet (PM) generator to provide the VSS signal. The PM generator is located in the transaxle and replaces the speedometer cable. The signal from the PM generator drives a stepper motor which drives the odometer. A failure in the VSS circuit should set a Code 24 for MFI vehicles and Code P0502 for SFI vehicles.

Throttle Position (TPS)

The Throttle Position Sensor (TPS) is connected to the throttle shaft and is controlled by the throttle mechanism. A 5 volt reference signal is sent to the TPS from the ECM/PCM. As the throttle valve angle is changed (accelerator pedal moved), the resistance of the TPS also changes. At a closed throttle position, the resistance of the TPS is high, so the output voltage to the ECM/PCM will be low (approximately 0.5 volt). As the throttle plate opens, the resistance decreases so that, at wide open throttle, the output voltage should be approximately 5 volts. At closed throttle position, the voltage at the TPS should be less than 1.25 volts.

By monitoring the output voltage from the TPS, the ECM/PCM can determine fuel delivery based on throttle valve angle (driver demand). The TPS can either be misadjusted, shorted, open or loose. Misadjustment might result in poor idle or poor wide-open throttle performance. An open TPS signals the ECM/PCM that the throttle is always closed, resulting in poor performance. This usually sets a Code 22 for MFI vehicles. A shorted TPS gives the ECM/PCM a constant wide-open throttle signal and should set a Code 21 on MFI vehicles. A loose TPS on MFI vehicles indicates to the ECM/PCM that the throttle is moving. This causes intermittent bursts of fuel from the injector and an unstable idle. Once the trouble code is set, the ECM/PCM will use an artificial default value for the TBI and some vehicle performance will return.

A problem in the 5 volt circuit of SFI vehicles should set off Codes P0122 or P0123 and a problem with the TPS sensor ground circuit may set Codes P0123 and P0117. Once the DTC is set on SFI vehicles, the ECM/PCM will use an artificial default value based on the mass air flow for the TPS sensor and some vehicle performance will return. A high idle on SFI vehicles may result in Codes P0122 or P0123 to be set.

Crankshaft

Some systems use a magnetic crankshaft sensor, mounted remotely from the ignition module, which protrudes into the block within approximately 0.050 in. (0.127mm) of the crankshaft reluctor. The reluctor is a special wheel cast into the crankshaft with 7 slots machined into it, 6 of which are equally spaced (60 degrees apart). A seventh slot is spaced approximately 10 degrees from one of the other slots and serves to generate a **SYNC PULSE** signal. As the reluctor rotates as part of the crankshaft, the slots change the magnetic field of the sensor, creating an induced voltage pulse.

Based on the crank sensor pulses, the ignition module sends 2X reference signals to the ECM/PCM which are used to indicate crankshaft position and engine speed. The ignition module continues to send these reference pulses to the ECM at a rate of 1 per each 180 degrees of the crankshaft rotation. This signal is called the 2X reference because it occurs 2 times per crankshaft revolution.

The ignition also sends a second, 1X reference signal to the ECM/PCM which occurs at the same time as the **SYNC PULSE** from the crankshaft sensor. This signal is called the 1X reference because it occurs 1 time per crankshaft revolution. The 1X reference and the 2X reference signals are necessary for the ECM/PCM to determine when to activate the

fuel injectors. Also known as the 3X Crankshaft Position Sensor.

By comparing the time between pulses, the ignition module can recognize the pulse representing the seventh slot (sync pulse) which starts the calculation of the ignition coil sequencing. The second crank pulse following the **SYNC PULSE** signals the ignition module to fire the No. 2-3 ignition coil and the fifth crank pulse signals the module to fire the No. 1-4 ignition coil.

24X Crankshaft Position Sensor

The 24X sensor is used to improve the idle spark control at engine speeds up to approximately 1200 rpm. Four 24X pulses to be seen between two 3X pulses. If the sequence of these pulses is not correct for 50 engine revolutions, the ECM/PCM will set off a Code of P0321.

Dual Crank/Combination

The dual crank sensor is mounted in a pedestal on the front of the engine near the harmonic balancer. The sensor consists of 2 Hall Effect switches, which depend on 2 metal interrupter rings mounted on the balancer to activate them. Windows in the interrupters activate the hall effect switches as they provide a patch for the magnetic field between the switches transducers and magnets. When one of the hall effect switches is activated, it grounds the signal line to the C_3I module, pulling that signal line's (Sync Pulse or Crank) applied voltage low, which is interpreted as a signal.

Because of the way the signal is created by the dual crank sensor, the signal circuit is always either at a high or low voltage (square wave signal). Three crank signal pulses and one **SYNC PULSE** are created during each crankshaft revolution. The crank signal is used by the C_3I module to create a reference signal which is also a square wave signal similar to the crank signal. The reference signal is used to calculate the engine rpm and crankshaft position by the ECM/PCM. The **SYNC PULSE** is used by the C_3I module to begin the ignition coil firing sequence starting with No. 3-6 coil. The firing sequence begins with this coil because either piston No. 3 or piston No. 6 is now at the correct position in compression stroke for the spark plugs to be fired. Both the crank sensor and the **SYNC PULSE** signals must be received by the ignition module for the engine to start. A misadjusted sensor or bent interrupter ring could cause rubbing of the sensor resulting in potential driveability problems, such as rough idle, poor performance, or a nor start condition.

➡️**Failure to have the correct clearance will damage the crankshaft sensor.**

The dual crank sensor is not adjustable for ignition timing but positioning of the interrupter ring is very important. A clearance of 0.025 in. (0.635mm) is required on either side of the interrupter ring. A dual crank sensor that is damaged, due to mispositioning or a bent interrupter ring, can result in a hesitation, sag stumble or dieseling condition.

To determine if the dual crank sensor could be at fault, scan the engine rpm with a suitable scan tool, while driving the vehicle. An erratic display indicates that a proper reference pulse has not been received by the ECM/PCM, which may be the result of a malfunctioning dual crank sensor.

Air Conditioning Pressure

The air conditioning (A/C) pressure sensor provides a signal to the computer control module (ECM/PCM) which indicates varying high side refrigerant pressure between approximately 0-450 psi (0-3102 kPa). The ECM/PCM used this input to the A/C compressor load on the engine to help control the idle speed with the IAC valve.

The A/C pressure sensor electrical circuit consists of a 5 volt reference line and a ground line, both provided by the ECM/PCM and a signal line to the ECM/PCM. The signal is a voltage that varies approximately 0.1 volt at 0 psi (0 kPa), to 4.9 volts at 450 psi (3102 kPa) or more. A problem in the A/C pressure circuits or sensor should set a Code 66 on MFI vehicles and Code P1530 on SFI vehicles, then will make the A/C compressor inoperative.

Non-Air Conditioning Program Input

Vehicles not equipped with air conditioning (A/C) have a circuit connecting the ECM/PCM terminal **BC3** to ground, to program to operate without A/C related components connected to it. Vehicles with A/C do not have a wire in ECM **BC3** terminal. If this circuit is open on a non-A/C vehicle it may cause false Codes 26 and/or Code 66. If terminal **BC3** is grounded on A/C equipped vehicles, it will cause the compressor relay to be on whenever the ignition is in the **ON** position.

Detonation (Knock)
▶ See Figure 62

This sensor is a piezoelectric sensor located near the back of the engine (transaxle end). It generates electrical impulses which are directly proportional to the frequency of the knock which is detected. A buffer then sorts these signals and eliminates all except for those frequency range of detonation. This information is passed to the ESC module and then to the ECM/PCM, so that the ignition timing advance can be retarded until the detonation stops.

SWITCHES

Park/Neutral Switch

➡**Vehicle should not be driven with the park/neutral switch disconnected as idle quality may be affected in park or neutral and a Code 24 (VSS) may be set.**

This switch indicates to the ECM/PCM when the transaxle is in **P** or **N**. the information is used by the ECM/PCM for control on the torque converter clutch, EGR, and the idle air control valve operation.

Air Conditioning Request Signal

This signal indicates to the ECM/PCM that an air conditioning mode is selected at the switch and that the A/C low pressure switch is closed. The ECM/PCM controls the A/C and adjusts the idle speed in response to this signal.

Torque Converter Clutch Solenoid
▶ See Figure 63

The purpose of the torque converter clutch system is to eliminate power loss (slippage) by the converter and increase fuel economy. By locking the converter clutch, a more effective coupling to the flywheel is achieved. The converter clutch is operated by the ECM/PCM controlled torque converter clutch solenoid.

Power Steering Pressure Switch

The power steering pressure switch is used so that the power steering oil pressure pump load will not effect the engine idle. Turning the steering wheel increase the power steering oil pressure and pump load on the engine. The power steering pressure switch will close before the load can cause an idle problem. The ECM/PCM will also turn the A/C clutch off when high power steering pressure is detected.

Oil Pressure Switch

The oil pressure switch is usually mounted on the back of the engine, just below the intake manifold. Some vehicles use

86814078

Fig. 62 A piezoelectric sensor is located near the back of the engine (transaxle end). It generates electrical impulses which are directly proportional to the frequency of the knock which is detected

86814077

Fig. 63 The torque converter clutch solenoid operates in conjunction with the ECM/PCM to control the converter clutch the oil pressure switch as a parallel power supply, with the fuel pump relay and will provide voltage to the fuel pump, after approximately 4 psi (28 kPa) of oil pressure is reached. This switch will also help prevent engine seizure by shutting off the power to the fuel pump and causing the engine to stop when the oil pressure is lower than 4 psi (28 kPa).

EMISSION CONTROL SYSTEMS

Various components are used to control exhaust emissions from a vehicle. These components are controlled by the ECM/PCM based on different engine operating conditions. These components are described in the following paragraphs. Not all components are used on all engines.

Exhaust Gas Recirculation (EGR) System
▶ See Figure 64

EGR is a oxides of nitrogen (NOx) control which recycles exhaust gases through the combustion cycle by admitting exhaust gases into the intake manifold. The amount of exhaust gas admitted is adjusted by a vacuum controlled valve in response to engine operating conditions. If the valve is open, the recirculated exhaust gas is released into the intake manifold to be drawn into the combustion chamber.

The integral exhaust pressure modulated EGR valve uses a transducer responsive to exhaust pressure to modulate the vacuum signal to the EGR valve. The vacuum signal is provided by an EGR vacuum port in the throttle body valve. Under conditions when exhaust pressure is lower than the control pressure, the EGR signal is reduced by an air bleed within the transducer. Under conditions when exhaust pressure is higher than the control pressure, the air bleed is closed and the EGR valve responds to an unmodified vacuum signal. Physical arrangement of the valve components will vary depending on whether the control pressure is positive or negative.

The newer models use what is called a digital EGR valve. The digital EGR valve is designed to accurately supply EGR to an engine, independently of the intake manifold vacuum. The valve controls EGR flow from the exhaust to the intake manifold through three orifices which increment in size to produce seven different combinations. When a solenoid is energized, the armature, with the attached shaft and swivel pintle is lifted, this opens the orifice. The flow accuracy is dependant on the metering orifice size only, which results in improved control.

The digital EGR is opened by the ECM/PCM QDM (quad driver), grounding each respective solenoid circuit. The EGR valve usually opens under certain conditions such as, a warm engine operation, and an above idle speed condition.

Positive Crankcase Ventilation (PCV) System
▶ See Figure 65

A closed Positive Crankcase Ventilation (PCV) system is used to provide more complete scavenging of crankcase vapors. Fresh air from the air cleaner is supplied to the crankcase, mixed with blow-by gases and then passed through a PCV valve into the induction system.

The primary mode of crankcase ventilation control is through the PCV valve, which meters the mixture of fresh air and blow-by gases into the induction system at a rate dependent upon manifold vacuum.

To maintain the idle quality, the PCV valve restricts the ventilation system flow whenever intake manifold vacuum is designed to allow excessive amounts of blow-by gases to backflow through the breather assembly into the air cleaner and through the throttle body to be consumed by normal combustion.

Evaporative Emission Control (EEC) Systems

The basic evaporative emission control system used on all vehicles uses the carbon canister storage method. This method transfers fuel vapor to an activated carbon storage device for retention when the vehicle is not operating. A ported vacuum signal is used for purging vapors stored in the canister.

CONTROLLED CANISTER PURGE

The ECM/PCM controls a solenoid valve which controls vacuum to the purge valve in the charcoal canister. In open loop, before a specified time has expired and below a specified rpm, the solenoid valve is energized and blocks vacuum to the purge valve. When the system is in closed loop, after a specified time and above a specified rpm, the solenoid valve is de-energized and vacuum can be applied to the purge valve. This releases the collected vapors into the intake manifold. On systems not using an ECM/PCM controlled solenoid, a Thermo Vacuum Valve (TVV) is used to control purge. See the appropriate vehicle sections for checking procedures.

Air Management Control

The air management system aids in the reduction of exhaust emissions by supplying air to either the catalytic converter, engine exhaust manifold, or to the air cleaner. The ECM/PCM controls the air management system by energizing or de-energizing an air switching valve. Operation of the air switching valve is dependent upon such engine operating characteristics as coolant temperature, engine load, and acceleration (or deceleration), all of which are sensed by the ECM/PCM.

PULSAIR REACTOR SYSTEM

The Pulsair Injection Reactor (PAIR) system utilizes exhaust pressure pulsations to draw air into the exhaust system. Fresh air from the clean side of the air cleaner supplies filtered air to avoid dirt build-up on the check valve seat. The air cleaner also serves as a muffler for noise reduction. The internal mechanism of the Pulsair valve reacts to 3 distinct conditions.

The firing of the engine creates a pulsating flow of exhaust gases which are of positive (+) or negative (-) pressure. This pressure or vacuum is transmitted through external tubes to the Pulsair valve.

1. If the pressure is positive, the disc is forced to the closed position and no exhaust gas is allowed to flow past the valve and into the air supply line.

2. If there is a negative pressure (vacuum) in the exhaust system at the valve, the disc will open, allowing fresh air to mix with the exhaust gases.

3. Due to the inertia of the system, the disc ceases to follow the pressure pulsations at high engine rpm. At this point, the disc remains closed, preventing any further fresh air flow.

1	BOLT/SCREW
2	DIGITAL EGR VALVE
3	GASKET
4	EGR PAD (PART OF THE UPPER INTAKE MANIFOLD)
5	GASKET
6	FOLDED TABS
7	BRACKET (PART OF THE EGR PIPE ASSEMBLY)
8	EXHAUST MANIFOLD

86814075

Fig. 64 Newer models use a digital EGR valve, which is designed to accurately supply EGR to an engine, independent of intake manifold vacuum

Catalytic Converter

Of all emission control devices available, the catalytic converter is the most effective in reducing tailpipe emissions. The major tailpipe pollutants are hydrocarbons (HC), carbon monoxide (CO), and oxides of nitrogen (NOx).

SERVICE PRECAUTIONS

When working around any part of the fuel system, take precautionary steps to prevent fire and/or explosion:
• Disconnect negative terminal from battery (except when testing with battery voltage is required).
• When ever possible, use a flashlight instead of a drop light.
• Keep all open flame and smoking material out of the area.
• Use a shop cloth or similar to catch fuel when opening a fuel system.

• Relieve fuel system pressure before servicing.
• Use eye protection.
• Always keep a dry chemical (class B) fire extinguisher near the area.

➡**Due to the amount of fuel pressure in the fuel lines, before doing any work to the fuel system, the fuel system should be depressurized.**

Electrostatic Discharge Damage

Electronic components used in the control system are often design to carry very low voltage and are very susceptible to damage caused by electrostatic discharge. It is possible for less than 100 volts of static electricity to cause damage to some electronic components. By comparison it takes as much as 4000 volts for a person to even feel the zap of a static discharge.

There are several ways for a person to become statically charged. The most common methods of charging are by friction and induction. An example of charging by friction is a person sliding across a car seat, in which a charge as much

⇨ CLEAN AIR

→ VOLATILE OIL FUMES

- - -→ MIXTURE OF AIR AND FUMES

1 CRANKCASE VENTILATION VALVE
2 TO THROTTLE BODY
3 CRANKCASE VENT HOSE
4 CRANKCASE VENTILATION VALVE HOSE
5 TO INTAKE MANIFOLD

86814076

Fig. 65 The primary mode of crankcase ventilation control is through the PCV valve, which meters the mixture of fresh air and blow-by gases into the induction system at a rate dependent upon manifold vacuum

as 25,000 volts can build up. Charging by induction occurs when a person with well insulated shoes stands near a highly charged object and momentarily touches ground. Charges of the same polarity are drained off, leaving the person highly charged with the opposite polarity. Static charges of either type can cause damage, therefore, it is important to use care when handling and testing electronic components.

➡ **To prevent possible electrostatic discharge damage to the ECM/PCM, do not touch the connector pins or soldered components on the circuit board. When handling a PROM, Mem-Cal or Cal-Pak, do not touch the component leads and remove the integrated circuit from the carrier.**

ECM/PCM LEARNING ABILITY

The ECM/PCM has a learning capability. If the battery is disconnected, the learning process has to begin all over again. A change may be noted in the vehicle's performance. To teach the ECM/PCM, insure the vehicle is at operating temperature

and drive at part throttle, with moderate acceleration and idle conditions, until performance returns.

DLC/CHECK CONNECTOR

♦ **See Figure 66**

The Data Link Connector or Assembly Line Diagnostic Link (DLC/ALDL), is a diagnostic connector located usually under the instrument panel, it is sometimes covered by a plastic cover labeled "DIAGNOSTIC CONNECTOR." The assembly plant were the vehicles originate use these connectors to check the engine for proper operation before it leaves the plant. The connector can also be used by a technician to identify stored codes using different procedures and to read the ECM/PCM data using a hand held scan tool, such as TECH 1. Although it is recommended to use as hand held scan tool to read diagnostic trouble codes, it may be possible to flash codes on certain vehicle. These vehicles have a 12 pin DLC.

READING CODES AND DIAGNOSTIC MODES

This information is able to be read by putting the ECM/PCM into 1 of 4 different modes. These modes are entered by inserting a specific amount of resistance between the DLC/ALDL connector terminals A and B. The modes and resistances needed to enter these modes are as follows:

Diagnostic Modes — 0 Ohms

When 0 resistance is between terminals A and B of the DLC/ALDL connector, the diagnostic mode is entered. There are 2 positions to this mode. One with the engine **OFF**, but the ignition **ON**; the other is when the engine is running called Field Service Mode.

If the diagnostic mode is entered with the engine in the **OFF** position, trouble codes will flash and the idle air control motor will pulsate in and out. Also, the relays and solenoids are energized with the exception of the fuel pump and injector.

As a bulb and system check, the SERVICE ENGINE SOON light will come on with the ignition switch **ON** and the engine not running. When the engine is started, the SERVICE ENGINE SOON light will turn off. If the SERVICE ENGINE SOON light remains on, the self-diagnostic system has detected a problem.

If the B terminal is then grounded with the ignition **ON**, engine not running, each trouble code will flash and repeat 3 times. If more than 1 problem has been detected, each trouble code will flash 3 times. Trouble codes will flash in numeric order (lowest number first). The trouble code series will repeat as long as the B terminal is grounded.

A trouble code indicates a problem in a given circuit (Code 14, for example, indicates a problem in the coolant sensor circuit, this includes the coolant sensor, connector harness, and ECM/PCM). The procedure for pinpointing the problem can be found in diagnosis. Similar charts are provided for each code.

Also in this mode all ECM/PCM controlled relays and solenoids except the fuel pump relay. This allows checking the circuits which may be difficult to energize without driving the

A GROUND   **F** TCC (IF USED)

B DIAGNOSTIC TERMINAL (IF USED)   **M** SERIAL DATA

E SERIAL DATA (IF USED)   **L** SERIAL DATA (IF USED)

TERMINAL IDENTIFICATION (12 PIN DLC)

16 PIN DLC — **TERMINAL IDENTIFICATION**

2 SERIAL DATA (CLASS 2) (IF USED)   **6** OUTPUT/FIELD SERVICE ENABLE (IF USED)

4 GROUND   **9** SERIAL DATA (UART)

5 GROUND   **16** B+

86814079

Fig. 66 The Data Link Connector (DLC) or Assembly Line Diagnostic Link (ALDL) is a diagnostic connector located usually under the instrument panel. It is sometimes covered by a plastic cover labeled "DIAGNOSTIC CONNECTOR"

vehicle and being under particular operating conditions. The IAC valve will move to its fully extended position on most vehicles, block the idle air passage. This is useful in checking the minimum idle speed.

Field Service Mode — 0 Ohms

When the DLC/ALDL connector terminal B is grounded with the engine running, the ECM/PCM goes into the field service mode. In this mode, the SERVICE ENGINE SOON light flashes closed or open loop and indicates the rich/lean status of the engine. The ECM/PCM runs the engine at a fixed ignition timing advanced above the base setting.

The SERVICE ENGINE SOON light will show whether the system is in Open Loop or Closed Loop. In Open Loop the SERVICE ENGINE SOON light flashes 2 times and one half times per second. In Closed Loop the light flashes once per second. Also in Closed Loop, the light will stay OUT most of the time if the system is too lean. It will stay ON most of the time if the system is too rich. In either case the Field Service mode check, which is part of the Diagnostic circuit check, will lead you into choosing the correct diagnostic chart to refer to.

Back-up Mode — 3.9 Kilo-Ohms

The backup mode is entered by applying 3.9 kilo-ohms resistance between terminals A and B of the DLC/ALDL connector with the ignition switch in the **ON** position. The DLC/ALDL scanner tool can now read 5 of the 20 parameters on the data stream. These parameters are as mode status, oxygen sensor voltage, rpm, block learn and idle air control. There are 2 ways to enter the backup mode. Using a scan tool is one way, putting a 3.9 kilo-ohms resistor across terminals A and B of the DLC/ALDL is another.

Special Mode — 10 Kilo-Ohms

This special mode is entered by applying a 10K ohms resistor across terminals A and B. When this happens, the ECM/PCM does the following:
- Allows all of the serial data to be read
- Bypasses all timers
- Adds a calibrated spark advance
- Enables the canister purge solenoid on some engines
- Idles at 1000 rpm fixed idle air control and fixed base pulse width on the injector
- Forces the idle air control to reset at part throttle (approximately 2000 rpm)
- Disables the Park/Neutral restriction functions

Open or Road Test Mode — 20 Kilo-Ohms

The system is in this mode during normal operation and is used by a scan tool to extract data while driving the vehicle.

DLC/ALDL Scan Tester Information

An DLC/ALDL display unit (DLC/ALDL tester, scanner, monitor, etc), allows a you to read the engine control system information from the DLC/ALDL connector under the instrument panel. It can provide information faster than a digital voltmeter or ohmmeter can. The scan tool does not diagnose the exact location of the problem. The tool supplies information about the ECM/PCM, the information that it is receiving and the commands that it is sending plus special information such as integrator and block learn. To use an DLC/ALDL display tool you should understand thoroughly how an engine control system operates.

An DLC/ALDL scanner or monitor puts a fuel injection system into a special test mode. This mode commands an idle speed of 1000 rpm. The idle quality cannot be evaluated with a tester plugged in. When a scanner is in a special test mode it commands a fixed spark with no advance. On vehicles with Electronic Spark Control (ESC), there will be a fixed spark, but it will be advanced. On vehicles with ESC, there might be a serious spark knock, this spark knock could be bad enough so as not being able to road test the vehicle in the DLC/ALDL test mode. Be sure to check the tool manufacturer for instructions on special test modes which should overcome these limitations.

When a tester is used with a fuel injected engine, it bypasses the timer that keeps the system in Open Loop for a certain period of time. When all Closed Loop conditions are met, the engine will go into Closed Loop as soon as the vehicle is started. This means that the air management system will not function properly and air may go directly to the converter as soon as the engine is started.

These tools cannot diagnose everything. They do not tell where a problem is located in a circuit. The diagnostic charts to pinpoint the problems must still be used. These testers do not let you know if a solenoid or relay has been turned on. They only tell the you the ECM/PCM command. To find out if a solenoid has been turned on, check it with a suitable test light or digital voltmeter, or see if vacuum through the solenoid changes.

Scan Tools For Intermittents

In some scan tool applications, the data update rate may make the tool less effective than a voltmeter, such as when trying to detect an intermittent problem which lasts for a very short time. Some scan tools have a snapshot function which stores several seconds or even minutes of operation to located an intermittent problem. Scan tools allow one to manipulate the wiring harness or components under the hood with the engine not running while observing the scan tool's readout.

The scan tool can be plugged in and observed while driving the vehicle under the condition when the SERVICE ENGINE SOON light turns on momentarily or when the engine driveability is momentarily poor. If the problem seems to be related to certain parameters that can be checked on the scan tool, they should be checked while driving the vehicle. If there does not seem to be any correlation between the problem and any specific circuit, the scan tool can be checked on each position. Watching for a period of time to see if there is any change in the reading that indicates intermittent operation.

The scan tool is also an easy way to compare the operating parameters of a poorly operating engine with typical scan data for the vehicle being serviced or those of a known good engine. For example, a sensor may shift in value but not set a trouble code. Comparing the sensor's reading with those of a known good parameters may uncover the problem.

The scan tool has the ability to save time in diagnosis and prevent the replacement of good parts. The key to using the scan tool successfully for diagnosis lies in the ability to understand the system being diagnosed, as well as the scan tool's operation and limitations.

CLEARING TROUBLE CODES

When the ECM/PCM detects a problem with the system, the SERVICE ENGINE SOON light will come on and a trouble code will be recorded in the ECM/PCM memory. If the problem is intermittent, the SERVICE ENGINE SOON light will go out after 10 seconds, when the fault goes away. However the trouble code will stay in the ECM/PCM memory until the battery voltage to the ECM/PCM is removed. Removing the battery voltage for 10 seconds will clear all trouble codes. Do this by disconnecting the ECM/PCM harness from the positive battery terminal pigtail for 10 seconds with the key in the **OFF** position, or by removing the ECM/PCM fuse for 10 seconds with the key **OFF**.

➡ **To prevent ECM/PCM damage, the key must be OFF when disconnecting and reconnecting ECM/PCM power.**

INTEGRATOR AND BLOCK LEARN

The integrator and block learn functions of the ECM/PCM are responsible for making minor adjustments to the air/fuel ratio on the fuel injected GM vehicles. These small adjustments are necessary to compensate for pinpoint air leaks and normal wear.

The integrator and block learn are 2 separate ECM/PCM memory functions which control fuel delivery. The integrator makes a temporary change and the block learn makes a more permanent change. Both of these functions apply only while the engine is in Closed Loop. They represent the on-time of the injector. Also, integrator and block learn controls fuel delivery on the fuel injected engines as does the MC solenoid dwell on the CCC carbureted engines.

Integrator

Integrator is the term applied to a means of temporary change in fuel delivery. Integrator is displayed through the DLC/ALDL data line and monitored with a scanner as a number between 0 and 255 with an average of 128. The integrator monitors the oxygen sensor output voltage and adds and subtracts fuel depending on the lean or rich condition of the oxygen sensor. When the integrator is displaying 128, it indicates a neutral condition. This means that the oxygen sensor is seeing results of the 14.7:1 air/fuel mixture burned in the cylinders.

➡ **An air leak in the system (a lean condition) would cause the oxygen sensor voltage to decrease while the integrator would increase (add more fuel) to temporarily correct for the lean condition. If this happened the injector pulse width would increase.**

Block Learn

Although the integrator can correct fuel delivery over a wide range, it is only for a temporary correction. Therefore, another control called block learn was added. Although it cannot make as many corrections as the integrator, it does so for a longer period of time. It gets its name from the fact that the operating range of the engine for any given combinations of rpm and load is divided into 16 cell or blocks.

The computer has a given fuel delivery stored in each block. As the operating range gets into a given block the fuel delivery will be based on what value is stored in the memory in that block. Again, just like the integrator, the number represents the on-time of the injector. Also, just like the integrator, the number 128 represents no correction to the value that is stored in the cell or block. When the integrator increases or decreases, block learn which is also watching the integrator will make corrections in the same direction. As the block learn makes corrections, the integrator correction will be reduced until finally the integrator will return to 128 if the block learn has corrected the fuel delivery.

Block Learn Memory

Block learn operates on 1 of 2 types of memories depending on application: non-volatile or volatile. The non-volatile memories retain the value in the block learn cells even when the ignition switch is turned **OFF**. When the engine is restarted, the fuel delivery for a given block will be based on information stored in memory.

The volatile memories lose the numbers stored in the block learn cells when the ignition is turned to the **OFF** position. Upon restarting, the block learn starts at 128 in every block and corrects from that point as necessary.

Integrator/Block Learn Limits

Both the integrator and block learn have limits which will vary from engine to engine. If the mixture is off enough so that the block learn reaches the limit of its control and still cannot correct the condition, the integrator would also go to its limit of control in the same direction and the engine would then begin to run poorly. If the integrators and block learn are close to or at their limits of control, the engine hardware should be checked to determine the cause of the limits being reached, vacuum leaks, sticking injectors, etc.

If the integrator is lied to, for example, if the oxygen sensor lead was grounded (lean signal) the integrator and block learn would add fuel to the engine to cause it to run rich. However, with the oxygen sensor lead grounded, the ECM/PCM would continue seeing a lean condition eventually setting a Code 44 and the fuel control system would change to open loop operations.

CLOSED LOOP FUEL CONTROL

The purpose of closed loop fuel control is to precisely maintain an air/fuel mixture 14.7:1. When the air/fuel mixture is maintained at 14.7:1, the catalytic converter is able to operate at maximum efficiency which results in lower emission levels.

Since the ECM/PCM controls the air/fuel mixture, it needs to check its output and correct the fuel mixture for deviations from the ideal ratio. The oxygen sensor feeds this output information back to the ECM/PCM.

ENGINE PERFORMANCE DIAGNOSIS

Engine performance diagnostic procedures are guides that will lead to the most probable causes of engine performance complaints. They consider the components of the fuel, ignition, and mechanical systems that could cause a particular complaint, and then outline repairs in a logical sequence.

It is important to determine if the SERVICE ENGINE SOON light is on or has come on for a short interval while driving. If the SERVICE ENGINE SOON light has come on, the Computer Command Control System should be checked for stored **TROUBLE CODES** which may indicate the cause for the performance complaint.

All of the symptoms can be caused by worn out or defective parts such as spark plugs, ignition wiring, etc. If time and/or mileage indicate that parts should be replaced, it is recommended that it be done.

➡**Before checking any system controlled by the Electronic Fuel Injection (EFI) system, the Diagnostic Circuit Check must be performed or misdiagnosis may occur. If the complaint involves the SERVICE ENGINE SOON light, go directly to the Diagnostic Circuit Check.**

Basic Troubleshooting

➡**The following explains how to activate the trouble code signal light in the instrument cluster and gives an explanation of what each code means. This is not a full system troubleshooting and isolation procedure.**

Before suspecting the system or any of its components as faulty, check the ignition system including distributor, timing, spark plugs and wires. Check the engine compression, air cleaner, and emission control components not controlled by the ECM/PCM. Also check the intake manifold, vacuum hoses and hose connectors for leaks.

The following symptoms could indicate a possible problem with the system:

- Detonation
- Stalls or rough idle-cold
- Stalls or rough idle-hot
- Missing
- Hesitation
- Surges
- Poor gasoline mileage
- Sluggish or spongy performance
- Hard starting-cold
- Objectionable exhaust odors (that rotten egg smell)
- Cuts out
- Improper idle speed

As a bulb and system check, the SERVICE ENGINE SOON light will come on when the ignition switch is turned to the **ON** position but the engine is not running. The SERVICE ENGINE SOON light will also produce the trouble code or codes by a series of flashes which translate as follows. When the diagnostic test terminal under the dash is grounded, with the ignition in the **ON** position and the engine not running, the SERVICE ENGINE SOON light will flash once, pause, then flash twice in rapid succession. This is a Code 12, which indicates that the diagnostic system is working. After a long pause, the Code 12 will repeat itself 2 more times. The cycle will then repeat itself until the engine is started or the ignition is turned **OFF**.

When the engine is started, the SERVICE ENGINE SOON light will remain on for a few seconds, then turn off. If the SERVICE ENGINE SOON light remains on, the self-diagnostic system has detected a problem. If the test terminal is then grounded, the trouble code will flash 3 times. If more than 1 problem is found, each trouble code will flash 3 times. Trouble codes will flash in numerical order (lowest code number to highest). The trouble codes series will repeat as long as the test terminal is grounded.

A trouble code indicates a problem with a given circuit. For example, trouble Code 14 indicates a problem in the cooling sensor circuit. This includes the coolant sensor, its electrical harness, and the ECM/PCM. Since the self-diagnostic system cannot diagnose every possible fault in the system, the absence of a trouble code does not mean the system is trouble-free. To determine problems within the system which do not activate a trouble code, a system performance check must be made.

In the case of an intermittent fault in the system, the SERVICE ENGINE SOON light will go out when the fault goes away, but the trouble code will remain in the memory of the ECM/PCM. Therefore, it a trouble code can be obtained even though the SERVICE ENGINE SOON light is not on, the trouble code must be evaluated. It must be determined if the fault is intermittent or if the engine must be at certain operating conditions (under load, etc.) before the SERVICE ENGINE SOON light will come on. Some trouble codes will not be recorded in the ECM/PCM until the engine has been operated at part throttle for about 5-18 minutes.

INTERMITTENT SERVICE ENGINE SOON LIGHT

An intermittent open in the ground circuit would cause loss of power through the ECM/PCM and intermittent SERVICE ENGINE SOON light operation. When the ECM/PCM loses ground, distributor ignition is lost. An intermittent open in the ground circuit would be described as an engine miss.

Therefore, an intermittent SERVICE ENGINE SOON light, no code stored and a driveability comment described as similar to a miss will require checking the grounding circuit and the Code 12 circuit as it originates at the ignition coil.

UNDERVOLTAGE TO THE ECM/PCM

An undervoltage condition below 9 volts will cause the SERVICE ENGINE SOON light to come on as long as the condition exist.

Therefore, an intermittent SERVICE ENGINE SOON light, no code stored and a driveability comment described as similar to a miss will require checking the grounding circuit, Code 12 circuit and the ignition feed circuit to terminal C of the ECM/PCM. This does nor eliminate the necessity of checking the normal vehicle electrical system for possible cause such as a loose battery cable.

OVERVOLTAGE TO THE ECM/PCM

The ECM/PCM will also shut off when the power supply rises above 16 volts. The overvoltage condition will also cause the SERVICE ENGINE SOON to come on as long as this condition exists.

A momentary voltage surge in a vehicle's electrical system is a common occurrence. These voltage surges have never presented any problems because the entire electrical system acted as a shock absorber until the surge dissipated. Voltage surges or spikes in the vehicle's electrical system have been known, on occasion, to exceed 100 volts.

The system is a low voltage (between 9 and 16 volts) system and will not tolerate these surges. The ECM/PCM will be shut off by any surge in excess of 16 volts and will come back on, only after the surge has dissipated sufficiently to bring the voltage under 16 volts.

A surge will usually occur when an accessory requiring a high voltage supply is turned off or down. The voltage regulator in the vehicle's charging system cannot react to the changes in the voltage demands quickly enough and surge occurs. The driver should be questioned to determine which accessory circuit was turned off that caused the SERVICE ENGINE SOON light to come on.

Therefore, intermittent SERVICE ENGINE SOON light operation, with no trouble code stored, will require installation of a diode in the appropriate accessory circuit.

TPS OUTPUT CHECK TEST

Due to the varied application of components, a general procedure is outlined. For the exact procedure for the vehicle being service use Code 21 or 22 chart the appropriate engine.

With Scan Tool

1. Use a suitable scan tool to read the TPS voltage.
2. With the ignition switch **ON** and the engine **OFF**, the TPS voltage should be less than 1.25 volts.
3. If the voltage reading is higher than specified, replace the throttle position sensor.

Without Scan Tool

1. Remove air cleaner. Disconnect the TPS harness from the TPS.
2. Using suitable jumper wires, connect a digital voltmeter J-29125-A or equivalent to the correct TPS terminals A and B.
3. With the ignition **ON** and the engine running, The TPS voltage should be 0.3-1.0 volts at base idle to approximately 4.5 volts at wide open throttle.
4. If the reading on the TPS is out of specification, check the minimum idle speed before replacing the TPS.
5. If the voltage reading is correct, remove the voltmeter and jumper wires and reconnect the TPS connector to the sensor.
6. Reinstall the air cleaner.

FUEL SYSTEM PRESSURE

Testing

When the ignition switch is turned **ON**, the in-tank fuel pump is energized for as long as the engine is cranking or running and the control unit is receiving signals from the HEI distributor or DIS. If there are no reference pulses, the control unit will shut off the fuel pump within 2 seconds. The pump will deliver fuel to the fuel rail and injectors and then to the pressure regulator, where the system pressure is controlled to maintain 26-46 psi (179-317 kPa). Each vehicle varies slightly in the amount of psi.

1. Connect pressure gauge J-34730-1, or equivalent, to fuel pressure test point on the fuel rail. Wrap a rag around the pressure tap to absorb any leakage that may occur when installing the gauge.
2. Turn the ignition **ON** and check that pump pressure is 24-40 psi (165-275 kPa). This pressure is controlled by spring pressure within the regulator assembly.
3. Start the engine and allow it to idle. The fuel pressure should drop to 28-32 psi (193-220 kPa) due to the lower manifold pressure.

➡**The idle pressure will vary somewhat depending on barometric pressure. Check for a drop in pressure indicating regulator control, rather than specific values.**

4. On turbocharged vehicles, use a low pressure air pump to apply air pressure to the regulator to simulate turbocharger boost pressure. Boost pressure should increase fuel pressure by 1 lb. for every lb. of boost. Again, look for changes rather

than specific pressures. The maximum fuel pressure should not exceed 46 psi (317 kPa).

5. If the fuel pressure drops, check the operation of the check valve, the pump coupling connection, fuel pressure regulator valve and the injectors. A restricted fuel line or filter may also cause a pressure drip. To check the fuel pump output, restrict the fuel return line and run 12 volts to the pump. The fuel pressure should rise to approximately 75 psi (517 kPa) with the return line restricted.

❄❄CAUTION

Before attempting to remove or service any fuel system component, it is necessary to relieve the fuel system pressure.

CRANKSHAFT SENSOR

Inspection

1. Disconnect the negative battery cable.
2. Rotate the harmonic balancer using a 28mm socket and pull on the handle until the interrupter ring fills the sensor slots and edge of the interrupter window is aligned with the edge of the deflector on the pedestal.
3. Insert feeler gauge adjustment tool J-36179 or equivalent into the gap between the sensor and the interrupter on each side of the interrupter ring.
4. If the gauge will not slide past the sensor on either side of the interrupter ring, the sensor is out of adjustment or the interrupter ring is bent.
5. The clearance should be checked again, at 3 positions around the interrupter ring approximately 120° apart.

TROUBLE CODE CHARTS

Following is a listing of the Diagnostic Trouble Code Charts for the various engine control systems covered in this manual. When using these charts along with the ECU self-diagnostic system, remember that a code only points to a faulty circuit, not necessarily to a faulty component. Loose, damaged or corroded connections may contribute to a fault code on a cir-

6. If found out of adjustment, the sensor should be removed and inspected for potential damage.

MFI SYSTEM DIAGNOSTIC CHARTS

To properly diagnose driveability problems, refer to the following trouble code charts. Make certain the charts cover the appropriate engine. If your check engine light is not lit, check for engine stored engine codes. If any codes are stored write them down for reference later. Clear the codes as described earlier. Road test the vehicle to see if any of the codes return. Never try to fix a code problem until you're sure that it comes back. It may have been an old code.

After clearing any codes and checking that they do not return. If the car drives fine you're finished. But if there are no codes and the car runs poorly you'll need to check the symptoms charts. The problem is most likely not the computer or the devices it controls but the ignition system or engine mechanical.

If you do have a code(s) that returns start with the lowest code and follow the proper chart. You must follow every step of the chart and not jump from test to test or you'll never be certain to find and fix the real problem.

Start with the lowest to highest code chart, making sure to use the charts for your engine. If you have a 50 series code, like code 54. Always check those out first. They are rare but usually indicate a problem with the computer itself or its ability to test itself properly.

➡**Whereas component repair and replacement are covered in Section 5, this section only deals with testing the system for driveability and emission problems.**

cuit when the sensor or component is operating properly. Be sure that the components are faulty before replacing them, especially the expensive ones. Since many of these codes vary from year-to-year, be sure to refer to the appropriate charts.

CARBURETED FUEL SYSTEM

DIAGNOSTIC ENGINE PERFORMANCE CHART

Preliminary Conditions: If the check engine light is not on, follow the procedures for checking a driveability complaint on any vehicle not equipped with a C4 system. When the generator or coolant light is on at the same time as the check engine light, check for a generator or coolant problem first. Inspect for poor connections at the coolant sensor, M/C solenoid and wiring. Check for loose vacuum hoses and connections and repair as needed.

Any time an engine is started, even a warm engine, it must be run at part throttle for 3 minutes or until the dwell starts to vary before proceeding with any checks.

Driver Complaint	Probable Cause	Correction or Additonal Testing
Intermittent check engine light but no trouble code stored	1. Engine runs below 200 rpm	1. No correction—code not stored when caused by low rpm condition
	2. Poor electrical connection ⊕ at the distributor tach to ECM "A" terminal	2. Repair or tighten connections
	3. Poor connection from the ⊕ "1" ignition to the ECM "V" terminal	3. Repair or tighten connections
	4. Poor connection from the ⊕ ECM "T" to terminal to ground	4. Repair or tighten connections
	5. Tach filter defective or faulty. The filter should have 14,000–18,000 ohms when checked with an end disconnected and an open circuit to ground	5. Replace tach filter
	6. Low battery voltage (less than 9 volts)	6. Recharge battery/repair charging system
Loss of long term memory	1. Defective 20 amp ECS fuse	1. Replace 20 amp ECS fuse
	2. Defective Electronic Control Module—ECM Momentarily ground the dwell lead with engine idling and test lead disconnected. This should produce a code 23, which should be retained after the engine is stopped and restarted. If voltage is present at the long term memory terminal "S" of the ECM, but the code is not stored, the ECM is defective	2. Replace the ECM
Backfire during warmup	1. A.I.R. pump diverter valve not shiting air to air cleaner for 5 seconds after engine start up or on quick deceleration	1. Replace the diverter valve
Poor gas mileage	1. Air management switch not shifting air pump output to the catalytic converter upon TVS signal after engine warmup	1. Replace air switch valve.
Full throttle performance complaint	1. Follow TPS chart number 4	1. Repair as check out indicates
All other complaints	1. Make systems perform-check on warm engine	1. Repair as check out indicates

NOTE: System performance checks should be performed after any repairs to the C4 system have been completed.
⊕ On 3.8L V6 trace the circuit: Distributor module terminal "R" to ECM terminal "10", Bat. to ECM terminal "C" and "R", and ECM terminal "U" to ground.

86814090

Fig. 67 Computer Controlled Catalatic Converter ("C4") system

Computer Controlled Catalytic Converter—C4

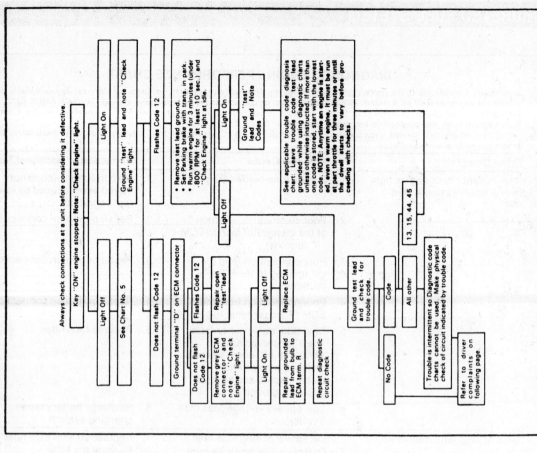

Always check connections at a unit before considering it defective.

Key "ON" engine stopped. Note: "Check Engine" light.

Light On
→ Light Off → See Chart No. 5

Light On
→ Ground "test" lead and note "Check Engine" light.
- Flashes Code 12
- Does not flash Code 12 → Ground terminal "D" on ECM connector
  - Flashes Code 12
  - Does not flash Code 12 → Remove grey ECM connector and note "Check Engine" light.
    - Light On → Repair grounded lead from bulb to ECM term. R
    - Light Off → Replace ECM
  - Repair open "test"lead → Repeat diagnostic circuit check

- Remove test lead ground.
- Set Parking brake with trans. in park.
- Run warm engine for 3 minutes (under 800 RPM for at least 10 sec.) and "Check Engine" light at idle.

Ground "test" lead and Note Codes

See applicable trouble code diagnosis chart. Leave trouble code test lead grounded while using diagnostic charts unless otherwise instructed. If more than one code is stored, start with the lowest code. NOTE: Anytime an engine is started, even a warm engine, it must be run at part throttle for three minutes or until the dwell starts to vary before proceeding with checks.

Ground test lead and check for trouble code.
- No Code → Trouble is intermittent so Diagnostic code charts cannot be used. Make physical check of circuit indicated by trouble code.
- Code
- All other → 13, 15, 44, 45
  - Refer to driver complaints on following page.

Computer Controlled Catalytic Converter—C4

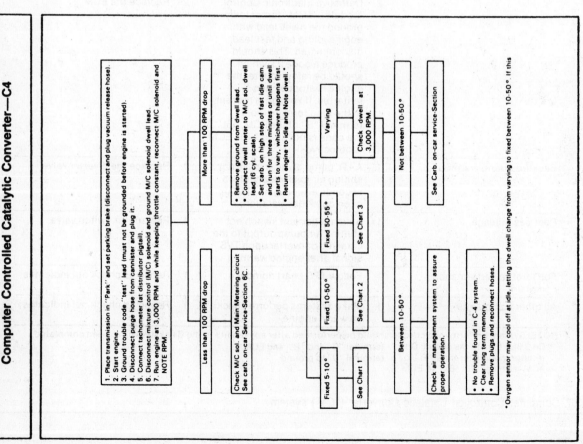

1. Place transmission in "Park" and set parking brake (disconnect and plug vacuum release hose).
2. Start engine.
3. Ground trouble code "test" lead (must not be grounded before engine is started).
4. Disconnect purge hose from cannister and plug it.
5. Connect tachometer (at distributor pigtail).
6. Disconnect mixture control (M/C) solenoid and ground M/C solenoid dwell lead.
7. Run engine at 3,000 RPM and while keeping throttle constant, reconnect M/C solenoid and NOTE RPM.

Less than 100 RPM drop
→ Check M/C sol. and Main Metering circuit See carb. on-car Service-Section 6C.

More than 100 RPM drop
- Remove ground from dwell lead.
- Connect dwell meter to M/C sol. dwell lead (6 cyl. scale).
- Set carb. on high step of fast idle cam and run for three minutes or until dwell starts to vary, whichever happens first.
- Return engine to idle and Note dwell. *

- Fixed 5-10° → See Chart 1
- Fixed 10-50° → See Chart 2
- Fixed 50-55° → See Chart 3
- Varying
  - Check dwell at 3,000 RPM.
    - Between 10-50° → Check air management system to assure proper operation.
      - No trouble found in C-4 system.
      - Clear long term memory.
      - Remove plugs and reconnect hoses.
    - Not between 10-50° → See Carb. on-car service-Section

*Oxygen sensor may cool off at idle, letting the dwell change from varying to fixed between 10-50°. If this

86814091

Computer Controlled Catalytic Converter—C4

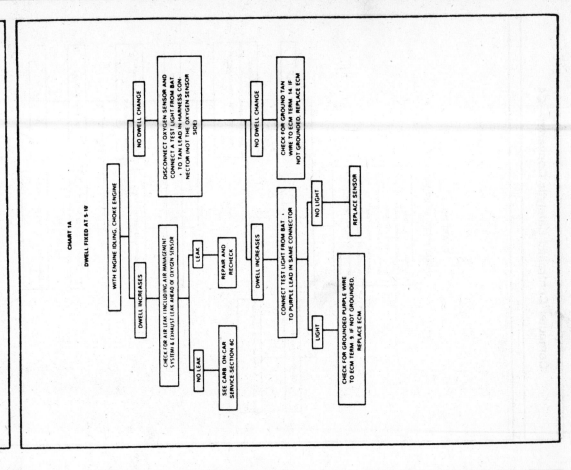

CHART 1A

DWELL FIXED AT 5-10°

WITH ENGINE IDLING, CHOKE ENGINE

DWELL INCREASES → CHECK FOR AIR LEAK (INCLUDING AIR MANAGEMENT SYSTEM) & EXHAUST LEAK AHEAD OF OXYGEN SENSOR

LEAK → REPAIR AND RECHECK

NO LEAK → SEE CARB ON-CAR SERVICE SECTION 6C

NO DWELL CHANGE → DISCONNECT OXYGEN SENSOR AND CONNECT A TEST LIGHT FROM BAT. + TO TAN LEAD IN HARNESS CONNECTOR (NOT THE OXYGEN SENSOR SIDE)

NO DWELL CHANGE → CHECK FOR GROUND TAN WIRE TO ECM TERM. 14 IF NOT GROUNDED, REPLACE ECM

DWELL INCREASES → CONNECT TEST LIGHT FROM BAT. + TO PURPLE LEAD IN SAME CONNECTOR

NO LIGHT → REPLACE SENSOR

LIGHT → CHECK FOR GROUNDED PURPLE WIRE TO ECM TERM. 9 IF NOT GROUNDED, REPLACE ECM

Computer Controlled Catalytic Converter—C4

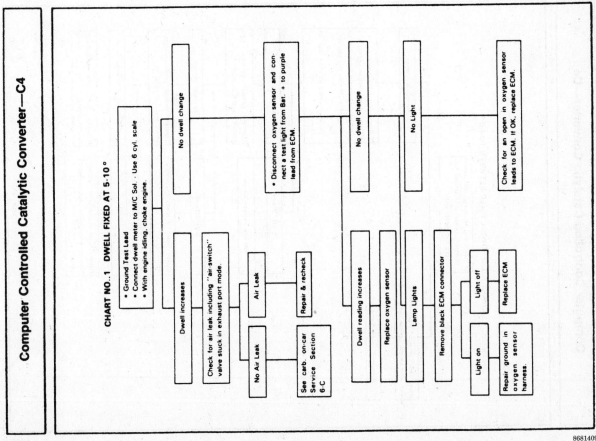

CHART NO. 1   DWELL FIXED AT 5-10°

- Ground Test Lead
- Connect dwell meter to M/C Sol. - Use 6 cyl. scale
- With engine idling, choke engine.

Dwell increases → Check for air leak including "air-switch" valve stuck in exhaust port mode.

Air Leak → Repair & recheck

No Air Leak → See carb. on-car Service Section 6-C

No dwell change → • Disconnect oxygen sensor and connect a test light from Bat. + to purple lead from ECM.

Dwell reading increases → Replace oxygen sensor

No dwell change → Lamp Lights → Remove black ECM connector

Light on → Repair ground in oxygen sensor harness.

Light off → Replace ECM

No Light → Check for an open in oxygen sensor leads to ECM. If OK, replace ECM.

Computer Controlled Catalytic Converter—C4

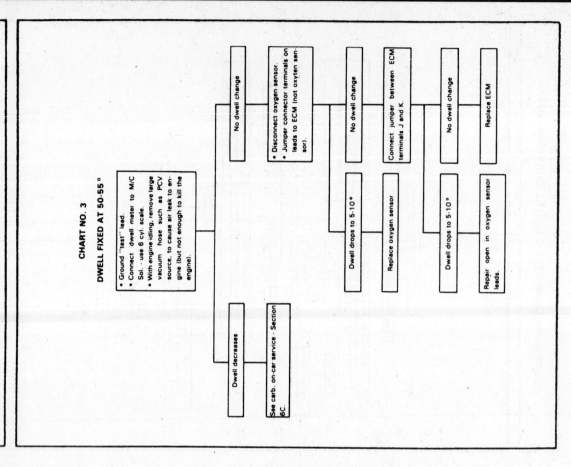

CHART NO. 3

DWELL FIXED AT 50-55°

- Ground "test" lead.
- Connect dwell meter to M/C Sol. - use 6 cyl. scale.
- With engine idling, remove large vacuum hose such as PCV source, to cause air leak to engine (but not enough to kill the engine).

Dwell decreases

See carb. on-car service - Section 6C.

No dwell change

- Disconnect oxygen sensor.
- Jumper connector terminals on leads to ECM (not oxyiten sensor).

Dwell drops to 5-10°

Replace oxygen sensor

No dwell change

Connect jumper between ECM terminals J and K.

Dwell drops to 5-10°

Repair open in oxygen sensor leads.

No dwell change

Replace ECM

Computer Controlled Catalytic Converter—C4

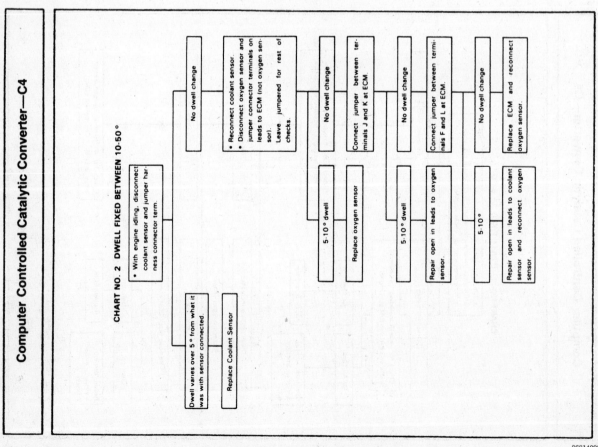

CHART NO. 2 DWELL FIXED BETWEEN 10-50°

- With engine idling, disconnect coolant sensor and jumper harness connector term.

Dwell varies over 5° from what it was with sensor connected.

Replace Coolant Sensor

No dwell change

- Reconnect coolant sensor.
- Disconnect oxygen sensor and jumper connector terminals on leads to ECM (not oxygen sensor).
  Leave jumpered for rest of checks.

5-10° dwell

Replace oxygen sensor

No dwell change

Connect jumper between terminals J and K at ECM.

5-10° dwell

Repair open in leads to oxygen sensor.

No dwell change

Connect jumper between terminals F and L at ECM.

5-10°

Repair open in leads to coolant sensor and reconnect oxygen sensor.

No dwell change

Replace ECM and reconnect oxygen sensor.

Computer Controlled Catalytic Converter—C4

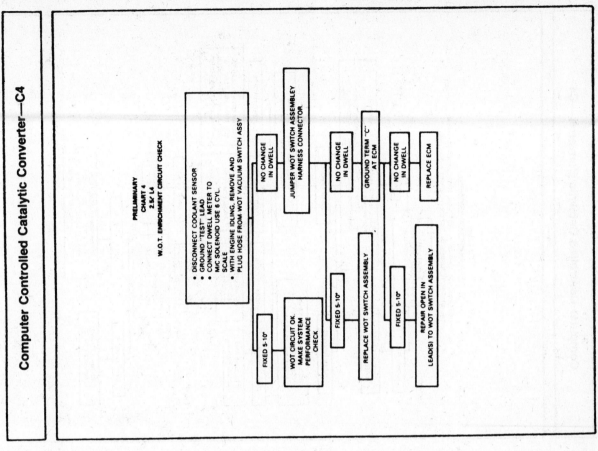

PRELIMINARY
CHART 4
2.5" L4
W.O.T. ENRICHMENT CIRCUIT CHECK

- DISCONNECT COOLANT SENSOR
- GROUND "TEST" LEAD
- CONNECT DWELL METER TO MC SOLENOID USE 6 CYL. SCALE
- WITH ENGINE IDLING, REMOVE AND PLUG HOSE FROM WOT VACUUM SWITCH ASSY

FIXED 5-10°	NO CHANGE IN DWELL

WOT CIRCUIT OK MAKE SYSTEM PERFORMANCE CHECK

JUMPER WOT SWITCH ASSEMBLEY HARNESS CONNECTOR.

FIXED 5-10°	NO CHANGE IN DWELL

REPLACE WOT SWITCH ASSEMBLY

GROUND TERM "C" AT ECM

FIXED 5-10°	NO CHANGE IN DWELL

REPAIR OPEN IN LEAD(S) TO WOT SWITCH ASSEMBLY

REPLACE ECM

Computer Controlled Catalytic Converter—C4

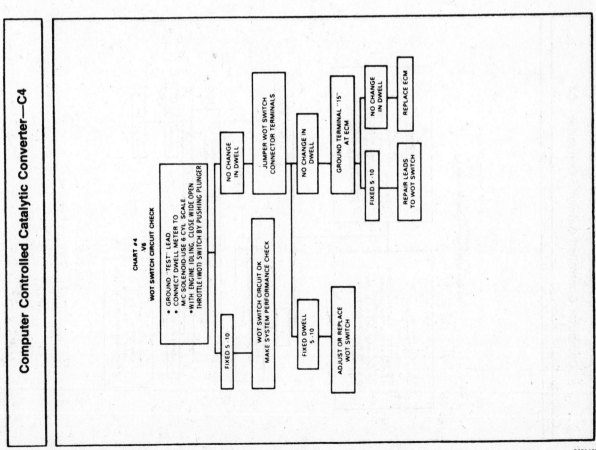

CHART #4
V6
WOT SWITCH CIRCUIT CHECK

- GROUND "TEST" LEAD
- CONNECT DWELL METER TO MC SOLENOID-USE 6 CYL. SCALE
- WITH ENGINE IDLING, CLOSE WIDE OPEN THROTTLE (WOT) SWITCH BY PUSHING PLUNGER

FIXED 5 -10	NO CHANGE IN DWELL

WOT SWITCH CIRCUIT OK MAKE SYSTEM PERFORMANCE CHECK

JUMPER WOT SWITCH CONNECTOR TERMINALS

FIXED DWELL 5 -10	NO CHANGE IN DWELL

ADJUST OR REPLACE WOT SWITCH

GROUND TERMINAL "15" AT ECM

FIXED 5 -10	NO CHANGE IN DWELL

REPAIR LEADS TO WOT SWITCH

REPLACE ECM

86814094

Computer Controlled Catalytic Converter—C4

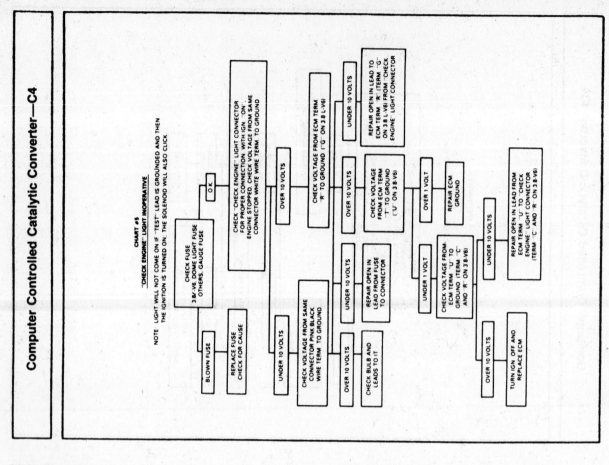

CHART #5
"CHECK ENGINE" LIGHT INOPERATIVE

NOTE LIGHT WILL NOT COME ON IF "TEST" LEAD IS GROUNDED AND THEN THE IGNITION IS TURNED ON. THE SOLENOID WILL ALSO CLICK

Computer Controlled Catalytic Converter—C4

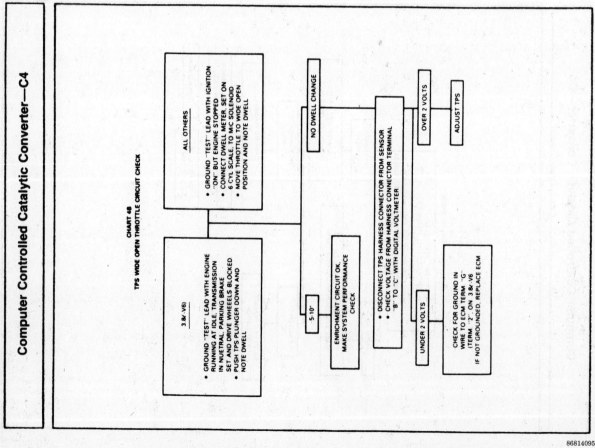

CHART 4B
TPS WIDE OPEN THROTTLE CIRCUIT CHECK

86814095

Computer Controlled Catalytic Converter—C4

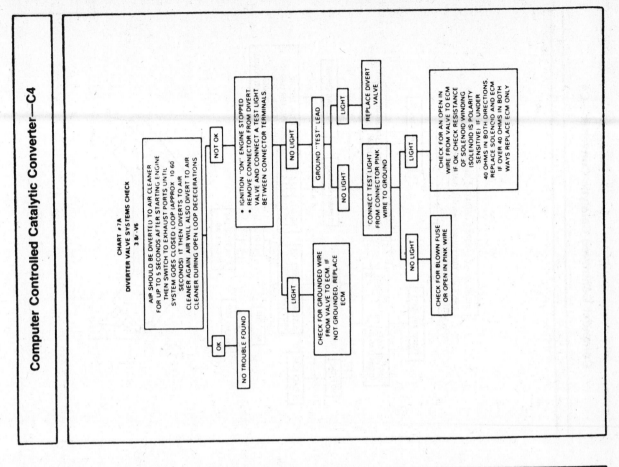

Computer Controlled Catalytic Converter—C4

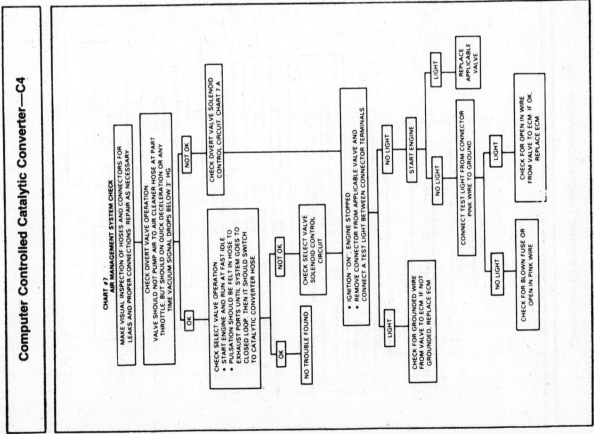

86814096

Computer Controlled Catalytic Converter—C4

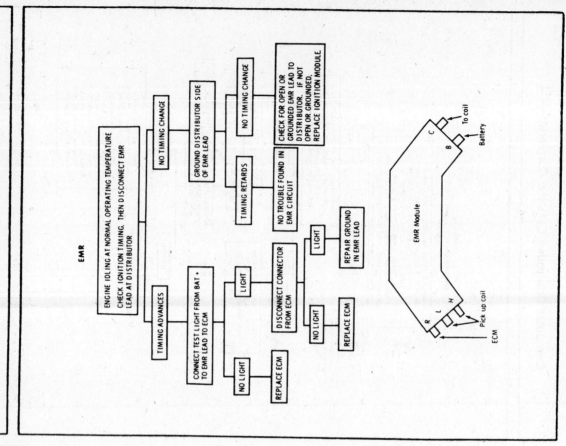

Computer Controlled Catalytic Converter—C4

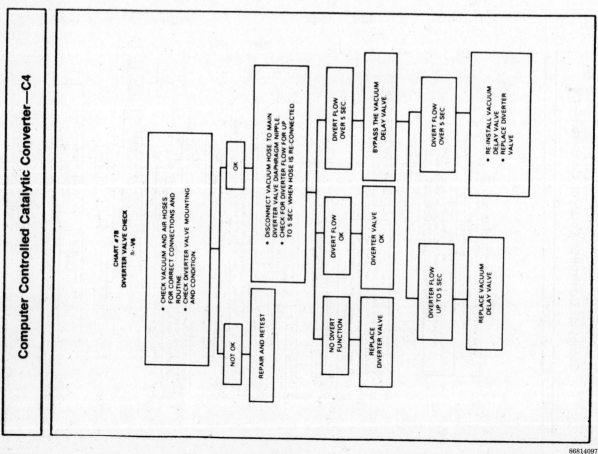

Computer Controlled Catalytic Converter—C4

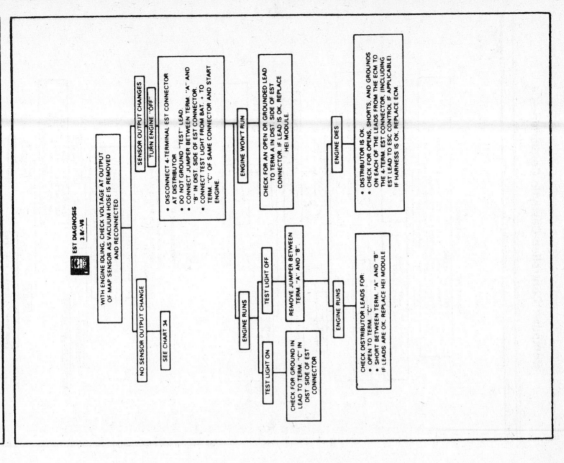

EST DIAGNOSIS
3.8ℓ-V6

WITH ENGINE IDLING, CHECK VOLTAGE AT OUTPUT OF MAP SENSOR AS VACUUM HOSE IS REMOVED AND RECONNECTED

SENSOR OUTPUT CHANGES
TURN ENGINE "OFF"

NO SENSOR OUTPUT CHANGE

SEE CHART 34

DISCONNECT 4-TERMINAL EST CONNECTOR AT DISTRIBUTOR
- DO NOT GROUND "TEST" LEAD
- CONNECT JUMPER BETWEEN TERM. "A" AND "B" IN DIST. SIDE OF EST CONNECTOR
- CONNECT TEST LIGHT FROM BAT. + TO TERM. "C" OF SAME CONNECTOR AND START ENGINE.

ENGINE RUNS

ENGINE WON'T RUN

TEST LIGHT ON

TEST LIGHT OFF

CHECK FOR GROUND IN LEAD TO TERM. "C" IN DIST. SIDE OF EST CONNECTOR

CHECK FOR AN OPEN OR GROUNDED LEAD TO TERM. A IN DIST. SIDE OF EST CONNECTOR. IF LEAD IS OK. REPLACE HEI MODULE.

REMOVE JUMPER BETWEEN TERM. "A" AND "B"

ENGINE RUNS

ENGINE DIES

CHECK DISTRIBUTOR LEADS FOR:
- OPEN TO TERM. "C"
- SHORT BETWEEN TERM. "A" AND "B"
IF LEADS ARE OK. REPLACE HEI MODULE

DISTRIBUTOR IS OK.
- CHECK FOR OPENS, SHORTS, AND GROUNDS ON EACH OF THE LEADS FROM THE ECM TO THE 4-TERM. EST CONNECTOR. (INCLUDING EST LEAD TO ESC CONTROL IF APPLICABLE) IF HARNESS IS OK. REPLACE ECM.

Computer Controlled Catalytic Converter—C4

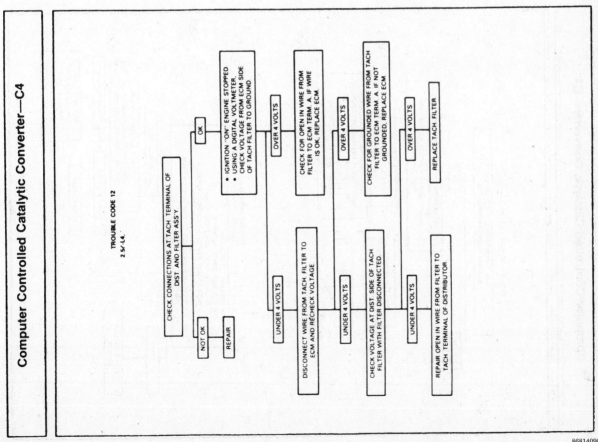

TROUBLE CODE 12
2.5ℓ-L4.

CHECK CONNECTIONS AT TACH TERMINAL OF DIST AND FILTER ASS'Y

NOT OK

REPAIR

OK
- IGNITION "ON" ENGINE STOPPED
- USING A DIGITAL VOLTMETER, CHECK VOLTAGE FROM ECM SIDE OF TACH FILTER TO GROUND

OVER 4 VOLTS

UNDER 4 VOLTS

DISCONNECT WIRE FROM TACH FILTER TO ECM AND RECHECK VOLTAGE

CHECK FOR OPEN IN WIRE FROM FILTER TO ECM TERM. A. IF WIRE IS OK. REPLACE ECM.

OVER 4 VOLTS

UNDER 4 VOLTS

CHECK VOLTAGE AT DIST SIDE OF TACH FILTER WITH FILTER DISCONNECTED

CHECK FOR GROUNDED WIRE FROM TACH FILTER TO ECM TERM. A. IF NOT GROUNDED, REPLACE ECM.

OVER 4 VOLTS

UNDER 4 VOLTS

REPLACE TACH FILTER

REPAIR OPEN IN WIRE FROM FILTER TO TACH TERMINAL OF DISTRIBUTOR

86814098

Computer Controlled Catalytic Converter—C4

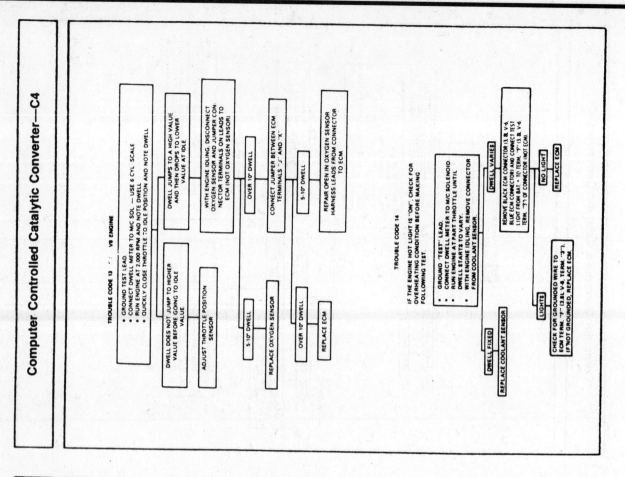

Computer Controlled Catalytic Converter—C4

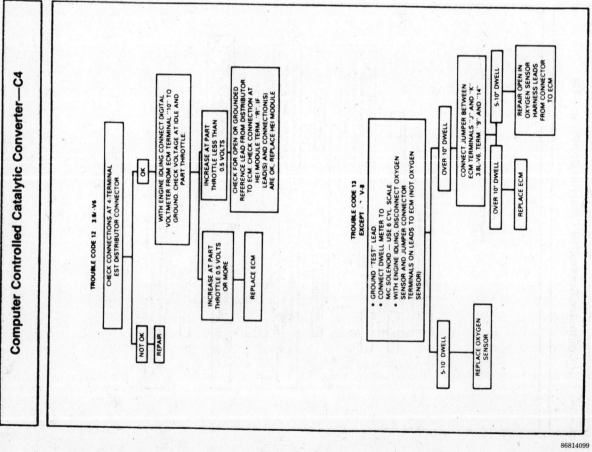

86814099

Computer Controlled Catalytic Converter—C4

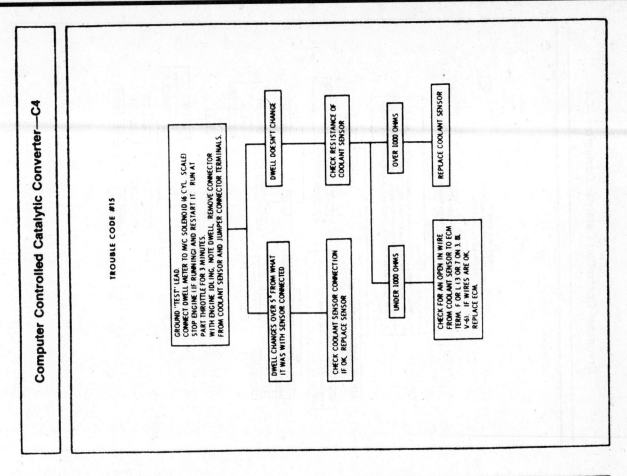

TROUBLE CODE #15

GROUND "TEST" LEAD.
CONNECT DWELL METER TO M/C SOLENOID (6 CYL. SCALE)
STOP ENGINE (IF RUNNING) AND RESTART IT. RUN AT
PART THROTTLE FOR 3 MINUTES.
WITH ENGINE IDLING, NOTE DWELL. REMOVE CONNECTOR
FROM COOLANT SENSOR AND JUMPER CONNECTOR TERMINALS.

DWELL DOESN'T CHANGE

CHECK RESISTANCE OF
COOLANT SENSOR

OVER 1000 OHMS

REPLACE COOLANT SENSOR

UNDER 1000 OHMS

CHECK FOR AN OPEN IN WIRE
FROM COOLANT SENSOR TO ECM
TERM. F OR L13 OR 7 ON 3. BL
V-6). IF WIRES ARE OK,
REPLACE ECM.

DWELL CHANGES OVER 5° FROM WHAT
IT WAS WITH SENSOR CONNECTED

CHECK COOLANT SENSOR CONNECTION
IF OK. REPLACE SENSOR

Computer Controlled Catalytic Converter—C4

TROUBLE CODE 21
3 BL. V6

• GROUND "TEST" LEAD
• CONNECT DWELL METER TO M/C
  SOLENOID — USE 8 CYL SCALE
• WITH ENGINE IDLING, DISCONNECT W0T SWITCH

OVER 10° DWELL

REPLACE W0T SWITCH

5-10° DWELL

CONNECT A TEST LIGHT FROM
BAT + TO LIGHT GREEN WIRE
TERM. OF W0T SW HARNESS

NO LIGHT

REPLACE ECM

REMOVE BLUE
ECM CONNECTOR
AND NOTE TEST
LIGHT

LIGHTS

LIGHT

REPAIR GROUND
IN W0T SWITCH
GREEN LEAD

TROUBLE CODE 21 & 22 AT SAME TIME   2 BL. L4 ENGINE

• GROUND "TEST" LEAD
• DISCONNECT COOLANT SENSOR LEAD
• CONNECT DWELL METER TO M/C SOLENOID (6 CYL SCALE)
• WITH ENGINE IDLING, DISCONNECT W0T SWITCH

OVER 10° DWELL

CHECK VACUUM AT W0T
SWITCH

OVER 10"

REPLACE
W0T SWITCH

UNDER 10"

REPAIR HOSE
OR HOSE
CONNECTIONS

5-10° DWELL

CONNECT A TEST LIGHT FROM
BAT + TO LIGHT GREEN WIRE
TERM. OF W0T SW HARNESS

NO LIGHT

REPLACE ECM

REMOVE BLACK
ECM CONNECTOR
AND NOTE TEST
LIGHT

LIGHTS

LIGHT

REPAIR GROUND
IN W0T SWITCH
GREEN LEAD

86814100

Computer Controlled Catalytic Converter—C4

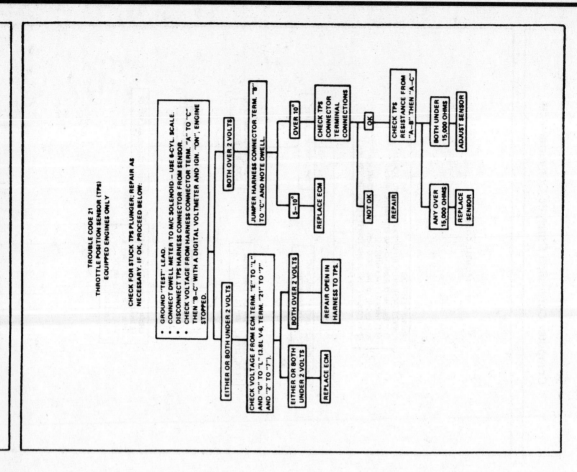

TROUBLE CODE 21
THROTTLE POSITION SENSOR (TPS)
EQUIPPED ENGINES ONLY

CHECK FOR STUCK TPS PLUNGER. REPAIR AS NECESSARY. IF OK, PROCEED BELOW:

- GROUND "TEST" LEAD.
- CONNECT DWELL METER TO M/C SOLENOID — USE 6-CYL. SCALE.
- DISCONNECT TPS HARNESS CONNECTOR FROM SENSOR.
- CHECK VOLTAGE FROM HARNESS CONNECTOR TERM. "A" TO "C" THEN "B-C" WITH A DIGITAL VOLTMETER AND IGN. "ON", ENGINE STOPPED.

EITHER OR BOTH UNDER 2 VOLTS

- CHECK VOLTAGE FROM ECM TERM. "E" TO "L" AND "G" TO "L" (3.8L V-6, TERM. "21" TO "7" AND "2" TO "7").

  EITHER OR BOTH UNDER 2 VOLTS → REPLACE ECM

  BOTH OVER 2 VOLTS → REPAIR OPEN IN HARNESS TO TPS.

BOTH OVER 2 VOLTS

JUMPER HARNESS CONNECTOR TERM. "B" TO "C" AND NOTE DWELL.

- **OVER 10°** → CHECK TPS CONNECTOR TERMINAL CONNECTIONS

  OK → CHECK TPS RESISTANCE FROM "A-B" THEN "A-C"

  - **BOTH UNDER 15,000 OHMS** → ADJUST SENSOR
  - **ANY OVER 15,000 OHMS** → REPLACE SENSOR

  NOT OK → REPAIR

- **5–10°** → REPLACE ECM

Computer Controlled Catalytic Converter—C4

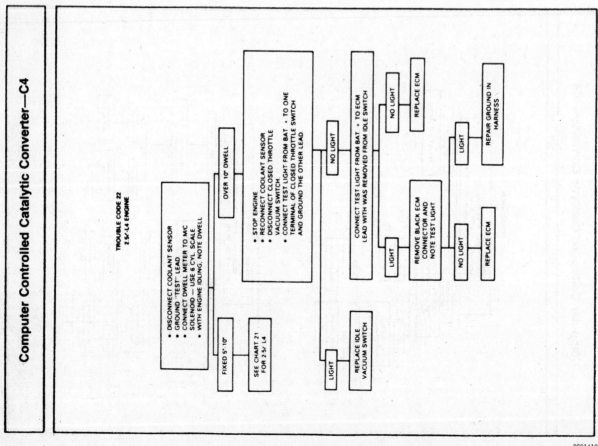

TROUBLE CODE 22
2.5/-L4 ENGINE

- DISCONNECT COOLANT SENSOR
- GROUND "TEST" LEAD
- CONNECT DWELL METER TO M/C SOLENOID — USE 6 CYL. SCALE WITH ENGINE IDLING, NOTE DWELL.

FIXED 5°-10° → SEE CHART 21 FOR 2.5/ L4

OVER 10° DWELL

- STOP ENGINE
- RECONNECT COOLANT SENSOR
- DISCONNECT CLOSED THROTTLE VACUUM SWITCH.
- CONNECT TEST LIGHT FROM BAT + TO ONE TERMINAL OF CLOSED THROTTLE SWITCH AND GROUND THE OTHER LEAD.

  LIGHT → REPLACE IDLE VACUUM SWITCH

  NO LIGHT → CONNECT TEST LIGHT FROM BAT + TO ECM LEAD WITH WAS REMOVED FROM IDLE SWITCH.

  - **NO LIGHT** → REPLACE ECM

  - **LIGHT** → REMOVE BLACK ECM CONNECTOR AND NOTE TEST LIGHT

    - **NO LIGHT** → REPLACE ECM
    - **LIGHT** → REPAIR GROUND IN HARNESS

86814101

Computer Controlled Catalytic Converter—C4

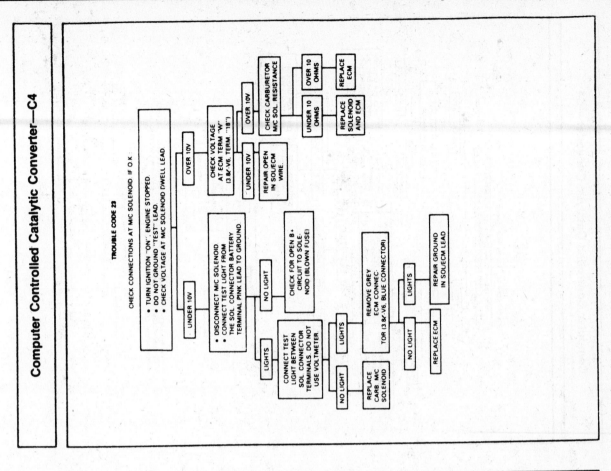

Computer Controlled Catalytic Converter—C4

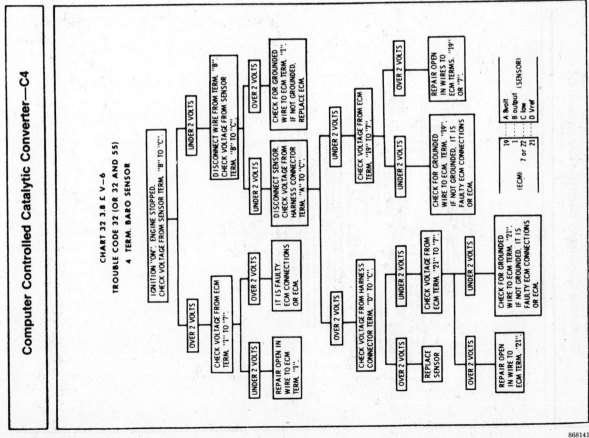

86814102

Computer Controlled Catalytic Converter—C4

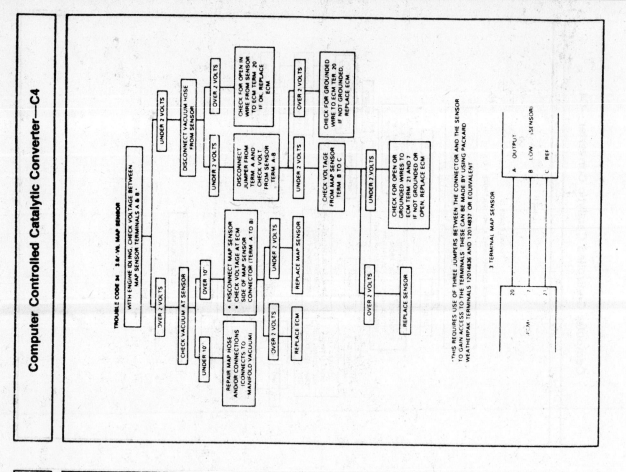

TROUBLE CODE 34   3.8L-V6. MAP SENSOR

WITH ENGINE IDLING, CHECK VOLTAGE BETWEEN MAP SENSOR TERMINALS A & B.

OVER 2 VOLTS → CHECK VACUUM AT SENSOR

- UNDER 10" → REPAIR MAP HOSE AND/OR CONNECTIONS (CONNECTS TO MANIFOLD VACUUM)
- OVER 10" → • DISCONNECT MAP SENSOR • CHECK VOLTAGE AT ECM SIDE OF MAP SENSOR CONNECTOR (TERM. A TO B.)
  - OVER 2 VOLTS → REPLACE ECM
  - UNDER 2 VOLTS → REPLACE MAP SENSOR

UNDER 2 VOLTS → DISCONNECT VACUUM HOSE FROM SENSOR

- UNDER 2 VOLTS → DISCONNECT JUMPER FROM TERM A AND CHECK VOLT FROM SENSOR TERM A-B
  - OVER 2 VOLTS → CHECK FOR OPEN IN WIRE FROM SENSOR TO ECM TERM. 20 IF OK, REPLACE ECM
  - UNDER 2 VOLTS → CHECK VOLTAGE FROM MAP SENSOR TERM. B TO C
    - OVER 2 VOLTS → REPLACE SENSOR
    - UNDER 2 VOLTS → CHECK FOR OPEN OR GROUNDED WIRES TO ECM TERM. 21 AND 7 IF NOT GROUNDED OR OPEN, REPLACE ECM
- OVER 2 VOLTS → CHECK FOR GROUNDED WIRE TO ECM TER. 20 IF NOT GROUNDED, REPLACE ECM

*THIS REQUIRES USE OF THREE JUMPERS BETWEEN THE CONNECTOR AND THE SENSOR TO GAIN ACCESS TO THE TERMINALS. THESE CAN BE MADE BY USING PACKARD WEATHERPAK TERMINALS 12014836 AND 12014837 OR EQUIVALENT

3 TERMINAL MAP SENSOR

A	OUTPUT
B	(SENSOR) LOW
C	REF

ECM: 20, 7, 21

Computer Controlled Catalytic Converter—C4

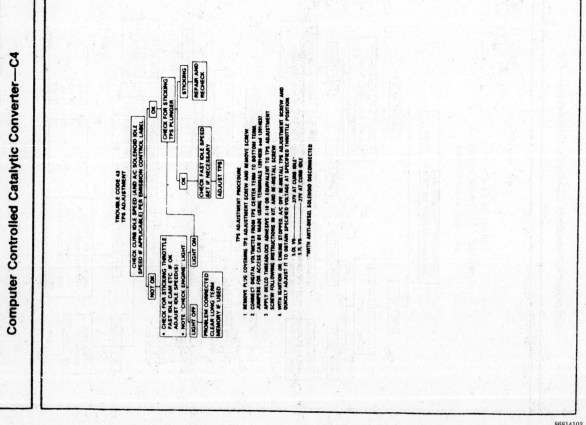

TROUBLE CODE 43
TPS ADJUSTMENT

CHECK CURB IDLE SPEED (AND A/C SOLENOID IDLE SPEED IF APPLICABLE) PER EMISSION CONTROL LABEL

- NOT OK → • CHECK FOR STICKING THROTTLE FAST IDLE CAM ETC. IF OK ADJUST IDLE SPEED(S) • NOTE "CHECK ENGINE" LIGHT
  - LIGHT OFF → PROBLEM CORRECTED CLEAR LONG TERM MEMORY IF USED
  - LIGHT ON
- OK → CHECK FOR STICKING TPS PLUNGER
  - OK → CHECK FAST IDLE SPEED SET IF NECESSARY → ADJUST TPS
  - STICKING → REPAIR AND RECHECK

TPS ADJUSTMENT PROCEDURE

1. REMOVE PLUG COVERING TPS ADJUSTMENT SCREW AND REMOVE SCREW
2. CONNECT DIGITAL VOLTMETER FROM TPS CENTER TERM. TO BOTTOM TERM. JUMPERS FOR ACCESS CAN BE MADE USING TERMINALS 12014836 and 12014837
3. APPLY DELCO THREADLOCK ADHESIVE X-10 OR EQUIVALENT TO TPS ADJUSTMENT SCREW FOLLOWING INSTRUCTIONS IN KIT, AND RE-INSTALL SCREW
4. WITH IGNITION ON, ENGINE STOPPED, A/C OFF. RE-INSTALL TPS ADJUSTMENT SCREW AND QUICKLY ADJUST IT TO OBTAIN SPECIFIED VOLTAGE AT SPECIFIED THROTTLE POSITION

   5.0L V6 .... .37V AT CURB IDLE
   3.7L V6 .... .27V AT CURB IDLE

*WITH ANTI-DIESEL SOLENOID DISCONNECTED

Computer Controlled Catalytic Converter—C4

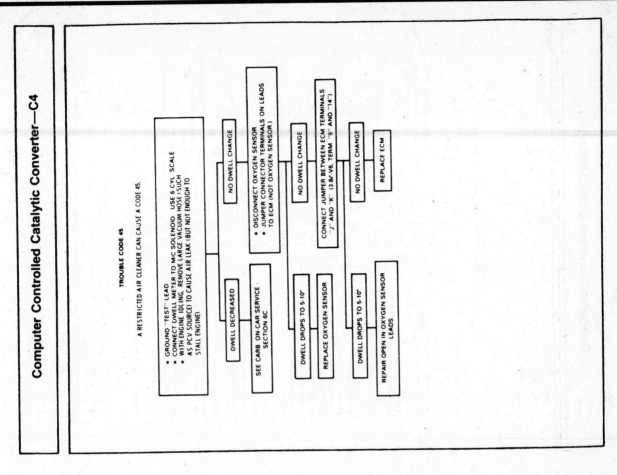

TROUBLE CODE 45

A RESTRICTED AIR CLEANER CAN CAUSE A CODE 45.

- GROUND "TEST" LEAD
- CONNECT DWELL METER TO M/C SOLENOID · USE 6 CYL · SCALE
- WITH ENGINE IDLING, REMOVE LARGE VACUUM HOSE (SUCH AS PCV SOURCE) TO CAUSE AIR LEAK (BUT NOT ENOUGH TO STALL ENGINE).

DWELL DECREASED

NO DWELL CHANGE

SEE CARB ON-CAR SERVICE · SECTION 6C

- DISCONNECT OXYGEN SENSOR
- JUMPER CONNECTOR TERMINALS ON LEADS TO ECM (NOT OXYGEN SENSOR)

DWELL DROPS TO 5-10°

NO DWELL CHANGE

REPLACE OXYGEN SENSOR

CONNECT JUMPER BETWEEN ECM TERMINALS "J" AND "K" (3.8/-V6, TERM. "9" AND "14")

DWELL DROPS TO 5-10°

NO DWELL CHANGE

REPAIR OPEN IN OXYGEN SENSOR LEADS.

REPLACE ECM

Computer Controlled Catalytic Converter—C4

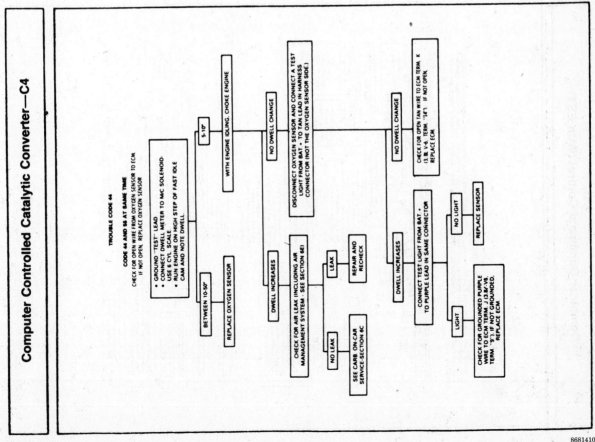

TROUBLE CODE 44

CODE 44 AND 56 AT SAME TIME

CHECK FOR OPEN WIRE FROM OXYGEN SENSOR TO ECM
IF NOT OPEN, REPLACE OXYGEN SENSOR

- GROUND "TEST" LEAD
- CONNECT DWELL METER TO M/C SOLENOID · USE 6 CYL · SCALE
- RUN ENGINE ON HIGH STEP OF FAST IDLE CAM AND NOTE DWELL.

BETWEEN 10-50°

5-10°

REPLACE OXYGEN SENSOR

WITH ENGINE IDLING, CHOKE ENGINE

DWELL INCREASES

NO DWELL CHANGE

CHECK FOR AIR LEAK (INCLUDING AIR MANAGEMENT SYSTEM · SEE SECTION 6E)

DISCONNECT OXYGEN SENSOR AND CONNECT A TEST LIGHT FROM BAT + TO TAN LEAD IN HARNESS CONNECTOR (NOT THE OXYGEN SENSOR SIDE)

LEAK

NO LEAK

REPAIR AND RECHECK

SEE CARB ON-CAR SERVICE-SECTION 6C

DWELL INCREASES

NO DWELL CHANGE

CONNECT TEST LIGHT FROM BAT + TO PURPLE LEAD IN SAME CONNECTOR

CHECK FOR OPEN TAN WIRE TO ECM TERM. K (3. 8L V-6, TERM. "14"). IF NOT OPEN, REPLACE ECM

NO LIGHT

LIGHT

REPLACE SENSOR

CHECK FOR GROUNDED PURPLE WIRE TO ECM TERM. L (3.8/-V6, TERM. "9"). IF NOT GROUNDED, REPLACE ECM

Computer Command Control (With EST)

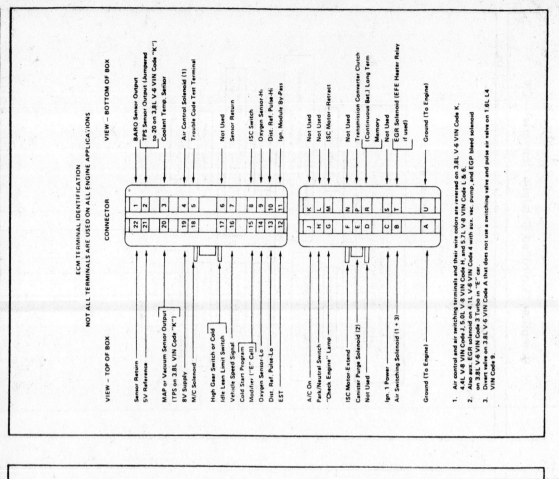

ECM TERMINAL IDENTIFICATION

NOT ALL TERMINALS ARE USED ON ALL ENGINE APPLICATIONS

VIEW – TOP OF BOX   CONNECTOR   VIEW – BOTTOM OF BOX

1. Air control and air switching terminals and their wire colors are reversed on 3.8L V-6 VIN Code K, 4.4L V-8 VIN Code J, 5.0L V-8 VIN Code H, and 5.7L V-8 VIN Code L & 6.
2. Also aux. EGR solenoid on 4.1L V-6 VIN Code 4 with aux. vac. pump, and EGP bleed solenoid on 3.8L V-6 VIN Code 3 Turbo in "E" car.
3. Divert valve on 3.8L V-6 VIN Code A that does not use a switching valve and pulse air valve on 1.6L L4 VIN Code 9.

Computer Command Control (With EST)

DIAGNOSTIC CIRCUIT CHECK

ALWAYS CHECK PROM FOR CORRECT APPLICATION AND INSTALLATION BEFORE REPLACING AN ECM. ALSO, REMOVE TERMINAL(S) FROM ECM CONNECTOR FOR CIRCUIT INVOLVED CLEAN TERMINAL CONTACT AND EXPAND IT SLIGHTLY TO INCREASE CONTACT PRESSURE AND RECHECK TO SEE IF PROBLEM IS CORRECTED.

Computer Command Control (With EST)

DRIVER COMPLAINT

ENGINE PERFORMANCE PROBLEM (ODOR, SURGE, FUEL ECONOMY . . . .)
EMISSION PROBLEM

IF THE "CHECK ENGINE" LIGHT IS NOT ON, NORMAL CHECKS THAT WOULD BE PERFORMED ON CARS WITHOUT THE SYSTEM SHOULD BE DONE FIRST.

IF GENERATOR OR COOLANT LIGHT IS ON WITH THE CHECK ENGINE LIGHT, THEY SHOULD BE DIAGNOSED FIRST.

INSPECT FOR POOR CONNECTIONS AT COOLANT SENSOR, M/C SOLENOID, ETC., AND POOR OR LOOSE VACUUM HOSES AND CONNECTIONS. REPAIR AS NECESSARY.

- Intermittent Check Engine light but no trouble code stored.
  Check for intermittent connection in circuit from:
  - Ignition coil to ground and arcing at spark plug wires or plugs
  - Bat to ECM Term. 'C' and 'R'.
  - ECM Term. 'A' and 'U' to engine ground.
- Loss of long-term memory.
  Grounding dwell lead for 10 seconds with "test" lead ungrounded should give Code 23 which should be retained after engine is stopped and ignition turned to "RUN" position.
  If it is not, ECM is defective.

- EST wires should be kept away from spark plug wires, distributor housing, coil and generator. Wires from ECM Term. 13 to dist. and the shield around EST wires should be a good ground.

- Open diode across A/C compressor clutch.

- Stalling, Rough Idle, or Improper Idle Speed.
  See idle speed control

- Detonation (spark knock)
  Check.
  MAP or Vacuum Sensor output.
  EGR operation.
  TPS enrichment operation.
  HEI operation.

- Poor Performance and/or Fuel Economy
  See EST diagnosis

- Poor Full Throttle Performance
  See Chart 4 if equipped with TPS.

- ALL OTHER COMPLAINTS
  Make system performance check on warm engine
  (upper radiator hose hot).

The system performance check should be performed after any repairs to the system has been made.

Computer Command Control (With EST)

SYSTEM PERFORMANCE CHECK

1. Start engine
2. Ground "test" term. (Must not be grounded before engine is started.)
3. Disconnect purge hose from canister and plug it. On E2SE carburetor, disconnect bowl vent at carburetor.
4. Connect tachometer.
5. Disconnect Mixture Control (M/C) Solenoid and ground M/C Solenoid dwell term.
6. Run engine at 3,000 RPM and, while keeping throttle constant, reconnect M/C Solenoid and note RPM
7. If car is equipped with an electric cooling fan, it may lower RPM when it engages.
   Remove ground from M/C Solenoid dwell term. before returning to idle.

Less than 100 RPM drop
- Check that pink wire is attached to right hand term. of M/C Solenoid Connector, as viewed from harness end.
- Check evaporator canister for being loaded with fuel and related valves, such as purge and bowl vents for leaks which would cause richness. Also check for fuel in crankcase. If OK, see Carb. On Car Service, Section 6C.

Fixed under 10° → See Chart #1

Fixed 10–50° → See Chart #2

More than 100 RPM drop
- Connect dwell meter to M/C sol. dwell term. (6-cyl. scale).
- Set carb. on high step of fast idle cam and run for one (1) minute or until dwell starts to vary, whichever happens first.
- Return engine to idle and note dwell.*

Fixed over 50° → See Chart #3

Varying → Check dwell at 3,000 RPM (on 2.8L V-6, Auto Trans. Only, disconnect and plug hose to vacuum sensor during check.)

Not between 10–50° → See Carb. Calibration Procedure including TPS adjust.

Between 10–50° → Check air management system.

- No trouble found in the "System."
- Clear long term memory **

*Oxygen sensors may cool off at idle and the dwell change from varying to fixed. If this happens, running the engine at fast idle will warm it up again

**See Code(s) Clearing Procedure

86814106

Computer Command Control (With EST)

CHART NO 1

DWELL FIXED UNDER 10°

Computer Command Control (With EST)

CHART P2

DWELL FIXED BETWEEN 10°-50°

(OPEN COOLANT OR OXYGEN SENSOR CIRCUIT)

CHECK FOR STICKING TPS PLUNGER AND ADJUSTMENT AND LOW COOLANT

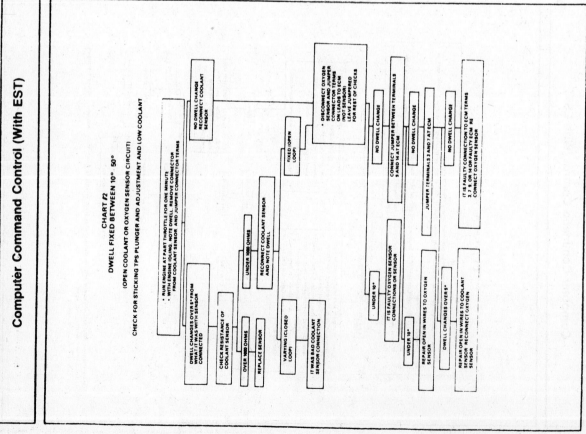

86814107

Computer Command Control (With EST)

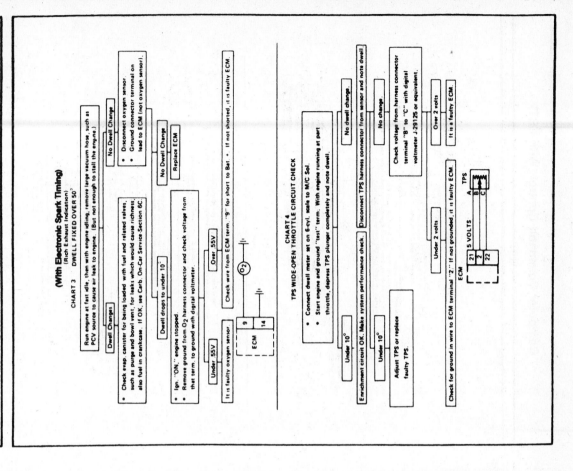

(With Electronic Spark Timing)
(Rich Exhaust Indication)
CHART 3   DWELL FIXED OVER 50°

CHART 4
TPS WIDE-OPEN THROTTLE CIRCUIT CHECK

Computer Command Control (With EST)

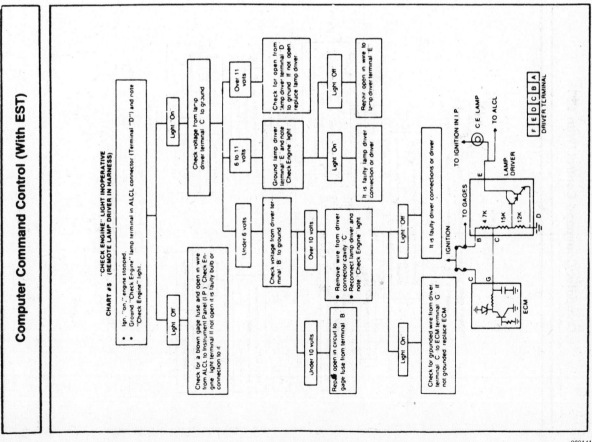

CHART #5   "CHECK ENGINE" LIGHT INOPERATIVE
(REMOTE LAMP DRIVER IN HARNESS)

86814108

Computer Command Control (With EST)

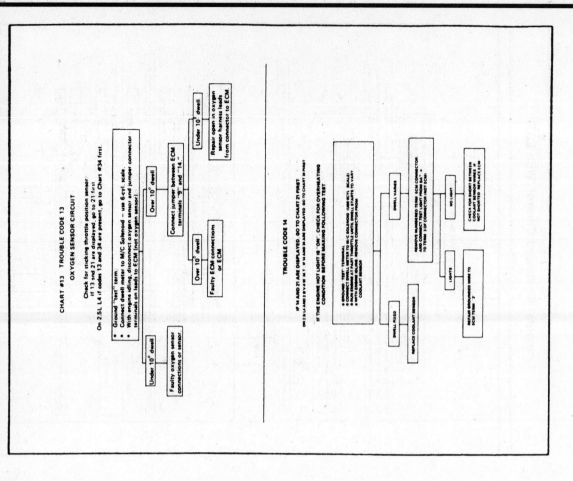

CHART #13 TROUBLE CODE 13
OXYGEN SENSOR CIRCUIT

Check for sticking throttle position sensor.
If 13 and 21 are displayed, go to 21 first.
On 2.5L L4 if codes 13 and 34 are present, go to Chart #34 first.

* Ground "test" term.
* Connect dwell meter to M/C Solenoid — use 6-cyl. scale.
* With engine idling, disconnect oxygen sensor and jumper connector
  terminals on leads to ECM (not oxygen sensor).

Under 10° dwell
Faulty oxygen sensor connections or sensor.

Over 10° dwell
Faulty ECM connection or ECM

Connect jumper between ECM terminals "9" and "14."

Under 10° dwell
Repair open in oxygen sensor harness leads from connector to ECM

TROUBLE CODE 14

IF 14 AND 21 ARE DISPLAYED, GO TO CHART 21 FIRST
ON 2.5 L4 VIEW M.Y. 14 AND 34 ARE DISPLAYED GO TO CHART 34 FIRST

IF THE ENGINE HOT LIGHT IS "ON," CHECK FOR OVERHEATING
CONDITION BEFORE MAKING FOLLOWING TEST

* GROUND "TEST" TERMINAL.
* CONNECT DWELL METER TO M/C SOLENOID (USE 6CYL. SCALE)
* WITH ENGINE AT PART THROTTLE NOTE DWELL STARTS TO VARY
* WITH ENGINE IDLING REMOVE CONNECTOR FROM
  COOLANT SENSOR

DWELL FIXED
REPLACE COOLANT SENSOR

DWELL VARIES
REMOVE REMAINDER TERM. ECM CONNECTOR AND CONNECT TEST LIGHT FROM BAT "+" TO TERM 3 OF CONNECTOR (NOT ECM)

LIGHTS
REPAIR GROUNDED WIRE TO ECM TERM "7"

NO LIGHT
CHECK FOR SHORT BETWEEN COOLANT SENSOR WIRES IF NOT SHORTED REPLACE ECM

Computer Command Control (With EST)

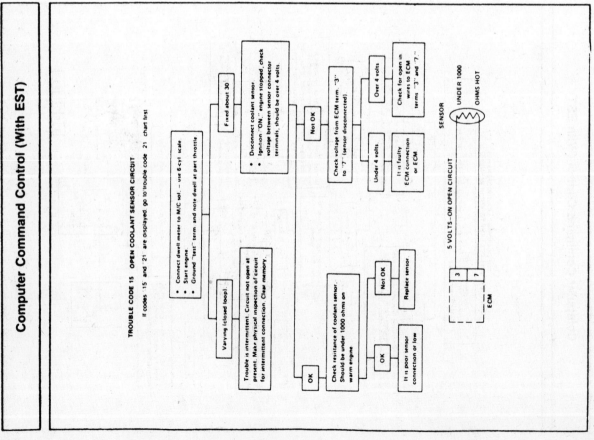

TROUBLE CODE 15 OPEN COOLANT SENSOR CIRCUIT

If codes 15 and 21 are displayed go to trouble code 21 chart first

* Connect dwell meter to M/C sol. — use 6-cyl. scale.
* Start engine
* Ground "test" term. and note dwell at part throttle.

Varying (closed loop)
Trouble is intermittent. Circuit not open at present. Make physical inspection of circuit for intermittent connection. Clear memory.

Fixed about 30
* Disconnect coolant sensor.
* Ignition "ON," engine stopped, check voltage between sensor connector terminals, should be over 4 volts.

Over 4 volts.
Check for open in wires to ECM terms. "3" and "7."

Under 4 volts.
It is faulty ECM connection or ECM

Check voltage from ECM term. "3" to "7" (sensor disconnected)

OK
Check resistance of coolant sensor. Should be under 1000 ohms on warm engine

OK
It is poor sensor connection or low

Not OK
Replace sensor.

Not OK

SENSOR

UNDER 1000 OHMS HOT

5 VOLTS—ON OPEN CIRCUIT

3
7
ECM

86814109

Computer Command Control (With EST)

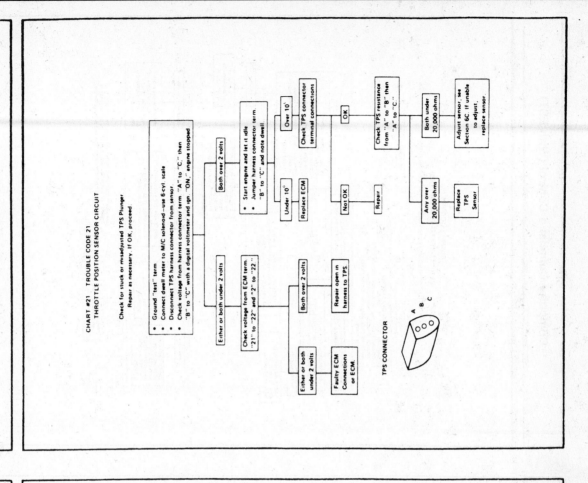

CHART #21   TROUBLE CODE 21
THROTTLE POSITION SENSOR CIRCUIT

Check for stuck or misadjusted TPS Plunger.
Repair as necessary. If OK, proceed.

- Ground "test" term
- Connect dwell meter to M/C solenoid—use 6-cyl. scale
- Disconnect TPS harness connector from sensor.
- Check voltage from TPS harness connector term. "A" to "C," then "B" to "C" with a digital voltmeter and ign. "ON," engine stopped

Both over 2 volts

Either or both under 2 volts

Start engine and let it idle
- Jumper harness connector term. "B" to "C" and note dwell

Over 10°

Under 10°

Replace ECM

Check TPS connector terminal connections

OK

Not OK

Repair

Check voltage from ECM term. "21" to "22" and "2" to "22"

Both over 2 volts

Either or both under 2 volts

Repair open in harness to TPS

Faulty ECM Connections or ECM.

Check TPS resistance from "A" to "B" then "A" to "C"

Both under 20,000 ohms

Any over 20,000 ohms

Adjust sensor, see Section 6C. If unable to adjust, replace sensor.

Replace TPS Sensor

TPS CONNECTOR

Computer Command Control (With EST)

TROUBLE CODE 24   M/C SOLENOID CIRCUIT (OPEN OR GROUNDED)
Check connections at M/C solenoid. If O.K. Clear memory* and recheck for code(s). If no code 23, circuit is OK

- Turn ignition "on", engine stopped
- Do not ground "Test" terminal
- Check voltage at M/C solenoid dwell lead

Over 10 Volts

Under 10 Volts

Check voltage at ECM term "18"

Over 10 Volts

Under 10 Volts

Check carburetor M/C Sol. Resistance

Repair open in SOL/ECM wire

Over 10 ohms

Under 10 ohms

Faulty ECM connections or ECM

Replace solenoid and ECM

- Disconnect M/C solenoid
- Connect test light from the sol. connector battery terminal pink lead to ground

Light Off

Light On

Check for open B+ circuit to solenoid (pink / black wire)

Connect test light between sol. harness connector terminals. Do not use voltmeter.

Light On

Light Off

Check for an open in wire from M/C Sol to dwell connector. If not open, it is a faulty M/C solenoid connection or Solenoid

Remove numbered term. ECM connector

Light On

Light Off

Repair ground in wire from solenoid to ECM terminal "18"

Replace ECM

DWELL CONNECTOR

M/C SOLENOID

IGN

M/C SOLENOID

ECM

*See Code(s) Clearing Procedure

86814110

Computer Command Control (With EST)

TROUBLE CODE 24

VEHICLE SPEED SENSOR (VSS)

SEE THAT SPEEDOMETER WORKS BEFORE PROCEEDING

Computer Command Control (With EST)

TROUBLE CODE 32

BARO SENSOR CIRCUIT LOW

86814111

Computer Command Control (With EST)

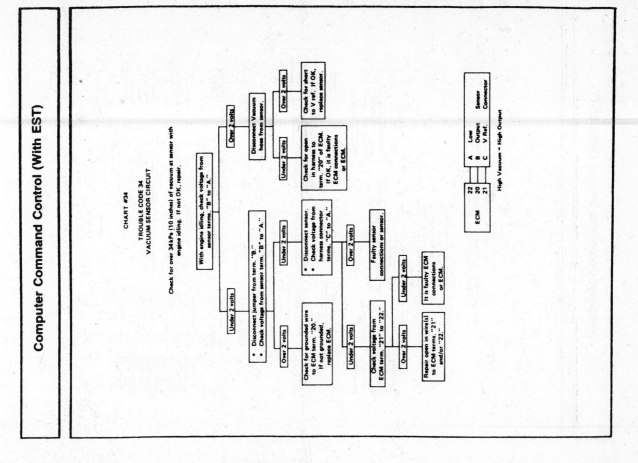

Computer Command Control (With EST)

Computer Command Control (With EST)

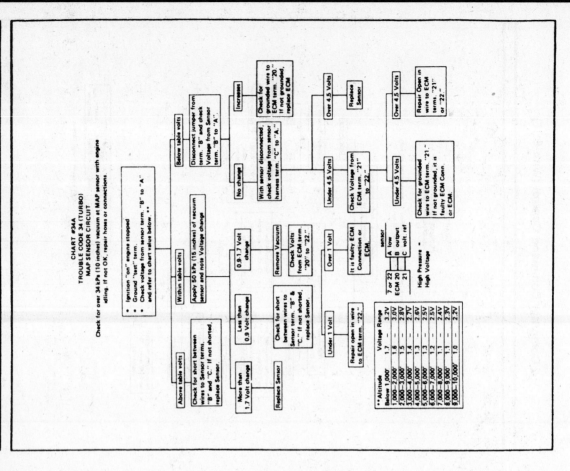

CHART #34A
TROUBLE CODE 34 (TURBO)
MAP SENSOR CIRCUIT

Check for over 34 kPa (10 inches) vacuum at MAP sensor with engine idling. If not OK, repair hoses or connections.

- Ignition "on" engine stopped
- Ground "test" term.
- Check voltage from sensor term. "B" to "A" and refer to chart value below. **

** Altitude	Voltage Range
Below 1,000'	1.7 – 3.2V
1,000–2,000'	1.6 – 3.0V
2,000–3,000'	1.5 – 2.8V
3,000–4,000'	1.4 – 2.7V
4,000–5,000'	1.3 – 2.6V
5,000–6,000'	1.3 – 2.5V
6,000–7,000'	1.2 – 2.5V
7,000–8,000'	1.1 – 2.4V
8,000–9,000'	1.1 – 2.3V
9,000–10,000'	1.0 – 2.2V

sensor
A low
B output
C volt ref

7 or 22	A low
ECM 20	B output
21	C volt ref

High Pressure = High Voltage

Computer Command Control (With EST)

TROUBLE CODE 35

SHORTED IDLE SPEED CONTROL (ISC) CIRCUIT
Check for sticking TPS plunger – repair as necessary

- Test terminal ungrounded
- Run engine at 3000 RPM for 5 seconds and note - check engine" light

Trouble is intermittent and system is OK at present. Make physical inspection of circuit. Clear memory.

- Ignition "OFF"
- Disconnect ISC connector
- Connect ohmmeter from Term. "A" to "B" on ISC motor assembly.
- Open throttle and note resistance.

- Ign. "ON," engine stopped
- Check voltage from terminal "A" to "B" on harness connector.

Check adjustment of TPS (see Section 6C). If OK, replace ECM.

Check for shorted or grounded wire from terminal "B" to ECM terminal "B". If not shorted or grounded, replace ECM.

86814113

Computer Command Control (With EST)

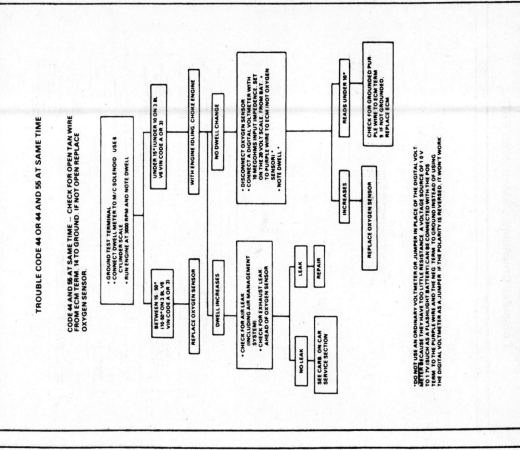

Computer Command Control (With EST)

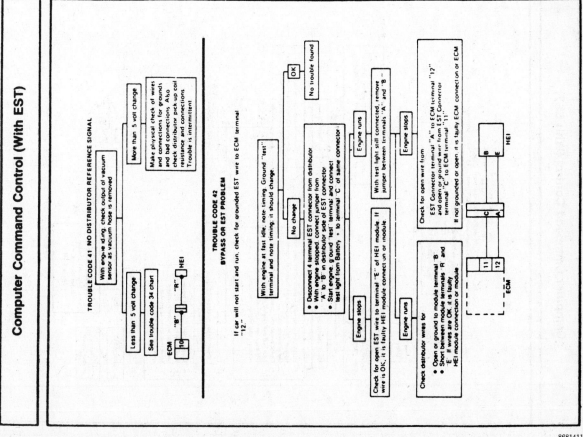

86814114

Computer Command Control (With EST)

TROUBLE CODES 51 - 54

CODE 51

CHECK THAT ALL PINS ARE FULLY INSERTED IN THE SOCKET. IF OK, REPLACE PROM. CLEAR MEMORY, AND RECHECK. IF CODE 51 REAPPEARS, REPLACE ECM.

CODE 52, 53
REPLACE ECM

CODE 54

CHECK M/C SOLENOID RESISTANCE

OVER 10 OHMS

UNDER 10 OHMS

- IGNITION "ON" ENGINE STOPPED
- CONNECT TEST LIGHT FROM GROUND TO DWELL LEAD AT M/C SOLENOID WITH SOL. DISCONNECTED
- DISCONNECT NUMBERED TERMINAL CONNECTOR AT ECM

LIGHT

NO LIGHT

REPAIR SHORT TO BATT. + BLUE WIRE TO ECM TERM. 18. CLEAR MEMORY AND CHECK FOR TROUBLE CODES

REPLACE ECM

- REPLACE SOLENOID
- CLEAR MEMORY
- START ENGINE AND CHECK FOR TROUBLE CODE

CODE

NO CODE

SEE APPLICABLE CODE CHART

MAKE SYSTEM PERFORM CHECK

Computer Command Control (With EST)

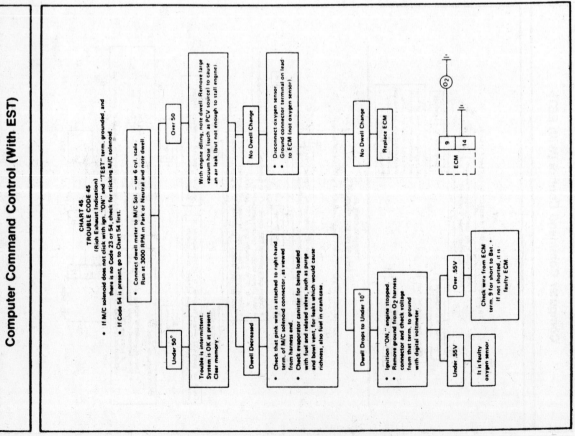

CHART 45
TROUBLE CODE 45
(Rich Exhaust Indication)

- If M/C solenoid does not click with ign. "ON" and "TEST" term. grounded, and there is no Code 23 or 54, check for sticking M/C solenoid.
- If Code 54 is present, go to Chart 54 first.

- Connect dwell meter to M/C Sol — use 6 cyl. scale
Run at 3000 RPM in Park or Neutral and note dwell.

Under 50°

Over 50°

Trouble is intermittent. System is OK at present. Clear memory.

With engine idling, note dwell. Remove large vacuum hose (such as PCV source) to cause an air leak (but not enough to stall engine)

Dwell Decreased

No Dwell Change

- Check that pink wire is attached to right hand term. of M/C solenoid connector, as viewed from harness end.
- Check evaporator canister for being loaded with fuel and related valves, such as purge and bowl vent, for leaks which would cause richness, also fuel in crankcase.

- Disconnect oxygen sensor
- Ground connector terminal on lead to ECM (not oxygen sensor).

Dwell Drops to Under 10°

No Dwell Change

- Ignition "ON" engine stopped
- Remove ground from O₂ harness connector and check voltage from that term. to ground with digital voltmeter.

Replace ECM

Over 55V

Under 55V

Check wire from ECM term. 9 for short to Bat. + If not shorted, it is faulty ECM.

It is faulty oxygen sensor.

O₂

9 14

ECM

86814115

Computer Command Control (With EST)

ENGINE CRANKS, BUT WILL NOT RUN (WITH INTEGRAL IGNITION COIL)

NOTE: Perform diagnostic circuit check before using this procedure. If a tachometer is connected to the tachometer terminal, disconnect it before proceeding with the test.

1   Check spark at plug with ST 125 while cranking (if no spark on one wire, check a second wire).
- Spark → Check fuel, spark plugs, etc.
- No Spark (Without EST)

2   Check voltage at distributor "bat" terminal while cranking.
- 7 volts or more → With ignition "on", check "tach" terminal voltage.
- Under 7 volts → Repair primary circuit to ignition switch.

3   With ignition "on", check "tach" terminal voltage.
- Under 1 Volt → It is faulty ign coil connection or coil.
- 10 Volts or More → Check for spark at coil output terminal with ST 125 while cranking.

4   Check for spark at coil output terminal with ST 125 while cranking.
- Spark → Check color match of pick up coil connector and ign coil lead. Inspect cap for water, cracks, etc. If OK replace rotor.
- No Spark → 1 to 10 Volts → Replace module and check for spark from coil as in Step 6.

5   Remove pick up coil leads from module. Check tach term voltage with "ign" "on". Watch voltmeter as test light is momentarily (not more than five (5) seconds) connected from bat + to module term.
- 4   Term Mod — Term "G"
- 5   Term Mod — Term "D"
- 7   Term Mod — Term "P"
  - Voltage Drops → 6 Check for spark from coil with ST 125 as test light is removed from module terminal.
  - No Drop in Voltage → Check module grnd and for open in wires from cap to distributor. If OK, replace mod.

6   Check for spark from coil with ST 125 as test light is removed from module terminal.
- Spark → 7 Check ign coil ground circuit. If OK, replace ign coil and repeat Step 6.
- No Spark → If no module tester is available.
  - If module tester is available, test module.
    - OK → Check ign coil ground. If OK, replace ign coil.
    - Bad → Replace mod.

7   Check ign coil ground circuit. If OK, replace ign coil and repeat Step 6.
- Spark → System OK.
- No Spark → It is pick up coil or connections. Coil resistance should be 500-1500 ohms and not grounded.
  - Replace ign coil. If it, too, is faulty.
  - System OK.
- Coil removed is OK, reinstall original coil and replace module.

PICK UP COIL — IGN COIL — RED WIRE — P/N 1876209
PICK UP COIL — IGN COIL — GREEN WIRE — WHITE WIRE — CLEAR, BLACK, BLUE CONNECTOR
IGN COIL — YELLOW WIRE — P/N 1875894
PICK UP COIL — GREEN WIRE — WHITE WIRE — RED WIRE — P, YELLOW WIRE — CONNECTOR

Computer Command Control (With EST)

Check for corrosion at ECM edgeboard connectors and terms. If present, check for coolant sensor, windshield or heater core leaks. Repair leaks, clean connector terms, and replace ECM. Also, check for 4 term. EST harness being too close to electrical signals, such as spark plug wires, distributor housing, generator, etc.

TROUBLE CODE 55 FAULTY OXYGEN SENSOR OR ECM

- Disconnect test terminal.
- Disconnect oxygen sensor and note "check engine" light with engine idling for less than one minute.
  - Light On
    - Ignition "ON," engine stopped. Check voltage from ECM Terminal "21" to "22."
      - Over 6 Volts
        - Turn Ign. "OFF."
        - Disconnect numbered connector from ECM.
        - Ign. "ON," check voltage from connector Term. "21" to "22."
          - Voltage → Check for short in B+ wire to Term. "21."
          - 0 Volts → Replace ECM.
      - Under 4 Volts
        - Check for ground in circuit to ECM Terminal "21" (includes shorted or grounded TPS Vacuum or Vehicle Speed Sensors). If not grounded or shorted, replace ECM.
      - 4 to 6 Volts
        - Disconnect O2 sensor.
        - Ign. "ON," engine stopped.
        - Check voltage from connector of purple wire disconnected from oxygen sensor.
          - Over 1 Volt → Turn "OFF" ign., disconnect numbered ECM connector and then turn ign. "ON." Check voltage from ECM, harness connector Term. "9" to ground.
            - Over 1 Volt → Check for short from wire to ECM Term. "9" to Bat.
            - Under 1 Volt → Check for open circuit from Term. "14" to ground. If not open, replace ECM.
          - Under 1 Volt → Check for intermittent ground in circuit to ECM Terminal "21" (includes TPS, MAP, BARO, and Vacuum Sensors). Clear codes and check for reoccurrence of Code 55. If it reappears, it could be faulty oxygen sensor (except on 4.3L VIN Code "F" and 5.0 VIN Code "Y").
  - Light Off

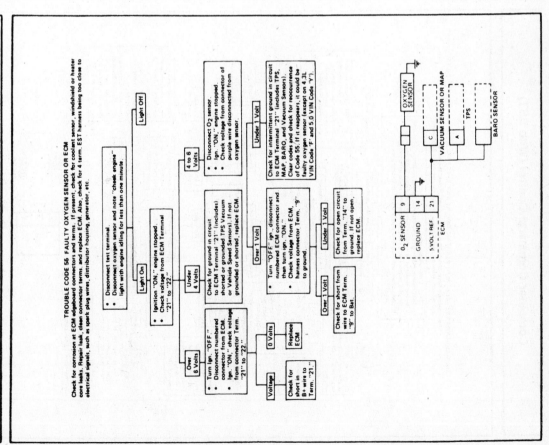

OXYGEN SENSOR
VACUUM SENSOR OR MAP — C — A — TPS
BARO SENSOR
O2 SENSOR — 9
GROUND — 14
5 VOLT REF — 21
ECM

Computer Command Control (With EST)

AIR MANAGEMENT SYSTEM CHECK

Engines which use dual bed converters and electric air control valves (EAC/ES)

On some applications, some air may divert to air cleaner, above 2000 RPM.

Make visual inspection of hoses and connectors for leaks and proper connections. Repair as necessary.

CHECK CONTROL VALVE OPERATION
- Start engine and do not ground "test" terminal.
- Quickly accelerate and decelerate engine. Valve should divert air to air cleaner outlet or atmosphere on deceleration only.

Check switching valve operation
- Run engine at part throttle (below 2000 rpm).
- Pulsations should be felt in outlet in exhaust ports until system goes closed loop, then switch to converter outlet.

Not OK → No divert → Check for at least 34 kPa (10") of vacuum at valve. If OK, replace valve.

Constant divert → Check control valve solenoid control circuit as follows.

OK → Ignition "ON," engine stopped check for a click at air control solenoid as "test" term. is grounded.

Clicks / No Click / No trouble found

Not OK → Check switching valve sol. control circuit as follows.

Ignition "ON," engine stopped check for a click at ELM Term. "4" for control valve or Term. "B" for switching valve. If not grounded replace ECM.

Ignition "ON," engine stopped. "TEST" term. ungrounded. Remove connector from applicable valve solenoid and connect a test light between harness connector terminals.

No light → Ground trouble code "test" term.
Light → It is faulty valve connections or valve.

No light → Light on one term.
Light on both term. → Repair short from bat. + to wire to ECM.
No light → Check for open in pink wire circuit.

Connect test light from each term. of connector to ground.

Check for open in wire to ECM Term. "4" for control valve or "B" for switching valve. If OK, check resistance of sol. If under 20 ohms, replace sol. and ECM. If not, it is faulty connection to ECM or ECM.

ECM — 4 / B — AIR CONT. / AIR SWITCH — IGN.

Computer Command Control (With EST)

AIR MANAGEMENT CHECK WITH ELECTRIC DIVERT AND ELECTRIC SWITCHING VALVE (ED/ES)

Check vacuum hoses condition and connection. Repair as necessary. On some applications, some air may divert to the air cleaner above 2000rpm.

- "Test" term. ungrounded.
- Start engine, running at part throttle, below 2000rpm, air should be felt at outlet to exhaust ports during Open Loop operation (from 8 seconds to 3 minutes on warm engine depending on application) and switch to converter when engine goes Closed Loop.

Constant divert to air cleaner → Check divert valve circuit as follows.

OK → No divert → No trouble found. Clear memory.

Ign. "ON," engine stopped. Disconnect Air Control solenoid electrical connector and connect test light between harness connector term. Note light.

Off → Replace air control valve.
On → Check for grounded wire from Air Control solenoid to ECM Term. "4." If wire is not grounded, replace E.C.M.

Constant converter air → Check air switching valve cir. as follows.

Ign. "ON," engine stopped. Ground "test" term. Disconnect applicable sol. electrical connector and connect test light between harness term. term. and note light.

Light On → Connect test light from both wire term. to ground and note light.

Light Off → Light On
Light on both term. → Repair short from Bat. + to wire to ECM Term. "B" for switching. If OK, check resistance of applicable sol. If under 20 ohms, replace sol. and ECM. If not, it is faulty ECM connection or ECM.

No light → Repair open in pink wire circuit to ign. switch.

Constant Port Air → Ign. "ON," engine stopped. "Test" term. not grounded. Disconnect air switching valve sol. electrical conn. and connect test light between harness conn. term. and note light.

Light Off → Replace air switching valve.
Light On → Check for grounded wire from air switching valve to ECM Term. "B." If not grounded, replace ECM.

Light on one term. → Check for open in wire from applicable sol. to ECM Term. "4" for air control or Term. "B" for air switching. If not open, check resistance of applicable sol. If under 20 ohms, replace sol. and ECM. If not, it is faulty ECM connection or ECM.

With integral sol. → With engine idling, check for at least 10" of vacuum at valve. If OK, it is faulty valve conn. or valve.

With remote sol. → With engine idling, check for at least 10" of vacuum at Air Control valve.
OK → It is faulty Air Control sol. conn. or sol.
Not OK → It is faulty Air Control valve.

ECM — 4 / B — AIR CONT. / AIR SW. — IGN.

86814117

Computer Command Control (With EST)

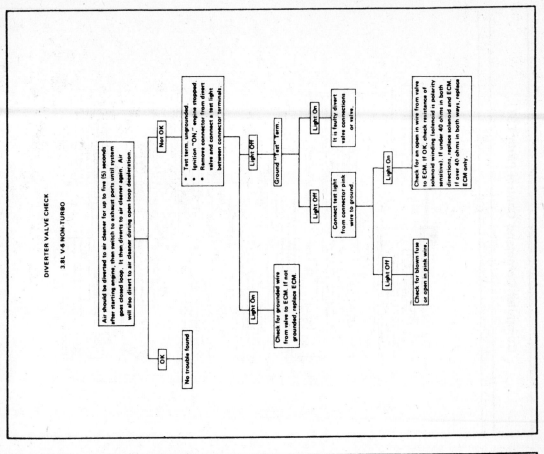

DIVERTER VALVE CHECK

3.8L V-6 NON-TURBO

Computer Command Control (With EST)

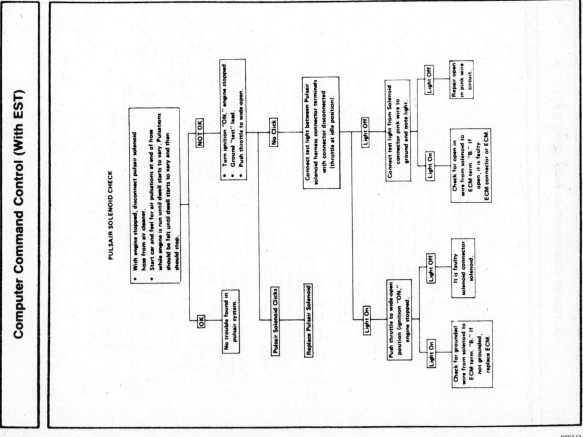

PULSAIR SOLENOID CHECK

86814118

Computer Command Control (With EST)

Computer Command Control (With EST)

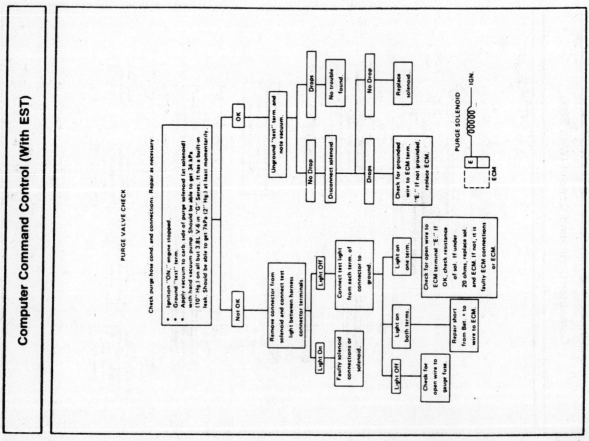

Computer Command Control (With EST)

Computer Command Control (With EST)

86814120

Computer Command Control (With EST)

EFE CHECK
(VACUUM SERVO TYPE)

- Check vacuum hoses and connections.
- Disconnect coolant sensor.
- Connect vacuum gage in place of EFE valve.
- Start engine and note vacuum at idle.
- Do not ground trouble code "test" term.

Under 34 kPa (10" Hg.)

- Stop engine.
- Disconnect EFE conn. and connect test light between conn. terms. "A" and "B."
- With ign. "ON," and "test" term. gn'ded, note test light.

Light Off

Connect test light from term. "B" (pink wire) to gn'd and note test light.

Light On

Check vac. source to solenoid. If OK, then it is faulty EFE solenoid connection or solenoid.

LIGHT OFF → Repair open in pink wire circuit.

LIGHT ON → Replace EFE solenoid.

Over 34 kPa (10" Hg.)

Reconnect coolant sensor and note vacuum. It should drop to zero within one minute.

No drop

Disconnect EFE connector and connect test light between conn. terms. "A" and "B." Ign. "ON," engine stopped, note test light.

LIGHT OFF → Check for gn'ded. wire to ECM term. "B." If not gn'ded. replace ECM.

LIGHT ON → Check for open in wire to ECM term. "B." If not open, it is faulty ECM conn. or ECM.

Drops

With engine stopped, apply 34 kPa (10" Hg.) of vacuum to EFE valve and listen for valve.

Doesn't Move

Did not have 34 kPa (10" Hg.) of vac.

Check for leak in line to EFE. If line OK, replace EFE valve.

Had 34 kPa (10" Hg.) of vacuum.

Check for restricted line to EFE. If line OK, replace EFE valve.

Moves

Disconnect vac. conn. and conn. from sol. assm. and conn. to hose containing check valve. Vacuum should rise quickly and fall slowly at engine is started and stopped.

Disconnect vac. conn. from sol. assm. and conn. to hose containing check valve. Vacuum should rise quickly and fall slowly as engine is started and stopped.

OK → No trouble found.

Not OK → Replace check valve.

Computer Command Control (With EST)

IDLE SPEED CONTROL (ISC) CHECK*

The ISC motor plunger is not used to adjust idle speed. Do not disconnect or connect ISC motor with ign. on, to do so may damage the ECM.

With engine idling in "Park" (auto. trans.) or "Neutral" (man. trans.) and high electrical load turned on, depress ISC plunger while holding throttle open to some speed above idle. Plunger should retract. Release plunger and slowly release throttle and plunger should return.

OK

Check idle speed against specs.

- **OK** → No trouble found.
- **Not OK** → See ISC plunger adj. in Sec. 6C.

Not OK

- Remove connector from motor.
- Connect test light from bat. + to term. "B" of motor assembly and ground terminal "A."
- Note test light while alternately depressing and extending plunger.

No light or constant light → Replace Motor

Light on and off

Operate motor by momentarily connecting 12V across two term's. closest to motor. Reverse polarity and recheck.**

Plunger doesn't extend and retract → It is faulty motor connections or motor.

Plunger extends & retracts

- Ignition "on," engine stopped.
- Check voltage from harness connector term. "B" to "A."

Under 6 volts → Check for open or grounded wires to ECM term's. "F" and "M." If wires are OK, it is faulty ECM connections or ECM.

Over 6 volts → Check for open or grounded wires to ECM term's. "J" with A/C clutch engaged.

Manual Trans.

Automatic trans.

- Ign. "on," engine stopped.
- Check voltage from ECM term. "H" to ground in each trans. Selector position. Should be under 3V in P/N position and over 3V in all other positions.

All over 3V or all under 3V

Over → Check for an open circuit from term. "H" thru P/N sw. to gn'd.***

Under → Check for grounded circuit from term. "H." If not grounded, it is faulty ECM conn. or ECM.

Not OK in some positions → adj. P/N switch

OK all positions

* Stalling or rough idle only with A/C "ON," there should be over 10 volts to ECM term. "J" with A/C clutch engaged. If there isn't, check for an open in the wire from the A/C clutch to ECM terminal "J."
** Do not leave battery voltage applied longer than necessary to retract plunger (not over 10 seconds).
*** The P/N switch grounds the circuit in P/N.

Computer Command Control (With EST)

EGR VALVE CHECK
(EXCEPT 5.0L V-8)

* Start warm engine with coolant sensor disconnected.
* Ground test terminal.
* Push up on underside of EGR to open it and note RPM change as valve opens.

Computer Command Control (With EST)

HEATED EFE OPERATION CHECK
* Ignition "on," engine stopped.
* Disconnect coolant sensor.
* Disconnect connector at heater.
* Connect test light between harness connector terminals.

86814122

ELECTRICAL DIAGNOSIS
(EXCEPT APPLICATIONS USING TCC/EGR BLEED SOLENOID)

Mechanical checks, such as linkage, oil level, etc., should be performed prior to using
this chart. Also, check for a Code "24." If present, see Chart 24.

• Connect test light from T.C.C. test point in Term. "F" in ALCL connector to ground (in fuse block to grnd on "J" car).
• With drive wheels off floor, trans. in gear, increase speed to 35 MPH and note light.

Light on
Hold throttle position. Test light should go out as brake pedal is momentarily depressed

Light off
Check for blown fuse. If OK, disconnect connector at trans. and connect test light from harness connector "A" to "B" term. on two term. connector ("A" to "D" on 4 term. connector) with ignition on, engine stopped, note test light.

Not OK
It is faulty brake switch or adj.

OK
Increase speed to 50-55 mph and note light.

Light off
Connect test light from term. "A" to ground.

Light on
Check for ground in wire to ECM term. "P." If not grounded, replace ECM.

Light on
Lightly depress parking brake and open throttle to maintain 50-55 mph for 5 sec. and note light.

Light off
Repair open in TCC brake switch circuit or adj. switch (3.0L V-6 check TCC cutout Relay)

Light on
Connect test light between harness connector term's. again. Ground trans. test point & note light.

Light on
Check volt. from ECM term. "2" to ground with digital V.M. with ign. on, eng. stopped, throttle wide open.

Light off
With 2 wires in trans. conn.

With 3 wires in trans. conn.

Light on
It is faulty conn. at trans. or trans. sol. circuit.

Light off
Repair open in wire from trans. to test point.

Under 1 volt

Over 1 volt

Check TPS adj. On 3.0L V-6 check TCC relay. If OK, no trouble found.

Ign. "on," eng. stopped, check voltage from ECM term. "N" to ground.

BRAKE SWITCH   3RD GEAR SWITCH

IGN

Check for gn'd. in wire to ECM term. "2." If not grounded, replace ECM.

Over 6 volts

Under 6 volts

P
N
ECM

Engine stopped. Ign. "ON," check volt from ECM term. "16" to gn'd. while turning one drive wheel by hand with the other on the floor. It should alternate from under 3 to over 10.

Check for open in wire from ECM term. "N" to trans. conn. term. "B." If not open, it is faulty conn. at trans. or open in trans. 4th gear sw.

Start engine and with trans. in "D," increase speed to 50-55 mph and note voltage reading.

TRANSMISSION

Over 6 volts

Under 6 volts

TRANS CONNECTOR

Check TPS adj. If OK, no elec. trouble found.

Ign. "ON," engine stopped. Disconnect trans. conn. and check volt from harness conn. term. "B" to ground.

A B
D C

OK
Check TPS adj. Check for low coolant level and higher than normal resistance in coolant sensor circuit. Check T.C.C. sol. resistance if under 20 ohms, replace sol. and ECM. If OK, it is faulty ECM connection or ECM.

Not OK
See Code chart 24.

Over 6 volts
Trans. 4th gear switch is grounded or not opening.

Under 6 volts
Check for grounded wire to ECM term. "17." If not grounded, it is faulty ECM conn. or ECM

86814123

Fig. 68 Torque Converter Clutch (TCC)

THROTTLE BODY FUEL INJECTION

THROTTLE BODY INJECTION DIAGNOSTIC CHARTS

86814125

THROTTLE BODY INJECTION DIAGNOSTIC CHARTS

86814126

THROTTLE BODY INJECTION DIAGNOSTIC CHARTS

CODE 13
OXYGEN (O₂) SENSOR CIRCUIT
(OPEN CIRCUIT)

Circuit Description:

The ECM supplies a voltage of about .45 volt between terminals "B2" and "B23". (If measured with a 10 megohm digital voltmeter, this may read as low as .32 volt).

When the O₂ sensor reaches operating temperature, it varies this voltage from about .1 volt (exhaust is lean) to about .9 volt (exhaust is rich).

The sensor is like an open circuit and produces no voltage when it is below 316°C (600°F). An open sensor circuit, or cold sensor, causes "Open Loop" operation.

Test Description: Numbers below refer to circled numbers on the diagnostic chart.

1. Code 13 will set under the following conditions:
   - Engine at normal operating temperature.
   - At least 40 seconds have elapsed since engine start-up.
   - O₂ signal voltage is steady between .35 and .55 volt.
   - Throttle angle is above 7%.
   - All above conditions are met for about 4 seconds.

   If the conditions for a Code 13 exist, the system will not operate in "Closed Loop."

2. This test determines if the O₂ sensor is the problem or if the ECM and wiring are at fault.

3. In doing this test, use only a 10 megohm digital voltmeter. This test checks the continuity of CKTs 412 and 413. If CKT 413 is open, the ECM voltage on CKT 412 will be over .6 volt (600 mV).

Diagnostic Aids:

Normal "Scan" tool O₂ sensor voltage varies between 100 mV to 999 mV (.1 and 1.0 volt) while in "Closed Loop." Code 13 sets in one minute if sensor signal voltage remains between .35 and .55 volt, but the system will go to "Open Loop" in about 15 seconds.

Verify a clean, tight ground connection for CKT 413. Open CKT(s) 412 or 413 will result in a Code 13. If Code 13 is intermittent, refer to "Symptoms."

CODE 13
OXYGEN (O₂) SENSOR CIRCUIT
(OPEN CIRCUIT)

ECM
- B2 — O₂ SENSOR SIGNAL
- B23 — O₂ SENSOR GROUND

412 PPL
413 TAN

OXYGEN (O₂) SENSOR
EXHAUST
ENGINE GROUND

The connector terminal identification on the Lumina may be different.

---

(1) ENGINE AT NORMAL OPERATING TEMPERATURE (ABOVE 80°C/176°F).
- RUN ENGINE ABOVE 1200 RPM FOR TWO MINUTES.
- DOES TECH 1 TOOL INDICATE "CLOSED LOOP"?

→ YES: CODE 13 IS INTERMITTENT

→ NO:
(2) DISCONNECT O₂ SENSOR.
- JUMPER HARNESS CKT 412 (ECM SIDE) TO GROUND.
- TECH 1 SHOULD DISPLAY O₂ VOLTAGE BELOW .2 VOLT (200 mV) WITH ENGINE RUNNING. DOES IT?

→ YES: FAULTY O₂ SENSOR CONNECTION OR SENSOR.

→ NO:
(3) REMOVE JUMPER.
- IGNITION "ON", ENGINE "OFF".
- CHECK VOLTAGE OF CKT 412 (ECM SIDE) AT O₂ SENSOR HARNESS CONNECTOR USING A DVM.

- .3-.6 VOLT (300 - 600 mV): FAULTY ECM.
- LESS THAN .3 VOLT (300 mV): OPEN CKT 412 OR FAULTY ECM CONNECTION OR FAULTY ECM.
- OVER .6 VOLT (600 mV): OPEN CKT 413 OR FAULTY CONNECTION OR FAULTY ECM.

"AFTER REPAIRS," REFER TO CODE CRITERIA   AND CONFIRM CODE DOES NOT RESET.

86814127

THROTTLE BODY INJECTION DIAGNOSTIC CHARTS

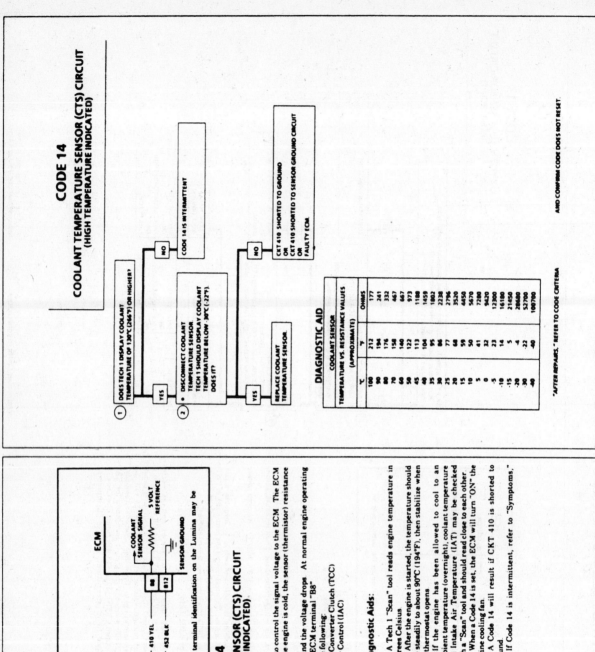

CODE 14
COOLANT TEMPERATURE SENSOR (CTS) CIRCUIT
(HIGH TEMPERATURE INDICATED)

(1) DOES TECH 1 DISPLAY COOLANT TEMPERATURE OF 130°C (266°F) OR HIGHER?

- NO → CODE 14 IS INTERMITTENT
- YES → **(2)** DISCONNECT COOLANT TEMPERATURE SENSOR. TECH 1 SHOULD DISPLAY COOLANT TEMPERATURE BELOW -30°C (-22°F). DOES IT?
  - NO → CKT 410 SHORTED TO GROUND OR CKT 410 SHORTED TO SENSOR GROUND CIRCUIT OR FAULTY ECM.
  - YES → REPLACE COOLANT TEMPERATURE SENSOR.

DIAGNOSTIC AID

COOLANT TEMPERATURE SENSOR
TEMPERATURE VS. RESISTANCE VALUES
(APPROXIMATE)

°C	°F	OHMS
100	212	177
90	194	241
80	176	332
70	158	467
60	140	667
50	122	973
45	113	1188
40	104	1459
35	95	1802
30	86	2238
25	77	2796
20	68	3520
15	59	4450
10	50	5670
5	41	7280
0	32	9420
-5	23	12300
-10	14	16180
-15	5	21450
-20	-4	28680
-30	-22	52700
-40	-40	100700

*"AFTER REPAIRS," REFER TO CODE CRITERIA

AND CONFIRM CODE DOES NOT RESET.

CODE 14
COOLANT TEMPERATURE SENSOR (CTS) CIRCUIT
(HIGH TEMPERATURE INDICATED)

ECM — COOLANT SENSOR SIGNAL — 5 VOLT REFERENCE — SENSOR GROUND

COOLANT TEMPERATURE SENSOR — A B

410 YEL — 452 BLK — TO TPS

B8 — B12

410 — 452

The connector terminal identification on the Lumina may be different.

Circuit Description:

The Coolant Temperature Sensor (CTS) uses a thermistor to control the signal voltage to the ECM. The ECM applies a reference voltage on CKT 410 to the sensor. When the engine is cold, the sensor (thermistor) resistance is high. The ECM will then sense a high signal voltage.

As the engine warms up, the sensor resistance decreases and the voltage drops. At normal engine operating temperature, the voltage will measure about 1.5 to 2.0 volts at ECM terminal "B8".

Coolant temperature is one of the inputs used to control the following:

- Fuel Delivery
- Torque Converter Clutch (TCC)
- Electronic Spark Timing (EST)
- Idle Air Control (IAC)
- Cooling Fan

Test Description: Numbers below refer to circled numbers on the diagnostic chart.

1. Checks to see if code was set as result of hard failure or intermittent condition. Code 14 will set if:
   - Signal voltage indicates a coolant temperature above 135°C (275°F) for 3 seconds.

2. This test simulates conditions for a Code 15. If the ECM recognizes the open circuit (high voltage) and displays a low temperature, the ECM and wiring are OK.

Diagnostic Aids:

A Tech 1 "Scan" tool reads engine temperature in degrees Celsius.

After the engine is started, the temperature should rise steadily to about 90°C (194°F), then stabilize when the thermostat opens.

If the engine has been allowed to cool to an ambient temperature (overnight), coolant temperature and Intake Air Temperature (IAT) may be checked with a "Scan" tool and should read close to each other.

When a Code 14 is set, the ECM will turn "ON" the engine cooling fan.

A Code 14 will result if CKT 410 is shorted to ground.

If Code 14 is intermittent, refer to "Symptoms."

86814128

THROTTLE BODY INJECTION DIAGNOSTIC CHARTS

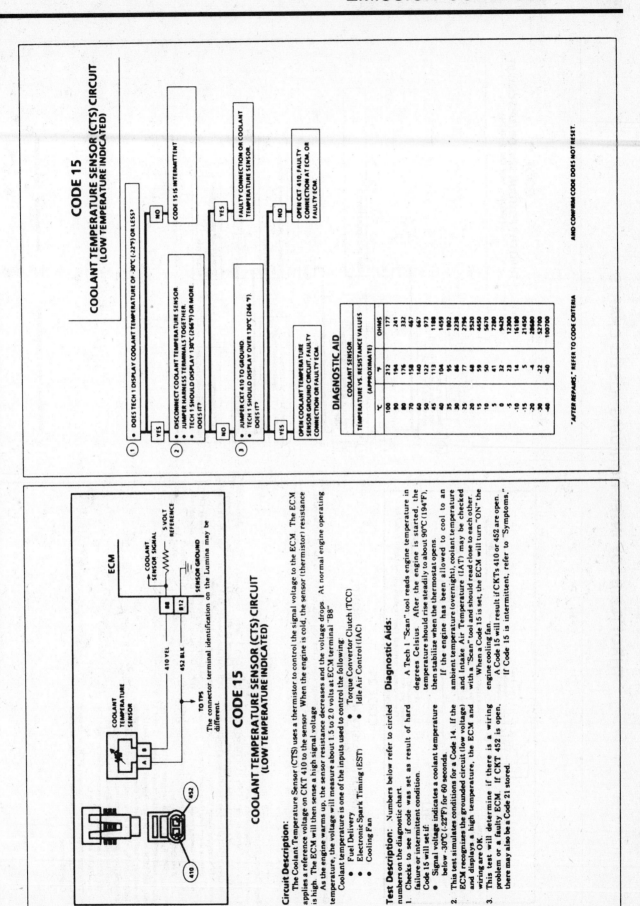

CODE 15
COOLANT TEMPERATURE SENSOR (CTS) CIRCUIT
(LOW TEMPERATURE INDICATED)

1. • DOES TECH 1 DISPLAY COOLANT TEMPERATURE OF -30°C (-22°F) OR LESS?

NO → CODE 15 IS INTERMITTENT

YES ↓

2. • DISCONNECT COOLANT TEMPERATURE SENSOR.
• JUMPER HARNESS TERMINALS TOGETHER.
• TECH 1 SHOULD DISPLAY 130°C (266°F) OR MORE. DOES IT?

YES → FAULTY CONNECTION OR COOLANT TEMPERATURE SENSOR.

NO ↓

3. • JUMPER CKT 410 TO GROUND
• TECH 1 SHOULD DISPLAY OVER 130°C (266°F) DOES IT?

NO → OPEN CKT 410, FAULTY CONNECTION AT ECM, OR FAULTY ECM.

YES → OPEN COOLANT TEMPERATURE SENSOR GROUND CIRCUIT, FAULTY CONNECTION OR FAULTY ECM.

DIAGNOSTIC AID

COOLANT SENSOR
TEMPERATURE VS. RESISTANCE VALUES
(APPROXIMATE)

°C	°F	OHMS
100	212	177
90	194	241
80	176	332
70	158	467
60	140	667
50	122	973
45	113	1188
40	104	1459
35	95	1802
30	86	2238
25	77	2796
20	68	3520
15	59	4450
10	50	5670
5	41	7280
0	32	9420
-5	23	12300
-10	14	16180
-15	5	21450
-20	-4	28680
-30	-22	52700
-40	-40	100700

"AFTER REPAIRS," REFER TO CODE CRITERIA   AND CONFIRM CODE DOES NOT RESET.

ECM
COOLANT SENSOR SIGNAL
5 VOLT REFERENCE
SENSOR GROUND
B8
B12
410 YEL
452 BLK
COOLANT TEMPERATURE SENSOR
TO TPS
A B
452
410

The connector terminal identification on the Lumina may be different.

CODE 15
COOLANT TEMPERATURE SENSOR (CTS) CIRCUIT
(LOW TEMPERATURE INDICATED)

Circuit Description:
The Coolant Temperature Sensor (CTS) uses a thermistor to control the signal voltage to the ECM. The ECM applies a reference voltage on CKT 410 to the sensor. When the engine is cold, the sensor (thermistor) resistance is high. The ECM will then sense a high signal voltage.

As the engine warms up, the sensor resistance decreases and the voltage drops. At normal engine operating temperature, the voltage will measure about 1.5 to 2.0 volts at ECM terminal "B8".

Coolant temperature is one of the inputs used to control the following:
• Fuel Delivery
• Electronic Spark Timing (EST)
• Cooling Fan
• Torque Convertor Clutch (TCC)
• Idle Air Control (IAC)

Test Description: Numbers below refer to circled numbers on the diagnostic chart.
1. Checks to see if code was set as result of hard failure or intermittent condition. Code 15 will set if:
• Signal voltage indicates a coolant temperature below -30°C (-22°F) for 60 seconds.
2. This test simulates conditions for a Code 14. If the ECM recognizes the grounded circuit (low voltage) and displays a high temperature, the ECM and wiring are OK.
3. This test will determine if there is a wiring problem or a faulty ECM. If CKT 452 is open, there may also be a Code 21 stored.

Diagnostic Aids:
A Tech 1 "Scan" tool reads engine temperature in degrees Celsius. After the engine is started, the temperature should rise steadily to about 90°C (194°F), then stabilize when the thermostat opens.

If the engine has been allowed to cool to an ambient temperature (overnight), coolant temperature and Intake Air Temperature (IAT) may be checked with a "Scan" tool and should read close to each other. When a Code 15 is set, the ECM will turn "ON" the engine cooling fan.

A Code 15 will result if CKTs 410 or 452 are open. If Code 15 is intermittent, refer to "Symptoms."

86814129

THROTTLE BODY INJECTION DIAGNOSTIC CHARTS

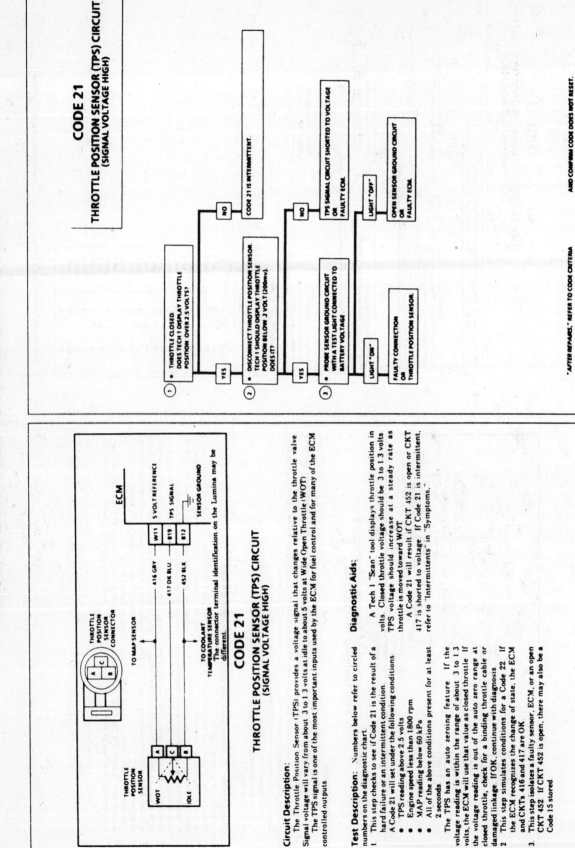

CODE 21

THROTTLE POSITION SENSOR (TPS) CIRCUIT
(SIGNAL VOLTAGE HIGH)

Circuit Description:

The Throttle Position Sensor (TPS) provides a voltage signal that changes relative to the throttle valve.
Signal voltage will vary from about 3 to 1.3 volts at idle to about 5 volts at Wide Open Throttle (WOT)

The TPS signal is one of the most important inputs used by the ECM for fuel control and for many of the ECM controlled outputs

Test Description: Numbers below refer to circled numbers on the diagnostic chart.

1. This step checks to see if Code 21 is the result of a hard failure or an intermittent condition.

   A Code 21 will set under the following conditions
   - TPS reading above 2.5 volts
   - Engine speed less than 1800 rpm
   - MAP reading below 60 kPa
   - All of the above conditions present for at least 2 seconds

   The TPS has an auto zeroing feature If the voltage reading is within the range of about 3 to 1.3 volts, the ECM will use that value as closed throttle If the voltage reading is out of the auto zero range at closed throttle, check for a binding throttle cable or damaged linkage. If OK, continue with diagnosis

2. This step simulates conditions for a Code 22 If the ECM recognizes the change of state, the ECM and CKTs 416 and 417 are OK.

3. This step isolates a faulty sensor, ECM, or an open CKT 452 If CKT 452 is open, there may also be a Code 15 stored

Diagnostic Aids:

A Tech 1 "Scan" tool displays throttle position in volts. Closed throttle voltage should be 3 to 1.3 volts TPS voltage should increase at a steady rate as throttle is moved toward WOT

A Code 21 will result if CKT 452 is open or CKT 417 is shorted to voltage If Code 21 is intermittent, refer to "Intermittents" in "Symptoms."

86814130

THROTTLE BODY INJECTION DIAGNOSTIC CHARTS

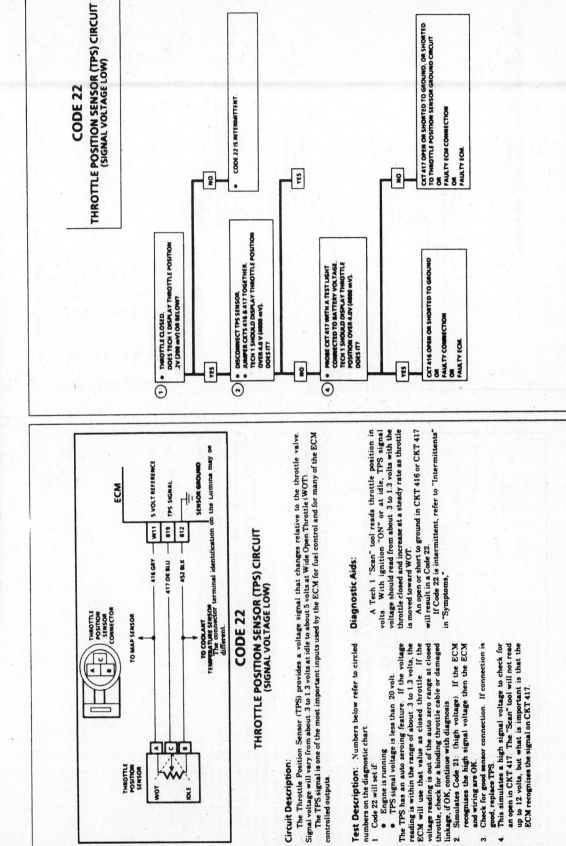

CODE 22
THROTTLE POSITION SENSOR (TPS) CIRCUIT
(SIGNAL VOLTAGE LOW)

Circuit Description:

The Throttle Position Sensor (TPS) provides a voltage signal that changes relative to the throttle valve. Signal voltage will vary from about 3 to 1.3 volts at idle to about 5 volts at Wide Open Throttle (WOT). The TPS signal is one of the most important inputs used by the ECM for fuel control and for many of the ECM controlled outputs.

Test Description: Numbers below refer to circled numbers on the diagnostic chart.

1. Code 22 will set if:
   - Engine is running
   - TPS signal voltage is less than .20 volt.

   The TPS has an auto zeroing feature. If the voltage reading is within the range of about 3 to 1.3 volts, the ECM will use that value as closed throttle. If the voltage reading is out of the auto zero range at closed throttle, check for a binding throttle cable or damaged linkage. If OK, continue with diagnosis.

2. Simulates Code 21: (high voltage). If the ECM recognizes the high signal voltage then the ECM and wiring are OK.

3. Check for good sensor connection. If connection is good, replace TPS.

4. This simulates a high signal voltage to check for an open in CKT 417. The "Scan" tool will not read up to 12 volts, but what is important is that the ECM recognizes the signal on CKT 417.

Diagnostic Aids:

A Tech 1 "Scan" tool reads throttle position in volts. With ignition "ON" or at idle, TPS signal voltage should read from about .3 to 1.3 volts with the throttle closed and increase at a steady rate as throttle is moved toward WOT.

An open or short to ground in CKT 416 or CKT 417 will result in a Code 22.

If Code 22 is intermittent, refer to "Intermittents" in "Symptoms."

86814131

THROTTLE BODY INJECTION DIAGNOSTIC CHARTS

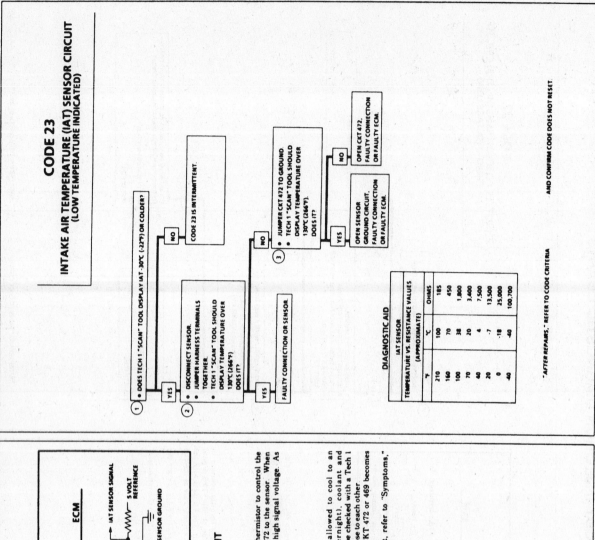

CODE 23

INTAKE AIR TEMPERATURE (IAT) SENSOR CIRCUIT
(LOW TEMPERATURE INDICATED)

Circuit Description:

The Intake Air Temperature (IAT) sensor, located on the intake manifold, uses a thermistor to control the signal voltage to the ECM. The ECM applies a reference voltage (4-5.5 volts) on CKT 472 to the sensor. When intake air is cold, the sensor (thermistor) resistance is high. The ECM will then sense a high signal voltage. As the air warms, the sensor resistance becomes less and the voltage drops.

Test Description: Numbers below refer to circled numbers on the diagnostic chart.

1. This step determines if Code 23 is the result of a hard failure or an intermittent condition. Code 23 will set when signal voltage indicates a IAT/MAT temperature less than -30°C and the engine is running for longer than 58 seconds

2. This test simulates conditions for a Code 25. If the "Scan" tool displays a high temperature, the ECM and wiring are OK.

3. This step checks continuity of CKTs 472 and 469 If CKT 469 is open there may also be a Code 33

Diagnostic Aids:

If the engine has been allowed to cool to an ambient temperature (overnight), coolant and IAT/MAT temperatures may be checked with a Tech 1 "Scan" tool and should read close to each other

A Code 23 will result if CKT 472 or 469 becomes open.

If Code 23 is intermittent, refer to "Symptoms,"

THROTTLE BODY INJECTION DIAGNOSTIC CHARTS

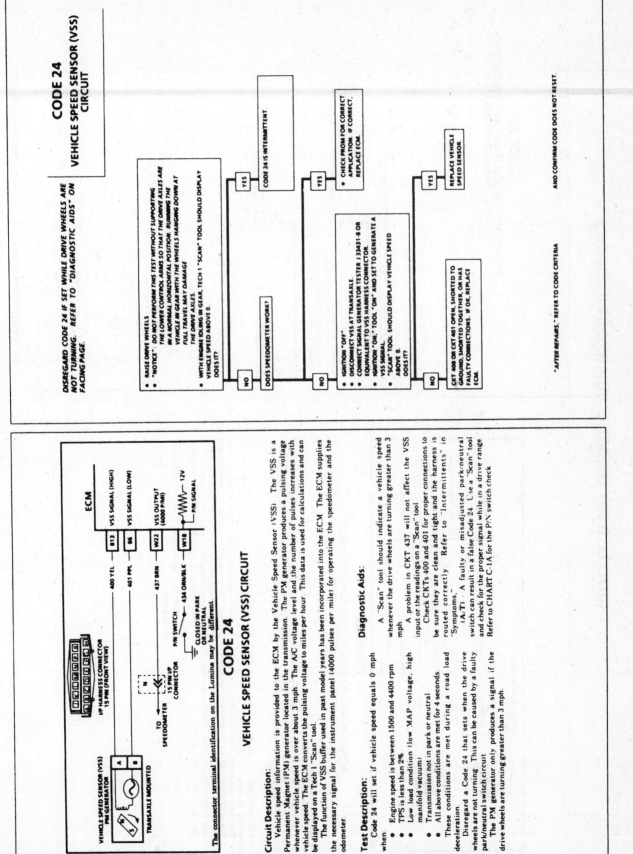

CODE 24
VEHICLE SPEED SENSOR (VSS) CIRCUIT

DISREGARD CODE 24 IF SET WHILE DRIVE WHEELS ARE NOT TURNING. REFER TO "DIAGNOSTIC AIDS" ON FACING PAGE.

- RAISE DRIVE WHEELS
- "NOTICE": DO NOT PERFORM THIS TEST WITHOUT SUPPORTING THE LOWER CONTROL ARMS SO THAT THE DRIVE AXLES ARE IN A NORMAL HORIZONTAL POSITION. RUNNING THE VEHICLE IN GEAR WITH THE WHEELS HANGING DOWN AT FULL TRAVEL MAY DAMAGE THE DRIVE AXLES.
- WITH ENGINE IDLING IN GEAR, TECH 1 "SCAN" TOOL SHOULD DISPLAY VEHICLE SPEED ABOVE 0.
  DOES IT?

NO | YES

YES → CODE 24 IS INTERMITTENT.

DOES SPEEDOMETER WORK?

NO | YES

- IGNITION "OFF".
- DISCONNECT VSS AT TRANSAXLE.
- CONNECT SIGNAL GENERATOR TESTER J 33431-B OR EQUIVALENT TO VSS HARNESS CONNECTOR.
- IGNITION "ON". TOOL "ON" AND SET TO GENERATE A VSS SIGNAL.
- "SCAN" TOOL SHOULD DISPLAY VEHICLE SPEED ABOVE 0.
  DOES IT?

NO | YES

YES → • CHECK PROM FOR CORRECT APPLICATION. IF CORRECT, REPLACE ECM.

NO → CKT 400 OR CKT 401 OPEN, SHORTED TO GROUND, SHORTED TOGETHER, OR HAS FAULTY CONNECTIONS. IF OK, REPLACE ECM.

YES → REPLACE VEHICLE SPEED SENSOR.

"AFTER REPAIRS," REFER TO CODE CRITERIA AND CONFIRM CODE DOES NOT RESET.

ECM

B13	VSS SIGNAL (HIGH)
B6	VSS SIGNAL (LOW)
W22	VSS OUTPUT (4000 P/MI)
W18	12V / PM SIGNAL

400 YEL
401 PPL
437 BRN
434 ORN/BLK

VEHICLE SPEED SENSOR (VSS) PM GENERATOR

TRANSAXLE MOUNTED

A B

VP HARNESS CONNECTOR 15 PIN (FRONT VIEW)

N

15 PIN VP CONNECTOR

TO SPEEDOMETER

P/N SWITCH

CLOSED IN PARK OR NEUTRAL

The connector terminal identification on the Lumina may be different.

CODE 24
VEHICLE SPEED SENSOR (VSS) CIRCUIT

Circuit Description:

Vehicle speed information is provided to the ECM by the Vehicle Speed Sensor (VSS). The VSS is a Permanent Magnet (PM) generator located in the transmission. The PM generator produces a pulsing voltage whenever vehicle speed is over about 3 mph. The A/C voltage level and the number of pulses increases with vehicle speed. The ECM converts the pulsing voltage to miles per hour. This data is used for calculations and can be displayed on a Tech 1 "Scan" tool.

The function of VSS buffer used in past model years has been incorporated into the ECM. The ECM supplies the necessary signal for the instrument panel (4000 pulses per mile) for operating the speedometer and the odometer.

Test Description:

Code 24 will set if vehicle speed equals 0 mph when:

- Engine speed is between 1500 and 4400 rpm
- TPS is less than 2%
- Low load condition (low MAP voltage, high manifold vacuum)
- Transmission not in park or neutral
- All above conditions are met for 4 seconds

These conditions are met during a road load deceleration.

Disregard a Code 24 that sets when the drive wheels are not turning. This can be caused by a faulty park/neutral switch circuit.

The PM generator only produces a signal if the drive wheels are turning greater than 3 mph.

Diagnostic Aids:

A "Scan" tool should indicate a vehicle speed whenever the drive wheels are turning greater than 3 mph.

A problem in CKT 437 will not affect the VSS input or the readings on a "Scan" tool.

Check CKTs 400 and 401 for proper connections to be sure they are clean and tight and the harness is routed correctly. Refer to "Intermittents" in "Symptoms."

(A/T) - A faulty or misadjusted park/neutral switch can result in a false Code 24. Use a "Scan" tool and check for the proper signal while in a drive range and check for the P/N switch check. Refer to CHART C-1A for the P/N switch check

86814133

THROTTLE BODY INJECTION DIAGNOSTIC CHARTS

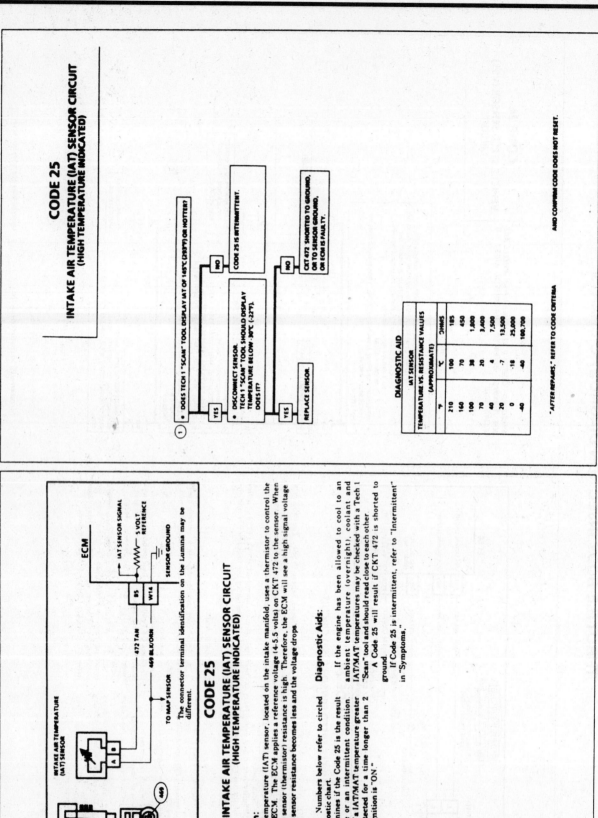

CODE 25

INTAKE AIR TEMPERATURE (IAT) SENSOR CIRCUIT
(HIGH TEMPERATURE INDICATED)

Circuit Description:

The Intake Air Temperature (IAT) sensor, located on the intake manifold, uses a thermistor to control the signal voltage to the ECM. The ECM applies a reference voltage (4-5.5 volts) on CKT 472 to the sensor. When intake air is cold, the sensor (thermistor) resistance is high. Therefore, the ECM will see a high signal voltage. As the air warms, the sensor resistance becomes less and the voltage drops.

Test Description: Numbers below refer to circled numbers on the diagnostic chart.

1. This check determines if the Code 25 is the result of a hard failure or an intermittent condition. Code 25 will set if a IAT/MAT temperature greater than 135°C is detected for a time longer than 2 seconds and the ignition is "ON."

Diagnostic Aids:

If the engine has been allowed to cool to an ambient temperature (overnight), coolant and IAT/MAT temperatures may be checked with a Tech 1 "Scan" tool and should read close to each other.

A Code 25 will result if CKT 472 is shorted to ground.

If Code 25 is intermittent, refer to "Intermittent" in "Symptoms."

The connector terminal identification on the Lumina may be different.

ECM

IAT SENSOR SIGNAL
5 VOLT REFERENCE
SENSOR GROUND

B5
W14

472 TAN
469 BLK/ORN

TO MAP SENSOR

INTAKE AIR TEMPERATURE (IAT) SENSOR

469
472

CODE 25

INTAKE AIR TEMPERATURE (IAT) SENSOR CIRCUIT
(HIGH TEMPERATURE INDICATED)

① • DOES TECH 1 "SCAN" TOOL DISPLAY IAT OF 145°C (293°F) OR HOTTER?

YES → • DISCONNECT SENSOR.
TECH 1 "SCAN" TOOL SHOULD DISPLAY TEMPERATURE BELOW -30°C (-22°F).
DOES IT?

NO → CODE 25 IS INTERMITTENT.

YES → REPLACE SENSOR.

NO → CKT 472 SHORTED TO GROUND, OR TO SENSOR GROUND, OR ECM IS FAULTY.

DIAGNOSTIC AID

IAT SENSOR		
TEMPERATURE VS. RESISTANCE VALUES (APPROXIMATE)		
°F	°C	OHMS
210	100	185
160	70	450
100	38	1,800
70	20	3,400
40	4	7,500
20	-7	13,500
0	-18	25,000
-40	-40	100,700

"AFTER REPAIRS," REFER TO CODE CRITERIA AND CONFIRM CODE DOES NOT RESET.

86814134

THROTTLE BODY INJECTION DIAGNOSTIC CHARTS

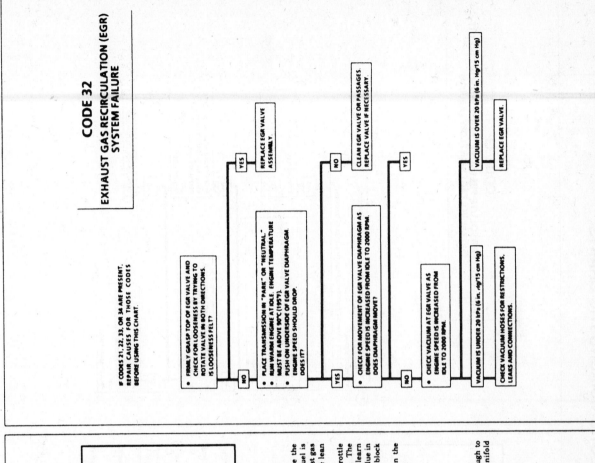

CODE 32
EXHAUST GAS RECIRCULATION (EGR) SYSTEM FAILURE

- IF CODES 21, 22, 33, OR 34 ARE PRESENT. REPAIR CAUSES FOR THOSE CODES BEFORE USING THIS CHART.

- FIRMLY GRASP TOP OF EGR VALVE AND CHECK FOR LOOSENESS BY TRYING TO ROTATE VALVE IN BOTH DIRECTIONS. IS LOOSENESS FELT?
  - YES → REPLACE EGR VALVE ASSEMBLY.
  - NO → PLACE TRANSMISSION IN "PARK" OR "NEUTRAL". RUN WARM ENGINE AT IDLE. ENGINE TEMPERATURE MUST BE ABOVE 90°C (195°). PUSH ON UNDERSIDE OF EGR VALVE DIAPHRAGM. ENGINE SPEED SHOULD DROP. DOES IT?
    - YES → CHECK FOR MOVEMENT OF EGR VALVE DIAPHRAGM AS ENGINE SPEED IS INCREASED FROM IDLE TO 2000 RPM. DOES DIAPHRAGM MOVE?
      - NO → CLEAN EGR VALVE OR PASSAGES. REPLACE VALVE IF NECESSARY.
      - YES → CHECK VACUUM AT EGR VALVE AS ENGINE SPEED IS INCREASED FROM IDLE TO 2000 RPM.
        - VACUUM IS UNDER 20 kPa (6 in. Hg/15 cm Hg) → CHECK VACUUM HOSES FOR RESTRICTIONS, LEAKS AND CONNECTIONS.
        - VACUUM IS OVER 20 kPa (6 in. Hg/15 cm Hg) → REPLACE EGR VALVE.

CODE 32
EXHAUST GAS RECIRCULATION (EGR) SYSTEM FAILURE

Circuit Description:

A properly operating EGR system will directly affect the air/fuel requirements of the engine. Since the exhaust gas introduced into the air/fuel mixture is an inert gas (contains very little or no oxygen), less fuel is required to maintain a correct air/fuel ratio. If the EGR system were to become inoperative, the inert exhaust gas would be replaced with air and the air/fuel mixture would be leaner. The ECM would compensate for the lean condition by adding fuel, resulting in higher block learn values.

The engine control system operates within two block learn cells, a closed throttle cell, and an open throttle cell. Since EGR is not used at idle, the closed throttle cell would not be affected by EGR system operation. The open throttle cell is affected by EGR operation and, when the EGR system is operating properly, the block learn values in both cells should be close to being the same. If the EGR system is inoperative, the block learn value in the open throttle cell would change (become higher) to compensate for the resulting lean system, but the block learn value in the closed throttle cell would not change.

This change or difference in block learn values is used to monitor EGR system performance. When the change becomes too great, a Code 32 is set.

Diagnostic Aids:

The Code 32 chart is a functional check of the EGR system. If the EGR system works properly, but a Code 32 has been set, check other items that could result in high block learn values in the open throttle cell, but not in the closed throttle cell.

CHECK:

EGR Passages
    Restricted or blocked

MAP Sensor
    A MAP sensor may shift in calibration enough to affect fuel delivery. Use CHART C-1D, "Manifold Absolute Pressure (MAP) Output Check."

86814135

THROTTLE BODY INJECTION DIAGNOSTIC CHARTS

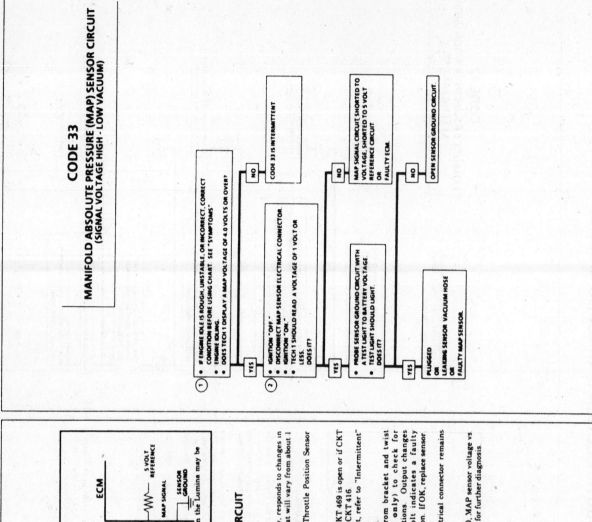

CODE 33

MANIFOLD ABSOLUTE PRESSURE (MAP) SENSOR CIRCUIT
(SIGNAL VOLTAGE HIGH - LOW VACUUM)

The connector terminal identification on the Lumina may be different.

Circuit Description:

The Manifold Absolute Pressure (MAP) sensor, located on the air cleaner assembly, responds to changes in manifold pressure (vacuum). The ECM receives this information as a signal voltage that will vary from about 1 to 1.5 volts at closed throttle (idle) to 4.5-4.8 volts at wide open throttle (low vacuum).

If the MAP sensor fails, the ECM will substitute a fixed MAP value and use the Throttle Position Sensor (TPS) to control fuel delivery.

Test Description: Numbers below refer to circled numbers on the diagnostic chart.

1. This step will determine if Code 33 is the result of a hard failure or an intermittent condition.

   A Code 33 will set under the following conditions:
   - MAP signal voltage is too high (low vacuum)
   - TPS less than 2%.
   - These conditions exist longer than 5 seconds.

2. This step simulates conditions for a Code 34. If the ECM recognizes the change, the ECM and CKTs 416 and 432 are OK.

A Code 33 will result if CKT 469 is open or if CKT 432 is shorted to voltage or to CKT 416.

If Code 33 is intermittent, refer to "Intermittent" in "Symptoms."
- Check all connections.
- Disconnect sensor from bracket and twist sensor (by hand only) to check for intermittent connections. Output changes greater than 1 volt indicates a faulty connector or connection. If OK, replace sensor.

NOTE: Make sure electrical connector remains securely fastened.

Diagnostic Aids:

With the ignition "ON" and the engine stopped, the manifold pressure is equal to atmospheric pressure and the signal voltage will be high. This information is used by the ECM as an indication of vehicle altitude. Comparison of this reading with a known good vehicle with the same sensor is a good way to check accuracy of a "suspect" sensor. Readings should be the same ± 4 volt.

- Refer to CHART C-1D, MAP sensor voltage vs. atmospheric pressure for further diagnosis.

ECM

5 VOLT REFERENCE
MAP SIGNAL
SENSOR GROUND

W11
B20
W14

416 GAY
432 LT GRN
469 BLK/ORN

TO TPS SENSOR
TO IAT SENSOR

MAP SENSOR
A B C

MANIFOLD ABSOLUTE PRESSURE (VACUUM)

---

①
- IF ENGINE IDLE IS ROUGH, UNSTABLE, OR INCORRECT, CORRECT CONDITION BEFORE USING CHART. SEE "SYMPTOMS".
- ENGINE IDLING.
- DOES TECH 1 DISPLAY A MAP VOLTAGE OF 4.0 VOLTS OR OVER?

↓ NO → CODE 33 IS INTERMITTENT

↓ YES

②
- IGNITION "OFF."
- DISCONNECT MAP SENSOR ELECTRICAL CONNECTOR.
- IGNITION "ON."
- TECH 1 SHOULD READ A VOLTAGE OF 1 VOLT OR LESS.
- DOES IT?

↓ NO → MAP SIGNAL CIRCUIT SHORTED TO VOLTAGE, SHORTED TO 5 VOLT REFERENCE CIRCUIT OR FAULTY ECM.

↓ YES

- PROBE SENSOR GROUND CIRCUIT WITH A TEST LIGHT TO BATTERY VOLTAGE.
- TEST LIGHT SHOULD LIGHT.
- DOES IT?

↓ NO → OPEN SENSOR GROUND CIRCUIT.

↓ YES

PLUGGED OR LEAKING SENSOR VACUUM HOSE OR FAULTY MAP SENSOR.

THROTTLE BODY INJECTION DIAGNOSTIC CHARTS

CODE 34

MANIFOLD ABSOLUTE PRESSURE (MAP) SENSOR CIRCUIT
(SIGNAL VOLTAGE LOW - HIGH VACUUM)

The connector terminal identification on the Lumina may be different

Circuit Description:

The Manifold Absolute Pressure (MAP) sensor, located on the air cleaner assembly, responds to changes in manifold pressure (vacuum). The ECM receives this information as a signal voltage that will vary from about 1 to 1.5 volts at closed throttle (idle) to 4.5-4.8 volts at wide open throttle (low vacuum).

If the MAP sensor fails, the ECM will substitute a fixed MAP value and use the Throttle Position Sensor (TPS) to control fuel delivery.

Test Description: Numbers below refer to circled numbers on the diagnostic chart.

1. This step determines if Code 34 is the result of a hard failure or an intermittent condition. A Code 34 will set under the following conditions:
   - Code 21 is not detected.
   - MAP signal voltage is too low.
   - Engine speed is less than 1200 rpm.
   OR
   - Engine speed is greater than 1200 rpm and throttle angle is greater than 20%.
   - All conditions above have been present for a period of time greater than 02 second.

2. Jumpering harness terminals "B" to "C" (5 volts to signal circuit) will determine if the sensor is at fault, or if there is a problem with the ECM or wiring.

3. The "Scan" tool may not display 5 volts. The important thing is that the ECM recognizes the voltage as more than 4 volts, indicating that the ECM and CKT 432 are OK.

With the ignition "ON" and the engine "OFF," the manifold pressure is equal to atmospheric pressure and the signal voltage will be high. This information is used by the ECM as an indication of vehicle altitude.

Comparison of this reading with a known good vehicle with the same sensor is a good way to check accuracy of a "suspect" sensor. Readings should be the same ± .4 volts. Also CHART C-1D can be used to test the MAP sensor. Refer to "Intermittents" in "Symptoms."

- Check all connections.
- Disconnect sensor from bracket and twist sensor (by hand only) to check for intermittent connections. Output changes greater than 1 volt indicates a faulty connector or connection. If OK, replace sensor.

NOTE: Make sure electrical connector remains securely fastened.

- Refer to CHART C-1D, MAP sensor voltage vs atmospheric pressure for further diagnosis

Diagnostic Aids:

An intermittent open in CKT 432 or CKT 416 will result in a Code 34. If CKT 416 is open or shorted to ground, there may also be a stored Code 22.

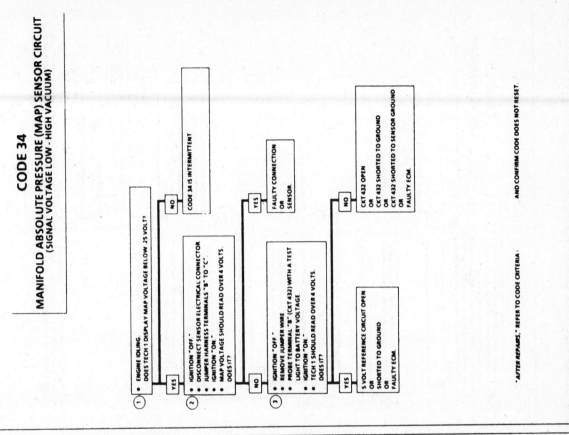

CODE 34
MANIFOLD ABSOLUTE PRESSURE (MAP) SENSOR CIRCUIT
(SIGNAL VOLTAGE LOW - HIGH VACUUM)

① ENGINE IDLING.
DOES TECH 1 DISPLAY MAP VOLTAGE BELOW .25 VOLT?

NO → CODE 34 IS INTERMITTENT

YES ↓

② IGNITION "OFF."
DISCONNECT SENSOR ELECTRICAL CONNECTOR.
JUMPER HARNESS TERMINALS "B" TO "C."
IGNITION "ON."
MAP VOLTAGE SHOULD READ OVER 4 VOLTS.
DOES IT?

YES → FAULTY CONNECTION OR SENSOR.

NO ↓

③ IGNITION "OFF."
REMOVE JUMPER WIRE.
PROBE TERMINAL "B" (CKT 432) WITH A TEST LIGHT TO BATTERY VOLTAGE.
IGNITION "ON."
TECH 1 SHOULD READ OVER 4 VOLTS.
DOES IT?

YES → 5 VOLT REFERENCE CIRCUIT OPEN
OR
SHORTED TO GROUND
OR
FAULTY ECM.

NO → CKT 432 OPEN
OR
CKT 432 SHORTED TO GROUND
OR
CKT 432 SHORTED TO SENSOR GROUND
OR
FAULTY ECM.

"AFTER REPAIRS," REFER TO CODE CRITERIA   AND CONFIRM CODE DOES NOT RESET.

86814137

THROTTLE BODY INJECTION DIAGNOSTIC CHARTS

ECM

441 LT BLU/WHT	W7	IAC COIL "A" HI
442 LT BLU/BLK	W17	IAC COIL "A" LO
443 LT GRN/WHT	W5	IAC COIL "B" HI
444 LT GRN/BLK	W8	IAC COIL "B" LO

The connector terminal identification on the Lumina may be different.

CODE 35
IDLE SPEED ERROR

Circuit Description:

The ECM controls engine idle speed with the IAC valve. To increase idle speed, the ECM retracts the IAC valve pintle away from its seat, allowing more air to bypass the throttle bore. To decrease idle speed, it extends the IAC valve pintle towards its seats, reducing bypass air flow. A Tech 1 "Scan" tool will read the ECM commands to the IAC valve in counts. Higher the counts indicate more air bypass (higher idle). The lower the counts indicate less air is allowed by bypass (lower idle). Code 35 will be set when the closed throttle speed is 100 rpm above or below the desired idle speed for 2.5 seconds.

Test Description: Numbers below refer to circled numbers on the diagnostic chart.

1. The IAC tester is used to extend and retract the IAC valve. Valve movement is verified by an engine speed change. If no change in engine speed occurs, the valve can be retested when removed from the throttle body.

2. This step checks the quality of the IAC movement in step 1. Between 700 rpm and about 1500 rpm, the engine speed should change smoothly with each flash of the tester light in both extend and retract. If the IAC valve is retracted beyond the control range (about 1500 rpm), it may take many flashes in the extend position before engine speed will begin to drop. This is normal on certain engines, fully extending IAC may cause engine stall. This may be normal.

3. Steps 1 and 2 verified proper IAC valve operation while this step checks the IAC circuits. Each lamp on the node light should flash red and green while the IAC valve is cycled. While the sequence of color is not important if either light is "OFF" or does not flash red and green, check the circuits for faults beginning with poor terminal contacts.

Diagnostic Aids:

A slow, unstable, or fast idle may be caused by a non-IAC system problem that cannot be overcome by the IAC valve. Out of control range IAC "Scan" tool counts will be above 60 if idle is too low, and zero counts if idle is too high. The following checks should be made to repair a non-IAC system problem.

• Vacuum Leak (High Idle)
If idle is too high, stop the engine. Fully extend (low) IAC with tester.

Start engine. If idle speed is above 800 rpm, locate and correct vacuum leak including PCV system. Also check for binding of throttle blade or linkage.

• System too lean (High Air/Fuel Ratio)
The idle speed may be too high or too low. Engine speed may vary up and down and disconnecting the IAC valve does not help. Code 44 may be set. "Scan" O2 voltage will be less than 300 mV (.3 volt). Check for low regulated fuel pressure, water in the fuel or a restricted injector.

• System too rich (Low Air/Fuel Ratio)
The idle speed will be too low. "Scan" tool IAC counts will usually be above 80. System is obviously rich and may exhibit black smoke in exhaust. "Scan" tool O2 voltage will be fixed above 800 mV (.8 volt).
Check for high fuel pressure, leaking or sticking injector. Silicone contaminated O2 sensor will "Scan" an O2 voltage slow to respond.

• Throttle Body
Remove IAC valve and inspect bore for foreign material.

• IAC Valve Electrical Connections
IAC valve connections should be carefully checked for proper contact.

• PCV System
An incorrect or faulty PCV system may result in an incorrect idle speed.

Refer to "Rough, Unstable, Incorrect Idle or Stalling" in "Symptoms."

If intermittent poor driveability or idle symptoms are resolved by disconnecting the IAC, carefully recheck connections, valve terminal resistance, or replace IAC.

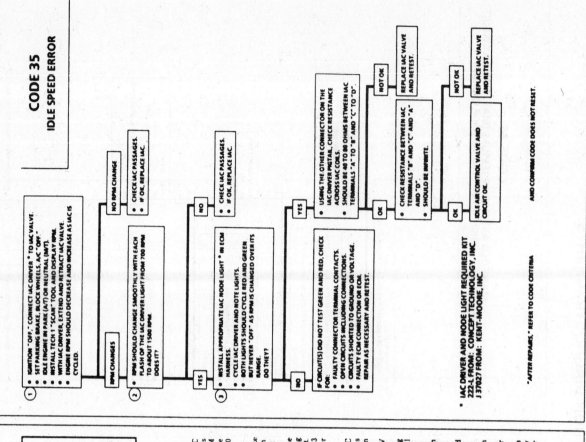

CODE 35
IDLE SPEED ERROR

1
• IGNITION "OFF." CONNECT IAC DRIVER* TO IAC VALVE.
• SET PARKING BRAKE, BLOCK WHEELS, A/C "OFF."
• IDLE ENGINE IN PARK (A/T) OR NEUTRAL (M/T).
• INSTALL TECH 1 "SCAN" TOOL AND DISPLAY RPM.
• WITH IAC DRIVER, EXTEND AND RETRACT IAC VALVE.
• ENGINE RPM SHOULD DECREASE AND INCREASE AS IAC IS CYCLED.

NO RPM CHANGE → CHECK IAC PASSAGES. IF OK, REPLACE IAC.

RPM CHANGES

2
• RPM SHOULD CHANGE SMOOTHLY WITH EACH FLASH OF THE IAC DRIVER LIGHT FROM 700 RPM TO ABOUT 1500 RPM. DOES IT?

NO → CHECK IAC PASSAGES. IF OK, REPLACE IAC.

YES

3
• INSTALL APPROPRIATE IAC NODE LIGHT* IN ECM HARNESS.
• CYCLE IAC DRIVER AND NOTE LIGHTS.
• BOTH LIGHTS SHOULD CYCLE RED AND GREEN BUT NEVER "OFF" AS RPM IS CHANGED OVER ITS RANGE. DO THEY?

YES → USING THE OTHER CONNECTOR ON THE IAC DRIVER PIGTAIL, CHECK RESISTANCE ACROSS IAC COILS.
• SHOULD BE 40 TO 80 OHMS BETWEEN IAC TERMINALS "A" TO "B" AND "C" TO "D".

OK → CHECK RESISTANCE BETWEEN IAC TERMINALS "B" AND "C" AND "A" AND "D".
• SHOULD BE INFINITE.

NOT OK → REPLACE IAC VALVE AND RETEST.

OK → IDLE AIR CONTROL VALVE AND CIRCUIT OK.

NOT OK → REPLACE IAC VALVE AND RETEST.

NO → IF CIRCUIT(S) DID NOT TEST GREEN AND RED, CHECK FOR:
• FAULTY CONNECTOR TERMINAL CONTACTS.
• OPEN CIRCUITS INCLUDING CONNECTIONS.
• CIRCUITS SHORTED TO GROUND OR VOLTAGE.
• FAULTY ECM CONNECTION OR ECM.
REPAIR AS NECESSARY AND RETEST.

• IAC DRIVER AND NODE LIGHT REQUIRED KIT
222-1 FROM: CONCEPT TECHNOLOGY, INC
J 37027 FROM: KENT-MOORE, INC.

*AFTER REPAIRS," REFER TO CODE CRITERIA AND CONFIRM CODE DOES NOT RESET.

86814138

THROTTLE BODY INJECTION DIAGNOSTIC CHARTS

CODE 42
ELECTRONIC SPARK TIMING (EST) CIRCUIT

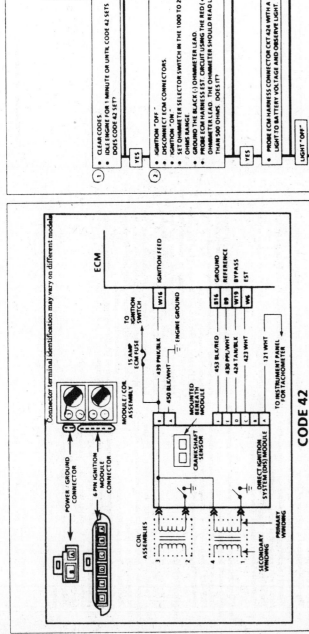

Connector terminal identification may vary on different models

ECM

IGNITION FEED — W16
TO IGNITION SWITCH

15 AMP ECM FUSE
ENGINE GROUND

439 PNK/BLK
450 BLK/WHT

MODULE / COIL ASSEMBLY

GROUND — B16
REFERENCE — B9
BYPASS — W19
EST — W6

453 BLK/RED
430 PPL/WHT
424 TAN/BLK
423 WHT

121 WHT
TO INSTRUMENT PANEL FOR TACHOMETER

CRANKSHAFT SENSOR
MOUNTED BENEATH MODULE

DIRECT IGNITION SYSTEM (DIS) MODULE

COIL ASSEMBLIES

SECONDARY WINDING
PRIMARY WINDING

POWER / GROUND CONNECTOR
6 PIN IGNITION MODULE CONNECTOR

CODE 42
ELECTRONIC SPARK TIMING (EST) CIRCUIT

Circuit Description:

The DIS module sends a reference signal to the ECM when the engine is cranking. While the engine speed is under 400 rpm, the DIS module controls the ignition timing. When the system is running on the ignition module (no voltage on the bypass line), the ignition module grounds the EST signal. The ECM expects to sense no voltage on the EST line during this condition. If it senses a voltage, it sets Code 42 and will not enter the EST mode.

When the engine speed exceeds 400 rpm, the ECM applies 5 volts to the bypass line to switch the timing to ECM control (EST). If the bypass line is open or grounded, once the rpm for EST control is reached, the ignition module will not switch to EST mode. This results in low EST voltage and the setting of Code 42. If the EST line is grounded, the ignition module will switch to EST, but because the line is grounded, there will be no EST signal. A Code 42 will be set.

Test Description: Numbers below refer to circled numbers on the diagnostic chart.

1. Code 42 means the ECM has sensed an open or short to ground in the EST or bypass circuits. This test confirms Code 42 and that the fault causing the code is present.

2. Checks for a normal EST ground path through the ignition module. An EST CKT 423, shorted to ground, will also read less than 500 ohms, but this will be checked later.

3. As the test light voltage contacts CKT 424, the module should switch, causing the ohmmeter to "overrange" if the meter is in the 1000-2000 ohms position. Selecting the 10-20,000 ohms position will indicate a reading above 5000 ohms. The important thing is that the module "switched."

4. The module did not switch and this step checks for:
   - EST CKT 423 shorted to ground
   - Bypass CKT 424 open
   - Faulty ignition module connection or module

5. Confirms that Code 42 is a faulty ECM and not an intermittent in CKT(s) 423 or 424

Diagnostic Aids:

The "Scan" tool does not have any ability to help diagnose a Code 42 problem.

If Code 42 is intermittent, refer to "Intermittent" in "Symptoms."

---

① • CLEAR CODES.
   • IDLE ENGINE FOR 1 MINUTE OR UNTIL CODE 42 SETS
   DOES CODE 42 SET?

   NO → CODE 42 INTERMITTENT.

   YES ↓

② • IGNITION "OFF".
   • DISCONNECT ECM CONNECTORS.
   • IGNITION "ON".
   • SET OHMMETER SELECTOR SWITCH IN THE 1000 TO 2000 OHMS RANGE.
   • GROUND THE BLACK (-) OHMMETER LEAD.
   • PROBE ECM HARNESS EST CIRCUIT USING THE RED (+) OHMMETER LEAD. THE OHMMETER SHOULD READ LESS THAN 500 OHMS. DOES IT?

   YES ↓

   • PROBE ECM HARNESS CONNECTOR CKT 424 WITH A TEST LIGHT TO BATTERY VOLTAGE AND OBSERVE LIGHT.

   LIGHT "ON" → OPEN CKT 423, FAULTY CONNECTION, OR FAULTY IGNITION MODULE.

   LIGHT "OFF" ↓

③ • WITH OHMMETER STILL CONNECTED TO ECM HARNESS CKT 423 AND GROUND AS DESCRIBED IN STEP #2, AGAIN PROBE ECM HARNESS CKT 424 WITH THE TEST LIGHT CONNECTED TO BATTERY VOLTAGE. AS TEST LIGHT CONTACTS CKT 424, RESISTANCE SHOULD SWITCH FROM HUNDREDS TO THOUSANDS OHMS. DOES IT?

   NO ↓

④ • DISCONNECT DIS 6-WAY CONNECTOR. NOTE OHMMETER THAT IS STILL CONNECTED TO CKT 423 AND GROUND. RESISTANCE SHOULD HAVE BECOME VERY HIGH (OPEN CIRCUIT). DOES IT?

   YES → CKT 424 OPEN, FAULTY CONNECTIONS, OR FAULTY IGNITION MODULE.

   NO → CKT 423 SHORTED TO GROUND.

   (from ③ YES) → • DISCONNECT IGNITION MODULE 6-WAY CONNECTOR.
   • PROBE ECM HARNESS CKT 424 WITH THE TEST LIGHT.

   LIGHT "OFF" → REPLACE IGNITION MODULE.

   LIGHT "ON" ↓

   • CKT 424 SHORTED TO GROUND.

⑤ • RECONNECT ECM AND IDLE ENGINE FOR ONE MINUTE OR UNTIL CODE 42 SETS. DOES CODE SET?

   YES → REPLACE ECM.

   NO → CODE 42 INTERMITTENT.

*"AFTER REPAIRS," REFER TO CODE CRITERIA AND CONFIRM CODE DOES NOT RESET.

86814139

THROTTLE BODY INJECTION DIAGNOSTIC CHARTS

CODE 44
OXYGEN SENSOR CIRCUIT
(LEAN EXHAUST INDICATED)

(1)
- RUN WARM ENGINE (75°C/167°F TO 95°C/203°F) AT 1200 RPM.
- DOES TECH 1 INDICATE O₂ SENSOR VOLTAGE FIXED BELOW .35 VOLT (350 mv)?

YES
- DISCONNECT O₂ SENSOR.
- WITH ENGINE IDLING, TECH 1 SHOULD DISPLAY O₂ SENSOR VOLTAGE BETWEEN .35 VOLT AND .55 VOLT (350 mV AND 550 mV). DOES IT?

NO → CODE 44 IS INTERMITTENT

YES

NO → CKT 412 SHORTED TO GROUND OR FAULTY ECM.

"AFTER REPAIRS," REFER TO CODE CRITERIA AND CONFIRM CODE DOES NOT RESET.

CODE 44
OXYGEN SENSOR CIRCUIT
(LEAN EXHAUST INDICATED)

The connector terminal identification on the Lumina may be different.

Circuit Description:

The ECM supplies a voltage of about .45 volt between terminals "B2" and "B23". (If measured with a 10 megohm digital voltmeter, this may read as low as .32 volt).

When the O₂ sensor reaches operating temperature, it varies this voltage from about 1 volt (exhaust is lean) to about .9 volt (exhaust is rich).

The sensor is like an open circuit and produces no voltage when it is below 316°C (600°F). An open sensor circuit, or cold sensor, causes "Open Loop" operation.

Test Description: Numbers below refer to circled numbers on the diagnostic chart.

1. Code 44 is set when the O₂ sensor signal voltage on CKT 412 remains below .2 volt for 60 seconds or more and the system is operating in "Closed Loop."

Diagnostic Aids:

Using the Tech 1 "Scan" tool, observe the block learn value at different engine speeds. If the conditions for Code 44 exists, the block learn values will be around 150 or higher.

Check the following possible causes
- O₂ Sensor A cracked or otherwise damaged O₂ sensor may cause an intermittent Code 44.
- O₂ Sensor Wire Sensor pigtail may be mispositioned and contacting the exhaust manifold. Check for ground in wire between connector and sensor.

- Fuel Contamination. Water, even in small amounts, near the in-tank fuel pump inlet can be delivered to the injector. The water causes a lean exhaust and can set a Code 44.
- Fuel Pressure. System will be lean if fuel pressure is too low. It may be necessary to monitor fuel pressure while driving the car at various road speeds and/or loads to confirm. See "Fuel System Diagnosis," CHART A-7.
- Exhaust Leaks. If there is an exhaust leak, the engine can cause outside air to be pulled into the exhaust and past the sensor. Vacuum or crankcase leaks can cause a lean condition.

If Code 44 is intermittent, refer to "Intermittents" in "Symptoms."

86814140

THROTTLE BODY INJECTION DIAGNOSTIC CHARTS

CODE 45
OXYGEN SENSOR CIRCUIT
(RICH EXHAUST INDICATED)

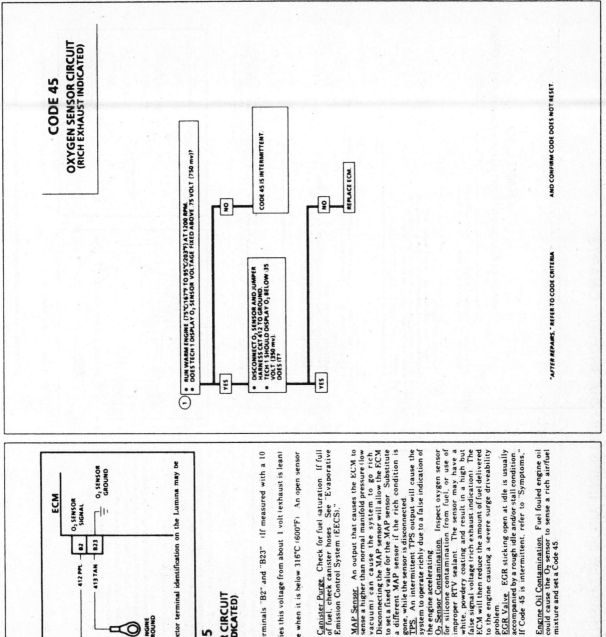

1. RUN WARM ENGINE (75°C(167°F) TO 95°C(203°F)) AT 1200 RPM.
   • DOES TECH 1 DISPLAY O₂ SENSOR VOLTAGE FIXED ABOVE .75 VOLT (750 mv)?

YES → DISCONNECT O₂ SENSOR AND JUMPER HARNESS CKT 412 TO GROUND. TECH 1 SHOULD DISPLAY O₂ BELOW .35 VOLT (350 mv). DOES IT?

NO → CODE 45 IS INTERMITTENT.

YES → REPLACE ECM.

NO → REPLACE ECM.

*AFTER REPAIRS, * REFER TO CODE CRITERIA AND CONFIRM CODE DOES NOT RESET.

ECM
O₂ SENSOR SIGNAL B2
O₂ SENSOR GROUND B23
412 PPL
413 TAN
OXYGEN (O₂) SENSOR
EXHAUST
ENGINE GROUND

The connector terminal identification on the Lumina may be different.

CODE 45
OXYGEN SENSOR CIRCUIT
(RICH EXHAUST INDICATED)

Circuit Description:

The ECM supplies a voltage of about .45 volt between terminals "B2" and "B23" (If measured with a 10 megohm digital voltmeter, this may read as low as .32 volt). When the O₂ sensor reaches operating temperature, it varies this voltage from about 1 volt (exhaust is lean) to about .9 volt (exhaust is rich).

The sensor is like an open circuit and produces no voltage when it is below 316°C (600°F). An open sensor circuit, or cold sensor, causes "Open Loop" operation.

Test Description: Numbers below refer to circled numbers on the diagnostic chart.

1. Code 45 is set when the O₂ sensor signal voltage on CKT 412 remains above 7 volt under the following conditions:
   • 50 seconds or more.
   • System is operating in "Closed Loop."
   • Engine run time after start is 1 minute or more.
   • Throttle angle is between 3% and 45%

Diagnostic Aids:

Code 45, or rich exhaust, is most likely caused by one of the following:

• **Fuel Pressure.** System will go rich, if pressure is too high. The ECM can compensate for some increase. However, if it gets too high, a Code 45 will be set. See "Fuel System Diagnosis," CHART A-7.

• **Leaking Injector.** See CHART A-7.

• **HEI Shielding.** An open ground CKT 453 may result in EMI, or induced electrical "noise." The ECM looks at this "noise" as reference pulses. The additional pulses result in a higher than actual engine speed signal. The ECM then delivers too much fuel causing the system to go rich. The engine tachometer will also show higher than actual engine speed, which can help in diagnosing this problem.

• **Canister Purge.** Check for fuel saturation. If full of fuel, check canister hoses. See "Evaporative Emission Control System (EECS)."

• **MAP Sensor.** An output that causes the ECM to sense a higher than normal manifold pressure (low vacuum) can cause the system to go rich. Disconnecting the MAP sensor will allow the ECM to set a fixed value for the MAP sensor. Substitute a different MAP sensor if the rich condition is gone, while the sensor is disconnected.

• **TPS.** An intermittent TPS output will cause the system to operate richly due to a false indication of the engine accelerating.

• **O₂ Sensor Contamination.** Inspect oxygen sensor for silicone contamination from fuel, or use of improper RTV sealant. The sensor may have a white, powdery coating and result in a high but false signal voltage (rich exhaust indication). The ECM will then reduce the amount of fuel delivered to the engine causing a severe surge driveability problem.

• **EGR Valve.** EGR sticking open at idle is usually accompanied by a rough idle and/or stall condition. If Code 45 is intermittent, refer to "Symptoms."

• **Engine Oil Contamination.** Fuel fouled engine oil could cause the O₂ sensor to sense a rich air/fuel mixture and set a Code 45.

86814141

THROTTLE BODY INJECTION DIAGNOSTIC CHARTS

CHART C-1D

MANIFOLD ABSOLUTE PRESSURE (MAP) OUTPUT CHECK

ECM

5 VOLT REFERENCE

W11 — 416 GRY — TO TPS SENSOR

B20 — 432 LT GRN — MAP SIGNAL

W14 — 469 BLK/ORN — SENSOR GROUND

MAP SENSOR

MANIFOLD ABSOLUTE PRESSURE (VACUUM)

A B C

TO IAT SENSOR

Circuit Description:

The Manifold Absolute Pressure (MAP) sensor measures the changes in the intake manifold pressure which result from engine load (intake manifold vacuum) and rpm changes; and converts these into a voltage output. The ECM sends a 5 volt reference voltage to the MAP sensor. As the manifold pressure changes, the output voltage of the sensor also changes. By monitoring the sensor output voltage, the ECM knows the manifold pressure. A lower pressure (low voltage) output voltage will be about 1 - 2 volts at idle. While higher pressure (high voltage) output voltage will be about 4 - 4.8 at Wide Open Throttle (WOT). The MAP sensor is also used, under certain conditions, to measure barometric pressure, allowing the ECM to make adjustments for different altitudes. The ECM uses the MAP sensor to control fuel delivery and ignition timing.

Test Description: Numbers below refer to circled numbers on the diagnostic chart.

⚠ Important

• Be sure to use the same Diagnostic Test Equipment for all measurements.

1. When comparing Tech 1 readings to a known good vehicle, it is important to compare vehicles that use a MAP sensor having the same color insert or having the same "Hot Stamped" number. See figures on facing page.

2. Applying 34 kPa vacuum to the MAP sensor should cause the voltage to change. Subtract second reading from the first. Voltage value should be greater than 1.5 volts. Upon applying vacuum to the sensor, the change in voltage should be instantaneous. A slow voltage change indicates a faulty sensor.

3. Check vacuum hose to sensor for leaking or restriction. Be sure that no other vacuum devices are connected to the MAP hose.

NOTE: Make sure electrical connector remains securely fastened.

4. Disconnect sensor from bracket and twist sensor (by hand only) to check for intermittent connection. Output changes greater than 1 volt indicate a faulty connector or connection. If OK, replace sensor.

CHART C-1D

MANIFOLD ABSOLUTE PRESSURE (MAP) OUTPUT CHECK

NOTE: THIS CHART ONLY APPLIES TO MAP SENSORS HAVING GREEN OR BLACK COLOR KEY INSERT (SEE BELOW).

① IGNITION "ON," ENGINE "OFF."
• "SCAN" TOOL SHOULD INDICATE A MAP SENSOR VOLTAGE.
• COMPARE THIS READING WITH THE READING OF A KNOWN GOOD VEHICLE. SEE FACING PAGE TEST DESCRIPTION, STEP 1.
• VOLTAGE READING SHOULD BE WITHIN, ± .4 VOLT.
IS IT?

YES →

② • DISCONNECT AND PLUG VACUUM SOURCE TO MAP SENSOR.
• CONNECT A HAND VACUUM PUMP TO MAP SENSOR.
• START ENGINE.
• NOTE MAP SENSOR VOLTAGE.
• APPLY 34 kPa (10" Hg) OF VACUUM AND NOTE VOLTAGE CHANGE.
• SUBTRACT SECOND READING FROM THE FIRST. VOLTAGE VALUE SHOULD BE GREATER THAN 1.5 VOLTS.
IS IT?

NO → REPLACE SENSOR

YES →

③ • NO TROUBLE FOUND. CHECK SENSOR VACUUM SOURCE FOR LEAKAGE OR RESTRICTION. BE SURE THIS SOURCE SUPPLIES VACUUM TO MAP SENSOR ONLY.

NO → ④ • CHECK SENSOR CONNECTION. IF OK, REPLACE SENSOR.

COLOR KEYED INSERT

Figure 1 - Color Key Insert

HOT-STAMPED NUMBER

XXX XXX

C B A ← XXX
C B A ← XXX

Figure 2 - Hot-Stamped Number

"AFTER REPAIRS," CONFIRM "CLOSED LOOP" OPERATION AND NO "SERVICE ENGINE SOON" LIGHT.

86814142

THROTTLE BODY INJECTION DIAGNOSTIC CHARTS

CHART C-2C
IDLE AIR CONTROL (IAC) SYSTEM CHECK

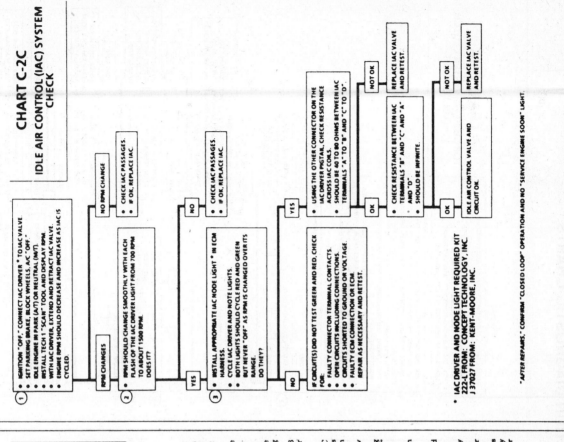

CHART C-2C
IDLE AIR CONTROL (IAC) SYSTEM CHECK

1.
- IGNITION "OFF". CONNECT IAC DRIVER * TO IAC VALVE.
- SET PARKING BRAKE. BLOCK WHEELS. A/C "OFF".
- IDLE ENGINE IN PARK (A/T) OR NEUTRAL (M/T).
- INSTALL TECH 1 "SCAN" TOOL AND DISPLAY RPM.
- WITH IAC DRIVER, EXTEND AND RETRACT IAC VALVE.
- ENGINE RPM SHOULD DECREASE AND INCREASE AS IAC IS CYCLED.

RPM CHANGES → NO RPM CHANGE → • CHECK IAC PASSAGES. IF OK, REPLACE IAC.

2.
- RPM SHOULD CHANGE SMOOTHLY WITH EACH FLASH OF THE IAC DRIVER LIGHT FROM 700 RPM TO ABOUT 1500 RPM. DOES IT?

YES / NO → NO → • CHECK IAC PASSAGES. IF OK, REPLACE IAC.

3.
- INSTALL APPROPRIATE IAC NODE LIGHT * IN ECM HARNESS.
- CYCLE IAC DRIVER AND NOTE LIGHTS.
- BOTH LIGHTS SHOULD CYCLE RED AND GREEN BUT NEVER "OFF" AS RPM IS CHANGED OVER ITS RANGE. DO THEY?

YES / NO

YES → • USING THE OTHER CONNECTOR ON THE IAC DRIVER PIGTAIL, CHECK RESISTANCE ACROSS IAC COILS.
- SHOULD BE 40 TO 80 OHMS BETWEEN IAC TERMINALS "A" TO "B" AND "C" TO "D".

OK / NOT OK
NOT OK → REPLACE IAC VALVE AND RETEST.
OK → • CHECK RESISTANCE BETWEEN IAC TERMINALS "B" AND "C" AND "A" AND "D".
- SHOULD BE INFINITE.

OK / NOT OK
OK → IDLE AIR CONTROL VALVE AND CIRCUIT OK.
NOT OK → REPLACE IAC VALVE AND RETEST.

NO → IF CIRCUIT(S) DID NOT TEST GREEN AND RED, CHECK FOR:
- FAULTY CONNECTOR TERMINAL CONTACTS.
- OPEN CIRCUITS INCLUDING CONNECTIONS.
- CIRCUITS SHORTED TO GROUND OR VOLTAGE.
- FAULTY ECM CONNECTION OR ECM.

REPAIR AS NECESSARY AND RETEST.

- IAC DRIVER AND NODE LIGHT REQUIRED KIT 222-L FROM: CONCEPT TECHNOLOGY, INC. J 37027 FROM: KENT-MOORE, INC.

* "AFTER REPAIRS." CONFIRM "CLOSED LOOP" OPERATION AND NO "SERVICE ENGINE SOON" LIGHT.

AIR FLOW — IAC CONNECTOR — D C B A — THROTTLE BODY

441 LT BLU/WHT
442 LT BLU/BLK
443 LT GRN/WHT
444 LT GRN/BLK

ECM

Terminal	Function
W7	IAC COIL "A" HI
W17	IAC COIL "A" LO
W9	IAC COIL "B" HI
W8	IAC COIL "B" LO

CHART C-2C
IDLE AIR CONTROL (IAC) SYSTEM CHECK

Circuit Description:

The ECM controls engine idle speed with the IAC valve. To increase idle speed, the ECM retracts the IAC valve pintle away from its seat, allowing more air to bypass the throttle bore. To decrease idle speed, it extends the IAC valve pintle towards its seat, reducing air flow. A Tech 1 "Scan" tool will read the ECM commands to the IAC valve in counts. Higher the counts indicate more air bypass (higher idle). The lower the counts indicate less air is allowed to bypass (lower idle).

Test Description: Numbers below refer to circled numbers on the diagnostic chart.

1. The IAC tester is used to extend and retract the IAC valve. Valve movement is verified by an engine speed change. If no change in engine speed occurs, the valve can be retested when removed from the throttle body.

2. This step checks the quality of the IAC movement in step 1. Between 700 rpm and about 1500 rpm, the engine speed should change smoothly with each flash of the tester light in both extend and retract. If the IAC valve is retracted beyond the control range (about 1500 rpm), it may take many flashes in the extend position before engine speed will begin to drop. This is normal on certain engines, fully extending IAC may cause engine stall. This may be normal.

3. Steps 1 and 2 verified proper IAC valve operation while this step checks the IAC circuits. Each lamp on the node light should flash red and green while the IAC valve is cycled. While the sequence of color is not important if either light is "OFF" or does not flash red and green, check the circuits for faults, beginning with poor terminal contacts.

Diagnostic Aids:

A slow, unstable, or fast idle may be caused by a non-IAC system problem that cannot be overcome by the IAC system. Out of control range IAC "Scan" tool counts will be above 60 if idle is too low, and zero counts if idle is too high. The following checks should be made to repair a non-IAC system problem

- **Vacuum Leak (High Idle)**
If idle is too high, stop the engine. Fully extend (low) IAC with tester

Start engine. If idle speed is above 800 rpm, locate and correct vacuum leak including PCV system. Also check for binding of throttle blade or linkage.

- **System too lean (High Air/Fuel Ratio)**
The idle speed may be too high or too low. Engine speed may vary up and down and disconnecting the IAC valve does not help. Code 44 may be set. "Scan" O_2 voltage will be less than 300 mv (.3 volt). Check for low regulated fuel pressure, water in the fuel or a restricted injector.

- **System too rich (Low Air/Fuel Ratio)**
The idle speed will be too low. "Scan" tool IAC counts will usually be above 80. System is obviously rich and may exhibit black smoke in exhaust.
"Scan" tool O_2 voltage will be fixed above 800 mv (.8 volt).
Check for high fuel pressure, leaking or sticking injector. Silicone contaminated O_2 sensors "Scan" voltage will be slow to respond.

- **Throttle Body**
Remove IAC valve and inspect bore for foreign material.

- **IAC Valve Electrical Connections**
IAC valve connections should be carefully checked for proper contact.

- **PCV System**
Incorrect or faulty PCV system components may result in an incorrect idle speed.
Refer to "Rough, Unstable, Incorrect Idle or Stalling" in "Symptoms".
If intermittent poor driveability or idle symptoms are resolved by disconnecting the IAC, carefully recheck connections, valve terminal resistance, or replace IAC

86814143

THROTTLE BODY INJECTION DIAGNOSTIC CHARTS

CHART C-8A
TORQUE CONVERTER CLUTCH (TCC) CIRCUIT

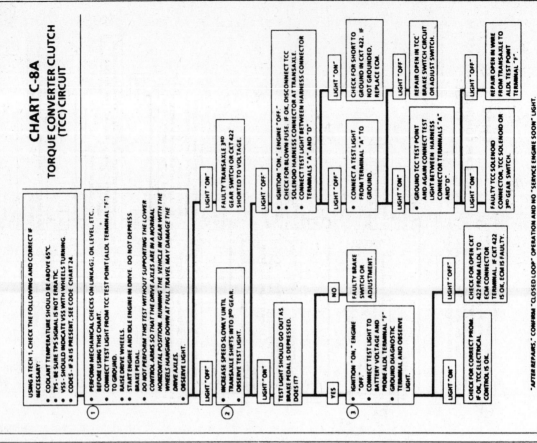

CHART C-8A

TORQUE CONVERTER CLUTCH (TCC) CIRCUIT

USING A TECH 1, CHECK THE FOLLOWING AND CORRECT IF NECESSARY:
- COOLANT TEMPERATURE SHOULD BE ABOVE 65°C.
- TPS - BE SURE TPS SIGNAL IS NOT ERRATIC.
- VSS - SHOULD INDICATE VSS WITH WHEELS TURNING.
- CODES - IF 24 IS PRESENT, SEE CODE CHART 24.

①
- PERFORM MECHANICAL CHECKS ON LINKAGE, OIL LEVEL, ETC., BEFORE USING THIS CHART.
- CONNECT TEST LIGHT FROM TCC TEST POINT (ALDL TERMINAL "F") TO GROUND.
- RAISE DRIVE WHEELS.
- START ENGINE AND IDLE ENGINE IN DRIVE. DO NOT DEPRESS BRAKE PEDAL.
- DO NOT PERFORM THIS TEST WITHOUT SUPPORTING THE LOWER CONTROL ARMS SO THAT THE DRIVE AXLES ARE IN A NORMAL HORIZONTAL POSITION. RUNNING THE VEHICLE IN GEAR WITH THE WHEELS HANGING DOWN AT FULL TRAVEL MAY DAMAGE THE DRIVE AXLES.
- OBSERVE LIGHT.

LIGHT "OFF" → FAULTY TRANSAXLE 3RD GEAR SWITCH OR CKT 422 SHORTED TO VOLTAGE.

LIGHT "ON"

②
- INCREASE SPEED SLOWLY UNTIL TRANSAXLE SHIFTS INTO 3RD GEAR.
- OBSERVE TEST LIGHT.

LIGHT "OFF" → TEST LIGHT SHOULD GO OUT AS BRAKE PEDAL IS DEPRESSED. DOES IT?
- NO → FAULTY BRAKE SWITCH OR ADJUSTMENT.
- YES

LIGHT "ON" →
- IGNITION "ON," ENGINE "OFF."
- CHECK FOR BLOWN FUSE. IF OK, DISCONNECT TCC SOLENOID HARNESS CONNECTOR AT TRANSAXLE.
- CONNECT TEST LIGHT BETWEEN HARNESS CONNECTOR TERMINALS "A" AND "D"

LIGHT "OFF" →
- CONNECT A TEST LIGHT FROM TERMINAL "A" TO GROUND.

LIGHT "ON" → CHECK FOR SHORT TO GROUND IN CKT 422. IF NOT GROUNDED, REPLACE ECM.

LIGHT "OFF" → REPAIR OPEN IN TCC BRAKE SWITCH CIRCUIT OR ADJUST SWITCH.

LIGHT "ON" →
- GROUND TCC TEST POINT AND AGAIN CONNECT TEST LIGHT BETWEEN HARNESS CONNECTOR TERMINALS "A" AND "D"

LIGHT "OFF" → FAULTY TCC SOLENOID CONNECTOR, TCC SOLENOID OR 3RD GEAR SWITCH.

LIGHT "ON" → REPAIR OPEN IN WIRE FROM TRANSAXLE TO ALDL TEST POINT TERMINAL "F."

③
- IGNITION "ON," ENGINE "OFF."
- CONNECT TEST LIGHT TO BATTERY VOLTAGE AND PROBE ALDL TERMINAL "F."
- GROUND DIAGNOSTIC TERMINAL AND OBSERVE LIGHT.

LIGHT "ON" → CHECK FOR CORRECT PROM. IF OK, TCC ELECTRICAL CONTROL IS OK.

LIGHT "OFF" → CHECK FOR OPEN CKT 422 FROM ALDL TO ECM CONNECTOR TERMINAL. IF CKT 422 IS OK, ECM IS FAULTY.

"AFTER REPAIRS," CONFIRM "CLOSED LOOP" OPERATION AND NO "SERVICE ENGINE SOON" LIGHT.

CHART C-8A

TORQUE CONVERTER CLUTCH (TCC) CIRCUIT

Circuit Description:

The purpose of the automatic transaxle torque converter clutch is to eliminate the power loss of the torque converter when the vehicle is in a cruise condition. This allows the convenience of the automatic transaxle and the fuel economy of a manual transaxle.

Fused ignition voltage is supplied to the TCC solenoid through the brake switch and transaxle third gear apply switch. The ECM will engage TCC by grounding CKT 422 to energize the solenoid. TCC will engage under the following conditions:
- Vehicle speed is above 56 km/h (35 mph) with A/C "OFF," or above 70 km/h (44 mph) with A/C "ON."
- Engine at normal operating temperature (above 70°C/158°F).
- Throttle position sensor output not changing, indicating a steady road speed.
- Transaxle third gear switch closed.
- Brake switch closed.

Test Description: Numbers below refer to circled numbers on the diagnostic chart.

1. Light "OFF" confirms transaxle third gear apply switch is open.
2. At approximately 48 km/h (30 mph), the transaxle third gear switch should close. This depends on throttle position. The minimum speed at which the third gear switch will close is approximately 34 km/h (21 mph). Test light will turn "ON" and confirm ignition voltage in the circuit and a closed brake switch.
3. Grounding the diagnostic terminal with the ignition "ON" and the engine "OFF" should light the test light. This test checks the capability of the ECM to control the solenoid.

Diagnostic Aids:

An engine coolant thermostat that is stuck open or opens at too low a temperature may result in an inoperative TCC.

86814144

MULTI-PORT FUEL INJECTION

DTC 13
OXYGEN SENSOR (O2S) CIRCUIT
(OPEN CIRCUIT)

Circuit Description:

The O2 sensor which is located in the exhaust stream near the engine monitors oxygen content of the engine's exhaust gases and produces a voltage. This voltage ranges from 100 mV (high O2 in exhaust-lean mixture) to 1V (low O2 in exhaust rich mixture).

The PCM always supplies a steady 450 mV bias voltage to the O2 sensor. When the sensor is cold, it either produces a very low voltage or a slow cycling unusable voltage. As the O2 sensor heats up, the voltage will begin cycling more rapidly above and below the 450 mV bias voltage which tells the PCM the voltage is ready to be used and then go into "Closed Loop."

DTC 13 Will Set When:
- Engine running at least 40 seconds.
- Coolant temperature at least 42.5°C (108°F).
- DTC 21 or 22 is not set.
- O2S signal voltage is steady between approximately .35 and .55 volt.
- The Throttle Position (TP) sensor angle is above 6%. (About .3 volt above closed throttle voltage.)
- All conditions are met for at least 20 seconds.

Action Taken (PCM will default to): The Malfunction Indicator Lamp (MIL) will illuminate, the O2S system will go into "Open Loop," and the cooling fan will enable.

DTC Chart Test Description:
Number(s) below refer to circled number(s) on the diagnostic chart.
1. During engine warm up, the O2S should warm up and its voltage should vary between 100 mV to 999 mV. When O2S voltage varies the engine will go into "Closed Loop." This step determines if the O2S is operating properly.
2. This will determine if the sensor, wiring, or PCM is the cause of the DTC 13.
3. Use only a high impedance digital volt ohmmeter for this test. This test checks the continuity of CKT 412 and CKT 413; because if CKT 413 is open, the PCM voltage on CKT 412 will be over .6 volt (600 mV).

Diagnostic Aids:
- Normal Tech 1 scan tool voltage varies between 100 mV to 999 mV (.1 volt to 1.0 volt) while in "Closed Loop."
- Always use at least a 10 megohm input impedance voltmeter when monitoring O2 voltage.
- Check condition of pigtail wire from O2 sensor for any opens or shorts. Also the O2 sensor louvered end should be free of any contaminants as this may cause a malfunction.

86814145

Fig. 69 MULTI-PORT FUEL INJECTION — DTC 13

DTC 13
OXYGEN SENSOR (O2S) CIRCUIT
(OPEN CIRCUIT)
2.2L (VIN 4) "A" CARLINE

1 ENGINE AT NORMAL OPERATING TEMPERATURE (ABOVE 80°C/176°F).
- RUN ENGINE ABOVE 1200 RPM FOR TWO MINUTES.
- DOES TECH 1 SCAN TOOL INDICATE "CLOSED LOOP"?

NO

YES

2
- DISCONNECT OXYGEN SENSOR (O2S).
- JUMPER HARNESS SIGNAL CIRCUIT (PCM SIDE) TO GROUND.
- TECH 1 SCAN TOOL SHOULD DISPLAY O2S VOLTAGE BELOW .2 VOLT (200 mV) WITH ENGINE RUNNING. DOES IT?

DTC IS INTERMITTENT. IF NO ADDITIONAL DTC(s) WERE STORED, REFER TO "DIAGNOSTIC AIDS"

NO

YES

3
- REMOVE JUMPER.
- IGNITION "ON," ENGINE "OFF."
- CHECK VOLTAGE OF SIGNAL CIRCUIT (PCM SIDE) AT O2S HARNESS CONNECTOR USING A DVM.

FAULTY O2S CONNECTION
OR
FAULTY O2S.

.3-.6 VOLT
(300 - 600 mV)

OVER .6 VOLT
(600 mV)

LESS THAN .3 VOLT (300 mV)

FAULTY PCM.

OPEN GROUND CIRCUIT
OR
FAULTY CONNECTION
OR
FAULTY PCM.

OPEN SIGNAL CIRCUIT
OR
FAULTY CONNECTION
OR
FAULTY PCM.

"AFTER REPAIRS," REFER TO DTC CRITERIA ON FACING PAGE AND CONFIRM DTC DOES NOT RESET.

86814147

Fig. 70 MULTI-PORT FUEL INJECTION — DTC 13

MULTI-PORT FUEL INJECTION — DTC 14

DTC 14

ENGINE COOLANT TEMPERATURE (ECT) SENSOR CIRCUIT
(HIGH TEMPERATURE INDICATED)
2.2L (VIN 4) "A" CARLINE

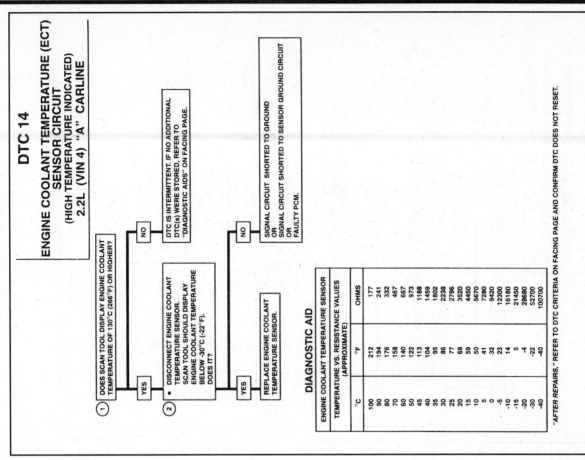

(1) DOES SCAN TOOL DISPLAY ENGINE COOLANT TEMPERATURE OF 130°C (266°F) OR HIGHER?

YES → (2) • DISCONNECT ENGINE COOLANT TEMPERATURE SENSOR. SCAN TOOL SHOULD DISPLAY ENGINE COOLANT TEMPERATURE BELOW -30°C (-22°F). DOES IT?

NO → DTC IS INTERMITTENT. IF NO ADDITIONAL DTC(s) WERE STORED, REFER TO "DIAGNOSTIC AIDS" ON FACING PAGE.

YES → REPLACE ENGINE COOLANT TEMPERATURE SENSOR.

NO → SIGNAL CIRCUIT SHORTED TO GROUND
OR
SIGNAL CIRCUIT SHORTED TO SENSOR GROUND CIRCUIT
OR
FAULTY PCM.

DIAGNOSTIC AID

ENGINE COOLANT TEMPERATURE SENSOR		
TEMPERATURE VS. RESISTANCE VALUES (APPROXIMATE)		
°C	°F	OHMS
100	212	177
90	194	241
80	176	332
70	158	467
60	140	667
50	122	973
45	113	1188
40	104	1459
35	95	1802
30	86	2238
25	77	2796
20	68	3520
15	59	4450
10	50	5670
5	41	7280
0	32	9420
-5	23	12300
-10	14	16180
-15	5	21450
-20	-4	28680
-30	-22	52700
-40	-40	100700

"AFTER REPAIRS," REFER TO DTC CRITERIA ON FACING PAGE AND CONFIRM DTC DOES NOT RESET.

86814149

MULTI-PORT FUEL INJECTION — DTC 14

DTC 14

ENGINE COOLANT TEMPERATURE (ECT) SENSOR CIRCUIT
(HIGH TEMPERATURE INDICATED)
2.2L (VIN 4) "A" CARLINE

PCM
5 VOLT REFERENCE
ECT SIGNAL
SENSOR GROUND
PC10
PB2
410 YEL
808 BLK
ENGINE COOLANT TEMPERATURE (ECT) SENSOR
B
A
C
TO TP SENSOR
135 DK GRN
TO COOLANT TEMPERATURE GAUGE

Circuit Description:

The Engine Coolant Temperature (ECT) sensor uses a thermistor to control the signal voltage to the Powertrain Control Module (PCM). The PCM supplies a 5 volt reference and a ground to the sensor. When the engine is cold the sensor (thermistor) resistance is high, therefore PCM terminal "PC10" voltage will be high.

As the engine warms, the sensor resistance becomes less, and the voltage drops. At normal engine operating temperature, the voltage will measure between 1.5 to 2.0 volts at PCM terminal "PC10".

Engine coolant temperature is one of the inputs used to control:

- Fuel delivery.
- Ignition Control (IC).
- Idle Air Control (IAC).
- Torque Convertor Clutch (TCC).
- Evaporative (EVAP) canister purge solenoid.
- Electric cooling fans.

DTC 14 Will Set When:

- Signal voltage indicates the engine coolant temperature is greater than 140°C (285°F).
- Engine run time is greater than 128 seconds.

Action Taken (PCM will default to):
The Malfunction Indicator Lamp (MIL) will illuminate, the PCM will default to 85°C for engine coolant temperature (Tech 1 scan tool will not show defaulted value), and the cooling fan will enable.

DTC Chart Test Description:
Number(s) below refer to circled number(s) on the diagnostic chart.

1. This checks to see if DTC 14 was set as a result of a hard failure or intermittent condition.
2. This test will determine if CKT 410 is shorted to ground which will cause the conditions for a DTC 14 to set.

Diagnostic Aids:

- Verify the engine is not overheating and has not been subjected to conditions which could create an overheating condition (i.e. overload, trailer towing, hilly terrain, heavy stop and go traffic, etc.).
- The "Temperature vs. Resistance Value" scale at the right may be used to test the sensor at various temperature levels to evaluate the possibility of a shifted (mis-scaled) sensor. A shifted sensor could result in poor driveability.

86814148

MULTI-PORT FUEL INJECTION — DTC 15

DTC 15
ENGINE COOLANT TEMPERATURE (ECT) SENSOR CIRCUIT
(LOW TEMPERATURE INDICATED)
2.2L (VIN 4) "A" CARLINE

① DOES TECH 1 SCAN TOOL DISPLAY IAT -30°C (-22°F) OR COLDER?

NO → DTC IS INTERMITTENT. IF NO ADDITIONAL DTC(s) WERE STORED, REFER TO "DIAGNOSTIC AIDS" ON FACING PAGE.

YES →

② DISCONNECT SENSOR. JUMPER HARNESS TERMINALS TOGETHER. TECH 1 SCAN TOOL SHOULD DISPLAY TEMPERATURE OVER 130°C (266°F). DOES IT?

YES → FAULTY CONNECTION OR SENSOR.

NO →

③ JUMPER SIGNAL CIRCUIT TO GROUND. TECH 1 SCAN TOOL SHOULD DISPLAY TEMPERATURE OVER 130°C (266°F). DOES IT?

YES → OPEN SENSOR GROUND CIRCUIT, FAULTY CONNECTION OR FAULTY PCM.

NO → OPEN SIGNAL CIRCUIT, FAULTY CONNECTION OR FAULTY PCM.

DIAGNOSTIC AID

INTAKE AIR TEMPERATURE SENSOR		
TEMPERATURE VS. RESISTANCE VALUES (APPROXIMATE)		
°C	°F	OHMS
100	212	177
90	194	241
80	176	332
70	158	467
60	140	667
50	122	973
45	113	1188
40	104	1459
35	95	1802
30	86	2238
25	77	2796
20	68	3520
15	59	4450
10	50	5670
5	41	7280
0	32	9420
-5	23	12300
-10	14	16180
-15	5	21450
-20	-4	28680
-30	-22	52700
-40	-40	100700

"AFTER REPAIRS," REFER TO DTC CRITERIA ON FACING PAGE AND CONFIRM DTC DOES NOT RESET.

86814151

MULTI-PORT FUEL INJECTION — DTC 15

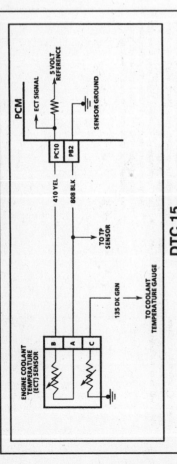

ENGINE COOLANT TEMPERATURE (ECT) SENSOR — B, A, C — PCM — ECT SIGNAL — 5 VOLT REFERENCE — SENSOR GROUND — PC10 — PB2 — 410 YEL — 808 BLK — 135 DK GRN — TO TP SENSOR — TO COOLANT TEMPERATURE GAUGE

DTC 15
ENGINE COOLANT TEMPERATURE (ECT) SENSOR CIRCUIT
(LOW TEMPERATURE INDICATED)
2.2L (VIN 4) "A" CARLINE

Circuit Description:

The Engine Coolant Temperature (ECT) sensor uses a thermistor to control the signal voltage to the Powertrain Control Module (PCM). The PCM supplies a 5 volt reference and a ground to the sensor. When the engine is cold, the sensor (thermistor) resistance is high, therefore, PCM terminal "PC10" voltage will be high.

As the engine warms, the sensor resistance becomes less, and the voltage drops. At normal engine operating temperature the voltage will measure between 1.5 to 2.0 volts at PCM terminal "PC10".

Engine coolant temperature is one of the inputs used to control:
- Fuel delivery.
- Ignition Control (IC).
- Idle Air Control (IAC).
- Torque Convertor Clutch (TCC).
- Evaporative (EVAP) canister purge valve.
- Electric cooling fan.

DTC 15 Will Set When:
- ECT signal voltage indicates the engine coolant temperature is less than -39°C (-38°F).
- Engine run time is greater than 60 seconds.

Action Taken (PCM will default to): The Malfunction Indicator Lamp (MIL) will illuminate, the PCM will default to 85°C for engine coolant temperature (Tech 1 scan tool will not display defaulted value), and the cooling fan will enable.

DTC Chart Test Description: Number(s) below refer to circled number(s) on the diagnostic chart.
1. This checks if DTC 15 was set as a result of a hard or intermittent condition.
2. This test simulates a DTC 14. If the PCM senses the low signal voltage (high temperature) and the scan reads 130°C, the PCM and wiring are OK.
3. This test will determine if CKT 410 is open. There should be 5 volts present at sensor connector.

Diagnostic Aids:
- After the engine is started, the temperature should rise steadily to about 90°C, and then stabilize when the thermostat opens. It is normal for engine coolant temperature to fluctuate slightly around 95°C. DTCs 15 and 21 stored at the same time could be the result of an open CKT 808.
- The "Temperature to Resistance Value" scale at the right may be used to test the sensor at various temperature levels to evaluate the possibility of a "shifted" (mis-scaled) sensor. A shifted sensor could result in poor driveability.

86814150

MULTI-PORT FUEL INJECTION — DTC 16

DTC 16
SYSTEM VOLTAGE HIGH
3300 (VIN N) "A" CARLINE (MFI)

- INSTALL TECH 1
- START ENGINE AND RUN ABOVE 800 RPM.
- OBSERVE "BATT/IGN VOLTS" ON TECH 1.

ABOVE 16 VOLTS → (1)

(1)
- INSTALL DVM ACROSS BATTERY.
- RUN ENGINE ABOVE 800 RPM.
- DOES DVM SHOW BATTERY VOLTAGE ABOVE 16 VOLTS?

NO
- REPLACE ECM.

YES
- REMOVE GENERATOR FOR REPAIR.

BELOW 16 VOLTS
- LOAD ELECTRICAL SYSTEM WITH HEADLAMPS AND HIGH A/C BLOWER.
- RAISE ENGINE RPM TO 2000.
- NOTE "BATT/IGN VOLTS" ON TECH 1.

ABOVE 16 VOLTS
- REMOVE GENERATOR FOR REPAIR.

BELOW 16 VOLTS
- FAULT IS NOT PRESENT.
- REFER TO "DIAGNOSTIC AIDS" ON FACING PAGE.

"AFTER REPAIRS," REFER TO DTC CRITERIA ON FACING PAGE AND CONFIRM DTC DOES NOT RESET.

86814193

MULTI-PORT FUEL INJECTION — DTC 16

DTC 16
SYSTEM VOLTAGE HIGH
3300 (VIN N) "A" CARLINE (MFI)

Circuit Description:

The ECM monitors system voltage on CKT 439 at terminal "BA6". If the ECM detects voltage above 16 volts for more than 10 seconds, it will turn the MIL (Service Engine Soon) "ON" and set DTC 16 in memory. DTC 16 will set if:
- Engine running.
- System voltage as monitored at ECM terminal "BA6" over 16 volts for at least 10 seconds.

Test Description: Number(s) refer to circled number(s) on the diagnostic chart.
1. Test generator output as outlined in "6D3" to determine proper operation of the voltage regulator. Run engine at moderate speed and measure voltage across the battery. If over 16 volts, repair generator as outlined in "6D3".

Diagnostic Aids:

Charging the battery with a battery charger and starting the engine may set DTC 16.

An intermittent may be caused by a poor connection, rubbed through insulation, a wire broken inside the insulation or poor ECM grounds.

Check For:
- Poor Connection or Damaged Harness. Inspect ECM harness connectors for improper mating, broken locks, improperly formed or damaged terminals, poor terminal to wire connection and damaged harness.

- Intermittent Test. If connections and harness checks OK, monitor battery voltage display while moving related connectors. If the failure is induced, the battery voltage will abruptly change. This may help to isolate the location of the malfunction.

Important
- If ECM and sensor grounds are located on the same stud at the transaxle as the battery ground you could have improper data to ECM or false DTC(s).

86814192

MULTI-PORT FUEL INJECTION — DTC 19

DTC 19

INTERMITTENT 7X REFERENCE CIRCUIT
2.2L (VIN 4) "A" CARLINE

86814153

① • IF OTHER DTC(s) ARE PRESENT, REFER TO THOSE CHARTS BEFORE PROCEEDING.
  • CLEAR DTC(s).
  • IDLE ENGINE FOR 5 MINUTES OR UNTIL MALFUNCTION INDICATOR LAMP (MIL) "SERVICE ENGINE SOON" TURNS "ON."
  DOES TECH 1 SCAN TOOL DISPLAY DTC 19?

YES

② • WITH ENGINE RUNNING, WIGGLE THE CONNECTIONS OF THE PCM, AND CKP SENSOR AND ASSOCIATED CIRCUITRY * WHILE LISTENING FOR ENGINE STUMBLE. ENGINE SHOULD NOT STUMBLE.
  DOES IT?

NO

③ • OBSERVE TECH 1 SCAN TOOL 7X RESYNC WHILE OPERATING ALL NON-ENGINE RELATED ELECTRONIC COMPONENTS ON THE VEHICLE. THERE SHOULD BE NO 7X RESYNC DURING THE OPERATION OF THE COMPONENTS.
  IS THERE?

YES / NO

YES
REPAIR FAULTY CIRCUIT(S) OR CONNECTOR(S) AND RETEST FOR DTC 19.

NO
INSPECT WIRING AND CONNECTORS BETWEEN PCM, AND CKP SENSOR. REPAIR IF FAULTY AND RETEST. IF DTC 19 IS STILL PRESENT, REPLACE CKP SENSOR AND RETEST. IF DTC 19 IS STILL PRESENT, REPLACE EPROM AND RETEST. IF DTC 19 IS STILL PRESENT, REPLACE PCM AND RETEST. IF NO ADDITIONAL DTC(s) WERE DISPLAYED, REFER TO "DIAGNOSTIC AIDS" ON FACING PAGE.

YES
REPAIR CIRCUIT(S) OF FAULTY COMPONENTS AND RETEST FOR DTC 19.

NO
WITH ENGINE RUNNING, WIGGLE THE CONNECTIONS OF THE PCM AND CKP SENSOR AND ASSOCIATED CIRCUITRY* WHILE LISTENING FOR ENGINE STUMBLE. ENGINE SHOULD NOT STUMBLE. DOES IT?

YES
REPAIR FAULTY CIRCUIT(S) OR CONNECTOR(S) AND RETEST FOR DTC 19.

NO
DTC 19 IS INTERMITTENT IF NO ADDITIONAL DTC(s) WERE DISPLAYED, REFER TO "DIAGNOSTIC AIDS" ON FACING PAGE.

CAUTION: WHEN WORKING AROUND A RUNNING ENGINE, AVOID CONTACT WITH MOVING PARTS AND HOT SURFACES TO PREVENT POSSIBLE BODILY INJURY.

"AFTER REPAIRS," REFER TO DTC CRITERIA ON FACING PAGE AND CONFIRM DTC DOES NOT RESET.

MULTI-PORT FUEL INJECTION — DTC 19

DTC 19

INTERMITTENT 7X REFERENCE CIRCUIT
2.2L (VIN 4) "A" CARLINE

86814152

Circuit Description:

The crankshaft position sensor sends a reference signal to the Powertrain Control Module (PCM) seven times per revolution to indicate crankshaft position and RPM so the PCM can determine when to pulse the ignition coils and control ignition timing. This signal is called the 7X reference because it occurs seven times per revolution. The seventh pulse is the sync pulse and is used for crankshaft position reference. The PCM applies 12 volts to terminal "PD10" through CKT 580 to crankshaft position sensor terminal "C".

DTC 19 Will Set When:
The PCM misses 15 or more resync pulses within 4 minutes and 16 seconds.

Action Taken (PCM will default to):
The Malfunction Indicator Lamp (MIL) will illuminate, and the cooling fan will enable.

DTC Chart Test Description:
Number(s) below refer to circled number(s) on the diagnostic chart.

1. This determines if the PCM recognizes a problem.
2. When a 7X resync occurs, engine stumble also occurs. If a component connection or circuitry is at fault, engine stumble may be induced by wiggling the circuit or connection. This step determines if a component connection or circuit is at fault.
3. Operating faulty non-engine related electronic components may emit Electromagnetic Interference (EMI) which may cause a 7X resync. This step determines if the non-engine related component is at fault.

Diagnostic Aids:

• An intermittent may be caused by a poor connection, rubbed through wire insulation, or a severed wire inside the insulation. Inspect PCM harness connector terminal "PD2" and ICM connector terminal "A" for improper mating, improperly formed or damaged terminals, or damaged harness.

• An intermittent may be the result of a defective reluctor wheel. Remove crankshaft sensor and inspect reluctor wheel through sensor mount hole. Check for porosity and condition of wheel.

• If complaint was "Cranks But Will Not Run," DTC 19 may be set when engine start is attempted more than 15 times and ignition is not turned "OFF" between attempts.

MULTI-PORT FUEL INJECTION — DTC 21

DTC 21
THROTTLE POSITION (TP) SENSOR CIRCUIT
(SIGNAL VOLTAGE HIGH)
2.2L (VIN 4) "A" CARLINE

(1) THROTTLE CLOSED.
DOES TECH 1 SCAN TOOL DISPLAY THROTTLE POSITION OVER 1.0 VOLT?

- NO → RUN ENGINE AT GREATER THAN 1500 RPM WHILE INCREASING THROTTLE. OBSERVE THROTTLE ANGLE ON TECH 1 SCAN TOOL. THE TECH 1 SHOULD DISPLAY THROTTLE ANGLE GREATER THAN 10%. DOES IT?
  - NO → FAULTY TP SENSOR.
  - YES → DTC IS INTERMITTENT. IF NO ADDITIONAL DTC(s) WERE STORED, REFER TO "DIAGNOSTIC AIDS" ON FACING PAGE.

- YES → (2) DISCONNECT THROTTLE POSITION SENSOR. TECH 1 SCAN TOOL SHOULD DISPLAY THROTTLE POSITION BELOW .2 VOLT (200 mV). DOES IT?
  - NO → TP SENSOR SIGNAL CIRCUIT SHORTED TO VOLTAGE OR FAULTY PCM.
  - YES → (3) PROBE SENSOR GROUND CIRCUIT WITH A TEST LIGHT CONNECTED TO BATTERY VOLTAGE. IS TEST LIGHT ON?
    - NO → OPEN SENSOR GROUND CIRCUIT OR FAULTY PCM.
    - YES → FAULTY CONNECTION OR THROTTLE POSITION SENSOR.

"AFTER REPAIRS," REFER TO DTC CRITERIA ON FACING PAGE AND CONFIRM DTC DOES NOT RESET.

86814155

MULTI-PORT FUEL INJECTION — DTC 21

PCM

5 V REF — PA3
THROTTLE POSITION (TP) SENSOR SIGNAL — PB7
SENSOR GROUND — PB2

416 GRY
417 DK BLU
808 BLK

THROTTLE POSITION (TP) SENSOR

A C B

TO ECT SENSOR

DTC 21
THROTTLE POSITION (TP) SENSOR CIRCUIT
(SIGNAL VOLTAGE HIGH)
2.2L (VIN 4) "A" CARLINE

Circuit Description:

The TP sensor provides an output voltage relative to throttle position angle. The PCM supplies a 5 volt reference and a ground to the TP sensor and monitors the voltage returned. The TP sensor voltage will vary from above .2V to .9V at idle or with ignition "ON" and engine "OFF" to over 4.5V at wide open throttle.

The TP sensor signal is one of the most important inputs used by the Powertrain Control Module (PCM) for fuel control and for most of the PCM control outputs.

DTC 21 Will Set When:

- Engine is running below 1500 RPM.
- DTC 33 or 34 is not set.
- MAP is less than 65 kPa.
- TP sensor signal voltage is greater than 3.9 volts.
- Above conditions exist for more than 5 seconds.

OR

- TP sensor voltage is greater than 4.7 volts.

Action Taken (PCM will default to): The Malfunction Indicator Lamp (MIL) will illuminate. TP sensor will read 0% if engine vacuum is less than 30 kPa. TP sensor will read 10% if engine vacuum is greater than 30 kPa or vehicle speed is greater than 2 mph. The cooling fan will enable.

DTC Chart Test Description: Number(s) below refer to circled number(s) on the diagnostic chart.

1. With throttle closed the TP sensor should read less than .900 volt. If it doesn't, check for sticking TP sensor or throttle linkage. If OK, replace TP sensor.
2. With the TP sensor disconnected, the TP sensor voltage should go low if the PCM and wiring are OK.
3. Probing CKT 808 with a test light checks the TP sensor ground circuit because an open or very high resistance ground circuit will cause a DTC 21.

Diagnostic Aids:

- DTCs 15 and 21 stored at the same time could be the result of an open CKT 808.
- Scan TP sensor while depressing accelerator pedal with engine "OFF" and ignition "ON." Display should vary between .2V to .9V when throttle is closed to over 4.5V at wide open throttle.
- Check condition of connector and sensor terminals for moisture or corrosion, and clean or replace as necessary. If corrosion is found, check condition of connector seal, repair or replace if necessary.

86814154

MULTI-PORT FUEL INJECTION — DTC 22

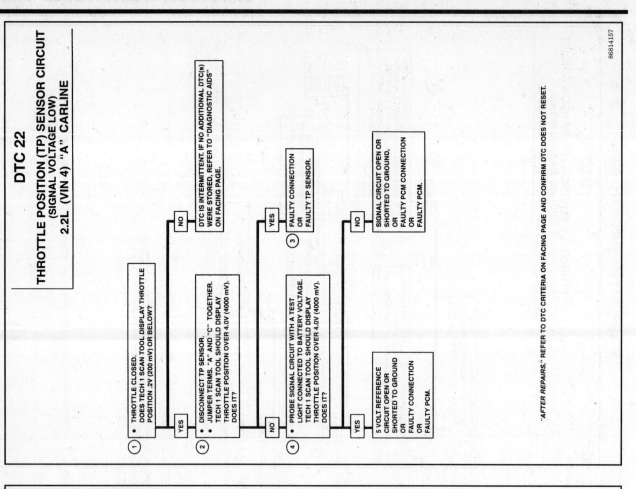

DTC 22

THROTTLE POSITION (TP) SENSOR CIRCUIT
(SIGNAL VOLTAGE LOW)
2.2L (VIN 4) "A" CARLINE

(1) • THROTTLE CLOSED.
• DOES TECH 1 SCAN TOOL DISPLAY THROTTLE POSITION .2V (200 mV) OR BELOW?

NO → DTC IS INTERMITTENT. IF NO ADDITIONAL DTC(s) WERE STORED, REFER TO "DIAGNOSTIC AIDS" ON FACING PAGE.

YES ↓

(2) • DISCONNECT TP SENSOR.
• JUMPER TERMS. "A" AND "C" TOGETHER.
• TECH 1 SCAN TOOL SHOULD DISPLAY THROTTLE POSITION OVER 4.0V (4000 mV). DOES IT?

YES → (3) FAULTY CONNECTION OR FAULTY TP SENSOR.

NO ↓

(4) • PROBE SIGNAL CIRCUIT WITH A TEST LIGHT CONNECTED TO BATTERY VOLTAGE. TECH 1 SCAN TOOL SHOULD DISPLAY THROTTLE POSITION OVER 4.0V (4000 mV). DOES IT?

NO → 5 VOLT REFERENCE CIRCUIT OPEN OR SHORTED TO GROUND OR FAULTY PCM CONNECTION OR FAULTY PCM.

YES → SIGNAL CIRCUIT OPEN OR SHORTED TO GROUND, OR FAULTY PCM CONNECTION OR FAULTY PCM.

"AFTER REPAIRS," REFER TO DTC CRITERIA ON FACING PAGE AND CONFIRM DTC DOES NOT RESET.

86814157

MULTI-PORT FUEL INJECTION — DTC 22

PCM
PA3 — 5 V REF — 416 GRY
PB7 — THROTTLE POSITION (TP) SENSOR SIGNAL — 417 DK BLU
PB2 — SENSOR GROUND — 808 BLK

THROTTLE POSITION (TP) SENSOR
A C B
TO ECT SENSOR

86814156

DTC 22
THROTTLE POSITION (TP) SENSOR CIRCUIT
(SIGNAL VOLTAGE LOW)
2.2L (VIN 4) "A" CARLINE

Circuit Description:
The TP sensor provides an output voltage relative to the throttle position angle. The PCM supplies a 5 volt reference and a ground to the TP sensor and monitors the voltage returned. The TP sensor voltage will vary from about .2V to .9V at idle or with ignition "ON" and engine "OFF" to over 4.5V at wide open throttle.
The TP sensor signal is one of the most important inputs used by the Powertrain Control Module (PCM) for fuel control and for a majority of the PCM control outputs.

DTC 22 Will Set When:
• TP sensor signal voltage is less than .21 volt.
• Above conditions are present for 5 seconds or more.

Action Taken (PCM will default to): The Malfunction Indicator Lamp (MIL) will illuminate. TP sensor will read 0% if engine vacuum is less than 30 kPa. TP sensor will read 10% if engine vacuum is greater than 30 kPa and vehicle speed is greater than 2 mph. The cooling fan will enable.

DTC Chart Test Description: Number(s) below refer to circled number(s) on the diagnostic chart.
1. The TP sensor has an auto zeroing feature. If the voltage reading is within the range of about .2 to .9 volt, the PCM will use that value as closed throttle. If the voltage reading is out of the auto zero range at closed throttle, check for a binding throttle cable or damaged linkage. if OK, continue with diagnosis.
2. Simulates DTC 21 (high voltage). If the PCM recognizes the high signal voltage then the PCM and wiring are OK.
3. Check for good sensor connection. If connection is good, replace TP sensor.
4. This simulates a high signal voltage to check for an open in CKT 417. The Tech 1 scan tool will not read up to 12 volts, but what is important is that the PCM recognizes the signal on CKT 417.

Diagnostic Aids:
• Scan TP sensor voltage while depressing accelerator pedal with engine "OFF" and ignition "ON." Display should be between .2 volt and .9V when throttle is closed to over 4.5V at wide open throttle.
• If DTCs 22 and 34 are set, check CKT 416 for faulty wiring or connections.
• Check condition of connector and sensor terminals for moisture or corrosion, and clean or replace as necessary. If corrosion is found, check condition of connector seal and repair or replace if necessary.

MULTI-PORT FUEL INJECTION — DTC 23

DTC 23
INTAKE AIR TEMPERATURE (IAT) SENSOR CIRCUIT
(LOW TEMPERATURE INDICATED)
2.2L (VIN 4) "A" CARLINE

1. DOES TECH 1 SCAN TOOL DISPLAY IAT -30°C (-22°F) OR COLDER?
   - NO → DTC IS INTERMITTENT. IF NO ADDITIONAL DTC(s) WERE STORED, REFER TO "DIAGNOSTIC AIDS" ON FACING PAGE.
   - YES →

2. • DISCONNECT SENSOR.
   • JUMPER HARNESS TERMINALS TOGETHER.
   TECH 1 SCAN TOOL SHOULD DISPLAY TEMPERATURE OVER 130°C (266°F). DOES IT?
   - YES → FAULTY CONNECTION OR SENSOR.
   - NO →

3. • JUMPER SIGNAL CIRCUIT TO GROUND. TECH 1 SCAN TOOL SHOULD DISPLAY TEMPERATURE OVER 130°C (266°F). DOES IT?
   - YES → OPEN SENSOR GROUND CIRCUIT, FAULTY CONNECTION OR FAULTY PCM.
   - NO → OPEN SIGNAL CIRCUIT, FAULTY CONNECTION OR FAULTY PCM.

DIAGNOSTIC AID

INTAKE AIR TEMPERATURE SENSOR		
TEMPERATURE VS. RESISTANCE VALUES (APPROXIMATE)		
°C	°F	OHMS
100	212	177
90	194	241
80	176	332
70	158	467
60	140	667
50	122	973
45	113	1188
40	104	1459
35	95	1802
30	86	2238
25	77	2796
20	68	3520
15	59	4450
10	50	5670
5	41	7280
0	32	9420
-5	23	12300
-10	14	16180
-15	5	21450
-20	-4	28680
-30	-22	52700
-40	-40	100700

"AFTER REPAIRS," REFER TO DTC CRITERIA ON FACING PAGE AND CONFIRM DTC DOES NOT RESET.

MULTI-PORT FUEL INJECTION — DTC 23

DTC 23
INTAKE AIR TEMPERATURE (IAT) SENSOR CIRCUIT
(LOW TEMPERATURE INDICATED)
2.2L (VIN 4) "A" CARLINE

Circuit Description:

The Intake Air Temperature (IAT) sensor uses a thermistor to control the signal voltage at the Powertrain Control Module (PCM). The PCM supplies a 5 volt reference and a ground to the sensor. When the air is cold the sensor (thermistor) resistance is high, therefore the PCM terminal "PC9" voltage will be high. If the air is warm the sensor resistance is low, therefore PCM terminal "PC9" voltage will be low.

DTC 23 Will Set When:

- IAT signal voltage indicates intake air temperature is below -40°C (-40°F).
- Engine run time is greater then 320 seconds.
- Vehicle speed is less than 15 mph.

Action Taken (PCM will default to):

The Malfunction Indicator Lamp (MIL) will illuminate, the PCM will default to 60°C for intake air temperature (Tech 1 scan tool will not show defaulted value), and the cooling fan will enable.

DTC Chart Test Description:

Number(s) below refer to circled number(s) on the diagnostic chart.

1. This checks if DTC 14 was set as a result of a hard or intermittent condition.
2. A DTC 23 will set due to an open sensor, wire, or connection. This test will determine if the wiring and PCM are OK.
3. This will determine if the signal CKT 472 or the sensor ground CKT 452 is open.

Diagnostic Aids:

- A Tech 1 scan tool displays temperature of the air entering the engine, which should be close to ambient air temperature when engine is cold, and rise as underhood temperature increases.
- If engine is at ambient temperature, compare IAT sensor to ECT sensor. They should be within a couple degrees of each other, or compare IAT sensor to a known good sensor. If DTCs 23, 33 and 66 are stored at the same time, it could be the result of an open CKT 452.
- The "Temperature vs. Resistance Values" scale at the right may be used to test the IAT sensor at various temperature levels to evaluate the possibility of a skewed (mis-scaled) sensor. A skewed sensor can result in poor driveability.

MULTI-PORT FUEL INJECTION — DTC 24

DTC 24

VEHICLE SPEED SENSOR (VSS) CIRCUIT
2.2L (VIN 4) "A" CARLINE

DISREGARD DTC 24 IF SET WHILE DRIVE WHEELS ARE NOT TURNING.

(1)
- RAISE DRIVE WHEELS.
- NOTICE: DO NOT PERFORM THIS TEST WITHOUT SUPPORTING THE LOWER CONTROL ARMS SO THAT THE DRIVE AXLES ARE IN A NORMAL HORIZONTAL POSITION. RUNNING THE VEHICLE IN GEAR WITH THE WHEELS HANGING DOWN AT FULL TRAVEL MAY DAMAGE THE DRIVE AXLES.
- WITH ENGINE IDLING IN GEAR, TECH 1 SCAN TOOL SHOULD DISPLAY VEHICLE SPEED ABOVE 0.

DOES IT?

NO → DOES SPEEDOMETER WORK?

YES → DTC IS INTERMITTENT. IF NO ADDITIONAL DTC(s) WERE STORED, REFER TO "DIAGNOSTIC AIDS" ON FACING PAGE.

DOES SPEEDOMETER WORK?

NO →
- IGNITION "OFF."
- DISCONNECT VSS HARNESS CONNECTOR AT TRANSAXLE.
- CONNECT SIGNAL GENERATOR TESTER J 33431-B, OR J 38522 OR EQUIVALENT TO VSS HARNESS CONNECTOR.
- IGNITION "ON," TESTER "ON." SET TESTER TO 60 Hz TO GENERATE A VSS SIGNAL.
- SCAN TOOL SHOULD DISPLAY VEHICLE SPEED ABOVE 0.

DOES IT?

YES → (2) CHECK EPROM FOR CORRECT CALIBRATION I.D. IF OK, REPLACE PCM.

NO → VSS "HIGH" OR VSS "LOW" OPEN, SHORTED TO GROUND, SHORTED TOGETHER, FAULTY CONNECTIONS, OR FAULTY PCM.

YES → REPLACE VEHICLE SPEED SENSOR.

NOTICE: BECAUSE THE VSS OUTPUT USES A 4000 PPM SIGNAL, THE TECH 1 SCAN TOOL WILL READ 9 MPH WITH THE TESTERS SET ON 60 Hz. USE SIGNAL GENERATOR ADAPTER J 41059 TO PERFORM THIS TEST.

"AFTER REPAIRS," REFER TO DTC CRITERIA ON FACING PAGE AND CONFIRM DTC DOES NOT RESET.

86814161

MULTI-PORT FUEL INJECTION — DTC 24

PCM

| BD13 | VSS SIGNAL "LOW" |
| BD14 | VSS SIGNAL "HIGH" |

401 PPL
400 YEL

VEHICLE SPEED SENSOR (VSS)

MOUNTED ON TRANSAXLE

7-09-94
SS 4424-0E

DTC 24

VEHICLE SPEED SENSOR (VSS) CIRCUIT
2.2L (VIN 4) "A" CARLINE

Circuit Description:

Vehicle speed information is provided to the Powertrain Control Module (PCM) by the Vehicle Speed Sensor (VSS) which is a permanent magnet generator that is mounted in the transaxle. The permanent magnet generator produces an AC pulsing voltage signal whenever vehicle speed is over 5 km/h (3 mph). The AC voltage level and the number of pulses increase with vehicle speed. The PCM then converts the pulsing voltage to mph and the mph can be displayed with a Tech 1 scan tool. Output of the VSS can also be measured by using a digital voltmeter on the AC scale while rotating the drive wheels.

The PCM then supplies the necessary signal to the instrument panel to operate the speedometer, odometer, and the cruise control module.

DTC 24 Will Set When:
- Vehicle speed is less than 2 mph (3 km/h).
- Engine speed is between 1700 and 3600 RPM.
- Not in park or neutral.
- DTC 21, 22, 33 or 34 is not set.
- Engine vacuum is between 72-80 kPa.
- All above conditions are met for 5 seconds.

Action Taken (PCM will default to): The Malfunction Indicator Lamp (MIL) will illuminate, and the cooling fan will enable.

DTC Chart Test Description: Number(s) below refer to circled number(s) on the diagnostic chart.
1. The permanent magnet generator only produces a signal if drive wheels are turning greater than 3 mph (5 km/h). This step checks for a hard or intermittent condition.
2. Check EPROM for correct application before replacing PCM.

Diagnostic Aids:
- A Tech 1 scan tool should indicate a vehicle speed whenever the drive wheels are turning greater than 3 mph (5 km/h).
- A faulty or misadjusted Park/Neutral Position (PNP) switch can result in a false DTC 24. Use a Tech 1 scan tool and check for proper signal while in drive (3T40). Refer to CHART C-1A for Park/Neutral Position (PNP) switch diagnosis check.
- DTC 24 can be falsely set if engine is "brake-torqued" in gear for 20 seconds. Output of the generator can be monitored using a digital voltmeter while rotating the tires.

86814160

MULTI-PORT FUEL INJECTION — DTC 25

DTC 25

INTAKE AIR TEMPERATURE (IAT) SENSOR CIRCUIT
(HIGH TEMPERATURE INDICATED)
2.2L (VIN 4) "A" CARLINE

PCM

IAT SENSOR SIGNAL

5 VOLT REFERENCE

SENSOR GROUND

PB1   452 BLK

PC9   472 TAN

TO A/C REFRIGERANT PRESSURE SENSOR

TO MAP SENSOR

INTAKE AIR TEMPERATURE (IAT) SENSOR

A
B

5-3-94
MB-12090

Circuit Description:

The Intake Air Temperature (IAT) sensor uses a thermistor to control the signal voltage at the Powertrain Control Module (PCM). The PCM supplies a 5 volt reference and a ground to the sensor. When the air is cold the sensor (thermistor) resistance is high, therefore the PCM terminal "PC9" voltage will be high. If the air is warm the sensor resistance will be low, therefore, PCM terminal "PC9" voltage will be low.

DTC 25 Will Set When:

* IAT sensor signal voltage indicates intake air temperature is greater than 151°C (304°F).
* Vehicle speed is greater than 15 mph.
* Engine run time is greater than 320 seconds.

Action Taken (PCM will default to): The Malfunction Indicator Lamp (MIL) will illuminate, the PCM will default to 60°C for intake air temperature (Tech 1 scan tool will not display defaulted value), and the cooling fan will enable.

DTC Chart Test Description: Number(s) below refer to circled number(s) on the diagnostic chart.

1. This checks if DTC 25 was set as an intermittent or a hard condition.

Diagnostic Aids:

* The "Temperature vs. Resistance Value" scale at the right may be used to test the IAT sensor at various temperature levels to evaluate the possibility of a skewed sensor. A skewed sensor can result in poor driveability.
* If engine is at ambient temperature, compare IAT sensor to ECT sensor. They should be within a couple degrees of each other, or compare against a known good sensor.

86814162

MULTI-PORT FUEL INJECTION — DTC 25

DTC 25

INTAKE AIR TEMPERATURE (IAT) SENSOR CIRCUIT
(HIGH TEMPERATURE INDICATED)
2.2L (VIN 4) "A" CARLINE

(1) DOES TECH 1 SCAN TOOL DISPLAY IAT OF 145°C (293°F) OR HOTTER?

YES → DISCONNECT SENSOR ELECTRICAL CONNECTOR. TECH 1 SCAN TOOL SHOULD DISPLAY TEMPERATURE BELOW -30°C (-22°F). DOES IT?

NO → DTC IS INTERMITTENT. IF NO ADDITIONAL DTC(s) WERE STORED, REFER TO "DIAGNOSTIC AIDS" ON FACING PAGE.

YES → FAULTY CONNECTION OR FAULTY SENSOR.

NO → SIGNAL CIRCUIT SHORTED TO GROUND OR FAULTY PCM.

DIAGNOSTIC AID

INTAKE AIR TEMPERATURE SENSOR		
TEMPERATURE VS. RESISTANCE VALUES (APPROXIMATE)		
°C	°F	OHMS
100	212	177
90	194	241
80	176	332
70	158	467
60	140	667
50	122	973
45	113	1188
40	104	1459
35	95	1802
30	86	2238
25	77	2796
20	68	3520
15	59	4450
10	50	5670
5	41	7280
0	32	9420
-5	23	12300
-10	14	16180
-15	5	21450
-20	-4	28680
-30	-22	52700
-40	-40	100700

"AFTER REPAIRS," REFER TO DTC CRITERIA ON FACING PAGE AND CONFIRM DTC DOES NOT RESET.

86814163

MULTI-PORT FUEL INJECTION — DTC 26

DTC 26
QUAD-DRIVER MODULE (QDSM) CIRCUIT
2.2L (VIN 4) "A" CARLINE

1. • INSTALL TECH 1 SCAN TOOL.
   • IGNITION "ON," ENGINE "OFF."
   • SCAN DTC(s).
   • IS DTC 26 SET?

   YES ↓

2. • ENGINE RUNNING.
   • USING TECH 1, COMMAND MIL "ON" AND "OFF."
   • DOES MIL GO "ON" AND "OFF" WHEN COMMANDED?

   NO → DTC 26 FAULT IS INTERMITTENT. CHECK FOR POOR TERMINAL CONTACT AT PCM AND QDM 1 CIRCUITRY.

   YES ↓

3. • IGNITION "ON."
   • USING TECH 1, COMMAND TEMP LIGHT "ON" AND THEN "OFF."
   • DOES TEMP LIGHT TURN "ON" AND "OFF" WHEN COMMANDED?

   NO → SEE SECTION "6E3-C16" TO DIAGNOSE PCM CONTROLLED TEMP LAMP CIRCUIT.

   YES ↓

   DTC 26 FAULT IS INTERMITTENT. CHECK FOR POOR TERMINAL CONTACT AT PCM AND QDM 1 CIRCUITRY. IF OK, CLEAR DTC(s) AND RE-CHECK. IF DTC 26 RESETS, REPLACE PCM.

"AFTER REPAIRS," REFER TO DTC CRITERIA ON FACING PAGE AND CONFIRM DTC DOES NOT RESET.

86814165

MULTI-PORT FUEL INJECTION — DTC 26

DTC 26
QUAD-DRIVER MODULE (QDSM) CIRCUIT
2.2L (VIN 4) "A" CARLINE

Circuit Description:

The Powertrain Control Module (PCM) controls most components with electronic switches which complete a ground circuit when turned "ON." These switches are arranged in groups of 4, called Quad-Driver Modules (QDMs) which can independently control up to 4 outputs (PCM terminals), although not all outputs are used. When an output is "ON," the terminal is grounded and its voltage normally will be low. When an output is "OFF," its terminal voltage normally will be high.

The QDSM is fault protected. If a relay or solenoid coil is shorted, having very low or zero resistance, or if the control side of the circuit is shorted to voltage, it would allow too much current into the QDSM. The QDSM senses this and the output turns "OFF" or its internal resistance increases to limit current flow and protect the QDSM. The result is high output terminal voltage when it should be low. If the circuit from B+ or the component is open, or the control side of the circuit is shorted to ground, terminal voltage will be low, even when output is commanded "OFF." Either of these conditions is considered to be a QDSM fault.

The QDSM has a separate fault line to indicate the presence of a current fault to the PCM's central processor. A scan tool displays the status of each of these fault lines as "Low" = OK, "High" = fault. QDSM should always read high when in Park or Neutral.

DTC 26 Will Set When:
• QDSM fault line:
  - Is "high" for 20 seconds or more.
  - Battery voltage is greater than 10.5 volts.

Action Taken (PCM will default to):
The cooling fan will enable.

DTC Chart Test Description:
Number(s) below refer to circled number(s) on the diagnostic chart.

1. This step checks to see if DTC 26 was set as a result of a hard failure or an intermittent condition.
2. This checks MIL operation.
3. This checks "temp" lamp operation.

Diagnostic Aids:
• A Tech 1 scan tool has the ability to command the MIL and "temp" lamp "ON" and "OFF" with engine running.
• A faulty connection or an open in CKT 419 or CKT 35 can result in a DTC 26.

86814164

MULTI-PORT FUEL INJECTION — DTC 26 (PAGE 1 OF 3)

DTC 26
(Page 1 of 3)
QUAD-DRIVER (QDM) CIRCUIT
3300 (VIN N) "A" CARLINE (MFI)

86814195

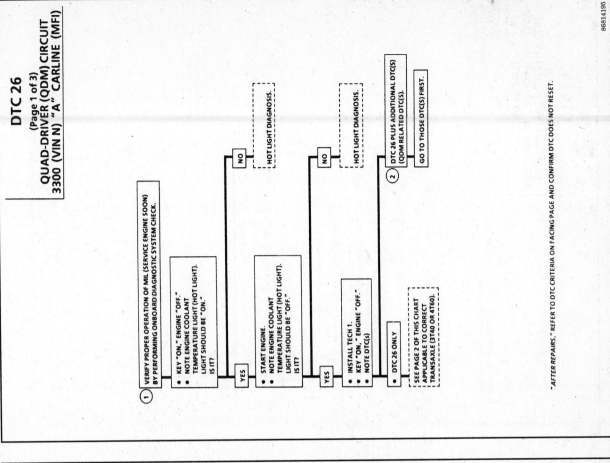

"AFTER REPAIRS," REFER TO DTC CRITERIA ON FACING PAGE AND CONFIRM DTC DOES NOT RESET.

MULTI-PORT FUEL INJECTION — DTC 26 (PAGE 1 OF 3)

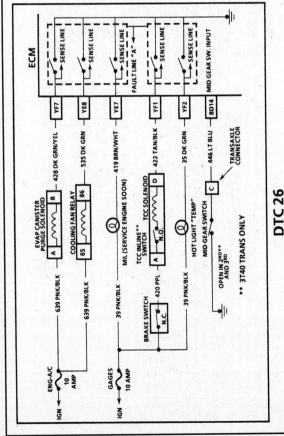

86814194

DTC 26
(Page 1 of 3)
QUAD-DRIVER (QDM) CIRCUIT
3300 (VIN N) "A" CARLINE (MFI)

Circuit Description:

Quad-Driver Modules (QDM) are used to control the components shown in the illustration above. When the ECM is commanding a component "ON," the QDM closes the switch completing the circuit to ground.

Each QDM output has a sense line. When a component is commanded "ON," the voltage potential on the sense line is low, and when the component is commanded "OFF" the voltage potential on the sense line is high. DTC 26 will set when the ECM is commanding a component "ON" and the voltage potential on a QDM "A" sense line is high, or if the component is commanded "OFF" and the voltage potential on a QDM "A" sense line is low. Either of these conditions will cause the QDM "A" fault line to display "HIGH" and set DTC 26.

On all vehicles, the QDM "A" fault status on the Tech 1 will display "HIGH" with the brake applied or if the engine is not running. On vehicles with a 3T40 transmission, the QDM "A" fault status on the Tech 1 will read "HIGH" until the TCC inline switch is closed. These conditions will not cause DTC 26 to set even though the fault line displays "HIGH." To simulate driving in second gear and change the QDM status to low, disconnect TCC connector and connect a test light between harness terminals "A" and "D".

DTC 26 will set if:
• The system is running in "Closed Loop."
• Brake switch is closed (brake not applied).
• Transaxle in mid or high gear.
• The ECM detects an improper voltage level on a QDM "A" controlled circuit for 10 seconds.

Test Description: Number(s) refer to circled number(s) on the diagnostic chart.

1. The ECM does not know which controlled circuit caused DTC 26 so this chart will go through each of the circuits to determine which is at fault. This test checks the MIL (Service Engine Soon) driver and the MIL (Service Engine Soon) circuit.

2. QDM symptoms:
   • TCC - Malfunctioning - DTC 39
   • Hot Light - "ON" all the time. - "OFF" during bulb check.
   • Cooling fan "ON" all the time or won't come "ON" at all
   • Poor driveability due to 100% canister purge.

MULTI-PORT FUEL INJECTION — DTC 26 (PAGE 2 OF 3 FOR THE 3T40 TRANS)

DTC 26
(Page 2 of 3)
QUAD-DRIVER (QDM) CIRCUIT
3300 (VIN N) "A" CARLINE (MFI)
(3T40 TRANS)

NOTICE: IF DTC 39 IS SET ALONG WITH DTC 26, DTC 39 MUST BE DIAGNOSED FIRST.

(3)
- KEY "OFF."
- DISCONNECT YELLOW ECM CONNECTOR.
- KEY "ON," ENGINE "OFF."
- DVM SET TO 2 AMP SCALE.
- PROBE ECM HARNESS TERMINALS "YF7", "YE8", "YF2", AND "YF7".
  - RED LEAD (+) TO ECM HARNESS.
  - BLACK LEAD (-) TO GROUND.
- EACH TERMINAL SHOULD MEASURE LESS THAN .75 AMP (BUT NOT 0 AMP).

OK → CHECK VOLTAGE AT ECM HARNESS TERMINAL "YF1" WITH A DVM TO GROUND. SHOULD READ NEAR 0 VOLTS. DOES IT?

NOT OK → SEE PAGE 3

NO → FAULTY TCC IN-LINE SWITCH OR CKT 422 SHORTED TO VOLTAGE.

YES → CHECK CKT 422 FOR A SHORT TO GROUND AND REPAIR IF GROUNDED. IF OK, REFER TO "DIAGNOSTIC AIDS" ON FACING PAGE.

"AFTER REPAIRS," REFER TO DTC CRITERIA ON FACING PAGE AND CONFIRM DTC DOES NOT RESET.

MULTI-PORT FUEL INJECTION — DTC 26 (PAGE 2 OF 3 FOR THE 3T40 TRANS)

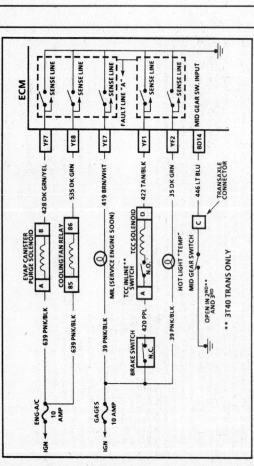

ECM
SENSE LINE
SENSE LINE
SENSE LINE
FAULT LINE "A"
SENSE LINE
SENSE LINE
MID GEAR SW. INPUT

YF7   YE8   YF7   YF1   YF2   BD14

IGN — ENG-A/C — 10 AMP — 639 PNK/BLK — 428 DK GRN/YEL — B — EVAP CANISTER PURGE SOLENOID — A
639 PNK/BLK — 535 DK GRN — 86 — COOLING FAN RELAY — 85
IGN — GAGES — 10 AMP — 39 PNK/BLK — 419 BRN/WHT — MIL (SERVICE ENGINE SOON)
BRAKE SWITCH — 420 PPL — N.C. — TCC INLINE SWITCH** — A — N.O. — TCC SOLENOID — D — 422 TAN/BLK
39 PNK/BLK — 35 DK GRN — HOT LIGHT "TEMP" — MID GEAR SWITCH
OPEN IN 2ND** AND 3RD
446 LT BLU — C — TRANSAXLE CONNECTOR

DTC 26 (Page 2 of 3)
QUAD-DRIVER (QDM) CIRCUIT
3300 (VIN N) "A" CARLINE (MFI)
(3T40 TRANS)

** 3T40 TRANS ONLY

Circuit Description:
Quad-Driver Modules (QDM) are used to control the components shown in the illustration above. When the ECM is commanding a component "ON," the QDM closes the switch completing the circuit to ground.

Each QDM output has a sense line. When a component is commanded "ON," the voltage potential on the sense line is low, and when the component is commanded "OFF" the voltage potential on the sense line is high. DTC 26 will set when the ECM is commanding a component "ON" and the voltage potential on a QDM "A" sense line is high, or if the component is commanded "OFF" and the voltage potential on a QDM "A" sense line is low. Either of these conditions will cause the QDM "A" fault line to display "HIGH" and set DTC 26.

On all vehicles, the QDM "A" fault status on the Tech 1 will display "HIGH" with the brake applied or if the engine is not running. On vehicles with a 3T40 transmission, the QDM "A" fault status on the Tech 1 will read "HIGH" until the TCC inline switch is closed. These conditions will not cause DTC 26 to set even though the fault line displays "HIGH." To simulate driving in second gear and change the QDM status to low, disconnect TCC connector and connect a test light between harness terminals "A" and "D."

DTC 26 will set if:
- The system is running in "Closed Loop."
- Brake switch is closed (brake not applied).
- Transaxle in mid or high gear.
- The ECM detects an improper voltage level on a QDM "A" controlled circuit for 10 seconds.

Test Description: Number(s) refer to circled number(s) on the diagnostic chart.
3. This test will determine which circuit is out of specifications.

Diagnostic Aids:
Monitor the voltage at each terminal while moving related harness connectors, including ECM harness.

If the failure is induced, the voltage will change. This may help locate the intermittent. Check for bent pins at ECM and ECM connector terminals. Also, ensure that the mid gear switch and CKT 446 is not open with the vehicle operating in park/neutral or first gear. This condition can cause a false DTC 26 to be set. Refer to DTC 27 chart for diagnosis. If DTC reoccurs with no apparent connector problem, replace ECM.

86814199

MULTI-PORT FUEL INJECTION — DTC 26 (PAGE 2 OF 3 FOR THE 4T60 TRANS)

DTC 26
(Page 2 of 3)
QUAD-DRIVER (QDM) CIRCUIT 3300 (VIN N) "A" CARLINE (MFI) (4T60 TRANS)

(3)

- KEY "OFF."
- DISCONNECT YELLOW ECM CONNECTOR.
- KEY "ON," ENGINE "OFF."
- DVM SET TO 2 AMP SCALE.
- PROBE ECM HARNESS TERMINALS "YE7", "YE8", "YF1", "YF2", AND "YF7."
  - RED LEAD (+) TO ECM HARNESS.
  - BLACK LEAD (-) TO GROUND.
  - EACH TERMINAL SHOULD MEASURE LESS THAN .75 AMP (BUT NOT 0 AMP).

OK → REFER TO "DIAGNOSTIC AIDS" ON FACING PAGE.

NOT OK → SEE PAGE 3

"AFTER REPAIRS," REFER TO DTC CRITERIA ON FACING PAGE AND CONFIRM DTC DOES NOT RESET.

MULTI-PORT FUEL INJECTION — DTC 26 (PAGE 2 OF 3 FOR THE 4T60 TRANS)

86814198

CANISTER PURGE SOLENOID

ENG CTRL
IGN — 10 AMP — 639 PNK/BLK — B — [SENSE LINE] — YF7 — 428 DK GRN/YEL

FAN/ELECT
IGN — 10 AMP — 250 BRN — COOLING FAN RELAY — F — [SENSE LINE] — YE8 — 535 DK GRN

GAGES
IGN — 10 AMP — 39 PNK/BLK — SES LIGHT — [SENSE LINE / FAULT LINE] — YE7 — 419 BRN/WHT

BRAKE SWITCH — 420 PPL — N.C.
**2ND GEAR SWITCH — A — N.O. — TCC SOLENOID — D — [SENSE LINE] — YF1 — 422 TAN/BLK

39 PNK/BLK — HOT LIGHT — [SENSE LINE] — YF2 — 35 DK GRN

QDM "A"

** 3T40 TRANS ONLY

CODE 26
(Page 2 of 3)
QUAD-DRIVER (QDM) CIRCUIT 3300 (VIN N) "A" CARLINE (PORT) (4T60 TRANS)

Circuit Description:

Quad-Driver Modules (QDM) are used to control the components shown in the illustration above. When the ECM is commanding a component "ON," the QDM closes the switch completing the circuit to ground.

Each QDM has a sense line and a fault line. When a component is commanded "ON," the voltage potential on the sense line is low and when the component is commanded "OFF" the voltage potential on the sense line is high.

Code 26 will set when the ECM is commanding a component "ON" and the voltage potential on the QDM "A" sense line is high, or if the component is commanded "OFF" and the voltage potential on the QDM "A" sense line is low. QDM "B" will not set a Code 26.

The QDM "A" fault status displayed on the Tech 1 will read "HI" with the brake applied or with the engine not running. Code 26 will not set under these conditions.

Code 26 will set if:
- The system is running in "Closed Loop."
- Brake switch is closed (brake not applied).
- Transaxle in mid or high gear.
- The ECM detects an improper voltage level on a QDM "A" controlled circuit for 10 seconds.

Test Description: Number(s) refer to circled number(s) on the diagnostic chart.

3. This test will determine which circuit is out of specifications.

Diagnostic Aids:

Monitor the voltage at each terminal while moving related harness connectors, including ECM harness. If the failure is induced, the voltage will change. This may help locate the intermittent. Check for bent pins at ECM and ECM connector terminals. If code reoccurs with no apparent connector problem, replace ECM.

MULTI-PORT FUEL INJECTION — DTC 26 (PAGE 3 OF 3)

DTC 26
(Page 3 of 3)
QUAD-DRIVER (QDM) CIRCUIT
3300 (VIN N) "A" CARLINE (MFI)

CIRCUIT ISOLATED FROM PRIOR CHARTS

④
- USE FACING PAGE WIRING DIAGRAM FOR SPECIFIC TERMINALS TO BE TESTED.
- RECONNECT ECM, IF APPLICABLE.
- KEY "ON," ENGINE "OFF," DLC DIAGNOSTIC REQUEST TERMINAL GROUNDED.
- REMOVE CONNECTOR FROM RELAY/SOLENOID IN AFFECTED CIRCUIT.
- PLACE TEST LIGHT ACROSS TERMINALS FOR COMPONENT IGNITION FEED AND ECM DRIVER CIRCUIT.
- LIGHT SHOULD BE "ON."
  IS IT?

YES | **NO**

(YES branch)
- REMOVE JUMPER AT DLC. NOTE LIGHT.

"ON" | "OFF"

("ON")
- DISCONNECT ECM CONNECTOR. NOTE LIGHT.

"ON" | "OFF"

REPAIR GROUNDED CIRCUIT. | CHECK FOR POOR CONNECTIONS. IF OK, REPLACE COMPONENT.

REPLACE ECM

(NO branch)
- CONNECT TEST LIGHT FROM COMPONENT IGNITION FEED CIRCUIT TO GROUND. NOTE LIGHT.

"ON" | "OFF"

("ON")
- DISCONNECT ECM CONNECTOR.
- CHECK FOR OPEN IN DRIVER CIRCUIT.

NOT OK | OK

REPAIR OPEN. | ECM CONN. OR ECM.

("OFF")
REPAIR OPEN IN COMPONENT IGNITION FEED CIRCUIT.

NOTICE: WITH THE INTRODUCTION OF GMP4 ECMS, DELCO ELECTRONICS CHANGED TO INTERNALLY PROTECTED QUAD DRIVERS. THIS INTERNAL PROTECTION CAN BE COMPARED TO THE ACTION OF A CIRCUIT BREAKER. IF TOO MUCH CURRENT FLOWS IN A CONTROLLED CIRCUIT, THIS TYPE OF QUAD DRIVER TURNS ITSELF "OFF." THIS ALLOWS THE QUAD DRIVER TO SURVIVE A SHORTED SOLENOID, RELAY, OR HARNESS. AND IT MEANS YOU DO NOT HAVE TO REPLACE THE ECM. JUST REPAIR THE FAULT IN THE OUTPUT CIRCUIT AND THE QUAD DRIVER WILL RETURN TO NORMAL OPERATION.

"AFTER REPAIRS," REFER TO DTC CRITERIA ON FACING PAGE AND CONFIRM DTC DOES NOT RESET.

86814201

MULTI-PORT FUEL INJECTION — DTC 26 (PAGE 3 OF 3)

 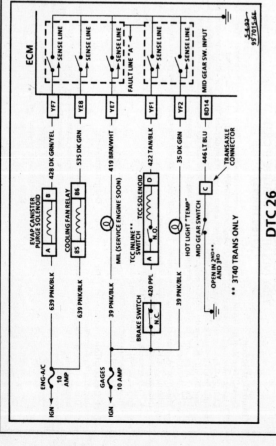

ECM
- SENSE LINE
- SENSE LINE
- SENSE LINE
- FAULT LINE "A"
- SENSE LINE
- SENSE LINE

YF7 — 428 DK GRN/YEL — B — EVAP CANISTER PURGE SOLENOID — A — 639 PNK/BLK — IGN — 10 AMP — ENG-A/C

YE8 — 535 DK GRN — 86 — COOLING FAN RELAY — 85 — 639 PNK/BLK — IGN — 10 AMP — GAGES

YE7 — 419 BRN/WHT — MIL (SERVICE ENGINE SOON) — 39 PNK/BLK

YF1 — 422 TAN/BLK — D — TCC SOLENOID — A — TCC INLINE SWITCH — N.O. — 420 PPL — BRAKE SWITCH — N.C. — 39 PNK/BLK

YF2 — 35 DK GRN — HOT LIGHT "TEMP" — MID GEAR SWITCH — OPEN IN 2ND** AND 3RD

BD14 — MID GEAR SW. INPUT — 446 LT BLU — C — TRANSAXLE CONNECTOR

** 3T40 TRANS ONLY

DTC 26
(Page 3 of 3)
QUAD-DRIVER (QDM) CIRCUIT
3300 (VIN N) "A" CARLINE (MFI)

Circuit Description:
Quad-Driver Modules (QDM) are used to control the components shown in the illustration above. When the ECM is commanding a component "ON," the QDM closes the switch completing the circuit to ground.

Each QDM output has a sense line. When a component is commanded "ON," the voltage potential on the sense line is low, and when the component is commanded "OFF" the voltage potential on the sense line is high.

DTC 26 will set when the ECM is commanding a component "ON" and the voltage potential on a QDM "A" sense line is high, or if the component is commanded "OFF" and the voltage potential on a QDM "A" sense line is low. Either of these conditions will cause the QDM "A" fault line to display "HIGH" and set DTC 26.

On all vehicles, the QDM "A" fault status on the Tech 1 will display "HIGH" with the brake applied or if the engine is not running. On vehicles with a 3T40 transmission, the QDM "A" fault status on the Tech 1 will read "HIGH" until the TCC inline switch is closed. These conditions will not cause DTC 26 to set even though the fault line displays "HIGH." To simulate driving in second gear and change the QDM status to low, disconnect TCC connector and connect a test light between harness terminals "A" and "D".

DTC 26 will set if:
- The system is running in "Closed Loop."
- Brake switch is closed (brake not applied).
- Transaxle in mid or high gear.
- The ECM detects an improper voltage level on a QDM "A" controlled circuit for 10 seconds.

Test Description: Number(s) refer to circled number(s) on the diagnostic chart.
4. This test will determine if the problem is the circuit or the component. As the factory installed ECM is protected with an internal fuse, it is highly unlikely that the ECM needs to be replaced.

86814200

MULTI-PORT FUEL INJECTION — DTC 27

DTC 27
QUAD-DRIVER MODULE (QDM 1) CIRCUIT
2.2L (VIN 4) "A" CARLINE

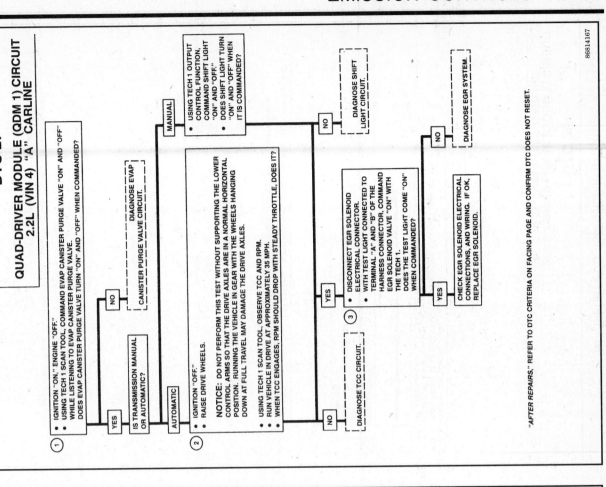

(1)
- IGNITION "ON," ENGINE "OFF."
- USING TECH 1 SCAN TOOL, COMMAND EVAP CANISTER PURGE VALVE "ON" AND "OFF" WHILE LISTENING TO EVAP CANISTER PURGE VALVE.
- DOES EVAP CANISTER PURGE VALVE TURN "ON" AND "OFF" WHEN COMMANDED?

YES | NO

NO → DIAGNOSE EVAP CANISTER PURGE VALVE CIRCUIT.

YES → IS TRANSMISSION MANUAL OR AUTOMATIC?

MANUAL →
- USING TECH 1 OUTPUT CONTROL FUNCTION, COMMAND SHIFT LIGHT "ON" AND "OFF."
- DOES SHIFT LIGHT TURN "ON" AND "OFF" WHEN IT IS COMMANDED?

NO → DIAGNOSE SHIFT LIGHT CIRCUIT.

AUTOMATIC →

(2)
- IGNITION "OFF."
- RAISE DRIVE WHEELS.

NOTICE: DO NOT PERFORM THIS TEST WITHOUT SUPPORTING THE LOWER CONTROL ARMS SO THAT THE DRIVE AXLES ARE IN A NORMAL HORIZONTAL POSITION. RUNNING THE VEHICLE IN GEAR WITH THE WHEELS HANGING DOWN AT FULL TRAVEL MAY DAMAGE THE DRIVE AXLES.

- USING TECH 1 SCAN TOOL, OBSERVE TCC AND RPM.
- RUN VEHICLE IN DRIVE AT APPROXIMATELY 35 MPH. WHEN TCC ENGAGES, RPM SHOULD DROP WITH STEADY THROTTLE, DOES IT?

YES → DIAGNOSE TCC CIRCUIT.

NO →

(3)
- DISCONNECT EGR SOLENOID ELECTRICAL CONNECTOR.
- WITH TEST LIGHT CONNECTED TO TERMINAL "A" AND "B" OF THE HARNESS CONNECTOR, COMMAND EGR SOLENOID VALVE "ON" WITH THE TECH 1.
- DOES THE TEST LIGHT COME "ON" WHEN COMMANDED?

NO → DIAGNOSE EGR SYSTEM.

YES → CHECK EGR SOLENOID ELECTRICAL CONNECTIONS, AND WIRING. IF OK, REPLACE EGR SOLENOID.

"AFTER REPAIRS," REFER TO DTC CRITERIA ON FACING PAGE AND CONFIRM DTC DOES NOT RESET.

86814167

MULTI-PORT FUEL INJECTION — DTC 27

PCM
TCC CONTROL — SENSE LINE — BC2 — 422 TAN/BLK — TO IGNITION SWITCH — TCC
SENSE LINE — 428 DK GRN/WHT — EVAP CANISTER PURGE VALVE — A B — TO IGNITION SWITCH
CANISTER PURGE — SENSE LINE — BC1 — TO IGNITION SWITCH
EGR SOLENOID VALVE — SENSE LINE — BC3 — 435 GRY — EGR SOLENOID VALVE — A B
QDM 1 — FAULT LINE B
6-5-94

DTC 27
QUAD-DRIVER MODULE (QDM 1) CIRCUIT
2.2L (VIN 4) "A" CARLINE

Circuit Description:
The PCM controls most components with electronic switches which complete a ground circuit when turned "ON." These switches are arranged in groups of 4, called Quad-Driver Modules (QDMs) which can independently control up to 4 outputs (PCM terminals), although not all outputs are used. When an output is "ON," the terminal is grounded and its voltage normally will be low. When an output is "OFF," its terminal voltage normally will be high, except for the TCC, as noted below, which depends on the brake and 3rd gear TCC switch.

QDMs are fault protected. If a relay or solenoid coil is shorted, having very low or zero resistance, or if the control side of the circuit is shorted to voltage, it would allow too much current into the QDM. The QDM senses this and the output turns "OFF" or its internal resistance increases to limit current flow and protect the QDM. The result is high output terminal voltage when it should be low. If the circuit from B+ or the component is open, or the control side of the circuit is shorted to ground, terminal voltage will be low, even when output is commanded "OFF." Either of these conditions is considered to be a QDM fault.

QDM 1 has a fault line to indicate the presence of a current fault to the PCM's central processor. A scan tool displays the status of the fault line as "Low" = OK, "High" = fault. Because of the brake and 3rd gear switch in the TCC circuit, DTC 27 is set under different conditions as follows:

DTC 27 Will Set When:
- QDM 1 fault line:
  - Is "high" for 20 seconds or more.
  - TCC is commanded "ON."
  - Battery voltage is greater than 10.5 volts.

Action Taken (PCM will default to): The Malfunction Indicator Lamp (MIL) will illuminate, and the cooling fan will enable.

DTC Chart Test Description: Number(s) below refer to circled number(s) on the diagnostic chart.
1. This checks to see if DTC 27 was set as a result of the EVAP canister purge valve circuit.
2. This checks TCC operation.
3. This checks the integrity of the EGR electrical circuit up to the solenoid.

Diagnostic Aids:
- If DTC 27 is intermittent, check all connections and wiring on QDM 1.

86814166

MULTI-PORT FUEL INJECTION — DTC 28

DTC 28

QUAD-DRIVER MODULE (QDM 2) CIRCUIT
2.2L (VIN 4) "A" CARLINE

86814169

(1) IGNITION "ON," ENGINE "OFF."
USING TECH 1 SCAN OUTPUT CONTROL FUNCTION, COMMAND COOLANT FAN RELAY "ON" AND THEN "OFF."
DOES COOLANT FAN TURN "ON" AND "OFF" WHEN RELAY IS COMMANDED?

- YES → (2)
- NO → DIAGNOSIS COOLANT FAN CIRCUIT.

(2) START ENGINE.
USING TECH 1 SCAN TOOL COMMAND A/C RELAY "ON" AND "OFF."
DOES A/C CLUTCH TURN "ON" AND "OFF" WHEN RELAY IS COMMANDED?

- NO → DIAGNOSE A/C CIRCUIT.
- YES → DTC 28 FAULT IS INTERMITTENT. CHECK FOR POOR TERMINAL CONTACT AT PCM AND QDM 3 CIRCUITRY. CLEAR DTCs AND RECHECK. IF DTC 28 RESETS, REPLACE PCM.

"AFTER REPAIRS," REFER TO DTC CRITERIA ON FACING PAGE AND CONFIRM DTC DOES NOT RESET.

MULTI-PORT FUEL INJECTION — DTC 27

86814168

DTC 28

QUAD-DRIVER MODULE (QDM 2) CIRCUIT
2.2L (VIN 4) "A" CARLINE

Circuit Description:

The Powertrain Control Module (PCM) controls most components with electronic switches which complete a ground circuit when turned "ON." These switches are arranged in groups of 4, called Quad-Driver Modules (QDMs) which can independently control up to 4 outputs (PCM terminals), although not all outputs are used. When an output is "ON," the terminal is grounded and its voltage normally will be low. When an output is "OFF," its terminal voltage normally will be high.

QDMs are fault protected. If a relay or solenoid coil is shorted, having very low or zero resistance, or if the control side of the circuit is shorted to voltage, it would allow too much current into the QDM. The QDM senses this and the output turns "OFF" or its internal resistance increases to limit current flow and protect the QDM. The result is high output terminal voltage when it should be low. If the circuit from B+ or the component is open, or the control side of the circuit is open, or the circuit is shorted to ground, terminal voltage will be low, even when output is commanded "OFF." Either of these conditions is considered to be a QDM fault.

QDM 2 has a fault line to indicate the presence of a current fault to the PCM's central processor. A scan tool displays the status of the fault line as "Low" = OK, "High" = fault.

DTC 28 Will Set When:

- QDM 2 fault line:
  - Is "high" for 20 seconds or more.
  - Battery voltage is greater than 10.5 volts.

Action Taken (PCM will default to): The cooling fan will enable.

DTC Chart Test Description: Number(s) below refer to circled number(s) on the diagnostic chart.

1. This checks the coolant fan circuit.
2. This checks the A/C clutch circuit (if equipped).

Diagnostic Aids:

- A Tech 1 scan tool has the ability to command the coolant fan and A/C clutch relays "ON" and "OFF."
- A faulty connection, or an open CKT 335, 459 or 473 can result in a DTC 28.

CONNECTOR 2 (J-2) PINK 24 PIN A-B CONNECTOR

PIN	WIRE COLOR	CIRCUIT	VOLTAGE KEY "ON"	VOLTAGE ENG. RUN
PA1	BLK/WHT	PCM GROUND	0*	0*
PA2				
PA3	GRY	+5V REFERENCE	5.0	5.0
PA4	GRY	+5V REFERENCE	5.0	5.0
PA5	ORN	KEEP ALIVE MEMORY	B+	B+
PA6				
PA7				
PA8	DK GRN/WHT	FUEL PUMP RELAY	B + (2)	B+
PA9				
PA10				
PA11				
PA12	PPL	O2S SIGNAL	.35 (1)	.1-.9 (1)
PB1	BLK	SENSOR GROUND	0*	0*
PB2	BLK	SENSOR GROUND	0*	0*
PB3	WHT	IGNITION CONTROL A (IC)(1)	0*	.5 (1)
PB4				
PB5				
PB6	TAN	O2S GROUND	0*	0*
PB7	DK BLU	TP SENSOR SIGNAL	.49	.5 (1)
PB8	DK GRN/WHT	4000 P/MI SPEED	8.3 (1)	9.4
PB9	LT GRN	MAP SIGNAL	4.7	1.4 (1)
PB10				
PB11				
PB12				

BLUE 32 PIN C-D CONNECTOR 3 (J-3)

PIN	WIRE COLOR	CIRCUIT	VOLTAGE KEY "ON"	VOLTAGE ENG. RUN
BC1	DK GRN/WHT	EVAP DRIVER	B+	.3
BC2	TAN/BLK	CONTROL/TCC	B+	"OFF"B+ "ON"0*
BC3	GRY	EGR CONTROL	B+	B+
BC4				
BC5	DK GRN	HOT LAMP		
BC6				
BC7				
BC8	BRN/WHT	MIL	0*	"ON"0* "OFF"B+
BC9	DK GRN	CLG FAN RELAY	B+	"ON"B+ "OFF"0*
BC10	DK BLU	AUX. COOLING FAN RELAY	B+	"OFF"B+ "ON"0*
BC11	DK GRN/WHT	A/C CLUTCH RELAY	0*	"OFF"B+ "ON"0*
BC12				
BC13	DK BLU	KNOCK SIGNAL	2.3	2.3
BC14				
BC15				
BC16				
BD1	ORN/BLK	P/N SWITCH		
BD2				
BD3				
BD4				
BD5				
BD6				
BD7				
BD8				
BD9				
BD10				
BD11				
BD12	ORN	DLC SERIES DATA		4.5
BD13	PPL	VSS "LOW"	4.2	0*
BD14	YEL	VSS "HIGH"	0*	0*
BD15				
BD16	PNK	IGNITION FEED	B+	B+

NOTICE: PA1 = PNK CONNECTOR, CAVITY A1, ETC. BC1 BLU CONNECTOR, CAVITY C1, ETC.

(1) VARIES FROM .60 TO BATTERY VOLTAGE DEPENDING ON POSITION OF DRIVE WHEELS.
(2) VARIES.
(3) B+ FIRST TWO SECONDS.
* LESS THAN .5 VOLT.

ENGINE 2.2L LN2
CARLINE - "A"

MULTIPORT FUEL INJECTION PCM CONNECTOR IDENTIFICATION

This PCM voltage chart is for use with a digital voltmeter to further aid in diagnosis. The voltages you get may vary due to low battery charge or other reasons, but they should be very close. The "B +" symbol indicates a nominal system voltage of 12-14 volts.

THE FOLLOWING CONDITIONS MUST BE MET BEFORE TESTING:
- Engine at operating temperature (upper rad. hose hot) • Engine idling in "Closed Loop" (For "Engine Run" column) in park or neutral

CONNECTOR (J1) — 32 PIN C-D CONNECTOR BACK VIEW OF CONNECTOR (PINK), PD1, PC1

CONNECTOR (J2) — 24 PIN A-B CONNECTOR BACK VIEW OF CONNECTOR (PINK), PB1, PA1

CONNECTOR (J3) — 32 PIN C-D CONNECTOR BACK VIEW OF CONNECTOR (BLUE), BD1, BC1

NOTICE: C/D cavity identification is visible on connector body with terminal retainer removed.

CONNECTOR 1 (J1) PINK 32 PIN C-D CONNECTOR

PIN	WIRE COLOR	CIRCUIT	VOLTAGE KEY "ON"	VOLTAGE ENG. RUN
PC1				
PC2				
PC3	LT BLU/WHT	IAC "A" HIGH	NOT USABLE	NOT USABLE
PC4	LT BLU/WHT	IAC "A" LOW	NOT USABLE	NOT USABLE
PC5	LT GRN/BLK	IAC "B" LOW	NOT USABLE	NOT USABLE
PC6	LT GRN/WHT	IAC "B" HIGH	NOT USABLE	NOT USABLE
PC7				
PC8				
PC9	TAN	IAT SIGNAL	2.33	1.5 (3)
PC10	YEL	ECT SIGNAL	1.2 (2)	2.0 (3)
PC11				
PC12	DK GRN	INJ DRIVER 2 & 3	B + (2)	B+
PC13	BLK/WHT	PCM GROUND	0*	0*
PC14				
PC15	ORN	IGNITION CONTROL (IC) MODULE "B"	0*	.5 (1)
PC16	DK BLU	INJ DRIVER 1 & 4	0*	B + (2)
PD1				
PD2	YEL	7X REF SIGNAL	0*	.6
PD3	RED/BLK	A/C REF PRESS SIGNAL		
PD4				
PD5				
PD6				
PD7				
PD8				
PD9				
PD10	ORN	CRANKSHAFT POSITION SENSOR FEED	0	B+
PD11	PPL	BRAKE SWITCH		
PD12	LT GRN	A/C REQUEST	0*	"ON"B+ "OFF"0*
PD13				
PD14	PPL	CKP GROUND	0*	0*
PD15				
PD16	DK BLU			

NOTICE: PC1-Pink connector, cavity C1; BC1-Blue connector, cavity C1, etc.

(1) VARIES.
(2) 12 VOLTS FIRST TWO SECONDS.
(3) VARIES WITH TEMPERATURE.

ENGINE - 2.2L/LN2
CARLINE - "A"

MULTI-PORT FUEL INJECTION DIAGNOSTIC CHARTS

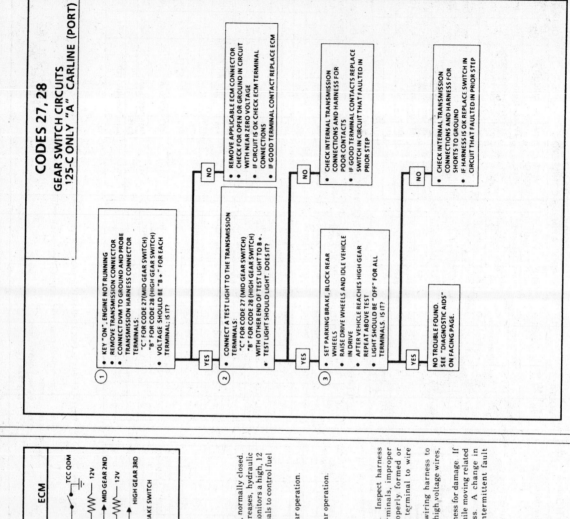

CODES 27, 28
GEAR SWITCH CIRCUITS
3300 (VIN N) 125-C ONLY "A" CARLINE (PORT)

Circuit Description:

The gear switches are located inside the transaxle. They are pressure operated switches, normally closed. The ECM supplies 12 volts through each selected circuit to the switch. As road speed increases, hydraulic pressure applies the specific gear clutches and the gear switch opens. At this time, the ECM monitors a high, 12 volt potential, and interprets this to indicate that gear is applied. The ECM uses the gear signals to control fuel delivery (and TCC)

Code 27 will set if

• CKT 108 indicates ground or closed switch for 10 seconds when vehicle is in 3rd gear operation.
• CKT 108 indicates an open (drive) when the engine is first started.

Code 28 will set if

• CKT 581 indicates ground or closed switch for 10 seconds when vehicle is in 3rd gear operation.
• CKT 581 indicates an open (drive) when the engine is first started.

Test Description: Numbers below refer to circled numbers on the diagnostic chart.

1. Must use a DVM. A test light will not light due to the very low current being supplied by the ECM.
2. Checks to see if circuit is grounded through the switch.
3. Checks for a good, properly operating switch and checks circuit within transaxle for an improper ground

Diagnostic Aids:

An intermittent may be caused by a poor connection, mis-routed harness, rubbed through wire insulation, or a wire broken inside the insulation.

Check For:

• **Poor Connection** at ECM pins. Inspect harness connectors for backed out terminals, improper mating, broken locks, improperly formed or damaged terminals, and poor terminal to wire connection.
• **Mis-routed Harness** Inspect wiring harness to insure that it is not too close to high voltage wires, such as spark plug leads.
• **Damaged Harness** Inspect harness for damage. If harness appears OK, "Scan" while moving related connectors and wiring harness. A change in display would indicate the intermittent fault location.

86814202

MULTI-PORT FUEL INJECTION DIAGNOSTIC CHARTS

CODES 28, 29

GEAR SWITCH CIRCUITS
440-T4 ONLY "A" CARLINE (PORT)

1
- KEY "ON", ENGINE NOT RUNNING
- REMOVE TRANSMISSION CONNECTOR
- CONNECT DVM TO GROUND AND PROBE TRANSMISSION HARNESS CONNECTOR TERMINALS:
  - "C" FOR CODE 28 (MID GEAR SWITCH)
  - "B" FOR CODE 29 (HIGH GEAR SWITCH)
- VOLTAGE SHOULD BE "B +" FOR EACH TERMINAL. IS IT?

(NO) → REMOVE APPLICABLE ECM CONNECTOR CHECK FOR OPEN OR GROUND IN CIRCUIT WITH NEAR ZERO VOLTAGE
- IF CIRCUIT IS OK CHECK ECM TERMINAL CONNECTIONS
- IF GOOD TERMINAL CONTACT REPLACE ECM

(YES) ↓

2
- CONNECT A TEST LIGHT TO THE TRANSMISSION CONNECTOR TERMINALS:
  - "C" FOR CODE 28 (MID GEAR SWITCH)
  - "B" FOR CODE 29 (HIGH GEAR SWITCH)
- WITH OTHER END OF TEST LIGHT TO B +
- TEST LIGHT SHOULD LIGHT. DOES IT?

(NO) → CHECK INTERNAL TRANSMISSION CONNECTIONS AND HARNESS FOR POOR CONTACTS
- IF GOOD TERMINAL CONTACTS REPLACE SWITCH IN CIRCUIT THAT FAULTED IN PRIOR STEP

(YES) ↓

3
- SET PARKING BRAKE, BLOCK REAR WHEELS
- RAISE DRIVE WHEELS AND IDLE VEHICLE IN DRIVE
- AFTER VEHICLE REACHES HIGH GEAR REPEAT ABOVE TEST
- LIGHT SHOULD BE "OFF" FOR ALL TERMINALS. IS IT?

(NO) → CHECK INTERNAL TRANSMISSION CONNECTIONS AND HARNESS FOR SHORTS TO GROUND
- IF HARNESS IS OK REPLACE SWITCH IN CIRCUIT THAT FAULTED IN PRIOR STEP

(YES) ↓

NO TROUBLE FOUND. SEE "DIAGNOSTIC AIDS" ON FACING PAGE.

CODES 28, 29

GEAR SWITCH CIRCUITS
3300 (VIN N) 440-T4 ONLY "A" CARLINE (PORT)

Circuit Description:

The gear switches are located inside the transaxle. They are pressure operated switches, normally closed. The ECM supplies 12 volts through each selected circuit to the switch. As road speed increases, hydraulic pressure applies the specific gear clutches and the gear switch opens. At this time, the ECM monitors a high, 12 volt potential, and interprets this to indicate that gear is applied. The ECM uses the gear signals to control fuel delivery (and TCC).

Code 28 will set if
- CKT 108 indicates ground or closed switch for 10 seconds when vehicle is in 4th gear operation.
- CKT 108 indicates an open (drive) when the engine is first started.

Code 29 will set if
- CKT 446 indicates ground or closed switch for 10 seconds when vehicle is in 4th gear operation.
- CKT 446 indicates an open (drive) when the engine is first started.

Test Description: Numbers below refer to circled numbers on the diagnostic chart.

1. Must use a DVM. A test light will not light due to the very low current being supplied by the ECM.
2. Checks to see if circuit is grounded through the switch.
3. Checks for a good, properly operating switch and checks circuit within transaxle for an improper ground.

Diagnostic Aids:

An intermittent may be caused by a poor connection, mis-routed harness, rubbed through wire insulation, or a wire broken inside the insulation.

Check For:

- **Poor Connection** at ECM pins. Inspect harness connectors for backed out terminals, improper mating, broken locks, improperly formed or damaged terminals, and poor terminal to wire connection.
- **Mis-routed Harness** Inspect wiring harness to insure that it is not too close to high voltage wires, such as spark plug leads.
- **Damaged Harness** Inspect harness for damage. If harness appears OK, "Scan" while moving related connectors and wiring harness. A change in display would indicate the intermittent fault location.

86814203

MULTI-PORT FUEL INJECTION DIAGNOSTIC CHARTS

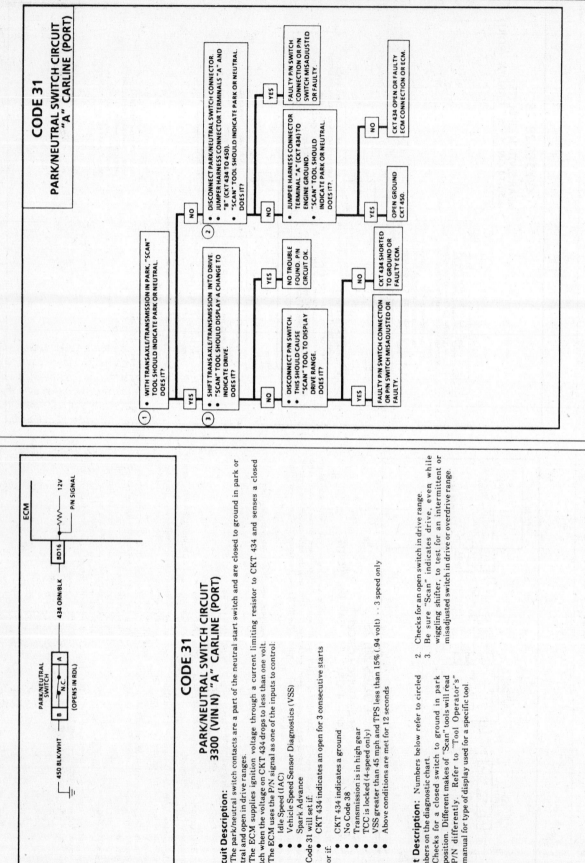

CODE 31

PARK/NEUTRAL SWITCH CIRCUIT
"A" CARLINE (PORT)

CODE 31

PARK/NEUTRAL SWITCH CIRCUIT
3300 (VIN N) "A" CARLINE (PORT)

Circuit Description:

The park/neutral switch contacts are a part of the neutral start switch and are closed to ground in park or neutral and open in drive ranges.

The ECM supplies ignition voltage through a current limiting resistor to CKT 434 drops to less than one volt.

switch when the voltage on CKT 434 drops to less than one volt.

The ECM uses the P/N signal as one of the inputs to control:

- Idle Speed (IAC)
- Vehicle Speed Sensor Diagnostics (VSS)
- Spark Advance

Code 31 will set if:

- CKT 434 indicates an open for 3 consecutive starts

or if:

- CKT 434 indicates a ground
- No Code 38
- Transmission is in high gear
- TCC is locked (4-speed only)
- VSS greater than 45 mph and TPS less than 15% (.94 volt) -- 3 speed only
- Above conditions are met for 12 seconds

Test Description: Numbers below refer to circled numbers on the diagnostic chart.

1. Checks for a closed switch to ground in park position. Different makes of "Scan" tools will read P/N differently. Refer to "Tool Operator's" manual for type of display used for a specific tool.

2. Checks for an open switch in drive range.

3. Be sure "Scan" indicates drive, even while wiggling shifter, to test for an intermittent or misadjusted switch in drive or overdrive range.

86814204

DTC 32
EXHAUST GAS RECIRCULATION (EGR) FLOW CHECK
2.2L (VIN 4) "A" CARLINE

Circuit Description:

A vacuum diaphragm in the EGR valve is connected to a timed vacuum signal port in the throttle body. As the throttle valve is opened, vacuum is applied through an exposed vacuum port to the EGR control solenoid valve. This valve which is located between the throttle body and the EGR valve commands vacuum to the EGR valve based on information from the certain input sensors.

The negative backpressure EGR valve is a normally closed valve and is opened against calibrated spring tension by a negative backpressure. If there is little or no vacuum in the diaphragm chamber from the timed vacuum supply, like idle or wide open throttle, the EGR valve will not open. However, if there is sufficient vacuum in the chamber, the pintle rises off its seat opening the EGR valve and allowing EGR to enter into the intake manifold.

When the EGR valve opens allowing EGR, the backpressure is reduced by interaction with manifold vacuum and creates a slight vacuum. This vacuum opens a control valve bleeding the vacuum from the diaphragm chamber causing the EGR valve to close.

DTC 32 Will Set When: The PCM does not see a change in MAP when EGR test is executed, based on current BARO value under the following conditions:

- Manifold vacuum is between 33 and 60 kPa.
- TCC is locked (A/T).
- VSS is greater than 40 mph.
- DTC(s) 21, 22, 33, or 34 is not set.

Action Taken (PCM will default to): The Malfunction Indicator Lamp (MIL) will illuminate, the EGR system will go into "Open Loop," and the cooling fan will enable.

DTC Chart Test Description: Number(s) below refer to circled number(s) on the diagnostic chart.

1. Intake passage: Shut the engine "OFF" and remove the EGR valve from the manifold. Plug the exhaust side hole with a suitable stopper. Leaving the intake side hole open, attempt to start the engine. If the engine runs at a high idle (up to 3000 RPM is possible) or starts and stalls, the EGR intake passage is not restricted. If the engine starts and idles normally, the EGR intake passage is restricted. Exhaust passage: With EGR valve still removed plug the intake side hole with a suitable stopper. With the exhaust side hole open, check for the presence of exhaust gas. If no exhaust gas is present, the EGR exhaust side passage is restricted.

2. The remaining test checks the ability of the EGR valve to interact with the exhaust system. This system uses a negative backpressure EGR valve which should hold vacuum with engine "OFF." **Be sure shop exhaust hose is not connected during Steps 2 and 3.**

3. When the engine is started, exhaust backpressure at the base of the EGR valve should open the valve's internal bleed and vent the applied vacuum allowing the valve to seat. **Because the shop exhaust hose is not installed at this time, do not allow the engine to run longer than 15 seconds.**

Diagnostic Aids:

- Vacuum lines should be thoroughly checked for proper routing. Refer to "Vehicle Emission Control Information" label.

86814170

Fig. 71 MULTI-PORT FUEL INJECTION — DTC 32

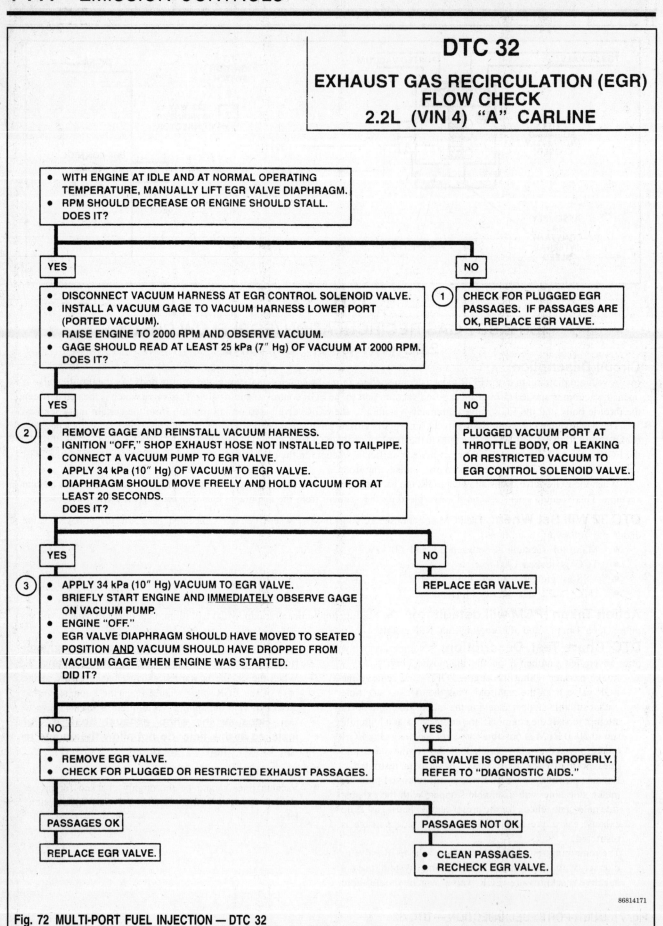

DTC 32

EXHAUST GAS RECIRCULATION (EGR) FLOW CHECK
2.2L (VIN 4) "A" CARLINE

- WITH ENGINE AT IDLE AND AT NORMAL OPERATING TEMPERATURE, MANUALLY LIFT EGR VALVE DIAPHRAGM.
- RPM SHOULD DECREASE OR ENGINE SHOULD STALL. DOES IT?

YES

- DISCONNECT VACUUM HARNESS AT EGR CONTROL SOLENOID VALVE.
- INSTALL A VACUUM GAGE TO VACUUM HARNESS LOWER PORT (PORTED VACUUM).
- RAISE ENGINE TO 2000 RPM AND OBSERVE VACUUM.
- GAGE SHOULD READ AT LEAST 25 kPa (7" Hg) OF VACUUM AT 2000 RPM. DOES IT?

NO

1. CHECK FOR PLUGGED EGR PASSAGES. IF PASSAGES ARE OK, REPLACE EGR VALVE.

YES

2.
- REMOVE GAGE AND REINSTALL VACUUM HARNESS.
- IGNITION "OFF," SHOP EXHAUST HOSE NOT INSTALLED TO TAILPIPE.
- CONNECT A VACUUM PUMP TO EGR VALVE.
- APPLY 34 kPa (10" Hg) OF VACUUM TO EGR VALVE.
- DIAPHRAGM SHOULD MOVE FREELY AND HOLD VACUUM FOR AT LEAST 20 SECONDS. DOES IT?

NO

PLUGGED VACUUM PORT AT THROTTLE BODY, OR LEAKING OR RESTRICTED VACUUM TO EGR CONTROL SOLENOID VALVE.

YES

3.
- APPLY 34 kPa (10" Hg) VACUUM TO EGR VALVE.
- BRIEFLY START ENGINE AND IMMEDIATELY OBSERVE GAGE ON VACUUM PUMP.
- ENGINE "OFF."
- EGR VALVE DIAPHRAGM SHOULD HAVE MOVED TO SEATED POSITION AND VACUUM SHOULD HAVE DROPPED FROM VACUUM GAGE WHEN ENGINE WAS STARTED. DID IT?

NO

REPLACE EGR VALVE.

NO

- REMOVE EGR VALVE.
- CHECK FOR PLUGGED OR RESTRICTED EXHAUST PASSAGES.

YES

EGR VALVE IS OPERATING PROPERLY. REFER TO "DIAGNOSTIC AIDS."

PASSAGES OK

REPLACE EGR VALVE.

PASSAGES NOT OK

- CLEAN PASSAGES.
- RECHECK EGR VALVE.

86814171

Fig. 72 MULTI-PORT FUEL INJECTION — DTC 32

DTC 33
MANIFOLD ABSOLUTE PRESSURE (MAP) SENSOR CIRCUIT
(SIGNAL VOLTAGE HIGH - LOW VACUUM)
2.2L (VIN 4) "A" CARLINE

Circuit Description:

The Manifold Absolute Pressure (MAP) sensor changes resistance based on manifold vacuum. The Powertrain Control Module (PCM) supplies a 5 volt reference and a ground. The MAP sensor voltage varies from 1.0 to 1.5V at idle (high vacuum) to 4.0-4.5V at wide open throttle (low vacuum). The MAP sensor is also used to measure barometric pressure, which allows the PCM to make adjustments for altitude changes.

DTC 33 Will Set When:
- MAP is greater than 80 kPa.
- TP sensor is less than 12%.
- VSS is less than 1 mph.
- DTC 21 or 22 is not set.
- Above conditions are met for 10 seconds.

Action Taken (PCM will default to): The Malfunction Indicator Lamp (MIL) will illuminate. The PCM will substitute a fixed MAP value and use the Throttle Position (TP) sensor to control fuel delivery. The cooling fan will enable.

DTC Chart Test Description: Number(s) below refer to circled number(s) on the diagnostic chart.
1. This step will determine if DTC 33 is the result of a hard failure or an intermittent condition.
2. This step simulates conditions for a DTC 34. If the PCM recognizes the change, the PCM, CKT 474 and CKT 432 are OK. If CKT 452 is open, there may also be a stored DTC 23.

Diagnostic Aids:
- With the ignition "ON" and the engine "OFF," the manifold pressure is equal to atmospheric pressure and the signal voltage will be high. This information is used by the PCM as an indication of vehicle altitude. Comparison of this reading with a known good vehicle with the same sensor is a good way to check accuracy of a "suspect" sensor. Readings should be the same ± .4 volt.
- Disconnect sensor from bracket and twist sensor by hand (only) to check for intermittent connections. Output changes greater than .1 volt indicates a bad connector or connection. If OK, replace sensor.

86814172

Fig. 73 MULTI-PORT FUEL INJECTION — DTC 33

DTC 33

MANIFOLD ABSOLUTE PRESSURE (MAP) SENSOR CIRCUIT
(SIGNAL VOLTAGE HIGH - LOW VACUUM)
2.2L (VIN 4) "A" CARLINE

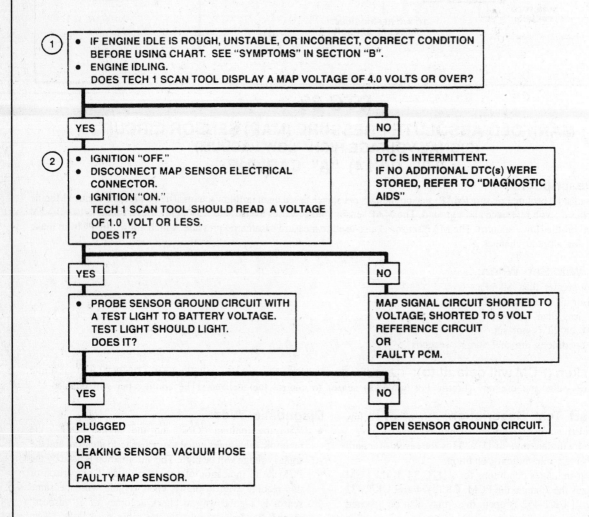

① ● IF ENGINE IDLE IS ROUGH, UNSTABLE, OR INCORRECT, CORRECT CONDITION BEFORE USING CHART. SEE "SYMPTOMS" IN SECTION "B".
● ENGINE IDLING.
DOES TECH 1 SCAN TOOL DISPLAY A MAP VOLTAGE OF 4.0 VOLTS OR OVER?

YES

NO

②
● IGNITION "OFF."
● DISCONNECT MAP SENSOR ELECTRICAL CONNECTOR.
● IGNITION "ON."
TECH 1 SCAN TOOL SHOULD READ A VOLTAGE OF 1.0 VOLT OR LESS.
DOES IT?

DTC IS INTERMITTENT.
IF NO ADDITIONAL DTC(s) WERE STORED, REFER TO "DIAGNOSTIC AIDS"

YES

NO

● PROBE SENSOR GROUND CIRCUIT WITH A TEST LIGHT TO BATTERY VOLTAGE.
TEST LIGHT SHOULD LIGHT.
DOES IT?

MAP SIGNAL CIRCUIT SHORTED TO VOLTAGE, SHORTED TO 5 VOLT REFERENCE CIRCUIT
OR
FAULTY PCM.

YES

NO

PLUGGED
OR
LEAKING SENSOR VACUUM HOSE
OR
FAULTY MAP SENSOR.

OPEN SENSOR GROUND CIRCUIT.

"*AFTER REPAIRS,*" REFER TO DTC CRITERIA ON FACING PAGE AND CONFIRM DTC DOES NOT RESET.

86814173

Fig. 74 MULTI-PORT FUEL INJECTION — DTC 33

DTC 34
MANIFOLD ABSOLUTE PRESSURE (MAP) SENSOR CIRCUIT
(SIGNAL VOLTAGE LOW - HIGH VACUUM)
2.2L (VIN 4) "A" CARLINE

Circuit Description:
The Manifold Absolute Pressure (MAP) sensor changes resistance based on manifold vacuum. The Powertrain Control Module (PCM) supplies a 5 volt reference and a ground. The MAP sensor voltage varies from 1.0 to 1.5V at idle (high vacuum) to 4.0-4.5V at wide open throttle (low vacuum). The MAP sensor is also used to measure barometric pressure, which allows the PCM to make adjustments for altitude changes.

DTC 34 Will Set When:
- DTC 21 is not set.
- MAP is less than 14 kPa.
- Engine speed is less than 1200 RPM or TP sensor is greater than 15.2%.
- Above conditions are met for .2 second.

Action Taken (PCM will default to):
The Malfunction Indicator Lamp (MIL) will illuminate. The PCM will substitute a fixed MAP value and use the Throttle Position (TP) sensor to control fuel delivery. The cooling fan will enable.

DTC Chart Test Description:
Number(s) below refer to circled number(s) on the diagnostic chart.
1. This step determines if <u>DTC 34</u> is the result of a hard failure or an intermittent condition.
2. Jumpering harness terminals "B" to "C" (5 volts to signal circuit) will determine if the sensor is at fault, or if there is a problem with the PCM or wiring.
3. The Tech 1 scan tool may not display 5 volts. The important thing is that the PCM recognizes the voltage as more than 4 volts, indicating that the PCM and CKT 432 are OK.

Diagnostic Aids:
- With the ignition "ON" and the engine "OFF," the manifold pressure is equal to atmospheric pressure and the signal voltage will be high. This information is used by the PCM as an indication of vehicle altitude.
- Comparison of this reading with a known good vehicle with the same sensor is a good way to check accuracy of a "suspect" sensor. Readings should be the same ± .4 volt.
- Disconnect sensor from bracket and twist sensor by hand (only) to check for intermittent connections. Output changes greater than .1 volt indicates a bad connector or connection. If OK, replace sensor.

86814174

Fig. 75 MULTI-PORT FUEL INJECTION — DTC 34

DTC 34

MANIFOLD ABSOLUTE PRESSURE (MAP) SENSOR CIRCUIT
(SIGNAL VOLTAGE LOW - HIGH VACUUM)
2.2L (VIN 4) "A" CARLINE

1
- ENGINE IDLING.
  DOES SCAN TOOL DISPLAY MAP VOLTAGE BELOW .25 VOLT?

YES

NO

2
- IGNITION "OFF."
- DISCONNECT SENSOR ELECTRICAL CONNECTOR.
- JUMPER HARNESS TERMINALS "B" TO "C".
- IGNITION "ON."
- MAP VOLTAGE SHOULD READ OVER 4.7 VOLTS.
  DOES IT?

DTC IS INTERMITTENT. IF NO ADDITIONAL DTC(s) WERE STORED, REFER TO "DIAGNOSTIC AIDS"

NO

YES

3
- IGNITION "OFF."
- REMOVE JUMPER WIRE.
- PROBE TERMINAL "B" WITH A TEST LIGHT TO BATTERY VOLTAGE.
- IGNITION "ON."
- SCAN TOOL SHOULD READ OVER 4 VOLTS.
  DOES IT?

FAULTY CONNECTION
OR
SENSOR.

YES

NO

5 VOLT REFERENCE CIRCUIT OPEN
OR
SHORTED TO GROUND
OR
FAULTY CONTROL MODULE.

SIGNAL CIRCUIT OPEN
OR
SIGNAL CIRCUIT SHORTED TO GROUND
OR
SIGNAL CIRCUIT SHORTED TO SENSOR GROUND
OR
FAULTY CONTROL MODULE.

"*AFTER REPAIRS*," REFER TO DTC CRITERIA ON FACING PAGE AND CONFIRM DTC DOES NOT RESET.

86814175

Fig. 76 MULTI-PORT FUEL INJECTION — DTC 34

DTC 35
IDLE SPEED ERROR
2.2L (VIN 4) "A" CARLINE

Circuit Description:

The Powertrain Control Module (PCM) controls idle speed to a calculated, "desired" RPM based on sensor inputs and actual engine RPM, determined by the time between successive 7X reference pulses from the ignition control. The PCM uses 4 circuits to move an Idle Air Control (IAC) valve, which allows varying amounts of air to flow into the intake manifold, controlling idle speed.

DTC 35 Will Set When:
- Engine speed is 175 RPM more or 200 RPM less than "desired idle."
- TP sensor angle indicates throttle is open less than 1%.
- IAC steps must be less than 10, or greater than 140.
- All above conditions are continuously met for 10 seconds or more.

Action Taken (PCM will default to):
The Malfunction Indicator Lamp (MIL) will illuminate, and the cooling fan will enable.

DTC Chart Test Description:
Number(s) below refer to circled number(s) on the diagnostic chart.

1. The Tech 1 scan tool is used to extend and retract the IAC valve. Valve movement is verified by an engine speed change. If no change in engine speed occurs, the valve can be retested when removed from the throttle body.

2. This step checks the quality of the IAC valve movement in Step 1. Between 900 RPM and about 1500 RPM, the engine speed should change smoothly with each flash of the test light in both extended and retracted position. If the IAC valve is retracted beyond the control range (about 1500 RPM), it may take many flashes in the extend position before engine speed will begin to drop. This is normal on certain engines. Fully extending the IAC valve may cause the engine to stall. This may be normal. Step 1 verifies proper IAC valve operation while this step checks the IAC valve circuits. Each lamp on the node light should flash red and green while the IAC valve is cycled. The sequence of color is not important. If either light is "OFF" or does not flash red and green, check the circuits for faults, beginning with poor terminal contact.

Diagnostic Aids:
- Check for vacuum leaks, disconnected or brittle vacuum hoses, cuts, etc. Examine manifold and throttle body gaskets for proper seal.
- Check for cracked intake manifold.
- Check open, shorts, chafed insulation or poor connections to IAC valve in CKTs 1747, 1748, 1749 and 444.
- An IAC valve which is stopped and cannot respond to the PCM, a throttle stop screw which has been tampered with, a damaged throttle body or linkage could cause a DTC 35.
- If DTC 35 is set and speedometer is not accurately reflecting correct vehicle speed, refer to DTC 24 (vehicle speed sensor circuit) diagnostics.

86814176

Fig. 77 MULTI-PORT FUEL INJECTION — DTC 35

DTC 35
IDLE SPEED ERROR
2.2L (VIN 4) "A" CARLINE

(1)
- INSTALL TECH 1 SCAN TOOL.
- ENGINE AT NORMAL OPERATING TEMPERATURE IN PARK/NEUTRAL WITH PARKING BRAKE SET.
- A/C "OFF."
- SELECT RPM CONTROL. (MISC. TESTS)
- CYCLE IAC VALVE THROUGH ITS RANGE FROM 900 RPM UP TO 1500 RPM. RPM SHOULD CHANGE SMOOTHLY. DOES IT?

NO

YES

(2)
- INSTALL IAC NODE LIGHT * IN IAC VALVE HARNESS.
- ENGINE RUNNING. CYCLE IAC VALVE WITH TECH 1 SCAN TOOL. EACH NODE LIGHT SHOULD CYCLE RED AND GREEN BUT NEVER "OFF." DO THEY?

- USING THE IAC DRIVER * OR OTHER CONVENIENT CONNECTOR, CHECK RESISTANCE ACROSS IAC VALVE COILS. SHOULD BE 40 TO 80 OHMS BETWEEN IAC VALVE TERMINALS "A" TO "B" AND "C" TO "D".

NO

IF CIRCUIT(S) DID NOT TEST RED AND GREEN, CHECK FOR:
- FAULTY CONNECTOR TERMINAL CONTACTS.
- OPEN CIRCUITS INCLUDING CONNECTORS.
- CIRCUITS SHORTED TO GROUND OR VOLTAGE. FAULTY PCM CONNECTIONS OR REPLACE PCM. REPAIR AS NECESSARY AND RETEST.

YES

- CHECK IAC VALVE CONNECTIONS.
- CHECK IAC VALVE PASSAGES. IF OK, REPLACE IAC VALVE.

OK

- CHECK RESISTANCE BETWEEN IAC VALVE TERMINALS "B" AND "C" AND "A" AND "D". SHOULD BE INFINITE.

NOT OK

REPLACE IAC VALVE AND RETEST.

OK

IDLE AIR CONTROL VALVE CIRCUIT OK. REFER TO "DIAGNOSTIC AIDS"

NOT OK

REPLACE IAC VALVE AND RETEST.

* IAC DRIVER AND NODE LIGHT REQUIRED KIT
222-L FROM: CONCEPT TECHNOLOGY, INC.
J 37027 FROM: KENT-MOORE, INC.

"AFTER REPAIRS," REFER TO DTC CRITERIA ON FACING PAGE AND CONFIRM DTC DOES NOT RESET.

86814177

Fig. 78 MULTI-PORT FUEL INJECTION — DTC 35

MULTI-PORT FUEL INJECTION DIAGNOSTIC CHARTS

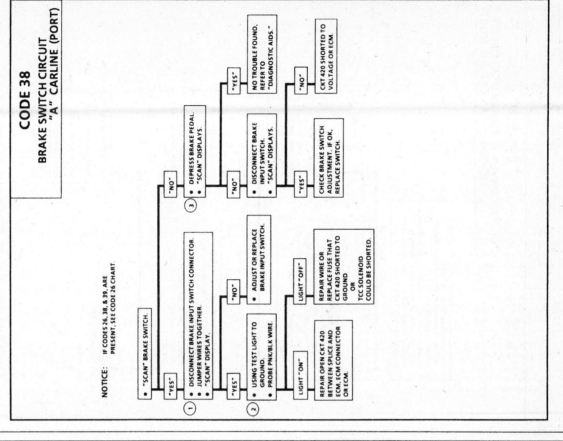

CODE 38
BRAKE SWITCH CIRCUIT "A" CARLINE (PORT)

NOTICE: IF CODES 26, 38, & 39, ARE PRESENT, SEE CODE 26 CHART.

CODE 38
BRAKE SWITCH CIRCUIT
3300 (VIN N) "A" CARLINE (PORT)

Circuit Description:
The ECM monitors the status of the brake switch circuits through ECM terminal "BC4".
Code 38 will set if:
- No Code 24 is present
- Status of CKT 420 has not changed state "high" to "low"
- Vehicle speed has been above 35 mph and back to 0 mph several (22) or more times

Test Description: Numbers below refer to circled numbers on the diagnostic chart.
1. By jumpering the brake switch this will determine if the ECM and the wiring for the brake circuit are OK.
2. Verifies the voltage to brake switch.
3. Test the brake switch for proper operation or misadjustment.

Diagnostic Aids:
- A Code 38 in combination with a Code 39 would mean a problem with one or more of the following components.
- Fuse, CKT 639, brake switch or wire before the splice.
- A single Code 38 is the result of a wire or CKT 420 problem between the splice and the ECM, poor connection to ECM connector, or possibly the ECM.

86814205

MULTI-PORT FUEL INJECTION DIAGNOSTIC CHARTS

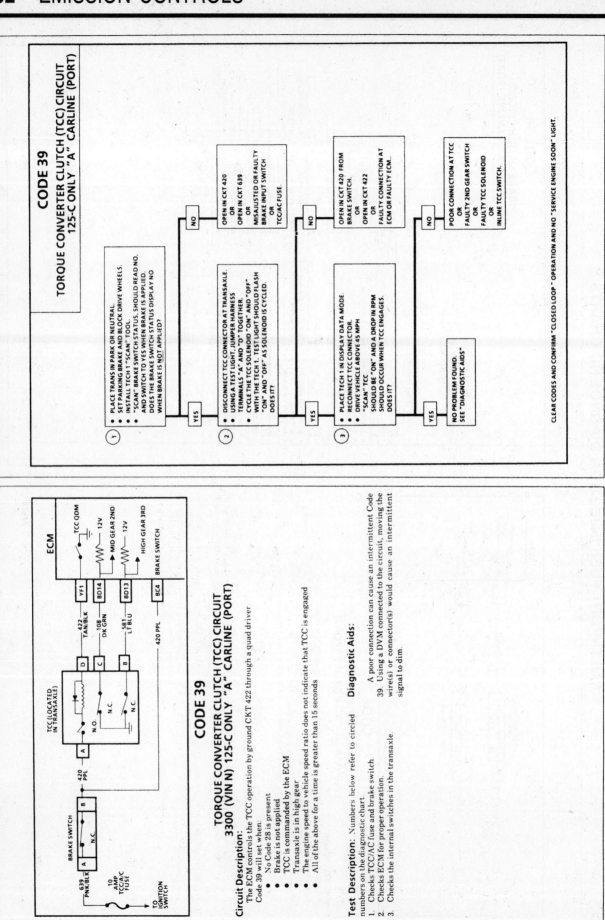

CODE 39

TORQUE CONVERTER CLUTCH (TCC) CIRCUIT
125-C ONLY "A" CARLINE (PORT)

CODE 39

TORQUE CONVERTER CLUTCH (TCC) CIRCUIT
3300 (VIN N) 125-C ONLY "A" CARLINE (PORT)

Circuit Description:
The ECM controls the TCC operation by ground CKT 422 through a quad driver.
Code 39 will set when:
• No Code 28 is present
• Brake is not applied
• TCC is commanded by the ECM
• Transaxle is in high gear
• The engine speed to vehicle speed ratio does not indicate that TCC is engaged
• All of the above for a time is greater than 15 seconds

Test Description: Numbers below refer to circled numbers on the diagnostic chart.
1. Checks TCC/AC fuse and brake switch.
2. Checks ECM for proper operation.
3. Checks the internal switches in the transaxle.

Diagnostic Aids:
A poor connection can cause an intermittent Code 39. Using a DVM connected to the circuit, moving the wire(s) or connector(s) would cause an intermittent signal to dim.

---

① • PLACE TRANS IN PARK OR NEUTRAL.
  • SET PARKING BRAKE AND BLOCK DRIVE WHEELS.
  • INSTALL TECH 1 "SCAN" TOOL.
  • "SCAN" BRAKE SWITCH STATUS. SHOULD READ NO. AND SWITCH TO YES WHEN BRAKE IS APPLIED.
  DOES THE BRAKE SWITCH STATUS DISPLAY NO WHEN BRAKE IS *NOT* APPLIED?

YES → ② • DISCONNECT TCC CONNECTOR AT TRANSAXLE.
  • USING A TEST LIGHT, JUMPER HARNESS TERMINALS "A" AND "D" TOGETHER.
  • CYCLE THE TCC SOLENOID "ON" AND "OFF" WITH THE TECH 1. TEST LIGHT SHOULD FLASH "ON" AND "OFF" AS SOLENOID IS CYCLED.
  DOES IT?

YES → ③ • PLACE TECH 1 IN DISPLAY DATA MODE.
  • RECONNECT TCC CONNECTOR.
  • DRIVE VEHICLE ABOVE 45 MPH
  • "SCAN" TCC
  SHOULD BE "ON" AND A DROP IN RPM SHOULD OCCUR WHEN TCC ENGAGES.
  DOES IT?

YES → NO PROBLEM FOUND.
  SEE "DIAGNOSTIC AIDS"

NO → OPEN IN CKT 420
  OR
  OPEN IN CKT 639
  OR
  MISAJUSTED OR FAULTY BRAKE INPUT SWITCH
  OR
  TCC/AC FUSE.

NO → OPEN IN CKT 420 FROM BRAKE SWITCH.
  OR
  OPEN IN CKT 422
  OR
  FAULTY CONNECTION AT ECM OR FAULTY ECM.

NO → POOR CONNECTION AT TCC
  OR
  FAULTY 2ND GEAR SWITCH
  OR
  FAULTY TCC SOLENOID
  OR
  INLINE TCC SWITCH.

CLEAR CODES AND CONFIRM "CLOSED LOOP" OPERATION AND NO "SERVICE ENGINE SOON" LIGHT.

86814206

MULTI-PORT FUEL INJECTION DIAGNOSTIC CHARTS

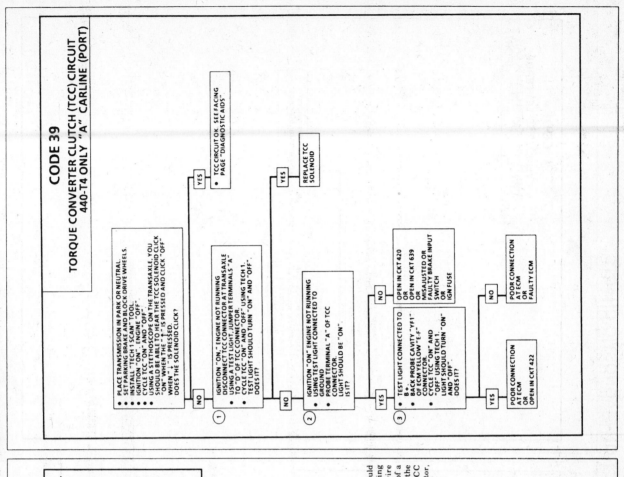

CODE 39
TORQUE CONVERTER CLUTCH (TCC) CIRCUIT 440-T4 ONLY "A" CARLINE (PORT)

- PLACE TRANSMISSION IN PARK OR NEUTRAL.
- SET PARKING BRAKE AND BLOCK DRIVE WHEELS.
- INSTALL "TECH 1 SCAN" TOOL.
- IGNITION "ON", ENGINE "OFF".
- CYCLE TCC "ON" AND "OFF".
- USING A STETHOSCOPE ON THE TRANSAXLE, YOU SHOULD BE ABLE TO HEAR THE TCC SOLENOID CLICK "ON" WHEN THE TCC IS PRESSED AND CLICK "OFF" WHEN "1" PRESSED.

DOES THE SOLENOID CLICK?

YES → TCC CIRCUIT OK. SEE FACING PAGE "DIAGNOSTIC AIDS".

NO (1)
- IGNITION "ON", ENGINE NOT RUNNING
- DISCONNECT TCC CONNECTOR AT TRANSAXLE
- USING A TEST LIGHT, JUMPER TERMINALS "A" TO "D" OF TCC CONNECTOR.
- CYCLE TCC "ON" AND "OFF" USING TECH 1.

TEST LIGHT SHOULD TURN "ON" AND "OFF". DOES IT?

YES → REPLACE TCC SOLENOID

NO (2)
- IGNITION "ON" ENGINE NOT RUNNING
- TEST LIGHT CONNECTED TO GROUND
- PROBE TERMINAL "A" OF TCC CONNECTOR.

LIGHT SHOULD BE "ON". IS IT?

YES (3)
- TEST LIGHT CONNECTED TO B+.
- BACK PROBE CAVITY "YF1" OF ECM YELLOW "E.F." CONNECTOR.
- CYCLE TCC "ON" AND "OFF" USING TECH 1.

LIGHT SHOULD TURN "ON". DOES IT?

NO → OPEN IN CKT 420 OR OPEN IN CKT 639 OR MISADJUSTED OR FAULTY BRAKE INPUT SWITCH OR IGN FUSE

NO → POOR CONNECTION AT ECM OR FAULTY ECM

YES → POOR CONNECTION AT ECM OR OPEN IN CKT 422

CODE 39
TORQUE CONVERTER CLUTCH (TCC) CIRCUIT 3300 (VIN N) 440-T4 ONLY "A" CARLINE (PORT)

Circuit Description:

The ECM controls TCC operation by grounding CKT 422 through the quad-driver.

Code 39 will set when

- No Code 28 & 29 is present
- Brake switch is closed, "OFF"
- TCC is commanded by the ECM
- Vehicle is in high gear (4th)
- The engine speed to vehicle speed ratio does not indicate that TCC is engaged
- All of the above for a time greater than 15 seconds

Test Description: Numbers below refer to circled numbers on the diagnostic chart.

1. Checks fuse, brake switch and B+ circuit to the TCC solenoid.
2. Checks availability of B+ on CKT 420.
3. Checks the ECM for proper operation.

Diagnostic Aids:

A Code 39 in combination with a Code 38 would mean a problem with one or more of the following components. Fuse, CKT 639, brake switch or wire before the splice. A single Code 39 is the result of a wire or CKT 420 problem between the splice and the TCC solenoid, CKT 422 problem between TCC solenoid and ECM, poor connection to ECM connector, or possibly the ECM.

4-27-89

86814207

MULTI-PORT FUEL INJECTION DIAGNOSTIC CHARTS

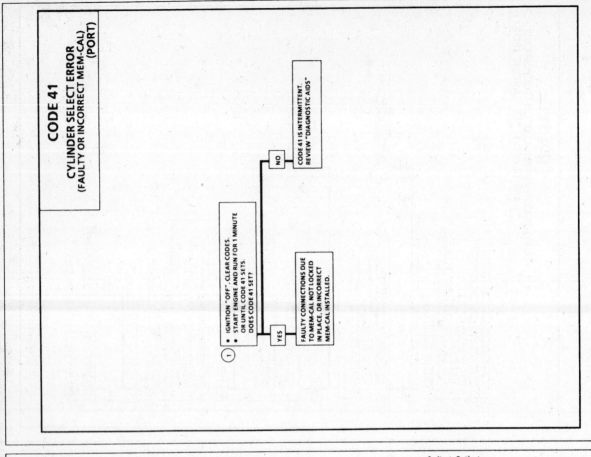

CODE 41
CYLINDER SELECT ERROR
(FAULTY OR INCORRECT MEM-CAL)
(PORT)

1 • IGNITION "OFF", CLEAR CODES.
• START ENGINE AND RUN FOR 1 MINUTE
OR UNTIL CODE 41 SETS.
DOES CODE 41 SET?

YES
FAULTY CONNECTIONS DUE
TO MEM-CAL NOT LOCKED
IN PLACE, OR INCORRECT
MEM-CAL INSTALLED.

NO
CODE 41 IS INTERMITTENT.
REVIEW "DIAGNOSTIC AIDS"

ACCESS COVER

MEM-CAL

ECM ASSEMBLY

9-21-87

CODE 41
CYLINDER SELECT ERROR
(FAULTY OR INCORRECT MEM-CAL)
3.1L (VIN T)   (PORT)

Test Description: Numbers below refer to circled
numbers on the diagnostic chart.
1. The ECM used for this engine can also be used for
other engines, and the difference is in the Mem-
Cal. If a Code 41 sets, the incorrect Mem-Cal has
been installed, or it is faulty and must be
replaced.

Diagnostic Aids:

Check Mem-Cal to be sure locking tabs are secure.
Also check the pins on both the Mem-Cal and ECM to
assure they are making proper contact.   Check the
Mem-Cal part number to assure it is the correct part.
If the Mem-Cal is faulty it must be replaced. It is also
possible that the ECM is faulty, however, it should not
be replaced until all of the above have been checked.
For additional information, refer to "Intermittents"

86814208

MULTI-PORT FUEL INJECTION DIAGNOSTIC CHARTS

CODE 42
ELECTRONIC SPARK TIMING (EST) CIRCUIT (PORT)

(1)
• CLEAR CODES.
• IDLE ENGINE FOR 1 MINUTE OR UNTIL CODE 42 SETS. DOES CODE 42 SET?

NO → CODE 42 INTERMITTENT. REFER TO "DIAGNOSTIC AIDS"

(2)
• IGNITION "OFF."
• DISCONNECT ECM CONNECTORS.
• IGNITION "ON."
• SET OHMMETER SELECTOR SWITCH IN THE 1000 TO 2000 OHMS RANGE.
• GROUND THE BLACK (−) OHMMETER LEAD
• PROBE ECM HARNESS EST. CIRCUIT USING THE RED (+) OHMMETER LEAD. THE OHMMETER SHOULD READ LESS THAN 500 OHMS. DOES IT?

NO → PROBE ECM HARNESS CONNECTOR CKT 424 WITH A TEST LIGHT TO BATTERY VOLTAGE AND OBSERVE LIGHT.

LIGHT "ON" → OPEN CKT 423, FAULTY CONNECTION, OR FAULTY IGNITION MODULE.

(3)
• WITH OHMMETER STILL CONNECTED TO ECM HARNESS CKT 423 AND GROUND AS DESCRIBED IN STEP #2, AGAIN PROBE ECM HARNESS CKT 424 WITH THE TEST LIGHT CONNECTED TO BATTERY VOLTAGE. AS TEST LIGHT CONTACTS CKT 424, RESISTANCE SHOULD SWITCH FROM HUNDREDS TO THOUSANDS OHMS. DOES IT?

LIGHT "OFF" → DISCONNECT IGNITION MODULE 6-WAY CONNECTOR.

LIGHT "OFF" → CKT 424 SHORTED TO GROUND

LIGHT "ON" → REPLACE IGNITION MODULE.

(4)
• DISCONNECT DIS 6-WAY CONNECTOR. NOTE OHMMETER THAT IS STILL CONNECTED TO CKT 423 AND GROUND. RESISTANCE SHOULD HAVE BECOME VERY HIGH (OPEN CIRCUIT). DOES IT?

NO → CKT 423 SHORTED TO GROUND.

YES → CKT 424 OPEN, FAULTY CONNECTIONS, OR FAULTY IGNITION MODULE.

(5)
• RECONNECT ECM AND IDLE ENGINE FOR ONE MINUTE OR UNTIL CODE 42 SETS. DOES CODE 42 SET?

YES → REPLACE ECM.

NO → CODE 42 INTERMITTENT. REFER TO "DIAGNOSTIC AIDS"

CLEAR CODES AND CONFIRM "CLOSED LOOP" OPERATION AND NO "SERVICE ENGINE SOON" LIGHT.

CODE 42
ELECTRONIC SPARK TIMING (EST) CIRCUIT 3.1L (VIN T)

Circuit Description:
When the system is running on the ignition module, that is, no voltage on the bypass line, the ignition module grounds the EST signal. The ECM expects to see no voltage on the EST line during this condition. If it sees a voltage, it sets Code 42 and will not go into the EST mode.

When the rpm for EST is reached (about 200 rpm), and bypass voltage applied, the EST should no longer be grounded in the ignition module so the EST voltage should be varying.

If the bypass line is open or grounded, the ignition module will not switch to EST mode, so the EST voltage will be low and Code 42 will be set.

If the EST line is grounded, the ignition module will switch to EST, but because the line is grounded, there will be no EST signal. A Code 42 will be set.

Test Description: Numbers below refer to circled numbers on the diagnostic chart.
1. Code 42 means the ECM has seen an open or short to ground in the EST or bypass circuits. This test confirms Code 42 and that the fault causing the code is present.
2. Checks for a normal EST ground path through the ignition module. An EST CKT 423 shorted to ground will also read less than 500 ohms. however, this will be checked later
3. As the test light voltage touches CKT 424, the module should switch causing the ohmmeter to "overrange" if the meter is in the 1000-2000 ohms position. Selecting the 10-20,000 ohms position will indicate above 5000 ohms. The important thing is that the module "switched." The module did not switch and this step checks for

• EST CKT 423 shorted to ground
• Bypass CKT 424 open
• Faulty ignition module connection or module

5. Confirms that Code 42 is a faulty ECM and not an intermittent in CKTs 423 or 424.

Diagnostic Aids:
The "Scan" tool does not have any ability to help diagnose a Code 42 problem.

A Mem-Cal not fully seated in the ECM can result in a Code 42.

86814209

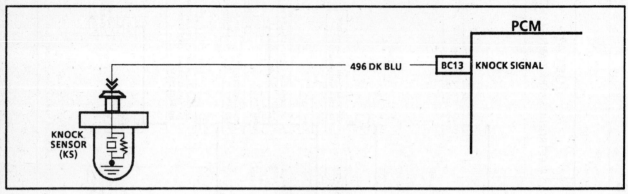

DTC 43
KNOCK SENSOR (KS) CIRCUIT
2.2L (VIN 4) "A" CARLINE

Circuit Description:

The knock sensor detects engine detonation and the Powertrain Control Module (PCM) retards the electronic spark timing based on the signal being received. The knock sensor produces an AC signal which is used for knock detection. The amplitude and signal frequency are dependent upon the knock level.

The PCM performs two tests on this circuit to determine if it is operating correctly.

DTC 43 Will Set When:
- ECT is above 56°C (133°F).
- TP angle is above 4.7%.
- Engine speed is between 2200 and 6375 RPM.
- There is an indication of knock for more than 4 seconds over a 6 second interval.
- Knock sensor activity does not increase with engine speed.

Action Taken (PCM will default to): The Malfunction Indicator Lamp (MIL) will illuminate, ignition timing will default to 3.95 degrees and the cooling fans will enable.

DTC Chart Test Description: Number(s) below refer to circled number(s) on the diagnostic chart.

1. If the conditions for the test as described above are met, DTC 43 will set and the MIL (Service Engine Soon) will be illuminated.
2. If the engines has an internal problem which is creating a knock, the knock sensor may be responding to the mechanical noise.
3. The Tech 1 scan tool displays knock sensor activity in counts, approximately 50 at idle. The counts should rise when engine speed increases or fall when engine speed decreases. This step checks knock sensor activity
4. This checks that the internal resistance of the knock sensor is within an acceptable range.
5. Check the knock sensor connection for loose terminals or corrosion. A faulty connection will set a DTC 43.

Diagnostic Aids:
- Mechanical engine knock can also cause a knock sensor signal. Abnormal engine noise must be corrected before using this chart.
- Check CKT 496 for a potential open or short to ground.
- Any circuit, that is suspected of causing the intermittent complaint, should be thoroughly checked for backed out terminals, broken locks or physical damage to the wiring harness.

86814178

Fig. 79 MULTI-PORT FUEL INJECTION — DTC 43

DTC 43
KNOCK SENSOR (KS) CIRCUIT
2.2L (VIN 4) "A" CARLINE

1
- START ENGINE.
- RUN ENGINE AT SLIGHTLY GREATER THAN 10% THROTTLE. IS THE MIL (SERVICE ENGINE SOON) ILLUMINATED?

YES

ARE ANY ADDITIONAL DTC(s) STORED?

NO

DTC IS INTERMITTENT. REFER TO "DIAGNOSTIC AIDS"

NO

YES

2 LISTEN TO ENGINE WHILE RAISING AND LOWERING ENGINE SPEED. IS AUDIBLE KNOCK PRESENT?

PROCEED TO STORED DTC CHARTS.

NO

YES

3 USING TECH 1 SCAN TOOL, OBSERVE KNOCK SENSOR ACTIVITY WHILE INCREASING ENGINE SPEED TO 2500 RPM. KNOCK SENSOR ACTIVITY SHOULD INCREASE WITH ENGINE SPEED. DOES IT?

REPAIR BASIC ENGINE PROBLEM AND REPEAT STEP #1.

NO

YES

4
- IGNITION "OFF."
- WITH A DVM CONNECTED TO GROUND, MEASURE THE RESISTANCE AT PCM CONNECTOR CAVITY. RESISTANCE SHOULD BE BETWEEN 90K-110K OHMS. IS IT?

CHECK FOR A FAULTY PCM CONNECTION. IF OK, REPLACE EPROM. IF CONDITION STILL EXISTS, REPLACE PCM.

YES

NO

5 INSPECT KNOCK SENSOR CONNECTION. IF OK, REPLACE KNOCK SENSOR AND REPEAT STEP #1. IF DTC RESETS, CHECK FOR A FAULTY PCM CONNECTION. IF OK, REPLACE EPROM. IF CONDITION STILL EXISTS, REPLACE PCM.

CHECK FOR OPEN OR SHORTED KNOCK SIGNAL CIRCUIT
OR
POOR CONNECTIONS AT PCM AND KNOCK SENSOR.
IF OK, REPLACE KNOCK SENSOR AND REPEAT STEP #1.

"AFTER REPAIRS," REFER TO DTC CRITERIA ON FACING PAGE AND CONFIRM DTC DOES NOT RESET.

86814179

Fig. 80 MULTI-PORT FUEL INJECTION — DTC 43

DTC 44
OXYGEN SENSOR (O2S) CIRCUIT
(LEAN EXHAUST INDICATED)
2.2L (VIN 4) "A" CARLINE

Circuit Description:

In order for the PCM to maintain the proper air/fuel ratio an O2 sensor is used to monitor combustion efficiency. The O2 sensor produces a voltage between .1V (indicating lean exhaust - high oxygen content) to 1V (rich exhaust - low oxygen content). When the O2 sensor voltage is low indicating lean exhaust the PCM will compensate by adding fuel (increasing injector pulse width) to maintain proper air/fuel ratio of 14.7 to 1. If the O2 sensor voltage does not increase when the PCM commands more fuel a DTC will set.

DTC 44 Will Set When:
- O2S signal voltage remains less then .3 volt for 50 seconds or more.
- The system is operating in "Closed Loop."
- DTC 33 or 34 is not set.

Action Taken (PCM will default to): The Malfunction Indicator Lamp (MIL) will illuminate, and the cooling fan will enable.

DTC Chart Test Description: Number(s) below refer to circled number(s) on the diagnostic chart.
1. This step determines if DTC 44 is the result of a hard failure or an intermittent condition.

Diagnostic Aids: DTC 44 or lean exhaust is most likely caused by one of the following:
- Fuel pressure - System will be lean if pressure is too low. It may be necessary to monitor fuel pressure while driving the vehicle at various road speeds and/or loads to confirm.
- MAP sensor - An output that causes the PCM to sense a lower than normal manifold pressure (high vacuum) can cause the system to go lean. Disconnecting the MAP sensor will allow the PCM to substitute a fixed (default) value for the MAP sensor. If the rich condition is gone when the sensor is disconnected, substitute a known good sensor and recheck.

- Fuel contamination - Water, even in small amounts, near the in-tank fuel pump inlet can be delivered to the injector.
- Sensor harness - Sensor pigtail may be mispositioned and contacting the exhaust manifold.
- Engine misfire - A cylinder misfire will result in unburned oxygen in the exhaust.

- Cracked Oxygen Sensor (O2S) - A cracked O2S or poor ground at the sensor.

- Plugged fuel filter
- Plugged Oxygen Sensor (O2S)
- Exhaust leak
- Vacuum leak
- Crankcase leak

86814180

Fig. 81 MULTI-PORT FUEL INJECTION — DTC 44

① • RUN WARM ENGINE (75°C/167°F TO 95°C/203°F) AT 1200 RPM.
• DOES TECH 1 SCAN TOOL INDICATE OXYGEN SENSOR (O2S) VOLTAGE FIXED BELOW .35 VOLT (350 mV)?

YES

• DISCONNECT O2S.
• WITH ENGINE IDLING, TECH 1 SCAN TOOL SHOULD DISPLAY O2S VOLTAGE BETWEEN .35 VOLT AND .55 VOLT (350 mV AND 550 mV). DOES IT?

NO

DTC IS INTERMITTENT.
IF NO ADDITIONAL DTC(s) WERE STORED, REFER TO "DIAGNOSTIC AIDS"

YES

REFER TO "DIAGNOSTIC AIDS" ON FACING PAGE.

NO

SIGNAL CIRCUIT SHORTED TO GROUND
OR
FAULTY PCM.

"AFTER REPAIRS," REFER TO DTC CRITERIA ON FACING PAGE AND CONFIRM DTC DOES NOT RESET.

86814181

Fig. 82 MULTI-PORT FUEL INJECTION — DTC 44

DTC 45

OXYGEN SENSOR (O2S) CIRCUIT
(RICH EXHAUST INDICATED)
2.2L (VIN 4) "A" CARLINE

Circuit Description:

In order for the PCM to maintain the proper air/fuel ratio an O2 sensor is used to monitor combustion efficiency. The O2 sensor produces a voltage between .1V (indicating lean exhaust - high oxygen content) to 1V (rich exhaust - low oxygen content). When the O2 sensor voltage is low indicating lean exhaust the PCM will compensate by adding fuel (increasing injector pulse width) to maintain proper air/fuel ratio of 14.7 to 1. If the O2 sensor voltage does not decrease when the PCM commands less fuel a DTC will set.

DTC 45 Will Set When:

- O2S voltage is greater than .75 volt.
- DTC 33 or 34 is not set.
- Fuel system is in "Closed Loop."

- Above conditions are met for 5 seconds or more.
- **OR**
- O2S voltage is above 1 volt for 5 seconds or more.

Action Taken (PCM will default to): The Malfunction Indicator Lamp (MIL) will illuminate, and the cooling fan will enable.

DTC Chart Test Description: Number(s) below refer to circled number(s) on the diagnostic chart.

1. This step determines if DTC 45 is the result of a hard failure or an intermittent condition.

Diagnostic Aids: DTC 45 or rich exhaust is most likely caused by one of the following:

- Fuel pressure - System will go rich if pressure is too high. The PCM can compensate for some increase. However, if it gets too high, a DTC 45 will set.

- Leaking injector
- EGR valve - A stuck open EGR valve will cause the O2 sensor to indicate a rich exhaust, causing DTC to set.
- EVAP canister purge - Check for fuel saturation. If full of fuel, check canister control and hoses.

- MAP sensor - An output that causes the PCM to sense a higher than normal manifold pressure (low vacuum) can cause the system to go rich. Disconnecting the MAP sensor will allow the PCM to set a fixed value for the MAP sensor. Substitute a different MAP sensor if the rich condition is gone while the sensor is disconnected.
- Pressure regulator - Check for leaking fuel pressure regulator diaphragm by checking for the presence of liquid fuel in the vacuum line to the regulator.
- TP sensor - An intermittent TP sensor output will cause the system to go rich due to a false indication of the engine accelerating.
- O2S contamination - Inspect O2S for silicone contamination from fuel or use of improper RTV sealant. The sensor may have a white powdery coating and result in a high but false signal voltage (rich exhaust indication). The PCM will then reduce the amount of fuel delivered to the engine causing a severe surge driveability problem.

86814182

Fig. 83 MULTI-PORT FUEL INJECTION — DTC 45

DTC 45

OXYGEN SENSOR (O2S) CIRCUIT
(RICH EXHAUST INDICATED)
2.2L (VIN 4) "A" CARLINE

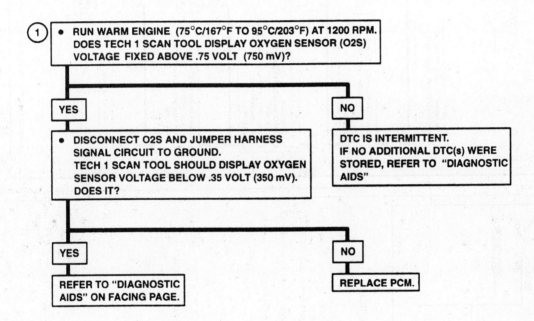

1
- RUN WARM ENGINE (75°C/167°F TO 95°C/203°F) AT 1200 RPM.
  DOES TECH 1 SCAN TOOL DISPLAY OXYGEN SENSOR (O2S)
  VOLTAGE FIXED ABOVE .75 VOLT (750 mV)?

YES

- DISCONNECT O2S AND JUMPER HARNESS
  SIGNAL CIRCUIT TO GROUND.
  TECH 1 SCAN TOOL SHOULD DISPLAY OXYGEN
  SENSOR VOLTAGE BELOW .35 VOLT (350 mV).
  DOES IT?

NO

DTC IS INTERMITTENT.
IF NO ADDITIONAL DTC(s) WERE
STORED, REFER TO "DIAGNOSTIC
AIDS"

YES

REFER TO "DIAGNOSTIC
AIDS" ON FACING PAGE.

NO

REPLACE PCM.

"*AFTER REPAIRS*," REFER TO DTC CRITERIA ON FACING PAGE AND CONFIRM DTC DOES NOT RESET.

86814183

Fig. 84 MULTI-PORT FUEL INJECTION — DTC 45

MULTI-PORT FUEL INJECTION DIAGNOSTIC CHARTS

CODE 46

POWER STEERING PRESSURE SWITCH (PSPS) CIRCUIT "A" CARLINE (PORT)

CODE 46

POWER STEERING PRESSURE SWITCH (PSPS) CIRCUIT
3300 (VIN N) "A" CARLINE (PORT)

Circuit Description:

The power steering pressure switch is normally open, and CKT 495 will be near battery voltage.

Turning the steering wheel increases power steering oil pressure and its load on an idling engine. The pressure switch will close before the load can cause an idle problem.

Closing the switch causes CKT 495 to read less than 1 volt. The electronic control module (ECM) will increase the idle air rate and disengage the A/C clutch.

- A pressure switch that will not close, or an open CKT 495 or 450, may cause the engine to stop when power steering loads are high.
- A switch that will not open, or a CKT 495 shorted to ground, may affect idle quality and will cause the A/C relay to be de-energized.

To set a Code 46, the following conditions must be met:
- Closed power steering switch. "LO" (low voltage potential)
- Vehicle speed is greater than 40 mph
- Both conditions existing for a time greater than 25 seconds

Test Description: Numbers below refer to circled numbers on the diagnostic chart.

1. Different makes of "Scan" tools may display the state of this switch in different ways. Refer to "Scan" tool operator's manual to determine how this input is indicated.

2. Checks to determine if CKT 495 is shorted to ground.

3. This should simulate a closed switch.

4-27-89

86814210

MULTI-PORT FUEL INJECTION DIAGNOSTIC CHARTS

CODE 48
MISFIRE DIAGNOSIS
3300 (VIN N) "A" CARLINE (PORT)

If multiple codes are set, go to the lowest code first.
Repairing for a Code 13, 44, or 45 may correct Code 48.

Test Description:

Code 48 will set if the following:
- TPS is between .58 and .93 volts
- Rpm is between 1500 and 2500
- Mph is between 50 and 60
- O₂ cross counts greater than 32-125C and 26-440 T₄
- All of the above for 30 seconds

O₂ Sensor Test:

Code 48 could be set if the O₂ sensor is degraded and cannot travel over the full rich to lean voltage range.
This narrowed range could allow O₂ cross counts to be above the value necessary to set the code.

- WITH "SCAN" TOOL INSTALLED, VERIFY ENGINE IS AT NORMAL OPERATING TEMPERATURE AND IN "CLOSED LOOP".

- ENGINE IDLING IN PARK.
- SELECT O₂ SENSOR POSITION ON "SCAN".
- RAPIDLY FLASH THE THROTTLE FROM IDLE TO NEAR WIDE OPEN THROTTLE AND BACK WHILE OBSERVING O₂ VOLTAGE. REPEAT IF NECESSARY TO CONFIRM VOLTAGE RANGE, AND "CLOSED LOOP".

VOLTAGE EXCEEDS 250-750 mV RANGE.

O₂ SENSOR OK. SEE "DIAGNOSTIC AIDS".

VOLTAGE REMAINS WITHIN 250-750 mV RANGE.

REPLACE O₂ SENSOR.

Diagnostic Aids:

1. **Ignition system checks:**
   Remove each spark plug and inspect (fouled, cracked, worn)
   Fouled -- check ignition wires (high resistance, damage, poor connections, grounds)
   check coil and module operation
   check basic engine problem (see 3 below)
   Cracked or worn -- replace as necessary

2. **Fuel system checks:**
   Restricted fuel system (injectors, fuel pump, lines, and filter)
   Injectors -- perform injector balance test.
   verify each injector circuit with tool J-34730-2 or equivalent
   Fuel Pump -- verify-proper fuel pressure and fuel quality
   Lines and Filter -- verify no restrictions in lines or filter

3. **Basic Engine Checks:**
   Unless spark plug(s) inspection identifies a specific cylinder(s), road test vehicle under test conditions to reverify Code 48 prior to engine disassembly.
   Basic engine (valves, compression, camshaft, lifters)
   Compression -- check rings, pistons, valves
   Valves -- check for burned, weak springs, broken parts, worn or loose guide
   Camshaft -- check for worn or broken
   Lifters -- check for worn, broken

CODE 51
MEM-CAL ERROR
(FAULTY OR INCORRECT MEM-CAL)
"A" CARLINE (PORT)

CHECK THAT ALL PINS ARE FULLY INSERTED IN THE SOCKET. IF OK, REPLACE MEM-CAL, CLEAR MEMORY AND RECHECK. IF CODE 51 REAPPEARS, REPLACE ECM.

NOTICE: To prevent possible Electrostatic Discharge damage to the ECM or MEM-CAL, Do Not touch the component leads, and Do Not remove integrated circuit from carrier.

86814211

DTC 51

EPROM ERROR
(FAULTY OR INCORRECT EPROM)
2.2L (VIN 4) "A" CARLINE

CHECK THAT ALL PINS ARE FULLY INSERTED IN THE SOCKET AND THAT EPROM IS PROPERLY LATCHED.

IF OK, REPLACE EPROM, CLEAR MEMORY, AND RECHECK. IF DTC 51 REAPPERAS, REPLACE PCM.

NOTICE: TO PREVENT POSSIBLE ELECTROSTATIC DISCHARGE DAMAGE TO THE PCM OR EPROM, DO NOT TOUCH THE COMPONENT LEADS, AND DO NOT REMOVE THE EPROM COVER OR THE INTEGRATED CIRCUIT FROM CARRIER.

"AFTER REPAIRS," CONFIRM "CLOSED LOOP" OPERATION AND NO MIL (SERVICE ENGINE SOON).

86814184

Fig. 85 MULTI-PORT FUEL INJECTION — DTC 51

CODE 51
CODE 52
CODE 53

2.8L (VIN W) "A" SERIES (PORT)

CODE 51

MEM-CAL ERROR
(FAULTY OR INCORRECT MEM-CAL)

CHECK THAT ALL PINS ARE FULLY INSERTED IN THE SOCKET AND THAT MEM-CAL IS PROPERLY LATCHED.
IF OK, REPLACE MEM/CAL, CLEAR MEMORY, AND RECHECK. IF CODE 51 REAPPEARS, REPLACE ECM.

CLEAR CODES AND CONFIRM "CLOSED LOOP" OPERATION AND NO "SERVICE ENGINE SOON" LIGHT.

CODE 52

CALPAK ERROR
(FAULTY OR INCORRECT CALPAK)

CHECK THAT THE MEM-CAL IS FULLY SEATED AND LATCHED INTO THE MEM-CAL
SOCKET. IF OK, REPLACE MEM-CAL, CLEAR MEMORY, AND RECHECK.
IF CODE 52 REAPPEARS, REPLACE ECM.

CLEAR CODES AND CONFIRM "CLOSED LOOP" OPERATION AND NO "SERVICE ENGINE SOON" LIGHT.

CODE 53

SYSTEM OVER VOLTAGE

THIS CODE INDICATES THERE IS A BASIC GENERATOR PROBLEM.
- CODE 53 WILL SET, IF VOLTAGE AT ECM IGNITION INPUT PIN IS GREATER THAN
  17.1 VOLTS FOR 2 SECONDS.
- CHECK AND REPAIR CHARGING SYSTEM.

CLEAR CODES AND CONFIRM "CLOSED LOOP" OPERATION AND NO "SERVICE ENGINE SOON" LIGHT.

86814212

Fig. 86 MULTI-PORT FUEL INJECTION — DTCs 51, 52 and 53

DTC 53
BATTERY VOLTAGE ERROR
2.2L (VIN 4) "A" CARLINE

Circuit Description:

DTC 53 will set when the ignition is "ON" and Powertrain Control Module (PCM) terminal "BD16" voltage is more than 17.1 volts for .2 second, or less than 10 volts for 240 seconds.

During the time the failure is present, all PCM outputs will be disabled.

DTC 53 Will Set When:
- Battery voltage is greater than 17.1 volts for about .2 second.
  OR
- Battery voltage is less than 10 volts for 240 seconds.

Action Taken (PCM will default to): The Malfunction Indicator Lamp (MIL) will illuminate, PCM outputs will be disabled, and the cooling fan will disable.

DTC Chart Test Description: Number(s) below refer to circled number(s) on the diagnostic chart.
1. Normal battery output is between 10 - 17.0 volts.
2. Checks if generator is faulty under load condition.

Diagnostic Aids:
- Charging the battery and then starting the engine, may set DTC 53.
- If DTC sets when an accessory is operated, check for poor connections or excessive current draw.

86814185

Fig. 87 MULTI-PORT FUEL INJECTION — DTC 53

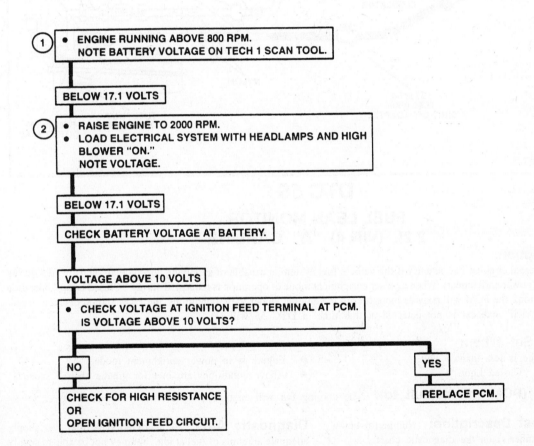

DTC 53

BATTERY VOLTAGE ERROR
2.2L (VIN 4) "A" CARLINE

1
• ENGINE RUNNING ABOVE 800 RPM.
  NOTE BATTERY VOLTAGE ON TECH 1 SCAN TOOL.

BELOW 17.1 VOLTS

2
• RAISE ENGINE TO 2000 RPM.
• LOAD ELECTRICAL SYSTEM WITH HEADLAMPS AND HIGH
  BLOWER "ON."
  NOTE VOLTAGE.

BELOW 17.1 VOLTS

CHECK BATTERY VOLTAGE AT BATTERY.

VOLTAGE ABOVE 10 VOLTS

• CHECK VOLTAGE AT IGNITION FEED TERMINAL AT PCM.
  IS VOLTAGE ABOVE 10 VOLTS?

NO

CHECK FOR HIGH RESISTANCE
OR
OPEN IGNITION FEED CIRCUIT.

YES

REPLACE PCM.

"AFTER REPAIRS," REFER TO DTC CRITERIA ON FACING PAGE AND CONFIRM DTC DOES NOT RESET.

86814187

Fig. 88 MULTI-PORT FUEL INJECTION — DTC 53

DTC 55
FUEL LEAN MONITOR
2.2L (VIN 4) "A" CARLINE

Circuit Description:

The PCM's internal circuitry can identify if the vehicle fuel system is capable of supplying adequate amounts of fuel during heavy acceleration (power enrichment). When a power enrichment mode of operation is requested during "Closed Loop" operation (by heavy acceleration), the PCM will provide more fuel to the engine. Under these conditions, the PCM should detect a "rich" condition. If this "rich" exhaust is not detected at this time, a DTC 55 will set.

DTC 55 Will Set When:
- O2S voltage is less than .3 volt.
- O2S is in "Closed Loop."
- Engine is in power enrichment mode.
- Above conditions are met for greater than 5 seconds.

Action Taken (PCM will default to): The cooling fan will enable.

DTC Chart Test Description: Number(s) below refer to circled number(s) on the diagnostic chart.

1. When the engine is idling or at steady cruise, the O2S voltage should vary, between approximately 100 mV to 900 mV. During power enrichment mode, more fuel is needed and O2S voltage should rise above 447 mV. This step checks if the O2S is operating properly.
2. Low fuel pressure or restricted fuel flow may cause a lean condition.

Diagnostic Aids: A restricted fuel filter can supply adequate amounts of fuel at idle, but may not be able to supply enough fuel during heavy acceleration.

Check for:
- Plugged injectors(s).
- Poor of contaminated fuel.
- Low fuel.
- Restricted fuel supply.
- A DTC 55 may set as a result of vehicle running out of fuel.

86814188

Fig. 89 MULTI-PORT FUEL INJECTION — DTC 55

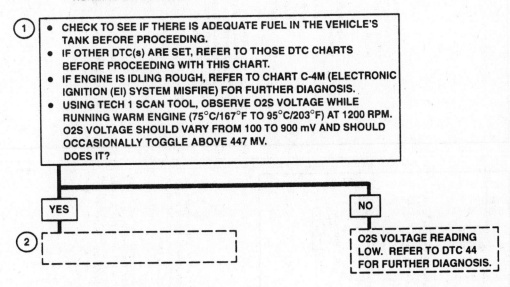

DTC 55

FUEL LEAN MONITOR
2.2L (VIN 4) "A" CARLINE

⚠ **Important**

- DTC MAY SET AS A RESULT OF THE VEHICLE
  RUNNING OUT OF FUEL.

1
- CHECK TO SEE IF THERE IS ADEQUATE FUEL IN THE VEHICLE'S
  TANK BEFORE PROCEEDING.
- IF OTHER DTC(s) ARE SET, REFER TO THOSE DTC CHARTS
  BEFORE PROCEEDING WITH THIS CHART.
- IF ENGINE IS IDLING ROUGH, REFER TO CHART C-4M (ELECTRONIC
  IGNITION (EI) SYSTEM MISFIRE) FOR FURTHER DIAGNOSIS.
- USING TECH 1 SCAN TOOL, OBSERVE O2S VOLTAGE WHILE
  RUNNING WARM ENGINE (75°C/167°F TO 95°C/203°F) AT 1200 RPM.
  O2S VOLTAGE SHOULD VARY FROM 100 TO 900 mV AND SHOULD
  OCCASIONALLY TOGGLE ABOVE 447 MV.
  DOES IT?

YES

NO

2

O2S VOLTAGE READING
LOW. REFER TO DTC 44
FOR FURTHER DIAGNOSIS.

"AFTER REPAIRS," REFER TO DTC CRITERIA ON FACING PAGE AND CONFIRM DTC DOES NOT RESET.

86814189

Fig. 90 MULTI-PORT FUEL INJECTION — DTC 55

MULTI-PORT FUEL INJECTION DIAGNOSTIC CHARTS

CODE 61
DEGRADED OXYGEN SENSOR

IF A CODE 61 IS STORED IN MEMORY THE ECM HAS DETERMINED THE OXYGEN SENSOR IS CONTAMINATED OR DEGRADED, BECAUSE THE VOLTAGE CHANGE TIME IS SLOW OR SLUGGISH.

THE ECM PERFORMS THE OXYGEN SENSOR RESPONSE TIME TEST WHEN:

COOLANT TEMPERATURE IS GREATER THAN 85°C.

MAT TEMPERATURE IS GREATER THAN 10°C.

IN CLOSED LOOP.

IN DECEL FUEL CUT-OFF MODE.

IF A CODE 61 IS STORED THE OXYGEN SENSOR SHOULD BE REPLACED. A CONTAMINATED SENSOR CAN BE CAUSED BY FUEL ADDITIVES, SUCH AS SILICON, OR BY USE OF NON-GM APPROVED LUBRICANTS OR SEALANTS. SILICON CONTAMINATION IS USUALLY INDICATED BY A WHITE POWDERY SUBSTANCE ON THE SENSOR FINS.

CLEAR CODES AND CONFIRM "CLOSED LOOP" OPERATION AND NO "SERVICE ENGINE SOON" LIGHT.

CODE 54
FUEL PUMP CIRCUIT
(LOW VOLTAGE)
3.1L (VIN T)   (PORT)

Circuit Description:

The status of the fuel pump CKT 120 is monitored by the ECM at terminal "YE13" and is used to compensate fuel delivery based on system voltage. This signal is also used to store a trouble code if the fuel pump relay is defective or fuel pump voltage is lost while the engine is running. There should be about 12 volts on CKT 120 for 2 seconds after the ignition is turned on or any time references pulses are being received by the ECM.

Code 54 will set if the voltage at terminal "YE13" is less than 4 volts for 4 second since the last reference pulse was received. This code is designed to detect a faulty relay, causing extended crank time, and the code will help the diagnosis of an engine that "Cranks But Will Not Run."

If a fault is detected during start-up, the "Service Engine Soon" light will stay "ON" until the ignition is cycled "OFF." However, if the voltage is detected below 4 volts with the engine running, the light will only remain "ON" while the condition exists.

86814213

MULTI-PORT FUEL INJECTION DIAGNOSTIC CHARTS

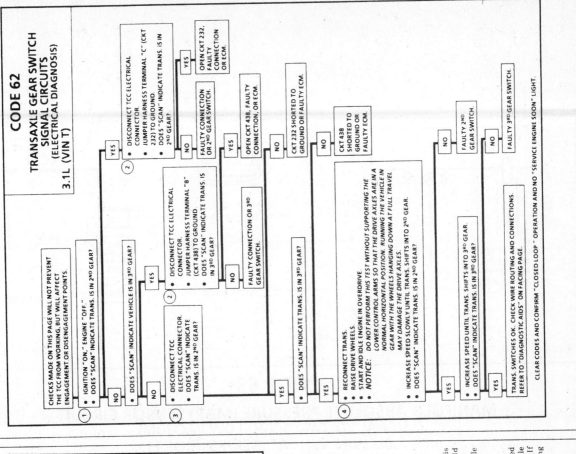

CODE 62
TRANSAXLE GEAR SWITCH SIGNAL CIRCUITS
(ELECTRICAL DIAGNOSIS)
3.1L (VIN T)

CODE 62
TRANSAXLE GEAR SWITCH SIGNAL CIRCUITS
(ELECTRICAL DIAGNOSIS)
3.1L (VIN T)

Circuit Description:
The 2nd gear signal switch in this vehicle should be open in 2nd and 3rd gear. The ECM uses this 2nd gear signal to disengage the TCC when downshifting.
The 3rd gear switch should be open in 3rd gear.

1st Gear = 2nd gear switch open
2nd gear signal switch closed
3rd gear signal switch closed

2nd Gear = 2nd gear switch closed
2nd gear signal switch opens
3rd gear signal switch closed

3rd Gear = 2nd gear switch closed
2nd gear signal switch opens
3rd gear signal switch opens

Test Description: Numbers below refer to circled numbers on the diagnostic chart.
1. Some "Scan" tools display the state of these switches in different ways. Be familiar with the type of tool being used. Since both switches should be in the closed state during this test, the tool should read the same for either the 2nd or 3rd gear switch.
2. Determines whether the switch or signal circuit is open. The circuit can be checked for an open by measuring the voltage (with a voltmeter) at the TCC connector (should be about 12 volts).
3. Because the switch(s) should be grounded in this step, disconnecting the TCC connector should cause the "Scan" switch state to change.
4. The switch state should change when the vehicle shifts into 2nd gear.

Diagnostic Aids:
If vehicle is road tested because of a TCC related problem, be sure the switch states do not change while in 3rd gear because the TCC will disengage. If switches change state, carefully check wire routing and connections.

10-11-88

86814214

9-21-87

CODE 63
MANIFOLD ABSOLUTE PRESSURE (MAP) SENSOR CIRCUIT
(SIGNAL VOLTAGE HIGH - LOW VACUUM)
2.8L (VIN W) "A" SERIES (PORT)

Circuit Description:

    The manifold absolute pressure sensor (MAP) responds to changes in manifold pressure (vacuum). The ECM receives this information as a signal voltage that will vary from about 1/1.5 volts at idle (high vacuum) to 4/4.5 volts at wide open throttle (low vacuum).

Test Description: Numbers below refer to circled numbers on the diagnostic chart.
1. Code 63 will set when:
   - Engine Running.
   - Manifold pressure greater than 75.3 kPa (A/C "OFF") 81.2 kPa (A/C "ON").
   - Throttle angle less than 2%.
   - Conditions met for 2 seconds.

   Engine misfire or a low unstable idle may set Code 63.
2. With the MAP sensor disconnected, the ECM should see a low voltage if the ECM and wiring are OK.

Diagnostic Aids:

    If idle is rough or unstable, refer to items which can cause an unstable idle.

    An open in CKT 455 or the connection will result in a Code 63.

    Ignition "ON" engine "OFF," voltages should be within the values shown in the table on the chart.

86814215

Fig. 91 MULTI-PORT FUEL INJECTION — DTC 63

CODE 64

MANIFOLD ABSOLUTE PRESSURE (MAP) SENSOR CIRCUIT
(SIGNAL VOLTAGE LOW - HIGH VACUUM)
2.8L (VIN W) "A" SERIES (PORT)

Circuit Description:

The manifold absolute pressure sensor (MAP) responds to changes in manifold pressure (vacuum). The ECM receives this information as a signal voltage that will vary from about 1/1.5 volts at idle (high vacuum) to 4/4.5 volts at wide open throttle (low vacuum).

Test Description: Numbers below refer to circled numbers on the diagnostic chart.

1. Code 64 will set if:
   - Engine rpm less than 600.
   - Manifold pressure reading less than 13 kPa.
   - Conditions met for 1 second.
   or
   - Engine rpm greater than 600.
   - Throttle angle over 20%.
   - Manifold pressure less than 13 kPa.
   - Conditions met for 1 second.
2. This test to see if the sensor is at fault for the low voltage, or if there is an ECM or wiring problem.
3. This simulates a high signal voltage to check for an open in CKT 432. If the test light is bright during this test, CKT 432 is probably shorted to ground. If "Scan" reads over 4 volts at this test, CKT 474 can be checked by measuring the voltage at terminal "C" (should be 5 volts).

Diagnostic Aids:

An intermittent open in CKTs 432 or 474 will result in a Code 64.

Ignition "ON" engine "OFF," voltages should be within the values shown in the table on the chart.

86814216

Fig. 92 MULTI-PORT FUEL INJECTION — DTC 64

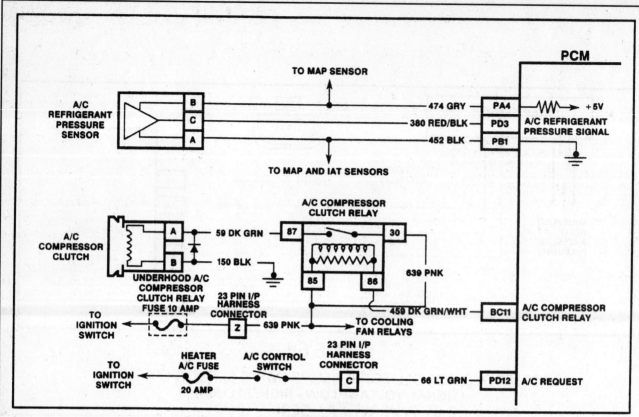

DTC 66

A/C REFRIGERANT PRESSURE SENSOR CIRCUIT
2.2L (VIN 4) "A" CARLINE

Circuit Description:

The A/C refrigerant pressure sensor responds to changes in A/C refrigerant system high side pressure. This input indicates how much load the A/C compressor is putting on the engine and is one of the factors used by the Powertrain Control Module (PCM) to determine IAC valve position for idle speed control. The circuit consists of a 5 volt reference and a ground, both provided by the PCM, and a signal line to the PCM. The signal is a voltage which is proportional to the pressure. The sensor's range of operation is 0 to 450 psi. At 0 psi, the signal will be about .1 volt, varying up to about 4.9 volts at 450 psi or above.

DTC 66 Will Set When:

- AC refrigerant pressure voltage is greater than 4.9 volts or less than .19 volt for 15 seconds.
  OR
- AC refrigerant pressure voltage is greater than 4.0 volts when A/C clutch is not requested.

Action Taken (PCM will default to): A/C clutch is disabled, and the cooling fan will enable.

DTC Chart Test Description: Number(s) below refer to circled number(s) on the diagnostic chart.

1. This checks the voltage signal being received by the PCM from the A/C refrigerant pressure sensor. The normal operating range is between .1 volt and 4.9 volts.
2. Checks if the high voltage signal is from a shorted sensor or a short to voltage in the circuit. Normally, disconnecting the sensor would make a normal circuit go to near zero volt.
3. Checks if low voltage signal is from the sensor or the circuit. Jumpering the sensor signal CKT 380 to 5 volts, checks the circuit, connections and PCM.
4. This checks if the low voltage signal was due to an open in the sensor circuit or the 5 volt reference circuit.

Diagnostic Aids:

- If problem is intermittent, check for opens or shorts in harness or for poor connections. If OK, replace A/C refrigerant pressure sensor.
- If DTC(s) 21, 22, or 34 are also set check CKT 474 for a short or open circuit.

86814190

Fig. 93 MULTI-PORT FUEL INJECTION — DTC 66

NOTICE: IF VEHICLE IS NOT EQUIPPED WITH AIR CONDITIONING, DO NOT USE THIS CHART, SEE "DIAGNOSTIC AIDS."

DTC 66
A/C REFRIGERANT PRESSURE SENSOR CIRCUIT
2.2L (VIN 4) "A" CARLINE

1
- KEY "ON," ENGINE NOT RUNNING.
- NOTE TECH 1 SCAN TOOL VOLTAGE FOR A/C REFRIGERANT PRESSURE.

ABOVE 3.9 VOLTS

BELOW .28 VOLT

BETWEEN .28 VOLT AND 3.9 VOLTS

2
- DISCONNECT A/C REFRIGERANT PRESSURE SENSOR.
  DOES SCAN TOOL DISPLAY LESS THAN 1 VOLT?

3
- DISCONNECT A/C REFRIGERANT PRESSURE SENSOR CONNECTOR.
- JUMPER TERMINALS "B" AND "C" TOGETHER.
  DOES SCAN TOOL DISPLAY ABOVE 4.6 VOLTS?

FAULT IS NOT PRESENT AT THIS TIME. SEE "DIAGNOSTIC AIDS."

NO

CHECK FOR SHORT TO VOLTAGE IN SENSOR GROUND CIRCUIT. IF NOT SHORTED, REPLACE PCM.

YES

CHECK FOR AN OPEN IN THE SENSOR GROUND CIRCUIT. IF NOT OPEN, CHECK FOR POOR SENSOR TERMINAL CONNECTIONS. IF OK, REPLACE A/C REFRIGERANT PRESSURE SENSOR.

NO

4
- REMOVE JUMPER.
- CONNECT VOLTMETER FROM TERMINAL "A" TO "B".
  IS VOLTAGE ABOUT 5 VOLTS?

YES

- CHECK SENSOR TERMINAL CONNECTIONS. IF OK, REPLACE A/C REFRIGERANT PRESSURE SENSOR.

NO

- BACKPROBE 5 VOLT REFERENCE CIRCUIT WITH VOLTMETER TO GROUND. IS VOLTAGE ABOUT 5 VOLTS?

YES

CHECK FOR OPEN IN SIGNAL CIRCUIT. CHECK FOR PROPER CONNECTION AT PCM TERMINAL. IF OK, REPLACE PCM.

NO

CHECK FOR PROPER CONNECTION AT PCM OR SHORT TO GROUND IN 5 VOLT REFERENCE CIRCUIT. IF OK, PCM IS FAULTY.

YES

REPAIR OPEN IN 5 VOLT REFERENCE CIRCUIT.

"AFTER REPAIRS," REFER TO DTC CRITERIA ON FACING PAGE AND CONFIRM DTC DOES NOT RESET.

86814191

Fig. 94 MULTI-PORT FUEL INJECTION — DTC 66

SEQUENTIAL FUEL INJECTION

DTC P0101
MASS AIR FLOW (MAF) SENSOR CIRCUIT
3100 (VIN M) "A" CARLINE (SFI) (MAF)

Circuit Description:

The Mass Air Flow (MAF) sensor measures the flow of air which passes through it in a given time. The PCM uses this information to monitor the operating condition of the engine for fuel delivery calculations. A large quantity of air movement indicates acceleration, while a small quantity indicates deceleration or idle.

The MAF sensor produces a frequency signal which cannot be easily measured. The sensor can be diagnosed using the procedures on this chart.

DTC P0101 Will Set When:
- Engine running.
- No MAF signal for over 4 seconds.

Action Taken (PCM will default to): With DTC P0101 set, the PCM will use a default value for airflow based on throttle position, IAC motor position and engine speed. The MIL (Service Engine Soon) will be illuminated.

DTC Chart Test Description: Number(s) below refer to circled number(s) on the diagnostic chart.
1. This step checks to see if PCM recognizes a problem.
2. A voltage reading at sensor harness connector terminal "A" of less than 4 or over 6 volts indicates a fault in CKT 492 or poor connection.
3. Verifies that both ignition feed voltage and a good ground circuit are available.

Diagnostic Aids: An intermittent may be caused by a poor connection, mis-routed harness, rubbed through wire insulation, or a wire broken inside the insulation. Check for:
- Poor connection at PCM pin - Inspect harness connectors for backed out terminals, improper mating, broken locks, improperly formed or damaged terminals, and poor terminal to wire connection.
- Mis-routed harness - Inspect MAF sensor harness to insure that it is not too close to high voltage wires, such as spark plug leads.
- Damaged harness - Inspect harness for damage. If harness appears OK, observe Tech 1 while moving related connectors and wiring harness. A change in display would indicate the intermittent fault location.
- Plugged air intake filter - A wide-open throttle acceleration from a stop should cause the MAF reading on the Tech 1 to range from about 4-7g/s at idle to 100 or greater at the time of the 1-2 shift. If not, check for restriction.

86814250

Fig. 95 SEQUENTIAL FUEL INJECTION — DTC P0101

SEQUENTIAL FUEL INJECTION — DTC P0112

PCM

BB3	5V REFERENCE
BB10	TP SENSOR SIGNAL
BA8	SENSOR(S) GROUND
BB9	ECT SIGNAL
BB7	IAT SIGNAL
BA8	SENSOR(S) GROUND
BB12	AC REFRIGERANT PRESSURE SIGNAL
BA3	5V REFERENCE
BB11	TRANS TEMP SIGNAL

416 GRY
417 DK BLU
452 BLK
410 YEL
472 TAN
452 BLK
380 RED/BLK
474 GRY
1227 YEL/BLK

THROTTLE POSITION (TP) SENSOR

FUEL INJECTOR IN-LINE HARNESS CONN
452 BLK

ENGINE COOLANT TEMPERATURE (ECT) SENSOR

INTAKE AIR TEMPERATURE (IAT) SENSOR

452 BLK

A/C REFRIGERANT PRESSURE SENSOR

TRANSAXLE CONNECTOR

452 BLK

TRANSMISSION FLUID TEMPERATURE SENSOR (INSIDE TRANS)

* DENOTES A COMMON SPLICE

DTC P0112

INTAKE AIR TEMPERATURE (IAT) SENSOR CIRCUIT
(LOW TEMPERATURE INDICATED)
3100 (VIN M) "A" CARLINE (SFI) (MAF)

Circuit Description:

The Intake Air Temperature (IAT) sensor is a thermistor. The PCM applies 5 volts on CKT 472 to the sensor. When the air is cold, the sensor resistance is high, and the PCM will measure a high signal voltage. If the air is warm, the sensor resistance is low causing the PCM to measure a low voltage.

DTC P0112 Will Set When:

- Engine coolant temperature above 60°C (140°F).
- Mass air flow less than 12 grams per second.
- Vehicle speed less than 25 mph.
- IAT signal voltage indicates an intake air temperature below -34°C (-29°F) for 5 seconds.

Action Taken (PCM will default to): With DTC P0112 set, the PCM will substitute a default value of 16°C (61°F) for intake air temperature. DTC P0112 does not illuminate the MIL (Service Engine Soon).

DTC P0112 Chart Test Description: Number(s) below refer to circled number(s) on the diagnostic chart.
1. A DTC P0112 will set due to an open sensor, wire, or connection. An open circuit would cause the Tech 1 to display approximately -40°C (-40°F). This test determines if the wiring and PCM are OK.

Diagnostic Aids: An intermittent may be caused by a poor connection, rubbed through wire insulation or a wire broken inside the insulation.

Check for:
- Poor connection or damaged harness - Inspect PCM

harness connectors for backed out terminals "BB7" and/or, "BA8", improper mating, broken locks, improperly formed or damaged terminals, poor terminal to wire connection, and damaged harness.
- Intermittent test - Observe Intake Air Temperature (IAT) on Tech 1 while moving related connectors and wiring harness with warm engine running. If the failure is induced, the IAT display will change to a -40° temperature reading. This may help to isolate the location of the malfunction.

86814252

SEQUENTIAL FUEL INJECTION — DTC P0101

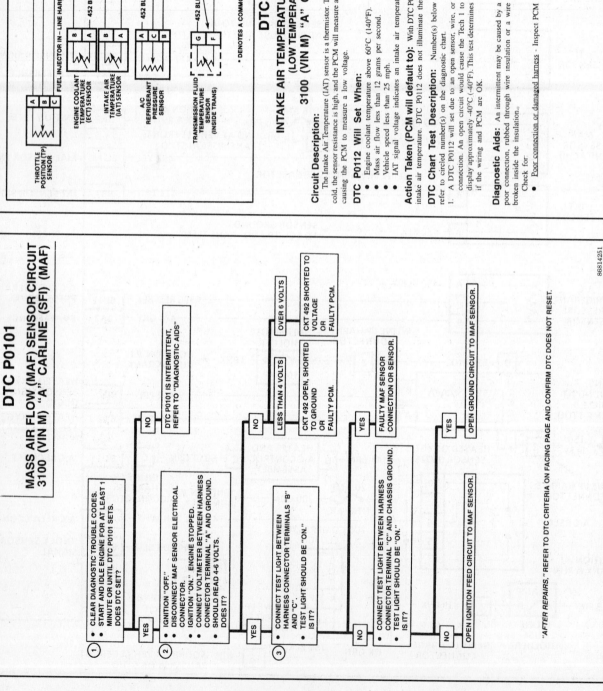

DTC P0101

MASS AIR FLOW (MAF) SENSOR CIRCUIT
3100 (VIN M) "A" CARLINE (SFI) (MAF)

(1)
- CLEAR DIAGNOSTIC TROUBLE CODES.
- START AND IDLE ENGINE FOR AT LEAST 1 MINUTE OR UNTIL DTC P0101 SETS.
  DOES DTC SET?

YES

NO → DTC P0101 IS INTERMITTENT, REFER TO "DIAGNOSTIC AIDS"

(2)
- IGNITION "OFF."
- DISCONNECT MAF SENSOR ELECTRICAL CONNECTOR.
- IGNITION "ON." ENGINE STOPPED.
- CONNECT VOLTMETER BETWEEN HARNESS CONNECTOR TERMINAL "A" AND GROUND. SHOULD READ 4-6 VOLTS.
  DOES IT?

YES

NO

OVER 6 VOLTS → CKT 492 SHORTED TO VOLTAGE OR FAULTY PCM.

LESS THAN 4 VOLTS → CKT 492 OPEN, SHORTED TO GROUND OR FAULTY PCM.

(3)
- CONNECT TEST LIGHT BETWEEN HARNESS CONNECTOR TERMINALS "B" AND "C".
- TEST LIGHT SHOULD BE "ON."
  IS IT?

YES → FAULTY MAF SENSOR CONNECTION OR SENSOR.

NO
- CONNECT TEST LIGHT BETWEEN HARNESS CONNECTOR TERMINAL "C" AND CHASSIS GROUND.
- TEST LIGHT SHOULD BE "ON."
  IS IT?

YES → OPEN GROUND CIRCUIT TO MAF SENSOR.

NO → OPEN IGNITION FEED CIRCUIT TO MAF SENSOR.

"AFTER REPAIRS," REFER TO DTC CRITERIA ON FACING PAGE AND CONFIRM DTC DOES NOT RESET.

86814251

SEQUENTIAL FUEL INJECTION — DTC P0113

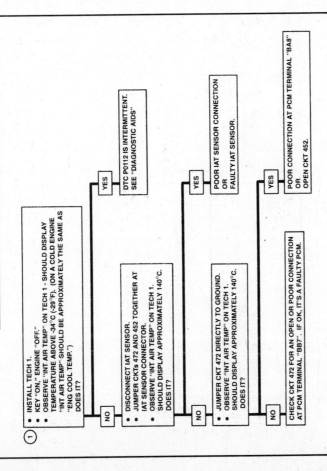

PCM

- BB3 — 416 GRY — 5V REFERENCE
- BB10 — 417 DK BLU — TP SENSOR SIGNAL
- BA8 — 452 BLK — SENSOR(S) GROUND
- BB9 — 410 YEL — ECT SIGNAL
- BB7 — 472 TAN — IAT SIGNAL
- BA8 — 452 BLK — SENSOR(S) GROUND
- BB12 — 380 RED/BLK — AC REFRIGERANT PRESSURE SIGNAL
- BA3 — 474 GRY — 5V REFERENCE
- BB11 — 1227 YEL/BLK — TRANS TEMP SIGNAL

FUEL INJECTOR IN-LINE HARNESS CONN

THROTTLE POSITION (TP) SENSOR

ENGINE COOLANT TEMPERATURE (ECT) SENSOR

INTAKE AIR TEMPERATURE (IAT) SENSOR

A/C REFRIGERANT PRESSURE SENSOR

TRANSMISSION FLUID TEMPERATURE SENSOR (INSIDE TRANS)

TRANSAXLE CONNECTOR

452 BLK

* DENOTES A COMMON SPLICE

DTC P0113

INTAKE AIR TEMPERATURE (IAT) SENSOR CIRCUIT
(HIGH TEMPERATURE INDICATED)
3100 (VIN M) "A" CARLINE (SFI) (MAF)

Circuit Description:

The Intake Air Temperature (IAT) sensor is a thermistor. The PCM applies a voltage (about 5 volts) on CKT 472 to the sensor. When air is cold, the sensor resistance is high and the PCM will measure a high signal voltage. If the air is warm, the sensor resistance is low causing the PCM to measure a low voltage.

DTC P0113 Will Set When:

- Signal voltage indicates an intake air temperature greater than 140°C (284°F).
- Vehicle speed is greater than 35 mph.
- Both of the above requirements are met for at least 5 seconds.

Action Taken (PCM will default to): With a current DTC P0113 set, the PCM will use a default value of 16°C (61°F) for intake air temperature. DTC P0113 does not illuminate the MIL (Service Engine Soon).

DTC P0113 Chart Test Description: Number(s) below refer to circled number(s) on the diagnostic chart.

1. A Tech 1 may be used to diagnose this fault since the PCM transmits "actual" values when the fault is present. A grounded circuit will cause the Tech 1 to display a temperature of approximately 147°C (297°F).
2. If the Tech 1 displays -40° with the IAT sensor disconnected, the PCM and wiring are OK and the IAT sensor must be replaced.

Diagnostic Aids: An intermittent may be caused by a poor connection, rubbed through wire insulation or a wire broken inside the insulation.

Check for:

- Poor connection or damaged harness - Inspect PCM harness for short to ground in CKT 472, improper mating, broken locks, improperly formed or damaged terminals, poor terminal to wire connection, and damaged harness.
- Intermittent test - Observe Intake Air Temperature (IAT) on Tech 1 while moving related connectors and wiring harness with warm engine running. If the failure is induced, the IAT display will change to a 147°C (297°F) temperature reading. This may help to isolate the location of the malfunction.

86814254

SEQUENTIAL FUEL INJECTION — DTC P0112

DTC P0112

INTAKE AIR TEMPERATURE (IAT) SENSOR CIRCUIT
(LOW TEMPERATURE INDICATED)
3100 (VIN M) "A" CARLINE (SFI) (MAF)

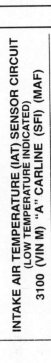

① • INSTALL TECH 1.
  • KEY "ON," ENGINE "OFF."
  • OBSERVE "INT AIR TEMP" ON TECH 1 - SHOULD DISPLAY TEMPERATURE ABOVE -34°C (-29°F). (ON A COLD ENGINE "INT AIR TEMP" SHOULD BE APPROXIMATELY THE SAME AS "ENG COOL TEMP.")
  DOES IT?

NO

• DISCONNECT IAT SENSOR.
• JUMPER CKTs 472 AND 452 TOGETHER AT IAT SENSOR CONNECTOR.
• OBSERVE "INT AIR TEMP" ON TECH 1. SHOULD DISPLAY APPROXIMATELY 140°C.
DOES IT?

NO

• JUMPER CKT 472 DIRECTLY TO GROUND.
• OBSERVE "INT AIR TEMP" ON TECH 1. SHOULD DISPLAY APPROXIMATELY 140°C.
DOES IT?

NO

CHECK CKT 472 FOR AN OPEN OR POOR CONNECTION AT PCM TERMINAL "BB7". IF OK, IT'S A FAULTY PCM.

YES → DTC P0112 IS INTERMITTENT. SEE "DIAGNOSTIC AIDS"

YES → POOR IAT SENSOR CONNECTION OR FAULTY IAT SENSOR.

YES → POOR CONNECTION AT PCM TERMINAL "BA8" OR OPEN CKT 452.

"AFTER REPAIRS," REFER TO DTC CRITERIA ON FACING PAGE AND CONFIRM DTC DOES NOT RESET.

86814253

SEQUENTIAL FUEL INJECTION — DTC P0117

PCM

Terminal	Signal
BB3	5V REFERENCE
BB10	TP SENSOR SIGNAL
BA8	SENSOR(S) GROUND
BB9	ECT SIGNAL
BB7	IAT SIGNAL
BA8	SENSOR(S) GROUND
BB12	AC REFRIGERANT PRESSURE SIGNAL
BA3	5V REFERENCE
BB11	TRANS TEMP SIGNAL

416 GRY
417 DK BLU
452 BLK
410 YEL
472 TAN
452 BLK
380 RED/BLK
474 GRY
1227 YEL/BLK

THROTTLE POSITION (TP) SENSOR — A B C

FUEL INJECTOR IN—LINE HARNESS CONN — E F

452 BLK

ENGINE COOLANT TEMPERATURE (ECT) SENSOR — B A

INTAKE AIR TEMPERATURE (IAT) SENSOR — B A

452 BLK

A/C REFRIGERANT PRESSURE SENSOR — A C B

452 BLK

TRANSMISSION FLUID TEMPERATURE SENSOR (INSIDE TRANS) — G F

TRANSAXLE CONNECTOR

452 BLK

* DENOTES A COMMON SPLICE

86814256

DTC P0117

ENGINE COOLANT TEMPERATURE (ECT) SENSOR CIRCUIT (LOW TEMPERATURE INDICATED)
3100 (VIN M) "A" CARLINE (SFI) (MAF)

Circuit Description:

The Engine Coolant Temperature (ECT) sensor uses a thermistor to control the signal voltage to the PCM. The PCM applies a voltage on CKT 410 to the sensor. When the engine is cold the sensor (thermistor) resistance is high; therefore, the PCM will see high signal voltage.

As the engine warms, the sensor resistance becomes less, and the voltage drops. At normal engine operating temperature (85°C to 95°C), the signal will measure about 1.5 to 2.0 volts.

DTC P0117 Will Set When:

- Engine is running over 15 seconds.
- Signal voltage indicates engine coolant temperature less than -39°C (-38°F) for at least .4 second.

Action Taken (PCM will default to): With a current DTC P0117 set, the PCM will turn the cooling fans "ON" and use a default engine coolant temperature value based on run time. The default value will rise to a maximum value of 90°C (194°F). The PCM will illuminate the MIL. (Service Engine Soon).

DTC Chart Test Description: Number(s) below refer to circled number(s) on the diagnostic chart.

1. Determines if conditions necessary to set DTC P0117 exist.
2. This test simulates DTC P0118. If the PCM recognizes the low signal voltage (high temperature), and the scan display reads 130°C (266°F) or more, the PCM and wiring are OK.
3. 5 volts present at sensor connector if measured with a DVM. There should be This test will determine if CKT 410 is open.

Diagnostic Aids: A Tech 1 displays engine coolant temperature in degrees. After engine is started the temperature should rise steadily to about 90°C (194°F) then stabilize when thermostat opens.

An intermittent may be caused by a poor connection, rubbed through wire insulation or a wire broken inside the insulation. Check for:

- Poor connection or damaged harness - Inspect PCM

harness connectors for backed out terminal "BB9" or "BA8", improper mating, broken locks, improperly formed or damaged terminals, poor terminal to wire connection and damaged harness.

- Intermittent test - With Tech 1, monitor engine coolant temperature while moving related connectors and wiring harness. If the failure is induced, the display will change. This may help to isolate the location of the malfunction.

- Shifted sensor - The "Temperature To Resistance Value" scale may be used to test the engine coolant temperature sensor at various temperature levels to evaluate the possibility of a "shifted" (mis-scaled) sensor which may result in driveability complaints. A faulty connection, or an open in CKT 410 or 452 will result in a DTC P0117.

SEQUENTIAL FUEL INJECTION — DTC P0113

DTC P0113

INTAKE AIR TEMPERATURE (IAT) SENSOR CIRCUIT (HIGH TEMPERATURE INDICATED)
3100 (VIN M) "A" CARLINE (SFI) (MAF)

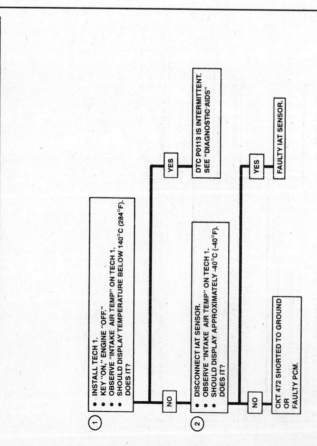

① INSTALL TECH 1.
- KEY "ON," ENGINE "OFF."
- OBSERVE "INTAKE AIR TEMP" ON TECH 1.
- SHOULD DISPLAY TEMPERATURE BELOW 140°C (284°F).
- DOES IT?

NO → ② DISCONNECT IAT SENSOR.
- OBSERVE "INTAKE AIR TEMP" ON TECH 1.
- SHOULD DISPLAY APPROXIMATELY -40°C (-40°F).
- DOES IT?

NO → CKT 472 SHORTED TO GROUND OR FAULTY PCM.

YES → DTC P0113 IS INTERMITTENT. SEE "DIAGNOSTIC AIDS"

YES → FAULTY IAT SENSOR.

86814255

"AFTER REPAIRS," "REFER TO DTC CRITERIA ON FACING PAGE AND CONFIRM DTC DOES NOT RESET.

SEQUENTIAL FUEL INJECTION — DTC P0118

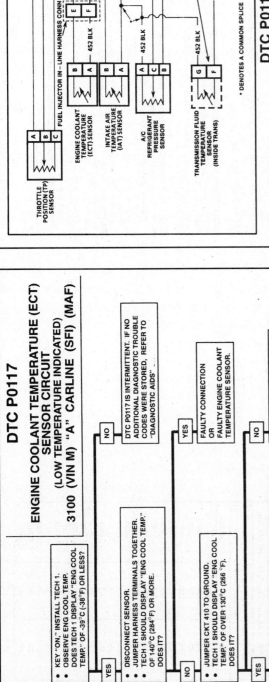

PCM

Terminal	Signal
BB3	5V REFERENCE
BB10	TP SENSOR SIGNAL
BA8	SENSOR(S) GROUND
BB9	ECT SIGNAL
BB7	IAT SIGNAL
BA8	SENSOR(S) GROUND
BB12	AC REFRIGERANT PRESSURE SIGNAL
BA3	5V REFERENCE
BB11	TRANS TEMP SIGNAL

416 GRY
417 DK BLU
452 BLK
410 YEL
472 TAN
452 BLK
380 RED/BLK
474 GRY
1227 YEL/BLK

FUEL INJECTOR IN-LINE HARNESS CONN

452 BLK

452 BLK

THROTTLE POSITION (TP) SENSOR

ENGINE COOLANT TEMPERATURE (ECT) SENSOR

INTAKE AIR TEMPERATURE (IAT) SENSOR

A/C REFRIGERANT PRESSURE SENSOR

TRANSAXLE CONNECTOR

452 BLK

TRANSMISSION FLUID TEMPERATURE SENSOR (INSIDE TRANS)

* DENOTES A COMMON SPLICE

DTC P0118

ENGINE COOLANT TEMPERATURE (ECT) SENSOR CIRCUIT
(HIGH TEMPERATURE INDICATED)
3100 (VIN M) "A" CARLINE (SFI) (MAF)

Circuit Description:

The Engine Coolant Temperature (ECT) sensor uses a thermistor to control the signal voltage to the PCM. The PCM applies a voltage on CKT 410 to the sensor. When the engine is cold the sensor (thermistor) resistance is high; therefore, the PCM will see high signal voltage.

As the engine warms, the sensor resistance becomes less and the voltage drops. At normal engine operating temperature (85°C to 95°C), the ECT signal will measure about 1.5 to 2.0 volts.

DTC P0118 Will Set When:
• Engine run time is greater than 15 seconds.
• Signal voltage indicates engine coolant temperature above 140°C for .4 second.

Action Taken (PCM will default to): With a current DTC P0118 set, the PCM will turn the cooling fans "ON" and use a default engine coolant temperature value based on run time. The default value will rise to a maximum value of 90°C (194°F). The PCM will illuminate the MIL (Service Engine Soon).

DTC Chart Test Description: Number(s) below refer to circled number(s) on the diagnostic chart.
1. Determines if conditions necessary to set DTC P0118 exist.
2. This test will determine if CKT 410 is shorted to ground which will cause the conditions for DTC P0118.

Diagnostic Aids: Tech 1 displays engine coolant temperature in degrees. After engine is started, the temperature should rise steadily to about 90°C (194°F) then stabilize when thermostat opens.

An intermittent may be caused by rubbed through wire insulation.

Check for:
• CKT 410 for a short to ground.
• Intermittent test - With Tech 1, monitor engine coolant temperature while moving related connectors and wiring harness. If the failure is induced, the "engine coolant temperature" display will change. This may help to isolate the location of the malfunction.
• Shifted sensor - The "Temperature To Resistance Value" scale may be used to test the engine coolant temperature sensor at various temperature levels to evaluate the possibility of a "shifted" (mis-scaled) sensor, which may result in driveability complaints.

86814258

SEQUENTIAL FUEL INJECTION — DTC P0117

DTC P0117

ENGINE COOLANT TEMPERATURE (ECT) SENSOR CIRCUIT
(LOW TEMPERATURE INDICATED)
3100 (VIN M) "A" CARLINE (SFI) (MAF)

1. • KEY "ON," INSTALL TECH 1.
   • OBSERVE ENG COOL TEMP.
   • DOES TECH 1 DISPLAY "ENG COOL TEMP." OF -39°C (-38°F) OR LESS?

   YES → DTC P0117 IS INTERMITTENT. IF NO ADDITIONAL DIAGNOSTIC TROUBLE CODES WERE STORED, REFER TO "DIAGNOSTIC AIDS".

   NO ↓

2. • DISCONNECT SENSOR.
   • JUMPER HARNESS TERMINALS TOGETHER.
   • TECH 1 SHOULD DISPLAY "ENG COOL TEMP." OF 140°C (284°F) OR MORE.
   • DOES IT?

   YES → FAULTY CONNECTION OR FAULTY ENGINE COOLANT TEMPERATURE SENSOR.

   NO ↓

3. • JUMPER CKT 410 TO GROUND.
   • TECH 1 SHOULD DISPLAY "ENG COOL TEMP." OF OVER 130°C (266°F).
   • DOES IT?

   NO → FAULTY CONNECTION AT PCM OR OPEN CKT 410 OR FAULTY PCM.

   YES → OPEN ENGINE COOLANT TEMPERATURE SENSOR GROUND CIRCUIT, FAULTY CONNECTION OR FAULTY PCM.

DIAGNOSTIC AID

ENGINE COOLANT TEMPERATURE SENSOR

TEMPERATURE VS. RESISTANCE VALUES (APPROXIMATE)

°C	°F	OHMS
100	212	177
90	194	241
80	176	332
70	158	467
60	140	667
50	122	973
45	113	1188
40	104	1459
35	95	1802
30	86	2238
25	77	2796
20	68	3520
15	59	4450
10	50	5670
5	41	7280
0	32	9420
-5	23	12300
-10	14	16180
-15	5	21450
-20	-4	28680
-30	-22	52700
-40	-40	100700

"AFTER REPAIRS", "REFER TO DTC CRITERIA ON FACING PAGE AND CONFIRM DTC DOES NOT RESET.

86814257

SEQUENTIAL FUEL INJECTION — DTC P0122

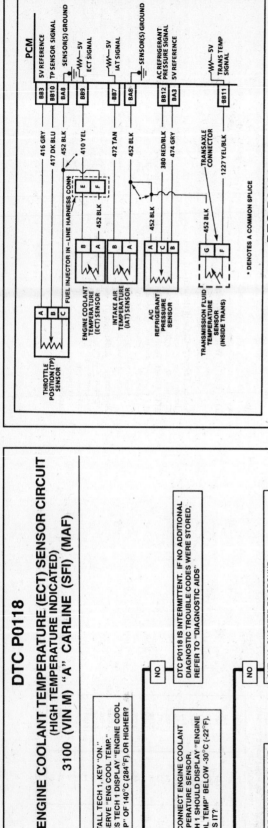

PCM

Terminal	Signal	Wire
BB3	5V REFERENCE	416 GRY
BB10	TP SENSOR SIGNAL	417 DK BLU
BA8	SENSOR(S) GROUND	452 BLK
BB9	ECT SIGNAL	410 YEL
BB7	IAT SIGNAL	472 TAN
BA7	SENSOR(S) GROUND	452 BLK
BB12	AC REFRIGERANT PRESSURE SIGNAL	380 RED/BLK
BA3	5V REFERENCE	474 GRY
BB11	TRANS TEMP SIGNAL	1227 YEL/BLK

THROTTLE POSITION (TP) SENSOR
FUEL INJECTOR IN-LINE HARNESS CONN
ENGINE COOLANT TEMPERATURE (ECT) SENSOR
INTAKE AIR TEMPERATURE (IAT) SENSOR
A/C REFRIGERANT PRESSURE SENSOR
TRANSMISSION FLUID TEMPERATURE SENSOR (INSIDE TRANS)
TRANSAXLE CONNECTOR
452 BLK

* DENOTES A COMMON SPLICE

DTC P0122

THROTTLE POSITION (TP) SENSOR CIRCUIT
(SIGNAL VOLTAGE LOW)
3100 (VIN M) "A" CARLINE (SFI) (MAF)

Circuit Description:

The Throttle Position (TP) sensor provides a voltage signal that changes relative to throttle blade angle. Signal voltage will vary from .2 - .74 volt at idle to above 4 volts at Wide Open Throttle (WOT).

The TP signal is one of the most important inputs used by the PCM for fuel control and for most of the PCM control outputs.

DTC P0122 Will Set When:
- Ignition "ON."
- TP sensor signal voltage is less than .16 volt for 4 seconds.

Action Taken (PCM will default to): If DTC P0122 is set, the Tech scan tool will continue to display the actual throttle sensor voltage, but ignore TP signal and read mass airflow value for other PCM and controlled functions, the PCM will not allow 4th gear, TCC or cruise control operation, 1st, 2nd and 3rd allowed. The MIL (Service Engine Soon) is illuminated.

If CKT 417 is open or grounded when the vehicle engine is started, a high idle may result. The Tech 1 may read the following with CKT 417 open or grounded:

TP = .16 volt or less, MIL (Service Engine Soon) "ON," DTC P0122 set.

DTC Chart Test Description: Number(s) below refer to circled number(s) on the diagnostic chart.
1. Determines if conditions necessary to set DTC P0122 exist.
2. Simulates DTC P0123: (high voltage) If PCM recognizes the high signal voltage and sets DTC P0123, the PCM and wiring are OK.
3. Simulates a high signal voltage. Checks CKT 417 for an open. The Tech 1 displays throttle position in volts. Voltage should increase at a steady rate as throttle is moved toward WOT.

Diagnostic Aids: The Tech 1 displays throttle position in volts. Voltage should vary from closed throttle TP sensor voltage when throttle is closed (.2 - .74 volt) to over 4.0 volts when throttle is held at Wide Open Throttle (WOT) position.

An open or short to ground in CKT 41o or 417 will result in DTC P0122.

Check for:
- Poor connection or damaged harness - Inspect PCM

harness connectors for backed out terminal "BB10" and/or "BB3", improper mating, broken locks, improperly formed or damaged terminals, poor terminal to wire connection, and damaged harness.
- Intermittent test - Monitor TP sensor voltage display while moving related connectors and wiring harness. If the failure is induced, the display will change. This may help to isolate the location of the malfunction.

TP sensor scaling - Observe TP sensor voltage display while depressing accelerator pedal with engine stopped and ignition "ON." Display should vary from closed throttle TP sensor voltage when throttle is closed (.2 - .74 volt) to over 4.0 volts when throttle is held at Wide Open Throttle (WOT) position.

86814260

SEQUENTIAL FUEL INJECTION — DTC P0118

DTC P0118

ENGINE COOLANT TEMPERATURE (ECT) SENSOR CIRCUIT
(HIGH TEMPERATURE INDICATED)
3100 (VIN M) "A" CARLINE (SFI) (MAF)

① INSTALL TECH 1, KEY "ON."
- OBSERVE "ENG COOL TEMP."
- DOES TECH 1 DISPLAY "ENGINE COOL TEMP" OF 140°C (284°F) OR HIGHER?

NO → DTC P0118 IS INTERMITTENT. IF NO ADDITIONAL DIAGNOSTIC TROUBLE CODES WERE STORED, REFER TO "DIAGNOSTIC AIDS"

YES ↓

② DISCONNECT ENGINE COOLANT TEMPERATURE SENSOR. TECH 1 SHOULD DISPLAY "ENGINE COOL TEMP" BELOW -30°C (-22°F). DOES IT?

NO → CKT 410 SHORTED TO GROUND
OR
CKT 410 SHORTED TO SENSOR GROUND CIRCUIT
OR
FAULTY PCM.

YES ↓

REPLACE ENGINE COOLANT TEMPERATURE SENSOR.

DIAGNOSTIC AID

ENGINE COOLANT TEMPERATURE SENSOR		
TEMPERATURE VS. RESISTANCE VALUES (APPROXIMATE)		
°C	°F	OHMS
100	212	177
90	194	241
80	176	332
70	158	467
60	140	667
50	122	973
45	113	1188
40	104	1459
35	95	1802
30	86	2238
25	77	2796
20	68	3520
15	59	4450
10	50	5670
5	41	7280
0	32	9420
-5	23	12300
-10	14	16180
-15	5	21450
-20	-4	28680
-30	-22	52700
-40	-40	100700

"AFTER REPAIRS," REFER TO DTC CRITERIA ON FACING PAGE AND CONFIRM DTC DOES NOT RESET.

86814259

SEQUENTIAL FUEL INJECTION — DTC P0123

DTC P0123

THROTTLE POSITION (TP) SENSOR CIRCUIT (SIGNAL VOLTAGE HIGH) 3100 (VIN M) "A" CARLINE (SFI) (MAF)

Circuit Description:

The Throttle Position (TP) sensor provides a voltage signal that changes relative to throttle blade angle. Signal voltage will vary from .2 - .74 volt at idle to about 5 volts at Wide Open Throttle (WOT).

The TP sensor signal is one of the most important inputs used by the PCM for fuel control and for most of the PCM control outputs.

DTC P0123 Will Set When:

- TP sensor voltage is greater than 4.8 volts at any time.
  OR
- Engine is running and air flow is less than 17 gm/sec.
  OR
- RPM greater than 600 RPM

- TP sensor signal voltage is greater than 1.06 volts.
- DTC P0101 not present.
- All conditions met for 5 seconds.

Action Taken (PCM will default to): If a DTC P0123 is set, the Tech 1 scan tool will continue to display the actual throttle sensor voltage. But ignore TP signal and read mass air flow value for other PCM controlled functions, the PCM will not allow cruise control, 4th gear or TCC operation, 1st, 2nd, and 3rd allowed. The MIL (Service Engine Soon) will be illuminated.

DTC Chart Test Description: Number(s) below

refer to circled number(s) on the diagnostic chart.

1. With closed throttle, ignition "ON" or at idle, voltage at "BB10" should be .2 - .74 volt.
2. With the TP sensor disconnected, the TP sensor voltage should go low and a DTC P0122 will set. This test verifies that the PCM and wiring are OK.
3. Probing CKT 452 with a test light checks the sensor ground circuit. A faulty sensor ground circuit will cause a DTC P0123.

Diagnostic Aids: The Tech 1 displays throttle position in volts. With closed throttle, ignition "ON" or at idle, voltage should be .2 - .74 volt. If not, refer to "Fuel Metering System," Section "6E3-C2" for replacement procedures.

An open in sensor ground CKT 452 may result in DTCs P0112, P0712, P0117 and P0123. Refer to "Intermittents," in "Symptoms," Section "6E3-B".

Check for:

- Poor connection or damaged harness.- Inspect PCM harness connectors for backed out terminal "BB10" or "BA8", improper mating, broken locks, improperly formed or damaged terminals, poor terminal to wire connection, and damaged harness.
- Intermittent test - Monitor TP sensor voltage on Tech 1 while moving related connectors and wiring harness. If the failure is induced, the display will change. This may help to isolate the location of the malfunction.
- TP sensor scaling- Observe TP sensor voltage display while depressing accelerator pedal with engine stopped and ignition "ON." Display should vary from closed throttle TP sensor voltage when throttle is closed (.2 - .74 volt) to over 4.0 volts when throttle is held at Wide Open Throttle (WOT) position.

86814262

SEQUENTIAL FUEL INJECTION — DTC P0122

DTC P0122

THROTTLE POSITION (TP) SENSOR CIRCUIT (SIGNAL VOLTAGE LOW) 3100 (VIN M) "A" CARLINE (SFI) (MAF)

1. THROTTLE CLOSED. DOES TECH 1 DATA DISPLAY INDICATE A THROTTLE POSITION OF .16 VOLT OR BELOW?
   - NO → DTC P0122 IS INTERMITTENT. IF NO ADDITIONAL DTC(s) WERE STORED, REFER TO "DIAGNOSTIC AIDS"
   - YES →

2. DISCONNECT THROTTLE POSITION SENSOR. JUMPER CKTs 416 AND 417 TOGETHER. TECH 1 DATA DISPLAY SHOULD INDICATE THROTTLE POSITION OVER 4.0 VOLTS. DOES IT?
   - YES → REPLACE TP SENSOR.
   - NO →

3. PROBE CKT 417 WITH A TEST LIGHT CONNECTED TO BATTERY VOLTAGE. TECH 1 DATA DISPLAY SHOULD INDICATE THROTTLE POSITION OVER 4.0V. DOES IT?
   - YES → CKT 416 OPEN OR SHORTED TO GROUND OR POOR CONNECTION AT PCM OR FAULTY PCM.
   - NO → CKT 417 OPEN OR SHORTED TO GROUND, OR SHORTED TO SENSOR GROUND CIRCUIT OR POOR CONNECTION AT PCM OR FAULTY PCM.

"*AFTER REPAIRS*," REFER TO DTC CRITERIA ON FACING PAGE AND CONFIRM DTC DOES NOT RESET.

86814261

SEQUENTIAL FUEL INJECTION — DTC P0131

PCM

HO2S SIGNAL LOW — BD2
HO2S SIGNAL HIGH — BD3

413 TAN
412 PPL
150 BLK

GROUND AT VEHICLE FRONT, TRANSMISSION STUD

A/C COMPRESSOR RELAY, CAMSHAFT POSITION SENSOR, 24X CRANKSHAFT POSITION SENSOR, COOLING FAN RELAYS #1 AND #2 AND EVAP CANISTER PURGE SOLENOID VALVE

A B C D

639 PNK

IN-LINE I/P HARNESS CONNECTOR

Z

10 AMP

IN-LINE FUSE HOLDER

HEATED OXYGEN SENSOR (HO2S)

3 PNK

TO IGNITION

86814264

DTC P0131

HEATED OXYGEN SENSOR (HO2S) CIRCUIT (LOW SIGNAL VOLTAGE) (FUEL CONTROL SYSTEM LEAN) 3100 (VIN M) "A" CARLINE (SFI) (MAF)

Circuit Description:
The PCM supplies a voltage of about 45 volt (450 mV) between terminals "BD2" and "BD3". (If measured with a 10 megohm digital voltmeter, this may read as low as .32 volt.) The Heated Oxygen Sensor (HO2S) varies the voltage within a range of about 1 volt (1000 mV) if the exhaust is rich, down to about .10 volt (100 mV) if exhaust is lean.

The sensor is like an open circuit and produces no voltage when it is below about 360°C (600°F). DTC P0131, P0132 or an open sensor circuit or cold sensor causes "Open Loop" operation.

DTC P0131 Will Set When:
• The HO2S signal voltage on CKT 412 remains below 248 mV for at least 4.2 minutes.
• The system is operating in "Closed Loop."

Action Taken (PCM will default to): A current DTC P0131 set will cause the system to operate in "Open Loop." With DTC P0131 set, the MIL (Service Engine Soon) will be illuminated.

DTC Chart Test Description: Number(s) below refer to circled number(s) on the diagnostic chart.
1. Running the engine at 1200 RPM keeps the oxygen sensor hot to ensure the oxygen sensor remains active and can read the exhaust oxygen content accurately.
2. Opening the HO2S signal circuit and grounding the HO2S low circuit should result in a displayed voltage between 350 and 550 mV. If the display is still fixed below 350 mV, the fault is a short to ground in CKT 412 or a faulty PCM.

Diagnostic Aids: Using the Tech 1, observe the L.T. fuel trim values at different RPM and air flow conditions. The Tech 1 also displays the fuel trim cells, so the L.T. fuel trim values can be checked in each of the cells to determine when DTC P0131 may have been set. If the conditions for DTC P0131 exist, the L.T. fuel trim values will be around 158 or greater.

• Heated oxygen sensor wire - Sensor pigtail may be mis-positioned and contacting the exhaust manifold.
• Check for intermittent ground in wire between connector and sensor.
• Poor PCM to engine block ground.

• MAF sensor - A Mass Air Flow (MAF) sensor output that causes the PCM to sense a lower than normal air flow will cause the system to go lean. Disconnect the MAF sensor. If the lean condition is gone, replace the MAF sensor.
• Lean Injector(s) - Perform injector balance test CHART C-2A.
• Fuel contamination - Water, even in small amounts, near the in-tank fuel pump inlet can be delivered to the injectors. The water causes a lean exhaust and can set a DTC P0131.
• Fuel pressure - System will be lean if pressure is too low. It may be necessary to monitor fuel pressure while driving the vehicle at various road speeds and/or loads to confirm.
• Exhaust leaks - If there is an exhaust leak, the engine can cause outside air to be pulled into the exhaust and past the sensor.
• Vacuum or crankcase leaks can cause a lean condition and/or possibly a high idle.
If the above are OK, it is a faulty heated oxygen sensor.
Faulty HO2S heater or heater circuit - See Diagnostic Aids DTC P0134

SEQUENTIAL FUEL INJECTION — DTC P0123

DTC P0123
THROTTLE POSITION (TP) SENSOR CIRCUIT (SIGNAL VOLTAGE HIGH) 3100 (VIN M) "A" CARLINE (SFI) (MAF)

1. THROTTLE CLOSED. DOES TECH 1 DATA DISPLAY INDICATE THROTTLE POSITION OVER 1.06 VOLTS?
— NO → DTC P0123 IS INTERMITTENT. IF NO ADDITIONAL DTC(s) WERE STORED, REFER TO "DIAGNOSTIC AIDS"
— YES ↓

2. DISCONNECT THROTTLE POSITION (TP) SENSOR. TECH 1 DATA DISPLAY SHOULD INDICATE THROTTLE POSITION BELOW .16 VOLT. DOES IT?
— NO → CKT 417 SHORTED TO VOLTAGE OR FAULTY PCM.
— YES ↓

3. PROBE SENSOR GROUND CIRCUIT AT TP SENSOR CONNECTOR WITH A TEST LIGHT CONNECTED TO BATTERY VOLTAGE. TEST LIGHT SHOULD BE "ON." IS IT?
— NO → OPEN SENSOR GROUND CIRCUIT TO TP SENSOR OR FAULTY PCM.
— YES → POOR CONNECTION AT TP SENSOR OR FAULTY TP SENSOR.

"AFTER REPAIRS," REFER TO DTC CRITERIA ON FACING PAGE AND CONFIRM DTC DOES NOT RESET.

86814263

SEQUENTIAL FUEL INJECTION — DTC P0132

DTC P0132

HEATED OXYGEN SENSOR (HO2S) CIRCUIT
(HIGH SIGNAL VOLTAGE) (FUEL CONTROL SYSTEM RICH)
3100 (VIN M) "A" CARLINE (SFI) (MAF)

Circuit Description:

The PCM supplies a voltage of about .45 volt (450 mV) between terminals "BD2" and "BD3". (If measured with a 10 megohm digital voltmeter, this may read as low as .32 volt.) The heated oxygen sensor varies the voltage within a range of between about 1 volt (1000 mV) if the exhaust is rich, to about .10 volt (100 mV) if exhaust is lean. The sensor is like an open circuit and produces no voltage when it is below about 360°C (600°F). DTC P0131, P0132, P0134 or a cold sensor causes "Open Loop" operation.

DTC P0132 Will Set When:

- The HO2S signal voltage on CKT 412 remains above 750 mV for 2 minutes while in "Closed Loop."
- Throttle angle between 6% and 40%.
- No DTC P0122 or P0123.

Action Taken (PCM will default to): A current DTC P0132 will cause the system to operate in "Open Loop." With DTC P0132 set, the MIL (Service Engine Soon) will be illuminated.

DTC Chart Test Description: Number(s) below refer to circled number(s) on the diagnostic chart.

1. Determines if conditions necessary to set DTC P0132 exist.
2. When grounding CKTs 412 and 413. The tech 1 scan tool should read below .35 volts. If not, CKT 412 may be shorted to voltage.

Diagnostic Aids:

- **Fuel pressure** - System will go rich if pressure is too high. The PCM can compensate for some increase. However, if it gets too high, DTC P0132 may be set.

Rich injector
- Leaking injector
- **EVAP canister purge** - Check for fuel saturation. If full of fuel, check canister control and hoses.

- **MAF sensor** - An output that causes the PCM to sense a higher than normal air flow can cause the system to go rich. Disconnecting the MAF sensor will allow the PCM to set a fixed value for the sensor. Substitute a different MAF sensor if the rich condition is gone while the sensor is disconnected.

- Check for leaking fuel pressure regulator diaphragm by checking vacuum line to regulator for fuel.
- **TP sensor** - An intermittent TP sensor output will cause the system to go rich due to a false indication of the throttle moving.

- False rich indication due to silicon contamination of the heated oxygen sensor. This will be indicated by DTC P0131 accompanied by lean driveability conditions and a powdery white deposit on the sensor.

- **Heated Oxygen Sensor (HO2S)** - If the HO2S is internally shorted the HO2S voltage displayed on a Tech 1 will be over 1 volt. Try disconnecting the HO2S with the key "ON," engine "RUNNING;" if the displayed voltage goes from over 1000 mV to around 450 mV, replace the HO2S. Faulty HO2S heater or heater circuit - See Diagnostic Aids DTC P0134.

86814266

SEQUENTIAL FUEL INJECTION — DTC P0131

DTC P0131

HEATED OXYGEN SENSOR (HO2S) CIRCUIT
(LOW SIGNAL VOLTAGE) (FUEL CONTROL SYSTEM LEAN)
3100 (VIN M) "A" CARLINE (SFI) (MAF)

① ▸ RUN WARM ENGINE (75°C/167°F TO 95°C/203°F) AT 1200 RPM.
▸ DOES TECH 1 DATA DISPLAY INDICATE HEATED OXYGEN SENSOR (HO2S) VOLTAGE FIXED BELOW .24 VOLT (240 mV)?

| YES | NO |

NO → DTC P0131 IS INTERMITTENT. IF NO ADDITIONAL DTC(s) WERE STORED, REFER TO "DIAGNOSTIC AIDS"

② ▸ KEY "OFF"
▸ DISCONNECT HO2S AND JUMPER CKT 413 (PCM SIDE) TO GROUND.
▸ KEY "ON" ENGINE RUNNING.
▸ WITH ENGINE IDLING TECH 1 DATA DISPLAY SHOULD INDICATE HO2S VOLTAGE BETWEEN .35 VOLT AND .55 VOLT (350 mV AND 550 mV) AND TOGGLING
▸ DOES IT?

| NO | YES |

YES → REFER TO "DIAGNOSTIC AIDS" ON FACING PAGE.

NO → CKT 412 SHORTED TO GROUND OR FAULTY PCM.

"AFTER REPAIRS," REFER TO DTC CRITERIA ON FACING PAGE AND CONFIRM DTC DOES NOT RESET.

86814265

SEQUENTIAL FUEL INJECTION — DTC P0134

86814268

DTC P0134

HEATED OXYGEN SENSOR (HO2S) CIRCUIT
(OPEN CIRCUIT)
3100 (VIN M) "A" CARLINE (SFI) (MAF)

Circuit Description:

The PCM supplies a voltage of about .45 volt between terminals "BD2" and "BD3". (If measured with a 10 megohm digital voltmeter, this may read as low as .32 volt.) The Heated Oxygen Sensor (HO2S) varies the voltage within a range of about 1 (1000 mV) volt if the exhaust is rich, to about .10 volt if exhaust is lean.

The sensor is like an open circuit and produces no voltage when it is below 360°C (600°F). DTC P0131, P0132, P0134 or a cold oxygen sensor causes "Open Loop" operation.

DTC P0134 Will Set When:

• Engine coolant temperature above 42.5°C (109°F).
• Engine run time more than 2 minutes.
• HO2S signal voltage is steady between 350 mV and 558 mV.
• Throttle angle above 3%.
• All conditions must be met for about 30 seconds.

Action Taken (PCM will default to): With a current DTC P0134 set, the system will operate in "Open Loop." The MIL (Service Engine Soon) will be illuminated.

DTC Chart Test Description: Number(s) below refer to circled number(s) on the diagnostic chart.

1. If the conditions for DTC P0134 exist, the system will not go into "Closed Loop."

2. This will determine if the sensor or the wiring is the cause of DTC P0134.

Diagnostic Aids: An intermittent may be caused by a poor connection, rubbed through wire insulation, or a wire broken inside the insulation.

Check for:

• Poor connection or damaged harness - Inspect harness connectors for backed out terminals, improper mating, broken locks, improperly formed or damaged terminals, poor terminal to wire connection, and damaged harness.

• Faulty HO2S heater or heater circuit - This can be detected using the Tech 1 Scan Tool, by taking a longer period of time to go "Closed Loop." Normal "Closed Loop" operation on cold running engine is 50 seconds or warm running engine is 2 seconds. Both conditions, engine RPM must be greater 850 for 2 seconds and coolant temperature greater than 20°C. A faulty HO2S heater element or heater circuit will delay closed loop operation on cold running engine 1-2 minutes. On warm running engine it will be hard to detect. If HO2S is suspected to be faulty, disconnect the HO2S and connect test light between harness terminals "C" and "D" if the test light does not light, repair open CKT 639 or 150. If the test light illuminates replace HO2S.

SEQUENTIAL FUEL INJECTION — DTC P0132

DTC P0132

HEATED OXYGEN SENSOR (HO2S) CIRCUIT
(HIGH SIGNAL VOLTAGE) (FUEL CONTROL SYSTEM RICH)
3100 (VIN M) "A" CARLINE (SFI) (MAF)

86814267

①
- RUN WARM ENGINE (75°C/167°F TO 95°C/203°F) AT 1200 RPM.
- DOES TECH 1 DATA DISPLAY INDICATE HEATED OXYGEN SENSOR (HO2S) VOLTAGE FIXED ABOVE .75 VOLT (750 mV)?

YES → **NO** → DTC P0132 IS INTERMITTENT. IF NO ADDITIONAL DTC(s) WERE STORED, REFER TO "DIAGNOSTIC AIDS"

②
- KEY "OFF"
- DISCONNECT HO2S AND JUMPER CKTS 412 AND 413 (PCM SIDE) TO GROUND.
- KEY "ON" ENGINE RUNNING
- WITH ENGINE IDLING TECH 1 DATA DISPLAY SHOULD INDICATE HO2S VOLTAGE BELOW .35 VOLT (350 mV).
- DOES IT?

YES → REFER TO "DIAGNOSTIC AIDS" ON FACING PAGE.

NO → REPLACE PCM.

"AFTER REPAIRS," REFER TO DTC CRITERIA ON FACING PAGE AND CONFIRM DTC DOES NOT RESET.

SEQUENTIAL FUEL INJECTION — DTC P0321

86814270

DTC P0321

IGNITION CONTROL 24X SIGNAL CIRCUIT
3100 (VIN M) "A" CARLINE (SFI) (MAF)

Circuit Description:

The 24X Crankshaft Position (CKP) sensor is used to improve idle spark control at low engine speeds. The 24X CKP sensor is located behind the harmonic balancer on the front of the engine where it picks up pulses from a reluctor wheel on the crankshaft. Its signal is conditioned by the PCM and used to more accurately control spark at lower engine speeds (under 1200 RPM) where spark control is critical for idle quality.

DTC P0321 Will Set When:
- Engine is running.
- Engine RPM below 1200 RPM.

Action Taken (PCM will default to): Four spark reference (24X) pulses to be seen between two fuel control (3X) pulses. If the sequence of these pulses is not correct for 50 engine revolutions, DTC P0321 will set. Once DTC P0321 is set, it latches and the PCM will ignore the 24X pulses (if it reappears) for the remainder of the ignition cycle. DTC P0321 does illuminate the MIL (Service Engine Soon).

DTC Chart Test Description: Number(s) below refer to circled number(s) on the diagnostic chart.
1. This test determines if signal voltage is present up to the PCM.
2. This will determine if 12 volts is present at the sensor input.
3. By applying 12 volts to the 24X crankshaft sensor pigtail circuit, pigtail and sensor integrity can be determined.
4. Ground path continuity is determined with this test.

Diagnostic Aids: An intermittent 24X signal error can be caused by poor connections. Ignition feed, reference low and the signal circuits should all be checked for poor connections.

SEQUENTIAL FUEL INJECTION — DTC P0134

DTC P0134

HEATED OXYGEN SENSOR (HO2S) CIRCUIT
(OPEN CIRCUIT)
3100 (VIN M) "A" CARLINE (SFI) (MAF)

① ENGINE AT NORMAL OPERATING TEMPERATURE (ABOVE 80°C/176°F).
- RUN ENGINE ABOVE 1200 RPM FOR TWO MINUTES.
- DOES TECH 1 INDICATE "CLOSED LOOP"?

→ YES → DTC P0134 IS INTERMITTENT. IF NO ADDITIONAL DIAGNOSTIC TROUBLE CODES WERE STORED, REFER TO "DIAGNOSTIC AIDS"

NO ↓

② KEY "OFF."
- DISCONNECT HEATED OXYGEN SENSOR (HO2S).
- JUMPER CKTS 412 AND 413 (PCM SIDE) TO GROUND.
- KEY "ON," ENGINE RUNNING.
- TECH 1 DATA DISPLAY SHOULD INDICATE HO2S VOLTAGE BELOW .35 VOLT (350 mV).
- DOES IT?

→ YES → FAULTY HO2S CONNECTION OR FAULTY HO2S.

NO ↓

KEY "OFF."
- REMOVE JUMPER AND RECONNECT HO2S.
- DISCONNECT GREEN PCM "C-D" CONNECTOR.
- KEY "ON."
- PROBE PCM HARNESS CONNECTOR TERMINAL "BD2" WITH A TEST LIGHT TO B+.
- TEST LIGHT SHOULD BE "ON."
- IS IT?

→ NO → OPEN CKT 413.

YES ↓

OPEN CKT 412
OR
POOR CONNECTION AT PCM
OR
FAULTY PCM.

"AFTER REPAIRS," "REFER TO DTC CRITERIA ON FACING PAGE AND CONFIRM DTC DOES NOT RESET."

86814269

SEQUENTIAL FUEL INJECTION — DTC P0325

PCM — KNOCK SIGNAL TO PROM — 5v — BB8 — 496 DK BLU — KNOCK SENSOR

DTC P0325
KNOCK SENSOR (KS) CIRCUIT
3100 (VIN M) "A" CARLINE (SFI) (MAF)

Circuit Description:

The Knock Sensor (KS) is used to detect engine detonation. The PCM receives the knock sensor signal and will retard Ignition Control (IC) timing until knock is not detected.

The circuitry within the KS will drop approximately half of the 5 volts applied to the sensor on CKT 496. When engine detonation occurs, the sensor produces an AC signal which rides on the 2.5 volt DC signal. The voltage amplitude and frequency is dependent upon the knock level emitted from the engine combustion process.

DTC P0325 Will Set When: The PCM detects above 3.56 volts or below 1.52 volts for 20 seconds.

Action Taken (PCM will default to): The MIL will become illuminated. Knock retard will be fixed at 15 degrees.

DTC Chart Test Description: Number(s) below refer to circled number(s) on the diagnostic chart.

1. If the conditions for DTC P0325, as described above, are being met, the Tech 1 scan tool will always indicate "Yes" when the knock signal position is selected. If an audible knock is heard from the engine, repair the internal engine problem, as normally no knock should be detected at idle.
2. The PCM applies a 5 volt signal to the sensor on CKT 496.

Diagnostic Aids: Check CKT 496 for an intermittent open or short to ground or short to voltage. Also, check for proper installation of KS module.

If the knock sensor CKT 496 is routed too close to secondary ignition wires, it may induce a voltage and cause a false knock signal.

86814272

SEQUENTIAL FUEL INJECTION — DTC P0321

DTC P0321
IGNITION CONTROL 24X SIGNAL CIRCUIT
3100 (VIN M) "A" CARLINE (SFI) (MAF)

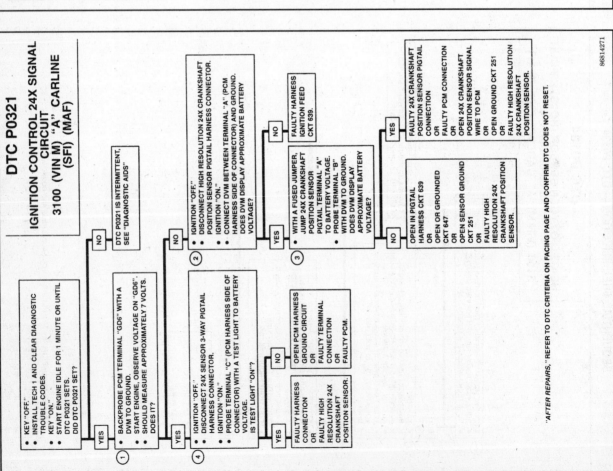

- KEY "OFF." INSTALL TECH 1 AND CLEAR DIAGNOSTIC TROUBLE CODES. KEY "ON." START ENGINE IDLE FOR 1 MINUTE OR UNTIL DTC P0321 SETS. DID DTC P0321 SET?
  - NO → DTC P0321 IS INTERMITTENT, SEE "DIAGNOSTIC AIDS"

(1) BACKPROBE PCM TERMINAL "GD6" WITH A DVM TO GROUND. START ENGINE. OBSERVE VOLTAGE ON "GD6." SHOULD MEASURE APPROXIMATELY 7 VOLTS. DOES IT?

(4) IGNITION "OFF." DISCONNECT 24X SENSOR 3-WAY PIGTAIL HARNESS CONNECTOR. IGNITION "ON." PROBE TERMINAL "C" (PCM HARNESS SIDE OF CONNECTOR) WITH A TEST LIGHT TO BATTERY VOLTAGE. IS TEST LIGHT "ON"?
  - YES → OPEN PCM HARNESS GROUND CIRCUIT OR FAULTY TERMINAL CONNECTION OR FAULTY PCM.
  - NO → FAULTY HARNESS CONNECTION OR FAULTY HIGH RESOLUTION 24X CRANKSHAFT POSITION SENSOR.

(2) IGNITION "OFF." DISCONNECT HIGH RESOLUTION 24X CRANKSHAFT POSITION SENSOR PIGTAIL HARNESS CONNECTOR. IGNITION "ON." CONNECT DVM BETWEEN TERMINAL "A" (PCM HARNESS SIDE OF CONNECTOR) AND GROUND. DOES DVM DISPLAY APPROXIMATE BATTERY VOLTAGE?
  - NO → FAULTY HARNESS IGNITION FEED CKT 639.

(3) WITH A FUSED JUMPER, JUMP 24X CRANKSHAFT POSITION SENSOR PIGTAIL TERMINAL "A" TO BATTERY VOLTAGE. PROBE TERMINAL "B" WITH DVM TO GROUND. DOES DVM DISPLAY APPROXIMATE BATTERY VOLTAGE?
  - NO → OPEN IN PIGTAIL HARNESS CKT 639 OR OPEN OR GROUNDED CKT 647 OR OPEN SENSOR GROUND CKT 251 OR FAULTY HIGH RESOLUTION 24X CRANKSHAFT POSITION SENSOR.
  - YES → FAULTY 24X CRANKSHAFT POSITION SENSOR PIGTAIL CONNECTION OR FAULTY PCM CONNECTION OR OPEN 24X CRANKSHAFT POSITION SENSOR SIGNAL WIRE TO PCM OR OPEN GROUND CKT 251 OR FAULTY HIGH RESOLUTION 24X CRANKSHAFT POSITION SENSOR.

"AFTER REPAIRS," REFER TO DTC CRITERIA ON FACING PAGE AND CONFIRM DTC DOES NOT RESET.

86814271

SEQUENTIAL FUEL INJECTION — DTC P0341

PCM

BA12 — CAM REFERENCE SIGNAL HIGH

GD6 — 24X REFERENCE SIGNAL HIGH

PIGTAIL CONNECTOR
B C A

CAMSHAFT POSITION SENSOR

630 BLK

251 BLK/WHT — GROUND(S) FOR DLC, FUEL PUMP RELAY, AND TRANSAXLE RANGE SWITCH

ENGINE GROUND VEHICLE FRONT, TRANS STUD

639 PNK

INLINE I/P HARNESS CONNECTOR
Z

24X CRANKSHAFT POSITION SENSOR
A C B
PIGTAIL CONNECTOR

647 LT BLU/BLK

10 AMP

INLINE FUSE HOLDER

3 PNK

TO IGNITION

DTC P0341
CAM/CRANK ERROR
3100 (VIN M) "A" CARLINE (SFI) (MAF)

Circuit Description:

During cranking, the ignition control module monitors the 3X crankshaft position sensor sync signal. The sync signal is used to determine the correct cylinder pair to spark first. After the sync signal has been processed by the ignition control module, it sends a fuel control reference pulse to the PCM on CKT 430. When the PCM receives this pulse it will command all six injectors to open for one priming shot of fuel in all cylinders. After the priming, the injectors are left "OFF" for the next six fuel control reference pulses from the ignition control module (two crankshaft revolutions). This allows each cylinder a chance to use the fuel from the priming shot. During this waiting period, a cam pulse will have been received by the PCM. Now the PCM begins to operate the injectors sequentially based on true camshaft position. With the engine running, the PCM monitors the cam and fuel control references pulses it receives and expects to see six fuel control pulses for each cam pulse.

DTC P0341 Will Set When:

- Ratio of fuel control pulses to cam pulses does not equal 6:1. (more cam pulses).
- Above condition for 10 occurrences during key cycle.

Action Taken (PCM will default to): With a current DTC P0341 set, the MIL (Service Engine Soon) will be illuminated for the remainder of the key cycle.

DTC Chart Test Description: Number(s) below refer to circled number(s) on the diagnostic chart.

1. Determines if conditions necessary to set DTC P0341 exist.
2. Determines if fault is in the wiring, camshaft sensor or PCM.

Diagnostic Aids: DTC P0341 may indicate an intermittent fault and may not set immediately or under all conditions. Customer comments of symptom experienced may help isolate the cause of the condition. A poor connection or fault in the camshaft position sensor CKTs 630, 639 or 251, or a faulty camshaft position sensor or faulty 3X crankshaft position sensor may cause the PCM to re-initialize injector sequence when the fault occurs, causing a possible stumble or miss.

If DTC P0341 does not set at idle, raise engine speed to about 3000 RPM. If engine stumbles or misfires and DTC P0341 sets, swap the 3X crankshaft position sensor with a known good one and retest.

86814274

SEQUENTIAL FUEL INJECTION — DTC P0325

DTC P0325
KNOCK SENSOR (KS) CIRCUIT
3100 (VIN M) "A" CARLINE (SFI) (MAF)

(1)
- INSTALL TECH 1.
- ENGINE IDLING, ENGINE COOLANT TEMP ABOVE 67°C.
- DOES TECH 1 INDICATE A FIXED VALUE OF KNOCK RETARD BETWEEN 4 AND 20 DEGREES?

NO → DTC P0325 IS INTERMITTENT. SEE "DIAGNOSTIC AIDS"

YES ↓

(2)
- DISCONNECT KNOCK SENSOR.
- IGNITION "ON."
- USING A DVM, MEASURE VOLTAGE BETWEEN HARNESS CKT 496 AND GROUND. VOLTAGE SHOULD BE 4–6 VOLTS. IS IT?

LESS THAN 4 VOLTS → CKT 496 OPEN, SHORTED TO GROUND OR FAULTY PCM.

OVER 6 VOLTS → CHECK FOR CKT 496 BEING ROUTED TOO CLOSE TO SECONDARY IGNITION WIRES OR CKT 496 SHORTED TO VOLTAGE OR FAULTY PCM.

YES ↓

- MEASURE RESISTANCE OF KNOCK SENSOR BY CONNECTING OHMMETER BETWEEN SENSOR TERMINAL AND ENGINE BLOCK. SHOULD BE BETWEEN 3.3kΩ AND 4.5kΩ. IS IT?

NO → REMOVE KNOCK SENSOR AND ENSURE THAT THREADS ON SENSOR AND BLOCK ARE CLEAN AND FREE OF CORROSION, TEFLON TAPE, ANTI-SEIZE COMPOUNDS, OR SEALANTS. IF OK, REPLACE FAULTY KNOCK SENSOR.

YES ↓

- CHECK HARNESS AND SENSOR CONNECTOR. IF OK,
- REMOVE PCM AND BE SURE PROM IS PROPERLY SEATED INTO PCM. IF OK,
- REPLACE PROM.

"AFTER REPAIRS," REFER TO DTC CRITERIA ON FACING PAGE AND CONFIRM DTC DOES NOT RESET.

86814273

SEQUENTIAL FUEL INJECTION — DTC P0342

DTC P0342

CAMSHAFT POSITION SENSOR (LOSS OF CAM PULSES) CIRCUIT
3100 (VIN M) "A" CARLINE (SFI) (MAF)

Circuit Description:

During cranking, the ignition control module monitors the 3X crankshaft position sensor sync signal. The sync signal is used to determine the correct cylinder pair to spark first. After the sync signal has been processed by the ignition control module, it sends a fuel control reference pulse to the PCM on CKT 430. When the PCM receives this pulse it will command all six injectors to open for one priming shot of fuel in all cylinders. After the priming, the injectors are left "OFF" for the next six fuel control reference pulses from the ignition control module (two crankshaft revolutions). This allows each cylinder a chance to use the fuel from the priming shot. During this waiting period, a cam pulse will have been received by the PCM. Now the PCM begins to operate the injectors sequentially based on true camshaft position. With the engine running, the PCM monitors the cam and fuel control references pulses it receives and expects to see six fuel control pulses for each cam pulse. If the sequence of these pulses is not correct for 10 occurrences.

DTC P0342 Will Set When: Cam reference pulses are not detected by the PCM for 5 seconds while the engine is running. DTC P0342 is looking for loss cam pulses.

Action Taken (PCM will default to): The PCM will pulse the injectors sequentially though possibly not in the correct sequence. The Malfunction Indicator Lamp (MIL) will be illuminated.

DTC Chart Test Description: Number(s) below refer to circled number(s) on the diagnostic chart.

1. Determines if conditions necessary to set DTC P0342 exist.
2. By repeatedly "bumping" the starter, the camshaft interrupter and the camshaft position sensor will align with each other. At this point, the voltage from the sensor applied to the PCM should drop to near zero temporarily. This indicates that the camshaft position sensor is capable of sending a signal to the PCM.

3. Before replacing the camshaft position sensor, inspect the sensor for proper installation.

Diagnostic Aids: An intermittent cam reference signal can be caused by poor connections, cracked sensor or internal engine problem.

SEQUENTIAL FUEL INJECTION — DTC P0341

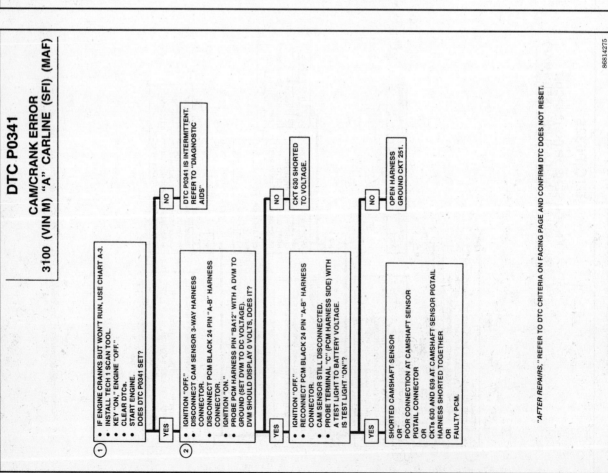

DTC P0341

CAM/CRANK ERROR
3100 (VIN M) "A" CARLINE (SFI) (MAF)

①
- IF ENGINE CRANKS BUT WON'T RUN, USE CHART A-3.
- INSTALL TECH 1 SCAN TOOL.
- KEY "ON," ENGINE "OFF."
- CLEAR DTCs.
- START ENGINE.
- DOES DTC P0341 SET?

YES

②
- IGNITION "OFF."
- DISCONNECT CAM SENSOR 3-WAY HARNESS CONNECTOR.
- DISCONNECT PCM BLACK 24 PIN "A-B" HARNESS CONNECTOR.
- IGNITION "ON."
- PROBE PCM HARNESS PIN "BA12" WITH A DVM TO GROUND (SET DVM TO DC VOLTAGE).
- DVM SHOULD DISPLAY 0 VOLTS, DOES IT?

YES

- IGNITION "OFF."
- RECONNECT PCM BLACK 24 PIN "A-B" HARNESS CONNECTOR.
- CAM SENSOR STILL DISCONNECTED.
- PROBE TERMINAL "C" (PCM HARNESS SIDE) WITH A TEST LIGHT TO BATTERY VOLTAGE.
- IS TEST LIGHT "ON"?

YES

SHORTED CAMSHAFT SENSOR
OR
POOR CONNECTION AT CAMSHAFT SENSOR PIGTAIL CONNECTOR
OR
CKTs 630 AND 639 AT CAMSHAFT SENSOR PIGTAIL HARNESS SHORTED TOGETHER
OR
FAULTY PCM.

NO → DTC P0341 IS INTERMITTENT. REFER TO "DIAGNOSTIC AIDS"

NO → CKT 630 SHORTED TO VOLTAGE.

NO → OPEN HARNESS GROUND CKT 251.

"AFTER REPAIRS," REFER TO DTC CRITERIA ON FACING PAGE AND CONFIRM DTC DOES NOT RESET.

SEQUENTIAL FUEL INJECTION — DTC P1350

DTC P1350

IGNITION CONTROL (IC) OPEN CIRCUIT
3100 (VIN M) "A" CARLINE (SFI) (MAF)

Circuit Description:

Ignition control spark timing is provided by the PCM on CKT 423. Inputs from a number of engine sensors allow the PCM to correctly calculate optimum spark timing. Engine load is calculated from the MAF sensor, engine RPM is derived from the 3X crankshaft position sensor, engine operating temperature from ECT and IAT sensors and engine knock activity from the knock sensor. Other engine functions modify spark to a lesser degree such as TCC engagement and EGR activity.

The bypass circuit controls an internal switch in the electronic Ignition Control Module (ICM). Unless the vehicle is in backup spark (base timing mode), the bypass circuit will have 5 volts applied to it. This 5 volt signal from the PCM allows a solid state switch to direct the IC timing pulses to the ICM for sequencing and energizing the coil packs. If the bypass circuit is not energized, the IC pulses from the ICM are shunted to ground and the electronic ICM uses it's own base timing schedule to time and energize the coil packs.

DTC P1350 Will Set When: Ignition Control (IC) pulses are detected on CKT 423 when the vehicle is in bypass (no voltage applied to bypass should allow IC pulses to be grounded by the electronic ICM). The test will either pass or fail within the first 100 milliseconds of engine running. If it passes, the test will not run until the next key cycle.

Action Taken (PCM will default to): The PCM will not allow the electronic ignition control module to control timing using it's own base timing schedule. The MIL will become illuminated.

DTC Chart Test Description: Number(s) below refer to circled number(s) on the diagnostic chart.

1. This test confirms DTC P1350 and that the fault causing the DTC is present.
2. Checks for a normal IC ground path through the ignition control module. A DTC P1350 indicates the PCM has detected an open or short to voltage in the IC circuit, or a short to voltage in the bypass circuit. An IC CKT 423 shorted to ground will also read less than 500 ohms; however, this should set a DTC P1361

Diagnostic Aids: The scan tool does not have any ability to help diagnose a DTC P1350 problem.

- Ignition control line - When CKT 423 is shorted voltage or open during crank will set DTC 1350; also if CKT 424 is shorted to voltage during crank DTC 1350 will set.
- Ignition control bypass line - During engine run operation CKT 424 opens or shorts to ground DTC 1361 will set. When DTC 1350 is stored, DTC 1350 will not be set. If DTC 1350 is stored, DTC 1361 also can be set.

86814278

SEQUENTIAL FUEL INJECTION — DTC P0342

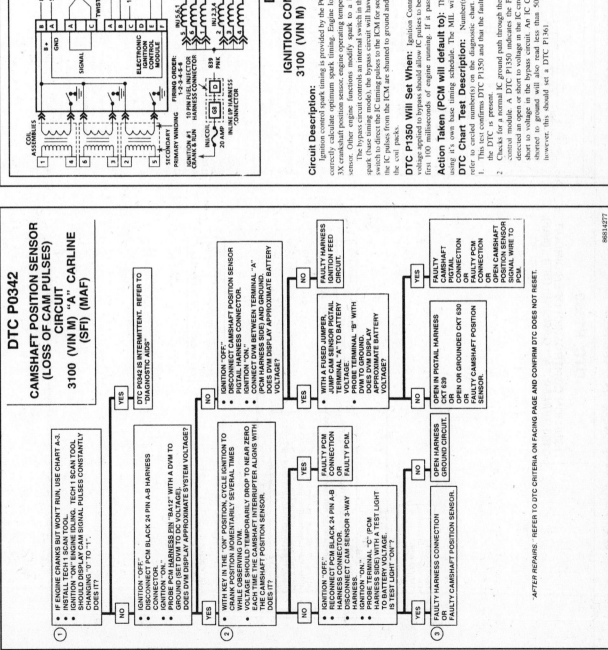

DTC P0342

CAMSHAFT POSITION SENSOR
(LOSS OF CAM PULSES)
CIRCUIT
3100 (VIN M) "A" CARLINE
(SFI) (MAF)

①
- IF ENGINE CRANKS BUT WON'T RUN, USE CHART A-3.
- INSTALL TECH 1 SCAN TOOL.
- IGNITION "ON" ENGINE IDLING. TECH 1 SCAN TOOL SHOULD DISPLAY CAM SIGNAL PULSES CONSTANTLY CHANGING "0" TO "1".
  DOES IT?

YES → DTC P0342 IS INTERMITTENT. REFER TO "DIAGNOSTIC AIDS"

NO →
- IGNITION "OFF."
- DISCONNECT PCM BLACK 24 PIN A-B HARNESS CONNECTOR.
- IGNITION "ON."
- PROBE PCM HARNESS PIN "BA12" WITH A DVM TO GROUND (SET DVM TO DC VOLTAGE).
  DOES DVM DISPLAY APPROXIMATE SYSTEM VOLTAGE?

YES → FAULTY PCM CONNECTION OR FAULTY PCM.

NO →
- IGNITION "OFF."
- DISCONNECT CAMSHAFT POSITION SENSOR PIGTAIL HARNESS CONNECTOR.
- IGNITION "ON."
- CONNECT DVM BETWEEN TERMINAL "A" (PCM HARNESS SIDE) AND GROUND.
  DOES DVM DISPLAY APPROXIMATE BATTERY VOLTAGE?

YES →
- WITH A FUSED JUMPER, JUMP CAM SENSOR PIGTAIL TERMINAL "A" TO BATTERY VOLTAGE.
- PROBE TERMINAL "B" WITH DVM TO GROUND.
  DOES DVM DISPLAY APPROXIMATE BATTERY VOLTAGE?

YES →
- IGNITION "OFF."
- RECONNECT PCM BLACK 24 PIN A-B HARNESS CONNECTOR.
- DISCONNECT CAM SENSOR 3-WAY HARNESS.
- IGNITION "ON."
- PROBE TERMINAL "C" (PCM HARNESS SIDE) WITH A TEST LIGHT TO BATTERY VOLTAGE.
  IS TEST LIGHT "ON"?

YES → FAULTY PCM CONNECTION OR FAULTY PCM.

NO → OPEN HARNESS GROUND CIRCUIT.

②
- WITH KEY IN THE "ON" POSITION, CYCLE IGNITION TO CRANK POSITION MOMENTARILY SEVERAL TIMES WHILE OBSERVING DVM.
  VOLTAGE SHOULD TEMPORARILY DROP TO NEAR ZERO EACH TIME THE CAMSHAFT INTERRUPTER ALIGNS WITH THE CAMSHAFT POSITION SENSOR.
  DOES IT?

YES → FAULTY HARNESS IGNITION FEED CIRCUIT.

NO →
- OPEN IN PIGTAIL HARNESS CKT 639
  OR
- OPEN OR GROUNDED CKT 630
  OR
- FAULTY CAMSHAFT POSITION SENSOR.

NO →
- OPEN IN PIGTAIL HARNESS CKT 639
  OR
- OPEN OR GROUNDED CKT 630
  OR
- FAULTY CAMSHAFT POSITION SENSOR.

③

YES → FAULTY CAMSHAFT PIGTAIL CONNECTION OR FAULTY PCM CONNECTION OR OPEN CAMSHAFT POSITION SENSOR SIGNAL WIRE TO PCM.

NO →
- FAULTY HARNESS CONNECTION OR FAULTY CAMSHAFT POSITION SENSOR.

AFTER REPAIRS: REFER TO DTC CRITERIA ON FACING PAGE AND CONFIRM DTC DOES NOT RESET.

86814277

SEQUENTIAL FUEL INJECTION — DTC P1361

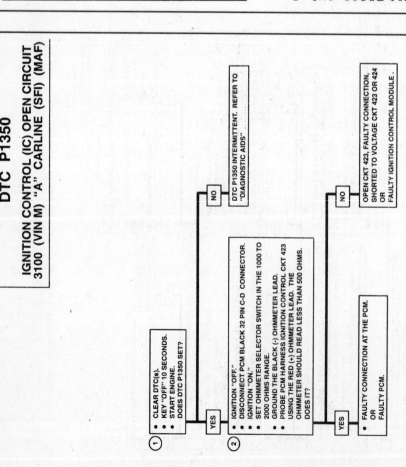

DTC P1361

IGNITION CONTROL (IC) BYPASS CIRCUIT
3100 (VIN M) "A" CARLINE (SFI) (MAF)

Circuit Description:

Ignition control spark timing is provided by the PCM on CKT 423. Inputs from a number of engine sensors allow the PCM to correctly calculate optimum spark timing. Engine load is calculated from the MAF sensor, engine RPM is derived from the 3X crankshaft position sensor, engine operating temperature from ECT and IAT sensors, and engine knock activity from the knock sensor. Other engine functions modify spark to a lesser degree such as TCC engagement and EGR activity.

The bypass circuit controls an internal switch in the electronic Ignition Control Module (ICM). Unless the vehicle is in backup spark (base timing mode), the bypass circuit will have 5 volts applied to it. This 5 volt signal from the PCM allows a solid state switch to direct the IC timing pulses to the ICM for sequencing and energizing the coil packs. If the bypass circuit is not energized, the IC pulses from the ICM are shunted to ground and the electronic ICM uses it's own base timing schedule to time and energize the coil packs.

DTC P1361 Will Set When: No pulses are detected on the IC circuit by the PCM.
Action Taken (PCM will default to): The PCM will allow the electronic ignition control module to control timing using its own base timing schedule. The MIL will become illuminated.
DTC Chart Test Description: Number(s) below refer to circled number(s) on the diagnostic chart.

1. This test confirms DTC P1361 and that the fault causing the DTC is present.
2. Checks for a normal IC ground path through the ignition control module. A DTC P1361 indicates the PCM has detected an open or short to voltage IC circuit, or the bypass circuit grounded or shorted to voltage. An IC CKT 423 shorted to ground will also read less than 500 ohms; however, this will be checked later.
3. As the test light voltage touches CKT 424, the module should switch causing the ohmmeter to "overrange" if the meter is in the 1000-2000 ohms position. Selecting the 10-20,000 ohms position will indicate above 5000 ohms. The important thing is that the module "switched."
4. The module did not switch and this step checks for

- IC CKT 423 shorted to ground.
- Bypass CKT 424 open.
- Faulty electronic ignition control module connection or module.
5. Confirms that DTC P1361 is a faulty PCM and not an intermittent in CKT 423 or 424.

Diagnostic Aids: The Tech 1 scan tool does not have any ability to help diagnose a DTC P1361 problem. Refer to "Intermittents" in "Symptoms," Section "6E3-B". EST line - When CKT 423 is shorted voltage or open during crank, will set DTC P1350 also if CKT 424 is shorted to voltage during crank DTC P1350 will set. Bypass line - during engine rune operation, if CKT 424 opens or shorts to ground DTC P1361 will set. When DTC P1361 is stored DTC P1350 will not be set. If DTC P1361 is stored DTC P1350 also can be set.

86814280

SEQUENTIAL FUEL INJECTION — DTC P1350

DTC P1350

IGNITION CONTROL (IC) OPEN CIRCUIT
3100 (VIN M) "A" CARLINE (SFI) (MAF)

1. CLEAR DTC(s).
- KEY "OFF" 10 SECONDS.
- START ENGINE.
- DOES DTC P1350 SET?

YES / NO

NO → DTC P1350 INTERMITTENT. REFER TO "DIAGNOSTIC AIDS"

2. - IGNITION "OFF."
- DISCONNECT PCM BLACK 32 PIN C-D CONNECTOR.
- IGNITION "ON."
- SET OHMMETER SELECTOR SWITCH IN THE 1000 TO 2000 OHMS RANGE.
- GROUND THE BLACK (-) OHMMETER LEAD.
- PROBE PCM HARNESS IGNITION CONTROL CKT 423 USING THE RED (+) OHMMETER LEAD. THE OHMMETER SHOULD READ LESS THAN 500 OHMS. DOES IT?

YES / NO

YES → - FAULTY CONNECTION AT THE PCM.
OR
- FAULTY PCM.

NO → OPEN CKT 423, FAULTY CONNECTION, SHORTED TO VOLTAGE CKT 423 OR 424
OR
FAULTY IGNITION CONTROL MODULE.

"AFTER REPAIRS," REFER TO DTC CRITERIA ON FACING PAGE AND CONFIRM DTC DOES NOT RESET.

86814279

SEQUENTIAL FUEL INJECTION — DTC P1361

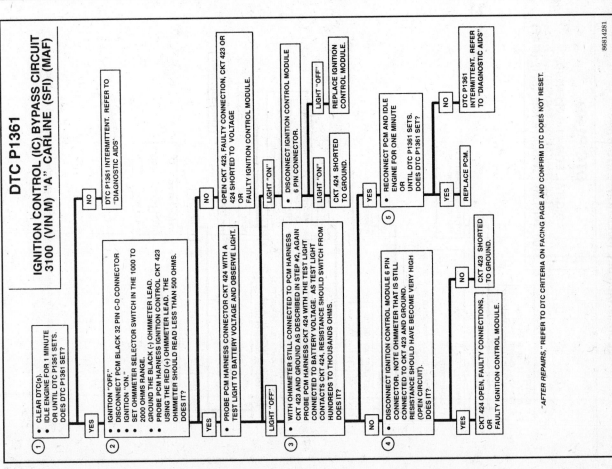

DTC P1361
IGNITION CONTROL (IC) BYPASS CIRCUIT
3100 (VIN M) "A" CARLINE (SFI) (MAF)

SEQUENTIAL FUEL INJECTION — DTC P1403

DTC P1403
DIGITAL EGR #1 SOLENOID
(ELECTRICAL DIAGNOSIS)
3100 (VIN M) "A" CARLINE (SFI) (MAF)

Circuit Description:

Exhaust gas recirculation (EGR) is administered through a digitally controlled three solenoid valve unit. Each of the three valves is controlled individually and can be open or closed in any combination during a long closed throttle deceleration. The PCM tests the EGR solenoids by momentarily commanding each solenoid "ON" while monitoring engine RPM. This test indicates if the EGR solenoids are operational electrically or if an EGR passage is obstructed. If the expected drop in RPM is not seen for a calibrated number of tests associated with solenoid #1 being commanded "ON." The PCM will illuminate the MIL (Service Engine Soon) and store DTC P1403.

DTC P1403 Will Set When:

- Engine run time greater than 5 seconds.
- Vehicle is in "Coast Down" condition.
- Fuel control system is "Closed Loop" and HO2S voltage greater than .6 volt.
- Vehicle not in decel fuel cutoff.
- Engine coolant temperature is over 84°C (183°F).
- Vehicle speed above 20 mph.
- A/C clutch not engaged.
- Engine RPM between 838 - 1050 for .10 seconds.

Action Taken (PCM will default to): EGR solenoid #1 is tested by energizing the solenoid and checking the RPM drop. There should be a drop of 50 RPM within 1.2 seconds. Solenoid #1 must fail 10 of 12 test to set the DTC P1403. Once 12 tests are run during an ignition cycle, the PCM will not run EGR solenoid test until the next ignition cycle. With a current DTC P1403 set. The PCM will illuminate the MIL (Service Engine Soon).

DTC P1403 Chart Test Description: Number(s) below refer to circled number(s) on the diagnostic chart.

1. This test determines if there is power to the EGR valve.
2. This test will determine if there is an open circuit in the EGR wiring or if the EGR valve is at fault.
3. This test will determine if there is a short to ground in CKT 697 going to the EGR valve or if the PCM is at fault.

Diagnostic Aids: An intermittent may be caused by a wire broken inside the insulation.

Check for:

- Poor connection or damaged harness - Inspect PCM harness connectors for backed out terminals, improper mating, broken locks, improperly formed or damaged terminals, poor terminal to wire connections and damaged harness.

Intermittent test - An intermittent may be caused by a poor connection, chaffed wire insulation, or a wire broken inside the insulation.

Intake plenum should be checked for possible plugged passages.

NOTICE: If the EGR valve shows signs of excessive heat, check the exhaust system for blockage (possibly a plugged converter).

If the exhaust system is restricted, repair the cause; one of which might be an injector which is open due to one of the following:

A. Stuck.
B. Grounded driver circuit.
C. Possible faulty PCM.

If this condition is found, the oil should be checked for possible fuel contamination.

86814282

86814281

"AFTER REPAIRS," REFER TO DTC CRITERIA ON FACING PAGE AND CONFIRM DTC DOES NOT RESET.

SEQUENTIAL FUEL INJECTION — DTC P1404

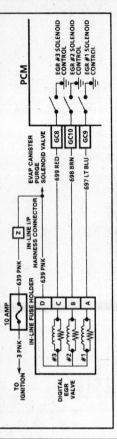

DTC P1404

DIGITAL EGR #2 SOLENOID
(ELECTRICAL DIAGNOSIS)
3100 (VIN M) "A" CARLINE (SFI) (MAF)

Circuit Description:

Exhaust Gas Recirculation (EGR) is administered through a digitally controlled three solenoid valve unit. Each of the three valves is controlled individually and can be open or closed in any combination. During a long closed throttle deceleration. The PCM tests the EGR solenoids by momentarily commanding each solenoid "ON" while monitoring engine RPM. This test indicates if the EGR solenoids are operational electrically or if an EGR passage is obstructed. If the expected drop in RPM is not seen for a calibrated number of tests associated with solenoid #2 being commanded "ON." The PCM will illuminate the MIL (Service Engine Soon) and store DTC P1404.

DTC P1404 Will Set When:

- Engine run time greater than 5 seconds.
- Vehicle is in "coast down" condition.
- Fuel control system is "Closed Loop" and HO2S voltage greater than .6 volt.
- Vehicle not in decel fuel cutoff.
- Engine coolant temperature is over 84°C (183°F).
- Vehicle speed above 20 mph.
- A/C Clutch not engaged.
- Engine RPM between 850 - 1075 for .10 seconds.

Action Taken (PCM will default to): EGR solenoid #2 is tested by energizing the solenoid and checking the RPM drop. There should be a drop of 50 RPM within .9 seconds. Solenoid #2 must fail 9 of 12 tests to set the DTC P1404. Once 12 tests are run during an ignition cycle, the PCM will not run EGR solenoid test until the next ignition cycle. With a current DTC P1404 set. The PCM will illuminate the MIL (Service Engine Soon).

DTC Chart Test Description: Number(s) below refer to circled number(s) on the diagnostic chart.

1. This test determines if there is power to the EGR valve.
2. This test will determine if there is an open circuit in the EGR wiring or if the EGR valve is at fault.
3. This test will determine if there is a short to ground in CKT 698 going to the EGR valve or if the PCM is at fault.

Diagnostic Aids: An intermittent may be caused by a wire broken inside the insulation.
Check for:

- Poor connection or damaged harness - Inspect PCM harness connectors for backed out terminals, improper mating, broken locks, improperly formed or damaged terminals, poor terminal to wire connections and damaged harness.

Intermittent test - An intermittent may be caused by a poor connection, chaffed wire insulation, or a wire broken inside the insulation. Intake plenum should be checked for possible plugged passages.

NOTICE: If the EGR valve shows signs of excessive heat, check the exhaust system for blockage (possibly a plugged converter) using the procedure found on CHART B-1. If the exhaust system is restricted, repair the cause; one of which might be an injector which is open due to one of the following:

A. Stuck.
B. Grounded driver circuit.
C. Possible faulty PCM.

If this condition is found, the oil should be checked for possible fuel contamination.

86814284

SEQUENTIAL FUEL INJECTION — DTC P1403

DTC P1403

DIGITAL EGR #1 SOLENOID
(ELECTRICAL DIAGNOSIS)
3100 (VIN M) "A" CARLINE (SFI) (MAF)

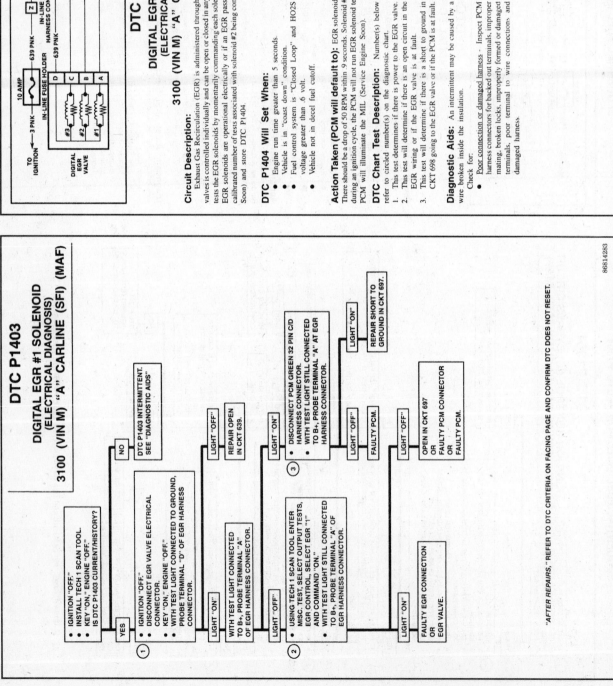

86814283

"AFTER REPAIRS," REFER TO DTC CRITERIA ON FACING PAGE AND CONFIRM DTC DOES NOT RESET.

SEQUENTIAL FUEL INJECTION — DTC P1405

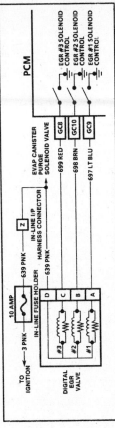

86814286

DTC P1405

DIGITAL EGR #3 SOLENOID
(ELECTRICAL DIAGNOSIS)
3100 (VIN M) "A" CARLINE (SFI) (MAF)

Circuit Description:

Exhaust Gas Recirculation (EGR) is administered through a digitally controlled three solenoid valve unit. Each of the three valves is controlled individually and can be open or closed in any combination. During a long closed throttle deceleration. The PCM tests the EGR solenoids by momentarily commanding each solenoid "ON" while monitoring engine RPM. This test indicates if the EGR solenoids are operational electrically, or if an EGR passage is obstructed. If the expected drop in RPM is not seen for a calibrated number of tests associated with solenoid #3 being commanded "ON," PCM will illuminate the MIL (Service Engine Soon) and store DTC P1405.

DTC P1405 Will Set When:

- Engine run time greater than 5 seconds.
- Vehicle is in "coast down" condition.
- Fuel control system is "Closed Loop" and HO2S voltage greater than .6 volt.
- Vehicle not in decel fuel cutoff.
- Engine coolant temperature is over 84°C (183°F).
- Vehicle speed above 20 mph.
- A/C Clutch not engaged.
- Engine RPM between 863 - 1113 for .07 seconds.

Action Taken (PCM will default to): EGR solenoid #3 is tested by energizing the solenoid and checking the RPM drop. There should be a drop of 63 RPM within .6 seconds. Solenoid #3 must fail 4 of 5 tests to set the DTC P1405. Once 12 tests are run during an ignition cycle, the PCM will not run EGR solenoid test until the next ignition cycle. With a current DTC P1405 set. The PCM will illuminate the MIL (Service Engine Soon).

DTC Chart Test Description: Number(s) below refer to circled number(s) on the diagnostic chart.

1. This test determines if there is power to the EGR valve.
2. This test will determine if there is an open circuit in the EGR wiring or if the EGR valve is at fault.
3. This test will determine if there is a short to ground in CKT 699 going to the EGR valve or if the PCM is at fault.

Diagnostic Aids: An intermittent may be caused by a wire broken inside the insulation.

Check for:

- Poor connection or damaged harness - Inspect PCM harness connectors for backed out terminals, improper mating, broken locks, improperly formed or damaged terminals, poor terminal to wire connections and damaged harness.

Intermittent test - An intermittent may be caused by a poor connection, chaffed wire insulation, or a wire broken inside the insulation.

Intake plenum should be checked for possible plugged passages.

NOTICE: If the EGR valve shows signs of excessive heat, check the exhaust system for blockage (possibly a plugged converter) using the procedure found on CHART B-1. If the exhaust system is restricted, repair the cause; one of which might be an injector which is open due to one of the following:

- A. Stuck.
- B. Grounded driver circuit.
- C. Possible faulty PCM.

If this condition is found. the oil should be checked for possible fuel contamination.

SEQUENTIAL FUEL INJECTION — DTC P1404

86814285

DTC P1404

DIGITAL EGR #2 SOLENOID
(ELECTRICAL DIAGNOSIS)
3100 (VIN M) "A" CARLINE (SFI) (MAF)

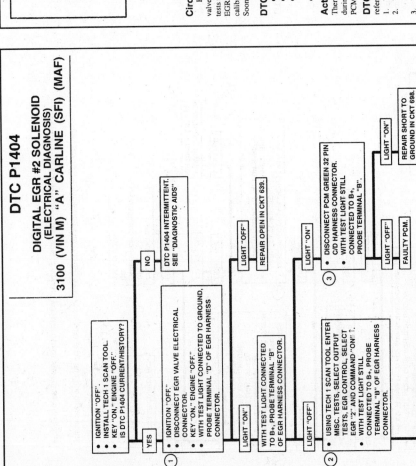

* THESE STEPS MUST BE DONE VERY QUICKLY AS THE PCM WILL COMPENSATE FUEL DELIVERY.

"AFTER REPAIRS," REFER TO DTC CRITERIA ON FACING PAGE AND CONFIRM DTC DOES NOT RESET.

SEQUENTIAL FUEL INJECTION — DTC P0501/0502

VEHICLE SPEED SENSOR (VSS) (TRANS MOUNTED)

TO CLUSTER MODULE →
TO CRUISE CONTROL MODULE →

PCM

400 YEL — GD14 VSS INPUT HIGH
401 PPL — GD13 VSS INPUT LOW
389 DK GRN — GD10 4 K/PPM (OUTPUT)

DTC P0501/P0502
VEHICLE SPEED SENSOR (VSS) CIRCUIT
3100 (VIN M) "A" CARLINE (SFI) (MAF)

Circuit Description:

Vehicle speed information is provided to the PCM by the vehicle speed sensor in the transaxle. The voltage level and the number of pulses increases with vehicle speed. The PCM converts the pulsing voltage to mph, and the mph can be displayed with a Tech 1.

The function of the VSS buffer, used in past model years, has been incorporated into the PCM. The PCM supplies the necessary signal for the instrument panel (4004 pulses per mile) for operating the speedometer and the odometer.

DTC P0501 Will Set When:
- Engine is running.
- No DTC P0703.
- Transmission is out of park or neutral for more than 4 seconds.
- Vehicle speed is greater than 18 mph.
- Brake not applied.
- All conditions met for 2 seconds.

DTC P0502 Will Set When:
- Vehicle speed goes from less than 3 to 0 mph in less than 2 seconds, brake not applied.
- Engine is running.
- Engine speed is greater than 3000 RPM.
- Transmission is out of park or neutral for more than 4 seconds.

Action Taken (PCM will default to): Cruise control operation will not be allowed with DTC P0501 or P0502 set. Also, DTC will remain set for rest of that ignition cycle and the PCM will command only 2nd and 3rd gear based on RPM and TPS. TCC will not be allowed to engage. Additionally, the cluster speedometer may be inoperative. The MIL (Service Engine Soon) will be illuminated.

DTC Chart Test Description: Number(s) below refer to circled number(s) on the diagnostic chart.
1. The VSS signal generator only produces a signal if drive wheels are turning greater then 3 mph.
2. Before replacing the PCM, check the PROM for correct application.

Diagnostic Aids: Tech 1 should indicate a vehicle speed whenever the vehicle is moving greater than 3 mph.

DTC P0502 indicates an intermittent problem and may not set immediately or under all conditions. Check CKTs 400 and 401 for proper connections to be sure they are clean and tight and the harness is routed correctly. Refer to "Intermittents," in "Symptoms." Section "6E3-B".

86814288

SEQUENTIAL FUEL INJECTION — DTC P1405

DTC P1405
DIGITAL EGR #3 SOLENOID
(ELECTRICAL DIAGNOSIS)
3100 (VIN M) "A" CARLINE (SFI) (MAF)

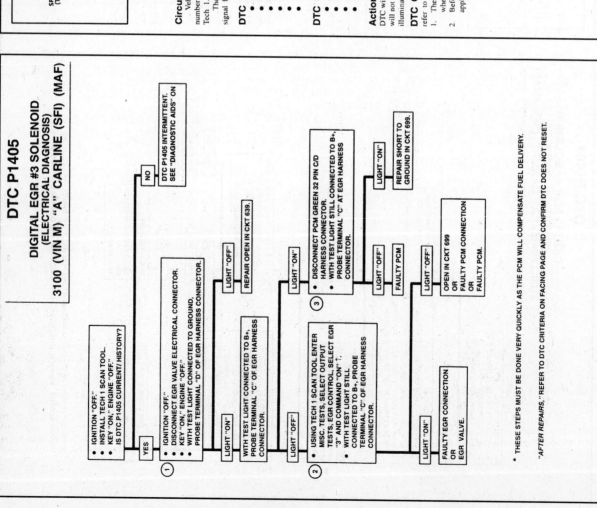

- IGNITION "OFF."
- INSTALL TECH 1 SCAN TOOL.
- KEY "ON," ENGINE "OFF."
- IS DTC P1405 CURRENT/HISTORY?

YES

NO → DTC P1405 INTERMITTENT. SEE "DIAGNOSTIC AIDS" ON

①
- IGNITION "OFF."
- DISCONNECT EGR VALVE ELECTRICAL CONNECTOR.
- KEY "ON," ENGINE "OFF."
- WITH TEST LIGHT CONNECTED TO GROUND, PROBE TERMINAL "D" OF EGR HARNESS CONNECTOR.

LIGHT "OFF" → REPAIR OPEN IN CKT 639.

LIGHT "ON"

WITH TEST LIGHT CONNECTED TO B+, PROBE TERMINAL "C" OF EGR HARNESS CONNECTOR.

LIGHT "OFF"

②
- USING TECH 1 SCAN TOOL ENTER MISC. TESTS, SELECT OUTPUT TESTS, EGR CONTROL, SELECT EGR "3" AND COMMAND "ON".
- WITH TEST LIGHT STILL CONNECTED TO B+, PROBE TERMINAL "C" OF EGR HARNESS CONNECTOR.

LIGHT "ON"

③
- DISCONNECT PCM GREEN 32 PIN C/D HARNESS CONNECTOR.
- WITH TEST LIGHT STILL CONNECTED TO B+, PROBE TERMINAL "C" AT EGR HARNESS CONNECTOR.

LIGHT "ON" → REPAIR SHORT TO GROUND IN CKT 699.

LIGHT "OFF" → FAULTY PCM

LIGHT "OFF" → OPEN IN CKT 699 OR FAULTY PCM CONNECTION OR FAULTY PCM.

LIGHT "ON" → FAULTY EGR CONNECTION OR EGR VALVE.

* THESE STEPS MUST BE DONE VERY QUICKLY AS THE PCM WILL COMPENSATE FUEL DELIVERY.

"AFTER REPAIRS," REFER TO DTC CRITERIA ON FACING PAGE AND CONFIRM DTC DOES NOT RESET.

86814287

SEQUENTIAL FUEL INJECTION — DTC P1530

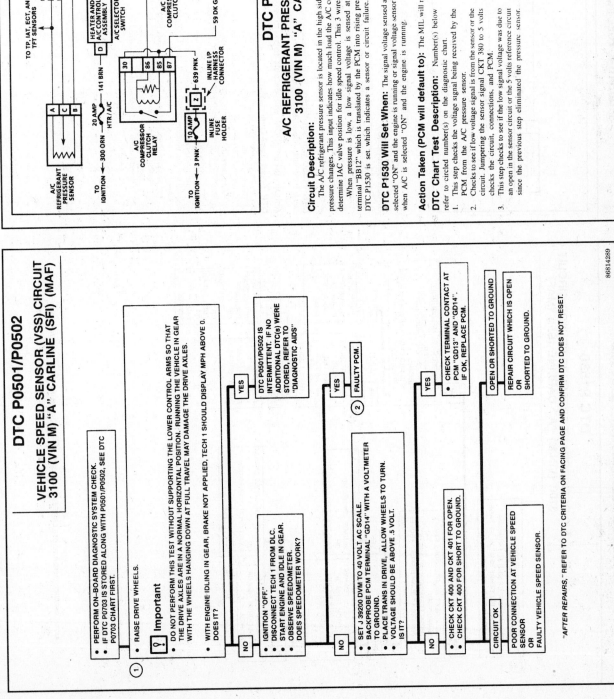

86814290

DTC P1530

A/C REFRIGERANT PRESSURE SENSOR CIRCUIT
3100 (VIN M) "A" CARLINE (SFI) (MAF)

Circuit Description:

The A/C refrigerant pressure sensor is located in the high side of the A/C cooling system and signals the PCM of refrigerant pressure changes. This input indicates how much load the A/C compressor is putting on the engine. The PCM uses this input to determine IAC valve position for idle speed control. This 3 wire sensor has a 5 volt reference input, a signal line and a ground.

When pressure is low, a low signal voltage is sensed at the PCM. As pressure rises, the voltage increases at PCM terminal "BB12" which is translated by the PCM into rising pressure. If the signal voltage remains below a calibrated value, a DTC P1530 is set which indicates a sensor or circuit failure.

DTC P1530 Will Set When: The signal voltage sensed at terminal "BB12" is below .1 volt for 25.4 seconds when A/C is selected "ON" and the engine is running or signal voltage sensor sensed at terminal "BB12" is above 4.92 volts for 25.4 seconds when A/C is selected "ON" and the engine is running.

Action Taken (PCM will default to): The MIL will not become illuminated and the A/C compressor will be disabled.

DTC Chart Test Description: Number(s) below refer to circled number(s) on the diagnostic chart.

1. This step checks the voltage signal being received by the PCM from the A/C pressure sensor.

2. Checks to see if low voltage signal is from the sensor or the circuit. Jumpering the sensor signal CKT 380 to 5 volts checks the circuit, connections, and PCM.

3. This step checks to see if the low signal voltage was due to an open in the sensor circuit or the 5 volts reference circuit since the previous step eliminated the pressure sensor.

4. Checks to see if the high voltage signal is from a shorted sensor or a short to voltage in CKT 380 or ground CKT 452 open. Normally, disconnecting the sensor would make a normal circuit go to near zero volts.

Diagnostic Aids: DTC P1530 sets when signal voltage falls outside the normal possible range of the sensor and is not due to a refrigerant system problem. If the problem is intermittent, check for opens or shorts in harness or poor connections.

SEQUENTIAL FUEL INJECTION — DTC P0501/0502

DTC P0501/P0502

VEHICLE SPEED SENSOR (VSS) CIRCUIT
3100 (VIN M) "A" CARLINE (SFI) (MAF)

①

- PERFORM ON-BOARD DIAGNOSTIC SYSTEM CHECK.
- IF DTC P0703 IS STORED ALONG WITH P0501/P0502, SEE DTC P0703 CHART FIRST.

- RAISE DRIVE WHEELS.

? Important

- DO NOT PERFORM THIS TEST WITHOUT SUPPORTING THE LOWER CONTROL ARMS SO THAT THE DRIVE AXLES ARE IN A NORMAL HORIZONTAL POSITION. RUNNING THE VEHICLE IN GEAR WITH THE WHEELS HANGING DOWN AT FULL TRAVEL MAY DAMAGE THE DRIVE AXLES.

- WITH ENGINE IDLING IN GEAR, BRAKE NOT APPLIED, TECH 1 SHOULD DISPLAY MPH ABOVE 0.
  DOES IT?

NO | YES

- DTC P0501/P0502 IS INTERMITTENT. IF NO ADDITIONAL DTC(s) WERE STORED, REFER TO "DIAGNOSTIC AIDS"

- IGNITION "OFF."
- DISCONNECT TECH 1 FROM DLC.
- START ENGINE AND IDLE IN GEAR.
- OBSERVE SPEEDOMETER.
  DOES SPEEDOMETER WORK?

NO | YES

② FAULTY PCM.

- SET J 39200 DVM TO 40 VOLT AC SCALE.
- BACKPROBE PCM TERMINAL "GD14" WITH A VOLTMETER TO GROUND.
- PLACE TRANS IN DRIVE, ALLOW WHEELS TO TURN.
- VOLTAGE SHOULD BE ABOVE .5 VOLT.
  IS IT?

NO | YES

- CHECK TERMINAL CONTACT AT PCM "GD13" AND "GD14".
- IF OK, REPLACE PCM.

- CHECK CKT 400 AND CKT 401 FOR OPEN.
- CHECK CKT 400 FOR SHORT TO GROUND.

OPEN OR SHORTED TO GROUND

REPAIR CIRCUIT WHICH IS OPEN OR SHORTED TO GROUND.

CIRCUIT OK

POOR CONNECTION AT VEHICLE SPEED SENSOR OR FAULTY VEHICLE SPEED SENSOR.

"AFTER REPAIRS," REFER TO DTC CRITERIA ON FACING PAGE AND CONFIRM DTC DOES NOT RESET.

86814289

SEQUENTIAL FUEL INJECTION — DTC P1550

DTC P1550
STEPPER MOTOR CRUISE CONTROL CIRCUIT
3100 (VIN M) "A" CARLINE (SFI) (MAF)

Circuit Description:

The stepper motor cruise system differs from the up integrated (PCM - controlled) cruise system previously used in that it is a stand-alone system. The PCM still retains the ability to disable cruise if conditions are detected which would make cruise control operation undesirable. The following conditions may cause cruise control to be inhibited by the PCM: Engine not running long enough for cruise operation; DTC P0705 OR P1630 set; engine speed too high or too low: Vehicle speed too high or too low: trans range input indicates park, neutral, low, or reverse gear selected. If the PCM detects any of these conditions, it will interrupt the ground at the cruise status signal (CKT 85) to request that cruise control be disengaged.

DTC P1550 Will Set When: The cruise status signal (CKT 85) indicates an open or a short to voltage while cruise is engaged and vehicle speed below 7 mph.

Action Taken (PCM will default to): DTC P1550 does not illuminate the MIL (Service Engine Soon).

DTC Chart Test Description: Number(s) below refer to circled number(s) on the diagnostic chart.
1. Ensures that the PCM is detecting a current fault.
2. Ensures that CKT 85 is not open or grounded, or shorted to voltage, and CKT 85 is being switched "ON" and "OFF" by the SMCC (I) cruise control module.

Diagnostic Aids: An intermittent may be caused by a poor connection, rubbed through wire insulation or a wire broken inside the insulation.

Check for:
- Poor connection or damaged harness - Inspect PCM harness for open or short to voltage in CKT 85. improper mating, broken locks, improperly formed or damaged terminals, poor terminal to wire connection, and damaged harness.

- **Intermittent test** - Observe SMCC (I) status on Tech 1 while moving related connectors and wiring harness with engine running. If the failure is induced, the SMCC (I) status display will change to engaged. This may help to isolate the location of the malfunction. SMCC (I) is a stand alone system, once the software has seen a valid cruise engagement, it has learned cruise is on the vehicle

86814292

SEQUENTIAL FUEL INJECTION — DTC P1530

DTC P1530
A/C REFRIGERANT PRESSURE SENSOR CIRCUIT
3100 (VIN M) "A" CARLINE (SFI) (MAF)

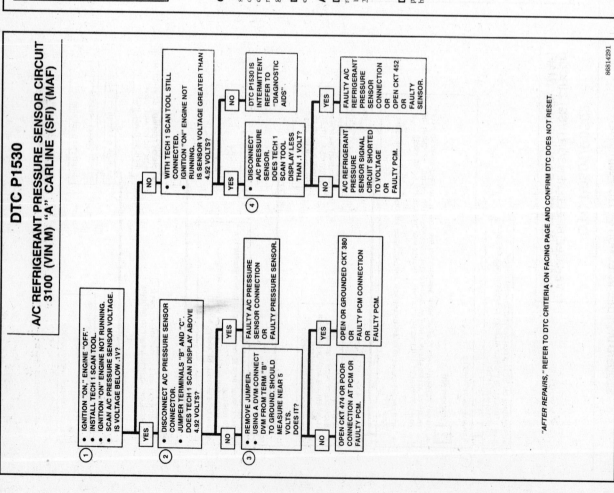

"AFTER REPAIRS," REFER TO DTC CRITERIA ON FACING PAGE AND CONFIRM DTC DOES NOT RESET.

86814291

SEQUENTIAL FUEL INJECTION — DTC P1623

DTC 1623

PROM ERROR
(FAULTY OR INCORRECT PROM)
3100 (VIN M) "A" CARLINE (SFI) (MAF)

CHECK THAT PROM IS CORRECTLY INSERTED IN THE SOCKET. (REFER TO SECTION "C1" "ON-VEHICLE SERVICE.") IF OK, REPLACE PROM, CLEAR MEMORY AND RECHECK. IF DTC P1623 REAPPEARS, REPLACE PCM.

NOTICE: To prevent possible Electrostatic Discharge damage to the PCM or PROM, Do Not touch the component leads. Do Not remove integrated circuit from carrier.

86814294

SEQUENTIAL FUEL INJECTION — DTC P1550

DTC P1550

STEPPER MOTOR CRUISE CONTROL CIRCUIT
3100 (VIN M) "A" CARLINE (SFI) (MAF)

NOTE: IF CRUISE IS INOP., REFER TO SECTION 8A FOR DIAGNOSIS.

(1)
- INSTALL TECH 1 SCAN TOOL.
- CLEAR DTC(s).
- KEY "ON," OBSERVE "SMCC STATUS" ON TECH 1.
- "SMCC STATUS" SHOULD DISPLAY "OFF"?
  DOES IT?

NO

- BACKPROBE PCM BLACK 32 PIN C-D CONNECTOR TERMINAL BD-9 WITH A DVM (DC VOLTS SCALE) TO GROUND.
  SHOULD MEASURE NEAR BATTERY VOLTAGE.
  DOES IT?

YES

FAULTY PCM.

NO

YES

(2)
- KEY "OFF."
- DISCONNECT CRUISE CONTROL MODULE CONNECTOR.
- KEY "ON."
- WITH A JUMPER WIRE CONNECT CKT 85 TERMINAL "J" HARNESS SIDE TO GROUND.
- WHILE GROUNDING OBSERVE TECH 1 SCAN TOOL. SMCC STATUS SHOULD GO FROM "OFF" TO "ON."
  DOES IT?

YES

POOR CONNECTION AT CRUISE CONTROL MODULE OR FAULTY CRUISE CONTROL MODULE.

NO

CKT 85 OPEN OR SHORTED TO VOLTAGE. POOR CONNECTION AT PCM OR FAULTY PCM.

"AFTER REPAIRS," REFER TO DTC CRITERIA ON FACING PAGE AND CONFIRM DTC DOES NOT RESET.

86814293

SEQUENTIAL FUEL INJECTION — DTC P1630

DTC P1630
SYSTEM VOLTAGE HIGH/LOW
3100 (VIN M) "A" CARLINE (SFI) (MAF)

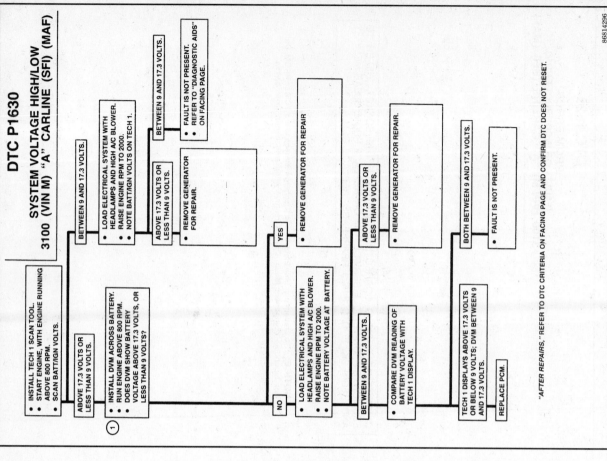

Flowchart:

- INSTALL TECH 1 SCAN TOOL.
- START ENGINE, WITH ENGINE RUNNING ABOVE 800 RPM.
- SCAN BATT/IGN VOLTS.

ABOVE 17.3 VOLTS OR LESS THAN 9 VOLTS.

- INSTALL DVM ACROSS BATTERY.
- RUN ENGINE ABOVE 800 RPM.
- DOES DVM SHOW BATTERY VOLTAGE ABOVE 17.3 VOLTS, OR LESS THAN 9 VOLTS?

(1)

BETWEEN 9 AND 17.3 VOLTS.

- LOAD ELECTRICAL SYSTEM WITH HEADLAMPS AND HIGH A/C BLOWER.
- RAISE ENGINE RPM TO 2000.
- NOTE BATT/IGN VOLTS ON TECH 1.

ABOVE 17.3 VOLTS OR LESS THAN 9 VOLTS.

- REMOVE GENERATOR FOR REPAIR.

BETWEEN 9 AND 17.3 VOLTS.

- FAULT IS NOT PRESENT.
- REFER TO "DIAGNOSTIC AIDS" ON FACING PAGE.

YES
- REMOVE GENERATOR FOR REPAIR.

NO
- LOAD ELECTRICAL SYSTEM WITH HEADLAMPS AND HIGH A/C BLOWER.
- RAISE ENGINE RPM TO 2000.
- NOTE BATTERY VOLTAGE AT BATTERY.

BETWEEN 9 AND 17.3 VOLTS.

- COMPARE DVM READING OF BATTERY VOLTAGE WITH TECH 1 DISPLAY.

ABOVE 17.3 VOLTS OR LESS THAN 9 VOLTS.

- REMOVE GENERATOR FOR REPAIR.

TECH 1 DISPLAYS ABOVE 17.3 VOLTS OR BELOW 9 VOLTS; DVM BETWEEN 9 AND 17.3 VOLTS.

- REPLACE PCM.

BOTH BETWEEN 9 AND 17.3 VOLTS.

- FAULT IS NOT PRESENT.

*"AFTER REPAIRS," REFER TO DTC CRITERIA ON FACING PAGE AND CONFIRM DTC DOES NOT RESET.

86814296

SEQUENTIAL FUEL INJECTION — DTC P1630

DTC P1630
SYSTEM VOLTAGE HIGH/LOW
3100 (VIN M) "A" CARLINE (SFI) (MAF)

Circuit Description:

The PCM monitors system voltage on CKT 439 to terminal "BA2."

DTC P1630 Will Set When: The PCM detects voltage above 17.3 volts or below 9 volts for more than 10 seconds while the engine is running.

Action Taken (PCM will default to): With a current DTC P1630 set, the transaxle will be forced to 3rd gear and TCC will not be allowed to engage. This is to avoid erratic shifting due to improper voltages. Also, the PCM will illuminate the MIL (Service Engine Soon).

DTC Chart Test Description: Number(s) below refer to circled number(s) on the diagnostic chart.

1 Test generator output _____ to determine proper operation of the voltage regulator. Run engine at moderate speed and measure voltage across the battery. If less than 9 or over 17.3 volts, repair generator

Diagnostic Aids: An intermittent may be caused by a poor connection, rubbed through insulation, a wire broken inside the insulation or poor PCM grounds.

Check for:
- Poor connection or damaged harness - Inspect PCM harness connectors for backed out terminal "BA2" "BA4" OR "BB4" improper mating, broken locks, improperly formed or damaged terminals, poor terminal to wire connection and damaged harness.

- Intermittent test - Monitor "SYSTEM VOLTS" display with a Tech 1 while moving related connectors. If the failure is induced, the display will abruptly change. This may help to isolate the location of the malfunction. An engine stall, while manipulating the harness indicates that the PCM has lost voltage at terminal "BA2." Check for loose connectors in CKT 439.

NOTICE:
- Charging with a battery charger while starting the engine may set a DTC P1630.
- When DTC P1630 is set, the transaxle will be forced to 3rd gear. This is to avoid erratic shifting due to improper voltages.

86814295

SEQUENTIAL FUEL INJECTION — DTC P1640

DTC P1640
QDM A CIRCUIT
3100 (VIN M) "A" CARLINE (SFI) (MAF)

1. INSTALL TECH 1. KEY "ON," ENGINE "OFF." NOTE DIAGNOSTIC TROUBLE CODES.

ONLY DTC P1640

QDM "A" DTC P1640 PLUS ADDITIONAL RELATED DTC P0740. WHICH DTC SET?
- YES → REFER TO DTC P0740.
- NO → REFER TO TCC SYSTEM.

2. REMOVE CANISTER HOSE FROM EVAP SOLENOID VALVE AND CONNECT A VACUUM GAGE TO THE CANISTER SIDE OF THE EVAP SOLENOID VALVE. IGNITION "ON," ENGINE RUNNING. WITH THE TECH 1 STILL INSTALLED, SELECT "MISC. TESTS" CCP SOLENOID CONTROL. CYCLE THE PURGE SOLENOID "ON" THEN "OFF." DOES THE VACUUM INCREASE AS THE SOLENOID IS CYCLED "ON" AND DECREASE WHEN IT IS CYCLED "OFF"?
- NO → REFER TO EVAP EMISSION CONTROL SYSTEM.
- YES → IGNITION "ON," ENGINE RUNNING. WITH TECH 1 STILL INSTALLED, SELECT "MISC. TEST" FAN CONTROL WITH TECH 1. SELECT FAN #2. CYCLE FAN #2 "ON," THEN "OFF." IS FAN #2 OPERATIONAL?
  - NO → REFER TO ELECTRIC COOLING FANS.
  - YES → DTC P1640 IS INTERMITTENT. SEE "DIAGNOSTIC AIDS" ON FACING PAGE.

"AFTER REPAIRS," REFER TO DTC CRITERIA ON FACING PAGE AND CONFIRM DTC DOES NOT RESET.

86814298

SEQUENTIAL FUEL INJECTION — DTC P1640

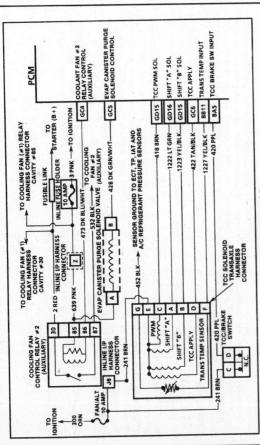

DTC P1640
QDM A CIRCUIT
3100 (VIN M) "A" CARLINE (SFI) (MAF)

86814297

Circuit Description:

The PCM is used to control several components such as those illustrated above. The PCM controls these devices through the use of a Quad-Driver Module (QDM). When the PCM is commanding a component "ON," the voltage potential of the output circuit will be "low" (near 0 volts). When the PCM is commanding the output circuit to a component "OFF," the voltage potential of the circuit will be "high" (near battery voltage). The primary function of the QDM is to supply the ground for the component being controlled. The fault line signal is available on the data stream for scan tool test equipment display on Tech 1. The PCM will compare the voltage at the QDM based on accepted values of the fault line. If the QDM A detection circuit senses a voltage other than the accepted value, the fault line will go from a "low" signal on the data stream to a "high" signal and DTC P1640 will set.

DTC P1640 Will Set When:
- The engine is running.
- The PCM detects an improper voltage level on a circuit connected to QDM A.
- If the brake is applied QDM A ignores fault.
- The above conditions met for 5 seconds.

Action Taken (PCM will default to): The PCM will illuminate the MIL (Service Engine Soon) with a current DTC P1640 set. QDM A controls EVAP canister purge solenoid valve, cooling fan #2, and TCC solenoid.

DTC Chart Test Description: Number(s) below refer to circled number(s) on the diagnostic chart.
1. If a QDM related DTC is stored, diagnose that DTC first. The repair made to the related DTC will repair DTC P1640 also.
2. This test will determine which QDM A control device has failed.

Diagnostic Aids: Monitor the voltage at each terminal shown above while moving related harness connectors, including PCM harness. If the failure is induced, the voltage will change. This may help locate an intermittent condition. Check for bent pins at PCM and PCM connector terminals. If DTC reoccurs with no apparent connector problem, replace PCM.

Important
- PCM is protected by an internal circuit breaker.
- PCM replacement is not necessary after repairing QDM A quad-driver controlled circuit or component.

SEQUENTIAL FUEL INJECTION — DTC P1650

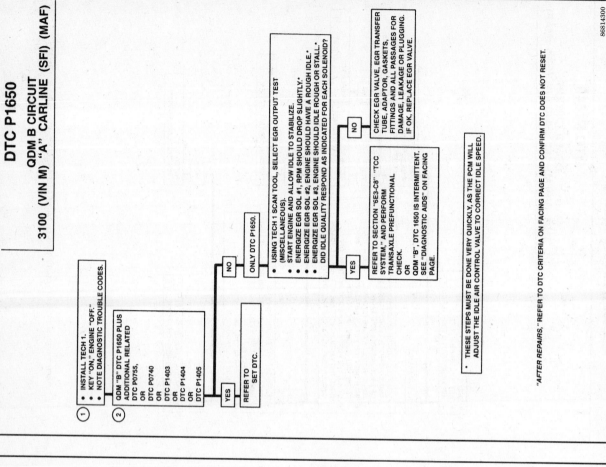

DTC P1650
QDM B CIRCUIT
3100 (VIN M) "A" CARLINE (SFI) (MAF)

1
- INSTALL TECH 1.
- KEY "ON," ENGINE "OFF."
- NOTE DIAGNOSTIC TROUBLE CODES.

2
- QDM "B" DTC P1650 PLUS
  ADDITIONAL RELATED
  DTC P0755,
  OR
  DTC P0740
  OR
  DTC P1403
  OR
  DTC P1404
  OR
  DTC P1405

YES — REFER TO SET DTC.

NO — ONLY DTC P1650.

- USING TECH 1 SCAN TOOL, SELECT EGR OUTPUT TEST (MISCELLANEOUS).
- START ENGINE AND ALLOW IDLE TO STABILIZE.
- ENERGIZE EGR SOL #1, RPM SHOULD DROP SLIGHTLY.
- ENERGIZE EGR SOL #2, ENGINE SHOULD HAVE A ROUGH IDLE.
- ENERGIZE EGR SOL #3, ENGINE SHOULD IDLE ROUGH OR STALL.
- DID IDLE QUALITY RESPOND AS INDICATED FOR EACH SOLENOID?

YES — REFER TO SECTION "6E3-C8" "TCC SYSTEM," AND PERFORM TRANSAXLE PREFUNCTIONAL CHECK.
OR
QDM "B", DTC 1650 IS INTERMITTENT. SEE "DIAGNOSTIC AIDS" ON FACING PAGE.

NO — CHECK EGR VALVE, EGR TRANSFER TUBE, ADAPTOR, GASKETS, FITTINGS AND ALL PASSAGES FOR DAMAGE, LEAKAGE OR PLUGGING. IF OK, REPLACE EGR VALVE.

- THESE STEPS MUST BE DONE VERY QUICKLY, AS THE PCM WILL ADJUST THE IDLE AIR CONTROL VALVE TO CORRECT IDLE SPEED.

"AFTER REPAIRS," REFER TO DTC CRITERIA ON FACING PAGE AND CONFIRM DTC DOES NOT RESET.

86814300

SEQUENTIAL FUEL INJECTION — DTC P1650

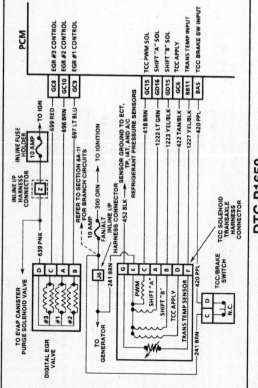

DTC P1650
QDM B CIRCUIT
3100 (VIN M) "A" CARLINE (SFI) (MAF)

Circuit Description:

The PCM is used to control several components such as those illustrated above. The PCM controls these devices through the use of a Quad-Driver Module (QDM). When the PCM is commanding a component "ON," the voltage potential of the output circuit will be "low" (near 0 volts). When the PCM is commanding the output circuit to a component "OFF," the voltage potential of the circuit will be "high" (near battery voltage). The primary function of the QDM is to supply the ground for the component being controlled. Each QDM has a fault line which is monitored by the PCM. The fault line signal is available on the data stream for scan tool test equipment display on Tech 1. The PCM will compare the QDM based on accepted values of the fault line. If the QDM B fault detection circuit senses a voltage other than the accepted value, the fault line will go from a "low" signal on the data stream to a "high" signal and DTC P1650 will set.

DTC P1650 Will Set When:

- The engine is running.
- The PCM detects an improper voltage level on a circuit connected to QDM B.
- The above conditions met for 5 seconds.

Action Taken (PCM will default to): The PCM will illuminate the MIL (Service Engine Soon) with a current DTC P1650 set. QDM B controls transaxle shift solenoid A and B, TCC PWM solenoid and three EGR solenoids.

DTC Chart Test Description: Number(s) below refer to circled number(s) on the diagnostic chart.

1. If a QDM related DTC is stored, diagnose that DTC first. The repair made to the related DTC will repair DTC P1650 also.
2. This test will determine which QDM B control device has failed.

Diagnostic Aids: Monitor the voltage at each terminal shown above while moving related harness connectors, including PCM harness. If the failure is induced, the voltage will change.

This may help locate an intermittent condition. Check for bent pins at PCM and PCM connector terminals. If DTC reoccurs with no apparent connector problem, replace PCM.

ℹ Important
- PCM is protected by an internal circuit breaker.
- PCM replacement is not necessary after repairing QDM B Quad driver controlled circuit or component

86814299

SEQUENTIAL FUEL INJECTION — DTC P0703

DTC P0703

TCC BRAKE SWITCH INPUT CIRCUIT
3100 (VIN M) "A" CARLINE (SFI) (MAF)

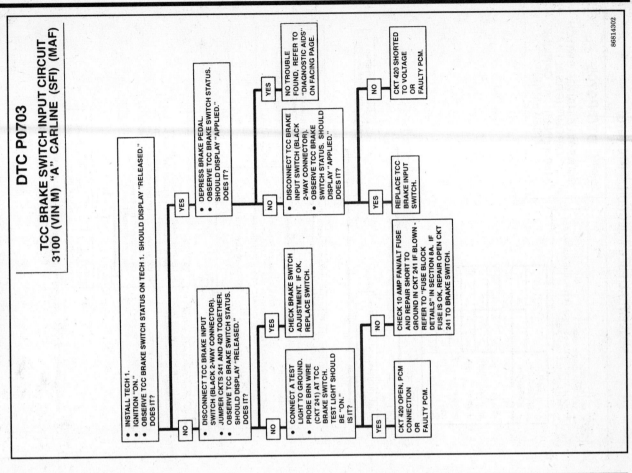

86814302

SEQUENTIAL FUEL INJECTION — DTC P0703

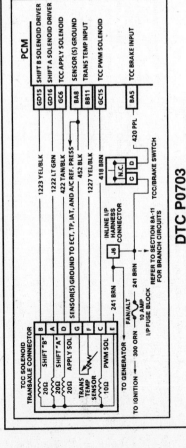

DTC P0703

TCC BRAKE SWITCH INPUT CIRCUIT
3100 (VIN M) "A" CARLINE (SFI) (MAF)

Circuit Description:

The PCM monitors the status of the TCC/Brake switch circuit through PCM terminal "BA5".

DTC P0703 Will Set When:

- No DTC P0501 is present.
- Vehicle speed has been above 35 mph for 10 seconds and back to 0 mph five times.
- TCC brake switch status has not changed from "Released" to "Applied," or "Applied," or "Released" as displayed on the Tech 1.

Action Taken (PCM will default to): When DTC P0703 is set, the PCM will not allow 4th gear, cruise control or TCC operation. DTC P0703 does not illuminate the MIL (Service Engine Soon).

Diagnostic Aids: An intermittent may be caused by a poor connection, rubbed through wire insulation or a wire broken inside the insulation.

Check for:

- Poor connection or damaged harness - Inspect PCM harness connectors for backed out terminals, improper mating, broken locks, improperly formed or damaged terminals, poor terminal to wire connection and damaged harness.
- Intermittent test - Monitor a Tech 1 while moving related connectors and wiring harness. If the failure is induced, the scan data will change from "Released" to "Applied," or "Applied" to "Released." This may help to isolate the location of the malfunction.

86814301

SEQUENTIAL FUEL INJECTION — DTC P0705

DTC P0705
TRANSAXLE RANGE SWITCH CIRCUIT (PRNDL) 3100 (VIN M) "A" CARLINE (SFI) (MAF)

(1)
- INSTALL TECH 1.
- KEY "ON," ENGINE "OFF."
- WHILE MOVING GEAR SELECTOR THROUGH ALL RANGES.
- TECH 1 SHOULD DISPLAY.

GEAR SELECTOR POSITION		TECH 1 DISPLAY		
		P	A	B	C
PARK	(P)	LO	LO	HI	HI
REVERSE	(R)	HI	LO	LO	HI
NEUTRAL	(N)	LO	HI	LO	HI
DRIVE 4	(D)	HI	HI	LO	LO
DRIVE 3	(3)	LO	LO	LO	LO
DRIVE 2	(2)	HI	LO	HI	LO
DRIVE 1	(1)	LO	HI	HI	LO

DOES IT?

NO → DO ALL TRANSAXLE RANGE SWITCH CIRCUITS STAY HIGH?

YES → NO TROUBLE FOUND REFER TO DIAGNOSTIC AIDS ON FACING PAGE.

YES → OPEN IN CKT 251 OR FAULTY TRANSAXLE RANGE SWITCH HARNESS CONNECTOR/CONNECTION OR FAULTY TRANSAXLE RANGE SWITCH OR FAULTY PCM.

NO →

(2)
- WHILE MOVING GEAR SELECTOR THROUGH ALL RANGES, OBSERVE WHICH CKT OR CKTs DID NOT CORRESPOND WITH TECH 1 SCAN TOOL DISPLAY CHART.
- KEY "OFF."
- DISCONNECT TRANSAXLE RANGE SWITCH 4-WAY HARNESS CONNECTOR.
- KEY "ON." TECH 1 SCAN TOOL STILL INSTALLED. BACKPROBE PCM SIDE OF TRANSAXLE RANGE SWITCH HARNESS CONNECTOR CIRCUITS (P) CKT 776, (A) CKT 771, (B) CKT 772, (C) CKT 773 ONE AT A TIME TO GROUND.
- TECH 1 SCAN TOOL SHOULD GO FROM HIGH TO LOW ONLY ON THAT CKT WHICH IS BEING GROUNDED.
- DOES IT?

YES → WIRING FROM TRANSAXLE RANGE SWITCH TO PCM AND PCM ARE OK. PROBLEM IS IN THE TRANSAXLE RANGE SWITCH. REPLACE TRANSAXLE RANGE SWITCH.

NO →
- KEY "OFF."
- LEAVING TRANSAXLE RANGE SWITCH 4-WAY HARNESS CONNECTOR DISCONNECTED, REMOVE PCM BLACK 32 PIN C-D HARNESS CONNECTOR.
- USE DVOM IN 100-200 OHM POSITION.
- CHECK CKTs 771, 772, 773, 776 FOR OPEN/GROUND OR GROUNDED TOGETHER.
- ARE CKT/CKTs OK?

NO → REPAIR OPEN/GROUND IN CKT/CKTs.

YES → CHECK FOR POOR CONNECTOR/CONNECTION AT PCM. IF OK REPLACE PCM.

"AFTER REPAIRS," REFER TO DTC CRITERIA ON FACING PAGE AND CONFIRM DTC DOES NOT RESET.

SEQUENTIAL FUEL INJECTION — DTC P0705

DTC P0705
TRANSAXLE RANGE SWITCH CIRCUIT (PRNDL) 3100 (VIN M) "A" CARLINE (SFI) (MAF)

GEAR SELECTOR POSITION		TECH 1 DISPLAY		
		P	A	B	C
PARK	(P)	LO	LO	HI	HI
REVERSE	(R)	HI	LO	LO	HI
NEUTRAL	(N)	LO	HI	LO	HI
DRIVE 4	(D)	HI	HI	LO	LO
DRIVE 3	(3)	LO	LO	LO	LO
DRIVE 2	(2)	HI	LO	HI	LO
DRIVE 1	(1)	LO	HI	HI	LO

Circuit Description:

The transaxle range switch is mounted on the transaxle assembly. It is a multi-signal switch sending information relative to gear selector position to the PCM. The PRNDL input consists of 4 discrete circuits to pull 4 PCM voltages low in various combinations to indicate each gear range. The voltage level of each of the circuits is represented as low = grounded circuit, high = open circuit. The 4 states displayed represent decoder Parity, A, B, and C inputs respectively.

DTC P0705 Will Set When:
- Ignition is "ON."
- PRNDL inputs status indicators (P, A, B, C) indicate an incorrect combination of low and high for a minimum of 10 seconds.

Action Taken (PCM will default to): When an invalid combination is detected (even before DTC P0705 is set) the PCM assumes the gear select lever is in the drive-4 position, scan data does not change.

1. This step checks for proper operation of the transaxle range switch.
2. This test checks for an open or grounded circuit. When DTC P0705 is present.

Diagnostic Aids: An intermittent may be caused by a poor connection, rubbed through wire insulation or a wire broken inside the insulation.

- Poor connection or damaged harness - Inspect PCM harness connectors for backed out terminals, improper mating, broken locks, improperly formed or damaged terminals, poor terminal to wire connection and damaged harness.
- Intermittent test - Monitor a Tech 1 while moving related connectors and wiring harness. If the failure is induced, the scan data will change from low to high or high to low. This may help to isolate the location of the malfunction.

VACUUM DIAGRAMS

Following is a listing of vacuum diagrams for most of the engine and emissions package combinations covered by this manual. Because vacuum circuits will vary based on various engine and vehicle options, always refer first to the vehicle emission control information label, if present. Should the label be missing, or should the vehicle be equipped with a different engine than the car's original equipment, refer to the following diagrams for the same or similar configuration.

If you wish to obtain a replacement emissions label, most manufacturers make the labels available for purchase. The labels can usually be ordered from a local dealer.

Fig. 98 A-Body 2.2L VIN 4 MFI — California 1993

Fig. 96 A-Body 2.2L VIN 4 MFI — Federal 1993

Fig. 99 A-Body 2.2L VIN 4 MFI — California 1993

Fig. 97 A-Body 2.2L VIN 4 MFI — Federal 1993

Fig. 100 A-Body 2.2L VIN 4 MFI — All 1994-95

Fig. 101 Chevrolet 2.5L VIN R TBI — Federal 1984

Fig. 104 Pontiac 2.5L VIN R TBI — Federal 1984

Fig. 102 Chevrolet 2.5L VIN R TBI — California 1984

Fig. 105 Pontiac 2.5L VIN R TBI — California 1984

Fig. 103 Chevrolet 2.5L VIN R TBI — Canada 1984

Fig. 106 Pontiac 6000 2.5L VIN R TBI — Federal 1985

Fig. 107 Pontiac 6000 2.5L VIN R TBI — California 1985

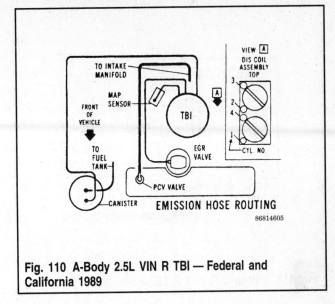

Fig. 110 A-Body 2.5L VIN R TBI — Federal and California 1989

Fig. 108 A-Body 2.5L VIN R TBI — Federal and California 1988

Fig. 111 A-Body 2.5L VIN R TBI — All 1990

Fig. 109 A-Body 2.5L VIN R TBI — Federal 1989

Fig. 112 A-Body 2.5L VIN R TBI — All 1990

Fig. 113 A-Body 2.5L VIN R TBI — All 1990

Fig. 116 A-Body 2.5L VIN R TBI — All 1991

Fig. 114 A-Body 2.5L VIN R TBI — All 1991

Fig. 117 A-Body 2.5L VIN R TBI — Federal 1992

Fig. 115 A-Body 2.5L VIN R TBI — All 1991

Fig. 118 A-Body 2.5L VIN R TBI — Federal 1992

Fig. 119 A-Body 2.5L VIN R TBI — California 1992

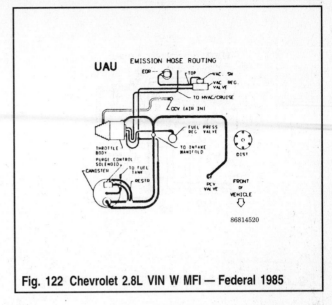

Fig. 122 Chevrolet 2.8L VIN W MFI — Federal 1985

Fig. 120 A-Body 2.5L VIN R TBI — California 1992

Fig. 123 Chevrolet 2.8L VIN W MFI — Police/Taxi Federal 1985

Fig. 121 Chevrolet 2.8L VIN W MFI — Federal 1985

Fig. 124 Chevrolet 2.8L VIN W MFI — Taxi California 1985

Fig. 125 Chevrolet 2.8L VIN W MFI — Canada 1985

Fig. 128 Chevrolet 2.8L VIN X 2BC — Taxi Canada 1985-86

Fig. 126 Chevrolet 2.8L VIN X 2BC — Federal 1985-86

Fig. 129 Chevrolet 2.8L VIN X 2BC — Taxi California 1985-86

Fig. 127 Chevrolet 2.8L VIN X 2BC — Taxi Federal 1985-86

Fig. 130 Chevrolet 2.8L VIN W TBI — Canada 1985-86

Fig. 131 A-Body 2.8L VIN W TBI — Manual, Federal and California 1988

Fig. 134 A-Body 2.8L VIN W TBI — Automatic, California 1989

Fig. 132 A-Body 2.8L VIN W TBI — Automatic, Federal and California 1988

Fig. 135 A-Body 2.8L VIN W TBI — no catalyst/export 1989

Fig. 133 A-Body 2.8L VIN W TBI — Automatic, Federal 1989

Fig. 136 A-Body 2.8L VIN W TBI — no catalyst/export 1989

Fig. 137 Buick 3.0L VIN E 2BC — Federal 1984

Fig. 140 Buick 3.0L VIN E — Federal 1985

Fig. 138 Buick 3.0L VIN E 2BC — California 1984

Fig. 141 Buick 3.0L VIN E — California 1985

Fig. 139 Buick 3.0L VIN E 2BC — California 1984

Fig. 142 Buick 3.0L VIN E — Federal 1985

Fig. 143 Buick 3.0L VIN E — California 1985

Fig. 146 A-Body 3.1L VIN T — Federal and without California/override 1989

Fig. 144 Buick 3.0L VIN E — Automatic Federal 1986

Fig. 147 A-Body 3.1L VIN T — Federal and California 1989

Fig. 145 Buick 3.0L VIN E — Automatic California 1986

Fig. 148 A-Body 3.1L VIN T — 1990

Fig. 149 A-Body 3.1L VIN T — 1990

Fig. 152 A-Body 3.1L VIN T — 1990

Fig. 150 A-Body 3.1L VIN T — 1990

Fig. 153 A-Body 3.1L VIN T — 1990

Fig. 151 A-Body 3.1L VIN T — 1990

Fig. 154 A-Body 3.1L VIN T — 1990

Fig. 155 A-Body 3.1L VIN T — 1990

Fig. 158 A-Body 3.1L VIN T — 1990

Fig. 156 A-Body 3.1L VIN T — 1990

Fig. 159 A-Body 3.1L VIN T — 1990

Fig. 157 A-Body 3.1L VIN T — 1990

Fig. 160 A-Body 3.1L VIN T MFI — 1990

Fig. 161 A-Body 3.1L VIN T MFI — Federal 1991

Fig. 164 A-Body 3.1L VIN M — Federal 1993

Fig. 162 A-Body 3.1L VIN T MFI — California 1991

Fig. 165 A-Body 3.1L VIN M — Federal 1993

Fig. 163 A-Body 3.1L VIN M — Federal 1993

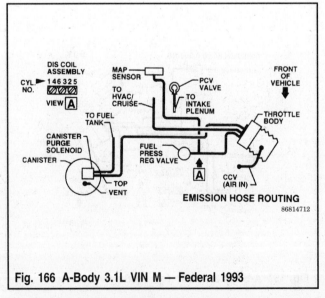

Fig. 166 A-Body 3.1L VIN M — Federal 1993

Fig. 167 A-Body 3.1L VIN M — Federal 1993

Fig. 168 A-Body 3.1L VIN M — California 1993

Fig. 169 A-Body 3.1L VIN M — California 1993

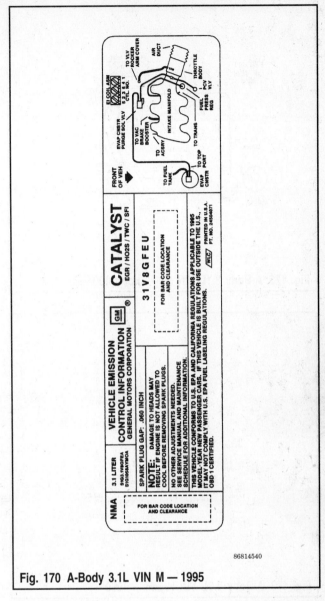

Fig. 170 A-Body 3.1L VIN M — 1995

Fig. 171 A-Body 3.1L VIN M — All 1994-95

Fig. 172 A-Body 3.1L VIN M — Export 1994-95

Fig. 175 A-Body 3.3L VIN N MFI — Federal 1991

Fig. 173 A-Body 3.3L VIN N MFI — 1990

Fig. 176 A-Body 3.3L VIN N MFI — Federal 1991

Fig. 174 A-Body 3.3L VIN N MFI — 1990

Fig. 177 A-Body 3.3L VIN N MFI — California 1991

Fig. 178 A-Body 3.3L VIN N MFI — California 1991

Fig. 181 A-Body 3.8L VIN X/Z 2BC — Federal 1984

Fig. 179 A-Body 3.8L VIN 3 TBI — Federal 1984

Fig. 182 Buick 3.8L VIN 3 TBI — California 1985-87

Fig. 180 A-Body 3.8L VIN 3 TBI — California 1984

Fig. 183 Buick 3.8L VIN 3 TBI — Federal 1985-87

Fig. 184 Buick 3.8L VIN 3 TBI — Canada 1985-87

Fig. 186 Buick 3.8L VIN X TBI — Federal 1985

Fig. 185 Buick 3.8L VIN X TBI — California 1985

Fig. 187 Buick 3.8L VIN X TBI — California 1985

Fig. 188 A-Body 3.8L VIN 3 MFI — Federal and California 1988

Fig. 189 A-Body 4.3L VIN T DSL — High Altitude 1982-85

Fig. 190 A-Body 4.3L VIN T DSL — Low Altitude, wagon with 4 speed trans 1982-85

86814531

Fig. 191 A-Body 4.3L VIN T DSL — Low Altitude, with 4 speed trans, exc. wagon 1982-85

Fig. 192 A-Body 4.3L VIN T DSL — Low Altitude, with 3 speed manual and automatic trans 1982-85

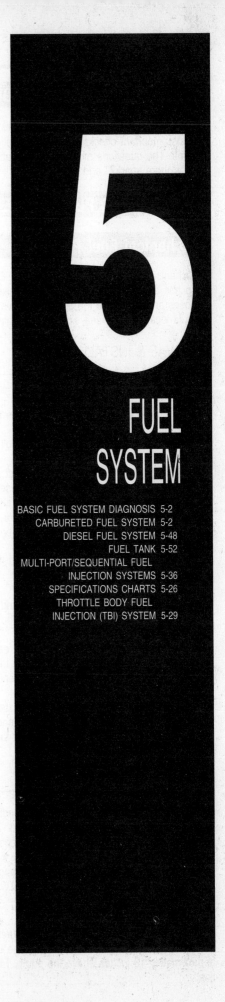

5

FUEL
SYSTEM

BASIC FUEL SYSTEM DIAGNOSIS

When there is a problem starting or driving a vehicle, two of the most important checks involve the ignition and the fuel systems. The questions most mechanics attempt to answer first, "is there spark?" and "is there fuel?" will often lead to solving most basic problems. For ignition system diagnosis and testing, please refer to Section 2 of this manual. If the ignition system checks out (there is spark), then you must determine if the fuel system is operating properly (is there fuel?).

CARBURETED FUEL SYSTEM

Mechanical Fuel Pump

Mechanical fuel pumps are used on 6-2.8L engines. The pump has a vapor return line for both emission control purposes and to reduce the likelihood of vapor lock. The fuel pump is located at the left side of the engine.

REMOVAL & INSTALLATION

▶ **See Figure 1**

1. Disconnect the negative cable at the battery. Raise and support the car.
2. Remove the pump shields and the oil filter, if so equipped.
3. With a shop towel handy, disconnect the inlet hose from the pump. Disconnect the vapor return hose, if equipped, then wrap the towel around the hose to catch any spilt fuel.
4. Loosen the fuel line at the carburetor, then disconnect the outlet pipe from the pump. Use another towel or the same one if possible for spilt fuel.
5. Remove the two mounting bolts and remove the pump from the engine.
   To install:
6. Place a new gasket on the pump and install the pump on the engine. Tighten the two mounting bolts alternately and evenly.
7. Install the pump outlet pipe. This is easier if the pipe is disconnected from the carburetor. Tighten the fitting while backing up the pump nut with another wrench. Install the pipe at the carburetor.
8. Install the inlet and vapor hoses. Install the shields (if equipped) and oil filter. Lower the car, connect the negative battery cable, start the engine, and check for leaks.

TESTING

To determine if the pump is in good condition, tests for both volume and pressure should be performed. The tests are made with the pump installed. Never replace a fuel pump without first performing these simple tests.

Be sure that the fuel filter has been changed at the specified interval. If in doubt, install a new filter first.

Pressure Test

1. Disconnect the fuel line at the carburetor and connect a fuel pump pressure gauge. Hold the gauge up so that it's approximately 16 inches above the pump. Pinch the fuel return line.

Fig. 1 Reinstalling the pipe fittings should be done carefully; make sure not to strip the ends or use the wrong size wrench

2. Start the engine and check the pressure with the engine at idle. If the pump has a vapor return hose, squeeze it off so that an accurate reading can be obtained. Pressure should measure 5.5-6.5 psi (38-45 kPa) consistently.
3. If the pressure is incorrect, replace the pump. If it is okay, go on to the volume test.

Volume Test

1. Disconnect the pressure gauge. Run the fuel line into a graduated container.
2. Run the engine at idle until one pint of gasoline has been pumped. One pint should be delivered in 30 seconds or less. There is normally enough fuel in the carburetor float bowl to perform this test, but refill it if necessary.
3. If the delivery rate is below the minimum, check the lines for restrictions or leaks, then replace the pump.

Carburetor

▶ **See Figures 2 and 3**

The Rochester E2SE is used on most 1982 and later A-body cars. It is a two barrel, two stage carburetor of downdraft design used in conjunction with the Computer Command Control system of fuel control. The carburetor has special design features for optimum air/fuel mixture control during all ranges of engine operation. In 1982 there was also the E2ME carburetor, it is a two barrel, single stage design carburetor. A triple venturi arrangement with plain tube nozzle is used in each bore which results in precise fuel metering control during the off idle and part of the throttle ranges of the engine operation.

The E2ME also uses the Computer Command Control system of fuel control. Like the E2SE the E2ME carburetor has special design features for optimum air/fuel mixture control during all periods of engine operation. All Rochester carburetors consist of 3 major assemblies: the air horn, the float bowl and the throttle body. They have 6 basic operating systems: float, idle, main metering, power, pump and choke.

MODEL IDENTIFICATION

▶ **See Figure 4**

General Motors Rochester carburetors are identified by their model code. The carburetor model identification number is stamped vertically on the float bowl, near the secondary throttle lever. The letters in the model name describe the specific features of the carburetor. For example: The first letter "E" indicates the the carburetor is Electronically controlled. The second and third digits, "2S" indicates the carburetor is a

member of the Varajet family. The last digit "E" indicates an integral Electric choke. The identification code is stamped on the float bowl.

ADJUSTMENTS

Fast Idle
▶ **See Figure 5**

1. Position the transaxle in the Park or Neutral position.
2. Set the ignition timing and curb idle speed, and disconnect and plug hoses as directed on the emission control decal.
3. Place the fast idle screw on the highest step of the cam, or what is specified on the emissions label.
4. Start the engine and adjust the engine speed to specification with the fast idle screw.

Choke Valve Angle Gauge
▶ **See Figure 6**

1. Attach the angle gauge magnet to the closed valve.
2. Rotator the degree scale until zero is opposite the pointer.
3. Center the leveling bubble, then rotate the scale to the specified angle.
4. Open the choke valve.
5. Adjust the linkage if the bubble is not recentered.

Float

1982-84 MODELS
▶ **See Figure 7**

1. Remove the air horn from the throttle body.
2. Use your fingers to hold the retainer in place, and to push the float down into light contact with the needle.
3. Measure the distance from the toe of the float (furthest from the hinge) to the top of the carburetor (gasket removed).
4. To adjust, remove the float and gently bend the arm to specification. After adjustment, check the float alignment in the chamber.

Fig. 2 Rochester E2SE carburetor assembly on the vehicle

Fig. 3 Rochester E2SE carburetor part locations

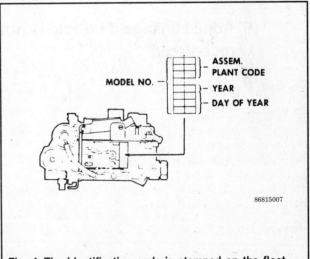

Fig. 4 The identification code is stamped on the float bowl

① PREPARE VEHICLE FOR ADJUSTMENTS - SEE EMISSION LABLE ON VEHICLE. PLACE TRANSMISSION IN PARK/NEUTRAL.

② PLACE FAST IDLE SCREW ON HIGHEST STEP OF FAST IDLE CAM.

③ TURN FAST IDLE SCREW IN OR OUT TO OBTAIN SPECIFIED FAST IDLE R.P.M. - (SEE LABEL).

86815010

Fig. 5 Fast idle adjustment for the E2SE carburetor

① Attach Angle Gage Magnet to closed Choke Valve.

② Rotate degree scale until zero is opposite pointer.

③ Center the leveling bubble.

④ Rotate scale to specified angle.

⑤ Open Choke Valve as described.

⑥ Adjust linkage if bubble is not recentered.

J-26701-A or BT-7704

86815020

Fig. 6 A choke valve angle gauge is used often in adjustments

Fig. 7 Float adjustment — 1982-84 models

1982-84 models diagram labels:
① HOLD RETAINER FIRMLY IN PLACE
(INSET)
GAUGE AT LARGE TOE OF FLOAT AT POINT FURTHEST AWAY FROM FLOAT HINGE PIN (SEE INSET)
③
④ REMOVE FLOAT AND BEND FLOAT ARM UP OR DOWN TO ADJUST
② PUSH FLOAT DOWN LIGHTLY AGAINST NEEDLE
⑤ VISUALLY CHECK FLOAT ALIGNMENT AFTER ADJUSTING
86815008

1985-86 MODELS

▶ See Figure 8

1. Remove the air horn, horn gasket, and upper float bowl insert.

2. Attach special tool J-34817-1 to the float bowl.

3. Place the J-34817-3 in the base of the carburetor, with the contact pin resting on the outer edge of the float lever.

4. Measure the distance from the top of the casting to the top of the float, at the point farthest from the float hinge, use tool J-9789-90.

5. If the gap is $\frac{2}{32}$ in. (1.59mm) or more different than specification (larger or smaller), use tool J-34817-20 to bend the lever up or down. Remove the bending tool, then measure repeating until it is within specification.

6. Check the float alignment, then reassemble the carburetor.

Pre-set Procedure

1. Remove the carburetor from the engine to gain access to the plug covering the idle mixture needle. Remove the plug, turn the mixture needle in until lightly seated and back out 4 turns.

2. If the plug in the air horn covering the idle air bleed has been removed, replace the air horn. If the plug is still in place, do not remove it.

3. Remove the vent stack screen assembly to gain access to the lean mixture screw. Be sure to reinstall the vent stack screen assembly after adjustment.

4. Using a special tool J-28696-10 or equivalent, turn the mixture screw in until it lightly bottoms, then back out $2\frac{1}{2}$ turns.

5. Reinstall the carburetor on the engine.

   a. Do not install the air cleaner and gasket.

   b. Disconnect the bowl vent line at the carburetor.

   c. Disconnect the EGR valve hose and the cannister purge hose at the carburetor, and cap the ports.

   d. Locate hose on port "D" on the emissions label to the temperature sensor and secondary vacuum break TVS. Disconnect the hose at the sensor on the air cleaner, then plug the open hose.

   e. Connect the positive lead of the dwell meter to the mixture control solenoid test lead (green). Connect the other meter lead to ground. Set the dwell meter to 6-cylinder position. Connect the tachometer to distributor lead (brown). The tachometer should be connected to the distributor side of the tach filter if the vehicle has a tachometer.

6. Block the drive wheels.

7. Place the vehicle in PARK (automatic transaxles) or NEUTRAL (manual transaxles), then set the Parking brake.

8. Proceed to the mixture adjustment procedure.

Mixture Adjustment

1. Preform the carburetor pre-set procedure.

2. Run the engine on high step of the fast idle cam. until the engine cooling fan starts to cycle.

3. Run the engine at 3,000 rpm and adjust the lean mixture screw slowly in small increments allowing time for dwell to stabilize after turning the screw to obtain an average dwell of 35°. If the dwell is too low, back the screw out, if too high, turn it in. If you are unable to adjust it to specifications, inspect the main metering circuit for leaks or restrictions.

4. Return to idle.

5. Adjust the mixture screw to obtain the average dwell of 25° with the cooling fan in the off cycle. If the reading is too low, back the screw out. If the reading is too high, turn it in. Allow time for reading to stabilize after each adjustment. Adjustment is very sensitive. Make a final check with the adjusting tool removed.

6. If you are unable to adjust to specifications, inspect the idle system for leaks, or restrictions.

7. Disconnect the mixture control solenoid when the cooling fan is in the off cycle, then check for an rpm change of at least 50 rpm. If the rpm does not change enough, inspect the idle air bleed circuit for restrictions or leaks.

8. Run the engine at 3,000 rpm for a few moments, then note the dwell reading. Dwell should be varying with the average reading of 35°.

9. If the 35° is not the average dwell, reset the lean mixture screw per step 3. Then reset the idle mixture screw to obtain a 25° dwell per steps 5 and 6.

10. If you have an average dwell, reconnect the systems disconnected (purge and vent hoses, EGR valve etc.), then reinstall the vent screen and set the idle speed.

Pump

The E2ME and the E2SE carburetors have a non-adjustable pump lever. No adjustments are either necessary or possible.

Choke Unloader

▶ See Figure 9

1. Connect a rubber band to the intermediate choke lever, then open the throttle valve to allow the choke valve to close.

2. Set up the angle gauge and the angle to specifications.

3. Position the fast idle screw on the second step of the fast idle cam (against the rise of the high step).

4. Turn the choke lever shaft to open the choke valve and make contact with the black closing tang.

5. Hold the primary throttle wide open.

6. If the engine is warm, close the choke valve by pushing in on the intermediate choke lever.

7. Bend the unloader tang until the bubble is centered.

1. REMOVE AIR HORN, AIR HORN GASKET AND UPPER FLOAT BOWL INSERT.

2. ATTACH J-34817-1 OR BT-8227A-1 TO FLOAT BOWL.

3. PLACE J-34817-3 OR BT-8227A IN BASE, WITH CONTACT PIN RESTING ON OUTER EDGE OF FLOAT LEVER.

4. MEASURE DISTANCE FROM TOP OF CASTING TO TOP OF FLOAT, AT POINT FARTHEST FROM FLOAT HINGE. USE J-9789-90 OR BT-8037.

5. IF MORE THAN ±1.59mm (2/32") FROM SPECIFICATION. USE J-34817-20 OR BT-8045A TO BEND LEVER UP OR DOWN. REMOVE BENDING TOOL AND MEASURE. REPEATING UNTIL WITHIN SPECIFICATION.

6. VISUALLY CHECK FLOAT ALIGNMENT.

7. REASSEMBLE CARBURETOR.

86815009

Fig. 8 Float adjustment — 1985-86 models

① ATTACH RUBBER BAND TO INTER-MEDIATE CHOKE LEVER.

② OPEN THROTTLE TO ALLOW CHOKE VALVE TO CLOSE.

③ SET UP ANGLE GAGE AND SET ANGLE TO SPECIFICATIONS.

④ HOLD THROTTLE LEVER IN WIDE OPEN POSITION.

⑤ PUSH ON CHOKE SHAFT LEVER TO OPEN CHOKE VALVE AND TO MAKE CONTACT WITH BLACK CLOSING TANG.

⑥ ADJUST BY BENDING TANG UNTIL BUBBLE IS CENTERED.

UNLOADER ADJUSTMENT

86815011

Fig. 9 The choke unloader adjustment can be made by following these steps

Choke Coil Lever
▶ **See Figure 10**

1. Remove the three retaining screws and remove the choke cover and coil. On models with a riveted choke cover, drill out the three rivets and remove the cover and choke coil.

➡**A choke stat cover retainer kit is required for reassembly.**

2. Place the fast idle screw on the high step of the cam.
3. Close the choke by pushing in on the intermediate choke lever.
4. Insert a drill or gauge of the specified size into the hole in the choke housing. The choke lever in the housing should be up against the side of the gauge.
5. If the lever does not just touch the gauge, bend the intermediate choke rod to adjust.

Fast Idle Cam-Choke Rod
▶ **See Figure 11**

➡**A special angle gauge should be used. If it is not available, an inch (millimeter) measurement can be made.**

1. Adjust the choke coil lever and fast idle first.
2. Rotate the degree scale until it is zeroed.
3. Close the choke and install the degree scale onto the choke plate. Center the leveling bubble.
4. Rotate the scale so that the specified degree is opposite the scale pointer.
5. Place the fast idle screw on the second step of the cam (against the high step). Close the choke by pushing in the intermediate lever.
6. Bend the fast idle cam rod at the U to adjust the angle to specifications.

Air Valve Rod
▶ **See Figure 12**

1. Close the air valve.

① IF RIVETED, DRILL OUT AND REMOVE RIVETS. REMOVE CHOKE COVER AND COIL ASSEMBLY.

② PLACE FAST IDLE SCREW ON HIGH STEP OF FAST IDLE CAM.

③ PUSH ON INTERMEDIATE CHOKE LEVER UNTIL CHOKE VALVE IS CLOSED.

④ INSERT .085" (2.18mm) PLUG GAGE IN HOLE.

⑤ EDGE OF LEVER SHOULD JUST CONTACT SIDE OF GAGE.

⑥ SUPPORT AT "S" AND BEND INTERMEDIATE CHOKE LINK TO ADJUST.

CHOKE COIL LEVER ADJUSTMENT

86815012

Fig. 10 The choke coil lever adjustment varies slightly on older models; you may need to drill out the rivets holding the cover — E2SE shown

Fig. 11 Fast idle cam choke rod relation

2. Insert the specified gauge between the rod and the end of the slot in the plunger.

3. Seat the vacuum diaphragm with an outside vacuum source. Tape over the purge bleed hole if present.

4. Rotate the air valve in the direction of the open air valve by applying a light pressure to the air valve shaft.

5. Bend the rod to adjust the clearance, notice the location of the bubble.

Air Valve Spring

▶ See Figure 13

1. To gain access to the lock screw, remove the intermediate choke link.

2. Using a ³⁄₃₂ in. (2.34mm) hex wrench, loosen the lock screw.

3. Turn the adjusting screw clockwise until the air valve opens slightly, then turn the screw counterclockwise until the valve closes and continue the number of specified turns.

4. Tighten the lock screw and apply lithium grease to the pin and the spring contact area.

Primary Side Vacuum Break

▶ See Figure 14

1. Connect a rubber band to the intermediate choke lever, then open the throttle valve to allow the choke valve to close.

2. Set up the angle gauge and the angle to specifications.

3. Position the fast idle screw on the second step of the fast idle cam (against the rise of the high step).

4. Turn the choke lever shaft to open the choke valve and make contact with the black closing tang.

5. Seat the choke vacuum diaphragm with an outside vacuum source.

6. Push in on the intermediate choke lever to close the choke valve, and hold closed during adjustment.

7. Adjust by using a ¹⁄₈ in. (3mm) hex wrench to turn the screw in the rear cover until the bubble is centered.

8. After adjusting, apply RTV silicone sealant over the screw to seal the setting.

⑤ SPECIFIED ANGLE (SEE SPECS.)

① DEGREE SCALE

④ LEVELING BUBBLE (CENTERED)

② AIR VALVE CLOSED

MAGNET

③ POINTER

FIGURE 1

⑦ ROTATE AIR VALVE IN THE DIRECTION OF OPEN AIR VALVE BY APPLYING A LIGHT PRESSURE TO THE AIR VALVE SHAFT.

⑥ SEAT VACUUM DIAPHRAGM USING OUTSIDE VACUUM SOURCE

FIGURE 2

⑧ TO ADJUST, BEND AIR VALVE ROD UNTIL BUBBLE IS CENTERED.

86815014

Fig. 12 Air valve rod adjustment

① IF NECESSARY, REMOVE INTER-MEDIATE CHOKE LINK, TO GAIN ACCESS TO LOCK SCREW.

② LOOSEN LOCK SCREW USING 3/32" (2.381mm) HEX WRENCH.

③ TURN TENSION-ADJUSTING SCREW ↻ UNTIL AIR VALVE OPENS SLIGHTLY.

TURN ADJUSTING SCREW ↺ UNTIL AIR VALVE JUST CLOSES. CONTINUE ↺ SPECIFIED NUMBER OF TURNS.

④ TIGHTEN LOCK SCREW.

⑤ APPLY LITHIUM BASE GREASE TO LUBRICATE PIN AND SPRING CON-TACT AREA.

② AND ④

AIR VALVE SPRING ADJUSTMENT

86815015

Fig. 13 Air valve spring adjustment

PRIMARY SIDE VACUUM BREAK ADJUSTMENT
(DUAL VACUUM BREAK UNITS)

86815016

Fig. 14 Primary side vacuum break adjustment

Secondary Vacuum Break

▶ See Figure 15

1. Connect a rubber band to the intermediate choke lever, then open the throttle valve to allow the choke valve to close.
2. Set up the angle gauge and the angle to specifications.
3. Position the fast idle screw on the second step of the fast idle cam (against the rise of the high step).
4. Turn the choke lever shaft to open the choke valve and make contact with the black closing tang.
5. Seat the choke vacuum diaphragm with an outside vacuum source.
6. Push in on the intermediate choke lever to close the choke valve, and hold closed during adjustment. Make sure the plunger spring is compressed and seated, if present.
7. Adjust by using a ⅛ in. (3mm) hex wrench to turn the screw in the rear cover until the bubble is centered.
8. After adjusting, apply RTV silicone sealant over the screw to seal the setting.

Secondary Throttle Lockout

▶ See Figure 16

1. Pull the choke wide open by pushing out on the intermediate choke lever.
2. Open the throttle until the end of the secondary actuating lever is opposite the toe of the lockout lever.
3. Gauge clearance between the lockout lever and secondary lever should be as specified.
4. To adjust, bend the lockout lever where it contacts the fast idle cam.

Choke Link/Fast Idle Cam

▶ See Figure 17

1. Connect a rubber band to the intermediate choke lever, then open the throttle valve to allow the choke valve to close.
2. Set up the angle gauge and the angle to specifications.
3. Position the fast idle screw on the second step of the fast idle cam (against the rise of the high step).
4. Turn the choke lever shaft to open the choke valve and make contact with the black closing tang.

SECONDARY SIDE VACUUM BREAK ADJUSTMENT

86815017

Fig. 15 The secondary vacuum break adjustment is basically the same as that for the primary vacuum break

① HOLD CHOKE VALVE WIDE OPEN BY PUSHING DOWN ON INTERMEDIATE CHOKE LEVER.

② OPEN THROTTLE LEVER UNTIL END OF SECONDARY ACTUATING LEVER IS OPPOSITE TOE OF LOCKOUT LEVER.

③ GAGE CLEARANCE - DIMENSION SHOULD BE TO SPECIFICATIONS.

④ IF NECESSARY TO ADJUST, BEND LOCKOUT LEVER TANG CONTACTING FAST IDLE CAM.

SECONDARY LOCKOUT ADJUSTMENT

Fig. 16 Secondary throttle lockout adjustment

① ATTACH RUBBER BAND TO INTERMEDIATE CHOKE LEVER.

② OPEN THROTTLE TO ALLOW CHOKE VALVE TO CLOSE.

③ SET UP ANGLE GAGE AND SET ANGLE TO SPECIFICATIONS.

④ PLACE FAST IDLE SCREW ON SECOND STEP OF CAM AGAINST RISE OF HIGH STEP.

⑤ PUSH ON CHOKE SHAFT LEVER TO OPEN CHOKE VALVE AND TO MAKE CONTACT WITH BLACK CLOSING TANG.

⑥ SUPPORT AT "S" AND ADJUST BY BENDING FAST IDLE CAM LINK UNTIL BUBBLE IS CENTERED.

CHOKE LINK - FAST IDLE CAM ADJUSTMENT

Fig. 17 Fast idle cam choke link

5. Support at the **S** point and bend the fast idle cam link until the bubble is centered.

REMOVAL & INSTALLATION

▶ See Figures 18, 19, 20, 21, 22, 23 and 24

1. Raise the hood and apply a cover on the fender.
2. Disconnect the battery cables and remove the battery.
3. Remove the air cleaner and gasket.
4. Disconnect the accelerator linkage.
5. Tag then disconnect the fuel pipes and hoses, then all the vacuum lines to the carburetor.
6. Tag and disconnect all electrical connections.
7. If equipped with an Automatic Transaxle, disconnect the downshift cable.
8. If equipped with cruise control, disconnect the linkage.
9. Unscrew the carburetor mounting bolts and remove the carburetor from the manifold.

Fig. 18 After removing the air cleaner, disconnect the accelerator linkage

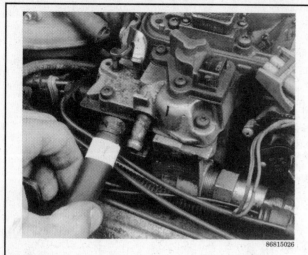

Fig. 19 Tag, then disconnect, the fuel lines and all vacuum lines to the carburetor

Fig. 20 Tag, then disconnect, all electrical connections to the carburetor, including the choke coil housing

Fig. 21 After removing all connections to the carburetor, unfasten the four mounting screws . . .

Fig. 22 . . . then remove the carburetor assembly from the manifold

10. Remove the EFE heater, then cover the fuel opening so that dirt can not enter.

To install:

11. Inspect the EFE heater for damage. Be sure that the throttle body and EFE mating surfaces are clean.

12. Install the new or rebuilt carburetor onto the manifold, then tighten the nuts alternately to 13 ft. lbs. (18 Nm).

13. Install the linkage connections for cruise, accelerator and the downshift cable.

14. Attach all the fuel lines and tagged vacuum lines.

15. Make sure all connections are intact, then install the battery and cable connections.

16. Start the engine and check for any fuel leaks. If any are present, turn the engine off immediately, fix the leak. If none are present proceed.

17. Remove the fender covers and lower the hood.

Fig. 23 Remove the EFE heater

Fig. 24 Cover the fuel opening so that dirt cannot enter

OVERHAUL

E2SE Carburetor

▶ See Figures 25 and 26

Efficient carburetion depends greatly on careful cleaning and inspection during overhaul, since dirt, gum, water, or varnish in or on the carburetor parts are often responsible for poor performance.

Overhaul your carburetor in a clean, dust-free area. Carefully disassemble the carburetor, referring often to the exploded views and directions packaged with the rebuilding kit. Keep all similar and look-alike parts segregated during disassembly and cleaning to avoid accidental interchange during assembly. Make a note of all jet sizes.

When the carburetor is disassembled, wash all parts (except diaphragms, electric choke units, pump plunger, and any other plastic, fiber, or rubber parts) in clean carburetor solvent. Do not leave parts in the solvent any longer than is necessary to sufficiently loosen the deposits. Excessive cleaning may remove the special finish from the float bowl and choke valve bodies, leaving these parts unfit for service. Rinse all parts in clean solvent and blow them dry with compressed air or allow them to air dry. Wipe clean all cork, plastic, and fiber parts with a clean, lint-free cloth.

Blow out all passages and jets with compressed air and be sure that there are no restrictions or blockages. Never use wire or similar tools to clean jets, fuel passages, or air bleeds. Clean all jets and valves separately to avoid accidental interchange.

Check all parts for wear or damage. If wear or damage is found, replace the defective parts. Especially check the following:

1. Check the float needle and seat for wear. If wear is found, replace the complete assembly.

2. Check the float hinge pin for wear and the float(s) for dents or distortion. Replace the float if fuel has leaked into it.

3. Check the throttle and choke shaft bores for wear or an out-of-round condition. Damage or wear to the throttle arm,

shaft, or shaft bore will often require replacement of the throttle body. These parts require a close tolerance of fit, wear may allow air leakage which could affect starting and idling.

➡**Throttle shafts and bushings are not included in overhaul kits. They can be purchases separately.**

4. Inspect the idle mixture adjusting needles for burrs or grooves. Any such condition requires replacement of the needle, since you will not be able to obtain a satisfactory idle.

5. Check the bowl cover for warped surfaces with a straightedge.

6. Closely inspect the accelerator pump plunger for wear and damage, replacing as necessary.

7. After the carburetor is assembled, check the choke valve for freedom of operation.

Carburetor overhaul kits are recommended for each overhaul. These kits contain all gaskets and new parts to replace those which deteriorate most rapidly. Failure to replace all parts supplied with the kit (especially gaskets) can result in poor performance later.

Some carburetor manufacturers supply overhaul kits for three basic types: minor repair, major repair, and gasket kits. Basically, they contain the following:

Minor Repair Kits:
- All gaskets
- Float needle valve
- All diagrams
- Spring for the pump diaphragm

Major Repair Kits:
- All jets and gaskets
- All diaphragms
- Float needle valve
- Pump ball valve
- Float
- Complete intermediate rod
- Intermediate pump lever
- Some cover hold-down screws and washers

Gasket Kits:
- All gaskets

After cleaning and checking all components, reassemble the carburetor, using new parts and referring to the exploded view. When reassembling, make sure that all screws and jets are tight in their seats, but do not overtighten as the tips will be distorted. Tighten all screws gradually, in rotation. Do not tighten needle valves into their seats, uneven jetting will result. Always use new gaskets. Be sure to adjust the float level when reassembling.

AIR HORN

▶ See Figures 27, 28, 29 and 30

1. Invert the carburetor, then remove the plug covering the idle mixture needle as previously described.

2. Install the carburetor in a suitable holding stand such as tool J-9789-118 or BT-30-15.

3. Remove the primary and secondary vacuum break assemblies. Be sure to take note of the linkage positions for installation.

4. Remove the three screws from the mixture control solenoid. Remove the mixture control solenoid with gasket and discard the gasket.

NOT ALL PARTS APPEAR ON ALL MODELS

IDLE SPEED DEVICES

86815033

Fig. 25 Model E2SE carburetor exploded view

EXPLODED VIEW - E2SE CARBURETOR

Parts Identification

1	Air Horn Assembly	38	Gasket - Air Horn to Float Bowl
2	Hose - Vacuum Break - Primary Side	39	Pump Assembly
3	Screw - Primary Side Vacuum Break Attaching	39A	Cup - Pump Plunger
3A	Screw Assembly - Primary Side Vacuum Break Attaching	39B	Spring - Pump Plunger
		40	Spring - Pump Return
4	Vacuum Break Assembly - Primary Side	41	Sensor - Throttle Position (TPS)
4A	Link - Primary Side Vacuum Break - Choke Lever	42	Spring - Sensor Adjusting
4B	Bushing - Link	42A	Screw - Sensor adjusting
4C	Retainer - Link	42B	Plug - Cup (TPS)
5	Link - Air Valve to Primary Side Vacuum Break	43	Upper Insert - Float Bowl
6	Retainer - Link	44	Hinge Pin - Float
7	Bushing - Link	45	Float
8	Washer - Tab Locking	46	Spring - Float Stabilizer
9	Nut - Solenoid Attaching	47	Lower Insert - Float Bowl
10	Solenoid - Idle Stop	48A	Needle - Float
10A	Throttle Kicker Assembly	48B	Clip - Float Needle Pull
10B	Washer - Tab Locking	48C	Seat - Float Needle
10C	Nut - Throttle Kicker Assembly Attaching	48D	Gasket - Float Needle Seat
11	Screw - Secondary Side Vacuum Break Attaching	49	Jet - Primary Metering
12	Vacuum Break Assembly - Secondary Side	49A	Needle - Lean Mixture Adjustment
12A	Link - Secondary Side Vacuum Break - Choke Lever	50	Guide - Pump Discharge Spring
12B	Bushing - Link	51	Spring - Pump Discharge Ball
12C	Retainer - Link	52	Ball - Pump Discharge
13	Retainer - Pump Link	53	Nut - Fuel Inlet
14	Lever - Pump	54	Gasket - Fuel Inlet Nut
15	Retainer - Link	55	Filter - Fuel Inlet
16	Bushing - Link	56	Spring - Fuel Filter
17	Screw - Vent Stack Attaching	57	Rivet - Choke Cover Attaching
18	Vent Stack and Screen Assembly	58	Retainer - Choke Cover
19	Screw Assembly - Solenoid Assembly Attaching	59	Electric Choke Cover and Stat Assembly
20	Mixture Control (M/C) Solenoid Assembly	60	Screw - Choke Stat Lever Attaching
21	Gasket - Air Horn to M/C Solenoid Assembly	61	Lever - Choke Stat
22	Retainer - Solenoid Seal	62	Intermediate Choke Shaft ,Lever and Link Assembly
23	Seal - Solenoid to Float Bowl	62A	Link - Intermediate Choke
24	Spacer - Solenoid Seal	63	Screw Assembly - Choke Housing Attaching
25	Screw Assembly - Air Horn to Float Bowl (Large)	64	Choke Housing
26	Screw Assembly - Air Horn to Float Bowl (Short)	65	Throttle Body Assembly
27	Screw Assembly - Air Horn to Float Bowl (Long)	65A	Valve - Primary Throttle
28	Cam - Fast Idle	65B	Valve - Secondary Throttle
28A	Lockout Lever and Bushing Assembly	66	Screw Assembly - Float Bowl to Throttle Body
29	Retainer - Link	67	Gasket - Float Bowl to Throttle Body
30	Bushing - Fast Idle Cam Link	68	Link - Pump
31	Link - Fast Idle Cam	69	Needle - Idle Mixture
32	Plunger - Sensor Actuator	69A	Plug - Idle Mixture Needle
33	Retainer - TPS Plunger Seal	70	Spring - Idle Mixture Needle
34	Seal - TPS Plunger	71	Screw - Throttle Stop
34A	Seal - TPS Plunger	72	Spring - Throttle Stop Screw
35	Retainer - Pump Stem Seal	73	Screw - Fast Idle Cam
36	Seal - Pump Stem	74	Clip - Fast Idle Cam Screw
37	Float Bowl Assembly		

86815034

Fig. 26 Model E2SE carburetor parts identification

Fig. 27 A handy device for working on carburetors is a holding stand like this one — tool J-9789-118 or BT-30-15

Fig. 28 The air horn is the top portion of the carburetor

5. Remove the two screws from the vent stack and remove the vent stack. Remove the intermediate choke shaft link retainer at the choke lever and discard it.

6. Remove the choke link and bushing from choke lever and save the bushing.

7. Remove the retainer and bushing from the fast idle cam link.

➡Do not remove fast idle cam screw and cam from the float bowl. If removed, the cam might not operate properly when reassembled. If needed, a replacement float bowl will include a secondary locknut lever, fast idle cam, and cam screw.

8. Remove the retainer from the pump link. Do not remove the screw attaching the pump lever to the air horn assembly. When reassembled, the screw might not hold properly.

9. Remove the seven screw assemblies of various length that retain the air horn to the carburetor and remove the air

Fig. 29 Remove the retainer and bushing from the fast idle cam link

horn assembly. Tilt the air horn to disconnect fast idle cam link from the slot in fast idle cam and the pump link from the hole in the pump lever.

10. Remove the cam link from the choke lever. Be sure to line up the "squirt" on link with slot in lever.

11. Invert the air horn and remove the Throttle Position Sensor (TPS) actuator plunger. The Throttle Position Sensor (TPS) adjusting screw and plug should not be removed.

12. Remove the stakings that holds the TPS plunger seal retainer and pump stem seal retainer.

13. Use a small prytool to remove the retainers and seals, then discard them.

14. Further disassembly of the air horn is not required for cleaning purposes. The choke valve and choke valve screws, the air valve and air valve shaft should not be removed.

➡Do not turn the secondary metering rod adjusting screw. The rod could come out of the jet and possibly cause damage.

Fig. 30 Use a small prytool to remove the Throttle Position Sensor (TPS) plunger seal

FLOAT BOWL

▶ **See Figure 31**

1. Remove the accelerator pump, air horn gasket and pump return spring.

2. Remove the Throttle Position Sensor (TPS) assembly and spring. Inspect the TPS connector wires for broken insulation, which could cause grounding of the TPS.

3. Remove the upper insert and the hinge pin. Remove the float and lever assembly with the float stabilizing spring if used. Remove the float needle and pull clip.

4. Remove the lower insert, if used.

5. Remove the float needle seat and seat gasket.

6. Remove the jet and lean mixture needle assembly.

➡**Do not remove or change the preset adjustment of calibration needle in the metering jet unless the Computer Command Control system performance check requires it.**

7. Remove the pump discharge spring guide, using a suitable slide hammer puller only.

➡**Do not pry the guide. Damage could occur to the sealing surfaces, and could require replacement of the float bowl.**

8. Remove the spring and check ball, by inverting the bowl and catching them as they fall.

9. Remove the fuel inlet nut and the fuel filter spring.

10. Remove the fuel filter assembly and discard it. Remove the filter gasket and discard it.

CHOKE ASSEMBLY AND THROTTLE BODY

▶ **See Figure 32**

1. Remove the choke cover as follows:

a. Use a ⁵⁄₃₂ in. (4 mm) drill bit to remove the heads (only) from the rivets.

b. Remove the choke cover retainers, then the remaining pieces of rivets, using drift and small hammer.

c. Remove the electric choke cover and stat assembly.

2. Remove the stat lever screw, stat lever, intermediate choke shaft, lever and link assembly.

3. Remove the two screws and the choke housing.

4. Remove the four screws, and the throttle body assembly from the inverted float bowl.

5. Remove the gasket, pump link and line up the "squirt" on link with the slot in the lever.

6. Count and make a record of the number of turns needed to lightly bottom the idle mixture needle, then back out and remove the needle and spring assembly using Idle Mixture Socket tool J-29030-B or BT-7610-B (or equivalent).

7. Do not disassemble throttle body further.

INSPECTION AND CLEANING

1. Place the metal parts in a cold immersion carburetor cleaner, such as Carbon X® or equivalent.

➡**Do not immerse idle stop solenoid, mixture control solenoid, throttle lever actuator, TPS, electric choke, rubber and plastic parts, diaphragms, and pump in the cleaner, as they may be damaged. Plastic bushing in throttle lever will withstand normal cleaning.**

2. Blow dry the parts with shop air. Be sure all fuel and air passages are free of burrs and dirt. Do not pass drill bits or wires through jets and passages.

3. Be sure to check the mating surfaces of casting for damage. Replace if necessary. Check for holes in levers for wear or out-of-round conditions. Check the bushings for damage and excessive wear. Replace if necessary.

CARBURETOR REASSEMBLY

▶ **See Figure 33**

1. Install the mixture needle and spring assembly using an Idle Mixture Socket tool J-29030-B/BT-7610-B or an equivalent. Lightly bottom the needle, then back it out the number of turns recorded during removal, as a preliminary adjustment. Refer to the idle mixture adjustment procedure in this section for the final idle mixture adjustment.

2. Install the pump link and a new gasket on the inverted float bowl.

3. Install the throttle body to the float bowl assembly and finger tighten the four retaining screws. If the secondary actuating lever engages the lockout lever, and the linkage moves without binding, tighten the retaining screws.

Fig. 31 Remove the pump discharge spring guide, using a suitable slide hammer puller only — E2SE shown

Fig. 32 Count and make a record of the number of turns needed to lightly bottom the idle mixture needle, then back out and remove the needle and spring assembly using Idle Mixture Socket tool J-29030-B, BT-7610-B or equivalent

4. If the float bowl assembly was replaced, stamp or engrave the model number on the new float bowl in the same location as on the old bowl.

5. Place the throttle body and float bowl together on a suitable carburetor holding stand.

6. Fasten the choke housing on the throttle body, with the retaining screws.

7. Install the intermediate choke shaft, lever and link assembly.

8. Attach the choke stat lever on the intermediate choke shaft. The intermediate choke lever must be upright.

9. Insert the choke lever attaching screw in the shaft.

10. Seat the gasket on the fuel inlet nut and install a new filter assembly in the nut.

11. Install the filter spring, then the fuel inlet nut. Tighten the fuel inlet nut to 18 ft. lbs. (24 Nm).

✳✳CAUTION

Tightening beyond this limit may damage gasket and could cause a fuel leak, which might result in personal injury.

12. Install the pump discharge ball and spring.

13. Install a new spring guide and tap it until the top is flush with the bowl casting.

14. Install the needle seat with gasket. If used, lower the insert.

15. Install the jet and lean mixture needle assembly. Using Lean Mixture Adjusting tool J-28696-10 or BT-7928 or equivalent, lightly bottom the lean mixture needle. Back it out 2½ turns, as a preliminary adjustment.

➡Only adjust the lean mixture needle screw if it was removed or touched during disassembly or if the Computer Command Control system performance check, made before disassembly, indicated an incorrect lean mixture needle setting:

16. Bend the float lever upward slightly at the notch.

17. If used, install the float stabilizing spring on float. Insert the hinge pin in float lever, with ends toward the pump well.

18. Install the needle with the pull clip assembly on the edge of the float lever. Install the float and lever assembly in float bowl.

➡Adjust the float level using Float Level T-Scale J-9789-90 or BT-8037 or equivalent.

19. Install the upper insert over the hinge pin, with the top flush with the bowl. Install the Throttle Position Sensor (TPS) spring and the TPS assembly. The parts must be below the surface of the bowl.

20. Install the gasket over the dowels. Install the spring and pump assembly.

21. Install a new pump stem seal with the lip facing outside of carburetor and install the retainer. Be sure to stake it at new locations.

22. Install a new TPS actuator plunger seal with the lip facing outside of carburetor, then install the retainer. Be sure to stake it at new locations.

23. Install the TPS plunger through the seal in the air horn. Use a lithium base grease, liberally to pin, if used, where contacted by spring.

J-28696-10 or BT-7928

86815053

Fig. 33 Install the jet and lean mixture needle assembly. Using Lean Mixture Adjusting tool J-28696-10, BT-7928 or equivalent, lightly bottom the lean mixture needle. Back it out 2½ turns, as a preliminary adjustment

24. Install the fast idle cam link in the choke lever. Be sure to line-up the "squirt" on the link with slot in the lever.

25. Rotate the cam to the highest position. The lower end of the fast idle cam link goes in the cam slot, and the pump link end goes into the hole in the lever.

26. Hold the pump down, then lower the air horn assembly onto the float bowl. Be sure to guide the pump stem through the seal.

27. Install one of the air horn retaining screws, then finger tighten it to hold the air horn in place.

28. Install the cam link in the slot of the cam. Install a new bushing and retainer to the link, with the large end of the bushing facing the retainer. Check for freedom of movement.

29. Install the rest of the air horn retaining screws.

30. Install the spacer and a new seal, then lightly coat the seal with automatic transmission fluid. Assemble the seal on the solenoid stem, touching the spacer.

31. Install a new retainer and gasket on the air horn. Install the mixture control solenoid lining up the stem with the recess in the bowl.

32. Install the solenoid retaining screws. Install the vent stack, with two retaining screws, (unless lean mixture needle requires on-vehicle adjustment).

33. Install a new retainer on the pump link. Adjust the air valve spring, if adjustable.

34. Install the bushing on the choke link. With the intermediate choke lever upright, install the link in the choke lever hole. Install the new link retainer.

35. The following procedures is for the reassembly of any small components that have been removed from the carburetor, replace any parts if necessary.

   a. Install the idle stop solenoid, retainer and nut to the secondary side vacuum break bracket. Bend the retainer tab to secure the nut.

   b. Install the bushing to the link, then the link to the vacuum break plunger. Install the retainer to the link.

   c. Rotate the assembly, insert the end of the link in the upper slot of the choke lever. Install the bracket screws.

   d. Install the idle speed device, retainer and nut to the primary side vacuum break bracket. Bend the retainer tab to secure the nut.

   e. Install the bushing to the vacuum break link. Install the link to vacuum break plunger. Install the retainer to the link and the bushing to the air valve link. Install the link to the plunger and the retainer to the link.

36. Rotate the vacuum break assembly (primary side) and insert the end of the air valve link into the air valve lever and the vacuum break link into the lower slot of the choke lever.

37. Install the bracket screws, then the vacuum hose between the throttle body tube and the vacuum break assembly.

38. Install the choke thermostat lever. Install the choke cover and thermostat assembly in the choke housing.

39. If the thermostat has a "trap" (box-shaped pick-up tang), the trap surrounds the lever.

40. Line up the notch in the cover with projection on the housing flange. Install the retainers and rivets with a rivet tool. If necessary, use an adapter. Adjust the choke as previously described.

E2ME Carburetor

▶ See Figures 34 and 35

In many cases, necessary service can be carried out and completed without removing the carburetor from the engine. The information that follows pertains to a complete overhaul. The carburetor first must be removed from the engine. A complete overhaul includes disassembly, through cleaning, inspection and replacement of all gaskets, diaphragms, seals, worn or damaged parts, and adjustment of individual systems.

Refer to exploded view for parts identification. Always replace internal gaskets that are removed. Base gasket should be inspected and replaced, only if damaged.

➡ Before performing any service on the carburetor, it is essential that it be placed on a suitable holding fixture, such as Tool J-9789-118, BY-30-15 or equivalent. Without the use of the holding fixture, it is possible to damage throttle valves or other parts of the carburetor.

IDLE SPEED SOLENOID REMOVAL

Remove the attaching screws, then remove the Idle Speed Solenoid. The Idle Speed Solenoid should not be immersed in any carburetor cleaner, and should always be removed before complete carburetor overhaul, as carburetor cleaner will damage the internal components.

IDLE MIXTURE NEEDLE PLUG REMOVAL

▶ See Figure 36

1. Invert the carburetor and drain the fuel into a suitable container. Place the carburetor on a holding fixture. Make sure to avoid damaging the linkage, tubes and parts protruding from the air horn.

2. Use hacksaw to make two parallel cuts in the throttle body, one on each side of the locator points near one idle mixture needle plug. The distance between the cuts will depend on the size of the punch to be used. Cuts should reach down to the steel plug, but should but extend more than $\frac{1}{8}$ in. (3mm) beyond the locator points.

3. Place a flat punch at a point near the ends of the saw marks in the throttle body. Hold the punch at a 45° angle, and drive it into the throttle body until the casting breaks away, exposing the hardened steel plug. The plug will break, rather than remaining intact. Remove all the loose pieces.

4. Repeat the procedure for the other idle mixture needle plug.

IDLE AIR BLEED VALVE COVER REMOVAL

▶ See Figure 37

1. Cover the internal bowl vents and the air inlets to the bleed valve with masking tape.

2. Carefully align a 0.110 in. (3mm) drill bit with the rivet head. Drill only enough to remove the head of each rivet holding the idle air bleed valve cover.

3. Use a suitably sized punch to drive out the remainder of the rivet from the castings. Repeat procedure with other rivet.

✳✳CAUTION

For the next operation, safety glasses must be worn to protect eyes from possible metal shaving damage.

4. Lift off the cover and remove any pieces of rivet still inside the tower. Use shop air to blow out any remaining chips.

5. Remove the idle air bleed valve from the air horn.

6. Remove and discard the O-ring seals from the valve. New O-ring seals are required for reassembly. The idle air bleed valve is serviced as a complete assembly only.

AIR HORN REMOVAL

1. Remove the upper choke lever from the end of the choke shaft by removing the retaining screw. Rotate the upper choke lever to remove the choke rod from the slot in the lever.

2. Remove the choke rod from the lower lever inside the float bowl casting. Remove the rod by holding the lower lever outward with small a flat-bladed tool and twisting the rod counterclockwise.

3. Remove the secondary metering rods by removing the small screw in the top of the metering rod hanger. Lift upward on the metering rod hanger until the secondary metering rods are completely out of the air horn. Metering rods may be disassembled from the hanger by rotating the ends out of the holes in the end of the hanger.

Fig. 34 Exploded view of the E2ME carburetor

HOT AIR
CHOKE MODELS

86815050

PART DESCRIPTION

AIR HORN PARTS

1. Air Horn Assembly
2. Gasket — Air Horn
3. Lever — Pump Actuating
4. Roll Pin — Pump Lever Hinge
5. Screw — Air Horn Short ( )
6. Screw — Air Horn Countersunk (2)
7. Gasket — Solenoid Connector to Air Horn
8. Valve — Idle Air Bleed
9. "O" Ring (Thick) — Idle Air Bleed Valve
10. "O" Ring (Thin) — Idle Air Bleed Valve
11. Plunger — TPS Actuator
12. Seal — TPS Plunger
13. Retainer — TPS Seal
14. Screw — TPS Adjusting
15. Plug — TPS Screw
16. Seal — Pump Plunger
17. Retainer — Pump Seal
18. Screw — Solenoid Plunger (Rich Stop)
19. Plug — Plunger Stop Screw (Rich Stop)
20. Plug — Solenoid Adjusting (Lean Mixture)

CHOKE PARTS

21. Vacuum Break Control & Bracket — Front
22. Screw — Control Attaching (2)
23. Hose — Vacuum
24. Lever — Choke Rod (Upper)
25. Screw — Choke Lever
26. Rod — Choke
27. Lever — Choke Rod (Lower)
28. Seal — Intermediate Choke Shaft
29. Link — Rear (Aux.) Vacuum Break
30. Int. Choke Shaft & Lever
31. Cam — Fast Idle
32. Seal — Choke Housing to Bowl (Hot Air Choke)
33. Kit — Choke Housing
34. Screw — Choke Housing to Bowl
35. Seal — Intermediate Choke Shaft (Hot Air Choke)
36. Lever — Choke Coil
37. Screw — Choke Coil Lever
38. Gasket — Stat Cover (Hot Air Choke)
39. Stat Cover & Coil Assy. (Hot Air Choke)
40. Stat Cover & Coil Assy. (Electric Choke)
41. Kit — Stat Cover Attaching
42. Rear Vacuum Break Assembly
43. Screw — Vacuum Break Attaching (2)

PART DESCRIPTION

FLOAT BOWL PARTS

44. Float Bowl Assembly
45. Jet — Primary Metering (2)
46. Ball — Pump Discharge
47. Retainer — Pump Discharge Ball
48. Baffle — Pump Well
49. Needle & Seat Assembly
50. Float Assembly
51. Hinge Pin — Float Assembly
52. Rod — Primary Metering (2)
53. Spring — Primary Metering Rod (2)
54. Insert — Float Bowl
55. Insert — Bowl Cavity
56. Screw — Connector Attaching
57. Mixture Control (M/C) Solenoid & Plunger Assy.
58. Spring — Solenoid Tension
59. Screw — Solenoid Adjusting (Lean Mixture)
60. Spring — Solenoid Adjusting Screw
61. Spring — Pump Return
62. Pump Assembly
63. Link — Pump
64. Throttle Position Sensor (TPS)
65. Spring — TPS Tension
66. Filter Nut — Fuel Inlet
67. Gasket — Filter Nut
68. Filter — Fuel Inlet
69. Spring — Fuel Filter
70. Screw — Idle Stop
71. Spring — Idle Stop Screw
72. Idle Speed Solenoid & Bracket Assembly
73. Bracket — Throttle Return Spring
74. Idle Load Compensator & Bracket Assembly
75. Idle Speed Control & Bracket Assembly
76. Screw — Bracket Attaching

THROTTLE BODY PARTS

77. Throttle Body Assembly
78. Gasket — Throttle Body
79. Screw — Throttle Body ( )
80. Idle Needle & Spring Assy. (2)
81. Screw — Fast Idle Adjusting
82. Spring — Fast Idle Screw
83. Tee — Vacuum Hose
84. Gasket — Flange

86815051

Fig. 35 Parts list for the E2ME exploded view

86815070

Fig. 36 Use a center punch to break away the casting of the throttle body, exposing the hardened steel plug

86815052

Fig. 37 Align a 0.110 in. (3mm) drill bit with the rivet head, then remove the head of each rivet while holding the air bleed valve cover

4. Remove the pump link retainer and remove the link from pump lever.

➡ **Do not attempt to remove the lever, as damage to the air horn could result.**

5. Remove the front vacuum break hose from tube on the float bowl.

6. Remove the eleven air horn-to-bowl screws; then remove the two countersunk attaching screws located next to the venturi. If used, remove secondary air baffle deflector from beneath the two center air horn screws.

7. Remove air horn from float bowl by lifting it straight up. The air horn gasket should remain on the float bowl for removal later.

➡ **When removing air horn from float bowl, use care to prevent damaging the mixture control solenoid connector, Throttle Position Sensor (TPS) adjustment lever, and the small tubes protruding from the air horn. These tubes are permanently pressed into the air horn casting. DO NOT remove them.**

8. Remove front vacuum break bracket attaching screws. The vacuum break assembly may now be removed from the air valve dashpot rod, and the dashpot rod from the air valve lever.

➡ **Do not place vacuum break assembly in carburetor cleaner, as damage to vacuum break will occur.**

9. Remove Throttle Position Sensor (TPS) plunger by pushing plunger down through seal in air horn.

10. Remove TPS seal and pump plunger stem seal by inverting air horn and using a small screwdriver to remove staking holding seal retainers in place. Remove and discard retainers and seals.

➡ **Use care in removing the TPS plunger seal retainer and pump plunger stem seal retainer to prevent damage to air horn casting. New seals and retainers are required for reassembly.**

11. Invert air horn, and use Tool J-28696-4, BT-7967A, or equivalent, to remove rich mixture stop screw and spring.

12. Use a suitable punch to drive the lean mixture screw plug and rich mixture stop screw plug out of the air horn. Discard the plugs.

13. Further disassembly of the air horn is not required for cleaning purposes.The choke valve and choke valve screws, the air valves and air valve shaft should not be removed. However, if it is necessary to replace the air valve closing springs or center plastic eccentric cam, a repair kit is available. Instructions for assembly are included in the repair kit.

FLOAT BOWL DISASSEMBLY

▶ **See Figure 38**

1. Remove the solenoid metering rod plunger by lifting straight up.

2. Remove the rubber seal from around the mixture control solenoid.

3. Remove the air horn gasket by lifting it from the dowel locating pins on the float bowl. Discard the gasket.

4. Remove the pump plunger from the pump well.

Fig. 38 Remove the solenoid metering rod plunger by lifting straight up

5. Remove the staking holding the Throttle Position Sensor (TPS) in the bowl as follows:

   a. Lay a flat tool or metal piece across the bowl casting to protect the gasket sealing surface.

   b. Use a small flat tool to depress the TPS sensor lightly and hold against spring tension.

   c. Observing safety precautions, pry upward with a small chisel or equivalent to remove the bowl staking, making sure the prying force is exerted against the metal piece and not against the bowl casting. Use care not to damage the TPS sensor.

   d. Push up from the bottom on the electrical connector, then remove the TPS and connector assembly from the bowl. Use care in removing the sensor and connector assembly to prevent damage to this critical electrical part.

   e. Remove the spring from the bottom of the TPS well in the float bowl.

6. Remove the plastic bowl insert from the float bowl.

7. Carefully lift each metering rod out of the guided metering jet, checking to be sure the return spring is removed with each metering rod.

➡ **Use extreme care when handling these critical parts to avoid damage to the metering rod and spring.**

8. Remove the mixture control solenoid from the float bowl as follows:

   a. Remove the screw attaching the solenoid connector to the float bowl. Do not remove the solenoid connector from the float bowl until called for in text.

   b. Use Tool J-28696-10, BT-7928, or equivalent, to remove the lean mixture (solenoid) screw. Do not remove the plunger return spring or the connector and wires from the solenoid body. The mixture control solenoid, with plunger and connector, is only serviced as a complete assembly.

   c. Remove the rubber gasket from the top of the solenoid connector, then discard.

   d. Remove the solenoid screw tension spring (next to float hanger pin).

9. Remove the float assembly and the float needle by pulling up on the retaining pin. Remove the needle, seat and

gasket using set remover Tool J-22769, BT-3006M, or equivalent.

10. Remove the large mixture control solenoid tension spring from the boss on the bottom of the float bowl located between the guided metering jets.

11. If necessary, remove the primary main metering jets using special Tool J-28696-4, BT-7928, or equivalent.

➡**Use care installing the tool on the jet, to prevent damage to the metering rod guide (upper area), and locating tool over vertical float sections on the lower area of the jet. Also, no attempt should be made to remove the secondary metering jets (metering orifice plates). These jets are fixed and, if damaged, entire bowl replacement is required.**

12. Remove the pump discharge check ball retainer and turn the bowl upside down, catching the discharge ball as if falls.

13. Remove the secondary air baffle, if replacement is required.

14. Remove the pump well fill slot baffle, only if necessary.

15. Remove the hose from the rear vacuum break assembly only if necessary. Then remove the two screws and rotate the assembly to remove the vacuum break link from the slot in the plunger head. The non-adjustable vacuum break link is not removed at this time, but is removed after removal of the choke assembly from the float bowl.

CHOKE DISASSEMBLY

▶ See Figures 39, 40 and 41

The tamper-resistant choke cover is used to discourage unnecessary readjustment of the choke thermostatic cover and coil assembly. However, if it is necessary to remove the cover and coil assembly during normal carburetor disassembly for cleaning and normal carburetor disassembly for cleaning and overhaul, the procedures below should be followed.

1. Support the float bowl and throttle body, as an assembly, on a suitable holding fixture such as Tool J-9789-118, BT-30-15, or equivalent.

2. Carefully align a $5/32$ in. (4mm) drill bit on the rivet head and drill only enough to remove rivet head. Drill the two remaining rivet heads, then use a drift and small hammer to drive the remainder of the rivets out of the choke housing.

➡**Use care in drilling to prevent damage to the choke cover or housing.**

3. Remove the two conventional retainers, retainer with tab, and choke cover assembly from choke housing.

4. Remove the choke housing assembly from the float bowl by removing the retaining screw and washer inside the choke housing. The complete choke assembly can be removed from the float bowl by sliding outward.

5. Remove the secondary throttle valve lock-out lever from the float bowl.

6. Remove the lower choke lever from inside the float bowl cavity by inverting the bowl.

7. To disassemble the intermediate choke shaft from the choke housing, remove the coil lever retaining screw at the end of the shaft inside the choke housing. Remove the ther-

Fig. 39 Removing the choke cover rivets with a drill

Fig. 40 Exploded view of a common choke assembly

mostatic coil lever from the flats on the intermediate choke shaft.

8. Remove the intermediate choke shaft from the choke housing by sliding it outward. The fast idle cam can now be removed from the intermediate choke shaft. On hot air choke models, remove the cup seal inside the choke housing shaft hole. Remove the cup seal from the float bowl cleaning purposes. DO NOT ATTEMPT TO REMOVE THE INSERT.

9. Remove the fuel inlet nut, gasket, check valve, filter assembly and spring. Discard the check valve filter assembly and gasket.

10. Remove the three throttle body-to-bowl attaching screws and lockwashers, then remove the throttle body assembly.

11. Remove the throttle body-to-bowl insulator gasket.

THROTTLE BODY DISASSEMBLY

1. Place the throttle body assembly on a carburetor holding fixture to avoid damage to the throttle valves.

FAST IDLE SCREW

THROTTLE BODY ATTACHING SCREWS

THROTTLE LEVER

THROTTLE VALVES

86815061

Fig. 41 Remove the three throttle body-to-bowl attaching screws and lockwashers, then remove the throttle body assembly

2. Remove the pump rod from the throttle lever by rotating the rod until the tang on the rod aligns with the slot in the lever.

➡**Do not remove the plugs covering the idle mixture needles during normal carburetor cleaning and servicing.**

3. If it is necessary to remove the idle mixture needles, see Idle Mixture Plug Removal.

4. Further disassembly of the throttle body is not required for cleaning purposes. The throttle valve screws are permanently staked in place and should not be removed. The throttle body is serviced as a complete assembly.

CARBURETOR REASSEMBLY

1. Install the lower end of the pump rod in the throttle lever by aligning the tang on the rod with the slot in the lever. The end of the rod should point outward toward the throttle lever.

2. Install the idle mixture needles and springs using Tool J-29030-B, BT07610B, or equivalent. Lightly seat each needle, then turn counterclockwise the number of specified turns, the final idle mixture adjustment is made on the vehicle.

3. If a new float bowl assembly is used, stamp or engrave the model number on the new float bowl. Install the new throttle body-to-bowl insulator gasket over two locating dowels on bowl.

4. Install throttle body making certain throttle body is properly located over dowels on float bowl. Install three throttle body-to-bowl screws and lockwashers and tighten evenly and securely.

5. Place carburetor on proper holding fixture such as J-9789-118, BT-30-15 or equivalent.

6. Install fuel inlet filter spring, a new check valve filter assembly, new gasket and inlet nut. Tighten nut to 18 ft. lbs. (24 Nm).

➡**When installing a service replacement filter, make sure the filter is the type that includes the check valve to meet government safety standard. New service replacement filters with check valve meet this requirement. When properly installed, the hole in the filter faces toward the inlet**

nut. Ribs on the closed end of the filter element prevent it from being installed incorrectly, unless forced. Tightening beyond the specified torque can damage the nylon gasket.

7. Install a new cup seal into the insert on the side of the float bowl for the intermediate choke shaft. The lip on the cup seal faces outward.

8. Install the secondary throttle valve lock-out lever on the boss of the float bowl, with the recess hole in the lever facing inward.

9. Install the fast idle cam on the intermediate choke shaft (steps on cam face downward).

10. Carefully install the fast idle cam and intermediate choke shaft assembly in the choke housing. Install the thermostatic coil lever on the flats on the intermediate choke shaft. Inside the thermostatic choke coil lever is properly aligned when both inside and outside levers face toward the fuel inlet. Install the inside lever retaining screw into the end of the intermediate choke shaft.

11. Install the lower choke rod (inner) lever into the cavity in the float bowl.

12. Install the choke housing to the bowl, sliding the intermediate choke shaft into the lower (inner) lever. Tool J-23417, BT-6911 or equivalent, can be used to hold the lower choke lever in the correct position while installing the choke housing. The intermediate choke shaft lever and fast idle cam are in the correct position when the tang on lever is beneath the fast idle cam.

13. Install the choke housing retaining screws and washers. Check the linkage for freedom of movement. Do not install the choke cover and coil assembly until the inside coil lever is adjusted.

14. If removed, install the air baffle in the secondary side of the float bowl with the notches towards the top. The top edge of the baffle must be flush with the bowl casting.

15. If removed, install the baffle inside of the pump well with the slot towards the bottom.

16. Install the pump discharge check ball and the retainer screw in the passage next to the pump well.

17. If removed, carefully install the primary main metering jets in the bottom of the float bowl using Tool J-28696-4, BT-7928, or equivalent.

➡**Use care in installing the jets to prevent damage to the metering rod guide.**

18. Install the large mixture control solenoid tension spring over the boss on the bottom of the float bowl.

19. Install the needle seat assembly, with gasket, using seat installer J-22769, BT-3006M, or equivalent.

20. To make the adjustment easier, carefully bend the float arm before assembly.

21. Install the float needle onto the float arm by sliding the float lever under the needle pull clip. Proper installation of the needle pull clip is to hook the clip over the edge of the float on the float arm facing the float pontoon.

22. Install the float hinge pin into the float arm with end of loop of pin facing pump well. Install the float assembly by aligning the needle in the seat, then the float hinge pin into locating channels in the float bowl. DO NOT install float needle pull clip into holes in float arm.

23. Make a float level adjustment as necessary.

24. Install the mixture control solenoid screw tension spring between the raised bosses next to the float hanger pin.

25. Install mixture control solenoid and connector assembly as follows:

a. Install the new rubber gasket on top of the solenoid connector.

b. Install the solenoid carefully in the float chamber, aligning pin on end of solenoid with hole in raised boss at bottom of bowl. Align solenoid connector wires to fit in slot in bowl.

c. Install the lean mixture (solenoid) screw through the hole in the solenoid bracket and the tension spring in the bowl, engaging the first six screw threads to assure the proper thread engagement.

d. Install the mixture control solenoid gauging Tool J-33815-1, BT-8253-A, or equivalent over the throttle side metering jet rod guide, and temporarily install solenoid plunger.

e. Holding the solenoid plunger against the Solenoid Stop, use Tool J-28696-10, BT-7928, or equivalent, to turn the lean mixture (solenoid) screw slowly clockwise, until the solenoid plunger just contacts the gauging tool. The adjustment is correct when the solenoid plunger is contacting BOTH the Solenoid Stop and the Gauging Tool.

f. Remove the solenoid plunger and gauging tool.

26. Install the connector attaching screw, but DO NOT overtighten, as that could cause damage to the connector.

27. Install the Throttle Position Sensor return spring in the bottom of the well in the float bowl.

28. Install the Throttle Position Sensor and connector assembly in the float bowl by aligning the groove in the electrical connector with the slot in the float bowl casting. Push down on the connector and the sensor assembly so that the connector and wires are located below bowl casting surface.

29. Install the plastic bowl insert over float valve, pressing downward until properly seated (flush with bowl casting surface).

30. Slide the metering rod return spring over the metering rod tip until the small end of the spring stops against the shoulder on the rod. Carefully install the metering rod and spring assembly through the holding in the plastic bowl insert, then gently lower the metering rod into the guided metering jet, until large end of spring seats on the recess on end of jet guide.

✳✳CAUTION

Do not force the metering rod down in jet. Use extreme care when handling these critical parts to avoid damage to rod and spring. if service replacement metering rods, springs and jets are installed, they must be installed in matched sets.

31. Install the pump return spring in the pump well.

32. Install the pump plunger assembly in the pump well.

33. Holding down on the pump plunger assembly against return spring tension, install the air horn gasket by aligning the pump plunger stem with the hole in the gasket, and aligning the holes in the gasket over the TPS plunger, solenoid plunger return spring metering rods, solenoid attaching screw and electrical connector. Position the gasket over the two dowel locating pins on the float bowl.

34. Holding down on air horn gasket and pump plunger assembly, install the solenoid-metering rod plunger in the solenoid, aligning slot in end of plunger with solenoid attaching screw. Be sure plunger arms engage top of each metering.

35. If a service replacement Mixture Control Solenoid package is installed, the solenoid and plunger MUST be installed as a matched set.

AIR HORN ASSEMBLY

1. If removed, install TPS adjustment screw in air horn using Tool J-28696-10, BT-7967A, or equivalent. Final adjustment of the Throttle Position Sensor is made on the vehicle.

2. Inspect the air valve shaft pin for lubrication. Apply a liberal quantity of lithium base grease to the air valve shaft pin, especially in the area contacted by the air valve spring.

3. Install new pump plunger and TPS plunger seals and retainers in air horn casting. The lip on the seal faces outward, away from the air horn mounting surface. Lightly stake seal retainer in three places, choosing locations different from the original stakings.

4. Install rich mixture stop screw and rich authority adjusting spring from bottom side of the air horn. Use Tool J-2869-4, BT-7967A, or equivalent, to bottom the stop screw lightly, then back out ¼ turn. Final adjustment procedure will be covered later in this section.

5. Install TPS actuator plunger in the seal.

6. Carefully lower the air horn assembly onto the float bowl while positioning the TPS Adjustment Lever over the TPS sensor and guiding pump plunger stem through the seal in the air horn casting. To ease installation, insert a thin screwdriver between the air horn gasket and float bowl to raise the TPS Adjustment Lever, positioning it over the TPS sensor.

7. Make sure that the bleed tubes and accelerating well tubes are positioned properly through the holes in the air horn gasket. Do not force the air horn assembly onto the bowl, but lower it lightly into place over the two dowel locating pins.

8. Install the two long air horn screws and lockwashers, nine short screws and lockwashers and two countersunk screws located next to the carburetor venturi area. Install secondary air baffle beneath the No. 3 and 4 screws. Tighten all screws evenly and securely.

9. Install the air valve rod into the slot in the lever on the end of the air valve shaft. Install the other end of the rod in hole in front vacuum break plunger. Install the front vacuum break and bracket assembly on the air horn, using two attaching screws. Tighten the screw securely. Connect the pump link to the pump lever and install the retainer.

➡**Use care installing the roll pin to prevent damage to the pump lever bearing surface and casting bosses.**

10. Install the two secondary metering rods into the secondary metering rod hanger (upper end of rods point toward each other). Install the secondary metering rod holder, with rods, onto the air valve cam follower. Install the retaining screw, then tighten securely. Work the air valves up and down several times to make sure they remove freely in both directions.

11. Connect the choke rod into the lower choke lever inside the bowl cavity. Install the choke rod in the slot in the upper choke lever, and position the lever on the end of the choke shaft, making sure the flats on the end of the shaft align with the flats in the lever. Install the attaching screw, then tighten

securely. When properly installed, the number on the lever will face outward.

12. Adjust the rich mixture stop screw:

a. Insert the external float gauging Tool J-34935-1,BT-8420A, or equivalent, in the vertical D-shaped vent hole in the air horn casting (next to the idle air bleed valve) and allow it to float freely.

b. Read (at eye level) the mark on the gauge, in inches, that lines up with the tip of the air horn casting.

c. Lightly press down on gauge, then again read and record the mark on the gauge that lines up with the top of the air horn casting.

d. Subtract the gauge UP dimension, found in Step b, from the gauge DOWN dimension, found in Step c, and record the difference in inches. This difference in dimension is the total solenoid plunger travel.

e. Insert Tool J-28696-10, BT-7928, or equivalent, in the access hole in the air horn, and adjust the rich mixture stop screw to obtain $\frac{4}{32}$ in. (3mm) total solenoid plunger travel.

13. With the solenoid plunger travel correctly set, install the plugs supplied in the service kit into the air horn to retain the setting and prevent fuel vapor loss:

a. Install the plug, hollow end down, into the access hole to the lean mixture (solenoid) screw and use a suitably sized punch to drive the plug into the air horn until top of plug is even with the lower edge of the hole chamber.

b. In a similar manner, install the plug over the rich mixture screw access hole and drive the plug into place so that the tip of the plug is $\frac{1}{16}$ in. (2mm) below the surface of the air horn casting.

14. Install the Idle Air Bleed Valve as follows:

a. Lightly coat the two new O-ring seals with automatic transmission fluid, to aid in their installation on the idle air bleed valve body. The thick seal goes in the upper groove and the thin seal goes in the lower groove.

b. Install the idle air bleed valve in the air horn, making sure that there is proper thread engagement.

c. Insert the idle air bleed valve gauging Tool J-33815-2, BT-8353B, or equivalent, in throttle side D-shaped vent hole of the air horn casting. The upper end of the tool should be positioned over the open cavity next to the idle air bleed valve.

d. Hold the gauging tool down lightly so that the solenoid plunger is against the solenoid stop, then adjust the idle air bleed valve so that the gauging tool will pivot over and just contact the top of the valve.

e. Remove the gauging tool.

f. The final adjustment of the idle air bleed valve is made on the vehicle to obtain idle mixture control.

15. Perform the Air Valve Spring Adjustment and Choke coil Lever Adjustment as previously described.

16. Install the cover and coil assembly in the choke housing, as follows:

a. Place the cam follower on the highest step of the fast idle cam.

b. Install the thermostatic cover and coil assembly in the choke housing, making sure the coil tang engages the inside coil pickup lever. Ground contact for the electric choke is provided by a metal plate located at the rear of the choke cover assembly. DO NOT install a choke cover gasket between the electric choke assembly and the choke housing.

c. A choke cover retainer kit is required to attach the choke cover to the choke housing. Follow the instructions found in the kit and install the proper retainer and rivets using a suitable blind rivet tool.

d. It may be necessary to use an adapter (tube) if the installing tool interferes with the electrical connector tower on the choke cover.

17. Install the hose on the front vacuum brake and on the tube on the float bowl.

18. Position the idle speed solenoid and bracket assembly on the float bowl, retaining it with two large countersunk screws.

19. Perform the Choke Rod-Fast Idle Cam Adjustment, Primary (Front) Vacuum Break Adjustment, Air Valve Rod Adjustment-Front, Unloader Adjustment and the Secondary Lockout Adjustment as previously described.

20. Reinstall the carburetor on the vehicle with a new flange gasket.

Carburetor Adjustments

PRELIMINARY CHECKS

The following should be observed before attempting any adjustments.

1. Thoroughly warm the engine. If the engine is cold, be sure that it reaches operating temperature.

2. Check the torque of all carburetor mounting nuts and assembly screws. Also check the intake manifold-to-cylinder head bolts. If air is leaking at any of these points, any attempts at adjustment will inevitably lead to frustration.

3. Check the manifold heat control valve (if used) to be sure that it is free.

4. Check and adjust the choke as necessary.

5. Adjust the idle speed and mixture. If the mixture screws are capped, don't adjust them unless all other causes of rough idle have been eliminated. If any adjustments are performed that might possible change the idle speed or mixture, adjust the idle and mixture again when you are finished.

Before you make any carburetor adjustments make sure that the engine is in tune. Many problems which are thought to be carburetor related can be traced to an engine which is simply out-of-tune. Any trouble in these areas will have symptoms like those of carburetor problems.

E2SE CARBURETOR SPECIFICATIONS

Year	Carburetor Identification	Float Level (in.)	Fast Idle Cam (deg.)	Choke Coil Lever (in.)	Air Valve Rod (deg.)	Primary Vacuum Break (deg.)	Secondary Vacuum Break (deg.)	Choke Unloader (deg.)
1982	17082196	5/16	18°	.096	—	21°	19°	27°
	17082316	1/4	17°	.090	10	26°	34°	35°
	17082317	1/4	17°	.090	10	29°	35°	35°
	17082320	1/4	25°	.142	10	30°	35°	33°
	17082321	1/4	25°	.142	10	29°	35°	35°
	17082640	1/4	17°	.090	10	26°	34°	35°
	17082641	1/4	17°	.090	10	29°	35°	35°
	17082642	1/4	25°	.142	10	30°	35°	33°
1983	17083356	13/32	22°	.085	1°	25°	35°	30°
	17083357	13/32	22°	.085	1°	25°	35°	30°
	17083358	13/32	22°	.085	1°	25°	35°	30°
	17083359	13/32	22°	.085	1°	25°	35°	30°
	17083368	1/8	22°	.085	1°	25°	35°	30°
	17083370	1/8	22°	.085	1°	25°	35°	30°
	17083450	1/8	28°	.085	1°	27°	35°	45°
	17083451	1/8	28°	.085	1°	27°	35°	45°
	17083452	1/8	28°	.085	1°	27°	35°	45°
	17083453	1/8	28°	.085	1°	27°	35°	45°
	17083454	1/8	28°	.085	1°	27°	35°	45°
	17083455	1/8	28°	.085	1°	27°	35°	45°
	17083456	1/8	28°	.085	1°	27°	35°	45°
	17083630	1/4	28°	.085	1°	27°	35°	45°
	17083631	1/4	28°	.085	1°	27°	35°	45°
	17083632	1/4	28°	.085	1°	27°	35°	45°
	17083633	1/4	28°	.085	1°	27°	35°	45°
	17083634	1/4	28°	.085	1°	27°	35°	45°
	17083635	1/4	28°	.085	1°	27°	35°	45°
	17083636	1/4	28°	.085	1°	27°	35°	45°
	17083650	1/8	28°	.085	1°	27°	35°	45°
1984	17072683	9/32	28°	.085	1°	25°	35°	45°
	17074812	9/32	28°	.085	1°	25°	35°	45°
	17084356	9/32	22°	.085	1°	25°	30°	30°
	17084357	9/32	22°	.085	1°	25°	30°	30°
	17084358	9/32	22°	.085	1°	25°	30°	30°
	17084359	9/32	22°	.085	1°	25°	30°	30°
	17084368	1/8	22°	.085	1°	25°	30°	30°
	17084370	1/8	22°	.085	1°	25°	30°	30°
	17084430	11/32	15°	.085	1°	26°	38°	42°

86815132

E2SE CARBURETOR SPECIFICATIONS

Year	Carburetor Identification	Float Level (in.)	Fast Idle Cam (deg.)	Choke Coil Lever (in.)	Air Valve Rod (deg.)	Primary Vacuum Break (deg.)	Secondary Vacuum Break (deg.)	Choke Unloader (deg.)
1984	17084431	11/32	15°	.085	1°	26°	38°	42°
	17084434	11/32	15°	.085	1°	26°	38°	42°
	17084435	11/32	15°	.085	1°	26°	38°	42°
	17084452	5/32	28°	.085	1°	25°	35°	45°
	17084453	5/32	28°	.085	1°	25°	35°	45°
	17084455	5/32	28°	.085	1°	25°	35°	45°
	17084456	5/32	28°	.085	1°	25°	35°	45°
	17084458	5/32	28°	.085	1°	25°	35°	45°
	17084532	5/32	28°	.085	1°	25°	35°	45°
	17084534	5/32	28°	.085	1°	25°	35°	45°
	17084535	5/32	28°	.085	1°	25°	35°	45°
	17084537	5/32	28°	.085	1°	25°	35°	45°
	17084538	5/32	28°	.085	1°	25°	35°	45°
	17084540	5/32	28°	.085	1°	25°	35°	45°
	17084542	1/8	28°	.085	1°	25°	35°	45°
	17084632	9/32	28°	.085	1°	25°	35°	45°
	17084633	9/32	28°	.085	1°	25°	35°	45°
	17084635	9/32	28°	.085	1°	25°	35°	45°
	17084636	9/32	28°	.085	1°	25°	35°	45°
1985	17084534	5/32	28°	.085	1°	25°	35°	45°
	17084535	5/32	28°	.085	1°	25°	35°	45°
	17084540	5/32	28°	.085	1°	25°	35°	45°
	17084542	1/8	28°	.085	1°	25°	35°	45°
	17085356	1/8	22°	.085	1°	25°	30°	30°
	17085357	9/32	22°	.085	1°	25°	30°	30°
	17085358	1/8	22°	.085	1°	25°	30°	30°
	17085359	9/32	22°	.085	1°	25°	30°	30°
	17085368	1/8	22°	.085	1°	25°	30°	30°
	17085369	9/32	22°	.085	1°	25°	30°	30°
	17085370	1/8	22°	.085	1°	25°	30°	30°
	17085371	9/32	22°	.085	1°	25°	30°	30°
	17085452	5/32	28°	.085	1°	28°	35°	45°
	17085453	5/32	28°	.085	1°	28°	35°	45°
	17085458	5/32	28°	.085	1°	28°	35°	45°
1986	17084534	5/32	28°	.085	1°	25°	35°	45°
	17084535	5/32	28°	.085	1°	25°	35°	45°
	17084540	5/32	28°	.085	1°	25°	35°	45°
	17084542	5/32	28°	.085	1°	25°	35°	45°

THROTTLE BODY FUEL INJECTION (TBI) SYSTEM

Description of System

The electronic throttle body fuel injection system is a fuel metering system with the amount of fuel delivered by the throttle body injector(s) determined by an electronic signal supplied by the Computer Control Module (ECM/PCM). The ECM/PCM monitors various engine and vehicle conditions to calculate the fuel delivery time (pulse width) of the injector(s). The fuel pulse may be modified by the ECM/PCM to account for special operating conditions, such as cranking, cold starting, altitude, acceleration, and deceleration.

The Throttle Body Injection (TBI) system provides a means of fuel distribution for controlling exhaust emissions within legislated limits. The TBI system, by precisely controlling the air/fuel mixture under all operating conditions, provides as near as possible complete combustion.

This is accomplished by using an Computer Control Module (ECM/PCM) (a small on-board microcomputer) that receives electrical inputs from various sensors about engine operating conditions. An oxygen sensor in the main exhaust stream functions to provide feedback information to the ECM/PCM as to the oxygen content, lean or rich, in the exhaust. The ECM/PCM uses this information from the oxygen sensor, and other sensors, to modify fuel delivery to achieve, as near as possible, an ideal air/fuel ratio of 14.7:1. This air/fuel ratio allows the 3-way catalytic converter to be more efficient in the conversion process of reducing exhaust emissions while at the same time providing acceptable levels of driveability and fuel economy.

Relieving the Fuel System Pressure

✳✳CAUTION

It is necessary to relieve the fuel system pressure to reduce the risk of fire or personal injury. Have a shop rag handy in case of any spilt fuel when disconnecting fuel lines.

1. Loosen the fuel filler cap on the vehicle.
2. Raise the vehicle, then disconnect the fuel pump electrical connector.
3. Lower the vehicle.
4. Start and run the engine until the fuel supply remaining in the fuel lines is consumed.
5. Engage the starter for three seconds to allow relief of any remaining pressure.
6. Disconnect the negative battery cable.

Electric Fuel Pump

REMOVAL & INSTALLATION

▶ See Figure 42

1. Relieve fuel system pressure.
2. Disconnect the negative battery cable.
3. Raise the vehicle and safely support.
4. Drain the fuel tank.
5. Disconnect wiring from the tank.
6. Remove the ground wire retaining screw from under the body.
7. Disconnect all hoses from the tank.
8. Support the tank on a jack and remove the retaining strap nuts.

1 Fuel tank meter assy.
2 Pulsator (port injection only)
3 Bumper
4 Fuel pump
5 Sound isolator sleeve
6 Sound insulator
7 Filter

86815071

Fig. 42 The electric fuel pump has an in-tank design

9. Lower the tank and remove it.

10. Notice the position of the filter for replacement. Support the pump with one hand and grasp the filter with the other. Rotate the filter in one direction, then pull off of the pump. Discard the filter.

11. Disconnect the fuel pump connector, on wagons it will not be necessary.

12. On all models excluding wagons:

a. Place the sending unit on a bench upside down, then pull the fuel pump downwards to remove from the mounting bracket. Tilt the pump outwards and remove from the pulsator.

13. On wagons proceed as follows:

a. Disconnect the negative terminal nut and lead (black) from the pump.

b. Disconnect the positive lead (gray) from the pump, then loosen the coupler clamps.

To install:

14. On all models excluding wagons:

a. Assemble the rubber bumper and insulator onto the pump.

b. Position the fuel sender assembly upside down and install the fuel pump between the pulsator and mounting bracket.

c. Connect the pump electrical connector.

15. On all wagon models:

a. Position the fuel sender assembly upside down and install the coupler and coupler clamps to the inlet tube, but do not tighten at this time.

b. Install the pump between the coupler and the mounting bracket, then tighten the clamps so that 5-8 teeth are engaged.

c. Attach the positive lead (gray) to its positive terminal with the nut, then attach the negative lead (black) to the negative terminal.

➡**Always install a new filter when installing a new pump.**

16. Position the pump filter on the new pump and push the outer edge of the ferrule until it is fully seated.

17. Install the sending unit.

18. Install the gas tank and check for leaks.

19. Reconnect the battery cable.

Throttle Body

REMOVAL & INSTALLATION

▶ **See Figures 43 and 44**

1. Relieve the fuel system pressure as described above.

2. Disconnect the negative battery cable.

3. Remove the air cleaner.

4. Disconnect all wiring from the idle air control valve, throttle position sensor, and the fuel injector.

5. Remove the grommet with wires from the throttle body.

6. Disconnect the linkage from the unit.

7. Mark and disconnect the vacuum lines from the unit.

8. Follow the CAUTION under the fuel Pressure Test above, then disconnect the fuel feed and return lines from the unit. Discard the fuel line O-rings.

9. Unbolt and remove the unit and flange gasket, then discard the gasket.

To install:

10. Place a cover over the throttle body opening on the manifold to prevent dirt from entering the engine.

11. Clean the gasket surface on the throttle body and the intake manifold.

12. Install a new flange gasket, then mount the TBI unit to the manifold.

13. Tighten the TBI attaching bolts to 10-18 ft. lbs. (13-24 Nm).

14. Slip the new O-rings onto the fuel lines, then attach the fuel feed and return lines to the throttle body. The use of a fuel line wrench is needed for tightening the lines.

15. Tighten the line nuts to 18-20 ft. lbs. (24-27 Nm).

16. Attach the marked vacuum lines to there proper locations, then connect the linkages.

17. Install the grommet with the wires to the throttle body, along with any other electrical connections. Make sure all the connections are properly seated.

18. Tighten the fuel filler cap, then connect the negative battery cable.

19. Inspect with the engine **OFF** to see that the accelerator pedal is free, depress the pedal to the floor and release. Until this is the case then you can proceed.

20. Turn the ignition switch **ON** for two seconds, then turn the ignition **OFF** for ten seconds. Again turn the ignition **ON** and check for leaks.

21. Attach the air cleaner assembly and gasket.

22. Reset the Idle Air Control valve pintle position.

a. Block the drive wheels, then apply the Parking brake.

b. Start the engine, then hold the idle speed above 2000 rpm. Ground the diagnostic test terminal (ALDL) for ten seconds, then remove the ground.

c. Turn the ignition **OFF**, then restart the engine and check for proper idle operation.

Injector

REPLACEMENT

▶ **See Figures 45, 46, 47, 48, 49 and 50**

1. Relieve fuel system pressure as described above.

2. Disconnect the negative battery cable.

3. Remove the air cleaner.

4. Remove the electrical connection to the injector. On Model 300, unfasten the injector connector by squeezing the two tabs together and pulling straight up.

5. On Model 300, remove the fuel metering cover.

6. Remove the fuel injector retaining screw and retainer on Model 700.

7. Place a small prytool under the ridge opposite the electrical connector of the injector, and carefully pry it out.

1	FUEL METER ASSEMBLY
2	GASKET – FUEL METER BODY
3	SCREW & WASHER ASSY – ATTACH. (3)
4	FUEL INJECTOR KIT
5	FILTER – FUEL INJECTOR NOZZLE
6	SEAL – SMALL "O" RING
7	SEAL – LARGE "O" RING
8	BACK-UP WASHER – FUEL INJECTOR
9	GASKET – FUEL METER COVER
10	DUST SEAL – PRESS, REGULATOR
11	GASKET – FUEL METER OUTLET
12	SCREW & WASHER ASSY – LONG (3)
13	SCREW & WASHER ASSY – SHORT (2)
14	NUT – FUEL INLET
15	GASKET – FUEL INLET NUT
16	NUT – FUEL OUTLET
17	GASKET – FUEL OUTLET NUT
18	FUEL METER BODY ASSEMBLY
19	THROTTLE BODY ASSEMBLY
20	SCREW – IDLE STOP
21	SPRING – IDLE STOP SCREW
22	LEVER – TPS
23	SCREW – TPS LEVER ATTACHING
24	SENSOR – THROTTLE POSITION KIT
25	SCREW – TPS ATTACHING (2)
26	IDLE AIR CONTROL ASSY-
27	GASKET – CONTROL ASSY- TO T.B.
28	GASKET – FLANGE MOUNTING

Fig. 43 Exploded view of the Model 300 TBI used on early A-body cars

86815072

1. Air cleaner gasket
2. Fuel line inlet nut o-ring
3. Fuel line outlet nut o-ring
4. Flange gasket
5. Fuel meter body assembly
6. Fuel meter body - throttle body attaching screw
7. Fuel meter body to throttle body gasket
8. Injector retainer attaching screw
9. Injector retainer
10. TBI injector assembly
11. Upper fuel injector o-ring
12. Lower fuel injector o-ring
13. Pressure regulator cover assembly
14. Pressure regulator attaching screw
15. Pressure regulator spring seat
16. Pressure regulator spring

17. Pressure regulator diaphragm assembly
18. Fuel inlet fitting
19. Fuel fitting seal
20. Fuel outlet fitting
21. Throttle body assembly
22. Idle stop screw plug
23. Idle stop screw assembly
24. Idle stop screw spring
25. Throttle position (TPS) sensor
26. TPS attaching screw assembly
27. Idle air control (IAC) valve assembly
28. IAC valve attaching screw
29. IAC valve o-ring
30. Tube module assembly
31. Tube module assembly attaching screw
32. Tube module assembly gasket

86815073

Fig. 44 Exploded view of the Model 700 TBI used on most A-body cars

Fig. 45 Remove the fuel metering cover to access the injector — TBI Model 300

1 Injector retainer screw
2 Injector retainer
3 Fuel meter assembly
4 Fuel injector o-ring (lower)
5 Fuel injector o-ring (upper)
6 Fuel injector assembly

Fig. 46 Remove the fuel injector retaining screw and retainer on Model 700

Fig. 47 Place a small prytool under the ridge opposite the electrical connector of the injector, and carefully pry it out — Model 300 shown

1 Fuel meter body
2 Fuel injector
A Prybar
B Fulcrum

Fig. 48 Place a small prytool under the ridge opposite the electrical connector of the injector, and carefully pry it out — Model 700 shown

8. Remove the two O-rings from the injector and discard them. Carefully rotate the injector fuel filter back and forth to remove the filter from the base of the injector.

✳✳CAUTION

Do not remove the four screws securing the pressure regulator to the meter cover. The pressure regulator includes a large spring under heavy tension.

To install:

9. Attach the filter to the injector, make sure the large end of the filter is facing the injector, so that the filter covers the raised rib at the base of the injector.

10. Lubricate the new O-rings with clean engine oil or transmission fluid, then place them on the injector. Make sure the upper O-ring is in the groove and the lower O-ring is up, flush against the filter.

11. If so equipped install the steel washer.

FUEL INJECTOR FILTER
FUEL INJECTOR ASSEMBLY
SMALL "O" RING
LARGE "O" RING
STEEL BACK-UP WASHER
FUEL METER BODY

Fig. 49 The Model 300 TBI unit has steel washers, unlike the Model 700 TBI unit

12. Install the fuel injector by positioning it in the throttle body with the electrical connector face cut-out for the wire grommet, then push the injector down to seat it in the cavity.

13. Install the injector retainer.

14. Apply Loctite-262 or an equivalent to the threads of the injector. Then install the injector retainer screw.

15. Tighten the retainer screw.

16. Tighten the fuel filler cap, the connect the negative battery cable.

Idle Air Control (IAC) Valve

♦ See Figures 51 and 52

REMOVAL & INSTALLATION

1. Remove the air cleaner.

2. Disconnect the electrical connection from the idle air control assembly (IAC).

3. Remove the idle air control assembly (IAC) from the throttle body.

➡ Before installing a new idle air control valve, measure the distance that the valve is extended. This measurement should be made from motor housing to end of the cone. The distance should be no greater than 1⅛ in. (28mm). If the cone is extended too far damage to the valve may result. The IAC valve pintle may also be retracted by using IAC/ISC Motor Tester J-37027/BT-8256K. It is recommended not to push or pull on the IAC pintle. The force required to move the pintle of a new valve should not cause damage. Do not soak the IAC valve in any liquid cleaner or solvent as damage may result.

1. Idle air control valve
A. Less than 28mm (1 ⅛ in.)
B. Type I (with collar)
C. Type II (without collar)
D. Gasket (part of IAC valve service kit)

86815080

Fig. 51 Model 300 TBI unit Idle Air Control valve; there are two types, one with a collar and one without

4. Be sure to identify the replacement idle air control valve and replace with an identical part. The IAC valve pintle shape and diameter are designed for specific applications.

➡ Shiny spots on the pintle or seat are normal and do not indicate misalignment or bend in the shaft.

To install:

5. Install a new O-ring and lubricate with engine oil onto the IAC valve.

6. Install the new idle air control valve with the attaching screws using a threadlocking material Loctite-262 or an equivalent.

7. Tighten the screws to 27 inch lbs. (3 Nm).

8. Reconnect all electrical connections.

9. Replace the air cleaner assembly.

INSTALLING FUEL INJECTOR

86815079

Fig. 50 Installing the fuel injector in Model 300. Push the injector down to seat it in the cavity

A. Distance of pintle extension
B. Diameter of pintle
C. IAC valve O-ring
D. IAC valve attaching screw

86815081

Fig. 52 The Model 700 TBI unit's IAC valve is basically the same as that for Model 300

10. The base idle will not be correct unit the ECM/PCM resets the IAC.

➡Be sure to clean the IAC valve O-ring sealing surface, pintle valve seat and air passage. Use a suitable carburetor cleaner (be sure it is safe to use on systems equipped with an oxygen sensor) and a parts cleaning brush to remove the carbon deposits. Do not use a cleaner that contains methyl ethyl ketone. It is an extremely strong solvent and not necessary for this type of deposits. Shiny spots on the pintle or on the seat are normal and do not indicate a misalignment or a bent pintle shaft. If the air passage has heavy deposits, remove the throttle body for a complete cleaning. Replace the IAC O-ring with a new one.

Resetting Procedure

1. If a repair has been made, reset the IAC before retesting.
2. Turn the ignition switch **OFF** for 10 seconds.
3. Start the engine for 5 seconds.
4. Turn the ignition switch **OFF** for 10 seconds.
5. Retest IAC system, as necessary.

Throttle Position Sensor

REMOVAL & INSTALLATION

▶ **See Figures 53 and 54**

1. Disconnect the negative battery cable. Remove the air cleaner assembly along with the necessary duct work.
2. Remove the TPS attaching screws. If the TPS is riveted to the throttle body, it will be necessary to drill out the rivets.
3. Remove the TPS from the throttle body assembly.

➡**The throttle position sensor is an electrical component and should not be immersed in any type of liquid solvent or cleaner, as damage may result.**

1. Throttle position sensor
2. Screw & washer
3. TPS pick up lever
4. Screw
5. Lever
6. Throttle body assembly

86815082

Fig. 53 Throttle Position Sensor (TPS) on a Model 300 TBI assembly

To install:

4. With the throttle valve closed, install the TPS onto the throttle shaft. Rotate the TPS counterclockwise to align the mounting holes. Install the retaining screws or rivets. Tighten the retaining screws to 18 inch lbs. (2 Nm).
5. Install the air cleaner assembly and connect the negative battery cable. Perform the TPS output check and adjust the TPS if applicable.

ADJUSTMENT

Not all vehicles provide for this adjustment. Generally, newer vehicles don't have adjustable throttle position sensors. If the sensor your car is equipped with does not have slots at the mounting screws, then it's not adjustable.

1. Remove air cleaner. Disconnect the TPS harness from the TPS.
2. Using suitable jumper wires, connect a digital voltmeter J-34029-A or equivalent from the TPS connector center terminal B to the outside terminal A. A suitable ALDL scanner can also be used to read the TPS output voltage.
3. With the ignition **ON** and the engine stopped, The TPS voltage should be less than 1.25 volts.
4. If the reading on the TPS is not within the specified range, rotate the TPS until 0.42-0.54 volts are obtained. If this specified voltage cannot be obtained, replace the TPS.
5. If the voltage reading is correct, remove the voltmeter and jumper wires and reconnect the TPS connector to the sensor. Re-install the air cleaner.

Idle Speed

ADJUSTMENT

This procedure should be performed only when the throttle body parts have been replaced. Newer models may not provide for this adjustment, as the computer is responsible for idle control.

➡**The following procedure requires the use of a special tool.**

1. Remove the air cleaner and gasket.
2. Plug the vacuum port on the TBI marked THERMAC.
3. If the car is equipped with a tamper resistant plug that covers the throttle stop screw, the TBI unit must be removed as previously described in order to remove the plug.
4. Remove the throttle valve cable from the throttle control bracket to allow access to the throttle stop screw.
5. Connect a tachometer to the engine.
6. Start the engine and run it to normal operating temperature.
7. Install tool J-33047 into the idle air passage of the throttle body. Be sure that the tool is fully seated and that no air leaks exist.
8. Using a #20 Torx bit (0.16 in.-4mm), turn the minimum air screw until the engine rpm is 675-725 with auto. trans. or 725-825 with manual trans. The AT should be in Park, the MT in Neutral.

9. Stop the engine and remove the special tool.
10. Install the cable on the throttle body.
11. Use RTV sealant to cover the throttle stop screw.

1. Fuel meter assembly
2. Throttle body assembly
3. Throttle position sensor
4. TPS attaching screw and washer assembly

86815083

Fig. 54 Throttle Position Sensor (TPS) on a Model 700 TBI assembly

MULTI-PORT/SEQUENTIAL FUEL INJECTION SYSTEMS

Description

The Multi-Port Injection (MFI) and Sequential Fuel Injection (SFI) systems are controlled by an Computer Control Module (ECM/PCM) which monitors engine operations and generates output signals to provide the correct air/fuel mixture, ignition timing and engine idle speed control. Input to the control unit is provided by an oxygen sensor, (heated on the SFI), coolant temperature sensor, detonation sensor, mass air flow sensor and throttle position sensor. The ECM/PCM also receives information concerning engine rpm, road speed, transaxle gear position, power steering and air conditioning.

The injectors are located, one at each intake port, rather than the single injector found on the earlier throttle body system. The injectors are mounted on a fuel rail and are activated by a signal from the electronic control module. The injector is a solenoid-operated valve which remains open depending on the width of the electronic pulses (length of the signal) from the ECM/PCM; the longer the open time, the more fuel is injected. The MFI system has fuel flowing to the injectors at a pulse time and the SFI system has fuel flowing to the injectors in sequence of the firing order. In other words, if the firing order is 1-2-3-4-5-6 the fuel will be sent to the injectors in that order. In this manner, the air/fuel mixture can be precisely controlled for maximum performance with minimum emissions.

Fuel is pumped from the tank by a high pressure fuel pump, located inside the fuel tank. It is a positive displacement roller vane pump. The impeller serves as a vapor separator and precharges the high pressure assembly. A pressure regulator maintains 28-36 psi (179-248 kPa) in the fuel line to the injectors and the excess fuel is fed back to the tank. A fuel accumulator is used to dampen the hydraulic line hammer in the system created when all injectors open simultaneously.

The Mass Air Flow (MAF) Sensor is used to measure the mass of air that is drawn into the engine cylinders. It is located just ahead of the air throttle in the intake system and consists of a heated film which measures the mass of air, rather than just the volume. A resistor is used to measure the temperature of the film at 75° above ambient temperature. As the ambient (outside) air temperature rises, more energy is required to maintain the heated film at the higher temperature and the control unit used this difference in required energy to calculate the mass of the incoming air. The control unit uses this information to determine the duration of fuel injection pulse, timing and EGR.

The throttle body incorporates an Idle Air Control (IAC) that provides for a bypass channel through which air can flow. It consists of an orifice and pintle which is controlled by the ECM through a step motor. The IAC provides air flow for idle and allows additional air during cold start until the engine reaches operating temperature. As the engine temperature rises, the opening through which air passes is slowly closed.

The Throttle Position Sensor (TPS) provides the control unit with information on throttle position, in order to determine injector pulse width and hence correct mixture. The TPS is connected to the throttle shaft on the throttle body and consists of as potentiometer with on end connected to a 5 volt source from the ECM and the other to ground. A third wire is connected to the ECM/PCM to measure the voltage output from the TPS which changes as the throttle valve angle is changed (accelerator pedal moves). At the closed throttle position, the output is low (approximately 0.4 volts); as the throttle valve opens, the output increases to a maximum 5 volts at Wide Open Throttle (WOT). The TPS can be misadjusted open, shorted, or loose and if it is out of adjustment, the idle quality or WOT performance may be poor. A loose TPS can cause intermittent bursts of fuel from the injectors and an unstable idle because the ECM/PCM thinks the throttle is moving. This should cause a trouble code to be set. Once a trouble code is set, the ECM/PCM will use a preset value for TPS and some vehicle performance may return. A small amount of engine coolant is routed through the throttle assembly to prevent freezing inside the throttle bore during cold operation.

Relieving Fuel System Pressure

✳✳CAUTION

Before opening any part of the fuel system, the pressure must be relieved. Follow the procedure below to relieve the pressure:

The fuel pressure release fitting is located at the top rear of the fuel injection rail. Use of a fuel pressure gauge, J-34730-1 or an equivalent.

1. Disconnect the negative battery cable to avoid possible fuel discharge.
2. Loosen the fuel filler cap to relieve the pressure.
3. Connect a fuel pressure gauge to the pressure valve, wrap a towel around the fitting while connecting a gauge to avoid spillage.
4. Install a bleed hose into an approved unbreakable container, then open the valve to bleed the pressure.
5. Drain any excess fuel in the gauge into the container.

Electric Fuel Pump

The electric fuel pumps are attached to the fuel sending unit, which is located in the fuel tank.

✳✳CAUTION

Before opening any part of the fuel system, the pressure must be relieved. Follow the procedure below to relieve the pressure:

REMOVAL & INSTALLATION

1. Relieve fuel system pressure.
2. Disconnect the negative battery cable.
3. Raise the vehicle and safely support.
4. Drain the fuel tank.
5. Disconnect wiring from the tank.
6. Remove the ground wire retaining screw from under the body.
7. Disconnect all hoses from the tank.
8. Support the tank on a jack and remove the retaining strap nuts.
9. Lower the tank and remove it.
10. Notice the position of the filter for replacement. Support the pump with one hand and grasp the filter with the other. Rotate the filter in one direction, then pull off of the pump. Discard the filter.
11. Disconnect the fuel pump connector, on wagons it will not be necessary.
12. On all models excluding wagons:
    a. Place the sending unit on a bench upside down, then pull the fuel pump downwards to remove from the mounting bracket. Tilt the pump outwards and remove from the pulsator.
13. On wagons proceed as follows:
    a. Disconnect the negative terminal nut and lead (black) from the pump.

b. Disconnect the positive lead (gray) from the pump, then loosen the coupler clamps.
To install:
14. On all models excluding wagons:
    a. Assemble the rubber bumper and insulator onto the pump.
    b. Position the fuel sender assembly upside down and install the fuel pump between the pulsator and mounting bracket.
    c. Connect the pump electrical connector.
15. On all wagon models:
    a. Position the fuel sender assembly upside down and install the coupler and coupler clamps to the inlet tube, but do not tighten at this time.
    b. Install the pump between the coupler and the mounting bracket, then tighten the clamps so that 5-8 teeth are engaged.
    c. Attach the positive lead (gray) to its positive terminal with the nut, then attach the negative lead (black) to the negative terminal.

➡**Always install a new filter when installing a new pump.**

16. Position the pump filter on the new pump and push the outer edge of the ferrule until it is fully seated.
17. Install the sending unit.
18. Install the gas tank and check for leaks.
19. Reconnect the battery cable.

TESTING

Pressure Test

1. Relive the fuel system pressure.
2. On MFI equipped engines, disconnect the fuel line from the EFI, then connect the fuel line to a pressure gauge.

➡**If the system is equipped with a fuel return hose, squeeze it off so that an accurate reading can be obtained.**

3. On the MFI equipped engines, connect a jumper wire from the positive battery terminal to the **G** terminal of the ALCL unit or on the carbureted engines, start the engine, then check the fuel pressure.
4. The fuel pressure should be about 34-46 psi.

➡**If the pressures do not indicate correctly, check the fuel line for restrictions or the pump for malfunctions.**

Volume Test

This test should be completed after the pressure test has been performed.

1. Disconnect the pressure gauge from the fuel line and connect a flexible tube from the fuel line to an unbreakable container.

➡**If the engine is equipped with a fuel return line, squeeze off the line to obtain an accurate reading.**

2. Connect a jumper wire from the positive battery cable to the **G** terminal of the ALCL unit.

3. In 15 seconds, the fuel pump should supply ½ pint of fuel.

➡**If the fuel volume is below minimum, check the fuel line for restrictions.**

4. After testing, reconnect the fuel line to the EFI unit.

Throttle Body

The throttle body is located at the front of the engine and is attached to the intake plenum.

REMOVAL & INSTALLATION

▶ **See Figures 55 and 56**

1. Disconnect the negative battery cable.
2. On MFI systems drain the coolant from the cooling system until the level is below the throttle body.
3. Remove the air inlet duct, the vacuum hoses and the coolant hoses from the throttle body.
4. Disconnect the accelerator and cruise control (if equipped) cables.
5. Remove the Idle Air Control (IAC) and the Throttle Position Sensor (TPS) electrical connectors from the throttle body.
6. Remove the nuts holding the throttle body to the upper intake manifold assembly.
7. Remove the throttle body and flange gasket, clean the gasket areas thoroughly.

To install:

8. Install a new flange gasket, then mount the throttle body assembly onto the intake manifold.
9. Install the retaining nuts, then tighten to 21 ft. lbs. (28 Nm).
10. Reinstall the coolant hose to the throttle body of the MFI system.
11. Attach all the control cables, then make adjustments accordingly.
12. Install the vacuum hoses and sensors, then attach the electrical connections to the sensors.
13. Install the air inlet duct. Connect the negative battery cable.
14. Add coolant to the system.
15. Reset the IAC pintle position:
   a. Turn the ignition **ON**.
   b. Ground the engine diagnostic lead for about five seconds.
16. Start the engine and check for proper idle and leaks.

Plenum/Upper Intake Manifold

The Plenum is the top portion of the intake manifold. This portion must be removed before servicing the injector system.

REMOVAL & INSTALLATION

MFI Engines — Except 3.1L (VIN T)

1. Disconnect the negative battery cable.

2. Tag and disconnect the vacuum lines.
3. Remove the EGR to plenum nuts.
4. Remove the two throttle body bolts.
5. Remove the throttle cable bracket bolts.
6. Remove the ignition wire plastic shield bolts.
7. Remove the plenum bolts.
8. Remove the plenum and gaskets from the engine.

To install:

9. Clean the gasket area, then install new gaskets.
10. Connect the plenum with the mounting bolts, then tighten them to 16 ft. lbs. (21 Nm).
11. Attach the ignition wire plastic shield bolts, then the throttle body bolts.
12. Tighten the throttle body bolts to 18 ft. lbs. (25 Nm).
13. Install the EGR to plenum nuts, then attach the throttle cable bracket bolts.
14. Hook up the vacuum lines, then connect the negative battery cable.
15. With the engine in the **OFF** position, make sure the accelerator pedal is free. Depress the pedal to the floor and release.
16. Reset the IAC pintle position:
   a. Turn the ignition **ON**.
   b. Ground the engine diagnostic lead for about five seconds.

3.1L Engine (VIN T)

▶ **See Figure 57**

1. Disconnect the negative battery cable.
2. Remove the air inlet duct at the throttle body and crankcase vent pipe at the valve cover grommet.
3. Disconnect the vacuum harness connector from the throttle body.
4. Remove the throttle cable bracket bolt.
5. Remove the throttle body attaching bolts. Remove the throttle body and gasket. Discard the gasket.
6. Remove the EGR transfer tube-to-plenum bolts. Remove the EGR transfer tube and gasket. Discard the gasket.
7. Remove the air conditioning compressor-to-plenum bracket attaching hardware. Remove the bracket.
8. Remove the plenum bolts and studs. Remove the plenum and gaskets. Discard the gaskets.

To install:

➡**Use care in cleaning old gasket material from machined aluminum surfaces. Sharp tool may damage gasket surfaces.**

9. Carefully, remove old gasket material from gasket sealing surfaces.
10. Install new plenum gaskets.
11. Install the plenum. Install the plenum bolts and studs. Tighten to 18 ft. lbs. (25 Nm).
12. Install the air conditioning compressor-to-plenum bracket and attaching hardware.
13. Install the EGR transfer tube with a new gasket. Install the EGR transfer tube bolts.
14. Install a new throttle body gasket. Install the throttle body and attaching bolts.
15. Install the throttle cable bracket bolt.
16. Connect the vacuum harness connector to the throttle body.

1 Flange gasket
2 Throttle body assembly
3 Idle stop screw plug
4 Idle stop screw assembly
5 Idle stop screw assembly spring
6 Throttle position sensor (TPS)
7 TPS attaching screw assembly
8 TPS attaching screw retainer
9 TPS lever
10 Coolant cavity cover
11 Coolant cover attaching screw assembly
12 Coolant cover to throttle body O-ring
13 Idle air/vacuum signal housing assembly
14 Idle air/vacuum signal assembly screw assembly
15 Idle air/vacuum signal assembly long screw assembly
16 Idle air/vacuum signal assembly gasket
17 Idle air control (IAC) valve assembly
18 IAC valve assembly gasket

86815090

Fig. 55 Throttle body component exploded view for a 3.8L engine

1 Nuts
2 Throttle body assembly
3 Gasket
4 Intake manifold assembly

86815091

Fig. 56 Before installing the throttle body assembly, remember to clean the gasket area, then install a new gasket

1 Plenum
2 Bolt (9)
3 Fuel rail asm.
4 Gasket
5 Bolt (4)

86815093

Fig. 57 Unfasten the plenum bolts and studs, then remove the plenum and gaskets. Discard the gaskets on the 3.1L (VIN T) engine

17. Connect the air inlet duct to the throttle body and crankcase vent pipe to the valve cover grommet.

18. Connect the negative battery cable.

19. With the ignition switch in the **OFF** position, ensure that the movement of the accelerator is free.

20. Perform the Idle Learn Procedure, as described in Section 1.

3.1 L Engine (VIN M)

▶ See Figure 58

1. Disconnect the negative battery cable.

2. Drain the coolant, then disconnect the air inlet duct.

3. Remove the accelerator and cruise control cables at the throttle body accelerator control cable bracket.

4. Disconnect the fuel pipe clip at the accelerator cable bracket, then remove the bracket.

5. Disconnect the vacuum lines, matchmarking them for installation.

6. Remove the EGR valve.

7. Unfasten the heater inlet hose clamps at the heater inlet pipe.

8. Remove the ignition coil front bolts, then loosen the rear bolts.

9. Remove the alternator braces.

10. Disconnect the electrical connections to the IAC valve, MAF and TPS sensors.

11. Remove the upper intake manifold bolts and studs, then remove the assembly. Discard of the gaskets.

12. Disassemble the throttle body from the upper intake manifold.

13. Remove the heater hoses from the upper intake manifold.

14. Disconnect the fuel pressure regulator vacuum line.

15. Clean the gasket surfaces.

To install:

16. Assemble the throttle body to the upper intake manifold.

17. Attach the heater hoses to the upper intake manifold.

18. Install new upper intake manifold gaskets, then connect the upper intake manifold by guiding the upper intake manifold heater hoses onto the heater inlet pipe.

19. Install the upper intake manifold bolts and studs, then tighten the bolts and studs to 18 ft. lbs. (25 Nm).

1 Studs
2 Bolts
3 Map sensor bracket
4 Gasket
5 Fuel rail

86815092

Fig. 58 Exploded view of the SFI upper intake manifold

20. Attach the heater hose clamps at the heater inlet pipe.
21. Install the alternator braces.
22. Insert the ignition coil front and rear bolts, then tighten.
23. Install the EGR valve bolts.
24. Connect the vacuum lines previously matchmarked.
25. Connect the electrical connections to the sensors and valves.
26. Attach the alternator control cable bracket, then connect the fuel pipe clip at the accelerator control cable bracket. Attach all the control cables.
27. Adjust the accelerator cable and cruise cables.
28. Attach the air inlet duct.
29. Install the negative battery cable, then refill the coolant.
30. Start the engine and check the coolant level, fill if needed.

Fuel Rail

REMOVAL & INSTALLATION

▶ See Figures 59 and 60

Before removal you should clean the fuel rail assembly. Use a special cleaner such as GM X-30 or an equivalent. Do not soak the rails in the solvent, follow the manufacturer's instructions.
1. Disconnect the negative battery cable.
2. Relieve the fuel system pressure.
3. Remove the intake manifold plenum, as required.
4. Disconnect the fuel feed and return lines at the fuel rail. Use a backup wrench, as required, to support the fuel rail tube fittings.
5. Remove the fuel line O-rings and discard.
6. Disconnect the vacuum line at the pressure regulator, then remove the regulator (if needed).
7. Disconnect the fuel injector electrical connectors, then the coolant temperature sensor connector.
8. Remove the fuel rail attaching bolts. Remove the fuel rail assembly. Note the location and routing of vacuum hoses around the fuel rail before removing the rail.
9. Remove the injector O-ring seal from the spray tip end of each injector. Discard the O-rings.
   To install:
10. Lubricate new injector O-ring seals with engine oil and install on the spray tip end of each injector.
11. Install the fuel rail assembly into the intake manifold. Tilt the rail assembly to install the injectors. Install the fuel rail attaching bolts and fuel rail bracket bolts. Tighten fuel rail attaching bolts.
12. Connect the electrical connection to the coolant temperature sensor, then the injector electrical connectors. Rotate the injectors, as required, to prevent stretching the wire harness.
13. Attach the main injector harness.
14. Install new O-rings on the fuel feed and return lines. Connect the fuel lines and tighten.
15. If removed, install the pressure regulator and connect the vacuum line.
16. Install the intake manifold plenum.
17. Connect the negative battery cable.
18. Tighten the fuel filler cap.

19. Turn the ignition switch to the **ON** position for 2 seconds, then turn to the **OFF** position for 10 seconds. Again, turn the ignition switch to the **ON** position and check for fuel leaks.
20. If equipped with the 3.1L (VIN T) engine, perform the Idle Learn Procedure, as described in Section 1.

Fuel Injectors

REMOVAL & INSTALLATION

▶ See Figures 61 and 62

1. Disconnect the negative battery cable.
2. Relieve fuel system pressure.
3. Remove the intake plenum and, if equipped, remove the runners.
4. Remove the fuel rail assembly.
5. Disconnect the injectors electrical connections.
6. Rotate the injector retaining clip to the release position, discard the clip.
7. Remove the injector from the fuel rail assembly.
8. Remove the O-rings from both ends of the injector and discard. Save the injector O-ring backups for use on assembly.
   To install:

➡ **When replacing fuel injectors, be sure the new injector is the same part number as the one removed from the engine.**

To install:
9. Install the injector backups, then lubricate new injector O-rings with engine oil and install on the injectors.
10. Put the new injector retainer clip on the injector. Position the open end of the clip facing the injector electrical connector.
11. Install injector into fuel rail injector socket with the electrical connectors facing out.
12. Rotate the injector clip to the locked position.
13. Make sure all electrical connections are intact.
14. Install the fuel rail assembly.
15. Check for fuel leaks by performing the following:
   a. Temporarily connect the negative battery cable.
   b. Turn the ignition switch to the **ON** position for 2 seconds. Turn the ignition switch to the **OFF** position for 10 seconds. Again turn the ignition switch to the **ON** position and check for fuel leaks.
   c. Disconnect the negative battery cable.
16. Install the plenum assembly.
17. Tighten the fuel filler cap.
18. Connect the negative battery cable.

Idle Air Control Valve

REMOVAL AND INSTALLATION

▶ See Figures 63 and 64

The idle air control valve is mounted to the throttle body and controls the bypass air around the throttle plate. It is used to

1 Fuel pressure connection cap
2 Fuel pressure connection valve assembly
3 RH fuel rail assembly
4 Retainer and spacer bracket
5 Filter screen
6 Pressure regulator inlet o-ring
7 Fuel pressure regulator assembly
8 Pressure regulator attaching screw
9 Upper injector (black) o-ring

10 Injector retainer clip
11 Fuel injector assembly
12 O-ring backup
13 Lower injector (brown) o-ring
14 Rail mounting bracket attaching screw
15 Rail mounting (2 ea.) bracket
16 LH fuel (with crossover tube) rail assembly
17 Crossover tube retainer clip
18 Crossover tube o-ring

86815094

Fig. 59 Exploded view of the SFI fuel rail

Fig. 60 Exploded view of the MFI fuel rail model R620

1 Fuel inlet line o-ring
2 Fuel return line o-ring
3 Fuel pressure connection assembly
4 Fuel pressure connection seal
5 Fuel pressure connection cap
6 Fuel inlet fitting
7 Fuel outlet fitting
8 Fuel fitting gasket
9 MPFI injector assembly
10 Injector o-ring seal
11 Injector retainer clip
12 Left hand fuel rail and plug assembly
13 Right hand fuel rail and plug assembly
14 Pressure regulator assembly
15 Base to rail connector
16 Connector o-ring seal
17 Fuel return o-ring seal
18 Pressure regulator mounting bracket
19 Pressure regulator bracket attaching screw assembly
20 Rail mounting bracket
21 Bracket attaching screw assembly

86815095

1 Fuel injector assembly
A Part number identification
B Build date code
C Month 1-9 (Jan-Sept) O, N, D, (Oct, Nov, Dec)
D Day
E Year

86815096

Fig. 61 When replacing fuel injectors, be sure the new injector is the same part number as the one removed from the engine. Note the location for identification

control the engine idle speed, to prevent stalls due to changes in the engine load.

1. Remove the electrical connector from the Idle Air Control (IAC) valve assembly.

2. Unscrew the IAC from the throttle body and discard the gasket.

➡**Do not remove the thread locking compound from the threads.**

To install:

3. Clean and inspect the IAC valve O-ring sealing surface, pintle seat and air passage. Do not soak the valve in any liquid cleaner or solvent, this will damage the valve. Use a carburetor cleaner and a parts cleaning brush to remove any carbon deposits. Shiny spots on the pintle or seat are normal and do not mean misalignment or a bent shaft.

4. If installing a new IAC valve, you will need to measure the distance between the tip of the pintle and the mounting flange. If it is greater than 1 inch (25mm), use finger pressure to slowly retract the pintle.

1 Fuel injector
2 Intake manifold
3 Intake valve
4 Electrical terminal
5 "O" ring
6 Fuel rail

86815099

Fig. 62 After the injector is installed, turn the ignition switch to the ON position for 2 seconds. Turn the ignition switch to the OFF position for 10 seconds. Again turn the ignition switch to the ON position and check for fuel leaks

SINGLE TAPER VALVE   DUAL TAPER VALVE

BLUNT PINTLE

86815097

Fig. 63 There are three types of Idle Air Control (IAC) valves

86815098

Fig. 64 If installing a new IAC valve, you will need to measure the distance between the tip of the pintle and the mounting flange. If it is greater than 1 inch (25mm), use finger pressure to slowly retract the pintle

    5. Lubricate the IAC valve O-ring with clean engine oil, then install the valve assembly.
    6. Attach the IAC with the mounting screws, tighten them to 27 inch lbs. (3 Nm).
    7. Connect the electrical connectors.
    8. Reset the OAC valve pintle:
      a. Turn the ignition **ON** for five seconds.
      b. Turn the ignition **OFF** for ten seconds.
      c. Start the engine, then check for proper idle operation.

Cold Start Valve

REMOVAL & INSTALLATION

▶ See Figure 65

    The cold start valve (not controlled by the ECM/PCM) provides additional fuel during the starting mode to improve cold start ups.
    1. Disconnect the negative battery cable.
    2. Remove the IAC pipe and the engine mount strut brace.
    3. Remove the fuel line from the fuel rail, the electrical connector from the valve and the valve retaining bolt.
    4. Pull the cold start valve from the fuel rail.
    5. Clean the areas around the valve and the connection with a suitable cleaner.
    6. Remove the valve from the tube and body assembly, then bend the tab back to permit unscrewing of the valve.
    To install:
    7. Coat the O-ring seals with engine oil, then install the new valve O-ring seal and body O-ring seal on the cold start valve.
    8. Install the tube O-ring seal on the tube and body assembly. Insert the cold start valve into the body assembly.

1 Cold start valve
2 Tube and body assembly
3 Valve o-ring seal
4 Body o-ring seal
5 Tube o-ring seal

86815100

Fig. 65 The cold start valve (not controlled by the ECM/PCM) provides additional fuel during the starting mode to improve cold start-ups

ADJUSTMENT

Cold Start Valve Assembly

This procedure is to be performed ONLY when installing the Cold Start Valve Assembly.

1. Turn the cold start valve completely into the body, until it seats.
2. Back out the valve one complete turn, until the electrical connector is at the top.
3. Bend the body tang forward to limit the rotation to less than a full turn.
4. Coat the new O-ring with engine oil and install it into the fuel rail.

Throttle Position Sensor (TPS)

REMOVAL & INSTALLATION

▶ **See Figure 66**

1. Disconnect the negative battery cable.
2. Unfasten the TPS electrical connector.
3. Remove the 2 mounting screws.
4. Remove the TPS and, if equipped, TPS seal from the throttle body.

To install:

5. Place the TPS in position. Align the TPS lever with the TPS drive lever on the throttle body.
6. Install the 2 TPS mounting screws.
7. Fasten the electrical connector.
8. Connect the negative battery cable.

1 Throttle body asm.
2 Throttle position sensor (TPS)
3 Retainer (2)
4 Screw (2) 2 Nm (18 in.lbs.)

86815101

Fig. 66 After unfastening the electrical connection on the TPS, remove the mounting screws

Mass Air Flow (MAF) Sensor

REMOVAL & INSTALLATION

▶ **See Figure 67**

1. Disconnect the negative battery cable.
2. Detach the electrical connector, then remove the MAF sensor.
3. On some vehicles you will need to loosen the clamps on the air inlet ducts, then remove the air inlet ducts and remove the MAF sensor.

To install:

➡**Take note that this is an expensive and fragile sensor. If it was defective try and find the cause so the new one will not be damaged by the same problem, especially the air filter, broken screen, defective charging system, etc.**

1. Mass Air Flow (MAF) sensor
2. Air cleaner assembly
3. Throttle body assembly

86815107

Fig. 67 On some vehicles you will need to loosen the clamps on the air inlet ducts, then remove the air inlet ducts and the MAF sensor — 3.8L engine shown

4. If removed install the air duct setup, then install the MAF sensor.

5. Mount with the attaching screws, then install the electrical connection to the sensor.

6. Reconnect the negative battery cable.

Crankshaft Sensor

REMOVAL & INSTALLATION

3.8L Engine

On vehicles with a manual transaxles, the crankshaft position sensor is easily accessed from beneath the engine. On vehicles with automatic transaxles, the rack and pinion heat shield and the converter intermediate exhaust assembly must be removed first.

1. Disconnect the negative battery cable.
2. Disconnect the electrical connector at the sensor.
3. Using a 28mm socket and pull handle, rotate the harmonic balancer until any window in the interrupter is aligned with the crank sensor.
4. Loosen the pinch bolt on the sensor pedestal until the sensor is free to slide.
5. Remove the pedestal to the engine mounting bolts.
6. While manipulating the sensor within the pedestal, carefully remove the sensor and pedestal as a unit.

To install:

7. Loosen the pinch bolt on the new sensor pedestal until the sensor is free to slide.
8. Verify that the window in the interrupter is still in the correct place.
9. Install the sensor and pedestal as a unit while making sure that the interrupter ring is aligned within the proper slot.
10. Install the pedestal and tighten the engine mounting bolts to 22 ft. lbs. (30 Nm).

3X Sensor

▶ **See Figure 68**

1. Disconnect the negative battery cable.
2. Remove the sensor harness connection to the sensor.
3. Unsecure the sensor block bolt.
4. Remove the Crankshaft Position (CKP) sensor from the vehicle. Inspect the O-ring for cracks and replace if needed.

To install:

5. Install the new O-ring if needed and lubricate with engine oil.
6. Install the sensor into the hole in the block.
7. Install the mounting screw and tighten to 71-88 inch lbs. (8-10 Nm).
8. Attach the sensor harness connector, then connect the negative battery cable.

Dual Crank Sensor

Sections 3 and 4 of this manual also cover testing, removal and installation, and adjustment of many computer controlled components.

1. Disconnect the negative battery cable.
2. Remove the belt(s) from the crankshaft pulley.

1 Engine block assembly
2 Crankshaft position (CKP) sensor

86815102

Fig. 68 Unsecure the harness, then unfasten the bolt to remove the CKP sensor

3. Raise and support the vehicle safely.
4. Remove the right front wheel and inner fender access cover.
5. Remove the crankshaft harmonic balancer retaining bolt, then remove the harmonic balancer.
6. Disconnect the sensor electrical connector.
7. Remove the sensor and pedestal from the engine block, then separate the sensor from the pedestal.

To install:

8. Loosely install the crankshaft sensor to the pedestal.
9. Using tool J-37089 or equivalent, position the sensor with the pedestal attached, on the crankshaft.
10. Install the pedestal-to-block retaining bolts. Tighten to 14-28 ft. lbs. (20-40 Nm).
11. Tighten the pedestal pinch bolt 30-35 inch lbs. (3-4 Nm).
12. Remove tool J-37089 or equivalent.
13. Place tool J-37089 or equivalent, on the harmonic balancer and turn. If any vane of the harmonic balancer touches the tool, replace the balancer assembly.

➡ **A clearance of 0.025 in. (0.635mm) is required on either side of the interrupter ring. Be certain to obtain the correct clearance. Failure to do so will damage the sensor. A misadjusted sensor of bent interrupter ring could cause rubbing of the sensor, resulting in potential driveability problems, such as rough idle, poor performance, or a no-start condition.**

14. Install the balancer on the crankshaft. Install the balancer retaining bolt. Tighten the retaining bolt to 200-239 ft. lbs. (270-325 Nm).
15. Install the inner fender shield.
16. Install the right front wheel assembly. Tighten the wheel nuts to 100 ft. lbs. (136 Nm).
17. Lower the vehicle.
18. Install the belt(s).
19. Reconnect the negative battery cable.

24X Crank Sensor

▶ **See Figure 69**

1. Disconnect the negative battery cable.
2. Remove the serpentine belt from the crankshaft pulley.

3. Raise and support the vehicle safely.

4. Remove the crankshaft harmonic balancer retaining bolt, then remove the harmonic balancer.

5. Disconnect the sensor electrical connector.

6. Unfasten the sensor bolts, then remove the sensor.

To install:

7. Install the crankshaft sensor to the engine with the two mounting bolts. Tighten the bolts to 8 ft. lbs. (10 Nm).

8. Attach the electrical harness to the sensor.

9. Using tool J-29113 or equivalent, install the harmonic balancer to the vehicle.

10. Apply a thread sealer such as GM 1052080 or an equivalent to the threads if the crankshaft balancer bolt, then tighten the bolt to 110 ft. lbs. (150 Nm).

11. Lower the vehicle.

12. Install the serpentine belt.

13. Reconnect the negative battery cable.

Camshaft Sensor

REMOVAL & INSTALLATION

▶ See Figure 70

1. Disconnect the negative battery cable.
2. Remove the serpentine drive belt.
3. Remove the power steering pump assembly.
4. Disconnect the electrical harness attached to the camshaft sensor.
5. Unfasten the bolt attaching the sensor, then remove the sensor.

To install:

6. Connect the camshaft sensor with the mounting bolt, then tighten the bolt to 8 ft. lbs. (10 Nm).
7. Attach the electrical harness to the sensor.
8. Install the power steering pump.
9. Install the serpentine drive belt, then connect the negative battery cable.

1 Camshaft position sensor
2 Bolt/screw - torque to 10 Nm (8 lb.ft.)
3 Engine block assembly
86815106

Fig. 70 Disconnect the electrical harness attached to the camshaft sensor

Minimum Idle Speed

ADJUSTMENTS

The engine should be at normal operating temperature before making this adjustment. Newer engines do not provide for this adjustment as the idle is completely computer controlled. If the computer cannot control the idle, the most likely cause a defective idle air control valve. Test the IAC valve, check the engine mechanical for basic tune-up, vacuum leaks, proper compression and the rest of the fuel control system. The least likely item bad is the computer itself, unless someone has recently working on the computer or the electrical system. For models that are adjustable following the following procedures:

1. Using an awl, pierce the idle stop screw plug (located on the side of the throttle body) and remove it by prying it from the housing.

1 Front engine cover
2 24x crankshaft position sensor assembly
3 Bolt (2)
86815103

Fig. 69 The 24X crankshaft sensor is secured by two bolts

2. Using a jumper wire, ground the diagnostic lead of the IAC motor.

3. Turn on the ignition, DO NOT start the engine and wait for 30 seconds, then disconnect the IAC electrical connector. Remove the diagnostic lead ground lead and start the engine. Allow the system to go to closed loop.

4. Adjust the idle set screw to 550 rpm for the automatic transaxle (in Drive) or 650 rpm for the manual transaxle (in Neutral).

5. Turn the ignition **OFF** and reconnect the IAC motor lead.

6. Using a voltmeter, adjust the TPS to 0.45-0.65 volt and secure the TPS.

7. Recheck the setting, then start the engine and check for proper idle operation.

8. Seal the idle stop screw with silicone sealer.

DIESEL FUEL SYSTEM

The diesel injection pump is mounted on top of the engine. It is gear driven by the camshaft and turns at camshaft speed. A light pressure rotary pump injects a metered amount of fuel into each cylinder at the precise time. Fuel delivery lines are the same length to prevent any difference in timing, from cylinder to cylinder. The timing advance is also controlled by the fuel pump. Engine rpm is controlled by the rotary fuel metering valve.

The fuel filter is located between the fuel pump and the injection pump at the left rear of the engine.

An electric fuel pump is used which is located at the front of the engine next to the fuel heater. Excess fuel returns to the tank via the fuel return line.

➡**Because of the exacting nature of the diesel injection system all major repairs should be referred to your local GM dealer.**

Injection Lines

REMOVAL & INSTALLATION

All lines may be removed without moving the injection pump. It is not necessary to use a back-up wrench.

1. Remove the air cleaner.

2. Remove the filters and pipes from the valve covers and air crossover.

3. Remove the air crossover. Cap the intake manifold with special cover J-29657 or its equal.

4. When working on the right rear bank of the engine it may be necessary to do the following:

   a. Rotate the intermediate steering shaft so that the steering gear stub shaft clamp bolt is in the up position, then remove the clamp bolt.

   b. Disconnect the intermediate shaft from the stub shaft.

✳✳CAUTION

Failure to disconnect the intermediate shaft from the rack of the pinion stub shaft can result in damage to the steering gear and the intermediate shaft. This can result in loss of steering control of the vehicle, which in turn may cause personal injury.

5. Remove the engine support strut, then place a floor jack under the front crossmember of the cradle, then raise the vehicle just enough to lift the car off the ground.

6. Remove the two front body mounts #1 and 3 bolts with the lower cushions and retainers. Remove the cushions from the bolts.

7. Thread the body mount bolts with the retainers a minimum of 3 turns into the cage nuts so that the bolts restrain the cradle movement.

8. Release the floor jack slowly until the crossmember contacts the body mount bolt retainers. When the jack is being lowered watch and fix any interference with hoses, lines, pipes and cables.

9. Reverse the above steps after completing the line replacement. Tighten the intermediate steering clamp bolt to 40 ft. lbs. (54 Nm) and the body mount bolts to 77 ft. lbs. (105 Nm).

10. Remove the injection pump line clamps. Remove the injection pump lines. Cap open lines, nozzles and pump fittings. Use a back-up wrench on the nozzle hex to prevent a fuel leak.

11. Installation is the reverse of removal.

Injector

REMOVAL & INSTALLATION

▸ See Figure 71

➡**When the lines are disconnected use a back-up wrench on the upper injection nozzle hex. It may also be necessary to jack up the engine to gain access to the back bank of injectors. Always cap the nozzle and lines to prevent damage of contamination.**

1. Remove the fuel injection lines.

2. Remove the injector nozzles by applying torque to the largest nozzle hex.

3. When working on the right rear bank of the engine it may be necessary to do the following:

   a. Rotate the intermediate steering shaft so that the steering gear stub shaft clamp bolt is in the up position, then remove the clamp bolt.

Fig. 71 Fuel injector nozzles on a diesel engine should be removed by tightening the body nut

b. Disconnect the intermediate shaft from the stub shaft.

❋❋CAUTION

Failure to disconnect the intermediate shaft from the rack of the pinion stub shaft can result in damage to the steering gear and the intermediate shaft. This can cause in loss of steering control of the vehicle which in turn causes possible personal injury.

4. Remove the engine support strut, then place a floor jack under the front crossmember of the cradle, then raise the vehicle just enough to lift the car off the ground.

5. Remove the two front body mounts #1 and 3 bolts with the lower cushions and retainers. Remove the cushions from the bolts.

6. Thread the body mount bolts with the retainers a minimum of 3 turns into the cage nuts so that the bolts restrain the cradle movement.

7. Release the floor jack slowly until the crossmember contacts the body mount bolt retainers. When the jack is being lowered watch and fix any interference with hoses, lines, pipes and cables.

8. Reverse the above steps after completing the nozzle replacement. Tighten the intermediate steering clamp bolt to 40 ft. lbs. (54 Nm) and the body mount bolts to 77 ft. lbs. (105 Nm).

➡ When replacing the injectors, be sure to use new copper gaskets.

To install:

9. When reinstalling the injectors special lubricant (GM part 9985462 or its equal) must be applied to the nozzle threads.

10. Remove the protective caps from the nozzle, then make sure the copper gasket is installed on the nozzle.

11. Install the nozzle and tighten to 25 ft. lbs. (34 Nm). The nozzle must be tightened at the largest nut hex.

12. Attach the lines using a backup wrench on the upper injection nozzle hex. Tighten the line nut to 25 ft. lbs. (34 Nm).

Fuel Supply Pump

REMOVAL & INSTALLATION

▸ **See Figure 72**

1. Disconnect the negative battery terminal.
2. Remove the air cleaner.
3. Unplug the electrical connection.
4. Using a ¾ in. (19mm) wrench to support the inlet fitting, use a ⅝ in. (16mm) wrench to unscrew the inlet tube.
5. Remove the outlet tube.

To install:

6. Remove the dust plugs from the inlet and outlet fitting of the pump.

7. Install the pump and bracket assembly onto the engine with the mounting bolts, tighten the bolts to 18 ft. lbs. (24 Nm).

8. Using 19 ft. lbs. (26 Nm) of torque, tighten the inlet and outlet fuel lines.

9. You may need to adjust the pump location somewhat, do this by loosening the bracket screw and turning the pump to get the location needed.

10. Connect the negative battery cable.

11. After the pump has been replaced disconnect the fuel line at the filter. Turn the ignition **ON** and bleed the lines. If the pump runs with a clicking sound, or air bubbles show up in the fuel, check the line for leaks. Check all connections to be sure they are dry. When the clicking noise disappears, tighten the line.

Injection Pump

REMOVAL & INSTALLATION

▸ **See Figure 73**

1. Disconnect the negative battery cable.
2. Remove the air cleaner.

Fig. 72 The diesel fuel pump is an easy access part for removal and installation

3. Remove the crankcase ventilation filter and pipes from the valve cover and air crossover.

4. Remove the air crossover and install special cover J-29657 or its equivalent. Remove the fuel lines, filter and fuel pump as an assembly. Cap all line openings.

5. Disconnect the throttle cable. Remove the return spring.

6. Remove the throttle and TV detent cables from the intake manifold brackets.

7. Disconnect the fuel return line from the injection pump.

8. Disconnect the injection line clamps, closest to the pump.

9. Disconnect the injection lines from the pump. Cap all openings. Carefully reposition the fuel lines.

10. Remove the two bolts retaining the injection pump.

11. Remove the pump. Discard the pump to adapter O-ring.

To install:

12. Installation is the reverse of removal, with the following recommendations. Position the number one cylinder to the firing position. Install a new O-ring, then install the pump fully, seating it by hand. If a new or intermediate adapter plate is used, set the pump at the center slots on the mounting flange. If the original adapter is used align the pump timing mark and the adapter mark. Tighten the pump bolts to 35 ft. lbs. (47 Nm).

13. Connect the negative battery cable.

CHECKING INJECTION TIMING

➡A special diesel timing meter is needed to check injection timing. There are a few variations of this meter, but the type desirable here uses a signal through a glow plug probe to determine combustion timing. The meter picks up the engine speed in RPM and the crankshaft position from the crankshaft balancer. This tool is available at automotive supply houses and from tool jobbers, and is the counterpart to a gasoline engine timing light, coupled with a tachometer. An intake manifold cover is also needed. The marks on the pump and adapter flange will normally be aligned within 0.050 in. (1.27mm).

HOUSING PRESSURE
COLD ADVANCE TERMINAL

THROTTLE SHAFT
ADVANCE CAM

FUEL SOLENOID
TERMINAL

PRESSURE TAP
PLUG AND SEAL

THROTTLE
SHAFT
PIN

GUIDE STUD

WASHER

ADVANCE CAM
ACTUATING ARM

86815109

Fig. 73 Right side view of the injection pump on a diesel engine

1. Place the transaxle shift lever in Park, apply the Parking brake and block the rear wheels.

2. Start the engine and let it run at idle until fully warm. Shut off the engine.

➡**If the engine is not allowed to completely warm up, the probe may soot up, causing incorrect timing readings.**

3. Remove the air cleaner assembly and carefully install cover J-26996-1. This cover over the intake is important. Disconnect the EGR valve hose.

4. Clean away all dirt from the engine probe holder (RPM counter) and the crankshaft balancer rim.

5. Clean the lens on both ends of the glow plug probe and clean the lens in the photoelectric pickup. Use a tooth pick to scrape the carbon from the combustion chamber side of the glow plug probe, then look through the probe to make sure it's clean. Cleanliness is crucial for accurate readings.

6. Install the probe into the crankshaft RPM counter (probe holder) on the engine front cover.

7. Remove the glow plug from No. 1 cylinder. Install the glow plug probe in the glow plug opening, and tighten to 8 ft. lbs. (11 Nm). Do not over tighten.

8. Set the timing meter offset selector to **A** (20).

9. Connect the battery leads, red to positive, black to negative.

10. Disconnect the two-lead connector at the generator.

11. Start the engine. Adjust the engine RPM to the speed specified on the emissions control decal.

12. Observe the timing reading, then observe it again in 2 minutes. When the readings stabilize over the 2 minutes intervals, compare that final stabilized reading to the one specified on the emissions control decal. The timing reading will be an ATDC (After Top Dead Center) reading when set to specifications.

13. Disconnect the timing meter and install the removed glow plug, tightening it to 15 ft. lbs. (20 Nm).

14. Connect the generator two-lead connection.

15. Install the air cleaner assembly and connect the EGR valve hose.

ADJUSTMENT

1. Shut off the engine.

2. Note the relative position of the marks on the pump flange and either the pump intermediate adapter.

3. Loosen the nuts or bolts holding the pump to a point where the pump can just be rotated. You may need a wrench with a slight offset to clear the fuel return line.

4. Rotate the pump to the left to advance the timing and to the right to retard the timing. The width of the mark on the intermediate adaptor is about ⅔°. Move the pump the amount that is needed and tighten the pump retaining nuts to 35 ft. lbs. (47 Nm).

5. Start the engine and recheck the timing as described earlier. Reset the timing if necessary.

6. Reset the fast and curb idle speeds.

➡**Wild needle fluctuations on the timing meter indicate a cylinder not firing properly. Correction of this condition must be made prior to adjusting the timing.**

7. If after resetting the timing, the timing marks are far apart and the engine still runs poorly, the dynamic timing could still be off. It is possible that a malfunctioning cylinder will cause incorrect timing. If this occurs, it is essential that timing be checked in cylinder 1 or 4. If different timing exists between cylinders, try both positions to determine which timing works best.

Glow Plugs

➡A burned out Fast Glow glow plug may bulge, then break off and drop into the pre-chamber when the plug is removed. When this occurs, the cylinder head must be removed and the pre-chamber removed from the head to extract the broken tip. When installing a glow plug, apply lubricant 1052771 or equivalent to the threads only if the engine is equipped with aluminum cylinder heads. It is important that the pre-chamber be fully installed flush to the surface of the cylinder head. If this is not done, cylinder head gasket or piston damage can occur. When servicing the right rear glow plugs, it may be necessary to utilize the following procedure.

REMOVAL & INSTALLATION

▶ See Figure 74

1. Remove the engine support strut.
2. Rotate the intermediate steering shaft so that the steering gear stub shaft clamp bolt is in the up position and remove

Fig. 74 Glow plugs need lubrication for installation; apply it to the threads only

21 N·m
(15 FT. LBS.)
APPLY LUBE TO THREADS ONLY
GLOW PLUG

86815113

the clamp bolt. Then disconnect the intermediate shaft from the stub shaft.

➡Whenever the body is going to be moved in relation to the cradle, the intermediate shaft should be disconnected from the rack and pinion steering gear stub shaft.

✳✳CAUTION

Failure to disconnect the intermediate shaft from the rack and pinion stub shaft can result in damage to the steering gear and/or intermediate shaft. This damage can cause loss of steering control which could result in a vehicle crash with possible bodily injury.

3. Place a floor jack under the front crossmember of the cradle and raise the jack until the jack just starts to raise the car.
4. Remove the front two body mount bolts with the lower cushions and retainers. Then remove the cushions from the bolts.

➡The removal of any one body mount requires the loosening of the adjacent body mounts to permit the cradle to separate from the body. Take care to prevent breaking the plastic fan shroud, or damaging frame attachments such as steering hoses and brake pipes, during replacement of body mounts.

5. Thread the body mount bolts with retainers a minimum of three turns into the cage nuts so that the bolts retain cradle movement.
6. Release the floor jack slowly until the crossmember contacts the body mount bolt retainers. As the jack is being lowered, watch and correct any interference with hoses, lines, pipes and cables.

✳✳CAUTION

Do not place your hands between the crossmember and body mount to remove objects or correct interference while the jack is lowering. Do not lower the cradle without it being restrained, as possible damage can occur to the body and underhood items.

7. Remove the glow plug lead, then the plug.
To install:
8. Install the new glow plug.
9. Jack up the front crossmember at the cradle until the jack just starts to raise the car.

➡When installing a body mount, take care to ensure that the body is seated properly in the frame mounting hole; otherwise, direct metal to metal contact will result between the frame and the body. The tube spacer should be in all bolt-in-body mounts. The insulator and metal washer should be positioned to prevent contact with the frame rail. Do not overtighten the body mount; otherwise, a collapsed tube spacer or stripped bolt may result.

10. Install the numbers 1 and 3 body bolt lower cushions and retainers. Tighten the bolts to 77 ft. lbs. (105 Nm).

➡ **Proper clamping by the mount depends on clean dry surfaces. If the body mount bolt doesn't screw in smoothly, it may be necessary to run a tap through the cage nut in the body to remove foreign material. Take care to ensure that the tap does not punch through the underbody.**

11. Lower the car.
12. Tighten the intermediate steering shaft clamp bolt to 40 ft. lbs. (54 Nm).
13. Install the engine support strut.

Diesel Idle Speed

ADJUSTMENT

1. Apply the Parking brake, then place the transaxle in Park and block the drive wheels.
2. Start the engine and allow it to reach operating temperature, then turn it **OFF**.
3. Remove the air cleaner cover and the MAP sensor retainer, then move the MAP sensor (with the leads and the hoses attached) aside.
4. Remove the air cleaner assembly and install tool J-26996-1 on the intake manifold.
5. Clean the rpm counter on the front cover and the crankshaft balancer rim. Install the magnetic pickup probe tool J-26925 into the rpm counter, then connect the power leads to the battery.
6. If equipped with A/C, disconnect the compressor clutch lead from the compressor. If equipped with cruise control, remove the servo cable retainer and disconnect the servo throttle cable from the servo blade.
7. Make sure all of the electrical accessories are turned Off.
8. Start the engine and place the transaxle in Drive, then check the slow idle speed reading.
9. Turn **OFF** the engine and unplug the engine coolant temperature sensor connector.

10. Start the engine and place the transaxle in Drive, then check the fast idle speed (allow the plunger to extend by opening the throttle slightly.
11. Connect the engine coolant temperature sensor connector and recheck and/or reset the slow idle speed.
12. Turn **OFF** the engine and reconnect the A/C compressor lead, if equipped.
13. To complete the installation, reverse the removal procedures.

Diesel Vacuum Regulator Valve

ADJUSTMENT

1. Disconnect the EGR valve pipe assembly from the air crossover, then remove the air crossover.
2. Disconnect the throttle cable and the TV cable from the pump throttle lever.
3. Loosen the vacuum regulator valve-to-injection pump bolts.
4. Install tool BT-7944 or J-26701-15 to the injection pump throttle lever, then place angle gauge tool BT-7704 or J-26701 on the adapter.

➡ **It may be necessary to file the tool so that it can fit on the pump's thicker throttle lever.**

5. Move the throttle lever to the wide open position and set the angle gauge to 0°.
6. Center the bubble in the level, then set the gauge to 49°. Rotate the throttle lever so that the bubble is centered.
7. Attach a vacuum source to port **A** and the vacuum gauge to port **B**, then apply 22 in. Hg (74 kPa) vacuum to port **A**.
8. Rotate the vacuum valve clockwise until 10.3-10.9 in. Hg (35-38 kPa) vacuum is obtained.
9. Tighten the vacuum bolts, then remove the vacuum source and the gauge.
10. Connect the throttle cable and the TV cables to the pump throttle lever, then remove the intake manifold screens.
11. Install the air crossover and the EGR valve pipe assembly to the crossover. Tighten the bolts to 19 ft. lbs. (26 Nm).

FUEL TANK

Tank Assembly

REMOVAL & INSTALLATION

▶ **See Figures 75, 76 and 77**

1. Relieve the fuel pressure from the vehicle, as is explained earlier in this section.
2. Disconnect the negative cable at the battery.
3. Raise and support the car.
4. Drain the tank. There is no drain plug, remaining fuel in the tank must be siphoned through the fuel feed line (the line to the fuel pump), because of the restrictor in the filler neck.

5. Disconnect the hose and the vapor return hose from the sending unit fittings.
6. Remove the ground wire screw.
7. Unplug the sending unit electrical connector.
8. Detach the vent hose. Disconnect any quick connect fittings.
9. If necessary, remove the exhaust pipe heat shield.
10. With an assistant supporting the tank, unbolt the retaining straps, and lower and remove the tank.
11. Remove the sending unit from the tank. Then remove the tank insulator pads, making note of where they are to be placed on the new tank.
   To install:
12. Attach the insulator pads to the new tank, then install the sending unit.

Fig. 75 After raising the car you will have a full view of the gas tank

13. With an assistant, position the tank and support it while attaching the retaining strap mounting bolts.

14. Tighten the front retaining strap bolts to 25 ft. lbs. (34 Nm) and the rear to 17 ft. lbs. (23 Nm).

15. If applicable, install the exhaust pipe heat shield.

16. Attach any quick connect fittings and all the EVAP connecting hoses.

17. Connect the sending unit electrical harness. Install the fuel filler vent hose and clamp, tighten the clamp to 22 inch lbs. (3 Nm).

18. Lower the vehicle.

19. Add fuel to the tank and install the filler cap.

20. Check for leaks. If non are present, connect the negative battery cable.

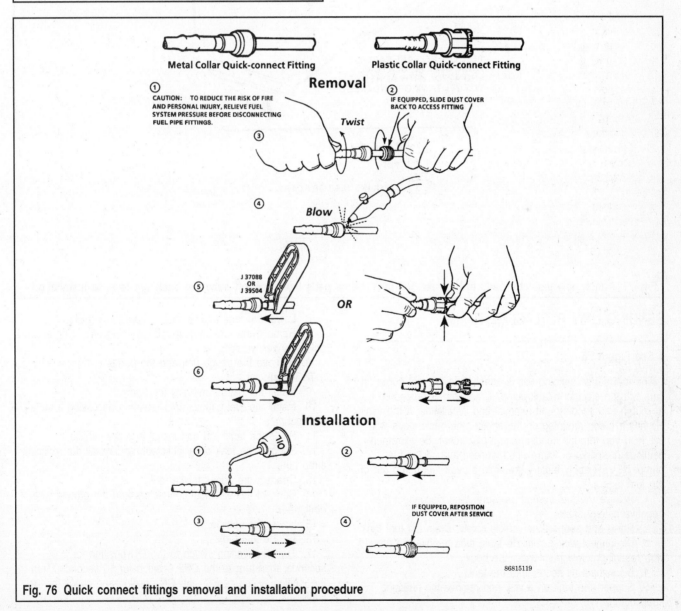

Fig. 76 Quick connect fittings removal and installation procedure

TAPE INSULATOR TO TANK IN THIS AREA WITH ONE PIECE 330.0mm LONG OR TWO PIECES 130.0mm LONG

PEEL OFF RELEASE PAPER FROM REAR INSULATORS AND APPLY WITH ADHESIVE TO FUEL TANK OR UNDERBODY.

FRT

1	TANK INSULATOR
2	TAPE
3	TANK INSULATOR REAR

86815115

Fig. 77 Attach new insulator pads to the new fuel tank. Some pads have peel-off adhesive backings to ease installation

SENDING UNIT REPLACEMENT

▶ **See Figure 78**

The fuel gauge sending unit is attached to the fuel pump on cars with an electric in-tank pump. The following procedure is for pump and sending unit removal and installation. If the vehicle has a pump mounted on the engine, the basic steps will still lead you through sending unit replacement. Be extremely cautious of sparks or flame when working around the fuel pump. NEVER apply battery power to a used fuel pump out of the fuel tank.

1. Relieve the fuel system pressure, then disconnect the negative battery cable.

2. Raise and support the vehicle safely. Drain the fuel tank.

3. Disconnect wiring from the tank, then remove the ground wire retaining screw from under the body.

4. Disconnect all hoses from the tank.

5. Support the tank on a jack and remove the retaining strap nuts.

6. Lower the tank and remove it from the vehicle.

7. Remove the fuel gauge/pump retaining ring using a suitable spanner wrench.

8. Remove the gauge unit and the pump.

To install:

9. Install the gauge unit and the pump.

10. Install the fuel gauge/pump retaining ring using a suitable spanner.

11. Raise the tank and and install it to the vehicle.

12. Support the tank on a jackstand and install the retaining strap nuts.

13. Connect the hoses to the tank.

14. Connect the electrical connectors and the ground wire, if equipped.

15. Lower the vehicle.

16. Fill the fuel tank.

17. Turn the ignition switch to the **ON** position for 2 seconds, then turn to the **OFF** position for 10 seconds. Turn the ignition switch back to the **ON** position and check for fuel leaks.

Fig. 78 Exploded view of a fuel sending unit

TORQUE SPECIFICATIONS

Component	US	Metric
Cam sensor:	8 ft. lbs.	10 Nm
Crankshaft bolt:		
3.3L engine	220 ft. lbs.	300 Nm
3.8L engine	220 ft. lbs.	300 Nm
Crankshaft sensor:		
3.8L vin-3	22 ft. lbs.	30 Nm
3X	71-88 inch lbs.	8-10 Nm
24X	8 ft. lbs.	10 Nm
dual	14-28 ft. lbs.	20-40 Nm
Carburetor monting nuts:	13 ft. lbs.	18 Nm
Carburetor fuel inlet nut:	18 ft. lbs.	24 Nm
Carburetor fuel line fuittings:	22 ft. lbs.	30 Nm
Diesel nozzle:	25 ft. lbs.	34 Nm
Diesel line nut:	25 ft. lbs.	34 Nm
Diesel inlet and outlet line:	18 ft. lbs.	24 Nm
Diesel fuel pump mounting bolts:	18 ft. lbs.	24 Nm
Diesel injection pump:	35 ft. lbs.	47 Nm
Fuel rail attaching nuts:	20 ft. lbs.	27 Nm
Fuel pressure regulator:		
2.5L engine	22 inch lbs.	2.5 Nm
excluding 2.5L engine	102 inch lbs.	11.5 Nm
Fuel tank straps:		
front	25 ft. lbs.	34 Nm
rear	17 ft. lbs.	23 Nm
Idle air control valve:		
screw in type	13 ft. lbs.	18 Nm
retaining screws	27 inch lbs.	3 Nm
Intake plenum:		
early EFI	16 ft. lbs.	21 Nm
SFI and 3.1L engine	18 ft. lbs.	25 Nm
Throttle position sensor:	18 inch lbs.	2 Nm
TBI fuel line nuts:	18-20 ft. lbs.	24-27 Nm
TBI injector retainer:	27 inch lbs.	3 Nm
TBI pessure regulator cover:	21 inch lbs.	2 Nm
TBI body bolts:	10-21 ft. lbs.	13-28 Nm
TBI tube module assembly:	27 inch lbs.	3 Nm

86815130

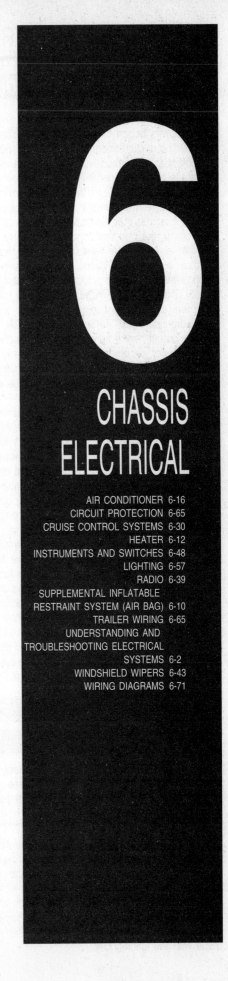

6

CHASSIS
ELECTRICAL

UNDERSTANDING AND TROUBLESHOOTING ELECTRICAL SYSTEMS

Over the years covered by this manual, import and domestic manufacturers began incorporating electronic control systems into their production lines. In fact, most (if not all) new vehicles sold today are equipped with one or more on-board computer. These electronic components (with no moving parts) should theoretically last the life of the vehicle, provided nothing external happens to damage the circuits or memory chips.

While it is true that electronic components should never wear out, in the real world malfunctions do occur. It is also true that any computer-based system is extremely sensitive to electrical voltages and cannot tolerate careless or haphazard testing/service procedures. An inexperienced individual can literally cause major damage looking for a minor problem by using the wrong kind of test equipment or connecting test leads/connectors with the ignition switch **ON**. When selecting test equipment, make sure the manufacturer's instructions state that the tester is compatible with whatever type of system is being serviced. Read all instructions carefully and double check all test points before installing probes or making any test connections.

The following section outlines basic diagnosis techniques for dealing with automotive electrical systems. Along with a general explanation of the various types of test equipment available to aid in servicing modern automotive systems, basic repair techniques for wiring harnesses and connectors are also given. Read the basic information before attempting any repairs or testing. This will provide the background of information necessary to avoid the most common and obvious mistakes that can cost both time and money. Although the replacement and testing procedures are simple in themselves, the systems are not, and unless one has a thorough understanding of all components and their function within a particular system, the logical test sequence these systems demand cannot be followed. Minor malfunctions can make a big difference, so it is important to know how each component affects the operation of the overall system to find the ultimate cause of a problem without replacing good components unnecessarily. It is not enough to use the correct test equipment; the test equipment must be used correctly.

Safety Precautions

✳✳CAUTION

Whenever working on or around any electrical or electronic systems, always observe these general precautions to prevent the possibility of personal injury or damage to electronic components.

• Never install or remove battery cables with the key **ON** or the engine running. Jumper cables should be connected with the key **OFF** to avoid power surges that can damage electronic control units. Engines equipped with computer controlled systems should avoid both giving and getting jump starts due to the possibility of serious damage to components from arcing in the engine compartment when connections are made with the ignition **ON**.

• Always remove the battery cables before charging the battery. Never use a high output charger on an installed battery or attempt to use any type of "hot shot" (24 volt) starting aid.

• Exercise care when inserting test probes into connectors to insure good contact without damaging the connector or spreading the pins. Always probe connectors from the rear (wire) side, NOT the pin side, to avoid accidental shorting of terminals during test procedures.

• Never remove or attach wiring harness connectors with the ignition switch **ON**, especially to an electronic control unit.

• Do not drop any components during service procedures and never apply 12 volts directly to any component (like a solenoid or relay) unless instructed specifically to do so. Some component electrical windings are designed to safely handle only 4 or 5 volts and can be destroyed in seconds if 12 volts are applied directly to the connector.

• Remove the electronic control unit if the vehicle is to be placed in an environment where temperatures exceed approximately 176°F (80°C), such as a paint spray booth or when arc/gas welding near the control unit location.

Add-On Electrical Equipment

The electrical system in your car is designed to perform under reasonable operating conditions without interference between components. Before any additional electrical equipment is installed, it is recommended that you consult your dealer or a reputable repair facility familiar with the vehicle and its systems.

If the vehicle is equipped with mobile radio equipment and/or mobile telephone, it may have an effect upon the operation of the ECM. Radio Frequency Interference (RFI) from the communications system can be picked up by the car's wiring harnesses and conducted into the ECM, giving it the wrong messages at the wrong time. Although well shielded against RFI, the ECM should be further protected by taking the following measures:

• Install the antenna as far as possible from the ECM. Since the ECM is located behind the center console area, the antenna should be mounted at the rear of the car.

• Keep the antenna wiring a minimum of eight inches away from any wiring running to the ECM and from the ECM itself. NEVER wind the antenna wire around any other wiring.

• Mount the equipment as far from the ECM as possible. Be very careful during installation not to drill through any wires or short a wire harness with a mounting screw.

• Insure that the electrical feed wire(s) to the equipment are properly and tightly connected. Loose connectors can cause interference.

• Make certain that the equipment is properly grounded to the car. Poor grounding can damage expensive equipment.

Organized Troubleshooting

When diagnosing a specific problem, organized troubleshooting is a must. The complexity of a modern automobile demands that you approach any problem in a logical, organized manner. There are certain troubleshooting techniques that are standard:

1. Establish when the problem occurs. Does the problem appear only under certain conditions? Were there any noises, odors, or other unusual symptoms?

2. Isolate the problem area. To do this, make some simple tests and observations; then eliminate the systems that are working properly. Check for obvious problems such as broken wires, dirty connections or split/disconnected vacuum hoses. Always check the obvious before assuming something complicated is the cause.

3. Test for problems systematically to determine the cause once the problem area is isolated. Are all the components functioning properly? Is there power going to electrical switches and motors? Is there vacuum at vacuum switches and/or actuators? Is there a mechanical problem such as bent linkage or loose mounting screws? Performing careful, systematic checks will often turn up most causes on the first inspection without wasting time checking components that have little or no relationship to the problem.

4. Test all repairs after the work is done to make sure that the problem is fixed. Some causes can be traced to more than one component, so a careful verification of repair work is important to pick up additional malfunctions that may cause a problem to reappear or a different problem to arise. A blown fuse, for example, is a simple problem that may require more than another fuse to repair. If you don't look for a problem that caused a fuse to blow, a shorted wire for example, may go undetected.

Experience has shown that most problems tend to be the result of a fairly simple and obvious cause, such as loose or corroded connectors or air leaks in the intake system. This makes careful inspection of components during testing essential to quick and accurate troubleshooting.

TEST EQUIPMENT

➡**Pinpointing the exact cause of trouble in an electrical system can sometimes only be accomplished by the use of special test equipment. The following describes commonly used test equipment and explains how to put it to best use in diagnosis. In addition to the information covered below, the manufacturer's instructions booklet provided with the tester should be read and clearly understood before attempting any test procedures.**

Jumper Wires

Jumper wires are simple, yet extremely valuable, pieces of test equipment. They are basically test wires which are used to bypass sections of a circuit. The simplest type of jumper wire is a length of multi-strand wire with an alligator clip at each end. Jumper wires are usually fabricated from lengths of standard automotive wire and whatever type of connector (alligator clip, spade connector or pin connector) that is required for the particular vehicle being tested. The well equipped tool box will have several different styles of jumper wires in several different lengths. Some jumper wires are made with three or more terminals coming from a common splice for special purpose testing. In cramped, hard-to-reach areas it is advisable to have insulated boots over the jumper wire

terminals in order to prevent accidental grounding, sparks, and possible fire, especially when testing fuel system components.

Jumper wires are used primarily to locate open electrical circuits, on either the ground (-) side of the circuit or on the hot (+) side. If an electrical component fails to operate, connect the jumper wire between the component and a good ground. If the component operates only with the jumper installed, the ground circuit is open. If the ground circuit is good, but the component does not operate, the circuit between the power feed and component may be open. By moving the jumper wire successively back from the lamp toward the power source, you can isolate the area of the circuit where the open is located. When the component stops functioning, or the power is cut off, the open is in the segment of wire between the jumper and the point previously tested.

You can sometimes connect the jumper wire directly from the battery to the hot terminal of the component, but first make sure the component uses 12 volts in operation. Some electrical components, such as fuel injectors, are designed to operate on about 4 volts and running 12 volts directly to the injector terminals can burn out the wiring.

By inserting an in-line fuse holder between a set of test leads, a fused jumper wire can be used for bypassing open circuits. Use a 5 amp fuse to provide protection against voltage spikes. When in doubt, use a voltmeter to check the voltage input to the component and measure how much voltage is normally being applied.

✳✳CAUTION

Never use jumpers made from wire that is of lighter gauge than used in the circuit under test. If the jumper wire is of too small gauge, it may overheat and possibly melt. Never use jumpers to bypass high resistance loads in a circuit. Bypassing resistances, in effect, creates a short circuit. This may, in turn, cause damage and fire. Jumper wires should only be used to bypass lengths of wire.

Unpowered Test Lights

The 12 volt test light is used to check circuits and components while electrical current is flowing through them. It is used for voltage and ground tests. Twelve volt test lights come in different styles but all have three main parts; a ground clip, a probe, and a light. The most commonly used 12 volt test lights have pick-type probes. To use a 12 volt test light, connect the ground clip to a good ground and probe wherever necessary with the pick. The pick should be sharp so that it can be probed into tight spaces.

✳✳CAUTION

Do not use a test light to probe electronic ignition spark plug or coil wires. Never use a pick-type test light to probe wiring on computer controlled systems unless specifically instructed to do so. Any wire insulation that is pierced by the test light probe should be taped and sealed with silicone after testing.

Like the jumper wire, the 12 volt test light is used to isolate opens in circuits. But, whereas the jumper wire is used to bypass the open to operate the load, the 12 volt test light is used to locate the presence of voltage in a circuit. If the test light glows, you know that there is power up to that point; if the 12 volt test light does not glow when its probe is inserted into the wire or connector, you know that there is an open circuit (no power). Move the test light in successive steps back toward the power source until the light in the handle does glow. When it glows, the open is between the probe and point which was probed previously.

➡**The test light does not detect that 12 volts (or any particular amount of voltage) is present; it only detects that some voltage is present. It is advisable before using the test light to touch its terminals across the battery posts to make sure the light is operating properly.**

Self-Powered Test Lights

The self-powered test light usually contains a 1.5 volt penlight battery. One type of self-powered test light is similar in design to the 12 volt unit. This type has both the battery and the light in the handle, along with a pick-type probe tip. The second type has the light toward the open tip, so that the light illuminates the contact point. The self-powered test light is a dual purpose piece of test equipment. It can be used to test for either open or short circuits when power is isolated from the circuit (continuity test). A powered test light should not be used on any computer controlled system or component unless specifically instructed to do so. Many engine sensors can be destroyed by even this small amount of voltage applied directly to the terminals.

Voltmeters

A voltmeter is used to measure voltage at any point in a circuit, or to measure the voltage drop across any part of a circuit. It can also be used to check continuity in a wire or circuit by indicating current flow from one end to the other. Voltmeters usually have various scales on the meter dial and a selector switch to allow the selection of different voltages. The voltmeter has a positive and a negative lead. To avoid damage to the meter, always connect the negative lead to the negative (-) side of circuit (to ground or nearest the ground side of the circuit) and connect the positive lead to the positive (+) side of the circuit (to the power source or the nearest power source). Note that the negative voltmeter lead will always be black and that the positive voltmeter will always be some color other than black (usually red). Depending on how the voltmeter is connected into the circuit, it has several uses.

A voltmeter can be connected either in parallel or in series with a circuit and it has a very high resistance to current flow. When connected in parallel, only a small amount of current will flow through the voltmeter current path; the rest will flow through the normal circuit current path and the circuit will work normally. When the voltmeter is connected in series with a circuit, only a small amount of current can flow through the circuit. The circuit will not work properly, but the voltmeter reading will show if the circuit is complete or not.

Ohmmeters

The ohmmeter is designed to read resistance (Ω) in a circuit or component. Although there are several different styles of ohmmeters, all will usually have a selector switch which permits the measurement of different ranges of resistance (usually the selector switch allows the multiplication of the meter reading by 10, 100, 1,000, and 10,000). A calibration knob allows the meter to be set at zero for accurate measurement. Since all ohmmeters are powered by an internal battery (usually 9 volts), the ohmmeter can be used as a self-powered test light. When the ohmmeter is connected, current from the ohmmeter flows through the circuit or component being tested. Since the ohmmeter's internal resistance and voltage are known values, the amount of current flow through the meter depends on the resistance of the circuit or component being tested.

The ohmmeter can be used to perform a continuity test for opens or shorts (either by observation of the meter needle or as a self-powered test light), and to read actual resistance in a circuit. It should be noted that the ohmmeter is used to check the resistance of a component or wire while there is no voltage applied to the circuit. Current flow from an outside voltage source (such as the vehicle battery) can damage the ohmmeter, so the circuit or component should be isolated from the vehicle electrical system before any testing is done. Since the ohmmeter uses its own voltage source, either lead can be connected to any test point.

➡**When checking diodes or other solid state components, the ohmmeter leads can only be connected one way in order to measure current flow in a single direction. Make sure the positive (+) and negative (-) terminal connections are as described in the test procedures to verify the one-way diode operation.**

In using the meter for making continuity checks, do not be concerned with the actual resistance readings. Zero resistance, or any reading, indicates continuity in the circuit. Infinite resistance indicates an open in the circuit. A high resistance reading where there should be none indicates a problem in the circuit. Checks for short circuits are made in the same manner as checks for open circuits except that the circuit must be isolated from both power and normal ground. Infinite resistance indicates no continuity to ground, while zero resistance indicates a dead short to ground.

Ammeters

An ammeter measures the amount of current flowing through a circuit in units called amperes or amps. Amperes are units of electron flow which indicate how fast the electrons are flowing through the circuit. Since Ohms Law dictates that current flow in a circuit is equal to the circuit voltage divided by the total circuit resistance, increasing voltage also increases the current level (amps). Likewise, any decrease in resistance will increase the amount of amps in a circuit. At normal operating voltage, most circuits have a characteristic amount of amperes, called "current draw" which can be measured using an ammeter. By referring to a specified current draw rating, measuring the amperes, and comparing the two values, one can determine what is happening within the circuit to aid in diagnosis. An open circuit, for example, will not allow any current to flow so the ammeter reading will be zero. More current flows through a heavily loaded circuit or when the charging system is operating.

An ammeter is always connected in series with the circuit being tested. All of the current that normally flows through the circuit must also flow through the ammeter; if there is any other path for the current to follow, the ammeter reading will not be accurate. The ammeter itself has very little resistance to current flow and therefore will not affect the circuit, but it will measure current draw only when the circuit is closed and electricity is flowing. Excessive current draw can blow fuses and drain the battery, while a reduced current draw can cause motors to run slowly, lights to dim and other components to not operate properly. The ammeter can help diagnose these conditions by locating the cause of the high or low reading.

Multimeters

Different combinations of test meters can be built into a single unit designed for specific tests. Some of the more common combination test devices are known as Volt/Amp testers, Tach/Dwell meters, or Digital Multimeters. The Volt/Amp tester is used for charging system, starting system or battery tests and consists of a voltmeter, an ammeter and a variable resistance carbon pile. The voltmeter will usually have at least two ranges for use with 6, 12 and/or 24 volt systems. The ammeter also has more than one range for testing various levels of battery loads and starter current draw. The carbon pile can be adjusted to offer different amounts of resistance. The Volt/Amp tester has heavy leads to carry large amounts of current and many later models have an inductive ammeter pickup that clamps around the wire to simplify test connections. On some models, the ammeter also has a zero-center scale to allow testing of charging and starting systems without switching leads or polarity. A digital multimeter is a voltmeter, ammeter and ohmmeter combined in an instrument which gives a digital readout. These are often used when testing solid state circuits because of their high input impedance (usually 10 megohms or more).

The tach/dwell meter that combines a tachometer and a dwell (cam angle) meter is a specialized kind of voltmeter. The tachometer scale is marked to show engine speed in rpm and the dwell scale is marked to show degrees of distributor shaft rotation. In most electronic ignition systems, dwell is determined by the control unit, but the dwell meter can also be used to check the duty cycle (operation) of some electronic engine control systems. Some tach/dwell meters are powered by an internal battery, while others take their power from the car battery in use. The battery powered testers usually require calibration much like an ohmmeter before testing.

TESTING

Open Circuits

To use the self-powered test light to check for open circuits, first isolate the circuit from the vehicle's 12 volt power source by disconnecting the battery or wiring harness connector. Connect the test light ground clip to a good ground and probe sections of the circuit sequentially with the test light. (start from either end of the circuit). If the light is out, the open is between the probe and the circuit ground. If the light is on, the open is between the probe and end of the circuit toward the power source.

Short Circuits

By isolating the circuit both from power and from ground, and using a self-powered test light, you can check for shorts to ground in the circuit. Isolate the circuit from power and ground. Connect the test light ground clip to a good ground and probe any easy-to-reach test point in the circuit. If the light comes on, there is a short somewhere in the circuit. To isolate the short, probe a test point at either end of the isolated circuit (the light should be on). Leave the test light probe engaged and open connectors, switches, remove parts, etc., sequentially, until the light goes out. When the light goes out, the short is between the last circuit component opened and the previous circuit opened.

➡ **The 1.5 volt battery in the test light does not provide much current. A weak battery may not provide enough power to illuminate the test light even when a complete circuit is made (especially if there are high resistances in the circuit). Always make sure that the test battery is strong. To check the battery, briefly touch the ground clip to the probe; if the light glows brightly the battery is strong enough for testing. Never use a self-powered test light to perform checks for opens or shorts when power is applied to the electrical system under test. The 12 volt vehicle power will quickly burn out the 1.5 volt light bulb in the test light.**

Available Voltage Measurement

Set the voltmeter selector switch to the 20V position and connect the meter negative lead to the negative post of the battery. Connect the positive meter lead to the positive post of the battery and turn the ignition switch **ON** to provide a load. Read the voltage on the meter or digital display. A well charged battery should register over 12 volts. If the meter reads below 11.5 volts, the battery power may be insufficient to operate the electrical system properly. This test determines voltage available from the battery and should be the first step in any electrical trouble diagnosis procedure. Many electrical problems, especially on computer controlled systems, can be caused by a low state of charge in the battery. Excessive corrosion at the battery cable terminals can cause a poor contact that will prevent proper charging and full battery current flow.

Normal battery voltage is 12 volts when fully charged. When the battery is supplying current to one or more circuits it is said to be "under load". When everything is off the electrical system is under a "no-load" condition. A fully charged battery may show about 12.5 volts at no load; will drop to 12 volts under medium load; and will drop even lower under heavy load. If the battery is partially discharged the voltage decrease under heavy load may be excessive, even though the battery shows 12 volts or more at no load. When allowed to discharge further, the battery's available voltage under load will decrease more severely. For this reason, it is important that the battery be fully charged during all testing procedures to avoid errors in diagnosis and incorrect test results.

Voltage Drop

When current flows through a resistance, the voltage beyond the resistance is reduced (the larger the current, the greater the reduction in voltage). When no current is flowing, there is no voltage drop because there is no current flow. All points in the circuit which are connected to the power source are at the same voltage as the power source. The total voltage drop always equals the total source voltage. In a long circuit with many connectors, a series of small, unwanted voltage drops due to corrosion at the connectors can add up to a total loss of voltage which impairs the operation of the normal loads in the circuit.

INDIRECT COMPUTATION OF VOLTAGE DROPS

1. Set the voltmeter selector switch to the 20 volt position.
2. Connect the meter negative lead to a good ground.
3. While operating the circuit, probe all resistances loads in the circuit with the positive meter lead and observe the voltage readings. There should be little or no voltage drop before the first load.

DIRECT MEASUREMENT OF VOLTAGE DROPS

1. Set the voltmeter switch to the 20 volt position.
2. Connect the voltmeter negative lead to the ground side of the resistance load to be measured.
3. Connect the positive lead to the positive side of the resistance or load to be measured.
4. Read the voltage drop directly on the 20 volt scale.

Too high a voltage indicates too high a resistance. If, for example, a blower motor runs too slowly, you can determine if there is too high a resistance in the resistor pack. By taking voltage drop readings in all parts of the circuit, you can isolate the problem. Too low a voltage drop indicates too low a resistance. Take the blower motor for example again. If a blower motor runs too fast in the MED and/or LOW position, the problem can be isolated in the resistor pack by taking voltage drop readings in all parts of the circuit to locate a possibly shorted resistor. The maximum allowable voltage drop under load is critical, especially if there is more than one high resistance problem in a circuit because all voltage drops are cumulative. A small drop is normal due to the resistance of the conductors.

HIGH RESISTANCE TESTING

1. Set the voltmeter selector switch to the 4 volt position.
2. Connect the voltmeter positive lead to the positive post of the battery.
3. Turn on the headlights and heater blower to provide a load.
4. Probe various points in the circuit with the negative voltmeter lead.
5. Read the voltage drop on the 4 volt scale. Some average maximum allowable voltage drops are:
   - FUSE PANEL: 0.7 volts
   - IGNITION SWITCH: 0.5 volts
   - HEADLIGHT SWITCH: 0.7 volts
   - IGNITION COIL (+): 0.5 volts
   - ANY OTHER LOAD: 1.3 volts

➡Voltage drops are all measured while a load is operating; without current flow, there will be no voltage drop.

Resistance Measurement

The batteries in an ohmmeter will weaken with age and temperature, so the ohmmeter must be calibrated or "zeroed" before taking measurements. To zero the meter, place the selector switch in its lowest range and touch the two ohmmeter leads together. Turn the calibration knob until the meter needle is exactly on zero.

➡All analog (needle) type ohmmeters must be zeroed before use, but some digital ohmmeter models are automatically calibrated when the switch is turned on. Self-calibrating digital ohmmeters do not have an adjusting knob, but its a good idea to check for a zero readout before use by touching the leads together. All computer controlled systems require the use of a digital ohmmeter with at least 10 megohms impedance for testing. Before any test procedures are attempted, make sure the ohmmeter used is compatible with the electrical system or damage to the on-board computer could result.

To measure resistance, first isolate the circuit from the vehicle power source by disconnecting the battery cables or the harness connector. Make sure the key is **OFF** when disconnecting any components or the battery. Where necessary, also isolate at least one side of the circuit to be checked in order to avoid reading parallel resistances. Parallel circuit resistances will always give a lower reading than the actual resistance of either of the branches. When measuring the resistance of parallel circuits, the total resistance will always be lower than the smallest resistance in the circuit. Connect the meter leads to both sides of the circuit (wire or component) and read the actual measured ohms on the meter scale. Make sure the selector switch is set to the proper ohm scale for the circuit being tested to avoid misreading the ohmmeter test value.

✳✳WARNING

Never use an ohmmeter with power applied to the circuit. Like the self-powered test light, the ohmmeter is designed to operate on its own power supply. The normal 12 volt automotive electrical system current could damage the meter!

Wiring Harnesses

The average automobile contains about ½ mile of wiring, with hundreds of individual connections. To protect the many wires from damage and to keep them from becoming a confusing tangle, they are organized into bundles, enclosed in plastic or taped together and called wiring harnesses. Different harnesses serve different parts of the vehicle. Individual wires are color coded to help trace them through a harness where sections are hidden from view.

Automotive wiring or circuit conductors can be in any one of three forms:

1. Single strand wire
2. Multi-strand wire
3. Printed circuitry

Single strand wire has a solid metal core and is usually used inside such components as alternators, motors, relays and other devices. Multi-strand wire has a core made of many small strands of wire twisted together into a single conductor. Most of the wiring in an automotive electrical system is made up of multi-strand wire, either as a single conductor or grouped together in a harness. All wiring is color coded on the insulator, either as a solid color or as a colored wire with an identification stripe. A printed circuit is a thin film of copper or other conductor that is printed on an insulator backing. Occasionally, a printed circuit is sandwiched between two sheets of plastic for more protection and flexibility. A complete printed circuit, consisting of conductors, insulating material and connectors for lamps or other components is called a printed circuit board. Printed circuitry is used in place of individual wires or harnesses in places where space is limited, such as behind instrument panels.

Since automotive electrical systems are very sensitive to changes in resistance, the selection of properly sized wires is critical when systems are repaired. A loose or corroded connection or a replacement wire that is too small for the circuit will add extra resistance and an additional voltage drop to the circuit. A ten percent voltage drop can result in slow or erratic motor operation, for example, even though the circuit is complete. The wire gauge number is an expression of the cross-section area of the conductor. The most common system for expressing wire size is the American Wire Gauge (AWG) system.

Gauge numbers are assigned to conductors of various cross-section areas. As gauge number increases, area decreases and the conductor becomes smaller. A 5 gauge conductor is smaller than a 1 gauge conductor and a 10 gauge is smaller than a 5 gauge. As the cross-section area of a conductor decreases, resistance increases and so does the gauge number. A conductor with a higher gauge number will carry less current than a conductor with a lower gauge number.

➡**Gauge wire size refers to the size of the conductor, not the size of the complete wire. It is possible to have two wires of the same gauge with different diameters because one may have thicker insulation than the other.**

12 volt automotive electrical systems generally use 10, 12, 14, 16 and 18 gauge wire. Main power distribution circuits and larger accessories usually use 10 and 12 gauge wire. Battery cables are usually 4 or 6 gauge, although 1 and 2 gauge wires are occasionally used. Wire length must also be considered when making repairs to a circuit. As conductor length increases, so does resistance. An 18 gauge wire, for example, can carry a 10 amp load for 10 feet without excessive voltage drop; however if a 15 foot wire is required for the same 10 amp load, it must be a 16 gauge wire.

An electrical schematic shows the electrical current paths when a circuit is operating properly. It is essential to understand how a circuit works before trying to figure out why it doesn't. Schematics break the entire electrical system down into individual circuits and show only one particular circuit. In a schematic, no attempt is made to represent wiring and components as they physically appear on the vehicle; switches and other components are shown as simply as possible. Face views of harness connectors show the cavity or terminal locations in all multi-pin connectors to help locate test points.

If you need to backprobe a connector while it is on the component, the order of the terminals must be mentally reversed. The wire color code can help in this situation, as well as a keyway, lock tab or other reference mark.

WIRING REPAIR

Soldering is a quick, efficient method of joining metals permanently. Everyone who has the occasion to make wiring repairs should know how to solder. Electrical connections that are soldered are far less likely to come apart and will conduct electricity much better than connections that are only "pig-tailed" together. The most popular (and preferred) method of soldering is with an electrical soldering gun. Soldering irons are available in many sizes and wattage ratings. Irons with higher wattage ratings deliver higher temperatures and recover lost heat faster. A small soldering iron rated for no more than 50 watts is recommended, especially on electrical systems where excess heat can damage the components being soldered.

There are three ingredients necessary for successful soldering; proper flux, good solder and sufficient heat. A soldering flux is necessary to clean the metal of tarnish, prepare it for soldering and to enable the solder to spread into tiny crevices. When soldering, always use a rosin core solder which is non-corrosive and will not attract moisture once the job is finished. Other types of flux (acid core) will leave a residue that will attract moisture and cause the wires to corrode. Tin is a unique metal with a low melting point. In a molten state, it dissolves and alloys easily with many metals. Solder is made by mixing tin with lead. The most common proportions are 40/60, 50/50 and 60/40, with the percentage of tin listed first. Low priced solders usually contain less tin, making them very difficult for a beginner to use because more heat is required to melt the solder. A common solder is 40/60 which is well suited for all-around general use, but 60/40 melts easier and is preferred for electrical work.

Soldering Techniques

Successful soldering requires that the metals to be joined be heated to a temperature that will melt the solder, usually 360-460°F (182-238°C). Contrary to popular belief, the purpose of the soldering iron is not to melt the solder itself, but to heat the parts being soldered to a temperature high enough to melt the solder when it is touched to the work. Melting flux-cored solder on the soldering iron will usually destroy the effectiveness of the flux.

➡**Soldering tips are made of copper for good heat conductivity, but must be "tinned" regularly for quick transference of heat to the project and to prevent the solder from sticking to the iron. To "tin" the iron, simply heat it and touch the flux-cored solder to the tip; the solder will flow over the hot tip. Wipe the excess off with a clean rag, but be careful as the iron will be hot.**

After some use, the tip may become pitted. If so, simply dress the tip smooth with a smooth file and "tin" the tip again. Flux-cored solder will remove oxides but rust, bits of insulation and oil or grease must be removed with a wire brush or emery cloth. For maximum strength in soldered parts, the joint must start off clean and tight. Weak joints will result in gaps too wide for the solder to bridge.

If a separate soldering flux is used, it should be brushed or swabbed on only those areas that are to be soldered. Most solders contain a core of flux and separate fluxing is unnecessary. Hold the work to be soldered firmly. It is best to solder on a wooden board, because a metal vise will only rob the piece to be soldered of heat and make it difficult to melt the solder. Hold the soldering tip with the broadest face against the work to be soldered. Apply solder under the tip close to the work, using enough solder to give a heavy film between the iron and the piece being soldered, while moving slowly and making sure the solder melts properly. Keep the work level or the solder will run to the lowest part and favor the thicker parts, because these require more heat to melt the solder. If the soldering tip overheats (the solder coating on the face of the tip burns up), it should be retinned. Once the soldering is completed, let the soldered joint stand until cool. Tape and seal all soldered wire splices after the repair has cooled.

Wire Harness Connectors

Most connectors in the engine compartment or otherwise exposed to the elements are protected against moisture and dirt which could create oxidation and deposits on the terminals. These special connectors are weather-proof. All repairs require the use of a special terminal and the tool required to service it. This tool is used to remove the pin and sleeve terminals. If removal is attempted with an ordinary pick, there is a good chance that the terminal will be bent or deformed. Unlike standard blade type terminals, these weather-proof terminals cannot be straightened once they are bent. Make certain that the connectors are properly seated and all of the sealing rings are in place when connecting leads. On some models, a hinge-type flap provides a backup or secondary locking feature for the terminals. Most secondary locks are used to improve connector reliability by retaining the terminals if the small terminal lock tangs are not positioned properly.

Molded-on connectors require complete replacement of the connection. This means splicing a new connector assembly into the harness. All splices should be soldered to insure proper contact. Use care when probing the connections or replacing terminals in them as it is possible to short between opposite terminals. If this happens to the wrong terminal pair, it is possible to damage certain components. Always use jumper wires between connectors for circuit checking and never probe through weatherproof seals.

Open circuits are often difficult to locate by sight because corrosion or terminal misalignment are hidden by the connectors. Merely wiggling a connector on a sensor or in the wiring harness may correct the open circuit condition. This should always be considered when an open circuit or a failed sensor is indicated. Intermittent problems may also be caused by oxidized or loose connections. When using a circuit tester for diagnosis, always probe connections from the wire side. Be careful not to damage sealed connectors with test probes.

All wiring harnesses should be replaced with identical parts, using the same gauge wire and connectors. When signal wires are spliced into a harness, use wire with high temperature insulation only. It is seldom necessary to replace a complete harness. If replacement is necessary, pay close attention to insure proper harness routing. Secure the harness with suitable plastic wire clamps to prevent vibrations from causing the harness to wear in spots or contact any hot components.

➡**Weatherproof connectors cannot be replaced with standard connectors. Instructions are provided with replacement connector and terminal packages. Some wire harnesses have mounting indicators (usually pieces of colored tape) to mark where the harness is to be secured.**

In making wiring repairs, its important that you always replace damaged wires with wires that are the same gauge as the wire being replaced. The heavier the wire, the smaller the gauge number. Wires are color-coded to aid in identification and whenever possible the same color coded wire should be used for replacement. A wire stripping and crimping tool is necessary to install solderless terminal connectors. Test all crimps by pulling on the wires; it should not be possible to pull the wires out of a good crimp.

Wires which are open, exposed or otherwise damaged are repaired by simple splicing. Where possible, if the wiring harness is accessible and the damaged place in the wire can be located, it is best to open the harness and check for all possible damage. In an inaccessible harness, the wire must be bypassed with a new insert, usually taped to the outside of the old harness.

When replacing fusible links, be sure to use fusible link wire, NOT ordinary automotive wire. Make sure the fusible segment is of the same gauge and construction as the one being replaced and double the stripped end when crimping the terminal connector for a good contact. The melted (open) fusible link segment of the wiring harness should be cut off as close to the harness as possible, then a new segment spliced in as described. In the case of a damaged fusible link that feeds two harness wires, the harness connections should be replaced with two fusible link wires so that each circuit will have its own separate protection.

➡**Most of the problems caused in the wiring harness are due to bad ground connections. Always check all vehicle ground connections for corrosion or looseness before performing any power feed checks to eliminate the chance of a bad ground affecting the circuit.**

Hard Shell Connectors

Unlike molded connectors, the terminal contacts in hard shell connectors can be replaced. Weatherproof hard-shell connectors with the leads molded into the shell have non-replaceable terminal ends. Replacement usually involves the use of a special terminal removal tool that depresses the locking tangs (barbs) on the connector terminal and allows the connector to be removed from the rear of the shell. The connector shell should be replaced if it shows any evidence of burning, melting, cracks, or breaks. Replace individual terminals that are burnt, corroded, distorted or loose.

➡**The insulation crimp must be tight to prevent the insulation from sliding back on the wire when the wire is pulled. The insulation must be visibly compressed under the crimp tabs, and the ends of the crimp should be turned in for a firm grip on the insulation.**

The wire crimp must be made with all wire strands inside the crimp. The terminal must be fully compressed on the wire strands with the ends of the crimp tabs turned in to make a firm grip on the wire. Check all connections with an ohmmeter to insure a good contact. There should be no measurable resistance between the wire and the terminal when connected.

Fusible Links

▶ See Figures 1 and 2

The fuse link is a short length of special, Hypalon (high temperature) insulated wire, integral with the engine compartment wiring harness and should not be confused with standard wire. It is several wire gauges smaller than the circuit which it protects. Under no circumstances should a fuse link replacement repair be made using a length of standard wire cut from bulk stock or from another wiring harness.

To repair any blown fuse link use the following procedure:

1. Determine which circuit is damaged, its location and the cause of the open fuse link. If the damaged fuse link is one of three fed by a common No. 10 or 12 gauge feed wire, determine the specific affected circuit.

2. Disconnect the negative battery cable.

3. Cut the damaged fuse link from the wiring harness and discard it. If the fuse link is one of three circuits fed by a single feed wire, cut it out of the harness at each splice end and discard it.

4. Identify and procure the proper fuse link with butt connectors for attaching the fuse link to the harness.

➡ **Heat shrink tubing must be slipped over the wire before crimping and soldering the connection.**

5. To repair any fuse link in a 3-link group with one feed:

a. After cutting the open link out of the harness, cut each of the remaining undamaged fuse links close to the feed wire weld.

b. Strip approximately ½ in. (13mm) of insulation from the detached ends of the two good fuse links. Insert two wire ends into one end of a butt connector, then carefully push one stripped end of the replacement fuse link into the same end of the butt connector and crimp all three firmly together.

Fig. 1 Good and damaged fusible links

Fig. 2 Fusible link repair

➡**Care must be taken when fitting the three fuse links into the butt connector as the internal diameter is a snug fit for three wires. Make sure to use a proper crimping tool. Pliers, side cutter, etc. will not apply the proper crimp to retain the wires and withstand a pull test.**

c. After crimping the butt connector to the three fuse links, cut the weld portion from the feed wire and strip approximately ½ in. (13mm) of insulation from the cut end. Insert the stripped end into the open end of the butt connector and crimp very firmly.

d. To attach the remaining end of the replacement fuse link, strip approximately ½ in. (13mm) of insulation from the wire end of the circuit from which the blown fuse link was removed, and firmly crimp a butt connector or equivalent to the stripped wire. Then, insert the end of the replacement link into the other end of the butt connector and crimp firmly.

e. Using rosin core solder with a consistency of 60 percent tin and 40 percent lead, solder the connectors and the wires at the repairs then insulate.

6. To replace any fuse link on a single circuit in a harness, cut out the damaged portion, strip approximately ½ in. (13mm) of insulation from the two wire ends and attach the appropriate replacement fuse link to the stripped wire ends with two proper size butt connectors. Solder the connectors and wires, then insulate.

7. To repair any fuse link which has an eyelet terminal on one end such as the charging circuit, cut off the open fuse link behind the weld, strip approximately ½ in. (13mm) of insulation from the cut end and attach the appropriate new eyelet fuse link to the cut stripped wire with an appropriate size butt connector. Solder the connectors and wires at the repair, then insulate.

➡**When attaching a single No. 16, 17, 18 or 20 gauge fuse link to a heavy gauge wire, always double the stripped wire end of the fuse link before inserting and crimping it into the butt connector for positive wire retention.**

SUPPLEMENTAL INFLATABLE RESTRAINT SYSTEM (AIR BAG)

General Information

▶ See Figure 3

The Supplemental Inflatable Restraint (SIR) system helps supplement the protection offered by the driver's seat belt by deploying an air bag from the center of the steering wheel during certain front end collisions. The bag deploys when the vehicle is involved in a frontal crash of a sufficient force within 30 degrees of the centerline of the vehicle. Testing and any needed repairs should only be performed by a professional. Take cautions seriously when working near this system. Lack of care could result in possible air bag deployment, personal injury, or other needed repairs to the SIR system.

※※CAUTION

Whenever carrying a live inflator module, make sure that the bag and opening is pointed away from you. Never carry the module by the wires or connector on the under side of the module. When placing the live inflator on a bench or any other surface, always face the bag and trim cover up, away from the surface. Never rest a steering column assembly on the steering wheel with the inflator module face down.

SYSTEM OPERATION

▶ See Figure 4

The main portions of the SIR system are the deployment loop and the Diagnostic Energy Reserve Module (DERM). The main function of the deployment loop is to supply current through the inflator module in the steering wheel. This will allow deployment of the air bag in the event of a frontal crash.

The arming sensor, SIR coil assembly, inflator module, and discriminating sensors make up the deployment loop. The arming sensor switches power to the inflator module on the high

Fig. 3 The bag deploys when the vehicle is involved in a frontal crash of a sufficient force within 30 degrees of the centerline of the vehicle

Fig. 4 The main function of the deployment loop is to supply current through the inflator module in the steering wheel

side of the loop. Either of the sensors can supply ground to the inflator module on the low side of the loop. The module is only supplied sufficient current to deploy when the arming sensor and at least one of the two discriminating sensors are closed simultaneously.

SYSTEM COMPONENTS

Diagnostic Energy Reserve Module (DERM)

※※WARNING

Do not open the DERM case for any reason. Touching the connector pins or soldered components may cause electrostatic discharge damage. Repair of a malfunctioning DERM is by the replacement only.

The DERM is designed to perform the following functions in the SIR system:

1. Energy Reserve — The DERM maintains a 36 Volt Loop Reserve (36 VLR) energy supply to provide deployment energy when the cars voltage is low or lost in a frontal collision.

2. Malfunction Detection — The DERM performs diagnostic monitoring of the SIR system electrical components.

3. Malfunction Recording — The DERM provides the SIR system diagnostic trouble code information through a scan tool.

4. Driver Notification — The DERM warns the driver of SIR malfunction by controlling the AIR BAG warning lamp.

5. Frontal Crash Recording — The DERM records the SIR system status during a frontal crash.

The DERM is connected to the SIR wiring harness by a 24-way connector. The harness connector uses a shorting bar across certain terminals in the contact area. The shorting bar connects the AIR BAG warning lamp to ground when the DERM harness connector is unplugged. This will cause the AIR BAG lamp to come on steadily whenever the ignition is in the **RUN** or **START** position with the DERM disconnected.

Air Bag Warning Lamp

Ignition voltage is applied to the AIR BAG warning lamp when the ignition switch is at the **RUN** or **START** positions. The DERM controls the lamp by providing ground with a lamp driver. The lamp is used in the SIR system to do the following:

1. Verify the lamp and DERM operation by flashing seven times when the ignition switch is **ON**.

2. Warn the driver of SIR electrical systems malfunctions which could potentially affect the operation of the SIR system. These malfunctions could cause a non-deployment of the air bag in a frontal crash, or deployment in cases less severe than intended.

Arming Sensor

The arming sensor is a protective switch that is located in the high side of the deployment loop. The sensor is calibrated to close at low level velocity changes, lower than the discriminating sensors. This will ensure that the inflator module is connected directly to the 36 VLR output of the DERM or **ignition 1** voltage when either of the sensors closes.

The arming sensor consists of a sensing element, normally open switch contacts, two diagnostic resistors, and two diodes. These sensing elements close the switch contacts when the velocity of the vehicle changes at a rate that indicates a potential need for deployment.

The 51K ohm diagnostic resistor is connected in parallel with the switch contacts allowing a small amount of voltage to pass operation. This current flow results in voltage drops across each component within the deployment loop. The DERM monitors these drops to detect circuit or component malfunctions. The 2.49K ohm diagnostic resistor is connected in parallel with the diodes allowing the DERM to monitor the voltage applied to the high side of the deployment loop. These two diodes in the arming sensor provide an isolation between the 36 VLR output of the DERM and IGNITION 1 voltage.

SIR Coil Assembly
▶ See Figure 5

The SIR coil assembly consists of two current carrying coils, which are attached to the steering column. The coils allow the rotation of the steering wheel while maintaining continuous contact of the deployment loop to the inflator module.

Inflator Module
▶ See Figure 6

The inflator module is located on the steering wheel hub. The module consists of an inflatable bag and an inflator which is a canister of gas generating material and an initiating device. When the car is in a frontal crash of sufficient force. Current passing through the initiator ignites the material in the inflator module. The gas produced from this reaction quickly inflates the air bag.

DISARMING THE SYSTEM

▶ See Figure 7

1. To disable the SIR system, turn the steering wheel so that the vehicles wheels are pointing straight ahead.

2. Turn the ignition key to the **LOCK** position and remove the key.

3. Remove the AIR BAG fuse from the fuse block.

4. Unsecure the left sound insulator by removing the screws and nuts.

5. Remove the Connector Position Assurance (CPA) and the yellow two-way connector from the base of the steering column.

➡When the AIR BAG fuse is removed from the fuse block, and the key is in the ON position, the AIR BAG warning lamp will be ON. This is a normal condition and does not mean that the SIR system is malfunctioning.

ENABLING THE SYSTEM

1. Engage the yellow two-way connector to the base of the steering column and the Connect Position Assurance (CPA).

2. Install the left sound insulator with the mounting screws and nuts.

3. Insert the AIR BAG fuse in the fuse block.

1 SIR COIL ASSEMBLY

2 INFLATOR MODULE CONNECTOR

3 STEERING COLUMN CONNECTOR

86816075

Fig. 5 The SIR coil assembly attaches to the steering column assembly

BUICK SHOWN
OLDSMOBILE SIMILAR

1   SIR COIL ASSEMBLY
2   CONNECTOR POSITION ASSURANCE (CPA)
3   INFLATOR MODULE HARNESS CONNECTOR
4   INFLATOR MODULE
5   HORN LEAD

86816076

Fig. 6 The inflator module is located on the steering wheel hub

1   YELLOW 2-WAY (SIR) CONNECTOR
2   CONNECTOR POSITION ASSURANCE (CPA)
3   STEERING COLUMN WIRING HARNESS
4   I/P WIRING HARNESS

86816071

Fig. 7 Unplug the Connector Position Assurance (CPA) and the yellow two-way connector from the base of the steering column

4. Turn the ignition switch to the **RUN** position and verify that the AIR BAG warning lamp flashes 7 times and then turns off. If it does not turn off have your SIR system checked by an authorized service center.

HEATER

The heating system provides heating, ventilation and defrosting for the windshield and side windows. The heater core is a heat exchanger supplied with coolant from the engine cooling system. Temperature is controlled by the temperature valve which moves an air door that directs air flow through the heater core for more heat or bypasses the heater core for less heat.

Vacuum actuators control the mode doors which direct air flow to the outlet ducts. The mode selector on the control panel directs engine vacuum to the actuators. The position of the mode doors determines whether air flows from the floor, panel, defrost or panel and defrost ducts (bi-level mode).

Blower Motor

REMOVAL & INSTALLATION

▶ See Figures 8, 9 and 10

➡This procedure is applicable for vehicles, with or without air conditioning.

1. Disconnect the negative cable at the battery.
2. On the 3.1L (VIN M) you will need to remove the serpentine belt and move the alternator aside. See Section 3 for removal and installation.
3. For the 2.2L (VIN 4), disconnect the air inlet resonator, then remove the torque strut from the engine. Rotate the engine slightly forward.

4. Working inside the engine compartment, disconnect the blower motor electrical leads.

5. Remove the motor retaining bolts. If there is a hose disconnect it, then remove the blower motor.

To install:

6. Position the blower motor on it's mount.

7. Install the mounting bolts and tighten until snug.

8. Attach the drain hose if removed, then engage the electrical connection to the motor.

9. On the 2.2L (VIN 4), properly position the engine and install the torque strut to the engine. Connect the air inlet resonator.

10. On the 3.1L (VIN M), install the alternator, if removed. Install the serpentine belt.

11. Connect the negative battery cable, tighten the cable bolt to 11 ft. lbs. (15 Nm).

12. Reset the radio, clock and any other applicable electronic devices.

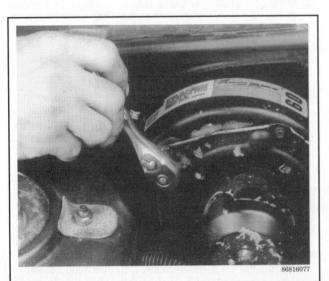

Fig. 8 Remove the blower motor retaining bolts . . .

Fig. 9 . . . then disconnect the hose

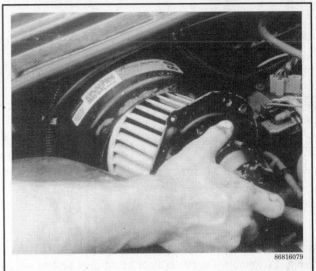

Fig. 10 The blower motor can now be removed

Heater Core

REMOVAL & INSTALLATION

Air Conditioned Models
▶ **See Figures 11, 12, 13 and 14**

✳✳CAUTION

When draining the coolant, keep in mind that cats and dogs are attracted by ethylene glycol antifreeze, and are quite likely to drink any that is left in an uncovered container or in puddles on the ground. This will prove fatal in sufficient quantity. Always drain the coolant into a sealable container. Coolant should be reused unless it is contaminated or several years old.

1. Disconnect the negative battery cable and drain the cooling system.

2. Disconnect the heater hoses from the heater core inlet and outlet connections in the engine compartment.

3. Allowing residual coolant from the heater core to drain. Cap the openings.

4. Working inside the vehicle, remove the lower instrument panel sound insulator.

5. Remove the heater floor outlet duct screws or clips and remove the duct.

6. Remove the heater core cover by removing the attaching screws and clips.

7. Remove the heater core cover.

8. Remove the heater core retainers and remove the heater core.

To install:

9. Position the heater core in the housing and install the retaining straps.

10. Position the heater core cover on the housing and install the attaching screws and clips.

11. Install the floor outlet duct and attaching screws or clips.

12. Install the lower instrument panel sound insulator.

Fig. 11 Remove the heater floor outlet duct screws or clips . . .

Fig. 12 . . . then remove the heater floor outlet duct

Fig. 13 Remove the mounting bolts which retain the heater core

13. Working in the engine compartment, connect the heater core inlet and outlet hoses.

14. Fill the cooling system.

15. Start the engine and check for coolant leaks. Allow the engine to warm up sufficiently to confirm the proper operation of the heater.

16. Recheck for leaks. Check the cooling system level.

Air Conditioned Models

◗ **See Figure 15**

1. Drain the cooling system.

✻✻CAUTION

When draining the coolant, keep in mind that cats and dogs are attracted by the ethylene glycol antifreeze, and are quite likely to drink any that is left in an uncovered container or in puddles on the ground. This will prove fatal in sufficient quantity. Always drain the coolant into a sealable container. Coolant should be reused unless it is contaminated or several years old.

2. If equipped with a diesel engine, raise and support the car on jackstands.

3. Disconnect the hoses at the core.

4. On diesels, remove the instrument panel lower sound absorber.

5. Remove the heater duct and lower side covers.

6. Remove the lower heater outlet.

7. Remove the two housing cover-to-air valve housing clips.

8. Remove the housing cover.

9. Remove the core restraining straps.

10. Remove the core tubing retainers and lift out the core.

To install:

11. Install the core, then attach the core tubing retainers.

12. Attach the core restraining straps.

13. Install the housing cover, then install the two housing cover-to-air valve housing clips.

14. Install the lower heater outlet, then attach the heater duct and lower side covers.

15. On diesels, install the lower instrument panel sound absorber.

16. Connect the hoses at the core.

17. Lower the vehicle if raised and supported.

18. Fill the cooling system.

19. Start the engine and check for coolant leaks. Allow the engine to warm up sufficiently to confirm the proper operation of the heater.

20. Recheck for leaks. Check the cooling system level.

Control Cables

REMOVAL & INSTALLATION

1. Disconnect the negative battery cable.

2. Remove the temperature control assembly from the dash.

3. Remove the lower instrument panel sound insulator.

4. Tag and disconnect the cable(s) at the module and control.

1. Fan ground terminal
2. Blower motor assembly
3. Fan support
4. Fan
5. Nut
6. Blower case
7. Clip
8. Mounting cable bracket
9. Temperature valve and seal assembly
10. Temperature shaft and lever assembly
11. Vent shaft and lever assembly
12. Heater case
13. Mounting cable bracket
14. Defroster valve and fitting assembly
15. Defroster shaft and lever assembly
16. Core clamp
17. Large air baffle
18. Valve seat
19. Plate cover
20. Core and fitting assembly
21. Seal tube

86816083

Fig. 14 Exploded view of the heater core and case assembly

1 MODULE ASSEMBLY, HEATER AND AIR CONDITIONING EVAPORATOR AND BLOWER
2 BOLT/SCREW, HEATER AND AIR CONDITIONING EVAPORATOR AND BLOWER MODULE
3 DASH PANEL
4 GASKET, HEATER AND AIR CONDITIONING EVAPORATOR AND BLOWER MODULE
5 MOTOR ASSEMBLY, BLOWER
6 BOLT/SCREW, BLOWER MOTOR

86816084

Fig. 15 Heater and air conditioning module assembly

5. Remove the cables.

To install:

6. Attach the cables in there proper locations, make sure any retaining clips are seated properly.

7. Install the lower instrument panel sound insulator.

8. Install the control assembly.

9. Adjust the cables as needed. Vehicles with sliding clips, proceed as follows:

   a. Place the control lever in the Cold position.

   b. Place the clip of the cable on the heater case temperature door post.

   c. Push the control head lever towards the Hot, until the temperature door seats and the spring back is out of the cable and control.

10. Connect the negative battery cable, tighten the cable bolt to 11 ft. lbs. (15 Nm).

11. Reset the radio, clock and any other electronic devises in need.

Control Panel

REMOVAL & INSTALLATION

1. Disconnect the negative battery cable.

2. Remove the radio knobs (if equipped) and the clock set knob (if equipped).

3. Remove the instrument bezel retaining screws.

4. Pull the bezel out to disconnect the rear defogger switch and the remote mirror control (if equipped).

5. Remove the instrument panel.

6. Remove the control head to dash screws and pull the head out.

7. Disconnect the electrical connectors and/or control cable(s) (if equipped), then remove the control head.

To install:

8. Attach the control head, then connect the electrical connectors and/or control cable(s) (if equipped).

9. Replace the control head in the dash and tighten down the dash screws.

10. Install the instrument panel.

11. Connect the rear defogger switch and the remote mirror control (if equipped).

12. Install the instrument bezel attaching it with the retaining screws.

AIR CONDITIONER

▶ See Figure 16

General Information

❄❄CAUTION

Some vehicles are equipped with the Supplemental Inflatable Restraint (SIR) system. This system must be disabled before performing service on or around the air bag, instrument panel components, wiring and sensors. Failure to

13. Reinstall the radio knobs (if equipped) and the clock set knob (if equipped).

14. Connect the negative battery cable, tighten the cable bolt to 11 ft. lbs. (15 Nm).

Defroster Vacuum Actuator

REMOVAL & INSTALLATION

1. Remove the instrument panel.

2. Disconnect the defroster nozzle. Remove the two clips securing mode valve and the housing assembly-to-case, then disconnect the vacuum hose connections at the defroster actuator and mode actuator.

3. Remove the mode valve housing assembly.

4. Remove the two defroster actuator retaining screws.

5. Release the actuator rod and remove the actuator assembly.

To install:

6. Install the defroster actuator with the retaining screws and connecting actuator rod.

7. Install the mode valve and housing assembly.

8. Connect the vacuum lines at the defroster actuator and the mode valve actuator.

9. Connect the defroster nozzle, then install the instrument panel assembly.

Temperature Valve

REMOVAL & INSTALLATION

1. Disassemble the mode valve housing.

2. Remove the temperature control cable and slide the valve pivot rod towards the passenger side of the vehicle.

3. Remove the valve.

To install:

4. Position the temperature valve in the case and slide the pivot rod back in place.

5. Connect the temperature control cable.

6. Install the mode valve housing, then adjust the temperature cable.

follow safety and disabling procedures could result in accidental air bag deployment, possible personal injury and unnecessary air bag system repairs.

The heater and air conditioning systems are controlled manually or electronically. The systems differ mainly in the way air temperature and the routing of air flow are controlled. The manual system controls air temperature through a cable-actuated lever and air flow through a vacuum switching valve and vacuum actuators. With Electronic Climate Control (ECC) systems, both temperature and air flow are controlled by the Body Control Module (BCM) through the Climate Control Panel

(CCP). There are 2 types of compressors used. The HR-6 compressor, used on Cycling Clutch Orifice Tube (CCOT) systems, is a 6-cylinder axial compressor consisting of 3 double-ended pistons actuated by a swash plate shaft assembly. The compressor cycles on and off according to system demands. The compressor driveshaft is driven by the serpentine belt when the electromagnetic clutch is engaged.

The V-5 compressor, used on Variable Displacement Orifice Tube (VDOT) systems, is designed to meet the demands of the air conditioning system without cycling. The compressor employs a variable angle wobble plate controlling the displacement of 5 axially oriented cylinders. Displacement is controlled by a bellows actuated control valve located in the rear head of the compressor. The electromagnetic compressor clutch connects the compressor shaft to the serpentine drive belt when the coil is energized.

Service Valve Locations

Refer to Section 1 for discharging and charging of the air conditioning system.

The high-side service valve is normally located in the refrigerant line near the discharge fitting of the compressor.

The low-side service valve is normally located on the accumulator or in the condenser-to-evaporator refrigerant line.

Compressor

REMOVAL & INSTALLATION

➡Procedures for discharging and servicing the air conditioning system is described in Section 1. If a refrigerant recovery/recycling machine is not available, this job should be performed at a dealer or a shop that has this equipment.

Except 2.2L (VIN 4) and 3.1L (VIN M)
▶ **See Figures 17 and 18**

1. Properly discharge the air conditioning system into a recovery/recycling machine.
2. Disconnect the negative battery cable.
3. Unplug the electrical connectors from the compressor.
4. Remove the coupled hose assembly from the rear of the compressor. Discard the O-rings.

➡Cap the refrigerant lines when opening the system to prevent the entry of dirt and moisture and the loss of refrigerant lubricant.

5. Release the drive belt tension and remove the belt from the compressor.
6. Remove the compressor attaching bolts.
7. Remove the compressor.
8. Drain and measure the refrigerant oil from the compressor. Discard the old oil.

To install:
9. If the compressor is to be replaced, drain the oil from the new compressor and discard. Add new refrigerant oil equivalent to the amount that was drained from the compressor upon removal.
10. Position the compressor in the vehicle.
11. Install the compressor attaching bolts.
12. Install new O-rings to the coupled hose assembly. Lubricate the O-rings with refrigerant oil.
13. Install the coupled hose assembly to the back of the compressor.
14. Install the drive belt.
15. Engage the electrical connectors to the compressor.
16. Connect negative battery cable.
17. Evacuate, recharge and leak test the system.

2.2L (VIN 4) Engine
▶ **See Figure 19**

1. Properly discharge the air conditioning system into a recovery/recycling machine.
2. Remove the drive belt on the vehicle.
3. Remove the air cleaner and resonator assembly.

Fig. 16 Air flow routing on air conditioned models

1. Bolt/Screw 25 ft. lbs. (33 Nm)
2. Hose and fitting assembly
3. O-ring
4. Accumulator
5. Condenser
6. Condenser outlet
7. Radiator support grommet
8. Condenser pipe
9. A/C compressor
10. Switch assembly

86816098

Fig. 17 Compressor and hose assembly on the 3.1L (VIN T) engine

1. A/C module
2. A/C hose assembly
3. A/C switches
4. Bolt/Screw 25 ft. lbs. (33 Nm)
5. Condenser pipe
6. Radiator support grommet
7. A/C compressor

86816099

Fig. 18 Compressor and hose assembly on the 2.5L (VIN R) engine

4. Unplug the electrical connections from the compressor.
5. Disconnect the negative battery cable.
6. Unfasten, then remove and cap the A/C hose from the compressor.

➡**Cap the refrigerant lines when opening the system to prevent the entry of dirt and moisture and the loss of refrigerant lubricant.**

7. Loosen the A/C compressor bolts, then raise and support the vehicle.
8. Remove the compressor.
To install:
9. Position the compressor on the vehicle.
10. Lower the vehicle.
11. Install the compressor bolts, then tighten the front bolts to 37 ft. lbs. (50 Nm) and the rear bolts to 22 ft, lbs. (30 Nm).
12. Attach the compressor hose using NEW sealing washers. Tighten the mounting bolts to 24 ft. lbs. (33 Nm).

➡**Lubricate O-rings with refrigerant oil.**

13. Engage the electrical connections to the compressor.
14. Install the air cleaner and resonator assembly.
15. Install the serpentine drive belt.
16. Connect negative battery cable.
17. Evacuate and charge the system.
18. Preform a leak test on the system.

3.1L (VIN M) Engine

▶ **See Figure 20**

1. Properly discharge the air conditioning system into a recovery/recycling machine.
2. Disconnect the negative battery cable.
3. Remove the serpentine drive belt.
4. Remove the front compressor bolts.
5. Raise and safely support the vehicle.
6. Remove the rear compressor bolts.

1 WATER PUMP ASSEMBLY
2 BOLT/SCREW, AIR CONDITIONING COMPRESSOR BRACKET
3 BOLT/SCREW, AIR CONDITIONING COMPRESSOR, REAR
4 BOLT/SCREW, AIR CONDITIONING COMPRESSOR BRACKET, REAR
5 COMPRESSOR ASSEMBLY, AIR CONDITIONING
6 BOLT/SCREW, LOWER COMPRESSOR BRACKET ENGINE MOUNT SUPPORT BRACKET
7 BRACKET ASSEMBLY, AIR CONDITIONING COMPRESSOR
8 BOLT/SCREW, AIR CONDITIONING COMPRESSOR, FRONT

86816096

Fig. 19 Compressor mounting on the 2.2L (VIN 4) engine

7. Unplug and cap the coupled hose assembly from the rear of the compressor.

➡ **Cap the refrigerant lines when opening the system to prevent the entry of dirt and moisture and the loss of refrigerant lubricant.**

8. Disconnect the electrical connection at the compressor.
9. Remove the compressor from the vehicle.

To install:

10. Install the compressor on the vehicle, engage the electrical connection to the compressor.
11. Install the coupled hose assembly to the rear of the compressor, with NEW sealing washers. Tighten the mounting bolt to 24 ft. lbs. (33 Nm).
12. Install the rear compressor bolts. Tighten the rear bolts to 8 ft. lbs. (25 Nm).
13. Lower the vehicle.
14. Install the front compressor bolts. Tighten them to 37 ft. lbs. (50 Nm).
15. Install the serpentine drive belt on the vehicle.
16. Connect the negative battery cable.
17. Evacuate and charge the system.
18. Preform a leak test.

Condenser

The condenser assembly is located in front of the radiator. It is made up of many tubes which carry the refrigerant, and cooling fins which provides a rapid transfer of heat. The air passing through the condenser cools the refrigerant vapors which causes it to condense to a high pressure liquid.

REMOVAL & INSTALLATION

➡ **Procedures for discharging and servicing the air conditioning system is described in Section 1. If a refrigerant recovery/recycling machine is not available, this job should be performed at a dealer or a shop that has the equipment.**

1 BOLT.SCREW, AIR CONDITIONING COMPRESSOR BRACKET POSITION #1
2 BOLT/SCREW, AIR CONDITIONING COMPRESSOR BRACKET POSITION #2
3 BRACKET ASSEMBLY, AIR CONDITIONING COMPRESSOR
4 BOLT/SCREW, AIR CONDITIONING COMPRESSOR, FRONT
5 BOLT/SCREW, AIR CONDITIONING COMPRESSOR BRACKET POSITION #6
6 BOLT/SCREW, AIR CONDITIONING COMPRESSOR BRACKET POSITION #3
7 COMPRESSOR ASSEMBLY, AIR CONDITIONING
8 BOLT/SCREW, AIR CONDITIONING COMPRESSOR BRACKET POSITION #5
9 BOLT/SCREW, AIR CONDITIIONING COMPRESSOR BRACKET POSITION #4

86816097

Fig. 20 Compressor mounting on the 3.1L (VIN M) engine

1982-93 Models

1. Properly discharge the air conditioning system into a recovery/recycling machine.
2. Disconnect the negative battery cable.
3. Disconnect the and cap the high-pressure and liquid lines at the condenser fittings. Discard the O-rings.

➡ **Use a backup wrench on the condenser fittings when removing the high-pressure and liquid lines. Cap both refrigerant lines when opening the system to prevent the entry of dirt and moisture and the loss of refrigerant lubricant.**

4. Remove the condenser attaching bolts from the center support.
5. Remove the engine strut bracket and upper radiator support. Lean the radiator back.
6. Remove the condenser.
To install:
7. Position the condenser in the vehicle.

➡ **If replacing the condenser or if the original condenser was flushed during service, add 1 fluid oz. (30ml) of refrigerant oil to the system.**

8. Install the upper radiator support and engine strut bracket.
9. Install the condenser attaching bolts.
10. Replace the condenser fitting O-rings. Lubricate the O-rings with refrigerant oil. Tighten until snug.
11. Connect the condenser high-pressure and liquid lines.

➡ **Use a backup wrench on the condenser fittings when tightening lines.**

12. Connect the negative battery cable.
13. Evacuate, charge and leak test the system.

1994-95 Models

▶ **See Figure 21**

1. Properly discharge the air conditioning system into a recovery/recycling machine.
2. Connect the negative battery cable.
3. Remove the grille center support retaining bolts.
4. Raise and support the vehicle safely.
5. Remove the center support lower retaining bolts and the support.
6. Unsecure the left side air inlet seal.
7. Disconnect and cap the inlet and outlet lines from the condenser.

➡ **Cap the refrigerant lines when opening the system to prevent the entry of dirt and moisture and the loss of refrigerant lubricant.**

8. Remove the lower condenser mounts and the condenser.
To install:
9. Install the condenser and lower condenser mounts.
10. Connect the inlet and outlet lines to the condenser.
11. Install the left side air inlet seal.
12. Attach the center support and lower retaining bolts.
13. Lower the vehicle.
14. Connect the negative battery cable.

1	RETAINER, UPPER TIE BAR
2	INSULATOR, A/C CONDENSER UPPER
3	RETAINER, A/C CONDENSER INSULATOR
4	NUT
5	BOLT/SCREW, A/C CONDENSER INSULATOR RETAINER
6	INSULATOR, A/C CONDENSER LOWER
7	CONDENSER ASSEMBLY, A/C
8	SEAL, A/C CONDENSER

86816100

Fig. 21 Condenser mounting used on 1994-95 models

15. Install the grille center support retaining bolts.
16. Evacuate and charge the system.
17. Preform a leak test on the vehicle.

Blower Motor Resistor

REMOVAL & INSTALLATION

▶ **See Figures 22 and 23**

1. Disconnect the negative battery cable.
2. Unplug the electrical connector at the resistor.
3. Remove the resistor attaching screws.
4. Remove the resistor from the evaporator case.
To install:
5. Position the resistor in the evaporator case. Install the attaching screws.
6. Engage the electrical connector.
7. Connect the negative battery cable. Tighten the cable bolt to 11 ft. lbs. (15 Nm).

86816101

Fig. 22 Unplug the electrical connector from the resistor

Fig. 23 After removing the attaching screws, pull the resistor from the case

8. Reset the radio, clock and any other applicable electronic devices.

Evaporator

The evaporator is a device which cools and dehumidifies the air before it enters the vehicle. A high pressure liquid refrigerant flows through the expansion tube, then becomes a low pressure liquid and enters the evaporator. The heat in the air passing through the core is transferred to the cooler surface of the core. Which then cools the air. As all the heat transfers from the air to the evaporator core surface, any moisture in the air is condensed on the outside surface of the core and drained off as condensate.

REMOVAL & INSTALLATION

➡Procedures for discharging and servicing the air conditioning system is described in Section 1. If a refrigerant recovery/recycling machine is not available, this job should be performed at a dealer or a shop that has the equipment.

✳✳CAUTION

Some vehicles are equipped with the Supplemental Inflatable Restraint (SIR) system. This system must be disabled before performing service on or around the air bag, instrument panel components, wiring and sensors. Failure to follow safety and disabling procedures could result in accidental air bag deployment, possible personal injury and unnecessary air bag system repairs.

1. Disconnect the negative battery cable.
2. Remove the air cleaner.
3. Properly discharge the air conditioning system into a recovery/recycling machine.
4. Unplug the module electrical connectors, disconnect the harness straps and move the harness aside.

5. On the 3.1L (VIN M) engine, remove the throttle modulator assembly.
6. Remove the heater hose routing bracket from the back of the cover.
7. Disconnect the liquid line at the evaporator inlet and low pressure line at the evaporator outlet.

➡Cap the refrigerant lines when opening the system to prevent the entry of dirt and moisture and the loss of refrigerant lubricant.

8. Remove the blower motor resistor from the top of the cover.
9. Unplug the blower motor electrical connector.
10. If equipped with the 2.8L MFI engine, remove the alternator bracket bolts, alternator rear brace bolt, alternator pivot bolt and move the alternator away from the module.
11. Remove the cover from the module.
12. Remove the evaporator core.
   To install:

➡If replacing the evaporator or if the original evaporator was flushed during service, add 2-3 fluid oz. (60-90ml) of refrigerant lubricant to the system.

13. Clean the old gasket material from the cowl.
14. Install the evaporator core in the module.
15. Apply permagum sealer to the case, then install the cover using a new gasket.
16. Install the cover attaching screws.
17. If equipped with the 2.8L MFI engine, position the alternator and install the pivot bolts, rear brace bolt and alternator bracket bolts.
18. Engage the blower motor electrical connector.
19. Install the resistor to the top of the cover.
20. Install new O-rings to the liquid and low pressure lines. Lubricate O-rings with refrigerant oil.
21. Connect the liquid line at the evaporator inlet and low pressure line at the evaporator outlet.
22. Install the heater hose routing bracket to the cover.
23. On the 3.1L (VIN M) install the throttle modulator assembly.
24. Route the cowl harness in the straps and connect the module electrical connectors.
25. Connect the negative battery cable. Tighten the cable bolt to 11 ft. lbs. (15 Nm).
26. Evacuate, recharge and leak test the system.
27. Reset the radio, clock and any other applicable electronic devices.

Accumulator

The sealed accumulator assembly is connected to the evaporator outlet pipe. It functions as a liquid/vapor separator the receives refrigerant vapor, some liquid refrigerant and refrigerant oil from the evaporator.

In the accumulator is a desiccant which acts as a drying agent for the moisture that may have entered the system. There is an oil bleed hole located in the bottom of the accumulator outlet pipe which provides an oil return path to the compensator.

REMOVAL & INSTALLATION

▶ See Figure 24

➡ Procedures for discharging and servicing the air conditioning system is described in Section 1. If a refrigerant recovery/recycling machine is not available, this job should be performed at a dealer or a shop that has the equipment.

1. Disconnect the negative battery cable.
2. Properly discharge the air conditioning system into a recovery/recycling machine.
3. On some models, you will need to remove the air cleaner and resonator assemblies.
4. Disconnect the low-pressure lines at the inlet and outlet fittings on the accumulator.

➡ Cap the refrigerant lines when opening the system to prevent the entry of dirt and moisture and the loss of refrigerant lubricant.

5. Unplug the pressure cycling switch connection and remove the switch, as required.
6. Loosen the lower strap bolt and spread the strap. Turn the accumulator and remove.
7. Drain and measure the oil in the accumulator. Discard the old oil.

To install:

8. Add new oil equivalent to the amount drained from the old accumulator. Add an additional 2-3 oz. (60-90ml) of oil to compensate for the oil retained by the accumulator desiccant.
9. Position the accumulator in the securing bracket, then tighten the clamp bolt to 88 inch lbs. (10 Nm).
10. Install new O-rings at the inlet and outlet connections on the accumulator. Lubricate the O-rings with refrigerant oil.
11. Connect the low-pressure inlet and outlet lines, tighten to 35 ft. lbs. (48 Nm).
12. Connect the negative battery cable. Tighten the cable bolt to 11 ft. lbs. (15 Nm).
13. Evacuate, charge and leak test the system.

1 ACCUMULATOR ASSEMBLY, A/C
2 INSULATOR, A/C ACCUMULATOR
3 BRACKET ASSEMBLY, A/C ACCUMULATOR
4 BOLT/SCREW, A/C ACCUMULATOR BRACKET
86816103

Fig. 24 The accumulator is secured in a strap bracket

14. Reinstall the air cleaner assembly if removed.
15. Reset the radio, clock and any other applicable electronic devices.

Refrigerant Lines

DISCONNECT & CONNECT

▶ See Figures 25, 26 and 27

1. Disconnect the negative battery cable.
2. Properly discharge the air conditioning system into a recovery/recycling machine.
3. Disconnect the refrigerant line connectors, using a backup wrench as required.
4. Remove the refrigerant line support or routing brackets, as required.
5. Remove the refrigerant line.

➡ Cap the refrigerant lines when opening the system to prevent the entry of dirt and moisture and the loss of refrigerant lubricant.

To install:

6. Position the new refrigerant line in place, leaving the protective caps installed until ready to connect.
7. Install new O-rings on refrigerant line connector fittings. Lubricate with refrigerant oil.
8. Connect the refrigerant line, using a backup wrench, as required.
9. Install the refrigerant line support or routing brackets, as required.
10. Connect the negative battery cable. Tighten the cable bolt to 11 ft. lbs. (15 Nm).
11. Evacuate, recharge and leak test the system.
12. Reset the radio, clock and any other applicable electronic devices.

Expansion Tube Orifice

Metal chips, flakes or silvers found on the expansion tube screen can usually be blown out with shop air once the tube is removed. Replace the tube only if one or more of the conditions is noticed:
- The plastic frame is broken
- The brass orifice tube is damaged or plugged
- The screen material is torn
- The screen is plugged with fine or gritty materials

The use of special tools will be needed for this procedure, J-26549-C the orifice tool remover and J-26549-D an extractor.

REMOVAL & INSTALLATION

▶ See Figures 28 and 29

1. Properly discharge the air conditioning system into a recovery/recycling machine.
2. Raise and support the vehicle.

1—A/C COMPRESSOR

2—O-RINGS

3—COUPLED FITTING

4—24 N•m (18 FT. LB.)

5—ENGINE COOLING FAN-HIGH PRESSURE SWITCH

6—LOW PRESSURE CYCLING SWITCH

7—40 N•m (30 FT. LB.)

8—ACCUMULATOR

9—LIQUID LINE ROUTING SAME AS ENGINE CODE R

10—CONDENSER INLET TUBE

11—ENGINE COOLING FAN-LO PRESSURE SWITCH

12—HIGH SIDE FITTING

13—A/C REFRIGERANT TUBES

14—BRACKET

15—LOCATE TAB ON BRACKET INTO HOLE IN SIDE RAIL

16—LEFT SIDE RAIL

17—LIQUID LINE (SEE ENGINE CODE R)

86816104

Fig. 25 Refrigerant lines and hose routing on the 4.3 (VIN T) engine

1 LOW SIDE FITTING

2 LIQUID LINE CONTINUED IN VIEW B

3 ORFICE TUBE LOCATION

4 EVAPORATOR CORE PIPE

5 TO RADIATOR

6 33 NM (24 FT LB)

7 COUPLED HOSE ASSY.

8 CONDENSER PIPES

9 O-RINGS

10 HIGH SIDE FITTING

11 TO RADIATOR

12 FITTINGS & HOSE ASM.

FRT

TYPICAL GASKET INSTALLATION

FRT

TO A/C MODULE

VIEW B

FWD

VIEW C

86816106

Fig. 26 Refrigerant lines and hose routing on the 2.5 (VIN R) engine

1—CAP
2—HOSE ASSEMBLY A/C
3—BOLT/SCREW
    9-11 N•m (7-8 LB. FT.)
4—CLAMP
5—RADIATOR HOSE
6—38-44 N•m (28-32 LB. FT.)
7—ACCUMULATOR
8—HEATER HOSE
9—SHOCK TOWER
10—BOLT/SCREW
    7-9 N•m (5-7 LB. FT.)
11—CLIP
12—BOLT/SCREW
13—BRACKET
14—BOLT/SCREW
    26-40 N•m (19-30 LB. FT.)
15—WASHER
16—"O" RING
17—CONDENSER ASSEMBLY
18—GROMMET
19—20-27 N•m (15-20 LB. FT.)
20—CLIP 11 IS TO BE ATTACHED TO
    BRACKET 12 BEFORE HOSE
    ASSEMBLY 2 IS ATTACHED TO
    ACCUMULATOR

86816105

Fig. 27 Refrigerant lines and hose routing on the 2.8 (VIN X and Z) engines

3. Disconnect the fitting, and the liquid line from the condenser outlet.

➡ **Cap the refrigerant lines when opening the system to prevent the entry of dirt and moisture and the loss of refrigerant lubricant.**

4. Remove the expansion tube (orifice) using the orifice remover. In the event of any difficulty in removal of a restricted or plugged tube (orifice), do the following:

  a. Remove as much of any impacted residue as possible.

  b. If the system has a pressure switch near the orifice tube location, it should be removed prior to the next step. This will prevent any damage to occur to the switch.

  c. Carefully apply heat with a heat gun (hair drier) approximately ¼ in. (6mm) from the dimples on the inlet pipe. Do not overheat the pipe.

  d. While applying heat, use the extractor tool to grip the orifice tube. Use a turning motion, along with a push-pull motion, to loosen the impacted orifice tube and remove it.
To install:

5. Install the orifice tube with the shorter screen end in first.

6. Connect the line to the condenser outlet, then tighten.

7. Lower the vehicle.

8. Evacuate, charge and preform a leak test on the system.

Manual Control Head

REMOVAL & INSTALLATION

▶ **See Figure 30**

1. Disconnect the negative battery cable.

2. Remove the hush panel, as required.

3. Remove the instrument panel trim plate.

4. Remove the control head attaching screws and pull the control head out.

5. Unplug the electrical and vacuum connectors at the back of the control head. Disconnect the temperature control cable.

6. Remove the control head.
To install:

7. Position the control head near the mounting location. Engage the electrical and vacuum connectors and cables to the back of the control head. Connect the temperature control cable.

8. Install the control head and attaching screws.

9. Install the instrument panel trim plate.

10. Install the hush panel, if removed.

11. Connect the negative battery cable. Tighten the cable bolt to 11 ft. lbs. (15 Nm).

12. Reset the radio, clock and any other applicable electronic devices.

Manual Control Cables

REMOVAL & INSTALLATION

▶ **See Figure 31**

1. Disconnect the negative battery cable.

2. Remove the temperature control assembly from the dash.

3. Remove the lower instrument panel sound insulator.

4. Tag and disconnect the cable(s) at the module.

5. Remove the cables.
To install:

6. Attach the cables in there proper locations, make sure any retaining clips are seated properly.

7. Install the lower instrument panel sound insulator.

8. Install the control assembly.

9. Adjust the cables as needed.

10. Connect the negative battery cable, tighten the cable bolt to 11 ft. lbs. (15 Nm).

11. Reset the radio, clock and any other applicable electronic devices.

VIEW A
& LB6

1	TUBE ASM. – EVAP. OUTLET & LB6
2	TUBE ASM – EVAP. INLET & LB6, LR8
3	BRACKET & LB6
4	CONDENSER OUTLET PIPE
5	ACCUMULATOR
6	EXPANSION TUBE (ORIFICE)

VIEW B

86816108

Fig. 28 Common location of an orifice in the A/C system

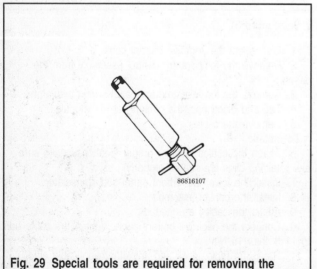

86816107

Fig. 29 Special tools are required for removing the orifice

ADJUSTMENT

Without Sliding Clips

1. Attach the cable to the control assembly.
2. Place the control lever in the **OFF** position.
3. Place the opposite loop of cable on the lever or actuator post.
4. Push the sheath toward the lever until the lever or actuator seats and the lash is out of the cable and control.
5. Tighten the screw to secure the cable.

With Sliding Clips

1. Place the control lever in the **COLD** position.
2. Place the clip of the cable on the heater case temperature door post.
3. Push the control head lever towards the **HOT** position, until the temperature door seats and the spring back is out of the cable and control.

1. NO BLOWER OPERATION WITH MODE LEVER IN "OFF" POSITION
2. IN THIS MODE LEVER POSITION, MAXIMUM COOLING IF OFFERED WITH THE CONDITIONED, RECIRCULATED AIR DISTRIBUTED THROUGH I/P. OUTLET.
3. CONDITIONED AIR IS DIRECTED THROUGH I.P.
4. CONDITIONED AIR IS DIRECTED THROUGH I.P. AND FLOOR DISTRIBUTOR OUTLETS WITH SOME ALSO TO WINDSHIELD
5. A NON-COMPRESSOR OPERATING POSITION, WITH OUTSIDE AIR DELIVERED THROUGH I.P. OUTLETS

6. A NON-COMPRESSOR OPERATING POSITION WITH OUTSIDE AIR DISTRIBUTED ABOUT 80% TO FLOOR (AND 20% TO WINDSHIELD AND SIDE WINDOWS).
7. CONDITIONED AIR DISTRIBUTED ABOUT 80% TO WINDSHIELD AND SIDE WINDOWS, AND 20% TO FLOOR
8. TEMPERATURE LEVER POSITION REGULATES TEMPERATURE OF THE AIR ENTERING THE PASSENGER COMPARTMENT BY CABLE OPERATION OF THE HEATER CORE TEMPERATURE DOOR
9. VACUUM OPERATED SYSTEM SELECTOR (MODE) LEVER
10. FAN CONTROL

86816109

Fig. 30 A/C manual control head

1. Defroster cable
2. Nut
3. Vent cable
4. Temperature cable
5. Control assembly
6. Bolt 13 inch lbs. (1.5 Nm)

VIEW A

86816113

Fig. 31 Control mounting and cable routing on the Pontiac wagon; others are similar

Electronic Climate Control Panel

REMOVAL & INSTALLATION

▶ See Figure 32

1. Disconnect the negative battery cable.
2. Remove the instrument panel trim plate(s) to gain access to the electronic control panel.
3. Remove the control panel attaching screws.
4. Pull the control panel out far enough to unplug the electrical connector. Remove control panel.

To install:

5. Engage the control panel electrical connector.
6. Install control panel attaching screws.
7. Install the instrument panel trim plate(s).
8. Connect the negative battery cable. Tighten the cable bolt to 11 ft. lbs. (15 Nm).
9. Reset the radio, clock and any other applicable electronic devices.

High-Pressure Compressor Cut-Off Switch

The function of the switch is to protect the engine from overheating in the event of excessively high compressor head pressure and to de-energize the compressor clutch before the high pressure relief valve discharge pressure is reached. The switch is mounted on the back of the compressor or on the refrigerant hose assembly near the back of the compressor. Servicing a switch mounted on the back of the compressor requires that the system be discharged. Switches mounted on the coupled hose assembly are mounted on Schrader-type valves and do not require discharging the system to be serviced.

1. Instrument panel assembly
2. Air conditioning and heater control
3. Radio
4. Screw

86816112

Fig. 32 The electronic climate control panel is located above the radio

REMOVAL & INSTALLATION

Compressor Mounted Switch

▶ See Figure 33

➡ Procedures for discharging and servicing the air conditioning system is described in Section 1. If a refrigerant recovery/recycling machine is not available, this job should be performed at a dealer or a shop that has the equipment.

1. Disconnect the negative battery cable.
2. Properly discharge the air conditioning system into a recovery/recycling machine.
3. Remove the coupled hose assembly at the rear of the compressor.
4. Unplug the electrical connector.
5. Remove the switch retaining ring using internal snapring pliers.
6. Remove the switch from the compressor. Discard the O-ring.

To install:

7. Lubricate a new O-ring with refrigerant oil. Insert into the switch cavity.
8. Lubricate the control switch housing with clean refrigerant oil and insert the switch until it bottoms in the cavity.
9. Install the switch retaining snapring with the high point of the curved sides adjacent to the switch housing. Ensure that the retaining ring is properly seated in the switch cavity retaining groove.
10. Engage the electrical connector.
11. Lubricate new coupled hose assembly O-rings with refrigerant oil. Install on the hose assembly fittings.
12. Connect the coupled hose assembly to the compressor.
13. Connect the negative battery cable. Tighten the cable bolt to 11 ft. lbs. (15 Nm).
14. Evacuate, recharge and leak test the system.
15. Operate the system to ensure proper operation and leak test the switch.
16. Reset the radio, clock and any other applicable electronic devices.

Refrigerant Line Mounted Switch

1. Disconnect the negative battery cable.
2. Unplug the electrical connector.
3. Remove the switch from the coupled hose assembly. Discard the O-ring.

To install:

4. Lubricate a new O-ring with refrigerant oil.
5. Install the O-ring on the switch and install the switch.
6. Engage the electrical connector.
7. Connect the negative battery cable. Tighten the cable bolt to 11 ft. lbs. (15 Nm).
8. Reset the radio, clock and any other applicable electronic devices.

1 A/C COMPRESSOR
2 A/C HIGH PRESSURE CUT-OUT SWITCH CONNECTOR
3 HARNESS RETAINER
4 BOLT/SCREW
5 POWER STEERING PIPES
6 RETAINER
7 BOLT/SCREW 10 N·m (88 LB. IN.)
8 A/C COMPRESSOR CLUTCH CONNECTOR

86816110

Fig. 33 Compressor mounted switch — 3.3L (VIN N) shown

Low-Pressure Compressor Cut-Off Switch

The function of the switch is to protect the compressor by de-energizing the compressor in the event of a low-charge condition. The switch may be mounted at the back of the compressor or on the coupled hose assembly near the compressor. Servicing the valve requires discharging the system.

REMOVAL & INSTALLATION

➡Procedures for discharging and servicing the air conditioning system is described in Section 1. If a refrigerant recovery/recycling machine is not available, this job should be performed at a dealer or a shop that has the equipment.

1. Disconnect the negative battery cable.
2. Properly discharge the air conditioning system into a recovery/recycling machine.

3. Unplug the electrical connector(s).
4. If the switch is mounted to the rear head of the compressor, remove the coupled hose assembly to gain access to the switch. Remove the switch.
5. If the switch is mounted to the coupled hose assembly, remove the switch from its mounting position.
   To install:
6. Install the switch.
7. Lubricate new O-rings with refrigerant oil.
8. If the switch is mounted to the rear head of the compressor, install the switch. Install new O-rings on the coupled hose assembly and install the assembly to the back of the compressor.
9. If the switch is mounted on the coupled hose assembly, install the switch.
10. Engage the electrical connector(s).
11. Connect the negative battery cable. Tighten the cable bolt to 11 ft. lbs. (15 Nm).
12. Evacuate, charge and leak test the system.
13. Reset the radio, clock and any other applicable electronic devices.

Idle Speed Power Steering Pressure Switch

Engine idle speed is maintained by cutting off the compressor when high power steering loads are imposed at idle. The switch is located on the pinion housing portion of the steering rack.

REMOVAL & INSTALLATION

1. Disconnect the negative battery cable.
2. Unplug the electrical connector.
3. Unscrew the switch.
   To install:
4. Install the switch.
5. Engage the electrical connector.
6. Connect the negative battery cable. Tighten the cable bolt to 11 ft. lbs. (15 Nm).
7. Allow the engine to reach normal operating temperature and confirm the proper operation of the switch.
8. Reset the radio, clock and any other applicable electronic devices.

Pressure Cycling Switch

The pressure cycling switch controls the refrigeration cycle by sensing low-side pressure as an indicator of evaporator temperature. The pressure cycling switch is the freeze-protection device in the system. The switch is mounted on a Schrader valve on the accumulator.

REMOVAL & INSTALLATION

◗ See Figure 34

➡ The system need not be discharged to remove the pressure cycling switch.

1. Disconnect the negative battery cable.
2. Unplug the electrical connector.
3. Remove the switch and O-ring seal. Discard the O-ring.

To install:

4. Install a new O-ring. Lubricate with refrigerant oil.
5. Install the switch to the accumulator.
6. Engage the electrical connector.
7. Connect the negative battery cable. Tighten the cable bolt to 11 ft. lbs. (15 Nm).
8. Reset the radio, clock and any other applicable electronic devices.

1	PRESSURE CYCLING SWITCH
2	ACCUMULATOR HOSE
3	ACCUMULATOR
4	CONDENSER HOSE
5	ENGINE WIRING HARNESS

86816111

Fig. 34 The pressure cycling switch is located on the accumulator

CRUISE CONTROL SYSTEMS

General Description

Cruise control is a speed control system which maintains a desired vehicle speed under normal driving conditions. Steep grades either up or down, may cause some variation in the set speed. Speed is maintained only by mechanically holding the throttle open or releasing it. The system cannot apply braking to slow the vehicle.

Most systems use vacuum to operate a throttle servo unit. The servo unit maintains a desired speed by trapping vacuum when the servo is at the desired position. The position of the servo and the vehicle speed are overseen by the controller or Cruise Control Module (CCM), this unit controls the input or release of vacuum within the servo, thus adjusting the throttle to maintain speed.

Some models may use an Electro Motor Cruise (EMC) system. The EMC uses an electric motor and connecting strap to vary the throttle angle according to directions from the CCM. The system is completely independent of vacuum and allows smoother throttle transitions.

Although the systems vary widely across GM's model line (component location, circuitry, interaction of computers, etc.) all cruise control units share certain common traits:
• The system will not engage until the vehicle exceeds a minimum speed, usually 25 mph (40 kph).
• The system provides several modes of operation including cruise, coast, resume/accelerate, most allow "tap up" and "tap down", an incremental increase or decrease in set speed.
• All have a system **ON/OFF** switch, the system must be turned **ON** before it will engage. Many have a pilot light on the dash which illuminates when the cruise control is engaged.
• All systems will disconnect if the brake and/or clutch pedal is depressed when the system is engaged. The vacuum sustained systems release vacuum as well as interrupting the electrical signal to the controller.

• The accelerator may be depressed at any time to override the chosen cruising speed. If the system receives no new orders, it will remember the previous cruising speed and return to it when the driver finishes accelerating.
• Failures in the cruise control may stem from electrical, mechanical and/or vacuum problems within the cruise control system or any combination of these.

➡**The use of the speed control is not recommended when driving conditions do not permit maintaining a constant speed. These conditions may include heavy or varying traffic, winding roads or slippery surfaces.**

The main parts of the vacuum systems are the:
• Mode control switches
• Cruise Control Module (CCM)
• Servo unit
• Vehicle Speed Sensor (VSS)
• Vacuum supply
• Electrical and vacuum release switches
• Electrical harness

SYSTEM OPERATION

For any of the following conditions to occur, the vehicle must be moving above 25 mph (40 kph) and the cruise control system switch must be switched **ON**. If either of these basics change, the system will cease to operate.

Set and Coast

When the vehicle is at the desired speed, engage the SET/COAST button momentarily. This button is usually at the end of the stalk and is pushed inward to engage it. Vehicle speed will be maintained within 1 mph (2 kph) of the speed the vehicle was traveling when the button was pushed. The system will maintain this speed until:

- The brake or clutch pedals move enough to disengage the system.
- A system control switch is used to send a new message to the controller.
- The system switch is turned **OFF**.
- The ignition is switched **OFF**.

If only the brake or clutch pedal is moved, the system disconnects the cruise function but remembers the set speed and can return to it. Pushing a system control button or turning the system off removes memory of the previous speed.

Once the vehicle is holding the desired speed, the SET/COAST button may be used to slow the vehicle. Holding the button in will disconnect the system as long as the button is held. Once the car has slowed to the new desired speed, releasing the button will cause the system to hold the new, slower speed.

If the driver accelerates beyond the set cruising speed, pushing the SET/COAST button causes the system to maintain the new higher speed. If the button is not engaged at the higher speed, the system will maintain the previous set speed after the vehicle slows.

Resume and Accelerate

The RESUME/ACCEL switch is used after braking to tell the system to return to the previous speed. The switch must be moved momentarily into engagement, less than one second for most systems. If held too long, the system enters the ACCEL mode.

The ACCEL mode, when engaged, will accelerate the vehicle from the present set speed, when the switch is released, the new (higher) speed will be set and maintained.

Tap-Up and Tap-Down

Many of the GM systems are programmed to obey momentary signals from the SET/COAST and RESUME/ACCEL switches. If the SET/COAST switch is tapped or engaged for less than one second, the controller will reduce the car speed by 1 mph (2 kph) per tap. Similarly, if the RESUME/ACCEL switch is momentarily engaged, the set speed will increase by 1 mph (2 kph) per tap. This is a particularly handy function for fine tuning vehicle speed to prevailing limits, weather or traffic conditions.

If either switch is held too long, the system enters either the COAST or ACCEL mode. When the driver next releases the switch, the system will note and maintain the new speed.

SYSTEM COMPONENTS

Vacuum Servo Unit

The servo operates the throttle in response to signals from the controller. The servo consists of a vacuum operated diaphragm, a normally open solenoid valve to vent the diaphragm chamber to atmosphere, a normally closed solenoid valve to connect the diaphragm chamber to the vacuum source, and a variable inductance position sensor. Under normal operating conditions, the controller reacts to 3 vehicle or system states.

STEADY CRUISE STATE

Both vacuum and vent valves are closed or sealed. The servo has a constant vacuum on the diaphragm and places no flow requirements on the vacuum source. Vacuum is trapped in diaphragm chamber.

VEHICLE LOSING SPEED

The controller energizes the vacuum solenoid, opening the vacuum valve to the vacuum source. This increases the vacuum level in the servo to increase the throttle opening. The vent remains closed.

VEHICLE GAINING SPEED

The controller de-energizes the vent solenoid, opening the vent valve to the atmosphere. This reduces vacuum in the servo and allows the throttle return spring to decrease the throttle opening. The vacuum inlet valve remains closed. When the controller senses an over or underspeed condition, it will pulse the opening of the vent or vacuum valve. The controller pulse will be repeated, as required, until the speed correction brings the vehicle to the set speed.

Under normal road conditions, the vacuum valve will remain in a completely open position when vehicle speed has dropped 5 mph (8 kph) below set speed. Likewise, if vehicle speed is 3 (5 kph) or more mph over the set speed, such as down a steep grade, the vent will go into full open position.

When the cruise system is on and operating with no input from the driver through the control switches, no correction to the speed will be made until the vehicle deviates 1/2 mph (.8 kph) from the set speed.

The servo incorporates a steel core which moves within a coil. Its resulting variable inductance provides a continuous voltage signal to the controller. The servo position signal is constantly compared to the vehicle speed signal. This comparison determines if the pulses issued have corrected the speed error or if additional pulses are required. This comparison is also used to lengthen the average pulse when it is not enough to compensate for the speed error, such as a steep grade.

EMC Controller/Actuator

The Electro-Motor Cruise (EMC) system eliminates the vacuum servo and incorporates the controller and actuator into a single unit. The control assembly consists of the electronic controller board, a solenoid operated clutch, the drum gear and strap (connected to the throttle linkage) and a stepper motor with 3-phase wiring and 4-pole stator.

When the vehicle speed is set or changed, the controller assembly adjusts throttle position by activating the stepper motor. The motor provides rotation in either direction through the use of 3 drive transistors. As the rotor turns, a pinion gear drives the drum gear assembly, causing the strap to wind or unwind on the drum. The strap pulls or releases the throttle linkage accordingly.

If the system is turned off or deactivated for any reason, the controller de-energizes the solenoid operated clutch. The spring on the clutch arm pushes the pinion away from the drum gear and a spring within the drum unwinds the strap. The throttle linkage is released and returns to the idle position until a new speed is set by the operator.

Electronic Controller (Module)

The controller interprets the position of the servo or electric motor, the position of the control switches and the output of the speed sensor. In response to these inputs, the controller electrically signals the opening or closing of the vent and vacuum solenoid valves in the servo or the rotation of the actuator motor.

The control functions may be performed by either a separate controller (stand alone system) or through the engine control module (integrated system). The stand alone controller uses a quartz crystal to produce clock signals for the integrated circuits within. The ECU/PCM can perform the same functions to control the system. Integrated systems also receive input from the neutral safety switch, many of these systems receive a throttle position signal instead of servo position signal.

Vehicle Speed Sensor (VSS)

OPTICAL VSS AND BUFFER AMPLIFIER

There are 2 types of VSS buffer amplifiers, single or dual output. The optic head portion of the VSS is located in the speedometer frame. A reflective blade is attached to the speedometer cable/head assembly. The blade spins like a propeller, with its blades passing through a light beam from a LED in the optic head. As each blade enters the LED light beam, light is reflected back to a photocell in the optic head, causing a low power speed signal to be sent to the buffer for amplification and signal conditioning. The switching transistor within the buffer provides the speed signal to the ECM/PCM and/or cruise control module.

PM GENERATOR

▶ See Figure 35

This device supplies the vehicle speed input to the controller on some cars. Vehicle speed information is provided to the controller by a Permanent Magnet (PM) generator driven by the transmission/transaxle. The PM generator produces an AC sine wave signal. Through use of an integrator and Schmitt Trigger, the signal is converted to square wave DC. Since cruise control is not the only function requiring VSS input, these signals are sent to various control units on the vehicle. Depending on the model, the speed signal may be used by the speedometer.

Vacuum Accumulator

Found on most systems (except those with diesel engines), the familiar ball-shaped vacuum accumulator is used to maintain satisfactory cruise control performance in vehicles with low manifold vacuum at normal road speeds. The accumulator is connected to the intake manifold through a one way check valve and "stores" the high vacuum level that is available during periods of low engine loading. The system operates on accumulator vacuum when it is higher than manifold vacuum.

System Service Precautions

✳✳CAUTION

Some vehicles are equipped with the Supplemental Inflatable Restraint (SIR) system. This system must be disabled before performing service on or around the air bag, instrument panel components, wiring and sensors. Failure to follow safety and disabling procedures could result in accidental air bag deployment, possible personal injury and unnecessary air bag system repairs.

• Never unplug any electrical connection with the ignition switch **ON**.
• Always wear a grounded wrist static strap when servicing any control module or component labeled with a Electrostatic Discharge (ESD) sensitive device symbol.
• Avoid touching module connector pins.
• Leave new components and modules in the shipping package until ready to install them.
• Always touch a vehicle ground after sliding across a vehicle seat or walking across vinyl or carpeted floors to avoid static charge damage.
• Never allow welding cables to lie on, near or across any vehicle electrical wiring.
• Do not allow extension cords for power tools or droplights to lie on, near or across any vehicle electrical wiring.
• Do not operate the cruise control or the engine with the drive wheels off the ground.

Electric Release Switch and Vacuum Release Valve

REMOVAL & INSTALLATION

▶ See Figure 36

1. At the brake switch, unplug either the 2 electrical connectors or the electrical connector and the vacuum hose.
2. Remove the cruise control switch and the stop lamp switch from the retainers.
3. Remove the tubular retainer from the brake pedal mounting bracket.

To install:

4. Install the tubular retainer to the brake pedal mounting bracket.
5. Press the brake pedal, then install the cruise control and stop lamp switch into the retainer until fully seated in the clips.
6. Connect the wiring and/or vacuum lines. Adjust the switch.

ADJUSTMENT

1. Depress the brake pedal and check that the release switch is fully seated in the clips.
2. Slowly pull the brake pedal back to the at-rest position. The switch and valve assembly will move within the clips to the adjusted position.

Fig. 35 The VSS permanent magnet generator (PM) electrical schematic

1 — PEDAL ASSEMBLY, BRAKE
2 — RETAINER, STOPLAMP SWITCH
3 — SWITCH ASSEMBLY, STOPLAMP
4 — SWITCH ASSEMBLY, CRUISE CONTROL
5 — RETAINER, CRUISE CONTROL SWITCH
6 — BRACKET, BRAKE PEDAL

86816115

Fig. 36 The stoplamp and cruise control switches are mounted on the pedal bracket

3. Measure the pedal travel and check switch engagement. The electric brake release switch contacts must open within 1/8-1/2 in. (3-13mm) of pedal travel when measured at the centerline of the pedal pad. The brake lights should illuminate after another 3/16 in. (5mm) of travel. The vacuum release should engage within 5/8-1 in. (16-25mm) of pedal travel.

Vacuum Servo Unit

REMOVAL & INSTALLATION

▶ See Figure 37

1. Unplug the electrical connector and vacuum hoses at the servo.
2. Disconnect the actuating chain, cable or rod from the servo.
3. Remove the screws securing the vacuum servo and solenoid unit to the bracket and remove the unit.

INTERNAL VIEW

TO VACUUM SUPPLY

TO VACUUM BRAKE RELEASE VALVE

1 — SERVO
2 — VACUUM SOLENOID AND VALVE (NORMALLY CLOSED)
3 — COIL
4 — VARIABLE INDUCTANCE POSITION SENSOR
5 — VENT SOLENOID AND VALVE (NORMALLY OPEN)
6 — STEEL CORE
7 — THROTTLE ATTACHMENT

86816116

Fig. 37 Cruise control servo unit components

To install:

4. Connect the large diameter brake release vacuum line to the servo unit. Connect the vacuum hose from the vacuum control valve to the servo unit.
5. Connect the actuating chain, rod or cable to the servo.
6. Install the servo unit to the bracket, then tighten the screws to 12 inch lbs. (1 Nm).
7. Engage the electrical connector to the servo.
8. Adjust the cable, rod or chain.

LINKAGE ADJUSTMENT

➡ Do not stretch cables or chains to make pins fit or holes align. This will prevent the engine from returning to idle.

Cable Type

▶ See Figure 38

1. Check that the cable is properly installed and that the throttle is closed to the idle position.
2. Pull the servo end of the cable toward the linkage bracket of the servo. Place the servo connector in one of the 6 holes in the bracket which allows the least amount of slack and does not move the throttle linkage.
3. Install the retainer clip. Check that the throttle linkage is still in the idle position.

Rod With Screw Adjuster

▶ See Figure 39

1. Inspect the rod assembly for proper attachment to the servo and throttle stud. Make certain the throttle is at idle.
2. Adjust the slotted bracket or the rod to obtain a clearance of 0.02-0.04 in. (0.5-1.0mm) between the throttle stud and the end of the bracket slot.
3. Install the retainer clip, then make certain the throttle is still at idle.

Rod With Adjustment Holes

1. Inspect the rod to be sure it is securely connected to the servo and throttle linkage, make certain that the throttle is at idle.
2. Install the retainer pin in the hole which provides the least slack between the servo bracket and the retainer.
3. Check the throttle, it must still be in the idle position.

Chain and Cable

▶ See Figures 40 and 41

1. If the chain is connected at the throttle perform the following:
   a. Check for proper installation of cable assembly. Inspect the throttle, it must be in the idle position.
   b. Install the chain in the swivel so that the slack does not exceed 1/2 the diameter of the ball stud.
   c. Install the retainer on the swivel and make sure the throttle has not move from idle.
2. If the chain is connected at the servo, perform the following:
   a. Check for proper installation of cable assembly. Inspect the throttle, it must be in the idle position.

Fig. 38 Cable type servo unit

Fig. 39 Rod type servo unit with the screw adjuster

Fig. 40 On some servo units, the chain is connected to the throttle lever

b. Install the cable on the third link of the chain, then adjust the jam nuts of the servo until there is no noticeable slack in the chain.

c. Tighten the jam nuts, then check that the throttle has not moved out of the idle position.

Cruise Control Multi Function Lever

REMOVAL & INSTALLATION

❋❋CAUTION

Some vehicles are equipped with the Supplemental Inflatable Restraint (SIR) system. This system must be disabled before performing service on or around the air bag, instrument panel components, wiring and sensors. Failure to follow safety and disabling procedures could result in accidental air bag deployment, possible personal injury and unnecessary air bag system repairs.

1. Disable the SIR system, if equipped.
2. Disconnect the negative battery terminal.
3. Unplug the cruise control switch connector at the base of steering column. It may be necessary to remove an under dash panel or trim piece for access.
4. Make sure the lever is in the **CENTER** or **OFF** position.
5. Pull the lever straight out of the retaining clip within the steering column.
6. Attach mechanic's wire or similar pull wire to the connector. Gently pull the harness through the column, leaving the pull wire in place.
   To install:
7. Place the transmission selector in **LOW** or **1**. Attach the mechanic's wire to the connector. Gently pull the harness into place, checking that the harness is completely clear of any moving or movable components such as tilt-column, telescoping column, brake pedal linkage, etc.
8. Position the lever and push it squarely into the retainer until it snaps in place.

Fig. 41 On other units, the chain is connected to the servo

9. Remove the mechanic's wire and engage the cruise control harness connector.

10. Reinstall any panels or insulation which were removed for access.

11. Connect the negative battery terminal.

12. Enable the SIR system.

13. Reset the radio, clock ect. as necessary.

Vehicle Speed Sensor (VSS)

REMOVAL & INSTALLATION

✴✴CAUTION

Some vehicles are equipped with the Supplemental Inflatable Restraint (SIR) system. This system must be disabled before performing service on or around the air bag, instrument panel components, wiring and sensors. Failure to follow safety and disabling procedures could result in accidental air bag deployment, possible personal injury and unnecessary air bag system repairs.

Optical Type With Buffer

1. Disable the SIR system, if equipped.
2. Disconnect the negative battery cable.
3. To gain access to the sensor and buffer behind the speedometer, the instrument cluster must be partially removed. When doing so, unplug the harness connector at the rear of the cluster. If the cluster is pulled too far outward with the harness attached, both may be damaged.
4. Unplug the amplifier connector.
5. Remove the speed sensor attaching screw and remove the sensor through the opening in the base of the instrument panel.

To install:
6. Route the sensor wire connector and harness through the opening in the base of the instrument panel.
7. Install the sensor on its bracket and install the retaining screw.
8. Engage the amplifier connector.
9. Reinstall the instrument cluster and connect the electrical harness.
10. Connect the negative battery cable. Tighten the cable bolt to 11 ft. lbs. (15 Nm).
11. Reset the radio, clock and any other applicable electronic devices.

Permanent Magnet Type
▶ See Figure 42

1. On some models, it will be easier to access the speed sensor with the wheel removed. If so, loosen the wheel lugs, then raise and support the vehicle. Remove the wheel.
2. Disconnect the wiring harness from the speed sensor. If the sensor also contains the speedometer cable, remove the cable.
3. Remove the retainer clip or screw depending on what your vehicle uses.
4. Carefully lift the sensor out of the transmission.

Fig. 42 Permanent magnet speed sensor location on the 4T60-E transaxle

5. Remove the O-ring.
To install:
6. Lubricate a new O-ring with appropriate transmission fluid and install the ring on the sensor.
7. Install the sensor and secure the retaining clip, or tighten the screw to 98 inch lbs. (11 Nm).
8. Connect the speedometer cable if it was removed, then engage the wiring harness. Make certain the harness is routed clear of moving or hot components.
9. If applicable, install the right front wheel, then lower the vehicle.

Vacuum Reservoir

REMOVAL & INSTALLATION

▶ See Figure 43

Disconnect the vacuum line, then remove the retaining screws and the reservoir. When reinstalling, tighten the retaining screws to 53-88 inch lbs. (6-10 Nm).

Cruise Control Module

REMOVAL & INSTALLATION

Accelerator Bracket Mounted
▶ See Figure 44

1. Disconnect the negative battery cable.
2. The cruise control module is located on a bracket mounted above the accelerator pedal. Disconnect the wiring harness from the module.
3. Remove the bracket and module assembly from the accelerator bracket.
4. Release the lock tab and remove the module.
To install:
5. Fit the module to its bracket and secure the lock tab.

1 CANISTER ASSEMBLY, VAPOR
2 BOLT/SCREW, HEATER AND A/C CONTROL VACUUM
3 TANK ASSEMBLY, HEATER AND A/C CONTROL VACUUM
4 NUT, HEATER AND A/C CONTROL VACUUM TANK

86816125

Fig. 43 Disconnect the vacuum line, remove the retaining screws and remove the reservoir

1 Bracket
2 Cruise control module
3 Accelerator bracket
4 Lock tab

86816127

Fig. 44 The cruise control module is mounted on a bracket above the accelerator pedal

6. Install the module assembly to the accelerator bracket.
7. Connect the module wiring harness.
8. Connect the negative battery cable, then reset the radio, clock ect. as necessary.

Under Dash Mounted
▶ See Figure 45

1. Disconnect the negative battery cable.
2. Remove the left side sound insulator.
3. Disconnect the electrical harness from the module.
4. Remove the push-in retainers, then pull the module out of it's mounting area.
To install:
5. Mount the module with the push-in retainers.
6. Connect the electrical harness on the module.
7. Install the left sound insulator.
8. Connect the negative battery cable, then reset the radio, clock ect. as necessary.

Wheelhousing Mounted
▶ See Figure 46

1. Open the hood, then disconnect the negative battery cable.
2. Remove the mounting bolts securing the module on the left wheelhousing.
3. Disconnect the wiring harness, then remove the module.
To install:
4. Attach the wiring harness to the module.
5. Mount the module in place using the mounting bolts, tighten the bolts to 36 inch lbs. (4 Nm).
6. Connect the negative battery cable, then reset the radio, clock ect. as necessary.

Cruise Control Basic Tests

PRELIMINARY CHECKS

Improper operation can be caused by any combination of mechanical, electrical and vacuum problems. In resolving any cruise system operating problem, always ensure there are no bare, broken, or disconnected wires or any pinched, damaged, or disconnected vacuum hoses. The servo and throttle linkage should operate freely and smoothly.

Since any problem in this system may be due to one or more causes, a quick visual inspection should always be made before beginning extended diagnosis. This can be done by eliminating an obvious vacuum, mechanical or electrical problem. Start the engine and use a vacuum gauge to confirm vacuum at the servo. Check the related fuse(s) and look for loose or corroded harness connectors. Inspect the brake and clutch switches for loose wires or hoses. Check that the switch plunger moves smoothly and is not stuck in the disconnect position. Inspect the throttle linkage from the servo for binding, breakage or excess slack.

➡If the speedometer is not operating correctly, vehicles using optic vehicle speed sensors will not provide the correct speed signal to the cruise control module.

ROAD TEST

1. With the cruise control switch **OFF**, drive the car to highway speeds. Depress the SET switch button, then release. The system should remain inoperative.
2. Set the cruise control system switch to **ON**.
3. Engage the system, by momentarily depressing the SET button, then releasing it at approximately 50 mph, then remove your foot from the accelerator. The vehicle should maintain speed.
4. Push the RESUME/ACCEL switch and hold. The vehicle should accelerate at a controlled rate. Release the slide to engage the system at a cruise speed of approximately 55 mph (88 kph). The system should now be set at this new speed, and the vehicle should maintain that speed.
5. Depress the brake pedal about ½ in. (13mm), the indicator light, if equipped, should go out. This confirms the action of the electric brake release switch, and the vehicle should start

1 RETAINER, CRUISE CONTROL MODULE BRACKET
2 BOLT/SCREW, CRUISE CONTROL MODULE BRACKET
3 MODULE ASSEMBLY, CRUISE CONTROL
4 BRACKET, CRUISE CONTROL MODULE
5 MODULE, DIAGNOSTIC ENERGY RESERVE

86816128

Fig. 45 On some models, the cruise control module is located under the dash behind the left sound insulator

1 BOLT/SCREW, CRUISE CONTROL MODULE BRACKET
2 BRACKET, CRUISE CONTROL MODULE
3 MODULE ASSEMBLY, CRUISE CONTROL
4 PANEL, LH WHEELHOUSE

86816126

Fig. 46 On 1994-95 models, the module is mounted on the wheelhousing

to slow down. Allow the vehicle to slow to approximately 45 mph, using the brakes if desired.

6. Momentarily push the RESUME/ACCEL switch, then release. The vehicle should accelerate at a controlled rate and resume previously set speed of about 55 mph (88 kph), and maintain that speed. The indicator light (if equipped) should come on when the slide switch is released.

7. Depress the SET/COAST button and hold. The indicator light (if equipped) should go out. Coast to 50 mph. with the button pressed.

8. Release the SET/COAST button to engage the system at 50 mph (81 kph). The vehicle should maintain the new speed.

9. Check the tap-down feature. Depress the SET/COAST button for less than ½ second (tap). The vehicle speed should drop about 1 mph (2 kph). Tap the button a couple more times to check incremental speed decreases.

10. Check the tap-up feature. Actuate the RESUME/ACCEL for less than ½ second (tap). The vehicle speed should increase about 1 mph (2 kph). Tap the switch a couple more times to check incremental speed increases.

11. If all functional conditions are met during this test, the system is O.K.

Cruise System Surges

1. The servo and throttle linkages should operate freely and smoothly. This linkage should be adjusted if necessary.
2. Check the hose routing for pinches, leaks or restrictions.

Cruise Set Speed High or Low

1. Check the vacuum hoses for proper routing, restrictions or leaks. Adjust or replace as required.
2. Check the servo linkage for excess slack and adjust, if necessary.
3. If no system problem is noted, replace the controller.

Excessive Cruise Speed Loss On Hills

1. Check all the hoses for vacuum leaks.
2. Determine if the check valve to the vacuum accumulator is functional.

Cruise Tap-Up and Tap-Down

If all other functions of cruise control are operating correctly except the tap-up and/or tap-down, the controller is faulty.

SYSTEM TESTING

▶ **See Figure 47**

The use of tool J-34185, Cruise Control Quick Checker or its equivalent is recommended for vacuum operated systems. The checker connects to the harness in place of the module. It allows manual system testing and can considerably reduce diagnostic time. A test lamp may be required during some tests.

➡ **All systems rely on proper battery voltage to operate. Ensure the battery is correctly charged before beginning diagnostics. Do not allow battery to drain during extended testing. Turn system switch or ignition switch OFF when not actively testing the system. Involved testing and special tools are required for most testing. This would be best left to a professional shop with the necessary test equipment, as the cost involved for the tools is usually more than the cost of the repairs.**

Fig. 47 Special tools are available to test the cruise control system

RADIO

Radio Receiver/Tape Player/CD Player

▶ **See Figure 48**

✳✳WARNING

Some vehicles are equipped with an anti-theft radio system. Please refer to your owners manual or consult a dealer about any special procedures applicable to your system.

1. Disconnect the negative battery cable.
2. Remove the instrument panel insulator mounting screws enough to remove the steering column trim cover.
3. On some models it will be necessary to:
   a. Remove the ash tray, then the ash tray/fuse block assembly. Separate the fuse block and the ash tray. Push forward to access the cigarette lighter and the rear defogger switch.
   b. Disconnect the lighter and the defogger switch connectors.
   c. Remove the cigarette lighter, the glove box.
4. Remove the instrument panel center trim mounting nuts and the trim panel enough to unplug the radio.
5. Remove the radio mounting screws from the bracket(s), then pull the radio out enough to remove the electrical harness and the antenna lead.
   To install:
6. Connect the electrical harness and the antenna lead.
7. Slide the radio into the mounting area, then install the radio attaching bolts to the bracket(s).
8. Install the instrument cluster trim plate.
9. Install the accessory trim plate.

1. Radio
2. Screw on side of radio fits here
3. Retainer
4. Grille
5. Speaker
6. Front speaker assembly
7. Front speaker assembly
8. Rear speaker wire
9. Antenna
10. Rear speakers
11. Front speakers
12. I.P. harness
13. Receiver assembly
14. I.P. harness

86816135

Fig. 48 Radio mounting on the Buick's; other models are similar

10. Connect the negative battery cable. Tighten the cable bolt to 11 ft. lbs. (15 Nm).

11. Reset the radio, clock and any other applicable electronic devices.

Fixed Antenna

REMOVAL & INSTALLATION

Fender Mounted

▶ **See Figures 49 and 50**

1. Remove the steel mast from the antenna base.

2. Loosen the antenna escutcheon nut on top of the fender using a special tool J-28641 or an equivalent.

3. Remove the two side mounting bolts through the engine compartment.

4. On some models you will need to remove the right sound insulator and shroud panel to access the antenna cable.

5. Disconnect the antenna lead in the cable.

6. On some models you will need to:

a. Raise and support the car, to remove the inner fender clips and screws.

b. Pull back the inner fender strip and remove the escutcheon nut. Remove the antenna base assembly.

7. Inspect the grommet in the fender wheel for cracks or distortion of any kind.

To install:

8. Replace the grommet if needed.

9. Slide the new antenna into place, with the antenna lead attached.

10. Install the escutcheon nut. Attach the inner fender clips and screws, then lower the vehicle.

11. Tighten the two mounting bolts in the engine compartment, then tighten the antenna escutcheon nut.

12. Install the antenna mast to the base.

13. Reinstall the right shroud panel and sound insulator.

J-28641
Antenna Nut Socket
86816137

Fig. 49 Loosen the antenna escutcheon nut on top of the fender using special tool J-28641 or an equivalent

Fig. 50 Exploded view of the fixed antenna components

Windsheild Mounted

▶ **See Figure 51**

The pigtail from the glass to the lead-in can be replaced by carefully cutting away the sealer, removing the pigtail and soldering a new pigtail to the copper plate. Use a rosin core solder and only enough heat to obtain a good solder joint. Reseal with RTV. Body sealer should not be used. To replace the lead-in:

1. Disconnect the lead-in from the radio.
2. Connect a 3 ft. length of wire to the lead-in connector to aid in pulling the new lead-in into place.
3. Remove the lower windshield reveal moulding and the air inlet grille.
4. Unplug the pigtail connector from the antenna lead-in connector at the cowl.
5. Remove the two attaching screws and the antenna lead-in to the cowl.
6. Pull the lead-in out until the wire attached in the previous step is accessible. Disconnect the wire from the lead-in.

To install:

7. Wrap the pull-in wire around the new antenna lead-in and start feeding the lead-in through the cowl.
8. Apply RTV sealer to the cowl where the lead-in attaches to the cowl.
9. Pull the lead-in into place, then install the attaching screws.
10. Engage the pigtail connector to the antenna lead-in.
11. Install the air inlet grille and the reveal moulding.
12. Remove the pull-in wire from the antenna lead-in connector, then plug the lead-in into the radio.

Power Antenna

REMOVAL & INSTALLATION

▶ **See Figure 52**

```
RADIO   ANTENNA
```

WINDSHIELD

Antenna wires (2) are laminated between the glass.

SIDE VIEW

RUBBER COVERED CONNECTOR FROM ANTENNA

INNER PLENUM SECTION OF DASH

CONNECTOR SOLDERED TO ANTENNA WIRES IN WINDSHIELD

ANTENNA LEAD-IN TO RADIO

IMPORTANT
For maximum efficiency, the antenna trimmer must be adjusted to exact peak (loudest signal) with radio tuned to a weak station near 1400 KHz (14) and volumn on full.
TO TEST ANTENNA FOR SHORT CIRCUIT
1. Remove antenna lead-in from radio.
2. Connect 12 volt test light to 12 volt source and to antenna lead-in center terminal.
   A. If test light is "OFF", antenna is not shorted.
   B. If test light is "ON", disconnect antenna from lead-in socket at base of windshield. If test light turns off, short circuit was in short wire to windshield.
      Tape it and position it to prevent short circuit from occuring. If test light stays on, remove lead-in and repair or replace as required.

A whip antenna can be adjusted to 25-30 inches and temporarily connected to the radio to determine if antenna or lead-in is at fault. If there is considerable improvement in reception, the connector at the base of the windshield should be inspected for corrosion and loose connections. The antenna wires can be visually inspected for breaks. A crack in the glass across one of the wires would probably break the wire. If the problem is in the antenna wires or wire to the connector and cannot be repaired, a whip antenna can be installed or the windshield replaced.

86816139

Fig. 51 Windshield antenna test

Front Mounted

1. Disconnect the negative battery cable.
2. Remove the instrument panel sound absorber pad.
3. Unplug the antenna lead-in and harness connector from the relay assembly.
4. Apply masking tape to the rear edge of the fender and door.
5. If required, remove the inner to outer fender retaining screws.
6. If required, raise the vehicle and support it safely, then remove the associated front wheel assembly.
7. Remove the lower rocker panel retaining screws, lower fender-to-body retaining bolt and remove the lower rocker panel, as required.
8. Remove the inner splash shield from the fender, as required.
9. Remove the upper antenna retaining nut, using an appropriately tool.
10. Remove the antenna-to-bracket retaining bolts, then remove the antenna.

To install:

11. Fit the antenna into position, then loosely install the antenna gasket and upper nut.
12. Loosely install the antenna to bracket retaining bolts.
13. Tighten the upper antenna retaining nut, using the appropriately tool, then tighten the antenna to bracket retaining bolts.

14. Complete installation in the reverse order of the removal procedure.
15. Apply silicone grease to the harness connector before reconnecting.
16. Check the operation of the antenna mast. Reset the radio and clock, if required.

Rear Mounted

1. Disconnect the negative battery cable.
2. From inside the trunk, remove the trim panel from either the right or left rear wheel area.
3. Remove the antenna mounting bracket retaining screws.
4. Remove the upper antenna nut and bezel from the antenna, using an appropriately tool.
5. Remove the lead-in cable and wiring connector.
6. Remove the antenna assembly from the vehicle.

To install:

7. Fit the antenna to the vehicle, then connect the lead-in cable.
8. Install the nut and bezel to the antenna and mounting bracket retaining screws.
9. Apply silicone grease to the harness connector before reconnecting.
10. Install the trim panel and reconnect the negative battery cable.
11. Check the operation of the antenna mast. Reset the radio and clock, if required.

1 Insulator
2 Bezel
3 Screw
4 Antenna assembly
5 Grommet
6 Bracket

86816140

Fig. 52 Power antenna assembly components

WINDSHIELD WIPERS

Windshield Wiper Blade and Arm

REMOVAL & INSTALLATION

▶ See Figure 53

Wiper blade insert replacement procedures are detailed in Section 1.

Removal of the wiper arms requires the use of a special tool, GM J-8966 or its equivalent prytool. Versions of this tool are generally available in auto parts stores.

1. With the wipers on, turn the ignition **OFF** when the blades get to the mid-wipe position.
2. Mark the position of the arms on the windshield.
3. Lift the wiper arm from the windshield, then insert the tool under the wiper arm. Pry the arm off the upper transmission drive shaft.
4. Disconnect the washer hose from the arm (if so equipped).
5. Remove the wiper blade assembly from the arm.
   To install:
6. Install the wiper blade on the arm. Align the arm with the mark made on the windshield.
7. Attach the wiper arm assembly to the transmission drive shaft, then push in the arm retaining latch, and return the wiper arm assembly to the windshield.
8. Turn the ignition in the **ON** position, then park the wipers.

ADJUSTMENT

The only adjustment for the wiper arms is to remove an arm from the transmission shaft, rotate the arm the required distance and direction and then install the arm back in position so it is in line with the blackout line on the glass. The wiper motor must be in the park position.

Fig. 53 Lift the wiper arm from the windshield, then insert the tool under the wiper arm

86816144

The correct blade-out wipe position on the driver's side is $1^1/_{32}$ in. (28mm) for 1982-85 models and $^{11}/_{16}$ in. (18mm) for 1986-95 models, from the tip of the blade to the left windshield pillar molding. The correct blade-down wipe position on the passenger side of the car is in line with the blackout line at the bottom of the glass.

Rear Wiper Arm and Blade

REMOVAL & INSTALLATION

▶ See Figure 54

Removal of the wiper arms requires the use of special tool, GM J-8966 or its equivalent prytool. Versions of this tool are generally available in auto parts stores.

1. Lift the wiper arm from the window, then insert the tool under the wiper arm. Lever the arm off the transmission drive shaft. Use care not to damage the paint on the vehicle.
2. Remove the wiper blade from the arm.
   To install:
3. Install the wiper blade onto the arm.
4. Position the wiper arm on the wiper motor drive shaft so that the blade assembly rests in the proper park position.
5. Press down on the wiper arm until it is fully seated on the drive shaft. The same special tool for removal can be used for installation.

Wiper Motor

REMOVAL & INSTALLATION

▶ See Figures 55, 56, 57, 58, 59 and 60

1. Disconnect the negative battery cable.
2. Remove the wiper arms.

J 8966

WIPER ARM ASSEMBLY

86816148

Fig. 54 The same tool for removal can be used for installation

3. Remove the cowl cover.

4. When lifting the cowl up disconnect the washer nozzle hoses.

5. Loosen (but do not remove) the drive link-to-crank arm attaching nuts and detach the drive link from the motor crank arm.

6. Unplug the wiper motor electrical connector.

7. Remove the wiper motor attaching bolts.

8. Remove the wiper motor, guiding the crank arm through the hole.

To install:

9. Insert the wiper motor, guiding the crank arm through the hole.

10. Guide the crank arm through the opening in the body and then tighten the mounting bolts to 4-6 ft. lbs. (5-8 Nm).

11. Install the drive link to the crank arm with the motor in the park position.

12. Install the wiper motor attaching bolts.

13. Engage the electrical connectors.

14. Connect the wiper arm drive link to the crank arm.

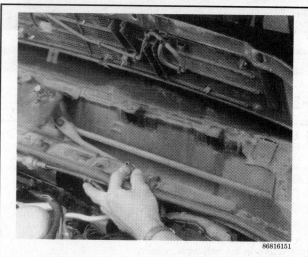
Fig. 57 Disconnect the washer nozzle hoses from the cowl

Fig. 55 Remove the cowl lower attaching bolts . . .

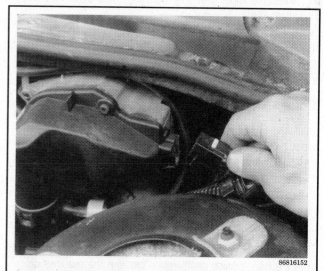
Fig. 58 Unplug the wiper motor electrical connector

Fig. 56 . . . and the upper screws

Fig. 59 Remove the wiper motor attaching bolts . . .

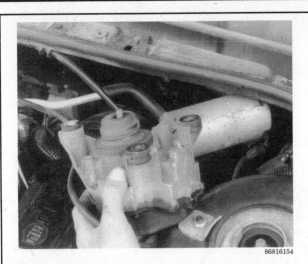

Fig. 60 Remove the wiper motor, guiding the crank arm through the hole

15. Install the cowl cover.
16. Install the wiper arms.
17. Connect the negative battery cable. Tighten the cable bolt to 11 ft. lbs. (15 Nm).
18. Reset the radio, clock and any other applicable electronic devices.

Rear Wiper Motor

REMOVAL & INSTALLATION

1. Disconnect the negative battery cable.
2. Remove the wiper arm assembly from the wiper motor drive shaft.
3. Remove the nut and washer from the wiper motor drive shaft.
4. Unfasten the liftgate glass opening upper finish moulding.
5. Remove the electrical harness from the motor.
6. Remove the two screws, then guide the motor out of the tailgate recess.

To install:

➡When fasteners are removed always reinstall them at the same location from which they were removed. If a fastener need replacing, always use the same fastener, or one of equal size and/or stronger that the original. If these conditions are not followed, parts or system damage could occur.

7. Install the wiper motor in the recess of the tailgate.
8. Tighten the two screws to 53 inch lbs. (6 Nm).
9. Apply the washer and nut to the wiper shaft, then tighten to 62 inch lbs. (7 Nm).
10. Connect the electrical harness to the motor assembly.
11. Install the liftgate glass upper moulding.
12. Connect the negative battery cable. Tighten the cable bolt to 11 ft. lbs. (15 Nm).

13. Attach the wiper arm to the motor drive shaft.
14. Reset the radio, clock ect. as necessary.

Wiper Linkage

REMOVAL & INSTALLATION

▶ See Figures 61, 62 and 63

1. Disconnect the negative battery cable.
2. Remove the wiper arms.
3. Remove the shroud top vent grille.
4. Loosen (but do not remove) the drive link-to-crank arm attaching nuts.
5. Loosen the two nuts, then separate the transmission drive link from the wiper motor crank arm using tool J-39232 or equivalent.
6. Unscrew the linkage-to-cowl panel retaining screws and remove the linkage by guiding it through the access hole in the shroud upper panel.
7. Some models you will need to unsnap the two water deflectors from the transmission assembly.

To install:

8. Attach the two water deflectors over the position marks on the transmission, then snap closed to secure.
9. Insert the transmission assembly by positioning it in the plenum chamber through the panel openings.
10. Install the screws loosely.
11. Connect the transmission drive link socket to the wiper motor crank arm ball using tool J-39529 or equivalent. Tighten the nuts to 62 inch lbs. (7 Nm).
12. Align the transmission assembly, then tighten the screws to 71 inch lbs. (8 Nm).
13. Attach the cowl panel.
14. Connect the negative battery cable. Tighten the cable bolt to 11 ft. lbs. (15 Nm).
15. Install the wiper arm assembly, check for operation, adjust the blades if needed.
16. Reset the radio and clock.

Washer Pump

REMOVAL & INSTALLATION

▶ See Figures 64 and 65

1. Disconnect the negative battery cable.
2. Disconnect the electrical harness on the pump.
3. Drain the washer solvent from the fluid reservoir.
4. Remove screws mounting the reservoir, then disconnect the fluid hoses.
5. Pull the reservoir from the engine compartment, then remove the pump from the reservoir.
6. Inspect the grommet which the pump is mounted into for dry-rot or any other deterioration.
7. Installation is the reverse of removal.

Fig. 61 Wiper motor and transmission assembly

Fig. 62 Separate the transmission drive link from the wiper motor crank arm using tool J-39232 or equivalent

Fig. 63 Connect the transmission drive link socket to the wiper motor crank arm ball using tool J-39529 or equivalent

1 SCREW (2)
2 CONTAINER, WASHER SOLVENT
3 SEAL, CONTAINER
4 PUMP, WASHER
5 HOSE, WASHER

86816165

Fig. 64 Front washer fluid reservoir

1 SCREW (2)
2 BRACKET, CONTAINER
3 CONTAINER, WASHER SOLVENT
4 CONNECTOR, ELECTRICAL
5 PUMP, WASHER
6 HOSE, WASHER

86816166

Fig. 65 Rear washer reservoir assembly

INSTRUMENTS AND SWITCHES

Instrument Cluster

REMOVAL & INSTALLATION

✳✳CAUTION

The instrument cluster contains all of the displays, lamps and indicators which provide the operating information to the driver. Be extra careful when working around electrical items in your vehicle, many solid state components can be damaged by electrostatic discharge. If you are working around the SIR system remember to disarm the system. Otherwise air bag deployment could occur and cause personal injury.

You may want to place a clean cloth over the steering column to prevent scratches. On vehicles with tilt steering, it will help to lower the wheel all the way then unscrew the tilt wheel lever.

Century

▶ See Figures 66 and 67

✳✳CAUTION

Some vehicles are equipped with the Supplemental Inflatable Restraint (SIR) system. This system must be disabled before performing service on or around the air bag, instrument panel components, wiring and sensors. Failure to follow safety and disabling procedures could result in accidental air bag deployment, possible personal injury and unnecessary air bag system repairs.

1. Disconnect the negative battery cable.
2. Disable the SIR, if equipped.
3. Disconnect the speedometer cable and pull it through the firewall.
4. Remove the left side hush panel retaining screws and nut.
5. Remove the right side hush panel retaining screws and nut.
6. Remove the shift indicator cable clip.
7. Remove the steering column trim plate.
8. Put the gear selector in **L** or **1**. Remove the retaining screws and gently pull out the instrument panel trim plate.
9. Disconnect the parking brake cable at the lever by pushing it forward and sliding it from its slot.
10. Unbolt and lower the steering column.
11. Remove the gauge cluster retaining screws. Pull the cluster out far enough to disconnect any wires, then remove the instrument cluster.
    To install:
12. Install the gauge cluster, then attach the electrical wires and install the retaining screws.

13. Position the steering column, then install the retaining bolts.
14. Connect the parking brake cable at the lever.
15. Put the gear selector in **L** or **P**. Install the instrument panel trim plate.
16. Install the steering column trim plate.
17. Install the shift indicator cable clip.
18. Install the right side hush panel retaining screws and nut.
19. Install the left side hush panel retaining screws and nut.
20. Pull the speedometer cable through the firewall and connect to the speedometer.
21. Connect the negative battery cable. Tighten the cable bolt to 11 ft. lbs. (15 Nm).
22. Enable the SIR, if equipped.
23. Reset the radio, clock and any other applicable electronic devices.

Celebrity

1. Disconnect the negative battery cable.
2. Remove instrument panel hush trim.
3. Remove vent control housing, as required.
4. On non-air conditioning vehicles, remove steering column trim cover screws and lower cover with vent cables attached. On air conditioning vehicles, remove trim cover attaching screws and remove cover.
5. Remove instrument cluster trim pad.
6. Remove ash tray, retainer and fuse block, disconnecting wires as necessary.
7. Remove headlight switch knob and instrument panel trim plate. Unplug electrical connectors of any accessory switches in trim plate.
8. Remove cluster assembly and disconnect speedometer cable, **PRNDL** and cluster electrical connectors.
   To install:
9. Install cluster assembly and connect speedometer cable, **PRNDL** and cluster electrical connectors.
10. Install headlight switch knob and instrument panel trim plate. Engage electrical connectors of any accessory switches in trim plate.
11. Install the ash tray, retainer and fuse block. Engage the electrical connectors.
12. Install instrument cluster trim pad.
13. On non-air conditioned vehicles, raise the cover with vent cables attached and install steering column trim cover screws. On air conditioned vehicles, install trim cover and attaching screws.
14. If removed, install vent control housing.
15. Install instrument panel hush panel.
16. Connect the negative battery cable. Tighten the cable bolt to 11 ft. lbs. (15 Nm).
17. Reset the radio, clock and any other applicable electronic devices.

Fig. 66 Instrument cluster used on US Buick models — 1994-95

Fig. 67 Instrument cluster used on Canadian/Japanese Buick models — 1994-95

Ciera and Cruiser

▶ **See Figures 68, 69 and 70**

> **✳✳CAUTION**
>
> **Some vehicles are equipped with the Supplemental Inflatable Restraint (SIR) system. This system must be disabled before performing service on or around the air bag, instrument panel components, wiring and sensors. Failure to follow safety and disabling procedures could result in accidental air bag deployment, possible personal injury and unnecessary air bag system repairs.**

1. Disconnect the negative battery cable.
2. Disable the SIR, if equipped.
3. Remove left instrument panel trim pad.
4. Remove instrument panel cluster trim cover.
5. Disconnect speedometer cable at transaxle or cruise control transducer, if equipped.
6. Remove steering column trim cover.
7. Disconnect shift indicator clip from steering column shift bowl.
8. Remove 4 screws attaching cluster assembly to instrument panel.
9. Pull assembly out far enough to reach behind cluster and disconnect speedometer cable.
10. Remove cluster assembly.

To install:

11. Install the cluster assembly.
12. Connect the speedometer cable.
13. Install the 4 screws attaching cluster assembly to instrument panel.
14. Connect shift indicator clip to steering column shift bowl.
15. Install the steering column trim cover.
16. Connect the speedometer cable at the transaxle or cruise control transducer, if equipped.
17. Install the instrument panel cluster trim cover.
18. Install the left instrument panel trim pad.
19. Connect the negative battery cable. Tighten the cable bolt to 11 ft. lbs. (15 Nm).

1. I.P. HARNESS ASSEMBLY
2. INSTRUMENT PANEL
3. CLUSTER ASSEMBLY

86816184

Fig. 68 Instrument cluster mounting for Oldsmobile — 1992-95 models

EXCEPT YP9

WITH YP9

86816182

Fig. 69 Instrument cluster for Canadian Oldsmobile models — 1992-95

EXCEPT YP9

WITH YP9

86816183

Fig. 70 Instrument cluster for US Oldsmobile models — 1992-95

20. Reset the radio, clock and any other applicable electronic devices.

6000

1. On the electronic instrument cluster you will need to call up and record the maintenance reminder mileages (DIC) before proceeding.

➡**The service button is located on the instrument panel, the mileages will display and pushing the system recall button momentarily.**

2. Disconnect the negative battery cable, and remove the center and left side lower instrument panel trim plate.
3. Remove the screws securing the instrument cluster to the instrument panel carrier.
4. Remove the instrument cluster lens to gain access to the speedometer head and gauges.
5. Remove right side and left side hush panels and steering column trim cover. Disconnect the parking brake cable and vent cables, if equipped.
6. Remove steering column retaining bolts and lower the steering column.
7. Disconnect temperature control cable, inner-to-outer air conditioning wire harness and inner-to-outer air conditioning vacuum harness, if equipped.
8. Disconnect the chassis harness behind the left lower instrument panel and ECM/PCM connectors behind glove box. Disconnect instrument panel harness at cowl.
9. Remove center instrument panel trim plate, radio, (if equipped) and disconnect the neutral switch and brake light switch.
10. Remove upper and lower instrument panel retaining screws, nuts and bolts.
11. Pull instrument panel assembly out far enough to disconnect ignition switch, headlight dimmer switch and turn signal switch. Disconnect all other accessory wiring and vacuum lines necessary to remove instrument panel assembly.
12. Remove instrument panel assembly with wiring harness.
To install:
13. Install instrument panel assembly with wiring harness.
14. Connect ignition switch, headlight dimmer switch and turn signal switch. Connect all other accessory wiring and vacuum lines.
15. Install upper and lower instrument panel retaining screws, nuts and bolts.
16. Connect neutral switch and brake light switch. Install the radio, if equipped, and install center instrument panel trim plate.
17. Connect chassis harness behind left lower instrument panel and ECM/PCM connectors behind glove box. Connect instrument panel harness at cowl.
18. Connect temperature control cable, inner-to-outer air conditioning wire harness and inner-to-outer air conditioning vacuum harness, if equipped.
19. Raise the steering column and install retaining bolts.
20. Install right side and left side hush panels, steering column trim cover and connect parking brake cable and vent cables, if equipped.
21. Install the instrument cluster lens.
22. Install the screws securing the instrument cluster to the instrument panel carrier.

23. Install the center and left side lower instrument panel trim plate.
24. Connect the negative battery cable. Tighten the cable bolt to 11 ft. lbs. (15 Nm).
25. Reset the radio, clock and any other applicable electronic devices.
26. Reset the service reminder:

    a. Sequence through the service items by momentarily depressing and releasing the button until the desired service item is displayed. When the desired item is displayed DO NOT release the button.

    b. After the button is held for 5-10 seconds, the service interval miles displayed will count down in 500 mile intervals. When the desired interval is reached, release the button.

Speedometer

REMOVAL & INSTALLATION

➡When replacing a speedometer head Federal law requires the odometer reading of the replacement unit be set to the reading of the unit being replaced. If this is not possible, it is required by law to apply a label in the drivers door stating the previous odometer reading and the date of replacement. The replacement reading must be set to zero.

Century

❊❊CAUTION

Some vehicles are equipped with the Supplemental Inflatable Restraint (SIR) system. This system must be disabled before performing service on or around the air bag, instrument panel components, wiring and sensors. Failure to follow safety and disabling procedures could result in accidental air bag deployment, possible personal injury and unnecessary air bag system repairs.

1. Disconnect the negative battery cable and disable the SIR system.
2. Remove the left side trim plate.
3. Remove the instrument cluster housing screws. Remove the instrument cluster. If the vehicle is equipped with tilt-wheel steering, working room can be gained by removing the tilt-wheel cover.
4. Remove the speedometer lens screws and remove the speedometer lens.
5. Disconnect the speedometer cable by pushing in on the retaining clip and pulling back on the cable.
6. Remove the screws securing the speedometer to the instrument panel, then remove the speedometer assembly.
   To install:
7. Install the speedometer assembly and the screws securing the speedometer assembly to the instrument panel.
8. Connect the speedometer cable.
9. Install the speedometer lens and retaining screws.
10. Install the instrument cluster housing and retaining screws. If equipped with tilt-wheel steering and the tilt-wheel cover was removed, replace the cover.
11. Install the left side trim plate.

12. Connect the negative battery cable. Tighten the cable bolt to 11 ft. lbs. (15 Nm).
13. Enable the SIR system.
14. Reset the radio, clock and any other applicable electronic devices.

Celebrity

1. Disconnect the negative battery cable.
2. Remove the cluster trim panel.
3. Remove the cluster lens screws. Remove the cluster lens.
4. Remove the speedometer-to-cluster attaching screws. Remove the speedometer from the instrument cluster.
5. Disconnect the speedometer cable and remove the speedometer assembly.
   To install:
6. Position the speedometer assembly and connect the speedometer cable.
7. Install the speedometer-to-instrument cluster and install the attaching screws.
8. Install the cluster lens and attaching screws.
9. Install the cluster trim panel.
10. Connect the negative battery cable. Tighten the cable bolt to 11 ft. lbs. (15 Nm).
11. Reset the radio, clock and any other applicable electronic devices.

Ciera and Cruiser

❊❊CAUTION

Some vehicles are equipped with the Supplemental Inflatable Restraint (SIR) system. This system must be disabled before performing service on or around the air bag, instrument panel components, wiring and sensors. Failure to follow safety and disabling procedures could result in accidental air bag deployment, possible personal injury and unnecessary air bag system repairs.

1. Disconnect the negative battery cable and disable the SIR system.
2. Remove the instrument cluster assembly.
3. Remove the vehicle speed sensor screw from the rear of the speedometer. Remove the vehicle speed sensor, if equipped.
4. Remove the speedometer lens screws and remove the speedometer lens. Remove the bezel.
5. Remove the screw that holds the speedometer to the instrument cluster.
6. Remove the speedometer head by pulling forward. Disconnect the speedometer cable by prying gently on the retainer and pulling the speedometer cable from the speedometer head.
   To install:
7. Position the speedometer head and connect the speedometer cable.
8. Install the screw that holds the speedometer to the instrument cluster.
9. Install the speedometer lens and attaching screws. Install the bezel.
10. Install the vehicle speed sensor and the attaching screw at the rear of the speedometer.

11. Install the instrument cluster assembly.

12. Connect the negative battery cable. Tighten the cable bolt to 11 ft. lbs. (15 Nm).

13. Enable the SIR system.

14. Reset the radio, clock and any other applicable electronic devices.

6000

1. Disconnect the negative battery cable.

2. Remove the center and left lower trim plates.

3. Remove the screws securing the instrument cluster assembly to the dash assembly. Remove the instrument cluster.

4. Remove the instrument cluster lens screws. Remove the instrument cluster lens.

5. Remove the screws securing the speedometer to the instrument cluster. Remove the speedometer.

6. Disconnect the speedometer cable from the rear of the speedometer.

To install:

7. Connect the speedometer cable at the rear of speedometer.

8. Install speedometer and the screws securing the speedometer to the instrument cluster.

9. Install the instrument cluster lens and attaching screws.

10. Install the instrument cluster and the screws securing the instrument cluster assembly to the dash assembly.

11. Install the center and left lower trim plates.

12. Connect the negative battery cable. Tighten the cable bolt to 11 ft. lbs. (15 Nm).

13. Reset the radio, clock and any other applicable electronic devices.

Tachometer

REMOVAL & INSTALLATION

▶ **See Figure 71**

1. Remove the shift indicator.

2. Unfasten the retainers securing the tachometer to the cluster, then remove the tachometer by pulling it out.

To install:

3. Insert the tachometer into the cluster. Using the screws attach the tachometer to the cluster assembly.

4. Install the shift indicator.

Speedometer Cable

REMOVAL & INSTALLATION

▶ **See Figure 72**

➡Removing the instrument cluster will give better access to the speedometer cable.

1. Remove the instrument cluster.

2. Slide the cable out from the casing. If the cable is broken, the casing will have to be unscrewed from the transaxle and the broken piece removed from that end.

1	TACHOMETER
2	GAGE CLUSTER
3	NUT

86816190

Fig. 71 The tachometer is secured to the back of the cluster

3. Before installing a new cable, slip a piece of cable into the speedometer and spin it between your fingers in the direction of normal rotation. If the mechanism sticks or binds, the speedometer should be repaired or replaced.

To install:

4. Inspect the casing. If it is cracked, kinked, or broken, the casing should be replaced.

5. Slide a new cable into the casing, engaging the transaxle end securely. Sometimes it is easier to unscrew the casing at the transaxle end, install the cable into the transaxle fitting, then screw the casing back into place. Install the instrument cluster.

Gages, Fuel, Clock, Temperature, Ect.

REMOVAL & INSTALLATION

1. Disconnect the negative battery cable.

2. Remove the instrument panel cluster trim pad.

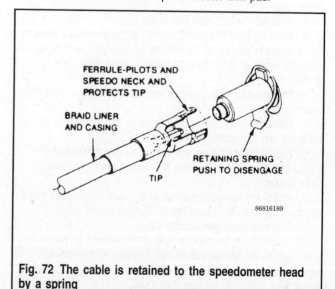

FERRULE-PILOTS AND
SPEEDO NECK AND
PROTECTS TIP

BRAID LINER
AND CASING

RETAINING SPRING
PUSH TO DISENGAGE

TIP

86816189

Fig. 72 The cable is retained to the speedometer head by a spring

3. Unfasten the cluster lens, then put aside on a clean cloth so not to scratch the lens.

4. The gauge can be taken off the cluster by removing the attaching screws.

To install:

5. Attach the new gauge on the cluster with the screws removed previously.

6. Attach the cluster lens with the mounting screws, then install the cluster trim pad.

7. Connect the negative battery cable. Tighten the cable bolt to 11 ft. lbs. (15 Nm).

8. Reset the radio, clock or any components which lost power while the battery cable was disconnected.

Windshield Wiper Switch

REMOVAL & INSTALLATION

1982-86 Models

1. Disconnect the negative battery cable.

2. Remove the steering wheel, the cover and the lock plate assembly.

3. Remove the turn signal actuator arm, the lever and the hazard flasher button.

4. Remove the turn signal switch screws, the lower steering column trim panel and the steering column bracket bolts.

5. Unplug the turn signal switch and the wiper switch connectors.

6. Pull the turn signal rearward 6-8 in. (15-20mm), then remove the key buzzer switch and the cylinder lock.

7. Remove and pull the steering column housing rearward, then remove the housing cover screw.

8. Remove the wiper switch pivot and the switch.

9. To install, reverse the removal procedures.

1987-95 Models

✳✳CAUTION

Some vehicles are equipped with the Supplemental Inflatable Restraint (SIR) system. This system must be disabled before performing service on or around the air bag, instrument panel components, wiring and sensors. Failure to follow safety and disabling procedures could result in accidental air bag deployment, possible personal injury and unnecessary air bag system repairs.

1. Disconnect the negative battery cable and disable the SIR system.

2. Remove the steering wheel and turn signal switch. It may be necessary to first remove the column mounting nuts and remove the bracket-to-mast jacket screws, then separate the bracket from the mast jacket to allow the connector clip on the ignition switch to be pulled from the column assembly.

3. Tag and unplug the washer/wiper switch lower connector.

4. Remove the screws attaching the column housing to the mast jacket. Be sure to note the position of the dimmer switch actuator rod for reassembly in the same position. Remove the column housing and switch as an assembly.

➡**Certain tilt columns are equipped with a removable plastic cover on the column housing. This provides access to the wiper switch without removing the entire column housing.**

5. Turn the assembly over and use a drift to remove the pivot pin from the washer/wiper switch. Remove the switch.

To install:

6. Place the switch into position in the housing. Install the pivot pin.

7. Position the housing onto the mast jacket and attach by installing the screws. Install the dimmer switch actuator rod in the same position as noted when removed. Check switch operation.

8. Reconnect lower end of the switch assembly.

9. Install the ignition switch connector clip to the column assembly.

10. Install the mast jacket to the bracket.

11. If removed, install the column mounting nuts and the retaining bolts.

12. Install the turn signal switch and steering wheel.

13. Connect the negative battery cable. Tighten the cable bolt to 11 ft. lbs. (15 Nm).

14. Enable the SIR system.

15. Reset the radio, clock and any other applicable electronic devices.

Headlight Switch

REMOVAL & INSTALLATION

Century

1. Disconnect the negative battery cable.

2. Remove the instrument panel trim plate.

3. Remove the left side instrument panel switch trim panel by removing the attaching screws. Gently rock the panel out.

4. Remove the switch screws, then pull the switch straight out.

To install:

5. Install the switch and the attaching screws.

6. Install the left side instrument panel switch trim panel and it's attaching screws.

7. Install the instrument panel trim plate.

8. Connect the negative battery cable. Tighten the cable bolt to 11 ft. lbs. (15 Nm).

9. Reset the radio, clock and any other applicable electronic devices.

Celebrity

1. Disconnect the negative battery cable.

2. Remove the headlight switch knob.

3. Remove the instrument panel trim pad.

4. Unbolt the switch mounting plate from the instrument panel carrier.

5. Disconnect the wiring from the switch.

6. Remove the switch.

To install:

7. Install the switch.

8. Connect the wiring to the switch.

9. Install the bolts attaching the switch mounting plate to the instrument panel carrier.

10. Install the instrument panel trim pad.

11. Install the headlight switch knob.

12. Connect the negative battery cable. Tighten the cable bolt to 11 ft. lbs. (15 Nm).

13. Reset the radio, clock and any other applicable electronic devices.

Ciera and Cruiser

1. Disconnect the negative battery cable.

2. Remove the left side instrument panel trim pad.

3. Unbolt the switch from the instrument panel.

4. Pull the switch rearward and remove it.

To install:

5. Install the switch and engage the electrical connectors.

6. Install the bolts attaching the switch to the instrument panel.

7. Install the left side instrument panel trim pad.

8. Connect the negative battery cable. Tighten the cable bolt to 11 ft. lbs. (15 Nm).

9. Reset the radio, clock and any other applicable electronic devices.

6000

1. Disconnect the negative battery cable.

2. Remove the steering column trim cover and headlight rod and knob by reaching behind the instrument panel and depressing the lock tab.

3. Remove the left instrument panel trim plate.

4. Unbolt and remove the switch and bracket assembly from the instrument panel.

5. Loosen the bezel and remove the switch from the bracket.

To install:

6. Install the switch to the bracket and install the bezel.

7. Install the switch and bracket assembly to the instrument panel and install the attaching bolts.

8. Install the left instrument panel trim plate.

9. Install the headlight rod and knob. Install the steering column trim cover.

10. Connect the negative battery cable. Tighten the cable bolt to 11 ft. lbs. (15 Nm).

11. Reset the radio, clock and any other applicable electronic devices.

Dimmer Switch

REMOVAL & INSTALLATION

✳✳CAUTION

Some vehicles are equipped with the Supplemental Inflatable Restraint (SIR) system. This system must be disabled before performing service on or around the air bag, instrument panel components, wiring and sensors. Failure to follow safety and disabling procedures could result in accidental air bag deployment, possible personal injury and unnecessary air bag system repairs.

1. Disable the SIR system if equipped.

2. Disconnect the negative battery cable.

3. Remove the steering wheel. Remove the trim cover.

4. Remove the turn signal switch assembly.

5. Remove the ignition switch stud and screw. Remove the ignition switch.

6. Remove the dimmer switch actuator rod by sliding it from the switch assembly.

7. Remove the dimmer switch bolts and remove the dimmer switch.

To install:

8. Install the dimmer switch and attaching bolts.

9. Install the dimmer switch actuator rod by sliding it into the switch assembly.

10. Adjust the dimmer switch by depressing the switch slightly and inserting a $\frac{3}{32}$ in. (2mm) drill bit into the adjusting hole. Push the switch up to remove any play and tighten the dimmer switch adjusting screw.

11. Install the ignition switch, stud and screw.

12. Install the turn signal switch assembly.

13. Install the trim cover. Install the steering wheel.

14. Connect the battery negative cable.

15. Enable the SIR system.

16. Reset the radio, clock and any other accessories.

Combination Switch

REMOVAL & INSTALLATION

▶ See Figures 73, 74 and 75

✳✳CAUTION

Some vehicles are equipped with the Supplemental Inflatable Restraint (SIR) system. This system must be disabled before performing service on or around the air bag, instrument panel components, wiring and sensors. Failure to follow safety and disabling procedures could result in accidental air bag deployment, possible personal injury and unnecessary air bag system repairs.

1. Disable the SIR system, if equipped.

2. Disconnect the negative battery cable.

3. Remove the steering wheel. Remove the trim cover.

4. Loosen the cover screws. Pry the cover off with a flat bladed tool, then lift the cover off the shaft.

5. Position the U-shaped lockplate compressing tool on the end of the steering shaft and compress the lock plate by turning the shaft nut clockwise. Pry the wire snaping out of the shaft groove.

6. Remove the tool and lift the lock plate off the shaft.

7. Slip the canceling cam, upper bearing preload spring, and thrust washer off the shaft.

8. Remove the turn signal lever. Push the flasher knob in and unscrew it. Remove the button retaining screw and remove the button, spring and knob.

Fig. 73 This U-shaped tool is used to compress the lockplate

1 Shaft lock
2 Turn sig cancel cam asm
3 Upper bearing spring
4 Upper brg inner race seat
5 Inner race

86818102

Fig. 74 Exploded view of the steering shaft lock components

1 Bndg cr recess screw
2 Rd wash hd screw
3 Signal switch arm
4 Turn signal switch

86818101

Fig. 75 Push the flasher knob in and unscrew it. Remove the button retaining screw and remove the button, spring and knob

9. Pull the switch connector out the mast jacket and tape the upper part to facilitate switch removal. Attach a long piece of wire to the turn signal switch connector. When installing the turn signal switch, feed this wire through the column first, then use this wire to pull the switch connector into position. On tilt wheels, place the turn signal and shifter housing in low position and remove the harness cover.

10. Remove the three switch mounting screws. Remove the switch by pulling it straight up while guiding the wiring harness cover through the column.

To install:

11. Install the replacement switch by working the connector and cover down through the housing and under the bracket. On tilt models, the connector is worked down through the housing, under the bracket, and then the cover is installed on the harness.

12. Install the switch mounting screws and the connector on the mast jacket bracket. Install the column-to-dash trim plate.

13. Install the flasher knob and the turn signal lever.

14. With the turn signal lever in neutral and the flasher now out, slide the thrust washer, upper bearing preload spring, and canceling cam onto the shaft.

15. Position the lock plate on the shaft and press it down until a new snapring can be inserted in the shaft groove. Always use a new snapring when assembling.

16. Install the cover and the steering wheel.

17. Connect the negative battery cable, then enable the SIR system, if equipped.

Clock

REMOVAL & INSTALLATION

1. Remove the instrument panel cluster bezel.
2. Remove the clock retaining screws and remove the clock.

Back-up Light Switch

REMOVAL & INSTALLATION

1. Working from underneath the dashboard, locate the back-up light switch on the steering column and remove the wiring harness.

2. Pull downward and remove the switch from the steering column.

To install:

3. Apply the parking brake and place the gear select lever in **N**.

4. Align the actuator on the switch with the hole in the shift tube.

5. Position the rearward portion of the switch (connector side) to fit into the cutout in the lower jacket.

6. Push up on the front of the switch, the two tangs on the housing back will snap into place in the rectangular holes in the jacket.

7. Adjust the switch by moving the gear selector to **P**. The main housing and the back should ratchet, providing proper switch adjustment.

Rear Defogger System

All systems operate on 12 volts. An instrument panel mounted switch with an integral indicator lamp is used to turn the system on.

Certain conditions such as outside temperature, vehicle speed, atmospheric pressure and even the number of passengers inside the vehicle affects the length of time required to remove fog from the glass.

The defogger is designed to turn off after approximately 10 minutes of operation. If the defogger is turn on again, it will only operate for approximately 5 minutes. You can however, turn the system off before the time is up by turning the defogger switch or ignition switch **OFF**.

REMOVAL & INSTALLATION

1. Disconnect the negative battery cable.
2. Remove the left side instrument panel or accessory trim plate, as required.
3. On some vehicles, it may be necessary to remove the steering column collar, steering column opening filler and cluster trim plate.
4. Remove the ash tray and sound insulator, as required.
5. On some vehicles, it may be necessary to remove the radio control knobs, air conditioning/heater control and/or cables.
6. Remove the rear defogger control retaining screws or clip and remove the switch.
7. Unplug the switch electrical connector.

To install:

8. Engage the electrical connector to the switch.
9. Fit the switch to the instrument panel and install the retaining screws.
10. Install the instrument panel or trim plate.
11. Reconnect the negative battery cable.
12. Reset the radio, clock and any other applicable accessories.

TESTING

▶ See Figure 76

1. Start the engine and pull out the defogger switch knob.
2. Using a test light, ground the end and touch the probe to each grid line. The test light should operate as indicated in the illustration.
3. If the test light remains bright at both ends of the grid lines, check for a loose ground.

➡The range zones may vary slightly from 1 glass to another. But, the test light brilliance will decrease proportionately as it is moved from left to right on the grid line.

4. If an abnormal reading is observed by the test light on any grid line, place the test light probe on the left of that bus bar and move the probe toward the right until the test lamp goes out. This will indicate a break in the continuity on that grid line.

REPAIR

▶ See Figures 77 and 78

1. Locate the break(s) on the grid line(s) and mark the outside of the glass, using a grease pencil.
2. Disconnect the negative battery cable.
3. Clean the area to be repaired. Buff with fine steel wool and wipe clean with a damped cloth with alcohol.
4. Position a strip of tape above and below the grid line area to be repair.
5. Repair the grid line break using defogger repair kit (GM part 1052858 or equivalent) and follow the manufacturer's instructions.
6. After the grid line has been repaired, carefully remove the strips of tape.

Fig. 76 Check the grid lines with a test light

Fig. 77 The grid lines can be repaired using a defogger repair kit (GM part 1052858 or equivalent)

7. Apply heat, (using a heat gun or blow dryer) to the repaired area for approximately 1-2 minutes. A minimum temperature of 300°F (149°C) is required.

➡To avoid damage to the interior trim, protect the trim near the area to be repair. Allow the repair materials to cure for at least 24 hours. Do not operate the unit until such time has passed.

8. Test the rear defogger operation to verify proper operation.

Fig. 78 Apply heat to the area with a blow dryer or heat gun

LIGHTING

❋❋CAUTION

Take care not to squeeze the bulbs too tightly, they can break in you hand and causes injury. If the bulbs are stuck, spray them with penetrating oil and allow them to soak for a few minutes. There are also tools on the market for gripping and removing bulbs.

Headlights

REMOVAL & INSTALLATION

Non-European Style

▶ See Figures 79, 80, 81, 82 and 83

1. Remove the headlamp trim panel attaching screws.
2. Remove the headlamp bulb retaining screws. Do not touch the two headlamp aiming screws, (at the top and side of the retaining ring), or the headlamp aim will have to be readjusted.
3. Using a screwdriver, remove the retaining ring screws.
4. Pull the bulb and ring forward then separate them. Unplug the electrical connector from the rear of the bulb.

To install:

5. Plug the new bulb into the electrical connector.
6. Install the bulb into the retaining ring and install the ring and bulb.
7. Install the trim panel.

European Style

1. Open the hood.

Fig. 79 Remove the headlamp trim panel attaching screws

2. Turn the bulb assembly counterclockwise ⅙ turn, pressing in firmly, until the flanges align with the slots in the retainer ring.
3. Pull out the bulb assembly. You may have to rock it up and down slightly to loosen it.
4. Disconnect the bulb base from the harness by lifting the plastic locking tab.

To install:

5. Snap a new bulb into the wiring harness. Make sure the locking tab is over the lock.
6. Install the bulb assembly by putting the small tab in the small notch in the retainer ring.
7. Turn the bulb assembly ⅙ turn clockwise to lock it in place.

Fig. 80 Remove the headlamp trim panel assembly from it's mounting location

Fig. 81 Using a screwdriver, remove the retaining ring screws

Fig. 82 Once the retaining ring screws are removed, the ring can be pulled away

Fig. 83 Pull the bulb out and unplug the electrical connector

AIMING

▶ See Figure 84

The head lamps should be aimed using a special alignment tool, however this procedure may be used for temporary adjustment. Local regulations may vary regarding head lamp aiming, consult with your local authorities.

1. Verify the tires are at their proper inflation pressure. Clean the head lamp lenses and make sure there are no heavy loads in the trunk. The gas tank should be filled.
2. Position the vehicle on a level surface facing a flat wall 25 ft. (7.7 m) away.
3. Measure and record the distance from the floor to the center of the head lamp. Place a strip of tape across the wall at this same height.
4. Place strips of tape on the wall, perpendicular to the first measurement, indicating the vehicle centerline and the centerline of both head lamps.
5. Rock the vehicle side-to-side a few times to allow the suspension to stabilize.
6. Turn the lights on, adjust the head lamps to achieve a high intensity pattern.

Signal and Marker Lights

REMOVAL & INSTALLATION

Front Turn Signal and Parking Lights
▶ See Figures 85, 86, 87, 88 and 89

1. On some models you will need to remove the headlight bezel mounting screws and the bezel.
2. Remove the mounting screws for the lamp assembly.
3. After the screws are removed, pull the assembly from the vehicle.

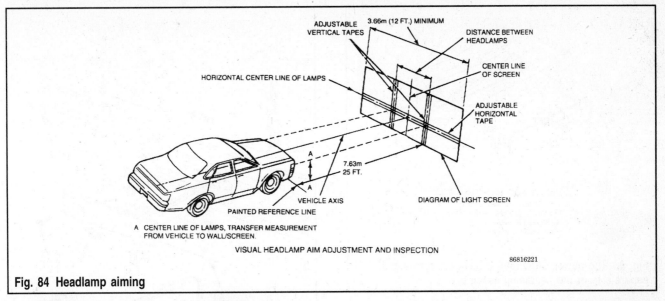

Fig. 84 Headlamp aiming

4. Disconnect the twist lock socket from the lens housing.

➡**To remove the bulb, turn the twist lock socket (at the rear of the housing) counterclockwise ¼ turn, then remove the socket with the bulb; replace the bulb if defective.**

To install:

5. Install the electrical harness to the back of the unit.

6. Position the signal assembly, then attach to the vehicle with the mounting screws. Tighten the screws to 54 inch lbs. (6 Nm).

7. Insert the socket to the back of the unit, then attach the headlamp bezel if removed.

Side Marker Lights
♦ **See Figure 90**

1. Remove the marker light housing screws and the housing.

Fig. 85 Remove the mounting screws securing the lamp assembly

Fig. 86 After the screws are removed, pull the assembly from the vehicle

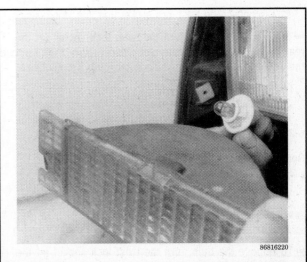

Fig. 87 Disconnect the twist lock socket from the lens housing

1 BAR ASSEMBLY, FRONT IMPACT BAR
2 BOLT/SCREW, PARKING LAMP
3 RETAINER, PARKING LAMP BOLT
4 NUT, PARKING LAMP
5 LAMP ASSEMBLY, PARKING

86816215

Fig. 88 The newer Oldsmobiles have the turn signal separate from the headlamp assembly . . .

1 HEADLAMP ASSEMBLY
2 NUT
3 NET HOLE
4 HEADLAMP HOUSING PANEL
5 STUD
6 SIDE MARKER LAMP ASSEMBLY

86816216

Fig. 89 . . . unlike the newer Buick's where the unit is attached to the headlamp

2. Disconnect the twist lock socket from the lens housing.

➡ To remove the bulb, turn the twist lock socket (at the rear of the housing) counterclockwise ¼ turn, then remove the socket with the bulb; replace the bulb if defective.

To install:

3. Connect the socket to the back of the lamp assembly.
4. Position the lamp housing to the vehicle, then attach with the mounting screws.

Rear Turn Signal, Brake and Parking Lights

▶ See Figures 91, 92 and 93

1. Remove the tail light assembly screws, then the assembly.
2. Disconnect the twist lock socket from the lens housing.

➡ To remove the bulb, turn the twist lock socket (at the rear of the housing) counterclockwise ¼ turn, then remove the socket with the bulb; replace the bulb if defective.

1 J-NUT
2 2 N·m (18 LB. IN.)
3 LAMP ASSEMBLY
4 WIRING HARNESS AND TAPE
5 REAR FASCIA

VIEW A

86816229

Fig. 90 The front and rear sidemarker lamps are removed using the same procedure

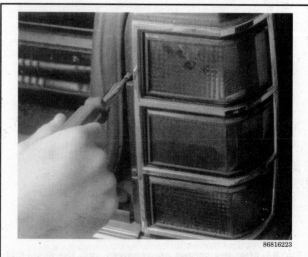

86816223

Fig. 91 Remove the tail light assembly screws, then the assembly — wagon shown

Fig. 92 Twist the socket counterclockwise to remove from the housing

Fig. 93 This type of bulb simply can be pulled out of the socket for replacement

To install:

3. Attach the socket assemblies to the back of the lamp unit.

4. Install the lamp assembly to the vehicle with the mounting screws.

License Plate Light

1. Remove the lens screws.

2. Once the lens is removed you, can access the bulb and replace if needed.

To install:

3. Install the new bulb, then attach the lens to the body of the vehicle.

Center High Mount Stoplamp

▶ **See Figure 94**

1. Remove the screws securing the lamp cover.

2. Remove the mounting nuts, then unplug the electrical harness to the lamp assembly.

3. The lamp now should come out.

To install:

4. Position the lamp assembly to the vehicle, then attach the electrical harness to the lamp.

5. Install the mounting nut, tighten to 62 inch lbs. (7 Nm).

6. Attach the lamp cover.

1	LIFT GATE GLASS
2	SCREW
3	COVER
4	NUT
5	CONNECTOR
6	STUD
7	STRIKER
8	WASHER
9	GASKET
10	HANDLE
11	GASKET
12	LAMP ASSEMBLY

Fig. 94 Exploded view of the center high mount stoplamp assembly — wagon shown

APPLICATION	BULB NO.	QUANTITY	RATING CANDLEPOWER
FRONT LAMPS			
Headlamp – Inner–Std.	4651	2	50W
– Inner–Halogen	H4651	2	50W
– Outer	4652	2	60/40W
Park	194NA	2	1.5CP
Park & Turn Signal	2057NA	2	1.5/24
Sidemarker	194	2	2
REAR LAMPS			
Backup – Sedan	2057	2	2/32
– Wagon	1156	2	32
License	194	1	2
Sidemarker	194	2	2
Tail – Sedan	194	2	2
Tail, Stop & Turn Signal	2057	4	2/32
High Mounted Stop – Sedan	1156	1	32
– Wagon	557	2	21
	212-2	1	12
INTERIOR ILLUMINATION			
A/C – Heater Control	194	1	2
Ash Tray	168	1	3
Auto Trans – Console	168	1	3
Courtesy Lamp – Front	194	2	2
– Console	212-2	1	6
Dome Lamp	561	1	12
Glove Box	194	1	2
Instrument Cluster	161/194	2/3	1/2
Luggage Compt. – Sedan	1003		
– Wagon	561	1	12
Radio Dial Exc. Graphic Equalizer	194	1	2
Graphic Equalizer	37	2	0.5
Reading Lamp	906	2	6
Underhood Lamp	93	1	15
WARNING LIGHTS & INDICATORS			
Brake	194	1	2
Service Engine Soon	194	1	2
Choke	194	1	2
High Beam	194	1	2
Low Fuel	194	1	2
Oil	194	1	2
Seat Belts	194	1	2
Tailgate Ajar	194	1	2
Temperature	194	1	2
Turn Signal	194	2	2
Upshift	194	1	2
Volts	194	1	2

86816237

Fig. 95 Light bulb application chart for all models with non-European headlamps

REPLACEMENT BULBS

Buick

	Trade No.
Exterior Lamps	
Back-up Lamps	1156
Center High-Mounted Stoplamp Without Luggage Carrier	1141
With Luggage Carrier	577
Front Parking/Turn Signal Lamps	2057
Headlamps Low-Beam	9006
High-Beam	9005
License Plate Lamps	194
Rear Tail/Stop/Turn Signal Lamps	2057
Taillamp Only	194
Tail/Stop	194
Sidemarker Lamps Front	194
Rear	24
Underhood Lamp	561

Interior Lamps

Air Conditioner/Heater Controls	T-1.0
Ashtray	194
Cluster Lighting	161
Courtesy Lamps	561
Door Courtesy	214-2
Dome	211-2
Dome/Reading Lamps	906
Gear Selector Indicator	194G
Headlamp High-Beam Indicator	194
Indicator Lamps	194
Indicator Lamp "SIR"	195
Instrument Panel Compartment	194
Map	168
Rear Compartment Lid Lamp	1003
Rear Dome (Wagon)	211-2
Turn Signal Indicators	194
Vanity Mirror	124

86816235

Fig. 96 Light bulb application chart for Buicks with European headlamps

REPLACEMENT BULBS

Oldsmobile

Exterior Lamps

Back-up Lamps 1156
Center High-Mounted Stoplamp   Luggage Carrier 57
    Sedan 577
    Station Wagon 577, 212-2
Front Parking/Turn Signal Lamps 207NA
Headlamps   Low-Beam..9006
    High-Beam..9005
License Plate Lamp 194
Sidemarkers Front 194
Taillamps/Stop/Turn Signals 2057
Underhood Lamp 089

Interior Lamps

Ashtray...194
Cluster...161
Courtesy Lamps...561
Dome Lamp   Without Reading Lamp(s) 586
    With Single Lens Reading Lamp 961
    Reading Lamps..906
    With Dual Lens Reading Lamp 961
    Reading Lamps..906
Rear Compartment Lid Lamp...1003
Instrument Panel Compartment Lamp..194
Heater & A/C Control 194
High-Beam Indicator 194
Indicator Lamps   "BRAKE" 194
    "CHARGE"..168
    "FASTEN BELTS" 194
    "OIL"..194
    "MALFUNCTION INDICATOR LAMP" 194
    "TAILGATE AJAR" 74
    "TEMP"...194
    "SIR" 195
Lighted Rearview Mirror 194
Lighted Visor Mirror..74
Rear Compartment Lamp (Wagon) 561
Rear Window Defogger Switch...2102
Turn Signal Indicators...194

86816236

Fig. 97 Light bulb application chart for Oldsmobiles with European headlamps

TRAILER WIRING

Wiring the car for towing is fairly easy. There are a number of good wiring kits available and these should be used, rather than trying to design your own. All trailers will need brake lights and turn signals as well as tail lights and side marker lights. Most states require extra marker lights for overly wide trailers. Also, most states have recently required back-up lights for trailers, and most trailer manufacturers have been building trailers with back-up lights for several years.

Additionally, some Class I, most Class II and just about all Class III trailers will have electric brakes.

Add to this number an accessories wire, to operate trailer internal equipment or to charge the trailer's battery, and you can have as many as seven wires in the harness.

Determine the equipment on your trailer and buy the wiring kit necessary. The kit will contain all the wires needed, plus a plug adapter set which included the female plug, mounted on the bumper or hitch, and the male plug, wired into, or plugged into the trailer harness.

When installing the kit, follow the manufacturer's instructions. The color coding of the wires is standard throughout the industry.

One point to note, some domestic vehicles, and most imported vehicles, have separate turn signals. On most domestic vehicles, the brake lights and rear turn signals operate with the same bulb. For those vehicles with separate turn signals, you can purchase an isolation unit so that the brake lights won't blink whenever the turn signals are operated, or, you can go to your local electronics supply house and buy four diodes to wire in series with the brake and turn signal bulbs. Diodes will isolate the brake and turn signals. The choice is yours. The isolation units are simple and quick to install, but far more expensive than the diodes. The diodes, however, require more work to install properly, since they require the cutting of each bulb's wire and soldering in place of the diode.

One final point, the best kits are those with a spring loaded cover on the vehicle mounted socket. This cover prevents dirt and moisture from corroding the terminals. Never let the vehicle socket hang loosely. Always mount it securely to the bumper or hitch.

➡ For more information on towing a trailer please refer to Section 1.

CIRCUIT PROTECTION

Fuses

▸ **See Figure 98**

REPLACEMENT

Fuses protect all the major electrical systems in the car. In case of an electrical overload, the fuse melts, breaking the circuit and stopping the flow of electricity.

If a fuse blows, the cause should be investigated and corrected before the installation of a new fuse. This, however, is easier to say than to do. Because each fuse protects a limited number of components, your job is narrowed down somewhat.

The amperage of each fuse and the circuit it protects are marked on the fusebox, which is located under the left side (driver's side) of the instrument panel and pulls down for easy access. To replace a fuse, simply pull it from the panel. Insert a new (same amp rating) fuse in its place.

GM PART NO.	RATING	COLOR
12004003	3 AMP	VIOLET
12004005	5 AMP	TAN
12004006	7.5 AMP	BROWN
12004007	10 AMP	RED
12004008	15 AMP	LIGHT BLUE
12004009	20 AMP	YELLOW
12004010	25 AMP	WHITE
12004011	30 AMP	LIGHT GREEN

86816240

Fig. 98 Fuses come in different colors which indicate different amperage ratings

Circuit Breakers

The headlights are protected by a circuit breaker in the headlamp switch. If the circuit breaker trips, the headlights will either flash on and off, or stay off altogether. The circuit breaker rests automatically after the overload is removed.

The windshield wipers are also protected by a circuit breaker. If the motor overheats, the circuit breaker will trip, remaining off until the motor cools or the overload is removed. One common cause of overheating is operation of the wipers in heavy snow.

The circuit breakers for the power door locks and power windows are located in the fuse box.

Flashers

REPLACEMENT

The hazard flasher is located in the convenience center, under the dash, on the left side kick panel. The turn signal flasher is installed in a clamp attached to the base of the steering column support inside the car. In all cases, replacement is made by unplugging the old unit and plugging in a new one.

FUSE PANEL

1. (10 AMP)
   GLOW PLUGS (DIESEL)
   FUEL INJECTORS (GAS
   L4 AND PFI V6)

2. (10 AMP)
   FUEL PUMP (GAS
   L4 AND PFI V6)

3. (20 AMP)
   STOP / HAZARD LAMPS

4. (20 AMP)
   CHOKE HEATER / (CARB
   V6) COOLANT FAN
   WARNING INDICATORS

5. (15 AMP)
   TURN SIGNAL LAMPS
   BACK-UP LAMPS

6. (10 AMP)
   ECM CRANK (GAS
   L4 AND PFIV6)

7. (20 AMP)
   PARK, SIDE MARKER,
   TAIL, LICENSE PLATE,
   STOP & TURN SIGNAL
   LAMPS, RADIO / DIGITAL
   CLOCK

8. (25 AMP)
   HEATER / AIR
   CONDITIONER

9. (10 AMP)
   GAGES / WARNING
   INDICATOR, AUDIBLE,
   WARNING SYSTEM,
   COMPUTER COMMAND
   CONTROL, RR WINDOW
   DEFOGGER, BRAKE
   WARNING INDICATOR,
   TORQUE CONVERTER
   CLUTCH, TRUNK RELEASE

10. (25 AMP)
    WIPER / WASHER

11. (20 AMP)
    COURTESY LAMP
    AUDIBLE WARNING
    SYSTEM, CIGAR LIGHTER
    UNDERHOOD LAMP,
    HORN, INTERIOR LAMPS

12. CIRCUIT BREAKER (30 AMP)
    POWER WINDOWS
    REAR WASHER / WIPER

13. (5 AMP)
    AUDIBLE WARNING
    SYSTEM, RR WINDOW
    DEFOGGER, INSTRUMENT
    PANEL LAMPS

14. (10 AMP)
    RADIO

15. CIRCUIT BREAKER (30 AMP)
    REAR WINDOW DEFOGGER,
    POWER DOOR LOCKS,
    POWER SEATS
    REAR WASHER / WIPER
    TAILGATE RELEASE

16. SPARE

17. (10 AMP)
    ECM COMPUTER
    COMMAND CONTROL
    (CARB V6)

86816242

Fig. 99 Fuse block assembly — 1982-85

Production changes may cause some of these fuse specifications to be revised. Always replace a fuse with one of the same amperage. If there is any question, see your Oldsmobile dealer.

A Computer Command Control (Ignition, CHECK ENGINE" Light) (10 Amp.)
B Cruise Control; Power Antenna; Sound System (10 Amp.)
C IP Clock; IP Lights; Auto-Calculator; Console Shift Indicator; Rear Defogger (5 Amp.)
D Chimes; Lighter; IP Clock; Electronic Level Control; Horn; Inside Lights; Power Antenna; Power Door Locks; Sound System; Auto-Calculator; Power Rear Lid Release (20 Amp.)
E Wiper and Washer (25 Amp.)
F Air Conditioning Compressor; Chimes; Fuel Injection (EFI & MFI); Brake Warning; Computer Command Control; Torque Converter Clutch; Electronic Level Control; Rear Defogger (10 Amp.)

G Heater; Air Conditioner (25 Amp.)
H Chimes; Electronic Instrument Cluster; Exterior Lights (except Headlights and Back-Up Lights); Sound System; Underhood Light (20 Amp.)
I Electronic Fuel Injection (10 Amp.)
J Back-Up Lights; Turn Signals; Power Rear Lid Release (15 Amp.)
K Choke Heater; Coolant Fan; Fuel Pump; Diesel Fuel Control (10 or 20 Amp – be sure to replace with a fuse of the same amperage)
L Stop/Turn/Parking Lights (20 Amp.)
M Electronic Fuel Injection (10 Amp.)
N Glow Plugs; Diesel Fuel Control; Computer Command Control; Fuel Injection (EFI and MFI); Torque Converter Clutch (10 Amp.)

86816243

Fig. 100 Fuse block assembly — 1986

FUSE BLOCK

DO NOT USE FUSES
OF HIGHER AMPERAGE RATING
THAN THOSE SPECIFIED.

1. Fuse - 10 Amp. (Red) (Ignition). (Electronic Control Module)
2. Fuse - 25 Amp. (White) (Starter Signal to Electronic Control Module)
3. Fuse - 10 Amp. (Red) (Fuel Pump Relay) (Oil Pressure Switch) Throttle Body Ignition
4. Fuse - 10 Amp. (Red) (Battery) (Computer Command Control - Electronic Control Module)
5. Fuse - 20 Amp. (Yellow) (Battery). (Tail Lights)
6. Fuse - 20 Amp. (Yellow) (Ignition)
7. Fuse - 25 Amp. (White) (Ignition). (Heater Air Conditioner and Electric Trunk Release)
8. Fuse - 20 Amp. (Yellow) (Battery). (Dome Lights, Horn Relay, Lighter, Glove Box, Air Conditioner Relay, Power Locks, Automatic Level Control, and Power Antenna)
9. Circuit Breaker (Ignition). (Power Window, Washer/Wiper, Tailgate on Wagons)
10. Circuit Breaker (Battery). (Power Seats, Electric Rear Window Defogger, Power Door Locks, Washer/Wiper, Tailgate on Wagons)
11. Fuse - 20 Amp. (Yellow) (Battery). (Stop Light Switch and Hazard Flasher Electronic Tone)
12. Fuse - 10 Amp. (Red) (Ignition). (Radio Feed and Cruise).
13. Blank
14. Fuse - 5 Amp. (Tan) (Instrument Panel Lights)
15. Fuse - 10 Amp. (Red) (Ignition). (Electric Rear Window Defogger Off-On Switch, Electronic Tones or Chimes, Gages, Vehicle Speed Sensor, Air Conditioner Relay, Transaxle Converter Clutch Brake Switch, Indicator Lights, Service Engine Soon Light, Vacuum Warning Module)
16. Fuse - 25 Amp. (White) (Ignition). (Windshield Wiper Motor)
17. Fuse - 15 Amp. (Light Blue) (Ignition). (Turn Flasher and Back-Up Lights)

86816244

Fig. 101 Fuse block assembly — 1987

FUSE SPECIFICATIONS

Production changes may cause some of these fuse specifications to be revised. Always replace a fuse with one of the same amperage. If there is any question, see your Oldsmobile dealer.

A. Wiper and Washer (25 Amp)

B. Cruise Control; Power Antenna; Music System (10 Amp)

C. IP Clock; IP Lights; Console Shift Indicator; Rear Defogger (5 Amp)

D. Chimes; Lighter; IP Clock; Electronic Level Control; Horn; Inside Lights; Power Antenna; Power Door Locks; Music System; Power Rear Lid Release (20 Amp)

E. Stop/Turn/Parking Lights (20 Amp)

F. Air Conditioning Compressor; Brake Warning; Chimes; Computer Command Control; Electronic Level Control; Fuel Injection; Instrument Panel; Rear Defogger (10 Amp)

G. Heater/Air Conditioner; Power Rear Lid Release (25 Amp)

H. Chimes; Electronic Instrument Cluster; Exterior Lights (except Headlights and Back-Up Lights); Music System; Underhood Light (20 Amp)

I. Not Used

J. Back-Up Lights; Fog Lights; Turn Signals; Power Rear Lid Release (15 Amp)

K. Charging System; Engine Coolant Fan; Fuel Pump; (10 Amp)

L. Computer Command Control (Ignition, Warning Light); Fuel Pump Relay (10 Amp)

M. Air Conditioning Compressor; Electronic Fuel Injection; Fuel Pump (20 Amp)

N. Computer Command Control; Fuel Injection; Torque Converter Clutch (15 Amp)

86816245

Fig. 102 Fuse block assembly — 1987-89

FRONT VIEW OF FUSE BLOCK

86816250

Fig. 104 Fuse block assembly — 1991

FRONT VIEW OF FUSE BLOCK

86816249

Fig. 105 Fuse block assembly — 1992

FRONT VIEW OF FUSE BLOCK

86816251

Fig. 103 Fuse block assembly — 1990

Fuse Usage

Fuse	Rating (AMPS)	Circuitry
A	15	ECM; MAF Sensor (3300 Engine only)
B	20	ECM Injectors/Coil
C	10	Eng. A/C Relay; EGR Solenoid; Canister Purge Solenoid
D	10	Fan/Elect; Generator; DRL Module
E	15	Turn Signal Flasher; Back-Up Lights; Trunk/Liftgate Release

Fuse	Rating (AMPS)	Circuitry
F	10	Supplemental Inflatable Restraint (Air Bag)
G	20	Tail; Park; Side Marker; License Plate; Stop/Turn Signal
H	20	Heater/Air Conditioner
I	10	Gages; Warning Indicators; Torque Convert Clutch; Audible Warning System; Computer Command Control; Trunk Release; Brake Warning Indicator; Rear Defog Switch; Speedometer
J	20	Stop Lights; Hazard Flashers
K	20	Interior, Underhood, Courtesy, I/P, Trunk Lights; Door Locks; Horn Relay, Passive Restraint System, Deck Lid Release, Power Antenna
L	30*	Liftgate Release; Power Windows
M	5	Illumination for: I/P, Radio, Pod Lights, Ashtray, Console Light, Heater-A/C Control, Defog Switch, Headlight Switch
N	10	Radio, Cruise Control
O	30*	Seats, Door Locks, Rear Defog
P	25	Windshield Wipe/Wash
Q	20	Cigarette Lighter
	15	Safety Belt/Chime (ICAM) Module (Located behind the fuse block, above the hush panel.)
	15	Remote Lock Control (Located behind the fuse block, above the hush panel.)
	15	Fuel Pump, ECM (Located under the hood.)

*Circuit Breaker

86816246

Fig. 106 Fuse block assembly — 1993

Fuse Usage

Fuse	Amp	Circuitry
1	15	ECM, MAF Sensor (3100 Engine only)
2	20	ECM Injectors/Coil
3	5	Automatic Door Lock/Unlock
4	15	Turn Signal Flasher, Back-Up Lights, Trunk/Liftgate Release
5	10	Supplemental Inflatable Restraint (Air Bag)
6	20	Tail, Park, Side Marker, License Plate, Stop/Turn Signal
7	20	Heater/Air Conditioner
8	10	Gages, Warning Indicators, Torque Convert Clutch, Audible Warning System, Computer Command Control, Trunk Release, Brake Warning Indicator, Rear Defog Switch, Speedometer
9	20	Stop Lights, Hazard Flashers
10	20	Interior, Underhood, Courtesy, I/P, Trunk Lights, Door Locks, Horn Relay, Passive Restraint System, Deck Lid Release, Power Antenna
11	30*	Liftgate Release, Power Windows
12	5	Illumination for: I/P, Radio, Pod Lights, Ashtray, Console Light, Heater-A/C Control, Defog Switch, Headlight Switch
13	10	Radio, Cruise Control
14	30*	Seats, Door Locks, Rear Defog
15	25	Windshield Wipe/Wash
16	20	Cigarette Lighter

*Circuit Breaker

86816247

Fig. 107 Fuse block assembly — 1994 Buick

Fuse Usage

Fuse	Rating (AMPS)	Circuitry
A	15	ECM
B	20	ECM Injectors/Coil
C	5	Auto Unlock (Remove this fuse to disable the automatic door unlock.)
D	10	Electric Fan; Generator; DRL Module
E	15	Turn Signal Flasher; Back-Up Lights; Trunk/Liftgate Release
F	10	Supplemental Inflatable Restraint (Air Bag)
G	20	Tail; Park; Side Marker; License Plate; Stop/Turn Signal
H	20	Heater/Air Conditioner
I	10	Gages; Warning Indicators; Torque Converter Clutch; Audible Warning System; Computer Command Control; Trunk Release; Brake Warning Indicator; Rear Defog Switch; Speedometer
J	20	Stop Lights; Hazard Flashers
K	20	Interior, Underhood, Courtesy, I/P, Trunk Lights; Door Locks; Horn Relay; Passive Restraint System; Deck Lid Release; Power Antenna
L	30*	Liftgate Release; Power Windows
M	5	Illumination for: I/P, Radio, Pod Lights, Ashtray, Console Light, Heater-A/C Control, Defog Switch, Headlight Switch
N	10	Radio, Cruise Control
O	30*	Seats, Door Locks, Rear Defog
P	25	Windshield Wiper/Washer
Q	20	Cigarette Lighter
	15	Seat Belt/Chime (ICAM) Module (Located behind the glove box. Have your dealer service.)
	10	Eng. A/C Relay; EGR Solenoid; Canister Purge Solenoid (Located behind the glove box. Have your dealer service.)
	15	SIR Crank (Located behind the glove box. Have your dealer service.)
	15	Fuel Pump, ECM (Located under the hood. Have your dealer service.)

*Circuit Breaker

86816248

Fig. 108 Fuse block assembly — 1994 Oldsmobile

WIRING DIAGRAMS

Fig. 109 Engine wiring — 1982 2.5L (VIN R)

Fig. 110 Engine wiring — 1982 2.8L (VIN X)

Fig. 111 Engine wiring — 1982 3.0L (VIN E)

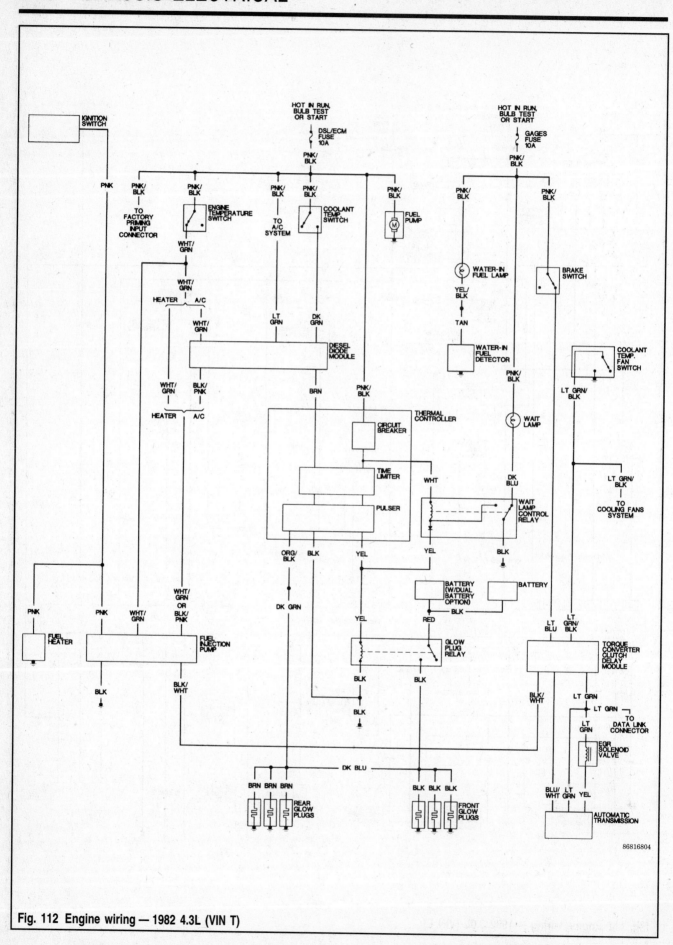

Fig. 112 Engine wiring — 1982 4.3L (VIN T)

86816804

Fig. 113 Chassis wiring — 1982 Century

Fig. 114 Chassis wiring — 1982 Century continued

86816806

Fig. 115 Chassis wiring — 1982 Ciera

86816807

Fig. 116 Chassis wiring — 1982 Ciera continued

Fig. 117 Chassis wiring — 1982 6000/Celebrity

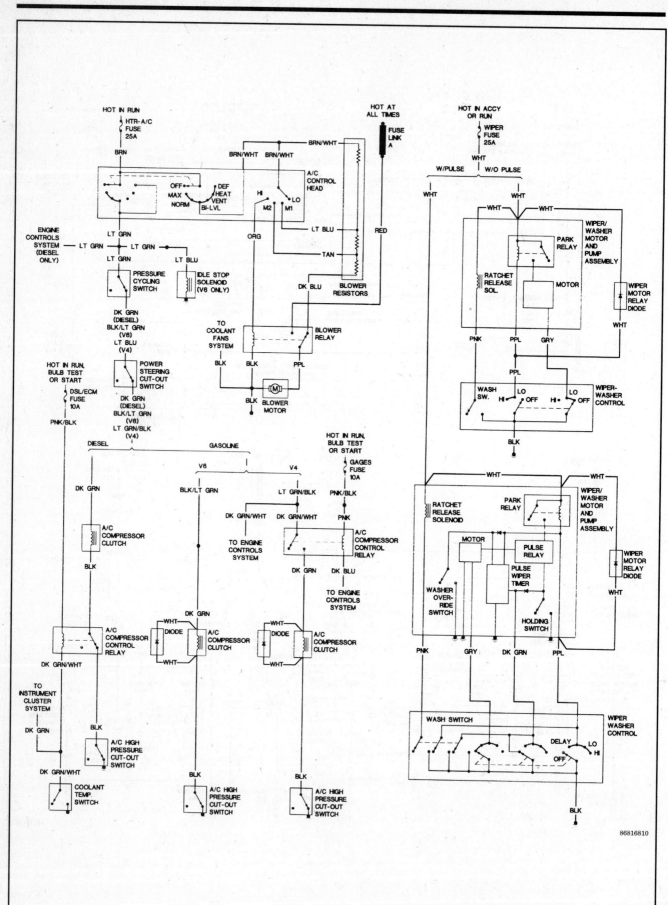

Fig. 118 Chassis wiring — 1982 6000/Celebrity continued

86816810

Fig. 119 Engine and chassis wiring — 1983 2.5L (VIN R)

86816812

Fig. 120 Engine and chassis wiring — 1983 2.8L (VIN X)

86816813

Fig. 121 Engine and chassis wiring — 1983 3.0L (VIN E)

86816814

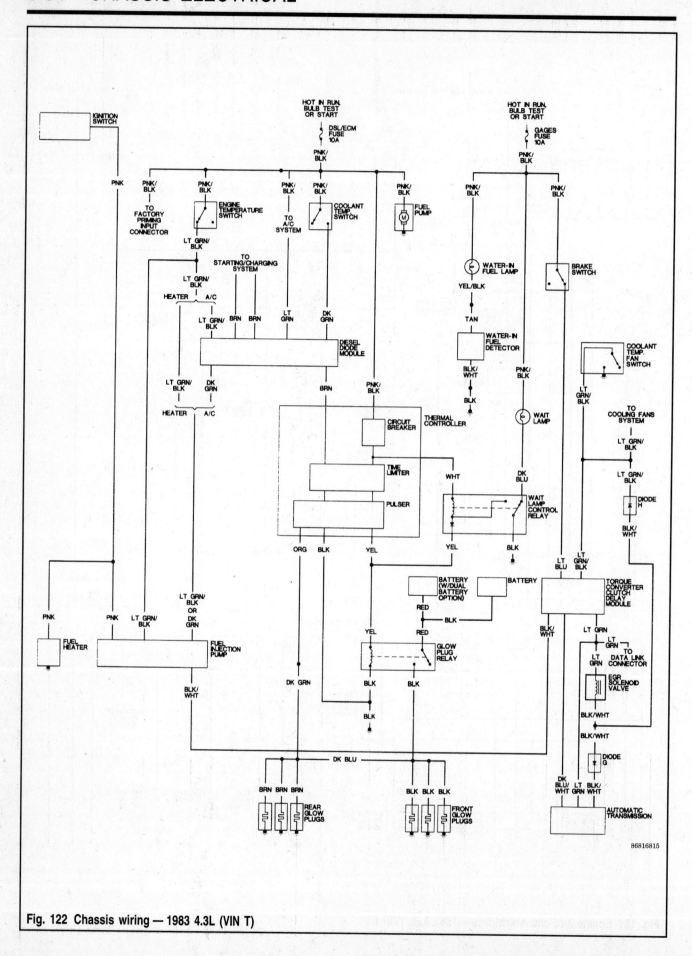

Fig. 122 Chassis wiring — 1983 4.3L (VIN T)

86816815

Fig. 123 Chassis wiring — 1983 Ciera/Century

Fig. 124 Chassis wiring — 1983 Ciera/Century continued

86816817

Fig. 125 Chassis wiring — 1983 6000/Celebrity

Fig. 126 Chassis wiring — 1983 6000/Celebrity continued

86816819

Fig. 127 Engine and chassis wiring — 1984 2.5L (VIN R)

Fig. 128 Engine and chassis wiring — 1984 2.8L (VIN X)

86816821

Fig. 129 Engine and chassis wiring — 1984 3.0L (VIN E)

Fig. 130 Engine and chassis wiring — 1984 4.3L (VIN T) 3spd Automatic

Fig. 131 Engine and chassis wiring — 1984 4.3L (VIN T) 4spd Automatic

Fig. 132 Chassis wiring — 1984 Ciera/Century

Fig. 133 Chassis wiring — 1984 Ciera/Century continued

86816826

Fig. 134 Chassis wiring — 1984 6000/Celebrity

86816827

Fig. 135 Chassis wiring — 1984 6000/Celebrity continued

Fig. 136 Engine and chassis wiring — 1985 2.5L (VIN R)

86816829

Fig. 137 Engine and chassis wiring — 1985 2.8L (VIN W)

86816830

Fig. 138 Engine and chassis wiring — 1985 3.0L (VIN E)

Fig. 139 Engine and chassis wiring — 1985 3.8L (VIN 3)

Fig. 140 Engine and chassis wiring — 1985 4.3L (VIN T)

86816833

Fig. 141 Chassis wiring — 1985 Ciera/Century

Fig. 142 Chassis wiring — 1985 Ciera/Century continued

86816835

Fig. 143 Chassis wiring — 1985 6000/Celebrity

86816836

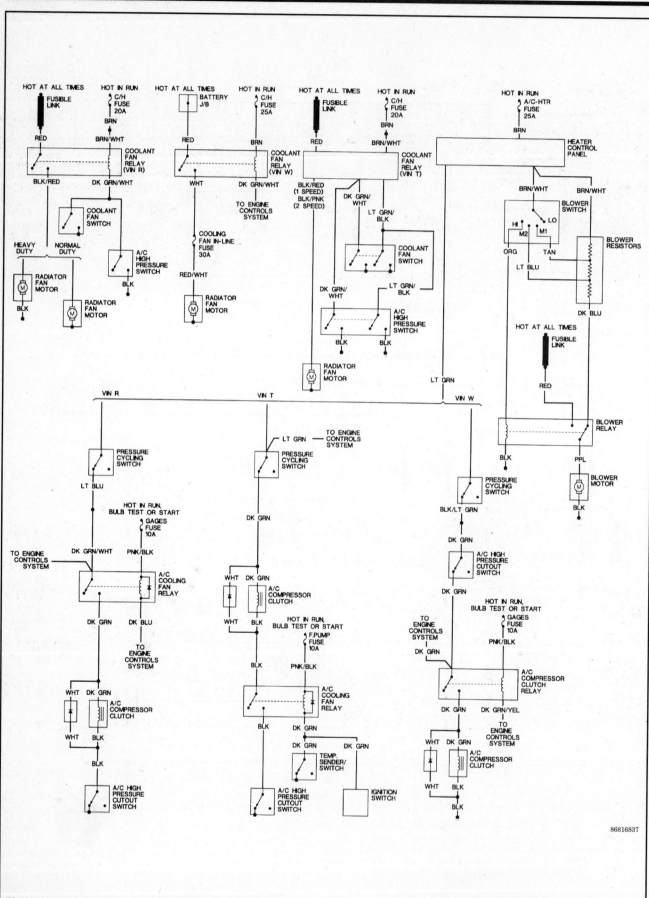

Fig. 144 Chassis wiring — 1985 6000/Celebrity continued

86816837

Fig. 145 Engine and chassis wiring — 1986 2.5L (VIN R)

86816838

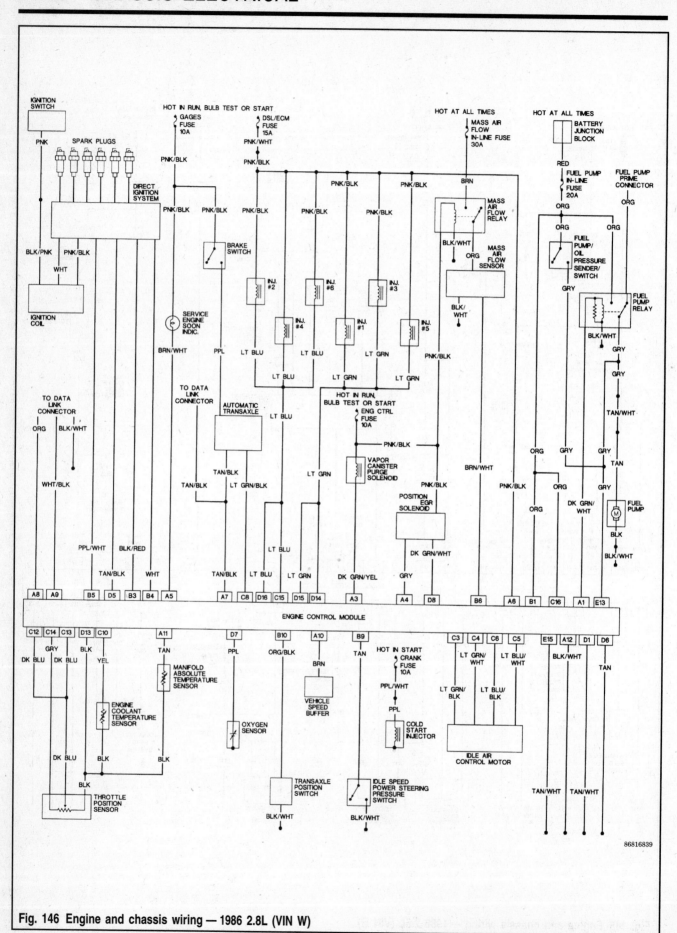

Fig. 146 Engine and chassis wiring — 1986 2.8L (VIN W)

Fig. 147 Engine and chassis wiring — 1986 2.8L (VIN X)

Fig. 148 Engine and chassis wiring — 1986 3.8L (VIN 3)

Fig. 149 Chassis wiring — 1986 Ciera/Century

86816842

Fig. 150 Chassis wiring — 1986 Ciera/Century continued

86816843

Fig. 151 Chassis wiring — 1986 6000/Celebrity

86816844

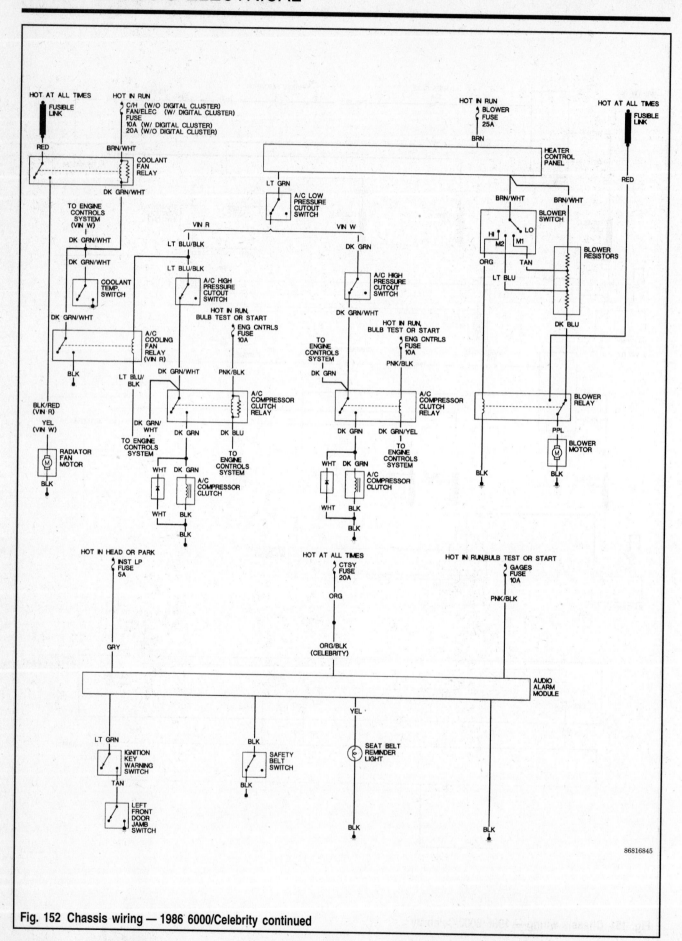

Fig. 152 Chassis wiring — 1986 6000/Celebrity continued

Fig. 153 Engine and chassis wiring — 1987-88 2.5L (VIN R)

86816846

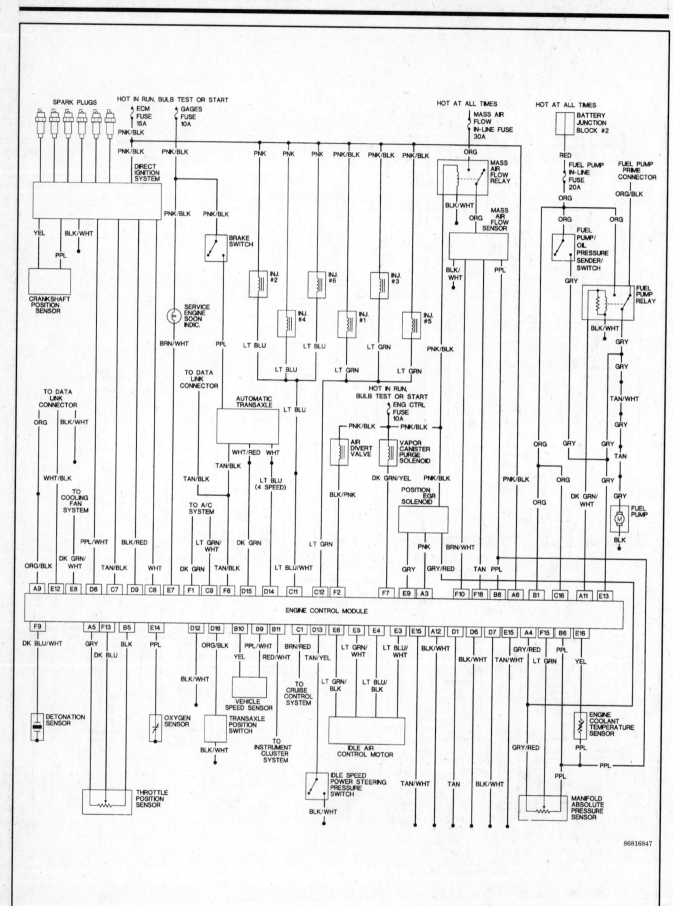

Fig. 154 Engine and chassis wiring — 1987-88 2.8L (VIN W)

86816847

Fig. 155 Engine and chassis wiring — 1987-88 3.8L (VIN 3)

86816848

Fig. 156 Chassis wiring — 1987-88 Ciera/Century

Fig. 157 Chassis wiring — 1987-88 Ciera/Century continued

86816850

Fig. 158 Chassis wiring — 1987-88 6000/Celebrity

Fig. 159 Chassis wiring — 1987-88 6000/Celebrity continued

Fig. 160 Engine and chassis wiring — 1989 2.5L (VIN R)

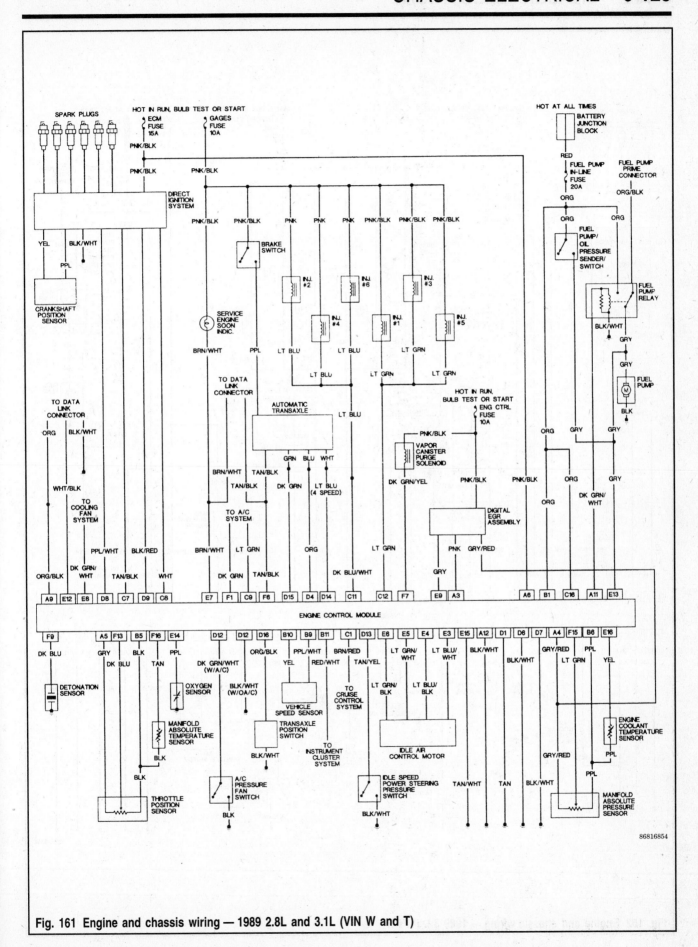

Fig. 161 Engine and chassis wiring — 1989 2.8L and 3.1L (VIN W and T)

86816854

Fig. 162 Engine and chassis wiring — 1989 3.L (VIN N)

86816855

Fig. 163 Chassis wiring — 1989 Ciera/Century

86816856

Fig. 164 Chassis wiring — 1989 Ciera/Century continued

86816850

Fig. 165 Chassis wiring — 1989 6000/Celebrity

86816859

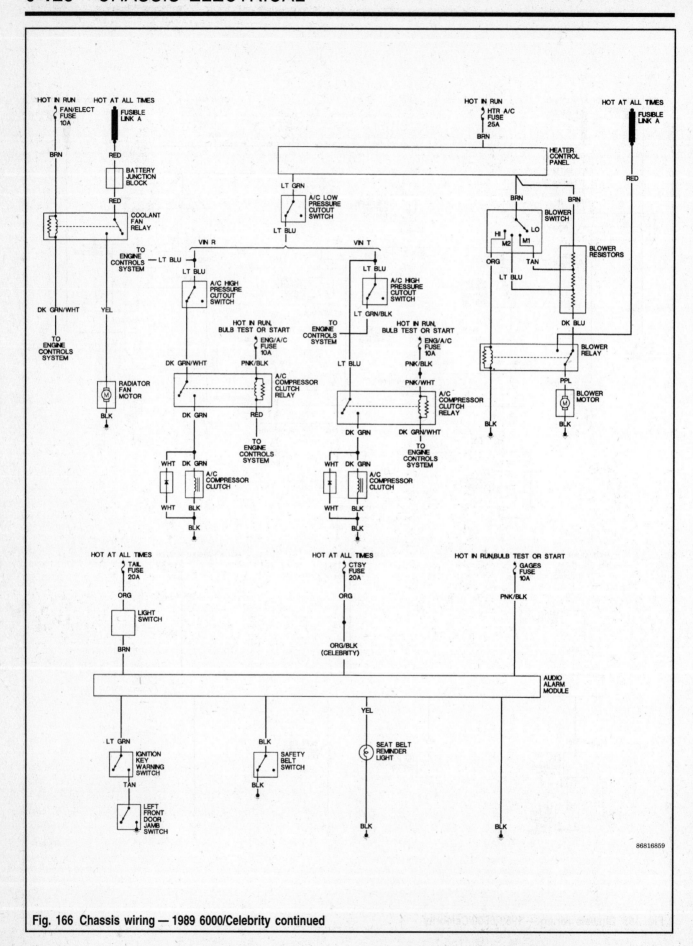

Fig. 166 Chassis wiring — 1989 6000/Celebrity continued

Fig. 167 Engine and chassis wiring — 1990-91 2.5L (VIN R)

86816860

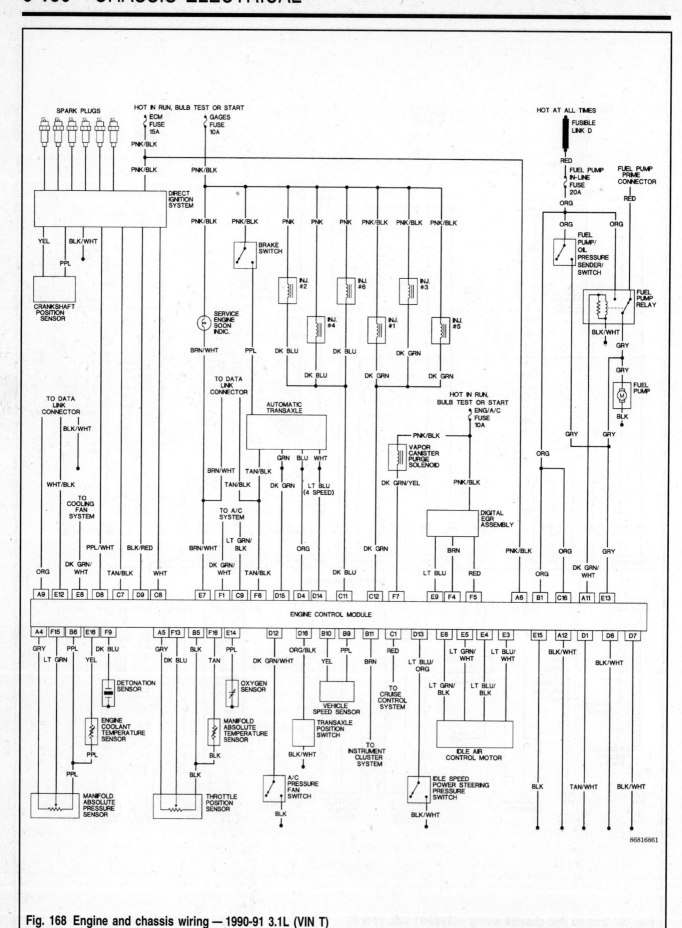

Fig. 168 Engine and chassis wiring — 1990-91 3.1L (VIN T)

Fig. 169 Engine and chassis wiring — 1990-91 3.3L (VIN N)

Fig. 170 Chassis wiring — 1990-91 Ciera/Century

Fig. 171 Chassis wiring — 1990-91 Ciera/Century continued

86816864

Fig. 172 Chassis wiring — 1990-91 6000/Celebrity

Fig. 173 Chassis wiring — 1990-91 6000/Celebrity continued

Fig. 174 Engine and chassis wiring — 1992 2.5L (VIN R)

Fig. 175 Engine and chassis wiring — 1992 3.3L (VIN N)

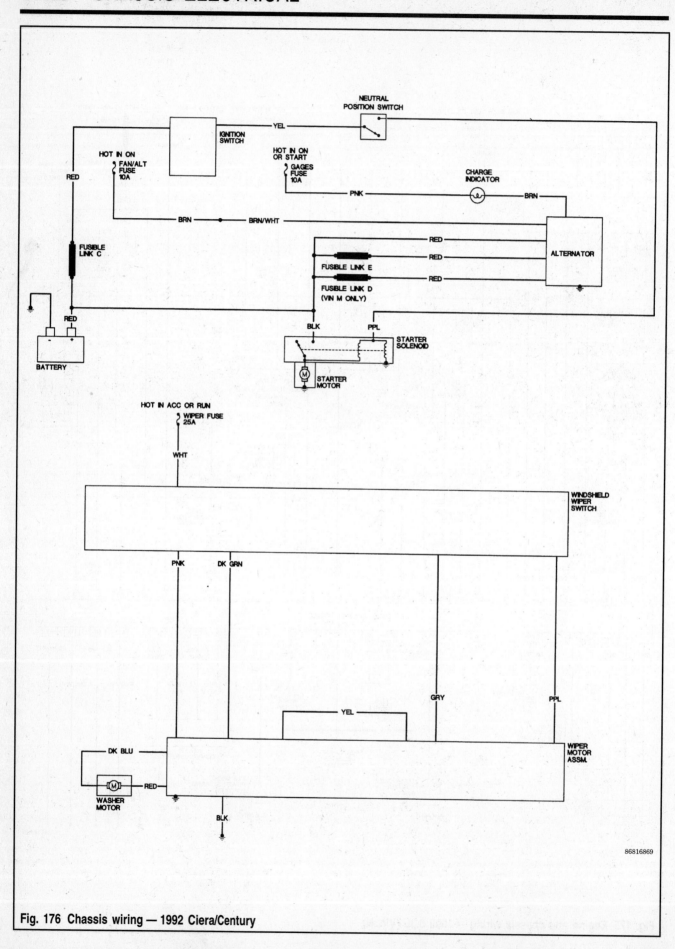

Fig. 176 Chassis wiring — 1992 Ciera/Century

Fig. 177 Chassis wiring — 1992 Ciera/Century continued

Fig. 178 Engine and chassis wiring — 1993 2.2L (VIN 4)

Fig. 179 Engine and chassis wiring — 1993-94 3.1L (VIN M)

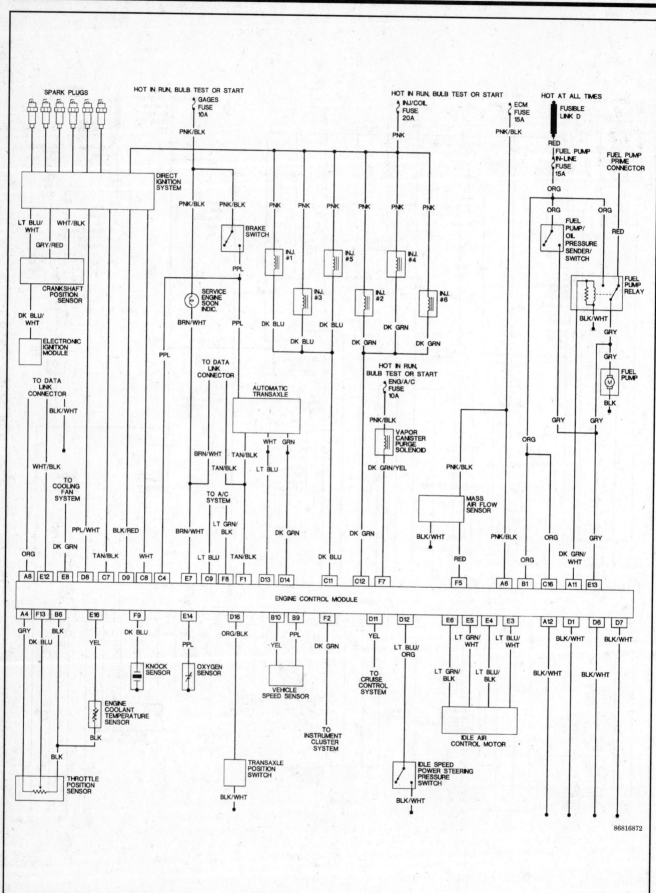

Fig. 180 Engine and chassis wiring — 1993 3.3L (VIN N)

86816872

Fig. 181 Chassis wiring — 1993 Ciera/Century

86816873

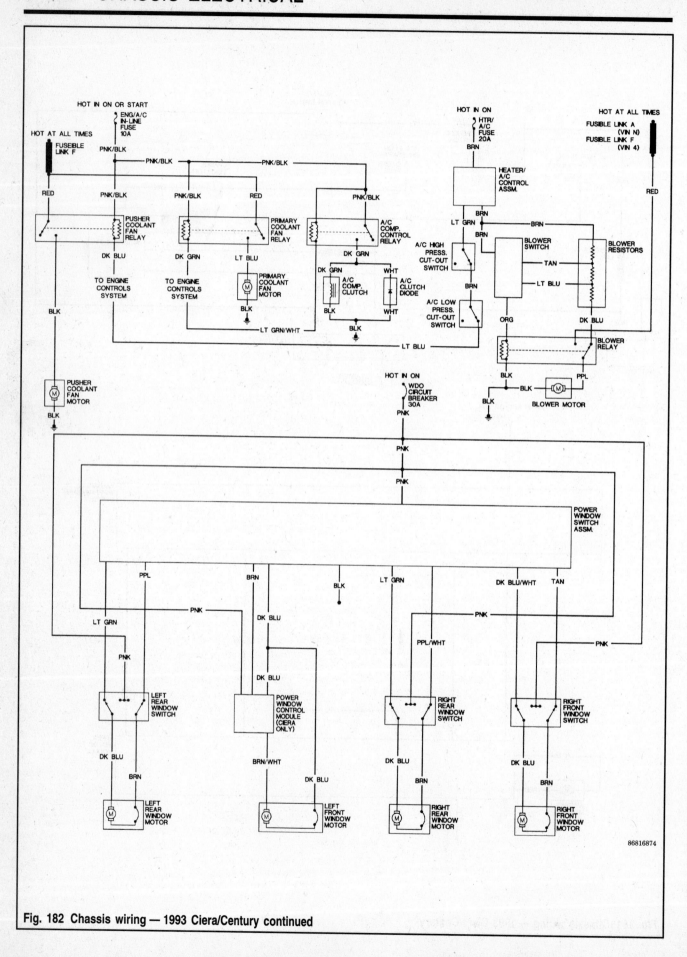

Fig. 182 Chassis wiring — 1993 Ciera/Century continued

86816874

Fig. 183 Engine and chassis wiring — 1994 2.2L (VIN 4)

Fig. 184 Chassis wiring — 1994 Ciera/Century

Fig. 185 Chassis wiring — 1994 Ciera/Century continued

Fig. 186 Engine and chassis wiring — 1995 2.2L (VIN 4)

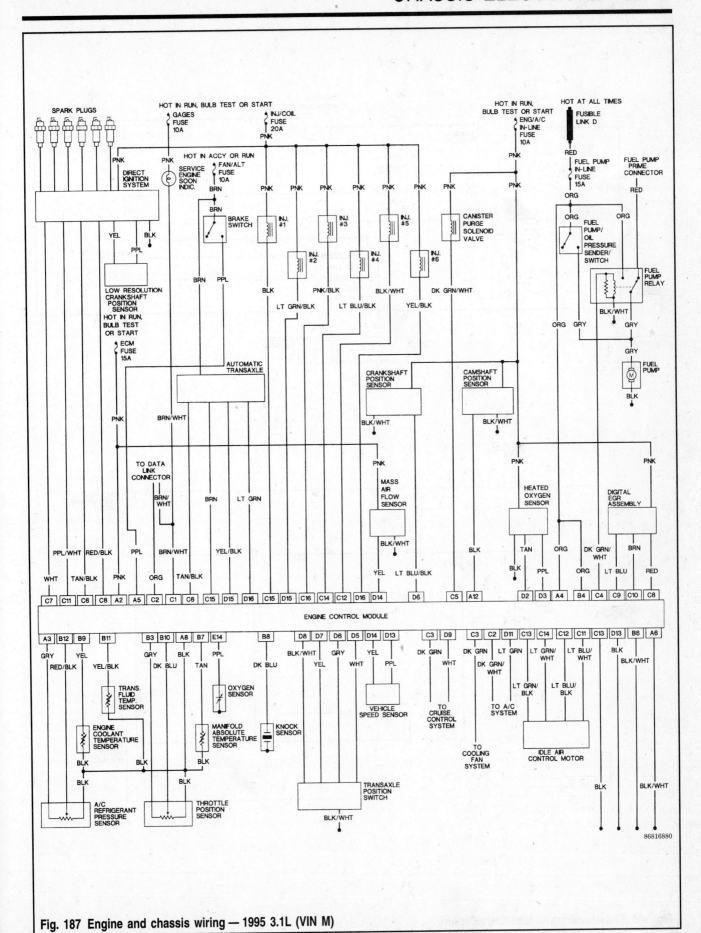

Fig. 187 Engine and chassis wiring — 1995 3.1L (VIN M)

86816880

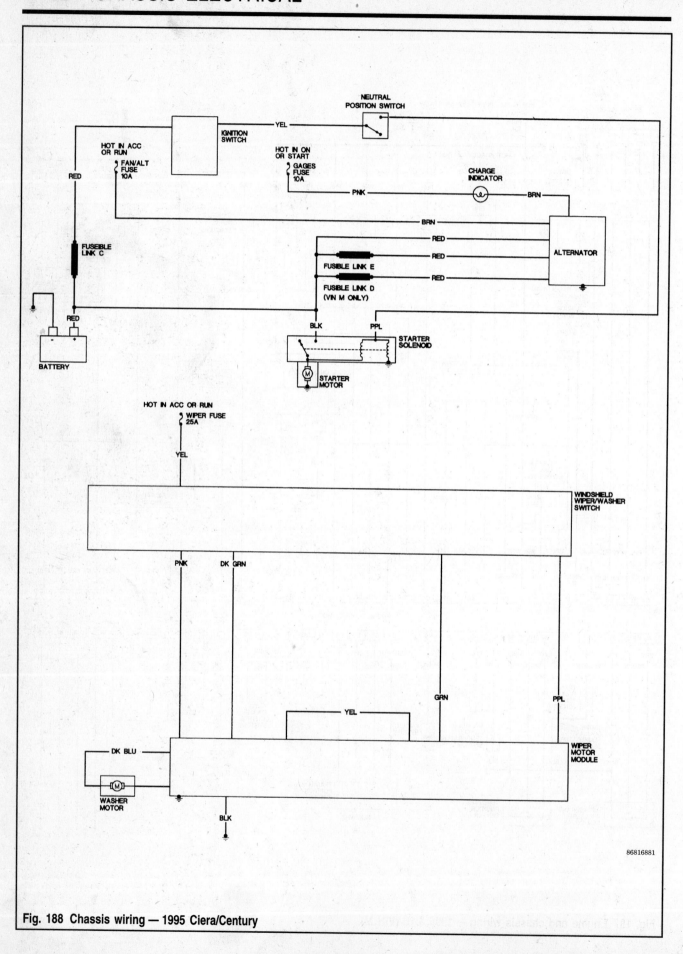

Fig. 188 Chassis wiring — 1995 Ciera/Century

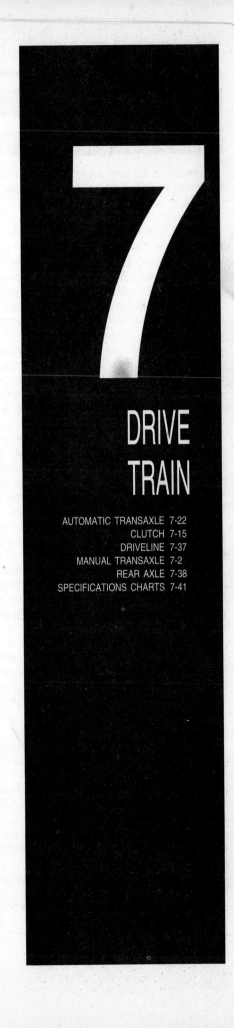

7

DRIVE TRAIN

MANUAL TRANSAXLE

General Information

Transaxle is the term used to identify a unit which combines the transmission and drive axle into one component. All 1982-86 models were equipped with MT-125 manual four speed transaxles. In 1987-88 Muncie five speed transaxles were used. The 4-speed transaxles use cable actuated clutches while the five speed clutches are hydraulically controlled utilizing a clutch master and slave cylinder.

All forward gears in this design are in constant mesh. Final drive from the transaxle is taken from the output gear, which is an integral part of the output shaft; the output gear transfers power to the differential ring gear and differential assembly. The differential is of conventional design.

The 4-speed transaxle assembly is a constant mesh design, combined with a differential unit and assembled in a single case, the forward gears are in constant mesh. For ease of shifting and gear selecting, synchronizers with blocker rings are controlled by shifting forks. A sliding idler gear arrangement is used for reverse gear.

The components consists of: an aluminum transaxle case, an aluminum clutch cover, input gear (shaft), output gear (shaft) and the differential assembly. Preloaded tapered roller bearings support the input gear, output gear and differential. Selective shims, used to establish the correct preload, are located beneath the right hand bearing cups.

The halfshafts which are attached to the front wheels, are turned by the differential and ring gear which are controlled by the final output gear.

The differential, consisting of a set of 4 gears, is a conventional arrangement that divides the torque between the halfshafts, allowing them to rotate at different speeds. Of the 4 gear set, 2 are known as differential side gears and the others are differential pinion gears.

The differential pinion gears, mounted on a differential pinion shaft, are free to rotate on the shaft. The pinion shaft, placed in the differential case bore, is at a right angle to the drive axle shaft. The Hydra-Matic Muncie 282 (HM-282) transaxle is a 5-speed unit. The gearing provides for 5 synchronized forward speeds, a reverse speed, a final drive with differential output and speedometer drive.

The input and output gear clusters are nested very close together, requiring extremely tight tolerances of shafts, gears and synchronizers.

The input shaft is supported by a roller bearing in the clutch and differential housing and a ball bearing in the transaxle case.

The output shaft is supported by a roller bearing in the clutch and differential housing and a combination ball-and-roller bearing in the transaxle case.

The differential case is supported by opposed tapered roller bearings which are under preload.

The speed gears are supported by roller bearings. A bushing supports the reverse idler gear.

Transaxle Identification

▶ **See Figure 1**

The transaxle identification stamp is located at the center top of the case. The transaxle identification tag is located on the left side near the left side cover.

Adjustments

LINKAGE

MT-125

▶ **See Figures 2, 3 and 4**

1. Disconnect the negative battery cable.
2. Remove the shifter boot, the console and retainer inside the car. Shift into first gear, then loosen the shift cable mounting nuts E at the transaxle D and F.
3. With the shift lever in first gear, position (pulled to the left and held against the stop) insert a yoke clip to hold the lever hard against the reverse lockout stop as shown in view D. Install two No. 22 drill bits, or two 5/32 in. (4mm) rods, into the two alignment holes in the shifter assembly to hold it in first gear. This is shown in view C.
4. Remove the lash from the transaxle by rotating the lever D in the direction of the arrow while tightening nut E. Tighten nut E on lever F.
5. Remove the two drill bits or pins from the shifter.
6. Connect the negative battery cable. Road test the vehicle to check for a good neutral gate feel during shifting. It may be necessary to fine tune the adjustment after road testing.

SHIFTER SHAFT WASHER

▶ **See Figures 5 and 6**

If a hang-up is experienced in the 1-2 gear range and the shift cables are properly adjusted, it may be necessary to change the shift selector washer.

1. From the end of the housing, remove the reverse inhibitor fitting spring and washer.
2. Position the shifter shaft into the **2nd** gear position.
3. Measure the end of housing-to-end of shifter shaft (dimension **A**).
4. On the opposite end of the shaft, apply a load of 8.8-13.3 lbs. (4-6 Kg) and measure the end of housing-to-end of shifter shaft (dimension **B**).
5. Subtract dimension **B** from dimension **A** and secure dimension **C**.
6. Using the dimension **C** and shifter shaft selective washer chart, select the correct shim washer to be used on the reinstallation.

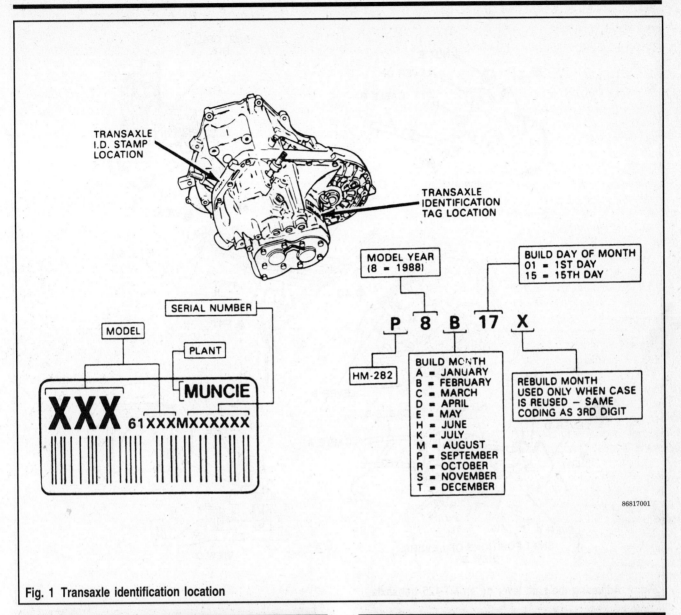

Fig. 1 Transaxle identification location

Back-up Light Switch

REMOVAL & INSTALLATION

1. Remove the shifter knob from the shifter by removing the retaining screw at the back of the knob.
2. Remove the screws at the sides and front of the console.
3. Open the console box, then remove the retaining screw inside the box.
4. Remove the ashtray at the rear of the console, then remove the retaining screw behind the ashtray.
5. Slide the console rearward slightly, then lift it over the shifter.
6. Disconnect the wiring harness at the back-up light switch.
7. Remove the switch from the base of the shifter.
8. Reverse steps to install the switch.

Shift Cable

REMOVAL & INSTALLATION

4-Speed Transaxle

1. Disconnect the negative battery cable.
2. At the transaxle, disconnect the shift cables, then remove the retaining clamp.
3. At the shift control, remove the knob, the control cover and the boot or console (if equipped).
4. Disconnect the shift cables from the shift control.
5. Remove the front sill plate and pull the carpet back to gain access to the cables.
6. Remove the cable grommet cover screws, the floor pan cover and cables.
   To install:
7. Route the cables into the vehicle, then install the cable cover and screws (at floor pan).

Fig. 2 Adjusting the shift lever on an MT-125 transaxle

Fig. 3 Control assembly on the MT-125 transaxle

Fig. 4 Shift cable assembly on the MT-125 transaxle

Fig. 5 Shift shaft assembly

SHIM PART NO.	DIM C (MM)	COLOR & NO OF STRIPES
14008235	1.8	3 WHITE
476709	2.1	1 ORANGE
476710	2.4	2 ORANGE
476711	2.7	3 ORANGE
476712	3.0	1 BLUE
476713	3.3	2 BLUE
476714	3.6	3 BLUE
476715	3.9	1 WHITE
476716	4.2	2 WHITE

86817007

Fig. 6 Selective washer chart

8. At the shift control assembly, connect the shift cables. Reposition the carpet and install the sill plate.

9. Raise and safely support the vehicle.

10. At the transaxle, position the cables and install the retaining clamps.

11. Lower the vehicle.

12. Connect and adjust the cables at the shift lever assembly.

13. Install the console, if equipped, the boot, the control cover and the knob.

14. Attach the negative battery cable.

5-Speed Transaxle

▸ **See Figure 7**

1. Disconnect the negative battery cable.

2. Disconnect the shift cables from the transaxle by removing the cable clamp at the transaxle.

3. Remove the cable ends from the ball studs at the shift levers by twisting a large flat blade tool between the nylon socket and the lever.

4. Remove the knob, console and shift boot.

5. Remove the cable ends from the ball studs of the shifter by twisting a large flat blade tool between the nylon socket and the shifter lever. Do not pry the socket off the stud using the cable end for leverage.

6. Remove the spring clip holding the cables to the shifter base and remove the cables from the shifter.

7. Remove the right front sill plate and pull the carpet back to gain access to the cables.

8. Remove the cable grommet cover screws and cover at the floor pan and remove the cables.

To install:

9. Route the cables, then install the cable grommet cover and attaching screws at the floor pan.

10. Install the shift cables at the control assembly. Snap the cable ends onto the ball studs using the channel locks.

11. Reposition the carpet and install the sill plate.

12. Raise and support the vehicle safely.

13. Route the cables to the transaxle.

14. Lower the vehicle.

Fig. 7 Shifter cable replacement on the Muncie 5-speed transaxle

15. Position the cables and install the retaining clamps at the transaxle. Connect the cables to the shift levers.

16. Install the shift boot, console and knob.

17. Connect the negative battery cable.

Transaxle

REMOVAL & INSTALLATION

When removing and installing a transaxle, special tools may be required for the job. Read the procedure completely before actually working on the vehicle.

1982-83 Models

MT-125

1. Disconnect the negative battery cable from the transaxle case.

2. Remove the two transaxle strut bracket bolts on the left side of the engine compartment, if equipped.

3. Remove the top four engine-to-transaxle bolts, and the one at the rear near the firewall. The one at the rear is installed from the engine side.

4. Loosen the engine-to-transaxle bolt near the starter, but do not remove.

5. Disconnect the speedometer cable at the transaxle, or at the speed control transducer on cars so equipped.

6. Remove the retaining clip and washer from the shift linkage at the transaxle. Remove the clips holding the cables to the mounting bosses on the case.

7. Support the engine with a lifting chain.

8. Unlock the steering column and raise and support the car. Drain the transaxle. Remove the two nuts attaching the stabilizer bar to the left lower control arm. Remove the four bolts which attach the left retaining plate to the engine cradle. The retaining plate covers and holds the stabilizer bar.

9. Loosen the four bolts holding the right stabilizer bracket.

10. Disconnect and remove the exhaust pipe and crossover if necessary.

11. Pull the stabilizer bar down on the left side.

12. Remove the four nuts and disconnect the front and rear transaxle mounts from the engine cradle. Remove the two rear center crossmember bolts.

13. Remove the three right side front cradle attaching bolts. They are accessible under the splash shield.

14. Remove the top bolt from the lower front transaxle shock absorber if equipped.

15. Remove the left front wheel. Remove the front cradle-to-body bolts on the left side, and the rear cradle-to-body bolts.

16. Pull the left side driveshaft from the transaxle using G. M. special tool J-28468 or the equivalent. The right side axle shaft will simply disconnect from the cage. When the transaxle is removed, the right shaft can be swung out of the way. A boot protector should be used when disconnecting the driveshafts.

17. Swing the cradle to the left side. Secure out of the way, outboard of the fender well.

18. Remove the flywheel and starter shield bolts, then remove the shields.

19. Remove the two transaxle extension bolts from the engine-to-transaxle bracket, if equipped.

20. Place a jack under the transaxle case. Remove the last engine-to-transaxle bolt. Pull the transaxle to the left, away from the engine, then down and out from under the car.

To install:

21. Place the transaxle on a jack and raise it into position. Position the right axle shaft into its bore as the transaxle is bolted to the engine.

22. Swing the cradle into position and install the cradle-to-body bolts immediately. Be sure to guide the left axle shaft into place as the cradle is moved back into position.

23. Install the two transaxle extension bolts into the engine-to-transaxle bracket.

24. Install the lower engine-to-transaxle bolts.

25. Install the flywheel to starter shield and retaining bolts.

26. Remove the boot protectors from the driveshafts.

27. Attach the top bolt to the lower front transaxle shock absorber.

28. Install the four nuts and connect the front and rear transaxle mounts to the engine cradle. Install the two rear center crossmember bolts.

29. Attach the stabilizer bar.

30. Install the exhaust pipe and crossover.

31. Secure the four bolts holding the right stabilizer bracket.

32. Install the two nuts attaching the stabilizer bar to the left lower control arm. Install the four bolts which attach the left retaining plate to the engine cradle.

33. Remove the transaxle jack, then disconnect the engine lifting chain and lower the vehicle.

34. Fill the transaxle with the recommended fluid.

35. Install the retaining clip and washer to the shift linkage at the transaxle. Install the clips holding the cables to the mounting bosses on the case.

36. Connect the speedometer cable at the transaxle, or at the speed control transducer on cars so equipped.

37. Tighten the engine-to-transaxle bolt near the starter.

38. Install the top four engine-to-transaxle bolts, and the one at the rear near the firewall. The one at the rear is installed from the engine side.

39. Remove the two transaxle strut bracket bolts on the left side of the engine compartment, if equipped.

40. Connect the negative battery cable to the transaxle case.

1984-86 Models

MT-125

1. Disconnect the battery ground cable from the transaxle and support it with a wire.

2. Disconnect the horn's electrical lead and remove the horn's mounting bolt. Remove the air cleaner.

3. Support the clutch pedal upward against the bumper stop to release the pawl from the quadrant. Disconnect the clutch cable from the release lever at the transaxle.

✳✳WARNING

DO NOT allow the clutch cable to snap rapidly toward the rear of the vehicle, for the quadrant in the adjusting mechanism can be damaged.

4. Lift the locking pawl away from the quadrant, then slide the cable out to the right side of the quadrant.

5. At the right side of the cowl, disconnect the cable retainer-to-upper stud nuts. Disconnect the cable from the transaxle bracket and remove the cable.

6. If equipped with a V6 engine, disconnect the fuel lines and clamps from the clutch cable bracket, then remove the exhaust crossover pipe.

7. At the transaxle, remove the shift linkage retaining clips and the shift cable retaining clips from the transaxle bosses.

8. Disconnect the speedometer cable at the transaxle. Remove the top engine-to-transaxle bolts.

9. Install and support the engine with tool J-22825-1. Raise the vehicle and drain the transaxle fluid.

10. Install the drive axle boot protector tool J-33162 to the drive axle boot. Remove the left front wheel and tire assembly.

11. Turn the steering wheel so that the intermediate shaft-to-steering gear stub shaft is in the upward position, then remove the bolt.

12. Position a floor jack under the engine to act as a support. Remove the power steering pressure line brackets.

13. Remove the steering gear mounting bolts, then support the steering gear. Disconnect the drive line vibration absorber, the front stabilizer from the left side lower control arm and the left side lower ball joint from the steering knuckle.

14. Remove both sides of the stabilizer bar reinforcements.

15. Using a ½ in. drill bit, drill through the spot weld (located between the rear holes of the left side front stabilizer bar mounting).

16. Disconnect the engine/transaxle mounts from the cradle. Remove the crossmember side bolts and the left side body bolts.

17. Remove the left side and the front crossmember assembly.

18. Using tools J-33008, J-29794 and J-261901, remove the left drive axle from the transaxle and the support.

➡**The right drive axle can be removed when the transaxle is removed from the vehicle.**

19. Remove the flywheel/starter shield bolts. Connect a transaxle jack to the transaxle, then remove the last engine-to-transaxle bolt.

20. Slide the transaxle away from the engine, lower the jack and move the transaxle away from the vehicle.

To install:

21. Place the transaxle on a jack and raise it into position. Position the right axle shaft into its bore as the transaxle is bolted to the engine.

22. Swing the cradle into position, then install the cradle-to-body bolts immediately. Be sure to guide the left axle shaft into place as the cradle is moved back into position.

23. Secure the flywheel/starter shield and bolts.

24. Attach the left side and front crossmember assembly.

25. Install the crossmember side bolts and the left side body bolts.

26. Connect the engine/transaxle mounts to the cradle.

27. Connect the left side lower ball joint to the steering knuckle.

28. Connect the front stabilizer to the left lower control arm.

29. Connect the drive line vibration absorber.

30. Install the stabilizer bar reinforcements, and the steering gear.

31. Install the power steering pressure line brackets.

32. Turn the steering wheel so that the intermediate shaft-to-steering gear stub shaft is in the upward position, then install the bolt.

33. Remove the drive axle boot protector tool J-33162 from the drive axle boot. Install the left front wheel and tire assembly.

34. Remove the engine support tool J-22825-1. Lower the vehicle and fill the transaxle with fluid.

35. Connect the speedometer cable at the transaxle. Install the top engine-to-transaxle bolts.

36. Install the shift linkage retaining clips and the shift cable retaining clips to the transaxle bosses.

37. If equipped with a V6 engine, connect the fuel lines and clamps to the clutch cable bracket, then install the exhaust crossover pipe.

38. At the right side of the cowl, connect the cable retainer-to-upper stud nuts. Install the cable to the transaxle bracket.

39. Lift the locking pawl away from the quadrant and slide the cable into the right side of the quadrant.

40. Connect the clutch cable to the release lever at the transaxle. Return the clutch pedal to its normal position.

41. Connect the horn's electrical lead and install the mounting bolt. Install the air cleaner.

42. Connect the battery ground cable to the transaxle.

1987-89 Models

MUNCIE

1. Disconnect the negative battery cable.
2. Remove the air cleaner and air intake duct assembly.
3. Detach the sound insulator from inside the car.
4. Remove the clutch master cylinder pushrod from the clutch pedal.
5. Remove the clutch slave cylinder from the transaxle.
6. Disconnect the exhaust crossover pipe.
7. Disconnect the shift cables at the transaxle.
8. Install the engine support fixture J-28467.
9. Remove the top engine to transaxle bolts.
10. Raise the car and suitably support it.
11. Remove the left-hand and right-hand front wheel and tire.
12. Install the drive axle boot seal protectors, Tool J-34754.
13. Remove the left-hand side frame and disconnect the rear transaxle mount from the bracket.
14. Drain the transaxle.
15. Disengage the right-hand and left-hand drive axles from the transaxle.
16. Remove the clutch housing cover bolts.
17. Disconnect the speedometer cable.
18. Attach a jack to the transaxle case.
19. Remove the remaining transaxle to engine bolts.
20. Slide the transaxle away from the engine. Carefully lower the jack while guiding the right-hand drive axle out of the transaxle.

To install:

21. Place the transaxle on a jack and guide it into the vehicle, position the right drive axle shaft into its bore as the transaxle is being installed. The right-hand shaft CANNOT be readily installed after the transaxle is connected to the engine.

22. Install the transaxle to engine bolts.

23. After the transaxle is fastened to the engine and the left drive axle is installed at the transaxle, position the left side frame and install the frame to body bolts.

24. Connect the transaxle to the front and rear mounts.

25. Connect the speedometer cable.

26. Install the clutch housing cover bolts.

27. Remove the drive axle boot seal protectors, Tool J-34754.

28. Fill the transaxle with the proper fluid.

29. Install the left side frame, then connect the rear transaxle mount to the bracket (if not already done).

30. Install the left and right front wheel and tire.

31. Remove the jack and safety supports and lower the car.

32. Install the top engine to transaxle bolts.

33. Remove the engine support fixture J-28467.

34. Connect the shift cables at the transaxle.

35. Connect the exhaust crossover pipe.

36. Install the clutch slave cylinder to the transaxle.

37. Install the clutch master cylinder pushrod from the clutch pedal.

38. Install the sound insulator inside the car.

39. Install the air intake duct assembly and the air cleaner.

40. Connect the negative battery cable.

Halfshafts

REMOVAL & INSTALLATION

▶ **See Figure 8**

✳✳WARNING

Use care when removing the drive axle. Tri-pots can be damaged if the drive axle is overextended.

Except Rear Axle — 6000 STE AWD
▶ **See Figures 9, 10, 11 and 12**

1. Remove the hub nut and discard. A new hub nut must be used for reassembly.

86817021

Fig. 8 A complete halfshaft assembly

2. Raise and safely support the vehicle. Remove the wheel and tire assembly.

3. Install an halfshaft boot seal protector onto the seal. The use of protector J-34754 or an equivalent is advised.

4. Disconnect the brake hose clip from the strut, but do not disconnect the hose from the caliper. Remove the brake caliper from the spindle and support the caliper with a length of wire. Do not allow the caliper to hang by the brake hose unsupported.

5. Mark the camber alignment cam bolt for reassembly. Remove the cam bolt and the upper attaching bolt from the strut and spindle.

6. Pull the steering knuckle assembly from the strut bracket.

7. Remove the halfshaft from the transaxle.

8. Using spindle remover tool J-28733 or equivalent, remove the halfshaft from the hub and bearing assembly. Do not allow the halfshaft to hang unsupported. If necessary, support using a length of wire in order to prevent component damage.

Fig. 11 With the other components disconnected from the axle shaft, it will slide out

To install:

9. If a new halfshaft is to be installed, a new knuckle seal should be installed first along with a boot seal protector when necessary.

10. Loosely install the halfshaft into the transaxle and steering knuckle.

11. Loosely attach the steering knuckle to the suspension strut.

12. The halfshaft is an interference fit in the steering knuckle. Press the axle into place, then install the hub nut. When the shaft begins to turn with the hub, insert a drift through the caliper into one of the cooling slots in the rotor to keep it from turning.

➡On some vehicles, the hub flange has a notch in it which can be used to prevent the hub and the shaft from turning, when one of the hub bearing retainer bolts is removed, by placing a longer bolt put in its place through the notch.

13. Tighten the hub nut to 70-75 ft. lbs. (95-103 Nm) to completely seat the shaft.

1 Remove tabs
2 Drive axle seal protector

Fig. 9 The use of protector J-34754 or an equivalent is advised

1 Drift punch
2 6 point deep well socket

Fig. 12 Position a drift through the caliper and into the rotor to hold it still while tightening the hub nut

Fig. 10 Apply the protector as shown on the shaft

14. Install the brake caliper. Tighten the caliper mounting bolts to 30 ft. lbs. (41 Nm).

15. Load the hub assembly by lowering it onto a jackstand. Align the camber cam bolt marks made during removal, install the bolt and tighten to 140 ft. lbs. (190 Nm). Tighten the upper nut to the same value.

16. Install the halfshaft all the way into the transaxle using a suitable tool inserted into the groove provided on the inner retainer. Tap the tool until the shaft seats in the transaxle. Remove the boot seal protector.

17. Connect the brake hose clip the the strut. Install the tire and wheel, lower the vehicle and tighten the hub nut to 192 ft. lbs. (260 Nm).

Rear Axle — 6000 STE AWD

▶ **See Figure 13**

1. Raise and safely support the vehicle.
2. Remove the tire and wheel assembly.
3. Disconnect the parking brake cable end from the bracket.
4. Remove the bolts securing the brake line and the Electronic Ride Control (ERC) sensor bracket to the control arm. Loosen the anti-lock brake sensor bolt and mover the sensor out of the way.
5. Insert a suitable tool through the caliper into the rotor to prevent the rotor from turning.
6. Remove the shaft nut and washer using special tool J-34826. Discard the shaft nut.
7. Remove the 2 brake caliper bolts and remove the caliper. Support the caliper using a length of wire.

➡ **Do not allow the caliper to hang by the brake hose unsupported.**

8. Remove the rotor from the hub and bearing assembly.
9. Install leaf spring compression tool J-33432 or equivalent.
10. Remove the 3 bolts mounting the hub and bearing to the knuckle.
11. Remove the hub and bearing assembly from the knuckle using special tool J-28733-A or equivalent.
12. Remove the bolts and nut plate attaching the lower strut mount to the knuckle. Scribe the position of the upper bolt prior removing.
13. Install a suitable CV-boot protector to prevent damage to the boot.
14. Swing the knuckle downward and away from the driveshaft.
15. Remove the drive axle from the differential using a suitable slide hammer.

To install:

16. Install the drive axle to the differential. Ensure positive engagement by pulling outward on the inner axle end. Grasp the housing only. Do not grasp and pull on the axle shaft.
17. Swing the knuckle up to the lower strut mount.
18. Position the nut plate and install the lower strut mount bolts to the knuckle. Align the top bolt with scribe marks before tightening the bolts. Tighten the bolts to 148 ft. lbs. (200 Nm).
19. Remove the CV-boot protector.

1 Outer joint
2 Knuckle
3 Hub and bearing assembly
4 Washer
5 61 ft. lbs. (84 Nm)
6 Washer
7 Shaft nut
   185 ft. lbs. (260 Nm)
   125 ft. lbs. (170 Nm)
8 125 ft. lbs. (170 Nm)
9 Differential
10 Inner joint
11 Slide hammer
12 Adapter
13 Adapter

86817013

Fig. 13 A slide hammer is used to remove the drive axle from the differential on the 6000 STE AWD

20. Secure the hub and bearing assembly to the knuckle and axle spline.
21. Install the hub and bearing attaching bolts. Tighten to 61 ft. lbs. (84 Nm).
22. Remove the leaf spring compression tool.
23. Install the rotor to hub and bearing assembly.
24. Install the brake caliper to the rotor and install the retaining bolts. Tighten the bolts to 38 ft. lbs. (51 Nm).
25. Install the anti-lock brake sensor to the knuckle and install the retaining bolt. Using a non-ferrous feeler gauge, adjust the sensor gap to 0.028 in. (0.7mm). Tighten the adjustment screw to 19 inch lbs. (2.2 Nm).
26. Connect the parking brake cable end into the bracket.
27. Install the shaft washer and new torque prevailing nut. Hold the rotor with a suitable to prevent the axle from turning while tightening. Tighten to 192 ft. lbs. (260 Nm).
28. Install the tire and wheel assembly.
29. Check the rear wheel camber. Adjust as necessary.

➡ **If the lower strut to knuckle bolts are properly aligned with the scribe marks, no camber adjustment should be necessary.**

30. Lower the vehicle.
31. Tighten the lugnuts.

OVERHAUL

Outer Joint

▶ **See Figures 14, 15, 16, 17, 18, 19 and 20**

1. Remove the axle shaft.
2. Cut off the seal retaining clamp. Using a brass drift and a hammer, lightly tap the seal retainer from the outside toward the inside of the shaft to remove from the joint.
3. Use a pair of snapring pliers to spread the retaining ring apart. Pull the axle shaft from the joint.
4. Using a brass drift and a hammer, lightly tap on the inner race cage until it has tilted sufficiently to remove one of the balls. Tilt the cage in the opposite direction to remove the opposing ball. Remove the other balls in the same manner.

1 Race retaining ring
2 C/V joint outer race

86817054

Fig. 14 Spread the ears on the race retaining ring with tool J-8059, then remove the CV-joint assembly from the axle shaft

A Land
B Windows
1 C/V joint cage
2 C/V joint outer race

86817056

Fig. 16 Position the cage and the inner race 90° to the centerline of the outer race, then align the cage windows with the lands of the outer race

1 Chrome alloy ball
2 C/V joint inner race
3 C/V joint cage
4 C/V joint outer race

86817055

Fig. 15 Using a brass drift and a hammer, lightly tap on the inner race cage until it has tilted sufficiently to remove one of the balls. Tilt the cage in the opposite direction to remove the opposing ball. Remove the other balls in the same manner

A Cage window
B Inner race land
1 C/V joint inner race
2 C/V joint cage

86817057

Fig. 17 Rotate the inner race 90° to the centerline of the cage with the lands of the inner race aligned with the windows of the cage

5. Position the cage and the inner race 90° to the centerline of the outer race, then align the cage windows with the lands of the outer race.

6. Rotate the inner race 90° to the centerline of the cage with the lands of the inner race aligned with the windows of the cage.

7. Pivot the inner race into the cage window and remove the inner race.

8. Clean all parts thoroughly and inspect for wear, make sure all parts are dry.

To install:

9. Assemble the new swage ring on the neck of the seal. DO NOT SWAGE.

10. Slide the swage ring onto the axle shaft, then position the neck of the seal in the seal groove on the axle shaft.

11. For the swage ring, mount the swage clamp tool, J-41048 in a vise and proceed:

    a. Position the outboard end of the shaft assembly in the tool.

J 41048

86817058

Fig. 18 Tool J-41048 or a suitable vise can be used for this procedure

b. Align the top of the seal neck on the bottom die using the indicator line.

c. Place the top half of the tool on the lower half of the tool.

d. Make sure there are no pinch points on the seal before proceeding. This could cause damage to the seal.

e. Insert the bolts, then tighten by hand until snug.

f. Make sure that the seal, housing and swage ring all remain in alignment.

g. Continue to tighten each of the bolts 180° at a time, alternating until; both of the sides are bottomed.

12. Put a light coat of the grease provided in the rebuilding kit onto the ball grooves of the inner race and outer joint.

13. Hold the inner race 90° centerline of the cage with the lands of the inner race aligned with the windows of the cage and insert the inner race into the cage.

14. Hold the cage and inner race 90° to centerline of the outer race, then align the cage windows with the lands of the outer race.

15. Assemble the cage and inner race into the outer race. Be sure that the retaining ring side of the inner race faces the axle shaft.

16. Insert the first chrome ball, then tilt the cage in the opposite direction to insert the opposing ball. Repeat this process until all of the balls are inserted.

17. Place approximately half of the grease from the service kit inside the seal, then pack the CV-joint with the remaining grease.

18. Push the CV-joint onto the axle shaft until the retaining ring is seated in the groove on the axle shaft.

19. Slide the large end of the seal with the a large seal clamp in place over the outside of the CV-joint race, then locate the seal lip in the groove on the race.

20. The seal must not be dimpled, stretched or out of shape in any way. If it is not in shape, equally pressurize the seal and shape it properly by hand.

21. Crimp the retaining ring clamp with tool J-35910 to 130 ft. lbs. (176 Nm).

22. Check the crimp profile for correct shape and ear gap.

1 Axle shaft
2 C/V joint outer race

86817059

Fig. 20 Push the CV-joint onto the axle shaft until the retaining ring is seated in the groove on the axle shaft

Outer Boot

▶ See Figures 21, 22 and 23

1. Raise and support the vehicle safely.
2. Remove the front tire and wheel assembly.
3. Remove the caliper bolts. Remove the caliper and support using a length of wire.
4. Remove the hub nut, washer and wheel bearing.
5. Using a brass drift, lightly tap around the seal retainer to loosen it. Remove the seal retainer.
6. Remove the seal retaining clamp or ring and discard.
7. Using snapring pliers, remove the race retaining ring from the halfshaft.
8. Pull the outer joint assembly and the outboard seal away from the halfshaft.
9. Flush the grease from the joint and repack with half of the grease provided. Put the remainder of the grease in the seal.

To install:

10. Check the boots for wear.

SEAL GROOVE
AXLE SHAFT
SEAL RETAINING CLAMP
OUTBOARD SEAL
SEAL RETAINER
COAT INSIDE OF SEAL LIP WITH GREASE
RACE RETAINING RING
JOINT ASSEMBLY

86817014

Fig. 19 Put a light coat of the grease provided in the rebuilding kit onto the ball grooves of the inner race and outer joint

TCCS7031

Fig. 21 Removing the outer band from the CV-boot

Fig. 22 Removing the inner band from the CV-boot

Fig. 23 Check the CV-boot for wear

11. Assemble the inner seal retainer, outboard seal and outer seal retainer to the halfshaft. Push the joint assembly onto the shaft until the retaining ring is seated in the groove.

12. Slide the outboard seal onto the joint assembly and secure using the outer seal retainer. Using seal clamp tool J-35910 or equivalent, tighten the outer clamp to 130 ft. lbs. (176 Nm) and the inner clamp to 100 ft. lbs. (136 Nm).

13. Install the wheel bearing, washer and hub nut. Tighten the hub nut to 192 ft. lbs. (260 Nm).

14. Secure the caliper with the caliper attaching bolts.

15. Install the front tire and wheel assembly.

16. Lower the vehicle.

17. Tighten the lugnuts.

Inner Joint

▶ **See Figures 24, 25, 26, 27 and 28**

1. Remove the axle shaft.

2. For swag ring removal use a hand grinder to cut through the ring.

3. Remove the larger seal retaining ring from the tri-pot joint with a side cutter and dispose.

4. Separate the seal from the trilobal tri-pot bushing at the large diameter, then slide the seal away from the joint along the axle shaft.

5. Remove the housing from the spider and shaft.

6. Spread the spacer ring with tool J-8059, then slide the spacer ring and spider back on the axle shaft.

7. Remove the shaft retaining ring from the groove on the axle shaft and slide the spider assembly off the shaft.

8. Clean the tri-pot balls, needle rollers and housing with clean solvent.

9. Remove the trilobal tri-pot bushing from the housing.

10. Remove the spacer ring and seal from the axle shaft.

11. Inspect all parts for wear.

To install:

12. Connect the new ring on the neck of the seal. DO NOT SWAGE.

13. Slide the seal on the shaft, then position the neck of the seal in the groove on the axle shaft.

1 Shaft retaining ring
2 Spacer ring
3 Axle shaft

Fig. 24 Full view of the spider on the axle shaft

1 Spacer ring
2 Axle shaft

Fig. 25 Spread the spacer ring with tool J-8059, then slide the spacer ring and spider back on the axle shaft

14. For the swag ring, mount the clamp tool in a vise, then proceed:

    a. Position the outboard end of the shaft assembly in the tool.

    b. Align the top of the seal neck on the bottom die using the indicator line.

    c. Place the top half of the tool on the lower half of the tool.

    d. Make sure there are no pinch points on the seal before proceeding. This could cause damage to the seal.

    e. Insert the bolts, then tighten by hand until snug.

    f. Make sure that the seal, housing and swage ring all remain in alignment.

    g. Continue to tighten each of the bolts 180° at a time, alternating until both of the sides are bottomed.

15. Install the spacer ring on the axle shaft and beyond the second groove.

16. Slide the spider assembly against the spacer ring on the shaft.

17. Be sure that the counterbored face of the spider faces the end of the shaft.

18. Install the shaft seating ring in the groove of the axle shaft with tool J-8059.

19. Slide the spider towards the end of the shaft, then reseat the spacer ring in the groove on the shaft.

20. Place approximately half of the grease from the service kit in the seal and use the remaining grease to repack the housing.

21. Install the trilobal tri-pot bushing to the housing.

22. Position the large clamp on the seal, then slide the housing over the spider assembly on the shaft.

23. Slide the large diameter of the seal, with the large clamp in place, over the outside of the trilobal tri-pot bushing, then locate the lip of the seal in the groove.

24. Position the joint assembly at the correct distance, as illustrated.

25. The seal must not be dimpled, stretched or out of shape in any way. If it is not in shape, equally pressurize the seal and shape it properly by hand.

26. Crimp the retaining ring clamp with tool J-35910 to 130 ft. lbs. (176 Nm).

27. Check the crimp profile for correct shape and ear gap.

Inner Boot

1. Raise and safely support the vehicle.

2. Remove the front tire and wheel assembly.

3. Unsecure the caliper bolts, then remove the caliper and support it using a length of wire.

4. Remove the hub nut, washer and wheel bearing.

5. Remove the halfshaft. Place in a suitable holding fixture being careful not place undue pressure on the halfshaft.

6. Remove the joint assembly retaining ring. Remove the joint assembly.

7. Remove the race retaining ring and remove the seal retainer.

8. Remove the inner seal retaining clamp. Remove the inner joint seal.

9. Flush the grease from the joint and repack with half of the grease provided. Put the remainder of the grease in the seal.

1 Retainer & housing asm.
2 Axle shaft

86817064

Fig. 26 Position the large clamp on the seal, then slide the housing over the spider assembly on the shaft

1 Retainer & housing asm.
2 Drive axle inboard seal
3 Axle shaft

125 mm (4.9")

86817065

Fig. 27 Position the joint assembly 4.9 in. (125mm) from the inner boot band

SEAL RETAINING CLAMP
BREAKER BAR
J 35910
TORQUE WRENCH
EAR GAP A

86817060

Fig. 28 Crimp the retaining ring clamp with tool J-35910 to 130 ft. lbs. (176 Nm)

To install:

10. Assemble the inner seal retainer, outboard seal and outer seal retainer to the halfshaft. Push the joint assembly onto the shaft until the retaining ring is seated in the groove.

11. Slide the outboard seal onto the joint assembly and secure using the outer seal retainer. Using seal clamp tool J-35910 or equivalent, tighten the outer clamp to 130 ft. lbs. (176 Nm) and the inner clamp to 100 ft. lbs. (136 Nm).

12. Insert the halfshaft assembly.
13. Secure the wheel bearing, washer and hub nut. Tighten the hub nut to 192 ft. lbs. (260 Nm).
14. Install the caliper and caliper attaching bolts.
15. Install the front tire and wheel assembly.
16. Lower the vehicle.

CLUTCH

✳✳CAUTION

The clutch driven disc may contain asbestos, which has been determined to be a cancer causing agent. Never clean clutch surfaces with compressed air! Avoid inhaling any dust from any clutch surface! When cleaning clutch surfaces, use a commercially available brake cleaning fluid.

Understanding the Clutch

The purpose of the clutch is to disconnect and connect engine power from the transaxle. A car at rest requires a lot of engine torque to get all that weight moving. An internal combustion engine does not develop a high starting torque (unlike steam engines), so it must be allowed to operate without any load until it builds up enough torque to move the car. Torque increases with engine rpm. The clutch allows the engine to build up torque by physically disconnecting the engine from the transaxle, relieving the engine of any load or resistance. The transfer of engine power to the transaxle (the load) must be smooth and gradual; if it weren't, drive line components would wear out or break quickly. This gradual power transfer is made possible by gradually releasing the clutch pedal. The clutch disc and pressure plate are the connecting link between the engine and transaxle. When the clutch pedal is released, the disc and plate contact each other (clutch engagement), physically joining the engine and transaxle. When the pedal is pushed in, the disc and plate separate (the clutch is disengaged), disconnecting the engine from the transaxle.

The clutch assembly consists of the flywheel, the clutch disc, the clutch pressure plate, the throwout bearing and fork, the actuating linkage and the pedal. The flywheel and clutch pressure plate (driving members) are connected to the engine crankshaft and rotate with it. The clutch disc is located between the flywheel and pressure plate, and splined to the transaxle shaft. A driving member is one that is attached to the engine and transfers engine power to a driven member (clutch disc) on the transaxle shaft. A driving member (pressure plate) rotates (drives) a driven member (clutch disc) on contact and, in so doing, turns the transaxle shaft. There is a circular diaphragm spring within the pressure plate cover (transaxle side). In a relaxed state (when the clutch pedal is fully released), this spring is convex; that it, it is dished outward toward the transaxle. Pushing in the clutch pedal actuates an attached linkage rod. Connected to the other end of this rod is the throwout bearing fork. The throwout bearing is attached to the fork. When the clutch pedal is depressed, the clutch linkage pushes the fork and bearing forward to contact the diaphragm spring of the pressure plate. The outer edges of the spring are secured to the pressure plate and are pivoted on rings so that when the center of the spring is compressed by the throwout bearing, the outer edges bow outward and, by so doing, pull the pressure plate in the same direction, away from the clutch disc. This action separates the disc from the plate, disengaging the clutch and allowing the transaxle to be shifted into another gear. A coil type clutch return spring attached to the clutch pedal arm permits full release of the pedal. Releasing the pedal pulls the throwout bearing away from the diaphragm spring resulting in a reversal of spring position. As bearing pressure is gradually released from the spring center, the outer edges of the spring bow outward, pushing the pressure plate into closer contact with the clutch disc. As the disc and plate move closer together, friction between the two increases and slippage is reduced until, when full spring pressure is applied (by fully releasing the pedal), The speed of the disc and plate are the same. This stops all slipping, creating a direct connection between the plate and disc which results in the transfer of power from the engine to the transaxle. The clutch disc is now rotating with the pressure plate at engine speed and, because it is splined to the transaxle shaft, the shaft now turns at the same engine speed. Understanding clutch operation can be rather difficult at first; if you're still confused after reading this, consider the following analogy. The action of the diaphragm spring can be compared to that of an oil can bottom. The bottom of an oil can is shaped very much like the clutch diaphragm spring and pushing in on the can bottom and then releasing it produces a similar effect. As mentioned earlier, the clutch pedal return spring permits full release of the pedal and reduces linkage slack due to wear. As the linkage wears, clutch free-pedal travel will increase and free-travel will decrease as the clutch wears. Free-travel is actually throwout bearing lash.

The diaphragm spring type clutches used are available in two different designs: flat diaphragm springs or bent spring. The bent fingers are bent back to create a centrifugal boost ensuring quick re-engagement at higher engine speeds. This design enables pressure plate load to increase as the clutch disc wears and makes low pedal effort possible even for a heavy-duty clutch. The throwout bearing used with the bent finger design is 1¼ in. (31.75mm) long and is shorter than the bearing used with the flat finger design. These bearings are not interchangeable. If the longer bearing is used with the bent finger clutch, free-pedal travel will not exist. This results in clutch slippage and rapid wear.

The transaxle varies the gear ratio between the engine and rear wheels. It can be shifted to change engine speed as driving conditions and loads change. The transaxle allows disengaging and reversing power from the engine to the wheels.

Adjustments

On 1982-86 models the only service adjustment necessary on the clutch is to maintain the correct pedal free play. Clutch pedal free play, or throwout bearing lash, decreases with driven disc wear. On 1987 and newer models a hydraulic clutch system provides automatic clutch adjustment.

LINKAGE AND PEDAL HEIGHT/FREE-PLAY

1982-86 Models

All cars use a self-adjusting clutch mechanism which may be checked as follows:

As the clutch friction material wears, the cable must be lengthened. This is accomplished by simply pulling the clutch pedal up to its rubber bumper. This action forces the pawl against its stop and rotates it out of mesh with the quadrant teeth, allowing the cable to play out until the quadrant spring load is balanced against the load applied by the release bearing. This adjustment procedure is required every 5,000 miles or less.

1. With engine running and brake on, hold the clutch pedal approximately ½ in. (13mm) from floor mat and move shift lever between first and reverse several times. If this can be done smoothly without clashing into reverse, the clutch is fully releasing. If shift is not smooth, clutch is not fully releasing and linkage should be inspected and corrected as necessary.

2. Check clutch pedal bushings for sticking or excessive wear.

3. Have an assistant sit in the driver's seat and fully apply the clutch pedal to the floor. Observe the clutch fork lever travel at the transaxle. The end of the clutch fork lever should have a total travel of approximately 1.5-1.7 in. (38-43mm).

4. If fork lever is not correct, check the adjusting mechanism by depressing the clutch pedal and looking for pawl to firmly engage with the teeth in the quadrant.

Clutch Pedal

REMOVAL & INSTALLATION

▶ See Figure 29

1. Support the clutch pedal upwards against the bumper stop to release the pawl from the quadrant. Disconnect the clutch cable from the release lever at the transaxle assembly. Be careful and prevent the cable from snapping rapidly towards the rear of the car. The quadrant in the adjusting mechanism can be damaged by allowing the cable to snap back.

2. From the inside of the car, disconnect the clutch cable from the quadrant. Lift the locking pawl away from the quadrant, then slide the cable away from the pedal along the right hand side of the quadrant.

3. Remove the neutral start switch from the pedal, then the pedal mounting bracket. Remove the pedal pivot nut, bolt and clutch pedal from the mounting bracket.

4. Carefully note the positions of the adjusting mechanism, the pawl and quadrant springs. Remove the E ring and disassemble the adjusting mechanism.

5. Clean all the surfaces of the pedal assembly that contact the quadrant and pawl. If there is tooth damage on either the pawl or quadrant, replace both parts.

To install:

6. Position the quadrant spring into the pocket and assemble the quadrant part-way onto the pedal with the spring tang inserted into the upper hole at the pedal. Rotate the quadrant 90° to wind up the spring and allow the quadrant to stop clear from the side of the pedal. Push the quadrant and pedal together hooking the quadrant stop on front of the pedal. Surfaces of the pedal and quadrant should be in contact with the spring load holding stop and pedal in contact.

7. Position the pawl spring over the pawl ends, then install onto the stud at the top of the pedal. The wide hook end of the spring must be assembled over the front of the pedal as the pawl is pushed onto the pedal stud with the teeth in mesh. The spring must force the pawl teeth into the teeth of the quadrant to prevent the forward rotation of the quadrant.

8. Position the support on the pedal stud and rotate clockwise to engage the narrow hook end of the pawl spring, loading the outer end of the pawl spring until the large hole in the support fits onto the large hub of the pedal groove. Look at the picture view C and E.

9. Lubricate only the inner and outer diameter surfaces of each bushing, then install the bushing and spacer into the pedal assembly.

10. Check the bracket to insure that the bumper is in place on the pedal stop. Position the pedal to the mounting bracket, then install the pivot bolt and nut. Tighten the nut to 35 ft. lbs. (50 Nm) Check the pedal to ensure it swings freely on its pivot bolt.

11. Check the operation of the pawl and quadrant, making sure the pawl disengages from the quadrant when the pedal is pulled to its upper position, and the quadrant rotates freely in both directions.

12. Route the cable end back on the right side between the quadrant and pedal. Lift the pawl and raise the cable into the quadrant groove and connect the cable to the quadrant as in F.

13. Support the pedal upwards against the bumper stop to release the pawl from the quadrant. Attach the other end of the cable to the clutch release lever.

14. Connect the neutral start switch to the pedal and bracket.

15. Check the clutch operation, then adjust by lifting the pedal up to allow the mechanism to adjust the cable length. Depress the pedal slowly several times to set the pawl into mesh with the quadrant teeth.

Clutch Cable

REMOVAL & INSTALLATION

▶ See Figures 29 and 30

1. Support the clutch pedal upward against the bumper stop to release the pawl from the quadrant. Disconnect the

end of the cable from the clutch release lever at the transaxle. Be careful to prevent the cable from snapping rapidly toward the rear of the car. The quadrant in the adjusting mechanism can be damaged by allowing the cable to snap back.

2. Disconnect the clutch cable from the quadrant. Lift the locking pawl away from the quadrant, then slide the cable out on the right side of the quadrant.

3. From the engine side of the cowl disconnect the two upper nuts holding the cable retainer to the upper studs. Disconnect the cable from the bracket mounted to the transaxle, and remove the cable.

4. Inspect the clutch cable for frayed wires, kinks, worn ends and excessive friction. If any of these conditions exist, replace the cable.

5. Inspect the clutch cable. Replace the cable if any of the conditions are found, frayed wires, kinked cable, worn end and excessive cable friction.

To install:

6. With the gasket in position on the two upper studs, position a new cable with the retaining flange against the bracket.

7. Attach the end of the cable to the quadrant, being sure to route the cable underneath the pawl.

8. Attach the two upper nuts to the retainer mounting studs, and tighten to specifications.

9. Attach the cable to the bracket mounted to the transaxle.

10. Support the clutch pedal upward against the bumper stop to release the pawl from the quadrant. Attach the outer end of the cable to the clutch release lever. Be sure not to yank on the cable, since overloading the cable could damage the quadrant.

11. Check clutch operation and adjust by lifting the clutch pedal up to allow the mechanism to adjust the cable length. Depress the pedal slowly several times to set the pawl into mesh with the quadrant teeth.

Driven Disc and Pressure Plate

REMOVAL & INSTALLATION

▶ See Figures 31, 32, 33, 34, 35, 36, 37, 38, 39, 40, 41 and 42

1. On 1987 and newer models, disconnect the negative battery cable, remove the hush panel from inside the vehicle, then disconnect the clutch master cylinder pushrod from the clutch pedal.

2. Remove the transaxle.

3. Mark the pressure plate assembly and the flywheel so that they can be assembled in the same position. They were balanced as an assembly at the factory.

4. Loosen the attaching bolts one turn at a time until spring tension is relieved.

5. Support the pressure plate and remove the bolts. Remove the pressure plate and clutch disc. Do not disassemble the pressure plate assembly, replace it if defective.

Fig. 30 Disconnect the end of the cable from the clutch release lever at the transaxle as shown

Fig. 29 Disconnect the clutch cable from the quadrant. Lift the locking pawl away from the quadrant, then slide the cable out on the right side of the quadrant as shown

Fig. 31 View of the clutch and pressure plate assembly

Fig. 32 Removing the clutch and pressure plate bolts

Fig. 33 Removing the clutch and pressure plate assembly

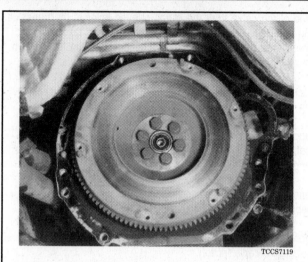

Fig. 34 View of the flywheel once the clutch assembly is removed

Fig. 35 Be sure that the flywheel surface is clean, before installing the clutch

Fig. 36 Check across the flywheel surface; it should be flat

Fig. 37 Checking the pressure plate for excessive wear

Fig. 38 Apply locking agent to clutch assembly bolts

Fig. 39 Install the clutch assembly bolts and tighten in steps, in an X pattern

Fig. 40 Be sure to use a torque wrench to tighten all the bolts

Fig. 41 Grease the throwout bearing assembly at the outer contact points

Fig. 42 Grease the throwout bearing assembly at the inner contact points

6. Inspect the flywheel, clutch disc, pressure plate, throwout bearing and the clutch fork and pivot shaft assembly for wear. Replace the parts as required. If the flywheel shows any signs of overheating, or if it is badly grooved or scored, it should be replaced.

To install:

7. Clean the pressure plate and flywheel mating surfaces thoroughly. Position the clutch disc and pressure plate into the installed position, and support with a dummy shaft or clutch aligning tool. The clutch plate is assembled with the damper springs offset toward the transaxle. One side of the factory supplied clutch disc is stamped "Flywheel side" on some vehicles.

8. Install the pressure plate-to-flywheel bolts. Tighten them gradually in a crisscross pattern.

9. Lubricate the outside groove and the inside recess of the release bearing with high temperature grease. Wipe off any excess. Install the release bearing.

10. Install the transaxle.

11. On 1987 and newer models connect the clutch master cylinder pushrod to the clutch pedal and install the retaining clip.

12. On 1987 and newer models, if equipped with cruise control, check the switch adjustment at the clutch pedal bracket.

13. Attach the clutch cable on older vehicles at the transaxle and clutch release lever.

➡**When adjusting the cruise control switch, do not exert an upward force on the clutch pedal pad of more than 20 lbs. (9 kg) or damage to the master cylinder pushrod retaining ring may result.**

14. On 1987 and newer models, install the hush panel and reconnect the negative battery cable.

15. Check the clutch operation. Adjust and add fluid as necessary.

Clutch Master and Slave Cylinder

➡**The clutch hydraulic system is removed and serviced as a complete assembly.**

REMOVAL & INSTALLATION

▶ **See Figure 43**

1. Disconnect the negative battery cable.
2. Remove the hush panel from inside the vehicle.
3. Remove the clutch master cylinder retaining nuts at the front of the dash.
4. Remove the slave cylinder retaining nuts at the transaxle.
5. Remove the hydraulic system as a unit from the vehicle.

To install:

6. Install the slave cylinder to the transaxle support bracket aligning the pushrod into the pocket on the clutch fork outer lever. Tighten the retaining nuts evenly to prevent damage to the slave cylinder. Tighten the nuts to 40 ft. lbs. (54 Nm).

➡**Do not remove the plastic pushrod retainer from the slave cylinder. The straps will break on the first clutch pedal application.**

7. Position the clutch master cylinder to the front of the dash. Tighten the nuts evenly to 20 ft. lbs. (27 Nm).

8. Remove the pedal restrictor from the pushrod. Lube the pushrod bushing on the clutch pedal. Connect the pushrod to the clutch pedal and install the retaining clip.

9. If equipped with cruise control, check the switch adjustment at the clutch pedal bracket.

➡**When adjusting the cruise control switch, do not exert an upward force on the clutch pedal pad of more than 20 lbs. or damage to the master cylinder pushrod retaining ring may result.**

10. Install the hush panel.

11. Press the clutch pedal down several times. This will break the plastic retaining straps on the slave cylinder pushrod. Do not remove the plastic button on the end of the pushrod.

12. Connect the negative battery cable.

OVERHAUL

This is a tedious, time consuming job. You can save yourself a lot of trouble by buying a rebuilt master cylinder from your dealer or parts supply house. The small difference in price between a rebuilding kit and a rebuilt part usually makes it more economical, in terms of time and work, to buy the rebuilt part.

1. Remove the master cylinder.
2. Remove the reservoir cover and drain the fluid.
3. Remove the pushrod and the rubber boot on non-power models.
4. Unbolt the proportioners and the failure warning switch from the side of the master cylinder body. Discard the O-rings found under the proportioners. Use new ones on installation. There may or may not be an O-ring under the original equipment failure warning switch. If there is, discard it. In either case, use a new O-ring upon assembly.
5. Clamp the master cylinder body in a vise, taking care not to crush it. Depress the primary piston with a wooden dowel and remove the lock ring with a pair of snapring pliers.
6. The primary and secondary pistons can be removed by applying compressed air into one of the outlets at the end of the cylinder and plugging the other three outlets. The primary piston must be replaced as an assembly if the seals are bad. The secondary piston seals are replaceable. Install these new seals with the lips facing outwards.
7. Inspect the bore for corrosion. If any corrosion is evident, the master cylinder body must be replaced. Do not attempt to polish the bore with crocus cloth, sandpaper or anything else. The body is aluminum, polishing the bore won't work.
8. To remove the failure warning switch piston assembly, remove the Allen head plug from the end of the bore and withdraw the assembly with a pair of needlenose pliers. The switch piston assembly seals are replaceable.
9. The reservoir can be removed from the master cylinder if necessary. Clamp the body in a vise by its mounting flange. Use a pry bar to remove the reservoir. If the reservoir is removed, remove the reservoir grommets and discard them. The quick take-up valves under the grommets are accessible

Fig. 43 Clutch hydraulic system

1. Clutch pedal assembly
2. Bolt
3. Bracket
4. Reservoir
5. Master cylinder
6. 20 ft. lbs.
7. Slave cylinder bracket
8. Bolt 40 ft. lbs.
9. Lever
10. Bolt 37 ft. lbs.
11. Nut
12. Nut 40 ft. lbs.
13. Slave cylinder
14. Master cylinder push rod.

86817024

after the retaining snaprings are removed. Use snapring pliers, no other tool will work.

10. Clean all parts in denatured alcohol and allow to air dry. Do not use anything else to clean and do not wipe dry with a rag, which will leaves bits of lint behind. Inspect all parts for corrosion or wear. Generally, it is best to replace all rubber parts whenever the master cylinder is disassembled and replace any metal part which shows any sign of wear or corrosion.

11. Lubricate all parts with fresh brake fluid before assembly.

12. Install the quick take-up valves into the master cylinder body and secure with the snaprings. Make sure the snaprings are properly seated in their grooves. Lubricate the new reservoir grommets with fresh brake fluid and press them into the master cylinder.

13. Install the reservoir into the grommets by placing the reservoir on its lid and pressing the master cylinder body down onto it with a rocking motion.

14. Lubricate the switch piston assembly. Install new O-rings and retainers on the piston. Install the piston assembly into the master cylinder and secure with the plug, using a new O-ring on the plug. Tighten to 40-140 inch lbs. (5-16 Nm.).

15. Assemble the new secondary piston seals onto the piston. Lubricate the parts, then install the spring, spring retainer and secondary piston into the cylinder. Install the primary piston, depress and install the lock ring.

16. Install new O-rings on the proportioners and the failure warning switch. Install the proportioners and tighten to 18-30 ft. lbs. (25-40 Nm.). Install the failure warning switch and tighten to 15-50 inch lbs. (2-6 Nm.).

17. Clamp the master cylinder body upright into a vise by one of the mounting flanges. Fill the reservoir with fresh fluid. Pump the piston with a dowel until fluid squirts from the outlet ports. Continue pumping until the expelled fluid is free of air bubbles.

18. Install the master cylinder and bleed the clutch. Check the clutch system for proper operation.

HYDRAULIC SYSTEM BLEEDING

Bleeding air from the system is necessary any time part of the system has been disconnected, or the fluid level in the reservoir has been allowed to fall so low that air has been drawn into the master cylinder.

✳✳WARNING

Never under any circumstance use fluid that has been bled from the system as it could be contaminated with air or moisture.

1. Clean the cap then remove the cap and diaphragm and fill the reservoir to the top with certified DOT 3 brake fluid.

AUTOMATIC TRANSAXLE

General Information

▶ **See Figures 44 and 45**

The automatic transaxle allows engine torque and power to be transmitted to the rear wheels within a narrow range of engine operating speeds. The transaxle's design allows the engine to turn fast enough to produce plenty of power and torque at very low speeds, while keeping it at a sensible rpm at high vehicle speeds. The transaxle performs this job entirely without driver assistance. The transaxle uses a light fluid as the medium for the transmission of power. This fluid also works in the operation of various hydraulic control circuits and as a lubricant. Because the transaxles fluid performs all of these three functions, trouble within the unit can easily travel from one part to another. For this reason, and because of the complexity and unusual operating principles of the transaxle, a very sound understanding of the basic principles of operation will simplify troubleshooting.

TORQUE CONVERTER

The torque converter replaces the conventional clutch. It has three functions:

1. It allows the engine to idle with the vehicle at a standstill, even with the transaxle in gear.
2. It allows the transaxle to shift from range to range smoothly, without requiring that the driver close the throttle during the shift.
3. It multiplies engine torque to an increasing extent as vehicle speed drops and throttle opening is increased. This has the effect of making the transaxle more responsive and reduces the amount of shifting required.

The torque converter is a metal case which is shaped like a sphere that has been flattened on opposite sides. It is bolted to the rear end of the engine's crankshaft. Generally, the entire metal case rotates at engine speed and serves as the engine's flywheel.

The case contains three sets of blades. One set is attached directly to the case. This set forms the torus or pump. Another set is directly connected to the output shaft, and forms the

2. Fully loosen the bleed screw which is in the slave cylinder body next to the inlet connection. Fluid will now begin to move from the master cylinder down the tube to the slave. It is important that for efficient gravity fill, the reservoir must be filled at all times.

3. At this point bubbles will be noticeable at the bleed screw outlet showing air is being expelled. When the slave is full, a steady stream of fluid will come from the slave outlet. At this point, tighten the bleed screw to 18 inch lbs. (2 Nm).

4. Install the diaphragm and cap to the reservoir. The fluid in the reservoir should be level with the step.

5. The hydraulic system should now be fully bled and should release the clutch. Check the vehicle by starting, then push the clutch pedal to the floor and selecting reverse gear. There should be no grinding of gears, if there is, the hydraulic system still contains air. If so, bleed the system again.

turbine. The third set is mounted on a hub which, in turn, is mounted on a stationary shaft through a one-way clutch. This third set is known as the stator.

A pump, which is driven by the converter hub at engine speed, keeps the torque converter full of transaxle fluid at all times. Fluid flows continuously through the unit to provide cooling.

Under low speed acceleration, the torque converter functions as follows:

The torus is turning faster than the turbine. It picks up fluid at the center of the converter and, through centrifugal force, slings it outward. Since the outer edge of the converter moves faster than the portions at the center, the fluid picks up speed.

The fluid then enters the outer edge of the turbine blades. It then travels back toward the center of the converter case along the turbine blades. In impinging upon the turbine blades, the fluid loses the energy picked up in the torus.

If the fluid were now to immediately be returned directly into the torus, both halves of the converter would have to turn at approximately the same speed at all times, and torque input and output would both be the same.

In flowing through the torus and turbine, the fluid picks up two types of flow, or flow in two separate directions. It flows through the turbine blades, and it spins with the engine. The stator, whose blades are stationary when the vehicle is being accelerated at low speeds, converts one type of flow into another. Instead of allowing the fluid to flow straight back into the torus, the stator's curved blades turn the fluid almost 90° toward the direction of rotation of the engine. Thus the fluid does not flow as fast toward the torus, but is already spinning when the torus picks it up. This has the effect of allowing the torus to turn much faster than the turbine. This difference in speed may be compared to the difference in speed between the smaller and larger gears in any gear train. The result is that engine power output is higher, and engine torque is multiplied.

As the speed of the turbine increases, the fluid spins faster and faster in the direction of engine rotation. As a result, the ability of the stator to redirect the fluid flow is reduced. Under cruising conditions, the stator is eventually forced to rotate on its one-way clutch in the direction of engine rotation. Under these conditions, the torque converter begins to behave almost

A T.V. CABLE AND/OR CASE SEAL
B REMOTE OR STANDARD VENT
C MANUAL SHAFT
D GOVERNOR OR SPEED SENSOR COVER
E SPEEDOMETER GEAR ASSEMBLY
F FILLER PIPE AND/OR SEAL
G RH AXLE

H CONVERTER TO CASE SEAL
I TORQUE CONVERTER
J OIL PAN (BOTTOM)
K ELECTRICAL CONNECTOR
L VALVE BODY COVER (SIDE PAN)
M COOLER FITTINGS
N LH AXLE

86817070

Fig. 44 Possible leak points on the 3T40 automatic transaxle

A BOTTOM PAN GASKET
B CASE (POROSITY/CRACKS)
C LINE PRESSURE TAP TO COOLER
  CONNECTOR
D FORWARD SERVO COVER SEAL
E OIL FILL TUBE SEAL
F CONVERTER SEAL ASSEMBLY

G REVERSE SERVO COVER SEAL
H CONVERTER (SEAMS/CRACKS)
I VENT
J ELECTRICAL CONNECTOR SEAL
K MANUAL SHAFT SEAL
L SPEED SENSOR SEAL
M VACUUM MODULATOR TO CASE
  SEAL

N SIDE COVER TO CASE GASKET
O SIDE COVER TO CHANNEL PLATE
  GASKET
P AXLE SEAL (LEFT HAND)
Q AXLE SEAL (RIGHT HAND)

86817071

Fig. 45 Possible leak points on the 4T60-E automatic transaxle

like a solid shaft, with the torus and turbine speeds being almost equal.

PLANETARY GEARBOX

The ability of the torque converter to multiply engine torque is limited. Also, the unit tends to be more efficient when the turbine is rotating at relatively high speeds. Therefore, a planetary gearbox is used to carry the power output of the turbine to the driveshaft.

Planetary gears function very similarly to conventional transmission gears. However, their construction is different in that three elements make up one gear system, and, in that all three elements are different from one another. The three elements are: an outer gear that is shaped like a hoop, with teeth cut into the inner surface; a sun gear, mounted on a shaft and located at the very center of the outer gear; and a set of three planet gears, held by pins in a ring-like planet carrier, meshing with both the sun gear and the outer gear. Either the outer gear or the sun gear may be held stationary, providing more than one possible torque multiplication factor for each set of gears. Also, if all three gears are forced to rotate at the same speed, the gearset forms, in effect, a solid shaft.

Most modern automatics use the planetary gears to provide either a single reduction ratio of about 1.8:1, or two reduction gears: a low of about 2.5:1, and an intermediate of about 1.5:1. Bands and clutches are used to hold various portions of the gearsets to the transaxle case or to the shaft on which they are mounted. Shifting is accomplished, then, by changing the portion of each planetary gearset which is held to the transaxle case or to the shaft.

SERVOS AND ACCUMULATORS

The servos are hydraulic pistons and cylinders. They resemble the hydraulic actuators used on many familiar machines, such as bulldozers. Hydraulic fluid enters the cylinder, under pressure, and forces the piston to move to engage the band or clutches.

The accumulators are used to cushion the engagement of the servos. The transaxle fluid must pass through the accumulator on the way to the servo. The accumulator housing contains a thin piston which is sprung away from the discharge passage of the accumulator. When fluid passes through the accumulator on the way to the servo, it must move the piston against spring pressure, and this action smooths out the action of the servo.

HYDRAULIC CONTROL SYSTEM

The hydraulic pressure used to operate the servos comes from the main transaxle oil pump. This fluid is channeled to the various servos through the shift valves. There is generally a manual shift valve which is operated by the transaxle selector lever and an automatic shift valve for each automatic upshift the transaxle provides: 2-speed automatics have a low/high shift valve, while 3-speeds have a 1-2 valve, and a 2-3 valve.

There are two pressures which effect the operation of these valves. One is the governor pressure which is affected by vehicle speed. The other is the modulator pressure which is affected by intake manifold vacuum or throttle position. Governor pressure rises with an increase in vehicle speed, and modulator pressure rises as the throttle is opened wider. By responding to these two pressures, the shift valves cause the upshift points to be delayed with increased throttle opening to make the best use of the engine's power output.

Most transaxles also make use of an auxiliary circuit for downshifting. This circuit may be actuated by the throttle linkage or the vacuum line which actuates the modulator, or by a cable or solenoid. It applies pressure to a special downshift surface on the shift valve or valves.

The transaxle modulator also governs the line pressure, used to actuate the servos. In this way, the clutches and bands will be actuated with a force matching the torque output of the engine.

Identification

▶ **See Figures 46, 47 and 48**

All automatic transaxles have a metal identification nameplate attached to the case exterior. The location of the nameplate is shown in the pictures. The information on the nameplate will help in the servicing and determination of replacement parts when ordered through your dealer or local parts house.

Fluid Pan

REMOVAL & INSTALLATION

1. Raise and support the vehicle on jackstands.
2. Place a drain pan under the transaxle bottom pan.
3. Loosen the pan bolts and drain the fluid.
4. Lightly tap the pan with a rubber mallet or pry the pan off loose with a suitable tool. This will remove the pan and the filter.

Fig. 46 Automatic transaxle THM 125C identification plate

Fig. 47 Automatic transaxle 4T60-E identification plate

Fig. 48 Automatic transaxle 3T40 identification plate

5. Clean the gasket mounting surfaces. The case and gasket surfaces should be cleaned with solvent and air dried. Some of the old gasket may adhere to the pan or the case itself, be sure to clean the areas well.

6. Inspect the pan for any metal particles, clutch facing materials, rubber particles, and engine coolant. If found determine the source of contamination, and fix the problem.

7. Check the pan for any distortion.

To install:

8. Always use a new gasket and filter. On the 3T40 coat the seal with a small amount of TRANSJEL J-36850, then reverse the removal procedures.

9. Tighten the pan bolts to the appropriate torque as follows:
- 3T40 transaxle: 98 inch lbs. (11 Nm)
- 4T60-E transaxle: 13 ft. lbs. (17 Nm)
- other transaxles: 10 ft. lbs. (14 Nm)

10. Lower the vehicle, and fill the transaxle with the proper and amount of fluid. Always use DEXRON III fluid.

11. Place the selector gear in park, start the engine, and run at as slow idle.

12. Inspect the fluid level, correct if needed, do not overfill. Check for leaks.

FILTER SERVICE

1. Raise and support the vehicle on jackstands.
2. Place a drain pan under the transaxle bottom pan.
3. Loosen the pan bolts and drain the fluid.
4. Lightly tap the pan with a rubber mallet or pry the pan off loose with a suitable tool. This will remove the pan and the filter.
5. On the 125C, 440-T4 and 3T40 transaxles, remove the oil filter and seal. The seal may be stuck to the case.
6. On the 4T60-E model, remove the screen/filter. The lip ring seal is pressed into the case and should be removed only if replacement is necessary.

7. Clean the gasket mounting surfaces. The case and gasket surfaces should be cleaned with solvent and air dried. Some of the old gasket may adhere to the pan or the case itself, be sure to clean the areas well.

8. Inspect the pan for any metal particles, clutch facing materials, rubber particles, and engine coolant. If found determine the source of contamination, and fix the problem.

9. Check the pan for any distortion.

To install:

10. Always use a new gasket and filter. On the 125C, 440-T4 and 3T40 coat the seal with a small amount of TRANSJEL J-36850, then reverse the removal procedures.

11. On most transaxles tighten the pan bolts to 10 ft. lbs. (14 Nm) on 3T40, 98 inch lbs. (11 Nm) and the 4T60-E, 13 ft. lbs. (17 Nm).

12. Lower the vehicle, and fill the transaxle with the proper and amount of fluid. Always use DEXRON III fluid.

13. Place the selector gear in park, start the engine, and run at as slow idle.

14. Inspect the fluid level, correct if needed, do not overfill. Check for leaks.

Adjustments

THROTTLE VALVE (TV) CABLE

▶ **See Figure 49**

1. Check to see that the cable is in the full non-adjustment position.

2. Without twisting or kinking the cable, insert the cable slug into the idler pulley (cam) slot.

3. The accelerator cable must be installed before adjustment.

4. Rotate the idler pulley (cam) in a counter clockwise direction to 65 inch lbs. (7.3 Nm).

5. Check that the cable is moving freely. The cable may appear to function properly with the engine stopped or cold. Recheck after the engine is hot.

6. Road test the vehicle.

Fig. 49 Throttle Valve (TV) adjuster

SHIFT LINKAGE

1. On some models you will need to lift up the locking button.

2. Place the shift lever into Neutral.

3. Disconnect the shift cable from the transaxle lever. Place the transaxle lever in Neutral, by moving the lever clockwise to the Low (L) detent, then counterclockwise through the Second (S) and Drive (D) detents to the Neutral detent.

4. Attach and tighten the shift cable to the pin on the transaxle lever. Check the shift operation.

5. On some models you will need to push down on the locking button.

✳✳CAUTION

Any inaccuracies in shift linkage adjustments may result in premature failure of the transaxle due to operation without the controls in full detent. Such operation results in reduced fluid pressure and in turn, partial engagement of the affected clutches. Partial engagement of the clutches, with sufficient pressure to permit apparently normal vehicle operation will result in failure of the clutches and/or other internal parts after only a few miles of operation.

Neutral Safety/Back-Up Light Switch

REMOVAL & INSTALLATION

Shifter Mounted

1. Apply the parking brake and block the wheels.
2. Place the vehicle in the neutral position.
3. Remove the shifter knob from the shifter by removing the retaining screw at the back of the knob.
4. Remove the screws at the sides and front of the console.
5. Open the console box and remove the retaining screw inside the box.
6. Remove the ashtray at the rear of the console and remove the retaining screw behind the ashtray.
7. Slide the console rearward slightly, then lift it over the shifter.
8. Disconnect the wiring harness at the back-up light switch.
9. Remove the switch from the base of the shifter.
10. Reverse to install the switch.
11. Adjust if needed, unblock the wheels.

Transaxle Mounted

▶ **See Figure 50**

1. Apply the parking brake and block the wheels.
2. Place the vehicle in the neutral position.
3. Remove the shifter linkage.
4. Disconnect the electrical harness to the switch.
5. Unfasten the switch, then lower from the vehicle.

To install:

6. Place the shift shaft in Neutral.
7. Align the flats of the shift shaft to flats in the switch.

1. Bolt – 21 ft. lbs. (28 Nm)
2. Switch assembly
3. Transaxle
4. Bracket (125C)
5. Bracket (440–T4)
6. Trans. shaft
7. ³/₃₂ inch. drill bit or 2.34 dia. gage pin

FRT

A

B

VIEW A

FRT

VIEW B

86817051

Fig. 50 Neutral safety switch location and adjustment

8. Install the switch assembly.

➡If the bolt holes do not align with the mounting boss on the transaxle, verify the sift shaft DO NOT ROTATE THE SWITCH. The switch is pinned in the neutral position. If the switch has been rotated and the pin broken or when using an old switch, adjust it.

9. Tighten the switch screw to 18 ft. lbs. (25 Nm).
10. Remove the gauge pin.
11. Attach the electrical connection, then connect the shifter linkage.

ADJUSTMENT

1. Place the transaxle control shifter in the neutral notch on the detent plate.
2. Loosen the switch attaching screws.
3. Rotate the switch on the shifter assembly to align the service adjustment hole with the carrier tang hole.
4. Insert a ³/₃₂ in. (2.34mm) maximum diameter gauge pin to a depth of ⁵/₈ in. (15mm).
5. Tighten the attaching screws.
6. Remove the gauge pin.

Transaxle

REMOVAL & INSTALLATION

✳✳WARNING

Do not use air powered tools to dissemble or assemble a transaxle. Such tools will negate the diagnostic value of precision torquing, and improper bolt tightness can contribute to transaxle problems.

THM 125C

➡Around September 1, 1991, the manufacturer changed the name of its THM 125C automatic transaxle to Hydra-Matic 3T40. However, 1989 and 1990 served as transitional years during which both names were in effect.

1. Disconnect the negative battery cable from the transaxle. Tape the wire to the upper radiator hose to keep it out of the way.
2. Remove the air cleaner and disconnect the detent cable. Slide the detent cable in the opposite direction of the cable to remove it from the carburetor.
3. Unbolt the detent cable attaching bracket at the transaxle.
4. Pull up on the detent cable cover at the transaxle until the cable is exposed. Disconnect the cable from the rod.
5. Detach the electrical connectors at the neutral safety switch, Torque Converter Clutch (TCC) and Vehicle Speed Sensor (VSS).
6. Remove the two transaxle strut bracket bolts at the transaxle, if equipped.
7. Remove all the engine-to-transaxle bolts except the one near the starter. The one nearest the firewall is installed from the engine side; you will need a short handled box wrench or ratchet to reach it.
8. Loosen, but do not remove the engine-to-transaxle bolt near the starter.
9. Disconnect the speedometer cable at the upper and lower coupling. On cars with cruise control, remove the speedometer cable at the transducer.
10. Remove the retaining clip and washer from the shift linkage at the transaxle. Remove the two shift linkage at the transaxle. Remove the two shift linkage bracket bolts.
11. Disconnect and plug the two fluid cooler lines at the transaxle. These are inch-size fittings; use a back-up wrench to avoid twisting the lines.
12. Install an engine holding chain or hoist. Raise the engine enough to take its weight off the mounts.
13. Unlock the steering column and raise the car.
14. Remove the two nuts holding the anti-sway (stabilizer) bar to the left lower control arm (driver's side).

15. Remove the four bolts attaching the covering plate over the stabilizer bar to the engine cradle on the left side (driver's side).

16. Loosen but do not remove the four bolts holding the stabilizer bar bracket to the right side (passenger's side) of the engine cradle. Pull the bar down on the driver's side.

17. Disconnect the front and rear transaxle mounts at the engine cradle.

18. Remove the two rear center crossmember bolts.

19. Remove the three right (passenger) side front engine cradle attaching bolts. The nuts are accessible under the splash shield next to the frame rail.

20. Remove the top bolt from the lower front transaxle shock absorber, if equipped (V6 engine only).

21. Remove the left (driver) side front and rear cradle-to-body bolts.

22. Remove the left front wheel. Attach an axle shaft removing tool (GM part no. J-28468 or the equivalent) to a slide hammer. Place the tool behind the axle shaft cones and pull the cones out away from the transaxle. Remove the right shaft in the same manner. Set the shafts out of the way. Plug the openings in the transaxle to prevent fluid leakage and the entry of dirt.

23. Swing the partial engine cradle to the left (driver) side and wire it out of the way outboard of the fender well.

24. Remove the four torque converter and starter shield bolts. Remove the two transaxle extension bolts from the engine-to-transaxle bracket.

25. Attach a transaxle jack to the case.

26. Use a felt pen to matchmark the torque converter and flywheel. Remove the three torque converter-to-flywheel bolts.

27. Remove the transaxle-to-engine bolt near the starter. Remove the transaxle by sliding it to the left, away from the engine.

To install:

28. Place the transaxle on a jack and raise it into the vehicle. As the transaxle is installed, slide the right axle shaft into the case.

29. Align the matchmarks and connect the torque converter to the flywheel. Install the transaxle-to-engine bolt near the starter.

30. Install the engine-to-transaxle bracket extension bolts. Install the torque converter and starter shield bolts.

31. Install the partial engine cradle.

32. Install the left axle shaft.

33. Install the drivers side front and rear cradle to body bolts.

34. Install the top bolt to the lower front transaxle shock absorber, if equipped (V6 engine only).

35. Install the three right (passenger) side front engine cradle attaching bolts.

36. Install the two rear center crossmember bolts.

37. Connect the front and rear transaxle mounts at the engine cradle.

38. Install the stabilizer bar. Tighten the four bolts holding the stabilizer bar bracket to the right side (passenger's side) of the engine cradle.

➡To aid in stabilizer bar installation, a pry hole has been provided in the engine cradle.

39. Install the four bolts attaching the covering plate over the stabilizer bar to the engine cradle on the left side (driver's side).

40. Install the two nuts holding the anti-sway (stabilizer) bar to the left lower control arm (driver's side).

41. Lower the vehicle and remove the engine support device.

42. Connect the two fluid cooler lines at the transaxle.

43. Install the two shift linkage bracket bolts.

44. Connect the two shift linkages at the transaxle and install the retaining clips and washers.

45. Connect the speedometer cable at the upper and lower coupling. On cars with cruise control, connect the speedometer cable at the transducer.

46. Tighten the engine-to-transaxle bolt near the starter.

47. Install all remaining engine-to-transaxle bolts. The one nearest the firewall is installed from the engine side, you will need a short handled box wrench or ratchet to reach it.

48. Install the two transaxle strut bracket bolts at the transaxle, if equipped.

49. Install the detent cable and air cleaner.

50. Connect the negative battery cable to the transaxle.

51. Fill the transaxle with fresh DEXRON III, then test drive.

Hydra-Matic 3T40

➡Around September 1, 1991, the manufacturer changed the name of its THM 125C automatic transaxle to Hydra-Matic 3T40. However, 1989 and 1990 served as transitional years during which both names were in effect.

1. Remove the air cleaner assembly from the vehicle.

2. Disconnect the shift cable from the lever and bracket at the transaxle.

3. Detach the TV cable at the transaxle and throttle bracket.

4. Detach the electrical connections at the neutral safety switch, Torque Converter Clutch (TCC), and Vehicle Speed Sensor (VSS).

5. Remove the upper transaxle-to-engine bolts, including the electrical grounds.

6. Install tool J-28467-A the engine support fixture.

7. Raise and support the vehicle safely.

8. Remove the left front tire and wheel assembly.

9. Remove the left engine splash shield.

10. Raise and support the vehicle, remove the left splash shield.

11. Remove the left lower pinch bolt.

✳✳CAUTION

Failure to disconnect the intermediate shaft from the rack and pinion stub shaft can result in damage to the steering gear and or the intermediate shaft. This damage can cause loss of steering control, which could result in personal injury.

12. Unsecure and remove the intermediate shaft-to-steering stub shaft retaining bolt.

13. Remove the stabilizer shaft bracket nuts and brackets from the left control arm.

14. Unfasten and remove the left and right stabilizer reinforcement bolts and reinforcement to frame.

15. Remove the center punch 2 spot welds at the frame crossmember near the left stabilizer bar-to-frame mount. Drill out the spot welds enough to separate the frame and crossmember.

16. Remove the left steering gear to frame bolt, then detach the left-to-right frame section retaining bolts.

17. Support the frame on jackstands, remove the left frame-to-body bolts.

18. Unfasten the transaxle mount nuts from the frame.

19. Remove the jackstand and frame assembly.

20. Disconnect and remove the starter and converter shield screws and the shield.

21. Unbolt there three flywheel-to-converter bolts.

22. Remove the transaxle oil cooler lines.

23. Detach the transaxle support bracket-to-transaxle bolt.

24. Attach the transaxle jack to the transaxle case.

25. Remove the left drive axle from the transaxle, then remove the remaining transaxle bolts.

26. Lower the transaxle with an assistant, including the right drive axle from the unit.

27. Clean and flush the cooler lines with J-35944-A or an equivalent whenever the transaxle has been removed.

28. Install the transaxle with the help of an assistant, make sure the case is fully engaged on both locating dowels.

29. Reverse to install. Tighten the flywheel bolts to 47 ft. lbs. (63 Nm), the converter cover screws to 89 inch lbs. (10 Nm).

30. Fill the transaxle with fresh DEXRON III, then test drive.

Hydra-Matic 440-T4

➡Around September 1, 1991, the manufacturer changed the name of its Hydra-Matic 440-T4 automatic transaxle to Hydra-Matic 4T60-E. However, 1989 and 1990 served as transitional years during which both names were in effect.

1. Disconnect the negative battery cable.

2. Remove the air cleaner and disconnect the TV cable at the throttle body.

3. Disconnect the shift linkage at the transaxle.

4. Remove the engine support fixture tool J-28467 or equivalent.

5. Unfasten all electrical connectors.

6. Remove the 3 bolts from the transaxle to the engine.

7. Disconnect the vacuum line at the modulator.

8. Raise and safely support the vehicle.

9. Remove the left front wheel and tire assembly.

10. Detach the left side ball joint from the steering knuckle.

11. Disconnect the brake line bracket at the strut.

➡A halfshaft seal protector tool J-34754 should be modified and installed on any halfshaft prior to service procedures on or near the halfshaft. Failure to do so could result in seal damage or joint failure.

12. Remove the halfshafts from the transaxle.

13. Disconnect the pinch bolt at the intermediate steering shaft. Failure to do so could cause damage to the steering gear.

14. Remove the frame to stabilizer bolts.

15. Unsecure the stabilizer bolts at the control arm.

16. Remove the left front frame assembly.

17. Disconnect the speedometer cable or wire connector from the transaxle.

18. Detach the extension housing to engine block support bracket.

19. Disconnect the cooler pipes.

20. Remove the converter cover and converter-to-flywheel bolts.

21. Remove all of the remaining transaxle-to-engine bolts except one.

22. Position a jack under the transaxle.

23. Remove the remaining transaxle-to-engine bolt and remove the transaxle.

To install:

24. Install the transaxle in the vehicle. Install the engine-to-transaxle bolt accessible from under the vehicle. Tighten to 55 ft. lbs. (75 Nm).

25. Insert all of the remaining transaxle-to-engine bolts. Tighten to 55 ft. lbs. (75 Nm).

26. Remove the jack.

27. Install the converter-to-flywheel bolts and the converter cover.

28. Connect the cooler pipes.

29. Install the extension housing to engine block support bracket.

30. Connect the speedometer cable or wire connector to the transaxle.

31. Install the left front frame assembly.

32. Attach the stabilizer bolts at the control arm.

33. Install the frame-to-stabilizer bolts.

34. Connect the pinch bolt at the intermediate steering shaft.

35. Install the halfshafts to the transaxle.

36. Connect the brake line bracket at the strut.

37. Install the left side ball joint to the steering knuckle.

38. Install the left front wheel and tire assembly.

39. Lower the vehicle.

40. Connect the vacuum line at the modulator.

41. Install the 3 bolts from the transaxle to the engine.

42. Connect all electrical connectors.

43. Remove the engine support tool.

44. Attach the shift linkage to the transaxle.

45. Connect the TV cable at the throttle body and adjust as necessary. Install the air cleaner.

46. Connect the negative battery cable.

47. Fill the transaxle with fresh DEXRON III, test drive.

Hydra-Matic 4T60-E

➡Around September 1, 1991, the manufacturer changed the name of its Hydra-Matic 440-T4 automatic transaxle to Hydra-Matic 4T60-E. However, 1989 and 1990 served as transitional years during which both names were in effect.

1. Remove the air cleaner assembly.

2. Remove the engine torque strut from the engine.

3. Disconnect the shift control cable bracket from the transaxle case.

4. Detach the Torque Converter Clutch (TCC) electrical connection from the unit.

5. Remove the vacuum hose form the modulator.

6. Unbolt the upper transaxle including grounds.

7. Install tool J-28467-A engine support.

8. Remove the engine splash shields.

9. Remove both front tires and wheels.

10. Remove the pinch bolts from the control arms.

11. Unbolt the stabilizer shaft bolts and the reinforcement plates from the frame.

12. Unfasten the stabilizer shaft nuts and bracket from the control arm.

13. Using a 7/16 in. drill bit, drill through the two spot welds located between the front and rear holes of the left front stabilizer shaft mounting.

14. Remove the front and rear transaxle mounting nuts.

15. Disconnect the power steering cooler line bolts.

16. Disconnect the electrical harness from the frame.

17. Detach the right frame-to-left frame retaining bolt, then position a jackstand under the frame for support.

18. Loosen the two frame bolts from the frame.

19. Remove the left frame assembly with help from an assistant.

20. Unfasten the right lower ball joint from the knuckle, then remove the bolts from the transaxle support bracket.

21. Disconnect the power steering cooler line support from the transaxle.

22. Remove the transaxle converter cover.

23. Remove the starter assembly from the engine, then remove the torque converter bolts.

24. Unsecure the transaxle mount bolts from the case, then remove the mount.

25. Disconnect the neutral safety switch connection.

26. Slide both drive axles from the vehicle.

27. Remove the Vehicle Speed Sensor (VSS) connection from the transaxle.

28. Install a transaxle jack.

29. Remove the oil cooler lines and plug the openings.

30. Remove the remaining bolts at the transaxle, then with help from an assistant, lower the transaxle.

31. Clean and flush the cooler lines with J-35944-A or an equivalent. This should be done whenever the transaxle has been removed.

32. Install the transaxle with the help of an assistant.

33. Reverse to install, tightening the transaxle mounting bolts-to-case 41 ft. lbs. (55 Nm), converter bolts 47 ft. lbs. (63 Nm), converter cover bolts 89 inch lbs. (10 Nm), transaxle support bracket and bolts-to-transaxle 32 ft. lbs. (43 Nm), left/right frame-to-body bolts 40 ft. lbs. (54 Nm), and transaxle rear mount-to-frame bolts 24 ft. lbs. (33 Nm).

34. Fill the transaxle with fresh DEXRON III, then test drive.

Halfshafts

REMOVAL & INSTALLATION

✳✳WARNING

Use care when removing the drive axle. Tri-pots can be damaged if the drive axle is overextended.

Except Rear Axle — 6000 STE AWD

1. Remove the hub nut and discard. A new hub nut must be used for reassembly.

2. Raise and safely support the vehicle. Remove the wheel and tire assembly.

3. Install an halfshaft boot seal protector onto the seal.

4. Disconnect the brake hose clip from the McPherson strut but do not disconnect the hose from the caliper. Remove the brake caliper from the spindle and support the caliper with a length of wire. Do not allow the caliper to hang by the brake hose unsupported.

5. Mark the camber alignment cam bolt for reassembly. Remove the cam bolt and the upper attaching bolt from the strut and spindle.

6. Pull the steering knuckle assembly from the strut bracket.

7. Remove the halfshaft from the transaxle.

8. Using spindle remover tool J-28733 or equivalent, remove the halfshaft from the hub and bearing assembly. Do not allow the halfshaft to hang unsupported. If necessary, support using a length of wire in order to prevent component damage.

To install:

9. If a new halfshaft is to be installed, a new knuckle seal should be installed first along with a boot seal protector when necessary.

10. Loosely install the halfshaft into the transaxle and steering knuckle.

11. Loosely attach the steering knuckle to the suspension strut.

12. The halfshaft is an interference fit in the steering knuckle. Press the axle into place, then install the hub nut. When the shaft begins to turn with the hub, insert a drift through the caliper into one of the cooling slots in the rotor to keep it from turning.

➡**On some vehicles, the hub flange has a notch in it which can be used to prevent the hub and the shaft from turning, when one of the hub bearing retainer bolts is removed, by placing a longer bolt put in its place through the notch.**

13. Tighten the hub nut to 70 ft. lbs. (95 Nm) to completely seat the shaft.

14. Install the brake caliper. Tighten the caliper mounting bolts to 30 ft. lbs. (41 Nm).

15. Load the hub assembly by lowering it onto a jackstand. Align the camber cam bolt marks made during removal, install the bolt and tighten to 140 ft. lbs. (190 Nm). Tighten the upper nut to the same value.

16. Install the halfshaft all the way into the transaxle using a suitable tool inserted into the groove provided on the inner retainer. Tap the tool until the shaft seats in the transaxle. Remove the boot seal protector.

17. Connect the brake hose clip the the strut. Install the tire and wheel, lower the vehicle and tighten the hub nut to 192 ft. lbs. (261 Nm).

Rear Axle — 6000 STE AWD

1. Raise and safely support the vehicle.

2. Remove the tire and wheel assembly.

3. Disconnect the parking brake cable end from the bracket.

4. Insert a suitable tool through the caliper into the rotor to prevent the rotor from turning.

5. Remove the shaft nut and washer using special tool J-34826. Discard the shaft nut.

6. Remove the anti-lock brake sensor bolt and move the sensor aside.

7. Remove the 2 brake caliper bolts and remove the caliper. Support the caliper using a length of wire.

➡**Do not allow the caliper to hang by the brake hose unsupported.**

8. Remove the rotor from the hub and bearing assembly.

9. Install leaf spring compression tool J-33432 or equivalent.

10. Remove the 3 bolts mounting the hub and bearing to the knuckle.

11. Remove the hub and bearing assembly from the knuckle using special tool J-28733-A or equivalent.

12. Remove the bolts and nut plate attaching the lower strut mount to the knuckle. Scribe the position of the upper bolt prior removing.

13. Install a suitable CV-boot protector to prevent damage to the boot.

14. Swing the knuckle downward and away from the driveshaft.

15. Remove the drive axle from the differential using a suitable slide hammer.

To install:

16. Install the drive axle to the differential. Ensure positive engagement by pulling outward on the inner axle end. Grasp the housing only. Do not grasp and pull on the axle shaft.

17. Swing the knuckle up to the lower strut mount.

18. Position the nut plate and install the lower strut mount bolts to the knuckle. Align the top bolt with scribe marks before tightening the bolts. Tighten the bolts to 148 ft. lbs. (200 Nm).

19. Remove the CV-boot protector.

20. Install the hub and bearing assembly to the knuckle and axle spline.

21. Install the hub and bearing attaching bolts. Tighten to 61 ft. lbs. (84 Nm).

22. Remove the leaf spring compression tool.

23. Install the rotor to hub and bearing assembly.

24. Install the brake caliper to the rotor and install the retaining bolts. Tighten the bolts to 38 ft. lbs. (51 Nm).

25. Install the anti-lock brake sensor to the knuckle and install the retaining bolt. Using a non-ferrous feeler gauge, adjust the sensor gap to 0.028 in. (0.7mm). Tighten the adjustment screw to 19 inch lbs. (2.2 Nm).

26. Connect the parking brake cable end into the bracket.

27. Install the shaft washer and new torque prevailing nut. Hold the rotor with a suitable to prevent the axle from turning while tightening. Tighten to 185 ft. lbs. (260 Nm).

28. Install the tire and wheel assembly.

29. Check the rear wheel camber. Adjust as necessary.

➡**If the lower strut to knuckle bolts are properly aligned with the scribe marks, no camber adjustment should be necessary.**

30. Lower the vehicle.
31. Tighten the lugnuts.

OVERHAUL

▶ See Figure 51

Outer Joint

▶ **See Figures 52, 53, 54, 55, 56 and 57**

1. Remove the axle shaft.

2. Cut off the seal retaining clamp. Using a brass drift and a hammer, lightly tap the seal retainer from the outside toward the inside of the shaft to remove from the joint.

3. Use a pair of snapring pliers to spread the retaining ring apart. Pull the axle shaft from the joint.

4. Using a brass drift and a hammer, lightly tap on the inner race cage until it has tilted sufficiently to remove one of the balls. Tilt the cage in the opposite direction to remove the opposing ball. Remove the other balls in the same manner.

5. Position the cage and the inner race 90° to the centerline of the outer race, then align the cage windows with the lands of the outer race.

6. Rotate the inner race 90° to the centerline of the cage with the lands of the inner race aligned with the windows of the cage.

7. Pivot the inner race into the cage window and remove the inner race.

8. Clean all parts thoroughly and inspect for wear, make sure all parts are dry.

To install:

9. Assemble the new swage ring on the neck of the seal. DO NOT SWAGE.

10. Slide the swage ring onto the axle shaft, then position the neck of the seal in the seal groove on the axle shaft.

11. For the swage ring, mount the swage clamp tool, J-41048 in a vise and proceed:

   a. Position the outboard end of the shaft assembly in the tool.

   b. Align the top of the seal neck on the bottom die using the indicator line.

   c. Place the top half of the tool on the lower half of the tool.

   d. Make sure there are no pinch points on the seal before proceeding. This could cause damage to the seal.

   e. Insert the bolts, then tighten by hand until snug.

   f. Make sure that the seal, housing and swage ring all remain in alignment.

   g. Continue to tighten each of the bolts 180° at a time, alternating until; both of the sides are bottomed.

12. Put a light coat of the grease provided in the rebuilding kit onto the ball grooves of the inner race and outer joint.

13. Hold the inner race 90° centerline of the cage with the lands of the inner race aligned with the windows of the cage and insert the inner race into the cage.

14. Hold the cage and inner race 90° to centerline of the outer race, then align the cage windows with the lands of the outer race.

15. Assemble the cage and inner race into the outer race. Be sure that the retaining ring side of the inner race faces the axle shaft.

16. Insert the first chrome ball, then tilt the cage in the opposite direction to insert the opposing ball. Repeat this process until all of the balls are inserted.

1 Retainer ring
2 Retainer & housing asm.
3 Shaft retaining ring
4 Tripot joint spider
5 Spacer ring
6 Seal retaining clamp
7 Trilobal tripot bushing
8 Drive axle inboard
9 Seal retaining clamp/ring
10 Axle shaft (RH shown, LH similar)
11 Drive axle outboard seal
12 Seal retaining clamp
13 Race retaining clamp
14 Chrome alloy ball
15 C/V joint inner race
16 C/V joint cage
17 C/V joint outer race

86817052

Fig. 51 Tri-pot design — exploded view

1 Race retaining ring
2 C/V joint outer race

86817054

Fig. 52 Spread the ears on the race retaining ring with tool J-8059, then remove the CV-joint assembly from the axle shaft

1 Chrome alloy ball
2 C/V joint inner race
3 C/V joint cage
4 C/V joint outer race

86817055

Fig. 53 Using a brass drift and a hammer, lightly tap on the inner race cage until it has tilted sufficiently to remove one of the balls. Tilt the cage in the opposite direction to remove the opposing ball. Remove the other balls in the same manner

A Land
B Windows
1 C/V joint cage
2 C/V joint outer race

86817056

Fig. 54 Position the cage and the inner race 90° to the centerline of the outer race, then align the cage windows with the lands of the outer race

A Cage window
B Inner race land
1 C/V joint inner race
2 C/V joint cage

86817057

Fig. 55 Rotate the inner race 90° to the centerline of the cage with the lands of the inner race aligned with the windows of the cage

J 41048

86817058

Fig. 56 Tool J-41048 or a suitable vise can be used for this procedure

17. Place approximately half of the grease from the service kit inside the seal, then pack the CV-joint with the remaining grease.

18. Push the CV-joint onto the axle shaft until the retaining ring is seated in the groove on the axle shaft.

19. Slide the large end of the seal with the a large seal clamp in place over the outside of the CV-joint race, then locate the seal lip in the groove on the race.

20. The seal must not be dimpled, stretched or out of shape in any way. If it is not in shape, equally pressurize the seal and shape it properly by hand.

21. Crimp the retaining ring clamp with tool J-35910 to 130 ft. lbs. (176 Nm).

22. Check the crimp profile for correct shape and ear gap.

Outer Boot

1. Raise and support the vehicle safely.

2. Remove the front tire and wheel assembly.

3. Remove the caliper bolts. Remove the caliper and support using a length of wire.

1 Axle shaft
2 C/V joint outer race

86817059

Fig. 57 Push the CV-joint onto the axle shaft until the retaining ring is seated in the groove on the axle shaft

1 Shaft retaining ring
2 Spacer ring
3 Axle shaft

86817061

Fig. 58 Full view of the spider on the axle shaft

4. Remove the hub nut, washer and wheel bearing.
5. Using a brass drift, lightly tap around the seal retainer to loosen it. Remove the seal retainer.
6. Remove the seal retaining clamp or ring and discard.
7. Using snapring pliers, remove the race retaining ring from the halfshaft.
8. Pull the outer joint assembly and the outboard seal away from the halfshaft.
9. Flush the grease from the joint and repack with half of the grease provided. Put the remainder of the grease in the seal.

To install:
10. Check the boots for wear.
11. Assemble the inner seal retainer, outboard seal and outer seal retainer to the halfshaft. Push the joint assembly onto the shaft until the retaining ring is seated in the groove.
12. Slide the outboard seal onto the joint assembly and secure using the outer seal retainer. Using seal clamp tool J-35910 or equivalent, tighten the outer clamp to 130 ft. lbs. (176 Nm) and the inner clamp to 100 ft. lbs. (136 Nm).
13. Install the wheel bearing, washer and hub nut. Tighten the hub nut to 192 ft. lbs. (260 Nm).
14. Secure the caliper with the caliper attaching bolts.
15. Install the front tire and wheel assembly.
16. Lower the vehicle.
17. Tighten the lugnuts.

Inner Joint

▶ **See Figures 58, 59, 60, 61 and 62**

1. Remove the axle shaft.
2. For swag ring removal use a hand grinder to cut through the ring.
3. Remove the larger seal retaining ring from the tri-pot joint with a side cutter and dispose.
4. Separate the seal from the trilobal tri-pot bushing at the large diameter, then slide the seal away from the joint along the axle shaft.
5. Remove the housing from the spider and shaft.
6. Spread the spacer ring with tool J-8059, then slide the spacer ring and spider back on the axle shaft.

7. Remove the shaft retaining ring from the groove on the axle shaft and slide the spider assembly off the shaft.
8. Clean the tri-pot balls, needle rollers and housing with clean solvent.
9. Remove the trilobal tri-pot bushing from the housing.
10. Remove the spacer ring and seal from the axle shaft.
11. Inspect all parts for wear.

To install:
12. Connect the new ring on the neck of the seal. DO NOT SWAGE.
13. Slide the seal on the shaft, then position the neck of the seal in the groove on the axle shaft.
14. For the swag ring, mount the clamp tool in a vise, then proceed:
    a. Position the outboard end of the shaft assembly in the tool.
    b. Align the top of the seal neck on the bottom die using the indicator line.
    c. Place the top half of the tool on the lower half of the tool.

J 8059

1 Spacer ring
2 Axle shaft

86817062

Fig. 59 Spread the spacer ring with tool J-8059, then slide the spacer ring and spider back on the axle shaft

d. Make sure there are no pinch points on the seal before proceeding. This could cause damage to the seal.

e. Insert the bolts, then tighten by hand until snug.

f. Make sure that the seal, housing and swage ring all remain in alignment.

g. Continue to tighten each of the bolts 180° at a time, alternating until both of the sides are bottomed.

15. Install the spacer ring on the axle shaft and beyond the second groove.

16. Slide the spider assembly against the spacer ring on the shaft.

17. Be sure that the counterbored face of the spider faces the end of the shaft.

18. Install the shaft seating ring in the groove of the axle shaft with tool J-8059.

19. Slide the spider towards the end of the shaft, then reseat the spacer ring in the groove on the shaft.

20. Place approximately half of the grease from the service kit in the seal and use the remaining grease to repack the housing.

21. Install the trilobal tri-pot bushing to the housing.

22. Position the large clamp on the seal, then slide the housing over the spider assembly on the shaft.

23. Slide the large diameter of the seal, with the large clamp in place, over the outside of the trilobal tri-pot bushing, then locate the lip of the seal in the groove.

24. Position the joint assembly at the correct distance, as illustrated.

25. The seal must not be dimpled, stretched or out of shape in any way. If it is not in shape, equally pressurize the seal and shape it properly by hand.

26. Crimp the retaining ring clamp with tool J-35910 to 130 ft. lbs. (176 Nm).

27. Check the crimp profile for correct shape and ear gap.

Inner Boot

1. Raise and safely support the vehicle.

2. Remove the front tire and wheel assembly.

3. Unsecure the caliper bolts, then remove the caliper and support it using a length of wire.

4. Remove the hub nut, washer and wheel bearing.

1 Retainer & housing asm.
2 Axle shaft

86817064

Fig. 60 Position the large clamp on the seal, then slide the housing over the spider assembly on the shaft

1 Retainer & housing asm.
2 Drive axle inboard seal
3 Axle shaft

86817065

Fig. 61 Position the joint assembly 4.9 in. (125mm) from the inner boot band

86817060

Fig. 62 Crimp the retaining ring clamp with tool J-35910 to 130 ft. lbs. (176 Nm)

5. Remove the halfshaft. Place in a suitable holding fixture being careful not place undue pressure on the halfshaft.

6. Remove the joint assembly retaining ring. Remove the joint assembly.

7. Remove the race retaining ring and remove the seal retainer.

8. Remove the inner seal retaining clamp. Remove the inner joint seal.

9. Flush the grease from the joint and repack with half of the grease provided. Put the remainder of the grease in the seal.

To install:

10. Assemble the inner seal retainer, outboard seal and outer seal retainer to the halfshaft. Push the joint assembly onto the shaft until the retaining ring is seated in the groove.

11. Slide the outboard seal onto the joint assembly and secure using the outer seal retainer. Using seal clamp tool J-35910 or equivalent, tighten the outer clamp to 130 ft. lbs. (176 Nm) and the inner clamp to 100 ft. lbs. (136 Nm).

12. Insert the halfshaft assembly.

13. Secure the wheel bearing, washer and hub nut. Tighten the hub nut to 192 ft. lbs. (260 Nm).

14. Install the caliper and caliper attaching bolts.

15. Install the front tire and wheel assembly.

16. Lower the vehicle.

DRIVELINE

Replacement of the driveshaft on the Pontiac 6000 AWD is covered in detail under the Automatic Transaxle Driveshaft removal and installation procedure.

Driveshaft and U-Joint

REMOVAL & INSTALLATION

Original Driveshaft

▶ See Figure 63

1. Raise and safely support the vehicle.

➡**The relationship between the center bearing support and the floor pan must be maintained. Established at the assembly plant, the relationship has an influence on the front joint stoke capacity and remains constant for the vehicle, regardless of the driveshaft installed.**

2. Scribe the transaxle output shaft flange opposite the "painted" marking on the front driveshaft. The rear pinion flange must be scribed opposite the "painted" marking on the rear driveshaft. Scribe the center support mounting plate to floor pan of the vehicle.

3. Remove the 4 bolts connecting the rear driveshaft to the rear axle pinion flange. Be sure to support the rear of the rear driveshaft while rem,moving the remainder of the driveshaft.

➡**Do not loosen, remove or disconnect the 4 bolts adjacent to the center double cardan joint. Disturbing these fasteners may result in a vibration.**

4. With the aid of an assistant, support the driveshaft while performing the following:

a. Remove the 3 nuts retaining the center bearing support to the underbody of the vehicle.

b. Remove the 4 bolts connecting the front driveshaft to the transaxle output shaft flange.

c. Remove the driveshaft from the vehicle.

To install:

5. With the aid of an assistant, perform the following:

a. Install the driveshaft to the vehicle.

b. Align the rear driveshaft flange to the rear axle pinion flange, aligning the scribe marks.

c. Loosely install the nuts to the center bearing support and bolts to the rear axle pinion flange. Tighten the rear driveshaft flange to the rear axle pinion flange bolts to 40 ft. lbs. (54 Nm).

d. Install the bolts to the front driveshaft-to-transaxle output flange, using the reference marks to align the front flange position and center bracket location. Tighten the center bearing support bolts using the scribed reference marks to 25 ft. lbs. (34 Nm); nuts to 20 ft. lbs. (27 Nm). Tighten the front propeller shaft-to-transaxle output flange bolts to 40 ft. lbs. (54 Nm).

➡**The center mount plate must be reinstalled at the scribed position so that the front CV-joint is correctly located within its travel limits.**

6. Remove the support and lower the vehicle.

7. Road test the vehicle.

New Driveshaft

1. Remove the original driveshaft from the vehicle.

1 Transmission
2 Driveshaft assembly
3 20 ft. lbs. (27 Nm)
4 Rear differential assembly
5 40 ft. lbs. (54 Nm)

86817066

Fig. 63 Driveshaft assembly on the 6000 STE AWD

To install:

2. Using a dial indicator, measure and mark the bolt hole corresponding to the high point of radial run-out on both the transaxle output flange and rear axle pinion flange.

3. Transfer the center bearing bracket from the old driveshaft to the new driveshaft assembly.

4. With the aid of an assistant, perform the following:

a. Install the driveshaft to the vehicle.

b. Align the point marks supplied on the flanges of the propeller shaft to the scribe marks made during removal.

c. Loosely install the nuts to the center bearing support and bolts to the rear axle pinion flange. Tighten the rear driveshaft flange to the rear axle pinion flange bolts to 40 ft. lbs. (54 Nm).

d. Push the propeller shaft forward until a click is heard. Temporarily install a 0.9 in. (23mm) thick spacer between the output flange and the front driveshaft flange. Clamp in this position.

5. Install the remaining center bracket nuts. Tighten to 20 ft. lbs. (27 Nm).

6. Remove the spacer, extend the front CV-joint to meet the output flange and tighten the bolts. Tighten the front propeller shaft-to-transaxle output flange bolts to 40 ft. lbs. (54 Nm).

7. Verify correct location of the front CV-joint plunge.

8. Remove the supports. Lower the vehicle.

U-JOINT REPLACEMENT

▶ **See Figure 64**

A universal joint is two Y-shaped yokes connected by a crossmember called a spider. The spider is shaped like a cross having arms of equal length called trunnions. These U-joints are designed to handle the effects of various loadings and the rear axle windup during acceleration. Unfortunately these U-joints are not replaceable in the driveshaft unit. If you have any U-joint problems, the driveshaft unit must be replaced.

CENTER BEARING

▶ **See Figure 65**

A center support bearing is used to support the driveline at the connection of the driveshafts. The center bearing is a ball-type bearing mounted in a rubber cushion that is attached to the under body of the vehicle. The bearing is pre-lubricated and is sealed during manufacture.

Fig. 64 The U-joint assembly on the 6000 STE AWD is not replaceable

Fig. 65 A center support bearing is used to support the driveline at the connection of the driveshafts

REAR AXLE

Hub and Bearing Assembly

REMOVAL & INSTALLATION

6000 STE AWD

▶ **See Figure 66**

1. Raise and support the car on a hoist.

2. Remove the wheel.

3. Remove the brake caliper assembly and suspend on a wire.

✳✳CAUTION

Do not hammer on the caliper, as damage to the bearing could result.

4. Remove the hub and bearing assembly to rear axle attaching bolts and remove the hub and bearing assembly.

➡**The bolts which attach the hub and bearing assembly also support the brake assembly. When removing these bolts, support the brake assembly with a wire or other means. Do not let the brake line support the brake assembly.**

To install:

5. Install the hub and bearing assembly to the rear axle, then tighten the hub and bearing bolts to 61 ft. lbs. (83 Nm).
6. Install the brake caliper.
7. Install the tire and wheel assembly, then lower the car.
8. Tighten the lugnuts.

Axle Assembly

REMOVAL & INSTALLATION

6000 STE AWD

▶ **See Figure 67**

1. Open the rear decklid.
2. Raise and safely support the vehicle.
3. Remove both tire and wheel assemblies.
4. Disconnect the parking brake cable end from the bracket.
5. Insert a suitable tool through the caliper into the rotor to prevent the rotor from turning.
6. Remove the shaft nut and washer using special tool J-34826.
7. Discard the shaft nut.

86817072

Fig. 66 Rear axle bearing assembly for the 6000 STE AWD

8. Remove the anti-lock brake sensor bolt and move the sensor aside.
9. Unfasten the Electronic Ride Control (ERC) electrical connections and air lines, and disconnect the height sensor arm from the bracket stud.
10. Detach the brake line/ERC sensor bracket to the left control arm.
11. Disconnect the exhaust support bolt (above the cradle).
12. Scribe the relationship of the propeller shaft to the rear axle pinion flange, then remove the four shaft-to-differential bolts and suspend the propeller shaft with wire.
13. Remove the cradle-to-underbody bracket bolts, 4 on each side.
14. Install a spring compressor tool J-33432 or an equivalent onto the leaf spring.
15. Disconnect the strut upper mount bolts and nuts.
16. Lower the vehicle slightly to gain access to the luggage compartment nuts.
17. Raise the vehicle to the previous position, then release the spring tension and remove the spring compression tool.
18. Install a transaxle jack under the jacking plate, then remove the 4 cradle mount bolts.
19. Lower the axle assembly slightly, then disconnect the differential vent tube, then lower completely.

To install:

20. Raise the axle enough to connect the differential vent tube, then raise completely to align the cradle mount bores.
21. Attach the four cradle mount bolts and tighten to 103 ft. lbs. (140 Nm).
22. Remove the transaxle jack.
23. Install the spring compression tool, then tighten it to compress the spring.
24. The strut upper mount bolts and nuts need to be tightened to 28 ft. lbs. (38 Nm). Then lower the vehicle and install the mount nuts in the luggage compartment.
25. Raise the vehicle again, then remove the spring compression tool.
26. Attach the cradle brace-to-underbody bracket bolts, then tighten to 28 ft. lbs. (38 Nm).
27. Connect the four propeller shaft-to-differential bolts, and tighten to 40 ft. lbs. (54 Nm).
28. Install the exhaust support bolt above the cradle, then tighten to 11 ft. lbs. (15 Nm).
29. Attach the bolt securing the brake line/ERC sensor bracket to the left control arm, then tighten to 18 ft. lbs. (24 Nm).
30. Attach the ERC electrical connection, air lines and the height sensor arm to the bracket stud.
31. Connect the anti-lock brake sensors using one bolt each.
32. Attach the brake calipers and attach the Torx® bolts.
33. Connect the parking brake cable at the tensioner.
34. Connect the parking brake brackets, bolts and springs.
35. Connect the parking brake cables at both ends.
36. Tighten the cables at the tensioner.
37. Install both of the wheels, then lower the vehicle.
38. Close the decklid.

1 Rear cradle assembly
2 Parking brake bracket and spring
3 Parking brake tensioner
4 Stabilizer bar
5 Cradle mount bolt 140 Nm (103 lbs. ft.)
6 Retainer
7 Insulator
8 Brake caliper
9 Cradle brace

10 Underbody bracket bolt
    38 Nm (28 lbs. ft.)
11 Under body bracket
12 Bolt 54 Nm (40 lbs. ft.)
13 Insulator
14 Spacer
15 Retainer
16 Cage nut
17 Body rail

86817085

Fig. 67 Rear axle assembly for the 6000 STE AWD

Disconnecting Air Lines

The Electronic Ride Control (ERC) system air lines use a spring clip connection with mounted sealing shoulders in the retainer and on the end of the air line with double "O" ring seals. Before disconnecting any air line, clean the connector and surrounding area. Squeeze the spring clip to release the connector. To reassemble, lubricate the "O" rings with petroleum jelly or an equivalent, then push the air line and the connector fully into the fitting.

Repairing Air Lines

▶ See Figure 68

Air lines used on the ERC system can be repaired by splicing in a coupling at the leaking area.
1. Inflate the system to 100 psi (600 kPa).
2. Locate the leaking area using a sop and water solution or a stethoscope.
3. Deflate the system.
4. Cut and remove the leaking line section.
5. Splice the replacement line to the existing line.
   a. Remove the plastic retainer pin from one of the nuts and slide the replacement line into the nut until it bottoms in the rubber seal.
   b. While holding the line in the position described in the previous step, tighten the nut to 70 inch lbs. (8 Nm).
   c. Attach the original line to the other end of the coupling as in steps a and b.
   d. Using a tie strap, secure the line to the vehicle in a location where it will not be pinched or contact the exhaust system.
6. Reinflate the system and check for leaks.

1 Service coupling
2 Rubber seal
3 Coupling sleeve
4 Internal metal sleeve
5 Air tube

86817084

Fig. 68 Repairing the air lines

Troubleshooting Basic Clutch Problems

Problem	Cause
Excessive clutch noise	Throwout bearing noises are more audible at the lower end of pedal travel. The usual causes are: · Riding the clutch · Too little pedal free-play · Lack of bearing lubrication A bad clutch shaft pilot bearing will make a high pitched squeal, when the clutch is disengaged and the transmission is in gear or within the first 2″ of pedal travel. The bearing must be replaced. Noise from the clutch linkage is a clicking or snapping that can be heard or felt as the pedal is moved completely up or down. This usually requires lubrication. Transmitted engine noises are amplified by the clutch housing and heard in the passenger compartment. They are usually the result of insufficient pedal free-play and can be changed by manipulating the clutch pedal.
Clutch slips (the car does not move as it should when the clutch is engaged)	This is usually most noticeable when pulling away from a standing start. A severe test is to start the engine, apply the brakes, shift into high gear and SLOWLY release the clutch pedal. A healthy clutch will stall the engine. If it slips it may be due to: · A worn pressure plate or clutch plate · Oil soaked clutch plate · Insufficient pedal free-play
Clutch drags or fails to release	The clutch disc and some transmission gears spin briefly after clutch disengagement. Under normal conditions in average temperatures, 3 seconds is maximum spin-time. Failure to release properly can be caused by: · Too light transmission lubricant or low lubricant level · Improperly adjusted clutch linkage
Low clutch life	Low clutch life is usually a result of poor driving habits or heavy duty use. Riding the clutch, pulling heavy loads, holding the car on a grade with the clutch instead of the brakes and rapid clutch engagement all contribute to low clutch life.

86817086

PROBLEM	PROBABLE CAUSE	CORRECTION
C.V./Universal joint noise.	1. Worn C.V. joint. 2. Worn center bearing. 3. Worn universal joint bearings. 4. Improper lubrication. 5. Loose flange bolts.	1. Replace propeller shaft. 2. Replace the propeller shaft. 3. Replace propeller shaft. 4. Lubricate as directed. 5. Tighten to "Specifications."
Ping, snap, or click in driveline (usually heard on initial load after the transmission is in gear; forward or reverse).	1. Loose rear module brace bolts or rear axle module hold down bolts. 2. Worn rear module brace bushings or rear axle module hold down bushings.	1. Tighten the bolts to specified torque. 2. Replace worn or damaged bushings.
Knocking or clunking in the driveline when operating the vehicle in a floating condition in high or neutral gear at 10 mph (16 km/h).	1. Worn or damaged universal joint. 2. Side gear hub counterbore in the differential is worn oversize. 3. Worn center bearing.	1. Replace the propeller shaft. 2. Replace the differential case and/or the side gears. 3. Replace the propeller shaft.
Roughness or vibration.	1. Bent or dented propeller shafts. 2. Undercoating on propeller shafts. 3. Tire unbalance, 30-55 mph (40-89 km/h). Not throttle conscious. 4. Tight universal joint. 5. Worn universal joint. 6. Burrs or gouges on companion flange. Check snap ring locating surfaces of flange yoke. 7. Propeller shaft or companion flange is unbalanced. 8. Excessive looseness at the slip spline. 9. Distorted or damaged yokes or flanges. 10. Yokes out of phase.	1. Replace propeller shafts. 2. Clean propeller shafts. 3. Balance or replace as required. 4. Impact yokes with a shaft hammer to free up. If unable to free up or if joint feels rough when rotated, replace propeller shafts. 5. Replace propeller shafts. 6. Rework or replace the companion flange. 7. Check for a missing balance weight on the propeller shaft. Rotate the companion flange 180°. 8. Replace necessary parts. 9. Install new yokes or flanges. 10. Remove companion flange, turn 180 degrees from the original position and install. Tighten bolts to specified torque.

86817087

PROBLEM	PROBABLE CAUSE	CORRECTION
	11. Propeller shaft runout at 50 mph (80 km/h). Throttle conscious.	11. Check propeller shaft runout at a front and rear. Should be less than specified. If above, rotate propeller shaft 180 degrees and recheck. Replace the propeller shaft if runout is still over specification.
Scraping Noise.	Slinger, companion flange, or end yoke rubbing on rear axle or center bearing.	Correct the interference.
Roughness above 35 mph (56 km/h) felt and/or heard.	1. Tires unbalanced or worn.	1. Balance or replace as required.
Squeak.	1. Lack of lubricant.	1. Lubricate joint and splines. Also check for worn or brinelled parts.
	2. Center bearing worn.	2. Replace propeller shafts.
	3. Worn universal joint.	3. Replace propeller shafts.
Whine or whistle.	1. Center bearing.	1. Place the vehicle on a hoist with rear wheels free to rotate and diagnose for source of noise, replace propeller shaft, if required.
Shudder on acceleration (low speed).	1. Loose or missing bolts at the center bearing or flanges.	1. Replace or tighten bolts to specified torque.
	2. Incorrectly set driveline angle.	2. Shim under the transmission support mount to change the driveline angle.
	3. Worn universal joint/ C.V. joint.	3. Replace propeller shafts.

86817088

TORQUE SPECIFICATIONS

Component	US	Metric
Clutch assemby:		
Cluth master cylinder	15-25 ft. lbs.	20-34 Nm
Clutch pedal-to-bracket	20-25 ft. lbs.	28-34 Nm
Clutch release lever	30-45 ft. lbs.	40-60 Nm
Clutch slave cylinder bleeder screw	18 inch lbs.	2 Nm
Clutch slave cylinder	14-20 ft. lbs.	18-26 Nm
Pressure plate-to-flywheel	12-18 ft. lbs.	16-24 Nm
4 Speed Transaxle:		
Case-to-cover bolts	16 ft. lbs.	21 Nm
Front support strut	48 ft. lbs.	65 Nm
Input shaft right bearing retainer	7 ft. lbs.	9Nm
Pinion shaft lock bolt	7 ft. lbs.	9 Nm
Output shaft left bearing retainer	45 ft. lbs.	65 Nm
Rear mount through bolt nut	80 ft. lbs.	108 Nm
Reverse idler shaft lock bolt	16 ft. lbs.	21 Nm
Shift control mount nuts	18 ft. lbs.	24 Nm
Transaxle-to-engine	47-62 ft. lbs.	65-85 Nm
5 Speed Transaxle:		
Clutch housing-to-gear housing	15 ft. lbs	21 Nm
Control box-to-case	11-16 ft. lbs.	15-22 Nm
Differential gear	61 ft. lbs.	83 Nm
Differential pin	84 inch lbs.	9 Nm
End plate-to-gear housing	15 ft. lbs.	21 Nm
Drain plug	18 ft. lbs.	24 Nm
Flywheel	44-60 ft. lbs.	60-80 Nm
Front strut-to-frame	50 ft. lbs.	68 Nm
Front strut-to-transaxle	40 ft. lbs.	54 Nm
Interlock plate	15 ft. lbs.	21 Nm
Neutral saftey switch	3 ft. lbs.	4-5 Nm
Output bearing race	15 ft. lbs.	21 Nm
Output shaft bearing support	50 ft. lbs.	70 Nm
Pressure plate-to-flywheel	14-18 ft. lbs.	18-24 Nm
Rear cover	11-16 ft. lbs.	15-22 Nm
Rear mount through bolt nut	80 ft. lbs.	108 Nm
Reverse idler shaft bolt	22-33 ft. lbs.	30-45 Nm
Reverse shift bracket	11-16 ft. lbs.	15-22 Nm
Ring gear bolts	73-79 ft. lbs.	98-107 Nm
Shift contol mount nuts	18 ft. lbs.	24 Nm
Transaxle case-to-clutch housing	22-33 ft. lbs.	30-45 Nm
Transaxle-to-engine	60 ft. lbs.	75 Nm

86817089

TORQUE SPECIFICATIONS

Component	US	Metric
3T40 Automatic Transaxle:		
Case-to-cover	18 ft. lbs.	24 Nm
Oil pan-to-valve body cover	8 ft. lbs.	11 Nm
Manual detent spring-to-case	8 ft. lbs.	11 Nm
Cooler connector	23 ft. lbs.	38 Nm
Parking lock bracket-to-case	18 ft. lbs.	24 Nm
Pipe retainer-to-case	18 ft. lbs.	24 Nm
Govener cover-to-case	8 ft. lbs.	11 Nm
TV cable-to-case	75 inch lbs.	9 Nm
Pressure switch	8 ft. lbs.	11 Nm
4T60-E Automatic Transaxle:		
Case extension-to-case	22-30 ft. lbs.	30-41 Nm
Speed sensor retainer-to-case	71-124 inch lbs.	8-14 Nm
Special trans oil pan-to-case	80-115 inch lbs.	9-13 Nm
Channel plate-to-case	15-20 ft. lbs.	20-27 Nm
Temperature sensor	58-66 inch lbs.	6.5-7.5 Nm
Hub nut:	70-75 ft. lbs.	95-103 Nm
Final	192 ft. lbs.	260 Nm
Failure warning switch:	15-50 inch lbs.	2-6 Nm

86817090

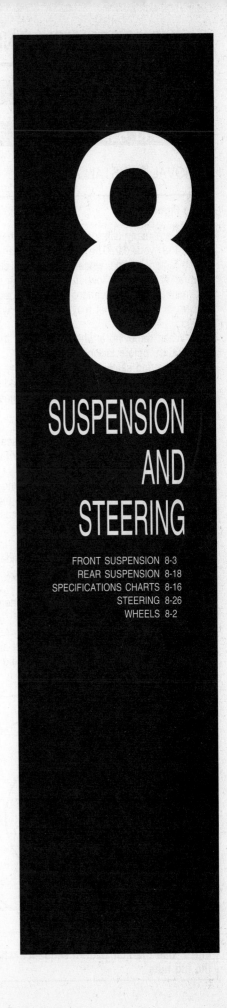

8

SUSPENSION AND STEERING

WHEELS

Front and Rear Wheel

REMOVAL & INSTALLATION

▶ See Figure 1

There are many different aftermarket wheels that can be installed on your car. The procedures given in this manual are for the factory original wheels. If your vehicle is equipped with aftermarket wheels, follow any special instructions given by that manufacturer. Pay attention to any special washers, spacers or adapters that may have come with aftermarket wheels.

1. When removing a wheel, loosen all the lug nuts at least one full turn, before jacking up the car.
2. Raise and safely support the car.
3. Finish removing the already loosened lug nuts. Sometimes applying slight pressure on wheel toward car will make it easy to screw them off by hand.
4. Remove the wheel.
5. If the wheel is stuck on the hub place at least two lug nuts back on. Only screw them on two or three turns, don't allow them to touch the wheel.
6. Lower the vehicle back on the ground and rock it side to side. This is safer than shaking a vehicle that is on a jack. After the wheel pops loose, repeat the steps after raise and support the vehicle.

To install:
7. Place the wheel on the vehicle, hand-tighten all of the lug nuts. If the studs or nuts are rusty, now is a good time to place some light lubricate on them.
8. After all of the nuts are hand-tightened, lower the vehicle.
9. Further tighten the nuts with a lug wrench until they are all snug. Use the "star pattern" method of skipping every other nut in the tightening sequence until all 5 lug nuts have been tightened.

10. Finally, using a torque wrench, tighten the lug nuts to specification. Although 100 ft. lbs. (136 Nm) may be suitable for factory-equipped steel wheels, aftermarket wheels may require a different amount. Be careful to observe the recommended torque value.

➡ **Uneven tightening of wheel lug nuts can cause early disc brake pad and rotor wear.**

Inspection

Wheels can be distorted or bent and not effect dry road handling to a noticeable degree. Out of round wheels will show up as uneven tire wear, or make it difficult to balance the tires. Without special tools it is difficult to check wheel radial runout. It would be best to ask the shop that balances the tires for you to do this. But a good visual inspection will usually reveal any problems.

Look for any bends or cracks. Not all repairs can be made to a wheel. If a wheel has any repair marks like welds or patches it should be discarded. Steel wheels that have slight bends where the tire meets the wheel doesn't mean the wheel is bad. Many times this is cause by the tire changing machine and can be hammered back into shape. This will only work on steel wheels not alloy or aluminum. If a wheel had a little bend in this area and had been repair it should be rebalanced and placed in a tank of water to check for leaks.

Another way to check for leaks where the wheel and tire meet is to lay the wheel flat on the ground. Place dish detergent and water solution around the wheel and wait a few minutes. If there is a slow leak you will see suds. Flip the tire over and repeat this procedure. If a leak is found the tire must be removed from the wheel. Then the tire bead and wheel rim must be cleaned, lubricated and reassembled. Always recheck to make sure the leak is fixed.

Wheel Lug Studs

REPLACEMENT

▶ See Figures 2 and 3

1. To remove the wheel, loosen all the lug nuts at least one full turn, before jacking up the car.
2. Raise and safely support the car.
3. Remove the wheel and tire assembly.
4. Remove the brake assembly components.
5. Remove the hub assembly.
6. Remove the damaged stud using a C-clamp and pressing it out the back.

To install:
7. Install the new stud by inserting the stud into the hole.
8. Place washers on the stud, then install a lug nut and tighten evenly to pull stud into place.
9. Make certain stud doesn't turn in the hub or it will strip out the hole. If stud doesn't fit very tight you'll need to replace the hub, too.
10. Remove the nut and washers after the stud is seated.

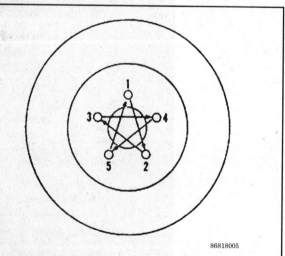

86818005

Fig. 1 Use the star pattern sequence when tightening the lug nuts

1 Front wheel hub
2 Wheel nut

J 6627-A

86818006

Fig. 2 Remove the damaged stud by using a C-clamp or tool J-6627-A, and pressing it out the back

11. Reinstall the hub and brake components.
12. Install the wheel, then hand-tighten the lug nuts.
13. Lower the vehicle and tighten the lug nuts to 100 ft. lbs. (136 Nm).

1 Hub and bearing assembly removed from vehicle
2 Insert washers over wheel stud
3 Tighten nut to draw wheel stud into correct position

86818007

Fig. 3 Place washers on the stud, then install a lug nut and tighten evenly to pull the stud into place

FRONT SUSPENSION

▶ **See Figures 4, 5 and 6**

The A-Bodies uses a MacPherson strut front suspension design. The MacPherson strut combines the functions of a shock absorber and an upper suspension member (upper arm) into one unit. The strut is surrounded by a coil spring, which provides normal front suspension functions.

The strut bolts to the body shell at its upper end, and to the steering knuckle at the lower end. The strut pivots with the steering knuckle by means of a sealed mounting assembly at the upper end which contains a preloaded, non-adjustable bearing.

The steering knuckle is connected to the chassis at the lower end by a conventional lower control arm, and pivots in the arm in a preloaded ball joint of standard design. The knuckle is fastened to the ball joint stud by means of a castellated nut and cotter pin.

Advantages of the MacPherson strut design, aside from its relative simplicity, include reduced weight and friction, minimal intrusion into the engine and passenger compartments, and ease of service.

➡**When removing any steering components, it is advisable to matchmark (scribe) the locations of the components**

MacPherson Struts and Coil Springs

TESTING

The purpose of a MacPherson strut, much like a shock absorber, is to dampen harsh spring movement and provide a means of dissipating the motion of the wheels. As a result, shocks encountered by the wheels are not totally transmitted

Fig. 4 Exploded view of the front suspension

86818021

1 Front wheel drive shaft kit
2 Front suspension strut mount washer
3 Front suspension strut mount nut
4 Prevailing torque nut (M 12 x 1.75)
5 Front suspension strut bolt
6 Front suspension strut nut
7 Front suspension strut mount
8 Front spring seat
9 Front suspension strut bumper
10 Front suspension strut shield
11 Front spring upper insulator
12 Front spring
13 Front suspension strut washer
15 Front suspension strut washer
16 Steering knuckle
17 Front wheel inner bearing seal
18 Front wheel hub
19 Front brake splash shield
20 Front brake splash shield bolt
21 Steering bolt
22 Front wheel drive shaft washer
23 Front wheel drive shaft nut

24 Front brake rotor
25 Wheel bolt
26 Steering knuckle nut
27 Front brake caliper
28 Front caliper bolt
29 Front wheel drive shaft kit
30 Front lower control arm reinforcement
31 Front lower control arm reinforcement bolt
32 Washer flat (M 12.2 x 24 x 3.38)
33 Front lower control arm bolt
34 Front lower control arm
35 Front lower control arm ball stud kit
36 Front stabilizer shaft insulator
37 Front stabilizer shaft insulator clamp
39 Prevailing torque nut
40 Front lower control arm bushing
41 Front stabilizer shaft insulator
42 Front stabilizer shaft
43 Front suspension nut
44 Drivetrain and front suspension frame reinforcement
45 Drivetrain and front suspension frame bolt

NOTE: BOLT/SCREWS MUST BE INSTALLED IN DIRECTION SHOWN

86818022

Fig. 5 Numbered list of the exploded view for the front suspension

STRUT DAMPER

DRIVE AXLES

LOWER CONTROL ARM

86818019

Fig. 6 The front suspension components are basically the same on both sides

to the body and, therefore, to you and your passengers. As the wheel moves up and down, the strut shortens and lengthens, thereby imposing a restraint on movement by its hydraulic action.

A good way to see if your struts are functioning correctly is to push one corner of the car until it is moving up and down for almost the full suspension travel, then release it and watch its recovery. If the car bounces slightly about one more time and comes to a rest, the strut is all right. If the car continues to bounce excessively, the struts will probably require replacement.

REMOVAL & INSTALLATION

▶ See Figures 7, 8, 9, 10, 11, 12 and 13

1. Remove the top strut-to-body mounting nuts.
2. Loosen the wheel nuts, then raise and support the vehicle on jackstands. Make sure the weight of the vehicle is not on the control arm.
3. Remove the wheel and tire assembly.

Fig. 7 Exploded view of a MacPherson strut assembly

4. Remove the brake line bracket from the strut assembly.

5. Install the boot protector tool J-28712 (Double-Offset joint) or J-33162 (Tri-Pot joint) over the drive axle boot.

➡️**If equipped with a Tri-Pot joint, disconnect the drive axle from the transaxle before separating the strut from the steering knuckle.**

6. If equipped, separate the ABS front brake sensor connection. These are on the 6000 STE models.

7. Before separating the strut from the steering knuckle, matchmark components by performing the following, as illustrated:

   a. Using a sharp tool, scribe the knuckle along the lower outboard strut radius.

   b. Scribe the strut flange on the inboard side, along the curve of the steering knuckle.

   c. Using a chisel, mark the strut-to-steering knuckle interface.

8. Remove the steering knuckle-to-strut bolts.

➡️**The steering knuckle should be supported after removing the bolts to prevent axle joint overextension.**

9. Remove the strut.

To install:

10. Install the strut to the body, then secure with the mounting nuts. Hand-tighten the nuts.

11. Place a jack under the lower arm. Raise the arm and install the lower strut-to-knuckle bolts. Align the strut-to-steering knuckle marks made during removal. Tighten the strut-to-knuckle bolts to 122-140 ft. lbs. (165-190 Nm), and the strut-to-body nuts to 16-18 ft. lbs. (22-24 Nm).

12. Reconnect the ABS sensor wiring.

13. Install the brake hose bracket to the strut.

14. Install the wheel, hand-tighten the lug nuts. Raise the vehicle slightly to allow removal of the jackstands.

15. Remove the jackstands and lower the car. Tighten the lug nuts to 100 ft. lbs. (136 Nm).

➡️**If a new strut dampener has been installed, the front end will have to be realigned.**

Fig. 9 Before removal, make scribe marks on the knuckle along the lower outboard strut radius (view A), the strut flange on the inboard side, along the curve of the steering knuckle (view B), and across the strut-to-steering knuckle interface (view C)

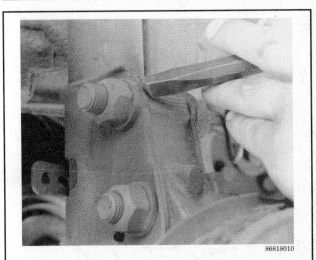

Fig. 10 Use a chisel to mark the strut-to-steering knuckle interface

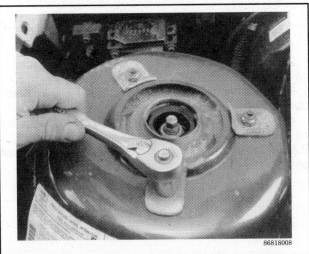

Fig. 8 Using a ratchet, remove the top strut-to-body mounting nuts

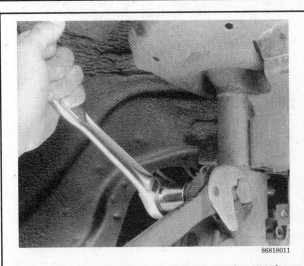

Fig. 11 With the use of two tools, remove the steering knuckle-to-strut bolts

Fig. 12 After removing the bolts connecting the steering knuckle to the strut, the strut can be extracted from the vehicle

DISASSEMBLY & ASSEMBLY

▶ See Figures 14 and 15

A MacPherson strut compressor tool J-34013-B or the equivalent must be used.

1. Mount the compressor tool J-34013-B in the holder J-3289-20.

2. Install the strut in the compressor J-34013-B, then install the compressor adapters, if used.

3. Compress the spring approximately ½ its height after initial contact with the top cap. **Do not bottom the spring or the dampener rod.**

4. Remove the nut from the strut dampener shaft and place the J-34013-27 on top of the dampener shaft. Using this alignment rod J-34013-27 guide the dampener shaft straight down through the bearing cap while decompressing the spring.

5. Remove the components.

Assembly:

6. Install the bearing cap into J-34013-B if previously removed. Mount the strut into J-34013-B using the bottom locking pin only, then extend the dampener shaft and install J-34013-20 on the shaft.

7. Install the spring over the dampener and swing the assembly up so that the locking pin can be installed. Install the upper insulator, shield, bumper, and upper spring seat. Make sure that the flat on the upper spring seat is facing in the proper direction. The spring should seat flat at 10° forward of the centerline of the strut assembly spindle.

8. Install tool J-34013-13 and turn, forcing the screw while J-34013-27 centers the assembly. When the threads on the dampener shaft are visible, remove tool J-34013-27, then install the nut.

9. Tighten the nut. Using a crow's foot line wrench while holding the dampener shaft with a socket.

10. Remove tool J-34013-20.

Lower Ball Joints

INSPECTION

1. Raise and safely support the car.

2. Grasp the tire at top and bottom and move the top to the tire in and out.

3. Observe for any horizontal movement of the knuckle relative to the control arm.

4. Ball joints must be replaced if there is any looseness in the ball joint and should be replaced if the seal is damaged. The ball joint may check good with a bad seal, but will not last long due to dirt and water entering the joint.

1 Strut assembly
2 Strut to body nuts 25 Nm (18 lbs. ft.)
3 Brake line bracket bolt 17 Nm (13 lbs.ft.)
4 Strut to steering knuckle nuts 190 Nm (140 lbs.ft.)
5 Retain steering knuckle with wire once strut assembly is removed

Fig. 13 Pontiac 6000 STE AWD strut mounting is slightly different than that of front wheel drive models

DISASSEMBLE AND ASSEMBLE STRUT

DISASSEMBLY	ASSEMBLY

NOTICE: CARE SHOULD BE TAKEN TO AVOID CHIPPING OR CRACKING THE SPRING COATING WHEN HANDLING THE FRONT SUSPENSION COIL SPRING.

86818016

Fig. 14 Disassembly and assembly of the strut

REMOVAL & INSTALLATION

▶ **See Figures 16 and 17**

Only one ball joint is used in each lower arm. The MacPherson strut design does not use an upper ball joint.

➡**Care must be exercised to prevent the halfshafts from being overextended. Support the lower arm.**

1. Loosen the wheel nuts, raise the car.
2. Place a jackstand under the vehicles frame or suspension support.
3. Lower the vehicle slightly, so that the weight of the vehicle rest on the jackstands and not on the control arms.
4. Remove the tire and wheel assembly.
5. Install a CV-boot protector.
6. Remove the steering knuckle bolts, then remove the ball joint nut and cotter pin from the steering knuckle.
7. Use a ⅛ in. (3mm) drill bit to drill a hole approximately ¼ in. (6mm) deep in the center of each of the three ball joint rivets.

8. Use a ½ in. (13mm) drill bit to drill off the rivet heads. Drill only enough to remove the rivet head.

✳✳WARNING

Take care not to drill through the halfshaft dust boots.

9. Use a hammer and punch to remove the rivets. Drive them out from the bottom.
10. Loosen the stabilizer shaft insulator nuts, then remove the ball joint assembly.
   To install:
11. Install the new ball joint into the control arm. Secure the three ball joint nuts, see your instructions supplied by the part supplier for tightening specifications.
12. Install the ball joint into the knuckle pinch bolt fitting. It should go in easily if not, check the stud alignment. Install the pinch bolt from the rear to the front. Tighten to 40 ft. lbs. (50 Nm) for 1982-84, 33 ft. lbs. (45 Nm) for 1985-93 and 38 ft. lbs. (52 Nm) for 1994-95.
13. Remove the CV-boot protector.

J 34013-B STRUT COMPRESSOR

J 3289-20 HOLDING FIXTURE BASE

J 34013-20 DAMPER ROD CLAMP

J 34658 FRONT KNUCKLE SEAL INSTALLER

J 34657-A HUB SEAL INSTALLER

J 34013-27 ALIGNMENT ROD

86818017

Fig. 15 Special tools used by GM for suspension work

86818031

Fig. 16 Use a ⅛ in. (3mm) drill bit to drill a hole approximately ¼ in. (6mm) deep in the center of each of the three ball joint rivets

BALL JOINT

86818030

Fig. 17 Install the new ball joint into the control arm, then secure the three ball joint nuts

14. Tighten the stabilizer shaft clamp insulator bolts to 32 ft. lbs. (43 Nm).

15. Install the wheel, hand-tighten the lug nuts.

16. Raise the vehicle slightly to allow removal of the jackstands.

17. Remove the jackstands, then lower the vehicle, tighten the lug nuts to 100 ft. lbs. (136 Nm).

Stabilizer Bar

REMOVAL & INSTALLATION

▶ See Figure 18

1. Raise and support the vehicle on jackstands.

2. Matchmark the stabilizer bar to the mounting bracket for installation.

3. Remove the two nuts attaching the clamps for the stabilizer bar to the lower control arms. Do not remove the studs from the control arm.

4. Remove the bolts which attach the retaining plates to the engine cradle on both sides. The retaining plate covers and holds the stabilizer bar.

5. Disconnect and remove the exhaust pipe and crossover if necessary.

6. Pull the stabilizer bar down and remove, then remove the insulators.

To install:

7. Install the insulators to the ends of the stabilizer bar.

8. Align the stabilizer bar to the matchmarks and attach the stabilizer to the frame.

➡ **To aid in stabilizer bar installation, a pry hole has been provided in the engine cradle.**

9. Install the reinforcements to each side at the frame, then tighten the reinforcement bolts to 40 ft. lbs. (55 Nm).

10. Secure the insulator clamps to the control arms and tighten the attaching nuts to 32 ft. lbs. (43 Nm).

11. Lower the vehicle.

Lower Control Arm

REMOVAL & INSTALLATION

▶ See Figures 19 and 20

1. Loosen the wheel nuts, raise the car.

2. Place jackstands under the frame, then lower the vehicle slightly so that the weight of the vehicle rests on the jackstands and not on the control arms.

3. Remove the tire and wheel assembly.

4. Place a boot protector over the axle boot.

5. Remove the stabilizer shaft to the control arm bolt.

6. Remove the steering knuckle pinch bolt.

7. Remove the control arm pivot bolts and the control arm from the vehicle.

8. If removal of the control arm bushings is required, refer to the accompanying illustration.

A Install insulator with slit toward
front of vehicles as shown
1 Frame
2 Stabilizer shaft frame bushing
3 Stabilizer shaft
4 Reinforcement plate
5 55 Nm (40 lbs.ft.)

86818060

Fig. 18 Front stabilizer bar mounting

To install:

9. Insert the control arm to the frame. Install the control arm bolts and nuts, but do not tighten the nuts yet.

10. Install the stabilizer shaft insulators, then secure the steering knuckle in place with new nuts and bolts.

11. Raise the vehicle slightly so that the weight is supported by the control arms while tightening the mounting nuts.

12. Install the stabilizer bar clamp. Tighten to 33 ft. lbs. (45 Nm).

13. Tighten the control arm nut to 61 ft. lbs. (83 Nm).

14. Tighten the pinch bolt nut to 40 ft. lbs. (50 Nm) for 1982-84, 33 ft. lbs. (45 Nm) for 1985-94 and 38 ft. lbs. (52 Nm).

15. Remove the boot protector.

16. Install the wheel and lug nuts. Raise the vehicle slightly to remove the jackstands from under the frame.

17. Lower the car, and tighten the lug nuts to 100 ft. lbs. (136 Nm).

NOTE: GROOVE IN STUD MUST BE ALIGNED WITH HOLE IN KNUCKLE BEFORE INSERTING

FRT

1 Steering knuckle bolt
2 Steering knuckle nut
3 Front lower control arm stud kit
4 Wheel speed sensor wire assembly
5 Wheel speed sensor wire bracket

86818040

Fig. 19 A pinch bolt is exactly what its name implies; the bolt, when tightened, literally pinches the knuckle to the ball joint end

FRT

1 Prevailing torque nut (M 12 x 1.75)
2 Front lower reinforcement control arm
3 Front lower control arm reinforcement bolt
4 Washer (M 12.2 x 24 x 3.38)
5 Front lower control arm bolt
6 Front lower control arm
7 Front stabilizer shaft insulator
8 Front stabilizer shaft insulator clamp
9 Prevailing torque nut (M 10 x 1.5)

86818041

Fig. 20 Lower control arm assembly exploded view

CONTROL ARM BUSHING REPLACEMENT

▶ **See Figure 21**

Refer to the accompanying picture for removal and installation of control arm bushings.

Knuckle

REMOVAL & INSTALLATION

1982-89 Models

1. Remove the hub nut.
2. Raise the front of the car. Remove the wheel and tire.
3. Install an axle shaft boot seal protector, GM special tool J-28712 or equivalent, onto the seal.
4. Disconnect the brake hose clip from the MacPherson strut, but do not disconnect the hose from the caliper. Remove the brake caliper, rotor and shield from the spindle, and hang the caliper out of the way by a length of wire. Do not allow the caliper to hang by the brake hose.
5. Matchmark the camber alignment cam bolt for reassembly. Remove the cam bolt and the upper attaching bolt from the strut and spindle.
6. Pull the steering knuckle assembly from the strut bracket.

To install:

Prior to installation, a new knuckle seal should be installed on the steering knuckle.

7. Loosely attach the steering knuckle to the suspension strut, then install the rotor and the hub nut. When the shaft begins to turn with the hub, insert a drift through the caliper into one of the cooling slots in the rotor to keep it from turning. Insert a long bolt in the hub flange to prevent the shaft from turning. Tighten the hub nut to 70 ft. lbs. (95 Nm).
8. Tighten the brake caliper bolts to 30 ft. lbs. (41 Nm).
9. Load the hub assembly by lowering it onto a jackstand. Align the camber cam bolt marks made during removal, then

REMOVE LOWER CONTROL ARM BUSHING

INSTALL LOWER CONTROL ARM BUSHING

1 J 21474-18-nut
2 Bearing
3 J 21058-12 (bushing remover)
4 J 21474-5 (bushing receiver)
5 J 21474-19-bolt
6 J 21474-25-spacer
7 J35561-3 (bushing installer)

86818042

Fig. 21 Lower control arm bushing replacement

install the bolt and tighten to 140 ft. lbs. (190 Nm). Tighten the upper nut to the same value.

10. Remove the boot seal protector.

11. Connect the brake hose clip to the strut. Install the tire and wheel, lower the car, and tighten the hub nut to 225 ft. lbs. (305 Nm) for 1981-82, 185 ft. lbs. (251 Nm) for 1983-89.

1990-95 Models

1. Loosen the lug nuts on the side of the vehicle from which you will be removing the knuckle.

2. Raise and support the vehicle, then remove the lug nuts.

3. Remove and discard the hub nut, then disconnect the drive axle.

4. Disconnect the outer tie rod from the end of the steering knuckle. Scribe the strut to the knuckle, then remove the strut to knuckle bolts.

5. Loosen and remove the steering knuckle bolt and nut, then remove the knuckle. Disassemble the bearing hub and rotor splash shield. Using a prytool, dislodge the inner dust seal.

To install:

6. Install a new inner dust seal, then reconnect the bearing hub and rotor splash shield.

7. Attach the knuckle assembly with its mounting nut and bolt, tighten the nut to 38 ft. lbs. (52 Nm).

8. Install the strut bolts, then tighten them to 122 ft. lbs. (165 Nm).

9. Reconnect the drive axle. Install the hub nut, wheel and lug nuts.

10. Lower the vehicle, tighten the lug nuts to 100 ft. lbs. (136 Nm). Inspect the wheel alignment.

Front Hub and Bearing

REPLACEMENT

▶ See Figures 22, 23, 24, 25 and 26

The front wheel bearings are sealed, non-adjustable units which require no periodic attention. They are bolted to the steering knuckle by means of an integral flange.

You will need a special tool to pull the bearing free of the halfshaft: tool J-28733 or equivalent. You should also use a halfshaft boot protector tool such as J-28712 (Double-Offset joint) or J-33162 (Tri-Pot joint) to protect the parts from damage.

1. Raise and support the vehicle on jackstands. Remove the wheel and tire assembly.

2. Install a drive axle boot protector over the inboard CV-joint, tools J-28712 (Double-Offset Joint) or J-33162 (Tri-Pot Joint) can be used.

3. Insert a drift punch through the caliper and into the brake rotor cooling fins. Clean the drive axle threads of all dirt and lubricant.

4. Remove the hub nut and washer, then discard the nut. Remove the drift punch. Remove the caliper and support it on a wire, then remove the rotor.

5. On ABS vehicles, disconnect the ABS sensor from the hub bearing.

Fig. 22 The hub bearing is part of the hub, so bearing replacement necessitates hub replacement

Fig. 23 Install a drive axle boot protector over the axle joint

Fig. 24 Use the appropriate size socket to remove the hub nut, then discard the nut

6. Remove the hub bearing-to-steering knuckle mounting bolts, remove the backing plate. Separate the halfshaft from the hub bearing assembly using tool J-28733. Remove the hub and bearing assembly, retaining bolts, shield and O-ring.

➡**If the bearing assembly is to be reused, mark the assembly and the steering knuckle so that the assembly can be reinstalled in the same position. To prevent damage to the bearing, DO NOT use heat or a hammer.**

7. Using a punch, tap the seal towards the engine. When the seal is removed from the steering knuckle, cut it off the drive axle using side cutters.

To install:

8. Clean the gasket and the seal mounting surfaces.

9. Using tool J-28671 on 1982-84 or J-34657 on 1985-88 heavy duty, install the new steering knuckle seal from the outboard side, use tool J-34658 on 1985-95 standard duty to install the seal from the inboard side. Grease the lip of the seal with wheel bearing grease.

10. Route the ABS sensor wire through the steering knuckle and connect it to the ABS harness.

11. Install a new O-ring around the hub bearing.

12. Guide the halfshaft spines into the hub bearing splines and make sure they engage properly.

13. Install the hub bearing onto the steering knuckle, install the backing plate and the bearing retaining bolts, then tighten the bolts to 63 ft. lbs. (85 Nm) standard duty or 77 ft. lbs. (104 Nm) for heavy duty.

14. Install the rotor and place the caliper assembly into position on the rotor, then tighten the caliper mounting bolts to 28 ft. lbs. (38 Nm) for 1982-84 and 38 ft. lbs. (51 Nm) for 1985-95.

15. Install the washer and new hub nut, then tighten the hub nut on the halfshaft partially to 74 ft. lbs. (100 Nm). If the rotor and hub starts to rotate as the hub nut is tightened, insert a drift through the caliper and into the rotor cooling fins to prevent rotation. Do not apply full torque to the hub nut at this time, just seat the bearing.

16. Remove the drive axle boot protector. Install the tire and wheel assembly.

Fig. 26 Depending on the application, install the new steering knuckle seal from the outboard side using tool J-28671 (1982-84) or J-34657 (1985-95 heavy duty); otherwise, install the seal from the inboard side using tool J-34658 (1985-95 standard duty). Be sure to grease the lip of the seal with wheel bearing grease

17. Lower the vehicle, then tighten the hub nut to 225 ft. lbs. (305 Nm) for 1982 and 185 ft. lbs. (251 Nm) for 1983-95.

Front End Alignment

Only camber and toe are adjustable on these cars, caster is preset and non-adjustable.

CAMBER

▶ **See Figure 27**

Camber is the inward or outward tilt from the vertical, measured in degrees, of the front wheels at the top. An outward tilt gives the wheel positive camber, an inward tilt is called negative camber. Proper camber is critical to assure even tire wear.

Camber angle is adjusted on the A-Bodies by loosening the through bolts which attach the MacPherson strut to the steering knuckle in or out. The bolts must be tightened afterwards.

Fig. 25 Remove the hub/bearing assembly-to-steering knuckle mounting bolts and the bearing assembly. The use of tool J-28733 or equivalent will aid in the removal

Fig. 27 Camber is the inward or outward tilt of the front wheels from the vertical plane, as measured in degrees

The bolts must be seated properly between the inner and outer guide surfaces on the strut flange. Measurement of the camber angle requires special alignment equipment, thus the adjustment of camber is not a do-it-yourself job, and not covered here.

CASTER

Caster is the forward or rearward tilting of the steering axis from the vertical. A rearward tilt (at the top) is called positive, and the forward tilt is negative. Zero caster indicates that the strut is directly above the ball joint. Caster influences the directional control of the steering but does not affect the tire wear. If you have weak springs or you overload your vehicle this will effect the caster. Caster affects the vehicles directional stability and steering effort.

Caster is measured in degrees like camber. If one wheel has more positive caster than the other, this will cause the wheel to pull towards the center of the vehicle, causing the vehicle to move or lead toward the side with the least amount of positive caster. Caster is not adjustable.

TOE-IN

▶ See Figure 28

Toe is the amount, measured in a fraction of a millimeter, that the wheels are closer together at one end than the other.

Toe-in means that the front wheels are closer together at the front than the rear. Toe-out means the rear of the front wheels are closer together than the front. A-Body cars are designed to have a slight amount of toe-in.

Toe is adjusted by turning the tie rods. It must be checked after camber has been adjusted, but it can be adjusted without disturbing the camber setting. You can make this adjustment without special equipment if you make very careful measurements. The wheels must be straight ahead.

1. Toe can be determined by measuring the distance between the centers of the tire treads, at the front of the tire and at the rear. If the tread pattern makes this impossible, you can measure between the edges of the wheel rims, but make sure to move the car forward and measure in a couple of places to avoid errors caused by bent rims or wheel runout.

2. If the measurement is not within specifications, loosen the nuts at the steering knuckle end of the tie rod, and remove the tie rod boot clamps. Rotate the tie rods to align the toe to specifications. Rotate the tie rods evenly, or the steering wheel will be crooked when you're done.

3. When the adjustment is correct, tighten the nuts to 44 ft. lbs. (60 Nm). Adjust the boots and tighten the clamps.

✳✳WARNING

If severely out of adjustment, a tire can wear out quite prematurely. It is advisable to have a front end alignment professionally done after replacing steering or suspension components to avoid costly tire wear.

LOOSEN NUT TO ADJUST
RE-TIGHTEN TO 60N·m (44 FT. LBS.)

ADJUST TOE — RE-ADJUST BOOTS

86818045

Fig. 28 Toe is adjusted by turning the tie rods

WHEEL ALIGNMENT

Year	Model		Caster Range (deg.)	Caster Preferred Setting (deg.)	Camber Range (deg.)	Camber Preferred Setting (deg.)	Toe-in (in.)	Steering Axis Inclination (deg.)
1982	All	F	1P-3P	2P	1/2N-1/2N	0	0	14.5
1983	All	F	1P-3P	2P	1/2N-1/2N	0	0	NA
1984	All	F	1P-3P	2P	1/2N-1/2N	0	0	NA
1985	Century	F	1P-3P	2P	1/2N-1/2P	0	0	NA
	Celebrity	F	1P-3P	2P	1/2N-1/2P	0	3/32N-3/32P	NA
	Cutlass Ciera	F	23/32P-2 23/32P	1 23/32P	1/2N-1/2P	0	0	14 1/2
	6000	F	23/32P-2 23/32P	1 23/32P	1/2N-1/2P	0	0	14 9/16
1986	Century	F	3/4P-2 3/4P	1 3/4P	1/2N-1/2P	0	0	NA
	Celebrity	F	1P-3P	2P	1/2N-1/2P	0	0	NA
	Cutlass Ciera	F	23/32P-2 23/32P	1 23/32P	1/2N-1/2P	0	0	14 1/2
	6000	F	23/32P-2 23/32P	1 23/32P	1/2N-1/2P	0	0	14 9/16
1987	Century	F	3/4P-2 3/4P	1 3/4P	1/2N-1/2P	0	0	NA
	Celebrity	F	23/32P-2 23/32P	1 23/32P	1/2N-1/2P	0	0	14 5/8
		R	-	-	1/4N-1/4P	0	0	-
	Cutlass Ciera	F	23/32P-2 23/32P	1 23/32P	1/2N-1/2P	0	0	14 1/2
	6000	F	23/32P-2 23/32P	1 23/32P	1/2N-1/2P	0	0	14 9/16
1988	Century	F	3/4P-2 3/4P	1 3/4P	1/2N-1/2P	0	0	NA
		R	-	-	1/4N-1/4P	0	0	-
	Celebrity	F	23/32P-2 23/32P	1 23/32P	1/2N-1/2P	0	0	14 5/8
		R	-	-	1/4N-1/4P	0	0	-
	Cutlass Ciera	F	3/4P-2 3/4P	1 3/4P	1/2N-1/2P	0	0	14 1/2
		R	-	-	1/4N-1/4P	0	0	-
	6000	F	23/32P-2 23/32P	1/23/32P	1/2N-1/.2P	0	0	14 9/16
		R	-	-	1/2N-1/2P	0	0	-
1989	Century	F	3/4P-2 3/4P	1 3/4P	1/2N-1/2P	0	0	NA
		R	-	-	1/4N-1/4P	0	0	-
	Celebrity	F	23/32P-2 23/32P	1 23/32P	1/2N-1/2P	0	0	14 5/8
		R	-	-	1/4N-1/4P	0	0	-
	Cutlass Ciera	F	3/4P-2 3/4P	1 3/4P	1/2N-1/2P	0	0	14 1/2
		R	-	-	1/4N-1/4P	0	0	-
	6000	F	11/16P-2 11/16P	1 11/16P	1/2N-1/2P	0	0	14 5./8
		R	-	-	1/4N-1/4P	0	0	-
	[3]	R	-	-	1N-0	1/2N	3/32P	-
1990	Century	F	3/4P-2 3/4P	1 3/4P	1/2N-1/2P	0	0	NA
		R	-	-	3/4N-1/2P	1/4N	1/8P	-
	Celebrity	F	11/16P-2 11/16P	1 11/16P	1/2N-1/2P	0	0	14 5/8
		R	-	-	[1]	[2]	0	
	Cutlass Ciera	F	3/4P-2 3/4P	1 3/4P	1/2N-1/2P	0	0	14 1/2
		R	-	-	1/4N-1/4P	0	0	-
	6000	F	11/16-2 11/16P	1 11/16P	1/2N-1/2P	0	0	14 5/8
		R	-	-	1/4N-1/4P	0	0	-
	[3]	R	-	-	1N-0	1/2N	3/32P	-
1991	Century	F	11/16P-2 11/16P	1 11/16P	1/2N-1/2P	0	0	NA
		R	-	-	5/16N-5/16P	0	0	-
	Cutlass Ciera	F	11/16P-2 11/16P	1 11/16P	1/2N-1/2P	0	0	14 1/2
		R	-	-	5/16N-5/16P	0	0	-

86818C01

WHEEL ALIGNMENT

Year	Model		Caster Range (deg.)	Caster Preferred Setting (deg.)	Camber Range (deg.)	Camber Preferred Setting (deg.)	Toe-in (in.)	Steering Axis Inclination (deg.)
1991	6000	F	11/16P-2 11/16P	1 11/16P	1/2N-1/2P	0	0	14 5/8
		R	-	-	1/4N-1/4P	0	0	-
1992	Century	F	11/16P-11/16P	1 11/16P	1/2N-1/2P	0	0	NA
		R	-	-	5/16N-5/16P	0	0	-
	Cutlass Ciera	F	11/16P-2 11/16P	1 11/16P	1/2N-1/2P	0	0	14 1/2
		R	-	-	5/16N-5/16P	0	0	-
1993	Century	F	11/16P-2 11/16P	1 11/16P	1/2N-1/2P	0	0	NA
		R	-	-	5/16N-5/16P	0	0	-
	Cutlass Ciera	F	11/16P-2 11/16P	1 11/16P	1/2N-1/2P	0	0	14 1/2
		R	-	-	5/16N-5/16P	0	0	-
1994	Century	F	2P-4P	3P	1/2N-1/2P	0	0	NA
		R	-	-	5/16N-5/16P	0	0	-
	Cutlass Ciera	F	2P-4P	3P	1/2N-1/2P	0	0	NA
		R	-	-	5/16N-5/16P	0	0	-
1995	Century	F	2P-4P	3P	1/2N-1/2P	0	0	NA
		R	-	-	1/16N-5/16P	0	0	-
	Cutlass Ciera	F	2P-4P	3P	1/2N-1/2P	0	0	NA
		R	0-3N	1N	5/16N-5/16P	0	0	-

NA - Not Available
F- Front
R - Rear
1   14" wheels: 3/16N-13/16P
     15", 16" wheels: 13/32N-19/32P
2   14" wheels: 5/16P
     15", 16" wheels: 3/32P
3   AWD

86818C02

REAR SUSPENSION

A Front Wheel Drive (FWD) rear suspension consists of a solid rear axle tube containing an integral, welded-in stabilizer bar, coil springs, shock absorbers, a lateral track bar, and trailing arms. The trailing arms (control arms) are welded to the axle, and pivot at the frame. Fore and after movement is controlled by the trailing arms; lateral movement is controlled by the track bar. A permanently lubricated and sealed hub and bearing assembly is bolted to each end of the axle tube, it is a non-adjustable unit which must be replaced as an assembly if defective.

The All Wheel Drive (AWD) rear suspension features a light-weight fiberglass transverse leaf spring which is mounted to the rear of the cradle. Other rear suspension components include struts, control arms, toe links, and a stabilizer bar. These components are all serviceable. The control arms, leaf springs and struts oppose the torque reaction on acceleration and braking and provides optimum handling. Each rear wheel has a spindle, a hub and bearing assembly, along with a knuckle which attaches to the outboard end of the control arm.

Coil Springs

REMOVAL & INSTALLATION

▶ See Figures 29 and 30

FWD Vehicles

✳✳CAUTION

The coil springs are under a considerable amount of tension. Be extremely careful when removing or installing them, since they can exert enough force to cause very serious injuries.

1. Raise and support the car on a hoist. Do not use twin-post hoist. The swing arc of the axle may cause it to slip from the hoist when the bolts are removed. If a suitable hoist is not available, raise and support the car on jackstands, and use a jack under the axle.

2. Support the rear axle with a jack that can be raised and lowered.

3. Remove the brake hose attaching brackets (right and left), allowing the hoses to hang freely. Do not disconnect the hoses.

4. Remove the track bar attaching bolts from the rear axle.

5. Remove both shock absorber lower attaching bolts from the axle.

6. Lower the axle. Remove the coil spring and insulator.

To install:

7. Position the spring and insulator on the axle. The leg on the upper coil of the spring must be parallel to the axle, facing the left hand side of the car.

8. Install the shock absorber and lower mounting bolts, then tighten to 43 ft. lbs. (58 Nm) for 1982-84, 35 ft. lbs. (47 Nm) for 1985-86, 44 ft. lbs. (59 Nm) for 1987-92, and 53 ft. lbs. (72 Nm) for 1993-95.

9. Install the track bar, tighten to 44 ft. lbs. (60 Nm) for 1982-92 and 53 ft. lbs. (72 Nm) for 1993-95.

10. Install the brake line brackets to the frame, then tighten to 8 ft. lbs. (11 Nm).

11. Remove the axle support and lower the vehicle.

Leaf Spring

REMOVAL & INSTALLATION

AWD Vehicles

The 6000 STE AWD vehicle has rear leaf spring suspension rather than the common coil spring.

1. Loosen the lug nuts from the rear wheels.

2. Raise the vehicle with a suitable hoist. Remove the tire and wheel assembly.

86818048

Fig. 29 With the vehicle in the air, access to the spring and shock absorber is much simpler

1 Underbody
2 Insulator upper
3 Spring
4 Lower insulator
5 Track bar

86818047

Fig. 30 Once you remove the track bar, you have better access to the coil spring

3. Remove the 4 bolts from the jacking plate, then remove the jacking plate.

4. Install the spring compression tool J-33432. Unfasten the 1 bolt securing the brake line at the electronic ride control (ERC) sensor bracket to the left hand control arm, then move the bracket out of the way.

5. Remove both of the control arm outer nuts and bolts at the knuckles.

➡It is not necessary to completely remove the control arms to permit removal of the leaf spring.

6. Disconnect and remove the outer stabilizer bar brackets, then loosen the spring compression tool J-33432 to allow the control arm to drop, then remove the tool.

7. Unsecure the 4 bolts (2 on each side) from the left and right spring-to-cradle brackets, then remove the brackets.

8. Remove the leaf spring by sliding it outwards.

To install:

9. Position the leaf spring to the cradle assembly. Make sure that the spring is properly seated in the control arms.

10. Insert the 2 leaf spring-to-cradle brackets, use the 4 bolts and tighten them to 61 ft. lbs. (83 Nm).

11. Attach the spring compression tool J-33432 on the spring and tighten to draw the outer control arm bolt bores up to the knuckle bores.

12. Install the outer stabilizer bar brackets. Fasten the bolts and nuts to the outer control arms and tighten the nuts to 125 ft. lbs. (170 Nm).

13. Reinstall the 1 bolt on the left control arm which secures the brake line/ERC sensor bracket, then tighten to 18 ft. lbs. (24 Nm).

14. Remove the spring compressor tool.

15. Install the tire and wheel, then hand-tighten the lug nuts.

16. Lower the vehicle, then tighten the lug nuts to 100 ft. lbs. (136 Nm).

Track Bar

REMOVAL & INSTALLATION

◆ See Figure 31

1. Raise the vehicle on a hoist and support the rear axle.

2. On some models it may be necessary to remove the right hand lower shock bolt, then swing the shock aside.

3. On wagons it will be necessary to remove the track bar brace.

4. Remove the nut and bolt from both the axle and body attachments, then remove the bar.

To install:

5. Position the track bar at the axle mounting bracket and loosely install the bolt and nut.

6. Place the other end of the track bar into the body reinforcement and install the bolt and nut. Tighten the nut at the axle bracket to 44 ft. lbs. (60 Nm) for 1982-92 and 53 ft. lbs. (72 Nm) for 1993-95. Tighten the nut at the body reinforcement to 35 ft. lbs. (47 Nm) for 1982-92 and 53 ft. lbs. (72 Nm) for 1993-95.

7. Remove the rear axle support and lower the vehicle.

1 Underbody bracket
2 47 Nm (35 lb.ft.)
3 Track bar
4 Axle asm
5 60 Nm (44 lb.ft.)
6 Track bar brace (wagon only)
7 47 Nm (35 lb.ft.)

86818050

Fig. 31 Rear track bar with torque specifications for 1982-92 models

Stabilizer Bar

REMOVAL & INSTALLATION

1. Loosen the rear lug nuts.

2. Raise and support the vehicle.

3. Remove the wheel and tire.

4. Unsecure the bolts and nuts attaching the outer stabilizer bar bracket to the control arm.

5. Remove the bolts attaching the inner stabilizer bar brackets to the cradle bracket.

6. Pull the stabilizer bar from the vehicle.

To install:

7. Position the stabilizer bar in the rear of the vehicle. Connect the stabilizer bar bracket to the cradle bracket with the bolts (on each side), then tighten them to 26 ft. lbs. (35 Nm).

8. Using the 3 bolts and nuts attach the outer stabilizer bar brackets (on each side) to the control arms, then tighten the bolts to 26 ft. lbs. (36 Nm).

9. Install the wheel and tire, then hand-tighten the lug nuts.

10. Lower the vehicle, then tighten the lug nuts to 100 ft. lbs. (136 Nm).

Shock Absorbers

REMOVAL & INSTALLATION

FWD Vehicles

▶ See Figures 32, 33, 34 and 35

➡If your vehicle is equipped with Electronic Ride Control (ERC) or super lift air shocks, you must bleed the system of air before disconnecting the hoses.

1. Open the hatch or trunk lid, remove the trim cover if present, and remove the upper shock absorber nut.

86818051

Fig. 33 Open the trunk or tailgate, then remove the shock absorber trim cover

1 Rear shock absorber
2 Rear shock absorber air tube assembly
3 Rear shock absorber air valve cap
4 Rear shock absorber air valve nut
5 Rear shock absorber air valve washer
6 Rear shock absorber air cross over tube assembly

86818056

Fig. 32 The super lift shock system and line routing. This system must be bled before disconnecting any lines

86818052

Fig. 34 Once the trim is removed, push the insulation aside and remove the shock nut cap. This will give you access to the upper shock nut

2. Raise and support the car at a convenient working height if you desire. It is not necessary to remove the weight of the car from the shock absorbers, however, so you can leave the car on the ground if you prefer.

3. If the car is equipped with ERC or the superlift shock absorbers, disconnect the air line.

4. Remove the lower attaching bolt, then remove the shock.

To install:

5. If new shock absorbers are being installed, repeatedly compress them while inverted and extend them in their normal upright position. This will purge them of air.

6. Insert the shock into position, then install the bolt and nut but do not tighten yet.

7. If super lift shocks are being installed, then connect the air hose to the shocks.

8. Lower the vehicle enough to guide the upper stud through the body opening, then install the upper nut loosely.

9. Tighten the lower mount nut and bolt to 43 ft. lbs. (58 Nm) for 1982-84 or 38 ft. lbs. (51 Nm) for 1985-92, and 50 ft. lbs. (72 Nm) for 1993-95. Tighten the upper nut to 13 ft. lbs.

86818055

Fig. 35 Unfasten the lower attaching bolt, then remove the shock absorber

(17 Nm) for 1982-83 or 28 ft. lbs. (37 Nm) for 1984-92, and 18 ft. lbs. (25 Nm).

10. Replace the upper nut cap, then the inner trim piece. Lower the vehicle the rest of the way, then close the trunk/liftgate.

11. Add air to the super lift shocks, approximately 80 kPa (12 psi), or see your owner's manual.

12. In the case of the ERC system, it automatically levels itself when the vehicle is on the ground and the key is turned on.

TESTING

Visually inspect the shock absorber. If there is evidence of leakage and the shock absorber is covered with oil, the shock is defective and should be replaced.

If there is no sign of excessive leakage (a small amount of weeping is normal) bounce the car at one corner by pressing down on the fender or bumper and releasing. When you have the car bouncing as much as you can, release the fender or bumper. The car should stop bouncing after the first rebound. If the bouncing continues past the center point of the bounce more than once, the shock absorbers are worn and should be replaced.

Rear Strut

REMOVAL & INSTALLATION

AWD Vehicles

▶ **See Figures 36, 37 and 38**

The following tools or equivalent will be needed to do this repair: J-33432 leaf spring compressor and J-37619 ball joint stud remover.

1. Loosen the lug nuts on the rear wheels.

2. Open the decklid and raise the vehicle securely.

3. Remove the wheel and tire assembly, then remove the lug nuts.

4. Support the lower control arm with a suitable stand or install the leaf spring compressor tool J-33432.

5. Remove the outer toe link cotter pin and the castellated nut at the strut.

6. Disconnect the toe link end from the lower strut mount assembly using tool J-37619.

7. Remove the parking brake cable from the strut mount bracket and move it out of the way.

8. Remove the bolts from the parking brake cable bracket and remove the bracket.

9. Loosen and remove the lower strut mount bolts that attach to the spindle, make sure to retain the nut plate for installation.

10. Disconnect the upper strut mount by removing the attaching bolts, then pull the strut assembly from the vehicle.

To install:

11. Position the strut to the upper strut mounting flange, install the upper strut mounting bolts and hand-tighten them.

J 33432 REAR MONO-LEAF
SPRING COMPRESSOR

J 37619 REAR BALL JOINT REMOVER

86818067

Fig. 36 A leaf spring compressor and ball joint stud remover are required for rear strut removal/installation

12. Position the lower strut mount to the spindle assembly. Position the nut plate into place, then install the 2 bolts into the lower strut mount assembly.

13. Tighten the lower mount bolts to 148 ft. lbs. (200 Nm).

14. Install the brake cable bracket to the lower strut mount and install the 2 attaching bolts. Connect the parking brake cable into the cable bracket.

15. Install the toe link end to the lower strut mount assembly.

16. Mount the castellated nut onto the outer toe link end at the lower strut mount, then tighten to 46 ft. lbs. (62 Nm).

17. Insert a new cotter pin at the castellated nut, tighten the upper strut mount bolts to 40 ft. lbs. (54 Nm).

18. Remove the leaf spring compression tool or stand supporting the control arm.

19. Install the wheel and tire, hand-tighten the lug nuts.

20. Lower the vehicle, tighten the lug nuts to 100 ft. lbs. (136 Nm). Close the decklid.

Outer Toe Link

REMOVAL & INSTALLATION

AWD Vehicles

▶ See Figure 39

1. Raise and support the vehicle.

2. Loosen the toe link sleeve outer tab nut and bolt.

3. Remove the cotter pin and castellated nut from the outer toe link end.

4. Disconnect the parking brake cable from the bracket. Remove the outer toe link end from the lower strut mount assembly using the ball joint stud remover J-37619 or an equivalent. Remove one parking brake bracket bolt and loosen the other. Swing the bracket out of the way to allow installation of tool J-37619.

5. Remove the outer toe link from the toe link sleeve.

To install:

6. Insert the outer toe link to the toe link sleeve. Install the outer end into the lower strut mount.

7. Put the castellated nut onto the outer toe link end at the lower strut mount, then tighten the nut to 46 ft. lbs. (62 Nm). Insert a new cotter pin to the outer toe link end.

8. Tighten the parking brake bracket bolts and route the cable into the bracket.

9. Adjust the rear wheel alignment as necessary, then tighten the tow link sleeve outer tab nut and bolt to 14 ft. lbs. (19 Nm).

10. Lower the vehicle.

Inner Toe Link

REMOVAL & INSTALLATION

AWD Vehicles

▶ See Figure 39

1. Raise and support the vehicle.

2. Loosen the toe link sleeve inner tab nut and bolt.

3. Remove the nut from the inner toe link end.

4. Disconnect the inner toe link end from the rear crossmember assembly using the ball joint stud remover J-37619 or an equivalent.

5. Remove the inner toe link from the sleeve.

To install:

6. Install the toe link to the sleeve, then position the inner toe link end to the rear crossmember support bar.

7. Connect with the nut to the inner toe link end, then tighten the nut to 61 ft. lbs. (83 Nm).

8. Adjust the rear wheel alignment as needed.

9. Tighten the toe link sleeve inner tab nut and bolt to 14 ft. lbs. (19 Nm).

10. Lower the vehicle.

1 RR hyp axle asm
2 Halfshaft asm
3 Hex bolt
4 Bolt head protector
5 Nut
6 Frame
7 Hex bolt
8 Knuckle brake & hub asm
9 Toe link asm
10 C/arm stab shaft isolator
11 Stabilizer shaft isolator
12 Stabilizer shaft
13 Stabilizer bar beam- mtg bracket
14 Bolt
15 Bolt
16 Jack support plate
17 Bolt
18 Spring retainer bracket
19 Insulator & pad spring asm
20 Nut
21 Parking brake cable asm

22 Lower cont arm bushing
23 R/suspension lower cont arm
24 Bolt
25 Parking brake cable asm
26 Inner toe link asm
27 Tube adjuster asm
28 Outer toe link asm
29 Cotter pin
30 Hex nut slotted
31 Washer
32 Nut
33 Nut
34 Lower bracket c/arm stb bar mtg
35 Upper bracket c/arm stb bar mtg

86818057

Fig. 37 The AWD rear suspension utilizes one leaf spring and two strut assemblies, rather than shock absorbers

1 Strut assembly
2 Bolt 200 Nm (148 lb.ft.)
3 Lower strut mount
4 Spindle
5 Parking brake cable bracket
6 Nut plate
7 Bolt 54 Nm (40 lb.ft.)
8 Upper strut mount
9 Nut 31 Nm (23 lb.ft.)
10 Strut tower
11 Outer toe link

86818070

Fig. 38 Rear strut mounting on the AWD 6000 STE

Lower Control Arm

REMOVAL & INSTALLATION

AWD Vehicles

1. Loosen the lug nuts on the rear wheels.
2. Raise and support the vehicle.
3. Support the control arm with a suitable stand or install tool J-33432 to neutralize the spring tension.
4. Remove the tire and wheel assembly.
5. Disconnect the 2 outer stabilizer bar bracket-to-control arm bolts and nuts.
6. Remove the one bolt connecting the brake line/ERC sensor bracket to the control arm (LH only), then move the bracket out of the way.
7. Remove the control arm-to-knuckle attaching bolt and nut.

8. Disconnect the lower control arm by slowly lowering the stand or loosening the spring compressing tool.
9. Unfasten the 2 control arm-to-cradle bolts and nuts.
10. Slide the control arm from the leaf spring.
To install:
11. Connect the control arm on the leaf spring, ensure that the leaf spring is in the correct position.
12. Attach the 2 control arm-to-cradle bolts and nuts, hand-tighten them only.
13. Raise the control arm or tighten the spring compressor to align the outer control arm bolt bore with the knuckle bore.
14. Install the control arm to knuckle with the attaching nuts and bolts.
15. Tighten the control arm nut at the knuckle to 125 ft. lbs. then the control arm at the cradle to 61 ft. lbs. (83 Nm).
16. Install the 1 bolt securing the brake line to the ERC sensor bracket to the control arm (LH only), then tighten the bolt to 18 ft. lbs. (24 Nm).
17. Connect the 2 outer stabilizer bar bracket to control arm bolts and nuts, then tighten them to 26 ft. lbs. (354 Nm).

1 Lower strut mount	6 Stabilizer bar
2 Outer toe link	7 Nut 83 Nm (61 lb.ft.)
3 Tab bolt	8 Cotter pin
4 Sleeve	9 Castellated nut
5 Inner toe link	62 Nm (46 lb.ft.)

86818069

Fig. 39 The toe link assembly, with its threaded sleeve and links, is much like a front tie rod assembly

18. Remove the stand or spring compressing tool that was used to support the arm.

19. Install the tire and wheel, hand-tighten the lug nuts.

20. Lower the vehicle, then tighten the lug nuts to 100 ft. lbs. (136 Nm).

Rear Hub and Bearing

REPLACEMENT

FWD Vehicles

1. Loosen the wheel lug nuts. Raise and support the car and remove the wheel.

2. Remove the brake drum. Removal procedures are covered in the next section, if needed.

➡**Do not hammer on the brake drum to remove, as damage to the bearing may result.**

3. Remove the four hub and bearing retaining bolts, then remove the assembly from the axle.

➡**The bolts which attach the hub and bearing assembly also support the brake assembly. When removing these bolts, be sure to support the brake assembly with a wire or something comparable. Do not allow the brake line to support the brake assembly.**

4. If equipped, disconnect the rear ABS wheel speed sensor.

To install:

5. Connect the ABS wheel speed sensor.

6. Install the hub and bearing assembly to the rear axle. Tighten the bolts to 45 ft. lbs. (60 Nm) for 1982-92 vehicles or 60 ft. lbs. (82 Nm) for 1983-95 vehicles.

7. Install the rear brake drum, then adjust the brakes. Install the wheel and lug nuts.

8. Lower the vehicle, then tighten the lug nuts to 100 ft. lbs. (136 Nm).

AWD Vehicles

▶ **See Figures 40 and 41**

1. Loosen the lug nuts, then raise and support the vehicle. Remove the wheel and tire assembly.

2. Disconnect the caliper assembly and suspend on a wire. Do not allow it to hang from the brake hose.

➡**Do not hammer on the brake caliper, as this could cause damage to the bearing.**

3. Remove the hub and bearing assembly from the axle. If necessary, use a special tool such as J-28733-A or equivalent.

➡**The bolts which attach the hub and bearing assembly also support the brake assembly. When removing these bolts, be sure to support the brake assembly with a wire or something comparable. Do not allow the brake line to support the brake assembly.**

To install:

4. Install the hub and bearing assembly into the rear axle. Tighten the hub and bearing bolts to 61 ft. lbs. (83 Nm).

5. Attach the brake caliper to the rear rotor.

6. Install the rear wheel, then hand-tighten the lug nuts.

7. Lower the car, then tighten the lug nuts to 100 ft. lbs. (136 Nm).

Rear End Alignment

When checking the rear alignment, the ELC system must have the superlift struts inflated with residual pressure only.

STEERING

The A-Body cars use an aluminum-housed Saginaw manual rack and pinion steering gear as standard equipment. The pi-

1 J 28733-A
2 Turn forcing screw until axle splines are just loose

86818066

Fig. 40 In order to remove the hub and bearing assembly from the axle, a special tool may be necessary

Always install the alignment equipment following the manufactures instructions. Measure the alignment angles and record the readings. If adjustments are needed, make them in the camber toe order. Camber is adjusted by moving the top of the rotor in or out. Toe-in can be increased or decreased by changing the length of the tie rods. A threaded sleeve is provided for this purpose.

nion is supported by and turns in a sealed ball bearing at the top and a pressed-in roller bearing at the bottom. The rack moves in bushings pressed into each end of the rack housing.

Wear compensation occurs through the action of an adjuster spring which forces the rack against the pinion teeth. This adjuster eliminates the need for periodic pinion preload adjustments. Preload is adjustable only at overhaul.

The inner tie rod assemblies are both threaded and staked to the rack. A special joint is used, allowing both rocking and rotating motion of the tie rods. The inner tie rod assemblies are lubricated for life and require no periodic attention.

Any service other than replacement of the outer tie rods or the boots requires removal of the unit from the car.

The optional power rack and pinion steering gear is an integral unit, and shares most features with the manual gear. A rotary control valve directs the hydraulic fluid to either side of the rack piston. The integral rack piston is attached to the rack and converts the hydraulic pressure into left or right linear motion. A vane-type constant displacement pump with integral reservoir provides hydraulic pressure. No in-car adjustments are necessary or possible on the system, except for periodic belt tension checks and adjustments for the pump.

1 Knuckle
2 Hub and bearing assembly
3 83 Nm (61 lb.ft.)
4 Hub nut - always replace- 260 Nm (192 lb.ft.)
5 170 Nm (125 lb.ft.)
6 Speed sensor bracket
7 Drive axle
8 10 Nm (89 lb.in.)

86818065

Fig. 41 The hub and bearing assembly slides directly into the axle shaft

Steering Wheel

REMOVAL & INSTALLATION

Without Air Bag

▶ See Figures 42, 43, 44, 45, 46, 47, 48 and 49

➡Disconnect the battery ground cable before removing the steering wheel. When installing a steering wheel, always make sure that the turn signal lever is in the neutral position.

1. Disconnect the negative battery cable.
2. If your vehicle is equipped with controls for the radio on the steering wheel proceed as follows:
    a. Pry out the control button assembly with a thin bladed tool along the top of the edge of the assembly.
    b. Disconnect the steering wheel control.
3. On vehicles without the radio controls on the steering pad, take a thin-bladed tool and pry the pad off the steering wheel. On wheels with a center cap, pull off the cap.
4. After lifting the trim off, pry the horn wires from the back of the pad. On some models gently push down on the horn lead and turn left, the wire and spring will then come out of the canceling cam tower.
5. Remove the retainer ring with a pair of ring expanders, then remove the steering wheel nut.
6. Mark the wheel-to-shaft relationship, and then remove the wheel with a threaded puller.

➡When removing a steering wheel with electronic accessory controls in the hub, take care to avoid damaging the electronic circuits. Wheel puller bolts used with the puller should be turned no more than 5 complete turns, in order to avoid contact with the sensitive circuits.

7. Now the steering wheel will slide off the shaft quite easily.
   To install:
8. Install the wheel on the shaft aligning the previously made marks.

1 Screw driver
2 Steering wheel
3 Steering wheel control assembly

86818072

Fig. 42 Pry out the control button assembly with a thin-bladed tool along the top of the edge, being careful not to damage the control assembly

9. Install the steering wheel nut, then tighten to 30 ft. lbs. (41 Nm).
10. Insert the retaining ring onto the steering shaft. Connect the horn wires into the canceling cam, pushing down and turning to the right into the lock position.
11. Install the center trim pad and reconnect the battery cable.

With Air Bag

▶ See Figure 50

Whenever you are working on a vehicle with the Supplemental Inflatable Restraint (SIR) System, it is recommended that an authorized service center do the work. This system can cause serious injury to one's self if the air bag deploys.

1. Disable the SIR system as follows:
    a. Turn the steering wheel so that the vehicles wheels are pointing straight ahead.
    b. Turn the ignition key to the **LOCK** position and remove the key.
    c. Remove the air bag fuse from the fuse block.
    d. Unsecure the left sound insulator by removing the screws and nuts.
    e. Remove the Connector Position Assurance (CPA) and the yellow two-way connector from the base of the steering column.

➡When the "AIR BAG" fuse is removed from the fuse block, and the key is in the ON position the "AIR BAG" warning lamp will be ON. This is a normal condition and does not mean that the SIR system is malfunctioning.

2. Loosen the screws in the back of the steering wheel using a T-30 Torx® driver or an equivalent until the inflator module can be released from the steering wheel.

✳✳CAUTION

Whenever carrying a live inflator module, make sure that the bag and opening are pointed away from you. Never carry the module by the wires or connector on the underside of the module. In case of an accidental deployment, the bag will deploy with minimal amount of injury. When placing the live inflator on a bench or any other surface, always face the bag and trim cover up, away from the surface. Never rest a steering column assembly on the steering wheel with the inflator module face down on the column vertical. This will allow free space for the bag to expand in case of accidental deployment. Otherwise, personal injury could result.

3. Disconnect the coil assembly and the Connector Position Assurance (CPA) from the inflator module.
4. Using a thin bladed tool gently pry the top of the pad away from the steering wheel.
5. Disconnect the horn lead from the steering column by gently pushing down on the lead and turning left. The wire and spring will come out of the cancelling cam.
6. Remove the retainer ring with a pair of retaining ring expanders, then remove the nut from the steering shaft.
7. Mark the wheel-to-shaft relationship.

1 Steering wheel
2 41 Nm (30 lb.ft.)
3 Horn lead
4 Horn pad
5 2 Nm (20 lb.in.)

Fig. 43 Common steering wheel pad types

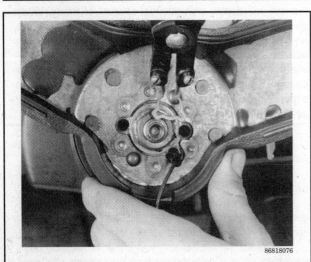

Fig. 44 Carefully pry the lead wire for the horn off of the horn pad

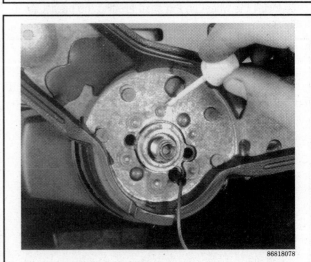

Fig. 46 Use a ratchet and socket to remove the steering wheel nut

Fig. 45 Remove the retainer ring with a pair of retaining ring expanders

Fig. 47 Mark the wheel-to-shaft relationship with some correction fluid or white paint

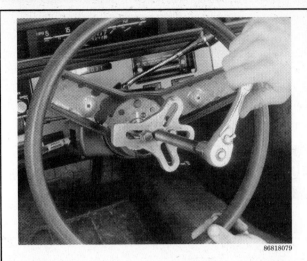

Fig. 48 Install a universal threaded puller to remove the steering wheel . . .

Fig. 49 . . . and the steering wheel will slide off the shaft quite easily

8. Attach a threaded universal puller to the steering wheel, do not screw the bolts in all the way this could cause damage to the coil assembly.

9. Remove the steering wheel assembly.

To install:

10. Install the steering wheel by aligning the mark on the steering wheel with the mark on the shaft.

11. Install the steering wheel nut, then tighten to 30 ft. lbs. (41 Nm). Install the retaining ring.

12. Connect the horn lead to the canceling cam tower by pushing down and turning right into the lock position.

13. Install the inflator module,

   a. Attach the coil assembly connector and connector position assurance (CPA) to the inflator module.

   b. Route the coil assembly lead around the mounting post and secure it under the clip.

   c. Attach the inflator module to the steering wheel. DO NOT use the module if it has been dropped from a height of 8.2 ft. (2.5m) or more.

   d. Ensure the wiring is not exposed or trapped between the inflator module and the steering wheel assembly on installation.

   e. Tighten the inflator module screws to 25 inch lbs. (3 Nm).

14. Enable the SIR system,

   a. Connect the yellow two-way connector to the base of the steering column and the connect position assurance (CPA).

   b. Install the left sound insulator with the mounting screws.

   c. Insert the AIR BAG fuse in the fuse block.

   d. Turn the ignition switch to the **RUN** position and verify that the "AIR BAG" warning lamp flashes 7 times and then turns OFF. If it does not turn off, have your SIR system checked by an authorized service center.

Turn Signal Switch

✳✳CAUTION

On vehicles equipped with an SIR (air bag) system, disable the system before proceeding, by following the instructions at the beginning of this section. Failure to do so could result in accidental inflation of the air bag and personal injury.

REMOVAL & INSTALLATION

▶ See Figures 51, 52 and 53

1. Disable the SIR system if equipped with an air bag.

2. Disconnect the negative battery cable.

3. On vehicles equipped with an air bag, follow the special instructions in this section on steering wheel removal.

✳✳CAUTION

Whenever carrying a live inflator module, make sure that the bag and opening are pointed away from you. Never carry the module by the wires or connector on the underside of the module. In case of an accidental deployment, the bag will deploy with minimal amount of injury. When placing the live inflator on a bench or any other surface, always face the bag and trim cover up, away from the surface. Never rest a steering column assembly on the steering wheel with the inflator module face down on the column vertical. This will allow free space for the bag to expand in case of accidental deployment. Otherwise, personal injury could result.

4. Remove the steering wheel as previously outlined. Remove the trim cover.

5. Loosen the cover screws. Pry the cover off with a flat-bladed tool, then lift the cover off the shaft.

6. Position the U-shaped lockplate compressing tool on the end of the steering shaft and compress the lock plate by turning the shaft nut clockwise, then pry the wire snapring out of the shaft groove.

7. Remove the tool and lift the lockplate off the shaft.

NOTICE To help avoid damage and possible malfunction of air bag system, do not rotate steering shaft with steering shaft disconnected. See GM Service Manual before disconnecting.

NOTICE To help avoid damage and possible malfunction of air bag system, do not rotate steering shaft with steering shaft disconnected. See GM Service Manual before disconnecting.

PRINTED IN U.S.A.
PT. NO. 10236194
86818400

Fig. 50 Label affixed to air bag equipped vehicles

SNAP RING

86818087

Fig. 51 Position the U-shaped lockplate compressing tool on the end of the steering shaft and compress the lockplate by turning the shaft nut clockwise, then pry the wire snapring out of the shaft groove

1 Shaft lock
2 Turn sig cancel cam asm
3 Upper bearing spring
4 Upper brg inner race seat
5 Inner race

86818102

Fig. 52 After removing the tool, lift the lockplate off the cam, then slip the canceling cam, upper bearing preload spring, and thrust washer off the shaft

8. Slip the canceling cam, upper bearing preload spring, and thrust washer off the shaft.

9. Remove the turn signal lever. Push the flasher knob in and unscrew it. Remove the button retaining screw and remove the button, spring and knob.

10. Pull the switch connector out the mast jacket and tape the upper part to facilitate switch removal. Attach a long piece of wire to the turn signal switch connector. When installing the turn signal switch, feed this wire through the column first, and then use this wire to pull the switch connector into position. On tilt wheels, place the turn signal and shifter housing in low position and remove the harness cover.

11. Remove the three switch mounting screws. Remove the switch by pulling it straight up while guiding the wiring harness cover through the column.

To install:

12. Install the replacement switch by working the connector and cover down through the housing and under the bracket. On tilt models, the connector is worked down through the housing, under the bracket, and then the cover is installed on the harness.

13. Install the switch mounting screws and the connector on the mast jacket bracket. Install the column-to-dash trim plate.

14. Install the flasher knob and the turn signal lever.

15. With the turn signal lever in neutral and the flasher know out, slide the thrust washer, upper bearing preload spring, and canceling cam onto the shaft.

16. Position the lock plate on the shaft and press it down until a new snapring can be inserted in the shaft groove. Always use a new snapring when assembling.

17. Install the cover and the steering wheel.

18. Enable the SIR system if an air bag is present.

MULTI-
FUNCTION
LEVER

HAZARD
KNOB

1 Bndg cr recess screw
2 Rd wash hd screw
3 Signal switch arm
4 Turn signal switch

86818101

Fig. 53 Push the flasher knob in and unscrew it. Unfasten the button retaining screw and remove the button, spring and knob

1 Strg col hsg jacket asm
2 Dimmer & ign sw mounting stud
3 Dimmer switch asm
4 Ignition switch asm
5 Hexagon nut
6 Wash hd screw
7 Dimmer switch rod

86818104

Fig. 54 Exploded view of the ignition switch removal

Ignition Switch

REMOVAL & INSTALLATION

▶ See Figure 54

The switch is located inside the channel section of the brake pedal support and is completely inaccessible without first lowering the steering column. The switch is actuated by a rod and rack assembly. A gear on the end of the lock cylinder engages the toothed upper end of the rod.

1. If your vehicle is equipped with the SIR system follow the instructions in Section 6 to disable the system before proceeding.
2. Lower the steering column, be sure to properly support it.
3. Put the switch in the **OFF**, unlocked position. With the cylinder removed, the rod is in the lock position when it is in the next to the uppermost detent. The **OFF**, unlocked position is two detents from the top.
4. Remove the two switch screws and remove the switch assembly.

To install:
5. Before installing, place the new switch in the **OFF**, unlocked position and make sure the lock cylinder and actuating rod are in the **OFF**, unlocked (third detent from the top) position.
6. Install the activating rod into the switch, then assemble the switch onto the column. Tighten the mounting screws. Use only the specified screws since overlength screws could impair the collapsibility of the column.
7. Reinstall the steering column.
8. Enable the SIR system.

Ignition Lock Cylinder

❊❊CAUTION

If the car is equipped with an air bag, do not service the steering column or dashboard components. Extreme danger of air bag deployment exists even with the battery removed! Serious injury could occur.

REMOVAL & INSTALLATION

Without Air Bag

1. Place the ignition switch in the **RUN** position.
2. Remove the lockplate, turn signal switch and buzzer switch.
3. Remove the screw and lock cylinder.

➡**If the screw is dropped on removal, it could fall into the column, requiring complete disassembly to retrieve the screw.**

To install:
4. Rotate the cylinder clockwise to align cylinder key with the keyway in the housing.
5. Push the lock all the way in.
6. Install the screw. Tighten the screw to 14 inch lbs. (2 Nm) for adjustable columns and 25 inch lbs. (3 Nm) for standard columns.

With Air Bag
▶ See Figures 55 and 56

❊❊CAUTION

Before proceeding, refer to Section 6 for information on disabling and enabling the SIR (air bag) system; otherwise, serious injury could occur.

1. Turn the steering wheel so the vehicles wheels are pointed straight ahead.

2. Place the ignition switch into the **LOCK** position to prevent undercentering of the coil assembly.

3. Disable the SIR system. Disconnect the negative battery cable.

4. Remove the coil assembly retaining ring, then disconnect the inflatable restraint coil assembly. Let the switch hang freely if removal is not needed. To remove the coil assembly proceed.

5. Remove the wave washer, then the shaft retaining lock ring with tool J-23653-SIR to push down on the shaft lock. Dispose of the ring, it is not reusable.

6. Remove the shaft lock, then disconnect the canceling cam assembly.

7. Remove the upper bearing spring, race seat and race.

8. Position the turn signal to the right turn (up) position.

9. Remove the multi-function lever and hazard knob assembly. Unsecure the round washer head screw and the signal switch arm and turn signal switch screws.

10. Remove the turn signal switch assembly by unfastening the connector from the bulkhead connector. Gently pull on the harness through the column and disconnect.

11. Make sure the coil assembly does not become uncentered, this could happen if the centering spring is pushed down letting the hub rotate while the coil is removed from the steering column.

12. Remove the inflatable restraint coil assembly with the wiring harness from the column assembly.

13. Remove the wire protector, then attach a length of mechanics wire to the coil terminal connector to aid in reassembly. Then gently pull the wire through the column.

14. Remove the key from the steering column lock cylinder set, then remove the buzzer switch assembly.

15. Reinsert the key into the lock cylinder, turn it to the **LOCK** position.

16. Remove the lock retaining screw, then the cylinder.
To install:

➡Make sure all fasteners are securely seated before applying the necessary torque. If you fail to do so, component damage or malfunctioning of the steering column may occur.

17. Install the lock cylinder assembly, insert the retaining screw, then tighten to 22 inch lbs. (2.5 Nm).

18. Insert the key into the lock cylinder. Install the buzzer switch assembly. Turn the key to the **LOCK** position.

19. Install the turn signal switch assembly wiring harness through the column, let the switch hang freely. Connect the wiring to the bulkhead.

20. Insert the coil assembly wiring harness through the column letting the coil hang freely. Attach the turn signal assembly with the binding head screws. Tighten the screws to 30 inch lbs. (3 Nm).

21. Attach the signal switch arm with the round washer head screw, tighten the screw to 20 inch lbs. (2 Nm).

22. Install the hazard knob assembly and the multi-function lever.

23. Install the inner race, upper bearing race seat and spring. Attach the turn signal cancelling cam assembly, apply grease for lubrication.

24. Replace the shaft lock and install a new shaft lock retaining ring. Use tool J-23653-SIR or equivalent to push down on the shaft lock. The ring must be firmly seated in the groove on the shaft.

➡Set the steering shaft so that the block tooth on the race and upper shaft is at the 12 o'clock position. The wheel on the car should be straight ahead. Set the ignition switch to the LOCK position, as this will ensure no damage to the coil assembly.

25. Install the wave washer, then attach the coil assembly, make sure it is centered correctly.

26. Attach the coil assembly retaining ring, the ring must be firmly seated in the groove on the shaft.

27. Gently pull the lower coil assembly, turn signal, and pivot (pulse) wires to remove any kinks that may be inside the steering column assembly. If you fail to do this you can damage the wiring.

28. Complete assembling the steering column assembly.

29. Attach the negative battery cable.

30. Check the functions of the turn signal, make sure it cancels when turned on and the steering wheel is turned.

31. Enable the SIR system.

Fig. 55 Special tool J-23653-SIR or equivalent is required for pushing down the shaft lock to remove the shaft ring

Fig. 56 Centering the coil assembly is important in assembling the column assembly

Steering Column

➡Once the steering column is removed from the car, the column is extremely susceptible to damage. Dropping the column assembly on its end could collapse the steering shaft or loosen the plastic injections which maintain column rigidity. Leaning on the column assembly could cause the jacket to bend or deform. Any of the above damage could impair the column's collapsible design. If it is necessary to remove the steering wheel, use a standard wheel puller. Under no condition should the end of the shaft be hammered upon, as hammering could loosen the plastic injection.

REMOVAL & INSTALLATION

▶ **See Figures 57 and 58**

1. If your vehicle is equipped with the SIR system, follow the instructions in Section 6 to disable the system before proceeding.
2. Remove the left instrument panel sound insulator. Next remove the left instrument trim pad and steering column trim collar.
3. If column repairs are to be made, remove the steering wheel.

✳✳CAUTION

Failure to disconnect the intermediate shaft from the rack and pinion stub shaft can result in damage to the steering gear and/or the intermediate shaft itself. This damage can cause loss of steering control which could result in personal injury.

4. Remove the steering column to intermediate shaft connection.
5. Remove the deflector and bracket.
6. Disconnect the shift indicator cable.
7. Disconnect all wiring harness connectors. Remove the dust boot mounting screws and column mounting bracket bolts.
8. Lower the column to clear the mounting bracket and carefully remove from the car.

To install:

➡If a service replacement steering column is being installed, do not remove the anti-rotation pin until after the steering column has been connected to the steering gear. Removing the anti-rotation pin before the steering column is connected to the steering gear could damage the SIR coil assembly.

9. Install the column into the vehicle and raise it into the mounting bracket.
10. Attach the shift cable to the actuator and housing holder.
11. Loosely install the column mounting bolts and all wiring harness connectors.

12. Attach the shift indicator cable, along with the deflector and brackets.

✳✳CAUTION

Failure to connect the intermediate shaft to the rack and pinion stub shaft can result in damage to the steering gear and/or the intermediate shaft itself. This damage can cause loss of steering control which could result in personal injury.

13. Connect the intermediate shaft to the steering column upper shaft pinch bolt. On SIR systems, tighten the steering column bolts to 22 ft. lbs. (30 Nm), steering column lower support nut to 22 ft. lbs. (30 Nm), steering column upper support stud to 21 ft. lbs. (29 Nm) and the intermediate shaft bolt to 35 ft. lbs. (48 Nm). On non-SIR systems, tighten the support bolts to 20 ft. lbs. (27 Nm), and the upper pinch bolts to 34 ft. lbs. (46 Nm).
14. Inspect the shift indicator adjustment.
15. Install the anti-rotation pin, if a service replacement steering column is being installed.
16. Install the steering wheel. Attach the steering column trim collar and the left instrument panel trim pad.
17. Replace the left sound insulator.
18. Enable the SIR system, then connect the negative battery cable.

Steering Linkage

REMOVAL & INSTALLATION

Tie Rod Ends

INNER

▶ **See Figures 59, 60 and 61**

1. Loosen the lug nuts.
2. Raise and support the vehicle safely.
3. Remove the tire and wheel assembly.
4. Remove the rack and pinion assembly from the vehicle.
5. Disconnect and remove the outer tie rod from the inner tie rod assembly.
6. Loosen the jam nut on the steering rack (inner tie rod).
7. Remove the tie rod end nut and the end clamp. Disconnect the boot clamp with side cutters and discard the boot.
8. Slide the shock dampener from the inner tie rod assembly and the other side of the rack.
9. Make sure you hold on to the rack during the inner tie rod removal to prevent rack damage.

➡In order to maintain proper front end alignment after installation, be sure to count the number of turns while removing the tie rod.

10. Separate the inner tie rod end from the rack. Place one wrench on the flat of the rack assembly. Then, place a wrench on the flats of the inner tie rod housing. Rotate the housing counterclockwise until the tie rod separates from the rack.

To install:

11. The rack must be held during the inner tie rod installation to prevent internal gear damage.

Fig. 57 Tilt steering column assembly exploded view

86818105

1- NUT, HEXAGON LOCKING (M14x1.5)
2- RING, RETAINING
3- COIL ASM, SIR
4- WASHER, WAVE
5- RING, RETAINING
6- LOCK, SHAFT
7- CAM ASM, TURN SIG CANCEL
8- SPRING, UPPER BEARING
9- SCREW, BNDG HD CR RECESS
10- SCREW, RD WASH HD (M4.2x1.41)
11- ARM, SIGNAL SWITCH
12- SWITCH ASM, TURN SIGNAL
13- SEAT, UPPER BRG INNER RACE
14- RACE, INNER
15- SCREW, PAN HD 6-LOBED SOC TAP
16- SWITCH ASM, BUZZER
18- SCREW, LOCK RETAINING
19- COVER & SLEEVE ASM, LOCK HSG
20- LOCK CYLINDER SET, STRG COL
21- ACTUATOR, DIMMER SW ROD
22- PIN, SWITCH ACTUATOR PIVOT
23- SWITCH ASM, PIVOT & (PULSE)
24- BASE PLATE, COL HSG CVR END
25- CAP, COL HSG COVER END
26- PROTECTOR, WIRING
28- SHROUD, CONNECTOR
30- HOUSING ASM, STRG COLUMN
31- BEARING ASM
32- BOLT, LOCK
33- SPRING, LOCK BOLT
34- SHOE, STEERING WHEEL LOCK
35- SHOE, STEERING WHEEL LOCK
36- SHIELD, WIRE PROTECTOR
37- SHAFT, DRIVE
38- PIN, DOWEL
39- PIN, PIVOT
40- SPRING, SHOE
41- SPRING, RELEASE LEVER
42- PIN, RELEASE LEVER
43- LEVER, SHOE RELEASE
44- RACK, SWITCH ACTUATOR
45- SPRING, RACK PRELOAD
46- HOUSING, STRG COLUMN
47- SECTOR, SWITCH ACTUATOR
48- SCREW, HEX WASHER HEAD
50- GUIDE, SPRING
51- SPRING, WHEEL TILT

52- RETAINER, SPRING
55- SHAFT ASM, STEERING
56- SHAFT ASM, RACE & UPPER
57- SPHERE, CENTERING
58- SPRING, JOINT PRELOAD
59- SHAFT ASM, LOWER
61- SCREW, SUPPORT
62- SUPPORT ASM, STRG COL
66- RING, SHIFT TUBE RETAINING
67- WASHER, THRUST
68- PLATE, LOCK
69- WASHER, WAVE
70- SPRING, SHIFT LEVER
71- BOWL ASM, GEARSHIFT LEVER
73- JACKET ASM, STRG COL
78- TUBE ASM, SHIFT
79- SWITCH ASM, IGN & DIMMER
80- STUD, DIMR & IGN SW MTG
82- NUT, HEXAGON (#10-24)
83- SCREW, WASH HD (#10-24X.25)
84- ROD, DIMMER SWITCH
85- ACTUATOR ASM, IGN SWITCH
86- BEARING ASM, ADAPTER &
87- SCREW, HEX WASHER HD TAP
88- SEAT, LOWER BEARING
89- SPRING, LOWER BEARING
90- RETAINER, LOWER SPRING
91- RETAINER, BEARING
94- CONN, AXIAL POSN ASSUR
95- SUPPORT, STEERING COL LOWER
96- BOLT, HEX FLANGED HD (M6X1X14)
97- ACTUATOR, ELECTRICAL (BTSI)
98- CLIP, ADJUSTMENT RETAINING
99- STRAP, WIRE HARNESS

Service Kits
201- RACK SERV KIT, COL SECTOR &
202- SPRING SERV KIT, TILT COLUMN
203- COIL SERV KIT, INFL RESTRAINT
204- SPHERE SERV KIT, TILT COLUMN
205- GREASE SERV KIT, (SYNTHETIC)

86818106

Fig. 58 Numbered list for the tilt steering column

86818088

Fig. 59 Loosen the jam nut on the steering rack (inner tie rod)

INNER TIE ROD HOUSING

1 R & P housing asm
2 Shock dampener ring
3 Inner tie (LT) rod asm
4 Piston & steering rack asm

86818090

Fig. 60 Place one wrench on the flat of the rack assembly. Place another wrench on the flats of the inner tie rod housing. Rotate the housing counter-clockwise until the tie rod separates from the rack

12. Install the rack and pinion assembly, then slide the shock dampener on top the rack.

13. Screw the tie rod end onto the steering rack (inner tie rod) the same number of turns as counted for removal. This will give approximately correct toe. Tighten the nut approximately 70 ft. lbs. (95 Nm).

14. Make sure that the tie rod rocks freely in the housing before staking the inner tie rod assembly or the rack.

15. Support the rack and housing of the inner tie rod assembly, then stake both sides of the inner rod housing to the flats on the rack.

16. Check both stakes by inserting a (0.25mm) 0.010 inch feeler gauge between the rack and the tie rod housing as shown in the picture. The feeler must not pass between the rack and the housing stake.

17. Slide the shock dampener over the housing until it engages, then install a new boot clamp onto the rack and pinion boot.

18. Apply grease to the inner tie rod and housing. Insert the elbow of the boot into the breather tube. Install the boot onto the housing until it seats in the housing groove.

➡**Do not twist or pucker the boot after installation.**

19. Position a new boot clamp on the boot and crimp, then position the tie rod end clamp with a pair of pliers on the boot.

20. Install a hex jam nut to the inner tie rod assembly and tighten, then install the outer tie rod.

21. Install the tie and wheel assembly, hand-tighten the lug nuts.

22. Lower the vehicle, then tighten the lug nuts to 100 ft. lbs. (136 Nm).

OUTER

▶ **See Figures 62, 63, 64 and 65**

1. Loosen the lug nuts, then raise and support the vehicle.
2. Remove the tire and wheel assembly.

1 Shock dampener ring
2 Inner tie (LT) rod asm
3 Piston & steering rack asm

86818092

Fig. 61 Support the rack and housing of the inner tie rod assembly, then stake both sides of the inner rod housing to the flats on the rack

86818095

Fig. 62 After loosening the jam nut, remove and discard the cotter pin

86818096

Fig. 63 Using a suitable tool, remove the hex nut holding the tie rod in place

3. Loosen the jam nut.
4. Remove and discard the cotter pin.
5. Using a suitable tool remove the hex nut holding the tie rod in place.
6. With a tie rod puller, the tie rod can be separated from the knuckle.
7. After separation, unscrew the end from the shaft.

To install:

8. Connect the new outer tie rod end onto the inner shaft, then connect the tie rod end to the knuckle.

9. Tighten the hex slotted nut to 31-52 ft. lbs. (42-70 Nm) to align the cotter pin into the slot, (¹/₆ turn maximum). Do not back off the nut to install the cotter pin.

10. Insert a new cotter pin into the tie rod stud.

11. Adjust the toe, then tighten the jam nut to 52 ft. lbs. (70 Nm).

86818097

Fig. 64 The tie rod can be separated from the knuckle with a tie rod puller

86818098

Fig. 65 After separation, unscrew the end from the shaft

Rack Bearing Preload

ADJUSTMENT

1. Make the adjustment with the front wheels raised and the steering wheel centered. Be sure to check the returnability of the steering wheel to the center after adjustment.
2. Loosen the adjuster plug locknut and turn the adjuster plug clockwise until it bottoms in the gear assembly, then back off 50°-70° (approximately ⅙ revolution).
3. Install the lock to the adjusting nut, then tighten the adjusting nut to 50 ft. lbs. (70 Nm) while holding the adjuster plug stationary.

Manual Rack and Pinion Steering Gear

REMOVAL & INSTALLATION

▶ See Figure 66

1. Raise the intermediate shaft seal and remove intermediate shaft-to-stub shaft pinch bolt.
2. Raise and support the vehicle on jackstands, then remove both front wheel and tire assemblies.
3. Remove the cotter pins and nuts from both tie rod ends. Using tool J-6627 or BT-7101, press the tie rod ends from the steering knuckle.
4. If equipped with an Air Management pipe, remove the bracket bolt from the crossmember.
5. Remove the 2 rear cradle mounting bolts and lower the rear of the cradle about 4-5 in. (102-127mm).

✳✳WARNING

If the rear of the cradle is lowered too far, the engine components nearest the cowl may be damaged.

6. If equipped, remove the rack and pinion heat shield.
7. Remove the rack and pinion mounting bolts, then the gear assembly through the left wheel opening.
   To install:
8. Install the gear assembly through the left wheel opening and install the mounting bolts.
9. Install the heat shield.
10. Raise the rear of the cradle and install the mounting bolts.
11. Install the bracket bolt to the crossmember under the air management pipe.
12. Install the tie rod ends to the steering knuckles, install the retaining nuts and insert new cotter pins.
13. Install the front wheels and lower the vehicle.
14. Install the intermediate shaft seal and the intermediate shaft-to-stub shaft pinch bolt.
15. Check and adjust the toe-in as necessary.

Power Rack and Pinion Steering Gear

REMOVAL & INSTALLATION

Except 2.2L and 1993-95 3.1L Engines
▶ See Figure 67

1. Raise the intermediate shaft seal and remove intermediate shaft-to-stub shaft pinch bolt.
2. Remove the air cleaner and disconnect the pressure hoses from the steering gear.
3. Raise and support the vehicle on jackstands, then remove both front wheel and tire assemblies.
4. Remove the cotter pins and nuts from both tie rod ends. Using tool J-6627 or BT-7101, press the tie rod ends from the steering knuckle.
5. If equipped with an Air Management pipe, remove the bracket bolt from the crossmember.

Fig. 66 Exploded view of the manual rack and pinion

6. Remove the 2 rear cradle mounting bolts and lower the rear of the cradle about 4-5 in. (102-127mm).

❋❋WARNING

If the rear of the cradle is lowered too far, the engine components nearest the cowl may be damaged.

7. If equipped, remove the rack and pinion heat shield.
8. Remove the rack and pinion mounting bolts, then the gear assembly through the left wheel opening.

To install:

9. Install the gear assembly through the left wheel opening and install the mounting bolts.
10. Install the heat shield.
11. Raise the rear of the cradle and install the mounting bolts.
12. Install the bracket bolt to the crossmember under the air management pipe.
13. Install the tie rod ends to the steering knuckles, install the retaining nuts and insert new cotter pins.

1 Steering gear
2 Bushing
3 Bolt
4 Nut
5 Nut
6 Cotter pin
7 Sleeve

86818115

Fig. 67 Power rack and pinion assembly

14. Install the front wheels and lower the vehicle.
15. Install the high pressure hoses to the steering gear and install the air cleaner.
16. Install the intermediate shaft seal and the intermediate shaft-to-stub shaft pinch bolt.

2.2L Engine

1. Disconnect the negative battery cable.
2. Install an engine support fixture J-28467-A, or the equivalent.
3. Raise and safely support the vehicle.
4. Remove the tire and wheel assembly.
5. Remove the intermediate shaft lower pinch bolt.
6. Disconnect the intermediate shaft from stub shaft.

❋❋CAUTION

Failure to disconnect the intermediate shaft from the rack and pinion stub shaft can result in damage to the steering gear and/or intermediate shaft. This damage can cause loss of steering control which could result in personal injury.

7. Remove the exhaust pipe hanger bracket near rear of frame including the brake line retainer and rubber exhaust pipe hangers.
8. Remove the engine and transaxle mount nuts at the subframe.
9. Support the rear of the subframe with jack stands.
10. Remove the rear subframe bolts and discard.
11. Lower the subframe for access to rack and pinion.

➡**Do not lower the rear of the cradle too far, as damage to engine components nearest the cowl may result.**

12. Remove the cotter pins and castle nuts from the outer tie rod ends and separate the tie rod ends from the steering knuckles using a suitable puller.
13. Disconnect the power steering lines from the steering gear.
14. Remove the rack and pinion mounting bolts and nuts.
15. Remove the rack and pinion through left wheel opening.

To Install:

16. Install the rack and pinion through left wheel opening.

17. Install the rack and pinion mounting bolts and nuts and tighten to 66 ft. lbs. (90 Nm).

18. Connect the power steering lines to the rack using new O-rings and tighten the fittings to 13 ft. lbs. (17 Nm) on the return line and 21 ft. lbs. (28 Nm) on the pressure line.

19. Install the power steering line clip to steering gear.

20. Connect the tie rod ends to the steering knuckles. Tighten the castle nuts to 31 ft. lbs. (42 Nm). Install new cotter pins.

21. Raise the subframe into position and install new frame mounting bolts. Tighten the bolts to 103 ft. lbs. (140 Nm).

22. Remove the jack.

23. Install the engine mount and transaxle mount nuts and tighten to 39 ft. lbs. (53 Nm).

24. Install the exhaust pipe hanger bracket near the rear of frame including brake line retainer and rubber exhaust pipe hanger.

25. Connect the intermediate shaft to the stub shaft and tighten the pinch bolt to 29 ft. lbs. (40 Nm).

26. Install the tire and wheel assembly.

27. Lower the vehicle.

28. Remove the support fixture.

29. Connect the negative battery cable.

30. Refill the power steering reservoir and bleed the system.

31. Check the front end alignment and adjust as necessary.

3.1L Engine (VIN M)

1. Disconnect the negative battery cable.

2. Remove engine torque strut from engine.

3. Install an engine support fixture J-28467-A, or the equivalent.

4. Raise and safely support the vehicle.

5. Remove the tire and wheel assembly.

6. Remove the cotter pins and castle nuts from the outer tie rod ends and separate the tie rod ends from the steering knuckles using a suitable puller.

7. Remove the center engine and rear transaxle mounts from the frame.

8. Remove the intermediate shaft lower pinch bolt.

9. Disconnect the intermediate shaft from stub shaft.

❋❋CAUTION

Failure to disconnect the intermediate shaft from the rack and pinion stub shaft can result in damage to the steering gear and/or intermediate shaft. This damage can cause loss of steering control which could result in personal injury.

10. Remove the brace bolts and brace, including brake line brace.

11. Support the rear of the subframe with jack stands.

12. Remove the rear subframe bolts and discard.

13. Lower the subframe for access to rack and pinion.

14. Remove the steering gear heat shield.

15. Remove the clip holding lines at rack assembly.

16. Disconnect the power steering lines and O-rings.

17. Remove the rack and pinion mounting bolts and nuts.

18. Remove the rack and pinion unit through the left wheel well.

To Install:

19. Install the rack and pinion through left wheel opening.

20. Install the rack and pinion mounting bolts and nuts and tighten the mounting bolts to 66 ft. lbs. (90 Nm).

21. Connect the power steering lines to the rack using new O-rings and tighten the fittings to 13 ft. lbs. (17 Nm) on the return line and 21 ft. lbs. (28 Nm). on the pressure line.

22. Install the power steering line clip to steering gear.

23. Install the steering gear heat shield.

24. Raise the subframe into position and install new frame mounting bolts. Tighten the bolts to 103 ft. lbs. (140 Nm).

25. Remove the jack.

26. Install the engine mount and transaxle mount nuts and tighten to 39 ft. lbs. (53 Nm).

27. Install the brace and bolts including brake line brace.

28. Connect the intermediate shaft to the stub shaft and tighten the pinch bolt to 29 ft. lbs. (40 Nm).

29. Connect the tie rod ends to the steering knuckles. Tighten the castle nuts to 31 ft. lbs. (42 Nm). Install new cotter pins.

30. Install the tire and wheel assembly.

31. Lower the vehicle.

32. Remove the support fixture.

33. Connect the negative battery cable.

34. Refill the power steering reservoir and bleed the system.

35. Check the front end alignment and adjust as necessary.

Power Steering Pump

REMOVAL & INSTALLATION

Gasoline Engines

▶ **See Figures 68, 69, 70, 71 and 72**

1. Disconnect the negative battery cable.

2. Remove the hoses at the pump and tape the openings shut to prevent contamination. Position the disconnected lines in a raised position to prevent leakage.

3. Remove the pump belt.

4. On some 4-cylinder models it may be necessary to:
   a. Remove the radiator hose clamp bolt.
   b. Remove the right side fender splash shield.

5. On 2.8L models:
   a. Remove the air cleaner assembly.
   b. Disconnect the electrical connector at the blower motor.
   c. Drain the cooling system, then remove the heater hose at the water pump.

6. On 3.0L models, remove the alternator.

➡**Removing a component such as the alternator may make the job easier on any model.**

7. Loosen the retaining bolts and any braces, then remove the pump.

8. Remove the pump pulley and attach it to the new pump, as illustrated.

To install:

9. Install the pump and brackets to the engine and hand-tighten the retaining bolts.

1 Pulley
2 Power steering pump
3 Tensioner
4 26 Nm (19 lb.ft.)

86818120

Fig. 68 Power steering pump assembly — 2.5L engine

GENERATOR
ADJUSTMENT
BRACKET

GENERATOR
SUPPORT

A

PUMP REAR
ADJUSTMENT
BRACKET

POWER STEERING PUMP

PULLEY

FRONT PUMP
ADJUSTMENT
BRACKET

VIEW A

TORQUE ALL FASTENERS SHOWN
TO 50 N·m (35 FT. LBS.)

86818122

Fig. 69 Power steering pump assembly — 3.0L engine

1 Belt tensioner asm.
2 Power steering pump
3 Bolt/screw
4 Belt tensioner brace
5 Pulley
6 Accessory drive belt
7 Bolt 27 Nm (20 lb.ft.)

FRT

86818121

Fig. 70 Power steering pump assembly — 3.3L engine

REMOVAL   INSTALLATION

30   30

BT-7185   BT-7005-A

A   B   A   B

30   30

J 25034-B   J 25033-B

A   A
B   B

A Hold tool here
B Turn tool here
30 P/S pump pulley

86818119

Fig. 71 Power steering pump pulley removal and installation tools

SPACER

BRACKET

BRACKET

50 N·m (35 FT. LBS.)

*

SPACER

PUMP ASSEMBLY

PULLEY

PIN

25 N·m (19 FT. LBS.)

*

50 N·m (35 FT. LBS.)

PUMP ASSEMBLY

"O" RING

27 N·m (20 FT. LBS.)

PRESSURE PIPE

CLAMP

RADIATOR HOSE

HOSE

RETURN LINE

CLAMP

86818123

Fig. 72 Power steering pump assembly — early model 2.5L engine

10. On 3.0L models:

a. Install the alternator support to the engine.

b. Position the alternator adjustment bracket over the front pump adjustment bracket.

c. Install the long bolt and alternator bracket, front pump bracket, rear pump bracket, and alternator support to the engine.

d. Attach the remaining alternator adjustment bracket bolt.

e. Install the power steering pump belt.

f. Raise the car, then install the rear pump adjustment bracket-to-pump nut.

11. Connect and tighten the hose fittings.

12. On 3.0L models, lower the vehicle, then install the alternator and belt.

13. On some 4-cylinder models, you will need to install the radiator hose clamp bolt.

14. On 2.8L models:

a. Connect the water hose to the water pump.

b. Install and connect the blower motor.

15. Refill the pump with fluid and bleed the system.

16. Install the pump belt and adjust the tension.

17. On 3.0L models, install the air cleaner assembly.

18. Connect the negative battery cable.

Diesel Engine

▶ **See Figure 73**

1. Remove the drive belt.

2. Raise and support the vehicle.

3. Remove the right front wheel.

4. Remove the front pulley and harmonic balancer.

5. Disconnect the hoses from the pump.

6. Drain the fluid from the power steering reservoir.

7. Disconnect the pressure line at the pump.

8. Remove the one bolt and two nuts from the rear bracket.

9. Remove the pump with the brackets.

10. Remove the pulley and brackets.

To install:

11. Install the brackets and pulley to the pump.

12. Attach the pump with the brackets on the engine.

13. Install the two nuts and one bolt on the rear bracket, then tighten.

14. Connect the pressure line and tighten. Then connect the reservoir line to the pump.

15. Install the harmonic balancer with the bolt and washer, tighten the bolt to 203-350 ft. lbs. (275-475 Nm).

16. Attach the pulley, tighten the four bolts to 30 ft. lbs. (41 Nm).

17. Install the right front wheel, install the lug nuts.

18. Lower the car, tighten the lug nuts.

19. Install the drive belt.

20. Fill the power steering reservoir.

21. Bleed the system.

Fig. 73 Power steering pump for the 4.3L diesel engine

BLEEDING

▶ **See Figure 74**

1. Turn the ignition switch to the **OFF** position.

2. Raise the front of the vehicle enough to get the wheels off the ground.

3. Turn the steering wheel completely to the left.

4. Fill the fluid reservoir to the FULL COLD level, make sure to leave the cap off.

5. Let the fluid stand undisturbed for two minutes, then crank the engine for about two seconds. Refill reservoir if necessary.

6. With an assistant checking the fluid level and condition, turn the steering wheel lock-to-lock at least 20 times, while the engine remains off.

7. Start the engine, then while idling maintain the fluid level. Install the cap.

8. Return the wheels to the center, then lower the front end to the ground.

9. Turn the wheels to the left and right, checking the fluid level and refilling if necessary.

Bleeding Air from Power Steering Systems

Before bleeding:
Inspect steering system. Check, and correct as needed:

 Hoses must not touch any other part of vehicle.

- Steering system noise could be caused by hose touching frame, body, or engine

All hose connections must be tight.

- Loose connections might not leak but could allow air into system

When to bleed:
After any component replacement
After disconnecting fluid line
In case of steering system noise

Why bleed?
To prevent pump damage
To ensure proper system operation
To stop steering system noise

Power Steering Fluid
Use only clean, new power steering fluid Fluid must be

Conventional Climate
GM #1052884 – 16 ounce
      #1050017 – 32 ounce

Cold Climate
GM #12345866 – 16 ounce
      #12345867 – 32 ounce

How to bleed:

1 Switch ignition off.

2 Raise front wheels off ground.

3 Turn steering wheel full left.

4 Fill fluid reservoir to "FULL COLD" level. Leave cap off

5 With assistant checking fluid level and condition, turn steering wheel lock-to-lock at least 20 times Engine remains off.

- On systems with long return lines or fluid coolers, turn steering wheel lock-to-lock at least 40 times
- Trapped air may cause fluid to overflow Thoroughly clean any spilled fluid to allow for leak check
- Keep fluid level at "FULL COLD "

6 While turning wheel, check fluid constantly

- No bubbles are allowed
- For any sign of bubbles, recheck connections Repeat step 5

7 Start engine. With engine idling, maintain fluid level. Reinstall cap

8 Return wheels to center Lower front wheels to ground.

9 Keep engine running for two minutes

10 Turn steering wheel in both directions

Verify
- ☑ Smooth power assist
- ☑ Noiseless operation
- ☑ Proper fluid level
- ☑ No system leaks
- ☑ Proper fluid condition
- No bubbles, no foam, no discoloration

11 If all proper conditions apply, procedure is complete

12 If any problem remains, see "Special Conditions "

Special Conditions:

Fluid

- **Foam or bubbles in fluid**
  Fluid must be completely free of bubbles In step 5, be alert to periodic bubbles that could indicate a loose connection or leaky O-ring seal in either the return hose or pressure hose
- **Discolored fluid**
  (milky, opaque, or light tan color)

Switch ignition off Wait two minutes Recheck hose connections Repeat steps 7-10 If condition still exists, replace and check a possible cause

- ☑ Return hose clamps
- ☑ Return hose O-ring
- ☑ Pressure hose O-rings
- ☑ Gear cylinder line O-rings

Fill system and repeat bleed procedure for each possible cause Repeat steps 7-10 to verify whether noise has been eliminated

Noise

- **Pump whine or groan**

With engine running, recheck hoses for possible contact with frame body or engine If no contact is found, follow either method below to cool down fluid and repressurize system

Method 1:
Normal Cool Down

Switch engine off
Wait for system to cool
Install reservoir cap

Method 2:
Partial Fluid Replacement

Switch engine off
Use a suction device to remove fluid from reservoir
Refill with cool, clean fluid
Install reservoir cap

After either method of cooling, start engine and allow engine to come up to operating temperature If noise persists, remove and replace power steering pump Repeat bleed procedure following pump replacement

86818107

Fig. 74 Bleeding air from the power steering system is very important when the system has been opened

Troubleshooting the Turn Signal Switch

Problem	Cause	Solution
Turn signal will not cancel	• Loose switch mounting screws • Switch or anchor bosses broken • Broken, missing or out of position detent, or cancelling spring	• Tighten screws • Replace switch • Reposition springs or replace switch as required
Turn signal difficult to operate	• Turn signal lever loose • Switch yoke broken or distorted • Loose or misplaced springs • Foreign parts and/or materials in switch • Switch mounted loosely	• Tighten mounting screws • Replace switch • Reposition springs or replace switch • Remove foreign parts and/or material • Tighten mounting screws
Turn signal will not indicate lane change	• Broken lane change pressure pad or spring hanger • Broken, missing or misplaced lane change spring • Jammed wires	• Replace switch • Replace or reposition as required • Loosen mounting screws, reposition wires and retighten screws
Turn signal will not stay in turn position	• Foreign material or loose parts impeding movement of switch yoke • Defective switch	• Remove material and/or parts • Replace switch
Hazard switch cannot be pulled out	• Foreign material between hazard support cancelling leg and yoke	• Remove foreign material. No foreign material impeding function of hazard switch—replace turn signal switch.
No turn signal lights	• Inoperative turn signal flasher • Defective or blown fuse • Loose chassis to column harness connector • Disconnect column to chassis connector. Connect new switch to chassis and operate switch by hand. If vehicle lights now operate normally, signal switch is inoperative • If vehicle lights do not operate, check chassis wiring for opens, grounds, etc.	• Replace turn signal flasher • Replace fuse • Connect securely • Replace signal switch • Repair chassis wiring as required

86818125

Troubleshooting the Turn Signal Switch (cont.)

Problem	Cause	Solution
Instrument panel turn indicator lights on but not flashing	• Burned out or damaged front or rear turn signal bulb • If vehicle lights do not operate, check light sockets for high resistance connections, the chassis wiring for opens, grounds, etc. • Inoperative flasher • Loose chassis to column harness connection • Inoperative turn signal switch • To determine if turn signal switch is defective, substitute new switch into circuit and operate switch by hand. If the vehicle's lights operate normally, signal switch is inoperative.	• Replace bulb • Repair chassis wiring as required • Replace flasher • Connect securely • Replace turn signal switch • Replace turn signal switch
Stop light not on when turn indicated	• Loose column to chassis connection • Disconnect column to chassis connector. Connect new switch into system without removing old.	• Connect securely • Replace signal switch
Stop light not on when turn indicated (cont.)	Operate switch by hand. If brake lights work with switch in the turn position, signal switch is defective. • If brake lights do not work, check connector to stop light sockets for grounds, opens, etc.	• Repair connector to stop light circuits using service manual as guide
Turn indicator panel lights not flashing	• Burned out bulbs • High resistance to ground at bulb socket • Opens, ground in wiring harness from front turn signal bulb socket to indicator lights	• Replace bulbs • Replace socket • Locate and repair as required
Turn signal lights flash very slowly	• High resistance ground at light sockets • Incorrect capacity turn signal flasher or bulb • If flashing rate is still extremely slow, check chassis wiring harness from the connector to light sockets for high resistance • Loose chassis to column harness connection • Disconnect column to chassis connector. Connect new switch into system without removing old. Operate switch by hand. If flashing occurs at normal rate, the signal switch is defective.	• Repair high resistance grounds at light sockets • Replace turn signal flasher or bulb • Locate and repair as required • Connect securely • Replace turn signal switch

Troubleshooting the Turn Signal Switch (cont.)

Problem	Cause	Solution
Hazard signal lights will not flash—turn signal functions normally	• Blow fuse • Inoperative hazard warning flasher • Loose chassis-to-column harness connection • Disconnect column to chassis connector. Connect new switch into system without removing old. Depress the hazard warning lights. If they now work normally, turn signal switch is defective. • If lights do not flash, check wiring harness "K" lead for open between hazard flasher and connector. If open, fuse block is defective	• Replace fuse • Replace hazard warning flasher in fuse panel • Conect securely • Replace turn signal switch • Repair or replace brown wire or connector as required

86818127

Troubleshooting the Power Steering Pump

Problem	Cause	Solution
Chirp noise in steering pump	• Loose belt	• Adjust belt tension to specification
Belt squeal (particularly noticeable at full wheel travel and stand still parking)	• Loose belt	• Adjust belt tension to specification
Growl noise in steering pump	• Excessive back pressure in hoses or steering gear caused by restriction	• Locate restriction and correct. Replace part if necessary.
Growl noise in steering pump (particularly noticeable at stand still parking)	• Scored pressure plates, thrust plate or rotor • Extreme wear of cam ring	• Replace parts and flush system • Replace parts
Groan noise in steering pump	• Low oil level • Air in the oil. Poor pressure hose connection.	• Fill reservoir to proper level • Tighten connector to specified torque. Bleed system by operating steering from right to left—full turn.
Rattle noise in steering pump	• Vanes not installed properly • Vanes sticking in rotor slots	• Install properly • Free up by removing burrs, varnish, or dirt
Swish noise in steering pump	• Defective flow control valve	• Replace part
Whine noise in steering pump	• Pump shaft bearing scored	• Replace housing and shaft. Flush system.
Low pump pressure	• Flow control valve stuck or inoperative • Pressure plate not flat against cam ring	• Remove burrs or dirt or replace. Flush system. • Correct

86818128

Troubleshooting the Power Steering Pump (cont.)

Problem	Cause	Solution
Hard steering or lack of assist	• Loose pump belt • Low oil level in reservoir **NOTE:** Low oil level will also result in excessive pump noise • Steering gear to column misalignment • Lower coupling flange rubbing against steering gear adjuster plug • Tires not properly inflated	• Adjust belt tension to specification • Fill to proper level. If excessively low, check all lines and joints for evidence of external leakage. Tighten loose connectors. • Align steering column • Loosen pinch bolt and assemble properly • Inflate to recommended pressure
Foaming milky power steering fluid, low fluid level and possible low pressure	• Air in the fluid, and loss of fluid due to internal pump leakage causing overflow	• Check for leaks and correct. Bleed system. Extremely cold temperatures will cause system aeriation should the oil level be low. If oil level is correct and pump still foams, remove pump from vehicle and separate reservoir from body. Check welsh plug and body for cracks. If plug is loose or body is cracked, replace body.
Momentary increase in effort when turning wheel fast to right or left	• Low oil level in pump • Pump belt slipping • High internal leakage	• Add power steering fluid as required • Tighten or replace belt • Check pump pressure. (See pressure test)
Steering wheel surges or jerks when turning with engine running especially during parking	• Low oil level • Loose pump belt • Steering linkage hitting engine oil pan at full turn • Insufficient pump pressure	• Fill as required • Adjust tension to specification • Correct clearance • Check pump pressure. (See pressure test). Replace flow control valve if defective.
Steering wheel surges or jerks when turning with engine running especially during parking (cont.)	• Sticking flow control valve	• Inspect for varnish or damage, replace if necessary
Excessive wheel kickback or loose steering	• Air in system	• Add oil to pump reservoir and bleed by operating steering. Check hose connectors for proper torque and adjust as required.
Low pump pressure	• Extreme wear of cam ring • Scored pressure plate, thrust plate, or rotor • Vanes not installed properly • Vanes sticking in rotor slots • Cracked or broken thrust or pressure plate	• Replace parts. Flush system. • Replace parts. Flush system. • Install properly • Freeup by removing burrs, varnish, or dirt • Replace part

86818129

TORQUE SPECIFICATIONS

Component		US	Metric
Brake line brackets:		8 ft. lbs.	11 Nm
Caliper retaining bolts:		38 ft. lbs.	51 Nm
Front crossmwmber-to-body bolts:		103 ft. lbs.	140 Nm
Halfshaft end nuts:		184-192 ft. lbs.	250-260 Nm
Knuckle camber cam bolt:		140 ft. lbs.	190 Nm
Knuckle attaching bolts:		38 ft. lbs.	52 Nm
Lower ball jopint pinch bolt:			
	1982-84	40 ft. lbs.	50 Nm
	1985-93	33 ft. lbs.	45 Nm
	1994-95	38 ft. lbs.	52 Nm
Lower control arm bolts:		61 ft. lbs.	83 Nm
MacPherson strut shaft nut:		65 ft. lbs.	85 Nm
MacPherson strut to fender:		18 ft. lbs.	24 Nm
MacPherson strut to knuckle:		122-140 ft. lbs.	165-190 Nm
Rear shock to lower mount:			
	1982-84	43 ft. lbs.	58 Nm
	1985-86	35 ft. lbs.	47 Nm
	1987-92	44 ft. lbs.	59 Nm
	1993-95	53 ft. lbs.	72 Nm
Rear shock to upper mount:		16 ft. lbs.	22 Nm
Rear axle top bolt 6000 AWD:		148 ft. lbs.	200 Nm
Rear control arm-to-bracket:		84 ft. lbs.	115 Nm
Rear control bracket-to-underbody:		28 ft. lbs.	38 Nm
Rear hub and bearing assembly:		44 ft. lbs.	60 Nm
Rear jack pad mounting bolts:		18 ft. lbs.	25 Nm
Rear track bar at brace or underebody:		35 ft. lbs.	47 Nm
Rear coil spring track bolt:			
	1982-92	44 ft. lbs.	60 Nm
	1993-95	53 ft. lbs.	72 Nm
Rear leaf spring-to-cradle bolts:		61 ft. lbs.	83 Nm
Rear strut lower mount bolts:		148 ft. lbs.	200 Nm
Spring retention plate bolts:		15 ft. lbs.	20 Nm
Stabilizer insulator clamps-to-control arms:		32 ft. lbs.	43 Nm
Steering column mounting bolts:		18 ft. lbs.	25 Nm
Steering rack mounting bolts:		59 ft. lbs.	80 Nm
Steering wheel retaining nut:		30 ft. lbs.	41 Nm
Tie rod adjustment jam nut:		52 ft. lbs.	70 Nm
Tie rod nut:		31-52 ft. lbs.	42-70 Nm
Toe link sleeve tab bolt:		14 ft. lbs.	19 Nm
Toe link inner nut:		61 ft. lbs.	83 Nm
Wheel lug nuts:		100 ft. lbs.	136 Nm

86818130

9

BRAKES

BRAKE SYSTEMS

Understanding The Brake System

HYDRAULIC SYSTEM

A hydraulic system is used to actuate the brakes. The system transports the power required to force the frictional surfaces of the braking system together from the pedal to the individual braking units at each wheel. A hydraulic system is used for three reasons. First, fluid under pressure can be carried to all parts of the automobile by small hoses, some of which are flexible, without taking up a significant amount of room or posing routine problems. Second, liquid is non-compressible, a hydraulic system can transport force without modifying or reducing that force. Third, a great mechanical advantage can be given to the brake pedal end of the system, and the foot pressure required to actuate the brakes can be reduced by making the surface area of the master cylinder pistons smaller than that of any of the pistons in the wheel cylinders or calipers.

The master cylinder consists of a fluid reservoir, a double cylinder and a piston assembly. Double type master cylinders are designed to separate the front and rear braking systems hydraulically in case of a leak.

Steel lines carry the brake fluid to a point on the vehicle's frame near each of the vehicle's wheels. The fluid is then carried to the slave cylinder by flexible tubes in order to allow for suspension and steering movements.

In drum brake systems, the slave cylinders are called wheel cylinders. Each wheel cylinder contains two pistons, one at either end, which push outward in opposite directions.

In disc brake systems, the slave cylinders are part of the calipers. One large cylinder is used to force the brake pads against the disc. All slave cylinder pistons employ some type of seal, usually made of rubber, to minimize the leakage of fluid around the piston. A rubber dust boot seals the outer end of the cylinder against dust and dirt. The boot fits around the outer end of the piston on disc brake calipers and around the brake actuating rod on wheel cylinders.

The hydraulic system operates as follows: When at rest, the entire system, from the pistons in the master cylinder to those in the wheel cylinders or calipers, is full of brake fluid. Upon application of the brake pedal, fluid trapped in front of the master cylinder pistons is forced through the lines to the slave cylinders. Here, it forces the pistons outward, (in the case of drum brakes), and inward toward the disc, (in the case of disc brakes). The motion of the pistons is opposed by return springs mounted outside the cylinders in drum brakes.

Upon release of the brake pedal, a spring located inside the master cylinder immediately returns the master cylinder pistons to the normal position. The pistons contain check valves and the master cylinder has compensating ports drilled in it. These are uncovered as the pistons reach their normal position. The piston check valves allow fluid to flow toward the wheel cylinders or calipers as the master cylinder pistons withdraw. Then, as the return springs force the shoes into the released position, the excess fluid returns to the master cylinder fluid reservoir through the compensating ports. It is during the time the pedal is in the released position that any fluid that has leaked out of the system will be replaced through the compensating ports.

Dual circuit master cylinders employ two pistons, located one behind the other, in the same cylinder. The primary piston is actuated by fluid trapped between the two pistons. If a leak develops in front of the secondary piston, it moves forward until it bottoms against the front of the master cylinder and the fluid trapped between the pistons will operate the rear brakes. If the rear brakes develop a leak, the primary piston will move forward until direct contact with the secondary piston takes place and it will force the secondary piston to actuate the front brakes. In either case, the brake pedal moves farther when the brakes are applied and less braking power is available.

All dual circuit system uses a switch to warn the driver when only half of the brake system is operational. This switch is located in a valve body which is mounted on the master cylinder. A hydraulic piston receives pressure from both circuits, each circuit's pressure being applied to one end of the piston. When the pressures are in balance, the piston remains stationary. When one circuit has a leak, however, the greater pressure in that circuit during application of the brakes will push the piston to one side, closing the switch and activating the brake warning light.

In disc brake systems, this valve body also contains a metering valve and, in some cases, a proportioning valve. The metering valve keeps pressure from traveling to the disc brakes on the front wheels until the brake shoes on the rear wheels have contacted the drums, ensuring that the front brakes will be used alone. The proportioning valve throttles the pressure to the rear brakes so as to avoid rear wheel lock-up during very hard braking.

These valves may be tested by removing the lines to the front and rear brake systems and installing special brake pressure testing gauge. Front and rear system pressures are then compared as the pedal is gradually depressed. Specifications vary with the manufacturer and design of the brake systems.

Brake warning lights may be tested by depressing the brake pedal and holding it while opening one of the wheel cylinder bleeder screws. If this does not cause the light to go on, substitute a new lamp, make continuity checks, and finally, replace the switch as necessary.

The hydraulic system may be checked for leaks by applying pressure to the pedal gradually and steadily. If the pedal sinks very slowly to the floor, the system has a leak. This is not to be confused with a springy or spongy feel due to the compression of air within the lines. If the system leaks, there will be a gradual change in the position of the pedal with a constant pressure.

Check for leaks along all lines and at wheel cylinder. If no external leaks are apparent, the problem is inside the master cylinder.

Disc Brakes

Instead of the traditional expanding brakes that press outward against a circular drum, disc brake systems utilize a cast iron disc with brake pads positioned on either side of it.

Braking effect is achieved in a manner similar to the way you would squeeze a spinning phonograph record between your fingers. The disc (rotor) is a one-piece casting with cooling fins between the two braking surfaces. This enables air to circulate between the braking surfaces making them less sensitive to heat buildup and more resistant to fade. Dirt and water do not affect braking action since contaminants are thrown off by the centrifugal action of the rotor or scraped off by the pads. Also, the equal clamp action of the two brake pads tends to ensure uniform, straightline stops. All disc brakes are self-adjusting.

Drum Brakes

Drum brakes employ two brake shoes mounted on a stationary backing plate. These shoes are positioned inside a circular cast iron drum which rotates with the wheel assembly. The shoes are held in place by springs, this allows them to slide toward the drums (when they are applied) while keeping the linings and drums in alignment. The shoes are actuated by a wheel cylinder which is mounted at the top of the backing plate. When the brakes are applied, hydraulic pressure forces the wheel cylinder's two actuating links outward. Since these links bear directly against the top of the brake shoes, the tops of the shoes are then forced outward against the inner side of the drum. This action forces the bottoms of the two shoes to contact the brake drum by rotating the entire assembly slightly (known as servo action). When pressure within the wheel cylinder is relaxed, return springs pull the shoes back away from the drum.

The drum brakes are designed to self-adjust during application when the car is moving in reverse. This motion causes both shoes to rotate very slightly with the drum, rocking an adjusting lever, thereby causing rotation of the adjusting screw by means of an actuating lever.

Power Brake Boosters

Power brakes operate just as standard brake systems except in the actuation of the master cylinder pistons. A vacuum diaphragm is located on the front of the master cylinder and assists the driver in applying the brakes, reducing both the effort and travel he must put into moving the brake pedal.

The vacuum diaphragm housing is connected to the intake manifold by a vacuum hose. A check valve is placed at the point where the hose enters the diaphragm housing, so that during periods of low manifold vacuum brake assist vacuum will not be lost.

Depressing the brake pedal closes off the vacuum source and allows atmospheric pressure to enter on one side of the diaphragm. This causes the master cylinder pistons to move and apply the brakes. When the brake pedal is released, vacuum is applied to both sides of the diaphragm, the return springs return the diaphragm and master cylinder pistons to the released position. If the vacuum fails, the brake pedal rod will butt against the end of the master cylinder actuating rod and direct mechanical application will occur as the pedal is depressed.

The hydraulic and mechanical problems that apply to conventional brake systems also apply to power brakes and should be checked if the following tests do not reveal the problem.

The hydraulic and mechanical problems that apply to conventional brake systems also apply to power brakes and should be checked if the following tests do not reveal the problem.

Test for a system vacuum leak as described below:

1. Operate the engine at idle with the transaxle in Neutral without touching the brake pedal for at least one minute.

2. Turn off the engine and wait one minute.

3. Test for the presence of assist vacuum by depressing the brake pedal and releasing it several times. Light application will produce less and less pedal travel, if vacuum was present. If there is no vacuum air is leaking into the system.

Test for system operation as follows:

4. Pump the brake pedal (with engine off) until the supply vacuum is entirely gone.

5. Put a light, steady pressure on the pedal.

6. Start the engine and operate it at idle with the transaxle in Neutral. If the system is operating, the brake pedal should fall toward the floor if constant pressure is maintained on the pedal. Power brake systems may be tested for hydraulic leaks just as ordinary systems are tested, except that the engine should be idling with the transaxle in neutral throughout the test.

BRAKE OPERATING SYSTEM

The A-Body cars have a diagonally split hydraulic system. This differs from conventional practice in that the left front and right rear brakes are on one hydraulic circuit, and the right front and left rear are on the other.

A diagonally split system necessitates the use of a special master cylinder design. The A-Body master cylinder incorporates the functions of a standard tandem master cylinder, plus a warning light switch and proportioning valves. Additionally, the master cylinder is designed with a quick take-up feature which provides a large volume of fluid to the brakes at low pressure when the brakes are initially applied. The lower pressure fluid acts to quickly fill the large displacement requirements of the system.

The front disc brakes are single piston sliding caliper units. Fluid pressure acts equally against the piston and the bottom

of the piston bore in the caliper. This forces the piston outward until the pad contacts the caliper to slide over, carrying the other pad into contact with the other side of the rotor. The disc brakes are self-adjusting.

Rear drum brakes are conventional duo-servo units. A dual piston wheel cylinder mounted to the top of the backing plate, actuates both brake shoes. Wheel cylinder force to the shoes is supplemented by the tendency of the shoes to wrap into the drum (servo action). An actuating link, pivot and lever serve to automatically engage the adjuster as the brakes are applied when the car is moving in reverse. Provisions for manual adjustment are also provided. The rear brakes also serve as the parking brakes; linkage is mechanical. Vacuum boost is an option. The booster is a conventional tandem vacuum unit.

Adjustments

DISC BRAKES

The front disc brakes are self-adjusting. No adjustments are necessary or possible.

DRUM BRAKES

The drum brakes are designed to self-adjust when applied with the car moving in reverse. However, they can also be adjusted manually. This manual adjustment should also be performed whenever the linings are replaced.

➡**Never adjust the parking brake cable, until after the regular service brakes have been adjusted.**

Adjustment Through Drum

1. To remove the wheel, loosen all the lug nuts at least one full turn, before raising the car.
2. Raise and support the vehicle.
3. Remove the lug nuts and the wheel.
4. Use a punch to knock out the stamped area on the brake drum. If this is done with the drum installed on the car, the drum must then be removed to clean out all metal pieces. After adjustments are complete, obtain a hole cover from your dealer (part no. 4874119 or the equivalent) to prevent entry of dirt and water into the brakes.
5. Use an adjusting tool especially made for the purpose to turn the brake adjusting screw star wheel.

➡**Keep turning the drum as you are adjusting it or you may overtighten the shoes against the drum.**

6. Expand the shoes until there is a slight drag.
7. Back off the adjusting screw a few notches, if too tight. If the shoes still are dragging lightly, back off the adjusting screw one or two additional notches. If the brakes still drag, the parking brake adjustment is incorrect or the parking brake is applied. Disengage the parking brake or loosen the adjusting nut as necessary.
8. Install the hole cover into the drum.
9. Check the parking brake adjustment.
10. Install the wheel, hand-tighten the lug nuts. Lower the vehicle, then tighten the lug nuts to 100 ft. lbs. (136 Nm).

Adjustment Through Backing Plate

On some models, no marked area or stamped area is present on the drum. In this case, a hole must be drilled in the backing plate:

1. To remove the wheel, loosen all the lug nuts at least one full turn, before raising the car.
2. Raise and support the vehicle.
3. Remove the lug nuts and the wheel.
4. These backing plates have two round flat areas in the lower half through which the parking brake cable is installed. Drill a ½ in. (13mm) hole into the round flat area on the backing plate opposite the parking brake cable. This will allow access to the star wheel.

5. After drilling the hole, remove the drum and remove all metal particles. Install a hole plug (part no. 4874119 or the equivalent) to prevent the entry of water or dirt.
6. Use an adjusting tool especially made for the purpose to turn the brake adjusting screw star wheel.

➡**Keep turning the drum as you are adjusting it or you may overtighten the shoes against the drum.**

7. Expand the shoes until there is a slight drag.
8. Back off the adjusting screw a few notches, if too tight. If the shoes still are dragging lightly, back off the adjusting screw one or two additional notches. If the brakes still drag, the parking brake adjustment is incorrect or the parking brake is applied. Disengage the parking brake or loosen the adjusting nut as necessary.
9. Install the hole cover into the drum.
10. Check the parking brake adjustment.

➡**Another option on these models is simply to remove the drum, adjust the shoe and try the drum on. If the drum fit is still loose, adjust the shoes out slightly more and repeat. Using this method may prove to be difficult, due to a ridge that forms on the outer edge of the drum.**

11. Install the wheel, hand-tighten the lug nuts. Lower the vehicle, then tighten the lug nuts to 100 ft. lbs. (136 Nm).

Brake Light Switch

REMOVAL & INSTALLATION

▶ **See Figure 1**

1. Disconnect the negative battery cable.
2. On some models you may need to remove the sound insulator on the left side.
3. Unplug the wiring connectors from the brake light switch.
4. Unscrew the brake light switch from the tubular retaining clip.

To install:

5. Insert the new switch into the retainer until the switch body seats against the clip.
6. Engage the wiring connectors.
7. Pull the brake pedal rearward against the pedal stop. The switch will be moved in the tubular clip providing proper adjustment.
8. Reinstall the left sound insulator. Connect the negative battery cable and reset the clock and radio.

Brake Pedal

REMOVAL & INSTALLATION

1. Remove the lower steering column panel, if needed.
2. Unfasten the pushrod from the brake pedal.
3. Remove the hinge bolt and bushing from the unit, then remove the pedal.

To install:

4. Attach the brake pedal with the bushing and hinge bolt.

1 Brake pedal assembly
2 Stoplamp switch retainer
3 Stoplamp switch assembly
4 Cruise control switch assembly
5 Cruise control switch retainer
6 Brake pedal bracket

86819001

Fig. 1 The brake light switch is positioned on the pedal bracket

5. Tighten the bolt to 25 ft. lbs. (34 Nm).
6. Install the pushrod to the pedal.
7. Attach the lower steering column panel, if removed.

Master Cylinder

REMOVAL & INSTALLATION

▶ **See Figures 2, 3 and 4**

1. For manual brakes, disconnect the master cylinder pushrod at the brake pedal inside the car. The pushrod is retained to the brake pedal by a clip. There is a washer under the clip, and a spring washer on the other side of the pushrod.
2. Unplug the electrical connector from the master cylinder.
3. Place a number of cloths or a container under the master cylinder to catch the brake fluid. Disconnect the brake tubes from the master cylinder, using a flare nut wrench, if one is available. Tape over or plug the open ends of the tubes.

➡**Brake fluid eats paint. Wipe up any spilled fluid immediately, then flush the area with clean water.**

4. Remove the two nuts attaching the master cylinder to the booster or firewall.
5. Remove the master cylinder.
To install:
6. Attach the master cylinder to the firewall or the booster with the nuts. Tighten to 29 ft. lbs. (40 Nm) for 1982-84 models, 22 ft. lbs. (27 Nm) for 1985-88 models, and 20 ft. lbs. (27 Nm) 1989-95 models.
7. Reconnect the pushrod to the brake pedal.
8. Remove the tape from the lines and connect the lines to the master cylinder. Tighten to 12 ft. lbs. (17 Nm) for 1982-84 models, 18 ft. lbs. (24 Nm) for 1985-88 models, 24 ft. lbs. (32 Nm) for 1989-95 models. Connect the electrical lead.
9. Fill the master cylinder to the proper level with clean fresh brake fluid.
10. Bleed the brakes.
11. Recheck the fluid level and add fluid if needed.

OVERHAUL

▶ **See Figures 5, 6, 7 and 8**

This is a tedious, time consuming job. You can save yourself a lot of trouble by buying a rebuilt master cylinder from your dealer or parts supply house. The small difference in price between a rebuilding kit and a rebuilt part usually makes it more economical, in terms of time and work, to buy the rebuilt part.

1. Remove the master cylinder from the vehicle.
2. Remove the reservoir cover and drain the fluid, inspect the cap for any cuts, cracks, nicks or deterioration.
3. Remove the pushrod and the rubber boot on non-power models.
4. Unbolt the proportioners and the failure warning switch from the side of the master cylinder body. Discard the O-rings found under the proportioners. Use new ones on installation. There may or may not be an O-ring under the original equipment failure warning switch. If there is, discard it. In either case, use a new O-ring upon assembly.
5. Clamp the master cylinder body in a vise, taking care not to crush it. Remove the snapring with a pair of snapring pliers or suitable tool.
6. The primary and secondary pistons can be removed by applying compressed air into one of the outlets at the end of the cylinder and plugging the other three outlets. The primary piston must be replaced as an assembly if the seals are bad. The secondary piston seals are replaceable. Install these new seals with the lips facing outwards.
7. Inspect the cylinder bore for scoring or corrosion. If any corrosion is evident, the master cylinder body must be replaced. Do not attempt to polish the bore with crocus cloth, sandpaper or anything else. The body is aluminum, polishing the bore won't work.
8. To remove the failure warning switch piston assembly, unfasten the allen head plug from the end of the bore and withdraw the assembly with a pair of needlenose pliers. The switch piston assembly seals are replaceable.
9. The reservoir can be removed from the master cylinder if necessary. Clamp the body in a vise by its mounting flange. Use a prytool to remove the reservoir. When the reservoir is removed, remove the reservoir grommets and discard them. The quick take-up valves under the grommets are accessible after the retaining snaprings are removed. Use snapring pliers, no other tool will work without damaging the component.
To assemble:
10. Clean all parts in denatured alcohol and allow to air dry. Do not use anything else to clean them, and do not wipe them dry with a rag, (which will leave bits of lint behind). Inspect all parts for corrosion or wear. Generally, it is best to replace all rubber parts whenever the master cylinder is disassembled and replace any metal part which shows any sign of wear or corrosion.
11. Lubricate all parts with clean brake fluid before assembly.
12. Install the quick take-up valves into the master cylinder body and secure with the snaprings. Make sure the snaprings are properly seated in their grooves. Lubricate the new reservoir grommets with clean brake fluid and press them into the master cylinder.

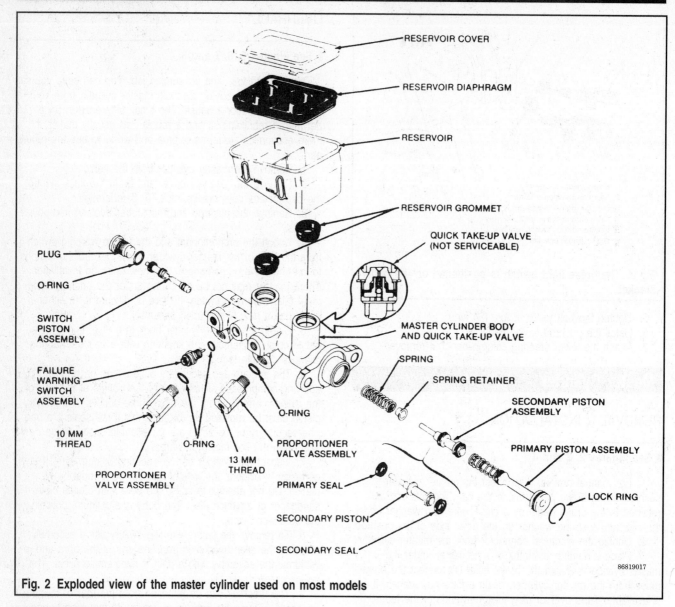

Fig. 2 Exploded view of the master cylinder used on most models

13. Install the reservoir into the grommets by placing the reservoir on its lid and pressing the master cylinder body down onto it with a rocking motion.

14. Lubricate the switch piston assembly with clean brake fluid. Install new O-rings and retainers on the piston. Install the piston assembly into the master cylinder and secure with the plug, using a new O-ring on the plug. Tighten to 40-140 inch lbs. (5-16 Nm).

15. Assemble the new secondary piston seals onto the piston. Lubricate the parts with clean brake fluid, then install the spring, spring retainer and secondary piston into the cylinder. Install the primary piston, depress and install the lockring.

16. Install new O-rings on the proportioners and the failure warning switch. Install the proportioners and tighten to 18-30 ft. lbs. (25-40 Nm). Install the failure warning switch, then tighten to 15-50 inch lbs. (2-6 Nm).

17. Clamp the master cylinder body upright into a vise by one of the mounting flanges. Fill the reservoir with fresh brake fluid. Pump the piston with a dowel until fluid squirts from the outlet ports. Continue pumping until the expelled fluid is free of air bubbles.

18. Install the master cylinder, then tighten the nuts to 29 ft. lbs. (40 Nm) for 1982-84 models or 20-22 ft. lbs. (28-30 Nm) for 1985-95 models. Bleed the brake system, then check the system for proper operation. Do not move the car until a "hard" brake pedal is obtained and the brake system has been thoroughly checked for soundness.

Power Brake Booster

REMOVAL & INSTALLATION

▶ See Figures 9 and 10

1. Remove the master cylinder from the booster. It is not necessary to disconnect the lines from the master cylinder. Just move the cylinder aside, make sure not to bend or distort any of the brake pipes.

2. Disconnect the vacuum booster pushrod from the brake pedal inside the car. It is retained by a bolt. A spring washer

1 Fluid level sensor
2 Proportioner valve cap assembly
3 O-ring
4 Spring
5 Proportioner valve piston
6 Proportioner valve seal
7 Reservoir cap
8 Diaphragm
9 Spring pin
10 Reservoir assembly
11 O-ring
12 O-ring
13 Retainer
14 Primary piston assembly
15 Secondary seal
16 Spring retainer
17 Primary seal
18 Secondary piston
19 Spring
20 Cylinder body

86819016

Fig. 3 Some later models use a slightly different master cylinder

86819003

Fig. 4 Disconnect the brake tubes from the master cylinder with a flare nut wrench

86819010

Fig. 5 A seal pick can be used to remove the snapring from the master cylinder

Fig. 6 When the master cylinder is completely disassembled, place the components on a clean workspace

Fig. 7 The seals on the secondary piston are replacable

Fig. 8 Always install the components by hand before tightening them with a wrench

1 Master cylinder
2 Vacuum booster assembly
3 Vacuum booster assembly nut
4 Master cylinder nut

Fig. 9 The brake booster is positioned behind the master cylinder

lies under the bolt head, and a flat washer goes on the other side of the pushrod eye, next to the pedal arm.

3. Remove the vacuum hose connected from the booster to the check valve.

4. Remove the four attaching nuts from inside the car. Remove the booster.

To install:

5. Install the booster on the firewall.

6. Connect the pushrod to the brake pedal. You may need to tilt the entire booster slightly to work the booster pushrod onto the pedal clevis pin without forcing unneeded side pressure on the pushrod.

7. Tighten the mounting nuts for the brake booster to 15-20 ft. lbs. (21-30 Nm).

8. Install the check valve and hose.

9. Install the master cylinder, then tighten the nuts to 29 ft. lbs. (40 Nm) for 1982-84 models or 20-22 ft. lbs. (28-30 Nm) for 1985-95 models. Bleed the brake system, then check the system for proper operation. Do not move the car until a "hard" brake pedal is obtained and the brake system has been thoroughly checked for soundness.

1 Booster
2 Pushrod
3 Vacuum check valve
4 Grommet

Fig. 10 Exploded view of the brake booster components

OVERHAUL

This job can be difficult, and requires a number of special tools which are expensive, (especially if they're to be used only once). Generally, it's better to leave this job to your dealer, or buy a rebuilt vacuum booster and install it yourself.

Diesel Engine Vacuum Pump

REMOVAL & INSTALLATION

Electrical Type
▶ See Figure 11

The electrical vacuum pump is mounted under the battery tray on the left hand side of the vehicle. The inlet hose is connected to the booster check valve and the booster outlet hose is connected to the intake manifold.

1. Disconnect the negative battery cable.
2. Raise and support the vehicle, then remove the splash shield on the left side.
3. Disconnect the hoses at the vacuum pump.
4. Unplug the electrical connection at the pump.
5. Remove the nuts which secure the pump assembly to the mounting bracket, then remove the pump.

To install:
6. Secure the pump assembly to the mounting bracket, tighten to 6 ft. lbs. (8 Nm).
7. Engage the electrical connection to the pump, then the hoses.
8. Install the left side splash shield. Lower the vehicle.
9. Connect the negative battery cable, reset the radio and clock.

Mechanical Type
▶ See Figure 12

1. Disconnect the negative battery cable.

2. Loosen the air pump drive belt.
3. Remove the three vacuum pump attaching bolts.
4. Remove the pump from the engine. With the pump removed, unfasten the pulley attaching bolts.
5. Remove the hub from the pump shaft by threading a ⅜ x ½ in. (10 x 13mm) bolt into the end if the shaft, then using a puller remove the hub.

To install:
6. Install the hub on the new pump by using tool J-25033 or an equivalent installer. It may be necessary to install a washer between the tool and the hub.
7. Install the hub and shaft so that the end if the shaft extends 0.15-0.17 in. (3.93-4.43mm) beyond the hub/pulley mating surfaces.
8. Attach the pump to the mounting bracket and tighten to 21 ft. lbs. (28 Nm).
9. Install the belt, then check the tension of the belt and the pulley alignment.

Fig. 12 Mechanical vacuum pump used on some diesel models

Fig. 11 Electric vacuum pump used on some diesel models

Proportioning Valves

REMOVAL & INSTALLATION

External Type

The external valves are used on 1982-86 models.
1. Disconnect and cap the brake line from the proportioning valve(s).
2. Using a suitable wrench remove the proportioning valve(s) from the master cylinder.

➡**If both proportioning valves are removed at the same time, make sure the proportioning valves are installed in the correct places. The threads on the two valves differ slightly and installation in the wrong port can damage the master cylinder or proportioning valves. If the valves are replaced both valves must be the same color code.**

3. Remove the old O-rings and discard.
To Install:
4. Install new O-rings on the proportioning valve(s).
5. Install the proportioning valve(s) and tighten to 24 ft. lbs. (32 Nm).
6. Connect the brake line(s) to the proportioning valve(s) and tighten the fittings to 24 ft. lbs. (32 Nm).
7. Bleed the brake system.

Internal Type

The internal proportioning valves are used on 1987-95 models.
1. Remove the master cylinder from the vehicle.
2. Remove the brake master cylinder reservoir.
3. Remove the proportioning valve cap assemblies.
4. Remove the O-rings from the caps and discard of them.
5. Remove the springs, then use needle nose pliers to remove the proportioning valve pistons. If you are not careful you could damage the piston stems.
6. Remove the piston seals and pistons from the cylinder.
To install:
7. Inspect the pistons for any corrosion or deformation, replace them if needed.
8. Clean all the parts in denatured alcohol, then dry with compressed air.
9. Lubricate the new O-rings, valve seals, stem, and valve pistons with silicone grease.
10. Install the new seals on the valve pistons with the seal lips facing upward toward the cap assembly.
11. Install the pistons and seals in the master cylinder body. Insert new O-rings in the grooves of the proportioning valve cap assemblies. Install the caps to the cylinder body.
12. Tighten the caps to 20 ft. lbs. (27 Nm). Install the reservoir assembly.
13. Bleed the brake system, then check the system for proper operation. Do not move the car until a hard brake pedal is obtained.
14. Close the hood.

Fluid Level Sensor

REMOVAL & INSTALLATION

▶ **See Figures 13 and 14**

1. Unplug the electrical connection on the fluid level sensor located on the master cylinder.
2. Remove the level sensor by using a pair of needle nose pliers to compress the locking tabs on the inboard side of the master cylinder.
To install:
3. Insert the fluid level sensor into position until the locking tabs snap into place.
4. Install the electrical connection to the sensor.

1. FLUID LEVEL SENSOR

86819026

Fig. 13 The fluid level sensor is located on the side of the master cylinder housing

86819025

Fig. 14 Use a pair of needle nose pliers to compress the switches locking tabs

Brake Hoses

Brake hoses are rubber covered flex hoses designed to transmit brake pressure from the metal tubes running along the frame to the calipers in front and wheel cylinders in the rear. The calipers and wheel cylinders are unsprung (ride along with the wheels) and the metal brake lines coming from the master cylinder are suspended by the vehicle's springs, along with the frame and body. The flex hoses permit the hydraulic force of the brake fluid to be transmitted to the wheels even though they are moving up and down in relation to the frame. The flexing can cause the hoses to wear, especially if the surface of a hose should rub against the frame or a suspension component. Inspect the hoses frequently and replace them if the rubber cover has cracked or deteriorated, or if there is any sign of leakage.

REMOVAL & INSTALLATION

▶ See Figure 15

1. Raise and support the vehicle.
2. Remove the through-bolt that fastens the hose to the caliper. Remove the washers, noting that there is one on either side of the fitting at the caliper end of the hose. Disconnect the hose.
3. If there is a clip retaining the connection at the frame, remove it. Now, unscrew the flare fitting located on the pipe running along the frame, using a backup wrench on the flats of the fitting at the end of the brake hose. Check for any other mounting brackets that would need removal. Remove the brake line.

To install:

4. Replace the old hose with a new one, using new washers, then tighten the connection at the caliper.
5. Install any retaining clips or mounting brackets back into position.
6. Lower the vehicle, then bleed the brake system.

Steel Lines

▶ See Figure 16

Loosen the steel brake line fittings using flare nut wrenches only. If the steel line starts to twist, stop and lubricate with penetrating oil. Move the wrench back and forth until the fitting turns freely. A backup wrench should be used when loosening steel-to-rubber brake hoses. Steel brake lines can be repaired by installing a double flare after the damaged portion has been removed. The tools needed for this procedure may be purchased at a local hardware or auto parts store. Steel brake lines MUST be double flared.

BRAKE PIPE FLAIRING

▶ See Figure 17

Flaring steel lines is a skill which needs to be practiced before it should be done on a line which is to be used on a vehicle. A special flaring kit with double flaring adapters is required. It is essential that the flare is formed evenly to prevent any leaks when the brake system is under pressure. Only steel lines, not copper lines, should be used. With the supply of parts available today, a pre-flared steel brake line should be available to fit your needs. Due to the high pressures in the brake system and the serious injuries that could occur if the flare should fail, it is strongly advised that pre-flared lines should be installed when repairing the braking system. If a line were to leak brake fluid due to a defective flare, and the leak were to go undetected, brake failure would result.

✳✳WARNING

A double flaring tool must be used, as single flaring tools cannot produce a flare strong enough to hold the necessary pressure.

1. Obtain the recommended tubing and the correct size steel fitting nuts. The outside diameter of the tubing is used to determine the size.
2. Cut the tubing to length. The correct length is determined by the measurement of the old pipe. You can use a piece of string to measure. Add 1/8 in. (3mm) for each flared end.
3. Make sure the fittings are installed before starting to flare. Chamfer the inside and outside diameter of the pipe with a deburring tool.
4. Remove all traces of lubricant from the pipe and flaring tool. Clamp the flaring tool body in a vise carefully.
5. Select the correct size collet, then the forming mandrel for the pipe size use, insert the proper forming mandrel into the tool body. While holding the mandrel in place with your finger, thread in the forcing screw until it makes contact, then begins to move the forming mandrel. When contact is made, turn the forcing screw back one complete turn.
6. Slide the clamping nut over the brake pipe into the correct collet. Leave approximately 0.75 in. (19mm) of tubing extending out the collet. Insert the assembly into the tool body The brake pipe end must make contact to the face of the forming mandrel.
7. Tighten the clamping nut into the tool body very tight or the pipe may push out. Wrench-tighten the forcing screw in until it bottoms. Do not overtighten the forcing screw or the flare may become oversized.
8. Next back the clamping nut out of the tool body and disassemble the clamping nut and collet assembly.
9. Bend the pipe to match the old pipe. Allow a clearance of at least 0.75 in. (19mm) from all moving parts and vibrations.

Bleeding

▶ See Figure 18

The purpose of bleeding the brakes is to expel air trapped in the hydraulic system. The system must be bled whenever the pedal feels spongy, indicating that compressible air has entered the system. It must also be bled whenever the system

1 Engine compartment outer side
2 Front brake hose assembly
3 Front brake hose clip bolt/screw
4 Front brake hose retainer
5 Front caliper assembly
6 Front brake hose fitting gasket
7 Front brake hose bolt/screw
8 Front brake hose assembly
9 Front brake hose bracket
10 Wheel speed sensor harness assembly

86819028

Fig. 15 Common front brake hose routing found on models covered in this manual

86819030

Fig. 16 Loosen the brake line fittings with a flare nut wrench

A. Single flare
B. Double flare

86819037

Fig. 17 Brake lines must be steel with double flared ends

has been opened or repaired. You will need an assistant for this procedure.

✳✳CAUTION

Never reuse brake fluid which has been bled from the brake system. Brake fluid should be changed every few years. It deteriotates due to moisture being absorbed which lowers the boiling point.

➡Old brake fluid is often the cause of spongy brakes returning a week or so after bleeding the system. If all parts are O.K., change the fluid by repeated bleeding.

1. Raise and support the vehicle securely. Your assistant should remain in the vehicle to apply the brake pedal when needed.

2. The sequence for bleeding is right rear, left front, left rear and right front. If the car has power brakes, bleed the vacuum by applying the brakes several times. Do not run the engine while bleeding the brakes.

3. Clean all the bleeder screws. You may want to give each one a shot of penetrating solvent to loosen it up. Seizure is a common problem with bleeder screws. They can break off, usually requiring replacement of the part to which they are attached.

4. Fill the master cylinder with DOT 3 brake fluid.

➡Brake fluid absorbs moisture from the air. Don't leave the master cylinder or the fluid container uncovered any longer than necessary. Be careful handling the fluid, it eats paint.

Check the level of the fluid often when bleeding, and refill the reservoirs as necessary. Don't let them run dry, or you will have to repeat the process.

5. Attach a length of clear vinyl tubing to the bleeder screw on the wheel cylinder. Insert the other end of the tube into a clear, clean jar half filled with brake fluid.

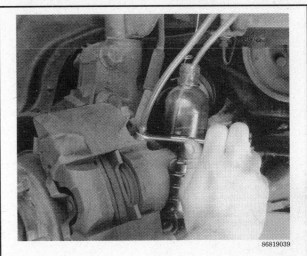

Fig. 18 An assitant can be helpful in bleeding the brake system

6. Have your assistant slowly depress the brake pedal. As this is done, open the bleeder screw $\frac{1}{3}$-$\frac{1}{2}$ of a turn and allow the fluid to run through the tube. Close the bleeder screw before the pedal reaches the end of its travel. Have your assistant slowly release the pedal. Repeat this process until no air bubbles appear in the expelled fluid.

7. Repeat the procedure on the other brakes, checking the level of fluid in the master cylinder reservoir often.

After you're done, there should be no sponginess in the brake pedal. If there is, either there is still air in the line, (in which case the process should be repeated) or there is a leak somewhere, (which of course must be corrected before the car is moved).

8. Lower the vehicle.

FRONT DISC BRAKES

✳✳CAUTION

Brake shoes may contain asbestos, which has been determined to be a cancer causing agent. Never clean the brake surfaces with compressed air! Avoid inhaling any dust from any brake surface! When cleaning brake surfaces, use a commercially available brake cleaning fluid.

Brake Pads

REMOVAL & INSTALLATION

Light Duty

▶ See Figures 19, 20, 21 and 22

1. Siphon $\frac{2}{3}$ of the brake fluid out of the master cylinder reservoir.

2. To remove the wheels, loosen all the lug nuts at least one full turn, before raising the car.

3. Raise and safely support the vehicle.

4. Remove the tire and wheel assembly.

5. Install two wheel nuts to secure the rotor in place.

6. Unstake the outboard pads using a hammer and chisel.

7. Remove the caliper mounting bolts.

8. Remove the caliper from the steering knuckle and support on a wire. DO NOT disconnect the brake hose or allow the brake hose to support the weight of the caliper.

9. Remove the outboard pad from the caliper.

10. Pull the top of the inboard pad out from the caliper to disengage the spring clip securing the inboard pad and remove the pad.

11. Using a suitable C-clamp compress the caliper piston fully into the caliper bore.

To Install:

12. Install a new spring clip on the back of the inboard pad. Make sure that the top tab in engaged in the pad before hooking the lower end.

1 Sleeve
2 Bushing
3 Outboard shoe & lining
4 Inboard shoe & lining
5 Shoe retainer spring
6 Caliper housing
7 Outboard shoe tab

86819031

Fig. 19 Brake pad components used on the light duty brake system

1 Inboard shoe & lining
2 Shoe retainer spring
3 Caliper housing

86819032

Fig. 21 Make sure that the top tab in engaged in the pad before hooking the lower end

1 Inboard shoe & lining
2 Shoe retainer spring
3 Retention lug

86819034

Fig. 20 A new spring clip should be used

1 Caliper body
2 Outboard shoe tab

86819033

Fig. 22 Stake the pad ears down until they are flat against the caliper. The pad ears must hold the pad firmly in place

13. Install the inboard pad with a new spring clip into the caliper piston. This can be done by locking the bottom edge of the spring clip into the piston and pushing the top of the pad back.

14. Install the outboard pad into the caliper.

15. Install the caliper on the steering knuckle and tighten the mounting bolts to 28 ft. lbs. (38 Nm) for 1982-84 models and 38 ft. lbs. (51 Nm) for 1985-95 models.

16. Pump up the brake pedal until the pads seat against the rotor. Using a suitable tool, secure the brake pedal in the down position keeping the front wheels locked.

17. Stake the pad ears down until they are flat against the caliper. The pad ears must secure the pad firmly in place.

18. Remove the two wheel nuts.

19. Install the tire and wheel assembly and tighten the lug nuts by hand.

20. Lower the vehicle. Then tighten the lug nuts to 100 ft. lbs. (136 Nm).

21. Check and top off the master cylinder.

Heavy Duty

▶ See Figures 23, 24, 25, 26 and 27

1. Siphon ⅔ of the brake fluid out of the master cylinder reservoir.

2. To remove the wheel, loosen all the lug nuts at least one full turn, before raising the car.

3. Raise and safely support the vehicle.

4. Remove the tire and wheel assembly.

5. Install two wheel nuts to secure the rotor in place.

6. Remove the caliper mounting bolts.

7. Remove the caliper from the steering knuckle and support on a wire. DO NOT disconnect the brake hose from the caliper or allow the caliper to hang by the brake hose unsupported.

8. Pull the top of the inboard pad out from the caliper to disengage the spring clip securing the inboard pad. Remove the pad.

9. Remove the outboard pad by pushing the pad inward to unseat the pad from the caliper. Once the pad alignment dow-

Fig. 23 Siphon 2/3 of the brake fluid out of the master cylinder reservoir

Fig. 24 A special socket is used to remove the caliper mounting bolts

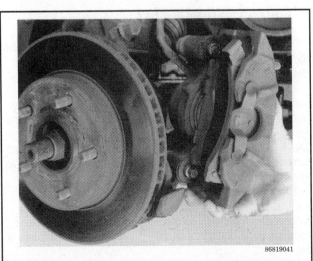

Fig. 25 Do not allow the caliper to hang freely by the brake hose. Support the caliper with a length of wire

Fig. 26 Pull the top of the inboard pad out from the caliper to disengage the spring clip securing the inboard pad

els are clear of the caliper body push the pad out of the caliper.

10. Using a suitable C-clamp compress the caliper piston fully into the caliper bore.

To Install:

11. Install the inboard pad with a new spring clip into the caliper piston. This can be done by locking the bottom edge of the spring clip into the piston and push the top of the pad back.

12. Install the outboard pad into the caliper making sure the dowels in the brake pad seat in the holes in the caliper.

13. Install the caliper on the steering knuckle and tighten the mounting bolts to 28 ft. lbs. (38 Nm) for 1982-84 models and 38 ft. lbs. (51 Nm) for 1985-95 models.

14. Remove the two wheel nuts.

15. Install the tire and wheel assembly and tighten the lug nuts by hand.

16. Lower the vehicle. Tighten the lug nuts to 100 ft. lbs (136 Nm).

17. Pump the brake pedal several times to seat the pads against the rotor.

Fig. 27 Now remove the outboard pad from the caliper

18. Check and top off the master cylinder.

INSPECTION

▶ **See Figure 28**

The pad thickness should be inspected every time that the tires are removed for rotation. The outer pad can be checked by looking in at each end, which is the point at which the highest rate of wear occurs. The inner pad can be checked by looking down through the inspection hole in the top of the caliper. If the thickness of the pad is worn to within 0.030 in. (0.76mm) of the rivet at either end of the pad, all the pads should be replaced. This is the factory recommended measurement, your state's automobile inspection laws may not agree with this.

➡ **Always replace all pads on both front wheels at the same time. Failure to do so will result in uneven braking action and premature wear.**

Brake Caliper

REMOVAL & INSTALLATION

▶ **See Figures 29, 30 and 31**

1. Siphon ⅔ of the brake fluid out of the master cylinder reservoir.
2. Release the parking brake.
3. Loosen the lug nuts, then raise and safely support the vehicle.
4. Remove the tire and wheel assembly.
5. Install two wheel nuts to secure the rotor in place.
6. Using a large C-clamp, position the clamp on the caliper housing and against the back of the outboard pad and lining. Tighten the clamp slowly to press the piston into the caliper bore.

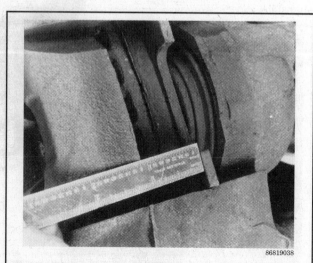

86819038

Fig. 28 The pad thickness should be inspected every time that the tires are removed for rotation

7. Remove the bolt attaching the hose fitting, only if the caliper is to be removed for overhaul. If only the pads are to be replaced, there is no need to disconnect the hose fitting.
8. Plug the opening in the caliper and the pipe to prevent fluid from seeping out and contamination.
9. Remove the allen head caliper mounting bolts. Inspect them for corrosion and replace them if necessary.
   To install:
10. Coat the bushings with silicone or grease.
11. Install the caliper and brake pads over the rotor, in the mounting bracket.
12. Install the mounting bolt and sleeve assembly, then tighten the mounting bolt to 28 ft. lbs. (38 Nm) for 1982-84 models and 38 ft. lbs. (51 Nm) for 1985-95 models.
13. Measure the clearance between the caliper and the bracket stops. If needed, remove the caliper and file down the ends of the bracket stops to provide clearance. The caliper may appear to be touching the lower abutment and still not be interfering. The caliper should slide freely on the mounting bolt and sleeve assemblies.
14. Install the brake hose to the caliper. The brake hose fitting should be tightened to 33 ft. lbs. (45 Nm). Always use new fasteners.
15. Install the wheel and tire, hand-tighten the lug nuts. Lower the vehicle, then tighten the lug nuts to 100 ft. lbs. (136 Nm).
16. Top off the brake fluid.

OVERHAUL

1. Remove the calipers.
2. Place some cloths or a slat of wood in front of the piston. Remove the piston by applying compressed air to the fluid inlet fitting. Use just enough air pressure to ease the piston from the bore.

✳✳CAUTION

Do not try to catch the piston with your fingers, which can result in serious injury.

3. Remove the piston dust boot.
4. Remove the bleeder screw and cap from the caliper.
5. Inspect the piston for scoring, nicks, corrosion, wear, and damaged or worn chrome plating. Replace the piston if any defects are found.
6. Remove the piston seal from the caliper bore groove using a scoul pick. Do not use a screwdriver, which will damage the bore. Inspect the caliper bore for nicks, corrosion and so on. Very light wear can be cleaned up with crocus cloth. Use finger pressure to rub the crocus cloth around the circumference of the bore, do not slide it in and out. More extensive wear or corrosion warrants replacement of the part.
   To assemble:
7. Clean any parts which are to be reused in denatured alcohol. Dry them with compressed or allow to air dry. Don't wipe the parts dry with a cloth, which will leave behind bits of lint.
8. Install the bleeder screw, tightening it to 110-120 inch lbs. (13-14 Nm)

* ON SOME MODELS THE RETAINER SPRING IS
ALREADY STAKED TO THE INBOARD SHOE.

1. Mounting bolt and
   sleeve assembly
2. Bushing
3. Bushing
4. Outboard shoe and
   lining
5. Inboard shoe and
   lining
6. Wear sensor
7. Shoe retainer spring
8. Boot
9. Piston

10. Piston seal
11. Bleeder valve
12. Caliper housing
13. Boot

86819053

Fig. 29 Exploded view of caliper model 3257

1. Bolt boot
2. Mounting bolt and
   sleeve assembly
3. Bushing
4. Bushing
5. Outboard shoe and
   lining

6. Wear sensor
7. Inboard shoe and
   lining
8. Boot
9. Piston
10. Piston seal
11. Bleeder valve
12. Caliper housing

86819054

Fig. 30 Exploded view of caliper model 3264, notice the bleeder screw is in a different location that in model 3257

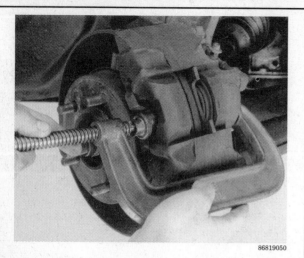

Fig. 31 A large C-clamp can be used to seat the piston in the caliper

9. Lubricate a new seal, with clean brake fluid. Install the seal in its groove, making sure it is fully seated and not twisted.

10. Install the new dust boot on the piston. Lubricate the bore of the caliper with clean brake fluid and insert the piston into its bore. Position the boot in the caliper housing and seat it with a seal driver of the appropriate size, or tool No. J-29077.

11. Install the caliper bushings. Lubricate the beveled end that is flush with the caliper, with silicone.

12. Install the pads, the caliper and bleed the brakes.

13. Install the wheel and tire assembly. Hand-tighten the lug nuts.

14. Lower the vehicle, then tighten the lug nuts to 100 ft. lbs. (136 Nm).

Brake Disc (Rotor)

REMOVAL & INSTALLATION

▶ See Figures 32 and 33

1. Remove the wheel cover.
2. To remove the wheel, loosen all the lug nuts at least one full turn, before raising the car.
3. Raise and support the car, then remove the front wheel.

To assemble:
4. Remove the allen head caliper mounting bolts and remove the brake caliper.
5. Remove the caliper from the knuckle and suspend from a length of wire. Do not allow the caliper to hang from the brake hose.
6. Pull the rotor from the knuckle.

To install:
7. Place the rotor onto the steering knuckle.
8. Place the caliper assembly into position on the rotor, then tighten the mounting bolt to 28 ft. lbs. (38 Nm) for 1982-84 models and 38 ft. lbs. (51 Nm) for 1985-95 models.
9. Install the tire and wheel, then tighten the lug nuts by hand.

10. Lower the car and tighten the lug nuts to 100 ft. lbs. (136 Nm).

11. Pump the brake pedal several times to seat the pads against the rotor.

INSPECTION

1. Check the rotor surface for wear or scoring. Deep scoring, grooves or rust pitting can be removed by refacing. This can be performed by your local machine shop or garage. Minimum thickness is stamped on the rotor, or see the brake specifications chart in this section. If the rotor is thinner than specifications after refinishing, it must be replaced.

2. Check the rotor parallelism with a micrometer. It must vary less than 0.0005 in. (0.0127mm) measured at four or more points around the circumference. Make all measurements at the same distance in from the edge of the rotor. Refinish the rotor if it fails to meet this specification.

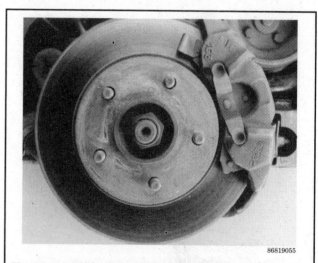

Fig. 32 It is necessary to remove the caliper in order to remove the rotor

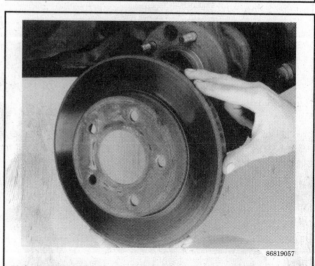

Fig. 33 With the caliper out of the way, the rotor can be removed from the hub

3. Measure the disc runout with a dial indicator. If runout exceeds 0.002 in. (0.051mm) for 1982-85 models, 0.004 in. (0.10mm) for 1985-87 models, and 0.002 in. (0.051mm) for 1988-95 models and the wheel bearings are OK (if runout is being measured with the disc on the car), the rotor must be refaced or replaced as necessary.

REAR DRUM BRAKES

✳✳CAUTION

Brake shoes may contain asbestos, which has been determined to be a cancer causing agent. Never clean the brake surfaces with compressed air! Avoid inhaling any dust from any brake surface! When cleaning brake surfaces, use a commercially available brake cleaning fluid.

Brake Drums

REMOVAL & INSTALLATION

▶ See Figures 34 and 35

1. Loosen the wheel lug nuts. Raise and support the car. Remove the wheel.
2. Clean the brake drum surface with a commercially available cleaning product, to remove the brake dust.
3. Remove the drum. If it cannot be slipped off easily, check to see that the parking brake is fully released. If so, the brake shoes are probably locked against the drum. If the drum will still not come off, spray some penetrating lubricant where the drum meets the hub. If necessary, tap gently using a rubber mallet on the outer rim of the drum and/or around the inner drum diameter by the hub.

To Install:
4. After removing the brake drum, wipe out the accumulated dust with a cloth saturated with brake cleaning fluid.

✳✳WARNING

Do not blow the brake dust out of the drums with compressed air or lung-power. Brake linings may contain asbestos, a known cancer causing substance. Dispose of the cloth used to clean the parts after use.

5. Inspect the drums for cracks, deep grooves, roughness, scoring, or out-of-roundness. Replace any drum which is cracked.
6. Install the drum. Install the wheel and hand-tighten the lug nuts.
7. Lower the vehicle, then tighten the lug nuts to 100 ft. lbs. (140 Nm).

INSPECTION

1. After removing the brake drum, wipe out the accumulated dust with a cloth saturated with brake cleaning fluid.

✳✳WARNING

Do not blow the brake dust out of the drums with compressed air or lung-power. Brake linings may contain asbestos, a known cancer causing substance. Dispose of the cloth used to clean the parts after use.

2. Inspect the drums for cracks, deep grooves, roughness, scoring, or out-of-roundness. Replace any drum which is cracked.

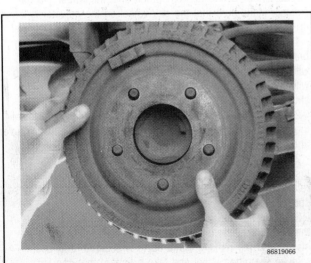

86819066

Fig. 34 Gently rock the drum side-to-side while pulling on it

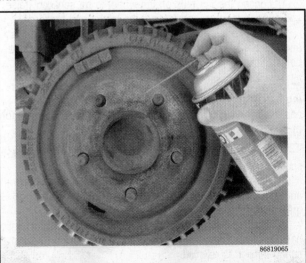

86819065

Fig. 35 If the drum will not come off, spray some penetrating lubricant where the drum meets the hub

3. Smooth any slight scores by polishing the friction surface with fine emery cloth. Heavy or extensive scoring will cause excessive lining wear and should be removed from the drum through resurfacing. This can be performed by your local machine shop or garage. The maximum finished diameter of the drums is 7.899 in. (200.6mm) for 1982-83 models, 8.920 in. (226.56mm) for 1984-85 models, 8.877 in. (25.47mm) for 1986-87 models, 8.880 in. (225.55mm) for 1988-95 models.

Brake Shoes

INSPECTION

After removing the brake drum, inspect the brake shoes. If the lining is worn down to within 0.030 in. (0.8mm) of a rivet, the shoes must be replaced.

➡**This figure may disagree with your state's automobile inspection laws. If the brake lining is soaked with brake fluid or grease, it must be replaced. If this is the case, the brake drum should be sanded with crocus cloth to remove all traces of brake fluid, and the wheel cylinders should be overhauled or replaced.**

If the lining is chipped, cracked or otherwise damaged, it must be replaced with a new lining.

➡**Always replace the brake linings in sets of two on both ends of the axle. Never replace just one shoe or both shoes on only one side.**

Check the condition of the shoes, retracting springs and hold-down springs for signs of overheating. If the shoes or springs have a slight blue color, this indicates overheating. Replacement of the shoes and springs is recommended.

REMOVAL & INSTALLATION

▶ **See Figures 36, 37, 38, 39, 40, 41, 42, 43, 44, 45 and 46**

1. Loosen the lug nuts on the wheel to be serviced, raise and support the car, and remove the wheel and brake drum.
2. Remove the hub and bearing assembly retaining bolts and remove the assembly from the axle. Reinstall two of the bolts to secure the backing plate.

➡**It is not necessary to remove the hub and wheel bearing assembly from the axle, but it does make the job easier. If you can work with the hub and bearing assembly in place, skip the step.**

3. Remove the return springs from the shoes. There are special brake spring pliers available for this job.
4. Remove the hold-down springs by pressing them down and turning 90 degrees. There are special tools available to grab and turn these parts, but pliers work fairly well.
5. Remove the shoe hold-down pins from behind the brake backing plate. They will simply slide out once the hold-down spring tension is relieved.
6. Lift up the actuator lever for the self-adjusting mechanism and remove the actuating link. Remove the actuator lever, pivot and the pivot return spring.

7. Spread the shoes apart to clear the wheel cylinder pistons, then remove the parking brake strut and spring.
8. If the hub and bearing assembly is still in place, spread the shoes far enough apart to clear it.
9. Remove the shoes, with the adjusting screw and spring. Disconnect the parking brake cable from the lever.
10. With the shoes removed, note the position of the adjusting spring, then remove the spring and screw.
11. Remove the C-clip from the parking brake lever and the lever from the secondary shoe.
    Inspection:
12. Use a damp cloth to remove all dirt and dust from the backing plate and brake parts.
13. Check the wheel cylinder by carefully pulling the lower edges of the wheel cylinder boots away from the cylinders. The inside of the cylinder may be moist with fluid. If excessive leakage exists, a wheel cylinder overhaul or replacement is in order. Do not delay, because brake failure could result.

➡**A small amount of fluid will be present to act as a lubricant for the wheel cylinder pistons. Fluid spilling from the boot, indicates excessive leakage and the necessity for cylinder overhaul or replacement.**

14. Use fine emery cloth to clean all rust and dirt from the shoe contact surfaces on the backing plate.
    To install:
15. Lubricate the fulcrum end of the parking brake lever with brake grease. Install the lever on the secondary shoe and secure with the C-clip.
16. Install the adjusting screw and spring on the shoes, connecting them together. The coils of the spring must not interfere with the star wheel on the adjuster. The left and right hand springs are not interchangeable. Do not mix them up.
17. Lubricate the shoe contact surfaces on the backing plate with the brake grease. Be certain that none of it actually gets on the linings or drums. Apply the same grease to the point where the parking brake cable contacts the plate. Use the grease sparingly.
18. Spread the shoe assemblies apart and connect the parking brake cable. Install the shoes on the backing plate, engaging the shoes at the top temporarily with the wheel cylinder pistons. Make sure that the star wheel on the adjuster is lined up with the adjusting hole in the backing plate, if back there.
19. Spread the shoes apart slightly and install the parking brake strut and spring. Make sure that the end of the strut without the spring engages the parking brake lever. The end with the spring engages the primary shoe (the one with the shorter lining).
20. Install the actuator pivot, lever and return spring. Install the actuating link in the shoe retainer. Lift up the actuator lever and hook the link into the lever.
21. Insert the hold-down pins through the back of the plate. Install the lever pivots and hold-down springs. Install the shoe return springs, careful not to stretch or otherwise distort these springs.
22. Take a look at everything. Make sure the linings are in the right place, the self-adjusting mechanism is correctly installed and the parking brake cable is secured. If in doubt, remove the other wheel and take a look at that one for comparison.

Fig. 36 Two slightly different types of drum brake assemblies are used. This one uses a spring to secure the wheel cylinder . . .

23. Measure the width of the linings, then measure the inside width of the drum. Adjust the linings by means of the adjuster so that the drum will fit onto the linings.

24. Install the hub and bearing assembly onto the axle, if removed. Tighten the retaining bolts to 45 ft. lbs. (60 Nm) without ABS, 60 ft. lbs. (82 Nm) with ABS.

25. Install the drum, adjust the brakes. Adjust the parking brake.

26. Install the wheel and hand-tighten the lug nuts.

27. Lower the car. Tighten lug nuts to 100 ft. lbs. (136 Nm).

28. Check the pedal for any sponginess or lack of a hard feel. Check the braking action and the parking brake.

Wheel Cylinders

REMOVAL & INSTALLATION

1. Loosen the wheel lug nuts. Raise and support the car, and remove the wheel. Remove the drum and brake shoes.

2. Remove any dirt from around the brake line fitting. Disconnect the brake line, then plug the opening to prevent fluid loss and contamination.

3. If the wheel cylinder is retained with bolts, simply remove the bolts. If retained with clips, remove the wheel cylinder retainer by using two awls or punches with a tip diameter of 1/8 in. (3mm) or less. Insert the awls or punches into the access slots between the wheel cylinder pilot and retainer locking tabs. Bend both tabs away simultaneously. Remove the wheel cylinder from the backing plate.

To install:

4. If retained with bolts, simply install wheel cylinder and tighten the bolts to 9-15 ft. lbs. (12-20 Nm). If retained with clips, position the wheel cylinder against the backing plate, then hold it in place with a wooden block between the wheel cylinder and the hub and bearing assembly.

1. Return spring
2. Return spring
3. Hold down spring
4. Lever pivot
5. Hold down pin
6. Actuator link
7. Actuator lever
8. Lever return spring
9. Parking brake strut
10. Strut spring
11. Primary (small) shoe & lining
12. Secondary (larger) shoe & lining
13. Adjusting screw spring
14. Socket
15. Pivot nut
16. Adjusting screw
17. Retaining ring
18. Pin
19. Parking brake lever
20. Bleeder valve
21. Bolt
22. Boot
23. Piston
24. Seal
25. Spring assembly
26. Wheel cylinder
27. Backing plate

86819081

Fig. 37 . . . while this type uses bolts to secure the wheel cylinder

86819068

Fig. 38 If you remove the hub, install two of the bolts to secure the backing plate

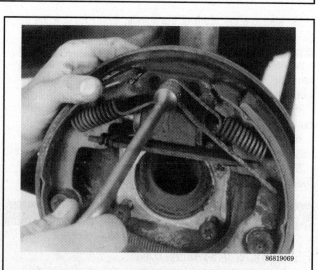

86819069

Fig. 39 Special tools are available for disengaging the return springs

Fig. 40 Remove the hold-down springs by pressing down and turning 90 degrees

Fig. 41 Removing the actuator lever, pivot and the pivot return spring

Fig. 42 Spread the shoes apart to clear the wheel cylinder pistons, then remove the parking brake strut and spring

Fig. 43 Remove the brake shoes. Note the parking brake cable is still attached to the lever

Fig. 44 Disconnecting the parking brake cable from the lever

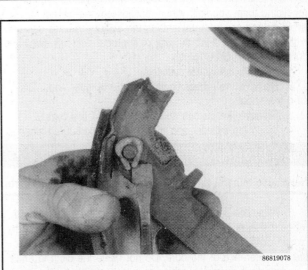

Fig. 45 Remove the C-clip from the parking brake lever using a small prytool

A. SETTING TOOL TO DRUM

B. SETTING BRAKE SHOES TO TOOL

86819079

Fig. 46 Measure the width of the linings, then measure the inside width of the drum

5. Install a new retainer over the wheel cylinder abutment on the rear of the backing plate by pressing it into place with a 1⅛ in. (1mm) 12-point socket and an extension.

6. Install a new bleeder screw into the wheel cylinder. Tighten the bleeder screw to 89 inch lbs. (10 Nm). Attach the brake line, then tighten to 10-15 ft. lbs. (14-20 Nm).

7. Install the brake shoes and drum. Adjust the brakes.

8. Install the tire and wheel assembly. Install the lug nuts hand-tight.

9. Lower the vehicle. Tighten the lug nuts to 100 ft. lbs. (136 Nm).

10. Bleed the brake system.

OVERHAUL

▶ See Figures 47, 48 and 49

As is the case with master cylinders, overhaul kits are available for the wheel cylinders, however it is usually more economical to simply buy new or rebuilt wheel cylinders rather rebuilding them yourself. When rebuilding wheel cylinders, avoid getting any contaminants in the system. Always use new high quality brake fluid; the use of improper fluid will swell and deteriorate the rubber parts.

1. Remove the wheel cylinders.

2. Remove the rubber boots from the cylinder ends. Discard the boots.

3. Remove the pistons and cups. Discard the cups.

4. Wash the cylinder and metal parts in denatured alcohol.

✳✳WARNING

Never use mineral based solvents to clean the brake parts.

5. Allow the parts to air dry and inspect the cylinder bore for corrosion or wear. Light corrosion can be cleaned up with crocus cloth. Use finger pressure and rotate the cloth around the circumference of the bore. Do not move the cloth in and out. Any deep corrosion, pitting or wear warrants replacement of the part(s).

86819083

Fig. 47 Remove the wheel cylinders, then remove the rubber boots from the cylinder ends.

86819084

Fig. 48 After the pistons are removed, the cup seals and spring can be removed

Fig. 49 Inspect the wheel cylinder for scoring, nicks, corrosion, and wear

6. Rinse the parts and allow to dry. Do not dry with a rag, which will leave bits of line behind.

7. Lubricate the cylinder bore with clean brake fluid. Insert the spring assembly.

8. Install new cups. Do not lubricate prior to assembly.

9. Install the pistons.

10. Press the new boots onto the cylinders by hand. Do not lubricate prior to assembly.

11. Install the wheel cylinder.

12. Install the brake shoes and drum. Adjust the brakes.

13. Install the tire and wheel assembly. Install the lug nuts.

14. Lower the vehicle. Tighten the lug nuts until snug.

REAR DISC BRAKES

✴✴CAUTION

Brake pads may contain asbestos, which has been determined to a cancer causing agent. Never clean the brake surfaces with compressed air! Avoid inhaling any dust from any brake surface! When cleaning brake surfaces, use a commercially available brake cleaning fluid.

Brake Pads

REMOVAL & INSTALLATION

▶ **See Figures 50, 51, 52, 53 and 54**

1. Siphon ⅔ of the brake fluid out of the master cylinder reservoir.

2. Release the parking brake, then raise and safely support the vehicle.

3. Remove the tire and wheel assembly.

---

15. Bleed the brake system.

Brake Backing Plate

REMOVAL & INSTALLATION

1. Disconnect the negative battery cable.

2. To remove the wheel, loosen all the lug nuts at least one full turn, before raising the car.

3. Raise and safely support the car.

4. Remove the wheel and tire assembly.

5. Remove the brake drum, shoes and springs as previously described.

6. Unsecure the brake line from the wheel cylinder, then remove the wheel cylinder.

7. Remove the parking brake cable.

8. Remove the hub and bearing assembly.

9. Remove the backing plate.

To install:

10. Install the backing plate to axle.

11. Install the hub and bearing assembly.

12. Connect the parking brake cable to the backing plate.

13. Install the wheel cylinder, following the procedures outlined.

14. Install the brake components.

15. Adjust and bleed the rear brakes.

16. Adjust the parking brake cables.

17. Install the wheel and tire assembly, hand-tighten the lug nuts.

18. Lower the vehicle, then tighten the lug nuts to 100 ft. lbs. (136 Nm).

Fig. 50 Exploded view of the rear brake pad components

4. Install two wheel nuts to secure the rotor in place.

✵✵CAUTION

Be prepared to catch the springs when you are removing the spring pins. The springs may fly out and can cause personal injury

5. Remove the spring pins using removal tool J 6125-1B and J 36620. The tool will thread into the spring pin. Using the tool remove the spring pins from the caliper.

6. Remove the outboard brake pad from the caliper. Loosen the parking brake cable adjustment if necessary to remove the pad.

7. Remove the inboard pad from the caliper. It may be necessary to slide the caliper in slightly to remove the pad.

8. Remove the two check valves from the end of the piston assembly, using a small flatbladed tool.

9. Bottom the piston in the caliper bore using a caliper spin back tool or tool J-36621. Turn the left caliper piston assembly counterclockwise and the right piston assembly clockwise. This is done to move the piston assembly back into the bore. Make sure the two notches in the caliper piston are at the 6 and 12 o'clock positions.

To install:

10. Install a new lubricated two way check valve into the piston assembly.

11. Install the inboard pad so the dowels on the back of the pad seat into the piston notches.

12. Install the outboard pad.

13. Install the pad spring over the outboard pad with the spring center section over the top of the pad. Slide the second spring pin into the caliper until the pad spring can be hooked under it.

14. Install the pad spring over the inboard pad with the spring center section over the top of the pad. Slide the second spring pin into the caliper until the pad spring can be hooked under it.

15. With both pad springs in place, drive the spring pins to the fully seated position in the caliper.

16. Install the tire and wheel. Hand-tighten the lug nuts.

Fig. 51 The spring pins are removed using this special tool

Fig. 53 Bottom the piston in the caliper bore using a caliper spin back tool

Fig. 52 Remove the inboard pad from the caliper. It may be necessary to push on the bridge, moving the caliper inboard to allow clearance for removing the pad

Fig. 54 Using a hammer and soft brass drift, install the spring pins

17. Lower the vehicle, then tighten the lug nuts to 100 ft. lbs. (136 Nm).

18. Pump the brake several times to seat the pads against the rotor. Top off the brake fluid.

INSPECTION

The pad thickness should be inspected every time that the tires are removed for rotation. The outer pad can be checked by looking in at each end, which is the point at which the highest rate of wear occurs. The inner pad can be checked by looking down through the inspection hole in the top of the caliper. If the thickness of the pad is worn to within 0.030 in. (0.76mm) of the rivet at either end of the pad, all the pads should be replaced. This is the factory recommended measurement, your state's automobile inspection laws may not agree with this.

➡Always replace all pads on both wheels at the same time. Failure to do so will result in uneven braking action and premature wear.

Brake Caliper

REMOVAL & INSTALLATION

1. To remove the wheel, loosen all the lug nuts at least one full turn, before raising the vehicle.
2. Raise and safely support the vehicle.
3. Remove the tire and wheel assembly.
4. Disconnect and cap the brake hose from the caliper.
5. Remove the brake pads.
6. Disconnect the parking brake cable from the parking brake lever and remove the return spring.
7. Remove the parking brake cable from the parking brake cable bracket. This can be done easily by inserting a 1/2 in. (13mm) wrench over the cable end lock tabs and pulling the cable out.
8. Remove the two caliper mounting bolts and remove the caliper from the vehicle.
To install:
9. Install the caliper over the rotor and install the caliper mounting bolts.
10. Tighten the mounting bolts to 74 ft. lbs. (100 Nm).
11. Install the parking brake cable into the cable mounting bracket.
12. Install the return spring and connect the cable end to the parking brake lever.
13. Install the brake pads.
14. Connect the brake hose to the caliper and tighten the mounting bolt to 33 ft. lbs. (45 Nm).
15. Bleed the brake system.
16. Install the tire and wheel. Hand-tighten the lug nuts.
17. Lower the vehicle, tighten the lug nuts to 100 ft. lbs. (136 Nm).

OVERHAUL

▶ **See Figures 55 and 56**

1. Raise and support the vehicle. Remove the wheel and tire assembly.
2. Remove the caliper.
3. Remove the parking brake lever and lever seal nut.
4. Inspect the bracket and bridge for cracks or distortion.
5. Disassemble the bridge bolts, bracket, and bridge, only if the bridge or bracket is suspected of being cracked or damaged in any way. The caliper can be overhauled without removing the bridge.
6. Inspect the piston for scoring, nicks, corrosion, wear and damaged or worn chrome plating. Replace the piston if any defects are found.
7. Remove the actuator screw by pressing on the threaded end. Inspect the actuator screw for cracks and thread damage.
8. Remove the balance spring, then unsecure the shaft seal and thrust washer from the actuator screw.
9. Remove the piston boot with a flatbladed tool, working carefully so that the piston bore is not scratched.
10. Remove the piston seal from the caliper bore groove using a piece of pointed wood or plastic. Do not use a metal tool, which will damage the bore. Inspect the caliper bore for nicks, corrosion and so on. Very light wear can be cleaned up with crocus cloth. Use finger pressure to rub the crocus cloth around the circumference of the bore, do not slide it in and out. More extensive wear or corrosion warrants replacement of the part.
11. Remove the bleeder screw and cap from the caliper.
To assemble:
12. Clean any parts which are to be reused in denatured alcohol. Dry them with compressed or allow to air dry. Don't wipe the parts dry with a cloth, which will leave behind bits of lint.
13. Assemble the bracket, bridge and bridge bolts, if they were removed. Tighten the bridge bolts to 74 ft. lbs (100 Nm).
14. Install the bleeder screw, tightening to 110-120 inch lbs. (13-14 Nm)
15. Lubricate the new seal (provided in a repair kit), with clean brake fluid. Install the seal in its groove, making sure it is fully seated and not twisted.
16. Mount the thrust washer onto the actuator screw, then install the copper side of the thrust washer toward the piston and the grayish side toward the housing.
17. Lubricate the shaft seal and insert on the actuator screw.
18. Install the new dust boot on the piston. Insert the lubricated screw with the shaft seal and thrust washer into the caliper housing. Install the balancer spring into the housing bore, with the end of the spring in recess at the bottom of the bore.
19. Lubricate the bore of the caliper with clean brake fluid and insert the piston into its bore. Make sure the piston is well lubricated before insertion. Position the boot in the caliper housing and seat with a seal driver of the appropriate size, or tool No. J-36623.
20. Turn the actuator screw as necessary to allow the piston assembly to move to the bottom of the caliper bore. Lubricate the lever seal and install over the end of the actuator screw.

1 Spring pin
2 Outboard shoe & lining
3 Inboard shoe & lining
4 Wear sensor
5 Spring
6 Mounting bolt
7 Sleeve boot
8 Sleeve
9 Nut
10 Lever
11 Return spring
12 Lever seal
14 Piston assembly
15 Two-way check valve
16 Boot
17 Piston seal
18 Actuator screw
19 Balance spring
20 Thrust washer
21 Shaft seal
22 Bleeder valve cap
23 Bleeder valve
24 Bridge bolt
25 Bracket
26 Bridge
27 Caliper housing

Fig. 55 Exploded view of the rear caliper assembly

The rubber sealing bead over the lever seal should be against the parking lever, and the copper end should be against the housing.

21. Hold the parking lever back against the stop on the caliper housing while tightening the nut. This will prevent any accidental application of the parking brake mechanism.

22. Insert the lever and nut, the hex hole in the lever must engage the hex hole in the actuator screw. Tighten the nut to 35 ft. lbs. (47 Nm).

23. Seat the caliper boot to the counterbore in the housing using tool No. J-36622 and J-36623.

24. Install the pads and the caliper, Bleed the brakes.

25. Lower the vehicle.

Fig. 56 Seat the caliper boot to the counterbore in the housing using tool No. J-36622 and J-36623

Brake Disc (Rotor)

REMOVAL & INSTALLATION

1. To remove the wheel, loosen all the lug nuts at least one full turn, before raising the car.
2. Raise and safely support the vehicle.
3. Remove the tire and wheel assembly.
4. Remove the two caliper mounting bolts and remove the caliper from the knuckle.
5. Using a piece of wire, support the caliper out of the way. DO NOT disconnect the brake hose or allow the caliper to hang from the brake hose.
6. Remove the brake rotor from the vehicle.

To Install:
7. Install the rotor on the vehicle.
8. Install the caliper onto the steering knuckle. Make sure the brake hose is not twisted.
9. Tighten the mounting bolts to 74 ft. lbs. (100 Nm).
10. Install the tire and wheel. Hand-tighten the lug nuts.
11. Lower the vehicle, then tighten the lug nuts to 100 ft. lbs. (136 Nm).

12. Pump the brake pedal several times to seat the pads against the rotor.

➡ **The brake pedal must be pumped prior to operating the vehicle or the vehicle will not stop on the initial pedal application.**

INSPECTION

1. Check the rotor surface for wear or scoring. Deep scoring, grooves or rust pitting can be removed by refacing. This can be performed by your local machine shop or garage. Minimum thickness is stamped on the rotor, or see the brake specifications chart in this section. If the rotor is thinner than specification, after refinishing, it must be replaced.
2. Check the rotor parallelism using a micrometer. It must vary less than 0.0005 in. (0.0127mm) measured at four or more points around the circumference. Make all measurements at the same distance in from the edge of the rotor. Refinish the rotor if it fails to meet this specification.
3. Measure the disc runout with a dial indicator. If runout exceeds 0.002 in. (0.051mm) for 1982-85 models, 0.004 in. (0.10mm) for 1985-87 models, and 0.002 in. (0.051mm) for 1988-95 models and the wheel bearings are OK (if runout is being measured with the disc on the car), the rotor must be refaced or replaced as necessary.

PARKING BRAKE

Cables

REMOVAL & INSTALLATION

Except Rear Disc Brakes

FRONT

▶ See Figures 57 and 58

1. Raise and safely support the vehicle.
2. Loosen the equalizer nut.
3. Disengage the front cable from the connector and equalizer.
4. Remove the clip at the frame.
5. Remove the cable from the hanger.
6. Lower the vehicle.
7. To remove the driver's side sound insulator panel, unsecure the screws and nuts. Remove the panel.
8. Remove the carpet finish molding, then lift the carpet.
9. Remove the cable retaining clip at the lever assembly.
10. Depress the retaining tangs and remove the cable and casing from the lever assembly.
11. Remove the cable from the retaining clips.
12. Remove the grommet retainer from the floor pan.
13. Unseat the grommet and pull the cable through the floor pan.

To install:
14. Insert the cable through the floor pan and grommet.
15. Seat the grommet. Install the grommet retainer to the floor pan.

Fig. 57 The parking brake control assembly is located under the dash on the drivers side

16. Fasten the cable in the retaining clips.
17. Connect the cable and casing to the lever assembly. Seat the retaining tangs.
18. Install the cable retaining clip at the lever assembly.
19. Place the carpet into position, then install the carpet finish molding.
20. Install the driver's side sound insulator panel with the attaching screws and nuts.
21. Raise and safely support the vehicle.
22. Fasten the cable to the hanger.
23. Install the clip to the frame.

Fig. 58 Parking brake cable routing on vehicles without rear disc brakes

24. Engage the front cable to the equalizer and connector.
25. Adjust the parking brake cable.
26. Lower the vehicle.

LEFT REAR

1. To remove the wheel, loosen all the lug nuts at least one full turn, before raising the car.
2. Raise and support the rear of the vehicle on jackstands.
3. Loosen the equalizer nut to relieve the cable tension, then remove the wheel and tire assembly.
4. Remove the brake drum, then insert a flatbladed tool between the brake shoe and the top of the brake adjuster bracket.
5. Push the bracket forward and release the top adjuster bracket rod. Remove the rear hold-down spring, the actuator lever and the lever return spring.
6. Remove the adjuster screw, spring and the top rear brake shoe return spring.
7. Remove the parking brake cable from the parking brake lever.

8. Depress the conduit fitting retaining tangs and remove the fitting from the backing plate.
9. Back off the equalizer nut and remove the left cable from the equalizer.
10. Depress the conduit fitting retaining tangs and remove the fitting from the axle bracket.
To install:
11. Install the cable through the rear of the backing plate. Seat the retaining tangs in the backing plate.
12. Connect the cable to the parking brake lever.
13. Install the brake drum, tire, wheel and lug nuts.
14. Engage the cable at the equalizer and connector.
15. Adjust the service brake shoes, then adjust the parking brake cable.
16. Install the wheel and tire, then hand-tighten the lug nuts.
17. Lower the vehicle, and tighten the lug nuts to 100 ft. lbs. (136 Nm).

RIGHT REAR

1. To remove the wheel, loosen all the lug nuts at least one full turn, before raising the car.

2. Raise and support the rear of the vehicle on jackstands.

3. Loosen the equalizer nut to relieve the cable tension, then remove the wheel and tire assembly.

4. Remove the brake drum, then insert a screwdriver between the brake shoe and the top of the brake adjuster bracket.

5. Push the bracket forward and release the top adjuster bracket rod. Remove the rear hold-down spring, the actuator lever and the lever return spring.

6. Remove the adjuster screw, spring and the top rear brake shoe return spring.

7. Remove the parking brake cable from the parking brake lever.

8. Depress the conduit fitting retaining tangs and remove the fitting from the backing plate.

9. Remove the cable button end from the connector.

10. Depress the conduit fitting retaining tangs and remove the fitting from the axle bracket.

To install:

11. Install the cable through the rear of the backing plate. Seat the retaining tangs in the backing plate.

12. Connect the cable to the parking brake lever.

13. Install the brake drum, wheel and hand-tighten the lug nuts.

14. Engage the cable at the equalizer and connector.

15. Adjust the regular service brake, then adjust the parking brake cable.

16. Lower the vehicle, then tighten the lug nuts to 100 ft. lbs. (136 Nm).

Rear Disc Brakes

FRONT

1. Raise and safely support the vehicle.

2. On the rear suspension member, loosen the nut on the parking brake cable equalizer.

3. Disconnect the front parking brake cable from the equalizer assembly.

4. Disconnect the parking brake cable from the frame clip at the left rear of the vehicle.

5. Pull the parking brake cable through the cable hanger in front of the clip mounting point.

6. Lower the vehicle.

7. Remove the drivers side sound insulator panel.

8. Remove the carpet finish moulding.

9. Pull the carpet back to uncover the parking brake cable.

10. Remove the cable retaining clip at the parking brake lever assembly.

11. Disengage the parking brake cable housing locking fingers from the parking brake assembly.

12. Disconnect the cable end from the parking brake lever assembly.

13. Remove the grommet retainer from the floor pan.

14. Pull the cable through the floor pan and remove.

To Install:

15. Pull the cable through the floor pan until the grommet can be seated in the hole in the floor.

16. Install the grommet retainer on the floor pan.

17. Connect the cable end to the parking brake assembly lever.

18. Seat the parking brake cable housing into the parking brake assembly until the locking fingers engage.

19. Install the cable retaining clip at the parking brake assembly.

20. Place the carpet back in place and install the carpet finish moulding.

21. Install the drivers side sound insulator cable.

22. Raise and safely support the vehicle.

23. Route the cable through the cable hanger at the rear of the vehicle.

24. Install the cable mounting clip at the left rear of the vehicle.

25. Connect the cable to the parking brake equalizer on the rear suspension member.

26. Adjust the parking brake.

27. Lower the vehicle.

REAR

▶ See Figure 59

1. Raise and safely support the vehicle.

2. On the rear suspension member, loosen the nut on the parking brake cable equalizer.

3. Disconnect the front parking brake cable from the equalizer assembly.

4. Disconnect the cable from the mounting bracket on the rear axle assembly.

5. Remove the tire and wheel assembly.

6. Disconnect the parking brake cable end from the parking brake lever on the caliper and remove the return spring.

7. Disconnect the cable guide from the strut mounting bracket.

To Install:

8. Connect the cable to the mounting bracket on the rear axle assembly.

9. Connect the cable end to the equalizer assembly.

10. Connect the cable to the cable guide on the strut.

11. Connect the cable to the bracket at the caliper, seat the locking fingers completely.

12. Install the return spring on the cable and connect the cable end to the caliper lever.

13. Install the tire and wheel assembly.

14. Adjust the parking brake cable.

15. Lower the vehicle.

ADJUSTMENT

Except ABS and Rear Disc Brakes

1. Adjust the brakes as described earlier.

2. Depress the parking brake pedal exactly three ratchet clicks.

3. Raise and support the car with both rear wheels off the ground.

4. Tighten the adjusting nut until the right rear wheel can just be turned backward using two hands, but cannot be turned forward.

5. Release the parking brake. Rotate the rear wheels, there should be no drag.

6. Lower the car.

1 – FRONT CABLE ASSEMBLY
2 – RIGHT REAR CABLE
3 – LEFT REAR CABLE
4 – EQUALIZER ASSEMBLY
5 – GUIDE
6 – CLIP

86819089

Fig. 59 Parking brake cable routing on vehicles with rear disc brakes

ABS Models

1. Adjust the rear brakes. Apply the parking brake to 10 clicks and release. Repeat this process 5 times.

2. Check the parking brake pedal for a full release.

   a. Turn the ignition to the **ON** position and note if the brake indicator light is off.

   b. If the light is on and the brake seems to be released, then operate the parking brake pedal lever and pull downwards on the front of the cable to remove any slack.

3. Raise and support the vehicle.

4. Adjust the parking brake by turning the nut on the equalizer while spinning both rear wheels. When either the rear wheels develops a drag, stop adjusting and back off the equalizer nut one full turn.

5. Apply the parking brake to 4 clicks, then check the rear wheel rotation. The wheel should not move when you attempt to rotate it by hand, in a forward direction. There should be wheel drag or no movement at all when you rotate the wheel in the rearward direction.

6. Release the parking brake and check for a free wheel rotation.

7. Lower the vehicle. Test drive the vehicle.

Rear Disc Brakes

1. Press the brake pedal 3 times with the force of approximately 175 ft. lbs. (237 Nm).

2. Apply and release the parking brake 3 times.

3. Check the parking brake pedals for full release.

   a. Turn the ignition to the **ON** position.

   b. The brake warning lamp should be off. If this is not the case, pull down on the front of the front parking brake cable with the hand lever completely released. This will remove any slack from the lever assembly.

4. Raise and support the vehicle.

5. Check that the parking brake levers on both of the calipers are against the lever stops on the housings. If the levers are not against the stops, then check for binding in the rear cables, and/or loosen the cable at each adjuster until both of the left and right levers are against there stops.

6. If the cables are binding, replace them.

7. Tighten the cable at the adjuster until either the left or right lever begins to move off the stop, then loosen the adjustment until the lever moves back to barely touch the stop.

8. Lower the vehicle.

9. Operate the parking brake several times to check the adjustment. After the cable adjustment, the brake parking brake pedal should not travel more than 16 ratchet clicks. The rear wheels should not rotate froward when the lever is applied 14 to 16 ratchet clicks.

TEVES ANTI-LOCK BRAKE SYSTEM

General Description

The Teves Anti-Lock Brake System used on the General Motors A-Body cars is manufactured by Alfred Teves Technologies of West Germany. The 4 wheel system uses a combination of wheel speed sensors and a microprocessor to determine impending wheel lock-up and adjust the brake pressure to maintain the best braking. This system helps the driver maintain the control of the vehicle under heavy braking conditions.

❊❊CAUTION

Some procedures in this section require that hydraulic lines, hoses and fitting be disconnected for inspection or testing purposes. Before disconnecting any hydraulic lines, hoses or fittings, be sure that the accumulator is fully depressurized. Failure to depressurize the hydraulic accumulator may result in personal injury.

➡️The use of rubber hoses or parts other than those specified for the ABS system may lead to functional problems and/or impaired braking or ABS function. Install all components included in repair kits for this system. Lubricate rubber pats with clean fresh brake fluid to ease assembly.

SYSTEM OPERATION

Under normal driving conditions the Anti-lock system functions the same as a standard brake system. The primary difference is that the power assist for normal braking is provided by the booster portion of the hydraulic unit through the use of pressurized brake fluid.

If a wheel locking tendency is noted during a brake application, the ABS system will modulate hydraulic pressure in the individual wheel circuits to prevent any wheel from locking. A separate hydraulic line and 2 specific solenoid valves are provided for each front wheel; both rear wheels share a set of solenoid valves and a single pipe from the master cylinder to the proportioner valve or tee. The proportioner valve splits the right and left rear brake circuits to the wheels.

➡️The Pontiac 6000 AWD incorporates a differential lock mounted on the transaxle transfer case. The lock is engaged when the vehicle is in all wheel drive and the transfer case differential is locked. Due to the rigid coupling of the front and rear axles through the drive train, the wheel speed sensors cannot relay accurate data to the controller. The differential lock disables the ABS system when the vehicle is in all wheel drive.

The ABS system can increase, decrease or hold pressure in each hydraulic circuit depending on signals from the wheel speed sensors and the electronic brake control module.

During an ABS stop, a slight bump or a kick-back will be felt in the brake pedal. This bump will be followed by a series of short pulsations which occur in rapid succession. The brake pedal pulsations will continue until there is no longer a need for the anti-lock function or until the vehicle is stopped. A slight ticking or popping noise may be heard during brake applications with anti-lock. This noise is normal and indicates that the anti-lock system is being used.

During anti-lock stops on dry pavement, the tires may make intermittent chirping noises as they approach lock-up. These noises are considered normal as long as the wheel does not truly lock or skid. When the anti-lock system is being used, the brake pedal may rise even as the brakes are being applied. This is normal. Maintaining a constant force on the pedal will provide the shortest stopping distance.

Anti-Lock Warning Light

Vehicles equipped with the ABS have an amber warning light in the instrument panel marked ANTILOCK. Additionally, some models using this system will flash other ABS related messages on the Graphic Control Center or other message panels. The warning light will illuminate if a malfunction in the anti-lock brake system is detected by the electronic controller. In case of an electronic malfunction, the controller will turn on the ANTILOCK warning light and disable some or all of the anti-lock system. If only the ANTILOCK light is on, normal braking with full assist is operational but there may be reduced or no anti-lock function. If the ANTILOCK warning light and the red BRAKE warning light come on at the same time, there may be a fault in the hydraulic brake system.

The ANTILOCK light will turn on during the starting of the engine and will usually stay on for approximately 3 seconds after the ignition switch is returned to the RUN position.

➡️Due to system de-pressurization over time, a vehicle not started in several hours may have the BRAKE and ANTILOCK warning lights stay on up to 30 seconds when started. This is normal and occurs because the ABS pump must restore the correct pressure within the hydraulic accumulator. Both lamps will remain on while this recharging is completed.

Brake System Warning Light

The Anti-lock Brake System uses a 2 circuit design so that some braking capacity is still available if hydraulic pressure is lost in 1 circuit. A BRAKE warning light is located on the instrument cluster and is designed to alert the driver of conditions that could result in reduced braking ability. Certain models may display brake related messages on screens or other panels, these messages supplement the brake warning light.

The BRAKE warning light should turn on briefly during engine starting and should remain on whenever the parking brake is not fully released. Additionally, the BRAKE warning lamp will illuminate if a sensor detects low brake fluid, if the pressure switch detects low accumulator pressure or if certain on-board computers run a self-check of the dashboard and instruments.

If the BRAKE warning light stays on longer than 30 seconds after starting the engine, or comes on and stays on while driving, there may be a malfunction in the brake hydraulic system.

SYSTEM COMPONENTS

▶ See Figure 60

Electronic Brake Control Module (EBCM)

The Electronic Brake Control Module (EBCM) monitors the speed of each wheel and the electrical status of the hydraulic unit. The EBCM's primary functions are to detect wheel lockup, control the brake system while in anti-lock mode and monitor the system for proper electrical operation. When 1 or more wheels approach lockup during a stop, the EBCM will command appropriate valve positions to modulate brake fluid pressure and provide optimum braking. It will continue to command pressure changes in the system until a locking tendency is no longer noted.

The EBCM is a separate computer used exclusively for control of the anti-lock brake system. The unit also controls the retention and display of the ABS trouble codes when in the diagnostic mode. As the EBCM monitors the system or performs a self-check, it can react to a fault by disabling the ABS system and illuminating the amber ANTILOCK warning light. The EBCM is located on the right side of the dashboard, generally behind the glove box.

VIEW A

A

1 Hydraulic unit
2 Electronic controller
3 Front wheel speed sensor
   wire routing
4 Relays and ground
5 Sensor connection to harness
6 Relays and fuse

86819101

Fig. 60 Teves anti-lock brake system main component locations

Wheel Speed Sensors

A wheel speed sensor at each wheel transmits speed information to the EBCM by generating a small AC voltage relative to the wheel speed. The voltage is generated by magnetic induction caused by passing a toothed sensor ring past a stationary sensor. The signals are transmitted through a pair of wires which are shielded against interference. The EBCM then calculates wheel speed for each wheel based on the frequency of the AC voltage received from the sensor.

Hydraulic Components

The ABS uses an integrated hydraulic unit mounted on the firewall or cowl. This unit functions as a brake master cylinder and brake booster. Additionally, the hydraulic unit provides brake fluid pressure modulation for each of the individual wheel circuits as required during braking. The hydraulic unit consists of several individual components:

MASTER CYLINDER/BOOSTER ASSEMBLY

This portion of the hydraulic unit contains the valves and pistons necessary to develop hydraulic pressure within the brake lines. Pressure in the booster servo circuit is controlled by a spool valve which opens in response to the amount of force applied to the brake pedal. The rate at which the vehicle decelerates depends on the type of road surface and the pressure applied to the brake pedal.

The master cylinder portion uses a 3-circuit configuration during normal braking; individual circuits are provided for each front wheel while a shared circuit is used for the rear wheels. The 3 circuits are isolated so that a leak or malfunction in one will allow continued braking on the others.

The master cylinder/booster is a non-serviceable component and should never be disassembled.

VALVE BLOCK

The valve block is attached to the right side of the hydraulic unit and includes the 6 solenoid valves used to modulate pressures in the 3 circuits during anti-lock braking. Each circuit is equipped with an inlet and outlet valve.

During normal braking, the inlet valves are open and the outlet valves are closed. When anti-lock control begins, the EBCM switches 12 volts to the appropriate valve circuit. This allows the fluid pressure in each circuit to be increased, decreased or held constant as the situation dictates. The position of the valves can be changed as quickly as 15 times per second when ABS is engaged.

The valve block may be serviced separately from the master cylinder/booster assembly but should never be disassembled.

MAIN VALVE

The main valve is a 2-position valve controlled by the Electronic Brake Control Module (EBCM). Except for testing, the valve is open only during ABS stops. When open, the valve allows pressurized brake fluid from the booster servo into the master cylinder front brake circuits to prevent excessive pedal travel.

The main valve is not serviceable as a component; the master cylinder/booster assembly must be replaced.

ACCUMULATOR

The hydraulic accumulator is used to store brake fluid at high pressure so that a supply of pressurized fluid is available for ABS operation and to provide power assist. The accumulator uses a rubber diaphragm to separate high-pressure nitrogen gas from the brake fluid.

Nitrogen in the accumulator is pre-charged to approximately 870 psi (6000 kPa). During normal operation, the pump and motor assembly charges the accumulator with brake fluid to an operation range of 2000-2600 psi (13,800-18,000 kPa).

Because of the high pressures in the system, it is extremely important to observe all safety and pressure reduction precautions before performing repairs or diagnosis.

PUMP/MOTOR ASSEMBLY

The ABS system uses a pump and motor assembly located on the left side of the hydraulic unit to pressurize fluid from the reservoir and store it in the accumulator. When pressure within the system drops, the pressure switch on the hydraulic unit grounds the pump motor relay which energizes the pump motor and pump.

The pump/motor assembly is serviceable only as an assembly; the pump must never be disconnected from the motor.

FLUID LEVEL SENSOR

Found in the fluid reservoir, this sensor is a float which operates 2 reed switches when low fluid level is detected. One switch will cause the red BRAKE warning light to illuminate; the other signals the EBCM and possibly other computers of the low fluid situation. Depending on model and equipment, other messages may be displayed to the driver. The Electronic Brake Control Module (EBCM) will engage the amber ANTILOCK warning light and disable the ABS function.

PRESSURE SWITCH

The pressure switch is mounted on the pump/motor assembly and serves 2 major functions, controlling the pump/motor and providing low pressure warning to the Electronic Brake Control Module (EBCM).

The switch will allow the pump/motor to run when system pressure drops below approximately 2030 psi (14,000 kPa) and will shut the pump/motor off when pressure in the accumulator is approximately 2610 psi (18,000 kPa). Should pressure within the accumulator drop below approximately 1500 psi (10,300 kPa), internal switches will both signal the EBCM and turn on the red BRAKE warning lamp. If the system re-pressurizes and reaches at least 1900 psi (13,100 kPa), the switches will reset.

PROPORTIONER VALVE

Included in the rear brake circuit is a proportioner valve or tee assembly which limits brake pressure build-up at the rear brake calipers. Since the front brakes do the majority of the braking, less pressure is required for the rear brakes under certain conditions. The proportioner valve improves front-to-rear brake balance during normal braking.

Troubleshooting

SERVICE PRECAUTIONS

✳✳CAUTION

This brake system uses a hydraulic accumulator which, when fully charged, contains brake fluid at very high pressure. Before disconnecting any hydraulic lines, hoses or fittings be certain that the accumulator pressure is completely relieved. Failure to depressurize the accumulator may result in personal injury and/or vehicle damage.

• If the vehicle is equipped with air bag (SIR) system, always properly disable the system before commencing work on the ABS system.

• Certain components within the ABS system are not intended to be serviced or repaired individually. Only those components with removal and installation procedures should be serviced.

• Do not use rubber hoses or other parts not specifically specified for the Teves ABS system. When using repair kits, replace all parts included in the kit. Partial or incorrect repair may lead to functional problems and require the replacement of the hydraulic unit.

• Lubricate rubber parts with clean, fresh brake fluid to ease assembly. Do not use lubricated shop air to clean parts, damage to rubber components may result.

• Use only brake fluid from an unopened container. Use of suspect or contaminated brake fluid can reduce system performance and/or durability.

• When any hydraulic component or line is removed or replaced, it may be necessary to bleed the entire system.

• A clean repair area is essential. Perform repairs after components have been thoroughly cleaned, then use only denatured alcohol to clean components. Do not allow ABS components to come into contact with any substance containing mineral oil, this includes used shop rags.

• Remove the lock pin before disconnecting Connector Position Assurance (CPA) connectors in the harnesses.

• The EBCM is a microprocessor similar to other computer units in the vehicle. Insure that the ignition switch is **OFF** before removing or installing controller harnesses. Avoid static electricity discharge at or near the Controller.

• Never disconnect any electrical connection with the ignition switch **ON** unless instructed to do so in a test.

• Always wear a grounded wrist strap when servicing any control module or component labeled with a Electrostatic Discharge (ESD) symbol.

• Avoid touching module connector pins.

• Leave new components and modules in the shipping package until ready to install them.

• To avoid static discharge, always touch a vehicle ground after sliding across a vehicle seat or walking across carpeted or vinyl floors.

• Never allow welding cables to lie on, near or across any vehicle electrical wiring.

• Do not allow extension cords for power tools or droplights to lie on, near or across any vehicle electrical wiring.

DEPRESSURIZING THE HYDRAULIC UNIT

The ABS pump motor assembly will keep the accumulator charged to a pressure between approximately 2000 psi (13,800 kPa) and 2600 psi (18,000 kPa) any time the ignition is in the **ON** or **RUN** position. The pump/motor cannot operate if the ignition is **OFF** or if a battery cable is disconnected.

1. With the ignition **OFF** and the negative battery cable disconnected, pump the brake pedal a minimum of 20 times using at least 50 ft. lbs. (68 Nm) of pedal force each time.

2. A definite increase in pedal effort will be felt as the accumulator becomes discharged.

3. After the increased pedal effort occurs, continue with 5-10 additional brake applications to release any remaining pressure.

VISUAL INSPECTION

Before any system diagnosis is begun, the brake system should be inspected visually for common faults which could disable the ABS or cause a code to set. Check the vehicle carefully for any sign of:

• Binding parking brake or faulty parking brake switch
• Low brake fluid
• System fluid leaks including pump/motor area
• Failed fuses or fusible links
• Failed ABS relay
• Loose or damaged wiring including connectors, harnesses, and insulation wear. Check the mounting and function of the brake calipers at each wheel

Carefully inspect the multi-pin connectors at the EBCM for pushouts or poor connections.

FUNCTIONAL CHECK

Once the visual check has been performed, perform the functional check (found in the diagnostic charts) to determine if the problem is truly ABS related or arising from common faults.

DISPLAYING ABS TROUBLE CODES

▶ See Figure 61

➡The 1st generation system found on the 6000 AWD does not display trouble codes; diagnosis is performed through symptom analysis and circuit testing.

Only certain ABS malfunctions will cause the EBCM to store diagnostic trouble codes. Failures causing a code will generally involve wheel speed sensors, main valve or the inlet and outlet valves. Conditions affecting the pump/motor assembly, the accumulator, pressure switch or fluid level sensor usually do not cause a code to set.

The EBCM will store trouble codes in a non-volatile memory. These codes remain in memory until erased through use of the correct procedure. The codes are NOT erased by disconnecting the EBCM, disconnecting the battery cable or turning off the ignition. Always be sure to clear the codes from the memory after repairs are made. To read stored ABS trouble codes:

1. Turn ignition switch to **ON**. Allow the pump to charge the accumulator. If fully discharged, the dash warning lights may stay on up to 30 seconds. If the ANTI-LOCK warning light does not go off within 30 seconds, make a note of it.

2. Turn ignition switch to **OFF**.

3. Remove the cover from the Assembly Line Diagnostic Link (ALDL) connector. Enter the diagnostic mode by using a jumper wire to connect pins H and A or to connect pin H to body ground.

➡On 1993 and later models the ALDL is also known as the Diagnostic Link Connector (DLC).

4. Turn the ignition switch to **ON** and count the light flashes for the first digit of the first code. The ANTI-LOCK light should illuminate for 4 seconds before beginning to flash. If, after 4 seconds, the light turns off and stays off, no codes are stored.

5. The light will pause for 3 seconds between the first and second digits of the first code and then continue flashing. When counting flashes, count only the ON pulses.

6. When the EBCM is finished transmitting the second digit of the first code, the ANTI-LOCK light will remain on. This last, constant ON should not be counted as a flash. Record the 2-digit code.

7. Without turning the ignition switch **OFF**, disconnect the jumper from pin H and reconnect it. If an additional code is present, it will be displayed in similar fashion to the first. Record the second code.

8. Repeat the disconnection and reconnection of pin H without changing the ignition switch position until no more codes are displayed. The system is capable of storing and displaying 7 codes, the ANTI-LOCK warning light will stay on continuously when all codes have been displayed.

ABS DIAGNOSTIC MODE

EXAMPLE:
- ABS CODE 34 PRESENT
- ALDL PIN H GROUNDED BEFORE KEY-ON

ON - - - - -
ANTI-LOCK LIGHT STATUS
OFF

IGNITION OFF | 4 SEC. DELAY | FIRST DIGIT OF CODE = 3 | 3 SEC. PAUSE | SECOND DIGIT OF CODE = 4 | CONTINUOUS LIGHT

KEY-ON

END OF CODE

86819102

Fig. 61 The codes are displayed through the ANTI-LOCK warning light

9. After recording each code, remove the jumper from the ALDL and replace the cover.

➡The ABS trouble codes are not specifically designated current or history codes. If the ANTI-LOCK light is on before entering the ABS diagnostic mode, at least 1 of the stored codes is current. It is impossible to tell which code is current. If the ANTI-LOCK light is off before entering the diagnostic mode, none of the codes are current.

INTERMITTENTS

Although the ABS trouble codes stored by the EBCM are not identified as current or history codes, these codes may still be useful in diagnosing intermittent conditions.

If an intermittent condition is being diagnosed:

1. Obtain an accurate description of the circumstances in which the failure occurs.

2. Display and clear any ABS trouble codes which may be present in the EBCM.

3. Test drive the vehicle, attempting to duplicate the failure condition exactly.

4. After duplicating the condition(s), stop the vehicle and display any ABS codes which have set.

5. If no codes have been stored, refer to the Symptom Diagnosis Charts. A good description of vehicle behavior can be helpful in determining a most likely circuit.

Most intermittent problems are caused by faulty electrical connections or wiring. Always check for poor mating of connector halves or terminals not fully seated in connector bodies, deformed or damaged terminals and poor terminal to wire connections.

Most failures within the ABS will disable the anti-lock function for the entire ignition cycle, even if the fault clears before the next key-off occurrence. There are 3 situations which will allow the ABS to re-engage if the condition corrects during the

ignition cycle. Each of these will illuminate 1 or both dash warning lights.

- Low system voltage: If the EBCM detects low voltage, the ANTI-LOCK warning lamp is illuminated. If the correct minimum voltage is restored to the EBCM, normal ABS function resumes.

- Low brake fluid level: Once detected by the fluid level sensor, this condition illuminates both the BRAKE and ANTI-LOCK warning lights; when the sensor indicates acceptable fluid level, the normal ABS function resumes.

- Low accumulator pressure: Should the accumulator lose or not develop correct pressure, both the BRAKE and ANTI-LOCK warning lights will illuminate. Full function is restored when the correct pressure is achieved.

- Any condition interrupting power to either the EBCM or hydraulic unit may cause the warning lights to come on intermittently. These circuits include the main relay, main relay fuse, EBCM fuse, pump motor relay and all related wiring.

CLEARING TROUBLE CODES

Stored ABS trouble codes should not be cleared until all repairs are completed. The control module will not allow any codes to be cleared until all have been read. After reading each stored code, drive the vehicle at a speed over 18 mph. (31 km/h)

Re-read the system, if codes are still present, then not all the codes were read previously or additional repair is needed.

➡In the following diagnostic charts, certain special tools may be required. Use of the J-35592 pinout box or equivalent, is required to avoid damage to the connectors at the EBCM. Use of J-35604 pressure gauge and J-35604-88 adapter (or equivalents) will be required to measure accumulator pressure. The use of a high-impedance Digital Volt/Ohmmeter (DVM or DVOM) is required at all times.

Speed Sensors

REMOVAL & INSTALLATION

Front Speed Sensor

PONTIAC 6000 AWD

▶ **See Figures 62 and 63**

1. To remove the wheel, loosen all the lug nuts at least one full turn, before raising the car.
2. Raise and safely support the vehicle.
3. Remove the tire and wheel.
4. Unplug the wheel sensor connector from the wiring harness.
5. Remove the sensor retaining screw.
6. Remove the wheel sensor and cable from the brackets.
7. Unseat the grommet and pull the cable and connector through the wheel housing.

To install:

8. Insert the cable and connector through the wheel housing, then seat the grommet in position.

➡ **New wheel sensors are equipped with a paper spacer that will properly gap the sensor when placed against the sensor ring.**

9. Install the sensor and cable to the bracket. Make certain the cable is clear of the steering and axle housing components.
10. Tighten the sensor retaining bolt to 53 inch lbs. (6 Nm).
11. If necessary, adjust the air gap to 0.028 in. (0.7mm) using a non-ferrous feeler gauge.
12. Tighten the sensor lockbolt to 18 inch lbs. (2 Nm).
13. Engage the wheel sensor connector.
14. Install the wheel and tire, hand-tighten the lug nuts.
15. Lower the vehicle, then tighten the lug nuts to 100 ft. lbs. (136 Nm).

PONTIAC 6000 STE

1. Unplug the sensor connector from the wiring harness.

1 Drive axle with toothed sensor ring
2 Bolt
3 Sensor bracket
4 Front wheel sensor
5 Bolt
6 Knuckle and hub assembly

86819104

Fig. 62 The front wheel speed sensor is secured by a retaining screw

1 Sensor wire
2 Grommet
3 Speed sensor

86819105

Fig. 63 When you install the sensor and cable to the bracket, make certain the cable is clear of the steering and axle components

2. To remove the wheel, loosen all the lug nuts at least one full turn, before raising the car.
3. Raise and safely support the vehicle.
4. Remove the wheel and tire.
5. Remove the sensor cables from the various clips and retainers.
6. Either remove the large cable grommets from there brackets or, if necessary, unbolt the bracket from the strut.
7. Remove the sensor retaining screw, then remove the sensor.

To install:

8. Coat the sensor body with anti-corrosion compound (GM 1052856 or an equivalent). Apply it where the sensor will contact the knuckle.
9. Install the sensor, then tighten the mounting bolt to 106 inch lbs. (12 Nm).
10. Position and install the cable into the grommets, clips and retainers. The cable must be secure in the retainers and clear of any moving parts. The cable must not be pulled too tight.
11. Connect the sensor to the wiring harness.
12. Install the wheel and tire, hand-tighten the lug nuts.
13. Lower the vehicle, then tighten the lug nuts to 100 ft. lbs. (136 Nm).

Rear Speed Sensor

PONTIAC 6000 AWD

▶ **See Figures 64 and 65**

1. Unplug the speed sensor connector in the front corner of the trunk compartment. If the right rear connector is to be disconnected, the spare wheel and tire must be removed.
2. Release the cable grommet. Carefully work the sensor cable and connector through the hole in the body panel.
3. To remove the wheel, loosen all the lug nuts at least one full turn, before raising the car.
4. Raise and safely support the vehicle.
5. Remove the wheel and tire.
6. Remove the sensor mounting bolt, then remove the sensor from the caliper. Slide the grommets out of the slots in the brackets and cable guide.

1 Rear wheel speed sensor
2 Mounting bolt
3 Grommet

86819106

Fig. 64 Remove the sensor mounting bolt, then remove the sensor from the caliper. Slide the grommets out of the slots in the brackets and cable guide

7. If the old sensor is to be reused, remove the paper spacer and any debris from the face of the sensor.
To install:
8. Install the sensor and tighten the retaining bolt to 80 inch lbs. (9 Nm). If reusing the old sensor, adjust the air gap.

➡**New wheel sensors are equipped with a paper spacer that will properly gap the sensor when placed against the sensor ring.**

9. Install the grommets into position on the brackets and cable guide.
10. Route the cable to avoid any contact with moving suspension components. Work the connector and cable up through the hole in the underbody, then fit the grommet into position in the hole.
11. Install the wheel and tire, hand-tighten the lug nuts. Lower the vehicle and tighten the lug nuts to 100 ft. lbs. (136 Nm).
12. Engage the wheel sensor connector to the wiring harness.

13. Install the spare wheel and tire if removed, then secure the trunk carpet.

Air Gap Adjustment

➡**Only the front and rear sensors on the Pontiac 6000 AWD are adjustable. On the Pontiac 6000 STE, the gap is not adjustable.**

1. To remove the wheel, loosen all the lug nuts at least one full turn, before raising the car.
2. Raise and safely support the vehicle.
3. Remove the wheel and tire.
4. Loosen the sensor adjustment bolt for the front or rear sensor.
5. Inspect the face of the sensor for abnormal wear or damage. If necessary, replace the sensor.

➡**New sensors come with a paper spacer which will properly gap the sensor when placed against the speed sensor ring.**

6. If the sensor is to be reused, clean the face of the sensor of all traces of the paper spacer, dirt, dust, etc.
To install:
7. Reposition the sensor, then adjust the air gap to 0.028 in. (0.7mm) using a non-ferrous feeler gauge.
8. Tighten the adjustment screw to 18 inch lbs. (2 Nm).
9. Install the wheel and tire, hand-tighten the lug nuts.
10. Lower the vehicle, then tighten the lug nuts to 100 ft. lbs. (136 Nm).

Hydraulic Unit

REMOVAL & INSTALLATION

Pontiac 6000 AWD
▶ See Figure 66

1. With the key **OFF**, disconnect the negative battery cable.
2. Depressurize the hydraulic accumulator.
3. Remove the wire clip from the return hose fitting and remove the return hose from the pump. Pull the return hose fitting out of the pump housing.
4. Remove the pressure hose bolt from the pump, then remove the hose and O-rings from the pump.
5. Remove the pump mounting bolt and separate the energy unit from the hydraulic unit.
6. Using 2 wrenches, disconnect the brake lines from the valve block and the hydraulic unit.
7. Disconnect the pushrod from the brake pedal.
8. Push the dust boot forward and off the rear half of the pushrod. Unscrew the 2 halves of the pushrod.
9. Remove the 2 hydraulic unit mounting bolts from the pushrod bracket.
10. Remove the hydraulic unit from the pushrod bracket. The front half of the pushrod will remain locked into the hydraulic unit.
To install:
11. Mount the hydraulic unit to the pushrod bracket and install the mounting bolts, then tighten the bolts to 37 ft. lbs. (50 Nm).

1 Right rear wheel sensor cable
2 Left rear wheel sensor cable
3 Wheel speed sensor
4 Grommet
5 Connector
6 EBCM wiring harness
7 Clip
8 Conduit

86819107

Fig. 65 Wiring harness routing for the rear speed sensors

12. Thread the 2 parts of the pushrod together and reposition the dust boot.

13. Connect the pushrod to the brake pedal then tighten the nut to 27 ft. lbs. (37 Nm).

14. Using 2 wrenches, connect the brake lines to the hydraulic unit and the valve block. Tighten to 11 ft. lbs (20 Nm).

15. Connect the energy unit to the pump unit, then install the pump mounting bolt.

16. Install the pressure hose and O-rings to the pump, then install the hose bolt and tighten it to 15 ft. lbs. (20 Nm).

17. Push the return hose fitting into the pump body and connect the return hose to the pump.

18. Install the wire clip to the return hose fitting.

19. Connect the wiring to the hydraulic unit.

20. Connect the negative battery cable.

21. Bleed the brake system.

✳✳CAUTION

Do not move vehicle until a firm brake pedal is achieved. Failure to obtain firm brake pedal may result in personal injury and/or property damage.

Pontiac 6000 STE

1. With ignition switch **OFF**, disconnect the negative battery cable.

2. Depressurize the hydraulic accumulator.

3. Unplug all electrical connections at the hydraulic unit.

4. Remove the cross-car brace if equipped.

5. Remove the pump bolt and then move pump motor assembly to allow access to the brake lines.

6. Using 2 wrenches, disconnect the brake lines from the hydraulic unit and the valve body.

7. Push the dust boot forward, past the hex on the pushrod. Separate the pushrod into 2 sections by unscrewing it.

1 Hydraulic unit
2 Bolt 50 Nm (37 lbs.ft.)
3 Pushrod assembly
4 Nut 20 Nm (177 lbs. in.)
5 Seal ring

86819108

Fig. 66 Hydraulic unit mounting on Teves systems

8. Remove the hydraulic unit mounting bolts at the pushrod bracket. Remove the hydraulic unit from the part of the pushrod may remain with the unit.

To Install:

9. Position the hydraulic unit, then install new retaining bolts at the pushrod bracket. Tighten the bolts to 37 ft. lbs. (50 Nm).

10. From inside car, thread pushrod halves together and tighten. Reposition the dust boot and connect the pushrod to the brake pedal.

11. Install the brake lines to the valve block, then tighten to 106 inch lbs. (12 Nm).

12. Position the pump motor assembly on the hydraulic unit. Install the mounting bolt, then tighten to 10 ft. lbs. (13 Nm).

13. Install the cross-car brace if one was removed.

14. Engage the electrical harness to the hydraulic unit.

15. Connect the negative battery cable.

16. Bleed the brake system.

❋❋CAUTION

Do not move vehicle until a firm brake pedal is achieved. Failure to obtain firm brake pedal may result in personal injury and/or property damage.

Valve Block Assembly

REMOVAL & INSTALLATION

▶ **See Figure 67**

1. With the ignition **OFF** disconnect the negative battery cable.

2. Depressurize the accumulator.

3. For Pontiac 6000 AWD, remove the hydraulic unit. For the Pontiac 6000 STE, drain or remove the brake fluid from the reservoir.

4. Unplug the electrical harness running to the valve block.

5. It may be necessary to disconnect the brake lines from the bottom of the valve block.

6. At the valve block, remove the nuts and the bolt with hex faces only. Remove the valve block assembly and O-rings by sliding the valve block off of the studs. Recover any O-rings or gaskets from the mounting points and/or the fluid line ports.

➡**Do not attempt to disassemble the valve block by removing the bolts with the recessed drive heads, the unit cannot be overhauled or repaired.**

To install:

7. Lubricate the O-rings with brake fluid.

8. Install the valve block and O-rings onto the master cylinder body.

9. Install the nuts and the bolt, then tighten to 18 ft. lbs. (25 Nm).

10. Connect the brake lines to the bottom of the valve block if they were removed.

11. Reinstall the hydraulic unit if it was removed.

REMOVE NUTS AND BOLT TO REMOVE VALVE BLOCK

86819109

Fig. 67 Remove the indicated nuts and bolt to remove the valve block

12. Connect the wiring harnesses.
13. Refill the system or reservoir to the correct level.
14. Connect the negative battery cable.
15. Bleed the brake system.

Pressure Warning Switch

REMOVAL & INSTALLATION

▶ See Figure 68

1. Disconnect the negative battery cable.
2. Depressurize the accumulator.
3. Unplug the electrical connector from the pressure warning switch.
4. Remove the pressure warning switch using tool J-35604 or an equivalent.
5. Remove the O-ring from the switch.

To install:

6. Lubricate a new O-ring with clean brake fluid.
7. Install the O-ring on the pressure warning switch.
8. Install the switch and tighten to 17 ft. lbs. (23 Nm). using the special tool.
9. Engage the electrical connector to the pressure warning switch.
10. Connect the negative battery cable.
11. Turn the ignition to the **ON** position. The BRAKE light should go out within 60 seconds.
12. Check for leakage around the switch.

Hydraulic Accumulator

REMOVAL & INSTALLATION

1. Disconnect the negative battery cable.
2. Depressurize the accumulator. Make certain the system is completely relieved of all hydraulic pressure.

86819110

Fig. 68 Unplug the electrical connector from the pressure warning switch, then remove the switch

3. Unscrew the hydraulic accumulator from the hydraulic unit.
4. Remove the O-ring from the accumulator.

To install:

5. Lubricate a new O-ring with clean brake fluid and install it on the accumulator.
6. Install the accumulator, then tighten to 32 ft. lbs. (43 Nm), except on 6000 AWD tighten to 17 ft. lbs. (23 Nm).
7. Connect the negative battery cable.
8. Turn the ignition switch to the **ON** position. The BRAKE light should go out within 60 seconds.
9. Check for leakage around the accumulator.

Brake Fluid Reservoir and Seal

REMOVAL & INSTALLATION

1. Disconnect the negative battery cable.
2. Depressurize the accumulator.
3. Remove the return hose and drain the brake fluid into a container. Discard the fluid properly.
4. Unplug the 2 wire connectors from the fluid level sensor assembly.
5. Remove the reservoir-to-block mounting bolt.
6. Remove the reservoir from the hydraulic unit by carefully prying between the reservoir and the hydraulic unit.
7. Remove the seals and O-ring from the unit.

To install:

8. Lubricate the new seals and O-ring with clean brake fluid, then install them into the unit.
9. Push the reservoir into the master cylinder until it is fully seated.
10. Connect the reservoir to the valve block with the mounting bolt, then tighten to 45 inch lbs. (5 Nm).
11. Engage the 2 wire connectors to the reservoir cap.
12. Connect the return hose to the reservoir.
13. Refill the reservoir with clean brake fluid.
14. Connect the negative battery cable.

Pump Motor

REMOVAL & INSTALLATION

1. Disconnect the negative battery cable.
2. Depressurize the accumulator.
3. Remove the fluid from the reservoir.

∗∗WARNING

Do not remove brake fluid from the reservoir using a syringe or other instrument which is contaminated with water, petroleum based fluids or any other foreign material. Contamination of the brake fluid may result.

4. Unplug the electrical connector from the pressure switch and the pump motor.
5. Remove the hydraulic accumulator and O-ring.

6. Disconnect the high pressure hose fitting connected to the pump.

7. Remove the pressure hose assembly and O-rings from the pump.

8. Disconnect the wire clip, then pull the return hose fitting out of the pump body.

9. Remove the pump mounting bolt and grommets attaching the pump motor assembly to the hydraulic unit.

10. Remove the pump motor assembly by sliding it off of the locating pin.

➡**Replace the insulators if damaged or deteriorated.**

To install:

11. Position the pump motor assembly to the hydraulic unit.

12. Install the bolt attaching the pump motor assembly to the hydraulic unit, tighten to 71 inch lbs. (8 Nm).

13. Connect the return pressure hose to the pump. Push the return hose fitting into the pump body.

14. Install the wire clip to the return hose fitting.

15. Install the O-rings and the pressure hose to the pump, attach the hose bolt to the pump. Tighten the bolt to 15 ft. lbs. (20 Nm).

16. Install the O-ring and the hydraulic accumulator, tighten the accumulator to 17 ft. lbs. (23 Nm).

17. Engage the electrical connector to the pressure switch and the pump motor.

18. Connect the negative battery cable.

19. Refill the fluid reservoir with clean brake fluid.

Filling and Bleeding the System

SYSTEM FILLING

➡**Do not allow the pump to run more than 60 seconds at 1 time. If the pump must run longer, allow the pump to cool several minutes between 60 second runs.**

With the ignition **OFF** and the negative battery cable disconnected, discharge the pressure within the accumulator. Remove the cap from the reservoir, then fill the reservoir to the correct level with DOT 3 fluid.

➡**Use only DOT 3 brake fluid from a clean, sealed container. The use of DOT 5 silicone fluid is not recommended. Internal damage to the pump components may result.**

SYSTEM BLEEDING

Front brake circuits should be bled using pressure bleeding equipment. The pressure bleeder must be of the diaphragm type and must have a rubber diaphragm between the air supply and brake fluid.

✷✷CAUTION

Do not move vehicle until a firm brake pedal is achieved. Failure to obtain firm brake pedal may result in personal injury and/or property damage

Front Brake Circuit

1. With the ignition switch **OFF**, disconnect the negative battery cable.

2. Depressurize the accumulator.

3. Remove the reservoir cap or disconnect the wiring sensor from the fluid level sensor and remove the sensor.

4. Install the special tool No. J-35798 in place of the cap or sensor.

5. Attach the brake bleeder to the adapter tool No. J-35798 and charge to 20 psi (138 kPa).

6. Attach a bleeder hose to one front bleeder valve and submerge the other end in a container of clean brake fluid.

7. Open the bleeder valve.

8. Allow the fluid to flow from the bleeder until no air bubbles are seen in the brake fluid.

9. Close the bleeder valve.

10. Repeat the previous steps on the other front bleeder valve.

11. Check the fluid level and fill as necessary.

12. Remove the brake bleeding equipment and adapters. Install the cap or sensor.

Rear Brake Circuit

1. Turn the ignition switch **OFF**.

2. Depressurize the accumulator.

3. Check the fluid level in the reservoir and fill as necessary.

4. Turn the ignition switch **ON** and allow the system to charge. (Listen for the pump motor, it will stop when the system is charged.)

5. Raise and safely support the vehicle.

6. Attach a clear bleeder hose to one of the rear bleeder valves and submerge the other end in a container of clean brake fluid.

7. Open the bleeder valve.

➡**Do not allow the pump to run more than 60 seconds at a time. If it must run longer, allow it to cool down for several minuets between the 60 second runs.**

8. With the ignition **ON**, slightly depress the brake pedal for at least 10 seconds.

9. Allow the fluid to flow from the bleeder until no air bubbles are seen in the brake fluid. Repeat the step as necessary.

10. Close the bleeder valve.

11. Repeat the procedure for the other side.

12. Lower the vehicle.

13. Fill the reservoir with clean fluid and check the pedal for sponginess. Repeat the entire bleeding procedure to correct a sponginess condition. Check the warning lamps for any indication of a low fluid level.

DIFFERENTIAL LOCK CONNECTOR FACES

CHART 15

ABS WIRING SCHEMATIC

CHART 16

DIFFERENTIAL LOCK ENGAGED
SWITCH JUMPER CONNECTORS

CIRCUIT NUMBER	WIRE COLOR	CIRCUIT DESCRIPTION
350	PINK-WHITE STRIPE	"ELEC BRK" FUSE TO PUMP MOTOR RELAY AND DIFFERENTIAL LOCK ENGAGED SWITCH
951	BLACK-WHITE STRIPE	DIFFERENTIAL LOCK ENGAGED SWITCH TO EBCM AND TO DIFFERENTIAL LOCK CONTROL RELAY AT CONSOLE VIA THE INSTRUMENT PANEL HARNESS

PIN B (951)

PIN A (350 E)

PIN A (350 E)

PIN B (951)

IGNITION ENABLE CIRCUIT

The ignition enable circuit provides power to the electronic brake control module (EBCM) for initialization and self checks.

A differential lock engaged switch is in series in this circuit. When the center differential in the transaxle transfer case is locked by the driver, the differential lock engaged switch opens the ignition enable circuit to deactivate the anti-lock brake system. When the center differential is released for normal operation, the ignition enable circuit is completed to the EBCM.

86819111

PRE-DIAGNOSIS INSPECTION

CHART 20

ITEM	INSPECT FOR:	CORRECTIVE ACTION
BRAKE FLUID RESERVOIR AND HYDRAULIC UNIT	– LOW FLUID LEVEL – EXTERNAL LEAKS	– FILL RESERVOIR – REPAIR LEAKS AS REQUIRED
PARKING BRAKE	– FULLY RELEASED – IMPROPERLY ADJUSTED	– RELEASE PARKING BRAKE – ADJUST CABLE
BATTERY	– ADEQUATE CHARGE	– CHARGE OR REPLACE BATTERY AS REQUIRED – SERVICE CHARGING SYSTEM AS REQUIRED
FUSES • 5 AMP ELECTRONIC BRAKE FUSE – LOCATED IN CONVENIENCE CENTER	– BLOWN FUSE	– REPLACE FUSE AND VERIFY OPERATION
• 10 AMP GAGES FUSE – LOCATED IN FUSE BLOCK	– BLOWN FUSE	– REPLACE FUSE AND VERIFY OPERATION
• 30 AMP MAIN RELAY FUSE – LOCATED ON MAIN RELAY BRACKET	– BLOWN FUSE	– REPLACE FUSE AND VERIFY OPERATION
• 30 AMP PUMP MOTOR FUSE – LOCATED ON PUMP MOTOR RELAY BRACKET	– BLOWN FUSE	– REPLACE FUSE AND VERIFY OPERATION
CONNECTORS • MAIN RELAY • PUMP MOTOR RELAY • PRESSURE SWITCH • PUMP MOTOR • MAIN VALVE • VALVE BLOCK • FLUID LEVEL SENSOR • ELECTRONIC BRAKE CONTROL MODULE (EBCM) • 4 SENSOR CONNECTORS (WITH ALL WHEEL DRIVE)	– PROPER ENGAGEMENT OF CONNECTOR – LOOSE WIRES IN CONNECTOR	– PROPERLY ENGAGE CONNECTORS – REPAIR LOOSE WIRES
• DIFFERENTIAL LOCK ENGAGED SWITCH CONNECTOR AT TRANSAXLE TRANSFER CASE • DIFFERENTIAL LOCK ENGAGED SWITCH JUMPER CONNECTOR TO EBCM WIRING HARNESS AT LEFT SIDE OF DASH PANEL	– PROPER ENGAGEMENT OF CONNECTOR – LOOSE WIRES IN CONNECTOR	– PROPERLY ENGAGE CONNECTORS – REPAIR LOOSE WIRES

ABS CIRCUIT INDEX

CHART 19

CIRCUIT NUMBER	WIRE COLOR	CIRCUIT LOCATION
002	RED	IGNITION ENABLE
003	PINK	IGNITION ENABLE
033	TAN-WHITE STRIPE	"BRAKE" WARNING LAMP
039	PINK-BLACK STRIPE	"BRAKE" WARNING LAMP
040	RED-WHITE STRIPE	PUMP MOTOR
155	BLACK	PUMP MOTOR. / MAIN RELAY / VALVE BLOCK AND MAIN VALVE / "BRAKE" WARNING LAMP
300	ORANGE	IGNITION ENABLE
350	PINK-WHITE STRIPE	IGNITION ENABLE, PUMP MOTOR
450	BLACK-WHITE STRIPE	IGNITION ENABLE, MAIN RELAY
640	RED-WHITE STRIPE	MAIN RELAY
850	ORANGE SPLICED TO PINK-WHITE	MAIN RELAY, "ANTILOCK" WARNING LAMP
852	BROWN-RED STRIPE	"ANTILOCK" WARNING LAMP
853	LT BLUE-ORANGE STRIPE	EBCM LOOP
854	RED	PUMP MOTOR
855	DARK BLUE	MAIN RELAY
856	PURPLE-WHITE STRIPE	VALVE BLOCK AND MAIN VALVE
857	BLACK-PINK STRIPE	VALVE BLOCK AND MAIN VALVE
858	DARK GREEN-YELLOW STRIPE	VALVE BLOCK AND MAIN VALVE
859	GRAY	VALVE BLOCK AND MAIN VALVE
861	BROWN-WHITE STRIPE	VALVE BLOCK AND MAIN VALVE
862	LIGHT BLUE-BLACK STRIPE	VALVE BLOCK AND MAIN VALVE
863	DARK BLUE-WHITE STRIPE	VALVE BLOCK AND MAIN VALVE
864	GRAY-RED STRIPE	PUMP MOTOR
865	PURPLE	EBCM LOOP
866	LIGHT GREEN	EBCM LOOP
901	RED-DOUBLE YELLOW STRIPE	EBCM TO EBCM CONNECT CIRCUIT
830	GREEN COAXIAL CABLE	WHEEL SPEED SENSOR
873	GREEN COAXIAL CABLE	WHEEL SPEED SENSOR
884	GREEN COAXIAL CABLE	WHEEL SPEED SENSOR
885	GREEN COAXIAL CABLE	WHEEL SPEED SENSOR
833	GREEN COAXIAL CABLE	WHEEL SPEED SENSOR
872	GREEN COAXIAL CABLE	WHEEL SPEED SENSOR
882	GREEN COAXIAL CABLE	WHEEL SPEED SENSOR
883	GREEN COAXIAL CABLE	WHEEL SPEED SENSOR

IGNITION ENABLE POWER CIRCUIT

When the ignition switch is "ON", the battery supplies a 12 volt signal to the EBCM through the junction block, fusible link, ignition switch, circuit 300 to the 5 amp electronic brake fuse in the convenience center, circuit 350E to the differential lock engaged switch, and circuit 951 to EBCM pin 2. The ignition enable circuit also supplies a 12 volt signal to the anti-lock brake system pump relay through a branch of circuit 350E, and to the differential lock control relay in the console through circuit 951.

When the ignition switch is turned to the "RUN" position, the "ANTI-LOCK" warning lamp will turn on for 3 to 5 seconds. If there is no voltage at EBCM pin 2, the anti-lock function will be disabled and the "ANTI-LOCK" warning lamp will remain on

IGNITION ENABLE GROUND CIRCUIT

Circuit 450 grounds the EBCM to the main relay bracket through EBCM pin 1

MAIN RELAY CIRCUIT

The main relay supplies switched battery power to the electronic brake control module (EBCM) to operate the main valve, solenoid valve, logic circuits and some self checks.

MAIN RELAY COIL CIRCUIT

The EBCM supplies 12 volts to the main relay coil through pin 8 of the EBCM and circuit 855 after the ignition switch is turned on, refer to "Ignition Enable Circuit" in this section. The main relay coil is grounded to the main relay bracket through circuit 450.

MAIN RELAY GROUND CIRCUIT

If the ignition system is on and power is not supplied to the main relay coil, circuit 850 will be grounded to the main relay bracket through circuit 155 and the "ANTI-LOCK" warning lamp will light, refer to "ANTI-LOCK Warning Lamp Circuit".

86819112

PRE-DIAGNOSIS INSPECTION (CONTINUED)

CHART 21

ITEM	INSPECT FOR:	CORRECTIVE ACTION
GROUNDS • BODY GROUNDS - LOCATED ON MAIN RELAY BRACKET • HYDRAULIC UNIT GROUND - ON HYDRAULIC UNIT	- LOOSE CONNECTIONS - BROKEN EYELETS - CORROSION	- TIGHTEN CONNECTIONS - REPAIR WIRE OR EYELET - CLEAN CONTACT SURFACES
JUNCTION BLOCK	- CORROSION - LOOSE JUNCTION BLOCK OR CONNECTIONS - BROKEN WIRES	- CLEAN CONTACT SURFACES - TIGHTEN CONNECTIONS - REPAIR OR REPLACE WIRES AS NECESSARY

WARNING AND INDICATOR LAMP SEQUENCES

CHART 22

WARNING/INDICATOR LAMP	COLOR	IGNITION "ON"	CRANKING*	RUNNING*	MOVING*	BRAKING*	STOPPED*	IDLE*	"LOCK-NORMAL" SWITCH MOVED TO "LOCK"	MOVED TO "NORMAL"
BRAKE	RED	OFF	ON	OFF	OFF	OFF	OFF	OFF	OFF	OFF
ANTI-LOCK	AMBER	ON THEN OFF	ON	ON THEN OFF	OFF	OFF	OFF	OFF	ON	ON THEN OFF
"LOCK-NORMAL" SWITCH "LOCK"	AMBER	OFF	OFF	OFF	OFF	OFF	OFF	OFF	ON	OFF
"NORMAL"	AMBER	OFF	OFF	OFF	OFF	OFF	OFF	OFF	FLASH	ON, THEN OFF
									OFF, THEN ON	ON, THEN OFF

NORMAL SEQUENCE

1. WITH IGNITION "ON", "ANTILOCK" WARNING LAMP WILL COME ON FOR 3.5 SECONDS IF ACCUMULATOR IS CHARGED. "ANTILOCK" WARNING LAMP MAY STAY ON FOR UP TO 30 SECONDS IF ACCUMULATOR IS DISCHARGED.

2. "BRAKE" AND "ANTILOCK" WARNING LAMPS WILL TURN ON DURING CRANKING.

3. IMMEDIATELY AFTER THE ENGINE STARTS, "ANTILOCK" WARNING LAMP WILL BE ON FOR 3.5 SECONDS.

4. WHEN "LOCK-NORMAL" SWITCH IS MOVED TO "LOCK", "ANTILOCK" INDICATOR LAMP WILL FLASH.

5. THE "LOCK" AND "ANTILOCK" LAMPS WILL TURN ON WHEN THE TRANSFER CASE DIFFERENTIAL VACUUM ACTUATED LOCK LOCKS THE DIFFERENTIAL.

6. WHEN "LOCK-NORMAL" SWITCH IS MOVED BACK TO "NORMAL", "ANTILOCK" WARNING LAMP WILL REMAIN ON FOR 3.5 SECONDS AND THEN GO OFF. "LOCK" INDICATOR LAMP WILL IMMEDIATELY STOP FLASHING AND REMAIN OFF.

7. THE "LOCK" INDICATOR LAMP WILL GO OFF WHEN THE TRANSFER CASE DIFFERENTIAL SPRING MECHANISM UNLOCKS THE DIFFERENTIAL.

8. ALL FOUR LAMPS WILL REMAIN OFF AT ALL OTHER TIMES.

* "LOCK-NORMAL" SWITCH SET TO "NORMAL"

LOW OR SPONGY PEDAL

CHART 24

- BLEED BRAKE SYSTEM AS DESCRIBED IN THIS SECTION
  - PEDAL FEELS NORMAL → CONDITION CORRECTED
  - PEDAL LOW OR SPONGY → CHECK CONDITION OF FRONT AND REAR BRAKES
    - BRAKES WORN → REPAIR AS REQUIRED
    - BRAKES IN GOOD CONDITION → INSPECT FOR FIRM PUSHROD ENGAGEMENT IN HYDRAULIC UNIT
      - PUSHROD IMPROPERLY ENGAGED → REPLACE HYDRAULIC UNIT
      - PUSHROD PROPERLY ENGAGED → CHECK HYDRAULIC UNIT MOUNTING → REMOUNT LOOSE OR MISADJUSTED COMPONENTS

WARNING AND INDICATOR LAMP SYMPTOM INDEX

CHART 23

WARNING LAMP SEQUENCE	SYMPTOM DESCRIPTION	SEE
	NORMAL WARNING LAMP SEQUENCE WITH - EXCESSIVE PEDAL TRAVEL OR SPONGY PEDAL - ANTI LOCK BRAKING OPERATION OR VALVE CYCLING DURING NORMAL STOPS ON DRY PAVEMENT - POOR VEHICLE TRACKING DURING ANTI-LOCK BRAKING	24 49 63
	CONTINUOUS "ANTI-LOCK" WARNING LAMP, CONTINUOUS "BRAKE" WARNING LAMP	
	"ANTI-LOCK" AND "BRAKE" WARNING LAMPS COME ON WHILE BRAKING	25
	NORMAL "ANTI-LOCK" WARNING LAMP, CONTINUOUS "BRAKE" WARNING LAMP	26
	NORMAL OR CONTINUOUS "ANTI-LOCK" WARNING LAMP, FLASHING "BRAKE" WARNING LAMP	26
	CONTINUOUS "ANTI-LOCK" WARNING LAMP, NORMAL "BRAKE" WARNING LAMP	28
	"ANTI-LOCK" WARNING LAMP COMES ON AFTER VEHICLE STARTS MOVING, NORMAL "BRAKE" WARNING LAMP	49
	NO "ANTI-LOCK" WARNING LAMP WHILE CRANKING, NORMAL "BRAKE" WARNING LAMP	68
	NO "ANTI-LOCK" WARNING LAMP, NORMAL "BRAKE" WARNING LAMP	68
	INTERMITTENT "ANTI-LOCK" WARNING LAMP WHILE DRIVING, NORMAL "BRAKE" WARNING LAMP	70

LAMP STATUS • SHADED AREAS = LAMP ON
• BLANK AREAS (NO SHADING) = LAMP OFF
• PARTIALLY SHADED AREAS = LAMP ON FOR PART OF TEST PERIOD

86819114

ENERGY UNIT: FUNCTIONAL CHECK (CONTINUED)

CHART 26

CONTINUE FROM 26

ACCUMULATOR LEAKDOWN TEST
- WITH IGNITION SWITCH IN "RUN" POSITION, PUMP BRAKE PEDAL UNTIL PUMP MOTOR STARTS. WHEN PUMP STOPS, TURN IGNITION SWITCH "OFF".
- AFTER WAITING APPROXIMATELY THREE MINUTES, RECORD ACCUMULATOR PRESSURE
- WAIT FIVE MINUTES AND RECORD ACCUMULATOR PRESSURE
- SUBTRACT SECOND PRESSURE READING FROM FIRST READING TO GET ACCUMULATOR LEAKDOWN

LEAKDOWN GREATER THAN 140 KPA (20 PSI) → SEE 29

LEAKDOWN LESS THAN 140 KPA (20 PSI)

ENERGY UNIT OPERATION IS NORMAL

REVERIFY SYSTEM OPERATION AND WARNING LAMP SEQUENCE

NORMAL WARNING LAMP SEQUENCE

CONTINUOUS "BRAKE" WARNING LAMP OPERATION → SEE 67

"BRAKE" WARNING LAMP TURNS ON DURING BRAKING → REPLACE HYDRAULIC UNIT

FLASHING "BRAKE" WARNING LAMP → SEE 67

SEE NOTE ON INTERMITTENTS

ENERGY UNIT: FUNCTIONAL CHECK

CHART 25

- DEPRESSURIZE HYDRAULIC ACCUMULATOR
- TURN IGNITION SWITCH TO "RUN" POSITION

PUMP RUNS

PUMP DOES NOT RUN → SEE 40

TURN IGNITION SWITCH "OFF"

IF COMPLAINT IS CONTINUOUS "BRAKE" WARNING LAMP OPERATION, CHECK FOR INOPERATIVE OR GROUNDED PARKING BRAKE SWITCH AND REPAIR AS REQUIRED

DETERMINE ACCUMULATOR PRE-CHARGE PRESSURE
- DEPRESSURIZE HYDRAULIC ACCUMULATOR
- INSTALL PRESSURE GAGE J 35604
- TURN IGNITION SWITCH TO "RUN" AND OBSERVE GAGE. PUMP MOTOR WILL START AND GAGE NEEDLE WILL QUICKLY JUMP TO THE PRE-CHARGE PRESSURE AND THEN SLOWLY RISE. RECORD PRECHARGE PRESSURE.

PRE-CHARGE PRESSURE LESS THAN 4000 KPA (580 PSI) OR GREATER THAN 8000 KPA (1160 PSI) → REPLACE ACCUMULATOR

PRE-CHARGE PRESSURE 4000-8000 KPA (580-1160 PSI)

DETERMINE ACCUMULATOR FINAL CHARGE PRESSURE
- TURN IGNITION SWITCH "OFF"
- DEPRESSURIZE HYDRAULIC ACCUMULATOR
- TURN IGNITION SWITCH TO "RUN" POSITION AND OBSERVE PUMP

PUMP CONTINUES TO RUN AFTER 45 SECONDS
- RECORD ACCUMULATOR PRESSURE
- TURN IGNITION SWITCH "OFF"
- SEE 28

PUMP STOPS WITHIN 45 SECONDS

RECORD FINAL CHARGE PRESSURE

FINAL CHARGE PRESSURE LESS THAN 17,200 KPA (2500 PSI) → SEE 41

FINAL CHARGE PRESSURE GREATER THAN 17,200 KPA (2500 PSI)

CONTINUE ON 27

86819115

HYDRAULIC UNIT LEAKDOWN

CHART 28

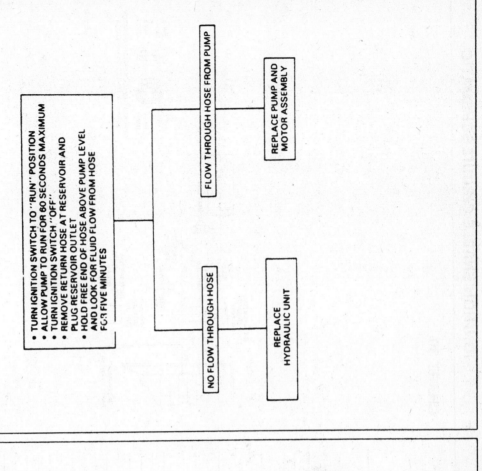

- TURN IGNITION SWITCH TO "RUN" POSITION
- ALLOW PUMP TO RUN FOR 60 SECONDS MAXIMUM
- TURN IGNITION SWITCH "OFF"
- REMOVE RETURN HOSE AT RESERVOIR AND PLUG RESERVOIR OUTLET
- HOLD FREE END OF HOSE ABOVE PUMP LEVEL AND LOOK FOR FLUID FLOW FROM HOSE FOR FIVE MINUTES

NO FLOW THROUGH HOSE → REPLACE HYDRAULIC UNIT

FLOW THROUGH HOSE FROM PUMP → REPLACE PUMP AND MOTOR ASSEMBLY

PUMP RUNS LONGER THAN 45 SECONDS

CHART 27

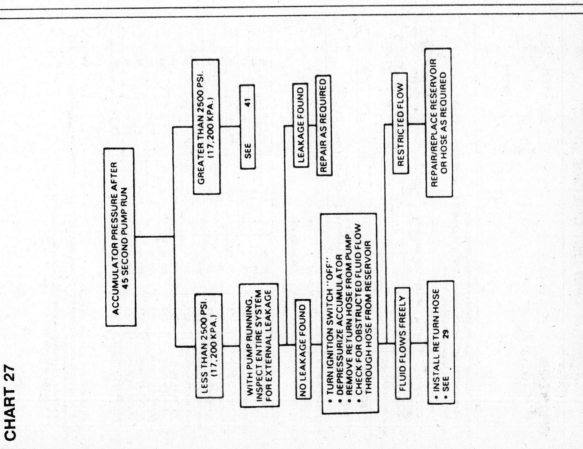

ACCUMULATOR PRESSURE AFTER 45 SECOND PUMP RUN

GREATER THAN 2500 PSI. (17,200 KPA.) → SEE 41

LESS THAN 2500 PSI. (17,200 KPA.)

WITH PUMP RUNNING, INSPECT ENTIRE SYSTEM FOR EXTERNAL LEAKAGE

LEAKAGE FOUND → REPAIR AS REQUIRED

NO LEAKAGE FOUND

- TURN IGNITION SWITCH "OFF"
- DEPRESSURIZE ACCUMULATOR
- REMOVE RETURN HOSE FROM PUMP
- CHECK FOR OBSTRUCTED FLUID FLOW THROUGH HOSE FROM RESERVOIR

RESTRICTED FLOW → REPAIR/REPLACE RESERVOIR OR HOSE AS REQUIRED

FLUID FLOWS FREELY

- INSTALL RETURN HOSE
- SEE 29

86819116

IGNITION ENABLE CIRCUIT SCHEMATIC

CHART 30

PIN OUT CHECKS

CHART 29

- CONNECT J 35592 TO 35-PIN EBCM HARNESS CONNECTOR.
- PERFORM CHECKS WITH HIGH IMPEDANCE DIGITAL MULTIMETER J 34029-A OR EQUIVALENT
- ALL CHECKS ARE MADE WITH ENGINE OFF

CIRCUIT TO BE TESTED	IGNITION SWITCH POSITION	MULTIMETER SCALE/RANGE	MEASURE BETWEEN PIN NUMBERS	SPECIFICATION	IF RESULT NOT WITHIN SPECIFICATION, SEE
IGNITION ENABLE	RUN	20 DCV	2(+)•,3(-)•	10 V MINIMUM	32 and 33
MAIN RELAY GROUND	OFF	200 ∧	1,3	CONTINUITY	35
MAIN RELAY COIL	OFF	200 ∧	1,20	CONTINUITY	36
		200 ∧	1,8	45-105 ∧	

BEFORE PERFORMING THIS TEST • REMOVE GAGE FUSE FROM FUSE BOX
• PLACE FUSED JUMPER BETWEEN J 35592 PINS 2 & 8

| MAIN RELAY POWER | ON | 20 DCV | 3(+),1(-) | 10 V MINIMUM | 37 |
| | ON | 20 DCV | 20(+),1(-) | 10 V MINIMUM | |

BEFORE PROCEEDING • REMOVE JUMPER FROM PINS 2 & 8
• INSTALL GAGE FUSE

EBCM SWITCH LOOP	OFF	200 ∧	9,10	LESS THAN 5 ∧	44
	OFF	200 ∧	1,9	NO CONTINUITY	45
RR SENSOR RESISTANCE	OFF	2k ∧	4,22	800-1400 ∧	47
LF SENSOR RESISTANCE	OFF	2k ∧	6,23	800-1400 ∧	48
LR SENSOR RESISTANCE	OFF	2k ∧	8,24	800-1400 ∧	49
RF SENSOR RESISTANCE	OFF	2k ∧	7,25	800-1400 ∧	50
MAIN VALVE SOLENOID	OFF	200 ∧	11,18	2-5 ∧	56
VALVE BLOCK GROUND	OFF	200 ∧	1,11	LESS THAN 2 ∧	58
RF INLET VALVE	OFF	200 ∧	11,15	5-7 ∧	59
LF INLET VALVE	OFF	200 ∧	11,35	5-7 ∧	60
REAR INLET VALVE	OFF	200 ∧	11,17	5-7 ∧	61
RF OUTLET VALVE	OFF	200 ∧	11,34	3-5 ∧	62
LF OUTLET VALVE	OFF	200 ∧	11,16	3-5 ∧	63
REAR OUTLET VALVE	OFF	200 ∧	11,33	3-5 ∧	64

*(+) OR (-) INDICATES MULTIMETER POLARITY
IF ALL TEST RESULTS ARE WITHIN SPECIFICATION, RECONNECT EBCM AND VERIFY CONTINUOUS "ANTILOCK" WARNING LAMP OPERATION
- IF NORMAL OPERATION RESUMES, SEE NOTE ON INTERMITTENTS
- IF LAMP REMAINS ON, SEE 69

86819117

CHECKING IGNITION ENABLE CIRCUIT

CHART 31

CHECKING IGNITION ENABLE CIRCUIT (CONTINUED)

CHART 32

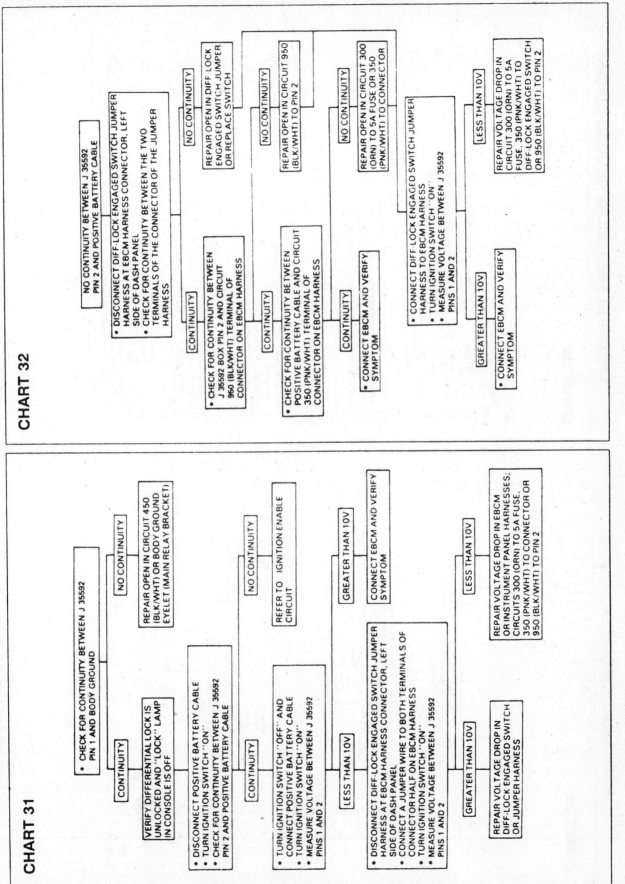

86819118

CHECKING MAIN RELAY GROUND CIRCUIT

CHART 34

MAIN RELAY CIRCUIT SCHEMATIC

CHART 33

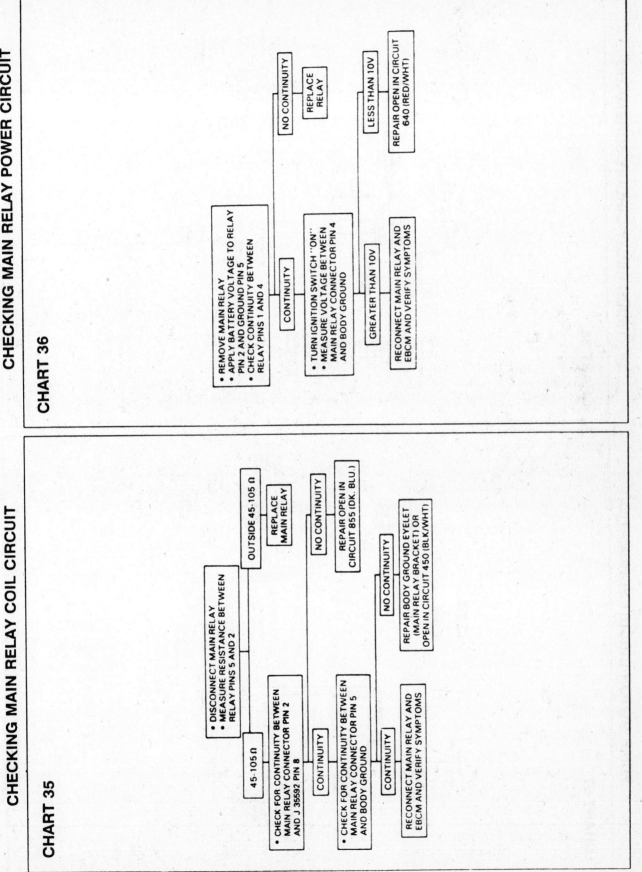

CHECKING MAIN RELAY POWER CIRCUIT

CHART 36

- REMOVE MAIN RELAY
- APPLY BATTERY VOLTAGE TO RELAY PIN 2 AND GROUND PIN 5
- CHECK CONTINUITY BETWEEN RELAY PINS 1 AND 4

NO CONTINUITY → REPLACE RELAY

CONTINUITY

- TURN IGNITION SWITCH "ON"
- MEASURE VOLTAGE BETWEEN MAIN RELAY CONNECTOR PIN 4 AND BODY GROUND

LESS THAN 10V → REPAIR OPEN IN CIRCUIT 640 (RED/WHT)

GREATER THAN 10V → RECONNECT MAIN RELAY AND EBCM AND VERIFY SYMPTOMS

CHECKING MAIN RELAY COIL CIRCUIT

CHART 35

- DISCONNECT MAIN RELAY
- MEASURE RESISTANCE BETWEEN RELAY PINS 5 AND 2

OUTSIDE 45-105 Ω → REPLACE MAIN RELAY

45-105 Ω

- CHECK FOR CONTINUITY BETWEEN MAIN RELAY CONNECTOR PIN 2 AND J 35592 PIN 8

NO CONTINUITY → REPAIR OPEN IN CIRCUIT 855 (DK. BLU.)

CONTINUITY

- CHECK FOR CONTINUITY BETWEEN MAIN RELAY CONNECTOR PIN 5 AND BODY GROUND

NO CONTINUITY → REPAIR BODY GROUND EYELET (MAIN RELAY BRACKET) OR OPEN IN CIRCUIT 450 (BLK/WHT)

CONTINUITY → RECONNECT MAIN RELAY AND EBCM AND VERIFY SYMPTOMS

86819120

MAIN RELAY CIRCUIT SCHEMATIC

CHART 38

PUMP MOTOR CIRCUIT SCHEMATIC

CHART 37

CHECKING PRESSURE SWITCH

CHART 40

I. SWITCH STATUS – PRESSURIZED

- TURN IGNITION SWITCH TO "RUN" UNTIL PUMP STOPS
- TURN IGNITION SWITCH "OFF"
  NOTE: IF PUMP CONTINUES TO RUN AFTER 45 SECONDS, TURN IGNITION SWITCH OFF AND PROCEED
- CHECK PRESSURE SWITCH PINS FOR THE FOLLOWING CONDITIONS USING HIGH IMPEDANCE DIGITAL MULTIMETER

MEASURE BETWEEN PINS	SCALE	SPECIFICATION
1, 2	200 Ω	NO CONTINUITY
1, 4	200 Ω	NO CONTINUITY
3, 5	200 Ω	CONTINUITY
ALL PINS AND BODY GROUND	200 Ω	NO CONTINUITY

IF ANY CONDITION IS NOT MET, REPLACE PRESSURE SWITCH

II. SWITCH STATUS – DEPRESSURIZED

- DEPRESSURIZE HYDRAULIC ACCUMULATOR AS DESCRIBED IN THIS SECTION
- CHECK PRESSURE SWITCH PINS FOR THE FOLLOWING CONDITIONS USING HIGH IMPEDANCE DIGITAL MULTIMETER

MEASURE BETWEEN PINS	SCALE	SPECIFICATION
1, 2	200 Ω	CONTINUITY
1, 4	200 Ω	CONTINUITY
3, 5	200 Ω	NO CONTINUITY
ALL PINS AND BODY GROUND	200 Ω	NO CONTINUITY

IF ANY CONDITION IS NOT MET, REPLACE PRESSURE SWITCH

CONTINUED

PUMP DOES NOT RUN

CHART 39

- TURN IGNITION SWITCH "OFF"
- DEPRESSURIZE HYDRAULIC ACCUMULATOR
- DISCONNECT PUMP MOTOR CONNECTOR
- TURN IGNITION SWITCH TO "RUN"
- MEASURE VOLTAGE ACROSS PINS OF PUMP MOTOR CONNECTOR

GREATER THAN 10V → REPLACE PUMP AND MOTOR ASSEMBLY

LESS THAN 10V →

- REMOVE PUMP RELAY
- CHECK FOR CONTINUITY BETWEEN RELAY PINS 2 AND 5

NO CONTINUITY → REPLACE RELAY

CONTINUITY → MEASURE VOLTAGE BETWEEN RELAY CONNECTOR PIN 4 AND BODY GROUND

LESS THAN 10V → REPAIR CIRCUIT 40 (RED/WHT)

GREATER THAN 10V → CHECK FOR CONTINUITY BETWEEN RELAY CONNECTOR PIN 1 AND PUMP MOTOR CONNECTOR PIN 1

NO CONTINUITY → REPAIR OPEN IN CIRCUIT 854 (RED)

CONTINUITY → CHECK FOR CONTINUITY BETWEEN RELAY CONNECTOR PIN 5 AND BODY GROUND

NO CONTINUITY → MEASURE VOLTAGE BETWEEN RELAY CONNECTOR PINS 2 AND 5

CONTINUITY → CHECK FOR CONTINUITY BETWEEN RELAY CONNECTOR PIN 5 AND PRESSURE SWITCH CONNECTOR PIN 4

LESS THAN 10V → REPAIR CIRCUIT 350 (PNK/WHT)

GREATER THAN 10V → REPLACE RELAY

NO CONTINUITY → REPAIR OPEN IN CIRCUIT 864 (GRY/RED)

CONTINUITY → CHECK FOR CONTINUITY BETWEEN PRESSURE SWITCH CONNECTOR PIN 1 AND BODY GROUND

NO CONTINUITY → REPAIR CIRCUIT 155 (BLK) AND CHECK BODY GROUND

CONTINUITY → REPLACE PRESSURE SWITCH

86819122

CHECKING PRESSURE SWITCH (CONTINUED)

CHART 41

III. SWITCH THRESHOLDS

- DEPRESSURIZE HYDRAULIC ACCUMULATOR
- INSTALL J 35604-A
- CONNECT PRESSURE SWITCH CONNECTOR AND TURN IGNITION SWITCH TO "RUN" UNTIL PUMP STOPS
- USING HIGH IMPEDANCE DIGITAL MULTIMETER J 34029-A OR EQUIVALENT, MONITOR FOR CONTINUITY BETWEEN PRESSURE SWITCH PINS AS SHOWN BELOW WHILE SLOWLY BLEEDING OFF ACCUMULATOR PRESSURE BY PUMPING THE BRAKE PEDAL. CONTINUITY SHOULD BE GAINED OR LOST AS INDICATED.
- PRESSURIZE SYSTEM BETWEEN EACH TEST BY RECONNECTING PRESSURE SWITCH AND TURNING IGNITION SWITCH TO "RUN" UNTIL PUMP STOPS

MEASURE BETWEEN PINS	SWITCH STATUS	PRESSURE RANGE
1, 4	CONTINUITY SHOULD BE GAINED AT:	1980-2080 PSI (13,650-14,350 KPA)
1, 2	CONTINUITY SHOULD BE GAINED AT:	1500-1550 PSI (10,350-10,700 KPA)
3, 5	CONTINUITY SHOULD BE LOST AT:	1500-1550 PSI (10,350-10,700 KPA)

- IF ANY CONDITION IS NOT MET, REPLACE PRESSURE SWITCH

- DEPRESSURIZE HYDRAULIC ACCUMULATOR AS DESCRIBED IN THIS SECTION
- WITH IGNITION "OFF," CONNECT PRESSURE SWITCH CONNECTOR
- TURN IGNITION TO "RUN" AND OBSERVE GAGE. "ANTILOCK" LAMP, "BRAKE" LAMP AND PUMP MOTOR EVENTS SHOULD OCCUR AT PRESSURES INDICATED IN CHART BELOW

EVENT	PRESSURE
"ANTILOCK" LAMP TURNS OFF	1900-1975 PSI (13,100-13,600 KPA)
"BRAKE" LAMP TURNS OFF	1900-1975 PSI (13,100-13,600 KPA)
PUMP MOTOR STOPS	2550-2670 PSI (17,580-18,400 KPA)

IF ANY CONDITION IS NOT MET, REPLACE PRESSURE SWITCH

EBCM LOOP CIRCUIT SCHEMATIC

CHART 42

FLUID LEVEL SENSOR

PUMP MOTOR

PRESSURE SWITCH

HYDRAULIC UNIT

ELECTRONIC BRAKE CONTROL MODULE (EBCM)

FLUID LEVEL SENSOR CONNECTOR
PIN 1 853 LT BLUE W/ORANGE STRIPE
PIN 2 866 LT GREEN

PRESSURE SWITCH CONNECTOR
PIN 1 155 BLACK
PIN 2 033 TAN W/WHITE STRIPE
PIN 3 853 LT BLUE W/ORANGE STRIPE
PIN 4 864 GRAY W/RED STRIPE
PIN 5 865 PURPLE

86819123

EBCM LOOP CIRCUIT SHORTED

CHART 44

EBCM LOOP CIRCUIT OPEN

CHART 43

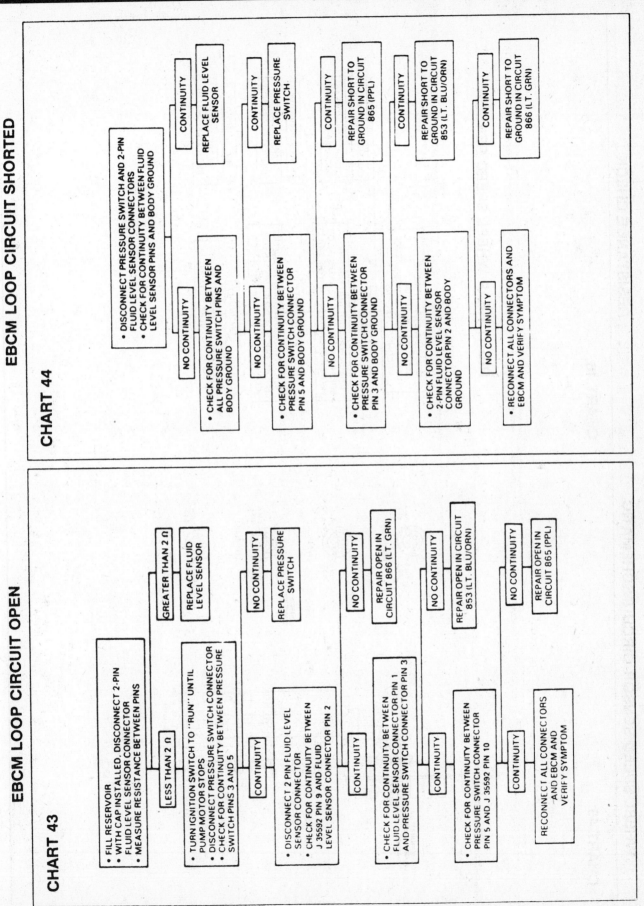

86819124

WHEEL SPEED SENSOR CIRCUIT SCHEMATIC

RESISTANCE CHECK

CHART 45

CHART 46

RIGHT REAR WHEEL SPEED SENSOR

- DISCONNECT RIGHT REAR SENSOR CONNECTOR
- MEASURE SENSOR RESISTANCE AT CONNECTOR PINS

800-1400 Ω

OUTSIDE 800-1400 Ω → REPLACE RIGHT REAR WHEEL SPEED SENSOR

CHECK FOR CONTINUITY BETWEEN BREAK-OUT BOX PIN 22 AND SENSOR CONNECTOR PIN B (HARNESS SIDE)

CONTINUITY

NO CONTINUITY → REPAIR CIRCUIT 882 (COAX CENTER)

CHECK FOR CONTINUITY BETWEEN BREAK-OUT BOX PIN 4 AND SENSOR CONNECTOR PIN A (HARNESS SIDE)

CONTINUITY

NO CONTINUITY → REPAIR CIRCUIT 883 (COAX SHIELD)

RECONNECT CONNECTOR AND EBCM AND VERIFY SYMPTOM

86819125

RESISTANCE CHECK

CHART 48

LEFT REAR WHEEL SPEED SENSOR

- DISCONNECT LEFT REAR SENSOR CONNECTOR
- MEASURE SENSOR RESISTANCE AT CONNECTOR PINS

800-1400 Ω

OUTSIDE 800-1400 Ω

REPLACE LEFT REAR WHEEL SPEED SENSOR

CHECK FOR CONTINUITY BETWEEN BREAK-OUT BOX PIN 24 AND SENSOR CONNECTOR PIN B (HARNESS SIDE)

NO CONTINUITY

CONTINUITY

REPAIR CIRCUIT 884 (COAX CENTER)

CHECK FOR CONTINUITY BETWEEN BREAK-OUT BOX PIN 6 AND SENSOR CONNECTOR PIN A (HARNESS SIDE)

NO CONTINUITY

CONTINUITY

REPAIR CIRCUIT 885 (COAX SHIELD)

RECONNECT CONNECTOR AND EBCM AND VERIFY SYMPTOM

RESISTANCE CHECK

CHART 47

LEFT FRONT WHEEL SPEED SENSOR

- DISCONNECT LEFT FRONT SENSOR CONNECTOR
- MEASURE SENSOR RESISTANCE AT CONNECTOR PINS

800-1400 Ω

OUTSIDE 800-1400 Ω

REPLACE LEFT FRONT WHEEL SPEED SENSOR

CHECK FOR CONTINUITY BETWEEN J 35592 PIN 23 AND SENSOR CONNECTOR PIN B (HARNESS SIDE)

NO CONTINUITY

CONTINUITY

REPAIR CIRCUIT 830 (COAX CENTER)

CHECK FOR CONTINUITY BETWEEN J 35592 PIN 5 AND SENSOR CONNECTOR PIN A (HARNESS SIDE)

NO CONTINUITY

CONTINUITY

REPAIR CIRCUIT 873 (COAX SHIELD)

RECONNECT CONNECTOR AND EBCM AND VERIFY SYMPTOM

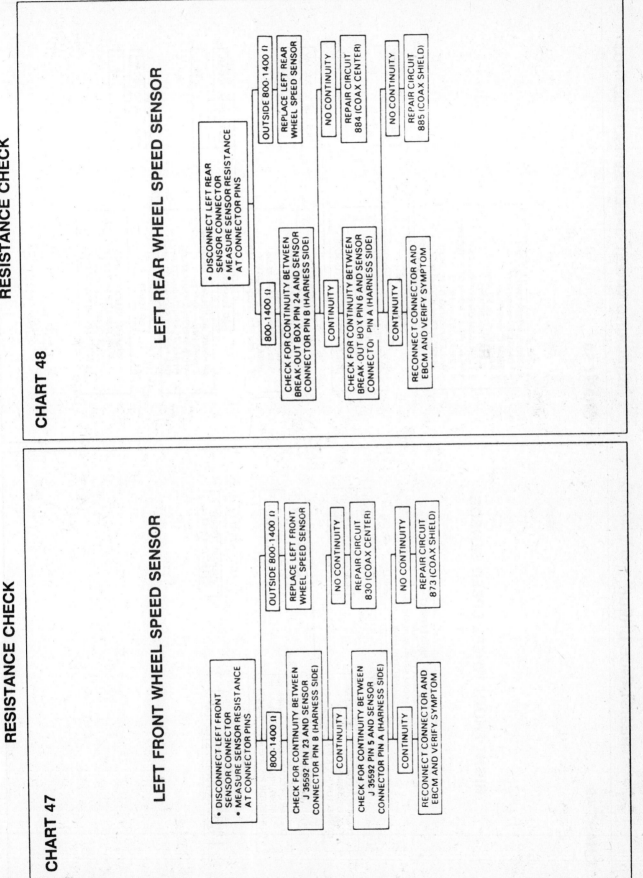

86819126

CHECKING WHEEL SPEED SENSOR OUTPUT

CHART 50

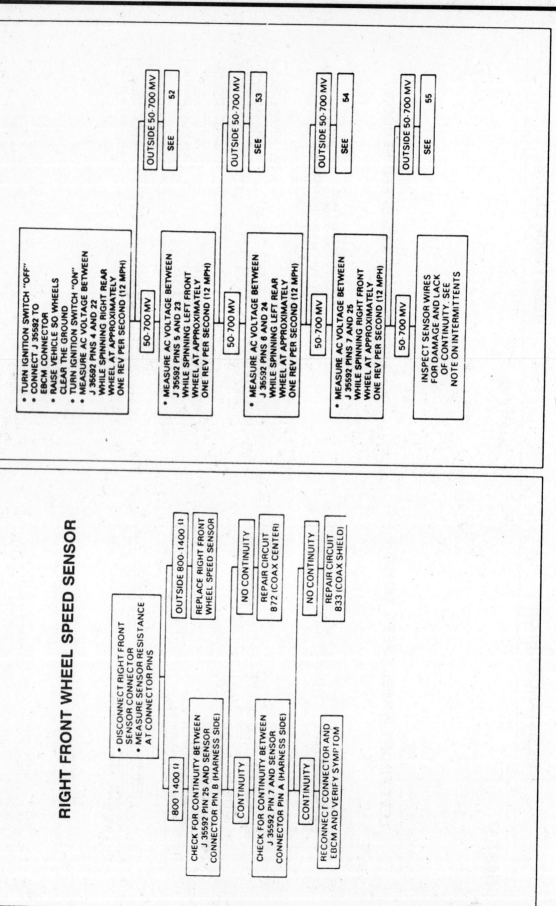

- TURN IGNITION SWITCH "OFF"
- CONNECT J 35592 TO EBCM CONNECTOR
- RAISE VEHICLE SO WHEELS CLEAR THE GROUND
- TURN IGNITION SWITCH "ON"
- MEASURE AC VOLTAGE BETWEEN J 35592 PINS 4 AND 22 WHILE SPINNING RIGHT REAR WHEEL AT APPROXIMATELY ONE REV PER SECOND (12 MPH)

50-700 MV → OUTSIDE 50-700 MV / SEE 52

- MEASURE AC VOLTAGE BETWEEN J 35592 PINS 5 AND 23 WHILE SPINNING LEFT FRONT WHEEL AT APPROXIMATELY ONE REV PER SECOND (12 MPH)

50-700 MV → OUTSIDE 50-700 MV / SEE 53

- MEASURE AC VOLTAGE BETWEEN J 35592 PINS 6 AND 24 WHILE SPINNING LEFT REAR WHEEL AT APPROXIMATELY ONE REV PER SECOND (12 MPH)

50-700 MV → OUTSIDE 50-700 MV / SEE 54

- MEASURE AC VOLTAGE BETWEEN J 35592 PINS 7 AND 25 WHILE SPINNING RIGHT FRONT WHEEL AT APPROXIMATELY ONE REV PER SECOND (12 MPH)

50-700 MV → OUTSIDE 50-700 MV / SEE 55

- INSPECT SENSOR WIRES FOR DAMAGE AND LACK OF CONTINUITY. SEE NOTE ON INTERMITTENTS

RESISTANCE CHECK

CHART 49

RIGHT FRONT WHEEL SPEED SENSOR

- DISCONNECT RIGHT FRONT SENSOR CONNECTOR
- MEASURE SENSOR RESISTANCE AT CONNECTOR PINS

800 1400 Ω → OUTSIDE 800-1400 Ω / REPLACE RIGHT FRONT WHEEL SPEED SENSOR

CHECK FOR CONTINUITY BETWEEN J 35592 PIN 25 AND SENSOR CONNECTOR PIN B (HARNESS SIDE)

CONTINUITY → NO CONTINUITY / REPAIR CIRCUIT 872 (COAX CENTER)

CHECK FOR CONTINUITY BETWEEN J 35592 PIN 7 AND SENSOR CONNECTOR PIN A (HARNESS SIDE)

CONTINUITY → NO CONTINUITY / REPAIR CIRCUIT 833 (COAX SHIELD)

RECONNECT CONNECTOR AND EBCM AND VERIFY SYMPTOM

86819127

LEFT FRONT WHEEL SPEED SENSOR OUTPUT

CHART 52

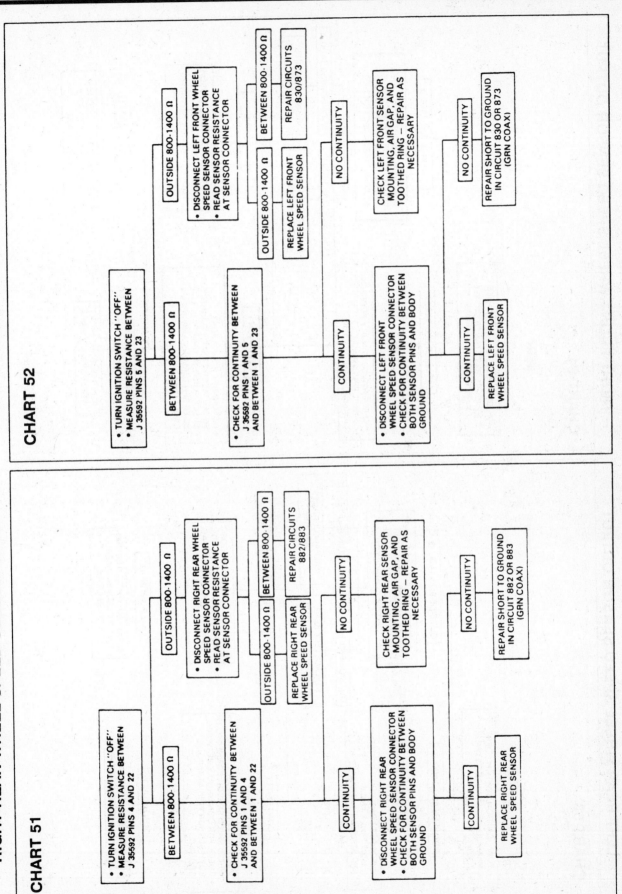

- TURN IGNITION SWITCH "OFF"
- MEASURE RESISTANCE BETWEEN J 35592 PINS 5 AND 23

↓ BETWEEN 800-1400 Ω → CHECK FOR CONTINUITY BETWEEN J 35592 PINS 1 AND 5 AND BETWEEN 1 AND 23

↓ OUTSIDE 800-1400 Ω → • DISCONNECT LEFT FRONT WHEEL SPEED SENSOR CONNECTOR • READ SENSOR RESISTANCE AT SENSOR CONNECTOR

BETWEEN 800-1400 Ω → REPAIR CIRCUITS 830/873

OUTSIDE 800-1400 Ω → REPLACE LEFT FRONT WHEEL SPEED SENSOR

CONTINUITY → • DISCONNECT LEFT FRONT WHEEL SPEED SENSOR CONNECTOR • CHECK FOR CONTINUITY BETWEEN BOTH SENSOR PINS AND BODY GROUND

NO CONTINUITY → CHECK LEFT FRONT SENSOR MOUNTING, AIR GAP, AND TOOTHED RING — REPAIR AS NECESSARY

CONTINUITY → REPLACE LEFT FRONT WHEEL SPEED SENSOR

NO CONTINUITY → REPAIR SHORT TO GROUND IN CIRCUIT 830 OR 873 (GRN COAX)

RIGHT REAR WHEEL SPEED SENSOR OUTPUT

CHART 51

- TURN IGNITION SWITCH "OFF"
- MEASURE RESISTANCE BETWEEN J 35592 PINS 4 AND 22

↓ BETWEEN 800-1400 Ω → CHECK FOR CONTINUITY BETWEEN J 35592 PINS 1 AND 4 AND BETWEEN 1 AND 22

↓ OUTSIDE 800-1400 Ω → • DISCONNECT RIGHT REAR WHEEL SPEED SENSOR CONNECTOR • READ SENSOR RESISTANCE AT SENSOR CONNECTOR

BETWEEN 800-1400 Ω → REPAIR CIRCUITS 882/883

OUTSIDE 800-1400 Ω → REPLACE RIGHT REAR WHEEL SPEED SENSOR

CONTINUITY → • DISCONNECT RIGHT REAR WHEEL SPEED SENSOR CONNECTOR • CHECK FOR CONTINUITY BETWEEN BOTH SENSOR PINS AND BODY GROUND

NO CONTINUITY → CHECK RIGHT REAR SENSOR MOUNTING, AIR GAP, AND TOOTHED RING — REPAIR AS NECESSARY

CONTINUITY → REPLACE RIGHT REAR WHEEL SPEED SENSOR

NO CONTINUITY → REPAIR SHORT TO GROUND IN CIRCUIT 882 OR 883 (GRN COAX)

86819128

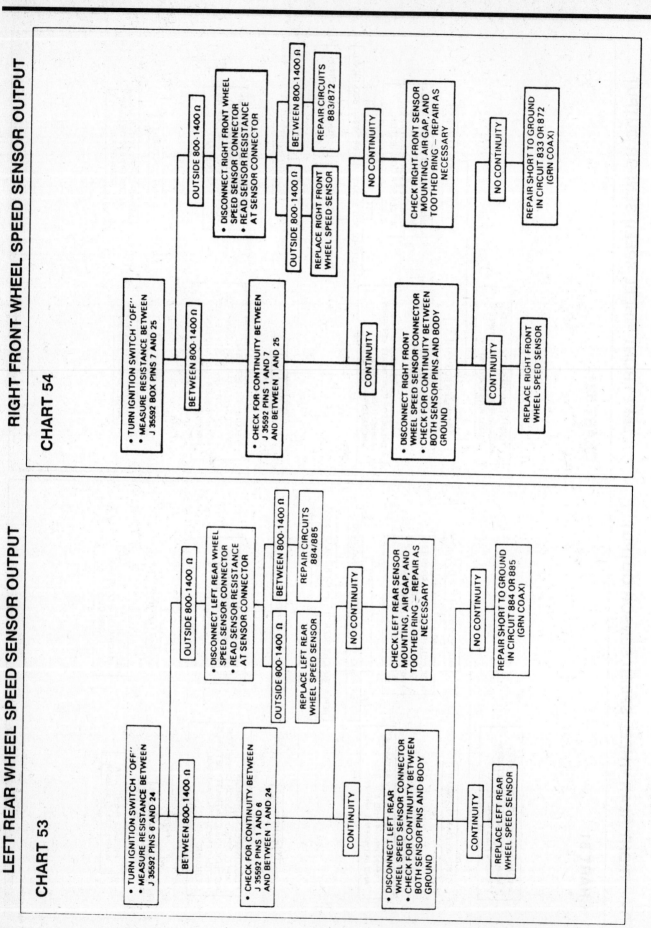

LEFT REAR WHEEL SPEED SENSOR OUTPUT

CHART 53

- TURN IGNITION SWITCH "OFF"
- MEASURE RESISTANCE BETWEEN J 35592 PINS 6 AND 24

BETWEEN 800-1400 Ω

- CHECK FOR CONTINUITY BETWEEN J 35592 PINS 1 AND 6 AND BETWEEN 1 AND 24

OUTSIDE 800-1400 Ω

- DISCONNECT LEFT REAR WHEEL SPEED SENSOR CONNECTOR
- READ SENSOR RESISTANCE AT SENSOR CONNECTOR

OUTSIDE 800-1400 Ω

REPLACE LEFT REAR WHEEL SPEED SENSOR

BETWEEN 800-1400 Ω

REPAIR CIRCUITS 884/885

CONTINUITY

- DISCONNECT LEFT REAR WHEEL SPEED SENSOR CONNECTOR
- CHECK FOR CONTINUITY BETWEEN BOTH SENSOR PINS AND BODY GROUND

NO CONTINUITY

CHECK LEFT REAR SENSOR MOUNTING, AIR GAP, AND TOOTHED RING — REPAIR AS NECESSARY

CONTINUITY

REPLACE LEFT REAR WHEEL SPEED SENSOR

NO CONTINUITY

REPAIR SHORT TO GROUND IN CIRCUIT 884 OR 885 (GRN COAX)

RIGHT FRONT WHEEL SPEED SENSOR OUTPUT

CHART 54

- TURN IGNITION SWITCH "OFF"
- MEASURE RESISTANCE BETWEEN J 35592 BOX PINS 7 AND 25

BETWEEN 800-1400 Ω

- CHECK FOR CONTINUITY BETWEEN J 35592 PINS 1 AND 7 AND BETWEEN 1 AND 25

OUTSIDE 800-1400 Ω

- DISCONNECT RIGHT FRONT WHEEL SPEED SENSOR CONNECTOR
- READ SENSOR RESISTANCE AT SENSOR CONNECTOR

OUTSIDE 800-1400 Ω

REPLACE RIGHT FRONT WHEEL SPEED SENSOR

BETWEEN 800-1400 Ω

REPAIR CIRCUITS 883/872

CONTINUITY

- DISCONNECT RIGHT FRONT WHEEL SPEED SENSOR CONNECTOR
- CHECK FOR CONTINUITY BETWEEN BOTH SENSOR PINS AND BODY GROUND

NO CONTINUITY

CHECK RIGHT FRONT SENSOR MOUNTING, AIR GAP, AND TOOTHED RING — REPAIR AS NECESSARY

CONTINUITY

REPLACE RIGHT FRONT WHEEL SPEED SENSOR

NO CONTINUITY

REPAIR SHORT TO GROUND IN CIRCUIT 833 OR 872 (GRN COAX)

86819129

VALVE BLOCK AND MAIN VALVE CIRCUIT SCHEMATIC

6000 AWD

CHART 55

CHECKING MAIN VALVE SOLENOID RESISTANCE

CHART 56

- DISCONNECT MAIN VALVE CONNECTOR
- MEASURE RESISTANCE BETWEEN MAIN VALVE SOLENOID PINS

```
2-5 Ω
```

CHECK FOR CONTINUITY BETWEEN J 35592 PIN 18 AND MAIN VALVE CONNECTOR PIN 2

CONTINUITY

CHECK FOR CONTINUITY BETWEEN BODY GROUND AND MAIN VALVE SOLENOID CONNECTOR PIN 1

CONTINUITY

RECONNECT CONNECTOR AND EBCM AND VERIFY SYMPTOM

```
OUTSIDE 2-5 Ω
```

REPLACE HYDRAULIC UNIT

NO CONTINUITY

REPAIR CIRCUIT 856 (PPL/WHT)

NO CONTINUITY

REPAIR CIRCUIT 155 (BLK). CHECK HYDRAULIC UNIT GROUND AND BODY GROUND (MAIN RELAY BRACKET)

CHECKING VALVE BLOCK GROUND CIRCUIT

CHART 57

RIGHT FRONT INLET VALVE RESISTANCE

CHART 58

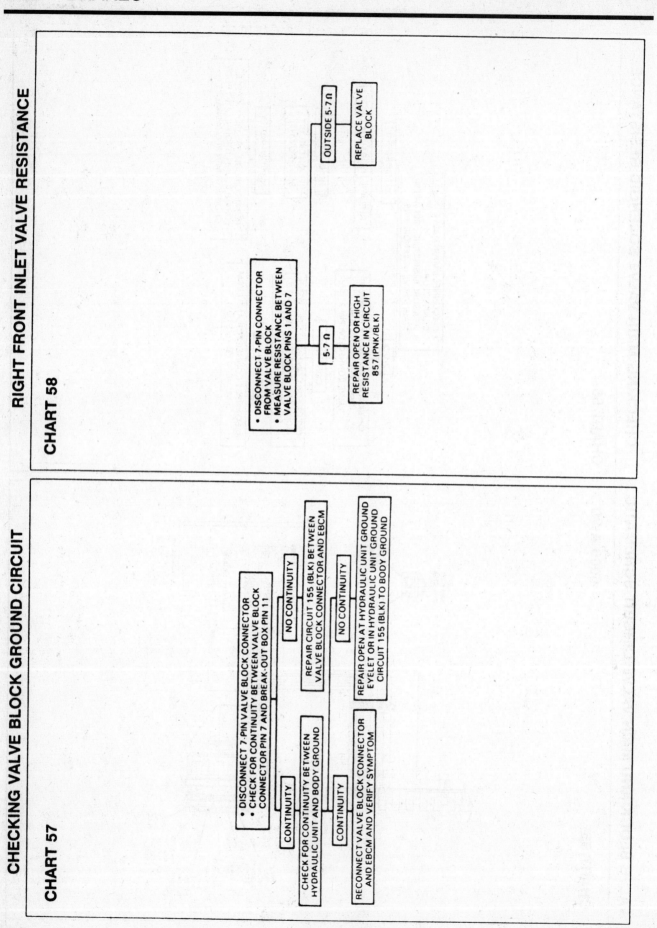

86819131

LEFT FRONT INLET VALVE RESISTANCE

REAR INLET VALVE RESISTANCE

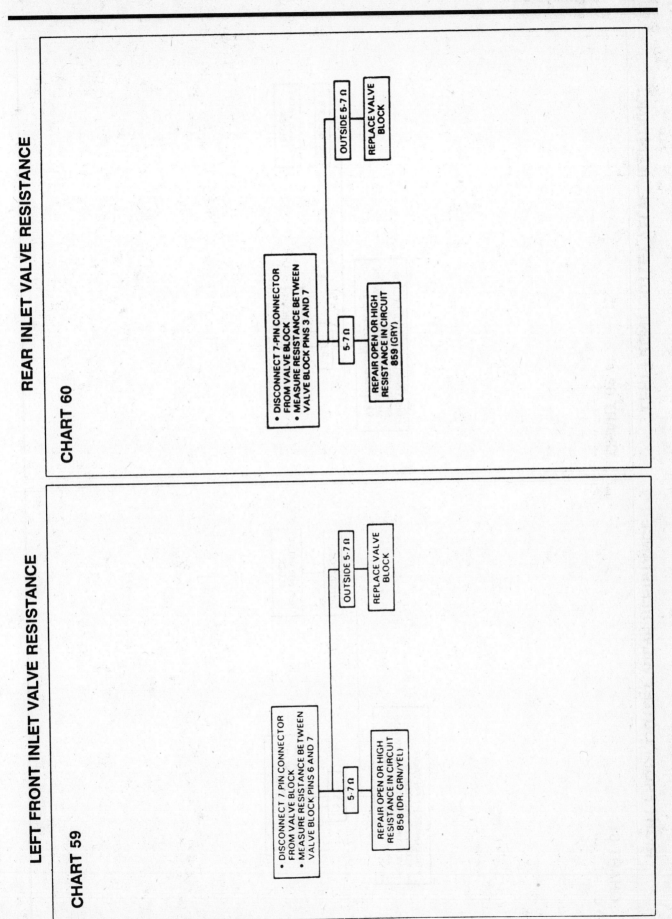

CHART 59

- DISCONNECT 7 PIN CONNECTOR FROM VALVE BLOCK
- MEASURE RESISTANCE BETWEEN VALVE BLOCK PINS 6 AND 7

5-7 Ω → OUTSIDE 5-7 Ω

REPAIR OPEN OR HIGH RESISTANCE IN CIRCUIT 858 (DR. GRN/YEL)

REPLACE VALVE BLOCK

CHART 60

- DISCONNECT 7-PIN CONNECTOR FROM VALVE BLOCK
- MEASURE RESISTANCE BETWEEN VALVE BLOCK PINS 3 AND 7

5-7 Ω → OUTSIDE 5-7 Ω

REPAIR OPEN OR HIGH RESISTANCE IN CIRCUIT 859 (GRY)

REPLACE VALVE BLOCK

86819132

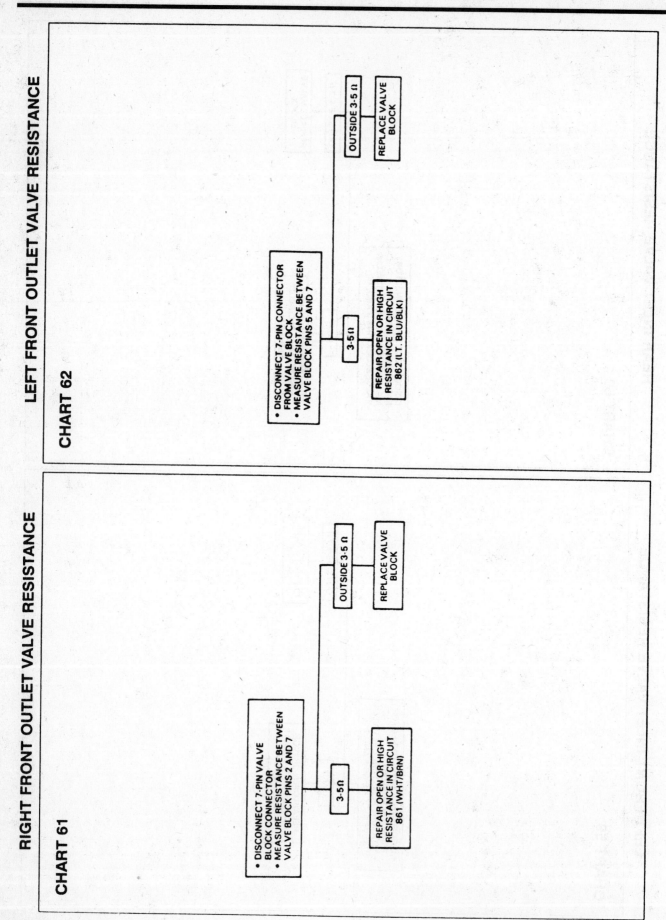

LEFT FRONT OUTLET VALVE RESISTANCE

CHART 62

- DISCONNECT 7-PIN CONNECTOR FROM VALVE BLOCK
- MEASURE RESISTANCE BETWEEN VALVE BLOCK PINS 5 AND 7

3-5 Ω

OUTSIDE 3-5 Ω

REPAIR OPEN OR HIGH RESISTANCE IN CIRCUIT 862 (LT. BLU/BLK)

REPLACE VALVE BLOCK

RIGHT FRONT OUTLET VALVE RESISTANCE

CHART 61

- DISCONNECT 7-PIN VALVE BLOCK CONNECTOR
- MEASURE RESISTANCE BETWEEN VALVE BLOCK PINS 2 AND 7

3-5 Ω

OUTSIDE 3-5 Ω

REPAIR OPEN OR HIGH RESISTANCE IN CIRCUIT 861 (WHT/BRN)

REPLACE VALVE BLOCK

86819133

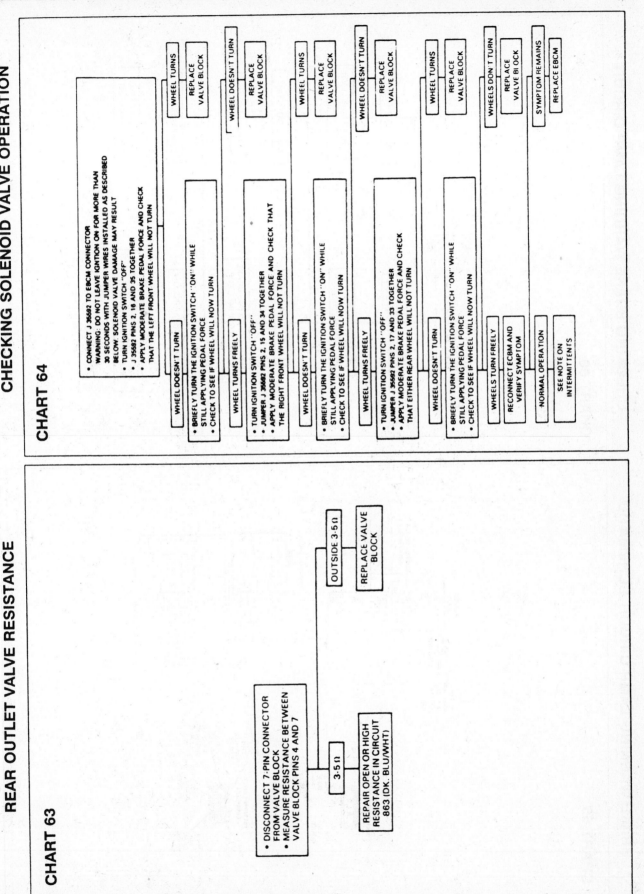

REAR OUTLET VALVE RESISTANCE

CHART 63

- DISCONNECT 7-PIN CONNECTOR FROM VALVE BLOCK
- MEASURE RESISTANCE BETWEEN VALVE BLOCK PINS 4 AND 7

- 3-5 Ω → REPAIR OPEN OR HIGH RESISTANCE IN CIRCUIT 863 (DK. BLU/WHT)
- OUTSIDE 3-5 Ω → REPLACE VALVE BLOCK

CHECKING SOLENOID VALVE OPERATION

CHART 64

- CONNECT J 35692 TO EBCM CONNECTOR
- WARNING: DO NOT LEAVE IGNITION ON FOR MORE THAN 30 SECONDS WITH JUMPER WIRES INSTALLED AS DESCRIBED BELOW. SOLENOID VALVE DAMAGE MAY RESULT
- TURN IGNITION SWITCH "OFF"
- J 35692 PINS 2, 16 AND 35 TOGETHER
- APPLY MODERATE BRAKE PEDAL FORCE AND CHECK THAT THE LEFT FRONT WHEEL WILL NOT TURN

WHEEL DOESN'T TURN
- BRIEFLY TURN THE IGNITION SWITCH "ON" WHILE STILL APPLYING PEDAL FORCE
- CHECK TO SEE IF WHEEL WILL NOW TURN
  - WHEEL TURNS → REPLACE VALVE BLOCK
  - WHEEL DOESN'T TURN → REPLACE VALVE BLOCK

WHEEL TURNS FREELY
- TURN IGNITION SWITCH "OFF"
- JUMPER J 35692 PINS 2, 15 AND 34 TOGETHER
- APPLY MODERATE BRAKE PEDAL FORCE AND CHECK THAT THE RIGHT FRONT WHEEL WILL NOT TURN

WHEEL DOESN'T TURN
- BRIEFLY TURN THE IGNITION SWITCH "ON" WHILE STILL APPLYING PEDAL FORCE
- CHECK TO SEE IF WHEEL WILL NOW TURN
  - WHEEL TURNS → REPLACE VALVE BLOCK
  - WHEEL DOESN'T TURN → REPLACE VALVE BLOCK

WHEEL TURNS FREELY
- TURN IGNITION SWITCH "OFF"
- JUMPER J 35692 PINS 2, 17 AND 33 TOGETHER
- APPLY MODERATE BRAKE PEDAL FORCE AND CHECK THAT EITHER REAR WHEEL WILL NOT TURN

WHEEL DOESN'T TURN
- BRIEFLY TURN THE IGNITION SWITCH "ON" WHILE STILL APPLYING PEDAL FORCE
- CHECK TO SEE IF WHEEL WILL NOW TURN
  - WHEELS DON'T TURN → REPLACE VALVE BLOCK

WHEELS TURN FREELY
- RECONNECT ECBM AND VERIFY SYMPTOM
  - SYMPTOM REMAINS → REPLACE EBCM
  - NORMAL OPERATION → SEE NOTE ON INTERMITTENTS

86819134

BRAKE WARNING LAMP CIRCUIT SCHEMATIC

CHART 65

CHECKING BRAKE WARNING LAMP CIRCUIT

CHART 66

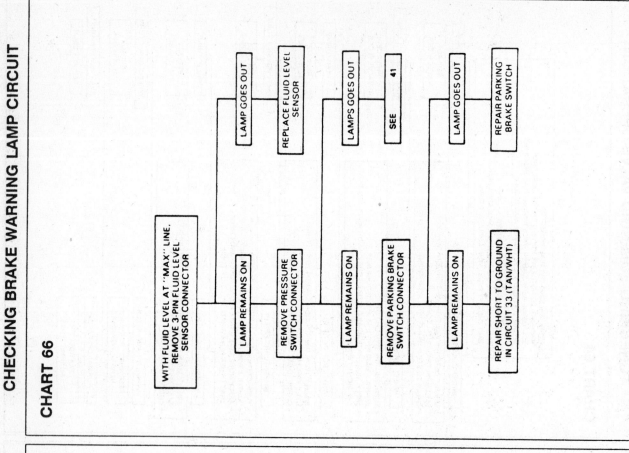

86819135

CHECKING ANTI-LOCK WARNING LAMP CIRCUIT

CHART 68

ANTI-LOCK WARNING LAMP CIRCUIT SCHEMATIC

CHART 67

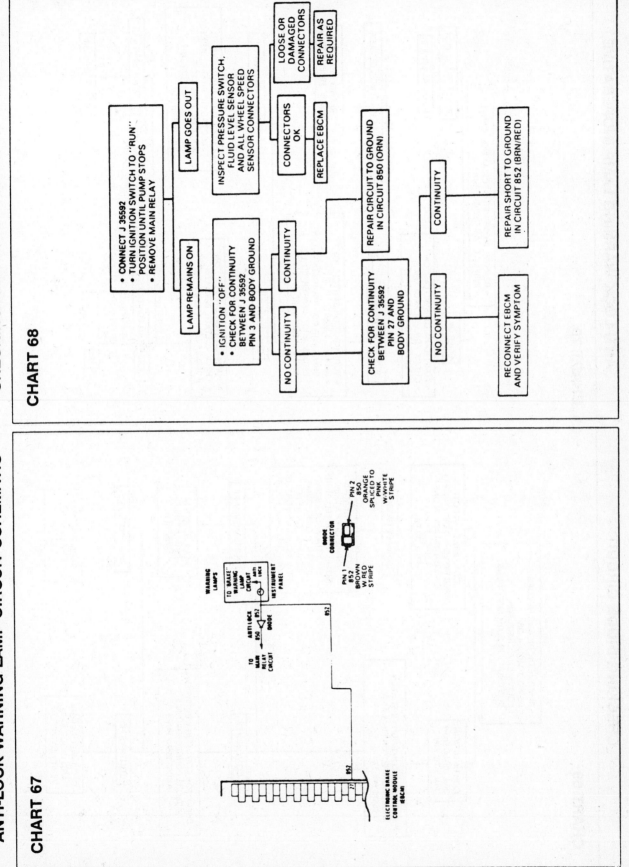

86819136

ANTI-LOCK WARNING LAMP INOPERATIVE

CHART 70

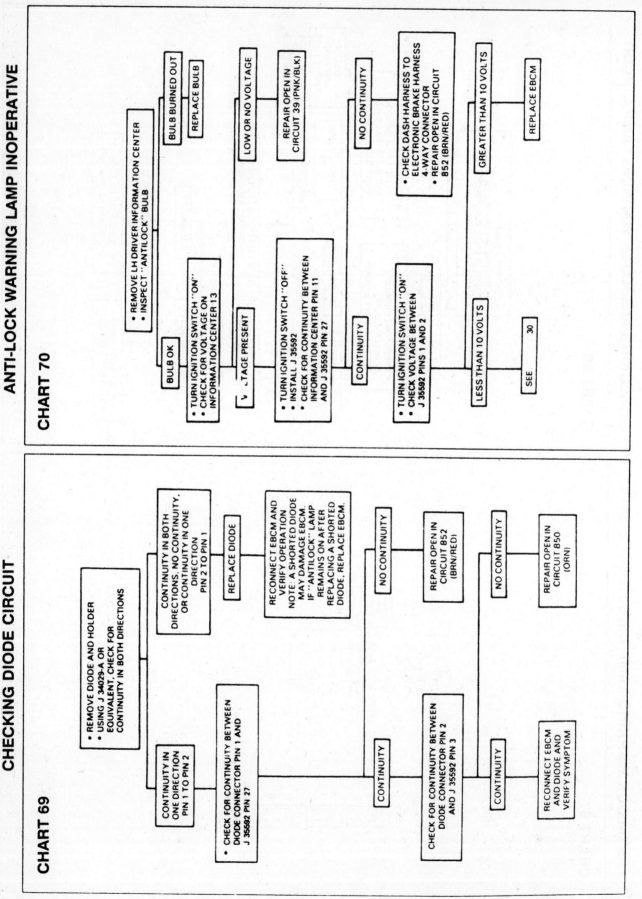

CHECKING DIODE CIRCUIT

CHART 69

86819137

ANTI-LOCK WARNING LAMP ON INTERMITTENTLY WHILE DRIVING

INTERRUPTIONS IN THE FOLLOWING CIRCUITS MAY CAUSE
THE "ANTILOCK" LAMP TO LIGHT INTERMITTENTLY. THIS
LIST DOES NOT INCLUDE ALL POSSIBILITIES, BUT
INCLUDES THOSE CIRCUITS MOST LIKELY TO CAUSE THE
"ANTILOCK" WARNING LAMP TO LIGHT INTERMITTENTLY.

- EBCM SWITCH LOOP, INCLUDING
  - CIRCUIT 866 (LT. GRN) FROM EB   TO FLUID LEVEL
    SENSOR
  - 2-PIN FLUID LEVEL SENSOR
  - CIRCUIT 853 (LT. BLU/ORN) FROM FLUID LEVEL SENSOR
    TO PRESSURE SWITCH
  - CIRCUIT 865 (PPL) FROM PRESSURE SWITCH TO EBCM

- IGNITION ENABLE CIRCUIT, INCLUDING
  - BRAKE FUSE (#5 IN CONVENIENCE CENTER 5A)
  - CIRCUIT 350 (PNK/WHT) FROM RELAY COIL TO GROUND
  - DIFFERENTIAL LOCK ENGAGED SWITCH AND JUMPER (AWD)
  - 951 CIRCUIT TO DIFFERENTIAL LOCK CONTROL RELAY IN THE
    CONSOLE (AWD)

- MAIN RELAY CIRCUITS, INCLUDING
  - CIRCUIT 855 (DK. BLU) FROM EBCM TO RELAY COIL
  - CIRCUIT 450 (BLK/WHT) FROM RELAY COIL TO GROUND

- ALL WHEEL SPEED SENSOR CIRCUITS

INSPECT CONNECTORS AND WIRES IN THESE CIRCUITS. IF
NO TROUBLE IS FOUND, SEE NOTE ON INTERMITTENTS

86819138

BRAKE SPECIFICATIONS
All measurements in inches unless noted

Year	Model		Master Cylinder Bore	Brake Disc			Brake Drum Diameter			Minimum Lining Thickness	
				Original Thickness	Minimum Thickness	Maximum Runout	Original Inside Diameter	Max. Wear Limit	Maximum Machine Diameter	Front	Rear
1982	All		0.874	NA	0.815	0.004	7.879	7.899	7.899	0.030	3
1983	All		0.874	NA	0.815	0.004	7.879	7.899	7.899	0.030	3
1984	All	1	0.874	NA	0.815	0.004	8.863	8.883	8.883	0.030	3
		2	0.944	NA	0.957	0.004	8.863	8.883	8.883	0.030	3
1985	Celebrity	1	0.875	0.885	0.815	0.004	7.879	7.929	7.899	0.030	3
		2	0.938	1.043	0.957	0.004	8.860	8.950	8.920	0.030	3
	Century	1	0.875	0.885	0.815	0.004	7.879	7.929	7.899	0.030	3
		2	0.938	1.043	0.957	0.004	8.860	8.950	8.920	0.030	3
	Cutlass Ciera	1	0.875	0.885	0.815	0.004	7.879	7.929	7.899	0.030	3
		2	0.938	1.043	0.957	0.004	8.860	8.950	8.920	0.030	3
1986	Celebrity	1	0.937	0.885	0.830	0.004	8.860	8.950	8.920	0.030	3
		2	0.937	1.043	0.972	0.004	8.860	8.950	8.920	0.030	3
	Century	1	0.875	0.885	0.815	0.004	8.860	8.909	8.880	0.030	3
		2	0.938	1.043	0.957	0.004	8.860	8.909	8.880	0.030	3
	Cutlass Ciera	1	0.875	0.885	0.815	0.004	8.860	8.909	8.880	0.030	3
		2	0.938	1.043	0.957	0.004	8.860	8.909	8.880	0.030	3
1987	Celebrity	1	0.937	0.885	0.830	0.004	8.860	8.950	8.920	0.030	3
		2	0.937	1.043	0.972	0.004	8.860	8.950	8.920	0.030	3
	Century	1	0.875	0.885	0.815	0.004	8.860	8.909	8.880	0.030	3
		2	0.937	1.043	0.957	0.004	8.860	8.909	8.880	0.030	3
	Cutlass Ciera	1	0.875	0.885	0.815	0.004	8.860	8.909	8.880	0.030	3
		2	0.938	1.043	0.957	0.004	8.860	8.909	8.880	0.030	3
1988	Celebrity	1	0.937	0.885	0.830	0.004	8.860	8.950	8.920	0.030	3
		2	0.937	1.043	0.972	0.004	8.860	8.950	8.920	0.030	3
	Century	1	0.874	0.885	0.815	0.004	8.866	8.946	8.920	0.030	3
		2	0.944	1.043	0.957	0.004	8.863	8.946	8.920	0.030	3
	Century wagon		0.944	1.043	0.957	0.004	8.863	8.909	8.877	0.030	3
	Cutlass Ciera	1	0.874	0.885	0.815	0.004	8.863	8.946	8.920	0.030	3
		2	0.944	1.043	0.957	0.004	8.863	8.946	8.920	0.030	3
	Cutlass Cruiser		0.944	1.043	0.957	0.004	8.863	8.909	8.877	0.030	3
1989	Celebrity	1	0.937	0.885	0.830	0.004	8.860	8.950	8.920	0.030	3
		2	0.937	1.043	0.972	0.004	8.860	8.950	8.920	0.030	3
	Century	1	0.874	0.885	0.815	0.004	8.866	8.946	8.920	0.030	3
		2	0.944	1.043	0.957	0.004	8.863	8.946	8.920	0.030	3
	Century wagon		0.944	1.043	0.957	0.004	8.863	8.909	8.877	0.030	3
	Cutlass Ciera	1	0.874	0.885	0.815	0.004	8.863	8.946	8.920	0.030	3
		2	0.944	1.043	0.957	0.004	8.863	8.946	8.920	0.030	3
	Cutlass Cruiser		0.944	1.043	0.957	0.004	8.863	8.909	8.877	0.030	3
	Cutlass Supreme	1	0.945	1.043	0.972	0.004	-	-	-	0.030	0.030
		2	0.945	0.492	0.429	0.004	-	-	-	0.030	0.030
1990	Celebrity	1	0.874	0.885	0.830	0.004	8.863	8.950	8.920	0.030	0.030
		2	0.944	1.043	0.972	0.004	8.863	8.950	8.920	0.030	0.030
	Century	1	0.874	0.885	0.815	0.004	8.866	8.946	8.920	0.030	3
		2	0.944	1.043	0.957	0.004	8.863	8.946	8.920	0.030	3
	Century wagon		0.944	1.043	0.957	0.004	8.863	8.909	8.877	0.030	3
	Cutlass Ciera	1	0.874	0.885	0.815	0.004	8.863	8.946	8.920	0.030	3
		2	0.944	1.043	0.957	0.004	8.863	8.946	8.920	0.030	3
	Cutlass Cruiser		0.944	1.043	0.957	0.004	8.863	8.909	8.877	0.030	3
	Cutlass Supreme		0.945	1.043	0.972	0.004	-	-	-	0.030	0.030
			0.945	0.492	0.429	0.004	-	-	-	0.030	0.030

86819600

BRAKE SPECIFICATIONS

All measurements in inches unless noted

Year	Model		Master Cylinder Bore	Brake Disc Original Thickness	Brake Disc Minimum Thickness	Brake Disc Maximum Runout	Brake Drum Diameter Original Inside Diameter	Brake Drum Diameter Max. Wear Limit	Brake Drum Diameter Maximum Machine Diameter	Minimum Lining Thickness Front	Minimum Lining Thickness Rear
1991	Century	1	0.874	0.885	0.815	0.004	8.866	8.946	8.920	0.030	3
		2	0.944	1.043	0.957	0.004	8.863	8.946	8.920	0.030	3
	Century wagon		0.944	1.043	0.957	0.004	8.863	8.909	8.877	0.030	3
	Cutlass Ciera	1	0.874	0.885	0.815	0.004	8.863	8.946	8.920	0.030	3
		2	0.944	1.043	0.957	0.004	8.863	8.946	8.920	0.030	3
	Cutlass Cruiser		0.944	1.043	0.957	0.004	8.863	8.909	8.877	0.030	3
	Cutlass Supreme		0.945	1.043	0.972	0.004	-	-	-	0.030	0.030
			0.945	0.492	0.429	0.004	-	-	-	0.030	0.030
1992	Century	1	0.874	0.885	0.815	0.004	8.866	8.946	8.920	0.030	3
		2	0.944	1.043	0.957	0.004	8.863	8.946	8.920	0.030	3
	Century wagon		0.944	1.043	0.957	0.004	8.863	8.909	8.877	0.030	3
	Cutlass Ciera	1	0.874	0.885	0.815	0.004	8.863	8.909	8.880	0.030	3
		2	0.944	1.043	0.957	0.004	8.863	8.909	8.880	0.030	3
	Cutlass Cruiser		0.944	1.043	0.957	0.004	8.863	8.950	8.877	0.030	3
	Cutlass Supreme		0.945	1.040	0.972	0.004	-	-	-	0.030	0.030
			0.945	0.492	0.429	0.004	-	-	-	0.030	0.030
1993	Century	1	0.874	0.885	0.815	0.004	8.866	8.946	8.920	0.030	3
		2	0.944	1.043	0.957	0.004	8.863	8.946	8.920	0.030	3
	Century wagon		0.944	1.043	0.957	0.004	8.863	8.909	8.877	0.030	3
	Cutlass Ciera	1	0.874	0.885	0.815	0.004	8.863	8.909	8.880	0.030	3
		2	0.944	1.043	0.957	0.004	8.863	8.909	8.880	0.030	3
	Cutlass Cruiser		0.944	1.043	0.957	0.004	8.863	3	8.877	0.030	3
	Cutlass Supreme		0.945	1.040	0.972	0.004	-	-	-	0.030	0.030
			0.945	0.492	0.492	0.004	-	-	-	0.030	0.030
1994	Century		0.944	1.028	0.957	0.002	8.863	8.946	8.920	0.030	3
	Cutlass Ciera		0.944	1.028	0.957	0.002	8.860	8.909	8.880	0.030	3
	Cutlass Cruiser		0.944	1.028	0.957	0.002	8.860	8.909	8.880	0.030	3
	Cutlass Supreme		0.945	1.039	0.972	0.003	-	-	-	0.030	0.030
			0.945	0.492	0.429	0.003	-	-	-	0.030	0.030
1995	Century		0.944	1.028	0.957	0.002	8.863	8.946	8.920	0.030	3
	Cutlass Ciera		0.944	1.028	0.957	0.002	8.863	8.909	8.920	0.030	3
	Cutlass Cruiser		0.944	1.028	0.957	0.002	8.863	8.909	8.920	0.030	3
	Cutlass Supreme		1.000	1.039	0.972	0.003	-	-	-	0.030	0.030
			1.000	0.492	0.429	0.003	-	-	-	0.030	0.030

1 Std.
2 Heavy duty
3 0.030 over rivet head: If bonded lining, use 0.062 from shoe
F - Front
R - Rear

86819601

TORQUE SPECIFICATIONS

Component	US	Metric
Brake line brackets:	8 ft. lbs.	11 Nm
Caliper retaining bolts:	38 ft. lbs.	51 Nm
Front crossmember-to-body bolts:	103 ft. lbs.	140 Nm
Halfshaft end nuts:	184-192 ft. lbs.	250-260 Nm
Knuckle camber cam bolt:	140 ft. lbs.	190 Nm
Knuckle attaching bolts:	38 ft. lbs.	52 Nm
Lower ball joint pinch bolt:		
1982-84	40 ft. lbs.	50 Nm
1985-93	33 ft. lbs.	45 Nm
1994-95	38 ft. lbs.	52 Nm
Lower control arm bolts:	61 ft. lbs.	83 Nm
MacPherson strut shaft nut:	65 ft. lbs.	85 Nm
MacPherson strut-to-fender:	18 ft. lbs.	24 Nm
MacPherson strut-to-knuckle:	122-140 ft. lbs.	165-190 Nm
Rear shock-to-lower mount:		
1982-84	43 ft. lbs.	58 Nm
1985-86	35 ft. lbs.	47 Nm
1987-92	44 ft. lbs.	59 Nm
1993-95	53 ft. lbs.	72 Nm
Rear shock-to-upper mount:	16 ft. lbs.	22 Nm
Rear axle top bolt 6000 AWD:	148 ft. lbs.	200 Nm
Rear control arm-to-bracket:	84 ft. lbs.	115 Nm
Rear control bracket-to-underbody:	28 ft. lbs.	38 Nm
Rear hub and bearing assembly:	44 ft. lbs.	60 Nm
Rear jack pad mounting bolts:	18 ft. lbs.	25 Nm
Rear track bar at brace or underebody:	35 ft. lbs.	47 Nm
Rear coil spring track bolt:		
1982-92	44 ft. lbs.	60 Nm
1993-95	53 ft. lbs.	72 Nm
Rear leaf spring-to-cradle bolts:	61 ft. lbs.	83 Nm
Rear strut lower mount bolts:	148 ft. lbs.	200 Nm
Spring retention plate bolts:	15 ft. lbs.	20 Nm
Stabilizer insulator clamps-to-control arms:	32 ft. lbs.	43 Nm
Steering column mounting bolts:	18 ft. lbs.	25 Nm
Steering rack mounting bolts:	59 ft. lbs.	80 Nm
Steering wheel retaining nut:	30 ft. lbs.	41 Nm
Tie rod adjustment jam nut:	45 ft. lbs.	60 Nm
Tie rod nut:	43 ft. lbs.	58 Nm
Toe link sleeve tab bolt:	14 ft. lbs.	19 Nm
Toe link inner nut:	61 ft. lbs.	83 Nm
Wheel lug nuts:	100 ft. lbs.	140 Nm

86819555

ABS-VI — ANTI-LOCK BRAKE SYSTEM (ABS)

Description and Operation

Anti-lock brakes provide the driver with 3 important benefits over standard braking systems: increased vehicle stability, improved vehicle steerability and potentially reduced stopping distances during braking.

The ABS-VI Anti-lock Braking System consists of a conventional braking system with a vacuum power booster, compact master cylinder, front disc brakes, rear drum brakes and interconnecting hydraulic brake lines augmented with the ABS components. The ABS-VI components consist of a hydraulic modulator assembly, Electronic Control Unit (ECU), a system relay, 4 wheel speed sensors, interconnecting wiring and an amber ABS warning light.

The ECU monitors inputs from the individual wheel speed sensors, then determines when a wheel or wheels are about to lock-up. The ECU controls the motors on the hydraulic modulator assembly to reduce brake pressure to the wheel about to lock-up. When the wheel regains traction, the brake pressure is increased until the wheel again approaches lock-up. The cycle repeats until either the vehicle comes to a stop, the brake pedal is released or no wheels are about to lock-up. The ECU also has the ability to monitor itself and can store diagnostic codes in a non-volatile (will not be erased if the battery is disconnected) memory. The ECU is serviced as an assembly.

The ABS-VI braking system employs 2 modes, the base (conventional) braking and the anti-lock braking. Under normal braking, the conventional part of the system stops the vehicle. When in the ABS mode, the system controls the 2 front wheels individually and the rear wheels together. If a rear wheel is about to lock-up, the hydraulic pressure to both wheels is reduced, controlling both wheels together. Since the vast majority of the braking is controlled by the front wheels, there is no adverse effect on vehicle control during hard braking.

PRECAUTIONS

Failure to observe the following precautions may result in system damage.

• Performing diagnostic work on the ABS-VI requires the use of a Tech I Scan diagnostic tool or equivalent. If unavailable, please refer diagnostic work to a qualified technician.

• Before performing electric arc welding on the vehicle, disconnect the Electronic Brake Control Module (EBCM) and the hydraulic modulator connectors.

• When performing painting work on the vehicle, do not expose the Electronic Brake Control Module (EBCM) to temperatures in excess of 185°F (85°C) for longer than 2 hrs. The system may be exposed to temperatures up to 200°F (95°C) for less than 15 min.

• Never disconnect or connect the Electronic Brake Control Module (EBCM) or hydraulic modulator connectors with the ignition switch ON.

• Never disassemble any component of the Anti-Lock Brake System (ABS) which is designated non-serviceable; the component must be replaced as an assembly.

• When filling the master cylinder, always use Delco Supreme 11 brake fluid or equivalent, which meets DOT-3 specifications; petroleum base fluid will destroy the rubber parts.

Onboard Diagnostics

The ABS-VI contains sophisticated onboard diagnostics that, when accessed with a bi-directional Scan tool, are designed to identify the source of any system fault as specifically as possible. There are many of diagnostic fault codes to assist the service technician with diagnosis. The last diagnostic fault code to occur is specifically identified, and specific ABS data is stored at the time of this fault. Additionally, using a bi-directional Scan tool, each input and output can be monitored, thus enabling fault confirmation and repair verification. Manual control of components and automated functional tests are also available when using a Scan tool. Details of many of these functions are contained in the following sections.

ENHANCED DIAGNOSTICS

Enhanced diagnostic information, found in the CODE HISTORY function of the bi-directional Scan tool, is designed to provide the service technician with specific fault occurrence information. For each of the first five (5) and the very last diagnostic fault codes stored, data is stored to identify the specific fault code number, the number of failure occurrences, and the number of drive cycles since the failure first and last occurred (a drive cycle occurs when the ignition is turned ON and the vehicle is driven faster than 10 mph). However, if a fault is present, the drive cycle counter will increment by turning the ignition ON and OFF. These first five (5) diagnostic fault codes are also stored in the order of occurrence. The order in which the first 5 faults occurred can be useful in determining if a previous fault is linked to the most recent faults, such as an intermittent wheel speed sensor which later becomes completely open.

During difficult diagnosis situations, this information can be used to identify fault occurrence trends. Does the fault occur more frequently now than it did during the last time when it only failed 1 out of 35 drive cycles? Did the fault only occur once over a large number of drive cycles, indication an unusual condition present when the fault occurred? Does the fault occur infrequently over a large number of drive cycles, indication special diagnosis techniques may be required to identify the source of the fault?

If a fault occurred 1 out of 20 drive cycles, the fault is intermittent and has not reoccurred for 19 drive cycles. This fault may be difficult or impossible to duplicate and may have been caused by a severe vehicle impact (large pot hole, speed bump at high speed, etc.) that momentarily opened an electrical connector or caused unusual vehicle suspension movement. Problem resolution is unlikely, and the problem may never reoccur. If the fault occurred 3 out of 15 drive cycles, the odds of finding the cause are still not good, but you know how often it occurs and you can determine whether or not the fault is becoming more frequent. If the fault occurred 10 out of 20 drive cycles, the odds of finding the cause are very good, as the fault may be easily reproduced.

By using the additional fault data, you can also determine if a failure is randomly intermittent or if it has not reoccurred for long periods of time due to weather changes or a prior repair. Say a diagnostic fault code occurred 10 of 20 drive cycles but has not reoccurred for 10 drive cycles. This means the failure occurred 10 of 10 drive cycles but has not reoccurred since. A significant environmental change or a repair occurred 10 drive cycles ago. A repair may not be necessary if a recent repair can be confirmed. If no repair was made, the service can focus on diagnosis techniques used to locate difficult to re-create problems.

DIAGNOSTIC PROCESS

When servicing the ABS-VI, the following steps should be followed in order. Failure to follow these steps may result in the loss of important diagnostic data and may lead to difficult and time consuming diagnosis procedures.

1. Using a bi-directional Scan tool, read all current and history diagnostic codes. Be certain to note which codes are current diagnostic code failures. DO NOT CLEAR CODES unless directed to do so.

2. Using a bi-directional Scan tool, read the CODE HISTORY data. Note the diagnostic fault codes stored and their frequency of failure. Specifically note the last failure that occurred and the conditions present when this failure occurred. This "last failure" should be the starting point for diagnosis and repair.

3. Perform a vehicle preliminary diagnosis inspection. This should include:

　a. Inspection of the master cylinder for proper brake fluid level.

　b. Inspection of the ABS hydraulic modulator for any leaks or wiring damage.

　c. Inspection of brake components at all four (4) wheels. Verify no drag exists. Also verify proper brake apply operation.

　d. Inspection for worn or damaged wheel bearings that allow a wheel to wobble.

　e. Inspection of the wheel speed sensors and their wiring. Verify correct air gap range, solid sensor attachment, undamaged sensor toothed ring, and undamaged wiring. Especially at vehicle attachment points.

　f. Verify proper outer CV-joint alignment and operation.

　g. Verify tires meet legal tread depth requirements.

4. If no codes are present, or mechanical component failure codes are present, perform the automated modulator test using the Tech 1, T-100 or equivalent scan tool to isolate the cause of the problem. If the failure is intermittent and not reproducible, test drive the vehicle while using the automatic snapshot feature of the bi-directional Scan tool.

Perform normal acceleration, stopping, and turning maneuvers. If this does not reproduce the failure, perform an ABS stop, on a low coefficient surface such as gravel, from approximately 30-50 mph (48-80 kph) while triggering on any ABS

code. If the failure is still not reproducible, use the enhanced diagnostic information found in CODE HISTORY to determine whether or not this failure should be further diagnosed.

5. Once all system failures have been corrected, clear the ABS codes. The Tech 1 and T-100, when plugged into the ALDL connector, becomes part of the vehicle's electronic system. The Tech 1 and T-100 can also perform the following functions on components linked by the Serial Data Link (SDL):

- Display ABS data
- Display and clear ABS trouble codes
- Control ABS components
- Perform extensive ABS diagnosis
- Provide diagnostic testing for Intermittent ABS conditions.

Each test mode has specific diagnosis capabilities which depend upon various keystrokes. In general, five keys control sequencing: YES, NO, EXIT, UP arrow and DOWN arrow. The FO through F9 keys select operating modes, perform functions within an operating mode, or enter trouble code or model year designations.

In general, the Tech 1 has five test modes for diagnosing the anti-lock brake system. The five test modes are as follows:

MODE FO: DATA LIST- In this test mode, the Tech 1 continuously monitors wheel speed data, brake switch status and other inputs and outputs.

MODE F1: CODE HISTORY- In this mode, fault code history data is displayed. This data includes how many ignition cycles since the fault code occurred, along with other ABS information. The first five (5) and last fault codes set are included in the ABS history data.

MODE F2: TROUBLE CODES- In this test mode, trouble codes stored by the EBCM, both current ignition cycle and history, may be displayed or cleared.

MODE F3: ABS SNAPSHOT- In this test mode, the Tech 1 captures ABS data before and after a fault occurrence or a forced manual trigger.

MODE F4: ABS TESTS- In this test mode, the Tech 1 performs hydraulic modulator functional tests to assist in problem isolation during troubleshooting. Included here is manual control of the motors which is used prior to bleeding the brake system.

Press F7 to covert from English to metric.

DISPLAYING CODES

Diagnostic fault codes can only be read through the use of a bi-directional Scan tool. There are no provisions for Flash Code diagnostics.

CLEARING CODES

The trouble codes in EBCM memory are erased in one of two ways:

- Scan tool "Clear Codes" selection.
- Ignition cycle default.

These two methods are detailed below. Be sure to verify proper system operation and absence of codes when clearing procedure is completed.The EBCM will not permit code clearing until all of the codes have been displayed. Also, codes cannot be cleared by unplugging the EBCM, disconnecting the battery cables, or turning the ignition **OFF** (except on an ignition cycle default).

Scan Tool Clear Codes Method

1. Select F2 for trouble codes.
2. After codes have been viewed completely, the scan tool will display "CLEAR ABS CODES". Answer yes.
3. The scan tool will then read "DISPLAY CODE HIST. DATA? LOST IF CODES CLEARED. NO TO CLEAR CODES". Answer no and codes will be cleared.

Ignition Cycle Default

If no diagnostic fault code occurs for 100 drive cycles (a drive cycle occurs when the ignition is turned **ON** and the vehicle is driven faster than 10 mph), any existing fault codes are cleared from the EBCM memory.

INTERMITTENT FAILURES

As with most electronic systems, intermittent failures may be difficult to accurately diagnose. The following is a method to try to isolate an intermittent failure especially wheel speed circuitry failures.

If an ABS fault occurs, the ABS warning light indicator will be ON during the ignition cycle in which the fault was detected. If it is an intermittent problem which seems to have corrected itself (ABS warning light OFF), a history trouble code will be stored. Also stored will be the history data of the code at the time the fault occurred. The Tech 1 must be used to read ABS history data.

Most intermittence are caused by faulty electrical connections or wiring, although occasionally a sticking relay or solenoid can be a problem. Some items to check are:

1. Poor mating of connector halves, or terminals not fully seated in the connector body (backed out).
2. Dirt or corrosion on the terminals. The terminals must be clean and free of any foreign material which could impede proper terminal contact.
3. Damaged connector body, exposing the terminals to moisture and dirt, as well as not maintaining proper terminal orientation with the component or mating connector.
4. Improperly formed or damaged terminals. All connector terminals in problem circuits should be checked carefully to ensure good contact tension. Use a corresponding mating terminal to check for proper tension.
5. The J 35616-A Connector Test Adapter Kit must be used whenever a diagnostic procedure requests checking or probing a terminal. Using the adapter will ensure that no damage to the terminal will occur, as well as giving an idea of whether contact tension is sufficient.
6. Poor terminal-to-wire connection. Checking this requires removing the terminal from the connector body. Some conditions which fall under this description are poor crimps, poor

solder joints, crimping over wire insulation rather than the wire itself, corrosion in the wire-to-terminal contact area, etc.

7. Wire insulation which is rubbed through, causing an intermittent short as the bare area touches other wiring or parts of the vehicle.

8. Wiring broken inside the insulation. This condition could cause a continuity check to show a good circuit, but if only 1 or 2 strands of a multi-strand-type wire are intact, resistance could be far too high.

Checking Terminal Contact

When diagnosing an electrical system that uses Metri-Pack 150/280/480/630 series terminals (refer to Terminal Repair Kit J 38125-A and instruction manual J 38125-4 for terminal identification), it is important to check terminal contact between a connector and component, or between in-line connectors, before replacing a suspect component.

Frequently, a diagnostic chart leads to a step that reads Check for poor connection. Mating terminals must be inspected to ensure good terminal contact. A poor connection between the male and female terminal at a connector may be the result of contamination or deformation.

Contamination is caused by the connector halves being improperly connected, a missing or damaged connector seal, or damage to the connector itself, exposing the terminals to moisture and dirt. Contamination, usually in underhood or underbody connectors, leads to terminal corrosion, causing an open circuit or an intermittently open circuit.

Deformation is caused by probing the mating side of a connector terminal without the proper adapter, improperly joining the connector halves or repeatedly separating and joining the connector halves. Deformation, usually to the female terminal contact tang, can result in poor terminal contact causing an open or intermittently open circuit.

Follow the procedure below to check terminal contact.

1. Separate the connector halves. Refer to Terminal Repair Kit J 38125-A instruction manual J 38125-4, if available.

2. Inspect the connector halves for contamination. Contamination will result in a white or green buildup within the connector body or between terminals, causing high terminal resistance, intermittent contact or an open circuit. An underhood or underbody connector that shows signs of contamination should be replaced in its entirety, terminals, seals, and connector body.

3. Using an equivalent male terminal from the Terminal Repair Kit J 38125-A, check the retention force of the female terminal in question by inserting and removing the male terminal to the female terminal in the connector body. Good terminal contact will require a certain amount of force to separate the terminals.

4. Using an equivalent female terminal from the Terminal Repair Kit J 38125-A, compare the retention force of this terminal to the female terminal in question by joining and separating the male terminal to the female terminal in question. If the retention force is significantly different between the two female terminals, replace the female terminal in question, using a terminal from Terminal Repair Kit J 38125-A.

ABS Hydraulic Modulator Assembly

REMOVAL & INSTALLATION

▸ **See Figure 69**

To avoid personal injury, use the Tech I scan tool or equivalent to relieve the gear tension in the hydraulic modulator. This procedure must be performed prior to removal of the brake control and motor assembly.

1. Disconnect the negative battery cable.
2. Unplug the 2 solenoid electrical connectors and the fluid level sensor connectors.
3. Unplug the 6-pin and 3-pin motor pack electrical connectors

4. Wrap a shop towel around the hydraulic brake lines and disconnect the 4 brake lines from the modulator.

➡**Cap the disconnected lines to prevent the loss of fluid and the entry of moisture and contaminants.**

5. Remove the 2 nuts attaching the ABS hydraulic modulator assembly to the vacuum booster.
6. Remove the ABS hydraulic modulator assembly from the vehicle.
   To install:
7. Install the ABS hydraulic modulator assembly to the vehicle. Install the 2 attaching nuts and tighten to 20 ft. lbs. (27 Nm).
8. Connect the 4 brake pipes to the modulator assembly. Tighten to 13 ft. lbs. (17 Nm).
9. Engage the 6-pin and 3-pin electrical connectors and the fluid level sensor connector.
10. Properly bleed the system.
11. Connect the negative battery cable.

1 Solenoid electrical connectors
2 Fluid level sensor connector
3 Motor pack connector
4 Hydraulic brake pipes(4)
5 Master cylinder attaching nuts (2)
6 Hydraulic modulator and master cylinder assembly
7 Vacuum booster

86819300

Fig. 69 The hydraulic modulator assembly is secured to the master cylinder

Control Unit

REMOVAL & INSTALLATION

1. Disconnect the negative battery cable.
2. Unplug the Electronic Control Unit (ECU) electrical connectors.
3. Remove the hex head screws attaching the ECU to the dash panel.
4. Remove the ECU from the dash panel.

To install:

5. Ensure all plastic grommets are properly located.
6. Install the ECU to the dash panel, aligning screw holes.
7. Install the hex head screws attaching the ECU.
8. Engage the ECU electrical connectors.
9. Connect the negative battery cable.

Speed Sensors

REMOVAL & INSTALLATION

Front Wheels

▶ **See Figure 70**

1. Disconnect the negative battery cable.
2. To remove the wheel, loosen all the lug nuts at least one full turn, before raising the car.
3. Raise and safely support the vehicle, then remove the wheel and tire.
4. Unplug the front speed sensor electrical connector.
5. Remove the hub and bearing assembly, then disconnect the speed sensor from the hub and bearing using a blunt flatbladed tool.

➡**When the speed sensor is removed it must be replaced, the sensor is damaged when being removed and cannot be reused. There are two parts to the speed sensor and they are only replaced as an assembly.**

To install:

6. Inspect the bearing for signs of water intrusion. If water has entered the bearing , the bearing must be replaced.
7. Alpply Loctite® 620 to the mating surfaces of the wheel speed sensor where it contacts the hub and bearing assembly.
8. Press the speed sensor onto the hub and bearing assembly with tool J-38764 or equivalent.
9. Install the hub and bearing assembly to the vehicle, then connect the speed sensor.
10. Install the wheel and tire. Hand-tighten the lug nuts.
11. Lower the vehicle, then tighten the lug nuts to 100 ft. lbs. (136 Nm).
12. Connect the negative battery cable.

Rear Wheels

➡**The rear integral wheel bearing and sensor assembly must be replaced as a unit.**

1. Disconnect the negative battery cable.

J 38764

86819305

Fig. 70 The speed sensor must be pressed onto the hub and bearing assembly. Tool J-38764 or its equivalent can be used to do this

2. To remove the wheel, loosen all the lug nuts at least one full turn, before raising the car.
3. Raise and safely support the vehicle.
4. Remove the rear wheels, then remove the brake drums.
5. Remove the bolts and nuts attaching the rear wheel bearing and speed sensor. Rotate the axle flange to align the large hole with each of the bolt locations. Remove the bolt while holding the nut.

➡**With the rear wheel bearing and speed sensor attaching bolts and nuts removed, the drum brake assembly is supported only by the brake line connection. To avoid bending or damage to the brake line, Install two of the wheel bearing assembly bolts to secure the brake.**

6. Remove the rear wheel bearing and speed sensor assembly.
7. Unplug the rear sensor electrical connection.

To install:

8. Engage the rear speed sensor electrical connector.
9. Secure the bolts and nuts, attaching the rear wheel bearing, speed sensor and drum assembly to the suspension bracket. Rotate the axle flange to align the large hole with each bolt location. Install the bolt while holding the nut. Tighten the bolts to 46 ft. lbs. (63 Nm).
10. Install the brake drums.
11. Install the rear wheels. Hand-tighten the lug nuts.
12. Lower the vehicle, then tighten the lug nuts to 100 ft. lbs. (136 Nm).
13. Connect the negative battery cable.

Brake Control Solenoid Assembly

REMOVAL & INSTALLATION

1. Disconnect the negative battery cable.
2. Unplug the solenoid electrical connector.
3. Remove the Torx® head bolt.
4. Remove the solenoid assembly.

To install:

5. Lubricate the O-rings on the new solenoid with clean brake fluid.

6. Position the solenoid so the connectors face each other.

7. Press down firmly by hand until the solenoid assembly flange seats on the modulator assembly.

8. Install the Torx® head bolts. Tighten to 39 inch lbs. (5 Nm).

9. Engage the solenoid electrical connector.

10. Properly bleed the brake system.

11. Connect the negative battery cable.

Filling and Bleeding

BRAKE CONTROL ASSEMBLY

➡**Only use brake fluid from a sealed container which meets DOT 3 specifications.**

1. Clean the area around the master cylinder cap.

2. Check fluid level in master cylinder reservoir and top-up, as necessary. Check fluid level frequently during bleeding procedure.

3. Attach a bleeder hose to the rear bleeder valve on the brake control assembly. Slowly open the bleeder valve.

4. Depress the brake pedal slowly until fluid begins to flow.

5. Close the valve and release the brake pedal.

6. Repeat for the front bleeder valve on the brake control assembly.

➡**When fluid flows from both bleeder valves, the brake control assembly is sufficiently full of fluid. However, it may not be completely purged of air. Bleed the individual wheel calipers/cylinders and return to the control assembly to purge the remaining air.**

WHEEL CALIPERS/CYLINDERS

▶ **See Figure 71**

1. Prior to bleeding the rear brakes, the rear displacement cylinder must be returned to the top-most position. This can be accomplished using the Tech I scan tool or equivalent, by entering the manual control function and applying the rear motor. If a scan tool is unavailable, bleed the front brakes. Ensure the pedal is firm. Carefully drive the vehicle to a speed above 4 mph to cause the ABS system to initialize. This will return the rear displacement cylinder to the top-most position.

2. Clean the area around the master cylinder cap.

3. Check fluid level in master cylinder reservoir and top-up, as necessary. Check fluid level frequently during bleeding procedure.

4. Raise and safely support the vehicle.

5. Attach a bleeder hose to the bleeder valve of the right rear wheel and submerge the opposite hose in a clean container partially filled with brake fluid.

6. Open the bleeder valve.

7. Slowly depress the brake pedal.

8. Close the bleeder valve and release the brake pedal.

9. Wait 5 seconds.

10. Repeat until the pedal begins to feel firm and no air bubbles appear in the bleeder hose.

11. Bleed the remaining wheels in the following order:
- left rear
- right front
- left front

12. Lower the vehicle.

Fig. 71 The Tech I scan tool or equivalent can be used to position the rear displacement cylinder

ABS TROUBLESHOOTING

DIAGNOSTIC PROCESS
(Page 2 of 3)

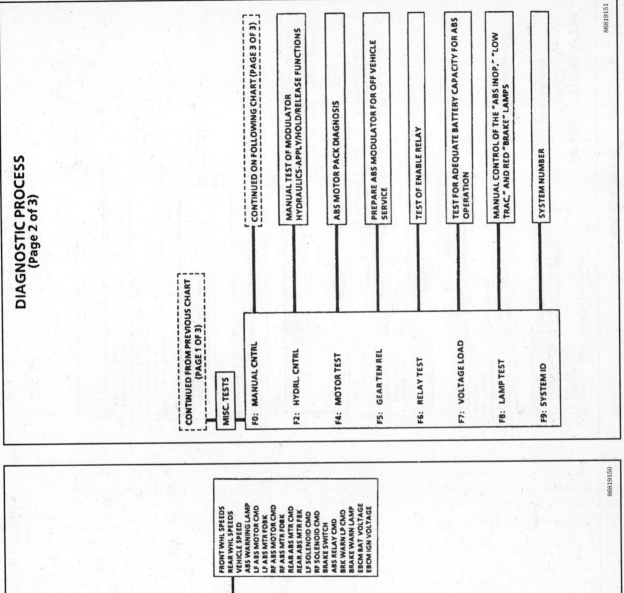

ABS TROUBLESHOOTING

DIAGNOSTIC PROCESS
(Page 1 of 3)

ABS TROUBLESHOOTING

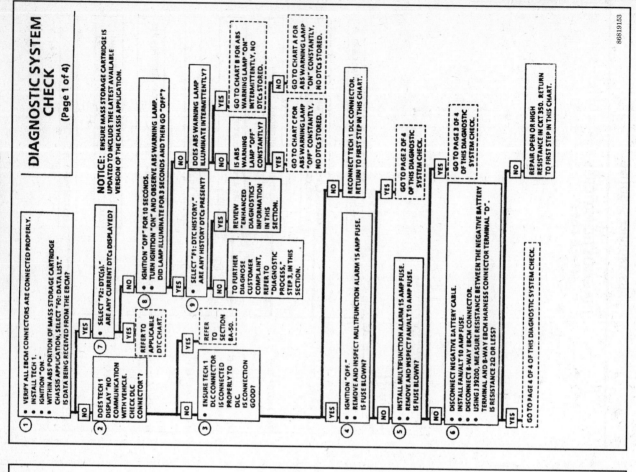

DIAGNOSTIC SYSTEM CHECK
(Page 1 of 4)

NOTICE: ENSURE MASS STORAGE CARTRIDGE IS UPDATED TO INCLUDE THE LATEST AVAILABLE VERSION OF THE CHASSIS APPLICATION.

(1)
- VERIFY ALL EBCM CONNECTORS ARE CONNECTED PROPERLY.
- INSTALL TECH 1.
- IGNITION "ON."
- WITHIN ABS PORTION OF MASS STORAGE CARTRIDGE CHASSIS APPLICATION, SELECT "F0: DATA LIST."
IS DATA BEING RECEIVED FROM THE EBCM?

(2) DOES TECH 1 DISPLAY "NO COMMUNICATION WITH VEHICLE. CHECK DLC CONNECTOR"?

(3) ENSURE TECH 1 DLC CONNECTOR IS CONNECTED PROPERLY TO DLC. IS CONNECTION GOOD?

REFER TO SECTION 8A-50.

(7)
- SELECT "F2: DTC(s)."
ARE ANY CURRENT DTCs DISPLAYED?

REFER TO APPLICABLE DTC CHART.

(8)
- IGNITION "OFF" FOR 10 SECONDS.
- TURN IGNITION "ON" AND OBSERVE ABS WARNING LAMP.
DID LAMP ILLUMINATE FOR 3 SECONDS AND THEN GO "OFF"?

DOES ABS WARNING LAMP ILLUMINATE INTERMITTENTLY?

GO TO CHART B FOR ABS WARNING LAMP "ON" INTERMITTENTLY, NO DTCs STORED.

IS ABS WARNING LAMP "OFF" CONSTANTLY?

GO TO CHART A FOR ABS WARNING LAMP "ON" CONSTANTLY, NO DTCs STORED.

GO TO CHART C FOR ABS WARNING LAMP "OFF" CONSTANTLY, NO DTCs STORED.

(9)
- SELECT "F1: DTC HISTORY."
ARE ANY HISTORY DTCs PRESENT?

REVIEW "ENHANCED DIAGNOSTICS" INFORMATION IN THIS SECTION.

TO FURTHER DIAGNOSE CUSTOMER COMPLAINT, REFER TO "DIAGNOSTIC PROCESS," STEP 3, IN THIS SECTION.

RECONNECT TECH 1 DLC CONNECTOR. RETURN TO FIRST STEP IN THIS CHART.

(4)
- IGNITION "OFF."
- REMOVE AND INSPECT MULTIFUNCTION ALARM 15 AMP FUSE.
IS FUSE BLOWN?

(5)
- INSTALL MULTIFUNCTION ALARM 15 AMP FUSE.
- REMOVE AND INSPECT FAN/ALT 10 AMP FUSE.
IS FUSE BLOWN?

(6)
- DISCONNECT NEGATIVE BATTERY CABLE.
- INSTALL FAN/ALT 10 AMP FUSE.
- DISCONNECT 8-WAY EBCM CONNECTOR.
- USING J 39200, MEASURE RESISTANCE BETWEEN THE NEGATIVE BATTERY TERMINAL AND 8-WAY EBCM HARNESS CONNECTOR TERMINAL "D."
IS RESISTANCE 2Ω OR LESS?

GO TO PAGE 2 OF 4 OF THIS DIAGNOSTIC SYSTEM CHECK.

GO TO PAGE 3 OF 4 OF THIS DIAGNOSTIC SYSTEM CHECK.

REPAIR OPEN OR HIGH RESISTANCE IN CKT 350. RETURN TO FIRST STEP IN THIS CHART.

GO TO PAGE 4 OF 4 OF THIS DIAGNOSTIC SYSTEM CHECK.

86819153

ABS TROUBLESHOOTING

DIAGNOSTIC PROCESS
(Page 3 of 3)

CONTINUED FROM PREVIOUS CHART (PAGE 2 OF 3)

MANUAL CONTROL OF SOLENOIDS AND MOTORS.

↑ = TURN ON
↓ = TURN OFF
YES TO CONTINUE

SELECT FUNCTION
F0: LF APPLY
F1: LF RELEASE
F2: LF SOLENOID
F4: RF APPLY
F5: RF RELEASE
F6: RF SOLENOID
F8: REAR APPLY
F9: REAR RELEASE

MOTOR APPLY
COMMAND: XX AMPS
FEEDBACK: XX AMPS
ABS RELAY: ON/OFF

MOTOR RELEASE
COMMAND: XX AMPS
FEEDBACK: XX AMPS
ABS RELAY: ON/OFF

SOLENOID
COMMAND: ON/OFF
ABS RELAY: ON/OFF

86819152

ABS TROUBLESHOOTING

DIAGNOSTIC SYSTEM CHECK
(Page 3 of 4)

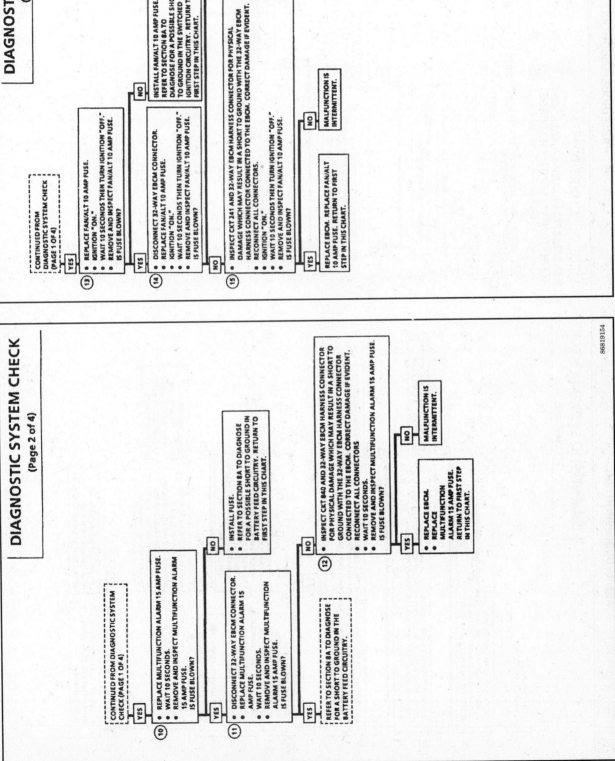

ABS TROUBLESHOOTING

DIAGNOSTIC SYSTEM CHECK
(Page 2 of 4)

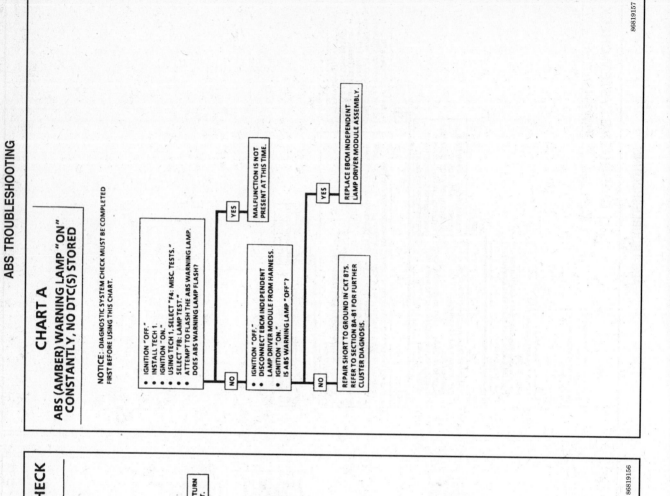

CHART A

ABS (AMBER) WARNING LAMP "ON" CONSTANTLY, NO DTC(S) STORED

NOTICE: DIAGNOSTIC SYSTEM CHECK MUST BE COMPLETED FIRST BEFORE USING THIS CHART.

- IGNITION "OFF."
- INSTALL "TECH 1"
- IGNITION "ON."
- USING TECH 1, SELECT "F4: MISC. TESTS."
- SELECT "F8: LAMP TEST."
- ATTEMPT TO FLASH THE ABS WARNING LAMP. DOES ABS WARNING LAMP FLASH?

NO

- IGNITION "OFF."
- DISCONNECT EBCM INDEPENDENT LAMP DRIVER MODULE FROM HARNESS.
- IGNITION "ON." IS ABS WARNING LAMP "OFF"?

NO

REPAIR SHORT TO GROUND IN CKT 875. REFER TO SECTION 8A-81 FOR FURTHER CLUSTER DIAGNOSIS.

YES

REPLACE EBCM INDEPENDENT LAMP DRIVER MODULE ASSEMBLY.

YES

MALFUNCTION IS NOT PRESENT AT THIS TIME.

86819157

DIAGNOSTIC SYSTEM CHECK
(Page 4 of 4)

CONTINUED FROM DIAGNOSTIC SYSTEM CHECK (PAGE 1 OF 4)

(16)
- DISCONNECT 32-WAY EBCM CONNECTOR.
- USING J 39200, MEASURE VOLTAGE BETWEEN GROUND AND 32-WAY EBCM HARNESS CONNECTOR TERMINAL "F10".
  IS VOLTAGE GREATER THAN 10 VOLTS?

YES

NO → REPAIR OPEN IN CKT 840. RETURN TO FIRST STEP IN THIS CHART.

(17)
- DISCONNECT POSITIVE BATTERY CABLE.
- USING J 39200, MEASURE RESISTANCE BETWEEN POSITIVE BATTERY CABLE TERMINAL AND 32-WAY EBCM HARNESS CONNECTOR TERMINAL "F10".
  IS RESISTANCE 2Ω OR LESS?

YES

NO → REPAIR HIGH RESISTANCE IN CKT 840. RETURN TO FIRST STEP IN THIS CHART.

(18)
- IGNITION "ON." (THIS IS DONE TO PROVIDE CIRCUIT CONTINUITY.)
- USING J 39200, MEASURE RESISTANCE BETWEEN POSITIVE BATTERY CABLE TERMINAL AND 32-WAY EBCM HARNESS CONNECTOR TERMINAL "F11".
  IS RESISTANCE 2Ω OR LESS?

YES

NO

(20)
- IGNITION "OFF."
- REMOVE FAN/ALT 10 AMP FUSE.
- USING J 39200, MEASURE RESISTANCE BETWEEN EACH FAN/ALT 10 AMP FUSE BLOCK TERMINAL AND 32-WAY EBCM HARNESS CONNECTOR TERMINAL "F11".
  IS RESISTANCE 2Ω OR LESS FOR EITHER MEASUREMENT?

YES

NO → REPAIR OPEN OR HIGH RESISTANCE IN CKT 241. INSTALL FAN/ALT 10 AMP FUSE. RETURN TO FIRST STEP IN THIS CHART.

REFER TO SECTION 8A TO REPAIR OPEN OR HIGH RESISTANCE BETWEEN POSITIVE BATTERY CABLE TERMINAL AND FAN/ALT 10 AMP FUSE BLOCK TERMINAL. RETURN TO THE FIRST STEP IN THIS CHART.

(19)
- INSPECT EBCM AND EBCM CONNECTOR TERMINALS FOR POOR TERMINAL CONTACT.
- INSPECT BATTERY TERMINALS AND BATTERY CABLE TERMINALS FOR A POOR CONNECTION. REFER TO SECTION 8A-4, "CHECKING TERMINAL CONTACT."
  IS POOR TERMINAL CONTACT OR A POOR CONNECTION EVIDENT?

YES → REPLACE TERMINALS OR REPAIR POOR CONNECTION INTEGRITY. RETURN TO FIRST STEP IN THIS CHART.

NO → RECONNECT EBCM CONNECTORS AND BATTERY CABLES. PROCEED TO SECTION 8A-50.

86819156

ABS TROUBLESHOOTING

CHART C

ABS (AMBER) WARNING LAMP "OFF" CONSTANTLY, NO DTCs STORED

NOTICE: DIAGNOSTIC SYSTEM CHECK MUST BE COMPLETED BEFORE USING THIS CHART.

- IGNITION "ON," ENGINE "OFF."
- USING TECH 1, SELECT LAMP TEST AND COMMAND THE ABS WARNING LAMP "ON."
- IS ABS WARNING LAMP "ON"?

YES → MALFUNCTION IS NOT PRESENT AT THIS TIME.

NO
- NOTICE: DTC 11 MAY BE SET DURING THIS TEST.
- IGNITION "OFF."
- DISCONNECT LAMP DRIVER MODULE (LDM) FROM HARNESS CONNECTOR.
- WITH A FUSED JUMPER, SUCH AS J 36169 WITH A 3 AMP FUSE, CONNECT TERMINAL "E" OF THE LDM HARNESS CONNECTOR TO GROUND.
- IGNITION "ON."
- IS ABS WARNING LAMP "ON"?

YES
- IGNITION "OFF."
- USING J 39200, MEASURE THE RESISTANCE BETWEEN GROUND AND TERMINAL "E" OF THE LDM HARNESS CONNECTOR.
- IS RESISTANCE 2Ω OR LESS?

YES → REPLACE LAMP DRIVER MODULE.

NO → REPAIR OPEN IN CKT 150.

NO
- REMOVE AND INSPECT JUMPER WIRE FUSE.
- IS FUSE BLOWN?

YES → REPAIR SHORT TO VOLTAGE IN CKT 875. REPLACE LAMP DRIVER MODULE.

NO
- INSPECT ABS WARNING LAMP BULB.
- IS BULB BLOWN?

YES → REPLACE BULB.

NO
- IGNITION "OFF."
- DISCONNECT CLUSTER HARNESS CONNECTOR.
- USING J 39200, MEASURE RESISTANCE BETWEEN TERMINAL "E" OF THE LDM CONNECTOR AND TERMINAL "C2-7" (BUICK) OR "C1-11" (OLDS), OF THE ABS WARNING LAMP ON THE CLUSTER HARNESS CONNECTOR.
- IS RESISTANCE 2Ω OR LESS?

YES → REFER TO SECTION 8A FOR FURTHER DIAGNOSIS OF VP CLUSTER.

NO → REPAIR OPEN OR HIGH RESISTANCE IN CKT 875.

86819159

ABS TROUBLESHOOTING

CHART B

ABS (AMBER) WARNING LAMP "ON" INTERMITTENTLY, NO DTCs STORED

NOTICE: DIAGNOSTIC SYSTEM CHECK MUST BE COMPLETED BEFORE USING THIS CHART.

(1)
- IGNITION "OFF."
- DISCONNECT 8-WAY EBCM CONNECTOR.
- DISCONNECT NEGATIVE BATTERY TERMINAL.
- DISCONNECT POSITIVE BATTERY TERMINAL.
- USING J 39200, MEASURE THE RESISTANCE BETWEEN THE NEGATIVE BATTERY CABLE TERMINAL AND TERMINAL "E" OF THE 8-WAY EBCM HARNESS CONNECTOR.
- OBSERVE MEASURED RESISTANCE WHILE "WIGGLING" WIRE HARNESS AND CONNECTORS.
- IS RESISTANCE ALWAYS 2Ω OR LESS?

NO → REPAIR INTERMITTENT OPEN OR HIGH RESISTANCE IN CKT 350. REFER TO SECTION 8A-4, "INTERMITTENTS AND POOR CONNECTIONS."

YES

(2)
- DISCONNECT 32-WAY EBCM CONNECTOR.
- USING J 39200, MEASURE THE RESISTANCE BETWEEN POSITIVE BATTERY CABLE TERMINAL AND TERMINAL "F10" OF THE 32-WAY EBCM HARNESS CONNECTOR.
- OBSERVE MEASURED RESISTANCE WHILE "WIGGLING" WIRE HARNESS AND CONNECTORS.
- IS RESISTANCE ALWAYS 2Ω OR LESS?

NO → REPAIR INTERMITTENT OPEN OR HIGH RESISTANCE IN CKTs 2 OR 840. REFER TO SECTION 8A-4, "INTERMITTENTS AND POOR CONNECTIONS."

YES

(3)
- TURN IGNITION SWITCH "ON" (THIS IS DONE TO COMPLETE THE IGNITION CIRCUIT).
- USING J 39200, MEASURE THE RESISTANCE BETWEEN POSITIVE BATTERY CABLE TERMINAL AND TERMINAL "E" OF THE 32-WAY EBCM HARNESS CONNECTOR.
- OBSERVE MEASURED RESISTANCE WHILE "WIGGLING" WIRE HARNESS AND CONNECTORS.
- IS RESISTANCE ALWAYS 2Ω OR LESS?

NO → REPAIR INTERMITTENT OPEN OR HIGH RESISTANCE IN CKTs 241 OR 300. REFER TO SECTION 8A-4, "INTERMITTENTS AND POOR CONNECTIONS."

YES

(4)
- CHECK POSITIVE BATTERY TERMINAL AND POSITIVE BATTERY CABLE TERMINAL FOR A POOR CONNECTION.
- INSPECT TERMINALS "F11" AND "F10" OF THE 32-WAY EBCM CONNECTOR AND TERMINAL "E" OF THE 8-WAY EBCM CONNECTOR FOR POOR TERMINAL CONTACT AND EVIDENCE OF CORROSION. REFER TO SECTION 8A-4, "CHECKING TERMINAL CONTACT."
- IS THERE EVIDENCE OF POOR TERMINAL CONTACT OR CORROSION?

YES → REPLACE TERMINALS THAT EXHIBIT POOR TERMINAL CONTACT OR SIGNS OF CORROSION. REPAIR CONNECTION INTEGRITY IF POOR CONTACT EXISTS AT BATTERY.

NO

(5)
- IGNITION "OFF."
- RECONNECT ALL CONNECTORS.
- IGNITION "ON."
- IS ABS WARNING LAMP "ON" INTERMITTENTLY WITH NO DTCs SET?

YES → REPLACE EBCM.

NO → MALFUNCTION IS NOT PRESENT AT THIS TIME. INTERMITTENTS MAY BE CAUSED BY INCORRECT WIRING HARNESS ROUTING OR LOOSE GROUND CONNECTIONS. REFER TO SECTION 8A-4, "INTERMITTENTS AND POOR CONNECTIONS."

86819158

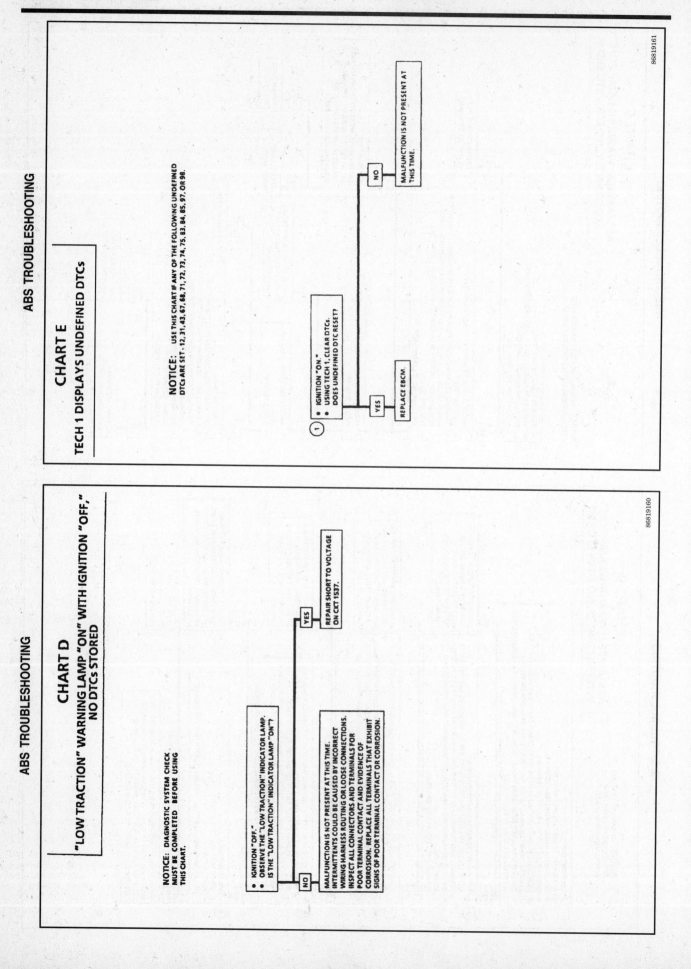

ABS TROUBLESHOOTING

CHART E
TECH 1 DISPLAYS UNDEFINED DTCs

NOTICE: USE THIS CHART IF ANY OF THE FOLLOWING UNDEFINED DTCs ARE SET - 12, 31, 43, 67, 68, 71, 72, 73, 74, 75, 83, 84, 85, 97, OR 98.

1.
- IGNITION "ON."
- USING TECH 1, CLEAR DTCs. DOES UNDEFINED DTC RESET?

YES → REPLACE EBCM.

NO → MALFUNCTION IS NOT PRESENT AT THIS TIME.

86819161

ABS TROUBLESHOOTING

CHART D
"LOW TRACTION" WARNING LAMP "ON" WITH IGNITION "OFF," NO DTCs STORED

NOTICE: DIAGNOSTIC SYSTEM CHECK MUST BE COMPLETED BEFORE USING THIS CHART.

- IGNITION "OFF."
- OBSERVE THE "LOW TRACTION" INDICATOR LAMP. IS THE "LOW TRACTION" INDICATOR LAMP "ON"?

YES → REPAIR SHORT TO VOLTAGE ON CKT 1537.

NO → MALFUNCTION IS NOT PRESENT AT THIS TIME. INTERMITTENTS COULD BE CAUSED BY INCORRECT WIRING HARNESS ROUTING OR LOOSE CONNECTIONS. INSPECT ALL CONNECTORS AND TERMINALS FOR POOR TERMINAL CONTACT AND EVIDENCE OF CORROSION. REPLACE ALL TERMINALS THAT EXHIBIT SIGNS OF POOR TERMINAL CONTACT OR CORROSION.

86819160

ABS TROUBLESHOOTING

DTC 11
(Page 2 of 2)
ABS WARNING LAMP CIRCUIT MALFUNCTION

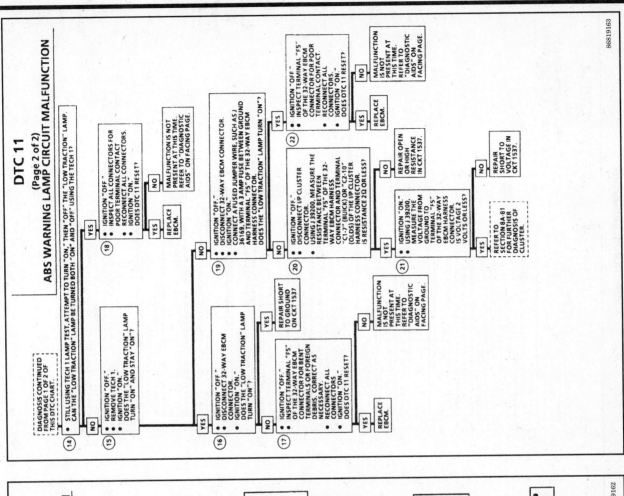

ABS TROUBLESHOOTING

DTC 11
(Page 1 of 2)
ABS WARNING LAMP
CIRCUIT MALFUNCTION

ABS TROUBLESHOOTING

DTC 14
(Page 2 of 3)
ABS ENABLE RELAY
CONTACT CIRCUIT OPEN

DTC 14
(Page 1 of 3)
ABS ENABLE RELAY
CONTACT CIRCUIT OPEN

86819165

86819164

ABS TROUBLESHOOTING

ABS TROUBLESHOOTING

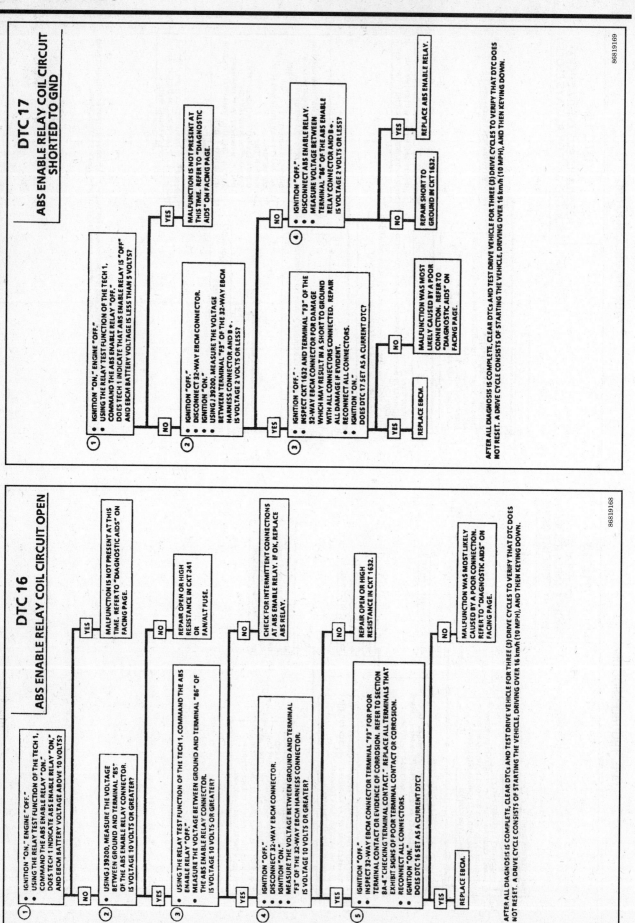

DTC 17
ABS ENABLE RELAY COIL CIRCUIT SHORTED TO GND

1
- IGNITION "ON," ENGINE "OFF."
- USING THE RELAY TEST FUNCTION OF THE TECH 1, COMMAND THE ABS ENABLE RELAY "OFF." DOES TECH 1 INDICATE THAT ABS ENABLE RELAY IS "OFF" AND EBCM BATTERY VOLTAGE IS LESS THAN 5 VOLTS?

YES → MALFUNCTION IS NOT PRESENT AT THIS TIME. REFER TO "DIAGNOSTIC AIDS" ON FACING PAGE.

2
- IGNITION "OFF."
- DISCONNECT 32-WAY EBCM CONNECTOR.
- IGNITION "ON."
- USING J 39200, MEASURE THE VOLTAGE BETWEEN TERMINAL "F3" OF THE 32-WAY EBCM HARNESS CONNECTOR AND B +. IS VOLTAGE 2 VOLTS OR LESS?

3
- IGNITION "OFF."
- INSPECT CKT 1632 AND TERMINAL "F3" OF THE 32-WAY EBCM CONNECTOR FOR DAMAGE WHICH MAY RESULT IN A SHORT TO GROUND WITH ALL CONNECTORS CONNECTED. REPAIR ALL DAMAGE IF EVIDENT.
- RECONNECT ALL CONNECTORS.
- IGNITION "ON."
- DOES DTC 17 SET AS A CURRENT DTC?

YES → REPLACE EBCM.

NO → MALFUNCTION WAS MOST LIKELY CAUSED BY A POOR CONNECTION. REFER TO "DIAGNOSTIC AIDS" ON FACING PAGE.

4
- IGNITION "OFF."
- DISCONNECT ABS ENABLE RELAY.
- MEASURE VOLTAGE BETWEEN TERMINAL "86" OF THE ABS ENABLE RELAY CONNECTOR AND B +. IS VOLTAGE 2 VOLTS OR LESS?

YES → REPLACE ABS ENABLE RELAY.

NO → REPAIR SHORT TO GROUND IN CKT 1632.

AFTER ALL DIAGNOSIS IS COMPLETE, CLEAR DTC's AND TEST DRIVE VEHICLE FOR THREE (3) DRIVE CYCLES TO VERIFY THAT DTC DOES NOT RESET. A DRIVE CYCLE CONSISTS OF STARTING THE VEHICLE, DRIVING OVER 16 km/h (10 MPH), AND THEN KEYING DOWN.

86819169

ABS TROUBLESHOOTING

DTC 16
ABS ENABLE RELAY COIL CIRCUIT OPEN

1
- IGNITION "ON," ENGINE "OFF."
- USING THE RELAY TEST FUNCTION OF THE TECH 1, COMMAND THE ABS ENABLE RELAY "ON." DOES TECH 1 INDICATE ABS ENABLE RELAY IS "ON," AND EBCM BATTERY VOLTAGE ABOVE 10 VOLTS?

YES → MALFUNCTION IS NOT PRESENT AT THIS TIME. REFER TO "DIAGNOSTIC AIDS" ON FACING PAGE.

2
- USING J 39200, MEASURE THE VOLTAGE BETWEEN GROUND AND TERMINAL "85" OF THE ABS ENABLE RELAY CONNECTOR. IS VOLTAGE 10 VOLTS OR GREATER?

NO → REPAIR OPEN OR HIGH RESISTANCE IN CKT 241 OR FAN/ALT FUSE.

3
- USING THE RELAY TEST FUNCTION OF THE TECH 1, COMMAND THE ABS ENABLE RELAY "OFF."
- MEASURE THE VOLTAGE BETWEEN GROUND AND TERMINAL "86" OF THE ABS ENABLE RELAY CONNECTOR. IS VOLTAGE 10 VOLTS OR GREATER?

NO → CHECK FOR INTERMITTENT CONNECTIONS AT ABS ENABLE RELAY. IF OK, REPLACE ABS RELAY.

4
- IGNITION "OFF."
- DISCONNECT 32-WAY EBCM CONNECTOR.
- IGNITION "ON."
- MEASURE THE VOLTAGE BETWEEN GROUND AND TERMINAL "F3" OF THE 32-WAY EBCM HARNESS CONNECTOR. IS VOLTAGE 10 VOLTS OR GREATER?

NO → REPAIR OPEN OR HIGH RESISTANCE IN CKT 1632.

5
- IGNITION "OFF."
- INSPECT 32-WAY EBCM CONNECTOR TERMINAL "F3" FOR POOR TERMINAL CONTACT OR EVIDENCE OF CORROSION. REFER TO SECTION 8A-4 "CHECKING TERMINAL CONTACT." REPLACE ALL TERMINALS THAT EXHIBIT SIGNS OF POOR TERMINAL CONTACT OR CORROSION.
- RECONNECT ALL CONNECTORS.
- IGNITION "ON."
- DOES DTC 16 SET AS A CURRENT DTC?

YES → REPLACE EBCM.

NO → MALFUNCTION WAS MOST LIKELY CAUSED BY A POOR CONNECTION. REFER TO "DIAGNOSTIC AIDS" ON FACING PAGE.

AFTER ALL DIAGNOSIS IS COMPLETE, CLEAR DTC's AND TEST DRIVE VEHICLE FOR THREE (3) DRIVE CYCLES TO VERIFY THAT DTC DOES NOT RESET. A DRIVE CYCLE CONSISTS OF STARTING THE VEHICLE, DRIVING OVER 16 km/h (10 MPH), AND THEN KEYING DOWN.

86819168

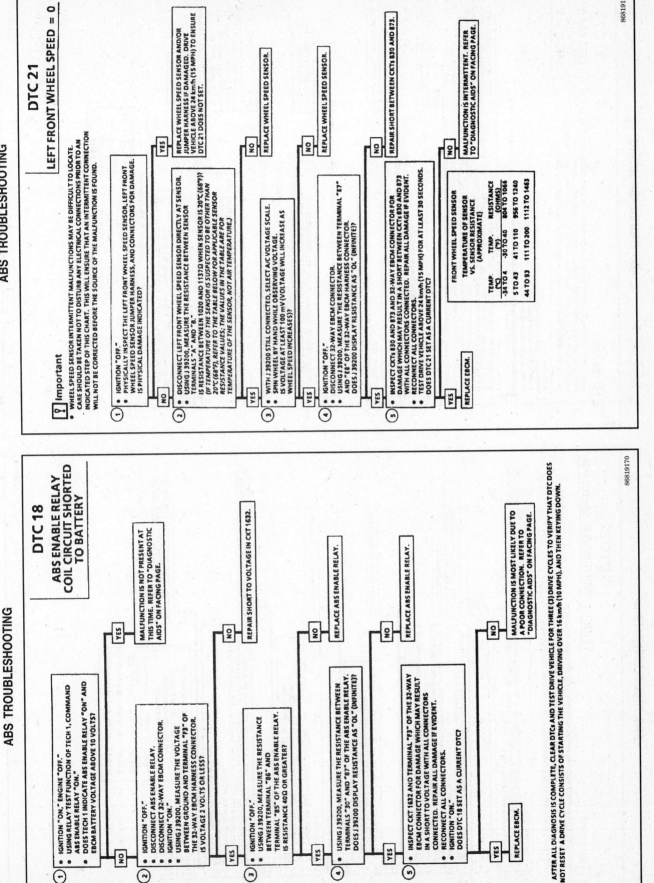

ABS TROUBLESHOOTING

DTC 21

LEFT FRONT WHEEL SPEED = 0

Important
- WHEEL SPEED SENSOR INTERMITTENT MALFUNCTIONS MAY BE DIFFICULT TO LOCATE. CARE SHOULD BE TAKEN NOT TO DISTURB ANY ELECTRICAL CONNECTIONS PRIOR TO AN INDICATED STEP OF THIS CHART. THIS WILL ENSURE THAT AN INTERMITTENT CONNECTION WILL NOT BE CORRECTED BEFORE THE SOURCE OF THE MALFUNCTION IS FOUND.

1.
- IGNITION "OFF."
- PHYSICALLY INSPECT THE LEFT FRONT WHEEL SPEED SENSOR, LEFT FRONT WHEEL SPEED SENSOR JUMPER HARNESS, AND CONNECTORS FOR DAMAGE. IS PHYSICAL DAMAGE INDICATED?

YES → REPLACE WHEEL SPEED SENSOR AND/OR JUMPER HARNESS IF DAMAGED. DRIVE VEHICLE ABOVE 24 km/h (15 MPH) TO ENSURE DTC 21 DOES NOT SET.

2.
- DISCONNECT LEFT FRONT WHEEL SPEED SENSOR DIRECTLY AT SENSOR.
- USING J 39200, MEASURE THE RESISTANCE BETWEEN SENSOR TERMINALS "A" AND "B."
- IS RESISTANCE BETWEEN 1020 AND 1137Ω WHEN SENSOR IS 20°C (68°F)? (IF TEMPERATURE OF THE SENSOR IS SUSPECTED TO BE OTHER THAN 20°C (68°F), REFER TO THE TABLE BELOW FOR APPLICABLE SENSOR RESISTANCE VALUES; THE VALUES IN THE TABLE ARE FOR TEMPERATURE OF THE SENSOR, NOT AIR TEMPERATURE.)

NO → REPLACE WHEEL SPEED SENSOR.

3.
- WITH J 39200 STILL CONNECTED, SELECT A/C VOLTAGE SCALE.
- SPIN WHEEL BY HAND WHILE OBSERVING VOLTAGE.
- IS VOLTAGE AT LEAST 100 mV (VOLTAGE WILL INCREASE AS WHEEL SPEED INCREASES)?

NO → REPLACE WHEEL SPEED SENSOR.

4.
- IGNITION "OFF."
- DISCONNECT 32-WAY EBCM CONNECTOR.
- USING J 39200, MEASURE THE RESISTANCE BETWEEN TERMINAL "E7" AND "E8" OF THE 32-WAY EBCM HARNESS CONNECTOR. DOES J 39200 DISPLAY RESISTANCE AS "OL" (INFINITE)?

YES → REPAIR SHORT BETWEEN CKTs 830 AND 873.

5.
- INSPECT CKTs 830 AND 873 AND 32-WAY EBCM CONNECTOR FOR DAMAGE WHICH MAY RESULT IN A SHORT BETWEEN CKTs 830 AND 873 WITH ALL CONNECTORS CONNECTED. REPAIR ALL DAMAGE IF EVIDENT.
- RECONNECT ALL CONNECTORS.
- TEST DRIVE VEHICLE ABOVE 24 km/h (15 MPH) FOR AT LEAST 30 SECONDS.
- DOES DTC 21 SET AS A CURRENT DTC?

NO → MALFUNCTION IS INTERMITTENT. REFER TO "DIAGNOSTIC AIDS" ON FACING PAGE.

YES → REPLACE EBCM.

FRONT WHEEL SPEED SENSOR
TEMPERATURE OF SENSOR
VS. SENSOR RESISTANCE
(APPROXIMATE)

TEMP. (°C)	TEMP. (°F)	RESISTANCE (OHMS)
-34 TO 4	-30 TO 40	604 TO 1066
5 TO 43	41 TO 110	956 TO 1240
44 TO 93	111 TO 200	1112 TO 1463

86819171

ABS TROUBLESHOOTING

DTC 18

ABS ENABLE RELAY COIL CIRCUIT SHORTED TO BATTERY

1.
- IGNITION "ON," ENGINE "OFF."
- USING RELAY TEST FUNCTION OF TECH 1, COMMAND ABS ENABLE RELAY "ON."
- DOES TECH 1 INDICATE ABS ENABLE RELAY "ON" AND EBCM BATTERY VOLTAGE ABOVE 10 VOLTS?

YES → MALFUNCTION IS NOT PRESENT AT THIS TIME. REFER TO "DIAGNOSTIC AIDS" ON FACING PAGE.

2.
- IGNITION "OFF."
- DISCONNECT ABS ENABLE RELAY.
- DISCONNECT 32-WAY EBCM CONNECTOR.
- IGNITION "ON."
- USING J 39200, MEASURE THE VOLTAGE BETWEEN GROUND AND TERMINAL "F3" OF THE 32-WAY EBCM HARNESS CONNECTOR. IS VOLTAGE 2 VOLTS OR LESS?

NO → REPAIR SHORT TO VOLTAGE IN CKT 1632.

3.
- IGNITION "OFF."
- USING J 39200, MEASURE THE RESISTANCE BETWEEN TERMINAL "86" AND TERMINAL "85" OF THE ABS ENABLE RELAY. IS RESISTANCE 40Ω OR GREATER?

NO → REPLACE ABS ENABLE RELAY.

4.
- USING J 39200, MEASURE THE RESISTANCE BETWEEN TERMINALS "30" AND "87" OF THE ABS ENABLE RELAY. DOES J 39200 DISPLAY RESISTANCE AS "OL" (INFINITE)?

NO → REPLACE ABS ENABLE RELAY.

5.
- INSPECT CKT 1632 AND TERMINAL "F3" OF THE 32-WAY EBCM CONNECTOR FOR DAMAGE WHICH MAY RESULT IN A SHORT TO VOLTAGE WITH ALL CONNECTORS CONNECTED. REPAIR ALL DAMAGE IF EVIDENT.
- RECONNECT ALL CONNECTORS.
- IGNITION "ON."
- DOES DTC 18 SET AS A CURRENT DTC?

NO → MALFUNCTION IS MOST LIKELY DUE TO A POOR CONNECTION. REFER TO "DIAGNOSTIC AIDS" ON FACING PAGE.

YES → REPLACE EBCM.

AFTER ALL DIAGNOSIS IS COMPLETE, CLEAR DTCs AND TEST DRIVE VEHICLE FOR THREE (3) DRIVE CYCLES TO VERIFY THAT DTC DOES NOT RESET. A DRIVE CYCLE CONSISTS OF STARTING THE VEHICLE, DRIVING OVER 16 km/h (10 MPH), AND THEN KEYING DOWN.

86819170

ABS TROUBLESHOOTING

DTC 22 — RIGHT FRONT WHEEL SPEED = 0

Important
- WHEEL SPEED SENSOR INTERMITTENT MALFUNCTIONS MAY BE DIFFICULT TO LOCATE. CARE SHOULD BE TAKEN NOT TO DISTURB ANY ELECTRICAL CONNECTIONS PRIOR TO AN INDICATED STEP OF THIS CHART. THIS WILL ENSURE THAT AN INTERMITTENT CONNECTION WILL NOT BE CORRECTED BEFORE THE SOURCE OF THE MALFUNCTION IS FOUND.

1. IGNITION "OFF."
   - PHYSICALLY INSPECT THE RIGHT FRONT WHEEL SPEED SENSOR, RIGHT FRONT WHEEL SPEED SENSOR JUMPER HARNESS, AND CONNECTORS FOR DAMAGE.
   IS PHYSICAL DAMAGE INDICATED?
   - YES → REPLACE WHEEL SPEED SENSOR AND/OR JUMPER HARNESS IF DAMAGED. DRIVE VEHICLE ABOVE 24 km/h (15 MPH) TO ENSURE DTC 22 DOES NOT SET.

2. DISCONNECT RIGHT FRONT WHEEL SPEED SENSOR DIRECTLY AT SENSOR.
   - USING J 39200, MEASURE THE RESISTANCE BETWEEN SENSOR TERMINALS "A" AND "B".
   IS RESISTANCE BETWEEN 1020 AND 1137Ω WHEN SENSOR IS 20°C (68°F)?
   (IF TEMPERATURE OF THE SENSOR IS SUSPECTED TO BE OTHER THAN 20°C (68°F), REFER TO THE TABLE BELOW FOR APPLICABLE SENSOR RESISTANCE VALUES; THE VALUES IN THE TABLE ARE FOR TEMPERATURE OF THE SENSOR, NOT AIR TEMPERATURE.)
   - NO → REPLACE WHEEL SPEED SENSOR.

3. WITH J 39200 STILL CONNECTED, SELECT A/C VOLTAGE SCALE.
   - SPIN WHEEL BY HAND WHILE OBSERVING VOLTAGE.
   IS VOLTAGE AT LEAST 100 mV (VOLTAGE WILL INCREASE AS WHEEL SPEED INCREASES)?
   - NO → REPLACE WHEEL SPEED SENSOR.

4. IGNITION "OFF."
   - DISCONNECT 32-WAY EBCM CONNECTOR.
   - USING J 39200, MEASURE THE RESISTANCE BETWEEN TERMINAL "E3" AND "E4" OF THE 32-WAY EBCM HARNESS CONNECTOR.
   DOES J 39200 DISPLAY RESISTANCE AS "OL" (INFINITE)?
   - NO → REPAIR SHORT BETWEEN CKTs 833 AND 872.

5. INSPECT CKTs 833 AND 872 AND 32-WAY EBCM CONNECTOR FOR DAMAGE WHICH MAY RESULT IN A SHORT BETWEEN CKTs 833 AND 872. WITH ALL CONNECTORS CONNECTED. REPAIR ALL DAMAGE IF EVIDENT.
   - RECONNECT ALL CONNECTORS.
   - TEST DRIVE VEHICLE ABOVE 24 km/h (15 MPH) FOR AT LEAST 30 SECONDS.
   DOES DTC 22 SET AS A CURRENT DTC?
   - YES → REPLACE EBCM.
   - NO → MALFUNCTION IS INTERMITTENT, REFER TO "DIAGNOSTIC AIDS" ON FACING PAGE.

FRONT WHEEL SPEED SENSOR — TEMPERATURE OF SENSOR VS. SENSOR RESISTANCE (APPROXIMATE)

TEMP. (°C)	TEMP. (°F)	RESISTANCE (OHMS)
-34 TO 4	-30 TO 40	804 TO 1066
5 TO 43	41 TO 110	956 TO 1240
44 TO 93	111 TO 200	1112 TO 1463

86819172

ABS TROUBLESHOOTING

DTC 23 — LEFT REAR WHEEL SPEED = 0

Important
- WHEEL SPEED SENSOR INTERMITTENT MALFUNCTIONS MAY BE DIFFICULT TO LOCATE. CARE SHOULD BE TAKEN NOT TO DISTURB ANY ELECTRICAL CONNECTIONS PRIOR TO AN INDICATED STEP OF THIS CHART. THIS WILL ENSURE THAT AN INTERMITTENT CONNECTION WILL NOT BE CORRECTED BEFORE THE SOURCE OF THE MALFUNCTION IS FOUND.

1. IGNITION "OFF."
   - PHYSICALLY INSPECT THE LEFT REAR WHEEL SPEED SENSOR, WHEEL SPEED SENSOR JUMPER HARNESS, AND CONNECTORS FOR DAMAGE.
   IS PHYSICAL DAMAGE INDICATED?
   - YES → REPLACE WHEEL SPEED SENSOR AND/OR WHEEL SPEED SENSOR JUMPER HARNESS IF DAMAGED. DRIVE VEHICLE ABOVE 24 km/h (15 MPH) TO ENSURE DTC 23 DOES NOT SET.

2. DISCONNECT LEFT REAR WHEEL SPEED SENSOR DIRECTLY AT SENSOR.
   - USING J 39200, MEASURE THE RESISTANCE BETWEEN SENSOR TERMINALS "A" AND "B".
   IS RESISTANCE BETWEEN 2059 AND 2353Ω WHEN SENSOR IS 20°C (68°F)?
   (IF TEMPERATURE OF THE SENSOR IS SUSPECTED TO BE OTHER THAN 20°C (68°F), REFER TO THE TABLE BELOW FOR APPLICABLE SENSOR RESISTANCE VALUES; THE VALUES IN THE TABLE ARE FOR TEMPERATURE OF THE SENSOR, NOT AIR TEMPERATURE.)
   - NO → REPLACE WHEEL SPEED SENSOR.

3. WITH J 39200 STILL CONNECTED, SELECT A/C VOLTAGE SCALE.
   - SPIN WHEEL BY HAND WHILE OBSERVING VOLTAGE.
   IS VOLTAGE AT LEAST 100 mV (VOLTAGE WILL INCREASE AS WHEEL SPEED INCREASES)?
   - NO → REPLACE WHEEL SPEED SENSOR.

4. IGNITION "OFF."
   - DISCONNECT 32-WAY EBCM CONNECTOR.
   - USING J 39200, MEASURE THE RESISTANCE BETWEEN TERMINAL "E1" AND "E2" OF THE 32-WAY EBCM HARNESS CONNECTOR.
   DOES J 39200 DISPLAY RESISTANCE AS "OL" (INFINITE)?
   - NO → REPAIR SHORT BETWEEN CKTs 884 AND 885.

5. INSPECT CKTs 884 AND 885 AND 32-WAY EBCM CONNECTOR FOR DAMAGE WHICH MAY RESULT IN A SHORT BETWEEN CKTs 884 AND 885 WITH ALL CONNECTORS CONNECTED. REPAIR ALL DAMAGE IF EVIDENT.
   - RECONNECT ALL CONNECTORS.
   - TEST DRIVE VEHICLE ABOVE 24 km/h (15 MPH) FOR AT LEAST 30 SECONDS.
   DOES DTC 23 SET AS A CURRENT DTC?
   - NO → REPLACE EBCM.

6. USING TECH 1, SELECT "F0: DATA LIST."
   - MONITOR WHEEL SPEEDS WHILE SLOWLY ACCELERATING TO 65 km/h (40 MPH) AND THEN SLOWLY DECELERATING TO 0 km/h (0 MPH).
   IS THE LEFT REAR WHEEL SPEED CONSTANTLY HIGHER THAN THE THREE REMAINING WHEEL SPEEDS?
   - YES → REPLACE INCORRECT OR MALFUNCTIONING LEFT WHEEL SPEED SENSOR/HUB AND BEARING ASSEMBLY WITH THE PROPER ASSEMBLY. REFER TO PARTS CATALOG FOR PROPER PART NUMBER.

REAR WHEEL SPEED SENSOR — TEMPERATURE OF SENSOR VS. SENSOR RESISTANCE (APPROXIMATE)

TEMP. (°C)	TEMP. (°F)	RESISTANCE (OHMS)
-34 TO 4	-30 TO 40	1622 TO 2205
5 TO 43	41 TO 110	1890 TO 2566
44 TO 93	111 TO 200	2245 TO 3028

86819173

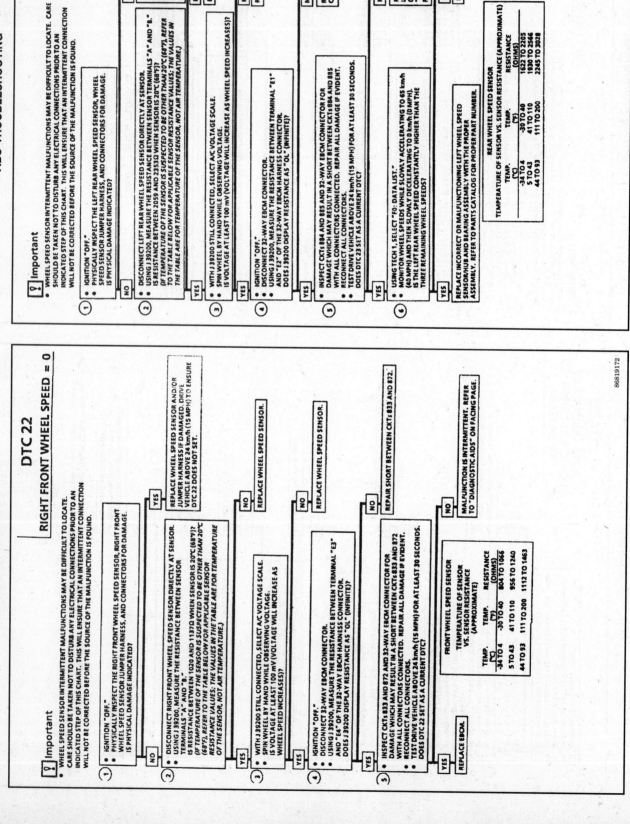

ABS TROUBLESHOOTING

DTC 25 — LEFT FRONT EXCESSIVE WHEEL SPEED VARIATION

Important
- WHEEL SPEED SENSOR INTERMITTENT MALFUNCTIONS MAY BE DIFFICULT TO LOCATE. CARE SHOULD BE TAKEN NOT TO DISTURB ANY ELECTRICAL CONNECTIONS PRIOR TO AN INDICATED STEP OF THIS CHART. THIS WILL ENSURE THAT AN INTERMITTENT CONNECTION WILL NOT BE CORRECTED BEFORE THE SOURCE OF THE MALFUNCTION IS FOUND.

1. IGNITION "OFF."
   - PHYSICALLY INSPECT THE LEFT FRONT WHEEL SPEED SENSOR, LEFT FRONT WHEEL SPEED SENSOR JUMPER HARNESS, AND CONNECTORS FOR DAMAGE. IS PHYSICAL DAMAGE INDICATED?
   - **YES** → REPLACE WHEEL SPEED SENSOR AND/OR WHEEL SPEED SENSOR JUMPER HARNESS IF DAMAGED. DRIVE VEHICLE ABOVE 24 km/h (15 MPH) TO ENSURE DTC 25 DOES NOT SET.

2. DISCONNECT LEFT FRONT WHEEL SPEED SENSOR DIRECTLY AT SENSOR.
   - USING J 39200, MEASURE THE RESISTANCE BETWEEN SENSOR TERMINALS "A" AND "B."
   - IS RESISTANCE BETWEEN 1020 AND 1137Ω WHEN SENSOR IS 20°C (68°F)? (IF TEMPERATURE OF THE SENSOR IS SUSPECTED TO BE OTHER THAN 20°C (68°F), REFER TO THE TABLE BELOW FOR APPLICABLE SENSOR RESISTANCE VALUES; THE VALUES IN THE TABLE ARE FOR TEMPERATURE OF THE SENSOR, NOT AIR TEMPERATURE.)
   - **NO** → REPLACE WHEEL SPEED SENSOR.

3. WITH J 39200 STILL CONNECTED, SELECT A/C VOLTAGE SCALE.
   - SPIN WHEEL BY HAND WHILE OBSERVING VOLTAGE.
   - IS VOLTAGE AT LEAST 100 mV (VOLTAGE WILL INCREASE AS WHEEL SPEED INCREASES)?
   - **YES** → REPLACE WHEEL SPEED SENSOR.

4. IGNITION "OFF."
   - DISCONNECT 32-WAY EBCM CONNECTOR.
   - USING J 39200, MEASURE THE RESISTANCE BETWEEN TERMINAL "E7" AND "E6" OF THE 32-WAY EBCM HARNESS CONNECTOR. DOES J 39200 DISPLAY RESISTANCE AS "OL" (INFINITE)?
   - **YES** → REPAIR SHORT BETWEEN CKTs 830 AND 873.

5. INSPECT CKTs 830 AND 873 AND 32-WAY EBCM CONNECTOR FOR DAMAGE WHICH MAY RESULT IN A SHORT BETWEEN CKTs 830 AND 873 WITH ALL CONNECTORS CONNECTED. REPAIR ALL DAMAGE IF EVIDENT.
   - RECONNECT ALL CONNECTORS.
   - TEST DRIVE VEHICLE ABOVE 24 km/h (15 MPH) FOR AT LEAST 30 SECONDS.
   - DOES DTC 25 SET AS A CURRENT DTC?
   - **YES** → REPLACE EBCM.
   - **NO** → MALFUNCTION IS INTERMITTENT. REFER TO "DIAGNOSTIC AIDS" ON FACING PAGE.

FRONT WHEEL SPEED SENSOR TEMPERATURE OF SENSOR VS. SENSOR RESISTANCE (APPROXIMATE)			
TEMP. (°C)	TEMP. (°F)		RESISTANCE (OHMS)
-34 TO 4	-30 TO 40		804 TO 1066
5 TO 43	41 TO 110		956 TO 1240
44 TO 93	111 TO 200		1112 TO 1463

86819175

ABS TROUBLESHOOTING

DTC 24 — RIGHT REAR WHEEL SPEED = 0

Important
- WHEEL SPEED SENSOR INTERMITTENT MALFUNCTIONS MAY BE DIFFICULT TO LOCATE. CARE SHOULD BE TAKEN NOT TO DISTURB ANY ELECTRICAL CONNECTIONS PRIOR TO AN INDICATED STEP OF THIS CHART. THIS WILL ENSURE THAT AN INTERMITTENT CONNECTION WILL NOT BE CORRECTED BEFORE THE SOURCE OF THE MALFUNCTION IS FOUND.

1. IGNITION "OFF."
   - PHYSICALLY INSPECT THE RIGHT REAR WHEEL SPEED SENSOR, WHEEL SPEED SENSOR JUMPER HARNESS, AND CONNECTORS FOR DAMAGE. IS PHYSICAL DAMAGE INDICATED?
   - **YES** → REPLACE WHEEL SPEED SENSOR AND/OR WHEEL SPEED SENSOR JUMPER HARNESS IF DAMAGED. DRIVE VEHICLE ABOVE 24 km/h (15 MPH) TO ENSURE DTC 24 DOES NOT SET.

2. DISCONNECT RIGHT REAR WHEEL SPEED SENSOR DIRECTLY AT SENSOR.
   - USING J 39200, MEASURE THE RESISTANCE BETWEEN SENSOR TERMINALS "A" AND "B." IS RESISTANCE BETWEEN 2059 AND 2353Ω WHEN SENSOR IS 20°C (68°F)? (IF TEMPERATURE OF THE SENSOR IS SUSPECTED TO BE OTHER THAN 20°C (68°F), REFER TO THE TABLE BELOW FOR APPLICABLE SENSOR RESISTANCE VALUES; THE VALUES IN THE TABLE ARE FOR TEMPERATURE OF THE SENSOR, NOT AIR TEMPERATURE.)
   - **NO** → REPLACE WHEEL SPEED SENSOR.

3. WITH J 39200 STILL CONNECTED, SELECT A/C VOLTAGE SCALE.
   - SPIN WHEEL BY HAND WHILE OBSERVING VOLTAGE.
   - IS VOLTAGE AT LEAST 100 mV (VOLTAGE WILL INCREASE AS WHEEL SPEED INCREASES)?
   - **YES** → REPLACE WHEEL SPEED SENSOR.

4. IGNITION "OFF."
   - DISCONNECT 32-WAY EBCM CONNECTOR.
   - USING J 39200, MEASURE THE RESISTANCE BETWEEN TERMINAL "E5" AND "E6" OF THE 32-WAY EBCM HARNESS CONNECTOR. DOES J 39200 DISPLAY RESISTANCE AS "OL" (INFINITE)?
   - **NO** → REPAIR SHORT BETWEEN CKTs 882 AND 883.

5. INSPECT CKTs 882 AND 883 AND 32-WAY EBCM CONNECTOR FOR DAMAGE WHICH MAY RESULT IN A SHORT BETWEEN CKTs 882 AND 883 WITH ALL CONNECTORS CONNECTED. REPAIR ALL DAMAGE IF EVIDENT.
   - RECONNECT ALL CONNECTORS.
   - TEST DRIVE VEHICLE ABOVE 24 km/h (15 MPH) FOR AT LEAST 30 SECONDS.
   - DOES DTC 24 SET AS A CURRENT DTC?
   - **NO** → MALFUNCTION WAS MOST LIKELY CAUSED BY A POOR CONNECTION. REFER TO "DIAGNOSTIC AIDS" ON FACING PAGE.

6. USING TECH 1, SELECT "F0: DATA LIST."
   - MONITOR WHEEL SPEEDS WHILE SLOWLY ACCELERATING TO 65 km/h (40 MPH) AND THEN SLOWLY DECELERATING TO 0 km/h (0 MPH). IS THE RIGHT REAR WHEEL SPEED CONSTANTLY HIGHER THAN THE THREE REMAINING WHEEL SPEEDS?
   - **YES** → REPLACE INCORRECT OR MALFUNCTIONING RIGHT WHEEL SPEED SENSOR/HUB AND BEARING ASSEMBLY WITH THE PROPER PART. ASSEMBLY. REFER TO PARTS CATALOG FOR PROPER PART NUMBER.
   - **NO** → REPLACE EBCM.

REAR WHEEL SPEED SENSOR TEMPERATURE OF SENSOR VS. SENSOR RESISTANCE (APPROXIMATE)			
TEMP. (°C)	TEMP. (°F)		RESISTANCE (OHMS)
-34 TO 4	-30 TO 40		1622 TO 2205
5 TO 43	41 TO 110		1930 TO 2566
44 TO 93	111 TO 200		2245 TO 3028

86819174

ABS TROUBLESHOOTING

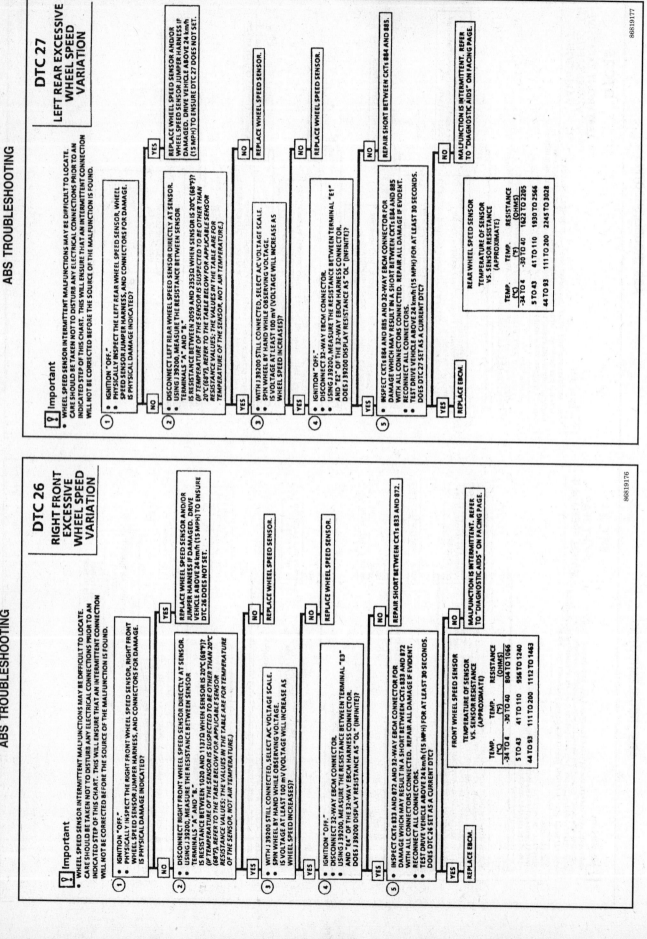

DTC 27 — LEFT REAR EXCESSIVE WHEEL SPEED VARIATION

Important
- WHEEL SPEED SENSOR INTERMITTENT MALFUNCTIONS MAY BE DIFFICULT TO LOCATE. CARE SHOULD BE TAKEN NOT TO DISTURB ANY ELECTRICAL CONNECTIONS PRIOR TO AN INDICATED STEP OF THIS CHART. THIS WILL ENSURE THAT AN INTERMITTENT CONNECTION WILL NOT BE CORRECTED BEFORE THE SOURCE OF THE MALFUNCTION IS FOUND.

1. IGNITION "OFF."
   - PHYSICALLY INSPECT THE LEFT REAR WHEEL SPEED SENSOR, WHEEL SPEED SENSOR JUMPER HARNESS, AND CONNECTORS FOR DAMAGE. IS PHYSICAL DAMAGE INDICATED?
   - YES → REPLACE WHEEL SPEED SENSOR AND/OR WHEEL SPEED SENSOR JUMPER HARNESS IF DAMAGED. DRIVE VEHICLE ABOVE 24 km/h (15 MPH) TO ENSURE DTC 27 DOES NOT SET.

2. DISCONNECT LEFT REAR WHEEL SPEED SENSOR DIRECTLY AT SENSOR. USING J 39200, MEASURE THE RESISTANCE BETWEEN SENSOR TERMINALS "A" AND "B." IS RESISTANCE BETWEEN 205Ω AND 2353Ω WHEN SENSOR IS 20°C (68°F)? (IF TEMPERATURE OF THE SENSOR IS SUSPECTED TO BE OTHER THAN 20°C (69°F), REFER TO THE TABLE BELOW FOR APPLICABLE SENSOR RESISTANCE VALUES; THE VALUES IN THE TABLE ARE FOR TEMPERATURE OF THE SENSOR, NOT AIR TEMPERATURE.)
   - NO → (go to step 1 side)
   - YES

3. WITH J 39200 STILL CONNECTED, SELECT A/C VOLTAGE SCALE. SPIN WHEEL BY HAND WHILE OBSERVING VOLTAGE. IS VOLTAGE AT LEAST 100 mV (VOLTAGE WILL INCREASE AS WHEEL SPEED INCREASES)?
   - NO → REPLACE WHEEL SPEED SENSOR.
   - YES

4. IGNITION "OFF."
   - DISCONNECT 32-WAY EBCM CONNECTOR. USING J 39200, MEASURE THE RESISTANCE BETWEEN TERMINAL "E1" AND "E2" OF THE 32-WAY EBCM HARNESS CONNECTOR. DOES J 39200 DISPLAY RESISTANCE AS "OL" (INFINITE)?
   - NO → REPLACE WHEEL SPEED SENSOR.
   - YES

5. INSPECT CKTs 884 AND 885 AND 32-WAY EBCM CONNECTOR FOR DAMAGE WHICH MAY RESULT IN A SHORT BETWEEN CKTs 884 AND 885 WITH ALL CONNECTORS CONNECTED. REPAIR ALL DAMAGE IF EVIDENT. RECONNECT ALL CONNECTORS. TEST DRIVE VEHICLE ABOVE 24 km/h (15 MPH) FOR AT LEAST 30 SECONDS. DOES DTC 27 SET AS A CURRENT DTC?
   - NO → REPAIR SHORT BETWEEN CKTs 884 AND 885.
   - YES → REPLACE EBCM.

- MALFUNCTION IS INTERMITTENT. REFER TO "DIAGNOSTIC AIDS" ON FACING PAGE.

REAR WHEEL SPEED SENSOR TEMPERATURE OF SENSOR VS. SENSOR RESISTANCE (APPROXIMATE)		
TEMP. (°C)	TEMP. (°F)	RESISTANCE (OHMS)
-34 TO 4	-30 TO 40	1622 TO 2205
5 TO 43	41 TO 110	1930 TO 2566
44 TO 93	111 TO 200	2245 TO 3028

86819177

ABS TROUBLESHOOTING

DTC 26 — RIGHT FRONT EXCESSIVE WHEEL SPEED VARIATION

Important
- WHEEL SPEED SENSOR INTERMITTENT MALFUNCTIONS MAY BE DIFFICULT TO LOCATE. CARE SHOULD BE TAKEN NOT TO DISTURB ANY ELECTRICAL CONNECTIONS PRIOR TO AN INDICATED STEP OF THIS CHART. THIS WILL ENSURE THAT AN INTERMITTENT CONNECTION WILL NOT BE CORRECTED BEFORE THE SOURCE OF THE MALFUNCTION IS FOUND.

1. IGNITION "OFF."
   - PHYSICALLY INSPECT THE RIGHT FRONT WHEEL SPEED SENSOR, RIGHT FRONT WHEEL SPEED SENSOR JUMPER HARNESS, AND CONNECTORS FOR DAMAGE. IS PHYSICAL DAMAGE INDICATED?
   - YES → REPLACE WHEEL SPEED SENSOR AND/OR WHEEL SPEED SENSOR JUMPER HARNESS IF DAMAGED. DRIVE VEHICLE ABOVE 24 km/h (15 MPH) TO ENSURE DTC 26 DOES NOT SET.

2. DISCONNECT RIGHT FRONT WHEEL SPEED SENSOR DIRECTLY AT SENSOR. USING J 39200, MEASURE THE RESISTANCE BETWEEN SENSOR TERMINALS "A" AND "B." IS RESISTANCE BETWEEN 102Ω AND 1137Ω WHEN SENSOR IS 20°C (68°F)? (IF TEMPERATURE OF THE SENSOR IS SUSPECTED TO BE OTHER THAN 20°C (69°F), REFER TO THE TABLE BELOW FOR APPLICABLE SENSOR RESISTANCE VALUES; THE VALUES IN THE TABLE ARE FOR TEMPERATURE OF THE SENSOR, NOT AIR TEMPERATURE.)
   - NO
   - YES

3. WITH J 39200 STILL CONNECTED, SELECT A/C VOLTAGE SCALE. SPIN WHEEL BY HAND WHILE OBSERVING VOLTAGE. IS VOLTAGE AT LEAST 100 mV (VOLTAGE WILL INCREASE AS WHEEL SPEED INCREASES)?
   - NO → REPLACE WHEEL SPEED SENSOR.
   - YES

4. IGNITION "OFF."
   - DISCONNECT 32-WAY EBCM CONNECTOR. USING J 39200, MEASURE THE RESISTANCE BETWEEN TERMINAL "E3" AND "E4" OF THE 32-WAY EBCM HARNESS CONNECTOR. DOES J 39200 DISPLAY RESISTANCE AS "OL" (INFINITE)?
   - NO → REPLACE WHEEL SPEED SENSOR.
   - YES

5. INSPECT CKTs 833 AND 872 AND 32-WAY EBCM CONNECTOR FOR DAMAGE WHICH MAY RESULT IN A SHORT BETWEEN CKTs 833 AND 872 WITH ALL CONNECTORS CONNECTED. REPAIR ALL DAMAGE IF EVIDENT. RECONNECT ALL CONNECTORS. TEST DRIVE VEHICLE ABOVE 24 km/h (15 MPH) FOR AT LEAST 30 SECONDS. DOES DTC 26 SET AS A CURRENT DTC?
   - NO → REPAIR SHORT BETWEEN CKTs 833 AND 872.
   - YES → REPLACE EBCM.

- MALFUNCTION IS INTERMITTENT. REFER TO "DIAGNOSTIC AIDS" ON FACING PAGE.

FRONT WHEEL SPEED SENSOR TEMPERATURE OF SENSOR VS. SENSOR RESISTANCE (APPROXIMATE)		
TEMP. (°C)	TEMP. (°F)	RESISTANCE (OHMS)
-34 TO 4	-30 TO 40	804 TO 1066
5 TO 43	41 TO 110	956 TO 1240
44 TO 93	111 TO 200	1112 TO 1463

86819176

ABS TROUBLESHOOTING

DTC 32
(Page 1 of 3)
LF WHEEL SPEED SNR CKT OPEN OR SHORT TO GND/BATT

Important
- WHEEL SPEED SENSOR INTERMITTENT MALFUNCTIONS MAY BE DIFFICULT TO LOCATE. CARE SHOULD BE TAKEN NOT TO DISTURB ANY ELECTRICAL CONNECTIONS PRIOR TO AN INDICATED STEP OF THIS CHART. THIS WILL ENSURE THAT AN INTERMITTENT CONNECTION WILL NOT BE CORRECTED BEFORE THE SOURCE OF THE MALFUNCTION IS FOUND.

① IGNITION "OFF."
- USING A 5% SALT WATER SOLUTION (TWO TEASPOONS OF SALT TO 12 OZ. WATER), THOROUGHLY SPRAY THE LEFT FRONT WHEEL SPEED SENSOR JUMPER HARNESS.
- DISCONNECT 32-WAY EBCM HARNESS CONNECTOR.
- USING J 39200, MEASURE THE RESISTANCE BETWEEN TERMINALS "E7" AND "E8" OF THE 32-WAY EBCM HARNESS CONNECTOR.
IS RESISTANCE BETWEEN 1020 AND 1137Ω WHEN SENSOR IS 20°C (68°F)? (IF TEMPERATURE OF SENSOR IS SUSPECTED TO BE OTHER THAN 20°C (68°F), REFER TO THE TABLE ON PAGE 2 OF 3 OF THIS DTC CHART FOR APPLICABLE SENSOR RESISTANCE VALUES; THE VALUES IN THE TABLE ARE FOR TEMPERATURE OF THE SENSOR, NOT AIR TEMPERATURE.)

NO → DIAGNOSIS CONTINUED ON PAGE 2 OF 3 OF THIS DTC CHART.

YES

② MEASURE THE RESISTANCE BETWEEN GROUND AND TERMINAL "E7" OF THE 32-WAY EBCM HARNESS CONNECTOR.
DOES J 39200 DISPLAY RESISTANCE AS "OL" (INFINITE)?

NO → DIAGNOSIS CONTINUED ON PAGE 3 OF 3 OF THIS DTC CHART.

YES

③ IGNITION "ON."
- USING J 39200, MEASURE THE VOLTAGE BETWEEN GROUND AND TERMINAL "E7" OF THE 32-WAY EBCM HARNESS CONNECTOR.
IS VOLTAGE 1 VOLT OR LESS?

NO → REPAIR SHORT TO VOLTAGE IN CKT 830.

YES

④ IGNITION "OFF."
- DISCONNECT LEFT FRONT WHEEL SPEED SENSOR DIRECTLY AT SENSOR.
- IGNITION "ON."
- USING J 39200, MEASURE THE VOLTAGE BETWEEN GROUND AND TERMINAL "E7" OF THE 32-WAY EBCM HARNESS CONNECTOR.
IS VOLTAGE 1 VOLT OR LESS?

NO → REPAIR SHORT TO VOLTAGE IN CKT 873.

YES

⑤ USING J 39200, MEASURE THE VOLTAGE BETWEEN GROUND AND TERMINAL "E8" OF THE 32-WAY EBCM HARNESS CONNECTOR.
IS VOLTAGE 1 VOLT OR LESS?

YES

⑥ IGNITION "OFF."
- INSPECT TERMINALS "E7" AND "E8" OF THE 32-WAY EBCM HARNESS CONNECTOR FOR POOR TERMINAL CONTACT AND CONTAMINATION. ALSO INSPECT CKTs 830 AND 873 FOR DAMAGE WHICH MAY RESULT IN AN OPEN CIRCUIT, SHORT TO GROUND, OR SHORT TO VOLTAGE. REPAIR ALL DAMAGE IF EVIDENT.
- RECONNECT ALL CONNECTORS.
- IGNITION "ON."
DOES DTC 32 SET AS A CURRENT DTC?

NO → MALFUNCTION IS INTERMITTENT. REFER TO "DIAGNOSTIC AIDS" ON FACING PAGE.

YES → REPLACE EBCM.

MALFUNCTION IS INTERMITTENT. INSPECT ALL CONNECTORS AND HARNESSES FOR DAMAGE WHICH MAY RESULT IN A SHORT TO VOLTAGE WHEN ALL COMPONENTS ARE CONNECTED. REPAIR ALL DAMAGE IF FOUND. REFER TO "DIAGNOSTIC AIDS" ON FACING PAGE FOR MORE INFORMATION.

ABS TROUBLESHOOTING

DTC 28
RIGHT REAR EXCESSIVE WHEEL SPEED VARIATION

Important
- WHEEL SPEED SENSOR INTERMITTENT MALFUNCTIONS MAY BE DIFFICULT TO LOCATE. CARE SHOULD BE TAKEN NOT TO DISTURB ANY ELECTRICAL CONNECTIONS PRIOR TO AN INDICATED STEP OF THIS CHART. THIS WILL ENSURE THAT AN INTERMITTENT CONNECTION WILL NOT BE CORRECTED BEFORE THE SOURCE OF THE MALFUNCTION IS FOUND.

① IGNITION "OFF."
- PHYSICALLY INSPECT THE RIGHT REAR WHEEL SPEED SENSOR, WHEEL SPEED SENSOR JUMPER HARNESS, AND CONNECTORS FOR DAMAGE.
IS PHYSICAL DAMAGE INDICATED?

YES → REPLACE WHEEL SPEED SENSOR AND/OR WHEEL SPEED SENSOR JUMPER HARNESS IF DAMAGED. DRIVE VEHICLE ABOVE 24 km/h (15 MPH) TO ENSURE DTC 28 DOES NOT SET.

NO

② DISCONNECT RIGHT REAR WHEEL SPEED SENSOR DIRECTLY AT SENSOR.
- USING J 39200, MEASURE THE RESISTANCE BETWEEN SENSOR TERMINALS "A" AND "B."
IS RESISTANCE BETWEEN 2059 AND 2353Ω WHEN SENSOR IS 20°C (68°F)? (IF TEMPERATURE OF THE SENSOR IS SUSPECTED TO BE OTHER THAN 20°C (68°F), REFER TO THE TABLE BELOW FOR APPLICABLE SENSOR RESISTANCE VALUES; THE VALUES IN THE TABLE ARE FOR TEMPERATURE OF THE SENSOR, NOT AIR TEMPERATURE.)

NO → REPLACE WHEEL SPEED SENSOR.

YES

③ WITH J 39200 STILL CONNECTED, SELECT A/C VOLTAGE SCALE.
- SPIN WHEEL BY HAND WHILE OBSERVING VOLTAGE.
IS VOLTAGE AT LEAST 100 mV (VOLTAGE WILL INCREASE AS WHEEL SPEED INCREASES)?

NO → REPLACE WHEEL SPEED SENSOR.

YES

④ IGNITION "OFF."
- DISCONNECT 32-WAY EBCM CONNECTOR.
- USING J 39200, MEASURE THE RESISTANCE BETWEEN TERMINAL "E5" AND "E6" OF THE 32-WAY EBCM HARNESS CONNECTOR.
DOES J 39200 DISPLAY RESISTANCE AS "OL" (INFINITE)?

YES → REPAIR SHORT BETWEEN CKTs 882 AND 883.

NO

⑤ INSPECT CKTs 882 AND 883 AND 32-WAY EBCM CONNECTOR FOR DAMAGE WHICH MAY RESULT IN A SHORT BETWEEN CKTs 882 AND 883 WITH ALL CONNECTORS CONNECTED. REPAIR ALL DAMAGE IF EVIDENT.
- RECONNECT ALL CONNECTORS.
- TEST DRIVE VEHICLE ABOVE 24 km/h (15 MPH) FOR AT LEAST 30 SECONDS.
DOES DTC 28 SET AS A CURRENT DTC?

NO → MALFUNCTION IS INTERMITTENT. REFER TO "DIAGNOSTIC AIDS" ON FACING PAGE.

YES → REPLACE EBCM.

REAR WHEEL SPEED SENSOR
TEMPERATURE OF SENSOR VS. SENSOR RESISTANCE (APPROXIMATE)

TEMP. (°C)	TEMP. (°F)	RESISTANCE (OHMS)
-34 TO 4	-30 TO 40	1622 TO 2205
5 TO 43	41 TO 110	1930 TO 2566
44 TO 93	111 TO 200	2245 TO 3028

ABS TROUBLESHOOTING

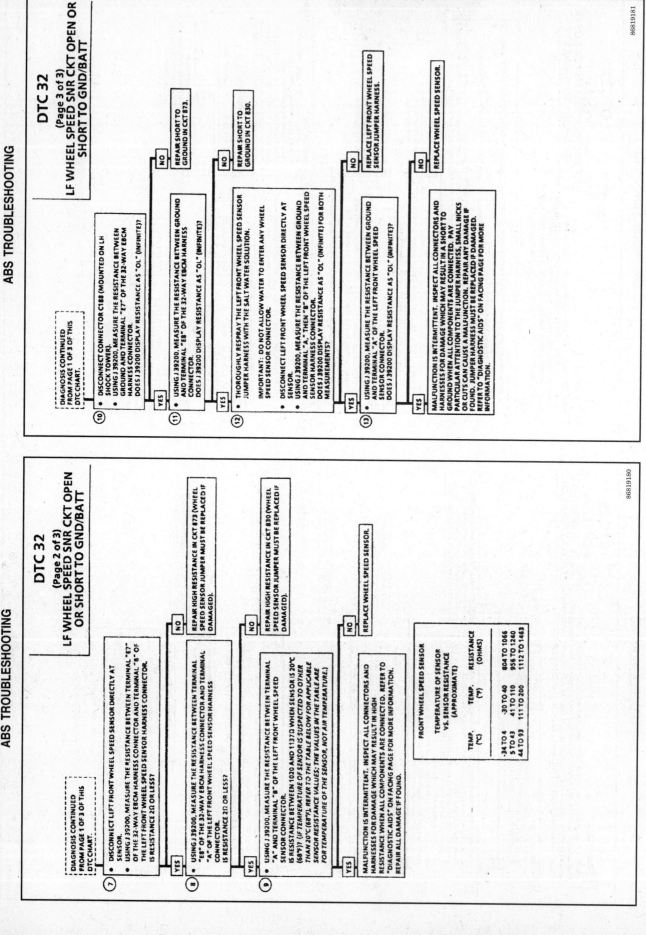

DTC 32

(Page 3 of 3)

LF WHEEL SPEED SNR CKT OPEN OR SHORT TO GND/BATT

DIAGNOSIS CONTINUED FROM PAGE 1 OF 3 OF THIS DTC CHART.

(10)
- DISCONNECT CONNECTOR C188 (MOUNTED ON LH SHOCK TOWER).
- USING J 39200, MEASURE THE RESISTANCE BETWEEN GROUND AND TERMINAL "E7" OF THE 32-WAY EBCM HARNESS CONNECTOR.
DOES J 39200 DISPLAY RESISTANCE AS "OL" (INFINITE)?

YES → NO → REPAIR SHORT TO GROUND IN CKT 873.

(11)
- USING J 39200, MEASURE THE RESISTANCE BETWEEN GROUND AND TERMINAL "E8" OF THE 32-WAY EBCM HARNESS CONNECTOR.
DOES J 39200 DISPLAY RESISTANCE AS "OL" (INFINITE)?

YES → NO → REPAIR SHORT TO GROUND IN CKT 830.

(12)
- THOROUGHLY RESPRAY THE LEFT FRONT WHEEL SPEED SENSOR JUMPER HARNESS WITH THE SALT WATER SOLUTION.

IMPORTANT: DO NOT ALLOW WATER TO ENTER ANY WHEEL SPEED SENSOR CONNECTOR.

- DISCONNECT LEFT FRONT WHEEL SPEED SENSOR DIRECTLY AT SENSOR.
- USING J 39200, MEASURE THE RESISTANCE BETWEEN GROUND AND TERMINAL "A", THEN "B" OF THE LEFT FRONT WHEEL SPEED SENSOR HARNESS CONNECTOR.
DOES J 39200 DISPLAY RESISTANCE AS "OL" (INFINITE) FOR BOTH MEASUREMENTS?

YES → NO → REPLACE LEFT FRONT WHEEL SPEED SENSOR JUMPER HARNESS.

(13)
- USING J 39200, MEASURE THE RESISTANCE BETWEEN GROUND AND TERMINAL "A" OF THE LEFT FRONT WHEEL SPEED SENSOR CONNECTOR.
DOES J 39200 DISPLAY RESISTANCE AS "OL" (INFINITE)?

YES → NO → REPLACE WHEEL SPEED SENSOR.

MALFUNCTION IS INTERMITTENT. INSPECT ALL CONNECTORS AND HARNESSES FOR DAMAGE WHICH MAY RESULT IN A SHORT TO GROUND WHEN ALL COMPONENTS ARE CONNECTED. PAY PARTICULAR ATTENTION TO THE JUMPER HARNESS, SMALL NICKS OR CUTS CAN CAUSE A MALFUNCTION. REPAIR ANY DAMAGE IF FOUND. JUMPER HARNESS MUST BE REPLACED IF DAMAGED. REFER TO "DIAGNOSTIC AIDS" ON FACING PAGE FOR MORE INFORMATION.

86819181

ABS TROUBLESHOOTING

DTC 32

(Page 2 of 3)

LF WHEEL SPEED SNR CKT OPEN OR SHORT TO GND/BATT

DIAGNOSIS CONTINUED FROM PAGE 1 OF 3 OF THIS DTC CHART.

(7)
- DISCONNECT LEFT FRONT WHEEL SPEED SENSOR DIRECTLY AT SENSOR.
- USING J 39200, MEASURE THE RESISTANCE BETWEEN TERMINAL "E7" OF THE 32-WAY EBCM HARNESS CONNECTOR AND TERMINAL "B" OF THE LEFT FRONT WHEEL SPEED SENSOR HARNESS CONNECTOR.
IS RESISTANCE 2Ω OR LESS?

YES → NO → REPAIR HIGH RESISTANCE IN CKT 873 (WHEEL SPEED SENSOR JUMPER MUST BE REPLACED IF DAMAGED).

(8)
- USING J 39200, MEASURE THE RESISTANCE BETWEEN TERMINAL "E8" OF THE 32-WAY EBCM HARNESS CONNECTOR AND TERMINAL "A" OF THE LEFT FRONT WHEEL SPEED SENSOR HARNESS CONNECTOR.
IS RESISTANCE 2Ω OR LESS?

YES → NO → REPAIR HIGH RESISTANCE IN CKT 830 (WHEEL SPEED SENSOR JUMPER MUST BE REPLACED IF DAMAGED).

(9)
- USING J 39200, MEASURE THE RESISTANCE BETWEEN TERMINAL "A" AND TERMINAL "B" OF THE LEFT FRONT WHEEL SPEED SENSOR CONNECTOR.
IS RESISTANCE BETWEEN 1020 AND 1137Ω WHEN SENSOR IS 20°C (68°F)? (IF TEMPERATURE OF SENSOR IS SUSPECTED TO OTHER THAN 20°C (68°F), REFER TO THE TABLE BELOW FOR APPLICABLE SENSOR RESISTANCE VALUES. THE VALUES IN THE TABLE ARE FOR TEMPERATURE OF THE SENSOR, NOT AIR TEMPERATURE.)

YES → NO → REPLACE WHEEL SPEED SENSOR.

MALFUNCTION IS INTERMITTENT. INSPECT ALL CONNECTORS AND HARNESSES FOR DAMAGE WHICH MAY RESULT IN HIGH RESISTANCE WHEN ALL COMPONENTS ARE CONNECTED. REFER TO "DIAGNOSTIC AIDS" ON FACING PAGE FOR MORE INFORMATION. REPAIR ALL DAMAGE IF FOUND.

FRONT WHEEL SPEED SENSOR

TEMPERATURE OF SENSOR VS. SENSOR RESISTANCE (APPROXIMATE)

TEMP. (°C)	TEMP. (°F)	RESISTANCE (OHMS)
-34 TO 4	-30 TO 40	804 TO 1066
5 TO 43	41 TO 110	956 TO 1240
44 TO 93	111 TO 200	1112 TO 1463

86819180

ABS TROUBLESHOOTING

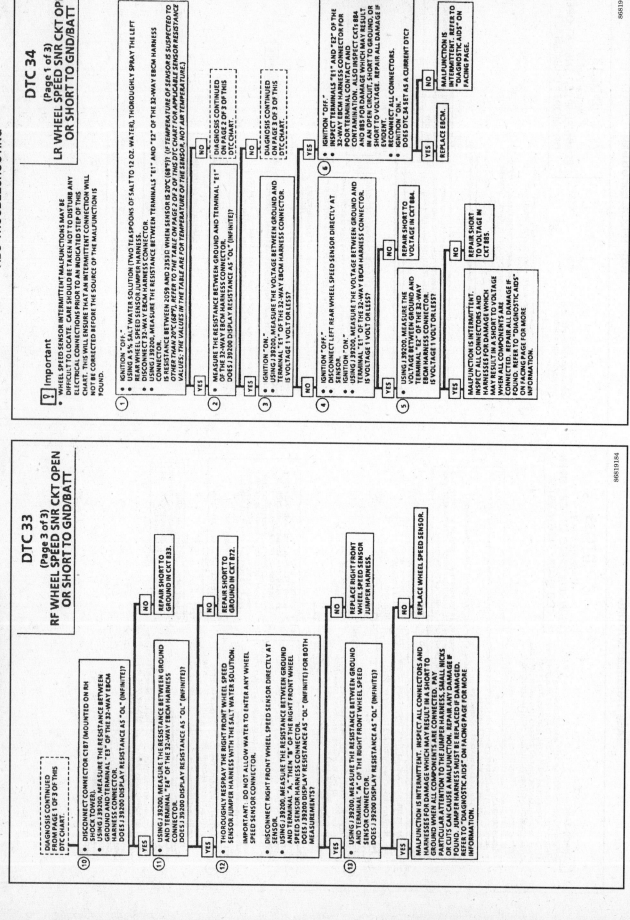

DTC 34
(Page 1 of 3)
LR WHEEL SPEED SNR CKT OPEN OR SHORT TO GND/BATT

DTC 33
(Page 3 of 3)
RF WHEEL SPEED SNR CKT OPEN OR SHORT TO GND/BATT

86819185

86819184

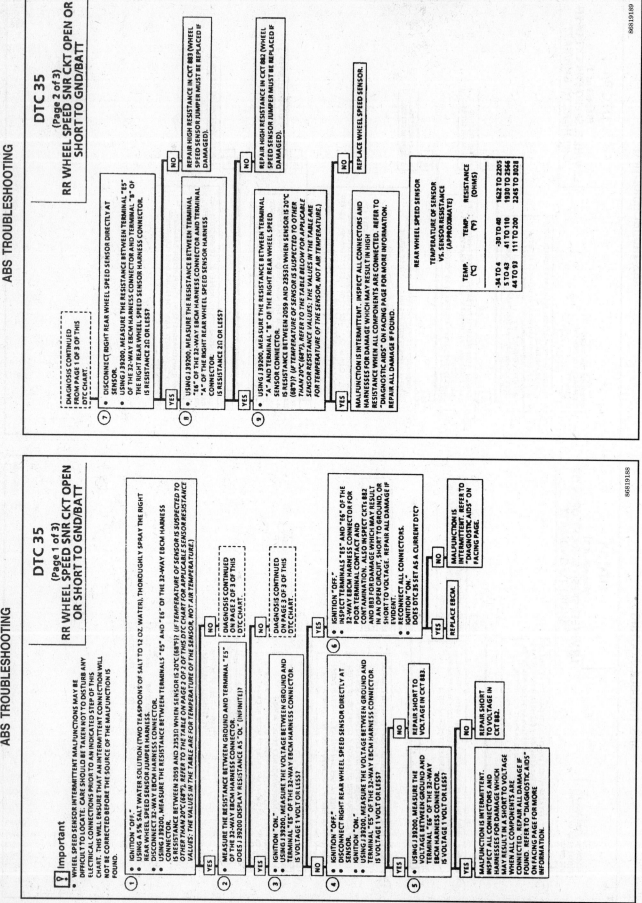

ABS TROUBLESHOOTING

DTC 35 (Page 2 of 3)
RR WHEEL SPEED SNR CKT OPEN OR SHORT TO GND/BATT

DIAGNOSIS CONTINUED FROM PAGE 1 OF 3 OF THIS DTC CHART.

7
- DISCONNECT RIGHT REAR WHEEL SPEED SENSOR DIRECTLY AT SENSOR.
- USING J 39200, MEASURE THE RESISTANCE BETWEEN TERMINAL "E5" OF THE 32-WAY EBCM HARNESS CONNECTOR AND TERMINAL "B" OF THE RIGHT REAR WHEEL SPEED SENSOR HARNESS CONNECTOR.
IS RESISTANCE 2Ω OR LESS?
YES / NO

NO → REPAIR HIGH RESISTANCE IN CKT 883 (WHEEL SPEED SENSOR JUMPER MUST BE REPLACED IF DAMAGED).

8
- USING J 39200, MEASURE THE RESISTANCE BETWEEN TERMINAL "E6" OF THE 32-WAY EBCM HARNESS CONNECTOR AND TERMINAL "A" OF THE RIGHT REAR WHEEL SPEED SENSOR HARNESS CONNECTOR.
IS RESISTANCE 2Ω OR LESS?
YES / NO

NO → REPAIR HIGH RESISTANCE IN CKT 882 (WHEEL SPEED SENSOR JUMPER MUST BE REPLACED IF DAMAGED).

9
- USING J 39200, MEASURE THE RESISTANCE BETWEEN TERMINAL "A" AND TERMINAL "B" OF THE RIGHT REAR WHEEL SPEED SENSOR CONNECTOR.
IS RESISTANCE BETWEEN 2059 AND 2353Ω WHEN SENSOR IS 20°C (68°F)? (IF TEMPERATURE OF SENSOR IS SUSPECTED TO OTHER THAN 20°C (68°F), REFER TO THE TABLE BELOW FOR APPLICABLE SENSOR RESISTANCE VALUES; THE VALUES IN THE TABLE ARE FOR TEMPERATURE OF THE SENSOR, NOT AIR TEMPERATURE.)
YES / NO

NO → REPLACE WHEEL SPEED SENSOR.

YES → MALFUNCTION IS INTERMITTENT. INSPECT ALL CONNECTORS AND HARNESSES FOR DAMAGE WHICH MAY RESULT IN HIGH RESISTANCE WHEN ALL COMPONENTS ARE CONNECTED. REFER TO "DIAGNOSTIC AIDS" ON FACING PAGE FOR MORE INFORMATION. REPAIR ALL DAMAGE IF FOUND.

REAR WHEEL SPEED SENSOR
TEMPERATURE OF SENSOR VS. SENSOR RESISTANCE (APPROXIMATE)

TEMP. (°C)	TEMP. (°F)	RESISTANCE (OHMS)
-34 TO 4	-30 TO 40	1622 TO 2205
5 TO 43	41 TO 110	1930 TO 2566
44 TO 93	111 TO 200	2245 TO 3028

86819189

ABS TROUBLESHOOTING

DTC 35 (Page 1 of 3)
RR WHEEL SPEED SNR CKT OPEN OR SHORT TO GND/BATT

Important
- WHEEL SPEED SENSOR INTERMITTENT MALFUNCTIONS MAY BE DIFFICULT TO LOCATE. CARE SHOULD BE TAKEN NOT TO DISTURB ANY ELECTRICAL CONNECTIONS PRIOR TO AN INDICATED STEP OF THIS CHART. THIS WILL ENSURE THAT AN INTERMITTENT CONNECTION WILL NOT BE CORRECTED BEFORE THE SOURCE OF THE MALFUNCTION IS FOUND.

1
- IGNITION "OFF."
- USING A 5% SALT WATER SOLUTION (TWO TEASPOONS OF SALT TO 12 OZ. WATER), THOROUGHLY SPRAY THE RIGHT REAR WHEEL SPEED SENSOR JUMPER HARNESS.
- DISCONNECT 32-WAY EBCM HARNESS CONNECTOR.
- USING J 39200, MEASURE THE RESISTANCE BETWEEN TERMINALS "E5" AND "E6" OF THE 32-WAY EBCM HARNESS CONNECTOR.
IS RESISTANCE BETWEEN 2059 AND 2353Ω WHEN SENSOR IS 20°C (68°F)? (IF TEMPERATURE OF SENSOR IS SUSPECTED TO OTHER THAN 20°C (68°F), REFER TO THE TABLE ON PAGE 2 OF 2 OF THIS DTC CHART FOR APPLICABLE SENSOR RESISTANCE VALUES: THE VALUES IN THE TABLE ARE FOR TEMPERATURE OF THE SENSOR, NOT AIR TEMPERATURE.)
YES / NO

2
- MEASURE THE RESISTANCE BETWEEN GROUND AND TERMINAL "E5" OF THE 32-WAY EBCM HARNESS CONNECTOR.
DOES J 39200 DISPLAY RESISTANCE AS "OL." (INFINITE)?
YES / NO

NO → DIAGNOSIS CONTINUED ON PAGE 2 OF 3 OF THIS DTC CHART.

3
- IGNITION "ON."
- USING J 39200, MEASURE THE VOLTAGE BETWEEN GROUND AND TERMINAL "E5" OF THE 32-WAY EBCM HARNESS CONNECTOR.
IS VOLTAGE 1 VOLT OR LESS?
NO / YES

NO → DIAGNOSIS CONTINUED ON PAGE 3 OF 3 OF THIS DTC CHART.

4
- IGNITION "OFF."
- DISCONNECT RIGHT REAR WHEEL SPEED SENSOR DIRECTLY AT SENSOR.
- IGNITION "ON."
- USING J 39200, MEASURE THE VOLTAGE BETWEEN GROUND AND TERMINAL "E5" OF THE 32-WAY EBCM HARNESS CONNECTOR.
IS VOLTAGE 1 VOLT OR LESS?
YES / NO

NO → REPAIR SHORT TO VOLTAGE IN CKT 883.

5
- USING J 39200, MEASURE THE VOLTAGE BETWEEN GROUND AND TERMINAL "E6" OF THE 32-WAY EBCM HARNESS CONNECTOR.
IS VOLTAGE 1 VOLT OR LESS?
YES / NO

NO → REPAIR SHORT TO VOLTAGE IN CKT 882.

YES → MALFUNCTION IS INTERMITTENT. INSPECT ALL CONNECTORS AND HARNESSES FOR DAMAGE WHICH MAY RESULT IN A SHORT TO VOLTAGE WHEN ALL COMPONENTS ARE CONNECTED. REPAIR ALL DAMAGE IF FOUND. REFER TO "DIAGNOSTIC AIDS" ON FACING PAGE FOR MORE INFORMATION.

6
- IGNITION "OFF."
- INSPECT TERMINALS "E5" AND "E6" OF THE 32-WAY EBCM HARNESS CONNECTOR FOR POOR TERMINAL CONTACT AND CONTAMINATION. ALSO INSPECT CKTs 882 AND 883 FOR DAMAGE WHICH MAY RESULT IN AN OPEN CIRCUIT, SHORT TO GROUND, OR SHORT TO VOLTAGE. REPAIR ALL DAMAGE IF EVIDENT.
- RECONNECT ALL CONNECTORS.
- IGNITION "ON."
- DOES DTC 35 SET AS A CURRENT DTC?
YES / NO

YES → REPLACE EBCM.

NO → MALFUNCTION IS INTERMITTENT. REFER TO "DIAGNOSTIC AIDS" ON FACING PAGE.

86819188

ABS TROUBLESHOOTING

DTC 36
(Page 1 of 2)
LOW SYSTEM VOLTAGE

1
- START ENGINE.
- USING TECH 1, SELECT "F3: SNAPSHOT."
- SELECT "F4: SINGLE DTC": THEN ENTER "36".
- DRIVE VEHICLE ABOVE 5 km/h (3 MPH).
- DID TECH 1 TRIGGER?

YES / NO
- WITH ENGINE RUNNING, USE TECH 1 AND SELECT "F4: MISC. TESTS."
- PERFORM "VOLTAGE LOAD" TEST.
- ARE IGNITION AND BATTERY VOLTAGES GREATER THAN 10 VOLTS?

YES
- MALFUNCTION IS NOT PRESENT AT THIS TIME. REFER TO "DIAGNOSTIC AIDS" ON FACING PAGE.

2
- REFER TO SECTION 6D3 TO DIAGNOSE CHARGING SYSTEM. IS CHARGING SYSTEM OK?

YES / NO
- REFER TO SECTION 6D3 TO CORRECT LOW VOLTAGE CONDITION.

3
- IGNITION "OFF."
- DISCONNECT 8-WAY AND 32-WAY EBCM CONNECTORS.
- DISCONNECT ABS ENABLE RELAY.
- USING J 39200 MEASURE RESISTANCE BETWEEN TERMINAL "87" OF THE ABS ENABLE RELAY HARNESS CONNECTOR AND TERMINAL "D" OF THE 8-WAY EBCM HARNESS CONNECTOR.
- IS RESISTANCE 2Ω OR LESS?

YES / NO
- REPAIR HIGH RESISTANCE IN CKT 1633.

4
- DISCONNECT NEGATIVE BATTERY CABLE.
- DISCONNECT POSITIVE BATTERY CABLE.
- USING J 39200 MEASURE RESISTANCE BETWEEN THE POSITIVE BATTERY CABLE TERMINAL AND TERMINAL "30" OF THE ABS ENABLE RELAY HARNESS CONNECTOR.
- IS RESISTANCE 2Ω OR LESS?

YES / NO
- REPAIR HIGH RESISTANCE IN CKTs 2 OR 1.

DIAGNOSIS CONTINUED ON PAGE 2 OF 2 OF THIS DTC CHART.

ABS TROUBLESHOOTING

DTC 35
(Page 3 of 3)
RR WHEEL SPEED SNR CKT OPEN OR SHORT TO GND/BATT

DIAGNOSIS CONTINUED FROM PAGE 1 OF 3 OF THIS DTC CHART.

10
- DISCONNECT CONNECTOR C106 (RH REAR UNDER BODY NEAR FRAME RAIL).
- USING J 39200, MEASURE THE RESISTANCE BETWEEN GROUND AND TERMINAL "E5" OF THE 32-WAY EBCM HARNESS CONNECTOR.
- DOES J 39200 DISPLAY RESISTANCE AS "OL" (INFINITE)?

YES / NO
- REPAIR SHORT TO GROUND IN CKT 883.

11
- USING J 39200, MEASURE THE RESISTANCE BETWEEN GROUND AND TERMINAL "E6" OF THE 32-WAY EBCM HARNESS CONNECTOR.
- DOES J 39200 DISPLAY RESISTANCE AS "OL" (INFINITE)?

YES / NO
- REPAIR SHORT TO GROUND IN CKT 882.

12
- THOROUGHLY RESPRAY THE RIGHT REAR WHEEL SPEED SENSOR JUMPER HARNESS WITH THE SALT WATER SOLUTION.
IMPORTANT: DO NOT ALLOW WATER TO ENTER ANY WHEEL SPEED SENSOR CONNECTOR.
- DISCONNECT RIGHT REAR WHEEL SPEED SENSOR DIRECTLY AT SENSOR.
- USING J 39200, MEASURE THE RESISTANCE BETWEEN GROUND AND TERMINAL "A," THEN "B" OF THE RIGHT REAR WHEEL SPEED SENSOR HARNESS CONNECTOR.
- DOES J 39200 DISPLAY RESISTANCE AS "OL" (INFINITE) FOR BOTH MEASUREMENTS?

YES / NO
- REPLACE RIGHT REAR WHEEL SPEED SENSOR JUMPER HARNESS.

13
- USING J 39200, MEASURE THE RESISTANCE BETWEEN GROUND AND TERMINAL "A" OF THE RIGHT REAR WHEEL SPEED SENSOR CONNECTOR.
- DOES J 39200 DISPLAY RESISTANCE AS "OL" (INFINITE)?

YES / NO
- REPLACE WHEEL SPEED SENSOR.

MALFUNCTION IS INTERMITTENT. INSPECT ALL CONNECTORS AND HARNESSES FOR DAMAGE WHICH MAY RESULT IN A SHORT TO GROUND WHEN ALL COMPONENTS ARE CONNECTED. PAY PARTICULAR ATTENTION TO THE JUMPER HARNESS. SMALL NICKS OR CUTS CAN CAUSE A MALFUNCTION. REPAIR ANY DAMAGE IF FOUND. JUMPER HARNESS MUST BE REPLACED IF DAMAGED. REFER TO "DIAGNOSTIC AIDS" ON FACING PAGE FOR MORE INFORMATION.

ABS TROUBLESHOOTING

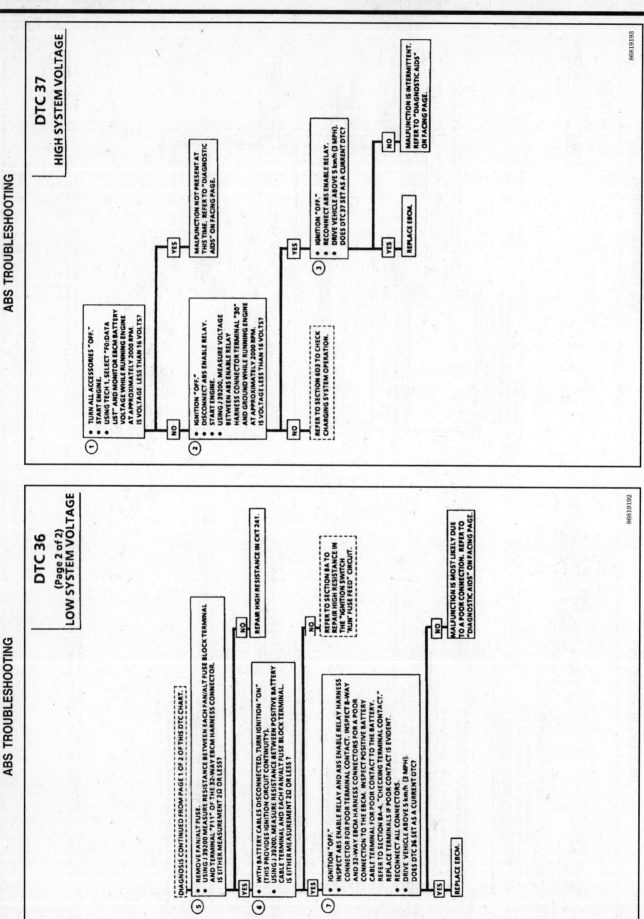

DTC 37
HIGH SYSTEM VOLTAGE

1
- TURN ALL ACCESSORIES "OFF."
- START ENGINE.
- USING TECH 1, SELECT "F0:DATA LIST" AND MONITOR EBCM BATTERY VOLTAGE WHILE RUNNING ENGINE AT APPROXIMATELY 2000 RPM. IS VOLTAGE LESS THAN 16 VOLTS?

YES → MALFUNCTION NOT PRESENT AT THIS TIME. REFER TO "DIAGNOSTIC AIDS" ON FACING PAGE.

2
- IGNITION "OFF."
- DISCONNECT ABS ENABLE RELAY.
- START ENGINE.
- USING J 39200, MEASURE VOLTAGE BETWEEN ABS ENABLE RELAY HARNESS CONNECTOR TERMINAL "30" AND GROUND WHILE RUNNING ENGINE AT APPROXIMATELY 2000 RPM. IS VOLTAGE LESS THAN 16 VOLTS?

NO → REFER TO SECTION 6D3 TO CHECK CHARGING SYSTEM OPERATION.

YES ↑

3
- IGNITION "OFF."
- RECONNECT ABS ENABLE RELAY.
- DRIVE VEHICLE ABOVE 5 km/h (3 MPH). DOES DTC 37 SET AS A CURRENT DTC?

NO → MALFUNCTION IS INTERMITTENT. REFER TO "DIAGNOSTIC AIDS" ON FACING PAGE.

YES → REPLACE EBCM.

86819193

ABS TROUBLESHOOTING

DTC 36
(Page 2 of 2)
LOW SYSTEM VOLTAGE

DIAGNOSIS CONTINUED FROM PAGE 1 OF 2 OF THIS DTC CHART.

5
- REMOVE FAN/ALT FUSE.
- USING J 39200 MEASURE RESISTANCE BETWEEN EACH FAN/ALT FUSE BLOCK TERMINAL AND TERMINAL "F11" OF THE 32-WAY EBCM HARNESS CONNECTOR. IS EITHER MEASUREMENT 2Ω OR LESS?

NO → REPAIR HIGH RESISTANCE IN CKT 241.

YES ↓

6
- WITH BATTERY CABLES DISCONNECTED, TURN IGNITION "ON" (THIS PROVIDES IGNITION CIRCUIT CONTINUITY).
- USING J 39200, MEASURE RESISTANCE BETWEEN POSITIVE BATTERY CABLE TERMINAL AND EACH FAN/ALT FUSE BLOCK TERMINAL. IS EITHER MEASUREMENT 2Ω OR LESS ?

NO → REFER TO SECTION 8A TO REPAIR HIGH RESISTANCE IN THE "IGNITION SWITCH RUN" FUSE FEED" CIRCUIT.

YES ↓

7
- IGNITION "OFF."
- INSPECT ABS ENABLE RELAY AND ABS ENABLE RELAY HARNESS CONNECTOR FOR POOR TERMINAL CONTACT. INSPECT B-WAY AND 32-WAY EBCM HARNESS CONNECTORS FOR A POOR CONNECTION TO THE EBCM. INSPECT POSITIVE BATTERY CABLE TERMINAL FOR POOR CONTACT TO THE BATTERY. REFER TO SECTION 8A-4, "CHECKING TERMINAL CONTACT." REPLACE TERMINALS IF POOR CONTACT IS EVIDENT.
- RECONNECT ALL CONNECTORS.
- DRIVE VEHICLE ABOVE 5 km/h (3 MPH). DOES DTC 36 SET AS A CURRENT DTC?

NO → MALFUNCTION IS MOST LIKELY DUE TO A POOR CONNECTION. REFER TO "DIAGNOSTIC AIDS" ON FACING PAGE.

YES → REPLACE EBCM.

86819192

ABS TROUBLESHOOTING

DTC 41
RIGHT FRONT ESB WILL NOT HOLD MOTOR

1.
- IGNITION "ON," ENGINE "OFF."
- PUMP BRAKE PEDAL UNTIL FIRM TO DEPLETE VACUUM RESERVE.
- USING TECH 1 MISC. TESTS, SELECT MANUAL CONTROL FUNCTION.
- SELECT ABS MOTOR APPLY FUNCTION OF THE RIGHT FRONT CHANNEL AND APPLY THE MOTOR.
- WAIT 5 SECONDS.
- APPLY FIRM PRESSURE ON BRAKE PEDAL.
- DID BRAKE PEDAL FALL?

YES → REPLACE ABS MOTOR PACK.

NO →

2.
- VISUALLY INSPECT THE 6-WAY ABS MOTOR PACK AND 8-WAY EBCM CONNECTORS FOR PROPER WIRE COLOR/CONNECTOR CAVITY COMBINATION.
- ARE THE PROPER WIRES LOCATED IN THE PROPER CONNECTOR CAVITIES?

NO → USING THE CIRCUIT DIAGRAMS LOCATED IN THE FRONT OF THIS SECTION, PLACE THE PROPER WIRES INTO THE PROPER CONNECTOR CAVITIES. CLEAR DTCs AND RECHECK SYSTEM.

YES →

3.
- EXIT TECH 1 MANUAL CONTROL FUNCTION.
- IGNITION "OFF."
- DISCONNECT 6-WAY ABS MOTOR PACK CONNECTOR AND 8-WAY EBCM CONNECTOR.
- USING J 39200, MEASURE THE RESISTANCE BETWEEN TERMINAL "E" OF THE 6-WAY ABS MOTOR PACK HARNESS CONNECTOR AND TERMINAL "G" OF THE 8-WAY EBCM HARNESS CONNECTOR.
- IS RESISTANCE 1.5Ω OR LESS?

NO → REPAIR HIGH RESISTANCE IN CKT 1282.

YES →

4.
- MEASURE THE RESISTANCE BETWEEN TERMINAL "F" OF THE 6-WAY ABS MOTOR PACK HARNESS CONNECTOR AND TERMINAL "H" OF THE 8-WAY EBCM HARNESS CONNECTOR.
- IS RESISTANCE 1.5Ω OR LESS?

NO → REPAIR HIGH RESISTANCE IN CKT 1283.

YES →

5.
- MEASURE THE RESISTANCE BETWEEN TERMINAL "E" AND TERMINAL "F" OF THE ABS MOTOR PACK CONNECTOR.
- IS RESISTANCE 1.5Ω OR LESS?

NO → REPLACE ABS MOTOR PACK.

YES →

6.
- INSPECT THE 6-WAY ABS MOTOR PACK CONNECTOR AND 8-WAY EBCM CONNECTOR FOR POOR TERMINAL CONTACT OR CORROSION. REFER TO SECTION 8A-4, "CHECKING TERMINAL CONTACT."
- DO ANY TERMINALS EXHIBIT POOR CONTACT OR EVIDENCE OF CORROSION?

YES → REPLACE TERMINALS THAT EXHIBIT POOR TERMINAL CONTACT OR EVIDENCE OF CORROSION.

NO →

7.
- IGNITION "OFF."
- RECONNECT ALL CONNECTORS.
- START ENGINE AND TEST DRIVE VEHICLE, ACHIEVING AT LEAST 16 km/h (10 MPH).
- REPEAT ABOVE DRIVE CYCLE SEQUENCE TWO MORE TIMES.
- DOES DTC 41 SET IN THE LAST THREE DRIVE CYCLES?

YES → REPLACE EBCM.

NO → MALFUNCTION IS INTERMITTENT. REFER TO "DIAGNOSTIC AIDS" ON FACING PAGE.

AFTER DIAGNOSIS IS COMPLETE, CLEAR DTCs AND TEST DRIVE VEHICLE FOR THREE (3) DRIVE CYCLES TO VERIFY THAT DTC DOES NOT RESET. A DRIVE CYCLE CONSISTS OF STARTING THE VEHICLE, DRIVING OVER 16 KM/H (10 MPH) AND THEN KEYING DOWN.

86819195

ABS TROUBLESHOOTING

DTC 38
LEFT FRONT ESB WILL NOT HOLD MOTOR

1.
- IGNITION "ON," ENGINE "OFF."
- PUMP BRAKE PEDAL UNTIL FIRM TO DEPLETE VACUUM RESERVE.
- USING TECH 1 MISC. TESTS, SELECT MANUAL CONTROL FUNCTION.
- SELECT ABS MOTOR APPLY FUNCTION OF THE LEFT FRONT CHANNEL AND APPLY THE MOTOR.
- WAIT 5 SECONDS.
- APPLY FIRM PRESSURE ON BRAKE PEDAL.
- DID BRAKE PEDAL FALL?

YES → REPLACE ABS MOTOR PACK.

NO →

2.
- VISUALLY INSPECT THE 6-WAY ABS MOTOR PACK AND 8-WAY EBCM CONNECTORS FOR PROPER WIRE COLOR/CONNECTOR CAVITY COMBINATION.
- ARE THE PROPER WIRES LOCATED IN THE PROPER CONNECTOR CAVITIES?

NO → USING THE CIRCUIT DIAGRAMS LOCATED IN THE FRONT OF THIS SECTION, PLACE THE PROPER WIRES INTO THE PROPER CONNECTOR CAVITIES. CLEAR DTCs AND RECHECK SYSTEM.

YES →

3.
- EXIT TECH 1 MANUAL CONTROL FUNCTION.
- IGNITION "OFF."
- DISCONNECT 6-WAY ABS MOTOR PACK CONNECTOR AND 8-WAY EBCM CONNECTOR.
- USING J 39200, MEASURE THE RESISTANCE BETWEEN TERMINAL "A" OF THE 6-WAY ABS MOTOR PACK HARNESS CONNECTOR AND TERMINAL "A" OF THE 8-WAY EBCM HARNESS CONNECTOR.
- IS RESISTANCE 1.5Ω OR LESS?

NO → REPAIR HIGH RESISTANCE IN CKT 1280.

YES →

4.
- MEASURE THE RESISTANCE BETWEEN TERMINAL "B" OF THE 6-WAY ABS MOTOR PACK HARNESS CONNECTOR AND TERMINAL "B" OF THE 8-WAY EBCM HARNESS CONNECTOR.
- IS RESISTANCE 1.5Ω OR LESS?

NO → REPAIR HIGH RESISTANCE IN CKT 1281.

YES →

5.
- MEASURE THE RESISTANCE BETWEEN TERMINAL "A" AND TERMINAL "B" OF THE MOTOR PACK CONNECTOR.
- IS RESISTANCE 1.5Ω OR LESS?

NO → REPLACE ABS MOTOR PACK.

YES →

6.
- INSPECT THE 6-WAY ABS MOTOR PACK CONNECTOR AND 8-WAY EBCM CONNECTOR FOR POOR TERMINAL CONTACT OR CORROSION. REFER TO SECTION 8A-4, "CHECKING TERMINAL CONTACT."
- DO ANY TERMINALS EXHIBIT POOR CONTACT OR EVIDENCE OF CORROSION?

YES → REPLACE TERMINALS THAT EXHIBIT POOR TERMINAL CONTACT OR EVIDENCE OF CORROSION.

NO →

7.
- IGNITION "OFF."
- RECONNECT ALL CONNECTORS.
- START ENGINE AND TEST DRIVE VEHICLE, ACHIEVING AT LEAST 16 km/h (10 MPH).
- REPEAT ABOVE DRIVE CYCLE SEQUENCE TWO MORE TIMES.
- DOES DTC 38 SET IN THE LAST THREE DRIVE CYCLE?

YES → REPLACE EBCM.

NO → MALFUNCTION IS INTERMITTENT. REFER TO "DIAGNOSTIC AIDS" ON FACING PAGE.

AFTER DIAGNOSIS IS COMPLETE, CLEAR DTCs AND TEST DRIVE VEHICLE FOR THREE (3) DRIVE CYCLES TO VERIFY THAT DTC DOES NOT RESET. A DRIVE CYCLE CONSISTS OF STARTING THE VEHICLE, DRIVING OVER 16 KM/H (10 MPH) AND THEN KEYING DOWN.

86819194

ABS TROUBLESHOOTING

ABS TROUBLESHOOTING

ABS TROUBLESHOOTING

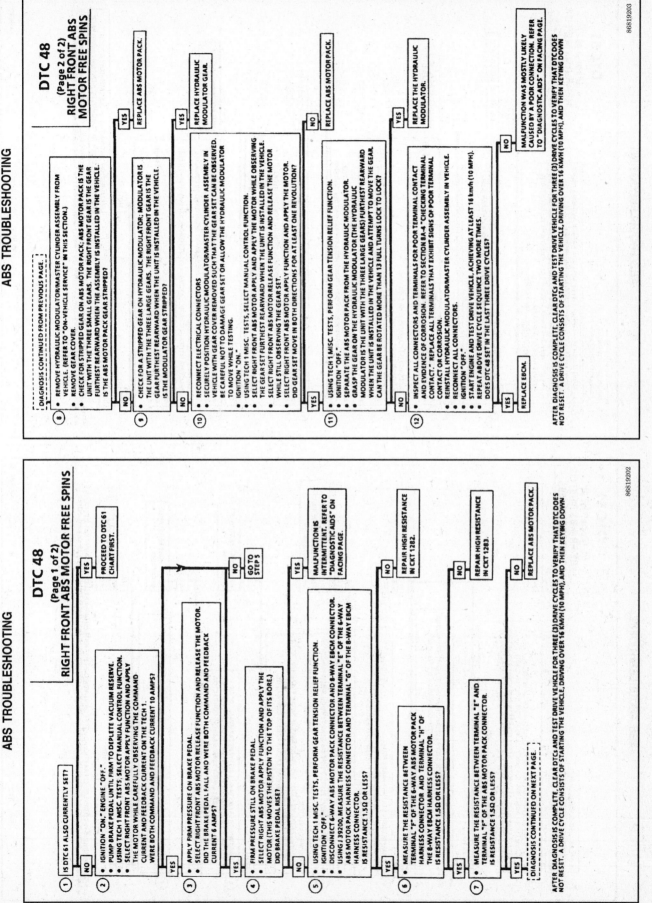

DTC 48
(Page 2 of 2)
RIGHT FRONT ABS
MOTOR FREE SPINS

86819203

ABS TROUBLESHOOTING

DTC 48
(Page 1 of 2)
RIGHT FRONT ABS MOTOR FREE SPINS

86819202

ABS TROUBLESHOOTING

DTC 51
(Page 2 of 2)
REAR ABS MOTOR
FREE SPINS

DTC 51
(Page 1 of 2)
REAR ABS MOTOR
FREE SPINS

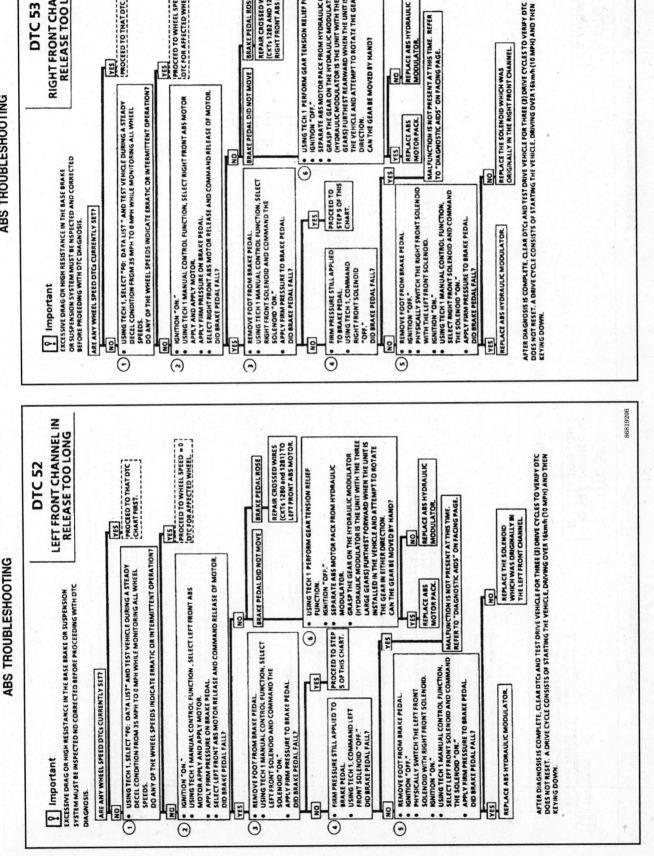

ABS TROUBLESHOOTING

DTC 55
EBCM MALFUNCTION

1. • IGNITION "ON," ENGINE "OFF."
   • USING TECH 1, READ DTCs.
   IS DTC 55 CURRENTLY SET?

   YES →

2. • USING TECH 1, CLEAR DTCs.
   • TEST DRIVE VEHICLE FOR THREE (3) DRIVE CYCLES. A DRIVE CYCLE CONSISTS OF KEY-ON, DRIVE VEHICLE OVER 16 km/h (10 MPH), THEN KEY DOWN.
   DOES DTC 55 RESET?

   NO → MALFUNCTION IS INTERMITTENT.

   YES → REPLACE EBCM.

   NO → MALFUNCTION IS INTERMITTENT.

86819209

ABS TROUBLESHOOTING

DTC 54
REAR CHANNEL IN RELEASE TOO LONG

💡 **Important**
• EXCESSIVE DRAG OR HIGH RESISTANCE IN THE BASE BRAKE OR SUSPENSION SYSTEM MUST BE INSPECTED AND CORRECTED BEFORE PROCEEDING WITH DTC DIAGNOSIS.

ARE ANY WHEEL SPEED DTCs CURRENTLY SET?

YES → PROCEED TO THAT DTC CHART FIRST.

1. • USING TECH 1, SELECT " F0: DATA LIST" AND TEST VEHICLE DURING A STEADY DECEL CONDITION FROM 35 MPH TO 0 MPH WHILE MONITORING ALL WHEEL SPEEDS. DO ANY OF THE WHEEL SPEEDS INDICATE ERRATIC OR INTERMITTENT OPERATION?

   NO ↓

   YES → PROCEED TO WHEEL SPEED = 0 DTC FOR AFFECTED WHEEL.

2. • RAISE REAR OF VEHICLE AND SUPPORT AS INDICATED IN SECTION 0A. SPIN BOTH REAR WHEELS AND CONFIRM PHYSICAL CONDITION OF BASE BRAKE SYSTEM.
   COULD BOTH REAR WHEELS BE SPUN FREELY BY HAND?

   NO → REPAIR SOURCE OF RESISTANCE IN BASE BRAKE SYSTEM.

3. • IGNITION "ON."
   • USING MANUAL CONTROL FUNCTION OF TECH 1, SELECT REAR AXLE ABS MOTOR APPLY.
   • APPLY FIRM PRESSURE ON BRAKE PEDAL.
   • COMMAND APPLY OF REAR ABS MOTOR AND TRY TO SPIN REAR WHEELS BY HAND.
   COULD REAR WHEELS BE SPUN BY HAND?

   YES ↓

   NO → MALFUNCTION IS NOT PRESENT AT THIS TIME. REFER TO "DIAGNOSTIC AIDS" ON FACING PAGE.

4. • WITH FIRM PRESSURE ON BRAKE PEDAL STILL APPLIED, COMMAND A RELEASE OF THE REAR AXLE ABS MOTOR. CAN WHEELS BE MOVED?

   YES ↓

   NO → REPAIR CROSSED WIRES AT REAR ABS MOTOR (CKTs 1284 AND 1285).

5. • USING TECH 1, PERFORM GEAR TENSION RELIEF FUNCTION.
   • SEPARATE ABS MOTOR PACK FROM HYDRAULIC MODULATOR.
   • CONNECT ABS MOTOR PACK WIRING.
   • IGNITION "ON."
   • USING TECH 1, PERFORM MOTOR TEST.
   DO ALL THREE ABS MOTOR PACK GEARS (SMALL GEARS) SPIN FREELY?

   NO → REPLACE ABS MOTOR PACK.

   YES → REPLACE ABS HYDRAULIC MODULATOR.

AFTER ALL DIAGNOSIS IS COMPLETE, CLEAR DTCs AND TEST DRIVE VEHICLE FOR THREE (3) DRIVE CYCLES TO VERIFY THAT DTC DOES NOT RESET. A DRIVE CYCLE CONSISTS OF STARTING THE VEHICLE DRIVING OVER 16 KM/H (10 MPH), AND THEN KEYING DOWN.

86819208

ABS TROUBLESHOOTING

DTC 57
LEFT FRONT ABS MOTOR CIRCUIT SHORTED TO GND

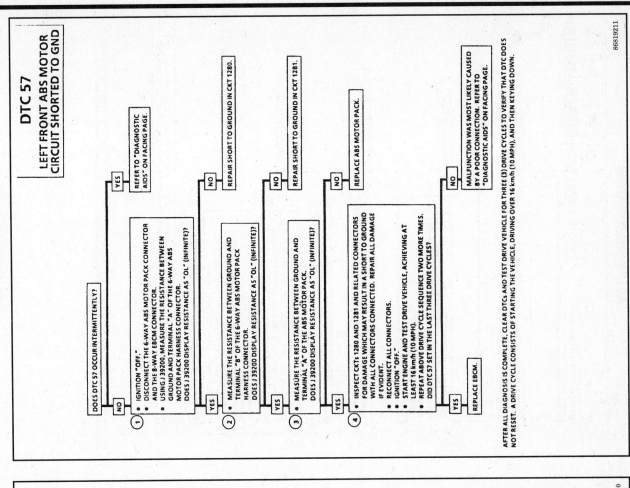

DOES DTC 57 OCCUR INTERMITTENTLY?

YES → REFER TO "DIAGNOSTIC AIDS" ON FACING PAGE.

NO

①
- IGNITION "OFF."
- DISCONNECT THE 6-WAY ABS MOTOR PACK CONNECTOR AND THE 8-WAY EBCM CONNECTOR.
- USING J 39200, MEASURE THE RESISTANCE BETWEEN GROUND AND TERMINAL "A" OF THE 6-WAY ABS MOTOR PACK HARNESS CONNECTOR.
DOES J 39200 DISPLAY RESISTANCE AS "OL" (INFINITE)?

NO → REPAIR SHORT TO GROUND IN CKT 1280.

YES

② MEASURE THE RESISTANCE BETWEEN GROUND AND TERMINAL "B" OF THE 6-WAY ABS MOTOR PACK HARNESS CONNECTOR.
DOES J 39200 DISPLAY RESISTANCE AS "OL" (INFINITE)?

NO → REPAIR SHORT TO GROUND IN CKT 1281.

YES

③ MEASURE THE RESISTANCE BETWEEN GROUND AND TERMINAL "A" OF THE ABS MOTOR PACK.
DOES J 39200 DISPLAY RESISTANCE AS "OL" (INFINITE)?

NO → REPLACE ABS MOTOR PACK.

YES

④
- INSPECT CKTS 1280 AND 1281 AND RELATED CONNECTORS FOR DAMAGE WHICH MAY RESULT IN A SHORT TO GROUND WITH ALL CONNECTORS CONNECTED. REPAIR ALL DAMAGE IF EVIDENT.
- RECONNECT ALL CONNECTORS.
- IGNITION "OFF."
- START ENGINE AND TEST DRIVE VEHICLE, ACHIEVING AT LEAST 16 km/h (10 MPH).
- REPEAT ABOVE DRIVE CYCLE SEQUENCE TWO MORE TIMES.
DID DTC57 SET IN THE LAST THREE DRIVE CYCLES?

NO → MALFUNCTION WAS MOST LIKELY CAUSED BY A POOR CONNECTION. REFER TO "DIAGNOSTIC AIDS" ON FACING PAGE.

YES → REPLACE EBCM.

AFTER ALL DIAGNOSIS IS COMPLETE, CLEAR DTCs AND TEST DRIVE VEHICLE FOR THREE (3) DRIVE CYCLES TO VERIFY THAT DTC DOES NOT RESET. A DRIVE CYCLE CONSISTS OF STARTING THE VEHICLE, DRIVING OVER 16 km/h (10 MPH), AND THEN KEYING DOWN.

86819211

ABS TROUBLESHOOTING

DTC 56
LEFT FRONT ABS MOTOR CIRCUIT OPEN

DOES DTC 56 OCCUR INTERMITTENTLY?

YES → REFER TO "DIAGNOSTIC AIDS" ON FACING PAGE.

NO

①
- IGNITION "OFF."
- DISCONNECT 6-WAY ABS MOTOR PACK CONNECTOR.
- USING J 39200, MEASURE RESISTANCE ACROSS ABS MOTOR PACK TERMINALS "A" AND "B."
IS RESISTANCE BELOW 2000Ω?

NO → REPLACE ABS MOTOR PACK.

YES

②
DISCONNECT 8-WAY CONNECTOR AT EBCM.
USING J 39200, MEASURE RESISTANCE BETWEEN TERMINAL "A" OF THE 8-WAY EBCM HARNESS CONNECTOR AND TERMINAL "A" OF THE 6-WAY ABS MOTOR PACK HARNESS CONNECTOR.
IS RESISTANCE 2Ω OR LESS?

NO → REPAIR OPEN OR HIGH RESISTANCE IN CKT 1280.

YES

③
USING J 39200, MEASURE RESISTANCE BETWEEN TERMINAL "B" OF THE 8-WAY EBCM HARNESS CONNECTOR AND TERMINAL "B" OF THE 6-WAY ABS MOTOR PACK HARNESS CONNECTOR
IS RESISTANCE 2Ω OR LESS?

NO → REPAIR OPEN OR HIGH RESISTANCE IN CKT 1281.

YES

④
- INSPECT THE 6-WAY ABS MOTOR PACK AND 8-WAY EBCM CONNECTORS FOR POOR TERMINAL CONTACT AND EVIDENCE OF CORROSION. REFER TO SECTION 8A-4, "CHECKING TERMINAL CONTACT." REPLACE ALL TERMINALS THAT EXHIBIT SIGNS OF POOR TERMINAL CONTACT OR CORROSION.
- RECONNECT ALL CONNECTORS.
- START ENGINE AND TEST DRIVE VEHICLE, ACHIEVING AT LEAST 16 km/h (10 MPH).
- REPEAT ABOVE DRIVE CYCLE SEQUENCE TWO MORE TIMES.
DID DTC 56 SET IN THE LAST THREE DRIVE CYCLES?

NO → MALFUNCTION WAS MOST LIKELY CAUSED BY A POOR CONNECTION. REFER TO "DIAGNOSTIC AIDS" ON FACING PAGE.

YES → REPLACE EBCM

AFTER DIAGNOSIS IS COMPLETE, CLEAR DTCs AND TEST DRIVE VEHICLE FOR THREE (3) DRIVE CYCLES TO VERIFY THAT DTC DOES NOT RESET. A DRIVE CYCLE CONSISTS OF STARTING THE VEHICLE, DRIVING OVER 16 KM/H (10 MPH), AND THEN KEYING DOWN.

86819210

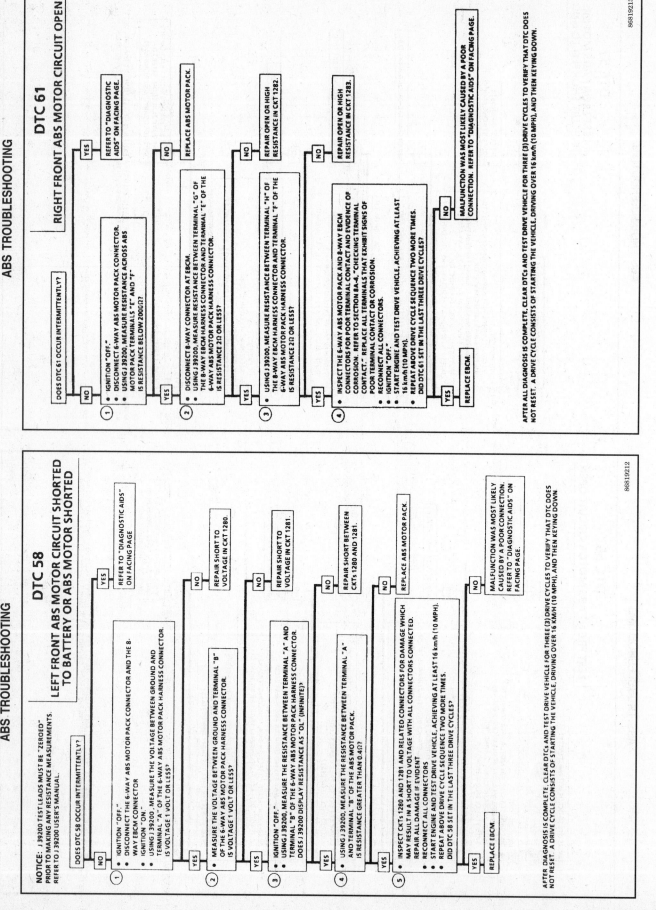

ABS TROUBLESHOOTING

DTC 61
RIGHT FRONT ABS MOTOR CIRCUIT OPEN

DOES DTC 61 OCCUR INTERMITTENTLY?

YES → REFER TO "DIAGNOSTIC AIDS" ON FACING PAGE.

NO

1.
- IGNITION "OFF."
- DISCONNECT THE 6-WAY ABS MOTOR PACK CONNECTOR.
- USING J 39200, MEASURE RESISTANCE ACROSS ABS MOTOR PACK TERMINALS "E" AND "F".

IS RESISTANCE BELOW 200Ω?

NO → REPLACE ABS MOTOR PACK.

YES

2.
- DISCONNECT 8-WAY CONNECTOR AT EBCM.
- USING J 39200, MEASURE RESISTANCE BETWEEN TERMINAL "G" OF THE 8-WAY EBCM HARNESS CONNECTOR AND TERMINAL "E" OF THE 6-WAY ABS MOTOR PACK HARNESS CONNECTOR.

IS RESISTANCE 2Ω OR LESS?

NO → REPAIR OPEN OR HIGH RESISTANCE IN CKT 1282.

YES

3.
- USING J 39200, MEASURE RESISTANCE BETWEEN TERMINAL "H" OF THE 8-WAY EBCM HARNESS CONNECTOR AND TERMINAL "F" OF THE 6-WAY ABS MOTOR PACK HARNESS CONNECTOR.

IS RESISTANCE 2Ω OR LESS?

NO → REPAIR OPEN OR HIGH RESISTANCE IN CKT 1283.

YES

4.
- INSPECT THE 6-WAY ABS MOTOR PACK AND 8-WAY EBCM CONNECTORS FOR POOR TERMINAL CONTACT AND EVIDENCE OF CORROSION. REFER TO SECTION 8A-4, "CHECKING TERMINAL CONTACT." REPLACE ALL TERMINALS THAT EXHIBIT SIGNS OF POOR TERMINAL CONTACT OR CORROSION.
- RECONNECT ALL CONNECTORS.
- IGNITION "OFF."
- START ENGINE AND TEST DRIVE VEHICLE, ACHIEVING AT LEAST 16 km/h (10 MPH).
- REPEAT ABOVE DRIVE CYCLE SEQUENCE TWO MORE TIMES.

DID DTC 61 SET IN THE LAST THREE DRIVE CYCLES?

YES → REPLACE EBCM.

NO → MALFUNCTION WAS MOST LIKELY CAUSED BY A POOR CONNECTION. REFER TO "DIAGNOSTIC AIDS" ON FACING PAGE.

AFTER ALL DIAGNOSIS IS COMPLETE, CLEAR DTCs AND TEST DRIVE VEHICLE FOR THREE (3) DRIVE CYCLES TO VERIFY THAT DTC DOES NOT RESET. A DRIVE CYCLE CONSISTS OF STARTING THE VEHICLE, DRIVING OVER 16 km/h (10 MPH), AND THEN KEYING DOWN.

86819213

ABS TROUBLESHOOTING

DTC 58
LEFT FRONT ABS MOTOR CIRCUIT SHORTED TO BATTERY OR ABS MOTOR SHORTED

NOTICE: J 39200 TEST LEADS MUST BE "ZEROED" PRIOR TO MAKING ANY RESISTANCE MEASUREMENTS. REFER TO J 39200 USER'S MANUAL.

DOES DTC 58 OCCUR INTERMITTENTLY?

YES → REFER TO "DIAGNOSTIC AIDS" ON FACING PAGE

NO

1.
- IGNITION "OFF."
- DISCONNECT THE 6-WAY ABS MOTOR PACK CONNECTOR AND THE 8-WAY EBCM CONNECTOR
- IGNITION "ON."
- USING J 39200, MEASURE THE VOLTAGE BETWEEN GROUND AND TERMINAL "A" OF THE 6-WAY ABS MOTOR PACK HARNESS CONNECTOR.

IS VOLTAGE 1 VOLT OR LESS?

NO → REPAIR SHORT TO VOLTAGE IN CKT 1280.

YES

2.
- MEASURE THE VOLTAGE BETWEEN GROUND AND TERMINAL "B" OF THE 6-WAY ABS MOTOR PACK HARNESS CONNECTOR.

IS VOLTAGE 1 VOLT OR LESS?

NO → REPAIR SHORT TO VOLTAGE IN CKT 1281.

YES

3.
- IGNITION "OFF."
- USING J 39200, MEASURE THE RESISTANCE BETWEEN TERMINAL "A" AND TERMINAL "B" OF THE 6-WAY ABS MOTOR PACK HARNESS CONNECTOR.

DOES J 39200 DISPLAY RESISTANCE AS "OL" (INFINITE)?

NO → REPAIR SHORT BETWEEN CKTs 1280 AND 1281.

YES

4.
- USING J 39200, MEASURE THE RESISTANCE BETWEEN TERMINAL "A" AND TERMINAL "B" OF THE ABS MOTOR PACK.

IS RESISTANCE GREATER THAN 0.4Ω?

NO → REPLACE ABS MOTOR PACK.

YES

5.
- INSPECT CKTs 1280 AND 1281 AND RELATED CONNECTORS FOR DAMAGE WHICH MAY RESULT IN A SHORT TO VOLTAGE WITH ALL CONNECTORS CONNECTED.
- REPAIR ALL DAMAGE IF EVIDENT
- RECONNECT ALL CONNECTORS
- START ENGINE AND TEST DRIVE VEHICLE, ACHIEVING AT LEAST 16 km/h (10 MPH).
- REPEAT ABOVE DRIVE CYCLE SEQUENCE TWO MORE TIMES.

DID DTC 58 SET IN THE LAST THREE DRIVE CYCLES?

YES → REPLACE EBCM.

NO → MALFUNCTION WAS MOST LIKELY CAUSED BY A POOR CONNECTION. REFER TO "DIAGNOSTIC AIDS" ON FACING PAGE.

AFTER DIAGNOSIS IS COMPLETE, CLEAR DTCs AND TEST DRIVE VEHICLE FOR THREE (3) DRIVE CYCLES TO VERIFY THAT DTC DOES NOT RESET. A DRIVE CYCLE CONSISTS OF STARTING THE VEHICLE, DRIVING OVER 16 KM/H (10 MPH), AND THEN KEYING DOWN

86819212

ABS TROUBLESHOOTING

DTC 63
RIGHT FRONT ABS MOTOR CIRCUIT SHORTED TO BATTERY OR ABS MOTOR SHORTED

NOTICE: J 39200 TEST LEADS MUST BE "ZEROED" PRIOR TO MAKING ANY RESISTANCE MEASUREMENTS. REFER TO J 39200 USER'S MANUAL.

DOES DTC 63 OCCUR INTERMITTENTLY?

YES → REFER TO "DIAGNOSTIC AIDS" ON FACING PAGE.

NO

1.
- IGNITION "OFF."
- DISCONNECT THE 6-WAY ABS MOTOR PACK CONNECTOR AND THE 8-WAY EBCM CONNECTOR.
- IGNITION "ON."
- USING J 39200, MEASURE THE VOLTAGE BETWEEN GROUND AND TERMINAL "E" OF THE 6-WAY ABS MOTOR PACK HARNESS CONNECTOR. IS VOLTAGE 1 VOLT OR LESS?

YES

2.
- MEASURE THE VOLTAGE BETWEEN GROUND AND TERMINAL "F" OF THE 6-WAY ABS MOTOR PACK HARNESS CONNECTOR. IS VOLTAGE 1 VOLT OR LESS?

NO → REPAIR SHORT TO VOLTAGE IN CKT 1282.

YES

3.
- IGNITION "OFF."
- USING J 39200, MEASURE THE RESISTANCE BETWEEN TERMINAL "E" AND TERMINAL "F" OF THE 6-WAY ABS MOTOR PACK HARNESS CONNECTOR. DOES J 39200 DISPLAY RESISTANCE AS "OL" (INFINITE)?

NO → REPAIR SHORT TO VOLTAGE IN CKT 1283.

YES

4.
- USING J 39200, MEASURE THE RESISTANCE BETWEEN TERMINAL "E" AND TERMINAL "F" OF THE ABS MOTOR PACK. IS RESISTANCE GREATER THAN 0.4Ω?

YES → REPAIR SHORT BETWEEN CKTS 1282 AND 1283

NO

5.
- INSPECT CKTs 1282 AND 1283 AND RELATED CONNECTORS FOR DAMAGE WHICH MAY RESULT IN A SHORT TO VOLTAGE WITH ALL CONNECTORS CONNECTED. REPAIR ALL DAMAGE IF EVIDENT.
- RECONNECT ALL CONNECTORS.
- START ENGINE AND TEST DRIVE VEHICLE, ACHIEVING AT LEAST 16 km/h (10 MPH).
- REPEAT ABOVE DRIVE CYCLE SEQUENCE TWO MORE TIMES. DID DTC 63 SET IN THE LAST THREE DRIVE CYCLES?

YES → REPLACE ABS MOTOR PACK.

NO → REPLACE EBCM.

→ MALFUNCTION WAS MOST LIKELY CAUSED BY A POOR CONNECTION. REFER TO "DIAGNOSTIC AIDS" ON FACING PAGE.

AFTER DIAGNOSIS IS COMPLETE, CLEAR DTCs AND TEST DRIVE VEHICLE FOR THREE (3) DRIVE CYCLES TO VERIFY THAT DTC DOES NOT RESET. A DRIVE CYCLE CONSISTS OF STARTING THE VEHICLE, DRIVING OVER 16 KM/H (10 MPH), AND THEN KEYING DOWN.

86819215

ABS TROUBLESHOOTING

DTC 62
RIGHT FRONT ABS MOTOR CIRCUIT SHORTED TO GND

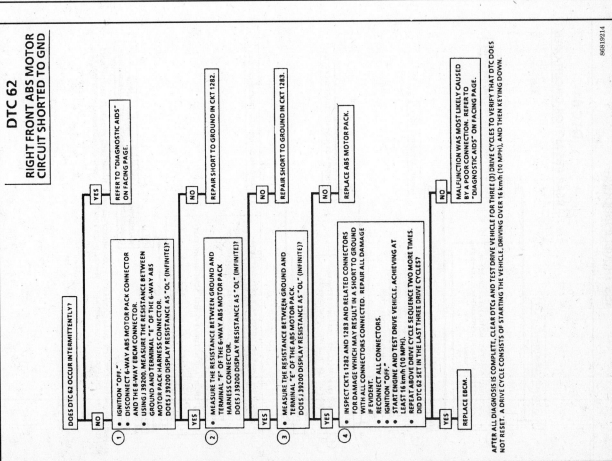

DOES DTC 62 OCCUR INTERMITTENTLY?

YES → REFER TO "DIAGNOSTIC AIDS" ON FACING PAGE.

NO

1.
- IGNITION "OFF."
- DISCONNECT 6-WAY ABS MOTOR PACK CONNECTOR AND THE 8-WAY EBCM CONNECTOR.
- USING J 39200, MEASURE THE RESISTANCE BETWEEN GROUND AND TERMINAL "E" OF THE 6-WAY ABS MOTOR PACK HARNESS CONNECTOR. DOES J 39200 DISPLAY RESISTANCE AS "OL" (INFINITE)?

YES

2.
- MEASURE THE RESISTANCE BETWEEN GROUND AND TERMINAL "F" OF THE 6-WAY ABS MOTOR PACK HARNESS CONNECTOR. DOES J 39200 DISPLAY RESISTANCE AS "OL" (INFINITE)?

NO → REPAIR SHORT TO GROUND IN CKT 1282.

YES

3.
- MEASURE THE RESISTANCE BETWEEN GROUND AND TERMINAL "E" OF THE ABS MOTOR PACK. DOES J 39200 DISPLAY RESISTANCE AS "OL" (INFINITE)?

NO → REPAIR SHORT TO GROUND IN CKT 1283.

YES

4.
- INSPECT CKTs 1282 AND 1283 AND RELATED CONNECTORS FOR DAMAGE WHICH MAY RESULT IN A SHORT TO GROUND WITH ALL CONNECTORS CONNECTED. REPAIR ALL DAMAGE IF EVIDENT.
- RECONNECT ALL CONNECTORS.
- IGNITION "OFF."
- START ENGINE AND TEST DRIVE VEHICLE, ACHIEVING AT LEAST 16 km/h (10 MPH).
- REPEAT ABOVE DRIVE CYCLE SEQUENCE TWO MORE TIMES. DID DTC 62 SET IN THE LAST THREE DRIVE CYCLES?

NO → REPLACE ABS MOTOR PACK.

YES → REPLACE EBCM.

→ MALFUNCTION WAS MOST LIKELY CAUSED BY A POOR CONNECTION. REFER TO "DIAGNOSTIC AIDS" ON FACING PAGE.

AFTER ALL DIAGNOSIS IS COMPLETE, CLEAR DTCs AND TEST DRIVE VEHICLE FOR THREE (3) DRIVE CYCLES TO VERIFY THAT DTC DOES NOT RESET. A DRIVE CYCLE CONSISTS OF STARTING THE VEHICLE, DRIVING OVER 16 km/h (10 MPH), AND THEN KEYING DOWN.

86819214

ABS TROUBLESHOOTING

ABS TROUBLESHOOTING

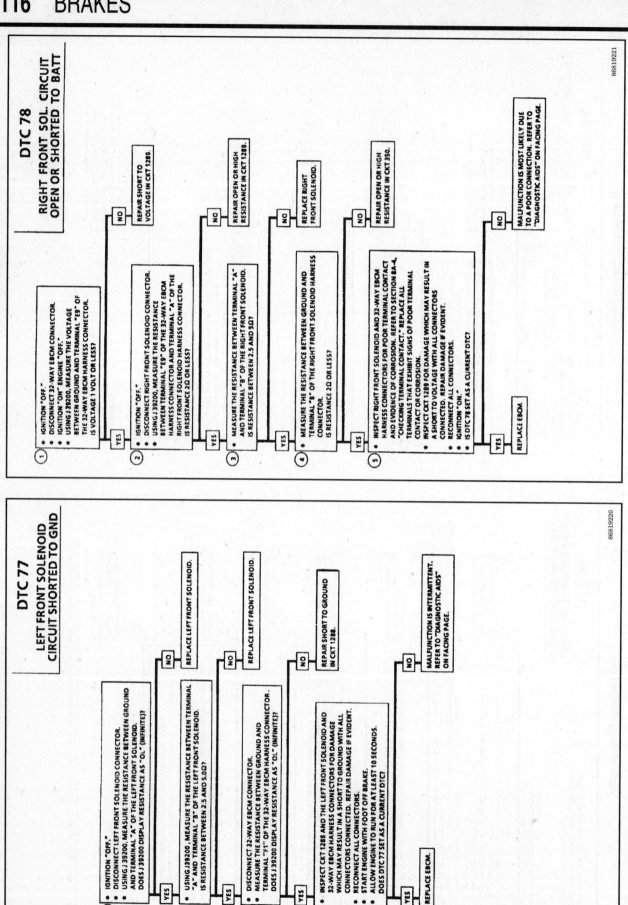

DTC 78

RIGHT FRONT SOL. CIRCUIT OPEN OR SHORTED TO BATT

1.
- IGNITION "OFF."
- DISCONNECT 32-WAY EBCM CONNECTOR.
- IGNITION "ON" ENGINE "OFF."
- USING J 39200, MEASURE THE VOLTAGE BETWEEN GROUND AND TERMINAL "E9" OF THE 32-WAY EBCM HARNESS CONNECTOR.
IS VOLTAGE 1 VOLT OR LESS?

NO → REPAIR SHORT TO VOLTAGE IN CKT 1289.

2.
- IGNITION "OFF."
- DISCONNECT RIGHT FRONT SOLENOID CONNECTOR.
- USING J 39200, MEASURE THE RESISTANCE BETWEEN TERMINAL "E9" OF THE 32-WAY EBCM HARNESS CONNECTOR AND TERMINAL "A" OF THE RIGHT FRONT SOLENOID HARNESS CONNECTOR.
IS RESISTANCE BETWEEN 2Ω OR LESS?

NO → REPAIR OPEN OR HIGH RESISTANCE IN CKT 1289.

3.
- MEASURE THE RESISTANCE BETWEEN TERMINAL "A" AND TERMINAL "B" OF THE RIGHT FRONT SOLENOID.
IS RESISTANCE BETWEEN 2.5 AND 5Ω?

NO → REPLACE RIGHT FRONT SOLENOID.

4.
- MEASURE THE RESISTANCE BETWEEN GROUND AND TERMINAL "B" OF THE RIGHT FRONT SOLENOID HARNESS CONNECTOR.
IS RESISTANCE 2Ω OR LESS?

NO → REPAIR OPEN OR HIGH RESISTANCE IN CKT 350.

5.
- INSPECT RIGHT FRONT SOLENOID AND 32-WAY EBCM HARNESS CONNECTORS FOR POOR TERMINAL CONTACT AND EVIDENCE OF CORROSION. REFER TO SECTION 8A-4, "CHECKING TERMINAL CONTACT." REPLACE ALL TERMINALS THAT EXHIBIT SIGNS OF POOR TERMINAL CONTACT OR CORROSION.
- INSPECT CKT 1289 FOR DAMAGE WHICH MAY RESULT IN A SHORT TO VOLTAGE WITH ALL CONNECTORS CONNECTED. REPAIR DAMAGE IF EVIDENT.
- RECONNECT ALL CONNECTORS.
- IGNITION "ON."
IS DTC 78 SET AS A CURRENT DTC?

YES → REPLACE EBCM.

NO → MALFUNCTION IS MOST LIKELY DUE TO A POOR CONNECTION. REFER TO "DIAGNOSTIC AIDS" ON FACING PAGE.

86819221

ABS TROUBLESHOOTING

DTC 77

LEFT FRONT SOLENOID CIRCUIT SHORTED TO GND

1.
- IGNITION "OFF."
- DISCONNECT LEFT FRONT SOLENOID CONNECTOR.
- USING J 39200, MEASURE THE RESISTANCE BETWEEN GROUND AND TERMINAL "A" OF THE LEFT FRONT SOLENOID.
DOES J 39200 DISPLAY RESISTANCE AS "OL" (INFINITE)?

NO → REPLACE LEFT FRONT SOLENOID.

2.
- USING J 39200, MEASURE THE RESISTANCE BETWEEN TERMINAL "A" AND TERMINAL "B" OF THE LEFT FRONT SOLENOID.
IS RESISTANCE BETWEEN 2.5 AND 5.0Ω?

NO → REPLACE LEFT FRONT SOLENOID.

3.
- DISCONNECT 32-WAY EBCM CONNECTOR.
- MEASURE THE RESISTANCE BETWEEN GROUND AND TERMINAL "F1" OF THE 32-WAY EBCM HARNESS CONNECTOR.
DOES J 39200 DISPLAY RESISTANCE AS "OL" (INFINITE)?

NO → REPAIR SHORT TO GROUND IN CKT 1288.

4.
- INSPECT CKT 1288 AND THE LEFT FRONT SOLENOID AND 32-WAY EBCM HARNESS CONNECTORS FOR DAMAGE WHICH MAY RESULT IN A SHORT TO GROUND WITH ALL CONNECTORS CONNECTED. REPAIR DAMAGE IF EVIDENT.
- RECONNECT ALL CONNECTORS.
- START ENGINE WITH FOOT OFF BRAKE.
- ALLOW ENGINE TO RUN FOR AT LEAST 10 SECONDS.
DOES DTC 77 SET AS A CURRENT DTC?

YES → REPLACE EBCM.

NO → MALFUNCTION IS INTERMITTENT. REFER TO "DIAGNOSTIC AIDS" ON FACING PAGE.

86819220

ABS TROUBLESHOOTING

DTC 82
CALIBRATION MALFUNCTION

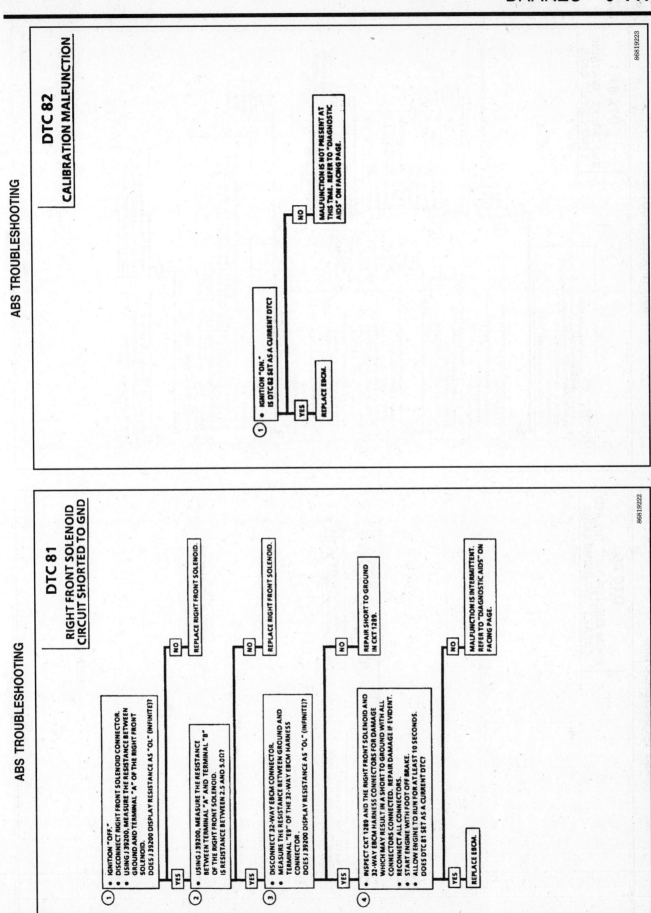

- IGNITION "ON."
  IS DTC 82 SET AS A CURRENT DTC?

YES → REPLACE EBCM.

NO → MALFUNCTION IS NOT PRESENT AT THIS TIME. REFER TO "DIAGNOSTIC AIDS" ON FACING PAGE.

ABS TROUBLESHOOTING

DTC 81
RIGHT FRONT SOLENOID
CIRCUIT SHORTED TO GND

1.
- IGNITION "OFF."
- DISCONNECT RIGHT FRONT SOLENOID CONNECTOR.
- USING J 39200, MEASURE THE RESISTANCE BETWEEN GROUND AND TERMINAL "A" OF THE RIGHT FRONT SOLENOID.
  DOES J 39200 DISPLAY RESISTANCE AS "OL" (INFINITE)?

NO → REPLACE RIGHT FRONT SOLENOID.

YES →

2.
- USING J 39200, MEASURE THE RESISTANCE BETWEEN TERMINAL "A" AND TERMINAL "B" OF THE RIGHT FRONT SOLENOID.
  IS RESISTANCE BETWEEN 2.5 AND 5.0Ω?

NO → REPLACE RIGHT FRONT SOLENOID.

YES →

3.
- DISCONNECT 32-WAY EBCM CONNECTOR.
- MEASURE THE RESISTANCE BETWEEN GROUND AND TERMINAL "E9" OF THE 32-WAY EBCM HARNESS CONNECTOR.
  DOES J 39200 DISPLAY RESISTANCE AS "OL" (INFINITE)?

NO → REPAIR SHORT TO GROUND IN CKT 1289.

YES →

4.
- INSPECT CKT 1289 AND THE RIGHT FRONT SOLENOID AND 32-WAY EBCM HARNESS CONNECTORS FOR DAMAGE WHICH MAY RESULT IN A SHORT TO GROUND WITH ALL CONNECTORS CONNECTED. REPAIR DAMAGE IF EVIDENT.
- RECONNECT ALL CONNECTORS.
- START ENGINE WITH FOOT OFF BRAKE.
- ALLOW ENGINE TO RUN FOR AT LEAST 10 SECONDS.
  DOES DTC 81 SET AS A CURRENT DTC?

NO → MALFUNCTION IS INTERMITTENT. REFER TO "DIAGNOSTIC AIDS" ON FACING PAGE.

YES → REPLACE EBCM.

ABS TROUBLESHOOTING

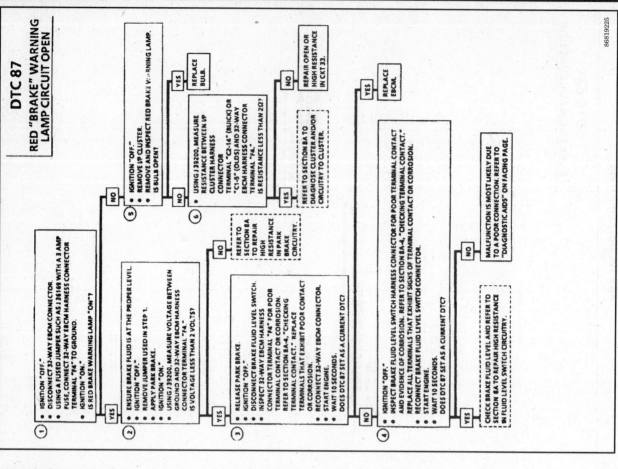

DTC 87
RED "BRAKE" WARNING LAMP CIRCUIT OPEN

1
- IGNITION "OFF."
- DISCONNECT 32-WAY EBCM CONNECTOR.
- USING A FUSED JUMPER SUCH AS J 36169 WITH A 3 AMP FUSE, CONNECT 32-WAY EBCM HARNESS CONNECTOR TERMINAL "F4" TO GROUND.
- IGNITION "ON."
- IS RED BRAKE WARNING LAMP "ON"?

YES → NO →

5
- IGNITION "OFF."
- REMOVE I/P CLUSTER.
- REMOVE AND INSPECT RED BRAKE WARNING LAMP.
- IS BULB OPEN?

YES → REPLACE BULB.
NO →

6
- USING J 39200, MEASURE RESISTANCE BETWEEN I/P CLUSTER HARNESS CONNECTOR TERMINAL "C2-14" (OLDS) OR "C1-5" (OLDS) AND 32-WAY EBCM HARNESS CONNECTOR TERMINAL "F4."
- IS RESISTANCE LESS THAN 2Ω?

NO → REPAIR OPEN OR HIGH RESISTANCE IN CKT 33.
YES → REFER TO SECTION 8A TO DIAGNOSE CLUSTER AND/OR CIRCUITRY TO CLUSTER.

2
- ENSURE BRAKE FLUID IS AT THE PROPER LEVEL.
- IGNITION "OFF."
- APPLY PARK BRAKE.
- IGNITION "ON."
- USING J 39200, MEASURE VOLTAGE BETWEEN GROUND AND 32-WAY EBCM HARNESS CONNECTOR TERMINAL "F4."
- IS VOLTAGE LESS THAN 2 VOLTS?

YES → NO → REFER TO SECTION 8A TO REPAIR HIGH RESISTANCE IN PARK BRAKE CIRCUITRY.

3
- RELEASE PARK BRAKE.
- IGNITION "OFF."
- DISCONNECT BRAKE FLUID LEVEL SWITCH.
- INSPECT 32-WAY EBCM HARNESS CONNECTOR TERMINAL "F4" FOR POOR TERMINAL CONTACT OR CORROSION. REFER TO SECTION 8A-4, "CHECKING TERMINAL CONTACT." REPLACE TERMINALS THAT EXHIBIT POOR CONTACT OR CORROSION.
- RECONNECT 32-WAY EBCM CONNECTOR.
- START ENGINE.
- WAIT 10 SECONDS.
- DOES DTC 87 SET AS A CURRENT DTC?

NO →

4
- IGNITION "OFF."
- INSPECT BRAKE FLUID LEVEL SWITCH HARNESS CONNECTOR FOR POOR TERMINAL CONTACT AND EVIDENCE OF CORROSION. REFER TO SECTION 8A-4, "CHECKING TERMINAL CONTACT." REPLACE ALL TERMINALS THAT EXHIBIT SIGNS OF TERMINAL CONTACT OR CORROSION.
- RECONNECT BRAKE FLUID LEVEL SWITCH CONNECTOR.
- START ENGINE.
- WAIT 10 SECONDS.
- DOES DTC 87 SET AS A CURRENT DTC?

YES → CHECK BRAKE FLUID LEVEL AND REFER TO SECTION 8A TO REPAIR HIGH RESISTANCE IN FLUID LEVEL SWITCH CIRCUITRY.
NO → MALFUNCTION IS MOST LIKELY DUE TO A POOR CONNECTION. REFER TO "DIAGNOSTIC AIDS" ON FACING PAGE.

YES → REPLACE EBCM.

86819225

ABS TROUBLESHOOTING

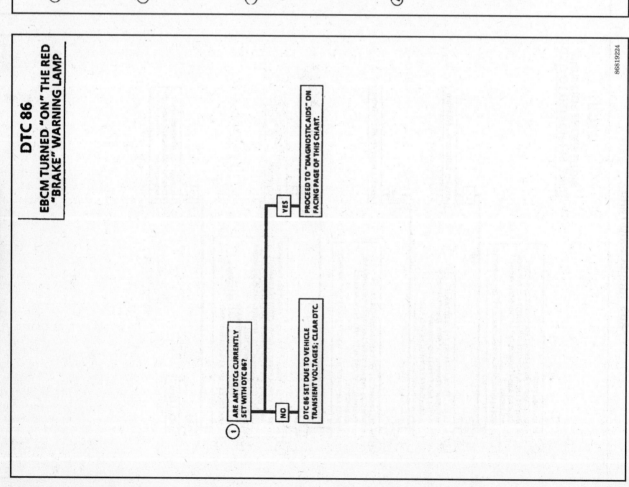

DTC 86
EBCM TURNED "ON" THE RED "BRAKE" WARNING LAMP

1
- ARE ANY DTCs CURRENTLY SET WITH DTC 86?

YES → PROCEED TO "DIAGNOSTIC AIDS" ON FACING PAGE OF THIS CHART.
NO → DTC 86 SET DUE TO VEHICLE TRANSIENT VOLTAGES; CLEAR DTC.

86819224

ABS TROUBLESHOOTING

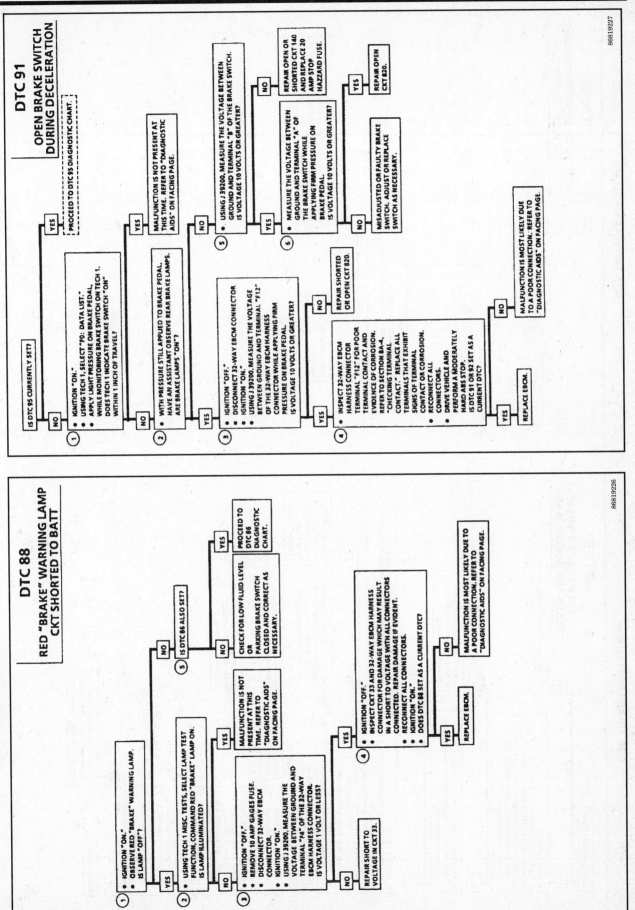

DTC 91
OPEN BRAKE SWITCH DURING DECELERATION

IS DTC 95 CURRENTLY SET?

YES → PROCEED TO DTC 95 DIAGNOSTIC CHART.

NO

① • IGNITION "ON."
• USING TECH 1, SELECT "F0: DATA LIST."
APPLY LIGHT PRESSURE ON BRAKE PEDAL,
WHILE MONITORING BRAKE SWITCH ON TECH 1.
DOES TECH 1 INDICATE BRAKE SWITCH "ON"
WITHIN 1 INCH OF TRAVEL?

YES

② • WITH PRESSURE STILL APPLIED TO BRAKE PEDAL,
HAVE AN ASSISTANT OBSERVE REAR BRAKE LAMPS.
ARE BRAKE LAMPS "ON"?

YES → MALFUNCTION IS NOT PRESENT AT THIS TIME. REFER TO "DIAGNOSTIC AIDS" ON FACING PAGE.

NO

③ • IGNITION "OFF."
• DISCONNECT 32-WAY EBCM CONNECTOR.
• IGNITION "ON."
• USING J 39200, MEASURE THE VOLTAGE
BETWEEN GROUND AND TERMINAL "F12"
OF THE 32-WAY EBCM HARNESS
CONNECTOR WHILE APPLYING FIRM
PRESSURE ON BRAKE PEDAL.
IS VOLTAGE 10 VOLTS OR GREATER?

NO → REPAIR SHORTED OR OPEN CKT 820.

YES

④ • INSPECT 32-WAY EBCM
HARNESS CONNECTOR
TERMINAL "F12" FOR POOR
TERMINAL CONTACT AND
EVIDENCE OF CORROSION.
REFER TO SECTION 8A-4,
"CHECKING TERMINAL
CONTACT." REPLACE ALL
TERMINALS THAT EXHIBIT
SIGNS OF TERMINAL
CONTACT OR CORROSION.
• RECONNECT ALL
CONNECTORS.
• DRIVE VEHICLE AND
PERFORM A MODERATELY
HARD ABS STOP.
IS DTC 91 OR 92 SET AS A
CURRENT DTC?

YES → REPLACE EBCM.

NO → MALFUNCTION IS MOST LIKELY DUE TO A POOR CONNECTION. REFER TO "DIAGNOSTIC AIDS" ON FACING PAGE.

⑤ • USING J 39200, MEASURE THE VOLTAGE BETWEEN
GROUND AND TERMINAL "B" OF THE BRAKE SWITCH.
IS VOLTAGE 10 VOLTS OR GREATER?

NO → REPAIR OPEN OR SHORTED CKT 140 AND REPLACE 20 AMP STOP HAZZARD FUSE.

YES

⑥ • MEASURE THE VOLTAGE BETWEEN
GROUND AND TERMINAL "A" OF
THE BRAKE SWITCH WHILE
APPLYING FIRM PRESSURE ON
BRAKE PEDAL.
IS VOLTAGE 10 VOLTS OR GREATER?

YES → REPAIR OPEN CKT 820.

NO → MISADJUSTED OR FAULTY BRAKE SWITCH. ADJUST OR REPLACE SWITCH AS NECESSARY.

86819227

ABS TROUBLESHOOTING

DTC 88
RED "BRAKE" WARNING LAMP CKT SHORTED TO BATT

① • IGNITION "ON."
• OBSERVE RED "BRAKE" WARNING LAMP.
IS LAMP "OFF"?

YES

② • USING TECH 1 MISC. TESTS, SELECT LAMP TEST
FUNCTION, COMMAND RED "BRAKE" LAMP ON.
IS LAMP ILLUMINATED?

YES

③ • IGNITION "OFF."
• REMOVE 10 AMP GAGES FUSE.
• DISCONNECT 32-WAY EBCM
CONNECTOR.
• IGNITION "ON."
• USING J 39200, MEASURE THE
VOLTAGE BETWEEN GROUND AND
TERMINAL "F4" OF THE 32-WAY
EBCM HARNESS CONNECTOR.
IS VOLTAGE 1 VOLT OR LESS?

NO → REPAIR SHORT TO VOLTAGE IN CKT 33.

YES → MALFUNCTION IS NOT PRESENT AT THIS TIME. REFER TO "DIAGNOSTIC AIDS" ON FACING PAGE.

NO (from ②) → CHECK FOR LOW FLUID LEVEL OR PARKING BRAKE SWITCH CLOSED AND CORRECT AS NECESSARY.

NO (from ①)

⑤ IS DTC 86 ALSO SET?

YES → PROCEED TO DTC 86 DIAGNOSTIC CHART.

④ • IGNITION "OFF."
• INSPECT CKT 33 AND 32-WAY EBCM HARNESS
CONNECTOR FOR DAMAGE WHICH MAY RESULT
IN A SHORT TO VOLTAGE WITH ALL CONNECTORS
CONNECTED. REPAIR DAMAGE IF EVIDENT.
• RECONNECT ALL CONNECTORS.
• IGNITION "ON."
• DOES DTC 88 SET AS A CURRENT DTC?

YES → REPLACE EBCM.

NO → MALFUNCTION IS MOST LIKELY DUE TO A POOR CONNECTION. REFER TO "DIAGNOSTIC AIDS" ON FACING PAGE.

86819226

ABS TROUBLESHOOTING

ABS TROUBLESHOOTING

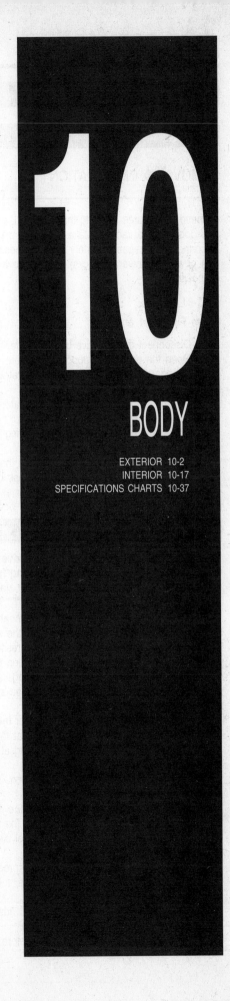

10

BODY

EXTERIOR

Doors

REMOVAL & INSTALLATION

These procedures apply to the front and, where applicable, rear doors of the vehicle. Make sure before you begin that you disconnect the negative battery cable (especially on vehicles with power windows and locks). The window should be in the up position.

1982-91 Models

▶ **See Figures 1 and 2**

1. Disconnect the negative battery cable.
2. Open the door and support it securely.
3. On doors equipped with power operated components, proceed as follows.

   a. Remove the door trim panel, insulator pad (if so equipped) and inner panel water deflector.

   b. Matchmark and disconnect the wiring harness from all components in door.

   c. Remove rubber conduit from door, then remove wire harness from door through conduit access hole.

4. Tape the area around the door pillar and body pillar (below the upper hinge) with cloth backed body tape.

✷✷CAUTION

Before performing the following step, cover the door spring with a towel to prevent the spring from flying out and possibly causing personal injury or damaging the car.

5. Insert a long flat-bladed lever underneath the pivot point of the hold-open link and over the top of the spring. The lever should be positioned so as not to apply pressure to the hold-open link. Cover spring with shop cloth, then lift the screwdriver to disengage spring. The spring can also be removed using tool No. J-28625, door hinge spring compressor tool, or equivalent. Proceed as follows:

   a. Install the two jaws of the tool over the spring. Put the jaw with the slot slides over the spring at the hold-open link. The jaw with the hole fits over the spring at the bubble on the door hinge pillar.

   b. Install the bolt to the jaws of the tool and tighten to compress the spring.

   c. Remove the tool and spring from the door hinge assembly. Do not remove the spring from the tool.

6. If replacement of the hinge pin barrel clips are not available, save the clips as follows:

   a. Using two small flat-bladed tools, spread each clip just enough to move the clip over the recess, then towards the pointed end of the pin.

   b. As the pin is removed, the clip will ride the shank of the pin and fall free.

   c. Reinstall the clips onto the pins before installing the door.

Fig. 1 Door hinge spring compressor tool J-28625 prior to installation on 1982-91 models

Fig. 2 Install the two jaws of tool J-28625 over the spring. Put the jaw with the slot slides over the spring at the hold-open link. The jaw with the hole fits over the spring at the bubble on the door hinge pillar

7. With the aid of an assistant, to support the door, remove the lower hinge pin using a soft headed hammer and locking type pliers. Your assistant can aid in the removal of the hinge pins by raising, then lowering the rear of the door.

8. Insert a 1¼ in. x 1½ in. bolt into the upper hole of the lower hinge to maintain the door attachment during the upper hinge pin removal.

9. Remove the upper hinge pin in the same manner as the lower. Remove the screw from the lower hinge, then remove the door from the body.

➡**Before installing the door, replace the hinge pin clips or reuse old clips as explained in the removal procedure.**

To install:

10. With the aid of an assistant, position the door, then insert a small bolt into the upper hole of the lower hinge.

11. The upper hinge pin is installed with the pointed end up. The lower hinge pin is installed with the pointed end down. With the door in the full open position, install the upper hinge pin using locking type pliers and a soft-headed hammer. Use a drift punch and hammer to complete the installation.

12. Remove the screw from the lower hinge and install the lower hinge pin. Use of tool No. J-28625, or use an equivalent for installing the hinge spring.

➡**If the spring is installed before installing the upper hinge pin, the hinge bushings may be damaged.**

13. If the spring was removed using a flat-bladed lever, then install as follows:
    a. Place the spring in tool No. J-28625, or an equivalent.
    b. Place the tool and spring in a bench vise.
    c. Compress the tool in vise, then install the bolt until the spring is fully compressed.
    d. Remove the tool (with compressed spring) from the vise, then install in the proper position in the door upper hinge. The slot in one jaw of the tool fits over the hold-open link. The hole on the other jaw fits over the bubble on the hinge.
    e. Remove the bolt from the tool to install the spring.
    f. Remove the tool from the door hinge (the tool will fall out in three pieces). Open and close the door to check for the proper operation of the spring.

➡**If tool No. J-28625 or equivalent was used to remove the spring, follow Steps d, e and f to install the spring.**

14. Remove the tape from the door and body pillars.

15. On doors with power operated components, install the wire harness to the door through the conduit access hole, then install the rubber conduit to the door.

16. Connect the wiring harness to each component in the door.

17. Install the inner panel water deflector.

18. Install the insulator pad and the door trim panel.

19. Connect the negative battery cable.

20. Reset the clock, radio and any other accessories if required.

1992-95 Models

▶ **See Figure 3**

1. Disconnect the negative battery cable.
2. Open the door and support it securely.
3. On doors equipped with power operated components, proceed as follows.
    a. Remove the door trim panel, insulator pad (if so equipped) and inner panel water deflector.
    b. Matchmark and disconnect the wiring harness from all components in door.
    c. Remove rubber conduit from door, then remove wire harness from door through conduit access hole.
4. Tape the area around the door pillar and body pillar (below the upper hinge) with cloth backed body tape.

✳✳CAUTION

Before performing the following step, cover the door spring with a towel to prevent the spring from flying out and possibly causing personal injury or damaging the car.

5. Insert a long flat-bladed lever underneath the pivot point of the hold-open link and over the top of the spring. The lever should be positioned so as not to apply pressure to the hold-open link. Cover spring with shop cloth, then lift the screwdriver to disengage spring. The spring can also be removed using tool No. J-36604, door hinge spring compressor tool, or equivalent.

6. If replacement of the hinge pin barrel clips are not available, save the clips as follows:
    a. Using two small flat-bladed tools, spread each clip just enough to move the clip over the recess, then towards the pointed end of the pin.
    b. As the pin is removed, the clip will ride the shank of the pin and fall free.
    c. Reinstall the clips onto the pins before installing the door.

7. With the aid of an assistant, to support the door, remove the lower hinge pin using a soft headed hammer and locking type pliers. Your assistant can aid in the removal of the hinge pins by raising, then lowering the rear of the door.

8. Insert a 1¼ in. x 1½ in. bolt into the upper hole of the lower hinge to maintain the door attachment during the upper hinge pin removal.

9. Remove the upper hinge pin in the same manner as the lower. Remove the screw from the lower hinge, then remove the door from the body.

➡**Before installing the door, replace the hinge pin clips or reuse old clips as explained in the removal procedure.**

To install:

10. With the aid of an assistant, position the door, then insert a small bolt into the upper hole of the lower hinge.

11. The upper hinge pin is installed with the pointed end up. The lower hinge pin is installed with the pointed end down. With the door in the full open position, install the upper hinge pin using locking type pliers and a soft-headed hammer. Use a drift punch and hammer to complete the installation.

12. Remove the screw from the lower hinge and install the lower hinge pin. Use of tool No. J-36604 or equivalent is the recommended method for installing the hinge spring.

13. Remove the tape from the door and body pillars.

86810102

Fig. 3 On 1992-95 models, use tool No. J-36604 or equivalent to remove the spring

14. On doors with power operated components, install the wire harness to the door through the conduit access hole, then install the rubber conduit to the door.

15. Connect the wiring harness to each component in the door.

16. Install the inner panel water deflector.

17. Install the insulator pad and the door trim panel.

18. Connect the negative battery cable, then reset the clock, radio and any other accessories if required.

STRIKER ADJUSTMENT

▶ See Figure 4

1. Make sure the door is aligned properly. Apply modeling clay or body calking compound to the lock bolt opening.

2. Close the door only enough so the striker bolt can form an impression into the clay/compound.

3. The impression should be centered fore and aft. The minimum allowance measurement for dimension is $\frac{3}{32}$ in. (2mm), the maximum allowance is $\frac{5}{32}$ in. (4mm). A spacer can be used to achieve the correct allowance, $\frac{3}{32}$ in. (2mm) or equivalent.

4. When adjustment is necessary, insert tool No. J-29843-9 or equivalent, into the star-shaped recess in the head of the striker retaining bolt and loosen. Repeat for the other striker bolts.

5. Shift the striker as required, then tighten the bolts to 34-46 ft. lbs. (46-62 Nm) for models through 1991, or 39 ft. lbs. (53 Nm) for 1992-95 models.

Hood

REMOVAL & INSTALLATION

▶ See Figures 5 and 6

1. Raise the hood. Install protective coverings over the fenders, to prevent damage to the paint and moldings.

2. Disconnect the underhood lamp wire.

3. Matchmark the position of the hinge on the hood to aid in alignment when hood is reinstalled.

4. With the hood supported, remove the hinge-to-hood screws on each side of the hood.

5. Remove the hood.

To install:

6. Align the hood with the marks made during removal.

7. Install the hood-to-hinge screws on each side of the hood, then tighten to 20 ft. lbs. (27 Nm).

8. Connect the underhood lamp wire.

9. Close the hood, then inspect for proper alignment. If not aligned properly, open the hood and repeat the previous tightening sequence.

Fig. 4 In order to loosen the striker, insert a specialized driver into the star-shaped recesses of the three striker bolts

Fig. 5 Matchmark the position of the hinge on the hood to aid in alignment when the hood is reinstalled

1. Pin
2. Nut
3. Washer
4. Bolt
5. Hinge bracket
6. Hinge strap

INBOARD

Fig. 6 Install the hood-to-hinge screws on each side of the hood, then tighten to 20 ft. lbs. (27 Nm)

ALIGNMENT

▶ **See Figure 7**

Fore and aft adjustment can be made at the hinge-to-hood attaching screws. Vertical adjustment at the front can be made by adjusting the rubber bumpers up or down.

Trunk Lid

REMOVAL & INSTALLATION

▶ **See Figure 8**

1. Prop the lid open, then place a protective covering along the edges of the rear compartment opening, this will prevent damage to the painted areas.
2. Where necessary, disconnect the wiring harness from the lid.
3. Matchmark the location of the hinge strap attaching bolts to lid.
4. While a helper supports the lid, remove the hinge to lid bolts and remove the lid.

To install:

5. Before installing the trunk lid, inspect the weatherstrip for any deterioration, replace if necessary.
6. With an assistant, replace the lid into position. Install the bolts for mounting.
7. Tighten the hinge-to-lid attaching bolts 18-20 ft. lbs. (25-27 Nm).
8. Replace the wire harness, remove the prop, close the lid.
9. Inspect the lid for proper alignment. If not, open the lid, then loosen the bolts and tighten, repeat until the lid is aligned.

1. Weatherstrip
2. Plug

VIEW A

86810111

Fig. 8 If replacement is necessary, lift off the old weatherstrip. Place the new strip into the rail, then seat it in place by applying pressure for a moulded fit. Apply sealer when necessary

ADJUSTMENT

Fore and aft adjustment of the lid assembly is controlled by the hinge-to-lid attaching bolts. To adjust the lid, loosen the hinge-to-lid attaching bolts and shift the lid to the desired position; then tighten the bolts to 20 ft. lbs. (27 Nm).

Liftgate/Hatch

REMOVAL & INSTALLATION

▶ **See Figures 9 and 10**

✳✳CAUTION

Do not attempt to remove or loosen the gas supports with the liftgate in any position other than fully open. This could cause personal injury.

HOOD LATCH BOLT ASM

54.0mm
(1¹⁄₈ INCH)

VIEW A

HOOD INR

30.0mm
1¹¹⁄₆₄ INCH

22.0mm
(⅞ INCH)

BUMPER ASM

HOOD BUMPER

VIEW C

RAD SUPT.   VIEW B

86810107

Fig. 7 Vertical adjustment at the front may be made by adjusting the rubber bumpers up or down

1. Open and support the liftgate in the full open position.
2. Remove the lid and body side retaining clips from the ends of the gas support assemblies.

3. Disengage the attachment at each end of the gas supports, then remove them from the body.
4. On styles with heated glass or rear wiper-washer system, disconnect the wiring harness and hose from the washer assembly. Remove the washer nozzle if needed.
5. Remove the clip tabs and the drive pin which go through the hinge. Using a $5/32$ in. (4mm) diameter rod, place the end of the rod against the pointed end of the hinge pin, then strike rod firmly to shear retaining clip tabs and drive pin through hinge. Repeat this operation on the opposite side hinge, then with the aid of a helper, remove the liftgate from the body.

To install:
6. Before installing the liftgate/hatch, inspect the weatherstrip for any deterioration, replace if necessary.

1 GAS SUPPORT
2 RETAINING CLIP
3 STUD
4 LIFT GATE

86810109

Fig. 9 Gas supports must be removed before removing the liftgate. Have a helper hold the liftgate in the up position while you remove the gas supports

1. Pinchweld Flange
2. Weatherstrip
3. Adhesive

Section A-A

86810110

Fig. 10 The liftgate/hatch weatherstrip needs to be inspected for any deterioration; replace if necessary

7. Prior to installing hinge pins, install new retaining clips in notches provided in hinge pins. Position retaining clips so that tabs point toward head of pin.
8. Reinstall the pins to the hinge.
9. Install the wire harness, hose, and nozzle for models with heated glass and rear wiper assemblies.
10. Replace the gas shock assemblies, insert the retaining clips. Install the connectors to the gas support (pivot glass only).
11. Close the liftgate or pivot glass.

Bumpers

REMOVAL & INSTALLATION

Front

1982-91 MODELS

1. Remove the usually 4 retaining screws in each of the head light bezels and remove the bezels.
2. Raise the car and support it securely.
3. Remove the usually 6 push-on retainers from the bottom of the bumper and remove the 6 screws holding the retainer to each fender.
4. Remove the usually 4 push-on retainers from the outer molding and partially remove the outer molding from the fenders.
5. Remove the usually 2 sheet metal screws from the center bumper retainer, then remove the front bumper.
6. Remove the usually 8 retaining screws and bolts from the impact bar and remove the impact bar from its reinforcements.
7. To install, reverse the procedure above.

1992-93 MODELS

1. Disconnect the negative battery cable.
2. Remove the front headlights and side marker lamps.
3. Remove the grille. Partially disengage each end of the rubber strip on the bumper fascia.
4. Raise the vehicle and support it safely.
5. Remove the push-on retainers from the front fascia, then the screws from the bottom side of the fascia-to-fender and valance panel.
6. Remove the nut from the fascia stud-to-fender. Remove the push-on retainers from the retainers fascia-to-fender.
7. Remove the fascia from the vehicle, then remove the nuts holding the bar to the absorber, then remove the bar.
8. The reinforcements and parking lamp housings need to be removed from the bar.
9. If the absorber is to be replaced, remove the bolts and nuts from the front of the unit and the bolt attaching the rear bracket to the frame.

To install:
10. Install the absorber to the car, if removed. Install the reinforcements and parking lamp housings to the bar.
11. Connect the impact bar and the nuts holding the bar to the absorber.
12. Tighten the bar nuts to 20 ft. lbs. (27 Nm).
13. Install the front fascia to the car aligning the fascia studs-to-fender.

14. Secure the retainers for the fascia-to-fender. Push on the retainers to the retainer.

15. Secure the nuts to the fascia studs.

16. Connect the push-on retainers to the fascia. Install the rubber strip, then insert the screws to the bottom side of the fascia and fender.

17. Tighten the fascia nuts to 53 inch lbs. (6 Nm), and fascia screws to 18 inch lbs. (2 Nm).

18. Lower the car, then connect the negative battery cable.

19. Reset the clock, radio and any other accessories if required.

1994-95 SEDAN — BUICK

▶ See Figure 11

1. Raise and support the vehicle.

2. Remove the nuts to the fascia-to-fender.

3. Unfasten the absorber-to-impact bar nuts.

4. Remove the impact bar as an assembly.

5. Remove the bumper guards, then unfasten the fascia-to-impact bar screws.

6. Loosen and remove the air inlet seals.

7. Unfasten the license plate bracket, if equipped.

8. Unlock the push-on retainers on the top and bottom that secure the fascia-to-bumper.

9. Remove the fascia from the impact bar.

To install:

10. Install the rubber strip if removed, then position the fascia on the impact bar.

11. Install the push-on retainers attaching the fascia-to-impact bar.

12. Install the air inlet seals.

13. Reinstall the license plate bracket, if removed.

14. Install the fascia-to-impact bar screws.

15. Reinstall the bumper guards.

16. Lower the vehicle.

1994-95 SEDAN — OLDSMOBILE

▶ See Figure 12

1. Raise the vehicle and support it safely.

2. Remove the push-on retainers from the front fascia, then the screws from the bottom side of the fascia-to-fender and valance panel.

3. Remove the nut from the fascia stud-to-fender. Remove the push-on retainers from the retainers fascia-to-fender.

4. Remove the fascia from the vehicle, then remove the nuts holding the bar to the absorber, then remove the bar.

5. The reinforcements and parking lamp housings need to be removed from the bar.

6. If the absorber is to be replaced, remove the bolts and nuts from the front of the unit and the bolt attaching the rear bracket to the frame.

To install:

7. Install the absorber to the car, if removed. Install the reinforcements and parking lamp housings to the bar.

8. Connect the impact bar and the nuts holding the bar to the absorber.

9. Tighten the bar nuts to 20 ft. lbs. (27 Nm).

10. Install the front fascia to the car aligning the fascia studs-to-fender.

11. Secure the retainers for the fascia-to-fender. Push on the retainers to the retainer.

12. Secure the nuts to the fascia studs.

13. Connect the push-on retainers to the fascia. Install the rubber strip, then insert the screws to the bottom side of the fascia and fender.

14. Tighten the fascia nuts to 53 inch lbs. (6 Nm), and fascia screws to 18 inch lbs. (2 Nm).

15. Lower the vehicle.

Rear

1982-91 MODELS

1. Raise and support the car to a suitable work height.

2. Remove the 2 push-on retainer clips from each end of the molding, then remove the molding.

3. Remove the 4 wing nuts and electrical connectors from each of the tail lamp assemblies and remove the left and right tail lamp assemblies.

4. Remove the 5 wing nuts, detach the electrical connector and remove the back-up light assembly.

5. Open the trunk and remove the 2 retaining nuts from the left and right side reflectors, then remove the reflectors.

6. Remove the 7 retaining pins from the valance panel and remove the panel.

7. Disconnect the electrical connector and remove the 8 retaining nuts, 4 retaining bolts and 11 retaining pins from the rear bumper and remove the bumper.

8. Disconnect the electrical connector, and remove the 8 retaining nuts from the impact bar and energy absorber.

9. Remove the 8 retaining clips and remove the impact bar from the mounting support bracket.

10. To install, reverse to install.

11. Lower the vehicle.

1992-95 SEDAN — BUICK

▶ See Figure 13

1. Raise and support the vehicle.

2. Matchmark the nuts for assembly purposes.

3. Remove the nuts on each side that attach the facia-to-rear quarter panel.

4. Support the rear bumper.

5. Unfasten the nuts which attach the impact bar to the absorber, then remove the fascia /impact bar assembly.

6. Remove the licence plate bracket from the fascia.

7. Remove the push retainers securing the fascia-to-impact bar, remove the fascia.

8. Remove the fascia pad along with the attaching screws.

To install:

9. Install the fascia pad and the retaining screws, then tighten to 35 inch lbs. (4 Nm).

10. Reinstall the fascia-to-impact bar, insert the push-on retainers to the fascia.

11. Secure the licence plate bracket to the fascia.

12. Install the impact bar/fascia to the absorber. Secure the attaching nuts to the scribed locations, then tighten the nuts to 20 ft. lbs. (27 Nm).

13. Insert the bumper fascia retaining nuts, then tighten to 89 inch lbs. (10 Nm).

14. Lower the vehicle.

1	FASCIA, FRONT BUMPER
2	BAR, FRONT BUMPER IMPACT
3	RETAINER, FRONT BUMPER FASCIA
4	SUPPORT, FRONT BUMPER FASCIA
5	STRIP, FRONT BUMPER RUB
6	PLATE, FRONT BUMPER IMPACT BAR BACKING
7	ABSORBER, FRONT BUMPER ENERGY
8	NUT, FRONT BUMPER IMPACT BAR REINFORCEMENT PLATE
9	REINFORCEMENT, FRONT BUMPER ENERGY ABSORBER
10	NUT, FRONT BUMPER ENERGY ABSORBER
11	SHIM, FRONT BUMPER ENERGY ABSORBER
12	NUT, FENDER
13	FENDER ASSEMBLY, FRONT
14	GUARD, FRONT BUMPER
15	RETAINER, FRONT BUMPER FASCIA
16	SUPPORT, FRONT BUMPER FASCIA LOWER
18	BOLT/SCREW, FRONT BUMPER ENERGY ABSORBER BRACKET
19	NUT, FRONT BUMPER GUARD
20	BOLT/SCREW, FRONT BUMPER GUARD

86810115

Fig. 11 Exploded view of Buick sedan front bumper — 1994-95 models

1 FASCIA, FRONT BUMPER
2 EXTENSION, FRONT BUMPER FASCIA
3 STRIP, FRONT BUMPER RUB
4 BAR, FRONT BUMPER IMPACT
5 BOLT/SCREW, FRONT BUMPER IMPACT
6 SUPPORT, FRONT BUMPER FASCIA
7 ABSORBER, FRONT BUMPER ENERGY
8 BRACKET, FRONT BUMPER ENERGY ABSORBER
9 BOLT/SCREW, FRONT BUMPER FASCIA EXTENSION
10 NUT, FRONT BUMPER FASCIA EXTENSION
11 PLATE, FRONT BUMPER IMPACT BAR REINFORCEMENT STUD
12 RETAINER, FRONT BUMPER FASCIA
13 RETAINER, FRONT BUMPER FASCIA

14 BOLT/SCREW, FRONT BUMPER ENERGY ABSORBER
15 RETAINER, FRONT BUMPER FASCIA
16 NUT, PUSH-ON
17 NUT, FRONT BUMPER IMPACT BAR REINFORCEMENT STUD PLATE
18 SHIM, FRONT BUMPER ENERGY ABSORBER
19 BOLT/SCREW, FRONT BUMPER ENERGY ABSORBER BRACKET
20 NUT, FRONT BUMPER ENERGY ABSORBER
21 NUT, FRONT BUMPER FASCIA
22 NUT, SPRING
23 NUT, PUSH-ON
24 BOLT/SCREW, FRONT BUMPER FASCIA
25 BRACKET, FRONT LICENSE

86810116

Fig. 12 Oldsmobile sedan front bumpers fasten together slightly differently than those on Buick sedans — 1994-95 models

1 NUT, REAR ENERGY ABSORBER BRACKET
2 BRACKET, REAR BUMPER ENERGY ABSORBER
3 ABSORBER, REAR BUMPER ENERGY
4 SHIM, REAR BUMPER ENERGY ABSORBER
5 NUT, REAR BUMPER IMPACT BAR STUD PLATE
6 PLATE, BACKING
7 BOLT/SCREW, REAR BUMPER ENERGY ABSORBER
8 BOLT/SCREW, REAR BUMPER ENERGY ABSORBER BRACKET

9 FASICA, REAR BUMPER
10 STRIP, REAR BUMPER RUB
11 PAD, REAR BUMPER FASCIA
12 BAR, REAR BUMPER IMPACT
13 RETAINER, PUSH IN
14 NUT, REAR BUMPER FASCIA RETAINER
15 BOLT/SCREW, REAR BUMPER FASCIA PAD
16 RETAINER, REAR BUMPER FASCIA

86810117

Fig. 13 Exploded view of Buick sedan rear bumper — 1992-95 models

1992-95 SEDAN — OLDSMOBILE

▶ See Figure 14

1. Raise and support the vehicle.
2. Unfasten the nuts from the end of the moulding, then remove the moulding.
3. Remove the tail lamp, back-up and side marker lamp assemblies.
4. Remove the retainers from the fascia-to-impact bar. Unfasten the screws, from the lower fascia-to-fender.
5. Loosen and remove the nuts from each side of the fascia studs to the fender.
6. Remove the screws from the fascia-to-fender. Unfasten the nuts from the reinforcement. Remove the impact bar and absorber from the vehicle.
7. Remove the rivets from the absorber, then the stud plates and retainers on the impact bar.

To install:

➡When installing the rear fascia, spread the outer "ears" by hand to prevent the ear mounting studs from scraping the paint surface.

8. Reattach the stud plates and retainers to the impact bar.
9. Insert the absorber into the impact bar, then replace the rivets onto the absorber. Tighten the impact bar nuts to 21 ft. lbs. (29 Nm).
10. Install the fascia to the vehicle, then install the retainers to the fascia and impact bar.
11. Insert the screws to the fascia-to-fender. Install and tighten the nuts for the fender-to-fascia studs.
12. Secure the screws to the lower fascia and fender. Tighten the fascia screws and nuts to 89 inch lbs. (10 Nm).
13. Reinstall the back-up, side marker, and tail lamp assemblies.
14. Reattach the moulding to the fascia, tighten with the nuts.
15. Lower the vehicle.

1992-95 WAGON — BUICK

▶ See Figure 15

1. Raise and support the vehicle. Scribe the locations of the nuts before disassembling for reassembly.

1 CAP, REAR BUMPER IMPACT BAR STUD PLATE
2 NUT, REAR BUMPER IMPACT BAR STUD PLATE
3 WASHER, REAR BUMPER IMPACT BAR STUD PLATE (TO BODY)
4 WASHER, REAR BUMPER IMPACT BAR STUD PLATE
5 NUT, REAR BUMPER IMPACT BAR STUD PLATE
6 PLATE, REAR BUMPER IMPACT BAR BACKING
7 SHIM, REAR BUMPER IMPACT BAR
8 PLATE, REAR BUMPER IMPACT BAR STUD

9 BRACKET, REAR BUMPER IMPACT BAR
10 BAR, REAR BUMPER IMPACT
11 ABSORBER, REAR BUMPER FASCIA ENERGY
12 RETAINER, REAR BUMPER FASCIA
13 FASCIA, REAR BUMPER
14 MOLDING, REAR BUMPER FASCIA
15 BOLT/SCREW, REAR BUMPER FASCIA
16 NUT, REAR BUMPER FASCIA
17 RIVET, REAR BUMPER FASCIA ENERGY ABSORBER

86810118

Fig. 14 Exploded view of Oldsmobile sedan rear bumper — 1992-95 models

2. Remove the filler panel attaching nuts from each side of the vehicle, then remove the panel.

3. Disconnect the nuts that attach the impact bar and bumper guards to the absorber.

4. Remove the impact bar and bumper guards.

5. Remove the step pad, rubber strip and guards.

To install:

6. Install the step pad, rubber strip and guards onto the impact bar.

7. Reattach the impact bar-to-absorber, then insert and tighten the nuts on each side of the impact bar and bumper guards. Tighten the absorber nuts to 21 ft. lbs. (29 Nm), and the bumper guard nuts to 20 ft. lbs. (27 Nm).

8. Install the filler panels and nuts on each side, then tighten the nuts to 53 inch lbs. (6 Nm).

1992-95 WAGON — OLDSMOBILE

▶ See Figure 16

1. Disconnect the left side storage panel screw and remove the panel.

2. Remove the left side filler nuts.

3. Remove the spare tire panel and tire. Unfasten the filler panel to quarter panel nuts.

4. Raise the vehicle and support securely.

5. Remove the filler panel push-in retainers, along with the filler panel-to-quarter panel nuts.

6. Loosen and remove the nuts attaching the absorber to the impact bar, then remove the impact bar.

7. Remove the rubber strip and step pad.

To install:

8. Reinstall the rubber strip and step pad.

9. Install the nuts for the absorber-to-impact bar, then align the assembly and tighten the nuts to 20 ft. lbs. (27 Nm).

10. Attach the nuts on the filler panels-to-quarter panel, tighten them to 27 inch lbs. (3 Nm).

11. Insert the push-in retainers to the filler panel.

12. Lower the vehicle, then install the spare tire and tire panel.

13. Insert the nuts for the filler panel, tighten them to 54 inch lbs. (6 Nm).

1 STRIP, MOLDING, REAR BUMPER RUB
2 NUT, REAR BUMPER IMPACT BAR
3 PAD, REAR BUMPER STEP
4 STRIP, REAR BUMPER RUB
5 EXTENSION, REAR BUMPER IMPACT BAR
6 BOLT/SCREW, ENERGY ABSORBER TO BODY
7 BODY
8 SHIM, REAR BUMPER ENERGY ABSORBER
9 ABSORBER, REAR BUMPER ENERGY
10 BOLT/SCREW, REAR BUMPER ENERGY ABSORBER
11 NUT, REAR BUMPER IMPACT BAR
12 INSULATOR, REAR BUMPER IMPACT BAR
13 NUT, PUSH-IN

14 BAR, REAR BUMPER IMPACT
15 BOLT/SCREW, REAR BUMPER IMPACT BAR
16 GUARD, REAR BUMPER
17 NUT, REAR BUMPER GUARD
18 NUT, REAR BUMPER RUB STRIP
19 RETAINER, REAR BUMPER IMPACT BAR EXTENSION
20 NUT, BODY
21 STUD, REAR BUMPER IMPACT BAR EXTENSION
22 WASHER, REAR BUMPER IMPACT BAR EXTENSION
23 NUT, REAR BUMPER IMPACT BAR EXTENSION

86810119

Fig. 15 Exploded view of Buick wagon rear bumper — 1992-95 models

1. ABSORBER, REAR BUMPER ENERGY
2. BOLT/SCREW, REAR BUMPER ENERGY ABSORBER
3. INSULATOR, REAR BUMPER IMPACT BAR
4. PANEL, REAR END
5. FILLER, REAR BUMPER CENTER
6. PAD, REAR BUMPER STEP
7. BAR, REAR BUMPER IMPACT
8. STRIP, REAR BUMPER RUB
9. BOLT/SCREW, REAR BUMPER ENERGY ABSORBER
10. EXTENSION, REAR BUMPER IMPACT BAR
11. MOLDING, REAR BUMPER IMPACT BAR EXTENSION

12. NUT, REAR BUMPER RUB STRIP
13. NUT, REAR BUMPER IMPACT BAR EXTENSION
14. NUT, REAR BUMPER ENERGY ABSORBER
15. SHIM, REAR BUMPER ENERGY ABSORBER
16. NUT, IMPACT BAR RETAINER
17. RETAINER, REAR BUMPER IMPACT BAR EXTENSION
18. RETAINER, IMPACT BAR EXTENSION
19. STUD, REAR BUMPER IMPACT BAR EXTENSION
20. NUT, REAR BUMPER IMPACT BAR EXTENSION

86810120

Fig. 16 Exploded view of Oldsmobile wagon rear bumper — 1992-95 models

14. Install the left side storage panel screw, then tighten to 21 ft. lbs. (29 Nm).

Grille

REMOVAL & INSTALLATION

▶ See Figure 17

1. Remove the retaining screws from the grille assembly.
2. Remove the grille from the front end panel.

To install:

3. Position the grille in the front end panel, then install the retaining screws.

86810170

Fig. 17 After the retaining screws are removed, the grille can be pulled off. Be careful not to cut your hands, as the metal is sharp

Outside Mirrors

REMOVAL & INSTALLATION

Standard

▶ **See Figure 18**

1. Remove the door trim panel and detach the inner panel water deflector. With the glass in the down position, pull out the front portion of the glass run weatherstrip.

2. Remove the attaching bolts and screws from the front glass run channel lower retainer to filler, then rotate retainer rearward.

3. Remove the noise control patch to gain access to the screw at the belt, then remove the screw.

4. Remove the filler attaching screws at the top front of the window frame, then remove the mirror and filler from the door.

5. Remove the attaching nuts from the mirror base studs, then remove the mirror.

To install:

6. Be sure that the mirror gasket is aligned.

7. Replace the mirror and filler on the door. Install the filler attaching screws at the top front of the window frame. Attach the nuts to the mirror studs and tighten.

8. Install the screw at the belt, then insert the noise control patch.

9. Insert the retainer, then install the attaching bolts and screws to the front glass run channel lower retainer to filler.

10. Replace the front portion of the glass run weatherstrip, insert the inner panel water deflector, then reinstall the door trim panel.

Manual Remote

1. Remove the mirror remote control escutcheons and door trim panel. Detach the inner panel water deflector.

➡**Right side remote mirror may require detaching part of the instrument panel.**

1. Front run channel retainer
2. Filler
3. Mirror gasket
4. Mirror

86810121

Fig. 18 Unfasten the attaching nuts from the mirror base studs, then remove the mirror

2. With the glass in the down position, pull out the front portion of the glass run weatherstrip.

3. Remove the attaching bolts and screws from the front glass run channel lower retainer to filler and rotate retainer rearward.

4. Remove the noise control patch to gain access to the 0.3 in. (7mm) screw at the belt and remove the screw.

5. Remove the filler attaching screws at the top front of the window frame.

6. Remove the mirror base with mirror and cable assembly from the door.

7. Remove the mirror to filler attaching nuts and remove the mirror and cable from filler.

To install:

8. Be sure cable is routed around front glass run channel retainer and installed to clip.

9. Install and connect the cable to the filler.

10. Attach the filler nuts to the mirror, then tighten to 72 inch lbs. (8 Nm).

11. Install the mirror base with the mirror and cable assembly to the door.

12. Insert the filler attaching screws to the top of the window frame, then install the screw to the belt.

13. Secure the noise control patch.

14. Attach the bolts and screws to the front of the glass run channel lower retainer and filler.

15. Install the glass run weatherstrip.

16. Attach the inner panel water deflector, door trim panel and mirror remote control escutcheon.

Electric Remote

1. Disconnect the negative battery cable.

2. Remove the mirror remote control escutcheons and door trim panel. Detach the inner panel water deflector and the electrical connector for the mirror.

➡**Right side remote mirror may require detaching part of the instrument panel.**

3. With the glass in the down position, pull out the front portion of the glass run weatherstrip.

4. Remove the attaching bolts and screws from the front glass run channel lower retainer to filler and rotate retainer rearward.

5. Remove the noise control patch to gain access to the 0.3 in. (7mm) screw at the belt and remove the screw.

6. Remove the filler attaching screws at the top front of the window frame.

7. Remove the mirror base with mirror and electric connector from the door.

8. Remove the mirror to filler attaching nuts and remove the mirror and electric wire from filler.

9. To install, reverse Steps 1 through 6. Be sure electric wire is routed around front glass run channel retainer and installed to the clip. Tighten the nuts to 72 inch lbs. (8 Nm).

10. Connect the negative battery cable, then reset the clock, radio and any other accessories if required.

Antenna

REMOVAL & INSTALLATION

Manual

1. Working from underneath the dash, disconnect the antenna cable from the radio.
2. Unscrew the antenna from the fender, then remove it from the car, with the cable attached.
   To install:
3. Insert the new antenna cable lead into the fender wheel, then route the lead towards the radio. Attach the lead into the back of the radio.
4. Screw the antenna mast into the fender. Check operation.

Fixed
▶ **See Figure 19**

1. Remove the antenna mast from the base. Remove the trim piece from the antenna housing.
2. Disconnect the antenna housing mounting screws.
3. Loosen and remove the antenna lead-in cable, routing the cable out through the engine compartment.
4. Remove the antenna base assembly.
   To install:
5. Install the base assembly. Route the lead-in cable through the engine compartment towards the radio.
6. Secure the antenna housing with the mounting screws and tighten to 18 inch lbs. (2 Nm).
7. Install the trim for the antenna housing. Install the antenna onto the base.

Power

Because of the varied applications of power antennas, the following general power antenna removal and installation procedures are outlined. These removal steps can be altered as necessary.

FRONT MOUNTED TYPE

1. Disconnect the negative battery cable.
2. Remove the instrument panel sound absorber pad.
3. Disconnect the antenna lead-in and harness connector from the relay assembly.
4. Apply masking tape to the rear edge of the fender and door.
5. If required, remove the inner to outer fender retaining screws.
6. If required, raise the vehicle and support it safely; then remove the associated front wheel assembly.
7. Remove the lower rocker panel retaining screws, lower fender to body retaining bolt and remove the lower rocker panel, as required.
8. Remove the inner splash shield from the fender, as required.
9. Remove the upper antenna retaining nut, using an appropriately tool.
10. Remove the antenna to bracket retaining bolts, then remove the antenna.
    To install:
11. Fit the antenna into position, then loosely install the antenna gasket and upper nut.
12. Loosely install the antenna to bracket retaining bolts.
13. Tighten the upper antenna retaining nut, using the appropriately tool, then tighten the antenna to bracket retaining bolts.
14. Complete installation in the reverse order of the removal procedure.
15. Apply silicone grease to the harness connector before reconnecting.
16. Connect the negative battery cable.
17. Check the operation of the antenna mast. Reset the clock, radio and any other accessories if required.

REAR MOUNTED TYPE

1. Disconnect the negative battery cable.
2. From inside the trunk, remove the trim panel from either the right or left rear wheel area.
3. Remove the antenna mounting bracket retaining screws.

1	BEZEL
2	ANTENNA CABLE ASSEMBLY
3	2 N·m (18 LB. IN.)
4	INSULATOR
5	R.H. FENDER
6	GROMMET
7	ANTENNA MAST
8	1.7 N·m (15 LB. IN.)
9	ANTENNA CABLE
10	INSTRUMENT PANEL HARNESS
11	RADIO ASSEMBLY

VIEW A

86810125

Fig. 19 Fixed antenna routing through the fender well, into the back of the radio

4. Remove the upper antenna nut and bezel from the antenna, using an appropriately tool.

5. Remove the lead-in cable and wiring connector.

6. Remove the antenna assembly from the vehicle.

To install:

7. Fit the antenna to the vehicle, then connect the lead-in cable.

8. Install the nut and bezel to the antenna and mounting bracket retaining screws.

9. Apply silicone grease to the harness connector before reconnecting.

10. Install the trim panel and reconnect the negative battery cable.

11. Check the operation of the antenna mast. Reset the clock, if required.

Fenders

REMOVAL & INSTALLATION

▶ **See Figure 20**

1. Disconnect the negative battery cable.

2. It will be easier to service the fender with the hood removed.

3. Remove the wiper arms.

4. Remove the cowl vent panel to gain access to the upper fender-to-cowl bolts.

➡**An outer fender panel with plastic inner panel may be used. Care must be taken in handling the unsupported fender due to the lack of rigidity prior to installation.**

5. Disconnect the headlamp wire connector.

6. Disconnect the side marker lamp connector.

7. Remove the rocker panel molding, if used.

8. Remove the wheelhouse panel.

9. Remove the screws attaching the front end panel to the fender.

10. Unfasten the lower valance panel, if used on your vehicle.

11. With the fender removed carefully remove the molding and name plates.

To install:

➡**If the fender is not primed or undercoated as you desire it may be better to have this procedure done to the fender before installation.**

12. Transfer fender moldings and nameplates to new fender.

13. Install the fender assembly and tighten attaching bolts to 88 inch lbs. (10 Nm).

14. Install the lower valance if removed and tighten bolts to 18 inch lbs. (2 Nm).

15. Install the wheelhouse panel and the rocker panel if used.

16. Secure the headlamp and marker lamp wiring and connectors.

17. Reinstall the cowl vent panel and wiper arms.

18. Install the hood if removed and connect the battery cable.

19. Reset the clock and radio, along with any other accessories.

1. Fender assembly
2. Retainer
3. Bolt/Screw 13 inch lbs. (1.5 Nm)
4. Cap
5. Wheel housing panel

VIEW A

86810126

Fig. 20 Remove the wheelhouse panel by unfastening a few bolts and screws

INTERIOR

Instrument Panel And Pad

REMOVAL & INSTALLATION

You may want to place a rag over the steering column to help prevent scratches. With vehicles equipped with tilt steering, it will help to lower the steering wheel all the way, then unscrew the tilt wheel lever. There is additional information on instrument panel and switches in Section 6 covering electrical components.

Century

▶ See Figure 21

1982-92 MODELS

1. Disconnect the negative battery cable.
2. Disconnect the speedometer cable and pull it through the firewall.
3. Remove the left side hush panel retaining screws and nut.
4. Remove the right side hush panel retaining screws and nut.
5. Remove the shift indicator cable clip.
6. Remove the steering column trim plate.
7. Put the gear selector in **L**. Remove the retaining screws and gently pull out the instrument panel trim plate.
8. Disconnect the parking brake cable at the lever by pushing it forward and sliding it from its slot.
9. Unbolt and lower the steering column.
10. Remove the gauge cluster retaining screws. Pull the cluster out far enough to disconnect any wires. Remove the instrument cluster.
To install:
11. Install the gauge cluster, connect the electrical connectors and install the retaining screws.

12. Position the steering column and install the retaining bolts.
13. Connect the parking brake cable at the lever.
14. Put the gear selector in **L**. Install the instrument panel trim plate.
15. Install the steering column trim plate.
16. Install the shift indicator cable clip.
17. Install the right side hush panel retaining screws and nut.
18. Install the left side hush panel retaining screws and nut.
19. Pull the speedometer cable through the firewall and connect to the speedometer.
20. Connect the negative battery cable.

1993-95 MODELS

1. Disconnect the negative battery cable.
2. Remove the left and right side sound insulators. Lower the steering column.
3. Disconnect the parking brake release cable.
4. Disconnect the harness connectors at the junction block.
5. Remove the speaker connections, then remove the A/C vacuum harness and temperature door cable.
6. Disconnect the engine harness connectors, then the antenna cable.
7. Remove the side window defogger hoses. Remove the bolts and screws holding the bulkhead connector.
8. Remove the bulkhead connector from the instrument panel.
9. Disconnect the windshield wiper motor and the brake master cylinder connectors, then unfasten the hoodlamp connection.
10. Disconnect the harness at the cowl by pulling the sides of the black clip out while pulling up on the clip.
11. To remove the harness, feed it throughout the cowl.
12. Unfasten the defroster/speaker grille by lifting up and out. Remove the two nuts on both inner sides of the steering column opening.

86810130

Fig. 21 Instrument panel mounting is similar on most A body cars — Century shown

13. Unscrew the three screws at the bottom of the instrument panel, then remove the six screws at the defroster opening on top of the instrument panel.

14. Remove the instrument panel.

15. Reverse to install. Connect the negative battery cable, reset the clock and radio.

Celebrity

1. Disconnect the negative battery cable.
2. Remove instrument panel hush panel.
3. Remove vent control housing, as required.
4. On non-air conditioning vehicles, remove steering column trim cover screws and lower cover with vent cables attached. On air conditioning vehicles, remove trim cover attaching screws and remove cover.
5. Remove instrument cluster trim pad.
6. Remove ash tray, retainer and fuse block, disconnect wires as necessary.
7. Remove headlight switch knob and instrument panel trim plate. Disconnect electrical connectors of any accessory switches in trim plate.
8. Remove cluster assembly and disconnect speedometer cable, **PRNDL** and cluster electrical connectors.

To install:

9. Install cluster assembly and connect speedometer cable, **PRNDL** and cluster electrical connectors.
10. Install headlight switch knob and instrument panel trim plate. Connect electrical connectors of any accessory switches in trim plate.
11. Install ash tray, retainer and fuse block, connect electrical connectors.
12. Install instrument cluster trim pad.
13. On non-air conditioned vehicles, raise the cover with vent cables attached and install steering column trim cover screws. On air conditioned vehicles, install trim cover and attaching screws.
14. If removed, install vent control housing.
15. Install instrument panel hush panel.
16. Connect the negative battery cable.

Ciera and Cruiser

1982-92 MODELS

1. Disconnect the negative battery cable. Remove left instrument panel trim pad.
2. Remove instrument panel cluster trim cover.
3. Disconnect speedometer cable at transaxle or cruise control transducer, if equipped.
4. Remove steering column trim cover.
5. Disconnect shift indicator clip from steering column shift bowl.
6. Remove 4 screws attaching cluster assembly to instrument panel.
7. Pull assembly out far enough to reach behind cluster and disconnect speedometer cable.
8. Remove cluster assembly.

To install:

9. Install the cluster assembly.
10. Connect the speedometer cable.
11. Install the 4 screws attaching cluster assembly to instrument panel.

12. Connect shift indicator clip to steering column shift bowl.
13. Install the steering column trim cover.
14. Connect the speedometer cable at the transaxle or cruise control transducer, if equipped.
15. Install the instrument panel cluster trim cover.
16. Install the left instrument panel trim pad.
17. Connect the negative battery cable.

1993-95 MODELS

1. Disconnect the negative battery cable.
2. Remove the left and right sound insulators. Unfasten the accessary trim plate and remove the ash tray assembly.
3. Unfasten the connection to the lighter. Remove the instrument cluster trim plate and cluster assembly.
4. Remove the shift indicator clip from the steering column shift bowl, then remove the shift trim collar and trim plate, along with the lower steering column.
5. Remove the speaker grilles by unfastening the mounting screws.
6. Disconnect the ventilation system, pull the control assembly from the dash, then disconnect the wiring harness from the control assembly. Unfasten the temperature control cables.
7. Unfasten the steering column wiring harness from the steering column.
8. Remove the parking brake release handle.
9. Disconnect the side window defogger hoses from the heater outlet. Unfasten the bolts which attach the wiper motor to the cowl.
10. Disconnect the bulkhead connector at the cowl panel. Remove the lower instrument panel bolts.
11. Loosen, then remove the defroster grille by carefully prying the grille with a small prytool.
12. Remove the upper instrument panel screws.
13. Open the hood, then remove the clip in the engine compartment that holds the wiring harness to the cowl. Disconnect the wiring harness connectors in the engine compartment, then pull it through the cowl on the passengers side.
14. Tilt the instrument panel forwards, then remove the remaining electrical connections. Remove the instrument panel.
15. Reverse to install, then connect the negative battery cable. Reset the clock and radio along with any other accessories.

6000

1. Disconnect the negative battery cable, and remove the center and left side lower instrument panel trim plate.
2. Remove the screws holding the instrument cluster to the instrument panel carrier.
3. Remove the instrument cluster lens to gain access to the speedometer head and gauges.
4. Remove right side and left side hush panels, steering column trim cover and disconnect parking brake cable and vent cables, if equipped.
5. Remove steering column retaining bolts and drop steering column.
6. Disconnect temperature control cable, inner-to-outer air conditioning wire harness and inner-to-outer air conditioning vacuum harness, if equipped.
7. Disconnect chassis harness behind left lower instrument panel and ECM/PCM connectors behind glove box. Disconnect instrument panel harness at cowl.

8. Remove center instrument panel trim plate, radio, if equipped, and disconnect neutral switch and brake light switch.

9. Remove upper and lower instrument panel retaining screws, nuts and bolts.

10. Pull instrument panel assembly out far enough to disconnect ignition switch, headlight dimmer switch and turn signal switch. Disconnect all other accessory wiring and vacuum lines necessary to remove instrument panel assembly.

11. Remove instrument panel assembly with wiring harness.

To install:

12. Install instrument panel assembly with wiring harness.

13. Connect ignition switch, headlight dimmer switch and turn signal switch. Connect all other accessory wiring and vacuum lines.

14. Install upper and lower instrument panel retaining screws, nuts and bolts.

15. Connect neutral switch and brake light switch. Install the radio, if equipped, and install center instrument panel trim plate.

16. Connect chassis harness behind left lower instrument panel and ECM/PCM connectors behind glove box. Connect instrument panel harness at cowl.

17. Connect temperature control cable, inner-to-outer air conditioning wire harness and inner-to-outer air conditioning vacuum harness, if equipped.

18. Raise the steering column and install retaining bolts.

19. Install right side and left side hush panels, steering column trim cover and connect parking brake cable and vent cables, if equipped.

20. Install the instrument cluster lens.

21. Install the screws holding the instrument cluster to the instrument panel carrier.

22. Install the center and left side lower instrument panel trim plate.

23. Connect the negative battery cable, then reset the clock and radio.

Console

REMOVAL & INSTALLATION

▶ **See Figures 22 and 23**

1. Remove the shifter knob from the shifter by removing the retaining screw at the back of the knob.

2. Remove the screws at the sides and front of the console.

3. Open the console box and remove the retaining screw inside the box.

4. Remove the electrical connectors for the ashtray light (if supplied) and lighter.

5. Remove the ashtray at the rear of the console and remove the retaining screw behind the ashtray.

6. Remove the power seat control (if supplied).

7. Slide the upper console from it's position, then disconnect the courtesy light.

8. Remove the screws holding the lower console into place, then slide the console rearward slightly and remove.

1. CONSOLE BASE
2. COMPARTMENT DOOR
3. COMPARTMENT
4. CENTER COMPARTMENT
5. SHIFTER PLATE
6. TAPE STORAGE
7. ASHTRAY

86810188

Fig. 22 Exploded view of center console assembly

To install:

9. Install the lower console by attaching the mounting screws, tighten them to 54 inch lbs. (6 Nm).

10. Connect the electrical harness to the courtesy light.

11. Attach the upper console with the mounting screws in the front.

12. Connect the electrical harness to the ashtray light and lighter.

13. Insert the power seat control into the console, then attach the trim console plate.

14. On column shift, install the center compartment.

15. On console shift, attach the electrical harness to the shifter light, then attach the shifter trim plate.

16. Mount the two screws at the rear of the center compartment or the shifter trim plate.

17. Tighten the two screws belonging in the ashtray opening.

18. On vehicles with shift console, screw on the shifter knob, then install the snap ring holding the shift knob.

19. Install the ashtray, then install the armrest compartment.

1. CONSOLE BASE
2. TRANSMISSION SHIFTER ASSEMBLY
3. 6 N·m (4 LBS. FT.)
4. PAD ASM.
5. COMPARTMENT ASM.
6. FULLY DRIVEN, SEATED AND NOT STRIPPED

86810189

Fig. 23 Mounting points for the center console

Door Panels

REMOVAL & INSTALLATION

▶ See Figures 24, 25, 26, 27, 28, 29, 30, 31 and 32

1. Disconnect the negative battery cable.
2. Remove all door inside handles.

3. Remove door inside locking rod knob.
4. Remove screws inserted through door armrest and pull handle assembly into door inner panel or armrest hanger support bracket.
5. On styles with remote control mirror assemblies, remove the remote mirror escutcheons and disengage the end of the mirror control cable.
6. On styles with power window controls located in the door trim assembly, disconnect the wire harness at the switch assembly.
7. Remove the remote control handle escutcheons screws.

VIEW A

SPRING CLIP

VIEW A

86810131

Fig. 24 A retaining spring clip fastens the window handle to the spindle

TOOL J—9886

RETAINING SPRING DISENGAGED

PUSH TOOL IN DIRECTION OF ARROW

INSIDE HANDLE

86810132

Fig. 25 Use tool J-9886 or equivalent to disengage the retaining spring from the window handle

VIEW A

1	ARMREST	5	PLUG
2	SCREW	6	BEZEL
3	PLUG	7	DOOR TRIM PANEL
4	TABS		

86810135

Fig. 26 Remove the armrest by dislodging the screw plugs, then unfastening the screws that secure the armrest

1. ESCUTCHEON ASSEMBLY – OUTSIDE
   REMOTE MIRROR
2. NUTS

86810136

Fig. 27 If your vehicle is equipped with a remote mirror, remove the mirror assembly, then the escutcheons. Disconnect the cable from the mirror head

| 1 | ESCUTCHEON | 3 | WINDOW PLATE |
| 2 | CONNECTOR | 4 | DOOR LOCK PLATE |

VIEW A

86810137

Fig. 28 On power window models, simply lift the switch assembly out of the mounting area and disconnect the harness from the switch

8. On styles with integral armrests, remove the screws inserted through the pull cup into the armrest hanger support.

9. Remove screws and plastic retainers from the perimeter of the door trim pad using tool BT-7323A or equivalent and a screwdriver. To remove the door trim panel, push trim upward and outboard to disengage it from the door inner panel at the belt line.

10. On styles with courtesy lamps located in the lower area of the trim panel, disconnect the wiring harness at the lamp assembly.

To install:

➡ Before installing the door trim panel, check that all trim retainers are securely installed to the panel and are not damaged. Replace damaged retainers as required.

11. Connect electrical components where present.

12. To install the door trim panel, pull door inside handle inward; then position the trim panel to the inner panel, inserting door handle through hole in panel.

13. Position the trim panel to the door inner panel so trim retainers are aligned with the attaching holes in the panel and tap the retainers into the holes with a clean rubber mallet.

14. Install the armrest into the inner panel or armrest hanger support brackets. Assemble the locking rod knob, then all inner door handles.

15. Connect the negative battery cable, reset the clock and radio.

Headliner

REMOVAL & INSTALLATION

◆ See Figures 33, 34 and 35

1. Disconnect the negative battery cable.

2. Remove the dome lamp, courtesy lamp, coat hooks and sunvisors. On wagons remove the rear courtesy lamp.

3. Remove the quarter upper trim finishing panels using tool J-24595-C.

4. Remove the rear seat roof mounted shoulder belt retainers, as needed.

5. Remove the windshield pillar upper side roof rail and garnish moldings.

6. Remove the headlining hook and loop strips along the front and on the rear using tool J-2772-C.

7. Remove the push-in retainers. On wagons, remove the retainers from the rear of the headliner.

8. Remove the assembly through the right front door opening.

To install:

9. Care must be taken not to overflex the new liner when installing. Load the rear portion of the lining diagonally through the right front door opening.

10. Align the headlining with holes for the sunvisors and the interior lamps. Press into place, along the areas with hook and loop strips.

11. Install the retainers and the push-in retainers, to the rear of the headlining, on wagons.

12. Install the sunvisors and the interior lamps.

Fig. 29 Remove the screws holding the escutcheon over the door handle assembly

1	BEZEL (WITHOUT POWER WINDOW)
2	SCREW
3	BEZEL (WITH POWER WINDOW)
4	INSIDE HANDLE
5	LOCKING ROD
6	BULB
7	CONNECTORS
8	KNOB

Fig. 30 Slide the escutcheon (bezel) forward to clear the inside locking rod, then slide the escutcheon rearward to disengage its tabs on the front from the trim panel. This will give you access to the wiring harness

| 1 | TRIM PANEL |
| 2 | COURTESY LAMP |

Fig. 31 The courtesy lamp can be removed by prying out with a suitable tool, then disconnecting the wiring harness leading to the lamp

13. Install the windshield pillar upper and side roof rail garnish moldings.

14. Install the rear shoulder belt retainers, on the wagon, if needed.

15. Install the quarter trim finishing panels.

16. Install the coat hooks.

17. Make certain no wires for the lamps are pinched or installed incorrectly.

18. Connect the negative battery cable, then reset the clock and radio.

86810139

Fig. 32 Make sure to align the door trim panel with the holes in the door before applying pressure to secure

J 2772-C

86810140

Fig. 33 Use tool J-2772-C or equivalent to remove the headlining hook and loop strips along the front and rear

Ventilation Ducts and Hoses

REMOVAL & INSTALLATION

Oldsmobile

DEFROSTER/LEFT AND CENTER DUCT

1. Disconnect the negative battery cable.
2. Remove the left and right sound insulators. Unassemble the steering column collar and trim cover, along with the lower column collar.
3. Remove the upper and lower instrument panel bolts, then tilt the instrument panel forwards and unfasten the screws holding the duct.
4. Remove the duct.
   To install:
5. Attach the duct with the mounting screws, tighten to 18 inch lbs. (2 Nm).

1. Dome lamp cutout
2. Sunvisor
3. Headlining
4. Retaining strips

SECTION A   VIEW B

86810141

Fig. 34 Align the headlining with holes for the sunvisors and the interior lamps. Press into place, along the areas with hook and loop strips

35 AND 69 STYLE

37 STYLE

1. Molding
2. Retaining clip
3. Tab
4. Fastener

SECTION A

SECTION B

86810142

Fig. 35 The windshield pillar upper and side roof rail garnish moldings are secured with fasteners and retaining clips. Be careful not to damage any of the mouldings

6. Insert the instrument panel into position and mount with the upper and lower bolts.

7. Install the steering column, then insert the column trim cover and collar. Reinstall the sound insulators.

8. Connect the negative battery cable, then reset the clock and radio.

RIGHT OUTLET DUCT

1. Disconnect the negative battery cable.
2. Remove the instrument panel, then remove the (usually) four screws mounting the duct.
3. Remove the duct.

To install:

4. Insert the duct into position, attach with the four screws.
5. Install the instrument panel.
6. Connect the negative battery cable, then reset the clock and radio.

Buick

1. Disconnect the negative battery cable.
2. Remove the instrument panel assembly.

3. Unfasten the hoses to the side window defoggers.
4. Unfasten the main duct bolts, then remove the duct.
5. Unfasten the side window defogger duct bolts, then remove the duct.

To install:

6. Install the side window defogger ducts and secure with bolts.
7. Insert the main duct with the bolts from removal. Install the hoses.
8. Install the instrument panel.
9. Connect the negative battery cable, then reset the clock and radio.

Door Locks

REMOVAL & INSTALLATION

1. Raise door window. Disconnect the negative battery cable.

2. Remove door trim panel and inner panel water deflector.

3. Disengage the inside lock rod, the inside handle-to-lock rod, lock cylinder-to-lock rod and the power lock actuator rod (power locks only) from the lock assembly.

4. On some models, remove the screw holding the door ajar switch-to-lock, then disconnect the connector from the lock.

5. Remove the lock screws, then lower the lock to disengage the outside handle-to-lock rod. Remove the lock from the door.

To install:

6. Align the lock cylinder gasket.

➡**Black lock cylinders should be lubricated with a light oil, all others should use a multi-purpouse grease.**

7. First install the spring clips to the lock assembly, then install the lock into the door.

8. Install the lock screws, lower lock-to-outside handle, and the lock rod. Tighten the screws to 62 inch lbs. (7 Nm).

9. Install the following rods at the lock assembly, check the rod clips for any weak points or breakage, replace if needed:

    a. The power lock actuator rod, for power locks only.

    b. The lock cylinder to the lock rod.

    c. The handle to the lock rod.

    d. Install the inside locking rod.

10. Attach the water deflector. Connect the negative battery cable, reset the clock and radio.

Tailgate Lock

REMOVAL & INSTALLATION

1. Remove the liftgate inner trim panel.

2. Using a flat bladed tool, remove the lock cylinder retainer.

3. On power locks, remove the screws and clip from the actuator.

4. Pull the lock cylinder out, unfasten the lock rods from the cylinder.

To install:

5. Attach the actuator to the lock cylinder with the screws and clip.

6. Lubricate the lock cylinder, then insert into mounting hole. Attach the rods to the cylinder.

7. Install the liftgate inner trim panel.

Power Door Lock Actuator

REMOVAL & INSTALLATION

1. Raise the window. Disconnect the negative battery cable.

2. Remove the door trim panel and water deflector.

3. Locate the rivets holding the actuator. Drive out the rivets center pins, then drill out the rivets using a ¼ in. (6mm) drill bit.

➡**Some vehicle's door lock actuator are retained with 16 in. rivets and will require the use of a 16 in. drill bit.**

4. Remove the actuator from the lock rod.

5. Disconnect the actuator electrical connector and remove the actuator from the door.

To install:

6. Fit the actuator through the door access hole and install the actuator to the lock rod.

7. Fastened the actuator to the inner panel using ¼ x ½ in. aluminum peel type rivets. If rivets are not available, install U-clips on the regulator at the metal retainer locations. Be certain to install the clips with the clinch nuts on the outboard side of the retainers.

8. Reconnect the electrical connector to the actuator.

9. Install the door trim panel and water deflector, as required.

10. Reconnect the negative battery cable, then reset the clock and radio.

Tailgate Lock Actuator

REMOVAL & INSTALLATION

▶ **See Figure 36**

1. Disconnect the negative battery cable.

2. Open the tailgate, then position the glass fully upwards.

3. Remove the tailgate handle, inner trim panel and water deflector.

4. Remove the right side access hole cover, then disconnect the actuator electrical connector.

5. Locate the rivets holding the actuator. Drive out the rivets center pins, then drill out the rivets using a ¼ in. (6mm) drill bit.

6. Remove the actuator and rod from the upper lock lever.

To install:

7. Install the actuator assembly, then reconnect the upper lock lever.

8. Secure the actuator using ¼ — 20 x 16 in. screws and nuts.

9. Reconnect the electrical connector, then install the access hole cover.

10. Install the water deflector, inner trim panel and tailgate handle.

11. Reconnect the negative battery cable, reset the radio and clock.

Door Glass and Regulator

REMOVAL & INSTALLATION

✳✳CAUTION

When working on vehicle glass, always wear eye protection and gloves to reduce the risk of injury.

Door Glass (Coupe)

1. Remove the door trim panel and inner panel water deflector.

1. Lift gate glass lock assembly
2. Nut
3. Bolt 44 inch lbs. (5 Nm)
4. Lift gate lock assembly
5. Lift gate
6. Clip
7. Actuator assembly
8. Solenoid assembly
9. Solenoid connector
10. Harness

VIEW A

VIEW B

VIEW C

VIEW D

86810144

Fig. 36 After removing the inner trim panel, the actuator, lock cylinder and other nearby components are accessible

2. Raise the window to the full up position, then tape the glass to the door frame using cloth-backed tape.

3. Remove the bolts holding the lower sash channel to the regulator sash.

4. Remove the rubber down stop at the bottom of the door by pulling carefully.

5. Attach the regulator handle and run the regulator to the full down position. Remove the regulator sash by rotating 90° (one-quarter turn) and pulling outward.

6. While supporting the glass, remove the tape and lower the window to the full down position. Disengage the front edge of the glass from the glass run channel retainer. Slide the glass forward and tilt slightly to remove the guide from the retainer in the run channel.

7. Using care, raise the glass while tilting forward and remove glass inboard of the upper frame.

8. To install, reverse the steps. Use liquid soap solution on the rubber down stop before installing the trim parts, then check the window for proper operation and alignment.

Door Glass (Sedan and Wagon)
▶ **See Figures 37 and 38**

1. Remove the door trim panel and inner panel water deflector.

2. Raise the window to the full up position, then tape the glass to the door frame using cloth-backed tape.

3. Remove the bolts holding the lower sash channel to the regulator sash.

4. Attach the regulator handle and run the regulator to the full down position.

5. While supporting the glass, remove the tape, then lower the window to the half down position.

6. Wrap tape around the blade of tool J-245895B or equivalent. Insert a tool between the guide and the glass at the fastener and carefully pry apart.

7. Using care, raise the glass while tilting forward and remove glass inboard of the upper frame.

8. Remove the guide from the rear of the run channel weatherstrip metal retainer and discard of the guide.

To install:

9. Replace the guide on the glass by using heat on the guide with a hot air gun, or soak it in hot water for about one minute.

10. Install the guide to the glass by aligning to hole in glass, then carefully press the guide together at the fastener location.

11. Install the glass and lower it about halfway.

12. With one hand on bottom edge, rotate the glass rearward to snap the guide into the retainer.

13. Reinstall the regulator handle, then bolt the lower sash channel (on the window) to the regulator sash.

14. Install the water deflector.

Regulator

MANUAL
▶ **See Figures 39, 40 and 41**

1. Remove the door trim panel and inner panel water deflector.

2. Raise the window to the full up position, then tape the glass to the door frame using cloth-backed tape.

3. Remove the lower sash bolts.

4. Punch out the center pins of the regulator rivet. Drill out the rivets using a ¼ in. (6mm) drill bit.

5. Remove the regulator through the rear access hole.

To install:

6. Use a hand rivet tool J-29022 or equivalent and install the regulator to the inner panel using ¼ in. x ½ in. aluminum peel type rivets, part No. 9436175 or equivalent.

7. If a hand rivet tool is not available, install U-clips on the regulator at the three attaching locations. Be sure to install the clips with cinch nuts on the outboard side of retainers.

8. Slide the regulator through the rear access hole, then align the regulator attaching clips with the holes in the inner panel. Attach regulator metal retainers with ¼ in. — 20 x ½ in. (6mm — 20 x 13mm) screws. Attach the housing part of the regulator with a ¼ in. — 20 x ½ in. screws into ¼ in. (6mm — 20 x 13mm) nuts with integral washers. Tighten the bolts to 90-125 inch lbs. (10-13 Nm).

9. Install the lower sash bolts.

10. Remove the tape from the door glass and frame.

Fig. 37 Use tool J-24595-B or equivalent to remove the door trim pad and garnishes

Fig. 38 Install the guide to the glass by aligning it with the hole in the glass, then carefully pressing the guide together at the fastener location

1. Door belt reveal molding with integral sealing strip
2. Window glass run channel assembly
3. Window guide
4. Door glass
5. Outside handle
6. Lock cylinder
7. Lock cylinder gasket
8. Lock cylinder retainer
9. Rear inner panel belt sealing strip filler
10. Lower sash channel
11. Filler assembly
12. Front inner panel belt sealing strip filler
13. Lock remote control handle assembly
14. Regulator sash
15. Manual window regulator assembly
16. Over slam bumper
17. Lock assembly
18. Window regulator handle
19. Electrical conduit hole plug
20. Outside handle to lock rod
21. Inside locking to lock rod shoe guide
22. Inside locking to lock rod
23. Lock remote control to lock rod
24. Inside locking knob
25. Lock cylinder to lock rod
26. Electric lock actuator
27. Electric window regulator assembly
28. Glass run channel lower front retainer

86810150

Fig. 39 Exploded view of the front door window glass assembly. Except for the motor and related components, manual and electric windows use virtually the same parts

Fig. 40 Hand rivet tools such as GM tool J-29022 are the easiest way to install rivets

11. Install the inner panel water deflector and door trim panel.

ELECTRIC

♦ See Figures 39, 40 and 41

1. Remove the door trim panel and inner panel water deflector.

2. Raise the window to the full up position. Make sure to disconnect the negative battery cable before working with your electric window regulator.

3. Tape the glass to the door frame using cloth-backed tape.

4. Remove the lower sash bolts.

5. Punch out the center pins of the regulator rivet. Drill out the rivets using a ¼ in. (6mm) drill bit.

Fig. 41 Remove the lower sash bolts, then punch out the center pins of the regulator rivet and drill out the rivets

6. Remove the glass as stated previously, then move the regulator and motor assembly rearward, and remove the electric connector. Remove the regulator and motor assembly through the rear access hole.

To install:

7. Use a hand rivet tool J-29022 or equivalent and install the regulator to the inner panel using ¼ in. x ½ in. (6mm x 13mm) aluminum peel type rivets, part No. 9436175 or equivalent.

8. If hand rivet tool is not available, install U-clips on regulator at three attaching locations. Be sure to install clips with cinch nuts on outboard side of retainers.

9. Slide the regulator through the rear access hole and align the regulator attaching clips with the holes in the inner panel. Attach regulator metal retainers with ¼ in. — 20 x ½ in. (6mm — 20 x 13mm) screws. Attach housing part of regulator with ¼ in. — 20 x ½ in. (6mm — 20 x 13mm) screws into ¼ in. (6mm) nuts with integral washers. Tighten the bolts to 90-125 inch lbs. (10-13 Nm).

10. Install the lower sash bolts.

11. Remove the tape from the door glass and frame.

12. Install the inner panel water deflector and door trim panel.

13. Connect the negative battery cable.

Electric Window Motor

REMOVAL & INSTALLATION

1. Remove the door trim panel and inner panel water deflector.

2. Raise the window to the full up position and tape the glass to the door frame using cloth-backed tape.

3. Disconnect the negative battery cable.

4. Remove the lower sash bolts.

5. Punch out the center pins of the regulator rivet. Drill out rivets using ¼ in. (6mm) drill bit.

6. Move regulator and motor assembly rearward, then remove the electrical connector.

7. With the regulator in the door, drill out the regulator-to-motor rivets using a ⅙ in. (4mm) drill bit, then remove the motor.

To install:

8. Install and connect the window motor.

9. Use ³⁄₁₆ in. (5mm) rivets or ³⁄₁₆ in. (5mm) nuts and bolts to install the motor to the regulator.

10. Connect the electrical wiring, then install the regulator and door inner panel using a ¼ in. (6mm) rivets.

11. Install the lower sash bolts, tighten to 62 inch lbs. (7 Nm).

12. Install the water deflector and remove the tape from the window.

13. Connect the negative battery cable, reset the clock and radio.

Windshield

➡Bonded windshields require special tools and procedures to ensure the windshield will be removed without being broken. Also it may be very difficult to provide a quite windshield air seal or water tight seal. For this reason it is recommended you refer to a qualified technician.

✳✳CAUTION

If you work on any vehicle glass always wear eye protection and gloves, to reduce the risk of injury.

REMOVAL & INSTALLATION

When replacing the windshield, check for the reason it was damaged in the first place. The cause of the crack may be an obstruction or high spot around the flange. This could cause the replacement to crack, especially after temperature changes when the windshield needs to flex and can't.

When a windshield is broken, the glass may have already fallen or been removed from the weatherstripping. Other times, it is necessary to remove a cracked windshield that is still intact. In this case, it is a good idea to crisscross the glass with strips of tape before removing it; this will help hold the glass together and minimize the risk of injury.

If a crack extends to the edge of the glass, mark the point where the crack meets the weatherstrip. Later examine the window flange at this point for the possible cause of the windshield crack.

The higher temperature of the work area, the more pliable the weatherstrip will be. The more pliable the weatherstrip, the easier the windshield can be removed.

There are 2 methods of windshield removal, depending on the method of windshield replacement chosen. When using the short method of installation, it is important to cut the glass from the urethane adhesive as close to the glass as possible. This is due to the fact that the urethane adhesive will be used to provide a base for the replacement windshield. When using the extended method, all the urethane adhesive must be removed from the pinchweld flange so the process of cutting the window from the adhesive is less critical.

Removal

▶ See Figures 42 and 43

➡The following procedure requires the use of a urethane glass sealant remover (hot knife) tool J-24709-1 or equivalent, and/or tool J-24402-A or equivalent.

1. Place the protective covering around the area will the glass will be removed.
2. Remove the wiper arms, cowl vent grille, windshield supports, rear view mirror and the interior garnish moldings.

➡If equipped with the radio antenna embedded in the windshield, disconnect the electrical connector at the base of the windshield.

3. Remove the exterior reveal molding from the urethane adhesive by prying one end of the molding from the adhesive.

✳✳CAUTION

If you work on any vehicle glass always wear eye protection and gloves, to reduce the risk of injury.

4. Using the urethane glass sealant remover (hot knife) J-24709 and the glass sealant remover tool J-24402-A or equivalents, cut the windshield from the urethane adhesive. If the short method of replacement is to be used, keep the knife as close to the glass as possible in order to leave a base for the replacement glass.
5. With the help of an assistant, remove the glass.
6. If the original glass is to be reinstalled, place it on a protected bench or make a holding device. Remove any remaining adhesive with a razor blade. Any remaining traces of

Fig. 42 Remove the exterior reveal molding from the urethane adhesive by prying one end of the molding away from the adhesive

Fig. 43 Using the urethane glass sealant remover (hot knife) J-24709-1 and the glass sealant remover tool J-24402-A, or equivalents, cut the windshield from the urethane adhesive. If the short method of replacement is to be used, keep the knife as close to the glass as possible, in order to leave a base for the replacement glass

adhesive material can be removed with denatured alcohol or lacquer thinner.

→**DO NOT use any petroleum based solvents, this will prevent the adhesion of the new material. Don't allow solvents to contact the plastic or any non-glass areas to avoid discoloration.**

Inspection

Inspect the opening for installation of the new glass. If there is no reason why known why the windshield broke, look carefully around the edges for any imperfections, then inspect the flange for any imperfections.

Check the replacement glass for chips or cracks. Small chips can be grounded off, restoring a smooth edge to the glass and minimizing concentrations of pressure that may cause breakage. Don't remove any more than necessary, you must maintain the original shape of the glass and the proper clearance between the glass and the flange opening. If not, leakage could occur. What a mess!

Short Method Installation

♦ **See Figure 44**

1. Using masking tape, apply the tape across the windshield pillar-to-windshield opening, then cut the tape and remove the windshield.

2. Using an alcohol dampened cloth, clean the metal flange surrounding the windshield opening. Allow the alcohol to air dry.

3. Using a pinchweld primer, found in the installation service kits, apply to the pinchweld area. Don't let any of the primer touch the exposed paint, it will damage the finish. Allow the primer to dry.

4. Cut the tip of the adhesive cartridge.

5. Apply adhesive first in and around the spacer blocks. Apply a smooth continuous bead into the gap between the glass edge and the sheet metal. Use a flat tool to paddle the material into position as necessary. Be sure the adhesive contacts the entire edge of the glass and extends to fill the gap between the glass and the solidified urethane base.

6. With aid from a helper, position the glass on the filler strips against the 2 support spacers.

→**The vehicle must remain at room temperature for at least 6 hours. It cannot be driven during that time.**

7. Spray a mist of water onto the urethane. Water will assist in the curing process. A mist, don't hose it down. Then dry the area where the reveal molding will contact the body glass.

8. Install new reveal moldings. Remove the protective tape covering the butyl adhesive on the underside of the molding. Push the molding caps onto each end of one of the reveal moldings. Press the lip of the molding into the urethane adhesive while holding it against the edge of the windshield. Take care to seat the moldings in the corners. The lip must fully contact the adhesive and the gap must be entirely covered by the crown of the molding. Slide the molding caps onto the adjacent moldings. Use tape to hold the molding in position until the adhesive cures.

9. Install the wiper arms, cowling and interior garnish moldings.

Fig. 44 With aid from a helper, position the glass on the filler strips against the 2 support spacers. After the windshield is in place, the vehicle must remain at room temperature for at least 6 hours. It cannot be driven during that time

Extended Method Installation

♦ **See Figures 45 and 46**

1. Using GM Strip Filler No. 20146247 or equivalent, install the sealing strip onto the pinchweld flange. The joint of the molding should be located a the bottom center of the molding.

2. Using masking tape, apply the tape across the windshield pillar-to-windshield opening, then cut the tape and remove the windshield.

3. Using an alcohol dampened cloth, clean the metal flange surrounding the windshield opening. Allow the alcohol to air dry.

4. Apply pinchweld primer, found in the installation service kits, to the pinchweld area. Don't let any of the primer touch the exposed paint, as it will damage the finish

5. With aid from a helper, position the glass on the filler strips against the 2 support spacers.

6. Cut the tip of the adhesive cartridge ⅜ in. (10mm) from end of tip.

7. Apply adhesive first in and around the spacer blocks. Apply a smooth continuous bead into the gap between the glass edge and the sheet metal. Use a flat tool to paddle the material into position as necessary. Be sure the adhesive contacts the entire edge of the glass and extends to fill the gap between the glass and the solidified urethane base.

→**The vehicle must remain at room temperature for at least 6 hours. If cannot be driven during that time.**

8. Spray a mist of water onto the urethane. Water will assist in the curing process. A mist, don't hose it down. Then dry the area where the reveal molding will contact the body glass.

9. Install the reveal molding onto the windshield and remove the masking tape from the inner surface of the glass.

10. Press the lip of the molding into the urethane adhesive while holding it against the edge of the windshield. Take care to seat the molding in the corners. The lip must fully contact the adhesive adhesive and the gap must be entirely covered by the crown of the molding. Slide the molding caps onto the adjacent moldings. Use tape to hold the molding in position until the adhesive cures.

Fig. 45 Apply pinchweld primer, found in the installation service kits, to the pinchweld area. Don't let any of the primer touch the exposed paint, as it will damage the finish. Allow the primer to dry

Fig. 46 Apply a smooth, continuous bead of adhesive into the gap between the glass edge and the sheet metal, as well as around the perimeter of the glass

11. Install the wiper arms, cowling and interior garnish moldings.

Inside Rear View Mirror

REPLACEMENT

The inside rear view mirror is permanently attached to the windshield. Should replacement become necessary, refer to your local dealer or a qualified technician for service. However, if the mirror simply falls off (due to faulty adhesive), reinstallation is possible using special rear view mirror adhesive, which is available at many automotive parts stores. Be sure to thoroughly clean the windshield and mirror mounting surfaces, and carefully follow the product's instructions.

Seats

REMOVAL & INSTALLATION

Front
▶ **See Figures 47, 48 and 49**

1. Position the seat in the full forward position. If the car is equipped with six-way power seats, place the seat in the full forward and up position. When necessary to gain access to the adjuster-to-floor pan attaching nuts, remove the adjuster rear foot covers and or carpet retainers.

2. Remove the track covers where necessary, then remove the adjuster-to-floor pan rear attaching nuts. Position the seat in the full rearward position.

3. Remove the adjuster front foot covers, then remove the adjuster to floor pan front attaching nuts. Tilt the seat rearward and disconnect the feed wire connector.

1 SEAT ASSEMBLY, FRONT
2 SEAT ASSEMBLY, REAR

Fig. 47 Common front bucket seats and rear bench seat

1 COVER, FRONT SEAT INNER ADJUSTER REAR TRACK
2 BOLT/SCREW, FRONT SEAT INNER ADJUSTER REAR TRACK COVER
3 SILENCER, FRONT SEAT DRIVER ADJUSTER RETURN SPRING
4 SPRING, FRONT SEAT DRIVER RETURN SPRING
5 SPACER, FRONT SEAT DRIVER OUTER ADJUSTER
6 COVER, FRONT SEAT DRIVER OUTER ADJUSTER REAR TRACK
7 BOLT/SCREW, FRONT SEAT
8 ADJUSTER ASSEMBLY, FRONT SEAT DRIVER OUTER
9 COVER, FRONT SEAT DRIVER OUTER ADJUSTER FRONT TRACK COVER
10 BOLT/SCREW, FRONT SEAT DRIVER OUTER ADJUSTER FRONT TRACK COVER
11 WIRE, FRONT SEAT DRIVER ADJUSTER
12 COVER, FRONT SEAT DRIVER INNER ADJUSTER FRONT TRACK
13 ADJUSTER ASSEMBLY, FRONT SEAT DRIVER INNER
14 BOLT/SCREW, FRONT SEAT DRIVER INNER ADJUSTER FRONT TRACK COVER
15 ADJUSTER ASSEMBLY, FRONT SEAT PASSENGER INNER

16 COVER, FRONT SEAT PASSENGER INNER ADJUSTER FRONT TRACK
17 BOLT/SCREW, FRONT SEAT PASSENGER INNER ADJUSTER FRONT TRACK COVER
18 WIRE, FRONT SEAT PASSENGER ADJUSTER
19 COVER, FRONT SEAT PASSENGER OUTER ADJUSTER FRONT TRACK
20 BOLT/SCREW, FRONT SEAT PASSENGER OUTER ADJUSTER FRONT TRACK COVER
21 ADJUSTER ASSEMBLY, FRONT SEAT PASSENGER OUTER
22 SPRING, FRONT SEAT PASSENGER RETURN SPRING
23 SILENCER, FRONT SEAT PASSENGER ADJUSTER RETURN SPRING
24 SPACER, FRONT SEAT PASSENGER OUTER ADJUSTER
25 COVER, FRONT SEAT PASSENGER OUTER ADJUSTER REAR TRACK
26 BOLT/SCREW, FRONT SEAT PASSENGER OUTER ADJUSTER REAR TRACK COVER
27 COVER, FRONT SEAT PASSENGER INNER ADJUSTER REAR TRACK
28 BOLT/SCREW, FRONT SEAT PASSENGER INNER ADJUSTER REAR TRACK COVER
29 BOLT/SCREW, FRONT SEAT DRIVER OUTER ADJUSTER REAR TRACK COVER

86810158

Fig. 48 Exploded view of the mounting for a common manual seat assembly

1 MOTOR ASSEMBLY, FRONT SEAT
2 CABLE, FRONT SEAT VERTICAL ADJUSTER
3 COVER, FRONT SEAT OUTER ADJUSTER REAR TRACK
4 ADJUSTER ASSEMBLY, FRONT SEAT OUTER
5 COVER, FRONT SEAT INNER ADJUSTER REAR TRACK
6 BOLT/SCREW, FRONT SEAT
7 COVER, FRONT SEAT OUTER ADJUSTER UPPER TRACK
8 COVER, FRONT SEAT OUTER ADJUSTER LOWER TRACK

9 BOLT/SCREW, FRONT SEAT OUTER ADJUSTER LOWER TRACK COVER
10 COVER, FRONT SEAT OUTER ADJUSTER FRONT TRACK
11 ADJUSTER ASSEMBLY, FRONT SEAT INNER
12 COVER, FRONT SEAT INNER ADJUSTER FRONT TRACK
13 COVER, FRONT SEAT INNER ADJUSTER LOWER TRACK
14 COVER, FRONT SEAT INNER ADJUSTER UPPER TRACK

86810156

Fig. 49 Exploded view of the mounting for a common power seat assembly

4. Remove the seat assembly from the car.

To install:

5. Reinstall the seat into the car, then connect the wire connection.

6. Attach the seat with the adjuster-to-floor pan front nuts, then tighten the nuts to 18 ft. lbs. (24 Nm).

7. Position the seat in the full forward and up position, then attach the adjuster-to-floor pan rear nuts. Tighten the nuts to 18 ft. lbs. (24 Nm).

8. Reinstall the track covers, if removed.

9. Install the rear foot covers and the carpet retainers, if they were removed.

➡**Inspect both seat adjusters making sure they are parallel and in phase with each other. This is where one adjuster reaches its maximum horizontal or vertical travel in a given direction, before the other adjuster. In the event they are out of phase.**

10. Check the operation of the seat assembly for a full limit of travel.

Rear Stationary

▸ **See Figures 50 and 51**

1. Push the lower forward edge of the seat cushion rearward.

2. Lift upward and pull forward on the seat cushion frame to disengage the cushion frame wires from the retainers on the rear seat pan.

3. Remove the lower seat cushion from the vehicle.

4. At the bottom of the seatback, remove the anchor bolts securing the rear seat wire retainers.

5. Grasp the bottom of the seatback and swing toward to disengage the offsets on the upper frame bar from the hangers.

6. Lift the seatback upward and remove from vehicle.

To install:

7. Install the seat back into the car, make sure to have the seat belts on the outer sides of the seat, so they are exposed for use.

8. Install the offsets to the hangers.

9. Secure all the anchor bolts, then tighten to 89 inch lbs. (10 Nm).

10. To install the rear seat cushion assembly, first pull the seat belts up so they will be exposed when the seat cushion is seated, then press down and rearward.

Folding Third Seat — Wagon

1. Remove the screws from the top side of the cushion.

2. Pull the top of the cushion outward and upward to remove.

To install:

3. Be sure to slot the lower rear of the cushion correctly into the back panel.

4. Install the cushion, then secure with the mounting screws.

Folding Split Second Seat — Wagon

1. Place the folding seatback into the down position, lift up the front flap of the carpet that covers the lower seatback.

2. Remove the cover(s) from the quarter inner trim panel(s).

Fig. 50 Install the offsets to the hangers, secure the anchor bolts, then tighten to 89 inch lbs. (10 Nm)

3. Remove the bolt(s) from the seatback support.

4. Separate the split seatback by lifting forward and outwards.

To install:

5. It may be necessary to loosen and realign the second seatback striker(s). Tighten the striker(s) to 18 ft. lbs. (24 Nm).

6. Install the split seatback to the car, then install the bolts to the supports. Tighten the bolts to 18 ft. lbs. (24 Nm).

7. Reinstall the covers to the quarter inner trim panels.

8. Install the carpet over the lower seatback.

Seat Belt Systems

REMOVAL & INSTALLATION

Floor Mount

1. Remove the cover from the anchor plate.

2. Remove the cover from the floor mounted retractor assembly.

3. Disconnect wiring from assembly, as needed.

4. Remove assembly.

To install:

5. Install the assembly. Tighten the retaining bolts to 31 ft. lbs. (42 Nm).

6. Connect the electrical wiring to the assembly.

7. Attach the cover to the floor mounted retractor assembly.

8. Attach the cover to the anchor plate.

Outboard Belts and Retractors

▸ **See Figure 52**

1. Remove door trim panel.

2. Remove screws securing intermediate guide to door.

3. Remove the intermediate guide.

4. Disconnect electrical connectors.

5. Unfasten the nut securing the lap retractor.

6. Remove the lap retractor.

7. Unfasten the nut and screw securing the shoulder retractor.

1. REAR SEAT BACK
2. RETAINER ON LOAD FLOOR
3. CUSHION FRAME WIRE
4. REAR SEAT CUSHION

VIEW A

86810160

Fig. 51 To install the rear seat cushion assembly, pull the seat belts up so they will be exposed when the seat cushion is in place, then press the seat down and rearward

1. Clevis
2. Nut 21 ft. lbs. (28 Nm)
3. Cover
4. Spacer
5. Connector
6. Intermediate guide
7. D-ring
8. Latch plate
9. Escutcheon
10. Door trim panel
11. Webbing
12. Nut
13. Screws
14. Screw
15. Lap retractor
16. Shoulder retractor
17. Stud

86810161

Fig. 52 Common front seat belt location and mounting for most sedans and wagons

4. Remove the seat assembly from the car.

To install:

5. Reinstall the seat into the car, then connect the wire connection.

6. Attach the seat with the adjuster-to-floor pan front nuts, then tighten the nuts to 18 ft. lbs. (24 Nm).

7. Position the seat in the full forward and up position, then attach the adjuster-to-floor pan rear nuts. Tighten the nuts to 18 ft. lbs. (24 Nm).

8. Reinstall the track covers, if removed.

9. Install the rear foot covers and the carpet retainers, if they were removed.

➡**Inspect both seat adjusters making sure they are parallel and in phase with each other. This is where one adjuster reaches its maximum horizontal or vertical travel in a given direction, before the other adjuster. In the event they are out of phase.**

10. Check the operation of the seat assembly for a full limit of travel.

Rear Stationary

▶ **See Figures 50 and 51**

1. Push the lower forward edge of the seat cushion rearward.

2. Lift upward and pull forward on the seat cushion frame to disengage the cushion frame wires from the retainers on the rear seat pan.

3. Remove the lower seat cushion from the vehicle.

4. At the bottom of the seatback, remove the anchor bolts securing the rear seat wire retainers.

5. Grasp the bottom of the seatback and swing toward to disengage the offsets on the upper frame bar from the hangers.

6. Lift the seatback upward and remove from vehicle.

To install:

7. Install the seat back into the car, make sure to have the seat belts on the outer sides of the seat, so they are exposed for use.

8. Install the offsets to the hangers.

9. Secure all the anchor bolts, then tighten to 89 inch lbs. (10 Nm).

10. To install the rear seat cushion assembly, first pull the seat belts up so they will be exposed when the seat cushion is seated, then press down and rearward.

Folding Third Seat — Wagon

1. Remove the screws from the top side of the cushion.

2. Pull the top of the cushion outward and upward to remove.

To install:

3. Be sure to slot the lower rear of the cushion correctly into the back panel.

4. Install the cushion, then secure with the mounting screws.

Folding Split Second Seat — Wagon

1. Place the folding seatback into the down position, lift up the front flap of the carpet that covers the lower seatback.

2. Remove the cover(s) from the quarter inner trim panel(s).

Fig. 50 Install the offsets to the hangers, secure the anchor bolts, then tighten to 89 inch lbs. (10 Nm)

3. Remove the bolt(s) from the seatback support.

4. Separate the split seatback by lifting forward and outwards.

To install:

5. It may be necessary to loosen and realign the second seatback striker(s). Tighten the striker(s) to 18 ft. lbs. (24 Nm).

6. Install the split seatback to the car, then install the bolts to the supports. Tighten the bolts to 18 ft. lbs. (24 Nm).

7. Reinstall the covers to the quarter inner trim panels.

8. Install the carpet over the lower seatback.

Seat Belt Systems

REMOVAL & INSTALLATION

Floor Mount

1. Remove the cover from the anchor plate.

2. Remove the cover from the floor mounted retractor assembly.

3. Disconnect wiring from assembly, as needed.

4. Remove assembly.

To install:

5. Install the assembly. Tighten the retaining bolts to 31 ft. lbs. (42 Nm).

6. Connect the electrical wiring to the assembly.

7. Attach the cover to the floor mounted retractor assembly.

8. Attach the cover to the anchor plate.

Outboard Belts and Retractors

▶ **See Figure 52**

1. Remove door trim panel.

2. Remove screws securing intermediate guide to door.

3. Remove the intermediate guide.

4. Disconnect electrical connectors.

5. Unfasten the nut securing the lap retractor.

6. Remove the lap retractor.

7. Unfasten the nut and screw securing the shoulder retractor.

1. REAR SEAT BACK
2. RETAINER ON LOAD FLOOR
3. CUSHION FRAME WIRE
4. REAR SEAT CUSHION

86810160

Fig. 51 To install the rear seat cushion assembly, pull the seat belts up so they will be exposed when the seat cushion is in place, then press the seat down and rearward

1. Clevis
2. Nut 21 ft. lbs. (28 Nm)
3. Cover
4. Spacer
5. Connector
6. Intermediate guide
7. D-ring
8. Latch plate
9. Escutcheon
10. Door trim panel
11. Webbing
12. Nut
13. Screws
14. Screw
15. Lap retractor
16. Shoulder retractor
17. Stud

86810161

Fig. 52 Common front seat belt location and mounting for most sedans and wagons

8. Remove the shoulder retractor.

9. Remove or lower window as necessary.

10. Remove the cover, nut and spacer from D-ring and remove the D-ring.

To install:

11. Install the D-ring, and tighten the bolt to 21 ft. lbs. (28 Nm).

12. Reposition and install the D-ring covers.

13. Secure the shoulder retractor, then tighten to 31 ft. lbs. (42 Nm).

14. Install the lap retractor, then tighten to 31 ft. lbs. (42 Nm).

15. Connect the electrical connectors to the retractors.

16. Secure the intermediate guide and tighten to 44 inch lbs. (5 Nm).

17. Install the door trim panels.

Power Seat Motor

REMOVAL & INSTALLATION

1. Position the seat in the full forward position. If the car is equipped with six-way power seats, place the seat in the full forward and up position. When necessary to gain access to the adjuster-to-floor pan attaching nuts, remove the adjuster rear foot covers and or carpet retainers.

2. Remove the track covers where necessary, then remove the adjuster-to-floor pan rear attaching nuts. Position the seat in the full rearward position.

3. Remove the adjuster front foot covers, then remove the adjuster to floor pan front attaching nuts. Tilt the seat rearward and disconnect the feed wire connector.

4. Remove the seat assembly from the car.

5. Place the seat up side down on a clean surface.

6. Disconnect the vertical and horizontal drive cables from the motor.

7. Remove the retainer nut from the motor support bracket.

8. Remove the motor from the seat.

To install:

9. Position the motor in the motor support bracket.

10. Connect the vertical and horizontal drive cables.

11. Place the seat into the vehicle and connect the feed wire.

12. Position the seat in the position that makes installation of the retaining nuts easiest. Install the adjuster to floor pan attaching nuts, tighten to 15-21 ft. lbs. (20-28 Nm), then install the foot covers.

SEAT BELT TORQUE CHART

	PART NAME	TYPE	THREAD	LENGTH	TORQUE N·m	Ft-Lb
	BOLT	1	M12-1.75	36 mm	35-48	26-35
	BOLT	2	M12-1.75	25 mm	35-48	26-35
	BOLT	3	M12-1.75	30 mm	35-48	26-35
	BOLT	4	M8-1.25	20 mm	20-24	15-17
	BOLT	5	M12-1.75	39 mm	35-48	26-35
	BOLT	6	M12-1.75	35 mm	35-48	26-35
	BOLT	7	M12-1.75	43 mm	35-48	26-35
	BOLT	8	M12-1.75	31 mm	35-48	26-35
	BOLT	9	M12-1.75	49 mm	35-48	26-35
	STUD	10	M6-1.00	15 mm	N/A	N/A
	BOLT	11	M12-1.75	53 mm	35-48	26-35
	NUT	12	M12-1.75		35-48	26-35
	NUT	13	M10-1.50		40-55	30-41
	NUT	14	M6-1.00		10-14	7-10
	NUT	15	M8-1.25		18-25	14-19
	STUD	16	M8-1.25	13 mm	N/A	N/A
	BOLT	18	5/16-18	1.25 N.S.	20-24	15-17
	BOLT	19	5/16-18	8.75 N.S.	20-24	15-17
	NUT	20	M6-1.00		9-12	7-9
	NUT	21	M10-1.50		30-40	22-30

86810166

How to Remove Stains from Fabric Interior

For best results, spots and stains should be removed as soon as possible. Never use gasoline, lacquer thinner, acetone, nail polish remover or bleach. Use a 3' x 3" piece of cheesecloth. Squeeze most of the liquid from the fabric and wipe the stained fabric from the outside of the stain toward the center with a lifting motion. Turn the cheesecloth as soon as one side becomes soiled. When using water to remove a stain, be sure to wash the entire section after the spot has been removed to avoid water stains. Encrusted spots can be broken up with a dull knife and vacuumed before removing the stain.

Type of Stain	How to Remove It
Surface spots	Brush the spots out with a small hand brush or use a commercial preparation such as K2R to lift the stain.
Mildew	Clean around the mildew with warm suds. Rinse in cold water and soak the mildew area in a solution of 1 part table salt and 2 parts water. Wash with upholstery cleaner.
Water stains	Water stains in fabric materials can be removed with a solution made from 1 cup of table salt dissolved in 1 quart of water. Vigorously scrub the solution into the stain and rinse with clear water. Water stains in nylon or other synthetic fabrics should be removed with a commercial type spot remover.
Chewing gum, tar, crayons, shoe polish (greasy stains)	Do not use a cleaner that will soften gum or tar. Harden the deposit with an ice cube and scrape away as much as possible with a dull knife. Moisten the remainder with cleaning fluid and scrub clean.
Ice cream, candy	Most candy has a sugar base and can be removed with a cloth wrung out in warm water. Oily candy, after cleaning with warm water, should be cleaned with upholstery cleaner. Rinse with warm water and clean the remainder with cleaning fluid.
Wine, alcohol, egg, milk, soft drink (non-greasy stains)	Do not use soap. Scrub the stain with a cloth wrung out in warm water. Remove the remainder with cleaning fluid.
Grease, oil, lipstick, butter and related stains	Use a spot remover to avoid leaving a ring. Work from the outisde of the stain to the center and dry with a clean cloth when the spot is gone.
Headliners (cloth)	Mix a solution of warm water and foam upholstery cleaner to give thick suds. Use only foam—liquid may streak or spot. Clean the entire headliner in one operation using a circular motion with a natural sponge.
Headliner (vinyl)	Use a vinyl cleaner with a sponge and wipe clean with a dry cloth.
Seats and door panels	Mix 1 pint upholstery cleaner in 1 gallon of water. Do not soak the fabric around the buttons.
Leather or vinyl fabric	Use a multi-purpose cleaner full strength and a stiff brush. Let stand 2 minutes and scrub thoroughly. Wipe with a clean, soft rag.
Nylon or synthetic fabrics	For normal stains, use the same procedures you would for washing cloth upholstery. If the fabric is extremely dirty, use a multi-purpose cleaner full strength with a stiff scrub brush. Scrub thoroughly in all directions and wipe with a cotton towel or soft rag.

86810165

TORQUE SPECIFICATIONS

Component	US	Metric
Adjuster to seat frame bolt:	18 ft. lbs.	24 Nm
Air deflector:	80 inch lbs.	9 Nm
Bumper to absorber bolts:	18-25 ft. lbs.	24-34 Nm
Door hinge to body:	15-20 ft. lbs.	20-28 Nm
Door striker:		
1982-91	34-46 ft. lbs.	46-62 Nm
1992-95	39 ft. lbs.	53 Nm
Fender bolts upper:	89 inch lbs.	10 Nm
Fender bolts lower:	18 ft. lbs.	25 Nm
Folding second seatback lock stricker to back support:	34 ft. lbs.	46 Nm
Front seat center armrest:	9 ft. lbs.	12 Nm
Front seatbelt to anchor plate:	31 ft. lbs.	42 Nm
Front seatbelt to rocker:	31 ft. lbs.	42 Nm
High mounted stop light:	49 inch lbs.	5.5 Nm
Hood hinge to hood bolts:	20 ft. lbs.	27 Nm
Interia lock to seat back panel:	89 inch lbs.	10 Nm
Interia lock to seat bottom frame:	89 inch lbs.	10 Nm
Lockout plate to seat bottom:	9 ft. lbs.	12 Nm
Luggage carrier deck lid:	13 inch lbs.	1.5 Nm
Luggage carrier rail:	13 inch lbs.	1.5 Nm
Outer seatback hinge upper and lower bolts:	18 ft. lbs.	5.5 Nm
Outer slat retaining nuts:	49 inch lbs.	9 Nm
Outside mirror retaining nuts:	72-80 inch lbs.	8-9 Nm
Pivot glass bolts:	80 inch lbs.	6 Nm
Pivot glass lock, solenoid and acuator:	53 inch lbs.	6 Nm
Pivot glass screws to deflector:	80 inch lbs.	9 Nm
Pivot glass striker to glass assembly:	80 inch lbs.	9 Nm
Rear compartment lid lock and solenoid screws:	53 inch lbs.	6 Nm
Rear seat cushion retainer to floor pan:	89 inch lbs.	10 Nm
Rear seatback bolt:	89 inch lbs.	10 Nm
Reclining to seatback bolt:	31 ft.lbs.	42 Nm
Reclining seatback actuator assembly to cushion frame:	13 ft. lbs.	18 Nm
Reveal moulding to liftgate:	13 ft. lbs.	18 Nm
Seat adjuster-to-floor bolt:	13 ft. lbs.	18 Nm
Seat bottom-to-back frame:	80 inch lbs.	9 Nm
Seat motor and trans. support:	18 ft. lbs.	24 Nm
Seatback frame-to-cushion:	89 inch lbs.	10 Nm
Seatback lock assembly screw:	106 inch lbs.	12 Nm
Seatback lock striker and inner side bar stop:	34 ft. lbs.	46 Nm
Trunk lid retaining bolts:	18-20 ft. lbs.	25-27 Nm

86810900

GLOSSARY

AIR/FUEL RATIO: The ratio of air-to-gasoline by weight in the fuel mixture drawn into the engine.

AIR INJECTION: One method of reducing harmful exhaust emissions by injecting air into each of the exhaust ports of an engine. The fresh air entering the hot exhaust manifold causes any remaining fuel to be burned before it can exit the tailpipe.

ALTERNATOR: A device used for converting mechanical energy into electrical energy.

AMMETER: An instrument, calibrated in amperes, used to measure the flow of an electrical current in a circuit. Ammeters are always connected in series with the circuit being tested.

AMPERE: The rate of flow of electrical current present when one volt of electrical pressure is applied against one ohm of electrical resistance.

ANALOG COMPUTER: Any microprocessor that uses similar (analogous) electrical signals to make its calculations.

ARMATURE: A laminated, soft iron core wrapped by a wire that converts electrical energy to mechanical energy as in a motor or relay. When rotated in a magnetic field, it changes mechanical energy into electrical energy as in a generator.

ATMOSPHERIC PRESSURE: The pressure on the Earth's surface caused by the weight of the air in the atmosphere. At sea level, this pressure is 14.7 psi at 32°F (101 kPa at 0°C).

ATOMIZATION: The breaking down of a liquid into a fine mist that can be suspended in air.

AXIAL PLAY: Movement parallel to a shaft or bearing bore.

BACKFIRE: The sudden combustion of gases in the intake or exhaust system that results in a loud explosion.

BACKLASH: The clearance or play between two parts, such as meshed gears.

BACKPRESSURE: Restrictions in the exhaust system that slow the exit of exhaust gases from the combustion chamber.

BAKELITE: A heat resistant, plastic insulator material commonly used in printed circuit boards and transistorized components.

BALL BEARING: A bearing made up of hardened inner and outer races between which hardened steel balls roll.

BALLAST RESISTOR: A resistor in the primary ignition circuit that lowers voltage after the engine is started to reduce wear on ignition components.

BEARING: A friction reducing, supportive device usually located between a stationary part and a moving part.

BIMETAL TEMPERATURE SENSOR: Any sensor or switch made of two dissimilar types of metal that bend when heated or cooled due to the different expansion rates of the alloys. These types of sensors usually function as an on/off switch.

BLOWBY: Combustion gases, composed of water vapor and unburned fuel, that leak past the piston rings into the crankcase during normal engine operation. These gases are removed by the PCV system to prevent the buildup of harmful acids in the crankcase.

BRAKE PAD: A brake shoe and lining assembly used with disc brakes.

BRAKE SHOE: The backing for the brake lining. The term is, however, usually applied to the assembly of the brake backing and lining.

BUSHING: A liner, usually removable, for a bearing; an anti-friction liner used in place of a bearing.

CALIPER: A hydraulically activated device in a disc brake system, which is mounted straddling the brake rotor (disc). The caliper contains at least one piston and two brake pads. Hydraulic pressure on the piston(s) forces the pads against the rotor.

CAMSHAFT: A shaft in the engine on which are the lobes (cams) which operate the valves. The camshaft is driven by the crankshaft, via a belt, chain or gears, at one half the crankshaft speed.

CAPACITOR: A device which stores an electrical charge.

CARBON MONOXIDE (CO): A colorless, odorless gas given off as a normal byproduct of combustion. It is poisonous and extremely dangerous in confined areas, building up slowly to toxic levels without warning if adequate ventilation is not available.

CARBURETOR: A device, usually mounted on the intake manifold of an engine, which mixes the air and fuel in the proper proportion to allow even combustion.

CATALYTIC CONVERTER: A device installed in the exhaust system, like a muffler, that converts harmful byproducts of combustion into carbon dioxide and water vapor by means of a heat-producing chemical reaction.

CENTRIFUGAL ADVANCE: A mechanical method of advancing the spark timing by using flyweights in the distributor that react to centrifugal force generated by the distributor shaft rotation.

OXIDES OF NITROGEN (NOx): Chemical compounds of nitrogen produced as a byproduct of combustion. They combine with hydrocarbons to produce smog.

OXYGEN SENSOR: Used with the feedback system to sense the presence of oxygen in the exhaust gas and signal the computer which can reference the voltage signal to an air/fuel ratio.

PINION: The smaller of two meshing gears.

PISTON RING: An open-ended ring which fits into a groove on the outer diameter of the piston. Its chief function is to form a seal between the piston and cylinder wall. Most automotive pistons have three rings: two for compression sealing; one for oil sealing.

PRELOAD: A predetermined load placed on a bearing during assembly or by adjustment.

PRIMARY CIRCUIT: The low voltage side of the ignition system which consists of the ignition switch, ballast resistor or resistance wire, bypass, coil, electronic control unit and pick-up coil as well as the connecting wires and harnesses.

PRESS FIT: The mating of two parts under pressure, due to the inner diameter of one being smaller than the outer diameter of the other, or vice versa; an interference fit.

RACE: The surface on the inner or outer ring of a bearing on which the balls, needles or rollers move.

REGULATOR: A device which maintains the amperage and/or voltage levels of a circuit at predetermined values.

RELAY: A switch which automatically opens and/or closes a circuit.

RESISTANCE: The opposition to the flow of current through a circuit or electrical device, and is measured in ohms. Resistance is equal to the voltage divided by the amperage.

RESISTOR: A device, usually made of wire, which offers a preset amount of resistance in an electrical circuit.

RING GEAR: The name given to a ring-shaped gear attached to a differential case, or affixed to a flywheel or as part of a planetary gear set.

ROLLER BEARING: A bearing made up of hardened inner and outer races between which hardened steel rollers move.

ROTOR: 1. The disc-shaped part of a disc brake assembly, upon which the brake pads bear; also called, brake disc. 2. The device mounted atop the distributor shaft, which passes current to the distributor cap tower contacts.

SECONDARY CIRCUIT: The high voltage side of the ignition system, usually above 20,000 volts. The secondary includes the ignition coil, coil wire, distributor cap and rotor, spark plug wires and spark plugs.

SENDING UNIT: A mechanical, electrical, hydraulic or electromagnetic device which transmits information to a gauge.

SENSOR: Any device designed to measure engine operating conditions or ambient pressures and temperatures. Usually electronic in nature and designed to send a voltage signal to an on-board computer, some sensors may operate as a simple on/off switch or they may provide a variable voltage signal (like a potentiometer) as conditions or measured parameters change.

SHIM: Spacers of precise, predetermined thickness used between parts to establish a proper working relationship.

SLAVE CYLINDER: In automotive use, a device in the hydraulic clutch system which is activated by hydraulic force, disengaging the clutch.

SOLENOID: A coil used to produce a magnetic field, the effect of which is to produce work.

SPARK PLUG: A device screwed into the combustion chamber of a spark ignition engine. The basic construction is a conductive core inside of a ceramic insulator, mounted in an outer conductive base. An electrical charge from the spark plug wire travels along the conductive core and jumps a preset air gap to a grounding point or points at the end of the conductive base. The resultant spark ignites the fuel/air mixture in the combustion chamber.

SPLINES: Ridges machined or cast onto the outer diameter of a shaft or inner diameter of a bore to enable parts to mate without rotation.

TACHOMETER: A device used to measure the rotary speed of an engine, shaft, gear, etc., usually in rotations per minute.

THERMOSTAT: A valve, located in the cooling system of an engine, which is closed when cold and opens gradually in response to engine heating, controlling the temperature of the coolant and rate of coolant flow.

TOP DEAD CENTER (TDC): The point at which the piston reaches the top of its travel on the compression stroke.

TORQUE: The twisting force applied to an object.

TORQUE CONVERTER: A turbine used to transmit power from a driving member to a driven member via hydraulic action, providing changes in drive ratio and torque. In automotive use, it links the driveplate at the rear of the engine to the automatic transmission.

TRANSDUCER: A device used to change a force into an electrical signal.

TRANSISTOR: A semi-conductor component which can be actuated by a small voltage to perform an electrical switching function.

TUNE-UP: A regular maintenance function, usually associated with the replacement and adjustment of parts and components in the electrical and fuel systems of a vehicle for the purpose of attaining optimum performance.

TURBOCHARGER: An exhaust driven pump which compresses intake air and forces it into the combustion chambers at higher than atmospheric pressures. The increased air pressure allows more fuel to be burned and results in increased horsepower being produced.

VACUUM ADVANCE: A device which advances the ignition timing in response to increased engine vacuum.

VACUUM GAUGE: An instrument used to measure the presence of vacuum in a chamber.

VALVE: A device which control the pressure, direction of flow or rate of flow of a liquid or gas.

VALVE CLEARANCE: The measured gap between the end of the valve stem and the rocker arm, cam lobe or follower that activates the valve.

VISCOSITY: The rating of a liquid's internal resistance to flow.

VOLTMETER: An instrument used for measuring electrical force in units called volts. Voltmeters are always connected parallel with the circuit being tested.

WHEEL CYLINDER: Found in the automotive drum brake assembly, it is a device, actuated by hydraulic pressure, which, through internal pistons, pushes the brake shoes outward against the drums.

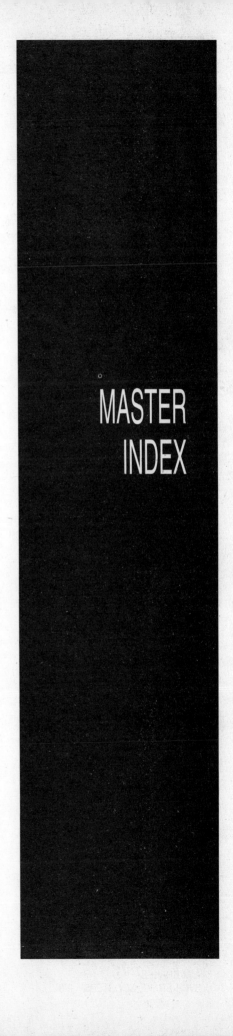

MASTER
INDEX